SEXUAL BEHAVIOR IN
THE HUMAN MALE

ALFRED C. KINSEY
Professor of Zoology, Indiana University

WARDELL B. POMEROY
Research Associate, Indiana University

CLYDE E. MARTIN
Research Associate, Indiana University

W. B. SAUNDERS COMPANY

PHILADELPHIA AND LONDON

1948

TO

the twelve thousand persons who
have contributed to these data

AND TO

the eighty-eight thousand more who,
someday, will help complete this study

PREFACE

Seen from the four points of the compass a great mountain may present aspects that are very different one from the other—so different that bitter disagreements can arise between those who have watched the mountain, truly and well, through all the seasons, but each from a different quarter. Reality, too, has many facets—some too readily disputed or denied by those who rely only on their own experience. Nor can science itself rightly lay claim to finality or the complete comprehension of reality, but only to honesty and accuracy of the additional facets it may be permitted to discover and report. I say "may be permitted" since the human race is familiar with the suppression of truth in both small matters and great. The history of science is part of the history of the freedom to observe, to reflect, to experiment, to record, and to bear witness. It has been a perilous and a passionate history indeed, and not yet ended.

Living creatures possess three basic characteristics or capacities—growth, adaptation, and reproduction. In human biology, the reproductive function has been the least and the last studied, scientifically. To the National Research Council's Committee for Research on Problems of Sex belongs the credit for sponsoring a more significant series of research studies on sex than has been accomplished perhaps by any other agency. Among these studies the findings of Dr. Alfred C. Kinsey and his associates at Indiana University deserve attention for their extent, their thoroughness, and their dispassionate objectivity. Dr. Kinsey has studied sex phenomena of human beings as a biologist would examine biological phenomena, and the evidence he has secured is presented from the scientist's viewpoint, without moral bias or prejudice derived from current taboos.

Certainly no aspect of human biology in our current civilization stands in more need of scientific knowledge and courageous humility than that of sex. The history of medicine proves that in so far as man seeks to know himself and face his whole nature, he has become free from bewildered fear, despondent shame, or arrant hypocrisy. As long as sex is dealt with in the current confusion of ignorance and sophistication, denial and indulgence, suppression and stimulation, punishment and exploitation, secrecy and display, it will be associated with a duplicity and indecency that lead neither to intellectual honesty nor human dignity.

These studies are sincere, objective, and determined explorations of a field manifestly important to education, medicine, government, and the integrity of human conduct generally. They have demanded from Dr. Kinsey and his colleagues very unusual tenacity of purpose, tolerance, analytical competence, social skills, and real courage. I hope that the reader will match the authors with an equal and appropriate measure of cool attention, courageous judgment, and scientific equanimity.

ALAN GREGG

The Medical Sciences
Rockefeller Foundation
New York City

ACKNOWLEDGMENTS

First of all, acknowledgment should be made to the 12,000 persons who have contributed histories, and particularly to the 5300 males who have provided the data on which the present volume is based. These persons represent each and every age, from children to the oldest groups; they represent every social level, of several racial groups. If these persons had not helped there would have been no study. It has taken considerable courage for many of them to discuss such intimate aspects of their histories, and to risk their confidences with the scientific investigators. They have contributed in order that there should be an increase in our knowledge of this important aspect of human biology and sociology. It is unfortunate that we cannot name each and every one involved. Those who have spent time in persuading their friends to cooperate have contributed in a very special way; and to them we are especially indebted for devoted and effective service.

Herman B Wells, the President of Indiana University, Fernandus Payne, Dean of the Graduate School of the University, the Trustees, and others in the Administration of the University have constantly encouraged, materially supported, and stoutly defended the importance of this research.

The Rockefeller Foundation has contributed a major portion of the cost of the program during the past six years. Dr. Alan Gregg, as Director for the Medical Sciences of The Foundation, has encouraged a wide-scale, long-time project which would adequately cover all social levels and all aspects of sexual behavior in our society.

The National Research Council's Committee for Research on Problems of Sex, as a part of the Medical Division of the Council, has administered the funds granted by The Rockefeller Foundation. It has encouraged and advised on many aspects of the research. Especial mention should be made of the cordial support given by Dr. Robert M. Yerkes, who has served as Chairman of the Research Council's Committee since its inception more than twenty-five years ago. Under Dr. Yerkes' guidance the Committee has contributed to a long list of notable projects on the sex endocrines; on the behavior of chimpanzees at the Yerkes Laboratories at Orange Park, Florida; on the behavior of lower mammals, particularly under the direction of Dr. Frank A. Beach, formerly at the American Museum of Natural History and now at Yale University; and on the human studies which were published by Peck and Wells (1923, 1925), by Hamilton (1929), by Katherine Davis (1929), by Terman et al. (1938), by Landis (1940, 1942), and by still others.

The statistical set-up of the research was originally checked by Dr. Lowell Reed of the School of Hygiene and Public Health at The Johns Hopkins University. A long list of persons experienced in sampling and in other aspects of statistics has been constantly available for consultation. We are especially indebted to Dr. Frank K. Edmondson, Chairman of the Department of Astronomy at Indiana University, for continual guidance and supervision of the details of the statistical methods which have been used.

Dr. R. L. Dickinson of the New York Academy of Medicine has rendered peculiar service based on his long experience with research projects in the field of human sex behavior. As the first head of the National Committee on Maternal Health, Dr. Dickinson encouraged a long list of pioneer studies, particularly on the clinical aspects of human reproduction and sexual behavior; and we have had the benefit of his accumulated experience, and his constant advice on many of the details of this research.

A number of other persons, additional to those whose names appear as authors of the present volume, have served for various periods of time as members of the full-time staff on this project. Dr. Glenn V. Ramsey, now of Princeton University, was responsible for a series of histories from younger boys and served on this staff for a short time before going into the Army as clinical psychologist during the recent war. Dr. Vincent Nowlis, now psychologist at the Child Welfare Research Station of the State University of Iowa, and Dr. Robert E. Bugbee, now of the Department of Biological Sciences at the University of Rochester, were formerly members of this staff, took some of the histories, and contributed to the laboratory handling of the data. Dr. Nowlis has critically reviewed the whole manuscript of this volume. Dr. Paul H. Gebhard, trained in anthropology at Harvard University, has been a member of the staff during the past year. Mrs. Elizabeth Murnan has given full time as statistical calculator during the past three years. Mrs. Velma Baldwin, Mrs. Enola Van Valer Trafford, and Mrs. Ellen Lauritzen Welch have served as secretaries and research assistants on the project. Mrs. Hedwig Gruen Leser has been the German translator on the staff.

Finally, much of the success of this project is to be attributed to our wives, without whose encouragement and specific help, and without whose support it would have been impossible to have carried this project through to its present point of development.

None of these persons is responsible for any of the errors which we, the authors, may have made in our calculations or in our interpretations of the data; but the credit for any merits which this volume may have should be shared by those to whom we have made acknowledgment.

THE AUTHORS

PUBLISHER'S FOREWORD

This volume is presented as an objective factual study of sexual behavior in the human male. It is based on surveys made by members of the staff of Indiana University, and supported by the National Research Council's Committee for Research on Problems of Sex by means of funds contributed by the Medical Division of The Rockefeller Foundation.

This book is intended primarily for workers in the fields of medicine, biology, psychology, sociology, anthropology and allied sciences and for teachers, social workers, personnel officers, law enforcement groups, and others concerned with the direction of human behavior.

W. B. SAUNDERS COMPANY

CONTENTS

Part I

HISTORY AND METHOD

Chapter 1

HISTORICAL INTRODUCTION

The present volume is a progress report from a case history study on human sex behavior. The study has been underway during the past nine years. Throughout these years, it has had the sponsorship and support of Indiana University, and during the past six years the support of the National Research Council's Committee for Research on Problems of Sex, with funds granted by the Medical Division of The Rockefeller Foundation. It is a fact-finding survey in which an attempt is being made to discover what people do sexually, and what factors account for differences in sexual behavior among individuals, and among various segments of the population.

For some time now there has been an increasing awareness among many people of the desirability of obtaining data about sex which would represent an accumulation of scientific fact completely divorced from questions of moral value and social custom. Practicing physicians find thousands of their patients in need of such objective data. Psychiatrists and analysts find that a majority of their patients need help in resolving sexual conflicts that have arisen in their lives. An increasing number of persons would like to bring an educated intelligence into the consideration of such matters as sexual adjustments in marriage, the sexual guidance of children, the pre-marital sexual adjustments of youth, sex education, sexual activities which are in conflict with the mores, and problems confronting persons who are interested in the social control of behavior through religion, custom, and the forces of the law. Before it is possible to think scientifically on any of these matters, more needs to be known about the actual behavior of people, and about the inter-relationships of that behavior with the biologic and social aspects of their histories.

Hitherto, there have not been sufficient answers to these questions, for human sexual behavior respresents one of the least explored segments of biology, psychology, and sociology. Scientifically more has been known about the sexual behavior of some of the farm and laboratory animals. In our Western European-American culture, sexual responses, more than any other physiologic activities, have been subject to religious evaluation, social taboo, and formal legislation. It is obvious that the failure to learn more about human sexual activity is the outcome of the influence which the custom and the law have had upon scientists as individuals, and of the not immaterial restrictions which have been imposed upon scientific investigations in this field,

3

There are cultures which more freely accept sexual activities as matters of everyday physiology (*e.g.*, Malinowski 1929), while maintaining extensive rituals and establishing taboos around feeding activities. One may wonder what scientific knowledge we would have of digestive functions if the primary taboos in our own society concerned food and feeding. Sexual responses, however, involve emotional changes which are more intense than those associated with any other sort of physiologic activity. For that reason it is difficult to comprehend how any society could become as concerned about respiratory functioning, about digestive functioning, about excretory functioning, or about any of the other physiologic processes. It is probable that the close association of sex, religious values, rituals, and custom in most of the civilizations of the world, has been primarily consequent on the emotional content of sexual behavior.

Sexual activities may affect persons other than those who are directly involved, or do damage to the social organization as a whole. Defenders of the custom frequently contend that this is the sufficient explanation of society's interest in the individual's sexual behavior; but this is probably a post factum rationalization that fails to take into account the historic data on the origin of the custom (May 1931, Westermarck 1936). It is ordinarily said that criminal law is designed to protect property and to protect persons, and if society's only interest in controlling sex behavior were to protect persons, then the criminal codes concerned with assault and battery should provide adequate protection. The fact that there is a body of sex laws which are apart from the laws protecting persons is evidence of their distinct function, namely that of protecting custom. Just because they have this function, sex customs and the sex laws seem more significant, and are defended with more emotion than the laws that concern property or person. The failure of the scientist to go further than he has in studies of sex is undoubtedly a reflection of society's attitudes in this field.

Scientists have been uncertain whether any large portion of the population was willing that a thoroughly objective, fact-finding investigation of sex should be made. It is quite probable that an investigation of the sort undertaken here would have been more difficult some years ago; but we have found that there is now an abundant and widespread interest in the possibilities of such a study. Thousands of persons have helped by contributing records of their own sexual activities, by interesting others in the research, and by providing the sort of constant support and encouragement without which the pursuit of this study would have been much more difficult, if not impossible. Even the scientist seems to have underestimated the faith of the man of the street in the scientific method, his respect for the results of scientific research, and his confidence that his own life and the whole of the social organization will ultimately benefit from the accumulation of scientifically established data.

OBJECTIVES IN THE PRESENT STUDY

The present study, then, represents an attempt to accumulate an objectively determined body of fact about sex which strictly avoids social or moral interpretations of the fact. Each person who reads this report will want to make interpretations in accordance with his understanding of moral values and social significances; but that is not part of the scientific method and, indeed, scientists have no special capacities for making such evaluations.

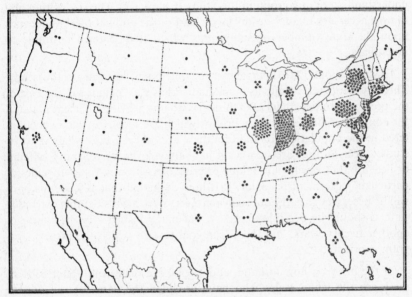

Figure 1. Sources of histories.

One dot represents 50 cases

The data in this study are being secured through first-hand interviews. These, so far, have been limited to persons resident in the United States. Histories have come from every state in the Union, but more particularly from the northeastern quarter of the country, in the area bounded by Massachusetts, Michigan, Tennessee, and Kansas (Figure 1). It is intended that the ultimate sample shall represent a cross-section of the entire population, from all parts of the United States. The study has already included persons who belong to the following groups:

Males, females	Various social levels
Whites, Negroes, other races	Urban, rural, mixed backgrounds
Single, married, previously married	Various religious groups
Ages three to ninety	Various degrees of adherence to reli-
Adolescent at different ages	gious groups, or with no religion
Various educational levels	Various geographic origins
Various occupational classes	

The study should ultimately include series of cases which will justify a description of the sexual patterns for each of these segments of the population. Whenever it is significant to have data for the American population as a whole, such calculations may be obtained by weighting and combining the figures for the individual groups (Chapter 3).

It is basically most important to know the story for each group in detail. By pragmatic tests of the effect of adding additional histories to the samples, it has been found that about 300 cases are necessary for a good understanding of any group in this study (Chapter 3). The size of the total sample necessary to analyze any larger part of the population thus depends upon the total number of sub-groups which it is deemed desirable to investigate.

To date, about 12,000 persons have contributed histories to this study. This represents forty times as much material as was included in the best of the previous studies; but 12,000 histories do not provide sufficient material for comprehending even those groups which are most frequently encountered in the population. In addition there are other groups which must be studied because they are significant in analyses of more general problems, or because they occupy an unique or critical position in the ontogenies of particular patterns of behavior. It is now estimated that 100,000 histories will be necessary to carry out such a project. With a considerably expanded staff, it should be possible to secure that many histories in the course of another twenty years, and this is the goal toward which the present program is oriented.

Of the histories now in hand, about 6300 are male, and about 5300 of these are the white males who have provided the data for the present publication. The generalizations reached in this volume are limited to those groups on which more or less adequate material is now available, or to those smaller groups which fall in line with the trends established for the whole series of data. But no generalizations can yet be made for many important elements in the population. For instance, it is not yet possible to give more than a suggestion of what happens among males beyond fifty years of age. We have only begun to accumulate data for the highly important chapter that involves infants and very young children. Older, unmarried males, and males who have previously been married, present an interesting situation which is only glimpsed in the present volume. The story for the rural population is quite incomplete, as is also the record for a number of the religious groups. Factory workers and manual labor groups are not sufficiently represented in the sample. Large sections of the country are not yet covered by the survey, although it is certain that there are striking geographic differences in patterns of sex behavior. The story for the Negro male cannot be told now, because the Negro sample, while of some size, is not yet sufficient for making analyses comparable to those made here for the white male. At no place has the sample been large enough to allow more than a six-way breakdown in the statistical analyses (Chapter 3), although enough important factors are now recognized to call for a twelve-way breakdown. A later revision of the present volume may be based on a further accumulation of male histories.

A volume on the female, comparable to the present volume on the male, should be possible in the not too distant future; and volumes on particular groups and on special problems in human sexuality can appear when there is a sufficient increase in the total accumulation of data. It is now planned to publish volumes on:

Sexual behavior in the human female
Sexual factors in marital adjustment
Legal aspects of sex behavior
The heterosexual-homosexual balance
Sexual adjustments in institutional populations
Prostitution
Sex education
Other special problems

All kinds of persons and all aspects of human sexual behavior are being included in this survey. No preconception of what is rare or what is common, what is moral or socially significant, or what is normal and what is abnormal has entered into the choice of the histories or into the selection of the items recorded on them. Such limitations of the material would have interfered with the determination of the fact. Nothing has done more to block the free investigation of sexual behavior than the almost universal acceptance, even among scientists, of certain aspects of that behavior as normal, and of other aspects of that behavior as abnormal. The similarity of distinctions between the terms normal and abnormal, and the terms right and wrong, amply demonstrates the philosophic, religious, and cultural origins of these concepts (Chapter 6); and the ready acceptance of those distinctions among scientific men may provide the basis for one of the severest criticisms which subsequent generations can make of the scientific quality of nineteenth century and early twentieth century scientists. This is first of all a report on what people do, which raises no question of what they should do, or what kinds of people do it. It is the story of the sexual behavior of the American male, as we find him. It is not, in the usual sense, a study of the normal male or of normal behavior, any more than it is a study of abnormal males, or of abnormal behavior. It is an unfettered investigation of all types of sexual activity, as found among all kinds of males.

There has not even been a distinction between those whom the psychiatrist would consider sexually well-adjusted persons and those whom he would regard as neurotic, psychotic, or at least psychopathic personalities. To have so limited the study would, as with moral evaluations, have constituted a pre-acceptance of the categories whose reality and existence were under investigation. That this agnostic approach has been profitable is evidenced throughout this report by the data we have obtained on the high incidences and considerable frequencies, among well-adjusted persons, of behavior which has usually been considered to be both rare and abnormal. The study should constitute a considerable brief for the avoidance of classifications until there is an adequate understanding of the phenomena involved, especially if such classifications reflect evaluations that have no scientific origins.

This is a study of all aspects of human sexual behavior, and not a study of its biologic aspects, or of its psychologic aspects, or of its sociologic aspects, as separate entities. What the human animal does sexually may be the concern of many academic departments, but the behavior in each case is a unit which must be comprehended as such and simultaneously on all of its several faces. Consequently, the persons involved in this research have been chosen because of their special backgrounds in a diversity of disciplines: anthropology, biology, psychology, clinical psychology, animal behavior, and the social sciences; and it is planned that persons trained in still other fields shall in time join in the research. Throughout the nine years of the study, many hours have been spent in consultation with specialists outside this staff, particularly in the following fields:

Anatomy	Neurology
Animal behavior	Obstetrics
Anthropology	Penology
Astronomy (statistical)	Psychiatry
Biology	Psychoanalysis
Child development	Psychology, general
Criminal law	Psychology, clinical
Endocrinology	Psychology, experimental
General physiology	Public health
Genetics	Public opinion polls
Gynecology	Sex education
Human physiology	Social work
Institutional management	Sociology
Law enforcement	Statistics
Marriage counseling	Urology
Medicine (various branches)	Venereal disease
Military authorities	

Rarely has any project had more specific help from specialists in so many contingent areas. It is unfortunate that the number of persons involved is too large to allow specific acknowledgment by name.

While the present volume may be of immediate use to many persons, its publication should emphasize the limitations of our present knowledge and should serve a most useful function if it enlists additional support for the continuance of the research and its pursuit to its ultimate goal. Eighty-eight thousand other persons will need to contribute histories if the survey is to cover the major segments of the population. It is further hoped that the publication of this over-all study will encourage specialists in various fields of biology, human physiology, psychology, sociology, and other disciplines to undertake research on problems which are little more than exposed by the present survey.

DEVELOPMENT OF PRESENT STUDY

The techniques of this research have been taxonomic, in the sense in which modern biologists employ the term. It was born out of the senior author's long-time experience with a problem in insect taxonomy. The transfer from insect to human material is not illogical, for it has been a transfer of a method that may be applied to the study of any variable population, in any field.

As a teacher in biology, the senior author had had his students bring him the usual number of questions about sex. On investigating biologic, psychologic, psychiatric, and sociologic studies to secure the answers to some of these questions, the author, as a taxonomist, was struck with the inadequacy of the samples on which such studies were being based, and the apparent unawareness of the investigators that generalizations were not warranted on the bases of such small samples. Stray individuals had been studied here, a few of them there, forty males in the next study, three hundred females in the most detailed of the case history studies (Landis et al. 1940). More extended samples had been used only in the questionnaire studies, but they were of doubtful validity in connection with a subject like sex (Chapter 2). All of the studies taken together did not begin to provide a sample of such size and so distributed as a taxonomist would demand in studying a plant or animal species, or a student of public opinion would need before he could safely describe public thinking or predict the future behavior of any portion of the population. The sex studies were on a very different scale from the insect studies where, in the most recent problem (preliminarily reported in Kinsey 1942), we had had 150,000 individuals available for the study of a single species of gall wasp.

In many of the published studies on sex there were obvious confusions of moral values, philosophic theory, and the scientific fact. In many of the studies, the interest in classifying types of sexual behavior, in developing broad generalizations, and in prescribing social procedures had far outrun scientific determinations of the objective fact. There seemed ample opportunity for making a scientifically sounder study of human sex behavior.

The difficulties that might be encountered in undertaking such a study promised to be greater than those involved in studying insects. The gathering of the human data would involve the learning of new techniques in which human personalities would be the obstacles to overcome and human memories would be the instruments whose use we would have to master. Analyses of the factors involved in the human behavior would be more difficult, because the sources of variation in behavior are much more complex than the sources of variation in structural characters in insects. The complexities of such a study constituted a test of the capacities of our science. However, enough success had been achieved in some of the previous sex studies to make it apparent that there were at least some people who could be persuaded to contribute records of their activities; and we had had enough contacts with persons of other social levels, in city communities, in farm areas, in the backwoods, and in the remote mountain areas from which we had collected gall wasps, to lead us to believe that we might be able to secure cooperation from a wide variety of people. The more recently published research provided a considerable basis for deciding what should be included in a sex history, and our background in both psychology and biology made it apparent that there were additional matters worth investigation. A few of our closer friends gave encouragement to the plan, and in July of 1938 we undertook to take the first histories.

It was a slow matter learning how to secure subjects and learning what interviewing techniques were most effective. Textbook prescriptions on how to conduct an interview did not prove effective. Our experience in teaching and in meeting people in the entomological field-work were better guides toward winning confidences and securing honest answers. It took six months to persuade the first sixty-two persons to contribute histories; but our techniques were developing, and we began to secure subjects more rapidly, as the following record will indicate:

Total Number of Histories

Year	Increment	Total
1938 (6 months)	62	62
1939	671	733
1940	959	1692
1941	843	2535
1942	816	3351
1943	1510	4861
1944	2490	7351
1945	2668	10019
1946	1467	11486
1947 (part)	728	12214

Our skills have been steadily developed, but the increasing ease with which we have found people willing to contribute their histories is largely the product of a spreading knowledge of the existence of the study among tens of thousands of people, and of an increasing understanding of its significance. For several years now it has been possible to find more histories than we have been able to handle. The first histories came largely from college students, because they were most available; but after the first year there has been a constant expansion of the sample to cover all segments of the population. The question of securing a sufficiently large and a well distributed sample, even with a hundred thousand histories as the goal, is no longer a problem.

Six persons have had a share in the gathering of the histories. The record is as follows:

Interviewers Involved

Interviewer	Histories taken	Percent of total histories
Kinsey	7036	57.6
Pomeroy	3808	31.2
Martin	890	7.3
Others	480	3.9

It has been necessary to develop techniques for coordinating the work of those associated in the research, so that the data secured by the several interviewers might fairly be added together; but this did not prove an impossible undertaking (Chapter 3). It has also been necessary to test the reliability of every other technique, at every point in the program (Chapter 3). During the first year the value of personal interviewing as opposed to the questionnaire technique was subjected to some testing. Since the first year, there has been an expansion of 22 per cent in the list of items covered in each history. A system was developed for coding the data taken in an interview. The basic problems of setting up a punch-card (Hollerith) system for analyzing the data were worked out. We learned how to make contacts that would bring histories from all segments of the population. By the end of the first nine months the scope of each history, the form of the record, and the techniques of the interview had been developed to very nearly their present form. Since then, there have been few changes except for the addition or deletion of some of the items included in a history.

Difficulties Encountered. Before undertaking the study it was understood that gathering human behavioral data would involve social questions that are not involved in the gathering of scientific material less directly affecting the emotional lives of people. During the first year or two we were repeatedly warned of the dangers involved in the undertaking, and were threatened with specific trouble. There was some organized opposition, chiefly from a particular medical group. There were attempts by the medical association in one city to bring suit on the ground that we were practicing medicine without a license, police interference in two or three cities, investigation by a sheriff in one rural area, and attempts to persuade the University's Administration to stop the study, or to prevent the publication of the results, or to dismiss the senior author from his university connection, or to establish a censorship over all publication emanating from the study. Through all of this, the Administration of Indiana University stoutly defended our right to do objectively scientific research, and to that defense much of the success of this project is due. In one city, a school board, whose president was a physician, dismissed a high school teacher because he had cooperated in getting histories outside of the school but in the same city. There were other threats of legal action, threats of political investigation, and threats of censorship, and for some years there was criticism from scientific colleagues. It has been interesting to observe how far the ancient traditions and social custom influence even persons who are trained as scientists.

There seem to have been two chief sources of these objections. Some of the psychologists contended that sexual behavior involved primarily psychological problems, and that no biologist was qualified to make such a study. Some of the sociologists felt that the problems were for the most part social, and that neither a biologist nor a psychologist was the right person to make a sex study. A few of the psychoanalysts felt that sexual behavior could not properly be studied by anyone but a psychoanalyst. One group of physicians objected that taking histories constituted clinical practice, and that all such studies should be made by clinicians inside of clinics.

The second type of objection came from some scientists who, while admitting that sex studies of other animals were desirable, doubted whether human studies could be put on the same objective bases as other scientific studies. They objected that however well established the data might be, it would be inexpedient to publish them, for society was not ready to face such facts. Various persons, particularly leaders in sex education, contended that human sex behavior was primarily a question of the emotions, that no scientific study had ever succeeded in measuring the emotions, and (anyway) that if it were possible to make such measurements the data were too dangerous to publish, at least until all of the hundred thousand histories were gathered. Well-meaning but still timid advisors suggested that the fact of the existence of the study should be kept secret until there was actual publication. Several scientists admitted that such a study might be desirable, but more or less openly intimated that even scientists should make moral evaluations as they interviewed subjects and analyzed data. Several scientific friends urged that the study be confined to "normal" sexual behavior, without raising any questions of the validity of the generally accepted distinctions between normal and abnormal behavior.

None of these scientific rationalizations, however, was as interesting as that of the hotel manager who refused to allow us to take histories—

"Because I do not intend that anyone should have his mind undressed in my hotel."

Withal, it is not certain that the persons who have objected to this study have offered more of a hazard than the deserts and the mudholes, the mountain walls and the chasms, and the sometimes hostile natives with whom we had to deal in the course of the insect surveys. Never has the interference materially slowed up the present study. There were always persons who were willing to cooperate, as against the few who tried to interfere. There have been 12,000 who have believed in the research strongly enough to contribute their histories; and there are tens of thousands more who are now ready to contribute, as soon as we have time to interview them.

After the first few years the interference largely passed, and the over-all history of the present study would be totally misunderstood if the emphasis were placed anywhere except on the remarkable record of cooperation from persons of every kind and from groups of every sort. For every scientist who has obstructed, there have been hundreds of others, in every field, who have helped. The list of consultants given above will indicate how diverse a group of specialists has been interested.

Cooperating Groups. Scores of psychiatrists and physicians have offered every sort of cooperation, including opportunities to lecture to medical groups, and to discuss the data with them in seminars and in clinical sessions; help in securing histories from medical students and from medical faculties; help in securing histories from patients; the free use of working space in medical school buildings and in private offices; access to library and laboratory facilities; and access to clinical records. It is doubtful if the medical and psychiatric group has ever contributed more generously to a study which was not primarily under medical direction and which was not wholly in the field of medicine. The history provides an outstanding instance of the sort of coordination of clinical experience and research science which will become increasingly necessary if either clinicians or research scientists are to gain any final understanding of human problems.

Medical and psychiatric groups, from some of whose numbers histories have been secured, include:

American Association of Marriage Counselors
Association for Psychoanalytic and Psychosomatic Medicine
Bellevue Psychiatric Hospital
Children's Hospital, Philadelphia
Cornell University Medical College
Frederick Douglass Memorial Hospital, Philadelphia
Hahnemann Medical College
Indiana University Medical School
Jefferson Medical College, Philadelphia
Margaret Sanger Research Bureau, New York

Menninger Clinic, Topeka, Kansas
New York Academy of Medicine
New York Medical College
New York Psychoanalytic Society and Institute
New York State Psychiatric Hospital and Institute
New York University Medical School
Psychiatric Institute, Philadelphia
Private Psychiatric Clinic, Chicago
Psychiatric Clinic for Chicago Courts
Temple University Medical School
University of Illinois Medical College
University of Pennsylvania Medical School
U. S. Army Training Program in Neuropsychiatry
U. S. Public Health Service
Womans Medical College, Philadelphia
Yale University Medical School

Hundreds of educators have cooperated, at every level of the educational system, from kindergarten schools, through public and private schools, to colleges, and the professional schools. Persons who have been students at 528 American colleges and universities have contributed histories to the record. The educational institutions which have been attended by these persons include the following:

Anderson, Indiana, High School
Bradley Institute (Illinois)
* Brooklyn College
* Bryn Mawr College
Butler University
California, University of
Chicago Junior Colleges (var.)
* Chicago, University of
College of City of New York
* Columbia University
* Cornell University
Depauw University
Drexel Institute (Philadelphia)
Franklin College (Indiana)
* Fort Hays State College (Kansas)
* Harvard University
Hunter College (New York)
* Illinois, University of
* Indiana University
Michigan, University of
Minnesota, University of
* New York University
Northwestern University
Ohio State University
Pennsylvania State College
* Pennsylvania, University of
Princeton University
Peoria, Illinois: Junior and Senior High Schools
Pestalozzi School (Chicago)
Philadelphia Public High Schools
Private schools: in Chicago, Wilmington, and Philadelphia (in the Germantown
     area, the Main-line area, and elsewhere)

* Institutions from which 100 or more subjects have contributed histories.

* Purdue University
ᵏ Swarthmore College
ᵏ Temple University
  Western Reserve University
  Wisconsin, University of
  Yale University

The administrations of penal and correctional institutions naturally questioned whether their inmates would be disturbed if we attempted to secure sex histories from them. However, a number of institutions have now cooperated, and others have extended invitations to work with their populations. Institutional heads, judges of courts, parole and probation officers, and police officers have expressed a considerable interest in the bearing of this research on problems of law enforcement. The inmate populations in these institutions have voluntarily cooperated in splendid fashion. From this material we shall ultimately publish a volume on the legal aspects of sexual behavior, and one on the problems of sexual adjustment within institutions. In addition, these prison populations have augmented our understanding of economically and educationally lower social levels, and of the broken marriages which are in the histories of a high proportion of the penal inmates. Groups from which histories have been secured include:

Central States Association of Parole and Probation Officers
Chicago: City Courts
Chicago: Randall House for Negro Boys
Cleveland: A suburban Court group
Delaware: Kruse School for Negro Girls
Indiana: State Penal Farm
Indiana: State Woman's Prison
Indianapolis: Board of Public Safety
Kansas: State Police
National Association of Superintendents of Women's Correctional Institutions
New York City: Courts
New York City: Florence Crittenton Home
New York City: Police Commissioner
New York State: Woman's Reformatory
Ohio: Bureau of Juvenile Research
Philadelphia: Probation officers
South Bend, Indiana: Courts

Other institutions, neither penal nor correctional, from which individuals have contributed histories include:

Michigan: State Training School (for feeble-minded) at Coldwater
Mishawaka, Indiana: Children's Home
Philadelphia: Salvation Army Home for Children
Philadelphia: Salvation Army Industrial Home
Philadelphia: Salvation Army Home for Unmarried Mothers
Philadelphia: Sheltering Arms, Home for Unmarried Mothers
St. Joseph County, Indiana: Department of Public Welfare

Persons not connected with any kind of institution have been more difficult to contact. Nevertheless, it has been possible to stir up considerable community interest in the study, and friends who tell their friends develop a geometrically expanding network of contacts which ultimately provide a broad sample of any community. The histories of such persons constitute a major source of the data used in this study. Individuals who have contributed histories have been associated with the following social or civic organizations:

American Museum of Natural History: Staff

Church Groups: Bloomington (Indiana), Nicodemus (Kansas), Chicago, Philadelphia, Edinburg (Indiana)

Conscientious Objectors: Philadelphia (3 groups), Bloomington

Family Groups: Philadelphia, New York, Chicago, Bloomington

Hitch-hikers

Homosexual Communities: Chicago, New York, Philadelphia, Indianapolis, St. Louis

Individual Histories: From all the communities in which we have worked

Journalists, Editorial, and Publishing Groups: Philadelphia, New York

Marriage Counseling Groups: New York, Philadelphia, Cleveland, State College (Pennsylvania)

Men's Service Clubs: Elkhart (Indiana)

Negro Lower Level Communities: Chicago, Indianapolis, Gary (Indiana)

Negro Professional and Middle Class Communities: Chicago, Columbus (Ohio), Philadelphia, Gary (Indiana), Hill City (Kansas), Nicodemus (Kansas), Peoria (Illinois)

Nurses' Groups: Philadelphia

N. Y. A.: Bloomington (Indiana)

Parent-Teacher Groups in Private Schools: Chicago, Philadelphia, Wilmington

Parent-Teacher Groups in Public Schools: Anderson (Indiana), Edinburg (Indiana), Philadelphia, Peoria (Illinois)

Physicians' Patients: New York, Chicago, Philadelphia

Probation, Parole, and Court Groups: Philadelphia, Cleveland, Chicago, South Bend (Indiana)

Professional Groups (various): New York, Chicago, Philadelphia

Salvation Army, Staff Workers and Clients: New York, Philadelphia, Chicago

Sex Education Groups: Philadelphia, New York, Cleveland

Social Worker Groups: Philadelphia, New York, Chicago, Southern Indiana, South Bend (Indiana), Cleveland

Travelers on Trains

Underworld Communities: Chicago, Peoria (Illinois), Indianapolis, New York City, Gary (Indiana)

University Woman's Group, AAUW: Wilmington (Delaware)

White, Lower Level Communities: Chicago, Peoria (Illinois)

White, Middle Class, and Upper Level Communities: Chicago, New York, Philadelphia, Bloomington, South Bend, Elkhart (Indiana), Anderson (Indiana)

Wistar Institute, Philadelphia

Y. M. C. A.: Peoria (Illinois), Indianapolis, Elkhart (Indiana)

Y. W. C. A.: Anderson (Indiana), Philadelphia, Chicago

Before undertaking this research, we had known something of people as they appear to their friends and to their neighbors; but now we have had a chance to learn more about them. Understanding something of their satisfactions and heartaches, and the backgrounds of their lives, has increased our sympathetic acceptance of people as they are.

THE TAXONOMIC APPROACH

Since the technique of this research has been taxonomic, a word needs to be said about the taxonomic method.

In Biology. Taxonomy is a development of systematic botany and systematic zoology. Historically, these are the oldest of the biologic sciences. Their original functions were those of naming, describing, and classifying species and the higher categories. Modern taxonomy still has those same functions, but its techniques are very different (Ahlstrom 1937, Crampton 1925, Dice 1932, Dobzhansky 1937, 1941, Erickson 1941, Hile 1937, Hubbs and Miller 1942, Hubbs and Johnson 1943, Huxley 1940, Kinsey 1942, Mayr 1942, Miller 1941). Since the differences between the present study and previous work on human sex behavior are essentially the same as the differences between modern taxonomy and the older systematics, it will be profitable to compare the two.

Modern taxonomy is the product of an increasing awareness among biologists of the uniqueness of individuals, and of the wide range of variation which may occur in any population of individuals. The taxonomist is, therefore, primarily concerned with the measurement of variation in series of individuals which stand as representatives of the species in which he is interested.

In order to have his sample representative the taxonomist must deal with much larger series than the older systematist ever thought of handling. Where the systematist used a single individual or a few individuals as the bases of his description and of his understanding of a species, the taxonomist undertakes population sampling on such a scale as may involve hundreds of individuals from each locality, and tens of thousands of individuals from the species as a whole. If individuals are collected in a fashion which eliminates all bias in their choosing, and in a fashion which includes material from every type of habitat and from the whole range of the species, it should be possible to secure a sample which, after measurement and classification, will indicate the frequency with which each type of variant occurs in each local population, or in the species as a whole. If the sample is adequate, the generalizations should apply not only to the individuals which were actually measured, but to those which were never collected and which were never measured at all. Obviously, the correctness of such an extension of the observed data depends upon the size of the sample, and upon the quality of the sample; and the capacity of the taxonomist is to be measured by the skill he demonstrates in choosing and securing that sample. The next two chapters will contain a description of the techniques by which the material for the present study has been obtained.

Beyond describing the groups involved, the taxonomist may also analyze some of the factors which account for differences between the individuals and between the populations of individuals which he is studying. These analyses depend upon comparisons of groups with backgrounds which are similar, except for some one item which may be identified as the source of the differences between the groups. This is the sort of analysis which an experimentalist makes when he compares an operated and a control group of animals. The experimentalist creates the backgrounds and controls the environmental factors which are the suspected agents of his results. The taxonomist finds the different backgrounds where they are already established in nature and, if his investigation is accurate, can reason as the experimentalist does about causal factors.

Descriptive taxonomy provides an over-all survey; the experimental techniques are better suited to the examination of ultimate details. The taxonomist charts the paths which specialists may subsequently follow. It is the function of the taxonomist to show the magnitude of the whole group which he has studied, so specialists will know how large an order must be satisfied if their generalizations are to apply to any significant portion of that group.

In Applied and Social Sciences. Medicine, psychiatry, psychology, sociology, economics, anthropology, and the other social sciences are, after all, faced with the same problems which have confronted biologists in their attempts to describe and classify basic phenomena. They, similarly, need to secure such an over-all understanding of their one, highly variable animal, the human, as will "show the magnitude of the whole group" and make it clear "how large an order must be satisfied if their generalizations are to apply to any significant portion of that group."

Unfortunately, it has not always been realized that problems in social fields involve the understanding of a whole species. Much of the publication in these fields is concerned with observations on a few individuals from whom generalizations are too often extended to any and to all other segments of the population. Observations on children, on senescent adults, on social groups, on gangs, or on whole towns are usually observations on *particular* groups, although they are presented as typical of life in all of America. Even when the data are experimentally derived, as in medicine and more recently in psychology, the problem of understanding the whole of the human species is still present. Experiments, whether operations, drug injections, physiologic tests, or psychologic manipulations, are usually limited to a few individuals when, in actuality, they should include persons of both sexes, of all ages, and from all sorts of socio-economic, educational, and religious backgrounds, if the conclusions are to be applied to the human species in general.

College students, of college age, mostly from middle-class and urban homes—often with the sex unrecorded—are the subjects for a high proportion of the observations and experiments of academic investigators. No caution is given the reader that individuals of other ages, with different educational backgrounds and different social origins, might react differently to the same sorts of experimental situations. Even among psychologists, the apparatus used in the experiment may be chosen with more care than the human subjects of the investigation.

In the medical, psychologic, and social sciences, there are a number of studies of single individuals who are described in elaborate detail (*e.g.*, Allport 1942, Blos 1941, Brown 1937, Carlson 1941, Conwell 1937, Hillyer 1927, Hoopes 1939, "Inmate" 1932, Johnson 1930, Judge Baker Fnd. 1922, Karpman 1935, 1944, Kellogg 1933, Prince 1905, Rogers 1942, Shaw 1930, Thomas and Znaniecki 1918–1920, Wright 1945). It is implied that the observations or the therapeutic techniques used in the one case are applicable to other individuals in the general population. Psychiatrists and psychoanalysts have been particularly involved in such publication, and the anthropologists have led in this field (*e.g.*, Barton 1938, Beers 1908, Dyk 1938, Ford 1941, Hatt 1931, Landes 1938, Linderman 1930, 1932, McGraw 1935, Radin 1920, 1926, Simmons 1942, Spott and Kroeber 1942, Underhill 1936, Washbourne 1940, etc.). The idea is old. Linnaeus extolled the lone moss which was worth a life-time of study, and Tennyson thought of the flower in the crannied wall as the key to the secrets of the universe. Such detailed studies of single individuals have often represented a certain high degree of industry and scholarship, but they are dangerous as sources of generalizations about larger segments of the population. Like descriptive systematics at its worst, such detailed studies of individual cases are the antitheses of analyses based on large and statistically well selected samples of the sort the modern taxonomist employs.

There are sociologic studies (*e.g.*, Burgess and Cottrell 1939), which appear statistical because they carefully define the group which was studied without, however, making any effort to select a sample which would be homogeneous and representative of any larger portion of the total population. Obviously, conclusions based on such studies are applicable only to the particular sample which was available to the particular investigator, and it is practically certain that no one will ever again meet, at any other time, in any other place, another group of persons similarly constituted.

Sometimes social scientists hobnob as tourists in some social milieu sufficiently removed from their own to make it possible for them to acquire "impressions" and "hunches" about "social patterns" and "motivations of behavior" in whole cultures. This method has the merit of requiring a minimum of time—much less than the public opinion polls or the taxonomists need for arriving at their generalizations. Nevertheless, to some students the day seems overdue when scientists studying human material will forsake barbershop techniques and attempt to secure some taxonomic understanding of the human population.

Some persons are appalled at the idea of having to undertake a large-scale coverage of thousands of individual cases before they are allowed to generalize about the whole. Contacts with the statistics of small samples have provided rationalizations for some of this inertia; but no statistical techniques can make a small sample represent any type of individual which was not present in the original body of data.

In the past dozen years, economic surveys, agricultural surveys, the public opinion polls, and a research group in the Census Bureau (McNemar 1940, 1946, Gallup and Rae 1940, Blankenship 1943, Gallup 1944, Cantril 1944) have shown the way in which a human population must be analyzed before there can be any understanding of any large segment of that population. Developed without benefit of the biologists' experience with taxonomy, the public opinion techniques are, nevertheless, an illustration of taxonomic procedure. During the recent war, problems of sampling in the field of social problems received increased attention from the statisticians and the biostatisticians. Public health surveys are now utilizing modern methods of sampling. With increasing frequency the business world has learned to depend upon analyses of consumer reactions in the commercial field. The predictions in such surveys usually lie within 1 to 5 per cent of the subsequent performance (Katz 1941, Gallup 1944). In contrast, we should guess that many of the generalizations coming from the traditional studies in the social sciences might prove erroneous in something between 20 and 90 per cent of the cases, if one attempted to apply them to any considerable portion of the population. It is unfortunate that the products of academic studies are not more often put to the dollars and cents tests which have provided the incentives for increasingly better techniques in economic and public opinion surveying.

Statistical Basis. Modern taxonomy is statistical in its approach. In many quarters there is an honest distrust of sampling techniques because there is a distrust of all statistical procedures. There is a widespread feeling that statistics are cold and that they cannot measure human emotions which, after all, are involved in all sexual activities as well as in many other human problems. It is objected that statistics can deal with incidences and frequencies and provide means for calculating average individuals, but that average individuals do not really exist, and that measurements of such hypothetic individuals provide no insight into the particular persons with whom the clinician must deal. Such objections involve, however, a misunderstanding of the utility of a statistical approach. It is, precisely, the function of a population analysis **to help in the understanding of particular individuals by showing their relation to the remainder of the group.** Given the range of variation, the mode, the mean, the median, and the shape of the frequency distribution for the whole group, the clinician can determine the averageness or uniqueness of any particular person, and comprehend the extent to which generalizations developed for the whole group may be applied to any particular case (see Clinical Tables, Chapter 23). Without such a background, each individual becomes unique and unexplainable except through an elaborate investigation of him as an isolated entity. On the other hand, if there are adequate data on the group, a major portion of the work involved in understanding a particular individual is thereby eliminated, even though it is true that he may still be so unique that he will need some special study.

The possession of some "statistical sense" would seem to be a fundamental requirement for anyone attempting to investigate any species, including the human. By "statistical sense" we refer to one's capacity to distinguish the specific from the universal and to recognize the difference between a phenomenon which is common and one which is rare. One shows a statistical sense when he is interested in knowing how often a particular thing is true, and how often something different might be so—in short, what the incidence of each variant is in the population as a whole. The investigator who is satisfied to report a single set of observations is lacking in a statistical sense. The clinician who has made a dozen tests of a particular therapeutic technique, and reports them as though they were applicable to anybody and everybody, is no scientist, for he lacks a statistical sense. Every scientist needs to cultivate his ability to distinguish between facts that are known to be true only for particular individuals, and facts which are known in such variety, for so many different kinds of individuals, that they may be added up to an understanding of a whole population.

The present study should provide an instance of the taxonomic method applied to a problem that lies primarily in the field of human behavior and sociology. If the results of this investigation seem significant, the study will have been justified not only because of its findings but, what may prove to be of as much import, because of its demonstration of a method that can be used in other fields of research on human problems.

STATUS OF PREVIOUS SEX STUDIES

Although we have said that scientists have largely avoided investigations of human sexuality, leaving this one of the most poorly explored fields in biology, psychology, or sociology, it should be emphasized that there is no aspect of human behavior about which there has been more thought, more talk, and more books written. From the dawn of human history, from the drawings left by primitive peoples, on through the developments of all civilizations, ancient, classic, Oriental, medieval, and modern, men have left a record of their sexual activities and their thinking about sex. The printed literature is tremendous, and the other material is inexhaustible. For bulk, the literature cannot be surpassed in many other fields; for scholarship, esthetic merit, or scientific validity it is of such mixed quality that it is difficult to separate the kernel from the chaff, and still more difficult to maintain any perspective during its perusal. It is, at once, an interesting reflection of man's absorbing interest in sex, and his astounding ignorance of it; his desire to know and his unwillingness to face the facts; his respect for an objective, scientific approach to the problems involved, and his overwhelming urge to be poetic, pornographic, literary, philosophic, traditional, and moral. Fortunately the scientific observer is not called upon to judge the merits of these diverse and contradictory approaches. All of them give evidence of what people think and do sexually, and that is sufficient to make them scientifically significant.

The data on most physiologic functions of the human animal are, for the most part, to be found in the scientific treatises and journal articles published by physiologists. In contrast, the data on sex are spread through every field of history, literature, art, science, the social sciences, philosophy, religion, and the academically not respectable but still important materials of pornography. These last, as any archeologist or anthropologist well knows, may be of considerable importance in the interpretation of a human culture. There is a surprisingly large body of unpublished manuscript material in this field. A sex library, and any scholarly review of it, would have to cover material drawn from practically all of the following fields:

Biology
    Anatomy
    Embryology
    Physiology
    Endocrinology
    Genetics
    Taxonomic method
    Human evolution
    Biostatistics
Psychology
    General
    Experimental
    Clinical
    Abnormal
    Social
    Child and adolescent
    Comparative (anthropoids and lower
        mammals)
Sociology
    General
    Criminology
    Penology
    Special problems
    Marriage and the family
Anthropology
    Cultural
    Physical
    Ethnography
    Archeology
    Classical
Medicine
    Obstetrics
    Gynecology
    Pediatrics
    Clinical endocrinology
    Urology
    Fertility and sterility

Contraception
    Pharmacology
    Public health
    Hygiene
    Social hygiene
    Psychiatry
    Psychoanalysis
Marriage Counseling
    Modern marriage manuals
    Classic manuals
Child Development
Personnel Programs
Public Opinion Surveying
Radio Programs
Philosophy
    Ethics
Religion
    Creeds
    Moral philosophy
    Sex cults
    History of religions
Education
    Child development
    Sex education
History
Law
    Legal procedure
    Criminal law
    Marriage law
    Paternity law
    History of law
Law Enforcement
    Police
    Parole and probation
    Censorship
    Military law
    Institutional management

Literature
    Fiction
    Essays
    Poetry
    Classical, of all cultures
    Biographies
    Travel
    Drama
    Journalistic, newspapers and magazines
    Propaganda
    Songs and ballads
    Folklore
    Linguistics
    Slangs and argots
Arts
    Graphic
    Sculpture
    Photography
    Moving pictures
    Music
    Dance
    Stage
Erotica, of Modern, Medieval, Classic, and Ancient Cultures
    Nude art
    Sculpture
    Art models
    Photographic materials
    Amateur drawings, stories, etc.
    Diaries

Cartoons
Moving pictures
China and pottery
Utensils
Household implements
Architectural designs
Symbolism
Music
    Songs and ballads
    Limericks
Wall inscriptions
Vocabularies
Literature
    Heterosexual
    Homosexual
    Flagellation, sadism, masochism
    Torture
    Religious persecution
    Corporal punishment
    Pseudo-psychologic
    Pseudo-anthropologic
    Love story magazines
    True confession magazines
    Physical culture magazines
    Nudist magazines
    Fetish magazines
    Scandal sheets
    Advertising materials
Fetishistic objects
Materials on sex cults

Obviously, it is impossible in any single volume to summarize the information contained in as diverse a body of material as is outlined above. Since the present volume is a taxonomic study of the frequencies and sources of sexual outlet among American males, we shall confine our review to those previous American studies which are (1) scientific, (2) based on more or less complete case histories, (3) based on series of at least some size, (4) involving a systematic coverage of approximately the same items on each subject, and (5) statistical in treatment. Many other studies which are not taxonomic have been important for comparison with our data, and they are cited throughout the present volume and listed in the Bibliography at the end of this book. There are only 19 studies of sex behavior (23 titles) which are in any sense taxonomic. They are:

1. Achilles, P. S. 1923. The effectiveness of certain social hygiene literature. New York, Amer. Soc. Hyg. Assoc., pp. 116.

    A group-administered questionnaire study of 1449 males and 483 females, made by a psychologist. All of the subjects were from the New York City area, including high school and college students and some lower middle-class and lower level groups, mostly of younger individuals, with a few of them Negro. The study was primarily concerned with the effectiveness of certain social hygiene literature in disseminating information about venereal disease, but some of the questions concerned the sex experiences of the subjects. The population is broader than in most studies, but not broken up into homogeneous groups for analyses. The conclusions, therefore, are not applicable to the whole American population, nor to any particular segment of it. The data are merely tabulated.

2. Bromley, D. D., and Britten, F. H. 1938. Youth and sex. A study of 1300 college students. New York and London, Harper and Bros., pp. XIII + 303.

A questionnaire and interview study of 1364 college students, made by two women with journalistic backgrounds. Forty-three per cent of the subjects were male, 57 per cent female. Questionnaires were filled out by students attending 46 colleges, spread throughout the United States, and the authors visited 15 colleges to supplement their questionnaires with partial and not so complete interviews. The contributors may have represented a somewhat select portion of each student body: only one-fifth of the questionnaires which were distributed were filled in, and no device was used to assure a good sample. The statistical treatment of the data is scant, arriving at totals and averages, with no breakdown of the sample for correlations. The data on petting and pre-marital intercourse agree fairly well with our own for college groups. On the other hand, the authors' suggestion (p. 27) that the conclusions may be safely transferred to the non-college segments of the population, because college students are the leaders and set the behavior patterns for the rest of the population, is incorrect (Chapter 10 in present volume). The males in the study evidently balked at telling the women investigators about their masturbatory and homosexual experiences, for the incidence figures on those points are lower than in any other published investigation.

3. Davis, K. B. 1929. Factors in the sex life of twenty-two hundred women. New York and London, Harper and Bros., pp. XX + 430.

A questionnaire study made by an experienced social worker and her collaborators, located in the New York City area. The 2200 women subjects represented the select segment which answered a questionnaire that was originally mailed to 20,000 persons. The sample was confined to "normal" women of good standing in their communities, most of them being college and club women. A high percentage of them were graduates of Eastern women's colleges. The ages ranged mostly between 25 and 55. Many of the women were teachers. The sample was, therefore, not broad, but neither was it strictly held to the group which was best represented in the study. Only a portion of the life history was covered. The treatment of the data is simple but statistical.

4. Dickinson, R. L., and Beam, L. 1931. A thousand marriages. Baltimore, Williams and Wilkins Co., pp. XXV + 482.
Dickinson, R. L., and Beam, L. 1934. The single woman. Baltimore, Williams and Wilkins Co., pp. XIX + 469.

Studies based on a gynecologist's half century of experience in private practice, dealing with over 5000 female patients from the New York City area. Publications of the National Committee on Maternal Health. The findings of the physical examinations are systematic, particularly as brought together in the same author's Human Sex Anatomy (1933, Baltimore, Williams and Wilkins Co., pp. XIII + 145 + 175 figs.). The data on sexual behavior vary from fairly complete life histories to single items. Most of the women came from middle-class or upper level homes. All age groups (except children) were included; and some of the cases were followed for scores of years. These pioneer studies have had considerable influence on later work, particularly among physicians, gynecologists, marriage counselors, students of fertility, and other clinical groups. There are only occasional tabulations of data, and the calculations of averages are sometimes inaccurate. There is no selection of the sample, and there are no analyses of the populations on which the various tabulations are based. The findings, therefore, cannot be transferred to other segments of the population.

5. Exner, M. J. 1915. Problems and principles of sex education. A study of 948 college men. New York, Association Press, pp. 39.

Apparently the pioneer attempt to secure statistical data on American sexual behavior. The author, a physician, was secretary of the Student Department of the

International Committee of the Y.M.C.A. A questionnaire study in which part of the questionnaires were group administered and part sent by mail. Answers were secured on a limited number of questions from 948 male students in colleges scattered widely over the United States. The treatment is simple tabulation. Since the population is homogeneously college male, the data should have been significant; but because of the inadequacies of questionnaires the incidence figures for various sexual activities are much too low. The most notable aspect of the study was the "100 per cent" sample secured by getting records from every one of the 673 males in a series of groups, this series providing material for comparison with the data secured from those in the remainder of the sample.

6. Finger, F. W. 1947. Sex beliefs and practices among male college students. J. Abn. Soc. Psych. 42:57–67.

An interesting and profitable questionnaire study of 111 males, all of whom were college students in three successive classes in advanced psychology. The author, as the instructor in the course, had previously given lectures to the group on psychological processes in general and on emotional behavior and on certain aspects of sex behavior in particular. All but ten of the subjects were premedical students. The group, in consequence, was uniquely prepared for cooperating in such a study, and this vitiates the author's contention that his results justify questionnaire studies as against more costly personal interview studies. It is probable that the same methods applied to college students who did not have such a preparation in biology and psychology would not have given comparable results, and the method would have been quite unworkable with most of the population that never goes to college. Of the 138 students to whom questionnaires were given, 111 (81%) made returns. Sixty of the students were given a duplicate questionnaire to fill out nine days later in an attempt to test the validity of the data. The study is unique among previous surveys of American sexual behavior in securing data on the incidence of the homosexual which are comparable to those reported in the present volume. Similarly, the data on masturbation and on heterosexual coitus compare well with those obtained by other investigators in this field. Since the population was homogeneous in its sex, its racial constitution, its age, marital status, and educational level, the data may be taken as indicative of what can be expected from similar groups.

7. Hamilton, G. V. 1929. A research in marriage. New York, A. and C. Boni, pp. XIII + 570.
Hamilton, G. V., and MacGowan, K. 1929. What is wrong with marriage. New York, A. and C. Boni, pp. XXI + 319.

A formalized interview study by a New York City psychiatrist whose earlier research experience had included studies of sexual behavior among apes. The project was undertaken at the suggestion and with the support of the National Research Council's Committee for Research on Problems of Sex. The study was based on 100 married females and 100 married males. Of this number 55 couples represented pairs of spouses, but no correlations of data were made on these pairs. The population was not selected to represent any particular segment of society, and its constitution is not even described in the original report. Nearly all of the subjects were college graduates, most of them nearer 30 and under 40 years of age, most of them the psychiatrist's patients or their friends, and most of them from the New York City area. An undue number (21%) of the subjects had been upset enough to have needed psychiatric help prior to their participation in the study. The data were obtained by personal "interviews" where the questions were typed on a card and handed without further discussion to the subject. The subject gave his answers orally, and they were recorded verbatim, without further questioning from the interviewer. There was considerable attention given to standardizing the questions and the interview, but none to standardizing the population, apparently on the assumption that if one standardizes one end of an experiment it does not matter what one throws in at the other end. The treatment involved simple tabulation and comparisons of male and female data. The small size of the sample also limits its usefulness, but there is a definitely systematic coverage of a large number of sexual items. The findings more or less match our own for white, married, college-bred, urban males between 30 and 35 years of age.

8. Hohman, L. B. and Schaffner, B. 1947. The sex life of unmarried men. Amer. J. Soc. 52: 501–507.

A study made by two psychiatrists on the basis of the interviews which they had with 4600 selectees at induction centers in New York City, upper New York State, and Baltimore during the recent war. Because of the very limited time available for each interview, the questions were few and, as pointed out in the report, not always well framed. The age, marital status, religious connections, educational level, and economic status of each individual were secured and the data on sexual activity were correlated with these background factors. A chief source of error was the fact that only two-way correlations were made. The data on the sexual activities of the several religious groups, for instance, probably would have led to different conclusions if the comparisons had been confined to persons of the same educational level, and if the devoutness of the religious connections had been taken into account. In all the other comparisons the results are badly distorted by the failure to take educational levels into account. The statements made concerning the Negroes are unwarranted, for that reason. The data on pre-marital intercourse are misleading because they represent ogives instead of the accumulative incidence curves (Chapter 3) that are needed to reach the conclusions which the authors are trying to make here. At several points (*e.g.*, in regard to the Negro histories, in regard to the high incidence of masturbation among adult males, etc.) the authors' own subjective responses become evident. They arrive at an incidence figure for the homosexual, as they define it, of 0.36 per cent and express the opinion that this figure is reliable "because we were specifically instructed by mobilization medical standards to exclude homosexuals." They seem to have no realization of the fact that the conditions under which three- to five-minute interviews were held in army induction centers were not conducive to winning admissions of socially taboo behavior, especially when the men had been informed beforehand that they would be punished by being excluded from the Armed Forces if they did admit such behavior. For our own data on the incidence of the homosexual in the sort of group which was involved here, see Chapter 21.

9. Hughes, W. L. 1926. Sex experiences of boyhood. J. Soc. Hyg. 12:262–273.

A group-administered questionnaire study of 1029 presumably unmarried males ranging for the most part between 15 and 20 years of age. The author was a biologist serving as a state health officer in North Carolina, and the sample represented a fair cross-section of both rural and urban populations of boys in high school, in grade school, and in employment in the mills of that state. Some comparisons of high school and mill boys were made with the caution that the sample was too small to warrant extended conclusions. Thus the set-up of the analyses was better than usual, but the dependence on the questionnaire was not good, and the choice of the questions was totally inadequate. Masturbation and nocturnal emissions were the only two, out of six possible sources of outlet, which were investigated; and at every point the study is loaded with moral evaluations (*e.g.*, "Has anyone ever tried to give you the mistaken idea that sex intercourse is necessary for the health of the young man?").

10. Landis, C., et al. 1940. Sex in development. A study of the growth and development of the emotional and sexual aspects of personality together with physiological, anatomical, and medical information on a group of 153 normal women and 142 female psychiatric patients. New York and London, Paul B. Hoeber, pp. XX + 329.

A study of approximately 300 females, personally interviewed by Mrs. Agnes T. Landis, the interviews standardized with formal questions which were carefully worded on the interviewing sheets. The study was supported by the National Research Council's Committee for Research on Problems of Sex. Approximately half of the sample was drawn from patients at the New York State Psychiatric

Institute and Hospital; the other half was obtained largely from a Y.W.C.A. and a Y.W.H.A. group. The ages lay between 18 and 25 years in 54 per cent of the sample; 54 per cent of the girls were Jewish, and 71 per cent had gone into high school but not beyond. The sample was largely from a particular sort of group but, unfortunately, it was not strictly confined to that group. The conclusions, consequently, are not transferable to the population as a whole, nor to a particular age, educational level, or religious group. After the breakdown for analyses, many of the ultimate groups contained only one or two to half a dozen individuals, and the statistical treatment is more elaborate than such small samples warrant. Practical experience shows that an additional three or four cases, or a dozen additional cases added to such small groups could have changed the conclusions which were drawn from such small samples.

11. Landis, C., and Bolles, M. M. 1942. Personality and sexuality of the physically handicapped woman. New York and London, Paul B. Hoeber, pp. XII + 171.

An interview study of 100 handicapped females (spastics, orthopedics, cardiacs, and epileptics), interviewed in the same way as in the previous study (Landis 1940), the interviewing done by Dr. Marjorie Bolles. The study was supported by the National Research Council's Committee for Research on Problems of Sex. The sample was drawn from a group of New York City institutions; most of the girls were between 18 and 25 years of age; half of them were Catholic. The statistical treatment is too detailed and open to much the same objections as in the previous Landis study (*q.v.* above).

12. Merrill, L. 1918. A summary of findings in a study of sexualism among a group of one hundred delinquent boys. J. Juv. Res. 3:255–267.

Data gathered by a probation officer who interviewed a hundred boys who were passing through a Juvenile Court in Seattle. The boys ranged in age between 8 and 18, and most of them probably came from lower social levels, as most court cases do. It is unfortunate that the social backgrounds were not held constant for the studied group, so the conclusions could have been utilized with more certainty. It is not entirely clear how systematically the sex items were covered on each history. The study is notable because it published the most definite record of pre-adolescent orgasm (for 6 boys in self masturbation), and gave the highest recorded incidence figures (31%) for younger boys involved with oral techniques in homosexual contacts. On both of these points, our own data substantiate those given by Merrill.

13. Pearl, R. 1925. The biology of population growth. New York, Alfred A. Knopf, pp. XIV + 260 (especially pp. 178–207).

A nicely analyzed study by a biostatistician using hospital data on 257 older, married, white males, most of them over 55 years of age. They had all undergone prostatic operation. Mailed questionnaires brought the information on frequencies of marital intercourse, which are the only sexual data actually given. The subjects may have come from the Baltimore area, or from elsewhere. The population is analyzed with a simultaneous age and occupational breakdown, which is instructive. On the whole, the samples in each ultimate breakdown are too small, but the age trends seem correct. Unfortunately, educational levels were not used in the calculations, and our present data show that Pearl's comparisons of rural and urban histories would have led to totally different conclusions if he had taken educational levels into account.

14. Peck, M. W., and Wells, F. L. 1923. On the psycho-sexuality of college graduate men. Ment. Hyg. 7:697–714.
Peck, M. W., and Wells, F. L. 1925. Further studies in the psycho-sexuality of college graduate men. Ment. Hyg. 9:502–520.

A directed questionnaire study of about 550 men with college backgrounds, the study made by a psychiatrist and a psychologist, with support from the National Research Council's Committee for Research on Problems of Sex. The study was made in the Boston area. Most of the subjects were between 21 and 30 years of age.

PUBLISHED STUDIES ON SEX

AUTHOR	BACKGROUND OF AUTHOR	NATURE OF INTERVIEW	GEOGRAPHIC ORIGIN	SIZE OF SAMPLE			CHIEF SOURCES	ITEMS COVERED (% of questions in present study)	BREAKDOWN OF SAMPLE	VALID TO EXTEND GENERALIZATION TO
				Male	Female	Total				
Exner 1915	Physician, YMCA	Qst'naire, group admst. and mailed	U. S., wide	948	0	948	College students	8 = 1.5%	None	Male college students
Merrill 1918	Probation Officer	Interview	Seattle	100	0	100	Juvenile delinquents, one court	Not recorded	None	None
Achilles 1923	Psychology	Qst'naire, group admst.	N. Y. C. area	1449	483	1932	YMCA, YWCA, Grade, H. S., College students	35 = 5.8%	None	None
Peck-Wells 1923, 1925	Psychiatry, Psychology	Qst'naire, directed	Boston area	550	0	550	College grad. group	32 = 6.1%	None	Coll. males under 30 yrs
Pearl 1925	Biology	Qst'naire, mailed; clin. records	Baltimore, etc.	257	0	257	Married hsptl. patients, prostate operations	?15 = 2.9%	Age, occupat.	None
Hughes 1926	Public Health	Qst'naire, group admst.	N. C.	1029	0	1029	H. S., grade school, mill workers	?25 = 4.8%	±Occupat.	None
Davis 1929	Social Work	Qst'naire, mailed	Northeast U. S., etc.	0	2200	2200	College alumnae, club lists	54 = 10.0%	None	None
Hamilton 1929	Psychiatry	Interview, directed	N. Y. C. area	100	100	200	Psychiatrist's patients, their friends	100 = 19.2%	Sex	None
Dickinson-Beam 1931, 1934	Gynecology	Interview, guided	N. Y. C. area	0	1448	1448	Gynecologist's patients	Usually limited	None	None
Taylor 1933	Psychology	Interview, guided	Mass., eastern	40	0	40	College students	13 = 2.5%	None	Doubtful for college males

Study	Field	Method	Location	Male	Female	Total	Population	N = %	Factors	Remarks
Strakosch 1934 —	Psychology	Clin. records	N. Y. C. area	0	700	700	State Psychiat. Hsptl.	18 = 3.5%	None	None
Bromley-Britten 1938	Journalism	Qst'naire, & partial interview	U. S, wide	592	772	1364	Students in 46 Colleges (+15?)	40 = 7.7%	Sex	Male and female college students
Terman 1938	Psychology	Qst'naire, group admst.	Calif., wide	1242	1242	2484	Marriage councils, clubs, college level, etc.	49 = 9.4%	Sex, age, occupat.	None
Peterson 1938	Education	Qst'naire, directed	Mid-West, Rocky Mt.	419	0	419	College students	28 = 5.4%	None	Male college students
Landis 1940	Psychology	Interview, directed	N. Y. C. area	0	295	295	State Psychiat. Hsptl, YWCA, YWHA	116 = 22.3%	Normal, psychiatric	None
Landis-Bolles 1942	Psychology	Interview, directed	N. Y. C. area	0	100	100	State Psychiat. Hsptl.	116 = 22.3%	None	None
Ramsey 1943	Psychology	Interview, guided	City in Illinois	291	0	291	Junior High School, YMCA, Boys' Clubs	218 = 41.9%	Age, adol.	Mid West urban white males of Jr. H. S. age
Finger 1947	Psychology	Qst'naire, directed	Virginia	111	0	111	College students	9 = 1.7%	None	Male college students
Hohman-Schaffner 1947	Psychiatrists	Interview	N. Y., Baltimore	4600	0	4600	Army inductees, all social levels	17 = 3.3%	Age, race, marital status, educ.level, relig., rural-urban	None
Kinsey-Pomeroy-Martin 1948	Biology, Psychology	Interview, guided	U. S., wide, esp. Mass. to Kans.	6200	5800	12,000	All social levels	521 = 100%	Sex, race, marital status, age, age at adol., educ., occupat. of subject, parents, rural-urban, religion	163 groups on which data are given

Table 1. Analyses of published studies on sex

Arranged chronologically.

29

The treatment was simple tabulation with no breakdown of the population; but since the study was confined to the one sort of group the generalizations may be extended to other college groups with a minimum possibility of error. The sex questions were limited to about 30 items, but as far as they go, the findings are close to those obtained in our own study. The second part of the study was expanded with about 80 more questions concerning the personality traits of the subjects, their recreational interests, etc.; but this added nothing to an understanding of the sexual data in the study.

15. Peterson, K. M. 1938. Early sex information and its influence on later sex concepts. Unpublished manuscript in Library of University of Colo., pp. 136.

A supervised questionnaire survey of 419 males who were still in college. The geographic locations of the colleges are not mentioned, but they were probably in Middle Western and Rocky Mountain areas. There is a simple tabulation of the data, most of which concern sex education, but there is some valuable information on adolescent developments and on later, overt experiences in sex. Some of the data were subsequently used in Kirkendall's volume on Sex Adjustments of Young Men (Kirkendall 1940). Since the population was uniformly male, of college level, and of college age, the data are transferable to other college male groups. The results, however, are not sufficient, because of the relative ineffectiveness of questionnaire studies.

16. Ramsey, G. V. 1943. The sex information of younger boys. Amer. J. Orthopsy- chiatry 13:347–352.
 Ramsey, G. V. 1943. The sexual development of boys. Amer. J. Psych. 56:217–23 4

Studies of 291 pre-adolescent and younger adolescent males, representing all of the boys (and some others) in a seventh and eighth grade group in a medium-large city in Illinois. Based on personal interviews which were coordinated with the list of questions and the techniques of the present study. The study is particularly valuable because of the age period covered, and further significant because of its hundred percent sample. The conclusions are not extensible to other groups of particular social levels, but the unselected sample is probably an approximation to the sort of group that occurs in any middle class junior high school in a medium- large city of the Middle West.

17. Strakosch, F. M. 1934. Factors in the sex life of seven hundred psychopathic women. Utica, N. Y., State Hospitals Press, pp. 102.

A doctor's thesis in psychology, based on the accumulated case history records in the New York State Psychiatric Institute and Hospital, in New York City. The data had been gathered by a number of psychiatrists, with possible variations in standards of recording. All of the 700 women were psychopathic. They represented a wide range of ages, and a variety of educational and social levels. There are tab- ulations and some simple but sometimes erroneous statistical treatments of the data, and comparisons of each item with similar calculations in the studies by Davis (1929), Hamilton (1929), and Dickinson and Beam (1931, 1934). These com- parisons are intended to show the similarities and differences between psychopathic and normal women. However, all of the other studies dealt with populations that were from more or less exclusively upper educational and social levels, and the Strakosch sample came from such different social levels that all comparisons in this study are invalid (see Chapter 10).

18. Taylor, W. S. 1933. A critique of sublimation in males: A study of 40 superior single men. Genet. Psych. Monogr. 13 (1):1–115.

The sample is fairly homogeneous. It is made up of single males, mostly between 21 and 30 years of age, who were for the most part superior graduate students from universities in Eastern Massachusetts. Because of the uniformity of the population, the results are better than such a small sample might be expected to give. The incidence and frequency data are tabulated and totalled, without further statistical analyses.

19. Terman, L. M., et al. 1938. Psychological factors in marital happiness. New York and London, McGraw Hill Book Co., pp. XIV + 474.

A group-administered questionnaire study of 2484 subjects representing nearly 1250 pairs of spouses. The study was made by a psychological group, supported by the National Research Council's Committee for Research on Problems of Sex. Most of the study was concerned with questions of personality and marital happiness, but there are data on pre-marital intercourse and on marital intercourse. The population came from various occupational groups, but chiefly from professional and semi-professional classes. Seventy-one per cent of the sample had gone to college; the mean age was near 39 years; the subjects came from various areas in California. The statistical treatment is better than in most studies, because the data are analyzed by age and by occupational class, although not simultaneously for the two factors because the populations were not large enough to warrant such a breakdown. The data would have been more reliable if they had been obtained by direct interviewing, and the conclusions would have been totally different at certain points if the analyses had been confined to particular educational levels.

In summarizing the taxonomic validity of the 19 studies reviewed above it is to be noted that:

1. The previous investigators of American sexual behavior have been, variously: Psychologists (in 9 cases), psychiatrists (in 4 cases), journalists (2 persons), a gynecologist, biologists (in 2 cases), a student of education, a public health officer, a social worker, a probation officer, and a physician who was an officer in the Y.M.C.A. The statistically most useful work has come from the two journalists (Bromley and Britten), the Y.M.C.A.'s physician (Exner), a psychiatrist (Peck), four psychologists (Ramsey, Finger, Taylor, and Wells), and the student of education (Peterson). Other studies have not been as sound because of the mixed or otherwise inadequate nature of the populations on which the generalizations were based.

2. The techniques of the studies have been questionnaire in 10 cases, and the examination of clinical records in 1 case. Gynecological examinations have been made in 2 studies. In less than half (8) of the cases has the investigator actually faced his subjects in actual interview, but in only 4 of the studies (Dickinson, Merrill, Ramsey, and Taylor) has the interviewer abandoned the limits of pre-formed questions and stilted formalities and talked as friends talk to friends (Chapter 2). The most serious error in these studies has been the wide use of questionnaires. They are used because they are easier to administer, and they save time. When distributed to a group of persons who simultaneously fill out the answers after they are brought together in a lecture room, a Y.M.C.A. gathering, or an Army mess hall, the investigator or his associates can secure a couple of hundred histories in the same amount of time that another person, using a personal interview technique, needs to contact, win, and secure a single history. However, the differences in values of the two techniques, especially when applied to a socially taboo subject like sex, more than justify the extra time and expense that go into an interview (Chapter 2).

3. More than a third (7) of the studies were based on material from the New York City area, and 5 others came from nearby points in the eastern United States. Our own data indicate that New York, in its sexual pattern, is one of the unique cities in the country; and, in spite of its importance, it does not give a picture which is typical of the United States as a whole. Three of the studies on college students (Bromley and Britten, Exner, and Peterson, all of them questionnaire studies) were the only ones which drew data from any wide area over the country.

4. Males and females have figured about equally in the published studies. In 10 cases only males were investigated; in 5 cases, only females; in 4 cases, both males and females. The sex distribution is fairly good, but there are few comparisons of the two sexes.

5. The previous studies were based wholly or primarily on individuals of college level in 10 of the 19 cases. In 6 studies most of the subjects belonged to groups that had not gone beyond high school, and in no study was the sample distributed through large portions of the population. In this field, as in many others, many of the studies have been "so limited by the campus-bound inertia of research that generalizations have tended to hold only for college students, rather than for man in general" (McNemar 1946). This has been particularly disastrous in considering questions of sexual behavior, for we now know (see later chapters) that different age groups, persons who stop their education at different levels, and persons from different social or occupational classes have very different sexual patterns, involving in some groups participation in certain types of activities with frequencies that may be 10 or 20 times higher than the frequencies in other portions of the population.

6. The number of questions asked in the various studies has varied from 8 in the earliest instance (Exner 1915) to 147 in the Hamilton study (1929). There were 218 in the Ramsey study (1943) which was coordinated with our own. There are 521 items which are systematically covered on each of the histories in the present study (Chapter 3). In the earlier studies there is evidence of a considerable hesitancy to ask direct questions about sex. The interviewer is evidently embarrassed, substitutes euphemisms, and completely avoids whole chapters of possible activity. In our own experience, direct questions on sex, asked as simply as questions about age, place of birth, etc., are answered as simply as they are asked, and get more honest answers. Either average men and women or the scientists have become more scientific in the thirty years that have elapsed since American sex surveys were first undertaken.

7. The size of the sample necessary for statistically sound generalizations depends on the variability of the phenomenon under investigation and the homogeneity of the population in respect to the factors which effect that variation. We have indicated that pragmatic tests show that about 300

cases are desirable for a sample in a group that is homogeneous for sex, age, educational level, and the various other factors (Chapter 3). The total number of cases gathered in most of the previously published studies falls above these minima, and seems impressive until it is realized that only five of the studies (Bromley and Britten, Exner, Finger, Peck and Wells, Peterson) were restricted to populations which were homogeneous for three or more of the factors listed above.

8. The possibility of extending the conclusions reached in any investigation is, after all, the chief excuse for doing research. A mastery of the realities of the universe, or of any particular corner of it, depends upon the capacity to find over-all formulae, over-all descriptions which will apply to the whole or to some appreciable portion of the whole. There is no use in studying particular rats or mice or men if one has to believe that information gained thereby will never again be of use, because one will never again meet exactly the same kinds of rats or mice or men. There is no use in tabulating and totalling and calculating means and other fine figures about the sexual doings of particular people who go to a clinic or to an office, or who fill out a questionnaire, if such calculations and totals give no reliable notion of what the next group is doing, because the next group is too different from the sample which was studied. One may, as Hamilton did (1929:8–9), disclaim any interest in even trying to get a sample that would be representative of any other group, and insist that one is simply studying a particular two hundred persons because of a "desire to obtain as many comparable case records as possible and a desire to make of each case record a comprehensive list of significant facts about the individuals under examination"; but no one is fooled, not even if it is a psychiatrist who tries to rationalize away the objectors which his conscience anticipates there will be among his "survey-minded readers." The book is entitled "A Research in Marriage" and there is no indication that it is supposed to end up as a study of the marriages of a particular group of two hundred people; but, rather, that it is a study of marriages in general, among people in general. No one would bother to study and to publish on the sexual behavior of particular persons if he did not expect that his generalizations would have some applicability to at least some other persons in the world.

The validity of extending generalizations derived from a study of any sample depends, fundamentally and unavoidably, upon the representativeness of that sample. Each segment which is studied must be precisely delimited, and all conclusions must be confined to such precisely defined groups. This is the principle on which modern taxonomic method, the agricultural and economic surveys, and the public opinion polls depend. Social scientists will have to pay as much attention to the way in which they select their subjects if they are ever to arrive at generalizations which are applicable to any large group of men. Unfortunately, such precise delimitations of the samples used have not been attempted in most of the previously published studies of sex. Davis, Hamilton, Dickinson, and Terman had populations which were largely college, and would have illuminated college populations very well if the samples had been strictly confined to college people; but the significance of the data in all these studies was impaired by the addition of cases from other social groups.

Beyond the specific studies which have been reviewed here, there are several which present tabulated data on series of European histories, mostly of Russian factory workers and Russian college students (see Willoughby 1937 for a bibliography and a summary of the data). The Continental European patterns of sex behavior are so distinct from the American (as our own European sampling already indicates), that no additions of the European to the American data should ever be made.

In addition, there are, of course, thousands of individual sex histories in the psychiatric and psychologic journals and texts, and in hundreds of other volumes. There are histories in the writings of Havelock Ellis, Freud, Stekel, Hirschfeld, Krafft-Ebing, Mantegazza, Marcuse, Moll, Block, Rohleder, Henry (1941), and a long list of others. In many ways these have been important contributions on sex. As pioneer studies they contributed materially to the development of a public realization that there were scientific aspects to human sexual behavior, and the present-day student finds it much simpler to undertake an investigation of sex because of the influence which these older studies had. But none of the authors of the older studies, in spite of their keen insight into the meanings of certain things, ever had any precise or even an approximate knowledge of what average people do sexually. They accumulated great bodies of sexual facts about particular people, but they did not know what people in general did sexually. They never knew what things were common and what things were rare, because their data came from the miscellaneous and usually unrepresentative persons who came to their clinics (Freud, Hirschfeld, et al.), or from persons from whom they happened to receive correspondence (Ellis), or from limited numbers of persons whom they interviewed in elaborate detail (as in the Henry study). None of the older authors, with the possible exception of Hirschfeld, attempted any systematic coverage of particular items in each history, and consequently there was nothing to be added or averaged, even for the populations with which they dealt.

Considering the importance which sexual problems have in the practice of psychiatry, medicine, psychology, and counseling of every sort, it is disconcerting to realize what scant bases there have been for over-all statements that have been made in this field. The present study is designed as a first step in the accumulation of a body of scientific fact that may provide the bases for sounder generalizations about the sexual behavior of certain groups and, some day, even of our American population as a whole.

Chapter 2

INTERVIEWING

The quality of a case history study begins with the quality of the interviewing by which the data have been obtained. If, in lieu of direct observation and experiment, it is necessary to depend upon verbally transmitted records obtained from participants in the activities that are being studied, then it is imperative that one become a master of every scientific device and of all the arts by which any man has ever persuaded any other man into exposing his activities and his innermost thoughts. Failing to win that much from the subject, no statistical accumulation, however large, can adequately portray what the human animal is doing. However satisfactory the standard deviations may be, no statistical treatment can put validity into generalizations which are based on data that were not reasonably accurate and complete to begin with. It is unfortunate that academic departments so often offer courses on the statistical manipulation of human material to students who have little understanding of the problems involved in securing the original data. Learning how to meet people of all ranks and levels, establishing rapport, sympathetically comprehending the significances of things as others view them, learning to accept their attitudes and activities without moral, social, or esthetic evaluation, being interested in people as they are and not as someone else would have them, learning to see the reasonable bases of what at first glance may appear to be most unreasonable behavior, developing a capacity to like all kinds of people and thus to win their esteem and cooperation—these are the elements to be mastered by one who would gather human statistics. When training in these things replaces or at least precedes some of the college courses on the mathematical treatment of data, we shall come nearer to having a science of human behavior.

Problems of interviewing have been particularly important in the present study because of the long-standing taboos which make it bad form and, for most people, socially or legally dangerous to discuss one's sexual activities in public or even in the presence of one's most intimate friends. It is astounding that anyone should agree to expose himself by contributing his sex history to an interviewer whom he has never before met, and to a research project whose full significance he, in most instances, cannot begin to understand. Still more remarkable is the fact that many of the histories in the present study have come from subjects who agreed to give histories within the first few minutes after they first met the interviewer. We are not sure that we completely comprehend why people have been willing to talk to us; but there may be some value in discussing the bases on which we have appealed for histories, and in describing some of the devices that we have employed to establish the quality of the record.

MAKING CONTACTS

Any study which depends upon obtaining data from large numbers of people must have an appeal which is sufficient to win the whole-hearted cooperation of persons of every sort. In the present instance, the chief appeal has been altruistic—an invitation to contribute to basic scientific research, an opportunity to help others by sharing one's experience. The appeal to professionally trained and other educated groups has involved a technical exposition of the scientific problems involved, and of the social significance of securing data which clinicians may utilize in their practice. The academic groups in psychology, biology, and sociology cooperated as soon as they saw broad, basic principles emerging from the study. Religious groups saw a need for information on the early training of children, and have shown an outstanding willingness to cooperate in any study which might contribute to an understanding of problems which affect the stability of the home and of marriage. More poorly educated and mentally dull individuals have responded to the simple and brief explanation that "The doctors need to know more about these things. They need your help, so they can help other people." The underworld requires only a gesture of honest friendship before it is ready to admit one as a friend, and to give histories "because you are my friend." For each group the mode of the appeal is different, but in each case it is based on the measure of altruism that is to be found—if one knows how to find it— in nearly all men.

In answer to our request for her history, the little, gray-haired woman at the cabin door, out on the Western plain, epitomized what we have heard now from hundreds of people: "Of all things—! In all my years I have never had such a question put to me! But—if my experience will help, I'll give it to you." This, in many forms, some of them simple, some of them sophisticated as scientists and scholars like them, some of them crude, incisive, and abrupt as the underworld makes them, is the expression of the altruistic bent (however philosophers and scientists may analyze it) which has been the chief motive leading people to cooperate in this study. We shall always be indebted "to the twelve thousand persons who have contributed to these data, and to the eighty-eight thousand more who, some day, will help complete this study." However involved the reader may become in the statistics, the fine points of the argument, and the grand intricacies of the minute details, he will never understand this study until he comprehends the human drama that has been involved in securing the data.

In an honest way, we have tried to make those who have contributed aware of our amazement at their willingness to help, and of our esteem for them because they have helped. This appreciation has, undoubtedly, been a factor in winning cooperation. Evident appreciation may, therefore, belong in the list of devices which may be employed to secure histories; but appreciation must be sincere, else it will not work.

More selfish interests have animated many of those who have contributed. This is understandable, too. Many of the subjects have welcomed the opportunity to obtain information about some item affecting their personal lives, their marriages, their families, friends, or social relations. The more frequent questions have concerned:

Possibly harmful effects from "excessive" sexual activity
Physical harm resulting from masturbation
Incidences of masturbation, pre-marital intercourse, extra-marital intercourse, mouth-genital contacts, homosexual relations, animal contacts
Comparisons of the individual's activities with averages for the group to which he belongs
"Am I normal?"
The physical and social significances of petting
The relation of pre-marital experience to subsequent adjustment in marriage
Items to consider in choosing a mate for marriage
Differences between male and female responsiveness
Techniques conducive to mutuality of response in marital intercourse
Medical aspects of contraception
Data on the sexual development and education of children
Problems arising from homosexual activity
Information about available medical, psychiatric, or other clinics to which persons with special problems may be referred
Impotency, heredity of physical defects, worries over genital characters, venereal disease, pregnancy (but these items only occasionally)

As scientists, the authors of this volume have given information when it was available and scientifically established, while refusing to advise on any choice of behavior. Nevertheless, many persons have felt that the information obtained was sufficient repayment for their own contributions to the study.

In a number of communities, public knowledge of this source of help has brought many histories. This does not mean that an undue number of neurotic or psychotic individuals has contributed. On the contrary, items of the sort listed above are the everyday sexual problems of the average individual; and the greatly disturbed type of person who goes to psychiatric clinics has been relatively rare in our sample. We have refused to take histories from recognizable psychotics who were handicapped with poor memories, hallucinations, or fantasies that distorted the fact.

The psychoanalyst will incline to the view that most of those who have given histories have obtained some inflation of their egos by doing so. This is undoubtedly true, whether the record was one of unusual prowess, of conformance with the norm, or of low rates of activity which were the result of some incapacity for which the individual wanted pity. Most clinicians find that people like to talk about themselves. On the other hand, there is no evidence that this human quality has distorted the record, and the exaltation of one's self has not seemed as significant as the altruistic motives which have animated most of the subjects—unless altruism is, of course, merely another means of self gratification.

There are some who have contributed histories in order to satisfy their curiosity as to the nature of the questions asked, and to learn how such an interview is conducted. Several hundred psychoanalysts, psychiatrists, physicians, clinical psychologists, social workers, and other professional persons have had an especial interest in observing the interviewing techniques. In communities where we have worked for periods of time, persons of every social level, even including the lowest, have volunteered in order to find out what sort of thing their friends were experiencing when they contributed histories.

In many instances, cooperation with the study may be made a group activity. To accomplish this, an interviewer must utilize the principles of mass psychology, mix them well with common sense, and add the skills of a patent medicine vendor and a Fuller brush man—while, withal, maintaining the community's esteem for the dignity of a science which has nothing to sell. Members of a college fraternity, a sorority, a church organization, a parent-teacher group, a service club, all of the inmates of a penal institution, the patients of a particular physician, all of the persons in some section of a city, all of the population in some rural community, may be persuaded to contribute as a matter of loyalty to an activity which is officially or tacitly supported by the group. In this way many persons have been reached who, as lone individuals, would have had little interest in the research. Loyalty to the group may also lead an individual to exercise more than usual care in providing a detailed and accurate record of his activity.

Lectures to college, professional, church, and other community groups have most frequently provided the entree to the better educated portions of the population. Hundreds of such lectures have been given. Perhaps 50,000 persons have heard about the research through lectures, and perhaps half of the histories now in hand have come in consequence of such contacts.

Practically all of the contacts at lower levels, and many of those at other levels, have depended upon introductions made by persons who had previously contributed their own histories. One who has not already given a history is not usually effective as a "contact man." Contact men and women

have often spent considerable time and have gone to considerable pains to
interest their friends and acquaintances. Many hundreds of such persons
have helped, but a short list of those who have helped most will show
something of the diversity of the backgrounds which have been represented:

Bootleggers	Ne'er-do-wells
Clergymen	Persons in the Social Register
Clerks	Physicians
Clinical psychologists	Pimps
College professors	Police court officials
College students	Prison inmates
Corporation officials	Prison officials
Editors	Professional women
Farmers	Psychiatrists
Female prostitutes	Public school teachers
Gamblers	Social workers
Headmasters of private schools	Thieves and hold-up men
Housewives	Y.M.C.A. secretaries
Lawyers	Y.W.C.A. secretaries
Male prostitutes	Welfare workers
Marriage counselors	Women's Club leaders

In securing histories through personal introductions, it is initially most
important to identify these key individuals, win their friendship, and
develop their interest in the research. Days and weeks and even some years
may be spent in acquiring the first acquaintances in a community. In a
sober rural area, the most highly esteemed of the local clergymen may be
the right person to sponsor the project. If it is a prison population, the
oldest-timer, the leading wolf, the kingpin in the inmate commonwealth,
or the girl who is the chief trouble-maker for the administration must be
won before one can go very far in securing the histories of other inmates.
If it is a good residential area in a large city, the quiet but steady young
housewife with a host of friends who know they can count on her, or the
sociable and reasonably successful middle-aged business man who is active
in service clubs and civic projects, is the person most likely to put us across
in that community. If it is the underworld, we may look for the man with
the longest FBI record and the smallest number of convictions, and set out
to win him. To get the initial introductions, it is necessary to become
acquainted with someone who knows someone who knows the person we
want to meet. Contacts may develop from the most unexpected sources. A
rich man may provide the introduction to a leader in the underworld, a
Salvation Army worker may serve as the contact for the Social Register.
The number of persons who can provide introductions has continually
spread until now, in the present study, we have a network of connections
that could put us into almost any group with which we wished to work,
anywhere in the country.

Having met these significant persons, and gotten their histories, we take
time to become acquainted with them and with their communities. They

must come to like us as individuals, and the whole community must know about us and about the research, if we expect to secure any large number of histories in the area. We go with them to dinner, to concerts, to night clubs, to the theater; we become acquainted with them at community dances, in poolrooms, in taverns, and in other places which they frequent. They in turn invite us to meet friends in their homes, at teas, at dinners, at other social events. For years we have maintained a considerable corre-spondence with persons who are likely sources of new contacts. In many cases we have developed friendships which are based upon mutual respect and upon our common interest in the success of this project. When, in the course of time, we turn to securing histories from the rest of the community, most of the people who then contribute do so because they are friends of our friends, because they accept the contact man's evaluation of the research, and because of their confidence that he would not involve them in difficulties. Among more poorly educated groups, and among such minority groups as rural populations, Negroes, segregated Jewish popula-tions, homosexual groups, penal institutional inmates, the underworld, etc., the community is particularly sensitive to the dangers of outside interfer-ence, and particularly dependent upon the advice of their leaders in decid-ing whether they should cooperate.

An element of competition may be introduced by working two groups simultaneously or in immediate succession. College A contributes because College B has also contributed. College B is persuaded to cooperate because College A has already contributed more histories than B. The principle works equally well for fraternity and sorority groups, for people living in different houses on a city block, for the inmates of a penal institu-tion, for the court judge and his staff, for groups of psychiatrists, and for many other groups.

There may be a certain amount of pressure employed in securing his-tories from the last persons in any group which is contributing a hundred percent to the study. Sometimes the pressure has originated from the investigators, more often it has been the group interest which has swayed the individual. There has been some constraint upon professional people, especially upon those who are involved in giving sexual advice in clinics, to contribute to a research project which will serve them in their profes-sional activities. Some of the histories obtained from inmates in institutions probably would not have been obtained except for the institutional tradi-tion of conformance to the administration's program, or to the group activity in which all the other inmates were cooperating. Where such indirect or more direct pressure is employed it becomes particularly important to establish a satisfactory rapport with each subject after he has actually come into conference for a history.

Payment for histories has been confined to the economically poorer elements in the population, to persons who are professionally involved in sexual activities (as prostitutes, pimps, exhibitionists, etc.) or to others who have turned from their regular occupation and spent considerable time in helping make contacts. The payment has never been large, rarely amounting to more than a dollar or two for the couple of hours involved in contributing; and equivalent amounts may be paid to persons who have helped make the contacts. There is no evidence that such payments have distorted the quality of the record, although the prospect of securing double payment leads an occasional individual to try to duplicate his contribution. In the latter case, it has been necessary to keep accurate records and require identification; but this has presented only a minor problem. On the whole, payment has worked well, for it has undoubtedly made it possible to secure many histories which otherwise would not have been obtainable; and it should be realized that even in the groups which are paid, men and women have contributed primarily because they respect us, because they appreciate our interest in them, and because they are willing to contribute for the sake of helping others. Certain it is that the remarkable body of confidential information that has been secured from some of these lower level and underworld groups would not have been available if there had been no other bases than money to interest them. Twelve thousand people have helped in this research primarily because they have faith in scientific research projects.

ESTABLISHING RAPPORT

There are, after all, only two reasons why anyone should hesitate to contribute his sex history to a scientific project. He may hesitate because he fears that the interviewer will object to something in his history, and he may fear a loss of social prestige, or legal penalties, if his history were to become a matter of public knowledge. An occasional individual has hesitated, in addition, because he did not want to stir up memories of old fears, old hurts, or old losses that were associated with his or her sexual life; occasionally a psychotic—or simply a contrary individual—has blocked at cooperating; but most persons who have hesitated have done so because they feared embarrassment before the interviewer, or feared public disclosure of their activities.

It is imperative, therefore, that the investigator be able to convince the subject:

1. That he, as a scientist, offers no objection to any type of sexual behavior in which the subject could possibly have been involved.

2. That the confidences of the record will be kept without question.

A scientist studying sex should be able to accept any type of sexual behavior objectively, listen to the record without adverse reaction, and record without social or moral evaluation. That much is expected of the student measuring the lengths of insect wings, recording the chemical changes that occur in a test tube, or observing the colors of the stars. It is not too much to expect similar objectivity of the student of human behavior.

But something more than cold objectivity is needed in dealing with human subjects. One is not likely to win the sort of rapport which brings a full and frank confession from a human subject unless he can convince the subject that he is desperately anxious to comprehend what his experience has meant to him. Sexual histories often involve a record of things that have hurt, of frustrations, of pain, of unsatisfied longings, of disappointments, of desperately tragic situations, and of complete catastrophe. The subject feels that the investigator who asks merely routine questions has no right to know about such things in another's history. The interviewer who senses what these things can mean, who at least momentarily shares something of the satisfaction, pain, or bewilderment which was the subject's, who shares something of the subject's hope that things will, somehow, work out right, is more effective, though he may not be altogether neutral.

The sympathetic interviewer records his reactions in ways that may not involve spoken words but which are, nonetheless, readily comprehended by most people. A minute change of a facial expression, a slight tensing of a muscle, the flick of an eye, a trace of a change in one's voice, a slight inflection or change in emphasis, slight changes in one's rate of speaking, slight hesitancies in putting a question or in following up with the next question, one's choice of words, one's spontaneity in inquiring about items that are off the usual routine, or any of a dozen and one other involuntary reactions betray the interviewer's emotions, and most subjects quickly understand them. Unlettered persons and persons of mentally lower levels are often particularly keen in sensing the true nature of another person's reactions.

If the interviewer's manner spells surprise, disapproval, condemnation, or even cold disinterest, he will not get the whole of the record. If his reactions add up right, then the subject is willing to tell his story. The interview has become an opportunity for him to develop his own thinking, to express to himself his own disappointments and hopes, to bring into the open things that he has previously been afraid to admit to himself, to work out solutions to his difficulties. He quickly comes to realize that a full and complete confession will serve his own interests. It becomes unthinkable that he should cover up, deny, or fail to relate anything that has happened.

These are the things that can be done in a person-to-person, guided interview that represents a communion between two deeply human individuals, the subject and the interviewer (McNemar 1946). These are the things that can never be done through a written questionnaire, or even through a directed interview in which the questions are formalized and the confines of the investigation strictly limited. In the present study, the number of persons who have admitted involvement in every type of sexual activity, and particularly in socially taboo types of activity, is much greater than has ever been disclosed in any questionnaire study; and comparisons of the data in this and in previously published studies should provide some measure of the possibilities of personal interviewing as a technique in case history studies.

It has been asked how it is possible for an interviewer to know whether people are telling the truth, when they are boasting, when they are covering up, or when they are otherwise distorting the record. As well ask a horse trader how he knows when to close a bargain! The experienced interviewer knows when he has established a sufficient rapport to obtain an honest record, in the same way that the subject knows that he can give that honest record to the interviewer. Learning to recognize these indicators, intangible as they may be, is the most important thing in controlling the accuracy of an interview. Beyond that there are cross-checks among the questions, inconsistencies to watch for, questions which demand proof, and other devices for testing the validity of the data (all of which are discussed in the last section of the present chapter).

At the beginning of an interview the subject must be assured that he can tell all, but it is not always possible to win complete rapport at the very start. The subject will need to be reassured many times in the course of the interview, and continually convinced by the evident sympathy of the interviewer. Often the subject begins by admitting only a small part of his activity, and adds more only gradually as he becomes more certain that he can do so without disapproval.—"Yes, I have been approached for such relations, but I did not pay attention."—"Yes, there were physical contacts, but they did not interest me."—"Yes, there were complete contacts—when I was asleep."—"Yes, there was one affair in which I responded, in a mild way."—"Yes, I liked it well enough, but I didn't think I wanted any more of it."—"Well, yes, I did try it again."—"Yes, since then I have become interested, and I have had a good deal of it lately."—So the history builds up. At each step the subject intended to stop with the minimum of information, and would have stopped completely if there had been any indication that the interviewer was surprised, was offended, or disapproved. After each essay, the additional bit of information was added because the subject discovered that he could tell more. If, at any point, the interviewer had failed, the story would have stopped there.

Sometimes the capacity of the investigator is severely tested. Whatever his sexual background, each person reaches the limit of things he can understand because of his own previous experience, the limit of things he can appear to understand because he has wanted them and would have had them if it had been socially expedient, and the limit of things he can sympathetically admit because he has glimpsed what they have meant to some

other people. Beyond that there are always things which seem esthetically
repulsive, provokingly petty, foolish, unprofitable, senseless, unintelligent,
dishonorable, contemptible, or socially destructive. Gradually one learns
to forego judgments on these things, and to accept them merely as facts
for the record. If one fails in his acceptance, he will know of it by the
sudden confusion or sudden tenseness of his subject, and the quick conclusion of the story. If the interviewer masters his own confusion, the subject may tell him about it, and congratulate him to boot for being able
and willing to "take it."

The many persons who have contributed to this study have done so
voluntarily and with a full understanding of what we were trying to learn
through our questioning. To have used any sort of devious device would
have ruined the subject's confidence in everything we were doing. It has
repeatedly been suggested that we try narcosynthesis, lie detectors, or
other such means for testing the reliability of at least some of the answers
of some of the subjects; but if we had coerced a single person by any such
means, we would have lost our capacity to win things from anyone else. In
any study which needs to secure quantities of data from human subjects,
there is no way except to win their voluntary cooperation through the
establishment of that intangible thing known as rapport.

THE CONFIDENCE OF THE RECORD

Our laws and customs are so far removed from the actual behavior of
the human animal that there are few persons who can afford to let their
full histories be known to the courts or even to their neighbors and their
best friends; and persons who are expected to disclose their sex histories
must be assured that the record will never become known in connection
with them as individuals. Each subject in this study has contributed only
because he has been thus assured by a friend whom he trusts, or by the
investigator at the beginning of the interview. It is important to note, however, that assuring one of the confidence of the record can be effective only
when that assurance is honest in its intent and never, under any circumstance, betrayed in its execution. If there were ever a single failure to maintain such confidence, then others would learn of it and refuse to contribute
histories. The care with which confidences have been guarded in the present
study has probably never been surpassed in any other project dealing with
human material.

Keeping confidence in this study has involved the development of a
cryptic code in which all of the data have been recorded (Chapter 3,
Figure 2). The code is never translated into words at any stage in the
analyses of the data. Each interviewer has memorized the code, and there
is no key to the code in existence. Only the six persons who have actually
taken histories have ever known any part of the code, and only four
persons are, at the present writing, acquainted with the whole code. None

of the other persons who have helped in the technical work in our laboratory knows the code. A few routine tabulations of non-sexual items have
been made by the technical assistants; but practically all of the handling
of the data, including the punching of the Hollerith cards and their manipulation in the IBM statistical machines, has been done by those of us who
have taken the histories. Never in the nine years of this research has any
other person had access to the information available on the histories of
particular individuals.

It has been necessary to preserve the identity of each history in order to
make subsequent additions, in order to compare re-takes of histories
(Chapter 4), and in order to coordinate data coming from two or more
persons involved in the same sexual activities (as spouses in a marriage or
heterosexual or homosexual companions in common sexual activities).
This identification has been accomplished by the use of a coded set of
symbols for which, again, there is no key in existence. The code was
developed with the help of an experienced cryptographer and involves,
simultaneously, the use of several devices designed to complicate possible
decoding. It is the judgment of the cryptographer who tried to break the
final form that decoding would be impossible unless one had access to all
of the histories and all of the files for a considerable period of time; and
that after identification the data would be practically unintelligible because
of the difficulty of deciphering such a position code as the one used here.
It should be added that the histories are kept behind locked doors and in
fireproof files with locks that are unique for this project.

To a very large degree, analyzing this material has involved additions
of data, summations of the numbers of persons engaged in particular
activities, tabulations of ages, tabulations of frequencies, totals of other
data, and correlations of facts and factors; and, as taxonomists interested
in the behavior of whole segments of the population, we do not foresee
that we will ever be concerned with the publication of the particular histories of particular individuals. It has, therefore, been possible to guaran-
tee that no history will ever be published in a form which would identify it
as an individual history. It has been possible to explain the safety of this
mode of publication even to uneducated and mentally duller individuals,
and thus to persuade them that they can safely contribute histories.

Individual histories in this project have been discussed only among the
research associates on this staff. They have not been discussed even with
professional friends outside of the staff. Particular histories have not been
used as illustrations in public lectures or in group conversation, although
examples have sometimes been synthesized from real cases. They have not
been discussed even when the individuals involved were geographically so
remote as to seem unidentifiable; for people travel about over the country,
and one often meets persons who are acquainted with one's subjects in
some distant town.

Few professional people seem to know what it means to preserve the absolute confidence of a record. Professional confidence too often refers to the discussion of individual cases with anyone in the professional fraternity. Such discussions, often in the hearing of secretaries or nurses, soon spread the information abroad, whence it returns to confound the subject who gave his history only after he was guaranteed strict confidence. Professional people connected with courts too often obtain confessions by promising the confidence of the record, which they promptly betray by carrying the data to the court. Academic persons doing research on human case histories regularly turn them over to graduate students to be studied, and on occasion exhibit them, with names attached, to whole classes of students for examination. Few clinical records are ever in code, and in very few cases is there any attempt to separate the name of the subject from the plainly written record. In many a social welfare agency there are more non-professional persons who see the confidential records than there are professional people in the organization. In penal institutions there are always inmates who are employed in clerical positions, where they have access to the "confidential" records; and information spreads through them to the whole of the inmate body. In some institutions the inmate population is better acquainted with the content of some of these records than the officials themselves. Persons who have been betrayed through such sources become, naturally enough, skeptical about contributing further data to any professional person, and it has often been difficult to convince them that our own records would be kept inviolate.

We have been pressed by many people for information about particular persons who have contributed histories. Husbands and wives often want data about their spouses, and in many cases such information would help them make better marital adjustments; but if such information were ever given, other husbands and wives would not be willing to give their histories. Parents ask about their children, and partners in common sexual activities often want advice which cannot be given without drawing upon the confidential record. While it has disappointed many persons not to secure such information, their esteem for the integrity of the records has inevitably increased and, in consequence, they are then willing to contribute their own histories, and to interest their friends in the project.

In penal and other institutions, we have maintained an invariable rule that no confidence given by an inmate would ever be passed on to the administration of the institution. We have worked only in institutions which have accepted us on these terms. No administration has ever asked us to break the rule. In a few cases where we have felt that some inmate would find it to his advantage to have the administration know more of his history, we have advised the subject to that effect and, if he has agreed, we have helped make such contacts—but only when he has voluntarily agreed to such a procedure.

There is probably no legal right for anyone to preserve the confidence of any information which has been given him. By custom the courts ordinarily recognize the rights of a priest or of a physician to preserve confidences obtained in the performance of their professional duties, but there is no statute law establishing such a right. If we were brought before a court we would have to hope that such precedents would be extended to scientists involved in the investigation of such a subject as human sex behavior. If the courts of all levels were to refuse to recognize such a privilege, there would be no alternative but to destroy our complete body of records and accept the consequences of such defiance of the courts. If law enforcement officials, students of law, and persons interested in social problems want scientific assistance in understanding such problems, they will have to recognize a scientist's right to maintain the absolute confidence of his records; for without that it would be impossible to persuade persons to contribute to this sort of study.

TECHNICAL DEVICES IN INTERVIEWING

The skillful interviewer will develop particular techniques which work for him, though they may not serve another investigator so well. But even though there are these differences in the applicability of particular methods, it may be of value to other persons who are interested in interviewing to know something of the technical devices that have proved effective in the present research.

1. Putting the subject at ease. Many of the persons who contribute to a sex study manifest some uneasiness at the beginning of an interview, and from the start particular attention needs to be given to putting the subject at ease. Interviews are held in places that are as attractive and comfortable as the subject's social background may demand. Many persons are considerably helped if they can smoke during the interview. Conversation is initiated as casually as possible, first about everyday affairs that may be remote from anything that is sexual. If the subject knows someone whom we have previously known, or has recreational interests which are in any way connected with our own, that provides a basis for conversation. One does the sort of things that a thoughtful host would do to make his guests comfortable, but always easily so that the subject is not aware that they are designed to put him at ease.

2. Assuring privacy. Places where the interviews are held should be reasonably soundproof, and there should be no unexpected interruptions from other persons entering the room.* From the very set-up of the interview, the subject must be reassured of confidence.

* In contrast, we have observed a psychiatrist interviewing a subject, who was under criminal indictment, in a small room in which a half dozen persons were continually moving about and listening to the whole of the conversation.

3. Establishing rapport. The subject should be treated as a friend or a guest in one's own home. The tottering old man who is a victim of his first penal conviction, appreciates the interviewer's solicitation about his health and his interest in seeing that he is provided with tobacco, candy, or the other things that the institution allows one who has sufficient funds. The inmate in a woman's penal institution particularly appreciates those courtesies which a male would extend to a woman of his own social rank, in his own home. The interviewer should be as interested in the subject as he is in recording the subject's history. It is important to look the subject squarely in the eye, while giving only a minimum of attention to the record that is being made. People understand each other when they look directly at each other.

4. Sequence of topics. Since, as already indicated, it is often necessary to build up rapport after an interview has actually started, it is advisable to begin a conference with the items that are non-sexual and least likely to disturb the subject, and to follow with a sequence which leads gradually into things that the subject may consider more difficult to discuss. Those things on which one may expect the maximum cover-up and blockage should be left until the end of the interview. By then the subject has acquired confidence, and it is possible to secure a record of things that could never have been secured at the beginning of the interview. In the present study we usually begin with a discussion of the subject's age, place of birth, educational history, recreational interests, physical health, parental background, brothers, sisters, and other non-sexual data. The first sexual items are those for which the subject is least responsible, namely the sources of his sex education. The record of overt sexual activities begins with the things that are most remote, such as the pre-adolescent sex play. From there on the sequence of topics is varied in accordance with the subject's social background, his age, and his educational level. For unmarried college males the sequence is nocturnal emissions, masturbation, pre-marital petting, pre-marital intercourse with companions, intercourse with prostitutes, animal contacts, and the homosexual. For males who have never gone beyond the tenth grade in school, pre-marital intercourse can be discussed much earlier in the interview, because it is generally accepted at that social level; but masturbation needs to be approached more carefully if one is to get the truth from that group. At that level, petting is secondary to intercourse in interest and in acceptance, and it is brought into an interview only after the discussion of intercourse.

With many females it is simpler to get a record of the homosexual than a record of masturbatory activity. For the older generation of males of every social level it is simpler to get a record of pre-marital intercourse than to get a record of masturbation. With persons who have publicly known homosexual histories, extensive masochistic or sadistic experience, histories as prostitutes, or other special sorts of sex experience, we get better cooperation when we take the record of the special experience before trying to get details on the more usual activities. It is often easier to get the professional record from a female prostitute than it is to get the record of her personal sex life with her boy friend or with her husband. In dealing with an uneducated and timid older woman from a remote farm area or mountain country, the sequence has to become most desultory, including only the simplest questions about each type of sexual experience, with no details on any point until the whole of the history has been covered in a preliminary way. By then the subject should have become more confident, and it will be possible to ask her such details about each type of activity as would have shocked her at the beginning of the interview. A good interviewer becomes very sensitive to the reactions of his subjects, immediately drops any line of inquiry which causes embarrassment, and stays with simpler matters until the subject is ready to talk in more detail. This technique, more than anything else, probably accounts for the fact that among the 12,000 persons who have been interviewed in the present study, all but three or four have completed their histories; and those few would not have been lost if we had known as much at the beginning of this study as we now know about a good sequence of questions in an interview.

5. Recognizing the subject's mental status. One should not attempt to take a history from a subject who is mentally incapacitated, whether permanently or temporarily so. Persons who are badly intoxicated cannot give reliable histories; and while it is impossible to rule out all who have been drinking, since that would rule out a high proportion of all persons in certain social groups, one must learn to identify the level of intoxication of his subjects and avoid taking a record that is below standard. Some individuals, of course, are more cooperative when they have had a small amount of alcohol. Persons who are under the immediate influence of drugs, particularly of some narcotic that induces sleep, are impossible as subjects. A person who is heavily intoxicated with marihuana (which is not a drug) is similarly unreliable. Benzedrine and some other drugs are not so likely to interfere with the individual's capacity to give an accurate record. Persons who are physically exhausted or mentally fatigued are difficult, and some older persons who are badly senile are hopeless.

Feeble-minded individuals vary considerably in their capacities to remember things. There are some whose memories are accurate on details, and this is also true of many uneducated persons who are not feeble-minded. Consequently, the interviewer must learn to identify a feeble-minded case and must preface the interview with such ordinary, everyday conversation as will allow him to determine the capacities of such an individual. It is possible to get a fair record from most feeble-minded individuals whose IQ's are not below 50, although interviewing any person with a rating below 70 becomes a slow process in which each idea must be given plenty of time to penetrate, with endless repetition, and with a vocabulary which is confined to the simplest of words, both in the sexual vernacular and in the references to commonplace activities.

6. Recording at time of interview. In the literature on interviewing, it is customary to advise that records should not be made in the presence of a subject, but that they should be made after the subject has left at the close of an interview. This is the commonest procedure among many psychiatrists, clinical psychologists, and among social workers. It is supposed that a subject is embarrassed at seeing his statements put on paper, and that he will talk more freely if he feels that he can say some things that are not recorded. It has been said that there is a loss of rapport when the interviewer records during the interview. For these reasons we attempted to follow standard practice early in this study and found that it introduced a tremendous error into the records. Much of the specific quotation which appears in psychiatric literature evidently represents the interviewer's notion of how the subject talked rather than a record of what the subject actually said. After the first few months of this study, we began to record all of the data directly in the presence of the subject, and there has been no indication that this has been responsible for any loss of rapport or interference with the subject's free exposure of confidences. We have become convinced that any loss of rapport which comes when data are recorded directly has been consequent upon the longhand method of writing out answers while the subject sits in silence waiting for the next question. This is the thing that is destructive to rapport. By using a code for recording, it has been possible in the present study to record as rapidly as one can carry on a conversation, without loss of rapport or blockage on the subject's part.

7. Systematic coverage. On each history in the present study there has been a systematic coverage of a basic minimum of about 300 items. This minimum is expanded for persons who have extended experience in premarital or extra-marital intercourse, who have extended homosexual histories, who have had experience as prostitutes or pimps, or who have had multiple marriages. The maximum history covers 521 items. One of the most fundamental aspects of the present survey is its systematic coverage of a uniform list of items on each history. Such coverage is not possible in a free association procedure where the subject records things as they happen to come to his mind and where, in consequence, each person may provide information on some items that are not covered by the next persons in the study, and where, in consequence, it is impossible to add together and secure incidence or frequency figures that would be applicable even to the sample population as a whole. The use of a standard form in coding the data (Figure 2) makes it possible to look over the history sheet at the end of an interview, and to make sure that every block in which there should be some record has been satisfactorily accounted for.

8. Supplementary exploration. While there may be a basic minimum of material that is covered on each history, the interviewer should not hesitate to secure additional data on special situations that are outside of the routine. For instance, about twenty questions are routinely asked about masturbation, but there are males who have developed elaborate techniques about which scores of additional questions should be put. Concerning the average individual's relations with his parents, the routine questions may give all the necessary information on most individuals, but an occasional individual may have had some complex relation with his parents which makes it valuable to get the record in more detail. In taking the histories of identical twins, especial inquiry is made about their emotional relations to each other, the extent to which they share common social activities, and other items which are not touched in the usual history. A highly intelligent individual who has had considerable experience in a socially taboo type of behavior may help analyze the situation in such detail as is never investigated in the average history. In the routine, there are only minor questions on masochism and sadism, but if there is any indication that a subject has been consciously and deliberately involved in such behavior, he should be questioned on scores of items which are not in the basic interview. Persons who are blind, deaf, crippled, or otherwise handicapped, persons who have lived in foreign countries, persons who have had experience in military groups or who have lived in other special situations, similarly become sources of special information. As scientific explorers, we, in the present study, have been unlimited in our search to find out what people do sexually. These, again, are the things that can be done in a guided interview and which cannot be touched in a questionnaire study or even in a directed interview.

9. Standardizing the point of the question. In the present study, the questions asked in the interviews have never been standardized in form, but the points which they cover have been strictly defined. When the subject is asked about his relations to his parents, there is a strict definition of the period to which the information should apply. When the question concerns the subject's experience in petting, petting is precisely defined so there is no confusion about the sort of experience which may be included under that head. When the subject's relations with prostitutes are the issue, a clear distinction is made between a prostitute and a girl who is merely promiscuous. Data about the health of an individual are designed to catch those illnesses which interfere with an individual's social adjustment. Each other question has had its point precisely defined, in order that the data secured from the many different subjects and by the several interviewers may fairly be added together. It is unfortunate that the limitations of space make it impossible to give the whole list of questions, with their precise definitions, anywhere in the present volume, although a list of items covered in each interview is shown in Chapter 3.

10. Adapting the form of the question. While the point of each question has been standardized, the form of each question has varied for the various social levels and for the various types of persons with whom the study has dealt. Standardized questions do not bring standardized answers, for the same question means different things to different people. In order to have questions mean the same thing to different people, they must be modified to fit the vocabulary, the educational background, and the comprehension of each subject. It is especially important to use a vocabulary with which the subject will feel at home, and which he will understand. The college-bred interviewer needs to go to considerable pains to limit his vocabulary to the relatively few words that are employed by persons in lower educational levels. Everyday terms, as well as sexual vernaculars, are involved: a lower level individual, for instance, is never ill or injured, though he may be sick or hurt. He does not wish to do a thing, though he wants to do it. He does not perceive, though he sees. He is not acquainted with a person, though he may know him. One needs a certain sensitivity to adapt his vocabulary to the limited usages of such subjects. Except among college graduates, there is little knowledge of the clinical terms that concern sex, and sexual vernaculars must be used in interviewing lower level individuals. Such vernaculars vary considerably among different groups.

One must know and use the vernacular terms with a fine sense of their proprieties and their exact meanings in each group. Their awkward use may damage instead of building rapport. Sexual vernaculars differ considerably in different sections of the country. One should take considerable pains to determine the precise meanings of the variant terms as soon as he starts work in a community. Negro and white groups differ in their usages even in the same city. There are differences between the vocabularies of older and younger generations in any social level. A volume could be written on the vernaculars that should be known by anyone attempting to deal with people outside of his own social level, and the training of interviewers for the present study has involved a considerable amount of work on that point. Everywhere questions must be varied so they will bring replies that pertain to exactly the same thing. In many instances, questions must be freely expanded in order to make their meanings clear to the subject. This again is the sort of thing which cannot be done with a questionnaire or with a directed interview in which the questions are standardized as to form.

11. Avoiding bias. In a study in which the forms of the questions are not standardized, there is a considerable responsibility on the interviewer to see to it that his spontaneous questions are not so phrased as to bias the subject's reply (McNemar 1946). In his tone of voice and in his choice of words, the interviewer must avoid giving the subject any clue as to the answers he expects. For instance, when the subject is at a loss to know how to estimate the frequencies with which he has engaged in a particular sort of activity, the interviewer can explain what sorts of frequencies are possible, provided he is careful not to give any idea what frequencies are common in the population, or what frequencies he, the subject, might be expected to have. What is actually done is to suggest to the subject that his activity might average once a week, three or four times a week, once a month, every day, or more often, or less often. The interviewer avoids suggesting an answer by avoiding any sequence in the illustrative list which he gives, and is careful not to attach particular importance to the last item in the list, which is the one that many persons will accept as their answer if the interviewer is not on his guard. Feeble-minded individuals and occasionally some other persons are highly suggestible, and then it becomes particularly important to avoid suggesting answers and important to test all answers for consistency.

12. Direct questions. When one is dealing with such a socially involved question as sex it becomes particularly important to ask direct questions, without hesitancy and without apology. If the interviewer shows any uncertainty or embarrassment, it is not to be expected that the subject will do better in his answers. Euphemisms should not be used as substitutes for franker terms. In some of the previous studies, many sexual terms are avoided: masturbation becomes "touching yourself"; a climax in masturbation becomes "securing a thrill through touching yourself"; and sexual intercourse becomes "relations with other persons," or "sex delinquency" (Ackerson 1931, 1942). With such questions the subject cannot help but sense the fact that the interviewer is not sure that sex is an honorable thing, and a thing that can be frankly talked about. Evasive terms invite dishonest answers. In one of the previous studies there was a long list of questions concerning the homosexual, but the approach was so indirect that a person who had had an abundance of such experience could have answered every one of the questions honestly, and still never have admitted that he had ever had an overt experience.

13. Placing the burden of denial on the subject. The interviewer should not make it easy for a subject to deny his participation in any form of sexual activity. It is too easy to say no if he is simply asked whether he has ever engaged in a particular activity. We always assume that everyone has engaged in every type of activity. Consequently we always begin by asking *when* they first engaged in such activity. This places a heavier burden on the individual who is inclined to deny his experience; and since it becomes apparent from the form of our question that we would not be surprised if he had had such experience, there seems to be less reason for denying it. It might be thought that this approach would bias the answer, but there is no indication that we get false admissions of participation in forms of sexual behavior in which the subject was not actually involved. Other techniques of modifying questions, particularly if they concern socially taboo behavior, may bring a considerable increase in the number of positive answers.

14. Avoiding multiple questions. Anyone experienced in teaching should have learned to avoid multiple questions. Multiple questions usually bring replies that are ambiguous, and their avoidance in a sex study is particularly important because they provide an opportunity for the subject to dodge one of the questions by giving his attention entirely to the other. For instance, the interviewer who asks the subject if he is erotically aroused "by seeing nude males or females," may get as an answer that he is always aroused by seeing females. Thereby the subject manages to evade the fact that he is to some degree aroused by seeing males.

15. Rapid-fire questioning. In order to cover the maximum amount of material in a single interview, it is necessary to ask questions as rapidly as the subject can possibly comprehend and reply. This method has the further advantage of forcing the subject to answer spontaneously without too much premeditation. Such a rapid fire of questions provides one of the most effective checks on fabrication, as detectives and other law-enforcement officials well know. It would be practically impossible for a person who was deliberately falsifying to answer the many questions that are asked concerning the details of his activity, when the questions come as rapidly as they do in our interviewing. Looking an individual squarely in the eye, and firing questions at him with maximum speed, are two of the best guarantees against exaggeration.

16. Cross-checks on accuracy. Cover-up is more easily accomplished than exaggeration in giving a history. The best protection against cover-up lies in the use of a considerable list of interlocking questions which provide cross-checks throughout the history, and particularly in regard to socially taboo items. There are, for instance, twelve questions concerning homosexual experience that appear in each interview before direct questions on that point are ever asked. The significance of some of these preliminary questions would not be recognized by anyone except a skilled psychiatrist. It would be difficult for most persons who had had anything more than incidental homosexual experience to deny that fact after they had answered the questions which provide the cross-checks on this point. There are similar cross-checks on various other aspects of a history. Such devices should be confined, however, to honest inquiries concerning items which are an integral part of the individual's history; and one should avoid setting traps that put the subject on the defensive because they are obvious devices for forcing him into an admission.

Probably the most effective system of cross-checks has been the use of vocabularies that are peculiar to persons with particular sorts of experience, and which are quite unknown to persons without such experience. For instance, when one asks a female subject "how many years she has been in the life," she must betray an honest confusion and inability to understand, or else she identifies herself as a prostitute. There are special argots for practically all of the socially taboo activities; and they may provide checks on many of the persons who must be included in a human case history study. Nevertheless, in spite of all that may be done, a certain amount of deliberate cover-up may slip by, and the investigator must find some means of measuring the extent of that cover-up in each part of his data.

17. Proving the answer. If it becomes apparent that the subject's first answer is not correct or sufficient, one should ask for additional information, and re-phrase the original question in a way that will make him prove his answer or expose the falsity of his reply. In a rapid fire of additional questions, it is difficult for a dishonest subject to be consistent. With uneducated persons, and particularly with feeble-minded individuals, it is sometimes effective to pretend that one has misunderstood the negative replies and ask additional questions, just as though the original answers were affirmatives; whereupon the subject may then expose the truth by answering as though he had never given a negative reply. "Yes, I know you have never done that, but how old were you the *first* time that you did it?" is a question which, amazingly enough, may break down the cover-up of a feeble-minded individual. With such a technique, on the other hand, it is especially important to make sure that the subject's final admissions are not fictions which the interviewer has suggested to him.

If the subject corrects his original answers, it should be made easy for him by ignoring the contradictions and receiving the new information as easily as though it were his first reply to the question. On a few occasions we have taken a complete history after we were convinced that it was a fraud, then laid it aside and suggested to the subject that he "now give it to us straight." If the interviewer is sure enough of his interpretation of the situation, the protests of the subject can be quickly silenced and he will proceed to give a full and correct history. These falsified histories, in conjunction with the corrected records, are especially valuable documents because of the insight they give into an individual's public acknowledgments, in contrast to his actual behavior.

18. Forcing a subject. There are some persons who offer to contribute histories in order to satisfy their curiosity, although they have no intentions of giving an honest record of their sexual activities. As soon as one recognizes such a case, he should denounce the subject with considerable severity, and the interviewer should refuse to proceed with the interview. Such an attack on a dishonest subject is quite contrary to the usual rules for interviewing, and a procedure which we at first hesitated to employ in the present study. We have, however, decided that it is a necessary technique in dealing with some individuals, particularly some older teen-age males and some females in underworld groups. Failure to command the situation in these cases would lower the community's respect for the investigator and make it impossible for him to secure honest histories from others in the group. It must be understood by all concerned that giving a history is a voluntary matter, but that as soon as an individual agrees to contribute he assumes the responsibility of serving scientific accuracy. If the falsification is not recognized until after the interview, and if the individual is of importance in his community, the interviewer may well return to him and demand that he correct the record. The list of persons who have been forced in this fashion, in the present study, has included individuals in the underworld, feeble-minded subjects, prison inmates, and one clergyman. No history has ever been lost as a result of such action, and the study has won a number of staunch friends because of our insistence on scientific honesty.

19. Limits of the interview. In spite of the long list of items included in the present study (Chapter 3) and in spite of the fact that each history has covered five times as much material as in any previous study, numerous students have suggested, and undoubtedly will continue to suggest after the publication of the present volume, that we should have secured more data in the fields of their special interests. Specifically it has been suggested that the following matters should have had more thorough investigation:

Anthropology: Racial ancestry for several generations. A companion study on some culture other than American. The correlation of somatotypes and behavior
Endocrinology: Hormonal assays of at least some series of homosexual cases
Gynecology: Physical examinations of the genitalia of each female subject
Marriage Counseling: Non-sexual factors in marital adjustment
Medicine: More complete histories of health and disease, and genital examinations of all male subjects
Psychoanalysis: More data on early childhood, parental relations, etc.
Psychology: More data on motivations and attitudes, and complete personality, intelligence, and masculinity-femininity tests
Sociology: More detailed studies of cultural and community backgrounds; a precise economic rating
Urology: Sperm counts, more detailed genital measurements and records of defects

We are quite conscious of the limitations of the data which we have secured, and would like to see intensive studies of all of the above subjects in their relations to sex. It is, however, physically impossible to undertake all collateral investigations while making a preliminary survey in any field. This is a taxonomic survey of the sexual behavior of a whole great section of mankind, and it has been necessary to limit the immediate study to those things which can be covered in the twenty-eight years assigned to the project. Specialists in psychoanalysis, in mental measurements, in gynecology, and in various other fields, are the ones best equipped to undertake intensive studies; but when we have made such suggestions, they properly enough respond that their techniques take too long, and that they are in consequence in no position to cover the tens of thousands of cases that we are handling in the present survey.

Early in the study it became apparent that it was highly desirable to cover each history in a single interview of limited duration. If an interview is interrupted, there is a considerable loss of rapport, and much time is wasted in trying to re-establish relations with a subject at a second meeting. If the interview extends beyond an hour and a half or two hours, the subject becomes fatigued and the quality of the record drops. If the average interview is to be kept within these limits, nothing can be added to the present schedule unless a corresponding number of other items is dropped out. The extension of each interview by even ten minutes would lower the quality of the intake and materially reduce the number of histories that could be secured in a year. To add such a thing as a good test of economic status, or a masculinity-femininity test, would nearly double the length of time needed for each individual.

20. Avoiding personal identifications. The subject will be considerably relieved if he does not have to name the other persons involved in his socio-sexual contacts; and it is well to go out of one's way to assure him that there is no desire to have such names. If the subject spontaneously includes them, make it apparent that they are not recorded on the history. We have secured thousands of confidences that could not have been obtained if we had insisted on having names of the other persons involved. Even then it is sometimes difficult to avoid identifications, and this is a prime reason why it is difficult to get histories from some married persons, from persons who have had sexual relations with relatives or with persons who are prominent in a community, and from persons involved in deeply emotional love affairs.

21. Avoiding controversial issues. The interviewer who makes moral appraisals of any type of sexual behavior is immediately forestalled from securing an honest record, and as scientists we have, of course, renounced our right to make such evaluations. The same principle applies to discussions of racial, religious, political, and economic issues, particularly among lower level, rural, and minority groups. It is not even possible to agree with the subject's attitudes or the attitudes of his community, for the limits of the interviewer's agreements are finally reached, and his silence on other issues names the things with which he disagrees. There is no way except to abstain from the discussion of all controversial social issues when one is making a scientific study of a human population.

22. Overt activities versus attitudes. To a large degree the present study has been confined to securing a record of the individual's overt sexual experience. This has been because we feel that there is no better evidence of one's attitudes on sex. Specific questions have been asked about each subject's attitudes toward his parents, toward masturbation, pre-marital intercourse, sexual relations with prostitutes, and homosexual experience; but we do not have much confidence in verbalizations of attitudes which each subject thinks are his own, when they are, in actuality, little more than reflections of the attitudes which prevail in the particular culture in which he was raised. Often the expressed attitudes are in striking contradiction to the actual behavior, and then they are significant because they indicate the existence of psychic conflict and they throw light on the extent to which community attitudes may influence an individual.

23. Interviewing young children. For children who are twelve or older, it is usually feasible to adapt the regular interview to their vocabulary and experience, securing quite satisfactory answers. For younger children, especially for those under eight years of age, it is necessary to use a totally different approach. An interview then becomes a social session involving participation in the child's ordinary activities. One of the parents has been present in all of our interviews with these younger children. The technique is one in which the interviewer looks at dolls, at toys of other sorts, joins in games, builds picture puzzles, romps and does acrobatics with the vigorous small boy, tells stories, reads stories, gets the child to tell stories, draws pictures, gets the child to draw pictures, shares candies and cookies, and withal makes himself an agreeable guest. Tucked into these activities are questions that give information on the child's sexual background. If the picture book shows kittens putting on nightgowns for bed, the child may be asked whether she wears nightgowns when she goes to bed. When the interviewer tussles with the four-year old boy, he may ask him whether he similarly tussles with the other boys in the neighborhood, and rapidly follows up with questions concerning tussling with the girls, whether he plays with any girls, whether he likes girls, whether he kisses girls.

There is no sequence of questions and one depends upon opportunities that the play activities create for leading off into particular questions. The child's drawings are highly significant, as psychologists will understand. Many a small child who cannot possibly describe the anatomical differences between males and females will draw pictures of boys and girls which make the distinction. An interview with a young child becomes an information test rather than an examination of the child's overt activity; and the reactions of the child to the questions are more important than the specific information which he supplies. The above-mentioned four-year old boy may talk freely and spontaneously about the other boys that he plays with. He may or may not so freely admit that there are girls in the neighborhood with whom he also plays, and his embarrassment, his hesitancy, his disturbed giggling, or his calm acceptance of the fact are the most important things for the student of sexual behavior to note. Many of the adult attitudes toward various items of sex are already discernible in the three-

or four-year old's history, and often the differences in attitudes of different social levels are already reflected in the reactions of these young children. A later volume will cover this aspect of the study.

THE INTERVIEWER'S BACKGROUND OF KNOWLEDGE

In general, it is difficult to explore effectively unless one has some understanding of the sort of thing that he is likely to find. One cannot intelligently push questions on sexual behavior if he does not comprehend what the possibilities of behavior may be. Inevitably these possibilities are beyond the personal experience that any interviewer is likely to have had, and consequently the prospective student of sexual behavior needs to learn a great deal from the very considerable literature on sex, and a great deal more from the experiences of the persons from whom he takes histories.

Specifically, one needs to comprehend the whole range of possible techniques in each possible type of sexual behavior, including masturbation, petting, intercourse, homosexual activities, animal contacts, relations with prostitutes, etc.; and one needs to understand the variety of psychic problems that may be involved and the considerable social complications that may develop in connection with each type of activity. There are hundreds of possible positions in intercourse, and although the original interview may be confined to questions concerning the six major possibilities, the interviewer should be prepared to investigate the full diversity of positions which an experimentally-inclined subject may use. There are scores of variant techniques in the homosexual which should be investigated when the opportunity comes to get such information. There are hundreds of things that need to be known about prostitution before one is ready to secure an adequate history from a prostitute. Lacking a knowledge of the possibilities, the interviewer will get only the most routine record from a person who in actuality could give a wealth of information.

Many of these variant and relatively rare situations provide most significant data on the backgrounds of human sexual behavior. In many instances variant types of behavior represent the basic mammalian patterns which have been so effectively suppressed by human culture that they persist and reappear only among those few individuals who ignore custom and deliberately follow their preferences in sexual techniques. In some instances sexual behavior which is outside the socially accepted pattern is the more natural behavior (Chapter 6) because it is less affected by social restraints. The clearest picture of learning in sexual behavior is to be found in the homosexual; and if the homosexual had been ignored in the present study, we should not have realized that similar learning processes are involved in the development of the heterosexual. Histories of extra-marital intercourse and the whole story of prostitution provide the best possible data on factors affecting orgasm in the female, and they are replete with striking instances of conditioning for particular situations. The interviewer who is satisfied with covering the routine, and who is not prepared to explore into the abundance of divergent fields, loses some of the scientifically richest material that can be obtained in a case history study.

The background of knowledge which the interviewer has is of great importance in establishing rapport with his subjects. The importance of this cannot be overemphasized. A subject is inevitably hesitant to discuss things which seem to be both outside of the experience of the interviewer, and beyond his knowledge. The narcissistic and masochistic male who has greatly elaborated his masturbatory techniques realizes that he is so unusual that he does not intend to admit anything beyond the simple fact of masturbation, when he first comes into the interview; but the experienced interviewer will discern that this is a special case when he asks the routine questions concerning the subject's interest in looking at his own genitalia during masturbation, his interest in observing himself in a mirror, his custom of nibbling or biting a partner during a sexual relation, his reactions to being similarly bitten, his reactions to stories of torture, and his reactions to being hurt himself. Although these questions do not come in a block, but are spread throughout the length of the interview, the investigator should be capable of putting the answers together and understanding what they mean. Ninety per cent of all masturbation in the male is by a single technique, but for this case that is now before him, the interviewer should know enough about other possible techniques to be able to convince the subject that he is talking with a person who understands. The subject must feel that the situation is not so new or so strange that the interviewer will be startled at these things. He must be convinced that the interviewer can take them as he did the routine material. The interviewer's background of knowledge is the key to obtaining a wealth of special material that a routine schedule of questions may completely miss.

It is particularly important that the interviewer understand socially taboo and illegal sexual activities, because these are the most difficult items on which to secure honest records. He needs to understand the sexual viewpoint of the culture to which each of his subjects belongs. For instance, it is impossible to get any number of histories from prostitutes, female or male, unless they realize that the interviewer understands both the sexual situations involved in prostitution, and the social organization of a prostitute's life. A single phrase from an understanding interviewer is often sufficient to make the subject understand this, and such an interviewer wins a record where none would have been disclosed to the uneducated investigator. A specific illustration will make this more apparent.

This is the case of the older Negro male whose first answers were wary and evasive. When questioned concerning his occupation, he listed a variety of minor jobs which, taken in connection with his manner of response,

seemed to spell underworld activities. We followed up our clue by immediately asking the subject whether he had ever been married. We were
not satisfied with his denial of marriage, and followed with a question as
to whether he had ever lived common law. The easy use of a vernacular
term made him feel freer to talk, and when he admitted that he had so
lived, we asked how old he was when he first lived common law. When he
said that he was then fourteen, our first suspicion concerning his underworld activity was confirmed, and we immediately followed up by asking
how old the woman was. At this, he smiled and admitted that she was
thirty-five. Then we remarked, easily and without surprise: "She was a
hustler, wasn't she?" This was the final step necessary for winning complete confidence. The subject stopped short in his reply, opened his eyes
wide, smiled in a friendly fashion, and said, "Well, sir, since you appear to
know something about these things, I'll tell you straight." The extraordinary record that we then got of his history as a pimp could not have been
obtained if the subject had not comprehended that we understood the
world in which he lived.

Very often the interviewer's capacity to secure an accurate history
depends upon his knowledge of the correlations that usually exist between
certain items, and his readiness to demand an explanation of any incon-
sistency that appears in a particular history. To illustrate again: one starts
by asking the girl how old she was when she turned her first trick (but one
does not ask how old she was when she was first paid as a prostitute). She
is then asked how many of the tricks return after their first contacts with
her. Considerably later in the interview there is a question concerning the
frequency with which she rolls her tricks (robs her customers). The girl
who reports that few of the men ever return, and who subsequently says
that she never robs any of the men, needs to be caught up abruptly and
assured that you know that it doesn't work that way. If she doesn't roll
any of the men, why don't they return to her? This question is likely to
bring a smile from the girl and an admission that since you appear to know
how these things work, she will tell you the whole story, which means that
she robs every time there is any possibility of successfully doing so.

The development of an interviewer is a long and slow process. In the
present study, for instance, it has involved a full year of training for each
interviewer before he was ready to go very far in taking histories. The code
had to be learned, and experience in its use was acquired by reading and
by re-recording histories that were already in the file. Further experience
was obtained by observing other interviewers in action and recording
simultaneously while they did the questioning. Conversely, the trainee was
given an opportunity to interview in the presence of the more experienced
members of the staff. Then there was an opportunity to re-take histories
which others had previously taken, and the trainee's own subjects were

given re-takes by a more experienced interviewer. When the new interviewer is able to secure a record that is practically a perfect duplicate of that obtained by the experienced person, he is in a position to take histories that can be added to those obtained by the older interviewers. Finally, each new interviewer has had to acquire a considerable knowledge of what people can do sexually and demonstrate that he can draw on that knowledge in the case of an unusual sort of history. After such a training program, one may, or may not, be ready to face the variety of situations that an investigator of human sexual behavior may meet.

The effectiveness of any interviewing technique is, in the last analysis, to be determined by the quality of the data that are obtained. We have described the techniques by means of which we have secured the data which are presented in the remainder of this volume. Whether the techniques which have been used in the present study would be equally effective with other persons engaged in studying other problems, is a question which must be answered empirically by each investigator in connection with his own special problems.

Chapter 3

STATISTICAL PROBLEMS

Students who are interested in population analyses will want to examine the technical procedures on which the present study has been based. Because of the scope of the project, it has been necessary to work out some original techniques in recording the material, in testing the validity of the record, and in analyzing the data statistically. These matters will be of less interest to those who are primarily concerned with the actual behavior of the human male, and such readers may prefer to pass over this and the next chapter and turn directly to the consideration of the sexual data which begins with Chapter 5.

NATURE OF THE DATA

It has already been explained (Chapter 1) that the data in the present study have all been gathered through personal interviews. In each history, 521 items have been explored; but since a subject is questioned only about those things in which he has had specific experience, the actual number of items covered in each case is usually nearer 300, and the number involved in the histories of younger and less experienced individuals is often less than that. The maximum list is shown in the following table. A few of the items (those marked with asterisks) call for information which is procurable only through physical examination or other special tests, and such items are being investigated only on certain individuals who are available for special study.

Items Covered on Sex Histories

I. SOCIAL AND ECONOMIC DATA
  1. Sex
  2. Age
  3. Date of birth
  4. Race
  5. Geographic origin
      State of subject's birth
      Countries, states of residence
        for a year or more
      Parents' place of birth
  6. Rural-urban background
  7. Religious background
      Denominations involved
      Degree of adherence
  8. Occupational history
  9. Economic status
  10. Educational history
      Years of schooling
      Colleges attended
      College majors
      Age upon leaving school
      Age while in high school
  *11. Psychological test ratings
  12. Recreational interests
      Extracurricular activities in
        school and college
      Moving pictures
      Dancing
      Cards
      Gambling
      Smoking
      Use of alcohol

* Items marked with asterisks (*) are checked only for selected series of individuals who are available for special study.

63

I. SOCIAL AND ECONOMIC DATA (*Cont'd*)
  12. Recreational interests (*Cont'd*)
      Use of narcotics
      Use of marihuana
      Hunting
      Fishing
      Reading
      Sewing
      Cooking
      Housework
      Special interest in music
      Special interest in sports
      Other special interests and sources of recreation
  13. Athletic experience
      On high school and college organized teams
  14. Fraternity or sorority membership in college
  15. Home background
      Parents' occupational status
      Parents' economic status
      Parents' educational background
      Parental marital history
        Happiness of adjustment
        Separation or divorce
      Parent-child relationships
        Attachment to father
        Attachment to mother
      Brothers, sisters
        Number
        Ages
      Companions at 10 and at 16
        Number
        Relative numbers, male and female
  16. Institutional history
      Prison, orphanage, etc.
      Army or Navy experience
  17. Personality traits

II. MARITAL HISTORIES (FOR EACH MARRIAGE)
  1. Marital status
  2. Spouse's history
      Age
      Length of previous acquaintance
      Length of engagement
      Religious affiliations
      Educational history
  3. Age of each spouse at marriage
  4. Years married, divorced, separated, or widowed
  5. Common law marriages
  6. Offspring
      Sex
      Ages
      Mother's age at first childbirth

  7. Abortions
      Spontaneous
      Induced
  8. Marital adjustment
      Rating
      Sources of conflict

III. SEX EDUCATION
  1. Sources of knowledge, ages when learned
      Pregnancy
      Coitus
      Fertilization
      Menstruation
      Venereal diseases
      Prostitution
      Contraception
      Abortions
      Male erection (in female histories)
  2. Parental contribution to sex education
  3. Experience in observing sex behavior
  4. Experience with graphic depictions of sexual activity
  5. Formal sex education in school and college
  6. Attitudes on nudity
      Of parents
      Of subject

IV. PHYSICAL AND PHYSIOLOGIC DATA
  1. General development and health
      Height
      Weight, and maximum ever reached
      *Pulse rate
      *Blood pressure and BMR
      Thickness of lips
      Handedness
      History of chronic illnesses and handicaps
      History of venereal disease
  2. Adolescence: ages at onset of
      Erotic responsiveness
      First orgasm (and its source)
      Pubic hair growth
      Breast development (in females)
      Breast knots (in adolescent males)
      Menstruation
      Voice change
      Onset of rapid growth
      Completion of growth
  3. Genital characters: male
      Testes
        Descent
        Position (of right and left)
      *Size
      History of injury

IV. PHYSICAL AND PHYSIOLOGIC DATA
  (*Cont'd*)
  3. Genital characters: male (*Cont'd*)
    Penis (subject's self measure-
      ment)
      Length and circumference,
        normal and erect
      Angle, erect
      Curvature, erect
      Direction of carriage, erect
    History of circumcision
      Age involved
      Presence of frenulum
      Extent of foreskin
      Phimosis
    Hypospadia
    Pre-coital mucous secretion
    *Sperm examination
    Erection
      Speed
      Presence of pulsation
      Potency in coitus
      Duration
      Morning erections, frequency
  4. Genital characters: female
    Clitoris
      *Size
      *Adherence of foreskin
    Hymen
      Status
      History of rupture
    Vaginal mucous secretions
      Amount
      Variation in menstrual cycle
  5. Menstruation
    Age at menarche
    Length and regularity of men-
      strual cycle
    Duration of flow
    Pains
    History of menopause
  6. Erotic responsiveness
    Auto-erótic
      Observing self in mirror
      Observing genitalia
      Exhibitionism
    Homo-erotic
      Thinking of own sex
      Observing own sex
      Observing erect genitalia
      Observing buttocks
      Burlesque shows
      Nude art
      Obscene stories
      Erotic literature
      Erotic moving pictures
      Erotic photographs and
        drawings
      Dancing

Hetero-erotic
  Thinking of other sex
  Observing other sex
  Nude art
  Burlesque shows
  Erotic pictures
  Obscene stories
  Erotic literature
  Moving pictures
  Dancing
  Physical contacts
  Biting
  Being bitten
Zoö-erotic
  Observing animal coitus
  Physical contacts with ani-
    mals
Non-sexual stimuli
  Music
  Alcohol
  Motion
  Pain
  Sadistic situations
  Masochistic situations
  Other emotional situation
    (especially in children)
V. NOCTURNAL SEX DREAMS
  1. Ages involved
  2. Frequencies of dreams with or-
    gasm
  3. Frequencies of dreams without
    orgasm
  4. Content of dreams
    Homo-, hetero-, or zoö-erotic
    Other
VI. MASTURBATION
  1. Ages involved, pre- and post-
    adolescent
  2. Sources of learning
    Conversation and reading
    Observation
    Participation, heterosexual or
      homosexual
    Self discovery
  3. Frequencies
    Maximum per week
    Means at each age
  4. Techniques
    For male
      Manual
      Frictional
      Oral
      Special devices
      Urethral insertions
    For female
      Breast
      Clitoral
      Vaginal insertion
      Frictional

VI. MASTURBATION (*Cont'd*)
  4. Techniques (*Cont'd*)
      Thigh pressure
      Urethral insertions
      With devices
  5. Time required for orgasm
  6. Accompanying imagery
      Self
      Homosexual
      Heterosexual
      Zoö-erotic
      Sado-masochistic
  7. Subject's evaluation
      Period involving fear or con-
        flict
      Sources of resolution of conflict
      Rejection: period involved,
        reasons for
      Estimate of moral, psychic,
        physical consequences
VII. HETEROSEXUAL HISTORY
  1. Pre-adolescent play
      Ages involved, frequencies
      Companions: ages and number
      Techniques
        Exhibition
        Physical exploration
        Vaginal insertion
        Urethral insertion
        Mouth-genital contact
        Coitus
  2. Pre-marital petting
      Ages involved
      Frequencies
      Companions
        Number in grade and high
          school
        Number between high school
          and marriage
      Techniques
        General body contact
        Lip kissing
        Tongue kissing
        Breast manipulation, manual
        Breast manipulation, oral
        Manual manipulation, male
          genitalia
        Manual manipulation, fe-
          male genitalia
        Mouth-genital contact on
          male, on female
        Genital apposition without
          entry
        Orgasm without intercourse,
          in male, in female
      Frequencies
      Ages involved
      After-effects
        Nervous disturbance

        Genital cramps
        Masturbation
  3. Attitudes on pre-marital coitus
      Sources of restraint
        Moral
        Lack of opportunity
        Lack of interest
        Fear of pregnancy
        Fear of venereal disease
        Fear of social disapproval
        Desire for virginity in fiancée
        Desire for marriage
        Desire for children, number
          desired
        Intention to have, or to con-
          tinue coitus
        Evaluation of own coital ex-
          perience
  4. Experience in pre-marital coitus
      Ages involved
      First experience
        Age and nature of partner
        Virginity of partner
        Speed of orgasm
        Physical satisfaction
      Frequencies in coitus
      Partners
        Total number
        Prostitutes or companions
        Age range
        Youngest since subject was
          eighteen
        Age preference
        Marital status
        Consanguinity
        Virginity
      Resulting pregnancies, births,
        abortions
        Ages involved
        Legal aspects
        Financial aspects
      Arrangements
        Places utilized for coitus
        Opportunity and desire for
          nudity
  5. Marital intercourse (separate rec-
      ords for each marriage)
      First experience
        Age of each spouse
        Virginity of partner
        Speed of orgasm
        Physical satisfaction
        Lapse between marriage and
          first coitus
      Frequencies
        Maximum ever
        Means at various periods
      Relation of sexual and marital
        adjustments

VII. HETEROSEXUAL HISTORY (*Cont'd*)

6. Extra-marital relations
   Ages involved
   Partners
     Number
     Age range
     Marital status
     Companions or prostitutes
   Frequencies
     Extra-marital coitus
     Extra-marital petting without intercourse
   Spouse's knowledge of the intercourse
   Effect on marriage
   Desire for further experience
7. Post-marital intercourse
   Ages involved
   Partners
     Number
     Age range
     Marital status
     Companions or prostitutes
   Frequencies
8. Intercourse with prostitutes
   Ages involved
   Number of prostitutes
   Frequencies
   Mouth-genital techniques
   Comparisons with non-prostitutes
9. Coital techniques
   Pre-coital play
     Duration
     Lip kissing
     Tongue kissing
     Breast manipulation: manual
     Breast manipulation: oral
     Genital manipulation: manual, by male and female
     Genital manipulation: oral, by male and female
     Frequency of orgasm
   Coital positions: relative frequencies and preferences
     Male superior
     Female superior
     Side
     Sitting
     Standing
     Rear entry
     Anal
     Other variations
   Male orgasm
     Duration of intromission
     Multiple climaces
   Female orgasm
     Frequency

Multiple climaces
Date of first orgasm in coitus
Relation to coital techniques
Nudity
  Frequency
  Attitudes
Preference for light or dark
Fantasies during coitus

10. Contraceptive history: pre-marital, marital, extra-marital; techniques employed, satisfaction and effectiveness
    Condom
      Source
      Testing
      Lubrication
      Breakage
    Diaphragm or cap
      Source
      Type
    Withdrawal
    Douche alone
      Materials employed
    Safe period
    Jelly alone
    Other techniques
11. Group heterosexual activities
    Circumstances, frequency
    Number and nature of partners
    Participation in strip poker
    Fraternal and other group initiation activities
    Observation of coitus
      Of parents
      Of friends
      Of professional exhibitionists
12. Heterosexual prostitution (the subject as prostitute; males or females as heterosexual prostitutes)
    Ages involved
    First experience
      Occasion
      Partner
      Pay involved
    Frequencies per week
      During first year
      During subsequent periods
    Maximum number of partners per day, per week
    Average number of partners per day and per week, at various periods
    Nature of partners
      Total number
      Age: range, average
      Number who return
      Longest affair

VIII. HOMOSEXUAL HISTORY (*Cont'd*)
  1. Pre-adolescent play (*Cont'd*)
    Mouth-genital contact
    Anal
  2. Post-adolescent experience
    Ages involved
    First experience
      Age
      Partner
        Age
        Race
        Relation to subject
      Circumstances
        Place of contact
        Initiation of approach
        Techniques employed, passive, active, or mutual
        Financial arrangements
        Satisfaction for subject
      Age of first experience with each technique, passive and active
        Manual
        Oral
        Anal
        Breast (for female)
        Femoral
        Full body contact
      Frequency
        During first year
        Maximum, ever, per day
        Maximum, ever, per week
        Average per week during each year
        Total number of contacts
      Partners
        Total number
        Age range
        Comparisons with age of subject
      Age preferences
      Reasons for age preferences
      Social position
        Students in grade school
        Students in high school
        Students in college
        Clergy
        Teachers
        Art groups
        Professional persons
        Business groups
        Armed forces
        Laboring groups
        Law enforcement officers
      Highest position held
      Number married
      Number without previous homosexual experience
      Number of oncers
      Duration of longest affairs
      Relations involving love and affection
      Percentage of approaches which are rejected
      Races involved: white, Negro, others
    Techniques
      Petting, passive and active
      Lip kissing
      Tongue kissing
      Body kissing
      Breast manipulation, manual
      Breast manipulation, oral
      Genital manipulation, manual
      Genital manipulation, oral
      Flagellation on back, buttocks, genitalia
      Urethral insertions
      Anilinctus
      Nudity
      Positions involved (including 69)
      Preference for light or dark
      Places involved
    Subject's orgasm
      Frequency by each technique or by spontaneous ejaculation
    Partner's orgasm
      Frequency by each technique or by spontaneous ejaculation
  3. Psychic reactions
    Preferences for
      Masculine or feminine type of partner
      Partner of particular height
      Partner of particular weight
      Partner of particular complexion
      Particular amount of body hair
      Particular genital characteristics
      Particular breast characteristics
      Circumcised partner
      Other physical qualities of partner
      Reaction to odor and taste, genitalia and semen
  4. Sources of contacts
    Personal friends
    Pick-ups
      Street

VIII. Homosexual History (Cont'd)
    4. Sources of contacts (Cont'd)
        Park
        Hotel
        Theatre
        Tavern
        Night club
        Restaurant
        Beach
        Transportation terminal
        Public bath
        Hitch hiking
        Other places
    5. Social conflicts
        Difficulties met in home, school, community, business
        Arrests, court action, penal history
        Blackmail, active and passive
        Robbery, active and passive
        Restriction to homosexual associates
    6. Homosexual prostitution
        Subject as prostitute
        Frequency
        Situations
        Amounts involved
        Long-time maintenance as prostitute
        Subject paying prostitutes
        Frequency
        Situations
        Amounts involved
        Long-time maintenance of prostitutes

    7. Subject's self analysis
        Recognition of physical stigmata
        Carriage and movements
        Voice
        Hip movements
        Walk
        Dress
        Make-up
        Interest in transvestism
        Other qualities
        Conflicts and regrets
        Expectancy for continuation
        Expectancy for transfer to heterosexual
        Recommendation of the homosexual for others
        Subject's analysis of factors involved
        Subject's estimate of extent of homosexuality
        Among males, females
        Among Negroes, whites
IX. Animal Contacts
    1. Ages involved
    2. Frequencies
        With orgasm
        Without orgasm
    3. Animal species involved, with preferences
    4. Techniques
        Masturbation of animal
        Vaginal coitus
        Mouth-genital contact
        Passive
        Active

Each item in the above list has been strictly defined in order to standardize the data used in the study; but the body of definitions is, unfortunately, too large to include in the present volume. As previously indicated (Chapter 2), the sequence of topics actually used in an interview is varied in accordance with the age, social background, and experience of the particular subject, and the sequence shown in the above list has never been used. Neither does the sequence in the list correspond with the one shown in the coded form of Figure 2. Although many of the items in the list are covered by single questions, and although an occasional question may elicit information on two or more points, it often takes more extended inquiry to secure particular answers. Consequently, the number of questions asked may considerably exceed the number of items which are covered. It has already been noted (Chapter 2) that additional questions may be asked of subjects who have been involved in activities which are not covered in the routine interviews. Persons with experience in particular situations, as in the armed forces, in prisons, CCC camps, and other institutions, are questioned in particular detail concerning those periods.

CODING

The data obtained in each interview are recorded directly in the sort of code which is shown in Figure 2. No record is kept in any other form, and the coded data have never been translated into any longhand or typewritten account. Coding at the time of the interview serves several functions: (1) It facilitates recording, making it possible to secure a complete history without slowing up an interview, and without losing rapport with the subject. (2) It preserves the confidence of the record, and this is particularly important in a sex study. (3) It facilitates the transference of the data from the original record sheet to punched cards for statistical analyses. (4) It increases the accuracy of the coding because the subject is present at the time of the operation. Where there is uncertainty about the classification of the data, additional questions may be asked and final determinations may be made on the spot. When coding is delayed until after a longhand record is carried back to the laboratory, the investigator too often finds that there are insufficient data to determine what classifications are involved. (5) Coding is of supreme importance in conserving space, making it possible to put the whole of the basic history on a single sheet, or on two sheets in the case of individuals who have especial experience in pre-marital intercourse, in extra-marital intercourse, in the homosexual, or in prostitution. Where the original record is made in longhand which is subsequently copied onto typewritten sheets, or even where the basic record is made in a standard or special system of shorthand, each history may extend over twenty, or thirty, or in some studies over a hundred or more pages. Coding and punching cards from such data are slow and some-times well-nigh impossible procedures. Moreover, it is always difficult for the investigator to comprehend the whole of such a history when it is spread over so many pages. If the record is confined to a single sheet, it is possible to correlate any item with any and every other item by a rapid sweep of one's eye over the page of simple and precisely placed symbols. (6) It facilitates and encourages the systematic coverage of the same items on each and every history. At the end of an interview, a rapid examination of the page will show what items have been missed, and the blank places can be filled before the subject has departed.

The specific code used in the present study cannot be explained because of the necessity for maintaining the confidence of the record. However, certain of the principles involved can be described for the benefit of those who are interested in developing coding devices in other studies:

1. The record is made on a ruled form which provides a number of blocks somewhat in excess of the number of items on the basic history (Figure 2). The form used in the present study is a standard Keuffel and Esser product (General Data Sheet No. 358–230), with over-printing done on our especial order.

2. Each aspect of the sex history is recorded in a particular block or portion of a particular block. The significance of any symbol depends, consequently, upon its position in a particular block on the page.

3. Each block has its own system of symbols, its own independent code.

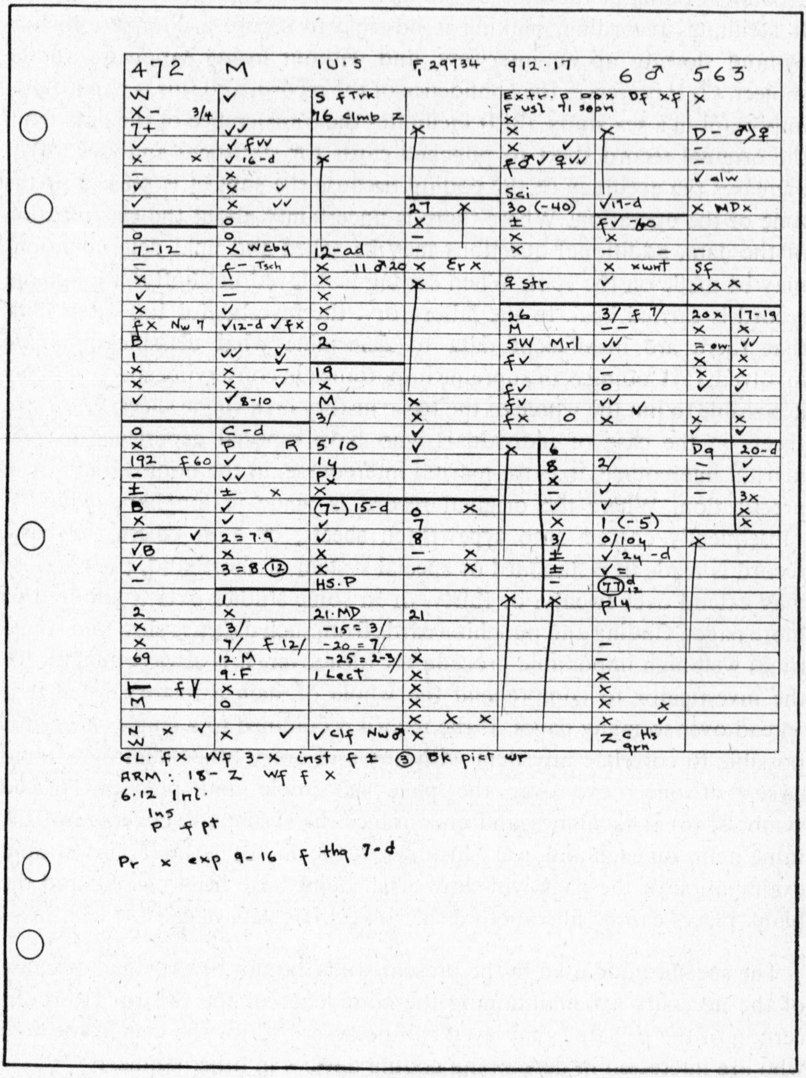

Figure 2. Sample history in code

4. In each block, the available symbols are sufficient in number to designate all of the categories into which the particular data will be classified during subsequent analyses. It is necessary to anticipate the whole array of possible classifications, including those that lie beyond usual

experience. The code used in the present study is so flexible that it has been possible to handle every type of overt activity and every sort of attitudinal situation which we have attempted to record in the 12,000 histories now at hand.

5. Since this study has been primarily concerned with percentages of incidence, with frequency distributions, graded scales of attitudes, intensities of response, and other questions of degree, the code provides for a considerable series of classifications of each item. Rarely is it a matter of alternative possibilities—of a yes or a no. It is the usual statistical experience that six to a dozen or twenty categories, and occasionally a few more, provide the number of points best designed to establish a curve; and in most instances there should be that many possibilities in the code for each item, in each block.

6. Where the nature of the code allows, as in using numbers to designate the ages or years involved, there is no objection to recording more detail than is used in the subsequent analyses. It not infrequently happens that such detail proves useful in making finer calculations than were originally planned.

7. The symbols used in coding data in the present study have included various mathematical signs ($\pm$, $-$, $\times$, $\sqrt{}$, 0, $\sqrt{}\sqrt{}$) and numbers for recording ages, the years involved, frequencies, and still other items. In addition, we have used numbers, letters, symbols derived from standard practice in biology, chemistry, physics, and the other sciences, and some unique symbols developed especially for this study.

8. There is no written key to the code that has been used in the present study, and the strict maintenance of that rule has been necessary for preserving the confidence of the record.

9. In consequence, each interviewer has had to memorize the code and learn, through considerable drilling, the significance of each block, and the symbols pertaining thereto.

10. In coding items that are not discrete in nature, it is necessary to make precise definitions to which each coded symbol should apply. The coding done by different interviewers on a project must constantly be checked to provide strict standardization. This is especially important in coding attitudes, intensities of response, and other non-discrete materials. For this reason in the present study a minimum of such items has been employed, and for these items the judgments made by the several interviewers have been repeatedly analyzed and coordinated.

SUPPLEMENTARY DATA

While most of the material in the present volume is based upon the data which have been routinely secured in the interviews, considerable attention has been given to securing supplementary information by other techniques.

These additional data have come from a considerable list of subjects with whom long-time social contacts have been maintained, in some cases for as long as seven and eight years. Time has been spent in their homes, and visits have been made with them to the homes of their friends, to theatres and to concerts, to night-clubs and to taverns, and to their other places of recreation. During these contacts, there have been abundant opportunities to observe how these individuals react to a variety of social, professional, academic, and other situations. With many of them there has been a considerable correspondence which now supplements their original histories with extensive day by day records of their activities, and of their thinking on various aspects of sex. In a number of cases there are several hundred pages, and in each of two cases there are over a thousand pages of such supplementary material. These latter constitute more extensive sexual histories than any which have yet been published on particular individuals. For some subjects there are photographic collections of their imaginative drawings, and scrapbooks; there are photographic collections of the complete artistic output of some of the artists who have contributed to the study, and complete collections of the books written by certain other subjects. For others who have had contact with public agencies, we have transcripts of the court records, institutional records, data from social agencies, and other material. While these supplementary records have contributed little to the statistical tabulations of data, they have provided a considerable portion of the detail which is given in this volume on the physical nature of sexual arousal and of orgasm, and on the psychologic and social concomitants of sexual behavior, particularly in relation to the factors which motivate and control the activities.

A number of persons have turned in sexual calendars and diaries showing their day to day activities over some period of time. The calendars now at hand cover periods which range from six months to more than thirty-five years in length. They admirably supplement the information routinely obtained on the standard histories. They provide data on the weekly periodicity which a seven-day calendar and the consequent social organization impose upon many human activities, as Havelock Ellis pointed out for a group of diaries which he studied (Ellis 1897, 1936 Edit.); and they clearly demonstrate the monthly periodicity of sexual responsiveness in the female, and the lack of any such periodicity in the male. As soon as there are enough of these calendars, it will be possible to run correlations between the precise records they supply and the estimated frequencies of activities obtained in the regular interviews; and it is unfortunate that there are not enough of the calendars yet available to make the analyses in the present volume. **Persons who have kept records or who are willing to begin keeping day by day calendars showing the frequencies and the sources of their sexual outlet, are urged to place the accumulated data at our disposal.**

Throughout this study, especial attention has been given to the communities in which the subjects of this study have lived. Contacts have been maintained with some of the communities for months or even several years. In that way it has been possible to win confidences from persons who hesitated to contribute their histories when we first arrived. In time one becomes accepted in the homes of a community and becomes acquainted with the daily lives of its individual members. One becomes acquainted with the general attitudes of the community on matters of sex and learns something about the community backgrounds which determine the early development of individual patterns of sexual behavior, and their fixation in the adult histories. One begins to understand how the church, the schools, political leaders, social agencies, and other groups affect the community's thinking on these matters. One learns how far each community goes in controlling the sexual activities of its individual members, and how its law enforcement officials act when sexual situations are involved. The communities with which we have maintained such long-time contacts include:

College communities connected with a variety of institutions
Several upper middle-class groups
Several professional groups
A remote and isolated rural community
A concentrated and rather large homosexual community in a large city
A Negro underworld community in a large city
Several penal institutional groups
A white male underworld group in a large city

THE TWELVE-WAY BREAKDOWN

It has previously been pointed out that the analyses in the present study have depended upon successive breakdowns of the total population on the basis of twelve biologic and socio-economic factors. Each of the ultimate groups resulting from these breakdowns is, in consequence, homogeneous in respect to these twelve items. The exact nature of each item involved is shown in the following tabulation.

1. Sex. A 2-way breakdown into male and female populations.

2. Race-cultural Group. An 11-way or further breakdown into groups which are:

(1) American and Canadian White
(2) American and Canadian Negro
(3) British (Great Britain)
(4) Western and Northern European
(5) Mediterranean European
(6) Latin American
(7) Slavic
(8) Oriental (Asia)

(9) Filipino
(10) Polynesian
(11) American Indian

There are still other groups to be considered and further breakdowns of the above which can be made whenever the material becomes available. The question is one of race-cultural backgrounds, rather than racial background in the exclusively biologic sense; and the subject's place of birth, his place of residence during childhood and adolescent years, and the ancestral home of the parents decide the race-cultural group to which he belongs. An individual may be placed in two or more of these groups if he has lived for appreciable periods of time in two or more of the areas, particularly if he has ever had an adolescent background which is definitely different from that of the United States in which he is now living.

The present volume is confined to a record on American and Canadian whites, but we have begun accumulating material which will make it possible to include the American and Canadian Negro groups in later publications. Several hundred histories from still other race-cultural groups begin to show the fundamental differences which exist between American and other patterns of sexual behavior, but the material is not yet sufficient for publication.

3. Marital Status. A 3-way breakdown into single, married, and post-marital groups. The single persons have never been married. The married persons were living, at the time they contributed their histories, either in formally consummated legal marriages or in common-law relations that had lasted for a year or more. The post-marital cases were widowed, divorced, or permanently separated from their former spouses.

4. Age. An 18-way breakdown by five-year periods, ranging from a group which has its maximum age at 5, to a group with a maximum age of 90. The chief difficulty involved here is the existence of three systems for designating age. Each system is more or less confined to a particular social level, persons of lower levels usually calculating in terms of their forthcoming birthdays, while better educated persons are in the habit of expressing their ages in terms of past birthdays. Some persons (perhaps most commonly in the middle classes) express their ages in terms of their nearest birthdays, and this is the system used by the insurance companies and by many government agencies. The error introduced by these diverse systems is rarely compensated for in the literature of the social sciences (Pearl 1940: 74). Ages given in institutional records are likely to be in error by a year, especially where the data apply to lower level inmates. Throughout the present study an attempt has been made to determine the precise year of birth and to calculate all ages as from the past birthday; but this has not always been possible and, consequently, differences in mean ages of two groups that are not more than a year apart are never to be taken as significant, because of the uncertainty involved in the original record (also *cf.* U. S. Census 1940: Populat. 4 (1):2–4).

5. Age at Adolescence. A 6-way or further breakdown based on the age of the subject at the time of the onset of adolescence. The determination of the year involved in the onset of adolescence is described in Chapters 5 and 9. The breakdown is as follows: Those who start adolescence at 10 or earlier, at 11, at 12, at 13, at 14, and at 15 and later.

6. Educational Level. A 9-way breakdown on the basis of the number of years in a completed educational history, by two-year periods. This classification can be made for those who have permanently stopped their schooling before contributing a history, but it cannot be made for those who are still in school. Specifically, the groups have had the following years of schooling: 0–2, 3–4, 5–6, 7–8, 9–10, 11–12, 13–14, 15–16, 17 plus. The last group includes all those who have done any graduate work. The classification depends upon the educational level attained by the individual, rather than upon the number of years required to reach that level. On the other hand, ever since state laws have required a minimum number of years of school attendance, there have been school systems which pass pupils through the grades and even into high school without respect to their actual achievements, and it is occasionally possible to find an illiterate or even a feeble-minded child who has been in the eighth or ninth grade in school. In such cases, the educational rating of the individual should be lowered to a grade approximating the one in which he could perform satisfactory work. In cases of persons who have acquired their education through private tutoring or through their own independent reading and travel, as sometimes happens in families of upper social levels, the educational rating should approximate the level to which the individual's achievements would have carried him in a formal school system. There are, however, few instances where it is necessary to make such arbitrary adjustments and, on the whole, the raw rating of an educational level is the best single indicator of the social stratum to which an individual belongs (Chapter 10).

7. Occupational Class of Subject. A 10-way breakdown based upon the classes developed by Chapin (1933) and W. Lloyd Warner (Warner and Lunt 1941, 1942, Warner and Srole 1945), and modified by other workers (Hollingshead 1939). This is an attempt to designate the social status of an individual by measuring the prestige of the work in which he is engaged. Persons within each occupational class not only work together, but carry on their social activities together. They are less often involved in social activities with persons of other occupational classes. The classification does not depend upon the individual's income. Warner's original classification has been adapted to the needs of the present study in the following manner:

(0) DEPENDENTS. If the subject is an adult who is dependent upon the State or upon a person other than a spouse for his or her support, the classification is 0. If the individual is a minor dependent upon his parents or other guardians, the classification is shown as a 0, with the classification of the parents shown in parenthesis, *e.g.*, 0 (5) for a minor from a home which belongs to class 5. The classification of a dependent wife is that of her husband.

(1) UNDERWORLD. Deriving a significant portion of the income from illicit activities: *e.g.*, bootleggers, con men, dope peddlers, gamblers, hold-up men, pimps, prostitutes, etc.

(2) DAY LABOR. Persons employed by the hour for labor which does not require special training: *e.g.*, construction labor, domestic help, factory labor, farm hands, junk and trash collectors, laundry help, maids, messenger boys, porters, railroad section hands, stevedores, WPA labor, etc.

(3) SEMI-SKILLED LABOR. Persons employed by the hour or on other temporary bases for tasks involving some minimum of training: *e.g.*, semi-skilled labor in factories or on construction jobs, bartenders, bell hops, blacksmiths, cooks (some), elevator operators, filling station attendants, firemen on railroads, firemen in cities, marines, miners, policemen, prize fighters, sailors, showmen, soldiers, stationary engineers, street car conductors, taxi drivers, truck drivers, ushers, etc.

(4) SKILLED LABOR. Persons involved in manual activities which require training and experience. Employed either by the hour or more often for piece work, or on salary: *e.g.*, skilled workmen as defined by labor unions, in factories or on construction jobs, athletes (professional), bakers, barbers, bricklayers (skilled), carpenters (skilled), cooks (skilled), dressmakers (skilled), electricians, farm owners (some), foremen in factories, linemen, machinists, masons, mechanics (skilled), plumbers, printers, radio technicians, tool and die makers, welders, etc.

(5) LOWER WHITE COLLAR GROUP. Persons involved in work which is not primarily manual but which more particularly depends upon their educational background and mental capacity: *e.g.*, army officers (some), bank clerks, bookkeepers, clergymen (in smaller churches), clerks in offices, clerks in better stores, express and postal agents, salesmen (some), secretaries, small store owners, small business operators, stenographers, farmers (some), insurance agents, musicians (some), nurses, navy officers (some), political officers (some), railroad conductors, teachers in grade schools, laboratory technicians, etc.

(6) UPPER WHITE COLLAR GROUP. Including persons of some importance in the business group, army officers (some), bank officials, certified public accountants, clergymen (most), better store owners, better actors, artists, and musicians, navy officers (some), school teachers in high schools,

school principals, farm and ranch owners (of better rank), management in construction and other businesses, higher political officers, some lawyers, some dentists, most salesmen, welfare workers, etc.

(7) PROFESSIONAL GROUP. Persons holding positions that depend upon professional training which is usually beyond the college level: *e.g.*, college professors, trained lawyers, physicians, dentists (with better training), trained engineers; some actors, artists, musicians, and writers; some clergymen, etc.

(8) BUSINESS EXECUTIVE GROUP. Primarily executive officers in larger businesses, and persons holding high social rank because of financial status or because of hereditary family position, including persons in the Social Register.

(9) EXTREMELY WEALTHY GROUP. Living primarily on income and occupying high social status because of their monied position and/or their family backgrounds.

8. Occupational Class of Parent. A 10-way breakdown on the same basis as that for the occupational class of the subject. Significant as a measure of the childhood and educational backgrounds of the subject.

9. Rural-Urban Background. A 5-way breakdown as follows:

(0) Never lived on an operating farm
(1) Incidental residence of at least a year, but not for any long period of years in rural areas
(2) Primarily rural, up to 11 years of age
(3) Primarily rural, between 12 and 18 years of age
(4) Primarily rural, after 18 years of age

The classification gives an opportunity to measure the effect of rural backgrounds during those periods in childhood and adolescence which are most important in the development of sexual patterns. A single individual may fall into more than one of these classes. Town farmers who live on farms which are operated for them by other persons, while they maintain businesses and social interests in the city, are not treated as rural.

10. Religious Groups. A 3-way or further breakdown into Protestant, Catholic, Jewish and other groups. Based upon membership, attendance, or any degree of activity or nominal connection with a religious group, in any period of the subject's life. A particular subject may belong to more than one such group within his lifetime.

11. Religious Adherence. A 4-way breakdown showing the degree of active connection with a particular religious group, as follows:

(1) Actively concerned in a religious group, either as a regular attendant or as an active participant in organized church activities. For devout Catholics, frequency of attendance at confession, and for Orthodox Jews,

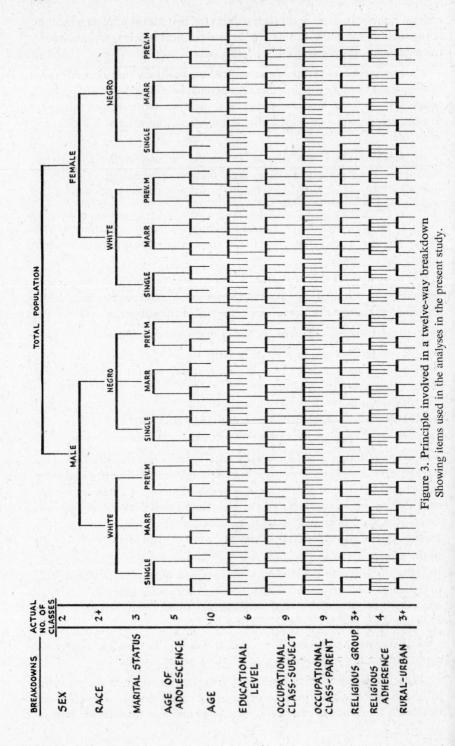

Figure 3. Principle involved in a twelve-way breakdown
Showing items used in the analyses in the present study.

frequency of attendance at the Synagogue and the extent to which the Orthodox observances are followed, provide measures of the individual's concern with his religion.

(2) Fairly frequent church attendance or activity.

(3) Infrequent church attendance or activity.

(4) Practically no church attendance or activity, although the individual's background may still be classifiable as Protestant, Catholic, or Jewish.

12. Geographic Origin. A breakdown which will be made as soon as the sample in the present study is sufficiently large. Residence is defined as continuous living in a given place for a period of at least twelve months. A single individual may, therefore, claim several places of residence in a lifetime. The state of residence for the most continuous period of time, and the place of residence during the childhood and adolescent years, will probably represent the most significant part of the data.

Successive breakdowns on these twelve items give a geometrically expanding array (Figure 3) which terminates in a great series of populations, each of which is homogeneous for all of the items involved in the breakdown. With only 12,000 cases now in hand, it has not been possible to make more than a 6- or 7-way breakdown at any point in the analysis, and there are some places at which it is impossible to make anything beyond a 5-way breakdown. As the study progresses, it should be possible and will be desirable to make the 12-way breakdowns outlined above.

Psychologic measurements of mental capacity have been available on two or three thousand of the persons who have contributed to this study. Unfortunately, the tests used have been so diverse, and administered by such a diversity of testers (in schools, colleges, and mental and penal institutions) that it has proved difficult to coordinate the measurements. An investigation of the possibility of a correlation between mental level and patterns of sexual behavior should be undertaken in the further development of the present research program.

The number of groups in the theoretic 12-way breakdown outlined above is nearly two billion, and a complete survey of the whole population would, obviously, be impossible if there were no means of reducing the problem. Fortunately, many of the theoretic groups are non-existent, or so rare in the American population that they are unimportant for study. For instance, it would never be possible to secure a statistically good sample of Orthodox Jewish males who were Negro, single, between the ages of eighty-five and ninety, illiterate, living in rural areas, and belonging to the Social Register. Again, the problem may be reduced by confining the study for the time being to American and Canadian white and Negro groups, and the theoretic eleven race-cultural groups are thus reduced to two. Since the age groups between 10 and 60 are the ones most frequently met with, the age breakdown may be limited to 11 instead of the theoretic 18 groups. In some other classifications, the problem can similarly be confined. Preliminary experience indicates that some groups are so similar that they may be thrown together for analyses. Thus the theoretic 9-way breakdown on the basis of the subject's educational history can become a 6-way breakdown into groups having 0–4, 5–8, 9–10, 11–12, 13–16, and 17 plus years of schooling; and for most purposes it can become a 3-way breakdown into groups having 0–8, 9–12, and 13 plus years of schooling. Finally, the problem is tremendously reduced because the history of each older person covers data for all the earlier 5-year age periods and, therefore, supplies cases for several of the breakdowns. This reduces the total problem to a small fraction of its theoretic magnitude, and brings it within the range of possible study.

SIZE OF SAMPLE

The number of factors which actually affect human sexual behavior must far exceed the twelve listed above. In spite of the degree of homogeneity which such a breakdown brings, there is a considerable amount of variation still to be found in each ultimate group. In order to understand any group it is necessary, therefore, to secure a sample of such size as will show the full range of the variation in the group, and show the frequency with which each type of variant occurs in the group. This is possible only with samples of some size.

In studies where an over-all picture of a total, undivided population is a chief objective, as in some of the Department of Agriculture surveys, and in most of the problems with which the Census Bureau has been concerned (Stephan, Deming, and Hansen 1940), the sampling has been considered sufficient when a small group of individuals represents each ultimate cell in the population. The validity of such a procedure may, however, be debatable even for over-all surveys, and it is certainly inadequate when an understanding of the variability within any sub-group is the prime concern. Persons who have recommended that we use pin-point sampling, and those who have urged that an elaboration of the techniques of factor analysis could accomplish the ends of this research with a sample of much smaller size, have failed to comprehend that the chief concern of the present study is an understanding of the sexual behavior of each segment of the population, and that it is only secondarily concerned with generalizations for the population as a whole. As subsequent chapters will indicate, there are segments of the population which engage in particular kinds of sexual activities with frequencies that average 10 or 20 times as high as the frequencies in other segments of the population. Scientifically and socially it is of the greatest importance to understand why populations differ as much as that. Pin-point sampling which is designed to secure an over-all picture of a total population provides no basis for analyzing factors which account for differences between groups, and it even obscures such differences, reducing all measures to the sort of mediocrity which a combination of high and low scores always gives.

It has, then, been of prime importance in the present study to determine the size of the sample needed in each ultimate group. Such a determination has been attempted through the strictly pragmatic procedure of making calculations on series of samples of different sizes. Means and medians* for both total and active populations, the incidences of active cases, the range, the height of the mode, and the locus of the mode have been calculated for each of the 698 samples which have been used in this study. Systematic comparisons of the results obtained from the populations of various sizes have provided information on the size of sample necessary for securing relatively stable results. The detailed data are shown in Tables 155 to 162, which form an Appendix in the present volume. A summary of the material shown in those tables is presented here as Table 2.

In every instance, the samples used in the present study have represented populations that were made homogeneous for sex, race, marital status, age, educational level, and either the rural-urban background or the religious background of the individual. The samples of various sizes have all been selected by a randomization performed on IBM machines. The successive samples in each problem contained 50, 100, 200, 300, 400, and (wherever the material was available) 600, 1000, and 1500 cases. Where there was still additional material, calculations were made for the total number of cases. In some instances more than 2700 histories were available for the final calculations.

The samples of successive size were all selected directly out of the total population, *i.e.*, the original sample of 50 cases was turned back into the total population after calculation, and the sample of 100 cases was then chosen from the total population. This process was repeated for each sample of subsequent size. In no instance was the larger sample obtained by adding cases to the smaller sample. If the latter procedure had been used, the results might have been confused because of variation in the increments which were added. The present method of selecting each sample has strictly confined the study to the problem of sample size.

Table 2 shows how many of the samples of various sizes (50, 100, 200, etc.) gave statistical calculations that were close enough to calculations derived from the largest samples to have been acceptable without the further accumulation of cases. The statistics derived from the largest sample in each series have been the bases for measuring the adequacy of the results obtained from the smaller samples. The smaller samples were identified as adequate whenever the statistics calculated from them came within 5 per cent, plus or minus (*i.e.*, within a total range of 10 per cent), of the corres-

---

* For definitions and explanations of the statistical terms used here, see later sections of the present chapter.

STATISTIC	PERCENT OF SAMPLES WHICH PROVE ADEQUATE WHEN SIZE OF SAMPLE IS:							
	50	100	200	300	400	600	1000	1500
MEAN FREQ., TOTAL POPULATION	%	%	%	%	%	%	%	%
All outlets	23	36	54	61	72	67	77	67
Masturbation	16	53	58	74	88	67	100	100
Nocturnal emissions	41	50	59	77	84	100	100	67
Pre-marital intercourse	16	16	37	21	65	50	50	33
Homosexual	5	11	37	32	12	17	33	33
MEAN FREQ., ACTIVE POPULATION								
All outlets	21	31	50	63	69	67	79	73
Masturbation	21	47	58	63	88	50	100	100
Nocturnal emissions	23	45	50	68	84	100	100	67
Pre-marital intercourse	26	16	26	37	53	50	50	33
Homosexual	0	0	32	47	24	33	67	67
MEDIAN FREQ., TOTAL POPULATION								
All outlets	14	34	49	64	67	75	90	50
Masturbation	5	42	47	63	65	67	100	33
Nocturnal emissions	18	22	33	61	63	100	100	67
Pre-marital intercourse	0	13	25	43	29	0	50	0
MEDIAN FREQ., ACTIVE POPULATION								
All outlets	21	31	48	52	71	67	73	67
Masturbation	11	32	37	58	71	67	100	67
Nocturnal emissions	32	36	59	50	89	100	100	100
Pre-marital intercourse	21	16	32	37	53	67	33	67
Homosexual	16	21	32	37	41	17	50	33
INCIDENCE								
All outlets	28	39	47	58	67	63	73	67
Masturbation	21	32	47	84	88	83	100	100
Nocturnal emissions	18	36	41	59	68	67	83	100
Pre-marital intercourse	11	11	26	26	41	33	67	...
Homosexual	5	11	21	16	29	33	17	33
RANGE (MINUS 1)								
All outlets	0	8	17	37	51	23	67	67
Masturbation	0	11	26	32	47	50	83	67
Nocturnal emissions	0	5	14	45	63	17	50	33
Pre-marital intercourse	0	11	11	26	35	33	67	67
Homosexual	0	11	16	47	41	17	83	100
MODE: HEIGHT								
All outlets	35	43	50	73	85	80	93	80
Masturbation	5	37	42	58	82	67	100	67
Nocturnal emissions	36	50	45	91	79	100	83	100
Pre-marital intercourse	42	53	53	74	100	83	100	100
Homosexual	68	58	84	95	100	100	100	100
All statistics	23%	35%	47%	60%	69%	63%	79%	69%
Number of samples studied	769	768	768	769	668	215	214	108

Table 2. Size of sample versus adequacy of sample

For an explanation, see the accompanying text.

ponding statistics derived from the largest samples. All comparisons shown in the table have been on this 5 per cent basis, except the comparisons of incidence data, for which a range of error of only 2 per cent was allowed. These definitions of adequacy have been, of course, quite arbitrary. It is obviously possible to calculate the adequacy of each sample when a larger range of error, or when only a smaller range of error, is allowed. A whole series of such calculations should be made before this sample study is completed; but such an extended statistical survey must be pursued elsewhere, rather than in the present volume.

An examination of Table 2 warrants a number of conclusions concerning the size of the sample that is needed for each of the ultimate cells in the present study. These generalizations will need to be modified before they are extended to problems in other fields; but they have served as guides in the set-up of the immediate problem, and should provide some help to others who are interested in setting up similar surveys.

1. Samples of 50 cases chosen at random after a 6-way breakdown of the total population occasionally give results which are within 5 per cent of those obtained from samples of 1000, 1500, or more cases. This happens in something between 5 and 60 per cent of all the problems which we have worked; but in most categories hardly 20 per cent of the samples of 50 prove adequate. If a sample of 50 is all that is used, the calculations of various statistics for various types of sexual outlet could not be depended upon in more than 1 in 5 cases.

2. A sample of 100 proves adequate, by the above definition, in a much larger number of cases. 1 in 3 or even 1 in 2 of the samples of 100 give results which are within 5 per cent, plus or minus, of those obtained from the largest samples.

3. There has been a corresponding increase in the quality of these samples when the cases were increased to 200.

4. There is a still more marked increase in adequacy when 300 cases are used. On most of the statistics calculated on populations of 300, two-thirds to three-fourths or more of all the samples give results which are nearly identical to those obtained from the largest samples.

5. Samples of 400 show still improved quality in regard to nearly all the calculated statistics except the frequency data; but the improvement is hardly enough to warrant the time and effort involved in gathering the last 100 cases—unless it is important to obtain greater precision than 300 cases afford.

6. Samples of various sizes between 400 and 1500, or even 2700 cases, fail to show any consistent improvement. By standard statistical theory, a steady albeit slow improvement in the quality of the calculations might have been expected as the size of the sample was increased. We fail to find that this is so in the present problem. On the contrary, the statistics calculated on the larger samples vary erratically from sample to sample, almost as much as they do between populations of two, three, and four hundred cases.

7. The incidence data are the most stable, and samples of 50 or 100 give results which, in many cases, are comparable to those obtained from the largest samples (Figures 4, 5). If samples of 200 or 300 are used, in half or more of these small samples the incidence data fall within 2 per cent of those obtained from the larger samples.

8. The locus of the mode is adequately determined in two-thirds of the samples of 50 cases, and in 80 or 90 per cent of the samples of 100 cases. This statement would be modified, of course, if the categories used in the frequency distributions were more or less extended than those which have been used in the present study (Figures 4, 5).

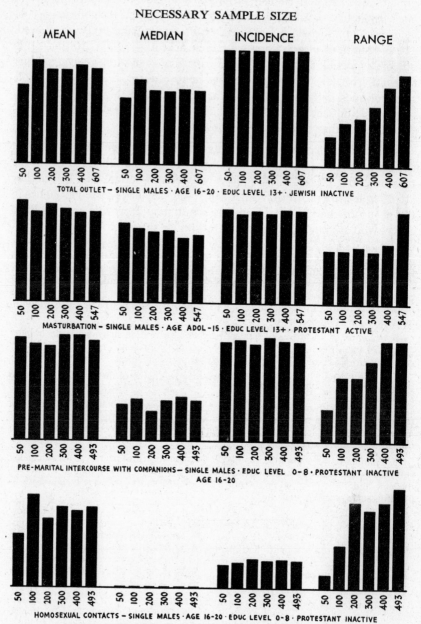

Figure 4. Relation of size of sample to statistical values

Size of each sample is shown in the figures at the base of each bar. Means and medians in each series are on the same scale, and therefore directly comparable.

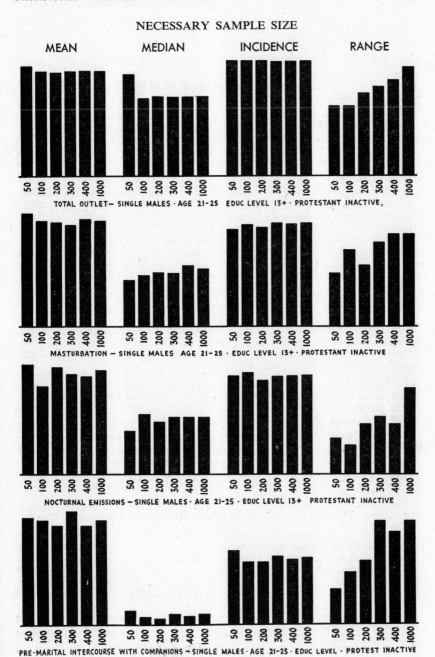

NECESSARY SAMPLE SIZE

Figure 5. Relation of size of sample to statistical values

Size of each sample is shown in the figures at the base of each bar. Means and medians in each series are on the same scale, and therefore directly comparable.

9. For most of the other statistics, samples of 300 are markedly better than samples of 200, except for the frequency data where samples of 400 are necessary to obtain consistent results (Figures 4, 5).

10. The range of variation which actually exists in a population is not adequately shown by any small sample. There is a steady extension of the range of variation through samples of 300 or 400, and in some cases the range is materially increased by still larger samples (Figures 4–7)

11. Frequency curves become increasingly smooth as the samples increase in size, at least up to 200 or 300 cases (Figures 6, 7). On some problems, they do not reach the ultimate degree of smoothness until 400 or 500 cases are used; but it is a waste of time and effort to secure a larger series of cases. Frequency curves never do reach the ideal in smoothness, at least with any large sample of the size (2700) which we have had for testing.

12. It is well known statistically that the adequacy of a sample depends upon its range of variation as well as upon its size. There are, therefore, some phenomena that may be sufficiently illustrated by samples that are inadequate for measuring other phenomena. The frequencies of masturbation, for instance, show a wider range of variation than the frequencies of nocturnal emissions, and the latter are sufficiently explored (Table 2) with a much smaller sample than would serve for describing masturbation in the same population. The size of a sample in a case history study, however, must be adequate for the examination of the most variable phenomenon which is to be studied.

13. Balancing the diverse considerations outlined above, we reach the conclusion that samples of 300 are desirable in each of the ultimate cells of the present study. Samples of 400 are enough better to warrant gathering that many histories when they are available. Samples of still larger size do not add enough information to warrant their use, and we have avoided going after such samples. The larger samples which are shown in a few places in the present volume have been obtained for the sake of an ultimate 7-, 8-, or even 12-way breakdown of the data.

14. While samples of 300 are more dependable than smaller samples, calculations based on samples of 100 or 200 have considerable significance, and calculations made in the present volume on samples of that size need not be dismissed as inadequate (Table 2, Figures 4, 5).

15. In a few cases, samples of 50 give a good indication of the results that a large sample would give. However, such small samples have been used in the present volume only when they belong to series for which most of the points are established by relatively large samples. Samples of 50 are used, for instance, to place older groups in age series for which larger samples of younger males have already established the trends.

16. Samples of less than fifty cases have not been used for any of the calculations in this volume. On occasion, incidental references have been made to such small groups.

17. All of the above conclusions apply to populations which are homogeneous for six of the factors which are used in the basic breakdown of the present problem. Preliminary calculations indicate that when seven or more breakdowns are made, the increasing homogeneity of each cell makes it possible to base analyses on something less than the three hundred cases called for above. Pragmatic tests of the size of sample necessary for these more complex breakdowns will have to be made as this research progresses.

It is customary in statistics to measure the accuracy of a calculated mean by computing its "standard deviation" (represented by the symbol σ_m), or by some similar measure of significance. This defines the limits on either side of the calculated mean, within which there is a 2 to 1 chance that the actual mean, the reality, may fall. Unfortunately, standard deviations of means are sometimes misinterpreted as measures of the adequacy of the samples on which they are based. In Tables 155–156 in the Appendix, standard deviations are attached to all of the means calculated for the samples of various sizes. Some idea of the effect of adding cases to originally smaller samples may be obtained from an examination of these standard deviations. More extensive comparisons of the significance of these statistical measures, in contrast to the results obtained by the pragmatic testing of sample size, will need to be made elsewhere at some later date.

Where the distribution of the variants in a population is fairly homogeneous (as in some physical universes), and where the range of variation is within limits which can be fairly well anticipated (again, as in some physical universes), a relatively small sample may be representative of the whole. But in the living world the distribution of the variants in any population is usually more irregular, and it is less often possible to anticipate the full range of variation. The number of factors affecting living protoplasm, and particularly the number of factors affecting the behavior of whole organisms, is infinitely greater than the number affecting most physical phenomena. There is, in consequence, much greater variation among living structures and biological phenomena. Behavior characters vary even more than physiologic characters, and these in turn vary more than morphologic characters (Pearl 1946: 43 ff.). Frequency distributions of physical phenomena often follow standard curves or simple permutations thereof; but frequency distributions in the living world are rarely normal, and usually fall into irregular curves that are sometimes not even smooth curves, as our own work on insect measurements has shown (preliminarily reported in Kinsey 1942), and as the frequency curves in the present volume will also demonstrate.

In such non-homogeneous populations, it is quite possible to collect a few individuals so nearly alike that the standard deviation of the mean is small. Unfortunately, in too many biologic, psychologic, sociologic, and anthropologic studies, including some of the published sex studies, such small standard deviations are taken as indicators of the adequacy of a sample, even though it may have only a half dozen or a dozen or a score or two individuals in it. Such a use of standard deviations or probable errors as measures of validity involves a misunderstanding of their real nature and function. The student with practical experience in taxonomy or in human surveying soon learns that the addition of a few more cases to such small samples may introduce data that are outside of the range of variation covered by the original specimens, and that such additions may alter the original calculations to an extent which would never have been anticipated through an examination of the standard deviations of the means. Each investigator must know the general order of the variation that may occur in the material with which he works, see to it that the sample is well spread through the whole range of variation, and learn

NECESSARY SAMPLE SIZE

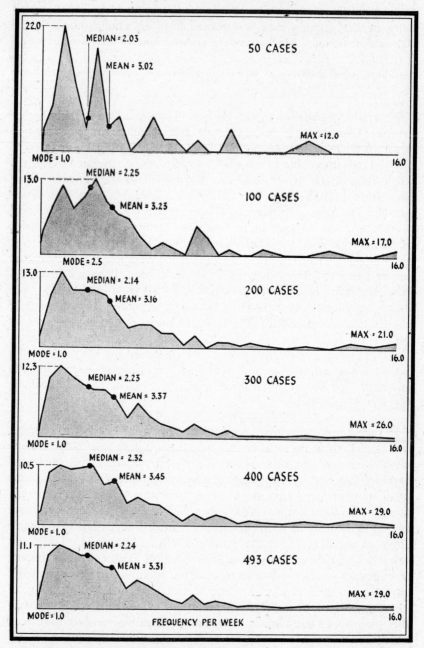

Figure 6. Relation of size of sample to form of frequency curve

Showing frequency distributions for total outlet. Based on single males, belonging to the age group 16–20, of grade school level (0–8), and inactive Protestant.

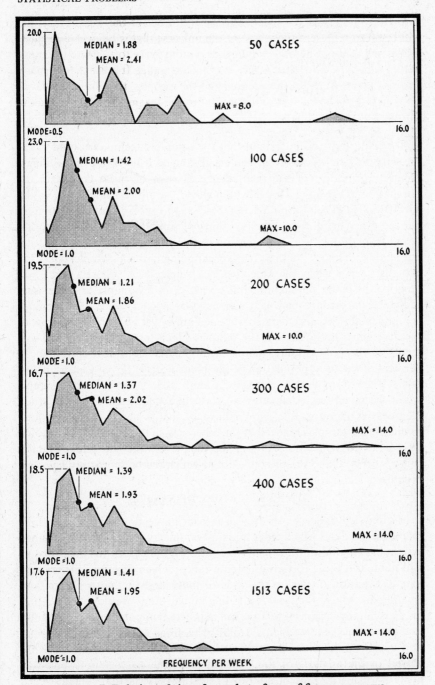

Figure 7. Relation of size of sample to form of frequency curve

Showing frequency distributions for masturbation. Based on single males belonging to the age group 16–20, of college level (13+), and inactive Protestant.

through some pragmatic means the general order of the sample size that will begin to represent the whole of the universe that is being sampled. At that point, and not before, standard deviations serve to indicate the range within which the calculated means may match reality. It is for that purpose, and not as measures of the adequacy of the samples, that standard deviations have been calculated and attached to the means shown in the tables throughout this volume.

It is important to understand that the sampling techniques used in the present study call for more or less **equal samples from each of the ultimate groups,** irrespective of the relative size of each of those groups in the population as a whole. This has been called "stratified sampling" (Snedecor 1946. See Whelpton and Kiser 1943–1945 for an instance of its use). On the other hand, many persons think of sampling as a technique that draws from each group in proportion to the size of that group in the total population. This is "representative sampling." Such samples may, in actuality, serve when the objective is a single set of figures which will describe the entire population. But whenever one attempts to understand the particular groups of which a population is composed, such a course is unacceptable because data so obtained are of variable reliability, due to the differences in the sizes of the samples which represent the several segments of the population. For instance, Negroes constitute less than 10 per cent of the total population of the United States (U. S. Census 1940); but a Negro sample that was only a tenth as large as the white sample would be much less adequate than the white sample. If one is to study Negroes as a group, one should have as many Negro cases as white. Similarly, the samples for each of the other cells in the present study should be more or less equal in size. This is a principle on which the public opinion surveys depend, and the principle about which the present study has been organized.

DIVERSIFICATION OF SAMPLE

In a physical universe, or even in measuring dead insects, it is possible to choose the cases which enter into any sample by some carefully planned system of randomization which avoids bias on the part of the investigator, and minimizes those fortuitous circumstances which account for the irregular distribution of particular kinds of individuals within a population. By the same token, the ideal set-up in a human study would involve a preliminary survey in which every person in the total population, or a randomized percentage of all persons, would be required to provide the information which would allow him to be classified on the basis of the items involved in the analysis of the problem (*e.g.,* the six-way or twelve-way breakdown in the present study). From the persons that fall into each ultimate cell, the necessary number of cases would then be selected by some thorough scheme of randomization, and persuaded or commanded to contribute the full and complete data necessary in the survey. A recent survey of factors affecting fertility, sponsored by the Milbank Foundation Fund, chose its sample in this way from white couples in the city of Indianapolis (Whelpton and Kiser 1943–1945).

Unfortunately, human subjects cannot be regimented as easily as cards in a deck, and the investigator of human behavior faces sampling problems which are not sufficiently allowed for by pencil and paper statisticians. In a nation-wide survey, it would be impossible to make the preliminary investigation necessary for classifying the population on a twelve-way, or even a six-way breakdown. Neither is it feasible to stand on a street corner, tap every tenth individual on the shoulder, and command him to contribute a full and frankly honest sex history. Theoretically less satisfactory but more practical means of sampling human material must be accepted as the best that can be done.

The first principle to observe in securing histories is that of diversifying each collection which enters into the sample. Even after a twelve-way breakdown, the population in each ultimate cell is still affected by a multiplicity of factors which cause variation in the group. Even after a twelve-way breakdown, a sample from one city cannot be taken as representative of cities in general. A study based on New York City (as nearly half of the previous sex studies have been) cannot be taken as representative of all other cities. The population in one city block differs from the population in the next block in the same city. A group from one church is not a duplicate of a group from the next church. The factory workers in one plant do not duplicate the factory workers in the next plant. Skilled carpenters must not be taken as representative of all skilled craftsmen. The students in one girls' college must not be depended upon for the total sample from exclusively girls' schools. The cases that are used to represent each ultimate cell in a human population should be drawn from a number of groups, widely distributed geographically, and including as great a diversity as is possible within the limits of the group.

HUNDRED PERCENT SAMPLES

Since it is impossible to secure a strictly randomized sample, the best substitute is to secure one hundred percent of the persons in each social unit from which the sample is drawn. One hundred percent of the members of a family group, all the persons living in a particular apartment house, all the members of a college sorority or fraternity, all the persons in some service club, all the members of some Sunday School class or some other church organization, all the persons in a city block, all the persons in a rural township, all the inmates of some penal or other institution, all the persons in some other unit, provided that unit has not been brought together by a common sexual interest.

HUNDRED PERCENT VERSUS PARTIAL SAMPLES
SINGLE WHITE MALES OF COLLEGE LEVEL

GROUP	SAMPLE	TOTAL POPULATION		ACTIVE POPULATION		
		Mean Frequency	Median Freq.	Incid. %	Mean Frequency	Median Freq.
AGE: ADOL.–15						
Total Outlet	100%	2.62 ± 0.11	1.96	95.6	2.74 ± 0.11	2.07
	Partial	2.89 ± 0.06	2.28	95.8	3.02 ± 0.06	2.40
Masturbation	100%	2.12 ± 0.09	1.52	82.7	2.56 ± 0.10	1.94
	Partial	2.25 ± 0.06	1.64	82.2	2.74 ± 0.06	2.11
Nocturnal Emissions	100%	0.30 ± 0.02	0.08	67.2	0.45 ± 0.03	0.26
	Partial	0.35 ± 0.02	0.11	70.7	0.49 ± 0.02	0.28
Pre-marital Coitus	100%	0.05 ± 0.02	0.00	9.5	0.56 ± 0.24	0.17
	Partial	0.08 ± 0.01	0.00	9.3	0.90 ± 0.11	0.30
Homosexual	100%	0.06 ± 0.01	0.00	17.9	0.32 ± 0.05	0.08
	Partial	0.10 ± 0.01	0.00	22.6	0.43 ± 0.04	0.09
AGE: 16–20						
Total Outlet	100%	2.38 ± 0.08	1.85	99.7	2.38 ± 0.08	1.85
	Partial	2.80 ± 0.05	2.20	99.8	2.81 ± 0.05	2.21
Masturbation	100%	1.61 ± 0.07	1.03	88.9	1.81 ± 0.07	1.29
	Partial	1.84 ± 0.05	1.24	88.5	2.08 ± 0.05	1.56
Nocturnal Emissions	100%	0.42 ± 0.02	0.24	91.3	0.46 ± 0.03	0.28
	Partial	0.42 ± 0.01	0.25	91.3	0.47 ± 0.01	0.29
Pre-marital Coitus	100%	0.18 ± 0.02	0.00	36.1	0.50 ± 0.05	0.23
	Partial	0.27 ± 0.02	0.00	39.6	0.67 ± 0.04	0.21
Homosexual	100%	0.03 ± 0.01	0.00	12.3	0.25 ± 0.04	0.08
	Partial	0.08 ± 0.01	0.00	17.1	0.44 ± 0.05	0.09
AGE: 21–25						
Total Outlet	100%	2.14 ± 0.09	1.64	100.0	2.14 ± 0.09	1.64
	Partial	2.57 ± 0.06	1.93	99.8	2.58 ± 0.06	1.94
Masturbation	100%	1.15 ± 0.07	0.66	88.8	1.30 ± 0.07	0.80
	Partial	1.34 ± 0.05	0.69	86.5	1.55 ± 0.05	0.88
Nocturnal Emissions	100%	0.40 ± 0.03	0.23	86.4	0.47 ± 0.04	0.30
	Partial	0.38 ± 0.02	0.22	87.2	0.43 ± 0.02	0.28
Pre-marital Coitus	100%	0.36 ± 0.05	0.01	52.3	0.68 ± 0.08	0.30
	Partial	0.47 ± 0.03	0.03	55.2	0.86 ± 0.05	0.31
Homosexual	100%	0.03 ± 0.01	0.00	5.7	0.57 ± 0.17	0.23
	Partial	0.10 ± 0.02	0.00	10.4	1.01 ± 0.12	0.32

Table 3. Comparisons of hundred percent and partial samples

The "partial samples" include both the hundred percent groups and the volunteers obtained outside of the hundred percent groups. Comparisons have been made on this basis in order that these "partial samples" should correspond with the samples on which calculations have been made throughout the present volume. Populations for the hundred percent samples in the three age groups are 655, 664, and 367, respectively; and for the partial samples, 2144, 2197, and 1531, respectively.

Securing a hundred percent of any group is, in actuality, more feasible than securing a good random sample of the same group; for, as already noted (Chapter 2), it is possible to develop a community interest in a group project, and this puts considerable pressure on each individual to contribute as a matter of loyalty or obligation to the group of which he is a part. It is, of course, easier to secure a hundred percent of a smaller group, unless it be a group of inmates in an institution, and it is ordinarily impossible to secure a hundred percent of any group unless the investigators can work with it for a period of weeks or months. Ordinarily it is not profitable to try to secure a complete sample until an appreciable portion (perhaps a half or more) of a group has contributed. Then the first persons who have given histories can help develop a group project by enlisting whatever organization there is to make it an official project. The time required to secure such a sample is costly, as calculated per history, and that is one reason why a larger number of hundred percent groups has not yet been secured for the present study. In some cases it has been necessary to work with the last few individuals in a group for as long as a year or two before they agree to contribute.

Of the 12,000 histories now at hand in the present study, 3104 ($= 26\%$) have come from hundred percent groups. These groups have come from the following sources:

Hundred Percent Groups

Type of Group	Number of Groups
College sororities	2
College fraternities	9
College student groups	6
College classes	7
College rooming houses, for unorganized	5
Professional groups	13
Conscientious objectors	2
NYA project	1
Junior high school classes	3
Speech clinic groups	3
Rooming houses, in town	3
Hitch-hikers (over a 3-year period)	1
Delinquent institutional groups	4
Penal institutional groups	2
Mental institutional group	1
Total	62

These hundred percent groups have come from some variety of sources, but only the college groups are well enough represented (by series of at least 300 cases) to allow their use in testing the validity of the partial sample in this study. The accumulation of many more histories in these complete

HUNDRED PERCENT VERSUS PARTIAL SAMPLES: ACCUMULATIVE INCIDENCE
DATA

EDUCATIONAL LEVEL 13+

| | MASTURBATION | | | | NOCTURNAL EMISSIONS | | | |
| AGE | Partial Sample | | 100% Sample | | Partial Sample | | 100% Sample | |
	Cases	% with Exper.	Cases	% with Exper.	Cases	% with Exper.	Cases	% with Exper.
8	2815	0.0	656	0.0	2811	0.0	656	0.0
9	2815	0.3	656	0.3	2811	0.0	656	0.0
10	2815	2.3	656	2.1	2811	0.5	656	0.6
11	2815	8.9	656	8.2	2811	3.2	656	3.2
12	2815	27.9	656	26.2	2811	11.6	656	10.4
13	2815	52.9	656	52.3	2811	29.1	656	25.3
14	2815	72.2	656	72.0	2811	52.2	656	47.1
15	2815	80.2	656	81.3	2811	68.9	656	67.2
16	2814	84.3	655	85.2	2810	80.7	655	79.8
17	2812	87.0	655	88.2	2808	87.0	655	86.9
18	2736	88.9	611	90.2	2732	91.0	611	92.0
19	2572	90.0	539	91.8	2568	92.6	539	93.9
20	2337	91.1	457	92.3	2333	93.6	457	95.4
21	2031	92.0	383	92.4	2027	94.5	383	95.0
22	1670	92.8	312	93.3	1668	94.7	312	95.2
23	1396	93.3	269	93.3	1395	94.8	269	95.2
24	1151	93.1	242	93.8	1150	95.7	242	95.9
25	1002	93.9	203	94.6	1001	96.2	203	97.0
26	884	94.9	163	95.7	883	96.5	163	97.5
27	774	95.3	124	96.0	773	96.2	124	97.6
28	699	95.3	110	95.5	698	96.6	110	97.3
29	634	95.0	94	94.7	633	96.8	94	97.9
30	573	95.6	79	96.2	572	97.2	79	97.5
31	529	95.3	73	95.9	528	97.3	73	97.3
32	492	95.5	67	98.5	491	97.6	67	98.5
33	448	95.3	58	98.3	447	97.5	58	98.3
34	412	95.9	51	98.0	411	98.1	51	98.0
35	382	95.8			381	98.4		
36	356	95.8			355	98.6		
37	323	95.7			322	98.4		
38	307	95.8			306	98.7		
39	280	95.4			279	98.6		
40	257	96.1			256	99.2		

Table 4. Comparisons of data obtained from partial and hundred percent samples
Based on males of the college level.

HUNDRED PERCENT VERSUS PARTIAL SAMPLES

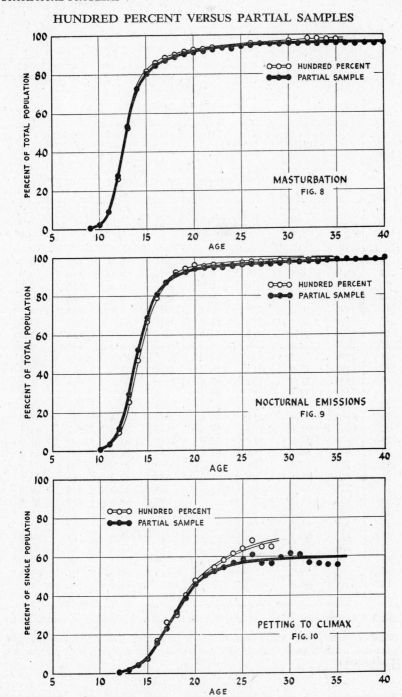

Figures 8–10. Comparisons of accumulative incidence curves based on hundred
percent and partial samples

For males of college level (13+).

	HUNDRED PERCENT VERSUS PARTIAL SAMPLES: ACCUMULATIVE INCIDENCE DATA						
	EDUCATIONAL LEVEL 13+						
AGE	PETTING TO CLIMAX				TOTAL INTERCOURSE		
	Partial Sample		100% Sample		Partial Sample		100% Sample	
	Cases	% with Exper.	Cases	% with Exper.	Cases	% with Exper.	Cases	% with Exper.
8	1596	0.0	276	0.0	2817	0.0	656	0.0
9	1596	0.0	276	0.0	2817	0.0	656	0.0
10	1596	0.0	276	0.0	2817	0.0	656	0.0
11	1596	0.0	276	0.0	2817	0.2	656	0.2
12	1596	0.3	276	0.4	2817	1.0	656	1.1
13	1596	1.6	276	1.8	2817	3.1	656	3.0
14	1596	4.1	276	3.6	2817	6.0	656	5.2
15	1596	7.6	276	8.0	2817	9.5	656	9.5
16	1596	15.5	276	16.3	2816	15.5	655	15.3
17	1593	23.0	275	26.2	2814	23.1	655	24.4
18	1534	31.2	245	30.6	2738	30.9	611	31.6
19	1474	38.4	232	40.1	2574	38.3	539	37.5
20	1389	46.0	227	47.6	2339	45.7	457	44.0
21	1240	50.1	214	50.9	2033	50.9	383	47.0
22	1047	52.8	193	54.4	1672	58.3	312	56.1
23	872	54.6	181	58.0	1397	63.0	269	61.0
24	688	56.3	164	61.6	1152	68.8	242	68.6
25	543	58.2	123	64.2	1002	75.0	203	72.9
26	437	60.6	97	68.0	884	80.1	163	77.3
27	321	56.7	60	65.0	774	82.6	124	79.8
28	255	56.5			699	85.1	110	81.8
29	204	59.3			634	87.1	94	85.1
30	161	61.5			573	89.5	79	87.3
31	122	60.7			529	90.9	73	89.0
32	100	57.0			492	91.3	67	89.6
33	89	56.2			448	91.1	58	89.7
34	72	55.6			412	92.5	51	94.1
35	61	55.7			382	93.2		

Table 5. Comparisons of data obtained from partial and hundred percent samples

Based on males of the college level. Petting is pre-marital. Total intercourse includes pre-marital, marital, extra-marital, and post-marital relations with both companions and prostitutes.

samples is one of the important things to be followed through in the future development of this project.

By means of Table 3 it is possible to compare the frequency and incidence figures for the 15 groups on which there are sufficient cases in the hundred percent sample. It will be seen that the active incidence figures (recording the number of persons who are involved in any particular period of time) show a remarkable conformance between the partial sample and the hundred percent portion of that sample. The same is true of the accumulative incidence figures (recording the number of persons who have ever been involved) (Tables 4–6, Figures 8–13). The differences usually involve 1 per cent to 5 per cent of the population. Throughout this study it may, therefore, be accepted that both the active and accumulative incidence data and curves show the general locus of the reality, though the curves may need correction of a few percent one way or the other. For instance, the actual, accumulative incidence figure for masturbation in the college segment of the population must lie within a few degrees of the 96 per cent figure given by the data; and whether it is in actuality 94 per cent or 98 per cent is not of much moment; but it is certain that it is not the 85 per cent nor 90 per cent figure given by some studies, nor the 100 per cent figure often guessed at, nor the 7 per cent figure found in one study (Bromley and Britten 1938). Similarly, there can be no question that the actual accumulative incidence figure for the homosexual in the college-bred group lies somewhere between the 28 per cent figure derived from the hundred per-cent sample and the 34 per cent figure derived from the partial sample of college histories, and that it is nowhere near the 1 per cent to 2 per cent figure which has been commonly published, nor even the 10 per cent figure which has been the maximum previously suggested.

There are greater discrepancies between the frequency figures (the number of times per week each type of activity is engaged in), as calculated from the hundred percent samples and from the partial samples. The figures derived from the partial samples are consistently higher for the total sexual outlet and for all the individual outlets except nocturnal emissions. For this, there are a number of possible explanations, and it seems impossible to identify the primary factors until we can secure more material for analysis. It is quite probable that a number of factors are really involved. The following considerations should be kept in mind:

1. The volunteers who make up the partial sample may represent a more active group of individuals, of the type which is aggressive, responds to a call for cooperation in a survey, and is more responsive and less inhibited sexually. It is true that the last persons to contribute in a hundred percent sample are sometimes the more prudish, restrained, apathetic, and sexually less active individuals. If this is often true, then the frequency figures throughout this volume should be reduced by some percentage, and

HUNDRED PERCENT VERSUS PARTIAL SAMPLES: ACCUMULATIVE INCIDENCE
DATA

EDUCATIONAL LEVEL 13+

AGE	INTERCOURSE WITH PROSTITUTES				HOMOSEXUAL OUTLETS			
	Partial Sample		100% Sample		Partial Sample		100% Sample	
	Cases	% with Exper.	Cases	% with Exper.	Cases	% with Exper.	Cases	% with Exper.
8	2816	0.0	656	0.0	2817	0.0	656	0.0
9	2816	0.0	656	0.0	2817	0.1	656	0.0
10	2816	0.0	656	0.0	2817	0.5	656	0.2
11	2816	0.0	656	0.0	2817	1.8	656	1.4
12	2816	0.0	656	0.0	2817	6.2	656	5.0
13	2816	0.1	656	0.0	2817	11.6	656	8.4
14	2816	0.8	656	0.2	2817	18.0	656	14.5
15	2816	2.3	656	1.8	2817	21.1	656	16.9
16	2815	4.8	655	4.4	2816	23.0	655	19.4
17	2813	9.1	655	9.8	2814	24.1	655	20.0
18	2737	13.6	611	13.1	2738	25.6	611	20.8
19	2573	17.4	539	15.4	2574	26.7	539	21.3
20	2338	20.6	457	19.7	2339	27.6	457	23.2
21	2032	22.2	383	24.8	2033	28.6	383	23.5
22	1672	24.9	312	26.3	1672	29.8	312	24.4
23	1397	25.7	269	21.9	1397	31.5	269	23.4
24	1152	26.6	242	23.6	1152	32.1	242	25.6
25	1002	28.6	203	25.1	1002	33.0	203	24.1
26	884	29.4	163	28.8	884	32.9	163	23.9
27	774	30.5	124	21.8	774	33.7	124	23.4
28	699	32.0	110	23.6	699	33.9	110	22.7
29	634	32.0	94	24.5	634	33.6	94	21.3
30	573	33.2	79	24.1	573	33.7	79	22.8
31	529	34.0	73	26.0	529	34.2	73	24.7
32	492	33.7	67	23.9	492	32.9	67	23.9
33	448	33.3	58	22.4	448	33.9	58	22.4
34	412	33.7	51	21.6	412	34.7	51	23.5
35	382	34.6			382	34.0		
36	356	35.7			356	33.7		
37	323	35.6			323	33.4		
38	307	36.2			307	33.2		
39	280	36.4			280	33.6		
40	257	36.6			257	32.7		

Table 6. Comparisons of data obtained from partial and hundred percent samples
Based on males of the college level.

HUNDRED PERCENT VERSUS PARTIAL SAMPLES

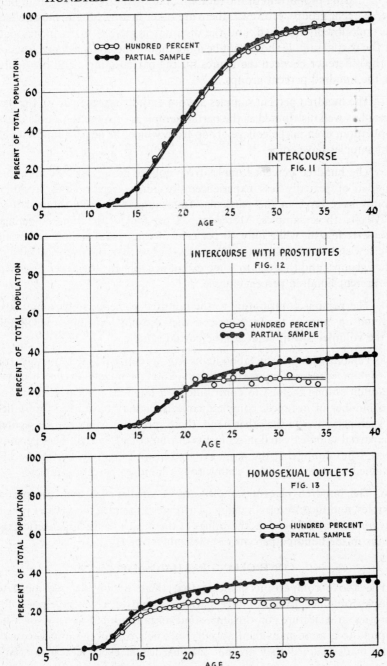

Figures 11-13. Comparisons of accumulative incidence curves based on hundred percent and partial samples

For males of college level (13+).

an increasing proportion of the future intake should be secured from hundred percent groups. However, there are other factors (given below) which are undoubtedly involved, and the discount made on the frequency data for the partial sample should not be more than some undetermined fraction of the difference between the figures for the partial sample and the figures for the hundred percent groups.

2. The hundred percent samples are not entirely representative, for they are not as well distributed as the partial sample is through the whole of the population, even in the college group from which the largest hundred percent samples have come.

3. The hundred percent samples from college groups include an undue number of sexually less experienced freshmen, because the freshmen groups were large in the particular fraternities which contributed most heavily to these samples. Moreover, 28 per cent of the hundred percent sample is Jewish, while only 10 per cent of the partial sample is Jewish. The Jewish histories (Chapter 13) are less active than the histories of some other groups, and this will to some extent account for the lower figures in the present hundred percent sample.

4. The persons contributing to the hundred percent samples may have covered up more of the fact, because they did not contribute as willingly as the volunteers who made up the partial sample.

5. Persons with socially taboo items (*e.g.*, pre-marital intercourse, extra-marital intercourse, homosexual activity, animal contacts) in their histories are often among the last to contribute to a hundred percent sample, and in a number of instances complete collections may have been forestalled by such persons. On the other hand, these special histories can be secured in a partial sample by making contacts through the friends of these persons. There is no doubt that the more extreme histories will always have to be obtained in some way other than through hundred percent samples.

6. The hundred percent samples are of smaller size than the partial samples, and therefore less reliable. The partial samples show wider ranges of variation, and this raises the values of the means. With larger series, the means in the hundred percent samples might be raised.

CONTROLLING PARTIAL SAMPLES

The above comparisons indicate that there is considerable merit to samples obtained from volunteers who respond to a general appeal for histories at a lecture, or through some organizational agency, or who respond to a more individual appeal. But such volunteer samples can be quite inadequate, if they are not safeguarded at every step in a study.

1. All general appeals for histories have emphasized the importance of securing every kind of history—"histories that have everything in them

and histories that are complete blanks"—"big histories and little histories and every other kind of history"—"histories that are quite usual and histories that have things in them that some people consider wrong or abnormal, but which we accept as objectively as any other kind of history." The restrained histories have, on the whole, been the more difficult to get, and it has been constantly necessary to reassure individuals with relatively inactive histories that they were contributing to the study in as important a way as the persons with more active histories.

2. Contact persons have had to be educated to understand that "a good history" is a history that accurately reports everything, rather than a history that has some special element in it. Especially at lower levels, where the contact men have been paid, it was difficult at first for them to understand that the forty-minute history of an inexperienced teen-ager is as important as the two- or three-hour history of an older person who has been involved in every conceivable sort of sexual activity.

3. Experience indicates that the first volunteers from any group are likely to be the extrovert, aggressive, sexually less inhibited, and often more active individuals; but if a group is worked with over a longer period of time the sample becomes more diversified. For that reason, we have, in general, avoided working with groups where only a single appeal could be made, or where the time for taking histories was limited to a few days or even a week or two. Also for that reason, we have concentrated on securing samples from a more limited number of cities and towns, and from particular groups to whom we might return over periods of months and even years. Some of these groups have been contributing throughout the eight or nine years of the research. In such places, some persons contribute even after two or three years of refusing—finally convinced by the reaction of the community that their socially irregular or utterly blank histories can be reported without embarrassment, and that the project is, after all, worth while. The partial sample employed in this study would never have been as representative as it is if we had not had such long-time contacts with most of the groups.

It is unfortunate that we do not yet have large enough populations to measure the differences between first samples and subsequent samples from the same community. It is possible, however, to report measurements on one college group where Maslow's dominance and security ratings were available on some of the females who contributed histories to the present study of sex behavior (see Maslow 1940, 1942a, 1942b; Maslow, Hirsh, Stein, and Honigmann 1945, for a detailed description of the tests). The first volunteers seemed to be more extrovert and assured individuals (though how that affects a sexual history is not yet clear). By staying nearly a month in the community, a sample was obtained from about 400 students, on 92 of whom dominance and/or security scores were available for comparison with about 80 students who were in the same psychology classes but who failed to volunteer for histories. The volunteer group showed the full range of variation in dominance and security ratings, from the most aggressive to the most timid levels. The mean dominance rating for the group that had volunteered for histories was about 10 per cent higher than for those who had not volunteered; the mean security score was about 3 per cent lower. We are indebted to Dr. A. H. Maslow for the data which allow this analysis.

4. Considerable attention must be given to securing an appreciable portion of each group from which histories are taken, even when it is not possible to secure a hundred percent sample. In many instances half to three-quarters or more of each group has been secured. We have an impression (but as yet insufficient data to test it) that such a sample is not so different from a complete sample. There is one statistical study (Shuttleworth 1941) that suggests that a sixty per cent sample is still insufficient to represent the whole.

Whenever, as in the present survey, it is not feasible to secure a strictly randomized sample, a combination of hundred percent sampling and controlled partial sampling seems the best that can be done. To attempt to base the entire study on hundred percent sampling would not be satisfactory, for it would be impossible to secure such complete samples in sufficient number from all of the diverse groups in a population. Sufficiently controlled partial samples seem to have considerable value, especially when they are offset by an even greater proportion of hundred percent samples than we have, as yet, utilized.

ORDER OF SAMPLING

The present study has been very much speeded up while the cost has been kept at a phenomenally low minimum—actually between 2 per cent and 4 per cent of the cost per history of the previous personal interview studies in this field. This has been primarily because of a policy of accepting whatever histories were immediately available, rather than going after particular sorts of histories in particular sequence. After securing the histories, they have been placed in the classificatory cells to which they belong. The value of such a policy was learned through our experience with insect sampling. The customary procedure of searching for particular persons to represent particular segments of the population is expensive because of the work involved in locating those particular cases. If one is satisfied to accept material in the order in which it appears, one sooner or later finds the particular cases which are necessary for the completion of a study. While we have always endeavored to secure some degree of diversity in our sample, we have not failed to seize the opportunity to take histories from the immediately available groups, until enough histories had been secured to satisfy the demands in those groups. At the present writing there are only two cells from which we have enough histories, and it is now a matter of avoiding cases that belong to those particular groups. In the course of time one has to go further out of his way to secure histories from certain other groups, and that will increase the cost; but the cost can always be kept relatively low if one bides his time and takes the material that is most available.

SYNTHESIZING A U. S. SAMPLE

While, as just indicated, data on each of the ultimate groups in the population are the first objectives of the present study, it has been desirable at certain points to calculate statistics which would be applicable to some larger group, as, for instance, all single white males in the U. S. population, or all married white males, or all white males of all sorts in the total American population. This has been accomplished by weighting the raw data from each of the ultimate groups in the study, in proportion to the size of that group in the U. S. Census, and totalling the weighted results for all the groups. The Census of 1940 shows the distribution of the total population by all the items which are involved in the six-way breakdown employed in the present volume: sex, race, marital status, age, number of years of schooling (without a clear distinction between current and completed educational histories), and the rural-urban background (on a slightly different basis than the one employed in the present study). At a few points where the Census breakdowns do not exactly match our own (*e.g.*, in their failure to indicate what proportion of the population is pre-adolescent, and in regard to the educational record as noted above), it has been possible to make estimates which cannot have introduced an error of more than a fraction of one per cent into the calculations. Tables 7 to 11 show the constants thus derived from the 1940 Census figures. They are the bases of the calculations which appear throughout the present volume as "U. S. Corrections" of the raw data. To make any correction from these tables, each item in the raw data should be multiplied by the figure shown at the appropriate point in the table. The products of all the items in any particular age group are then totalled and divided by the "age weight" figure (the second column in each table).

An examination of the tables and charts throughout this volume will show how far apart raw data and "U. S. Corrections" may be. Since the smaller groups in stratified sampling should be represented by samples of the same size as those used for the larger groups, they unduly affect the calculations made for a total population. Therefore, in the case of phenomena which occur most frequently in groups which constitute only a small proportion of the population (*e.g.*, masturbation, nocturnal dreams, and petting in the college population), the raw data for the total population give higher averages than the U. S. corrected data (*e.g.*, Figures 38–42, 53–57, 59–63). Conversely, in the case of phenomena which are more

TABLE FOR U. S. CORRECTION: MALES, WHITE

AGE GROUP	EDUCATIONAL LEVEL / MARITAL STATUS	0–8			9–12			13+			No Educ. Rpt.
		S	M	W&D	S	M	W&D	S	M	W&D	
				URBAN AND RURAL NON-FARM							
Adol.–14	Age Weight (4.59)	(1.03)			(1.83)			(0.48)			
15–19	12.33	2.46	0.03	0.00	6.01	0.08	0.00	0.35	0.00	0.00	0.06
20–24	11.43	1.58	0.56	0.01	3.79	1.36	0.02	1.07	0.38	0.01	0.07
25–29	10.93	1.05	1.82	0.03	1.58	2.74	0.05	0.54	0.95	0.02	0.08
30–34	10.24	0.69	2.64	0.06	0.70	2.74	0.07	0.28	1.10	0.04	0.09
35–39	09.51	0.57	3.21	0.12	0.39	2.18	0.08	0.17	0.95	0.03	0.10
40–44	08.92	0.50	3.39	0.17	0.27	1.81	0.08	0.12	0.79	0.03	0.11
45–49	08.57	0.48	3.58	0.21	0.19	1.45	0.08	0.09	0.66	0.03	0.12
50–54	07.72	0.46	3.32	0.28	0.14	1.07	0.10	0.07	0.51	0.04	0.11
55–59	06.23	0.36	2.65	0.31	0.10	0.76	0.09	0.05	0.36	0.04	0.09
60+	14.12	0.82	5.40	1.74	0.16	1.08	0.35	0.09	0.58	0.19	0.26
Total	100.00	8.97	26.60	2.93	13.33	15.27	0.92	2.83	6.28	0.43	1.09
				FARM							
Adol.–14	(4.59)	(0.38)			(0.69)			(0.18)			
15–19	12.33	1.68	0.03	0.00	1.53	0.03	0.00	0.05	0.00	0.00	0.02
20–24	11.43	0.98	0.34	0.01	0.79	0.27	0.01	0.12	0.04	0.00	0.02
25–29	10.93	0.48	0.73	0.02	0.29	0.43	0.01	0.04	0.06	0.00	0.01
30–34	10.24	0.28	0.89	0.02	0.13	0.39	0.01	0.02	0.07	0.00	0.02
35–39	09.51	0.21	1.01	0.03	0.06	0.30	0.01	0.01	0.06	0.00	0.02
40–44	08.92	0.17	1.04	0.03	0.04	0.27	0.01	0.01	0.06	0.00	0.02
45–49	08.57	0.15	1.12	0.05	0.03	0.23	0.01	0.01	0.06	0.00	0.02
50–54	07.72	0.15	1.09	0.07	0.02	0.19	0.01	0.01	0.06	0.00	0.02
55–59	06.23	0.13	0.96	0.09	0.02	0.14	0.01	0.01	0.04	0.00	0.02
60+	14.12	0.30	2.07	0.58	0.03	0.22	0.06	0.01	0.09	0.02	0.07
Total	100.00	4.53	9.28	0.90	2.94	2.47	0.14	0.29	0.54	0.02	0.24

Table 7. Six-way breakdown, U. S. Census, 1940

Weights to be used for correcting raw data on populations resulting from a 6-way successive breakdown on MALES where RACE, RURAL-URBAN BACKGROUND, EDUCATIONAL LEVEL, MARITAL STATUS, and AGE are known. Classification based on 44,743,534 white males aged 15 and over. Estimated number of single white adolescent males through 14 years of age = 2,052,793. These are not included in totals because the data are not segregated in the U. S. Census; but estimates are shown in parentheses on the first line of figures in the table.

AGE GROUP	EDUCATIONAL LEVEL	0–8			9–12			13+		
	MARITAL STATUS	S	M	W&D	S	M	W&D	S	M	W&D
	Age Weight									
Adol.–14	(4.59)	(1.41)	0.00	0.00	(2.52)	0.00	0.00	(0.66)	0.00	0.00
15–19	12.25	3.70	0.06	0.00	6.64	0.10	0.00	1.75	0.00	0.00
20–24	11.34	2.56	0.90	0.02	4.58	1.63	0.03	1.19	0.42	0.01
25–29	10.84	1.53	2.55	0.05	1.87	3.17	0.06	0.58	1.01	0.02
30–34	10.13	0.97	3.53	0.08	0.83	3.13	0.08	0.30	1.17	0.04
35–39	9.39	0.78	4.22	0.15	0.45	2.48	0.09	0.18	1.01	0.03
40–44	8.79	0.67	4.43	0.20	0.31	2.08	0.09	0.13	0.85	0.03
45–49	8.43	0.63	4.70	0.26	0.22	1.68	0.09	0.10	0.72	0.03
50–54	7.59	0.61	4.41	0.35	0.16	1.26	0.11	0.08	0.57	0.04
55–59	6.13	0.49	3.61	0.40	0.12	0.91	0.10	0.06	0.40	0.04
60+	13.79	1.12	7.47	2.32	0.19	1.30	0.41	0.10	0.67	0.21
Total	98.68	13.06	35.88	3.83	15.37	17.74	1.06	4.47	6.82	0.45

Table 8. Five-way breakdown, U. S. Census, 1940

Weights to be used for correcting raw data on populations resulting from a 5-way successive breakdown on MALES where RACE, EDUCATIONAL LEVEL, MARITAL STATUS, and AGE are the items involved in the analyses. For males who are under 19 years of age and still in grade or high school, estimates have been made of the educational levels which they will ultimately attain. Persons who did not report their education in the Census are eliminated from this calculation. Cf. legend on Table 7.

AGE GROUP	RURAL-URBAN EDUC. LEVEL	Urban and Rural Non-Farm				Farm			
		0–8	9–12	13+	No Educ. Rpt.	0–8	9–12	13+	No Educ. Rpt.
	Age Weight								
15–19	12.33	2.49	6.09	0.35	0.06	1.71	1.56	0.05	0.02
20–24	11.43	2.15	5.17	1.46	0.07	1.33	1.07	0.16	0.02
25–29	10.93	2.90	4.37	1.51	0.08	1.23	0.73	0.10	0.01
30–34	10.22	3.39	3.51	1.42	0.09	1.19	0.53	0.09	0.02
35–39	9.51	3.90	2.65	1.15	0.10	1.25	0.37	0.07	0.02
40–44	8.93	4.06	2.16	0.94	0.11	1.24	0.32	0.07	0.02
45–49	8.59	4.27	1.72	0.78	0.12	1.32	0.27	0.07	0.02
50–54	7.71	4.06	1.31	0.62	0.11	1.31	0.22	0.07	0.02
55–59	6.24	3.32	0.95	0.45	0.09	1.18	0.17	0.05	0.02
60+	14.11	7.96	1.59	0.86	0.26	2.95	0.31	0.12	0.07
Total	100.00	38.50	29.52	9.54	1.09	14.71	5.55	0.85	0.24

Table 9. Five-way breakdown, U. S. Census, 1940

Weights to be used for correcting raw data on populations resulting from a 5-way successive breakdown on MALES where RACE, RURAL-URBAN BACKGROUND, EDUCATIONAL LEVEL, and AGE are the items involved in the analyses.

TABLES FOR U. S. CORRECTION: MALES, WHITE

AGE GROUP	RURAL-URBAN	Urban and Rural Non-Farm			Farm		
	MARITAL STATUS	S	M	W&D	S	M	W&D
	Age Weight						
15–19	12.32	8.86	0.13	0.00	3.27	0.06	0.00
20–24	11.44	6.49	2.32	0.04	1.92	0.66	0.01
25–29	10.93	3.19	5.55	0.11	0.82	1.24	0.02
30–34	10.22	1.68	6.55	0.17	0.43	1.36	0.03
35–39	9.52	1.15	6.42	0.24	0.29	1.38	0.04
40–44	8.94	0.90	6.09	0.30	0.22	1.38	0.05
45–49	8.58	0.77	5.77	0.35	0.19	1.43	0.07
50–54	7.73	0.69	4.99	0.43	0.18	1.35	0.09
55–59	6.23	0.52	3.84	0.44	0.16	1.16	0.11
60+	14.11	1.10	7.24	2.33	0.35	2.41	0.68
Total	100.02	25.35	48.90	4.41	7.83	12.43	1.10

Table 10. Five-way breakdown, U. S. Census, 1940

Weights to be used for correcting raw data on populations resulting from a 5-way successive breakdown on MALES where RACE, AGE, the RURAL-URBAN BACKGROUND, and MARITAL STATUS are the items involved in the analyses. *Cf.* legend on Table 7.

AGE GROUP	AGE WEIGHT	RURAL-URBAN		EDUCATIONAL LEVEL				MARITAL STATUS		
		Non-farm	Farm	0–8	9–12	13+	No Rpt.	S	M	W&D
15–19	12.33	8.99	3.33	4.20	7.70	0.40	0.1	12.09	0.16	0.00
20–24	11.43	8.85	2.59	3.48	6.24	1.62	0.1	8.33	2.95	0.06
25–29	10.93	8.85	2.08	4.13	5.10	1.61	0.1	3.98	6.73	0.13
30–34	10.22	8.38	1.81	4.58	4.04	1.51	0.1	2.10	7.83	0.20
35–39	9.51	7.81	1.71	5.15	3.02	1.22	0.1	1.41	7.71	0.27
40–44	8.93	7.29	1.65	5.30	2.48	1.01	0.1	1.11	7.36	0.32
45–49	8.59	6.89	1.69	5.59	1.99	0.85	0.1	0.95	7.10	0.38
50–54	7.71	6.11	1.62	5.37	1.53	0.69	0.1	0.85	6.24	0.50
55–59	6.24	4.80	1.43	4.50	1.13	0.50	0.1	0.67	4.12	0.54
60+	14.11	10.67	3.44	10.91	1.90	0.98	0.3	1.41	9.44	2.94
Total	100.00	78.65	22.35	53.21	35.13	10.39	1.2	32.90	60.44	5.34

Table 11. Four-way breakdown, U. S. Census, 1940

Weights to be used for correcting data on populations resulting from a 4-way successive breakdown on MALES where RACE, AGE, and *either* the RURAL-URBAN BACKGROUND, *or* the EDUCATIONAL LEVEL, *or* the MARITAL STATUS are the only items involved in the analyses.

common in groups that constitute a larger segment of the population (*e.g.*, pre-marital intercourse and the homosexual in a population that has gone into high school but not beyond) the raw data are distinctly lower than the U. S. Corrections (*e.g.*, Figures 71–75, 77–81, 83–87). The public opinion polls and most of the government surveys are aware of this problem, but it is most unfortunate that students in psychology and the social sciences regularly publish raw data without corrections for the Census distributions of their populations. As these figures and many others will show, the raw data are sometimes as much as 34 per cent removed from the corrected data, and the general shape of the curve may be considerably changed by the corrections. Throughout the present volume, the figures given in the body of the text and the heavier lines shown in all the charts represent U. S. Corrections of the raw data, except in those relatively few instances where corrections have been impossible because of insufficient information in the Census.

STATISTICAL ANALYSES

All mathematical calculations on this project have been performed twice, independently by each of two persons. Computations have been set up on standard ruled forms, and these are all filed for consultation by any qualified student who needs to check the method or accuracy of the calculations.

The statistical manipulation of the data in this study has been kept at an absolute minimum. The incidence data (the record of the number of persons involved in the various sexual activities) are subject to error because of deliberate or unconscious cover-up, especially in regard to socially taboo items. The frequency data (the number of times the activities are engaged in) cannot be more than approximations to the actual fact, because sexual activities are more often irregular in their distribution, with days or weeks of high frequency alternating with days and weeks of low frequency, and only the persons accustomed to the handling of averages (as few people are) can estimate their mean frequencies in more than very approximate terms. Individuals who have kept diaries or calendars may have more accurate bases for their estimates; but few people have as yet turned in such records (see p. 74). For these reasons, the calculations in the present study are likely to involve greater errors than if it were a study of some other kind of phenomenon. In large series of cases, errors which are overestimates are sometimes compensated for by errors which are understatements, provided there is no bias which accumulates the errors primarily in one direction; but even then there can be no great precision to the calculations.

In consideration of the approximate nature of the original data, it would then be misleading to subject them to more than relatively simple mathematical treatment. For that reason, only the following statistical operations have been performed on each history and on each series of histories.

Individual Frequencies. Average frequencies of orgasm have been calculated on each history for each type of sexual activity, namely, masturbation, nocturnal dreams, heterosexual petting, heterosexual coitus, homosexual contacts, and contacts with animals of other species. Heterosexual relations have been calculated as pre-marital coitus with prostitutes, pre-marital coitus with females who are not prostitutes, marital coitus, extra-marital coitus with prostitutes, extra-marital coitus with other females, post-marital coitus with prostitutes, or post-marital coitus with other females. For the purposes of the present volume, only sexual activities which have led to orgasm have been included in these frequency calculations, although there are many other aspects of human sexual behavior which will also be considered in this and in later volumes. Throughout this volume all frequency figures have been calculated for each individual as average frequencies per week. In some of the previously published studies, such activities have been recorded as rates per month; but except for low frequencies, few persons are capable of estimating average rates for such a period of time. The social organization imposes a weekly periodicity on various human activities, including the sexual (Ellis 1901 (1936): 85 ff.), and weekly rates are consequently better known to most persons.

In summarizing the record on individuals and on groups, frequencies have been standardized as average frequencies per week extending over five-year periods involving ages 11–15 (inclusive), 16–20, 21–25, 26–30, etc. In these periods, weeks or years which were without sexual outlet have been averaged with the active periods, and in that way seasons of inactivity have lowered the weekly rates for the whole of a particular five-year period. Since the calculations apply only to the activities which occur after the onset of adolescence, the first age period really extends from adolescence to 15, and is usually something less than a five-year period. In the latter case, the averages shown are based on the active years, and are not reduced by being averaged with the pre-adolescent years. The last age period—the period in which the subject contributes his history— is treated in the same fashion, if it is less than a full five-year period.

For each outlet, average frequencies per week, per five-year period, have been calculated precisely to the first decimal place. Group averages have consequently been calculated to the second decimal place. Because of the approximate nature of the raw data, finer calculations have not seemed warranted.

Group Frequencies. The nature of any population has been found by classifying all of the individuals in it into frequency classes which have been named for their upper limits. The ranges of each class and the class means used for calculations have been as follows:

Class	Range	Mean Value
0	0	0
—	0.01– 0.09	0.05
0.5	0.1 – 0.5	0.3
1.0	0.6 – 1.0	0.8
1.5	1.1 – 1.5	1.3
2.0	1.6 – 2.0	1.8
2.5	2.1 – 2.5	2.3
etc.		
10.0	9.6 –10.0	9.8
11.0	10.1 –11.0	10.5
12.0	11.1 –12.0	11.5
etc.		
28.0	27.1 –28.0	27.5
29.0+	28.1 and higher	28.5

Frequency Curves. The number of individuals which fall into each of these frequency classes has been translated into percents of the whole population involved. Frequency curves throughout this volume have been based on such percents, rather than on the absolute number of cases in each frequency class. Many of the curves shown in psychologic and sociologic literature are uninterpretable because they are based on the absolute number, instead of upon the percentages of cases involved. All of the frequency curves in this volume are based on the actual calculations, and in no instance have they been smoothed by any process or approximated by interpolations or other sorts of estimates or predictions.

Group Averages. These have been calculated for each type of sexual outlet for the 5-year periods described above, for each population which has had 50 or more cases in it after 4-, 5-, or 6-way breakdowns of the total sample. All tabulations of data by groups, and all correlations, have been made by putting the data onto standard punch cards (Hollerith, IBM system), and all manipulations of cards have been performed on IBM machines. Both the punching of the cards and the handling of the machines on this project have been done by members of the research staff, in order that there be no betrayal of the confidence of the record. Each series of punch cards has carried a particular portion of each history, *e.g.*, the frequencies and sources of outlet on one set, the record of the pre-adolescent material on another set, the accumulative incidence data on another, etc. Thirteen sets of cards (*i.e.*, thirteen or more cards for each of the histories) have been punched for the calculation of the data presented in the present volume. Each of the thirteen cards in each set has carried the identical record of the age, educational level, occupational class, and other social backgrounds of the subject, mechanically reproduced on the thirteen cards to insure identity. Thus it has been possible to correlate all of the data on the thirteen sets with the same educational and social items. By a gang punch technique, it is possible to correlate the material on one card with the material on each other card.

Means. The averages which have been calculated have included mean frequencies for the population in each group, and means for the "active populations" in each group (*i.e.*, for those individuals who had any activity in that five-year period, in that particular type of sexual outlet). Means have been calculated by the formula:

$$M = \frac{\Sigma fv}{n}$$

For those who are not familiar with statistical practice, it may be pointed out that a mean represents the total number of measurements (in the present instance, the total number of orgasms) in each group divided by the number of individuals in the group. The mean represents the midpoint of the measurements. Its position (in contrast to the position of the median, which is described below) is therefore materially affected by the presence of even a few high-rating individuals in a population; and although the arithmetic mean is the average which is most commonly employed, both by most people in their everyday affairs and by the trained statistician, it may give a distorted picture because a few high-rating individuals affect the means more than a large population of low-rating individuals. Since nearly all of the distribution curves on human sex behavior are strongly skewed to the right (to the high frequency end of the curve), the means are quite regularly higher than the location of the body of the population would lead one to expect. Conversely, inactive cases in a population (*i.e.*, in the 0 class of frequencies) have a minimum effect on the position of the mean.

Standard Deviation of the Mean. This is also known as the standard error of the mean, and as the sigma of the mean. It is represented by the symbol σ_m. The standard deviation of each mean has been calculated in every instance, using the formula:

$$\sigma_m = \frac{\sigma}{\sqrt{n}} = \frac{\sqrt{\dfrac{\Sigma fv^2 - \dfrac{(\Sigma fv)^2}{n}}{n-1}}}{\sqrt{n}}$$

This formula is generally considered precise, and has the advantage of being calculable with maximum efficiency on a calculating machine. For the general reader, it may be pointed out that the standard deviation is attached to each mean shown in this volume, as follows:

$$2.36 \pm 0.04$$
$$\text{Mean} \quad \sigma_m$$

The σ_m is supposed to indicate the size of the error which may be involved in the mean—the limits, plus or minus, within which the true mean (as distingushed from the calculated mean) stands a 2 to 1 chance of lying. The size of σ_m in relation to the size of the mean indicates the degree of reliability of the calculated mean, and the smaller the σ_m, the less the probable error.

Medians. Median frequencies have been calculated, in every group, for the total sample population, and for the active population. Medians have been calculated by the formula:

$$Md = \frac{n+1}{2}$$

If all the individuals in a group are arranged linearly in accordance with the average frequencies of orgasm, the median designates the frequency of the individual who stands exactly midway in that series. Half of the individuals in the population have less frequent orgasm, half the individuals have more frequent orgasm. While the median is an average which is less often calculated by people in their everyday affairs, and while it is a statistic which has often been neglected by statisticians, it answers the very common question: "How frequently does the average individual engage in such activity?" and it provides, therefore, a most useful type of information. Recently statisticians have paid more attention to its significance. The location of a median is determined solely by the sequence of the individuals in a population, and it is unaffected by the low or high rates of particular individuals. Means and medians are averages which summarize two very different ideas, and in consequence their relative importance cannot properly be discussed. Means measure average frequencies, medians describe the average individuals.

Persons not familiar with these matters should understand that where most of the individuals in a sample belong in a frequency class which is midway between the extremes of the distribution, and where an equal number of individuals lie in symmetrical distribution on either side of the mid-point, the mean becomes identical with the median. Where the curve is asymmetric, the median becomes removed from the mean, sometimes by a very considerable distance. The median is lower than the mean when there are high-rating individuals who stand apart from the mass of the population; and this is almost always true as regards nearly all types of human sexual activity. The distance between the median and the mean is a measure of the extent to which the frequency distribution for the population (the frequency curve) is skewed in the direction of higher activity (extends to the right of the area which includes the body of the population). When a large portion of a population falls into the zero class (is without activity) in any particular calculation, the median for that population is so lowered that it loses significance. If more than 50 per cent of the population falls into the zero class, the mean is in the zero class and is useless for any understanding of the situation. In the same instance, however, a median calculated on the *active* portion of the population may have significance.

Percents of Individual Outlet. On each history, calculations have been made showing (in percents) the portion of his total sexual outlet which the individual has derived from each possible source (masturbation, dreams, coitus, etc.). The calculations have been made for the same five-year periods as were involved in the calculations of frequencies of total outlet.

Percents of Group Outlet. Similarly, frequency distributions have been plotted for these percents of outlets; and means, standard errors of the means, and medians have been routinely calculated on these percents for the total population and for the active portion of each population. When means are calculated in the usual way, the figures are the averages of all these percentages. When medians are calculated in this way, they show the percentage of the total outlet which the average individual derives from each of the possible sources. Neither of these calculations, however, answers the more usual question: "What percentage of the total orgasms of the population as a whole is derived from each kind of sexual activity?" In order to answer that question, it is necessary to compare the means of the absolute frequencies (not the percentage frequencies) for each type of out et in each group, with the mean of the absolute frequency of total outlet in the same group. The sum of the percentages so derived should total 100 per cent, which is the total outlet for the population.

Correlation Coefficients. At special points in the investigation, correlation coefficients and still other statistics have been calculated by standard procedures. Unless otherwise indicated the correlation coefficients represent the **Pearsonian r,** calculated by the formula:

$$r = \frac{(n \cdot \Sigma xy) - (\Sigma fx \cdot \Sigma fy)}{\sqrt{(n \cdot \Sigma fx^2) - ((\Sigma fx)^2) \cdot ((n \cdot \Sigma fy^2) - (\Sigma fy)^2)}}$$

In correlating data for which only two classes are possible, as with a *yes* or *no* situation, or with a record of presence or absence, the calculated coefficients represent the **tetrachoric r** derived from the tables published by Cheshire, Saffir, and Thurstone (1933).

Accumulative Incidence Curves. The one new statistical tool which we have had to develop for this study has been a curve which will show the number of persons who have ever had sexual experience of a particular sort up to any particular age of their lives. One of the questions most commonly asked is: "How many people do this— or that?" Specifically, it is "How many people masturbate?"—"How many people have homosexual experience?"—"What percentage of college students (or some other group) have intercourse before they marry?"—etc., etc. The question does not concern the number of persons having experience in any particular year (which is the *active* incidence figure), as often as it involves a question about the number of persons who *ever* have such experience in their lives, or in some portion of it. The answers usually given in both popular and technical literature are often incorrect because they are derived from curves based on cumulations of percentages. Such curves show the percentage increase of experienced persons (the increments) in each successive age group, the increments being totalled up to the end of the period of time under consideration. The cumulated percentages shown in Tables 28, 33, 35–37, and in Figures 15, 26, 27, 29, covering data on the ages involved in adolescent developments among boys, are examples of such calculations. Such curves are known as integral curves or ogives (the two "are fundamentally the same," according to Pearl 1940:143), and these are the curves that are ordinarily used in growth studies, learning studies, studies of social developments, etc.

But ogives are satisfactory only when the activity under consideration has involved a hundred percent of the population which is being studied, or when the histories of all the individuals in the study are concluded as far as that particular chapter in their lives is concerned. Cumulative percentage figures are quite sufficient in the cases cited above because all of the individuals on which they are based were adolescent when the data were gathered, *i.e.*, a hundred percent of the population was ultimately involved, and all of the individuals had the experience (onset of adolescence) which was being studied. An ogive would be correctly used if the ages of first pre-marital intercourse were being studied, and the curve were based on persons all of whom were married. In an ogive, the size of the basic population is constant for each and every age group, since all of the persons are either experienced or past the age at which they could possibly begin experience, and the total sample in an ogive is the basis for calculating the percentage of experienced individuals at each particular age.

Ogives, however, do not answer the question when only a portion of a population is eligible for experience, or when the histories of any of the individuals are not complete at the time the data are gathered. For instance, if the question is one of determining how many people have extra-marital intercourse, the real issue concerns the number of *married* people who ever *will* have such experience before they die. This could be determined by the use of an ogive if all persons in the study had been married, and if all the histories were taken after each person had terminated his marriage by separation or divorce, or after he had died. But since that is not easily effected, a technique must be used which will show the number of experienced persons in each age group, in relation to the number of persons in

ACCUMULATIVE INCIDENCE DATA: COITUS WITH PROSTITUTES
WHITE MALES, OF COLLEGE LEVEL

Age	*1 Age, first exper.	2 Σ of 1	*3 Age at report, exper. individ.	4 Σ of 3 Ages not reached	5 2 − 4 Freq.	*6 Age at report, inexper. individ.	7 3 + 6 Total population	8 Σ of 7, up. Years involved	9 5/8 Curve %	10 Increment
13	3	3			3			2816	0.1	
14	19	22			22			2816	0.8	+0.7
15	42	64			64	1	1	2816	2.3	+1.5
16	72	136			136	2	2	2815	4.8	+2.5
17	119	255	8		255	68	76	2813	9.1	+4.3
18	125	380	25	8	372	139	164	2737	13.6	+4.5
19	100	480	44	33	447	191	235	2573	17.4	+3.8
20	78	558	70	77	481	236	306	2338	20.6	+3.2
21	41	599	74	147	452	286	360	2032	22.2	+1.6
22	38	637	78	221	416	197	275	1672	24.9	+2.7
23	21	658	64	299	359	181	245	1397	25.7	+0.8
24	12	670	31	363	307	119	150	1152	26.6	+0.9
25	11	681	36	394	287	82	118	1002	28.6	+2.0
26	9	690	29	430	260	81	110	884	29.4	+0.8
27	5	695	18	459	236	57	75	774	30.5	+1.1
28	6	701	23	477	224	42	65	699	32.0	+1.5
29	2	703	17	500	203	44	61	634	32.0	+0.0
30	4	707	10	517	190	34	44	573	33.2	+1.2
31		707	16	527	180	21	37	529	34.0	+0.8
32	2	709	18	543	166	26	44	492	33.7	−0.3
33	1	710	11	561	149	25	36	448	33.3	−0.4
34	1	711	12	572	139	18	30	412	33.7	+0.4
35	5	716	8	584	132	18	26	382	34.6	+0.9
36	3	719	14	592	127	19	33	356	35.7	+1.1
37	2	721	5	606	115	11	16	323	35.6	−0.1
38	1	722	9	611	111	18	27	307	36.2	+0.6
39		722	9	620	102	14	23	280	36.4	+0.2
40	1	723	6	629	94	13	19	257	36.6	+0.2
41		723	10	635	88	7	17	238	37.0	+0.4
42		723	12	645	78	17	29	221	35.3	−1.7
43		723	2	657	66	13	15	192	34.4	−0.9
44		723	2	659	64	14	16	177	36.2	+1.8
45		723	3	661	62	7	10	161	38.5	+2.3
46		723	3	664	59	7	10	151	39.1	+0.6
47		723	11	667	56	14	25	141	39.7	+0.6
48		723	3	678	45	3	6	116	38.8	−0.9
49		723	1	681	42	12	13	110	38.2	−0.6
50+	1	724	42	682	42	55	97	97	43.3	+5.1
Total	724		724	724		2092	2816			

Table 12. Form for calculation of an accumulative incidence curve

Starred columns (*) are derived from punch cards; other columns are calculations based on the starred columns. The curve derived from this table is shown in Figure 14.

Explanation of an Accumulative Incidence Curve

Coitus with Prostitutes

Age.

1. Age of first experience.
2. Summation of Column 1. This is the **ogive**. It is based on the fictitious conception that the number of experienced persons in this population cannot be increased beyond the number now shown.
3. Ages at reporting, of experienced individuals.
4. Summation of Column 3, one step in advance. This represents the ages which the experienced individuals had not yet reached at the time they contributed their histories.
5. Subtraction of Column 4 from Column 2. This represents the years actually lived by the experienced individuals.
6. Ages at reporting, of inexperienced individuals.
7. Addition of Columns 3 + 6. This is the age distribution of all subjects (both experienced and inexperienced) at time of reporting.
8. Summation of Column 7, in reverse. This is the basic population for incidence calculations at each age.
9. Division of Column 5 by Column 8. This is the percent of the population at each age with experience in that year, or in any previous year.
10. Increment, calculated from Column 9.

NOTE: Pre-adolescent experience was eliminated from this calculation by punching cards only for experience that had occurred after the onset of adolescence.

The problem was restricted at the lower ages by adolescence. If the problem had been restricted at the upper ages to a particular portion of the life span, *e.g.*, to pre-marital years, Column 1 would have been corrected by sorting the experienced married individuals by age of marriage, and eliminating those whose first experience with prostitutes occurred after marriage. Column 3 would then have represented the sum of two groups of data: (1) the ages at marriage of the experienced population, and (2) the ages at reporting of the unmarried individuals who are experienced with prostitutes. Column 6 would then have represented the same sort of sum for the population which is not experienced with prostitutes.

each group who are eligible for such experience. This is the technique of the accumulative incidence curves which we have used in the present study.

Similarly, an accumulative incidence curve should be used when the ages of first pre-marital coital experience are to be determined for a population which contains some individuals who are not yet married. In such a problem, each point on the curve is based on a population which is independently calculated for each age. Each point is fixed by determining the number of persons in the sample who were not yet married, and by subtracting the persons who are no longer available for such experience because of marriage, or because the calculation has passed the ages at which those persons had contributed histories.

In order to build an accumulative incidence curve, two or more sets of data are needed on each individual involved in the study:

1. Age of first experience, for each subject.
2. Age of each subject at time of reporting.
3. In some cases, the age at which each subject became eligible for the sort of experience which is being studied (*e.g.*, the age of adolescence, for the study of post-adolescent experience; the age of marriage, for the study of experience as a married person; etc.).
4. In some cases, the age at which each subject became ineligible for experience (*e.g.*, the age at adolescence, as the end of the period at which the subject could have pre-adolescent experience; the age of marriage as an upper limit to pre-marital experience).

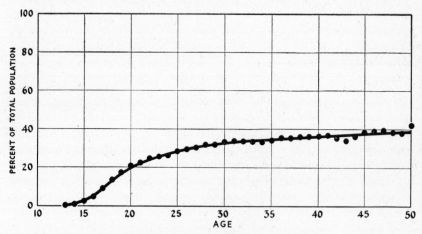

Figure 14. An accumulative incidence curve

Showing percentages of college males who have ever had intercourse with prostitutes by each of the indicated ages. Based on data in Table 12.

The derivation of an accumulative incidence curve was first worked out for a small sample by a hand manipulation of 1058 actual history sheets, adding them to piles as each individual became eligible, withdrawing them as each individual became ineligible for experience. It took some time to devise a procedure for Hollerith machine manipulation of punch cards on the problem, but a remarkably simple set-up has now been arrived at. It is shown in Table 12 where a specific problem is worked out in full detail (Figure 14). Since this seems to be a statistical procedure which has not been published before, it has seemed desirable to describe it at some length.

The usefulness of an accumulative incidence curve cannot be over-emphasized. It supplies the answer to the commonest of questions: "How many people have such experience?" From such a curve, one may at a glance determine the percentage of the population which has ever had experience by any given age. At the same time, the curve gives the best possible basis for predicting what percentage of any group will ever, in its lifetime, have such experience. This use of the curve for making predictions is one of its most significant values. As already indicated, it is of prime concern in any research that the conclusions be extensible to wider areas than those covered by the particular sample which has been investigated, and accumulative incidence curves are the most effective tools for so translating data. An accumulative incidence curve can be built on data from subjects whose histories are not yet complete, and thus it utilizes a large body of data which is not available for building an ogive (which depends upon completed histories). An accumulative incidence curve is less accurate nearer its end, because the populations which establish the successive points on the curve become smaller in these upper age levels. However, the area in which the curve becomes unreliable is well enough indicated by the wider scatter of the individual points, which is in sharp contrast to the smooth trends in the more reliable portions of the curve.

In conclusion, it should be emphasized that, after all of this statistical manipulation, the calculations given in the present volume still should be taken as approximations which are not to be pushed in detail, although they undoubtedly show the general locus of the incidence and frequency figures, with plus or minus errors of some few percent. In the next chapter data will be given to show the size of the corrections that may need to be made.

Chapter 4

VALIDITY OF THE DATA

Throughout research of the sort involved here, one needs to be continuously conscious, as already pointed out, that it is impossible to get more than approximations of the fact on the incidences and frequencies of various types of human sexual behavior. Memory cannot be wholly accepted as a source of information on what has actually happened in an individual's history. There is both deliberate and unconscious cover-up, especially of the more taboo items, and in dealing with people of diverse mental levels and educational backgrounds, there are differences in their ability to comprehend and to answer questions with any precision in an interview.

Moreover, it is difficult for a person who has not kept a diary, and especially for one who is not accustomed to thinking in statistical terms, to know how to average events which occur as irregularly as sexual activities usually do. The mass of the population is not often called upon to estimate the frequencies with which they engage in any sort of activity, sexual or otherwise. This is most obvious in dealing with poorly educated persons, and with mentally low grade individuals. Most persons are inclined to remember frequencies for periods when the activities were regular, and to forget those periods in which there was material interference with activity. In marital intercourse, for instance, there are menstrual periods, periods of illness, periods of travel when spouses are apart, periods of preoccupation with special duties which, affecting either of the two partners, interfere with the regularity of intercourse for both of them. While other sources of outlet may fill in some of these gaps, there are situations in which no kind of sexual outlet is readily available; but these blank periods are not always taken into account by a subject who is estimating averages for a history.

It has, therefore, been important to secure some measure of the size of the error for which allowance must be made on the calculations in the present volume. A number of techniques have been used for these tests, and a considerable body of information is now available on the validity of the data. We shall want to continue with these tests as the study expands.

In Chapter 2 it was pointed out that the techniques of the interviewing have provided a considerable control against exaggeration, but that there is a greater likelihood of understatement and cover-up getting by without being detected. In Chapter 3 the relation of validity to size of sample has been discussed. The present chapter covers the special devices which have been used to test the significance of the calculated data.

RE-TAKES

In order to test the constancy of memory, re-takes of whole histories have been made on 162 of the males and females who have contributed to the present study. It is unfortunate that a larger series is not now available, and this is one of the programs that should be expanded in the future progress of the research. In every case there has been a minimum lapse of eighteen months between the original history and the re-take, and in many cases three to seven years have intervened. The mean lapse has been 38.5 months. Re-takes, of course, cover activities which had not been engaged in until after the time of the original history; but with allowance for that fact, correlations have been made between the two records, for a diverse list of representative items. The results are shown in Table 13. There are no calculations of reliability which are more illuminating than these, and the table merits detailed study.

The analysis indicates that memory and/or cover-up, or other chance factors, introduce errors on certain items and on certain whole groups of items, while there is greater validity on other items. The incidence data are the most consistent. The coefficients of correlation (tetrachoric) on incidences are better than 0.9 in every case and better than 0.95 in all but three of the cases. The number of identical responses is better than 90 per cent, in every instance. The differences between the means calculated for the original histories, and the means calculated for the re-takes, are less than 2.4 per cent in most cases. The differences are larger only in regard to masturbation and to the homosexual, where the error is about 4 per cent. Throughout this volume, the incidence figures may, therefore, be accepted as very reliable. Many persons will find it difficult to believe that the high incidences shown for several types of sexual activity are not exaggerations of the fact, but every calculation indicates that they are understatements, if they are in error at all.

The next most accurate material covers the vital statistics of the population. There are data on the age of the subject, his marital status, the ages of his parents, the number of his brothers and sisters, his educational and religious background, etc. The coefficients of correlation (Pearsonian) are higher than 0.8 in every instance, and in six cases out of eight they are higher than 0.9. There are identical responses on the original histories and re-takes for better than 80 per cent of the subjects, on eight out of twelve items. The lowest scores concern the ages of the mother, of the father, of the wife at marriage, and of the husband at marriage—in that descending order. The differences between the means for the original histories, taken as a group, and the means for the re-takes are, however, immaterial, and the averages shown throughout the present volume can be accepted with

Comparing Originals and Re-takes on 162 Subjects

CASES	ITEMS INVOLVED	UNIT OF MEASUREMENT	IDENT. REPLIES %	WITHIN 1 UNIT OF IDENT. %	COEFFIC. OF CORREL.	ORIG. HIST.: MEANS	RE-TAKES: MEANS	DIFF. OF MEANS: RE-TAKE—ORIG.
	Incidences				Tetrachoric r	Incid. %	Incid. %	
104	Masturbation	Yes, No	96.2		> 0.95	90.4	94.2	+3.8
103	Nocturnal emissions	Yes, No	98.0		> 0.95	89.3	89.3	0.0
104	Petting experience	Yes, No	95.2		0.90	94.3	93.3	−1.0
92	Petting to climax	Yes, No	91.3		> 0.95	32.6	30.5	−2.1
105	Coitus, with compan.	Yes, No	99.0		> 0.95	67.6	68.6	+1.0
104	Coitus, with prostit.	Yes, No	95.2		> 0.95	37.5	38.5	+1.0
34	Coitus, extra-marital	Yes, No	94.2		> 0.95	67.6	67.6	0.0
104	Homosexual	Yes, No	90.4		> 0.95	46.2	50.0	+3.8
104	Animal	Yes, No	94.3		0.94	10.6	12.5	+1.9
	Vital Statistics				Pearsonian r			
152	Age of subject	1 year	89.5	98.0	0.99	25.46 ± 0.61	25.53 ± 0.62	+0.07 ± 0.03
104	Marital status	Yes, No	98.1					
61	Age ♂ at marriage	1 year	63.9	90.2	0.85	22.83 ± 0.46	23.25 ± 0.47	+0.42 ± 0.25
60	Age ♀ at marriage	1 year	53.3	81.7	0.89	21.55 ± 0.45	21.72 ± 0.46	+0.17 ± 0.22
73	Age of father	2 years	50.7	79.5	0.96	57.38 ± 1.29	56.67 ± 1.26	−0.71 ± 0.35
82	Age of mother	2 years	47.6	79.3	0.97	53.29 ± 1.16	52.85 ± 1.22	−0.44 ± 0.28
107	No. of brothers	1	96.3	98.1	0.96	2.44 ± 0.17	2.44 ± 0.15	0.00 ± 0.05
97	No. of sisters	1	89.7	95.9	0.91	2.25 ± 0.10	2.37 ± 0.12	+0.12 ± 0.05
102	Rural-urban	Yes, No	97.1					
160	Educational level	2	90.0	99.4	0.99	14.90 ± 0.33	14.96 ± 0.33	+0.06 ± 0.05
101	Religious group	1 of 3	99.0					
100	Religious devoutness	Yes, No	81.0					

Table 13. Comparisons of data on original histories and re-takes

	Frequencies				Pearsonian r	Frequency	Frequency	
278	Total outlet	1.0/wk.	30.9	65.8	0.67	3.52 ± 0.16	3.83 ± 0.15	+0.31 ± 0.13
212	Masturbation	0.5/wk.	26.4	48.1	0.60	1.96 ± 0.11	2.17 ± 0.12	+0.21 ± 0.10
209	Nocturnal emissions	0.1/wk.	53.1	69.4	0.65	0.28 ± 0.03	0.27 ± 0.03	−0.01 ± 0.02
43	Petting to climax	0.1/wk.	27.9	34.9	0.58	0.44 ± 0.06	0.37 ± 0.06	−0.07 ± 0.06
94	Coitus, with compan.	0.5/wk.	54.3	68.1	0.59	1.45 ± 0.19	1.26 ± 0.17	−0.19 ± 0.16
183	Coitus, total	0.5/wk.	37.2	59.0	0.66	2.19 ± 0.15	2.41 ± 0.16	+0.22 ± 0.13
84	Homosexual	0.5/wk.	54.8	73.8	0.67	1.14 ± 0.13	1.25 ± 0.14	+0.11 ± 0.11
	Age at first knowledge of:							
121	Pregnancy	2 years	43.0	85.1	0.66	11.58 ± 0.25	11.55 ± 0.24	−0.03 ± 0.20
134	Coitus	2 years	46.3	80.6	0.62	10.36 ± 0.23	10.48 ± 0.24	+0.12 ± 0.21
84	Fertilization	2 years	39.3	84.5	0.59	14.21 ± 0.27	13.90 ± 0.27	−0.31 ± 0.24
115	Menstruation	2 years	45.2	86.1	0.59	12.87 ± 0.27	13.43 ± 0.26	+0.56 ± 0.24
51	Abortion	2 years	45.1	80.4	0.43	15.24 ± 0.28	15.51 ± 0.41	+0.27 ± 0.38
55	Prostitution	2 years	40.0	81.8	0.44	13.85 ± 0.30	14.00 ± 0.31	+0.15 ± 0.33
65	Venereal disease	2 years	36.9	76.9	0.41	14.38 ± 0.29	14.54 ± 0.31	+0.16 ± 0.33
59	Condoms	2 years	32.2	78.0	0.58	14.02 ± 0.38	14.22 ± 0.37	+0.20 ± 0.35
	Age at first experience in:							
76	Pre-adol. heterosex. play	1 year	31.6	67.1	0.59	8.03 ± 0.27	8.01 ± 0.27	−0.02 ± 0.24
77	Pre-adol. homosex. play	1 year	13.0	59.7	0.50	8.37 ± 0.23	8.34 ± 0.26	−0.03 ± 0.25
157	Adolescence	1 year	56.7	87.3	0.72	13.07 ± 0.10	13.08 ± 0.09	+0.01 ± 0.07
105	First ejaculation	1 year	47.6	83.8	0.58	13.44 ± 0.13	13.64 ± 0.16	+0.20 ± 0.14
95	Masturbation	1 year	48.4	82.1	0.59	13.51 ± 0.21	13.74 ± 0.33	+0.23 ± 0.26
80	Nocturnal emissions	1 year	23.8	53.8	0.54	15.70 ± 0.29	15.38 ± 0.25	−0.32 ± 0.28
133	Petting	1 year	32.2	65.4	0.63	15.58 ± 0.23	15.68 ± 0.21	+0.10 ± 0.19
98	Coitus, any kind	1 year	43.9	72.4	0.81	16.90 ± 0.38	17.29 ± 0.42	+0.39 ± 0.25
28	Coitus, with prostitutes	1 year	39.3	64.3	0.81	18.46 ± 0.67	18.32 ± 0.65	−0.14 ± 0.41
21	Coitus, extra-marital	1 year	57.1	85.7				
48	Homosexual	1 year	41.7	64.6	0.60	15.63 ± 0.44	15.67 ± 0.40	+0.04 ± 0.38

108 males and 54 females are involved. The lapse between originals and re-takes ranged between 18 and 88 months (7 years and 4 months). The mean lapse is 38.5 months. The more than 200 "cases" in the frequency data depend on the fact that a single history may contribute data on more than one 5-year period.

little reservation. On the other hand, wherever the vital statistics on an individual history are to be used in a calculation, there should be allowances of a year, plus or minus.

Reports on ages of first experience in each type of sexual activity are much less accurate. The coefficients of correlation vary between 0.5 and 0.8. The number of precisely identical responses is quite low, ranging from 13 per cent to 57 per cent on most items. The number of responses that are identical within one year, plus or minus, is much higher, lying between 70 and 87 per cent on more than half of the items. However, in spite of the inadequacies of individual histories, the means for the whole population may be accepted with less question. The differences between the means for the originals and the means for the re-takes ordinarily constitute 5 per cent or less of the quantity involved. The lowest scores on memory of first experience pertain to the pre-adolescent sex play and to the first experiences in nocturnal emissions and heterosexual petting. These items are more indefinite and therefore more difficult to remember than such things as first ejaculation, first coitus, or first experience in other socio-sexual activities.

Reports on frequencies of sexual activity give correlations which run close to 0.6 on all of the items. This is a significant correlation, but not as reliable as that obtained on incidences or on many of the other items. The percents of identical responses are low, lying between 25 and 50 percent, and the percents of identical responses plus or minus one unit of measurement are still less than 65 per cent in most cases. The error on the means lies between 5 and 10 per cent on most items, and that much allowance should be made on any statement in this volume concerning frequencies of sexual activity. While the frequency data on any individual history are undoubtedly approximations to the fact, they are not accurate enough to be pushed in detail.

The poorest memory applies to the ages at which the individual first learns particular things, e.g., the age at which he first learns there is such a thing as intercourse, pregnancy, prostitution, etc. Even when a leeway of two years is allowed as identity, the coefficients of correlation are no higher than 0.4 and 0.5, and the number of identical responses is under 50 per cent. If an additional allowance is granted of plus or minus two more years, the number of identical responses is brought up to something over 80 per cent on most items. This means that a five-year allowance must be made for any answer in this area, i.e., an allowance of plus or minus 2.5 on the given answer. Here again, however, the means calculated for whole populations are much better, and a correction of something between 1 and 5 per cent seems a sufficient allowance.

There is no way of knowing whether the responses are more accurate on the first histories or on their re-takes, or whether either of them represents identity with the fact. Re-takes test the constancy of memory and the constancy of the degree of cover-up, rather than the validity of the record. There is reason for believing that memory which stays as fixed as it does on most of the items in this study is not wholly capricious, but allowance must be made for the fact that one may come to believe in a fiction on which he has decided at some time in his life. In general, the re-takes raise the incidence figures and, strikingly enough, they raise the record of age of first experience, first knowledge, etc. This suggests that as the individual grows older the period of beginning any type of activity seems to him to move up, to some degree. These are matters of broad import in psychology, but their more extensive examination has not yet been possible within the confines of the present study.

COMPARISONS OF SPOUSES

The histories of the two spouses in any marriage should contain a certain number of identities, and comparisons of such pairs of histories have given some insight into the validity of memory. Therefore, in this study, especial attention has been given to securing histories from spouses, and 231 pairs of spouses are the bases of the comparisons shown in Table 14. The items analyzed in the table include some vital statistics, the record of coital frequencies, and details concerning the foreplay, positions, and other techniques employed in the marital coitus. On the whole, the record shows an amazing agreement between the statements of the husbands and of the wives in each marriage, although allowance must be made for the possibility that there may have been collusion between some of the partners, and a conscious or unconscious agreement to distort the fact.

The coefficients of correlation between the replies of the husbands and the replies of the respective wives have the following values:

Correlations in Replies of Spouses

Coefficients	Items	Percentage of Items	Cumulated Percentages
0.50–0.59	2	6.3	100.0
0.60–0.69	6	18.8	93.7
0.70–0.79	10	31.2	74.9
0.80–0.89	5	15.6	43.7
0.90–0.99	9	28.1	28.1
Totals	32	100.0	

In regard to three-quarters of the items, the coefficient of correlation between the replies of the husbands and of the wives is 0.7 or better; for nearly half of the items it is 0.8 or better; and for more than a quarter of the

COMPARING DATA FROM 231 PAIRS OF SPOUSES

CASES	ITEMS INVOLVED	UNIT OF MEASURE-MENT	IDENT. RSPNS. %	WITH-IN 1 UNIT OF IDENT. %	COFFFIC. OF CORREL.	MEAN OF HUSBAND'S REPORTS	MEAN OF WIFE'S REPORTS	DIFF. OF MEANS: ♂ − ♀
	Vital Statistics				Pears. r			
229	Years married	1 year	88.6	96.1	0.99	6.35 ± 0.42	6.40 ± 0.42	−0.05
214	Pre-marital acquaint.	12 mon.	57.9	86.9	0.88	42.11 ± 2.83	40.88 ± 2.74	+1.23
156	Engagement	4 mon.	57.1	78.2	0.83	12.64 ± 1.03	12.85 ± 1.07	−0.21
226	Age, ♂ at marr.	1 year	68.6	97.3	0.99	27.27 ± 0.37	27.17 ± 0.37	+0.10
228	Age, ♀ at marr.	1 year	61.8	92.5	0.63	24.88 ± 0.32	24.75 ± 0.32	+0.13
231	No. children	1 child	99.6	100.0	0.99	0.90 ± 0.09	0.90 ± 0.09	0.00
185	No. abortions	1 event	90.3	98.4	0.76	0.32 ± 0.06	0.41 ± 0.08	−0.09
227	Lapse, first coitus—marr.	6 mon.	74.4	89.4	0.85	5.09 ± 0.88	4.72 ± 0.86	+0.37
87	Lapse, marr.—first birth	6 mon.	66.7	89.7	0.96	28.05 ± 1.99	28.19 ± 2.01	−0.14
220	Educ. level, ♂	2 years	84.1	99.1	0.97	16.23 ± 0.26	16.16 ± 0.25	+0.07
223	Educ. level, ♀	2 years	79.4	97.8	0.92	14.41 ± 0.21	14.67 ± 0.21	−0.26
219	Occup. class, ♂	1 of 9	91.8	98.6	0.98	5.32 ± 0.14	5.27 ± 0.14	+0.05
	Coital Freq.							
223	Max. freq., marit. coitus	2/wk.	33.2	68.2	0.54	6.72 ± 0.31	6.74 ± 0.31	−0.02
225	Av. freq., early marr.	1/wk.	34.7	73.3	0.50	2.73 ± 0.13	3.00 ± 0.14	−0.27
226	Av. freq., now	1/wk.	56.6	88.1	0.60	1.91 ± 0.11	2.21 ± 0.13	−0.30
218	% with orgasm, ♀	10%	55.0	71.1	0.75	69.82 ± 2.16	66.83 ± 2.26	+2.99
	Techniques in coital foreplay				Tetra-choric r	% Husbands ReportingYes	% Wives ReportingYes	
229	Kiss	Yes, No	97		0.92	95.6 ± 1.35	99.1 ± 0.62	−3.5
228	Deep kiss	Yes, No	85		0.72	85.1 ± 2.36	82.0 ± 2.54	+3.1
228	Hand—♀ breast	Yes, No	95		0.78	95.6 ± 1.36	96.5 ± 1.22	−0.9
228	Mouth—♀ breast	Yes, No	89		0.79	90.4 ± 2.04	86.0 ± 2.43	+4.4
229	Hand—♀ genitalia	Yes, No	90		0.61	92.6 ± 1.73	92.2 ± 1.77	+0.4
226	Hand—♂ genitalia	Yes, No	85		0.70	83.6 ± 2.46	85.8 ± 2.32	− .2
220	Mouth—♀ genitalia	Yes, No	82		0.84	35.9 ± 3.23	37.3 ± 3.26	−1.4
226	Mouth—♂ genitalia	Yes, No	85		0.93	33.6 ± 3.14	35.4 ± 3.18	−1.8
	Coital techniq.							
228	Male above	Yes, No	93		0.75	94.3 ± 1.54	93.5 ± 1.63	+0.8
228	Female above	Yes, No	76		0.74	54.8 ± 3.30	49.1 ± 3.31	+5.7
224	On side	Yes, No	76		0.68	39.3 ± 3.26	37.1 ± 3.23	+2.2
221	Sitting	Yes, No	81		0.63	19.0 ± 2.64	17.6 ± 2.56	+1.4
227	Standing	Yes, No	89		0.64	10.1 ± 2.00	7.9 ± 1.79	+2.2
224	Rear entrance	Yes, No	83		0.77	24.6 ± 2.88	17.4 ± 2.53	+7.2
186	Coitus nude	Yes, No	90		0.82	87.1 ± 2.46	89.2 ± 2.28	−2.1
223	Multiple orgasm, ♂	Yes, No	95		0.74	4.9 ± 1.45	4.1 ± 1.33	+0.8

Table 14. Comparisons of data obtained from spouses

items it is 0.9 or better. These are very high scores, as correlations go in social and psychological studies.

The number of identical replies received from the two spouses in each marriage is as follows:

Percents of Identical Replies	Exact Identity			Within One Unit (±) of Identity		
	No. of Items Involved	Percentage of Items	Cumulated Percentages	Cases	Percentage of Cases	Cumulated Percentages
30–39	2	6.2	100.0			
40–49	0	0.0	93.8			
50–59	4	12.5	93.8			
60–69	3	9.4	81.3	1	6.2	100.0
70–79	4	12.5	71.9	3	18.8	93.8
80–89	10	31.3	59.4	4	25.0	75.0
90–99	9	28.1	28.1	8	50.0	50.0
Totals	32	100.0		16	100.0	100.0

In regard to nearly 60 per cent of the items, the replies were identical for 80 per cent or more of the couples. In regard to three-quarters of the items, they were within one unit of identity for 80 per cent of the couples. These close identities are particularly impressive when it is remembered that in many instances there were intervals of two to six years or more between the interviews with the two spouses. On half of the items, there is near identity in something between 90 and 100 per cent of the histories. In most instances, near identity is about all that a student of behavior is interested in; it rarely matters whether the age of the spouse is a year one way or the other of the reported age, whether the other spouse has had six years or eight years of schooling, whether the male is a semi-skilled or a more skilled mechanic. Allowances are also to be made for the fact that some persons calculate their ages as from the last birthday, and some persons from the forthcoming birthday, and that a difference of a year in two reports may, in actuality, mean identity.

Averages for the entire group of histories are still closer than the correlations on individual histories. The differences between the means calculated for all the males and the means calculated for all the females are quite insignificant on all but a few items, as an examination of Table 14 will show.

The coefficients of correlation and the percentages of identical replies are low only in regard to the frequencies of marital coitus, and in regard to the percentage of the time in which the female reaches orgasm during the marital coitus. On the latter point, the male believes that his female partner experiences orgasm more often than she herself reports; but it is to be noted that the wife sometimes deceives her husband deliberately on that point. In regard to the frequencies of marital intercourse, there is an interesting psychological element involved. It is often the female who reports the higher frequencies, and this is undoubtedly related to the fact that females often complain of their husbands' desire for more coitus. Consequently, the females may be overestimating the actual frequencies. Similarly, the husbands regularly complain of their wives' lack of desire for coitus and, in consequence, are probably underestimating the frequencies with which they do have it. On individual histories, errors on this particular point may be expected in as many as two-thirds of the cases; but in regard to averages for whole populations, the correction is, again, remarkably small.

For most items of the sort covered in this study, it may be expected that something between 80 and 99 per cent of the subjects will give replies that will be verified, independently, by the partners in their marriages.

OTHER CROSS-CHECKS

In addition to re-takes and pairs of histories from spouses, a variety of other cross-checks have provided some further measure of the accuracy of memory. For instance, the internal consistency of a history, as it is pieced together in an interview, is of considerable significance as a test of validity. In each case, the subject is asked to supply a great many dates and records of ages in a sequence which is far from chronologic. Nevertheless, there is usually considerable coherence in the chronology that comes out of such a tabulation. Some time, it may be possible to reduce this matter to more precise calculation.

In Chapter 2, in connection with a discussion of interviewing techniques, it was pointed out that a skillful interviewer develops a certain ability to recognize falsification and cover-up when taking a history, and does have a considerable measure of the validity of the record he is getting, even though it may not be possible to reduce such a measure to statistical terms.

In Chapter 2 it was also pointed out that the trained interviewer must have a considerable fund of information concerning patterns of sexual behavior in different segments of the population. The constancy with which such patterns are followed in individual histories is very high, as later chapters (particularly Chapter 10) in the present volume will show. While it may be questioned whether a subject sometimes reports what he thinks is usual and acceptable in his social group, it should be emphasized that exceedingly few subjects have any idea of the patterns of behavior of other persons in their group. The histories cover such a mass of detail as few persons have ever discussed with their friends, and they simply do not know how those friends or any other persons in the same group are answering such questions. When 90 to 95 per cent of the persons in any social level report histories which agree with the patterns shown in Chapter 10, they not only establish the nature of the group patterns, but establish the validity of their own reports as well.

Further cross-checks are provided by sexual partners other than spouses. Whether they are involved in heterosexual or homosexual relations, each partner may supply some information about the other individual's history. The cross-references have been kept, and it may be possible to subject the material to statistical comparisons when the series are large enough. Now it can be reported that the secondhand information secured in this way has proved to be surprisingly accurate in most cases where there has been a chance to check it. Although none of this secondhand material has been used in any of the calculations in the present volume, it has been of value as a means of testing the accuracy of the related histories. Within the confines of the present chapter, a single example of this sort will have to suffice.

This example concerns the accuracy of the incidence data on the homosexual experience had by men in penal institutions and reported by them while they are under confinement in such institutions. This is material about which it is especially difficult to secure information, although in nearly all prisons there is a continuous undercurrent of gossip concerning such activity. The gossip reflects a mixture of desire for experience and bitter condemnation of such activity—a conflict between the individual's personal needs, and his training in the social traditions on matters of sex. There is, of course, official condemnation of such activity; and this may involve, especially in institutions for men, severe corporal punishment, loss of privileges, solitary confinement, and often an extension by a year or more of the sentence of an inmate who is discovered, suspected, or merely accused of homosexual relations. To persuade such an inmate to contribute a record of his activity while he is still in prison, is a considerable test of the ability of an interviewer. Nonetheless, we have gotten such records from something between 35 and 85 per cent of the inmates of every institution in which we have worked.

In one prison, a male who was well acquainted with the institution agreed to take the list of three hundred and fifty men who had contributed histories to this study, and to indicate which of them were, to his knowledge, currently having homosexual relations. About most of these men he knew nothing, but from the list he picked 32 with whom he claimed to have had relations, or whom he had actually seen in such relations. The informant never knew how his record compared with the data we had secured in the interviewing, but the histories showed that 27 of the 32 men (*i.e.*, about 85 per cent!) had admitted their experience when they were first interviewed. Two of the others had left the institution before they could be interviewed again, but the remaining three readily admitted their activity when they were called back for a second conference. This provided a check on the validity of secondhand reports and, incidentally, gave some measure of the extent of the cover-up that we are getting in the histories. Considering the nature of the item involved, this 15 per cent failure probably approaches the maximum which will be found anywhere in this study.

MEMORY VERSUS PHYSICAL FINDINGS

It is possible to make comparisons of certain of the data obtained by interviews in the present study, and data obtained in some other studies

AGE	PERCENT OF BOYS BEGINNING PUBIC HAIR DEVELOPMENT							
	CRAMPTON 1908		DIMOCK 1937		SCHONFELD 1943		PRESENT STUDY	
	%	Cumu-lated %	%	Cumu-lated %	%	Cumu-lated %	%	Cumu-lated %
9							0.2	0.2
10			2.0	2.0			2.0	2.2
11	7.0	7.0	15.0	17.0	12.0	12.0	7.7	9.9
12	24.0	31.0	21.0	38.0	30.0	42.0	25.5	35.4
13	28.0	59.0	22.0	60.0	25.0	67.0	33.5	68.9
14	25.0	84.0	27.0	87.0	12.0	79.0	22.8	91.7
15	11.0	95.0	11.0	98.0	19.0	98.0	5.5	97.2
16	4.0	99.0	2.0	100.0	1.0	99.0	2.0	99.2
17	1.0	100.0			1.0	100.0	0.7	99.9
18								99.9
19								99.9
20							0.1	100.0
Cases	3835		1406		1475		2511	
Mean	13.44 ± 1.51		13.08				13.45 ± 0.03	
Median					13.17		13.43	

Table 15. Comparisons of data obtained in four studies on pubic hair development

The data from the Crampton, Dimock, and Schonfeld studies were based upon physical examinations of young boys. The present study has been dependent upon the memory of older persons recalling their adolescent experiences.

from direct observations on similar groups of males. The readiest body of such material corcerns adolescent developments. In Table 15 and Figure 15, data on pubic hair development, drawn from three of the observational studies (Crampton 1908, Dimock 1937, Schonfeld 1943), are compared with data contributed by the subjects in the present study, on the basis of recall. The near identity of the recall curve and the other curves is remarkable, especially in consideration of the fact that many subjects protest that such an item as pubic hair development is recalled with less certainty than most other items. The larger series in the present study gives a growth curve which is smoother and more usual in type than the curves which some of the smaller series give. It is to be noted, again, that though this comparison goes a long way to justify recall as a source of averages for whole groups, it does not demonstrate how accurate the memory of any particular individual may be concerning his own individual history.

There are a number of other observational studies of adolescent developments (cited in Chapter 5), but unfortunately none of them provides data

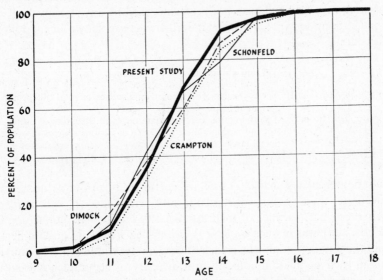

Figure 15. Comparison of memory with observational data

Record for age of onset of growth of pubic hair. The Crampton, Dimock, and Schonfeld studies based upon physical examinations of boys. The present study based on memory of older persons recalling adolescent experience.

which can be used in comparison with data from the present study. Some of these other studies are based on populations which are too small to be significant. Some of them appear to involve gross errors. In several cases, the other studies have used definitions of adolescent characters which are different from those used in the present study, *e.g.*, voice change is defined in some of the studies as the first sign of deepening voice (which is in reality often a pre-adolescent development), and pubic hair is defined as kinky hair (which may not appear until sometime after the first distinct but straight hair develops in the pubic area). It will, therefore, be necessary to wait until further observational data are available for further testing of the validity of recall on these characters.

SMOOTH TRENDS

It is to be said again that a major portion of the present volume is concerned with incidence figures and with average frequencies of the various types of sexual activity, calculated for groups which represent whole portions of the total population. In many instances the data have been calculated for series of such groups, as, for instance, successive age groups, groups representing successive levels of educational attainment, groups representing series of social levels, etc. In such series the incidence data and the means for the successive groups fall into straight lines or into curves which are remarkably smooth. This is to be seen in many of the charts shown in this volume. It is to be noted again that all of these curves are based on raw data and have not been smoothed by any statistical device. Some striking instances of such smooth trends are shown in the following charts:

Fig. 35.	Age and number of sources of outlet.
Fig. 37.	Age and incidence of impotence.
Figs. 38–88 (in part).	Age and mean and median frequencies of total outlet, and of particular sources of outlet.
Figs. 38–88 (in part).	Age and active incidence data on various sources of outlet.
Figs. 14–24.	Age and accumulative incidence of various sources of outlet.
Figs. 98–105.	Social levels and mean frequencies of various sources of outlet.
Figs. 136–160.	Individual variation in frequencies of various sources of outlet.

While irregularly shaped curves are not to be ruled out as necessarily inaccurate, there is some warrant for considering that smooth trends in such curves are evidence of their approach to reality. The population on which each point in such a curve is established is usually quite different from the population on which each other point is established. The individuals in each population come from a diversity of geographic and social backgrounds. They have been contributing now over a period of nine years. For the most part, no individual has had any way of knowing what other persons in the same group have done in their lives or reported in their interviews. In the majority of cases the subjects in this study have not known enough about the statistical breakdown of the population to have any precise idea of the confines of the groups to which they themselves belonged. When data obtained under such circumstances give averages which show such smooth trends, there is considerable warrant for believing that the vagaries of capricious memory have not been involved as often as the realities, namely the biologic and social factors which operate with steadily increasing or steadily diminishing force at successive points on the curve.

When the cases which establish particular points on these curves become too few, the points no longer fall within the smooth trend, and this exposes the extent of the deviations which too small samples may introduce.

HUNDRED PERCENT SAMPLES

When a study of everyday people discloses such unexpected behavior as the present study has disclosed, it is natural enough that one should wonder whether there has been some bias in the investigator's choice of subjects or his emphasis in interviewing. On this point, it has already been explained (Chapter 3) that the persons who have contributed histories have represented considerable samples and, whenever possible, hundred percent samples of each group that has been involved in the study. There has been next to no selection of subjects on the basis of anything that was previously known about their histories. The only exceptions have come in regard to a few extreme items which, as already explained (Chapter 3), could not have been obtained by way of hundred percent samples; and most of the histories have come from unselected individuals in whole groups. Such unselected series have been the prime bases for the incidence figures in this volume. See the preceding chapter for more detailed comparisons of the data obtained from hundred percent samples, and from the remainder of the population.

COMPARISONS OF INTERVIEWERS

One of the questions most frequently raised about the present research, and a thoroughly legitimate question about any research, concerns the possibility of another investigator duplicating the results. Moreover, in any project which has involved two or more investigators, it is important to compare the results obtained by each, before one can fairly add together the data obtained by the several interviewers. In consequence, throughout the years of this investigation repeated comparisons of that sort have been made.

Comparisons of the data obtained by different investigators can be significant only when the persons contributing histories to each investigator belong to the same sex, race, marital status, age, educational level, rural-urban group, religious group, etc. It is meaningless to compare data drawn from quite different sorts of groups. Even when comparisons are made for groups that are the products of six-way breakdowns, which is the limit possible with the sample now at hand, there are certainly many other factors which affect variation within each group. Consequently, it is not to be expected that the material obtained by two interviewers working with two different populations, even after a six-way breakdown, should be quite identical.

Table 16 compares the data obtained by the three authors of the present volume. The table includes all of those groups from which each of the interviewers has obtained at least 300 histories. To compare smaller populations would have introduced errors consequent on size of sample (Chapter 3). The senior author began accumulating histories some years before

COMPARISONS OF FREQUENCY DATA OBTAINED BY THREE INTERVIEWERS

GROUP	INTER-VIEWER	CASES	TOTAL POPULATION		ACTIVE POPULATION		
			Mean Frequency	Median Freq.	Incid. %	Mean Frequency	Median Freq.
Age 11–15							
Total Outlet	Kinsey	644	3.05 ± 0.14	2.11	93.9	3.24 ± 0.15	2.30
	Pomeroy	607	2.58 ± 0.11	1.83	97.2	2.65 ± 0.11	1.90
	Martin	325	2.69 ± 0.16	2.12	96.0	2.80 ± 0.17	2.23
Masturbation	Kinsey	644	2.36 ± 0.12	1.46	77.8	3.03 ± 0.14	2.17
	Pomeroy	607	2.01 ± 0.10	1.21	81.7	2.46 ± 0.12	1.75
	Martin	325	2.32 ± 0.17	1.70	82.5	2.82 ± 0.19	2.28
Nocturnal Emiss.	Kinsey	644	0.43 ± 0.03	0.15	74.1	0.58 ± 0.04	0.31
	Pomeroy	607	0.37 ± 0.03	0.17	76.3	0.49 ± 0.03	0.29
	Martin	325	0.28 ± 0.02	0.12	74.8	0.37 ± 0.03	0.26
Pre-mar. Coitus	Kinsey	644	0.09 ± 0.03	0.00	6.8	1.27 ± 0.46	0.17
	Pomeroy	607	0.03 ± 0.01	0.00	4.9	0.54 ± 0.16	0.20
	Martin	325	0.04 ± 0.02	0.00	6.8	0.63 ± 0.27	0.14
Homosexual	Kinsey	644	0.09 ± 0.02	0.00	21.1	0.43 ± 0.06	0.10
	Pomeroy	607	0.10 ± 0.02	0.00	21.3	0.45 ± 0.08	0.09
	Martin	325	0.02 ± 0.004	0.00	17.5	0.12 ± 0.02	0.07
Age 16–20							
Total Outlet	Kinsey	662	3.05 ± 0.12	2.30	99.7	3.06 ± 0.12	2.31
	Pomeroy	612	2.50 ± 0.09	1.87	99.8	2.50 ± 0.09	1.88
	Martin	331	2.66 ± 0.13	2.17	100.0	2.66 ± 0.13	2.17
Masturbation	Kinsey	662	2.11 ± 0.10	1.33	88.1	2.40 ± 0.11	1.66
	Pomeroy	612	1.72 ± 0.08	0.99	86.9	1.98 ± 0.09	1.40
	Martin	331	1.99 ± 0.13	1.48	89.4	2.22 ± 0.14	1.76
Nocturnal Emiss.	Kinsey	662	0.47 ± 0.03	0.27	91.2	0.51 ± 0.03	0.31
	Pomeroy	612	0.43 ± 0.02	0.27	91.5	0.47 ± 0.02	0.31
	Martin	331	0.36 ± 0.02	0.24	89.7	0.40 ± 0.03	0.28
Pre-mar. Coitus	Kinsey	662	0.26 ± 0.04	0.00	37.3	0.70 ± 0.11	0.19
	Pomeroy	612	0.15 ± 0.02	0.00	35.5	0.44 ± 0.05	0.15
	Martin	331	0.19 ± 0.03	0.00	38.4	0.49 ± 0.07	0.11
Homosexual	Kinsey	662	0.08 ± 0.02	0.00	14.8	0.50 ± 0.09	0.09
	Pomeroy	612	0.06 ± 0.01	0.00	17.6	0.33 ± 0.06	0.08
	Martin	331	0.02 ± 0.005	0.00	11.8	0.15 ± 0.04	0.07
Age 21–25							
Total Outlet	Kinsey	533	2.64 ± 0.12	1.79	99.6	2.65 ± 0.13	1.80
	Pomeroy	432	2.18 ± 0.09	1.70	100.0	2.18 ± 0.09	1.70
Masturbation	Kinsey	533	1.43 ± 0.09	0.62	86.3	1.66 ± 0.10	0.87
	Pomeroy	432	1.12 ± 0.06	0.59	87.7	1.27 ± 0.07	0.74
Nocturnal Emiss.	Kinsey	533	0.39 ± 0.03	0.23	87.1	0.45 ± 0.03	0.29
	Pomeroy	432	0.38 ± 0.02	0.25	87.7	0.43 ± 0.02	0.30
Pre-mar. Coitus	Kinsey	533	0.49 ± 0.06	0.04	57.4	0.85 ± 0.11	0.29
	Pomeroy	432	0.40 ± 0.04	0.03	54.6	0.72 ± 0.07	0.30
Homosexual	Kinsey	533	0.11 ± 0.03	0.00	10.7	1.05 ± 0.22	0.34
	Pomeroy	432	0.08 ± 0.02	0.00	8.8	0.96 ± 0.20	0.37

Table 16. Comparisons of data obtained by different interviewers

Comparisons confined to groups with over 300 histories, of same background for sex, race, marital status, educational level (all of college level), and age. Based on histories taken during last four years of the research.

the other two authors were involved; and on the chance that the first investigator's techniques of interviewing and his methods of recording may have varied in that time, the comparisons in Table 16 are confined to the data obtained by each of the three interviewers during the same period of time, namely, the more recent four years of this study.

The most important conclusions to be drawn from these comparisons are:

1. Three different interviewers have obtained very similar data from three different populations. Out of the 75 sets of calculations which appear in Table 16, 35 are so similar that the differences are immaterial—closer than any person could calculate about his own history. Such identity is amazing. There seems no reason to doubt that any other group of investigators could duplicate these results if their scientific objectivity and their methods in interviewing were comparable to those which have been used in the present study. In about 10 of the 75 sets of calculations, there are more or less material differences between the lowest and the highest figures.

2. The incidence data are more nearly identical for the three interviewers than the frequency data. There is close identity in incidences even for such a taboo item as the homosexual where, it will be noted, the active incidence figures in each of the five-year periods prove to be five to ten times as high as any which have previously been published. Whether the actual incidence figure for the homosexual in any particular group is 17.5 per cent or 21.3 per cent is of no great moment. The fact remains that the general locus of this, and of all the other figures, is established by the independent interviewing of three persons drawing their samples very largely at random, or from hundred percent groups which (especially in the case of the college level) constituted a considerable portion of the sample.

3. Some selection has been involved in assigning subjects to interviewers. Older persons, persons with more promiscuous histories (whether heterosexual or homosexual), and persons who were expected to prove reticent because of socially unusual items which were known to be in their histories, have more often been interviewed by the senior investigator, especially during the early years in the training of the younger members of the staff. This undoubtedly accounts for some of the differences between interviewers: for the lower homosexual incidence and frequency figures for the third interviewer, for the higher frequency data on pre-marital intercourse for the first interviewer, etc.

4. The frequency data for masturbation and for pre-marital intercourse (and in consequence for total outlet) are highest in every age group for the first interviewer and lowest for the second interviewer. The incidence and

COMPARISONS OF DATA OBTAINED BY THREE INTERVIEWERS

AGE	ACCUMULATIVE INCIDENCE: MASTURBATION EDUCATIONAL LEVEL 13+					
	HISTORIES TAKEN BY KINSEY		HISTORIES TAKEN BY POMEROY		HISTORIES TAKEN BY MARTIN	
	Cases	% with Exper.	Cases	% with Exper.	Cases	% with Exper.
8	1783	0.0	595	0.2	324	0.0
9	1783	0.3	595	0.5	324	0.0
10	1783	2.3	595	2.7	324	1.9
11	1783	8.1	595	11.4	324	9.3
12	1783	26.4	595	31.1	324	29.0
13	1783	52.3	595	56.3	324	50.0
14	1783	72.4	595	72.8	324	69.1
15	1783	79.6	595	80.8	324	81.5
16	1782	83.6	595	83.4	324	88.3
17	1781	86.6	594	86.0	324	90.4
18	1756	88.7	573	88.7	306	90.8
19	1642	90.0	548	89.2	283	91.5
20	1472	90.6	522	90.8	255	93.3
21	1273	91.4	472	91.7	216	94.0
22	1038	92.2	413	92.7	167	94.6
23	874	92.6	370	93.5	127	96.1
24	740	92.7	314	93.3	86	94.2
25	663	93.5	275	94.2	56	96.4
26	582	94.2	250	96.0		
27	512	94.7	222	96.4		
28	467	94.6	202	96.5		
29	432	94.2	179	96.6		
30	400	95.0	154	96.8		
31	378	94.7	135	96.3		
32	353	94.9	125	96.8		
33	322	94.7	114	96.5		
34	299	95.0	101	98.0		
35	277	94.9	95	97.9		
36	261	95.0	86	97.7		
37	233	94.8	81	97.5		
38	222	95.0	78	97.4		
39	207	94.7	66	97.0		
40	191	95.3	60	98.3		

Table 17. Comparisons of data obtained by different interviewers, on masturbation

Based on males of the college level.

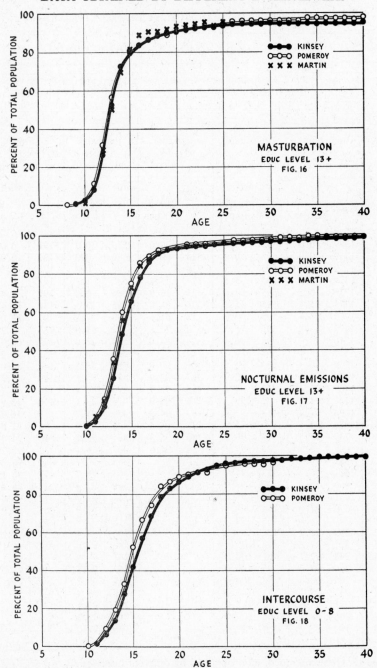

Figures 16–18. Comparing accumulative incidence data obtained by different interviewers

Data on masturbation, nocturnal emissions, and intercourse of any sort.

COMPARISONS OF DATA OBTAINED BY THREE DIFFERENT INTERVIEWERS

	ACCUMULATIVE INCIDENCE DATA				
	NOCTURNAL EMISSIONS EDUC. LEVEL 13+			TOTAL INTERCOURSE EDUC. LEVEL 0–8	
AGE	HISTORIES TAKEN BY KINSEY	HISTORIES TAKEN BY POMEROY	HISTORIES TAKEN BY MARTIN	HISTORIES TAKEN BY KINSEY	HISTORIES TAKEN BY POMEROY
	Cases / % with Exper.	Cases / % with Exper.	Cases / % with Exper.	Cases / % with Exper.	Cases / % with Exper.
8	1779 / 0.0	595 / 0.0	324 / 0.0	586 / 0.0	191 / 0.0
9	1779 / 0.0	595 / 0.0	324 / 0.0	586 / 0.0	191 / 0.0
10	1779 / 0.4	595 / 0.5	324 / 1.2	586 / 0.0	191 / 0.5
11	1779 / 2.6	595 / 3.5	324 / 5.2	585 / 1.2	191 / 1.0
12	1779 / 10.2	595 / 14.6	324 / 13.9	585 / 6.2	191 / 9.4
13	1779 / 25.7	595 / 35.8	324 / 34.6	585 / 13.5	191 / 19.4
14	1779 / 48.6	595 / 60.0	324 / 55.6	583 / 27.8	191 / 33.0
15	1779 / 65.8	595 / 75.3	324 / 72.8	582 / 41.8	186 / 52.2
16	1778 / 78.0	595 / 86.1	324 / 84.0	574 / 57.0	177 / 66.7
17	1777 / 86.1	594 / 89.2	324 / 87.7	556 / 68.2	155 / 74.2
18	1752 / 90.5	573 / 92.5	306 / 90.8	536 / 78.5	144 / 84.0
19	1638 / 92.4	548 / 92.9	283 / 92.9	514 / 83.1	129 / 86.8
20	1468 / 93.4	522 / 94.1	255 / 93.7	493 / 86.8	116 / 89.7
21	1269 / 94.2	472 / 95.3	216 / 94.9	475 / 89.1	110 / 90.9
22	1036 / 94.4	413 / 95.6	167 / 94.6	459 / 91.7	99 / 91.9
23	873 / 94.5	370 / 95.9	127 / 94.5	443 / 93.0	95 / 91.6
24	739 / 95.5	314 / 96.2	86 / 95.3	425 / 95.1	90 / 94.4
25	662 / 96.1	275 / 97.1	56 / 94.6	407 / 96.1	83 / 95.2
26	581 / 96.2	250 / 98.0		395 / 96.7	81 / 96.3
27	511 / 96.1	222 / 97.7		383 / 97.7	77 / 96.1
28	466 / 96.4	202 / 98.0		369 / 97.8	76 / 96.1
29	431 / 96.5	179 / 97.8		347 / 97.7	72 / 95.8
30	399 / 97.0	154 / 98.1		334 / 97.9	65 / 96.9
31	377 / 96.8	135 / 99.3		318 / 97.8	59 / 98.3
32	352 / 97.2	125 / 99.2		306 / 98.4	57 / 98.2
33	321 / 97.2	114 / 99.1		290 / 98.6	53 / 98.1
34	298 / 97.7	101 / 100.0		281 / 98.9	53 / 98.1
35	276 / 98.2	95 / 100.0		269 / 99.3	50 / 98.0
36	260 / 98.5	86 / 100.0		257 / 99.2	
37	232 / 98.3	81 / 100.0		242 / 99.2	
38	221 / 98.6	78 / 100.0		235 / 99.1	
39	206 / 98.5	66 / 100.0		215 / 99.1	
40	190 / 98.9	60 / 100.0		196 / 99.0	

Table 18. Comparisons of data obtained by different interviewers, on nocturnal emissions and on heterosexual coitus

The coitus data include intercourse from any source, pre-marital, marital, extra-marital, or post-marital, with companions or with prostitutes.

COMPARISONS OF DATA OBTAINED BY THREE DIFFERENT INTERVIEWERS

AGE	ACCUMULATIVE INCIDENCE DATA									
	TOTAL PRE-MARITAL INTERCOURSE EDUC. LEVEL 13+						TOTAL INTERCOURSE WITH PROSTITUTES EDUC. LEVEL 0–8			
	HISTORIES TAKEN BY KINSEY		HISTORIES TAKEN BY POMEROY		HISTORIES TAKEN BY MARTIN		HISTORIES TAKEN BY KINSEY		HISTORIES TAKEN BY POMEROY	
	Cases	% with Exper.	Cases	% with Exper.	Cases	% with Exper.	Cases	% with Exper.	Cases	% with Exper.
8	1783	0.0	595	0.0	324	0.0	587	0.0	191	0.0
9	1783	0.0	595	0.0	324	0.3	587	0.0	191	0.0
10	1783	0.0	595	0.0	324	0.3	586	0.0	191	0.0
11	1783	0.2	595	0.0	324	0.3	585	0.2	191	0.0
12	1783	1.1	595	0.7	324	0.6	585	0.5	191	1.0
13	1783	3.6	595	2.4	324	1.9	585	1.0	191	1.0
14	1783	7.0	595	4.0	324	3.7	583	3.4	191	4.2
15	1783	11.2	595	5.9	324	6.5	582	7.6	186	7.5
16	1782	17.3	595	11.9	324	11.4	574	18.5	177	14.7
17	1781	25.4	592	18.1	324	19.1	556	30.0	155	22.6
18	1755	32.8	570	25.8	306	27.8	536	42.2	144	36.1
19	1638	40.3	545	34.9	282	35.5	514	47.3	129	39.5
20	1452	46.7	517	39.7	251	42.2	493	50.9	116	49.1
21	1243	50.4	461	46.9	210	47.1	475	54.9	110	52.7
22	985	54.7	388	51.0	159	57.2	459	58.2	99	57.6
23	777	56.5	336	55.1	113	61.1	443	59.4	95	60.0
24	623	58.6	267	59.2	68	63.2	425	61.6	90	63.3
25	506	64.4	210	61.9			407	64.9	83	68.7
26	398	63.6	171	65.5			395	66.6	81	69.1
27	295	63.4	115	67.0			383	67.4	77	68.8
28	224	64.3	88	71.6			369	67.8	76	68.4
29	179	65.4	69	72.5			347	67.7	72	66.7
30	140	65.0	53	75.5			334	69.8	65	70.8
31	107	65.4					318	70.4	59	69.5
32	92	65.2					306	71.6	57	70.2
33	79	65.8					290	71.7	53	71.7
34	60	68.3					281	72.6	53	71.7
35	53	66.0					269	72.9	50	74.0

Table 19. Comparisons of data obtained by different interviewers, on pre-marital intercourse and on intercourse with prostitutes

Total pre-marital intercourse includes the coitus had with companions and with prostitutes. Total intercourse with prostitutes includes pre-marital, extra-marital, and post-marital data.

COMPARISONS OF DATA OBTAINED BY THREE INTERVIEWERS

AGE	ACCUMULATIVE INCIDENCE: HOMOSEXUAL OUTLETS EDUC. LEVEL 13+					
	HISTORIES TAKEN BY KINSEY		HISTORIES TAKEN BY POMEROY		HISTORIES TAKEN BY MARTIN	
	Cases	% with Exper.	Cases	% with Exper.	Cases	% with Exper.
8	1783	0.0	595	0.2	324	0.0
9	1783	0.1	595	0.2	324	0.0
10	1783	0.5	595	0.7	324	0.0
11	1783	1.9	595	2.4	324	0.9
12	1783	6.1	595	7.6	324	4.3
13	1783	11.5	595	12.9	324	9.6
14	1783	18.6	595	17.8	324	14.8
15	1783	21.6	595	21.3	324	18.2
16	1782	23.5	595	23.2	324	20.7
17	1781	24.8	594	24.1	324	21.6
18	1756	26.1	573	26.0	306	22.9
19	1642	27.3	548	27.4	283	23.7
20	1472	28.1	522	28.9	255	23.9
21	1273	28.4	472	30.7	216	26.4
22	1038	29.4	413	31.2	167	29.9
23	874	30.8	370	33.0	127	33.1
24	740	32.3	314	32.2	86	32.6
25	663	33.8	275	31.6	56	32.1
26	582	33.7	250	32.4		
27	512	34.0	222	33.8		
28	467	34.5	202	33.7		
29	432	34.0	179	35.2		
30	400	34.5	154	33.8		
31	378	34.9	135	34.1		
32	353	33.7	125	32.0		
33	322	34.8	114	32.5		
34	299	35.5	101	33.7		
35	277	35.0	95	31.6		
36	261	35.2	86	29.1		
37	233	33.9	81	32.1		
38	222	33.8	78	32.1		
39	207	34.3	66	31.8		
40	191	33.0	60	33.3		
41	180	31.1	53	35.8		

Table 20. Comparisons of data obtained by different interviewers, on total homosexual outlets

Based on males of the college level. Includes pre-marital, extra-marital, and post-marital experience in the homosexual.

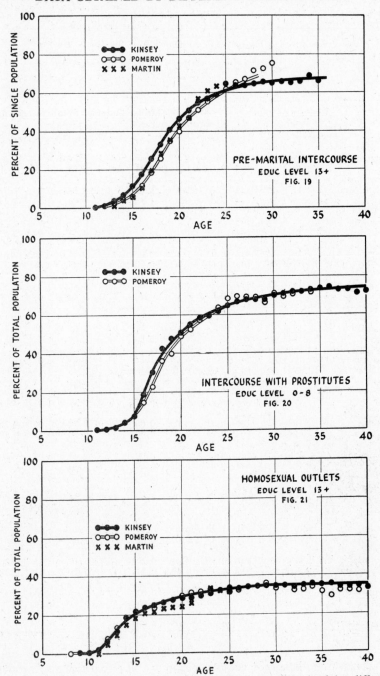

Figures 19–21. Comparing accumulative incidence data obtained by different interviewers

Data on pre-marital intercourse, intercourse with prostitutes, and homosexual outlets.

COMPARISONS OF FREQUENCY DATA OBTAINED IN SUCCESSIVE PERIODS

GROUP	PERIOD	CASES	TOTAL POPULATION		ACTIVE POPULATION		
			Mean Frequency	Median Freq.	Incid. %	Mean Frequency	Median Freq.
Age 11-15 Total Outlet	1938–42	1113	2.92 ± 0.07	2.46	96.1	3.04 ± 0.07	2.58
	1943–46	644	3.05 ± 0.14	2.11	93.9	3.24 ± 0.15	2.30
Masturbation	1938–42	1113	2.25 ± 0.06	1.82	85.2	2.64 ± 0.07	2.18
	1943–46	644	2.36 ± 0.12	1.46	77.8	3.03 ± 0.14	2.17
Nocturnal Emiss.	1938–42	1113	0.29 ± 0.02	0.06	61.8	0.47 ± 0.03	0.25
	1943–46	644	0.43 ± 0.03	0.15	74.1	0.58 ± 0.04	0.31
Pre-mar. Coitus	1938–42	1113	0.11 ± 0.02	0.00	13.7	0.81 ± 0.10	0.34
	1943–46	644	0.09 ± 0.03	0.00	6.8	1.27 ± 0.46	0.17
Homosexual	1938–42	1113	0.11 ± 0.01	0.00	23.4	0.46 ± 0.06	0.10
	1943–46	644	0.09 ± 0.02	0.00	21.1	0.43 ± 0.06	0.10
Age 16–20 Total Outlet	1938–42	1146	2.64 ± 0.06	2.14	99.7	2.65 ± 0.06	2.15
	1943–46	662	3.05 ± 0.12	2.30	99.7	3.06 ± 0.12	2.31
Masturbation	1938–42	1146	1.59 ± 0.05	1.12	89.4	1.77 ± 0.05	1.38
	1943–46	662	2.11 ± 0.10	1.33	88.1	2.40 ± 0.11	1.66
Nocturnal Emiss.	1938–42	1146	0.41 ± 0.02	0.22	91.3	0.45 ± 0.02	0.26
	1943–46	662	0.47 ± 0.03	0.27	91.2	0.51 ± 0.03	0.31
Pre-mar. Coitus	1938–42	1146	0.31 ± 0.03	0.00	41.9	0.74 ± 0.06	0.28
	1943–46	662	0.26 ± 0.04	0.00	37.3	0.70 ± 0.11	0.19
Homosexual	1938–42	1146	0.08 ± 0.01	0.00	17.8	0.47 ± 0.07	0.09
	1943–46	662	0.08 ± 0.02	0.00	14.8	0.50 ± 0.09	0.09
Age 21–25 Total Outlet	1938–42	691	2.58 ± 0.08	1.99	99.9	2.58 ± 0.08	2.00
	1943–46	533	2.64 ± 0.12	1.79	99.6	2.65 ± 0.13	1.80
Masturbation	1938–42	691	1.26 ± 0.05	0.74	86.3	1.46 ± 0.06	0.91
	1943–46	533	1.43 ± 0.09	0.62	86.3	1.66 ± 0.10	0.87
Nocturnal Emiss.	1938–42	691	0.40 ± 0.03	0.19	86.1	0.46 ± 0.03	0.26
	1943-46	533	0.39 ± 0.03	0.23	87.1	0.45 ± 0.03	0.29
Pre-mar. Coitus	1938–42	691	0.50 ± 0.05	0.02	52.4	0.95 ± 0.08	0.36
	1943–46	533	0.49 ± 0.06	0.04	57.4	0.85 ± 0.11	0.29
Homosexual	1938–42	691	0.10 ± 0.02	0.00	10.6	0.95 ± 0.17	0.28
	1943–46	533	0.11 ± 0.03	0.00	10.7	1.05 ± 0.22	0.34

Table 21. Comparisons of data obtained in two successive four-year periods

Comparing results obtained by the same interviewer (Kinsey) in the earlier half and in the later half of the study. All data from groups of college level ("educational level 13+").

the frequency data on all of the other items and the incidence data even on masturbation and pre-marital intercourse are very closely duplicated by the two interviewers. On the item which is most difficult to uncover, namely, the homosexual, the two interviewers secured almost exactly the same results. The differences in their findings on masturbation and pre-marital intercourse may be due to some selection of the subjects who have contributed the histories, or to real differences in the populations with which the two interviewers dealt; but this does not seem a sufficient explanation. On this point, further investigation needs to be made.

5. The accumulative incidence curves (Chapter 3), derived from the data gathered by the three interviewers (Tables 17–20, Figures 16–21), provide a striking demonstration of the capacities of different investigators to secure similar results, even on such intangible material as must be dealt with in the study of human sex behavior. In most cases, the incidence data obtained by the several interviewers are so nearly in accord that the curves lie precisely on top of each other. In those cases where there are differences, the general loci of the data are still confirmed, although there may be some question of the precise position of the fact between the two calculations, or to one or the other side of the extreme calculations.

STABILITY OF TECHNIQUES

The question involved here concerns the capacity of an interviewer to obtain uniform results over any long period of years. Is there a possibility that one's methods of recording change, particularly in regard to evaluations of items that are not strictly measurable? Is there a possibility that changes have entered in the methods of calculating from the raw data, since the first procedures were devised nine years ago? As a study of these problems, comparisons are shown in Table 21 between the data obtained by the senior author during the first four years of the research (1938–1942), and the data obtained by the same interviewer in the last four years (1943–1946). The two junior authors have not been involved in interviewing long enough to make such comparisons possible. Table 21 includes calculations on every group for which 300 or more cases were available from the interviewing done by the senior author in each and both of the periods. Comparisons of the accumulative incidence curves for masturbation, nocturnal emissions, pre-marital intercourse, and the homosexual in the two periods are shown in Tables 22 and 23, and Figures 22–24.

A study of the data leads to the following conclusions:

1. The active incidence data are phenomenally close in the two successive four-year samples. They leave no doubt of the general locus of the fact for every type of sexual behavior, and they even suggest that there can be considerable precision in determining these facts.

COMPARISONS OF ACCUMULATIVE INCIDENCE DATA OBTAINED IN SUCCESSIVE PERIODS

SINGLE MALES, EDUC. LEVEL 13+

AGE	MASTURBATION				NOCTURNAL EMISSIONS			
	HISTORIES TAKEN 1938–1942		HISTORIES TAKEN 1943–1946		HISTORIES TAKEN 1938–1942		HISTORIES TAKEN 1943–1946	
	Cases	% with Exper.	Cases	% with Exper.	Cases	% with Exper.	Cases	% with Exper.
8	1166	0.0	637	0.0	1163	0.0	636	0.0
9	1166	0.2	637	0.6	1163	0.0	636	0.0
10	1166	1.7	637	3.5	1163	0.4	636	0.5
11	1166	6.9	637	9.1	1163	2.1	636	3.1
12	1166	26.5	637	25.3	1163	8.6	636	12.7
13	1166	54.0	637	49.1	1163	21.5	636	33.5
14	1166	74.3	637	68.6	1163	44.5	636	56.1
15	1166	81.6	637	75.7	1163	62.8	636	71.7
16	1166	84.8	637	81.6	1163	75.7	636	83.0
17	1165	87.6	637	84.9	1162	85.2	636	88.5
18	1147	89.7	629	87.0	1144	90.4	628	91.4
19	1047	91.2	612	88.1	1044	92.4	611	93.1
20	878	91.1	594	89.9	875	93.6	593	94.1
21	705	92.1	558	91.0	702	94.6	557	94.6
22	502	92.6	503	91.8	501	94.8	502	94.8
23	351	91.5	445	92.8	351	94.3	444	94.8
24	256	91.8	385	92.5	256	95.7	384	95.6
25	199	93.0	320	92.2	199	95.0	319	96.2
26	154	93.5	256	92.6	154	95.5	255	96.9
27	102	94.1	204	93.1	102	95.1	203	96.6
28	68	94.1	163	92.6	68	95.6	162	95.7
29	51	92.2	134	94.0	51	96.1	133	95.5
30			107	95.3			106	96.2
31			82	93.9			82	95.1
32			72	94.4			72	94.4
33			61	93.4			61	95.1

Table 22. Comparisons of data obtained at two different periods, on masturbation and nocturnal emissions

Accumulative incidence data based on the pre-marital histories of males of the college level, taken by one interviewer (Kinsey) in two successive four-year periods.

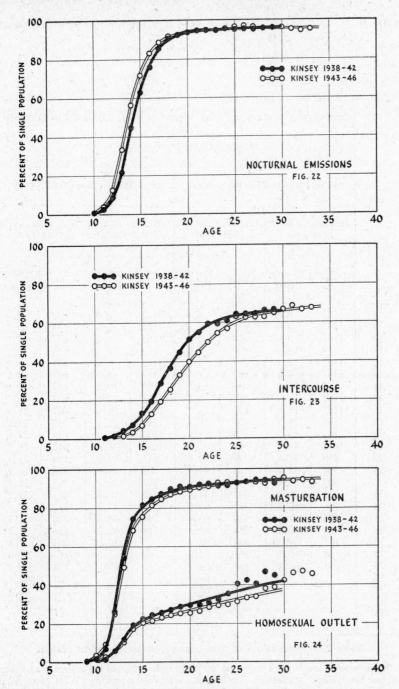

Figures 22–24. Comparing accumulative incidence data obtained by one interviewer in successive four-year periods

Data on nocturnal emissions, pre-marital intercourse, masturbation, and homosexual
contacts. All calculations based on males of college level (13+).

145

	COMPARISONS OF ACCUMULATIVE INCIDENCE DATA OBTAINED IN SUCCESSIVE PERIODS SINGLE MALES, EDUC. LEVEL 13+							
AGE	TOTAL PRE-MARITAL INTERCOURSE				PRE-MARITAL HOMOSEXUAL OUTLETS			
	HISTORIES TAKEN 1938–1942		HISTORIES TAKEN 1943–1946		HISTORIES TAKEN 1938–1942		HISTORIES TAKEN 1943–1946	
	Cases	% with Exper.	Cases	% with Exper.	Cases	% with Exper.	Cases	% with Exper.
8	1167	0.0	637	0.0	1163	0.0	637	0.0
9	1167	0.0	637	0.0	1163	0.0	637	0.2
10	1167	0.0	637	0.0	1163	0.2	637	1.1
11	1167	0.3	637	0.0	1163	1.5	637	2.2
12	1167	1.5	637	0.2	1163	5.9	637	5.7
13	1167	4.5	637	1.7	1163	12.0	637	10.2
14	1167	7.1	637	3.5	1163	19.3	637	17.1
15	1167	13.4	637	6.8	1163	22.2	637	20.7
16	1167	19.6	637	12.7	1163	24.6	637	21.5
17	1166	28.6	637	19.2	1162	25.6	637	23.1
18	1148	36.7	629	25.4	1144	27.0	629	24.6
19	1048	44.9	612	32.5	1044	28.3	612	25.5
20	879	51.4	594	39.6	875	29.3	594	25.8
21	706	55.0	558	44.4	702	29.6	558	26.7
22	503	59.4	503	49.9	501	30.7	503	28.2
23	351	59.3	445	54.4	351	32.8	445	29.2
24	256	60.9	385	56.9	256	35.2	385	29.9
25	199	64.3	320	63.4	199	40.7	320	31.3
26	154	64.3	256	62.5	154	42.2	256	33.2
27	102	64.7	204	62.3	102	40.2	204	33.8
28	68	66.2	163	62.6	68	47.1	163	38.0
29	51	66.7	134	64.9	51	45.1	134	38.8
30			107	66.4			107	42.1
31			82	68.3			82	46.3
32			72	66.7			72	47.2
33			61	67.2			61	45.9

Table 23. Comparisons of data obtained at two different periods

Accumulative incidence data based on histories of males of the college level, taken by one interviewer (Kinsey) in two successive four-year periods. Total pre-marital intercourse includes relations with companions and with prostitutes.

2. The accumulative incidence data are so nearly identical for the two different periods that it is highly improbable that two groups obtained in the same period would ever compare more closely. There is practically identity in regard to masturbation, nocturnal emissions, and the homosexual. The curves for pre-marital intercourse are about a year and a half apart during most of their rise, but reach nearly identical levels.

3. The conformance of frequency data, in the successive four-year samples, is quite close. In general, the medians are closer than the means. Since the values of means are affected by a few high-rating individuals, as the values of medians are not, this greater constancy of the medians indicates that the frequencies of persons with unusually high rates of outlet vary in successive samples, while the frequencies of the individuals in the mass of the population do not vary so much. This is obviously due to the fact that there are fewer extreme individuals and that they are not picked up in any process of sampling as regularly as the more average persons in the population. Only large samples can smooth out the effects of high-rating cases.

4. Some of the differences that do exist between the successive four-year samples may be the product of instability in the techniques of recording and calculating data, but it is just as likely that they are due to actual differences in the samples which have been involved. The comparisons in Table 21 have been made for populations resulting from a five-way breakdown (sex, race, marital status, age, and educational level), but there are many other factors that can modify the picture for particular groups.

5. The differences in calculations on successive four-year periods are not consistently higher nor lower. This means that no consistent bias has entered into the processes of the study.

6. There was, inevitably, some experimentation and some trial and error in developing the techniques of interviewing and in the manipulation of the data in the early years of the research. However, the errors that may have entered in this way do not appear to have been so large that the earlier histories need be eliminated from calculations which are based on the total body of histories. Throughout the present volume the data from the two four-year periods have, of course, been combined in all of the calculations, and the consequent statistics may (or may not) be nearer the realities of behavior than either of the sets of calculations shown in Table 21.

7. The comparisons in Tables 21–23 seem to indicate that methods of securing subjects, proficiency in interviewing, skill in using the code in which the data are recorded, and calculations and judgments which the data undergo in their statistical treatment, can be maintained at such uniform levels as many persons would have considered impossible in a case history study which is liable to error from so many sources, and which deals with as taboo a subject as sex.

IMMEDIATE VERSUS REMOTE RECALL

Any consideration of the validity of case history data involves the question of the relative accuracy of immediate memory versus remote recall. Does the subject, in an interview, give a more accurate record of his more recent or of his more remote activities? Since the subjects were of various ages when they contributed their histories, the data shown for any particular age period have been obtained partly from the more immediate recall of younger persons, and partly from the more remote—sometimes the quite remote—memory of older persons. Can data obtained by such different processes fairly be added together?

It has not been possible to undertake any study which would go into all of the complexities of this situation, although we have some measurements toward such a study. In the course of the interviewing, we have acquired certain impressions that may be worth recording in anticipation of the time when there will be enough material to make more precise determinations. These impressions cover the following points:

1. More recent events seem, in general, to be recalled more easily, and more remote events are recalled with greater difficulty. This seems reasonable enough, but it proves nothing concerning the validity of the recall. It seems reasonable to believe that more immediate and more easily recalled events would be reported with greater accuracy, but there are at least certain circumstances where that is clearly not so.

2. Pre-adolescent children, as young as three or four years of age, are ordinarily capable enough of recalling very immediate events, but often fail to recall activities and knowledge acquired only a few months or a year or two before. How much of this forgetting is a simple lapse of memory, and how much is psychologic blockage, is not readily determined. The psychoanalysts are undoubtedly correct in seeing considerable significance in the sometimes deliberate but more often unconscious repressions that develop in these early years, but they do not sufficiently allow for the simple failures of memory which seem sufficient explanation of some of the inadequacies of recall among younger subjects. There is no doubt that the analysts are correct in believing that more of this early experience is lost to memory than of the experience of any other segment of the life cycle.

3. Older persons seem to recall remote events, in many cases in minute detail, while forgetting what happened in recent weeks. This is rather generally accepted, and our own experience seems to confirm this. There are some psychologic studies that show the poor quality of the immediate recall of the aged (Thorndike 1928, Gilbert 1941), but apparently no precise studies on the validity of their remote recall.

4. While the quality of memory may show some degree of correlation with intelligence and with the extent of the individual's formal education,

there appears to be considerable accuracy of memory among some less intelligent and many poorly educated persons. Illiterate persons may remember such an amazing amount of detail about dates, names, and places, as is rarely found among educated persons whose minds are continually preoccupied with what they read in newspapers, magazines, and books. We still need precise measures of the accuracy of memory among these lower levels, but the data secured on the histories from such persons show consistencies in the chronology that are often remarkable. On the other hand, some professionally trained persons, for some reason still to be analyzed, may be much confused in attempting to construct a chronology of their own activities, and the most extreme and absurd disparities secured on any of our re-takes have come from graduate students and university instructors who had especial interest in the research and were doing their best to cooperate.

5. As usual, incidence figures are more accurate than frequency data. Estimates of average frequencies are especially difficult for children, for individuals of low mentality, and for most poorly educated individuals. Frequencies are more difficult to estimate when they concern remote periods of time.

6. The possibly greater accuracy of recent memory is at least partially offset by the greater extent of cover-up on recent events. Legal statutes of limitation are in line with the general human tendency to forgive something that is more remote, while reacting violently to more recent happenings. Consequently many subjects in a case history study will admit participation in the more taboo sexual activities at some time in the past, while insisting that such activities are no part of their current histories, or that the frequencies are now very much reduced. An undue number of persons have discontinued masturbation, pre-marital coitus, extra-marital coitus, mouth-genital contacts, homosexual activities, prostitution, or animal intercourse the year before they contributed their histories—or a few months or even weeks before! Re-takes have subsequently shown that the year of the first history was in actuality involved, although the activities are again supposed to have terminated before the date of the re-take.

7. Certain items are minimized, certain items played up, depending upon the immediate mental state of the subject. Re-takes, especially series of re-takes on the same person, and histories which can be compared with the precise records of a diary, show that these reactions fluctuate, rather than erring always in the same direction. For instance, the pre-marital heterosexual experiences which were reported on the first history may be minimized on the re-takes, while the report of the homosexual experience may be extended. A second re-take on the same individual may play up the heterosexual and minimize the homosexual experience, especially if the subject is now in the army and conscious of official attitudes on that

subject. Six months after being released from the army, the homosexual record may again be obtained in something like the form which was reported on the earlier histories.

The generalization to be drawn from these several impressions is that the memory of more recent events may be more accurate (except in the aged), but its accuracy is more or less offset by a considerable amount of cover-up on more immediate activities. What is the final effect on the quality of the individual record, and on the averages calculated for whole groups of individuals? The quality of the individual record is the clinician's constant problem, but one on which we, unfortunately, can contribute nothing more at this time. That the individual record is not wholly specious, the data elsewhere in this chapter, especially the data on re-takes, definitely show. We shall hope to make still further studies on this point as soon as we have the large series of histories which such a study will demand.

OLDER VERSUS YOUNGER GENERATIONS

As a further comparison of more immediate versus remote recall, the data in Chapter 11 bear on this point. The tables and charts in that chapter compare the younger half with the older half of the population which has entered into this study. The younger half is, of course, reporting more immediate experience. The older half, averaging about 22 years older than the first group, is recalling its early years from a distance which is that much more remote. While these data were originally calculated to study possible changes in behavior in successive generations, they also provide one more test of memory of recent versus more remote events. An examination of Chapter 11 will show that the incidence data for the two groups are, in most cases, almost precise duplicates. The frequency data are further apart in some groups but, again, precise duplicates in other groups. The factors involved in these diverse results are discussed in Chapter 11.

CONCLUSIONS

Throughout the whole period of this study, a variety of techniques has been employed to test the effectiveness of the methods of interviewing, the validity of the data which are obtained in an interview, and the appropriateness of the statistical techniques by which the data have been manipulated. It is unfortunate that these studies of method are not yet complete and, indeed, that they could not have been completed before the central problems of the research were laid out and their study initiated. But such investigations of method often demand more material than is needed to solve the problems which are central to the main study. In order to determine the necessary size of sample, for instance, it has been necessary to study some samples that were larger than those that have ultimately proved adequate. In order to compare results obtained by different interviewers, it is necessary that each interviewer have secured a sample as large as may be needed in the combined sample from all the interviewers.

Moreover, finished studies of method have to be made with populations which are homogeneous for at least the major items on the twelve-way breakdown used in this study; and the methodological investigations which are reported here in Chapters 3 and 4 are still restricted to a certain few segments of the population, chiefly to the college groups, because we do not yet have enough histories from other groups to make studies there. It will be highly important to secure some measure of the differences in validity of the data obtained from persons of different ages, of different educational and social levels, of different mental capacity, and different in still other respects. To that end, we shall continue this study of method as this research progresses.

The materials now in hand seem to justify the following conclusions concerning the validity of data obtained through personal interviewing in a case history study:

1. The accuracy varies considerably with different individuals. The inaccuracies are the product of simple forgetting, the deliberate or unconscious suppression of memory, and deliberate cover-up. Definite allowances must be made for such errors on individual histories obtained in the concentrated, relatively short interviews which have been used in the present investigation. Careful studies of the effectiveness of other types of interviewing—for instance, of the effectiveness of the psychoanalytic technique, with its two hundred or more hours spent on each individual—have never been made; and it is as yet impossible to make comparisons of the relative effectiveness of the methods used in the present study and in these other types of interviewing. It is not sufficient to depend upon the optimistic claims of each clinician for his own technique; and we hope, in time, to make joint studies with some other groups that will throw more light on these problems of interviewing.

2. In the present study, the validity of the individual histories varies with particular items and for different segments of the population. On the whole, the accuracy of the individual history is far greater than might have been expected, with correlation coefficients ranging above 0.7 in most cases, and percents of identical responses ranging between 75 and 99 on particular items. There are some low correlations which are highly significant because they give some insight into the factors which are responsible for errors and falsifications in reporting.

3. It is unfortunate that there is, as yet, insufficient experience to allow us to identify, in more than a part of the cases, those individuals who are least accurate in their reporting. The clinician needs this information, for he is most often concerned with the validity of the individual history, and

less often with the validity of the data from any group of individuals. But further studies will need to be made before we are able to say how one can identify those particular individuals who are more accurate, and those who are less accurate as reporters of the events that have occurred in their lives.

4. The accuracy of the averages calculated for whole groups of individuals is definitely higher than the accuracy of the individual histories, as statisticians will readily understand. Where there is no bias which accumulates errors in a particular direction, errors on one side will compensate for errors on the other side and the averages come nearer the fact, as the various tests in this chapter indicate.

5. For all types of sexual activity, in all segments of the population, the incidence data are more accurate than the frequency data. The incidence data are the most accurate of all. The actualities must lie within 1 to 10 per cent, plus or minus, of the published incidence figures, and within 1 to 5 per cent of most of them. In regard to nearly all types of sexual activity there has undoubtedly been some cover-up, and the actual incidences are probably higher than the published figures. This applies especially to masturbation at lower social levels, to pre-marital and extra-marital intercourse at upper levels, and to the homosexual and animal intercourse at all levels. There is little likelihood that the calculated figures on any of these items are too high. There are abundant social reasons why an individual should deny or minimize the frequency of any activity which is taboo and, in the last analysis, all sexual activities except marital intercourse may, in some social groups, fall under that head.

6. Data concerning such individual and social statistics as age, education, events concerned with marriage, parents, siblings, etc., are the next most accurate. The averages for whole groups are so close to the averages obtained by direct observation that they may be accepted as precise statements of fact, although they are not so dependable on individual histories.

7. The frequency data are much less accurate than the incidence data. On individual histories they may be removed by as much as 50 per cent from the reality. Nevertheless, mean frequencies and median frequencies calculated for whole groups will not need more than a 5 to 10 per cent allowance, plus or minus. Since differences in frequencies of sexual behavior in different segments of the population may amount to something between 100 and 800 per cent, the comparisons will not be materially affected by the necessary corrections. The statements made concerning mean and median frequencies for whole groups are much more accurate than the best trained individual could be in reporting his own individual frequencies.

8. The least accurate data are those that concern an individual's first knowledge of an event. This is true of the individual histories, but the

averages calculated for whole groups are still reliable. The inaccuracies on these points are obviously dependent upon the indefinite nature of the educational processes by which one finally becomes conscious of the fact that he has definite knowledge on some subject. On individual histories an allowance of 2.5 years, plus or minus, should be made on the reported data. The means calculated for whole groups will not need more than a 4 or 5 per cent correction, plus or minus, on these items.

9. Again it should be emphasized that most of these calculations of validity have been based on the college segment of the population, which is the only group represented now by large enough series to warrant such examination. Comparable studies are needed to determine the validity of the data obtained from other segments of the population, and we plan to undertake such studies as soon as sufficient re-takes, pairs of spouses, series from different interviewers, etc., are available. Preliminary examinations of data from lower social levels suggest that variations in the quality of such reports are wider than the variations among college males. Consequently quite large series will be needed before it will be possible to make satisfactory validity studies on the more poorly educated groups.

Throughout the remainder of this volume, the raw data and the calculations based on the raw data are treated with a precision that must not be misunderstood by the statistically inexperienced reader. It has not been practical to carry this warning in every paragraph of every chapter. Neither has it been possible to qualify every individual statistic, as every statistic in any study of the human animal should be qualified. For the remainder of the volume it should, therefore, be recognized that the data are probably fair approximations, but only approximations of the fact.

Part II

FACTORS AFFECTING SEXUAL OUTLET

Chapter 5

EARLY SEXUAL GROWTH AND ACTIVITY

The present volume is concerned, for the most part, with the record of the frequency and sources of sexual outlet in the biologically mature male, *i.e.*, in the adolescent and older male. This chapter, however, will discuss the nature of sexual response, and will show something of the origins of adult behavior in the activities of the younger, pre-adolescent boy.

The sexual activity of an individual may involve a variety of experiences, a portion of which may culminate in the event which is known as orgasm or sexual climax. There are six chief sources of sexual climax. There is self stimulation (masturbation), nocturnal dreaming to the point of climax, heterosexual petting to climax (without intercourse), true heterosexual intercourse, homosexual intercourse, and contact with animals of other species. There are still other possible sources of orgasm, but they are rare and never constitute a significant fraction of the outlet for any large segment of the population.

EROTIC AROUSAL AND ORGASM

Sexual contacts in the adolescent or adult male almost always involve physiologic disturbance which is recognizable as "erotic arousal." This is also true of much pre-adolescent activity, although some of the sex play of younger children seems to be devoid of erotic content. Pre-adolescent sexual stimulation is much more common among younger boys than it is among younger girls. Many younger females and, for that matter, a certain portion of the older and married female population, may engage in such specifically sexual activities as petting and even intercourse without discernible erotic reaction.

Erotic arousal is a material phenomenon which involves an extended series of physical, physiologic, and psychologic changes. Many of these could be subjected to precise instrumental measurement if objectivity among scientists and public respect for scientific research allowed such laboratory investigation. In the higher mammals, including the human, tactile stimulation is the chief mechanical source of arousal; but the higher mammal, especially the human, soon becomes so conditioned by his experience, or by the vicariously shared experiences of others, that psychologic stimulation becomes the major source of arousal for many an older person, especially if he is educated and his mental capacities are well trained. There is an occasional individual who comes to climax through psychologic stimulation alone.

Erotic stimulation, whatever its source, effects a series of physiologic changes which, as far as we yet know, appear to involve adrenal secretion, typically autonomic reactions, increased pulse rate, increased blood pressure, an increase in peripheral circulation and a consequent rise in the surface temperature of the body; a flow of blood into such distensible organs as the eyes, the lips, the lobes of the ears, the nipples of the breast, the penis of the male, and the clitoris, the genital labia and the vaginal walls of the female; a partial but often considerable loss of perceptive capacity (sight, hearing, touch, taste, smell); an increase in so-called nervous tension, some degree of rigidity of some part or of the whole of the body at the moment of maximum tension; and then a sudden release which produces local spasms or more extensive or all-consuming convulsions. The moment of sudden release is the point commonly recognized among biologists as orgasm.

The person involved in a sexual situation may be more or less conscious of some of the physiologic changes which occur although, unless he is scientifically trained, much of what is happening escapes his comprehension. Self observation may be especially inadequate because of the considerable (and usually unrecognized) loss of sensory capacities during maximum arousal. The subject's awareness of the situation is summed up in his statement that he is "emotionally aroused"; but the material sources of the emotional disturbances are rarely recognized, either by laymen or by scientists, both of whom are inclined to think in terms of passion, a sexual impulse, a natural drive, or a libido which partakes of the mystic more than it does of solid anatomy and physiologic function.

The most important consequence of sexual orgasm is the abrupt release of the extreme tension which preceded the event and the rather sudden return to a normal or subnormal physiologic state after the event. In the mature male, ejaculation of the liquid secretions of the prostate and seminal vesicles, through the urethra of the penis, is a usual consequence of the convulsions produced by orgasm in those particular organs; and such ejaculation usually provides the most ready proof that the individual has passed through climax. But orgasm may occur without the emission of semen. This latter situation is, of course, the rule when orgasm occurs among pre-adolescent males and among females. It also occurs among a few adult males (11 out of 4,102 adult males in our histories) who either are afflicted with ejaculatory impotence (6 cases: 2 operative, 2 hormonal, 1 after severe illness, 1 in an apparently normal individual), or who deliberately constrict their genital muscles (5 cases) in the contraceptive technique which is known as coitus reservatus. These males experience real orgasm, which they have no difficulty in recognizing, even if it is without ejaculation.

Among pre-adolescent boys, however, and among younger females, orgasm is not so readily recognized, partly because of the lack of an ejaculate, and partly because the inexperienced individual is without a background from which to judge the event. In the younger boy there is no ejaculate because the prostate and seminal vesicles are not yet functionally developed, and in the female those glands are rudimentary and never develop. Nevertheless, erotic arousal and orgasm where it occurs among younger boys and among females appears to involve the same sequence of physiologic events that has been described for the older, ejaculating males; and many of the younger boys and most of the older females who have contributed to the present study have been able to supply apparently reliable records of such experience.

While climax is thus clearly possible without ejaculation, it is doubtful if ejaculation can ordinarily occur without a preceding climax. There are some (the implication is in Reich 1942; also in Wolfe 1942) who consider that this latter situation does occur, and not infrequently, among some males. Subjects are quoted who have had erections and who have ejaculated under conditions which they insist brought them no satisfaction. But in our histories there are many subjects who make similar statements. There are husbands who report unsatisfactory intercourse with unresponsive wives; there are other males who so characterize their intercourse with prostitutes; and there are males who insist that they are "not at all aroused" in the stray homosexual relations which they have. Most of these individuals do, however, erect and ejaculate in such situations; and these reports probably amount to little more than records of varying degrees of physiologic disturbance during arousal and orgasm; or they are merely evidence of minimal psychic components with good enough physical responses, or, sometimes, of good enough psychic reactions that are inhibited, disguised, or rationalized in order to evade moral responsibility for socially taboo behavior. To repeat: the biologist thinks of ejaculation as the product of the convulsions which result from the physiologic event commonly known as orgasm; and, except under laboratory experimental conditions (as in the direct, electrical stimulation of erectile centers in the spinal cord) it is difficult to understand what mechanisms could produce ejaculation without a precedent orgasm. The confusion in the literature seems to be the result of making the term orgasm and orgastic pleasure synonymous. It is, of course, quite possible to recognize many degrees of physiologic change, and many degrees of satisfaction among sexual experiences, and there are admittedly occasions when there is little pleasure accompanying an ejaculation. But we have no statistics on the frequencies of physiologic differences, or of the various degrees of satisfaction, and, in the present study, all cases of ejaculation have been taken as evidence of orgasm, without regard to the different levels at which the orgasms have occurred.

Behavior during orgasm varies considerably with different individuals just as all other aspects of sexual behavior differ in any population (Chapter 6). The descriptions of orgasm in clinical texts, marriage manuals, and other literature are, however, remarkably uniform, partly because of each author's limited experience, and chiefly because of his failure to search for variation in securing data from clinical subjects. In consequence, there has been little comprehension of the complexity of the problem involved in advising different persons about their sexual adjustments, and about sexual techniques in marriage. There is great variety among adult males; and, it is interesting to note, there is as great variety and the same sort of variety among pre-adolescent boys. One of our subjects, who has had contacts with certain males over long periods of years (as many as sixteen years in some cases), from their early pre-adolescence into their late teens and twenties, states that the particular type of orgasm experienced by a younger boy remains as his particular type into his adult years. The variation in pattern of orgastic response thus seems to depend, at least to some degree (and in the limited number of cases so far studied), on inherent differences in the biologic constitution of different individuals.

Our several thousand histories have included considerable detail on the nature of orgasm; and these data, together with the records supplied by some older subjects who have had sexual contacts with younger boys, provide material for describing the different sorts of reactions which may occur. In the pre-adolescent, orgasm is, of course, without ejaculation of semen. In the descriptions which follow, the data supplied by adult observers for 196 pre-adolescent boys are the sources of the percentage figures indicating the frequency of each type of orgasm among such young males. While six types are listed, it should be understood that all gradations occur between the situations which are herewith described.

1. Reactions primarily genital: Little or no evidence of body tension; orgasm reached suddenly with little or no build-up; penis becomes more rigid and may be involved in mild throbs, or throbs may be limited to urethra alone; semen (in the adult) seeps from urethra without forcible ejaculation; climax passes with minor after-effects. A fifth (22%) of the pre-adolescent cases on which there are sufficient data belong here, and probably an even higher proportion of older males.

2. Some body tension: Usually involving a tension or twitching of one or both legs, of the mouth, of the arms, or of other particular parts of the body. A gradual build-up to a climax which involves rigidity of the whole body and some throbbing of the penis; orgasm with a few spasms but little after-effect. This is the most common type of orgasm, involving nearly

half (45%) of the pre-adolescent males, and perhaps a corresponding number of adult males.

3. Extreme tension with violent convulsion: Often involving the sudden heaving and jerking of the whole body. Descriptions supplied by several subjects indicate that the legs often become rigid, with muscles knotted and toes pointed, muscles of abdomen contracted and hard, shoulders and neck stiff and often bent forward, breath held or gasping, eyes staring or tightly closed, hands grasping, mouth distorted, sometimes with tongue protruding; whole body or parts of it spasmodically twitching, sometimes synchronously with throbs or violent jerking of the penis. The individual may have some, but little, control of these involuntary reactions. A gradual, and sometimes prolonged, build-up to orgasm, which involves still more violent convulsions of the whole body; heavy breathing, groaning, sobbing, or more violent cries, sometimes with an abundance of tears (especially among younger children), the orgasm or ejaculation often extended, in some individuals involving several minutes (in one case up to five minutes) of recurrent spasm. After-effects not necessarily more marked than with other types of orgasm, and the individual is often capable of participating in a second or further experience. About one sixth (17%) of the pre-adolescent boys, a smaller percentage of adult males.

4. As in either type 1 or 2; but with hysterical laughing, talking, sadistic or masochistic reactions, rapid motions (whether in masturbation or in intercourse), culminating in more or less frenzied movements which are continued through the orgasm. A small percentage (5%) of either pre-adolescent or adult males.

5. As in any of the above; but culminating in extreme trembling, collapse, loss of color, and sometimes fainting of subject. Sometimes happens only in the boy's first experience, occasionally occurs throughout the life of an individual. Regular in only a few (3%) of the pre-adolescent or adult males. Such complete collapse is more common and better known among females.

6. Pained or frightened at approach of orgasm. The genitalia of many adult males become hypersensitive immediately at and after orgasm, and some males suffer excruciating pain and may scream if movement is continued or the penis even touched. The males in the present group become similarly hypersensitive before the arrival of actual orgasm, will fight away from the partner and may make violent attempts to avoid climax, although they derive definite pleasure from the situation. Such individuals quickly return to complete the experience, or to have a second experience if the first was complete. About 8 per cent of the younger boys are involved here, but it is a smaller percentage of older boys and adults which continues these reactions throughout life.

AGE	AGES INVOLVED, PRE-ADOLESCENT SEX PLAY								
	TOTAL POPULATION, U. S. CORRECTION					EDUC. LEVEL 0–8			
	Cases	Any Sex Play %	Het-ero-sexual %	Co-itus %	Homo-sex-ual %	Cases	Any Sex Play %	Het-ero-sexual %	Co-itus %	Homo-sex-ual %
5	4321	9.8	6.5	2.6	5.7	822	7.9	4.7	2.8	5.7
6	4321	15.6	10.1	4.4	10.0	821	13.4	7.8	4.8	10.4
7	4320	20.0	13.2	6.7	13.5	819	17.6	11.2	7.4	14.0
8	4316	26.9	17.0	8.7	18.4	820	25.7	16.0	10.9	20.1
9	4302	28.5	16.7	8.7	21.4	817	28.4	17.0	11.5	22.9
10	4216	36.6	20.8	11.2	27.5	812	36.3	21.4	15.0	28.6
11	3933	37.4	22.0	12.3	27.9	784	36.7	21.7	15.2	29.0
12	2975	38.8	22.7	12.8	29.4	677	37.4	21.9	14.9	29.8
13	1610	35.0	20.2	12.9	26.5	491	33.4	18.1	13.2	26.7
14	424	33.6	17.8	9.3	27.6	181	36.5	16.6	11.6	29.8
15	112	24.1	16.0	5.0	19.9	40	17.5	7.5	5.0	15.0

AGE	EDUC. LEVEL 9–12					EDUC. LEVEL 13+			
	Cases	Any Sex Play %	Het-ero-sexual %	Co-itus %	Homo-sex-ual %	Cases	Any Sex Play %	Het-ero-sexual %	Co-itus %	Homo-sex-ual %
5	637	9.7	6.6	2.8	5.2	2862	14.0	10.2	1.5	7.3
6	637	16.5	11.0	4.6	9.9	2863	16.5	11.3	2.4	9.8
7	638	21.8	14.7	7.4	13.6	2863	18.5	11.7	2.8	11.8
8	637	28.1	18.2	8.8	17.7	2859	24.8	14.8	3.5	17.1
9	634	29.5	17.4	8.4	21.3	2851	24.6	13.2	3.5	18.2
10	623	38.2	21.8	10.9	27.8	2781	31.4	15.7	4.2	24.2
11	593	39.6	24.5	13.0	28.2	2556	30.2	13.3	3.7	24.5
12	467	41.5	25.9	14.1	30.0	1831	31.4	12.3	3.2	26.3
13	270	38.5	24.1	15.2	27.8	849	25.3	10.0	3.5	21.4
14	59	35.6	22.0	10.2	28.8	184	19.6	4.3	1.1	18.5

Table 24. Ages involved in pre-adolescent sex play

"Educ. level 0–8" are the males who never go beyond grade school. "9–12" are the males who enter high school but never go beyond. "13+" are the males who will ultimately go to college.

PRE-ADOLESCENT SEX PLAY

It has been assumed that the development of sexual attitudes and the first overt sexual activities occur in the early history of the infant, but there have been few specific data available. Recently we have begun the accumulation of information through conferences with quite young children and with their parents; and in addition we now have material obtained by some of our subjects through the direct observation of infants and of older pre-adolescents. These histories emphasize the early development of the attitudes which largely determine the subsequent patterns of adult sexual behavior; but this material must be analyzed in a later volume, after we have accumulated a great many more specific data. For the time being we can report only on the specifically genital play and overt socio-sexual behavior which occurs before adolescence.

We are not in a position to discuss the developing child's more generalized sensory responses which may be sexual, but which are not so specific as genital activities are. Freud and the psychoanalysts contend that all tactile stimulation and response are basically sexual, and there seems considerable justification for this thesis, in view of the tactile origin of so much of the mammalian stimulation. This, however, involves a considerable extension of both the everyday and scientific meanings of the term sexual, and we are not now concerned with recording every occasion on which a babe brings two parts of its body into juxtaposition, every time it scratches its ear or its genitalia, nor every occasion on which it sucks its thumb. If all such acts are to be interpreted as masturbatory, it is, of course, a simple matter to conclude that masturbation and early sexual activity are universal phenomena; but it is still to be shown that these elemental tactile experiences have anything to do with the development of the sexual behavior of the adult. There is now a fair list of significant and in many cases observational studies of this "pre-genital" level of reaction among infants and young children (Bell 1902, Blanton 1917, Hattendorf 1932, Isaacs 1933, Dudycha 1933, Halverson 1938, 1940, Campbell 1939, Conn 1939, 1940, Levy 1940. See Sears 1943 for a summary).

Adult behavior is more obviously a product of the specifically genital play which is found among children, and on which we can now provide a statistical record. Our own interviews with children younger than five, and observations made by parents and others who have been subjects in this study, indicate that hugging and kissing are usual in the activity of the very young child, and that self manipulation of genitalia, the exhibition of genitalia, the exploration of the genitalia of other children, and some manual and occasionally oral manipulation of the genitalia of other children occur in the two- to five-year olds more frequently than older persons ordinarily remember from their own histories. Much of this earliest sex play appears to be purely exploratory, animated by curiosity, and as devoid of erotic content as boxing, or wrestling, or other non-sexual physical contacts among older persons. Nevertheless, at a very early age the child learns that there are social values attached to these activities, and his emotional excitation while engaged in such play must involve reactions to the mysterious, to the forbidden, and to the socially dangerous performance, as often as it involves true erotic response (Sears 1943). Some of the play in the younger boy occurs without erection, but some of it brings erection and may culminate in true orgasm.

In pre-adolescent and early adolescent boys, erection and orgasm are easily induced. They are more easily induced than in older males. Erection may occur immediately after birth and, as many observant mothers (and few scientists) know, it is practically a daily matter for all small boys, from earliest infancy and up in age (Halverson 1940). Slight physical stimulation of the genitalia, general body tensions, and generalized emotional situations bring immediate erection, even when there is no specifically sexual situation involved. The very generalized nature of the response becomes evident when one accumulates a list of the apparently non-sexual stimuli which bring erection. Ramsey (1943) has published such a list gathered from a group of 291 younger boys which he had interviewed, and his histories provide part of the data which we have used in the present volume. A complete tabulation, based on the total sample now available on all cases, is as follows:

NON-SEXUAL SOURCES OF EROTIC RESPONSE
AMONG PRE-ADOLESCENT AND YOUNGER ADOLESCENT BOYS

Chiefly Physical

Sitting in class	Airplane rides
Friction with clothing	A sudden change in environment
Taking a shower	Sitting in church
Punishment	Motion of car or bus
Accidents	A skidding car
Electric shock	Sitting in warm sand
Fast elevator rides	Urinating
Carnival rides, Ferris wheel	Boxing and wrestling
Fast sled riding	High dives
Fast bicycle riding	Riding horseback
Fast car driving	Swimming
Skiing	

Chiefly Emotional

Being scared	Big fires
Fear of a house intruder	Setting a field afire
Near accidents	Hearing revolver shot
Being late to school	Anger
Reciting before a class	Watching exciting games
Asked to go front in class	Playing in exciting games
Tests at school	Marching soldiers
Seeing a policeman	War motion pictures
Cops chasing him	Other movies
Getting home late	Band music
Receiving grade card	Hearing "extra paper" called

Chiefly Emotional (*Cont'd*)

Harsh words	Adventure stories
Fear of punishment	National anthem
Being yelled at	Watching a stunting airplane
Being alone at night	Finding money
Fear of a big boy	Seeing name in print
Playing musical solo	Detective stories
Losing balance on heights	Running away from home
Looking over edge of building	Entering an empty house
Falling from garage, etc.	Nocturnal dreams of fighting, accidents,
Long flight of stairs	wild animals, falling from high places,
	giants, being chased, or frightened

Among these younger boys, it is difficult to say what is an erotic response and what is a simple physical, or a generalized emotional situation.

Specifically sexual situations to which the younger boys respond before adolescence include the following:

SEXUAL SOURCES OF EROTIC RESPONSE AMONG
212 PRE-ADOLESCENT BOYS

Seeing females	107	Physical contact with females	34
Thinking about females	104	Love stories in books	32
Sex jokes	104	Seeing genitalia of other males	29
Sex pictures	89	Burlesque shows	23
Pictures of females	76	Seeing animals in coitus	21
Females in moving pictures	55	Dancing with females	13
Seeing self nude in mirror	47		

The above table is based on the histories of 212 boys who were pre-adolescent at the time of interview. Since the questions were not systematically put in all the pre-adolescent cases, the figures represent frequencies of answers in particular boys, and should not be taken as incidence figures for the population as a whole.

The record suggests that the physiologic mechanism of any emotional response (anger, fright, pain, etc.) may be the basic mechanism of sexual response. Originally the pre-adolescent boy erects indiscriminately to the whole array of emotional situations, whether they be sexual or non-sexual in nature. By his late teens the male has been so conditioned that he rarely responds to anything except a direct physical stimulation of genitalia, or to psychic situations that are specifically sexual. In the still older male even physical stimulation is rarely effective unless accompanied by such a psychologic atmosphere. The picture is that of the psychosexual emerging from a much more generalized and basic physiologic capacity which becomes sexual, as an adult knows it, through experience and conditioning.

The most specific activities among younger boys involve genital exhibition and genital contacts with other children. Something more than a half (57%) of the older boys and adults recall some sort of pre-adolescent sex play. This figure is much higher than some other students have found

| | DURATION OF PRE-ADOLESCENT SEX PLAY | | | | | | | |
| NO. OF YEARS IN-VOLVED | TOTAL POPULATION U.S. CORRECTION | | EDUC. LEVEL 0–8 | | EDUC. LEVEL 9–12 | | EDUC. LEVEL 13+ | |
	%	Cumu-lated %	%	Cumu-lated %	%	Cumu-lated %	%	Cumu-lated %
				Any Sex Play				
1	24.3	100.0	18.6	100.0	24.0	100.0	37.9	100.0
2	17.9	75.7	11.8	81.4	20.1	76.0	22.8	62.1
3	10.4	57.8	10.3	69.6	10.2	55.9	11.1	39.3
4	11.2	47.4	11.5	59.3	11.6	45.7	8.8	28.2
5	11.0	36.2	14.3	47.8	10.4	34.1	6.1	19.4
6	9.5	25.2	12.0	33.5	9.2	23.7	5.3	13.3
7	7.2	15.7	10.8	21.5	5.9	14.5	4.3	8.0
8	5.7	8.5	8.2	10.7	5.2	8.6	2.3	3.7
9+	2.8	2.8	2.5	2.5	3.4	3.4	1.4	1.4
Cases	2749		426		404		1919	
Mean	3.72 years		4.32 years		3.63 years		2.76 years	
Median	2.82 years		3.83 years		2.60 years		1.53 years	
				Any Heterosexual Play				
1	36.3	100.0	25.6	100.0	37.6	100.0	54.0	100.0
2	15.8	63.7	12.2	74.4	17.1	62.4	18.6	46.0
3	9.4	47.9	8.5	62.2	10.1	45.3	8.7	27.4
4	10.2	38.5	11.5	53.7	10.4	35.2	6.4	18.7
5	7.4	28.3	9.6	42.2	7.1	24.8	3.9	12.3
6	7.3	20.9	10.4	32.6	6.7	17.7	3.0	8.4
7	7.7	13.6	13.7	22.2	5.7	11.0	2.7	5.4
8	3.3	5.9	5.9	8.5	2.3	5.3	1.6	2.7
9+	2.6	2.6	2.6	2.6	3.0	3.0	1.1	1.1
Cases	1850		270		298		1282	
Mean	3.23 years		4.00 years		3.06 years		2.22 years	
Median	2.11 years		3.34 years		1.74 years		0.93 years	
				Heterosexual Coitus				
1	39.2	100.0	32.7	100.0	38.3	100.0	56.3	100.0
2	13.6	60.8	9.0	67.3	15.6	61.7	15.7	43.7
3	10.2	47.2	6.0	58.3	13.0	46.1	8.8	28.0
4	10.2	37.0	15.1	52.3	8.5	33.1	6.0	19.2
5	7.1	26.8	9.6	37.2	6.5	24.6	4.1	13.2
6	7.4	19.7	7.0	27.6	8.4	18.1	4.7	9.1
7	9.2	12.3	14.6	20.6	7.8	9.7	2.8	4.4
8	1.6	3.1	3.5	6.0	0.6	1.9	1.3	1.6
9+	1.5	1.5	2.5	2.5	1.3	1.3	0.3	0.3
Cases	671		199		154		318	
Mean	3.09 years		3.72 years		2.97 years		2.19 years	
Median	2.07 years		3.17 years		1.77 years		0.89 years	

(*Table continued on next page*)

NO. OF YEARS IN-VOLVED	DURATION OF PRE-ADOLESCENT SEX PLAY							
	TOTAL POPULATION U.S. CORRECTION		EDUC. LEVEL 0–8		EDUC. LEVEL 9–12		EDUC. LEVEL 13+	
	%	Cumu-lated %	%	Cumu-lated %	%	Cumu-lated %	%	Cumu-lated %
	Homosexual Play							
1	27.1	100.0	20.0	100.0	26.9	100.0	43.2	100.0
2	17.8	72.9	11.2	80.0	20.9	73.1	19.8	56.8
3	10.0	55.1	11.2	68.8	9.1	52.2	11.1	37.0
4	10.8	45.1	8.8	57.6	12.8	43.1	7.7	25.9
5	11.5	34.3	14.7	48.8	11.1	30.3	6.0	18.2
6	8.8	22.8	12.9	34.1	7.4	19.2	5.1	12.2
7	6.7	14.0	10.9	21.2	5.1	11.8	3.8	7.1
8	5.2	7.3	8.2	10.3	4.4	6.7	2.1	3.3
9+	2.1	2.1	2.1	2.1	2.3	2.3	1.2	1.2
Cases	2096		340		297		1459	
Mean	3.54 years		4.24 years		3.39 years		2.63 years	
Median	2.63 years		3.88 years		2.26 years		1.35 years	

Table 25. Number of years involved, pre-adolescent sex play

(*e.g.*, Hamilton 1929); but it is probably still too low, for 70 per cent of the pre-adolescent boys who have contributed to the present study have admitted such experience, and there is no doubt that even they forget many of their earlier activities. It is not improbable that nearly all boys have some pre-adolescent genital play with other boys or with girls. Only about one-fifth as many of the girls have such play.

Most of this pre-adolescent sex play occurs between the ages of eight and thirteen (Table 24, Figure 25), although some of it occurs at every age from earliest childhood to adolescence. For a quarter of the boys who have such play, the activity is limited to a single year (24.3%) or two (17.9%) or three (10.4%) in pre-adolescence (Table 25). For many of them there is only a single experience. A third of the active males (36.2%) continue the play for five years or more. That the activity does not extend further is clearly a product of cultural restraints, for pre-adolescent sex play in the other anthropoids is abundant and continues into adult performance (Bingham 1928). Most of the play takes place with companions close to the subject's own age. On the other hand, the boy's initial experience is often (although not invariably) with a slightly older boy or girl. Older persons are the teachers of younger people in all matters, including the sexual. The record includes some cases of pre-adolescent boys involved in sexual contacts with adult females, and still more cases of pre-adolescent boys involved with adult males. Data on this point were not systematically gathered from all histories, and consequently the frequency of contacts with adults cannot be calculated with precision.

Homosexual Play. On the whole, the homosexual child play is found in more histories, occurs more frequently, and becomes more specific than the pre-adolescent heterosexual play. This depends, as so much of the adult homosexual activity depends, on the greater accessibility of the boy's own sex (Table 26). In the younger boy, it is also fostered by his socially encouraged disdain for girls' ways, by his admiration for masculine prowess, and by his desire to emulate older boys. The anatomy and functional capacities of male genitalia interest the younger boy to a degree that is not

COMPANIONS OF PRE-ADOLESCENT BOYS

AT SUBJECT'S AGE 10–11

CLASSIFICATION	TOTAL U. S. POPULATION %	EDUCATIONAL LEVEL		
		0–8 %	9–12 %	13+ %
Males predominate	72.3	73.8	69.2	80.7
Males many, females some	36.0	32.7	34.3	49.4
Males many, females none	32.8	37.1	31.4	29.0
Males some, females none	3.5	4.0	3.5	2.3
Males equal females	23.0	22.8	24.8	16.7
Males many, females many	17.6	17.4	18.8	13.7
Males some, females some	3.3	2.0	4.3	2.3
Males none, females none	2.1	3.4	1.7	0.7
Females predominate	4.7	3.4	6.0	2.6
Males none, females some	0.3	0.0	0.6	0.1
Males none, females many	0.4	0.4	0.5	0.1
Males some, females many	4.0	3.0	4.9	2.4
Cases	4311	820	633	2858

Table 26. Sex of companions of pre-adolescent boys

A record of the boy's associates, in his play and social activities, when he is 10–11 years of age.

appreciated by older males who have become heterosexually conditioned and who are continuously on the defensive against reactions which might be interpreted as homosexual.

About half of the older males (48%), and nearer two-thirds (60%) of the boys who were pre-adolescent at the time they contributed their histories, recall homosexual activity in their pre-adolescent years. The mean age of the first homosexual contact is about nine years, two and a half months (9.21 years) (Table 28, Figures 25, 26).

The order of appearance of the several homosexual techniques is: exhibition of genitalia, manual manipulation of genitalia, anal or oral contacts with genitalia, and urethral insertions (Table 27). Exhibition is much the most common form of homosexual play (in 99.8 per cent of all the histories which have any activity). It appears in the sex play of the youngest children, where much of it is incidental, definitely casual, and quite fruitless as far as erotic arousal is concerned. The most extreme development of exhibitionism occurs among the older pre-adolescents and the younger adolescent males who have discovered the significance of self masturbation and may have acquired proficiency in effecting orgasm. By that time there is a social value in establishing one's ability, and many a

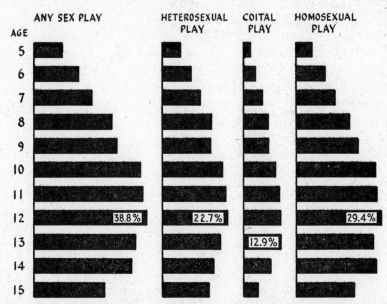

Figure 25. Percent of males involved in sex play at each pre-adolescent age
Data all corrected for U. S. Census distribution.

boy exhibits his masturbatory techniques to lone companions or to whole groups of boys. In the latter case, there may be simultaneous exhibition as a group activity. The boy's emotional reaction in such a performance is undoubtedly enhanced by the presence of the other boys. There are teen-age boys who continue this exhibitionistic activity throughout their high school years, some of them even entering into compacts with their closest friends to refrain from self masturbation except when in the presence of each other. In confining such social performances to self masturbation, these boys avoid conflicts over the homosexual. By this time, however, the psychic reactions may be homosexual enough, although it may be difficult to persuade these individuals to admit it.

Exhibitionism leads naturally into the next step in the homosexual play, namely the mutual manipulation of genitalia. Such manipulation occurs in the play of two-thirds (67.4%) of all the pre-adolescent males who have any homosexual activity (Table 27). Among younger pre-adolescents the manual contacts are still very incidental and casual and without any recognition of the emotional possibilities of such experience. Only a small portion

EDUC. LEVEL	CASES	ANY HETERO-SEXUAL PLAY, % OF TOTAL POPULATION	TECHNIQUES IN PRE-ADOLESCENT SEX PLAY % OF ACTIVE POPULATION				
			HETEROSEXUAL PLAY				
			Exhibition	Manual	Coital	Oral	Vaginal Insertions
Total	1843	39.6	99.6	81.4	55.3	8.9	49.1
0–8	270	30.0	99.6	91.7	74.4	17.0	59.3
9–12	295	44.0	99.7	80.0	52.4	5.8	49.8
13+	1277	43.0	99.0	64.8	25.7	3.4	24.4

EDUC. LEVEL	CASES	ANY HOMO-SEXUAL PLAY, % OF TOTAL POPULATION	HOMOSEXUAL PLAY				
			Exhibition	Manual	Anal	Oral	Urethral Insertions
Total	2102	44.0	99.8	67.4	17.0	15.9	6.0
0–8	341	38.0	100.0	66.7	17.5	13.3	4.8
9–12	298	45.0	99.7	67.4	16.7	16.8	6.9
13+	1463	53.0	99.5	69.2	16.9	17.7	5.3

Table 27. Techniques in pre-adolescent sex play

In order to determine the percent of the total pre-adolescent male population which has experience with any particular technique, multiply the figure in Column 3 (which shows the percent of the total population which has any kind of heterosexual or homosexual experience) by the incidence figure for the particular technique under consideration.

of the cases leads to the sort of manipulation which does effect arousal and possibly orgasm in the partner. Manual manipulation is more likely to become so specific if the relation is had with a somewhat older boy, or with an adult. Without help from more experienced persons, many pre-adolescents take a good many years to discover masturbatory techniques that are sexually effective.

Anal intercourse is reported by 17 per cent of the pre-adolescents who have any homosexual play. Anal intercourse among younger boys usually fails of penetration and is therefore primarily femoral. Oral manipulation is reported by nearly 16 per cent of the boys (Table 27). Among younger boys, erotic arousal is less easily effected by oral contacts, more easily effected by manual manipulation. The anal and oral techniques are limited as they are because even at these younger ages there is some knowledge of the social taboos on these activities; and it is, in consequence, probable that the reported data are considerable understatements of the activities which actually occur.

Pre-adolescent homosexual play is carried over into adolescent or adult activity in something less than a half of all the cases (Table 29). There are

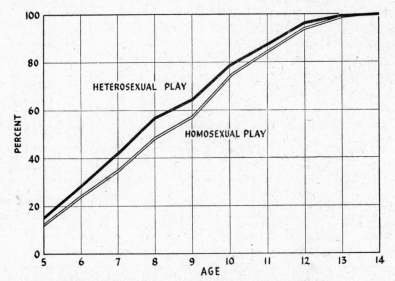

Figure 26. Age of first pre-adolescent sexual experience

Each curve an ogive, where 100 per cent is the total number of boys who ever have such experience.

differences between social levels. In lower educational levels, the chances are 50–50 that the pre-adolescent homosexual play will be continued into adolescence or later. For the group that will go to college, the chances are better than four to one that the pre-adolescent activity will not be followed by later homosexual experience. In many cases, the later homosexuality stops with the adolescent years, but many of the adults who are actively and more or less exclusively homosexual date their activities from pre-adolescence. In a later volume these data will be examined in more detail, in connection with an analysis of the factors involved in the development of a heterosexual-homosexual balance.

AGE	FIRST PRE-ADOLESCENT SEXUAL EXPERIENCE											
	TOTAL U.S. POPULATION		EDUC. LEVEL 0–8			EDUC. LEVEL 9–12			EDUC. LEVEL 13+		
	%	Cumu-lat. %	Cases	%	Cumu-lat. %	Cases	%	Cumu-lat. %	Cases	%	Cumu-lat. %
Any Sex Play											
5	16.1	16.1	65	15.2	15.2	62	15.3	15.3	401	20.9	20.9
6	13.9	30.0	56	13.1	28.3	58	14.4	29.7	260	13.5	34.4
7	11.5	41.5	46	10.6	38.9	49	12.1	41.8	215	11.2	45.6
8	14.5	56.0	67	15.7	54.6	55	13.6	55.4	298	15.5	61.1
9	8.0	64.0	38	8.9	63.5	30	7.4	62.8	166	8.6	69.7
10	15.1	79.1	68	15.9	79.4	60	14.9	77.7	270	14.1	83.8
11	8.1	87.2	26	6.1	85.5	38	9.4	87.1	145	7.5	91.3
12	8.5	95.7	35	8.2	93.7	37	9.2	96.3	129	6.7	98.0
13	3.4	99.1	19	4.4	98.1	13	3.2	99.5	33	1.7	99.7
14	0.9	100.0	8	1.9	100.0	2	0.5	100.0	4	0.3	100.0
Cases	2753		428			404			1921		
Mean	8.81 years		8.93 years			8.84 years			8.45 years		
Median	7.59 years		7.69 years			7.61 years			7.29 years		
Heterosexual Play											
5	15.4	15.4	39	14.4	14.4	42	14.1	14.1	292	22.8	22.8
6	13.2	28.6	34	12.5	26.9	39	13.1	27.2	194	15.1	37.9
7	13.5	42.1	34	12.5	39.4	43	14.4	41.6	153	11.9	49.8
8	14.9	57.0	44	16.3	55.7	41	13.8	55.4	206	16.1	65.9
9	7.4	64.4	21	7.8	63.5	21	7.0	62.4	105	8.2	74.1
10	14.1	78.5	41	15.1	78.6	41	13.8	76.2	166	13.0	87.1
11	8.8	87.3	19	7.0	85.6	31	10.4	86.6	86	6.7	93.8
12	9.2	96.5	26	9.6	95.2	30	10.1	96.7	62	4.8	98.6
13	2.7	99.2	11	4.1	99.3	7	2.3	99.0	17	1.3	99.9
14	0.8	100.0	2	0.7	100.0	3	1.0	100.0	1	0.1	100.0
Cases	1851		271			298			1282		
Mean	8.81 years		8.91 years			8.91 years			8.20 years		
Median	7.33 years		7.66 years			7.22 years			7.01 years		
Homosexual Play											
5	12.4	12.4	47	13.7	13.7	33	11.1	11.1	208	14.2	14.2
6	12.0	24.4	43	12.6	26.3	36	12.1	23.2	153	10.5	24.7
7	10.5	34.9	37	10.8	37.1	31	10.4	33.6	145	9.9	34.6
8	13.5	48.4	51	14.9	52.0	37	12.4	46.0	217	14.9	49.5
9	9.1	57.5	29	8.5	60.5	27	9.1	55.1	146	10.0	59.5
10	16.9	74.4	56	16.4	76.9	51	17.0	72.1	257	17.6	77.1
11	10.2	84.6	23	6.7	83.6	36	12.1	84.2	156	10.7	87.8
12	9.5	94.1	29	8.5	92.1	30	10.1	94.3	138	9.4	97.2
13	4.7	98.8	18	5.3	97.4	15	5.0	99.3	34	2.3	99.5
14	1.2	100.0	9	2.6	100.0	2	0.7	100.0	8	0.5	100.0
Cases	2102		342			298			1462		
Mean	9.21 years		9.10 years			9.31 years			9.06 years		
Median	8.22 years		7.87 years			8.46 years			8.06 years		

Table 28. Age of first pre-adolescent sex play

The cumulated percentages (ogives) are based on the total number of individuals who ever have such sexual experience (the active population). They do not represent percents of the total population.

172

Heterosexual Play. The average age for beginning pre-adolescent heterosexual play is about eight years and ten months (a mean of 8.81 years)
(Table 28, Figures 25, 26). This is approximately five months earlier than the
average age for the beginning of homosexual play; but heterosexual activity,
nonetheless, does not occupy quite as much of the attention of the pre-
adolescent boys. It is found in 40 per cent of the pre-adolescent histories.

Just as with the homosexual, the heterosexual play begins with the
exhibition of genitalia; and of those pre-adolescent boys who have any
sex play with girls, about 99 per cent engage in such exhibition (Table 27).
For nearly 20 per cent of the boys, this is the limit of the activity. There is
considerable curiosity among children, both male and female, about the
genitalia of the opposite sex, fostered, if not primarily engendered, by the
social restrictions on inter-sexual display. The boy is incited by the greater
care which many parents exercise in covering the genitalia of the girls in
the family—a custom which reaches its extreme in some other cultures where
the boys may go completely nude until adolescence, while the girls are
carefully clothed at least from the ages of four or five.

Of those pre-adolescent boys who have any heterosexual play, 81.4 per
cent carry it to the point of manually manipulating the genitalia of the
female (Table 27). For many of the youngest boys this is even more incidental than the manual manipulation which occurs in homosexual contacts.
Among certain groups, particularly in upper social levels, the children
sometimes lack information on coitus, and there may be no comprehension
that there are possibilities in heterosexual activity other than those afforded
by manual contacts. There are vaginal insertions which involve objects of
various sorts, but most often they are finger insertions. Pre-adolescent
attempts to effect genital union occur in nearly 22 per cent of all male
histories, which is over half (55.3%) of the histories of the boys who have
any pre-adolescent play. On this point, there are considerable differences
between social levels (Table 27). Three-quarters (74.4%) of the boys who
will never go beyond eighth grade try such pre-adolescent coitus, but such
experience is had by only one-quarter (25.7%) of the pre-adolescent boys
of the group which will ultimately go to college (Chapter 10).

The lower level boy has considerable information and help on these
matters from older boys or from adult males, and in many cases his first
heterosexual contacts are with older girls who have already had experience. Consequently, in this lower level, pre-adolescent contacts often
involve actual penetration and the children have what amounts to real
intercourse. The efforts of the upper level boys are less often successful, in
many cases amounting to little more than the apposition of genitalia. With
the lower level boy, pre-adolescent coitus may occur with some frequency,
and it may be had with a variety of partners. For the upper level boy, the
experience often occurs only once or twice, and with a single partner or

two. These differences between patterns at different social levels, even in pre-adolescence, are of the utmost significance in any consideration of a program of sex education (Chapter 10).

Oral contacts with females occur in only 8.9 per cent of the boys who have pre-adolescent heterosexual play. Oral contacts are more likely to occur where the girl is older, or where an adult woman is involved. There is considerable evidence that oral contacts are recognized as taboo, even at pre-adolescent ages.

POPULATION	CONTINUITY OF PRE-ADOLESCENT SEX PLAY % OF ACTIVE POPULATIONS					
	HETEROSEXUAL PETTING		HETEROSEXUAL COITUS		HOMOSEXUAL PLAY	
	Cases	% with Continuity	Cases	% with Continuity	Cases	% with Continuity
Total (U. S. Correction)	1227	64.9	628	54.7	1412	42.1
Educ. level 0–8	243	77.0	196	73.5	243	50.6
Educ. level 9–12	221	67.4	147	53.7	207	42.5
Educ. level 13+	763	29.8	285	18.6	962	22.5

Table 29. Continuity of pre-adolescent sex play with adolescent activity

Pre-adolescent heterosexual play is carried over into corresponding adolescent activities in nearly two-thirds of the cases (Table 29). There is a somewhat higher carry-over of heterosexual petting, a lesser carry-over of heterosexual coitus. Again there are tremendous differences between social levels. If coitus is had by a pre-adolescent boy who will never go beyond eighth grade in school, the chances are three to one that he will continue such activity, without any major break, in his adolescent and adult years. If the boy who has pre-adolescent coitus belongs to the group that will ultimately go to college, the chances are more than four to one that the activity will not be continued in his adolescent years. Community attitudes on these matters are already exerting an influence on the pre-adolescent boy.

Animal Contacts. Animal contacts are largely confined to farm boys. Of the boys who will ever be involved, a third have had their first contacts by nine years of age; but between 10 and 12 there is a more rapid increase in the active incidence figures. The level which is reached in these years is never again equalled, either in pre-adolescence or in adolescent or in later years. In about a third of the cases, there is direct continuity between the pre-adolescent and the adolescent experiences with animal intercourse.

PRE-ADOLESCENT ORGASM

In the technical literature there seem to be only a few references (*e.g.*, Moll 1912, Merrill 1918, Moses 1922, Krafft-Ebing 1924, Rohleder 1921, Hamilton 1929:427) to the possibility of the pre-adolescent child experiencing orgasm. But, as we have already indicated, orgasm is not at all

AGE	FIRST PRE-ADOLESCENT EROTIC AROUSAL AND ORGASM NUMBER OF CASES						
	EROTIC AROUSAL			ORGASM			
	In Any Sex Play	In Hetero-sexual Play	In Homo-sexual Play	Data from Present Study	Data from Other Subjects	Total Cases	% of Total
1					12	12	2.5
2					8	8	1.6
3				2	7	9	1.8
4	10	9	2		12	12	2.5
5	30	23	8	5	9	14	2.9
6	26	21	8	15	19	34	7.0
7	32	29	6	21	17	38	7.8
8	38	29	12	27	21	48	9.9
9	38	37	3	24	26	50	10.3
10	83	71	17	56	26	82	16.8
11	72	67	13	54	22	76	15.6
12	92	84	13	51	23	74	15.2
13	37	37	3	15	9	24	4.9
14	10	10		3	3	6	1.2
15	3	2	1				
Total	471	419	86	273	214	487	100.0
Mean Age	10.28	10.41	9.62	10.40	8.51	9.57	
Median Age	9.75	9.87	9.26	9.77	8.10	9.23	

Table 30. Pre-adolescent eroticism and orgasm

All data based on memory of older subjects, except in the column entitled "data from other subjects." In the later case, original data gathered by certain of our subjects were made available for use in the present volume. Of the 214 cases so reported, all but 14 were subsequently observed in orgasm (see Table 31).

rare among pre-adolescent boys, and it also occurs among pre-adolescent girls. Since this significant fact has not been well established in scientific publication, it will be profitable to record here the nature of the data for the male in some detail.

Pre-adolescent boys, since they are incapable of ejaculation, may be as uncertain as some inexperienced females in their recognition of orgasm. In consequence, the record on such early experience is incomplete in most of the histories, and it is as yet impossible to make any exact calculation of

AGE WHEN OBSERVED	PRE-ADOLESCENT EXPERIENCE IN ORGASM					
	TOTAL POPULA- TION	CASES NOT REACHING CLIMAX	CASES REACHING CLIMAX	CUMU- LATED POPULA- TION	CUMU- LATED CASES TO CLIMAX	PERCENT OF EACH AGE REACHING CLIMAX
2 mon.	1	1	0			
3 mon.	2	2	0			
4 mon.	1	1	0			
5 mon.	2	1	1			
8 mon.	2	1	1			
9 mon.	1	1	0			
10 mon.	4	1	3			
11 mon.	3	1	2			
12 mon.	12	10	2			
Up to 1 yr.	28	19	9	28	9	32.1
Up to 2 yr.	22	11	11	50	20	
Up to 3 yr.	9	2	7	59	27	57.1
Up to 4 yr.	12	5	7	71	34	
Up to 5 yr.	6	3	3	77	37	
Up to 6 yr.	12	5	7	89	44	
Up to 7 yr.	17	8	9	106	53	
Up to 8 yr.	26	12	14	132	67	63.4
Up to 9 yr.	29	10	19	161	86	
Up to 10 yr.	28	6	22	189	108	
Up to 11 yr.	34	9	25	223	133	
Up to 12 yr.	46	7	39	269	172	80.0
Up to 13 yr.	35	7	28	304	200	
Up to 14 yr.	11	5	6	315	206	
Up to 15 yr.	2	2	0	317	206	
Total	317	111	206	317	206	65.0

Table 31. Ages of pre-adolescent orgasm

Based on actual observation of 317 males.

the incidence or frequency in the population as a whole. Nevertheless, some of the younger boys who have contributed to the present study have described what is unmistakably sexual orgasm in their pre-adolescent histories, and a larger number of adults remember such experience (Table 30).

Better data on pre-adolescent climax come from the histories of adult males who have had sexual contacts with younger boys and who, with their adult backgrounds, are able to recognize and interpret the boys' experiences. Unfortunately, not all of the subjects with such contacts in their histories were questioned on this point of pre-adolescent reactions; but 9 of our adult male subjects have observed such orgasm. Some of these adults are technically trained persons who have kept diaries or other records which have been put at our disposal; and from them we have secured information on 317 pre-adolescents who were either observed in self masturbation, or who were observed in contacts with other boys or older adults. The record so obtained shows a considerable sexual capacity among these boys. Before presenting the data, however, it should be emphasized that this is a record of a somewhat select group of younger males and not a statistical representation for any larger group. These records are based on more or less uninhibited boys, most of whom had heard about sex and seen sexual activities among their companions, and many of whom had had sexual contacts with one or more adults. Most of them knew of orgasm as the goal of such activity, and some of them, even at an early age, had become definitely aggressive in seeking contacts. Most boys are more inhibited, more restricted by parental controls. Many boys remain in ignorance of the nature of a complete sexual response until they become adolescent.

Orgasm has been observed in boys of every age from 5 months to adolescence (Table 31). Orgasm is in our records for a female babe of 4 months. The orgasm in an infant or other young male is, except for the lack of an ejaculation, a striking duplicate of orgasm in an older adult. As described earlier in this chapter, the behavior involves a series of gradual physiologic changes, the development of rhythmic body movements with distinct penis throbs and pelvic thrusts, an obvious change in sensory capacities, a final tension of muscles, especially of the abdomen, hips, and back, a sudden release with convulsions, including rhythmic anal contractions—followed by the disappearance of all symptoms. A fretful babe quiets down under the initial sexual stimulation, is distracted from other activities, begins rhythmic pelvic thrusts, becomes tense as climax approaches, is thrown into convulsive action, often with violent arm and leg movements, sometimes with weeping at the moment of climax. After climax the child loses erection quickly and subsides into the calm and peace that typically follows adult orgasm. It may be some time before erection can be induced again after such an experience. There are observations of 16 males up to 11 months of age, with such typical orgasm reached in 7 cases. In 5 cases of young pre-adolescents, observations were continued over periods of months or years, until the individuals were old enough to make it certain that true orgasm was involved; and in all of these cases the later reactions were so similar to the earlier behavior that there could be no doubt of the orgastic nature of the first experience.

While the records for very young boys are fewer than for boys nearer the age of adolescence, and while the calculations for these youngest cases are consequently less reliable, the data do show a gradual increase, with advancing age, in the percentage of cases able to reach climax: 32 per cent of the boys 2 to 12 months of age, more than half (57.1%) of the 2- to 5-year olds, and nearly 80 per cent of the pre-adolescent boys between 10 and 13 years of age (inclusive) came to climax. Half of the boys had reached climax by 7 years of age (nearly half of them by 5 years), and two-thirds of them by 12 years of age. The observers emphasize that there are some of these pre-adolescent boys (estimated by one observer as less than one-quarter of the cases), who fail to reach climax even under prolonged and varied and repeated stimulation; but, even in these young boys, this probably represents psychologic blockage more often than physiologic incapacity.

TIME	CASES TIMED	PERCENT OF POPULATION	CUMULATED PERCENT
Up to 10 sec.	12	6.4	6.4
10 sec. to 1 min.	46	24.5	30.9
1 to 2 min.	40	21.3	52.2
2 to 3 min.	23	12.2	64.4
3 to 5 min.	33	17.5	81.9
5 to 10 min.	23	12.2	94.1
Over 10 min.	11	5.9	100.0
Total	188	100.0	

Mean time to climax: 3.02 minutes
Median time to climax: 1.91 minutes

Table 32. Speed of pre-adolescent orgasm

Duration of stimulation before climax; observations timed with second hand or stop watch. Ages range from five months of age to adolescence.

In the population as a whole, a much smaller percentage of the boys experience orgasm at any early age, because few of them find themselves in circumstances that test their capacities; but the positive record on these boys who did have the opportunity makes it certain that many infant males and younger boys are capable of orgasm, and it is probable that half or more of the boys in an uninhibited society could reach climax by the time they were three or four years of age, and that nearly all of them could experience such a climax three to five years before the onset of adolescence.

Erection is much quicker in pre-adolescent boys than in adults, although the speed with which climax is reached in pre-adolescent males varies considerably in different boys (Table 32), just as it does in adults. There are two-year olds who come to climax in less than 10 seconds, and there are two-year olds who may take 10 or 20 minutes, or more. There is a similar range among pre-adolescents of every other age. The mean time required to reach climax was almost exactly 3 minutes, and the median time was under 2 minutes. From earliest infancy until the middle twenties there is no effect of age on this point, although beyond that older males slow up in speed of response (Chapter 6).

The most remarkable aspect of the pre-adolescent population is its capacity to achieve repeated orgasm in limited periods of time. This capacity definitely exceeds the ability of teen-age boys who, in turn, are much more capable than any older males (Tables 33, 34, 48, Figure 36). Among 182 pre-adolescent boys on whom sufficient data are available, more than

NO. OF ORGASMS	CASES OB-SERVED	PERCENT OF POPULA-TION	CUMU-LATED PERCENT	TIME BETWEEN ORGASMS	CASES TIMED	PERCENT OF POPULA-TION	CUMU-LATED PERCENT
1	81	44.5	100.0	Up to 10 sec.	3	4.7	4.7
2	17	9.3	55.5	11 to 60 sec.	15	23.5	28.2
3	18	9.9	46.2	Up to 2 min.	8	12.5	40.7
4	10	5.5	36.3	Up to 3 min.	10	15.6	56.3
5	14	7.7	30.8	Up to 5 min.	7	10.9	67.2
6–10	30	16.5	23.1	Up to 10 min.	11	17.2	84.4
11–15	9	4.9	6.6	Up to 20 min.	7	10.9	95.3
16–20	2	1.1	1.7	Up to 30 min.	1	1.6	96.9
21+	1	0.6	0.6	Over 30 min.	2	3.1	100.0
Total	182	100.0	100.0	Total	64	100.0	100.0

Mean No. of Orgasms: 3.72   Mean Time Lapse: 6.28 minutes
Median No. of Orgasms: 2.62   Median Time Lapse: 2.25 minutes

Table 33. Multiple orgasm in pre-adolescent males

Based on a small and select group of boys. Not typical of the experience, but suggestive of the capacities of pre-adolescent boys in general.

half (55.5%, 138 cases) readily reached a second climax within a short period of time, and nearly a third (30.8%) of all these 182 boys were able to achieve 5 or more climaces in quite rapid succession (Tables 32–34). It is certain that a higher proportion of the boys could have had multiple orgasm if the situation had offered. Among 64 cases on which there are detailed reports, the average interval between the first and second climaces ranged from less than 10 seconds to 30 minutes or more, but the mean interval was only 6.28 minutes (median 2.25 minutes) (Table 33). There are older males, even in their thirties and older, who are able to equal this performance, but a much higher proportion of these pre-adolescent males are so capable. Even the youngest males, as young as 5 months in age, are capable of such repeated reactions. Typical cases are shown in Table 34. The maximum observed was 26 climaces in 24 hours, and the report indicates that still more might have been possible in the same period of time.

About a third of these boys remain in erection after the first orgasm and proceed directly to a second contact. There is another third that stays in erection but experiences some physical and erotic let-down before trying to achieve a second orgasm. In another third, the erection quickly subsides and there is a complete disappearance of arousal as soon as orgasm is reached. Any repetition depends upon new arousal, and that may not be possible for some minutes or hours after the original experience. Among

AGE	NO. OF ORGASMS	TIME INVOLVED	AGE	NO. OF ORGASMS	TIME INVOLVED
5 mon.	3	?	11 yr.	11	1 hr.
11 mon.	10	1 hr.	11 yr.	19	1 hr.
11 mon.	14	38 min.	12 yr.	7	3 hr.
2 yr.	{ 7 11	9 min. 65 min.	12 yr.	{ 3 9	3 min. 2 hr.
2½yr.	4	2 min.	12 yr.	12	2 hr.
4 yr.	6	5 min.	12 yr.	15	1 hr.
4 yr.	17	10 hr.	13 yr.	7	24 min.
4 yr.	26	24 hr.	13 yr.	8	2½ hr.
7 yr.	7	3 hr.	13 yr.	9	8 hr.
8 yr.	8	2 hr.	13 yr.	{ 3 11 26	70 sec. 8 hr. 24 hr.
9 yr.	7	68 min.			
10 yr.	9	52 min.			
10 yr.	14	24 hr.	14 yr.	11	4 hr.

Table 34. Examples of multiple orgasm in pre-adolescent males

Some instances of higher frequencies.

adult males, more individuals belong to this last class, and a much smaller number remains in erection until there is a repetition of the sexual contact.

These data on the sexual activities of younger males provide an important substantiation of the Freudian view of sexuality as a component that is present in the human animal from earliest infancy, although it gives no support to the Freudian concept of a pre-genital stage of generalized erotic response that precedes more specific genital activity; nor does it show any necessity for a sexually latent or dormant period in the later adolescent years, except as such inactivity results from parental and social repressions of the growing child. It would seem that analysts have been correct in considering these capacities for childhood sexual development, or their suppression, as prime sources of adult patterns of sexual behavior and of many of the characteristics of the total personality. There are, of course, some who have questioned the truly sexual nature of the child's experiences. Moore, for instance, remarks (1943, p. 45): "One would think that psychoanalysts would have confirmed their theories of infantile emotionality by a careful observation and study of large numbers of children . . . but I have been unable to find any such study by a member of the psychoanalytic school." And again (p. 48): "As to the presence of specific sexual experience in infancy and early childhood, we shall never be able to solve the problem by appealing to the introspection of the infant and the child. Neither does the memory of the adult reach back to those early years so that he can tell us whether or not it is really true that in infancy and early childhood he experienced specific sexual excitement, and that this was repressed and became latent, as Freud maintained."

Moore leans heavily on Bridges (1936) and Bühler (1931) to argue (pp. 46–48) that the earliest manifestations of emotion may be labelled *distress* or *delight;* but that, although young children may perform "acts similar to masturbation" and seek a partner for genital manipulation, "there is no evidence . . . that these acts are accompanied by specific sexual pleasure . . . even though there are signs that the child in some manner enjoys them." The conclusion is that although the child is capable of a tender personal love, it is of a non-erotic character and has nothing to do with the beginnings of sexuality. Adding data from endocrinologic sources, he concludes that specifically sexual behavior is the product of biologic growth and of experience.

Complying with the scientifically fair demand for records from trained observers, and answering Moore's further demand (p. 71) that "writers . . . test their theories . . . by empirical study and statistical procedures," we have now reported observations on such specifically sexual activities as erection, pelvic thrusts, and the several other characteristics of true orgasm in a list of 317 pre-adolescent boys ranging between infants of five months and adolescence in age. Adding the records based on the memories of older subjects concerning their own, and often clearly established, early experiences, there is a record of orgasm in 604 pre-adolescent boys (Tables 30 and 31 combined). The existence of such an early capacity is exactly what students of animal behavior have reported for other mammals (Beach 1947), and it is, therefore, not surprising to find it in the human infant. Important as learning and conditioning may be in the later development of specific types of sexual techniques and in the socio-sexual adjustments of the adolescent and adult, it must be accepted as a fact that at least some and probably a high proportion of the infant and older pre-adolescent males are capable of specific sexual response to the point of complete orgasm, whenever a sufficient stimulation is provided.

ADOLESCENCE

While the sexual history of the human male thus begins in earliest infancy and develops continuously to its maximum activity somewhere between the middle teens and twenty years of age (Chapter 7), the steady progress of the development is, among primates, accelerated in a period of growth which is known as adolescence.

During adolescence the young male rather suddenly acquires physical stature and adult conformation, and he begins to produce an ejaculate which contains mature sperm and which can, therefore, effect fertilization when in contact with the egg of a mature female. These are the most obvious and the biologically significant developments of the period; but the student of human sexual behavior is concerned with adolescence, and must consider its physical signs and stigmata, not because the physical developments are in themselves of prime importance, but because adolescence marks what is, in most individuals, a considerable break between the patterns of sexual activity of the pre-adolescent boy and the patterns of the older boy or adult. The sexual life of the younger boy is more or less a part of his other play; it is usually sporadic, and (under the restrictions imposed by our social structure) it may be without overt manifestation in a fair number of cases. The sexual life of the older male is, on the other hand, an end in itself, and (in spite of our social organization) in nearly all boys its overt manifestations become frequent and regular, soon after the onset of adolescence.

In a portion of the cases the pre-adolescent sexual activities have provided the introduction to adult activities: simple heterosexual play turns into more sophisticated petting; pre-adolescent attempts at intercourse lead to adult coitus; some of the pre-adolescent homosexual play leads into similar adult contacts. This is true in about 50 per cent of all male histories which include any pre-adolescent play (Table 29). In an equal number of the cases the pre-adolescent play ends well before or with the onset of adolescence, and adolescent and more adult sexual activities must start from new points, newly won social acquirements, newly learned techniques of physical contact. In many cases the newly adolescent boy's capacity to ejaculate, his newly acquired physical characters of other sorts, do something to him which brings child play to an end and leaves him awkward about making further socio-sexual contacts. The psychologic and social factors involved in this break between pre-adolescent sexuality and adult sexual activity are questions that will deserve considerable study by some qualified student. Those boys in whom child play does merge directly into adult activity are more often from less inhibited, lower social levels (Table 29).

For all boys, the experiences of pre-adolescence, whether directly continued or not, must provide considerable conditioning which encourages or inhibits their sexual development in adolescent and in more adult years.

Adolescence is a period of time, and not a particular point in the life of the growing boy. It involves a whole series of developmental changes, some of which come earlier, some later in the course of events. Individuals differ materially in the ages at which they experience the first of these events, and somewhat in the sequence in which the other transformations follow (Table 35, Figure 27).

Among most boys, the physical changes of adolescence come on more or less abruptly, usually between the ages of 11 and 14, and in that period their sexual activities are suddenly stepped up until, within another few years, most of them reach the maximum rate of their whole lives (Chapter 7). Among most females, as the data in another volume will show, sexual development comes on more gradually than in the male, is often spread over a longer period of time, and does not reach its peak until a good many years after the boy is sexually mature.

Chiefly within the past decade, several studies based on physical examinations of boys and girls have given precise information on the variation and average ages involved in the developmental changes of adolescence. Some of the studies (Baldwin 1916, Crampton 1908, 1944, Dimock 1937, Kubitschek 1932, Schonfeld 1943) have been cross-sectional, based on examinations of numbers of children of each age group; some, utilizing a longitudinal approach, have involved the more exact task of following the development of individual cases over a period of successive years (Boas 1932, Dearborn and Rothney 1941, Greulich et al. 1938, Jones 1944, Meredith 1935, 1939, Shuttleworth 1937, 1939). The latter, however, are not always the more fruitful studies, for such observations are tedious, and long-time contacts so often fail that only a few subjects can be followed through to conclusion.

The studies which are based on direct physical examinations may be accepted as more accurate than our own, for we have relied for the most part on the memory of persons who were removed by various and sometimes long periods of years from the events which they were recalling; but it is interesting to find that our records give averages and total curves which are not significantly different from the data in the observational studies (Chapter 4, Table 15, Figure 15). According to the memory of our subjects, physical changes in the adolescent boy usually proceed as follows: Beginning of development of pubic hair, first ejaculation, voice change, initiation of rapid growth in height, and, after some lapse of time, completion of growth in height (Table 35, Figure 27). Similar data have been previously published from our laboratory (Ramsey 1943a) for a small sample of 291 younger males who were in or near the beginning of adolescence at the time of the study. Our present, larger sample gives curves that

ADOLESCENT PHYSICAL DEVELOPMENT

AGE	PUBIC HAIR	FIRST EJACUL.	VOICE CHANGE	BODY GROWTH	COMPLETION OF GROWTH
			Percent Beginning		
8		0.1		0.1	
9	0.2	0.2		0.0	
10	2.0	1.8	0.6	3.0	0.1
11	7.7	6.1	2.9	3.8	0.2
12	25.5	19.5	14.0	14.3	1.3
13	33.5	29.2	26.4	19.4	3.4
14	22.8	25.1	26.0	22.7	8.2
15	5.5	10.2	14.3	15.9	11.5
16	2.0	4.2	9.1	11.4	18.6
17	0.7	1.8	3.3	6.4	17.1
18		0.8	1.6	2.3	17.9
19		0.4	0.7	0.5	8.4
20	0.1	0.1	0.4	0.2	7.5
21		0.1	0.3		3.1
22		0.1	0.3		1.8
23		0.1			0.4
24		0.1	0.1		0.2
25					0.2
Cases	2511	3573	2279	1355	2621
Mean Age	13.45	13.88	14.44	14.49	17.47
Median Age	13.43	13.77	14.23	14.42	17.40
AGE			Cumulated Percent		
8		0.1		0.1	
9	0.2	0.3		0.1	
10	2.2	2.1	0.6	3.1	0.1
11	9.9	8.2	3.5	6.9	0.3
12	35.4	27.7	17.5	21.2	1.6
13	68.9	56.9	43.9	40.6	5.0
14	91.7	82.0	69.9	63.3	13.2
15	97.2	92.2	84.2	79.2	24.7
16	99.2	96.4	93.3	90.6	43.3
17	99.9	98.2	96.6	97.0	60.4
18	99.9	99.0	98.2	99.3	78.3
19	99.9	99.4	98.9	99.8	86.7
20	100.0	99.5	99.3	100.0	94.2
21		99.7	99.6		97.3
22		99.8	99.9		99.1
23		99.9	99.9		99.5
24		100.0	100.0		99.7
25					100.0
Cases	2511	3573	2279	1355	2621

Table 35. Adolescent developments

are in most respects in close agreement with the Ramsey series; but his records show voice change beginning sooner after the onset of pubic hair growth and before the first ejaculation (also see Jerome 1937, Curry 1940, Pedrey 1945). The Ramsey data indicate that "breast knots," or subareolar nodes which are homologous to those which regularly occur in the female, are found in at least one-third of these boys between the ages of 12 to 14 (Jung and Shafton 1935, Ramsey 1943). Physical examinations (Meredith 1935, 1939) on limited and selected series of males have shown that sudden body growth may begin nearer the time of pubic hair development than our older subjects recall. There are many individual differences in the sequence of events.

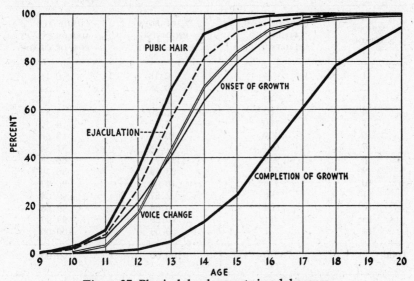

Figure 27. Physical developments in adolescence

The published studies of younger boys almost completely lack data on the most significant of all adolescent developments, the occurrence of the first ejaculation. There have been several attempts to secure information by indirect methods, including a technique of examining for sperm in early morning samples of urine (Baldwin 1928). These methods will not soon supply any quantity of data; and the only other sources of information on this point have been the records obtained from the recall of subjects in the previously published case history studies. This material is now augmented by a considerable record based on the memory of persons who have contributed to the present study, and on an important body of data from certain of our subjects who have observed first ejaculation in a list of several hundred boys.

The earliest ejaculation remembered by any of our apparently normal males was at 8 (three males). We have the history of one unusual boy (a

Negro, interviewed when he was 12) who fixed 6 as his age at first ejaculation. The boy had been diagnosed by the clinician as "idiopathically precocious in development." In the literature (*e.g.*, Ford and Guild 1937, Young 1937, Weinberger and Grant 1941) there are clinical cases for still younger ages, most of them involving endocrine pathologies. Pubic hair has been recorded for one year of age and non-motile sperm in urine after prostate massage at four and a half years. Eight, however, is the earliest age of first ejaculation known for apparently normal males.

Except for the 6 cases of life-long ejaculatory impotence referred to earlier in the present chapter, the latest ages of first ejaculation reliably

SCHOOL GRADE	NO. OF BOYS BEGINNING ADOLESCENCE	% OF BOYS BEGINNING ADOLESCENCE	CUMULATED % ADOLESCENT AT END OF GRADE
1	6	0.16	0.16
2	14	0.38	0.54
3	42	1.13	1.67
4	82	2.20	3.87
5	180	4.83	8.70
6	409	10.96	19.66
7	667	17.88	37.54
8	959	25.71	63.25
9	863	23.14	86.39
10	376	10.08	96.47
11	96	2.57	99.04
12	24	0.64	99.68
13	11	0.29	99.97
14	1	0.03	100.00
Total	3730	100.00	100.00

Mean grade at onset of adolescence: 8.33 $\pm$ 0.028
Median grade at onset of adolescence: 8.49

Table 36. School grade at adolescence

Most of the boys reaching adolescence in the lowest grades are retarded individuals of more advanced age than the average in the grade.

recorded in the histories are 21 for two apparently healthy males, 24 for a religiously inhibited individual, and 22 and after 24 for two males with hormonal deficiencies. The spread between the youngest and the oldest non-endocrine case is 16 years. A variety of educational and social problems arise out of these differences between chronologic and sexual age. For instance, an occasional boy in third or fourth grade is sexually as mature as an occasional senior in college (Table 36, Figure 28).

In spite of this spread in the population as a whole, the record shows (Table 35, Figure 27) that about 90 per cent of the males ejaculate for the first time between the ages of 11 and 15 (inclusive). This is an age range of 5 years. At the end of the seventh grade in school, about a third (37.5%) of the boys are adolescent; by the end of the tenth grade, nearly all of them (96.5%) are so (Table 36, Figure 28). The average boy turns adolescent in the eighth grade (a mean grade of 8.33).

The mean age of first orgasm resulting in ejaculation is 13 years, 10½ months (13.88 years). On this point, the male data are in striking contrast with preliminary calculations on the female. By 15 years of age, 92 per cent of the males have had orgasm, but at that same age less than a quarter of the females have had such experience; and the female population is 29

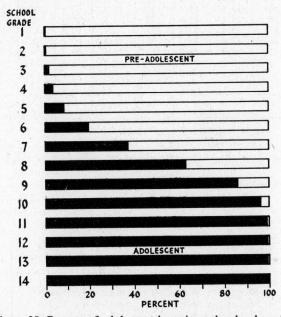

Figure 28. Percent of adolescent boys in each school grade

years old before it includes as high a percentage of experienced individuals as is to be found in the male curve at 15. Precise data on the female must await the publication of a later volume.

In the male the age of first ejaculation varies by nearly a year between different educational (social) levels: the mean is 14.58 for boys who never go beyond eighth grade in school, 13.97 for boys who go into high school but not beyond, and 13.71 for boys who will go to college (Table 37). The differences are probably the outcome of nutritional inequalities at different social levels, and they are in line with similar differences in mean ages of females at menarche, where nutrition is usually considered a prime factor effecting variation.

AGES AT ONSET OF ADOLESCENCE

AGE	EDUCATIONAL LEVEL 0–8			EDUCATIONAL LEVEL 9–12			EDUCATIONAL LEVEL 13+		
	Cases	% of Population	Cumulated Percent	Cases	% of Population	Cumulated Percent	Cases	% of Population	Cumulated Percent
8				1	0.2	0.2	2	0.1	0.1
9	1	0.1	0.1	2	0.3	0.5	7	0.3	0.4
10	7	0.9	1.0	11	1.8	2.3	70	2.5	2.9
11	22	2.9	3.9	32	5.2	7.5	221	7.8	10.7
12	104	13.6	17.5	123	19.9	27.4	707	25.1	35.8
13	185	24.1	41.6	189	30.5	57.9	980	34.8	70.6
14	275	35.8	77.4	205	33.0	90.9	647	23.0	93.6
15	137	17.8	95.2	39	6.3	97.2	126	4.5	98.1
16	31	4.0	99.2	13	2.1	99.3	37	1.3	99.4
17	5	0.7	99.9	3	0.5	99.8	15	0.5	99.9
18	1	0.1	100.0	1	0.2	100.0	2	0.1	100.0
19							1	—	100.0
Total	768	100.0		619	100.0		2815	100.0	
Mean Median	14.14 ± 0.044 14.24 years			13.67 ± 0.049 13.75 years			13.39 ± 0.023 13.41 years		

AGE	TOTAL SAMPLE POPULATION			CORRECTED FOR U. S. POPULATION	
	Cases	% of Population	Cumulated Percent	% of Population	Cumulated Percent
8	3	0.1	0.1	0.1	0.1
9	10	0.2	0.3	0.2	0.4
10	93	2.0	2.3	1.6	2.0
11	304	6.6	8.9	4.9	6.9
12	1035	22.5	31.4	18.7	25.6
13	1507	32.8	64.2	29.1	54.7
14	1209	26.3	90.5	32.4	87.1
15	316	6.9	97.4	9.6	96.7
16	85	1.9	99.3	2.6	99.3
17	23	0.5	99.8	0.6	99.9
18	4	0.1	99.9	0.2	100.0
19	1	0.1	100.0	—	100.0
Total	4590	100.0		100.0	
Mean Median	13.55 ± 0.018 13.56 years				

Table 37. Ages at onset of adolescence

Comparing development for three groups defined in accordance with the years of schooling ultimately attained. Figures for the U. S. population are based on the figures for the sample population corrected for the educational distribution shown ih the U. S. Census for 1940.

Since so many developments are involved, it is difficult to mark a single point at which an individual may be said to have begun adolescence. In the case of the male, it is not customary to attach that distinction to the very first appearance of any adolescent change, but to pay more attention to the time of first ejaculation, or to evidence that the boy would be capable of ejaculation if the proper opportunity were at hand. We have, to a large degree, followed this convention, in order that the calculations may be compared with other published figures. If the year of first ejaculation coincides with the year in which the pubic hair first appears, with the time of onset of growth in height, or with other developments, there is no question involved. If first ejaculation follows these other events by a year

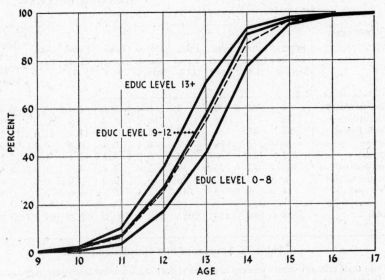

Figure 29. Age at onset of adolescence, by three educational levels

Curve for total population, on the basis of the U. S. Correction, is shown in the broken line.

or more, the record must be examined to see whether there was overt sexual behavior which would have provided previous opportunity for orgasm, and the reliability of the record on the other adolescent characters must be checked. First ejaculation which is derived from nocturnal dreams usually occurs a year or more after the onset of other adolescent characters and after ejaculation would have been possible by other means, if circumstances had allowed. Taking these several things into account, "adolescent ages" have been assigned to each of the subjects in the present study, and the distribution is shown in Table 37, Figure 29. When computed thus the average age of onset of adolescence in the white male is about 13 years and 7 months.

For the U. S. population, the sources of first ejaculation (Table 38, Figure 30) are, in order of frequency, masturbation (in about two-thirds of the males), nocturnal emissions (in an eighth of the cases), heterosexual coitus (in one boy out of eight), and homosexual contacts (in one boy out of twenty), with spontaneous ejaculation, petting to climax, and inter- course with other animals as less frequent stimuli for the initial experience (*cf.* Rohleder 1921). There are considerable differences in first sources in different educational levels. The highest incidence of masturbation as the first source of ejaculation occurs among the boys who will leave school

SOURCE	NUMBER OF ADOLESCENT MALES				PERCENT OF POPULATION				
	Popu- lat. in Sample	Educ. Level 0–8	Educ. Level 9–12	Educ. Level 13+	Popu- lat. in Sample	Educ. Level 0–8	Educ. Level 9–12	Educ. Level 13+	Total U. S. Popu- lation
No Ejaculation	14	4	2	3	0.4	0.6	0.4	0.1	0.42
Masturbation	2378	455	346	1293	66.2	68.2	70.1	62.2	68.39
Noct. Emiss.	798	47	58	654	22.2	7.1	11.7	31.4	13.11
Petting	13	2	2	9	0.4	0.3	0.4	0.4	0.37
Coitus	222	123	60	29	6.2	18.5	12.1	1.4	12.53
Homosexual	103	32	23	39	2.9	4.8	4.7	1.9	4.33
Animal Coitus	6	0	0	6	0.2	0.0	0.0	0.3	0.04
Spontaneous	54	3	3	48	1.5	0.5	0.6	2.3	0.81
Total	3588	666	494	2081	100.0	100.0	100.0	100.0	100.00

Table 38. Sources of first ejaculation

The final column shows percent involved if each educational level were represented in the proportions shown in the 1940 Census.

between the ninth and twelfth grades, the highest incidence of nocturnal emissions as the first source occurs among the boys who will subsequently go to college, and the highest incidence of heterosexual intercourse as the first source occurs among the boys who never get beyond the eighth grade in school.

While "spontaneous" ejaculation, meaning ejaculation without specific genital contact, is the first source of experience for only a small percentage of the boys (0.81%), the items which stimulate such response constitute an interesting list which includes non-sexual and more definitely sexual emotional situations, and a variety of circumstances which involve physical tension. In a number of cases (*e.g.*, wrestling, prolonged sitting while reading a book) both physical tension and psychologic stimulation are probably involved. The list includes a number of the non-sexual sources of erotic stimulation listed earlier in this chapter, but the following tabulation shows items which are responsible for actual ejaculation among these early adolescent boys.

SOURCES OF FIRST SPONTANEOUS EJACULATION

Chiefly Physical Stimulation

Sitting at desk	Sliding on chair
Sitting in classroom	Sliding down a bannister
Lying still on floor	Tension in gymnastics
Lying still in bed	Chinning on bar
Urination	Climbing tree, pole or rope
At toilet	(A rather common source)
General stimulation in bath	Wrestling with female
Moving water in bath	Wrestling with male
General stimulation with towel	Riding an automobile
General skin irritation	Tight clothing
Vibration of a boat	

Chiefly Emotional Stimulation

Day dreaming	Milking a cow
Reading a book	When scared at night
Walking down a street	When bicycle was stolen
In vaudeville	A bell ringing
In movies	An exciting basketball game
Kissed by female	Trying to finish an examination in
Watching petting	school
Peeping at nude female	Reciting in front of class
Sex discussion at YMCA	Injury in a car wreck

Beyond earliest adolescence, it is a rare male who ejaculates when no physical contact is involved. Many teen-age and even older males come to climax in heterosexual petting that may not involve genital contacts; but general body contact, or at least lip contact, is usually included in such situations. There are stray cases of males of college age ejaculating under the excitement of class recitation or examination, in airplanes during combat, and under other rare circumstances. There are two cases of older males who could reach climax by deliberate concentration of thought on erotic situations; but such spontaneous ejaculation is almost wholly confined to younger boys just entering adolescence.

After the initial experience in ejaculation, practically all males become regular in their sexual activity. This involves monthly, weekly, or even daily ejaculation, which occurs regularly from the time of the very first experience. Among approximately 4600 adolescent males, less than one per cent (about 35 cases) record a lapse of a year or more between their first experience and the adoption of a regular routine of sexual activ-

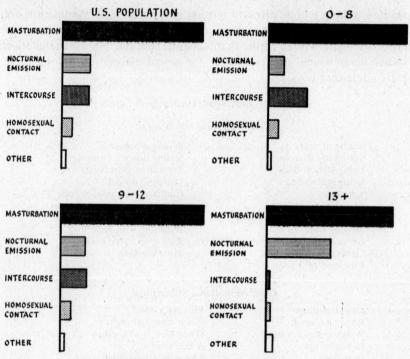

Figure 30. Sources of first ejaculation

Calculated for total population corrected for U. S. Census distribution, and for boys of the grade school (0–8), high school (9–12), and college (13+) levels.

ity. This means that more than 99 per cent of the boys begin regular sexual lives immediately after the first ejaculation. In this respect, the male is again very different from the female, for there are many women who go for periods of time ranging from a year to ten or twenty years between their earlier experiences and the subsequent adoption of regularity in activity. The male, in the course of his life, may change the sources of his sexual outlet, and his frequencies may vary through the weeks and months, and over a span of years, but almost never is there a complete cessation of his activity until such time as old age finally stops all response.

Chapter 6

TOTAL SEXUAL OUTLET

As previously noted, the six chief sources of orgasm for the human male are masturbation, nocturnal emissions, heterosexual petting, heterosexual intercourse, homosexual relations, and intercourse with animals of other species. The sum of the orgasms derived from these several sources constitutes the individual's total sexual outlet.

Since practically all of the sexual contacts of the mature male involve emotional changes, all of which represent expenditures of energy, all adult contacts might be considered means of outlet, even though they do not lead to orgasm. These emotional situations are, however, of such variable intensity that they are difficult to assess and compare; and, for the sake of achieving some precision in analysis, the present discussion of outlets is confined to those instances of sexual activity which culminate in orgasm.

FREQUENCY OF TOTAL OUTLET

There are some individuals who derive 100 per cent of their outlet from a single kind of sexual activity. Most persons regularly depend upon two or more sources of outlet; and there are some who may include all six of them in some short period of time. The mean number of outlets utilized by our more than 5000 males is between 2 and 3 (means of 2.5 or 2.2) (Table 39). This number varies considerably with different age groups and with different social levels (Figure 35; Chapters 7, 10).

There are, both theoretically and in actuality, endless possibilities in combining these several sources of outlet and in the extent to which each of them contributes to the total picture (Figure 31). The record of a single sort of sexual activity, even though it be the one most frequently employed by a particular group of males, does not adequately portray the whole sexual life of that group. Published figures on the frequency of marital intercourse, for instance (Pearl 1925), cannot be taken to be the equivalent of data on the frequency of total outlet for the married male; for marital intercourse may provide as little as 62 per cent of the orgasms of certain groups of married males (Table 97). Similarly, studies of masturbation among college and younger students are not the equivalents of studies of total sexual outlet for such a group. Again, many persons who are rated "homosexual" by their fellows in a school community, a prison population, or society at large, may be deriving only a small portion of their total outlet from that source. The fact that such a person may have had hundreds of

193

heterosexual contacts will, in most cases, be completely ignored. Even psychologic studies have sometimes included, as "homosexual," persons who were not known to have had more than a single overt experience. In assaying the significance of any particular activity in an individual history, or any particular type of sexual behavior in a population as a whole, it is necessary to consider the extent to which that activity contributes to the total picture. Since all previously published rates on human sexual activity have been figures for particular outlets, such as masturbation or marital intercourse, the figures given in the present study on total outlet are higher than previous data would have led one to expect.

NO. OF SOURCES	SAMPLE POPULATION			U. S. POPULATION		
	Cases	% of Population	Cumulated Percent	Cases per 10,000	% of Population	Cumulated Percent
0	263	2.2	100.0	199	1.99	100.00
1	2,169	18.4	97.8	2,579	25.79	98.01
2	3,834	32.4	79.4	3,314	33.14	72.22
3	3,478	29.5	47.0	2,742	27.42	39.08
4	1,690	14.3	17.5	974	9.74	11.66
5	342	2.9	3.2	179	1.79	1.92
6	33	0.3	0.3	13	0.13	0.13
Total	11,809			10,000		
Mean	2.45 ± 0.01			2.22		
Median	2.91			2.67		

Table 39. Number of sources of outlet in any 5-year period

Computed for the whole population involved in the present study, and computed for a theoretic adult male population with the age distribution found in the U. S. Census for 1940.

The average (mean) frequency of total sexual outlet for our sample of 3905 white males ranging between adolescence and 30 years of age is nearly 3.0 per week. It is precisely 2.88 for the total population of that age, or 2.94 for the sexually active males in that population (Table 40, Figure 32). For the total population, including all persons between adolescence and 85 years of age, the mean is 2.74 (Figure 33).

These average figures, however, are not entirely adequate, for they are based upon the particular groups of males who have contributed so far to this study. Subsequent analyses will show that there are differences in mean frequencies of sexual activity, dependent upon such factors as age, marital status, educational, religious, and rural-urban backgrounds, and on still other biologic and social factors. In order to be intelligible, any discussion of sexual outlet should be confined to a particular group of persons whose biologic condition, civil status, and social origins are homogeneous. Most of the present volume is concerned with the presentation of data for such homogeneous groups. If there is any advantage in having a generalized figure for the population of the country as a whole, that figure is best calculated by determining the frequencies for a variety of these homogeneous groups, determining the relative size of each of these groups in the national census, and then, through a process of weighting of means, reconstructing the picture for a synthetic whole (Chapter 3, Tables 7–11).

For this synthesized population, which more nearly represents the constitution of the nation as a whole, we arrive at a figure of 3.27 per week for the total sexual outlet of the average white American male under thirty years of age (Table 40). For all white males up to age 85, the corrected mean is 2.34 per week. The latter figure is lower because of the inactivity of the older males.

INDIVIDUAL VARIATION

While approximately 3.3 is the mean frequency of total outlet for younger males, no mean nor median, nor any other sort of average, can be significant unless one keeps in mind the range of the individual variation and the distribution of these variants in the population as a whole. This is particularly true in regard to human sexual behavior, because differences in behavior, even in a small group, are much greater than the variation in physical or physiologic characters (Table 40, Figures 32, 33). There are a few males who have gone for long periods of years without ejaculating: there is one male who, although apparently sound physically, had ejaculated only once in thirty years. There are others who have maintained average frequencies of 10, 20, or more per week for long periods of time: one male (a scholarly and skilled lawyer) has averaged over 30 per week for thirty years (Table 43). This is a difference of several thousand times.

In considering structural characters of plants and animals, such as total height in the human, or length of wings, legs or other parts in other animals, a maximum that was two or three times the size of the minimum would command considerable attention (Bateson 1894, Wechsler 1935, Thorndike 1940). One of us has published data (Kinsey 1942) on individual variation in populations of insects. The populations represented individuals of single species, from single localities. There were many characters which varied. Extreme wing lengths, for instance, varied between 10 and 180 micrometer units. This difference of 18 times probably represents as extreme a linear variation as is known in any population of adults of any species of plant or animal. But differences between the extreme frequencies of sexual outlet in the human (Figures 32–33) range far beyond these

COMBINATIONS OF SEXUAL OUTLET

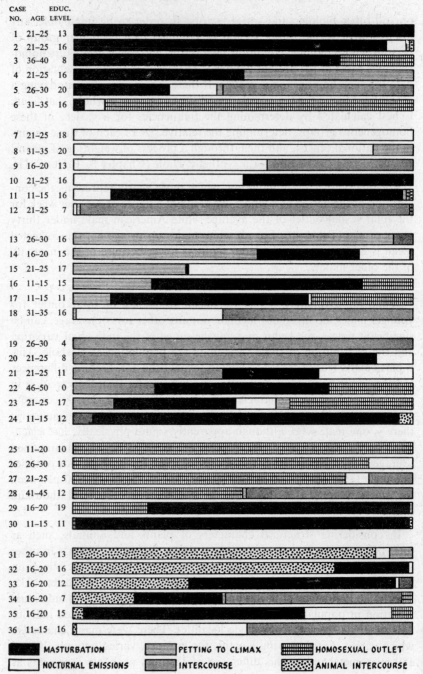

Figure 31. Diverse examples of combinations of six sources of outlet

Each bar shows a combination of outlets used by one individual.

morphologic differences. Calculation will show that the difference between one ejaculation in thirty years and mean frequencies of, say, 30 ejaculations per week throughout the whole of thirty years, is a matter of 45,000 times. This is the order of the variation which may occur between two individuals who live in the same town and who are neighbors, meeting in the same place of business, and coming together in common social activities. These sexually extreme individuals may be of equal significance, or insignificance, in the societal organization. They may be considered as very similar sorts of persons by their close friends who do not know their sexual histories. It has been notable throughout our field collections that a sample of as few as a hundred histories is likely to show a considerable portion of this full range of variation.

These differences in frequency of sexual activity are of great social importance. The publicly pretended code of morals, our social organization, our marriage customs, our sex laws, and our educational and religious systems are based upon an assumption that individuals are much alike sexually, and that it is an equally simple matter for all of them to confine their behavior to the single pattern which the mores dictate. Even in such an obviously sexual situation as marriage, there is little consideration, under our present custom, of the possibility that the two persons who have mated may be far apart in their sexual inclinations, backgrounds, and capacities. Persons interested in sex education look for a program which will satisfy children—meaning all the children—at some particular educational level, overlooking the fact that one individual may be adapted to a particular, perhaps relatively inactive, sort of sexual adjustment, while the next would find it practically impossible to confine himself to such a low level of activity. In institutional management, there has been almost complete unawareness of these possible differences between inmates. The problems of sexual adjustment for persons committed to penal, mental, or other institutions, the problems of sexual adjustment for men and women in the army, the navy, or other armed forces, are a thousand different problems for any thousand of the persons involved.

While the curve shows three-quarters (77.7%) of the males with a range of variation that lies between 1.0 and 6.5 per week, there is still nearly a quarter (22.3%) of the males who fall into extreme ranges (total population, U. S. Correction). There are, for instance, 7.6 per cent of all the males whose outlets may average 7 or more per week for periods of at least five years in some part of their lives. Daily and more than daily arousal and sexual activity to the point of complete orgasm must occur among some of the friends and acquaintances which any person has. When the data on the female are subsequently published, they will show that there is even a wider range of variation there, although a larger number of the females are in the lower portion of the curve.

FRE-QUENCIES PER WEEK	YOUNGER AGES: ADOLESCENT TO 30			ALL AGES: ADOLESCENT TO 85		
	Cases	Sample Population %	U. S. Population %	Cases	Sample Population %	U. S. Population %
0.0	232	2.0	1.7	291	2.1	1.3
—	192	1.7	1.2	260	1.8	1.3
0.5	1136	9.9	8.3	1491	10.6	12.1
1.0	1397	12.2	11.3	1852	13.2	14.8
1.5	1235	10.8	11.2	1579	11.2	11.4
2.0	1240	10.8	10.4	1606	11.4	13.3
2.5	1066	9.3	9.6	1299	9.2	9.6
3.0	979	8.5	7.6	1194	8.5	7.7
3.5	910	7.9	8.1	1049	7.4	6.2
4.0	622	8.5	5.2	717	5.1	4.3
4.5	455	4.0	4.1	529	3.8	3.1
5.0	411	3.6	3.5	446	3.2	2.3
5.5	267	2.3	2.2	298	2.1	1.7
6.0	249	2.2	2.5	279	2.0	2.3
6.5	158	1.4	1.5	169	1.2	1.0
7.0	189	1.6	1.9	208	1.5	1.2
7.5	122	1.1	1.2	127	0.9	0.7
8.0	99	0.9	1.4	105	0.7	0.7
8.5	65	0.6	0.7	69	0.5	0.4
9.0	33	0.3	0.2	44	0.3	0.2
9.5	40	0.3	0.3	46	0.3	0.3
10.0	68	0.6	0.8	71	0.5	0.6
11.0	61	0.5	0.9	67	0.5	0.5
12.0	43	0.4	0.5	49	0.3	0.3
13.0	30	0.3	0.6	39	0.3	0.4
14.0	31	0.3	0.5	36	0.3	0.4
15.0	25	0.2	0.4	33	0.2	0.3
16.0	19	0.2	0.3	23	0.2	0.5
17.0	18	0.2	0.4	20	0.1	0.2
18.0	10	0.1	0.1	12	0.1	0.1
19.0	10	0.1	0.2	12	0.1	0.1
20.0	9	0.1	0.2	11	0.1	0.2
21.0	5	—	0.2	6	0.1	0.1
22.0	8	0.1	0.1	10	0.1	0.1
23.0	6	—	0.1	6	—	—
24.0	2	—	—	2	—	—
25.0	6	—	0.1	6	—	0.1
26.0	4	—	0.2	5	—	0.1
27.0	3	—	0.1	3	—	—
28.0	0	0	—	0	0	—
29.+	12	0.1	0.2	14	0.1	0.1
Total	11467	100.0	100.0	14083	100.0	100.0
Mean	2.88 ± 0.027		3.27	2.74 ± 0.024		2.34
Median	2.14			1.99		

Table 40. Individual variation in frequency of total sexual outlet

Raw data, based on the available sample, are corrected for a population of the same age, marital status, and educational level as that shown for the total population in the U. S. Census of 1940.

The possibility of any individual engaging in sexual activity at a rate that is remarkably different from one's own, is one of the most difficult things for even professionally trained persons to understand. Meetings of educators who are discussing sex instruction and policies to be followed in the administration of educational institutions, may bring out extreme differences of opinion which range from recommendations for the teaching of complete abstinence to recommendations for frank acceptance of almost any type of sexual activity. No other subject will start such open dissension in a group, and it is difficult for an observer to comprehend how objective reasoning can lead to such different conclusions among intelligent men and women. If, however, one has the histories of the educators involved, it may be found that there are persons in the group who are not ejaculating more than once or twice a year, while there may be others in the same group who are experiencing orgasm as often as ten or twenty times per week, and regularly. There is, inevitably, some correlation between these rates and the positions which these persons take in a public debate. On both sides of the argument, the extreme individuals may be totally unaware of the possibility of others in the group having histories that are so remote from their own. In the same fashion, we have listened to discussions of juvenile delinquency, of law enforcement, and of recommendations for legislative action on the sex laws, knowing that the policies that ultimately come out of such meetings would reflect the attitudes and sexual experience of the most vocal members of the group, rather than an intelligently thought-out program established on objectively accumulated data.

Even the scientific discussions of sex show little understanding of the range of variation in human behavior. More often the conclusions are limited by the personal experience of the author. Psychologic and psychiatric literature is loaded with terms which evaluate frequencies of sexual outlet. But such designations as infantile, frigid, sexually under-developed, under-active, excessively active, over-developed, over-sexed, hypersexual, or sexually over-active, and the attempts to recognize such states as nymphomania and satyriasis as discrete entities, can, in any objective analysis, refer to nothing more than a position on a curve which is continuous. Normal and abnormal, one sometimes suspects, are terms which a particular author employs with reference to his own position on that curve.

The most significant thing about this curve (Figures 32, 33) is its continuity. It is not symmetrical, with a particular portion of the population set off as "normal," "modal," "typical," or discretely different. No individual has a sexual frequency which differs in anything but a slight degree from the frequencies of those placed next on the curve. Such a continuous and widely spread series raises a question as to whether the terms "normal" and "abnormal" belong in a scientific vocabulary. At

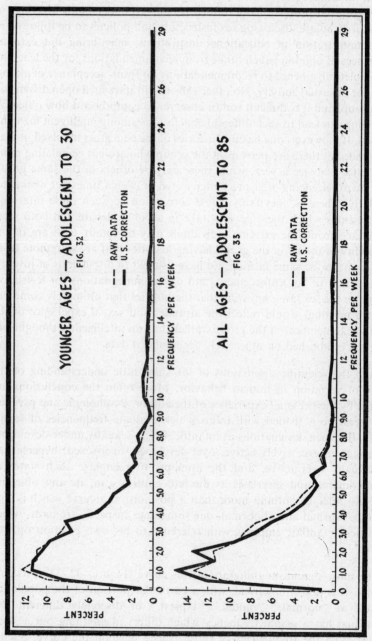

Figures 32–33. Individual variation in frequency of total sexual outlet

the best, abnormal may designate certain individuals whose rates of activity are less frequent, or whose sources of sexual outlet are not as usual in the population as a whole; but in that case, it is preferable to refer to such persons as rare, rather than abnormal. Moreover, many items in human sexual behavior which are labelled abnormal, or perversions, in textbooks, prove, upon statistical examination, to occur in as many as 30 or 60 or 75 per cent of certain populations (see later chapters). It is difficult to maintain that such types of behavior are abnormal because they are rare.

The term "abnormal" is applied in medical pathology to conditions which interfere with the physical well-being of a living body. In a social sense, the term might apply to sexual activities which cause social maladjustment. Such an application, however, involves subjective determinations of what is good personal living, or good social adjustment; and these things are not as readily determined as physiologic well-being in an organic body. It is not possible to insist that any departure from the sexual mores, or any participation in socially taboo activities, always, or even usually, involves a neurosis or psychosis, for the case histories abundantly demonstrate that most individuals who engage in taboo activities make satisfactory social adjustments. There are, in actuality, few adult males who are particularly disturbed over their sexual histories. Psychiatrists, clinical psychologists, and others who deal with cases of maladjustment, sometimes come to feel that most people find difficulty in adjusting their sexual lives; but a clinic is no place to secure incidence figures. The incidence of tuberculosis in a tuberculosis sanitarium is no measure of the incidence of tuberculosis in the population as a whole; and the incidence of disturbance over sexual activities, among the persons who come to a clinic, is no measure of the frequency of similar disturbances outside of clinics. The impression that such "sexual irregularities" as "excessive" masturbation, pre-marital intercourse, responsibility for a pre-marital pregnancy, extra-marital intercourse, mouth-genital contacts, homosexual activity, or animal intercourse, always produce psychoses and abnormal personalities is based upon the fact that the persons who do go to professional sources for advice are upset by these things.

It is unwarranted to believe that particular types of sexual behavior are always expressions of psychoses or neuroses. In actuality, they are more often expressions of what is biologically basic in mammalian and anthropoid behavior, and of a deliberate disregard for social convention. Many of the socially and intellectually most significant persons in our histories, successful scientists, educators, physicians, clergymen, business men, and persons of high position in governmental affairs, have socially taboo items in their sexual histories, and among them they have accepted nearly the whole range of so-called sexual abnormalities. Among the socially most successful and personally best adjusted persons who have contributed to the present study, there are some whose rates of outlet are as high as those in any case labelled nymphomania or satyriasis in the literature, or recognized as such in the clinic.

Clinical subjects who have such unusual items in their histories often do present psychopathologies—that is why they have gone to the clinics. But the presence of particular behavior, or the existence of a high rate, is not the abnormality which needs explanation. The real clinical problem is the discovery and treatment of the personality defects, the mental difficulties, the compulsions, and the schizophrenic conflicts which lead particular individuals to crack up whenever they depart from averages or socially accepted custom, while millions of other persons embrace the very same behavior, and may have as high rates of activity, without personal or social disturbance. It has been too simple a solution to discover the sexual items in a patient's history, to consider them symptoms of a neurosis, and to diagnose the disturbance as the outcome of the departure from the established mores. It is much more difficult to discover the bases of the unstable personalities that are upset by such sexual departures, and to treat the basic defects rather than to patch up the particular issues over which the disturbances occur. Clinicians would have more incentive for using such an approach if they were better acquainted with the normal frequencies of the so-called abnormal types of activity, and if, at least as far as sex is concerned, they could acquire a wider acquaintance with the sexual histories of well-adjusted individuals.

Most of the complications which are observable in sexual histories are the result of society's reactions when it obtains knowledge of an individual's behavior, or the individual's fear of how society would react if he were discovered. In various societies, under various circumstances, and (as we shall later show) even at various social levels of the population living in a particular town, the sex mores are fundamentally different. The way in which each group reacts to a particular sort of history determines the "normality" or "abnormality" of the individual's behavior—in that particular group (Benedict 1934). Whatever the moral interpretation (as in Moore 1943), there is no scientific reason for considering particular types of sexual activity as intrinsically, in their biologic origins, normal or abnormal. Yet scientific classifications have been nearly identical with theologic classifications and with the moral pronouncements of the English common law of the fifteenth century. This, in turn, as far as sex is concerned, was based on the medieval ecclesiastic law which was only a minor variant of the tenets of ancient Greek and Roman cults, and of the Talmudic law (Angus 1925, May 1931). Present-day legal determinations of sexual acts which are acceptable, or "natural," and those which are "contrary to nature" are not based on data obtained from biologists, nor from nature herself. On the contrary, the ancient codes have been accepted by laymen, jurists, and scientists alike as the ultimate sources of moral evaluations, of present-day legal procedure, and of the list of subjects that may go into a textbook of abnormal psychology. In no other field of science have scientists been satisfied to accept the biologic notions of ancient jurists and theologians, or the analyses made by the mystics of two or three thousand years ago. Either the ancient philosophers were remarkably well-trained psychologists, or modern psychologists have contributed little in defining abnormal sexual behavior.

The reactions of our social organization to these various types of behavior are the things that need study and classification. The mores, whether they concern food, clothing, sex, or religious rituals, originate neither in accumulated experience nor in scientific examinations of objectively gathered data. The sociologist and anthropologist find the origins of such customs in ignorance and superstition, and in the attempt of each group to set itself apart from its neighbors. Pyschologists have been too much concerned with the individuals who depart from the group custom. It would be more important to know why so many individuals conform as they do to such ancient custom, and what psychology is involved in the preservation of these customs by a society whose individual members would, in most cases, not attempt to defend all of the specific items in that custom. Too often the study of behavior has been little more than a rationalization of the mores masquerading under the guise of objective science.

While this problem will be met again in other places, the present discussion of frequencies of total sexual outlet provides a good opportunity for understanding the futility of classifying individuals as normal or abnormal, or well-adjusted or poorly adjusted, when in reality they may be nothing more than frequent or rare, or conformists or non-conformists with the socially pretended custom.

FACTORS EFFECTING VARIATION

Morphologic differences between individuals are the product of both hereditary and environmental factors. Differences in behavior, on the other hand, are dependent not only upon hereditary morphology and upon the direct effects of environment on that anatomy, but upon psychologic conditioning and social pressures as well. Because of the larger number of factors involved, variation in behavior is much greater than variation in anatomic structures.

The most important biologic factors affecting the nature and frequency of sexual response in the human animal are the hereditary forces which account for the differences between male and female. Within either of these sexes, heredity must also account for some of the variation in sensory structures and in the mechanisms which are concerned with emotional response; but there is little precise information on this point. Variation within the lifetime of a single individual is effected by such biologic factors as age, general metabolic level, nutrition (Miles 1919, Jackson 1925), vitamins (Biskind and Falk 1943, Moore 1942), general health, changes in neurologic conditions, and still other situations. Age is the one biologic factor that most strongly affects variation in the sex life of an individual and which, therefore, accounts for the differences between populations of different age (Chapter 7). Sex hormones are the biologic factors with which there has been the most experimentation. In general, an increased avail-ability of male hormone (up to the point of its optimum effect) increases the frequency of sexual activity (Hamilton 1937, Moore 1942, Pratt 1942, Lisser and Curtis 1943, Heller, Nelson and Roth 1943). Less often noted in the literature and less widely utilized for experimentation, thyroid hormones produce, if anything, more marked results, and our histories include some persons who have had the intensity of their sex drive and the frequency of their activity considerably increased by the administration of thyroid extracts. Since thyroid so directly affects the general metabolic level, it is probable that its influence on sexual frequencies is by way of its relation to metabolism in general rather than through any immediate action of the hormone. The master gland of the hormonal system, the pituitary, regulates both thyroid and sex glands and thus (probably in this indirect fashion only) affects the sexual activity of the individual.

Psychologic conditioning accounts for a larger part of the variation in behavior in a population. All living organisms, from the lowest to the highest, are modified by the experiences through which they pass. This modifiability is one of the intrinsic qualities of living protoplasm. In any creature with a central nervous system which is as highly developed as that found in the vertebrates, particularly in the primates, this conditioning becomes a paramount factor in determining the animal's behavior. Whether an individual is located at some lower point or at a higher point on the total curve of outlets depends in part upon the experience which he has previously had and the incentive which that experience provides for a repetition or avoidance of further activity. Whether an individual depends upon masturbation or heterosexual intercourse for his pre-marital outlet depends in part upon the early experience he happens to have had. Whether exclusively heterosexual or exclusively homosexual patterns are followed, or whether both heterosexual and homosexual outlets are utilized in his history, depends in part upon the circumstance of early experience.

A third group of factors effecting variation in human sexual behavior is the sociologic group. As later chapters in this volume will show, the mores are the prime forces which produce variation in the sources of sexual outlet in different groups. Patterns of sexual behavior are, in an astonishingly high percentage of the cases, merely reflections of the patterns of the particular social level to which an individual belongs. In most cases, the individual rationalizes his particular pattern and thinks that he himself has logically chosen the regimen which is most satisfactory, socially profitable, or morally right; but mores which are many hundreds of years old are, in reality, the sources of most of these decisions.

There are, then, a variety of factors which may modify the frequency and sources of sexual activity within the lifetime of a single individual; but within any limited period of time—within a five-year period, for instance—changes are effected chiefly by physical health and by modifications of situations which affect the opportunity for sexual contact. Most individuals maintain a surprisingly constant position on the outlet curve for periods of several years, changing mostly because of advancing age.

LOW FREQUENCIES AND SUBLIMATION

It is not simple to determine the extent to which an individual's total outlet represents something less than the rate to which he would rise if there were no restrictions on his behavior. In a few cases, however, it is possible to make some analyses. The rates of unmarried males between the ages of 16 and 20 average 3.35 (based on 2868 histories, corrected for the U. S. Census distribution) while the rates for married males of the same age group average 4.83 (Table 60). The difference of 1.5 ejaculations per week is to a considerable extent dependent upon the social restrictions on pre-marital activity (Chapter 8). It is probable that the biologic capacity of the average younger male is even higher than 4.8 per week, for even in marriage there is considerable interference with sexual performance. Periods of menstruation and pregnancy cause interruption of activity. Most males would have intercourse more frequently if their spouses were more interested, if other occupations did not interfere, if business routines that take precedence over intercourse did not leave one physically and mentally fatigued by the time sexual contacts are available. The human animal usually demands a certain privacy which is not always available when intercourse or other outlets are most desired; society tries to restrict all sexual activities to monogamous relations; and moral codes put a taint on many sorts of sexual gratification. It seems safe to assume that daily orgasm would be within the capacity of the average human male, and that the more than daily rates which have been observed for some primate species (Sokolowsky 1923, Bingham 1928, Yerkes and Elder 1936, Carpenter 1942, Young and Orbison 1944), could be matched by a large portion of the human population if sexual activity were unrestricted. The males who are astounded to find that 7.6 per cent of the population does, in actuality, have daily or more than daily outlet are, in most cases, simply unaware of their own capacities. Since this percentage of the males already has daily rates, in spite of the restrictions on their behavior, it is probable that such a percentage of the population would, under optimal conditions, be involved in still more frequent activity during the first five or ten years of their adolescent and adult lives.

In another study we will present data on the relation of sexual and physical activity. There is no invariable correlation, and the list of top athletes includes persons with both low and high rates of sexual outlet. On the whole it is evident that general good health and, therefore, the physical activity which engenders good health, may contribute to an increase in the frequency of sexual performance. Only physical exercise which is carried to the point of exhaustion interferes with sexual as well as other sorts of reactions.

Sexual abstinence for short periods of time, such as a few days or weeks, is of common occurrence; but average frequencies as low as once in two weeks, or lower, occur in only 11.2 per cent of the males under 31 years of age (Table 40). Average frequencies ranging between 0.0 and once in ten weeks (for any five-year period under 31 years of age) occur in only about 2.9 per cent of the population. There is a steady increase in the number of low-rating males after age 35. The list may include some whose pruderies led them to understate the frequency of their sexual activity; but this is more likely to be true among the females, and it is probably not true of more than an insignificantly small portion of the male population, for most males are inclined to be ashamed of very low rates of activity. On the other hand, the list of inactive males includes some persons of such superior scientific and other professional training that there can be no question that their statements were as complete and accurate as could be made. The low-rating males have all sorts of educational, religious, and social backgrounds (Table 41). Larger segments of the low-rating population come, however, from persons with lower grade school education (many of whom are of lower intellectual capacity and dull sexually as well as mentally); from persons who are religiously most active (especially devout Catholics and Orthodox Jews); and particularly from males who are late in arriving at adolescence (Chapter 9).

An examination of these cases of low outlet should give some information on the incidence of so-called sublimation. The concept, ascribed by the psychoanalysts to Freud (Brill, in Freud 1938), implies that it is possible for an individual to divert his sexual energies to such "higher levels" of activity as art, literature, science, and other socially more acceptable channels. The concept is, of course, much older than Freud. Its affinity to Christian, Hebraic, Greek, and more ancient asceticism is betrayed by its recognition of social values, and confirmed by the speed with which moral leaders of all denominations have adopted the term to cover everything that Freud originally intended, and abstinence, self-control, stern suppression, and the rest of the ascetic virtues as well. One can hardly object if a supposedly scientific concept has been turned into a moral issue, when the supposedly scientific concept amounted, in the first place, to little more than a formalization of an age-old tenet of several religions. Its original presentation (Freud, 1938 transl.) was dogmatic and without supporting data, and its subsequent treatment has usually involved little more than a faithful acceptance of the doctrine (*e.g.*, Henry 1938, Brown 1940, Allen 1940, Young 1940, Brill 1944).

The importance of a soundly scientific critique of the whole theory of sublimation can hardly be over-emphasized. A great many persons have tried to establish their sexual lives on the assumption that sublimation is possible and the outcome desirable. In the histories available in the present study there are many cases of individuals who make definite and distinct, and sometimes heroic, efforts (also see Brockman 1902) to control their responses and who, in actuality, reduce the frequencies of their orgasms considerably below the levels which they otherwise would attain. But it still remains to be determined whether these persons turn their sexual energies into "higher" things, as nervous energy is shunted from one to another portion of a nervous system, or electricity short-circuited into new paths and channels. If sublimation is a reality, it should be possible to find individuals whose erotic responses have been reduced or eliminated, *without nervous disturbance*, as a result of an expenditure of energy in utterly non-sexual activities. It does not suffice to cite artists, or statesmen, or other busy persons as cases of sublimation, merely because they are energetic in the pursuit of their non-sexual professions. Certainly no one who actually knew the sexual histories of particular artists would have thought of using them as illustrations of sexually sublimated people. It is not sufficient to cite sexually apathetic or frigid women as examples of sublimation with no regard to the high incidence of relatively unresponsive females who never had any appreciable amount of sexual energy to be diverted. There must be a determination, based on an objective and thorough psychologic, psychoanalytic, and physiologic examination, of the incidence of persons of proved sexual capacity who have expended at least part of that energy in non-sexual activities, and whose energies are not merely dulled or suppressed.

We, in the present study, are not qualified to make all of these necessary analyses. It is possible, however, to draw attention to the sorts of cases that might conceivably serve as instances of sublimation, and to show the presence of other factors that must be taken into account in analyzing such histories. The most likely cases are those with unusually low rates of outlet. There are 179 males in our series who are under 36 years of age and whose rates have averaged once in two weeks, or lower, for periods of at least five years. These are the males whose histories would be most likely to show evidence of sublimation. There may be high-rating individuals whose activities would be still more frequent if they were not sublimated, but such cases will be more difficult to recognize and to analyze.

179 MALES WITH LOW OUTLET

GROUP	POPULATION IN TOTAL STUDY	LOW RATING CASES	% OF POPULATION
AGES INVOLVED			
Adol.–15	4102	138	3.4
16–20	3836	80	2.1
21–25	2642	47	1.8
26–30	1405	25	1.8
31–35	950	22	2.3
EDUCATIONAL LEVEL			
Grades 0–4	173	19	11.0
5–8	729	45	6.2
High School 9–12	724	25	3.5
College 13–16	1413	43	3.0
Professional 17+	1063	47	4.4
OCCUPATIONAL CLASS			
1. Underworld	81	2	2.5
2. Day Laborers	708	44	6.2
3. Semi-skilled Laborers	839	54	6.4
4. Skilled Laborers	287	21	7.3
5. Lower White Collar	1116	41	3.7
6. Upper White Collar	1288	45	3.5
7. Professional	595	29	4.9
8. Business Executive	26	1	3.8
RELIGION			
Protestant: Inactive	2310	89	3.9
Protestant: Active	834	51	6.1
Catholic: Inactive	303	9	3.0
Catholic: Active	173	13	7.5
Jewish: Inactive	436	10	2.3
Jewish: Active	64	6	9.4
Total: Inactive	3049	108	3.5
Total: Active	1071	70	6.5
AGE AT ONSET OF ADOLESCENCE			
9–12	1252	25	2.0
13	1339	40	3.0
14	1093	74	6.8
15	281	19	6.8
16+	104	8	7.7

Table 41. Social backgrounds of low-rating males

Every age and every educational, religious, and social background are represented. Larger segments of the low-rating population come from poorly educated and religiously devout persons, and from males who became adolescent at late ages.

(1) Among these 179 males with the lowest rates, there are a few individuals (9 males = 5.0%) who are in such poor health, or otherwise so incapacitated by structural, hormonal, or other physical deficiencies, that all heavy expenditures of energy are impossible or held at a minimum. At ages over 45 there is a fair number of cases of impotency, and at younger ages there are a few males (4 cases cited in the previous chapter) who have been totally impotent throughout their lives for physical or physiologic reasons. There are more cases of younger males who are impotent under particular situations; but at ages under 36, neither erectal nor ejaculatory impotence accounts for more than a few stray cases of low rates of outlet. Other physical deficiencies are involved in the 9 cases which belong in this list.

(2) There is another group of males (at least 52.5% of the above tabulation) who are apathetic. They never, at any time in their histories, have given evidence that they were capable of anything except low rates of activity. These are persons who would be described, figuratively, as "low in sex drive." Whether the factors are biologic, psychologic, or social, it is certain that such persons exist. After these apathetic persons have had orgasm, they may go for some days or weeks without further arousal. There are few if any psychologic stimuli which will excite them, and even when these males deliberately put themselves in erotic situations which involve active petting and genital manipulation they may be unable to respond more than once in several weeks. This situation is even more often found among females, 30 per cent of whom are more or less sexually unresponsive. Such fundamentally apathetic persons are the ones who are most often moral (conforming with the mores), most insistent that it is a simple matter to control sexual response, and most likely to offer themselves as examples of the possibility of the diversion of probably nonexistent sexual energies. But such inactivity is no more sublimation of sex drive than blindness or deafness or other perceptive defects are sublimation of those capacities.

There is an inclination among psychiatrists to consider all unresponding individuals as inhibited, and there is a certain scepticism in the profession of the existence of people who are basically low in capacity to respond. This amounts to asserting that all people are more or less equal in their sexual endowments, and ignores the existence of individual variation. No one who knows how remarkably different individuals may be in morphology, in physiologic reactions, and in other psychologic capacities, could conceive of erotic capacities (of all things) that were basically uniform throughout a population. Considerable psychiatric therapy can be wasted on persons (especially females) who are misjudged to be cases of repression when, in actuality, at least some of them never were equipped to respond erotically.

(3) In this list of relatively inactive males there are 35 cases (19.6%) who were delayed in starting activity, but whose rates were abruptly and materially increased as soon as they made their first socio-sexual contacts. As their later performances demonstrated, their earlier rates were low only because their capacities had not been awakened. Having once been conditioned by sexual experience, these males subsequently found it difficult to get along without regular sexual outlet. Such histories are not cases of sublimation.

(4) There are many cases of males of proved sexual capacity who are suddenly forced into relative inactivity by being deprived of opportunities for outlet. Sometimes this results in nervous disturbance; but where the individuals are effectively removed from sources of erotic arousal, most of them are able to adjust to the lower rates. This is best illustrated by the many hundreds of histories which we have from men who have been confined to penal institutions, some of them for periods of as much as twenty or twenty-five years. In a prison, there may be opportunity for such outlets as masturbation, nocturnal emission, the homosexual, or a stray experience of some other sort; but the sum total of sexual activity is very much below that found in similar groups outside of an institution. In a short-time prison, the majority of the men do not accept homosexual contacts, and there are a great many who, coming from a social level in which masturbation is taboo (Chapter 10) and from a social level where nocturnal emissions are at a minimum (Chapters 10, 15), may go for long periods of months, or for a year or more, without ejaculation. A few of these men are nervously disturbed as a result of their lack of outlet; but most of them live comfortably enough, apparently because there is little erotic arousal which needs to be relieved by orgasm. The men in such institutions regularly insist that there is very little if any arousal from conversation, printed pictures, descriptions in literature, or anything short of actual contact with a sexual partner. Educated persons are commonly misled by the constant discussion of sex for which prisons, armies, factories, and other places of partial restraint are notorious. Academically trained students are too prone to interpret such situations in terms of their own, highly conditioned, responses. For the more poorly educated portion of the population, however, there is a minimum of erotic fantasy, and 91.5 per cent of all of those committed to penal institutions never go beyond high school in their education (U. S. Census 1940). In consequence, these prison males do not illustrate sublimation, for they have little or no aroused sexual energy which needs dissipation. This is such a special situation that prison cases are not included in the above list of low-rating cases, and frequencies in prison have not entered into any of the calculations of the rates of outlet in the present volume.

There are, however, males who represent cases of deprivation under more usual situations, such as divorce, the illness of the wife, and other causes; and these constitute 8.3 per cent of the low-rating list given above.

(5) Finally there are timid or inhibited individuals in this low-rating list, who are afraid of approaching other persons for sexual relations, afraid of condemnation were they to engage in such socially taboo behavior as masturbation, pre-marital intercourse, or the homosexual; or afraid of their own self condemnation if they were to engage in almost any sort of sexual activity. This accounts for more than half of the low-rating list (58.1%). Some of these individuals become paranoid in their fear of moral transgression, or its outcome. There are 9 cases of attempted suicide among the histories of males who were trying to suppress some aspect of their sexual activity. These individuals readily acquire and accept every super-stitious tale concerning the consequences of masturbation; ascribe every pimple and stomach ache, their limitations in height and their failures in school or business to their occasional departures from the moral code; and seek religious confession, penance, and introverted solitude as means of avoiding further sin. Many of these individuals in actuality reduce the frequencies of their orgasms considerably below the level of the rest of the population.

If they are better educated persons, and especially if they have some command of psychology, these inhibited persons rationalize more adroitly, admit that masturbation does no physical harm, but reason that it is bad to continue a habit that may subsequently make one unfit for normal marital relations, decide that pre-marital intercourse similarly unfits one for making satisfactory sexual adjustments in marriage, that the homo-sexual is a biologic abnormality, and that extra-marital intercourse inevitably destroys homes. Even among scientifically trained persons, these propositions are offered as excuses for their sexual inactivity. Of 58 male psychologists who have contributed histories to the present study, 57 have defended one or more of these theses, in spite of the fact that no one of these conclusions has ever been justified by objective data that would satisfy scientists in any field that did not have a moral (traditional) impli-cation. Out of 74 male psychiatrists who have contributed, 70 defend one or more of these same prejudices. These are all rationalizations, clutched at in support of a sexual suppression that is too often mistaken for sublimation.

Recently we have secured histories from a segregated group of males, a high percentage of whom are sexually restrained. This has provided an unusual opportunity to see the results of suppression on a large scale. The group is not at all typical of the American population as a whole. It is drawn largely (82.8%) from males in their twenties (Table 42), almost wholly from college trained (90.3%) and white collar levels (93.3%), and almost wholly from Protestant religious groups (96.3%), with 43.3 per cent of the group actively religious, which is about double the number of actively religious persons in the total population on which the present study is based. The mean frequencies of total outlet of the segregated group, both in the single and the married histories, are between a half and two-thirds of the frequencies for corresponding age groups in the total population. The incidences of masturbation and of homosexual contacts in the group are almost identical with those found in the total population, but the incidence of pre-marital intercourse is definitely less (74% of the figure for the total population). The group has been honored by several religious organizations for its idealism and its refusal to allow any interference with

OUTLET	CASES IN RESTRAINED GROUP	A RESTRAINED GROUP OF 134 MALES COMPARED WITH U. S. POPULATION	
		RESTRAINED GROUP	U. S. POPULATION
Total outlet		Mean frequency	Mean frequency
Single males, at age:			
Adol.–15	130	2.26	3.17
16–20	132	2.11	3.30
21–25	115	1.68	3.04
26–30	36	1.65	2.94
Married males, at age:			
21–25	22	3.10	4.14
26–30	24	2.58	3.51
		Accumulative incidence %	Accumulative incidence %
Masturbation	124	92.5	93.0
Pre-marital intercourse	60	44.8	85.0
Homosexual	44	32.8	35.0

Table 42. Sexual outlet in a restrained group of males
Compared with the U. S. population of same age and marital status.

its ideals. Many of these males are belligerently defensive of their sexual philosophy. Some of them are vociferous in claiming that they are perfect examples of sublimation, and many outsiders look on the group as sexually sublimated. However, several of the members of the group were receiving psychiatric attention at the time of our interviews, and several psychiatrists have reached the conclusion that a high percentage of the whole group is neurotic.

If then, from the list of low-rating males, one removes those who are physically incapacitated, natively low in sexual drive, sexually unawakened in their younger years, separated from their usual sources of sexual stimulation, or timid and upset by their suppressions, there are simply no cases which remain as clear-cut examples of sublimation. Whether there is partial sublimation among individuals with higher rates of outlet, it would be much harder to determine. Whether there is more real sublimation among certain groups, as among celibate priests, is a matter that cannot be known until we have an adequate sample of histories from such groups. Certain it is that among the many males who have contributed to the present sample, sublimation is so subtle, or so rare, as to constitute an academic possibility rather than a demonstrated actuality. In view of the widespread and easy acceptance of the theory, and the efforts that such a large proportion of the population has made to achieve this goal, one might have expected better evidence of its existence, at least among the sexually least active 5 per cent of the males in the population.

HIGH FREQUENCIES OF OUTLET

Since most people have only average rates of sexual outlet, many of them will question the accuracy of the data on persons with high frequencies. Pearl, for instance (1925), considered high frequencies as "extremely rare," although he emphasized the fact that "they do occur often enough to show that apparently there really does exist a small but definite 'sexual athlete' class of men, of which Casanova may be regarded as the classic prototype in literature." However, our large sample shows that, far from being rare, individuals with frequencies of 7 or more per week constitute a not inconsiderable segment (7.6%) of any population.

There are high-rating persons of every sort, including some who are scientifically trained, and other reliable individuals whose records cannot be doubted. This high-rating population is described in Table 43. In each age group under 30, there are more than four times as many males as in any group over 50. More or less equal percentages of the high-rating males come from single, married, and previously married groups. Every age, educational, and social group is included. It is important to realize that an individual may be very active sexually, and of considerable significance socially. All religious groups, Protestant, Catholic, and Jewish, are duly represented by both their inactive and devout members. Nearly half (49.4%) of all the underworld males who have contributed to this study appear in this high-rating group, and this is further evidence for believing that most individuals could be much more active sexually if they were as unrestrained as the group that openly and regularly defies the law and the social convention. Fewer high-rating males come from the college level, but a somewhat larger number comes from the group that has professional training. Upper white-collar classes are rather less often represented. The boys who are earliest adolescent, by age twelve at the latest, are the ones who most often have the highest rates of outlet in the later years of their lives.

GROUP	POPULAT. IN TOTAL STUDY	OUTLETS 7–13 PER WK.		OUTLETS 14–20 PER WK.		OUTLETS 21+ PER WK.		TOTAL WITH HIGH RATES	
		Cases	%	Cases	%	Cases	%	Cases	%
AGES INVOLVED									
Adol.–15	4102	224	5.5	45	1.1	13	0.3	282	6.9
16–20	3836	209	5.4	45	1.2	17	0.4	271	7.1
21–25	2642	148	5.6	33	1.3	16	0.6	197	7.5
26–30	1405	76	5.4	21	1.5	10	0.7	107	7.6
31–35	950	27	2.8	12	1.3	6	0.6	45	4.7
36–40	690	16	2.3	6	0.9	4	0.6	26	3.8
41–45	473	9	1.9	6	1.3	0		15	3.2
46–50	320	9	2.8	3	0.9	0		12	3.8
51–55	206	3	1.5	1	0.5	0		4	1.9
56–60	117	2	1.7	0		0		2	1.7
61+	134	2	1.5	0		0		2	1.5
MARITAL STATUS									
Single	8159	545	6.7	113	1.4	35	0.4	693	8.5
Married	2665	179	6.7	56	2.1	30	1.1	265	9.9
Post-Marital	754	45	6.0	14	1.9	8	1.1	67	8.9
EDUCATIONAL LEVEL									
Grades 0–4	173	17	9.8	10	5.8	3	1.7	19	11.0
5–8	729	84	11.5	33	4.5	11	1.5	109	15.0
H. S. 9–12	724	88	12.2	19	2.6	9	1.2	99	13.7
College 13–16	1413	121	8.6	14	1.0	4	0.3	126	8.9
Professional 17+	1063	100	9.4	11	1.0	6	0.6	109	10.3
OCCUPATIONAL CLASS									
1. Underworld	81	31	38.3	15	18.5	7	8.6	40	49.4
2. Day Laborers	708	87	12.3	32	4.5	12	1.7	109	15.4
3. Semi-skilled	839	102	12.2	46	5.5	18	2.2	135	16.1
4. Skilled Laborers	287	34	11.8	8	2.8	0		35	12.2
5. Lower White Collar	1116	108	9.7	18	1.6	7	0.6	119	10.7
6. Upper White Collar	1288	106	8.2	15	1.2	6	0.5	115	8.9
7. Professional	595	72	12.1	7	1.2	5	0.8	74	12.4
AGE, ONSET ADOL.									
9–10	91	13	14.3	1	1.1	1	1.1	13	14.3
11–12	1161	147	12.7	43	3.7	16	1.4	175	15.1
13	1339	117	8.7	23	1.7	6	0.4	131	9.8
14	1093	94	8.6	17	1.6	9	0.8	103	9.4
15	281	30	10.7	2	0.7	1	0.4	31	11.0
16+	104	7	6.7	1	1.0	0	0.0	8	7.7
RELIGION									
Protestant, Inactive	2310	242	10.5	54	2.3	20	0.9	271	11.7
Protestant, Active	834	54	6.5	12	1.4	3	0.4	62	7.4
Catholic, Inactive	303	54	17.8	11	3.6	5	1.7	62	20.5
Catholic, Active	173	10	5.8	4	2.3	0	0.0	14	8.1
Jewish, Inactive	436	50	11.5	6	1.4	5	1.1	53	12.2
Total Inactive	3049	346	11.3	71	2.3	30	1.0	386	12.7
Total Active	1071	64	6.0	16	1.5	3	0.3	76	7.1

Table 43. Social backgrounds of high-rating males

Every age and every educational, religious, and social background are represented. Higher percentages come from younger age groups, from religiously less active groups, and from the underworld.

In explanation of these high rates of outlet, it is to be noted that it is a common pattern for many persons to engage in intercourse every night or practically every night in the week; and there are many married persons, especially at lower social levels, who have intercourse quite regularly both in the evening upon retiring and in the morning upon awakening. Where the occupation allows the male spouse to return home at noon, contacts may also occur at that hour of the day and, consequently, there is a regular outlet of fourteen to twenty-one times per week. In the same fashion, masturbation, the homosexual, and still other sorts of sexual activities may acquire daily or more than daily frequencies.

An even larger portion of this high-rating group secures its outlet in multiple ejaculations during a limited number of sexual contacts. The existence of multiple orgasm in the pre-adolescent male has been discussed in Chapter 5. A similar situation occurs, although less frequently, in the adult (Table 48, Figure 36). Most males occasionally ejaculate more than once; but there are males who regularly do so, practically every time there is a socio-sexual contact. Of the white males who have contributed to the present study and who have had experience in intercourse, 380 have had a history of regular, multiple ejaculation at some period in adolescence or in adult years. Sometimes these ejaculations, totaling two or three or more, are spread over several hours in a single evening, with more or less continuous sex play; but in a fair number of cases it is habitual for a male to ejaculate two or more times in continuous intercourse and while maintaining a continuous erection (it is mentioned in Kahn 1939:110). Some physiologists have questioned the possibility of such a performance. Since multiple ejaculation in the male depends upon glandular secretion, there are complications which are not involved in the female, where multiple orgasm is better known. Nevertheless, scepticism over the possibility of repeated response in the male merely emphasizes the incapacity of even scientifically trained persons to comprehend that others may be made differently from themselves. Both the testimony of the performing husbands and the collaborative record obtained from their wives or other female partners, leave no doubt that multiple orgasm, usually with ejaculation, is the regular routine in a fair number of cases. Data from males with homosexual experience indicate that in such relations it is not at all infrequent for a younger male to proceed to a second or a third orgasm in a matter of five or ten minutes. Most of these multiple climaces occur in younger males, but not all of them do so, as the age distribution in Table 48 will show. Very few adult males are able to reach more than four or five climaces in any limited period of time; an occasional teen-age boy will reach six or more; and a quarter of the pre-adolescents for whom we have any record of orgasm were able to go beyond five, and in some cases to as many as ten, twenty, or more in a few hours' time (Table 33). Wherever there is multiple orgasm, the total frequencies of outlet are multiplied, and these cases account for nearly 30 per cent of the population which lies on the higher portions of the curve.

Among the more active cases in our histories, there are male prostitutes whose capacity to perform may determine the level of their income. Male prostitutes may be involved in heterosexual prostitution, which is rare, or in homosexual prostitution, which is much more frequent. In male prostitution, the prostitute usually experiences orgasm. This is in contrast to the situation among female prostitutes, most of whom go into prostitution for the sake of the money that may be earned. In most cases the female prostitute is not aroused and does not experience orgasm during a

SIX MOST ACTIVE MALES

Maximum frequencies during 30 continuous years, in best authenticated cases

Marital status during maximum activity
    Married (4), single (2)
Religion
    Active Protestant (1), inactive Protestant (4), inactive Jewish (1)
Educational level in years
    3, 16, 17, 20 (3 cases)
Occupations
    WPA and labor, physician (2), scientific worker, educator, lawyer
Ages at onset of adolescence
    11 (2 cases), 12, 13 (2 cases), 14
30-year period involved
    11–40 (2 cases), 12–41, 13–42, 16–45, 21–50
Years of maximum frequency
    At ages 11–15, 12–15, 13–15, 21–25, 36–40 (2 cases)
Average rates per week for 30-year period
    10.6, 11.7, 13.6, 14.0, 17.8, 33.1
Range in rate during 30-year period
    5.3 to 19.6, 11.6 to 31.6, 9.0 to 13.0, 14.7 to 15.7, 10.0 to 21.5, 25.6 to 37.8
Multiple ejaculation
    1–2, 2 when younger, 2–5, 3 and 4, in each coitus. Two cases never multiple
Chief sources of outlet
    Masturbation, marital intercourse, and extra-marital intercourse
    Masturbation, marital intercourse, and homosexual contacts
    Masturbation and extra-marital intercourse
    Masturbation and pre-marital intercourse
    Masturbation and homosexual outlets
    Marital intercourse only

professional contact. In male prostitution, on the contrary, in some of the techniques that are employed, capacity to achieve erection and ejaculate is a requisite part of the arrangement. Some male prostitutes ejaculate five, six, or more times per day with regularity over long periods of years. While the amount of semen per ejaculation is thereby reduced, there is usually emission, even with such frequent orgasms. The validity of the data on this point depends not only upon the records of the several hundred male prostitutes who have contributed their histories, but also upon the observations of persons who have had contact with them. In a few cases, there are records made by persons who have observed the actual performance of particular male prostitutes from hour to hour, over periods of time, and there is no question that there is frequent arousal and actual ejaculation of semen five or more times per day in some of these cases. One such set of observations concerns a 39-year-old Negro male who had averaged more than three per day from 13 to 39 years of age, and at the latter age was still capable of 6 to 8 ejaculations when the occasion demanded. The average frequencies of such an individual carry the curve of total sexual outlet to unusually high points.

The six white males with the highest long-time averages for a continuous 30-year period deserve further examination, although it should be understood that there is a continuous list of others who grade into these highest cases. The males included in this list all went to considerable pains to give details for each of the periods involved; one is a lawyer, one is an educator, three of them are scientifically trained persons, two of whom had kept diaries or other records; and we have had such extended contact with three of these individuals that we feel considerable reliance can be placed on their data. The six cases are strikingly different in regard to ages involved, in the variability of the rate during the 30-year period, and in the sources of most of the sexual outlet.

Outside of penal institutions and cloistered halls, there are ever-present stimuli to heterosexual response. For the educated portion of the male population, for instance, there are persons of the opposite sex, female wearing apparel which emphasizes and suggests sexual situations, the constant portrayal of these things in magazines, in moving pictures, on billboards, in decorative art, in the plots of printed fiction and stage drama, in the emphasis given to radio performances, in advertisements everywhere, in most poetry and songs, and, more subtly but even more effectively, in all those forms and ceremonies which are accepted as courtesies between the sexes, and in the social traditions connected with marriage. There is, in consequence, constant arousal and regular sexual activity in most males, particularly younger males who are conditioned by any experience, or by the vicariously shared experiences of their fellows. While all males must have known of the regularity of sexual activity in their own histories, the significance of the fact for the population as a whole has never been fully appreciated. The assumption that the unmarried male has only occasional outlet, or that he may go for long periods of time without any sexual activity, is not in accord with the fact. The assumption that there can be such sublimation of erotic impulse as to allow an appreciable number of males to get along for considerable periods of time without sexual activity is not yet substantiated by specific data. For most males, whether single or married, there are ever-present erotic stimuli, and sexual response is regular and high.

Chapter 7

AGE AND SEXUAL OUTLET

In physiology, endocrinology, genetics, and still other fields, biologists often go to considerable pains to restrict their experimental material to animals of particular species, to particular age groups, and to individuals that are reared on a uniform diet and kept under strictly controlled laboratory conditions. Different hereditary strains of a single species may give different results in a physiologic experiment; and, in many laboratories, stocks are restricted to the progeny of particular pairs of pedigreed ancestors. In studies of human behavior, there is even more reason for confining generalizations to homogeneous populations, for the factors that affect behavior are more abundant than those that affect simpler biologic characters, and there are, in consequence, more kinds of populations to be reckoned with. Nevertheless, restrictions of psychologic and sociologic studies to clearly defined groups have rarely been observed (McNemar 1940), perhaps because we have not, heretofore, known what things effect variability in a human population and how important they are in determining what people do.

There are at least eleven factors which are of primary importance in determining the frequency and sources of human sexual outlet. They are sex, race, age, age at onset of adolescence, marital status, educational level, the subject's occupational class, the parental occupational class, rural-urban backgrounds, religious affiliations, and the extent of the subject's devotion to religious affairs. The effects of these factors on the sexual histories of white males are discussed in the present volume. In view of the conclusions that these analyses now afford, it becomes apparent that generalizations concerning any aspect of human sexual behavior are uninterpretable unless they are limited to populations which are clearly defined in regard to the more important of the eleven items listed above.

In the sexual history of the male, there is no other single factor which affects frequency of outlet as much as age. Age affects the source of sexual outlet only indirectly, by way of its relation to marital status, to the availability of social contacts, to the liability to physical fatigue, and to the psychologic fatigue that comes as a result of the repetition of a particular sort of activity. But age more directly affects frequency of outlet. Age is so important that its effects are usually evident, whatever the marital status, the educational level, the religious background, or the other factors which

218

enter the picture. It is logical, therefore, to begin the present analyses with a consideration of this factor.

ADOLESCENT SEXUAL ACTIVITY

As we have previously indicated (Chapter 5), there is sexual activity in the pre-adolescent male which may involve definite erotic arousal and actual orgasm; but the onset of regular sexual performance is usually coincidental with the onset of adolescence. Throughout the remainder of this volume, descriptions of sexual activity will apply to age periods that begin with adolescence and which extend, in the first instance, through 15 years of age, and which are five year periods from that point through the remainder of the individual's history.

Over 95 per cent of the adolescent males are regularly active by 15 years of age (Table 44). Over 99 per cent of the adolescent and older males are active throughout the whole period from 16 to 45. In those 30 years, only 1 or 2 per cent of the male population is without regular and usually frequent outlet. After 45 there is a gradual but distinct drop in the number of active cases. These generalizations apply to all white males, whether single or married, and whatever their educational level or social background.

Maximum Activity. The maximum sexual frequencies (total outlet) occur in the teens. Frequencies then drop gradually but steadily into old age (Table 44, Figure 34). Considering the active, single males in the population, the maximum mean frequencies are almost 3.4 per week (calculated for the U. S. population), which is almost exactly every other day in the week, month, or year (Tables 45, 60, Figures 50–52). This rate is reached between adolescence and 20 years of age.

The means for the married males begin at their highest point, 4.8 per week, between 16 and 20 (Tables 45, 60, Figures 50–52). Few males are married prior to 16, and there is not enough material to calculate statistically significant averages for any married group prior to that age. It is probable that in a population which married at an earlier age, the highest frequency on the curve would come in the earlier adolescent group; but, in our society as it is, the high point of sexual performance is, in actuality, somewhere around 16 or 17 years of age. It is not later. The data which have already been given on the sexual capacity of the pre-adolescent boy (Chapter 5) indicate that the peak of *capacity* occurs in the fast-growing years prior to adolescence; but the peak of *actual performance* is in the middle or later teens.

The earliest serious attempt to determine the age of maximum sexual activity, and the effect of age on sexual performance in the human male, was made by Pearl (1925). For his study, he had data from 213 men (average age 64.53 years) who felt they could recall the frequencies of marital intercourse in their earlier histories. The point of maximum sexual activity

AGE GROUP	CASES	TOTAL OUTLET: FREQUENCY PER WEEK							
		TOTAL SAMPLE POPULATION			ACTIVE IN SAMPLE POPULATION			U. S. POPULATION	
		Range (minus 1)	Mean	Median	% of Total	Mean	Median	Mean: Total Popul.	Mean: Active Popul.
Adol. −15	3905	0.0–29+	2.86± 0.05	2.11	95.1	3.00± 0.05	2.26	3.17	3.36
16–20	3750	0.0–29+	2.87± 0.05	2.17	99.3	2.89± 0.05	2.19	3.32	3.37
21–25	2502	0.0–29+	2.85± 0.06	2.10	99.6	2.86± 0.06	2.11	3.35	3.40
26–30	1310	0.0–29+	3.01± 0.09	2.24	99.5	3.03± 0.09	2.25	3.35	3.38
31–35	879	0.0–29+	2.64± 0.10	1.91	99.7	2.65± 0.10	1.92	2.89	2.90
36–40	628	0.0–22.0	2.36± 0.10	1.73	99.5	2.37± 0.10	1.73	2.36	2.36
41–45	440	0.0–15.0	1.98± 0.11	1.41	99.1	2.00± 0.11	1.42	1.96*	1.98*
46–50	285	0.0–12.0	1.78± 0.12	1.10	97.5	1.82± 0.12	1.15	1.75*	1.78*
51–55	173	0.0–10.0	1.50± 0.14	0.90	96.0	1.57± 0.14	0.96		
56–60	106	0.0–9.0	1.20± 0.15	0.73	95.3	1.26± 0.15	0.79		
61–65	58	0.0–4.0	0.84± 0.16	0.52	81.0	1.04± 0.19	0.71		
66–70	30	0.0–3.0	0.65± 0.24	0.30	73.3	0.88± 0.31	0.48		
71–75	12	0.0–0.5	0.13± 0.07	0.00	41.7	0.30± 0.14	0.30		
76–80	4	0.0– scant	0.01± 0.01	0.00	25.0	0.05	0.10		
81–85	2	0.0	0.00	0.00	0.0	0.00	0.00		
Total	14084	0.0–29+	2.74± 0.02	1.99	97.9	2.80± 0.02	2.04		
Adol. −30	11467	0.0–29+	2.88± 0.03	2.14	98.0	2.94± 0.03	2.20		

Table 44. Total sexual outlet in relation to advancing age

These data are based on the total population, including single, married, and previously married groups. For each group calculated separately, see Table 60. Data for the U. S. population are based on a theoretic group with the marital status and educational levels shown in the U. S. Census for 1940. *Starred items are corrected for marital status only.

for this population was located in the 30–39 year period. For the younger ages, Pearl recorded definitely lower frequencies; but he concluded, as we have with our own data, that "the low frequency exhibited in this [younger] age period is in part and probably mainly an expression of an essentially social factor—lack of opportunity—rather than of anything physiological." Of the men who were married in their twenties, 67 essayed to recall frequencies in that period; and 9 of the men who were married in their teens supplied data for that age. On these limited bases, Pearl concluded that "with approximate equality of opportunity at the different ages the peak of activity is in the 20-29 decade and that thereafter there is a steady decline"; but after inspecting the curve, he theoretically adds that "with unrestricted

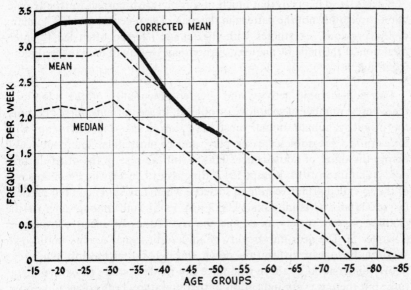

Figure 34. Frequency of total outlet in relation to age

Based on total population, including single, married, and previously married groups. Broken lines represent raw data; the solid black line represents the mean corrected for the U. S. Census distribution.

legitimate opportunity the peak of sex activity is prior to age 20." Our own abundant data push the peak of the curve back, as Pearl predicted, into the late teens. Unfortunately, the conclusions which are more often quoted from the Pearl study are those based on his total population, with its maximal frequency between 30 and 39 years; whereas the curve which he derived from the smaller sample of married males, and his prediction that the maximum activity occurs before the twenties, prove to be the more correct.

Social Significance. The identification of the sexually most active period as late adolescence will come as a surprise to most persons. General opinion would probably have placed it in the middle twenties or later. Certainly the average college student and the town boy of corresponding age will be startled to learn that their younger brothers who are still in high school surpass them in capacity and ofttimes in performance. By law, society provides a source of regular sexual outlet in marriage, in part because it recognizes the sexual need of the older male; but it fails to recognize that the teen-age boys are potentially more capable and often more active than their 35-year old fathers. Even among physicians and biologists, there has been a general opinion that sexual capacity develops gradually in early adolescence, reaches its maximum in the thirties or forties (the "prime of life"), passes a peak somewhere in a period which is considered a male climacteric, and drops abruptly into the inactivity and complete impotence of old age. It so happens that much of this picture is correct for the female, but it is certainly not the pattern in the male. The preoccupation of so many of the previous sex studies with the female has too often led to interpretation of the male by analogy, rather than by way of data taken directly from him.

This considerable activity and greater potentiality of the adolescent male pose a number of sociologic problems. In the normal course of events, the primitive human animal must have started his sexual activities with unrestrained pre-adolescent sex play, and begun regular intercourse well before the onset of adolescence. This is still the case in the other anthropoids (Hamilton 1914, Kempf 1917, Bingham 1928, Nowlis 1941), in some of the so-called primitive human societies which have not acquired particular sex taboos (Malinowski 1929, Ford 1945), and among such of the children in our society as escape the restrictions of social conventions (Chapter 5). The near-universality of adolescent sexual activity in our own Western European civilization down through the eighteenth century is poorly understood by those who have not made a study of earlier literature; but there is every indication in that literature, both sober and erotic, that the high capacity of the younger male was recognized and rather widely accepted until near the Victorian day in England. The problem of sexual adjustment for the younger male is one which has become especially aggravated during the last hundred years, and then primarily in England and in America, under an increasing moral suppression which has coincided with an increasing delay in the age of marriage. This has resulted in an intensification of the struggle between the boy's biologic capacity and the sanctions imposed by the older male who, to put it objectively, is no longer hard-pressed to find a legalized source of sexual contact commensurate with his reduced demand for outlet.

The fact that the unmarried male still manages to find an outlet of 3.4 per week demonstrates the failure of the attempt to impose complete abstinence upon him. The sources of this outlet must be a matter of bewilderment to those who have supposed that most males remained continent until marriage. Nocturnal emissions do not provide any considerable portion of the orgasms (Chapter 15), in spite of the fact that many persons have wished that to be the case. Masturbation is a more frequent outlet among the upper social level males where, during the last two or three decades, it has been allowed as a not too immoral substitute for pre-marital intercourse; but most of the less-educated 85 per cent of the population still consider masturbation neither moral nor normal. For the mass of the unmarried boys, intercourse still provides the chief sexual activity (Chapter 10). This means that the majority of the males in the sexually most potential and most active period of their lives have to accept clandestine or illegal outlets, or become involved in psychologic conflicts in attempting to adjust to reduced outlets. With the data now available, biologists, psychologists, physicians, psychiatrists, and sociologists should be enabled to make better analyses of the problem which has heretofore been imposed on this unmarried male in his middle and late teens, and in his twenties.

The situation is complicated by the fact that the average adolescent girl gets along well enough with a fifth as much sexual activity as the adolescent boy, and the frequency of outlet of the female in her twenties and early thirties is still below that of the average adolescent male. As mothers, as school teachers, and as voting citizens, women are primarily responsible for the care of these boys; and, to a large degree, they are the ones who control moral codes, schedules for sex education, campaigns for law enforcement, and programs for combating what is called juvenile delinquency. It is obviously impossible for a majority of these women to understand the problem that the boy faces in being constantly aroused and regularly involved with his normal biologic reactions.

The mean rate of outlet for the women who are young mothers and high school teachers lies between 0.7 and 2.1 per week (as indicated by preliminary calculations from our unpublished material on the female). Many of these women, including some high school biology teachers, believe that the ninth or tenth grade boy is still too young to receive any sex instruction when, in actuality, he has a higher rate of outlet and has already had a wider variety of sexual experience than most of his female teachers ever will have. Whether there should be sex instruction, and what sort of instruction it should be, are problems that lie outside the scope of an objective scientific study; but it is obvious that the development of any curriculum that faces the fact will be a much more complex undertaking than has been realized by those who think of the adolescent boy as a beginner, relatively inactive, and quite capable of ignoring his sexual development.

Institutional Problems. The legal approach to this problem is, as usual, even less realistic. By making illegal all pre-marital sexual activities except nocturnal emissions and solitary masturbation, English and American law forces most boys, as indicated above, into illicit activity. The chief exceptions are largely in that group that goes on to college, and which, coincidentally, accepts masturbation as a chief source of outlet. Precise incidence figures for the various types of sexual behavior which are illegal are given in later chapters of the present volume. On a specific calculation of our data, it may be stated that at least 85 per cent of the younger male population could be convicted as sex offenders if law enforcement officials were as efficient as most people expect them to be. The stray boy who is caught and brought before a court may not be different from most of his fellows, but the public, not knowing of the near universality of adolescent sexual activity, heaps the penalty for the whole group upon the shoulders of the one boy who happens to be apprehended. This situation presents a considerable dilemma for law enforcement officials and for students of the social organization as a whole.

The problem of sexual adjustment for a younger male who is confined to a mental, penal, or other sort of institution is even more difficult than the problem of the boy who lives outside in society. Administrators who have these younger males in their care are generally bewildered and at a loss to know how to handle their sexual problems. In many cases, the situation is simply tolerated or ignored, and the administrator would prefer not to be aware of the actualities. For this, many people would condemn him; but the problem in an institution for teen-age boys is far more complex than the public or the administration or scientific students have realized. It is obvious that lifetime patterns of sexual behavior are greatly affected by the experiences of adolescence, not only because they are the initial experiences, but because they occur during the age of greatest activity and during the time of the maximum physical capacity of the male. This is the period in which the boy's abilities to make social adjustments, to develop any sort of socio-sexual contacts, and to solve the issues of a heterosexual-homosexual balance, are most involved. Since younger boys have not acquired all of the social traditions and taboos on sex, they are more impressionable, more liable to react *de novo* to any and every situation that they meet. If these adolescent years are spent in an institution where there is little or no opportunity for the boy to develop his individuality, where there is essentially no privacy at any time in the day, and where all his companions are other males, his sexual life is very likely to become permanently stamped with the institutional pattern. Long-time confinement for a younger male is much more significant than a similar period of confinement for an older adult.

The situation is aggravated by the more recent development of the juvenile court. Abundant as the merits of such an institution may be, there are complications involved when a court assumes control of a juvenile for a long period of years, until he is twenty or twenty-one, without, at the same time, considering the problems of sexual adjustment for its ward. The practice of the juvenile court is based on a realization that a child may need long-time training; but it ignores these other aspects of the child's development. The juvenile court protects many a boy from the more severe sentences of the adult laws; but it sometimes holds a juvenile for several years in a correctional institution, or under probation with the court, when the crime involved would have brought only a few months' sentence on an adult criminal charge. Adult institutions often have young inmates who have falsified their age in order to draw the lesser time of a penal commitment. The juvenile court structure is disguised by a verbiage which avoids references to "convictions," "sentences," "penalties," "years to serve," "prisons," or "penal institutions." But in spite of the legal fiction, the fact remains that teen-age boys may, by order of a court, be held in custody, sometimes for several years, in institutions which may be no less repressive and punitive than the average of adult prisons. It is doubtful if many of these committing judges ever consider the juvenile's sexual adjustment when he is sent to such an institution. Within recent years there has been a movement to extend the jurisdiction of the juvenile court to persons as old as eighteen or twenty. There are commendable objectives back of such moves, but no one seems to have considered the sexual problems that will arise from the commitment of a still larger portion of the teen-age population to what are in essence long-time institutions.

The problem is not solved by the common practice of releasing juveniles from institutions on long-time parole; for the terms of the parole are, in most states, practically as strict in regard to sexual activities as the rules of the institution itself. We have numerous histories of boys who have been paroled from such institutions to elderly persons, often on farms, who have no understanding of the problems of sexual adjustment of a younger boy, who do not comprehend the significance of his socio-sexual development during that period, and who believe that such a boy should be kept from making even the simplest sort of social contacts with individuals of the opposite sex. If any large portion of the male population had been raised under such conditions, the implications of the situation would be apparent to everyone; but since the boys who get into institutions represent a small portion and a socially limited portion of the whole population, most people do not have firsthand contacts with them, and have not, therefore, considered the problem of sexual adjustment for institutionalized boys.

Boys who live in private boarding schools, and even boys who attend public or private day schools that are restricted to the single sex, face some of the same sexual problems as the boys in a penal institution.

SEXUAL AGING

Having reached its peak in adolescence, sexual activity in the male drops steadily from then into old age (Tables 44–45, Figures 34–37). As far as human sexuality is concerned, aging begins at least with the onset of adolescence; and if the capacity (rather than the performance) of the

TOTAL OUTLET, MARITAL STATUS, AND AGE

| AGE GROUP | CASES | TOTAL OUTLET: SAMPLE POPULATION | | | | | TOTAL OUTLET: U. S. POPULATION | | |
| | | TOTAL POPULATION | | ACTIVE POPULATION | | | TOTAL POPUL. | ACTIVE POPULATION | |
		Mean Frequency	Median Freq.	Incid. %	Mean Freq.	Median Freq.	Mean Freq.	Incid. %	Mean Freq.
Single Males									
Adol. −15	3012	2.91 ± 0.05	2.18	95.1	3.06	2.33	3.17	94.2	3.36
16–20	2868	2.88 ± 0.05	2.19	99.2	2.90	2.22	3.30	98.8	3.35
21–25	1535	2.67 ± 0.07	1.95	99.1	2.70	1.97	3.04	97.9	3.11
26–30	550	2.63 ± 0.11	1.90	99.3	2.65	1.92	2.94	98.6	2.98
31–35	195	2.38 ± 0.21	1.58	99.0	2.40	1.60	2.44	99.2	2.46
36–40	97	2.07 ± 0.21	1.36	97.9	2.12	1.39	2.00	98.5	2.04
41–45	56	1.79 ± 0.28	0.98	96.4	1.85	1.05	....	....	....
46–50	39	1.88 ± 0.43	1.00	92.3	2.04	1.13	....	....	....
Married Males									
16–20	272	4.67 ± 0.29	3.21	100.0	4.67	3.21	4.83	100.0	4.83
21–25	751	3.90 ± 0.14	2.81	100.0	3.90	2.81	4.14	100.0	4.14
26–30	737	3.27 ± 0.12	2.47	100.0	3.27	2.47	3.51	100.0	3.51
31–35	569	2.73 ± 0.11	2.08	100.0	2.73	2.08	2.90	100.0	2.90
36–40	390	2.46 ± 0.13	1.89	99.7	2.47	1.89	2.42	99.9	2.42
41–45	272	1.95 ± 0.12	1.61	100.0	1.95	1.61	1.95	100.0	1.95
46–50	175	1.79 ± 0.16	1.18	98.9	1.81	1.20	1.80	98.1	1.83
51–55	109	1.54 ± 0.18	1.00	98.2	1.57	1.04	1.54	97.2	1.58
56–60	67	1.08 ± 0.12	0.79	98.5	1.09	0.81	....	....	....

Table 45. Total sexual outlet, marital status, and age

For explanations, see the legend with Table 51 on masturbation.

pre-adolescent is taken into account (Chapter 5), it seems more correct to think of aging as a process that sets in soon after the initiation of growth. The sexagenarian—or octogenarian—who suddenly becomes interested in the problems of aging is nearly a lifetime beyond the point at which he became involved in that process.

It will be interesting to know how many of the other physical and physiologic functions of the human animal reach their prime before the twenties. There are a few studies of physiologic aging, and the data (just as with sexual aging) show a steady degeneration of capacities from the age of the youngest child studied. This, for instance, has been shown for such phenomena as basal heart rate, resting oxygen intake and intake during maximum work, respiratory quotient, and carbon dioxide and lactic acid relations during work (data and references in Robinson 1938). In everyday affairs, it is to be noted that armies and navies, and others who depend on manpower to accomplish work, know that the male in his late teens has physical quality, nervous coordination, and capacity for recovery that are beyond those of the even slightly older man. But research on aging has concerned itself primarily with very old individuals, and too often failed to consider such fundamentals as might be seen only in the beginnings of the processes. Aging studies need to be re-oriented around the origins of biologic decline, and that will mean around pre-adolescence or early adolescence in regard to at least some aspects of human physiology.

From the early and middle teens, the decline in sexual activity is remarkably steady, and there is no point at which old age suddenly enters the picture. The calculations become more significant when the single and married males are analyzed separately (Table 45, Figures 50–52). There are no calculations in all of the material on human sexuality which give straighter slopes than the data showing the decline with age in the total outlet of the single males, or the similar curve showing the decline in outlet for the married males. Starting from a high point of 3.2 for the single males, or 4.8 for the married males, in the middle teens, the mean for both groups drops steadily to about the same point, 1.8 per week at 50 years of age, to 1.3 per week at 60 years, and to 0.9 per week at 70 years of age.

Individual males may show variations from this picture, but departures from a steady decline are exceptions in the population as a whole. There are some clinical studies (Norbury 1934, Mead and Stith 1940, Heller and Myers 1944, Bauer 1944, Werner 1945, et al.) which seem to show that some males reach a period in middle life that may be recognized as a climacteric, accompanied by an abrupt reduction in the frequency of sexual activity; but our own data show no such phenomena for the population as a whole, nor for most of the individuals in the population.

The decline in sexual activity of the older male is partly, and perhaps primarily, the result of a general decline in physical and physiologic capacity. It is undoubtedly affected also by psychologic fatigue, a loss of interest in repetition of the same sort of experience, an exhaustion of the possibilities for exploring new techniques, new types of contacts, new situations. Evidence of this is to be found in numerous cases of older males whose frequencies had dropped materially until they met new partners,

AGE AND NUMBER OF SOURCES OF OUTLET

AGE GROUP	CASES	% OF POPULATION UTILIZING EACH NUMBER OF SOURCES							MEAN NO. OF SOURCES
		NUMBER OF SOURCES							
		0	1	2	3	4	5	6	
Adol.–15	3,378	5.4	25.3	36.7	22.0	8.3	2.0	0.3	2.10 ± 0.02
16–20	3,206	0.8	8.6	27.5	34.1	22.3	6.1	0.6	2.89 ± 0.02
21–25	2,106	0.5	10.5	28.6	35.3	22.8	2.2	0.1	2.77 ± 0.02
26–30	1,062	0.6	15.6	35.3	33.8	13.0	1.6	0.1	2.48 ± 0.03
31–35	704	0.4	23.0	37.5	32.1	6.1	0.8	0.1	2.24 ± 0.04
36–40	511	1.2	30.4	36.5	27.4	3.3	1.2	0.0	2.05 ± 0.04
41–45	358	1.7	36.3	33.5	25.4	2.5	0.6	0.0	1.92 ± 0.05
46–50	235	3.0	38.8	38.7	17.4	1.7	0.4	0.0	1.77 ± 0.06
51–55	151	3.2	43.8	31.1	19.9	1.3	0.7	0.0	1.74 ± 0.07
56–60	98	7.2	50.2	26.6	12.3	3.7	0.0	0.0	1.56 ± 0.10
Adol.–60	11,809	2.2	18.4	32.4	29.5	14.3	2.9	0.3	2.45
U.S.Popul.	10,000	2.0	25.8	33.1	27.4	9.7	1.8	0.1	2.22

AGE GROUP	CASES	ACCUMULATED % WITH EACH NUMBER OF SOURCES						MEDIAN NO. OF SOURCES
		NUMBER OF SOURCES						
		1	2	3	4	5	6	
Adol.–15	3,378	94.6	69.3	32.6	10.6	2.3	0.3	2.53
16–20	3,206	99.2	90.6	63.1	29.0	6.7	0.6	3.38
21–25	2,106	99.5	89.0	60.4	25.1	2.3	0.1	3.30
26–30	1,062	99.4	83.8	48.5	14.7	1.7	0.1	2.96
31–35	704	99.6	76.6	39.1	7.0	0.9	0.1	2.71
36–40	511	98.8	68.8	31.9	4.5	1.2	0.0	2.51
41–45	358	98.3	62.0	28.5	3.1	0.6	0.0	2.36
46–50	235	97.0	58.2	19.5	2.1	0.4	0.0	2.22
51–55	151	96.8	53.0	21.9	2.0	0.7	0.0	2.11
56–60	98	92.8	42.6	16.0	3.7	0.0	0.0	1.87
Adol.–60	11,809	97.8	79.4	47.0	17.5	3.2	0.3	2.91
U. S. Popul.	10,000	98.0	72.2	39.1	11.7	1.9	0.1	2.67

Table 46. Age and number of sources of outlet

Effect of age on the number of different kinds of sexual outlet (masturbation, dreams, intercourse, etc.) utilized in each age period. Based on the whole population involved in the study. Calculations of means for the U. S. population are based on a theoretic population with the age distribution found in the U. S. Census for 1940.

adopted new sexual techniques, or embraced totally new sources of outlet. Under new situations, their rates materially rise, to drop again, however, within a few months, or in a year or two, to the old level. How much of the over-all decline in the rate for the older male is physiologic, how much is based on psychologic situations, how much is based on the reduced availability of contacts, and how much is, among educated people, dependent upon preoccupation with other social or business functions in the professionally most active period of the male's life, it is impossible to say at the present time.

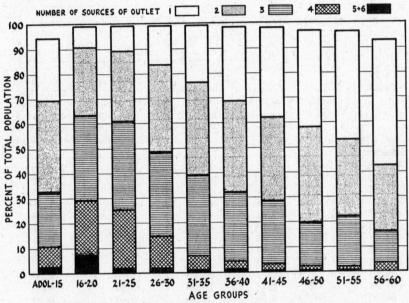

Figure 35. Number of sources of outlet in relation to age

In addition to the decrease in frequency of total outlet, there is a more or less corresponding decrease in frequency for each type of outlet (Tables 51–59, Figures 38–49, 53–88).

The number of sources contributing to the total outlet is highest in the 16–20 year period. After that, some of the sources of outlet are abandoned in some of the histories. From the teens into old age there is a steady decline in number of sources utilized (Table 46, Figure 35). The mean number of sources of outlet for the older teen-age males is 2.9 (a median of 3.4), and there is a fair number of individuals (6.7%) of that age who have five or six kinds of outlet. By 60 years of age, the mean number of sources has dropped to 1.6 (the median is 1.9), and none of these 60-year olds has more than four sources of outlet.

Throughout the life span, there is a steady decline in erotic responsiveness (Table 47). As measured by reactions to particular stimuli, each history in the present study has been rated on a scale which allows some comparison of persons of different degrees of responsiveness. Ratings for the entire white male population average, for instance, 16.4 at 26–30 years of age. The ratings then steadily drop, until they reach a median erotic rating of 3.6 between 66 and 70 years of age.

Frequencies of morning erection show some decline from younger to older age groups (Table 47). The frequency is probably highest in pre-adolescent or early adolescent boys, where we do not have sufficient data.

AGE GROUP	EROTIC RATING	MORNING ERECTIONS, FREQUENCIES PER WEEK	DURATION OF ERECTION, MINUTES	ANGLE OF ERECTION (HIGHER ANGLES INDICATED BY LARGER FIGURES)	MUCOUS SECRETION (GREATER ABUNDANCE INDICATED BY LARGER FIGURE)
Adol.–15	13.64	0.97	12.00	0.74	0.00
16–20	14.51	1.40	42.88	1.02	1.07
21–25	15.82	1.41	54.43	1.06	1.37
26–30	16.35	1.77	53.09	1.10	1.26
31–35	13.92	2.05	47.24	0.94	1.08
36–40	12.60	1.68	40.62	0.91	0.97
41–45	10.31	1.47	31.07	0.95	0.72
46–50	8.73	1.33	29.02	0.78	0.57
51–55	6.44	1.29	21.62	0.81	0.80
56–60	8.17		26.67		0.00
61–65	4.75	1.18	19.50	0.81	0.00
66–70	3.60	0.50	7.00	0.64	0.00
71+	0.00		0.00		0.00

The table heading: AGE AFFECTING PHYSICAL AND PHYSIOLOGIC CHARACTERS — MEDIANS

Table 47. Age affecting physiologic capacities

Data for angle of erection and for mucous secretion were coded, and calculations based on the figures so obtained.

The highest recorded median frequency is 2.05 per week between 31 and 35 years of age. By age 70 the median frequency is down to 0.50, and it drops still lower in older groups. There are a number of cases of persons who were able to record the amount of decrease in frequency of morning erections in their individual histories. There are some data that indicate that the frequency of morning erection is correlated with general physical vigor and, consequently, with frequency of sexual activity (e.g., Hamilton 1937), and that the steady decline in morning erections over the life span is therefore some measure of the decline in intensity of the sex drive in the male.

There is evidence of greater speed in reaching full erection during earlier years, and slower erection during later years, although this has been a difficult matter on which to secure calculable data. We have already drawn attention to the high sensitivity of pre-adolescent boys (Chapter 5). Older adults are definitely slower than youths in their teens and twenties. A number of our adults were able to estimate the changes which had occurred in the course of their lives. This gradual loss in speed of erection of the male becomes evident ten or twenty years before he becomes totally impotent.

The length of time over which erection can be maintained during continuous erotic arousal and before there is an ejaculation, drops from an average of nearly an hour in the late teens and early twenties to 7 minutes in the 66–70 year old group (Table 47). Under prolonged stimulation, as in heterosexual petting or group activities or in protracted homosexual activities, many a teen-age male will maintain a continuous erection for several hours, even when the physical contacts are at a minimum and, in some cases, even after two or three ejaculations have occurred. Very few middle-aged males, and no older ones, are capable of such a performance. A considerable loss in ability to maintain an erection becomes evident some years before the onset of complete impotence.

In any age group there is considerable variation in the angle at which the erect penis is carried on the standing male. The average position, calculated from all ages, is very slightly above the horizontal, but there are approximately 15 to 20 per cent of the cases where the angle is about 45° above the horizontal, and 8 to 10 per cent of the males who carry the erect penis nearly vertically, more or less tightly against the belly. The angle of erection is, in general, higher for males in the early twenties, and lower in more advanced ages (Table 47). Average angles become definitely reduced in males past fifty. It has been difficult to secure quite dependable estimates of angles from the subjects in this study, and it is probable that the changes in medians shown in the table do not express the full extent of the change with advancing age. There are records of 106 older males who recalled a change through the years of their own histories; and these cases indicate a more considerable drop in angle, even from near the vertical to the horizontal or, at later ages, to something below a horizontal position.

With advancing age there is a steady reduction in the amount of precoital mucus which is, in a portion of the population, secreted from the urethra during sexual arousal and before ejaculation. In each age group there are about a third of the males who do not secrete such a mucus. Usually the secretion forms only a single clear drop; but for some males it amounts to several drops, or it is enough to wet the whole glans of the penis, or enough to drip. The greater abundance is found in the twenty-

AGE GROUP	TOTAL POPULATION ACTIVE IN COITUS OR HOMOSEXUAL	CAPACITIES FOR MULTIPLE ORGASM						
		ORGASMS PER CONTACT: NUMBER OF CASES INVOLVED						
		1–2	2	2–3	3	4	5+	Total
Pre-adol.	182		17		18	10	56	101
Adol.–15	792	53	66	14	14	8	3	158
16–20	2092	91	155	32	28	10	2	318
21–25	2886	65	115	30	22	6	2	240
26–30	1225	43	44	15	7	2	1	112
31–35	866	21	20	10	2	3	0	56
36–40	630	13	6	7	2	1	0	29
41–45	431	3	3	2	1	1	0	10
46–50	278	2	3	2	1	1	0	9
51–55	172	2	3	1	1	1	0	8
56–60	101	1	1	0	1	0	0	3
Total	9655	294	433	113	97	43	64	1044

AGE GROUP	TOTAL POPULATION	ORGASMS PER CONTACT. % OF ACTIVE POPULATION INVOLVED						
		1–2	2	2–3	3	4	5+	Total
Pre-adol.	182		9.3		9 9	5.5	30 8	55.5
Adol.–15	792	6.7	8.3	1.8	1.8	1.0	0 4	20.0
16–20	2092	4.3	7.4	1.5	1.3	0.5	0.1	15 2
21–25	2886	2.3	4.0	1.0	0 8	0.2	0.1	8.3
26–30	1225	3.5	3.6	1.2	0.6	0.2	0.1	9.1
31–35	866	2.4	2.3	1 2	0 2	0.3	0.0	6.5
36–40	630	2.1	1.0	1 1	0.3	0.2	0.0	4.6
41–45	431	0.7	0.7	0 5	0.2	0.2	0.0	2 3
46–50	278	0.7	1.1	0.7	0.4	0.4	0.0	3.2
51–55	172	1.2	1.7	0.6	0.6	0.6	0.0	4.7
56–60	101	1.0	1.0	0.0	1.0	0.0	0.0	3.0

Table 48. Multiple orgasm and age

Capacity to have multiple orgasm in each sexual contact rapidly decreases with age the capacities of the pre-adolescent males and males in their teens being far beyond those of older adults. Table includes 380 males who regularly have multiple climax in intercourse.

year old males, and there is a steady decline among the older males (Table 47). There are a few males who have been able to indicate the amount of reduction in their histories; but the record accumulated for the current ages (at time of reporting) gives a more definite picture of the decline The amount of mucus varies in any individual with the intensity of the erotic arousal, and it is probable that the lessened secretion of the older male is as much a measure of a reduction in the degree of arousal, as it may be of degenerating glands.

The capacity to reach repeated climax in a limited period of time definitely decreases with advancing age. Occasional multiple climax occurs in

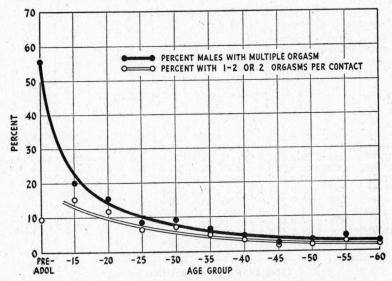

Figure 36 Capacity for multiple orgasm in relation to age

most of the histories, but regular multiple climax is characteristic of only a smaller number of males. The capacity is highest among those pre-adolescent boys (55.5%) who have sufficient sexual contact to test their capacities (Chapter 5), but multiple climax is still frequent among males (15% to 20%) in their teens and twenties (Table 48). While a few males (perhaps 3%) retain this capacity until they are 60 or older, most men lose it by 35 or 40 years of age.

Individuals differ in the way in which they age just as they differ in their frequencies and in their choices of sexual outlet Generalizations which are based on averages of any sort must always be tempered with an understanding of the range of variation in each age group Data on means and medians must not be confused with data on particular individuals, many of whom represent wide departures from any average.

It is important to note that the range of variation in physical and behavioral characters is greatest in the youngest groups and is gradually reduced in successive periods (Table 49). This means that older populations are more homogeneous than younger groups. This is true in regard to the frequency of total sexual outlet, and in connection with most but not all of the individual sources of outlet.

Masturbation, nocturnal emissions, total pre-marital intercourse, and animal intercourse follow the general picture in having their maximum

AGE GROUP	CASES STUDIED	MAXIMUM FREQUENCIES PER WEEK (NOT INCLUDING THE ONE MOST EXTREME CASE IN EACH GROUP)									
		TOTAL OUTLET	MASTURBATION	NOCTURNAL EMISSIONS	PRE-MARITAL INTERCOURSE	MARITAL INTERCOURSE	ANIMAL INTERCOURSE	PETTING TO CLIMAX	INTERCOURSE WITH PROSTITUTES	HOMOSEXUAL	EXTRA-MARITAL INTERCOURSE
Adol. −15	3012	29.0	23.0	12.0	25.0		8.0	3.5	2.0	7.0	
16–20	2868	28.0	15.0	6.5	25.0	25.0	4.0	4.5	4.0	10.0	7.5
21–25	1535	29.0	12.0	6.5	25.0	29.0	1.0	7.0	7.0	11.0	18.0
26–30	550	29.0	9.0	4.0	16.0	25.0	0.1	4.0	4.0	15.0	6.0
31–35	195	29.0	7.0	3.0	13.0	20.0		1.0	3.0	4.5	4.0
36–40	97	22.0	7.0	2.0	8.5	20.0		0.5	2.5	4.0	4.0
41–45	56	15.0	7.0	1.0	6.5	14.0		0.5	1.5	5.0	2.0
46–50	39	14.0	6.0	1.0	3.5	14.0		0.1	2.5	5.0	2.5
51–55	173	7.0	1.5	1.0		6.0			1.0	0.1	2.0
56–60	106	4.5	0.5	0.5		3.0				0.1	2.0
61–65	58	4.0				5.0					2.0

Table 49. Range of variation and age

Data based on histories of single (unmarried) males, except for marital and extra-marital intercourse. The lower limits of the ranges are 0 or near 0, and the maximum case is therefore a measure of the range of variation in each case. Differences between the least active and most active individuals in each age group decrease with advancing age, *i.e.*, the range of varaition becomes less, the homogeneity of the population increases, with advancing age. Only the last 4 sources have the maximum cases in anything but the youngest groups.

range of variation in the youngest years, and narrower ranges in the older years. On the other hand, pre-marital petting, pre-marital intercourse with prostitutes, homosexual activity, and extra-marital intercourse reach their maximum range of variation ten or more years beyond adolescence. The magnitudes of the ranges in these latter cases increase through the first age groups (in spite of reductions in sample size). The latter cases, it is to be noted, include more or less taboo activities. In these cases, the restriction of these ranges in the younger groups is probably due to the impact of the social tradition; and the achievement of maximum range and maximum mean frequency at a later period represents the gradual emancipation of the individual from the social tradition, and his final acceptance of a pattern which suits him (Chapter 21). Many of the individual histories support such an interpretation. After reaching the maximum range, each of these outlets then follows the rule in having the range of variation drop in successive age periods.

OLD AGE AND IMPOTENCE

We have the histories of 87 white males (and 39 Negro males) past 60 years of age. The number is too small to allow statistical analyses of the sort employed for the other age groups. Nevertheless, there is such interest in the sexual fate of the older male that it seems valuable to summarize the data even for these few cases.

The most important generalization to be drawn from the older groups is that they carry on directly the pattern of gradually diminishing activity which started with 16-year olds. Even in the most advanced ages, there is no sudden elimination of any large group of individuals from the picture. Each male may reach the point where he is, physically, no longer capable of sexual performance, and where he loses all interest in further activity; but the rate at which males slow up in these last decades does not exceed the rate at which they have been slowing up and dropping out in the previous age groups. This seems astounding, for it is quite contrary to general conceptions of aging processes in sex. The mean frequencies of these older white males who are still active range from 1.0 per week in the 65-year old group to 0.3 in the 75-year olds, and less than 0.1 in the 80-year old group (Table 44).

At 60 years of age, 5 per cent of these males were completely inactive sexually. By 70, nearly 30 per cent of them were inactive. From there on, the incidence curve (as far as our few cases allow us to judge) continues to drop. There is, of course, tremendous individual variation. There is the history of one 70-year old white male whose ejaculations were still averaging more than 7 per week. Among the Negro males, there was one aged 88 who was still having intercourse with his 90-year old wife, with frequencies varying from one per month to one per week. In the latter case, both of the spouses were still definitely responsive.

Heterosexual intercourse continues longer than any other outlet, but masturbation still occurs in some of the histories of men between 71 and 86 years of age, and nocturnal dreams with emission persist into the 76–80 year period. Among these cases, there is no male over 75 who has more than a single source of outlet. Erotic response at age 75 has a rating which is one-quarter of the mean rating for age 65.

Among these particular males, the mean frequency of morning erections had been 4.9 per week in the earlier years of their lives. In the 65-year period, it had dropped to 1.8, and at 75 years of age it had dropped to 0.9

AGE	TOTAL POPULATION	CASES IMPOTENT	% IMPOTENT	INCREMENT %
10	4108	0	0	
15	3948	2	0.05	0.05
20	3017	3	0.1	0.05
25	1627	6	0.4	0.3
30	1025	8	0.8	0.4
35	741	10	1.3	0.5
40	513	10	1.9	0.6
45	347	9	2.6	0.7
50	236	16	6.7	4.1
55	134	9	6.7	0.0
60	87	16	18.4	11.7
65	44	11	25.0	6.6
70	26	7	27.0	2.0
75	11	5	55.0	28.0
80	4	3	75.0	20.0

Table 50. Age and erectile impotence

An accumulative incidence curve; based on cases which are more or less totally and, to all appearances, permanently impotent.

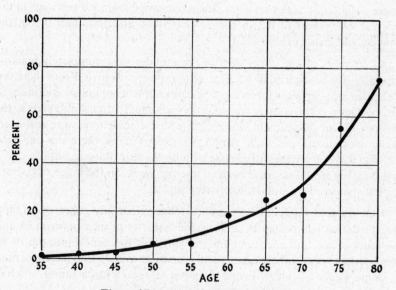

Figure 37. Age of onset of impotence

Percent of total population which is impotent is shown for each age.

per week. Morning erections usually persist for several years, even as long as five or ten years, after a male has become completely impotent in other situations.

The data on impotence will command especial interest. True ejaculatory impotence (incapacity to ejaculate even when aroused and in erection) is a very rare phenomenon (in 6 out of 4108 cases). Erectal impotence, on the other hand, is not uncommon. It appears occasionally in younger cases and is, of course, the ultimate outcome of the sexual picture in a portion of the older histories. Early erectal impotence occurs in only a few cases (0.4 per cent of the males under 25, and less than 1 per cent of the males under 35 years of age). In only a small portion of these is it a lifelong and complete incapacity. Sometimes the situation is complicated by a normal development of erotic responsiveness without an ability to perform. In some of these males, ejaculation may occur without erection as a result of the utilization of special techniques in intercourse. In many older persons, erectile impotence is, fortunately, accompanied by a decline in and usually complete cessation of erotic response.

Out of 4108 adult males on whom adequate data are available, there are 66 cases which have reached more or less permanent erectile impotence. Ruling out instances of temporary incapacity in younger individuals, the ages involved in onset of permanent impotence and the incidence data for each of the subsequent age groups are shown in Table 50 and Figure 37.

It will be seen that there are stray cases of impotence between adolescence and 35 years of age. Between 45 and 50, more males become incapacitated, and after 55 the number of cases increases rapidly. By 70 years of age, about one-quarter (27.0%) of the white males have become impotent; by 75 more than one-half (55.0%) are so; and 3 out of the 4 white males in the 80-year group are impotent. Two Negro males were still potent at 80. We have three histories of Negroes 88 years of age, and one aged 90. One of these males had been impotent for fifteen years. Two had not tried to have intercourse for some years, but morning erections made them believe they would still be potent if aroused; they were, however, no longer responding to erotic stimulation. The oldest potent male in our histories was the 88-year old Negro, who was still having regular intercourse with his 90-year old wife. Only a portion of the population ever becomes impotent before death, although most males, but not all of them, would become so if they all lived into their eighties.

A problem which deserves noting is that of the old men who are apprehended and sentenced to penal institutions as sex offenders. These men are usually charged with contributing to delinquency by fondling minor girls or boys; often they are charged with attempted rape. Among the older sex offenders who have given histories for the present study, a considerable number insist that they are impotent, and many of them give a history of long-standing impotence. A few of these men may have falsified the record, and many courts incline to the belief that all of them perjure themselves. We find, however, definite evidence in the histories that many of these men are in actuality incapable of erection. The usual professional interpretation describes these offenders as sexually thwarted, incapable of winning attention from older females, and reduced to vain attempts with children who are unable to defend themselves. An interpretation which would more nearly fit our understanding of old age would recognize the decline in erotic reaction, the loss of capacity to perform, and the reduction of the emotional life of the individual to such affectionate fondling as parents and especially grandparents are wont to bestow upon their own (and other) children. Many small girls reflect the public hysteria over the prospect of "being touched" by a strange person; and many a child, who has no idea at all of the mechanics of intercourse, interprets affection and simple caressing, from anyone except her own parents, as attempts at rape. In consequence, not a few older men serve time in penal institutions for attempting to engage in a sexual act which at their age would not interest most of them, and of which many of them are undoubtedly incapable.

MASTURBATION AND AGE

Masturbation is primarily a phenomenon of younger and unmarried groups, although it does occur in a fair number of the married histories. Later analyses will show that the incidence and frequency of masturbation are particularly affected by social backgrounds and correlated with educational levels and occupational status (Chapter 10).

The highest incidence for masturbation among single males (in the population taken as a whole) lies between 16 and 20 years of age, when 88 per cent is involved (Table 51, Figures 53–58). If the population is broken down into three groups on the basis of the amount of schooling they receive before they finally leave school (Table 82), it becomes apparent that the highest frequencies of masturbation really occur in the period between adolescence and age 15. The incidence steadily drops from that point. About half of the single population (53.8%) is still masturbating at 50 years of age. Among married males, the highest incidence (42.1%) occurs between 21 and 25 years of age, and the figures for these males similarly drop steadily into old age. In the middle fifties, hardly more than a tenth of the married males (11.4%) is involved. Masturbation is the first major source of outlet to disappear from the histories. A stray male is still involved at 75 years of age, but there is no complete masturbation to orgasm in any of the older histories.

Individuals differ tremendously in the frequencies with which they masturbate. There are boys who never masturbate. There are boys who masturbate twice or thrice in a lifetime; and there are boys and older youths who masturbate two and three times a day, averaging 20 or more per week throughout periods of some years. The population is most variable (the range of masturbatory frequencies is greatest, the differences between the least active and most active males are greatest) in the 11–15-year old group (Table 49). From this point on, the population becomes more homogeneous (there is a steady decline in range of frequencies) with advancing age. The highest rating individual at 15 years of age has a masturbatory rate which is two and a half times that of the highest rating individual at 30 years of age, and four times the rate of the highest individual at 50 years of age.

For the single population, the maximum average frequencies of masturbation are in the very youngest group (Table 51, Figures 53–58). In this group the boy who is masturbating at all ejaculates more than twice a week from this source (a mean of 2.1 and a median of 1.8 for the active population). By the middle teens the frequencies have dropped to approximately two-thirds of the figures in the younger group, and they continue to drop steadily into old age. By 50 years of age, there is about half as much masturbation among single males as in the younger adolescent boys. The decline in frequencies is dependent upon the fact that masturbation is, to a certain extent, a substitute for heterosexual or homosexual intercourse which replaces it in older groups; but it is to be emphasized that throughout the lives of many males, including married males especially of upper social levels, masturbation remains as an occasional source of outlet that is deliberately chosen for variety and for the particular sort of pleasure involved. Among the married males who do masturbate the frequencies are usually not high, averaging about once in three weeks for the active population as a whole. The frequencies are much higher for married males of upper educational levels. For the total married population, the mean frequencies are highest in the youngest age groups, dropping steadily into old age; but in the active portion of the married population, the frequencies hardly vary between 16 and 55 years of age. Here the effect of age is not in the direction of reducing rates among individuals who do masturbate, but by way of reducing the number of males who are involved.

In the youngest adolescent group, considering the population as a whole, the average boy is drawing nearly two-thirds (60.2%) of his total sexual outlet from masturbation. The figures drop steadily into old age. By 50, the average unmarried male who has any masturbation in his history derives only about a third (37.9%) of his outlet from that source. Among the married males who draw at all on this outlet, about 8 per cent of the total number of ejaculations comes from masturbation between 16 and 20 years of age; and, interesting to note, the figure rises in the later married years until it reaches 16 per cent at 50 years of age.

MASTURBATION AND AGE

Single Males

AGE GROUP	CASES	MASTURBATION: SAMPLE POPULATION							MASTURBATION: U. S. POPULATION				
		TOTAL POPULATION			ACTIVE POPULATION				TOTAL POPULATION		ACTIVE POPULATION		
		Mean Frequency	Median Freq.	% of Total Outlet	Incid. %	Mean Frequency	Median Freq.	% of Total Outlet	Mean Freq.	% of Total Outlet	Incid. %	Mean Freq.	% of Total Outlet
Adol.–15	3012	2.02 ± 0.04	1.44	70.33	85.4	2.36 ± 0.04	1.79	77.94 ± 0.53	1.86	60.22	87.2	2.14	71.02
16–20	2868	1.46 ± 0.03	0.89	51.28	88.4	1.66 ± 0.03	1.09	60.23 ± 0.64	1.23	38.50	87.7	1.40	47.76
21–25	1535	1.10 ± 0.04	0.53	41.95	80.7	1.37 ± 0.04	0.80	54.40 ± 0.94	0.86	29.52	73.6	1.16	43.12
26–30	550	0.94 ± 0.06	0.38	36.40	77.1	1.22 ± 0.07	0.66	47.34 ± 1.63	0.75	26.94	73.9	1.02	39.12
31–35	195	0.73 ± 0.09	0.25	31.29	71.3	1.02 ± 0.12	0.49	40.43 ± 2.81	0.59	24.94	67.6	0.88	34.03
36–40	97	0.76 ± 0.15	0.20	37.32	62.9	1.20 ± 0.21	0.63	47.06 ± 4.28	0.58	29.09	57.7	1.01	41.30
41–45	56	0.61 ± 0.19	0.08	35.19	60.7	1.01 ± 0.29	0.37	43.66 ± 6.31	....	....	....	....	....
46–50	39	0.62 ± 0.25	0.07	33.13	53.8	1.15 ± 0.45	0.50	37.88 ± 7.05	....	....	....	....	....

Age	Cases												
16–20	272	0.17 ± 0.03	0.00	3.63	39.0	0.43 ± 0.08	0.11	9.91 ± 1.53	0.14	2.95	37.1	0.38	8.29
21–25	751	0.21 ± 0.02	0.00	5.52	47.8	0.45 ± 0.04	0.17	12.15 ± 0.97	0.17	4.40	42.1	0.42	9.40
26–30	737	0.20 ± 0.02	0.00	6.19	47.9	0.42 ± 0.04	0.14	12.50 ± 0.97	0.16	4.57	36.5	0.43	11.34
31–35	569	0.16 ± 0.02	0.00	6.03	45.5	0.36 ± 0.04	0.10	12.44 ± 1.15	0.11	3.79	32.8	0.34	10.25
36–40	390	0.13 ± 0.02	0.00	5.22	36.7	0.35 ± 0.05	0.10	12.41 ± 1.66	0.07	2.95	22.2	0.33	13.17
41–45	272	0.11 ± 0.02	0.00	5.64	32.7	0.34 ± 0.06	0.10	12.66 ± 2.14	0.05	2.43	15.0	0.32	11.80
46–50	175	0.09 ± 0.02	0.00	5.11	30.9	0.30 ± 0.06	0.10	14.94 ± 2.92	0.05	2.53	13.6	0.33	16.29
51–55	109	0.10 ± 0.03	0.00	6.35	25.7	0.38 ± 0.11	0.10	18.18 ± 4.18	0.03	2.13	11.4	0.34	12.09
56–60	67	0.04 ± 0.02	0.00	4.06	19.4	0.22 ± 0.10	0.09	20.86 ± 7.86	....	....	....	....	....

Table 51. Masturbation and age

In this, and in the succeeding charts in this and the following chapter, means and medians represent average frequencies per week.

"% of Total Outlet" in the TOTAL POPULATION shows what portion of the total number of orgasms is derived from masturbation in the total population. A total of such figures for all the possible sources of outlet equals 100%, which is the total outlet of the group.

"% of Total Outlet" for the ACTIVE POPULATION represents the mean of the figures showing the percentage of the total outlet which is derived from this source by each individual who has any masturbation in his history, in that particular age period. The percents for the several possible outlets do not total 100% because different individuals are involved in the populations utilizing each type of outlet.

U. S. population figures are corrections of the raw data for a population whose age, marital status, and educational level are the same as those shown in the U. S. Census for 1940.

241

NOCTURNAL EMISSIONS AND AGE

AGE GROUP	CASES	NOCTURNAL EMISSIONS: SAMPLE POPULATION							NOCTURNAL EMISSIONS: U. S. POPULATION				
		TOTAL POPULATION			ACTIVE POPULATION				TOTAL POPULATION		ACTIVE POPULATION		
		Mean Frequency	Median Freq.	% of Total Outlet	Incid. %	Mean Frequency	Median Freq.	% of Total Outlet	Mean Freq.	% of Total Outlet	Incid. %	Mean Freq.	% of Total Outlet
Single Males													
Adol.–15	3012	0.22 ± 0.01	0.01	7.80	52.2	0.43 ± 0.02	0.21	26.49 ± 0.88	0.14	4.55	39.1	0.36	19.97
16–20	2868	0.32 ± 0.01	0.12	11.29	80.3	0.40 ± 0.01	0.23	21.72 ± 0.58	0.23	7.41	70.2	0.33	15.53
21–25	1535	0.33 ± 0.02	0.12	12.40	80.8	0.40 ± 0.02	0.23	23.47 ± 0.81	0.24	8.30	70.9	0.34	17.36
26–30	550	0.28 ± 0.02	0.10	10.67	78.7	0.35 ± 0.02	0.22	22.98 ± 1.38	0.22	7.92	69.9	0.32	17.86
31–35	195	0.19 ± 0.02	0.07	8.11	70.8	0.27 ± 0.03	0.15	21.68 ± 2.51	0.17	7.34	64.3	0.27	21.50
36–40	97	0.12 ± 0.02	0.03	5.93	59.8	0.20 ± 0.03	0.10	19.12 ± 3.63	0.10	5.17	56.4	0.18	16.17
41–45	56	0.08 ± 0.03	0.00	4.73	48.2	0.17 ± 0.05	0.08	19.48 ± 5.49	....	....	....	....	....
Married Males													
16–20	272	0.13 ± 0.02	0.01	2.85	52.9	0.25 ± 0.04	0.09	5.57 ± 0.88	0.12	2.52	53.3	0.23	5.17
21–25	751	0.14 ± 0.01	0.03	3.68	59.0	0.24 ± 0.02	0.09	6.49 ± 0.54	0.12	3.09	58.4	0.21	5.45
26–30	737	0.14 ± 0.01	0.03	4.29	62.6	0.22 ± 0.02	0.08	6.49 ± 0.51	0.13	3.65	50.8	0.23	6.00
31–35	569	0.12 ± 0.01	0.03	4.54	60.6	0.20 ± 0.02	0.08	7.18 ± 0.70	0.11	3.73	51.5	0.21	6.56
36–40	390	0.11 ± 0.01	0.01	4.40	53.3	0.20 ± 0.02	0.08	6.80 ± 0.70	0.08	3.24	42.1	0.19	5.99
41–45	272	0.09 ± 0.01	0.01	4.50	54.4	0.16 ± 0.02	0.08	7.49 ± 1.02	0.07	3.55	41.1	0.18	6.08
46–50	175	0.07 ± 0.01	0.00	3.91	48.0	0.15 ± 0.02	0.07	9.40 ± 1.81	0.06	2.97	34.9	0.15	9.79
51–55	109	0.07 ± 0.02	0.00	4.42	44.0	0.15 ± 0.03	0.07	7.90 ± 1.91	0.06	3.50	30.4	0.18	10.06
56–60	67	0.03 ± 0.01	0.00	2.73	28.4	0.10 ± 0.02	0.07	13.79 ± 6.03	....	....	....	....	....

Table 52. Nocturnal emissions and age

For explanations, see the legend with Table 51 on Masturbation.

Age is, obviously, a factor which affects masturbation in most of its aspects. Its influences are to be noted in the steady reductions in the numbers of persons involved (the incidences); in similar reductions in the frequencies (rates per week) with which masturbation occurs, both in the single and in the married portions of the population; in the reduction in the range of frequency. The percentage of the total outlet which is supplied by masturbation is reduced in the total population, both single and married; but among those who continue to draw on this source, masturbation remains a fairly constant portion of the outlet during the single years, even if they extend into old age. For the married males who masturbate it is an increasingly important source of orgasm with the advancing years.

NOCTURNAL EMISSIONS AND AGE

Nocturnal emissions enter the picture somewhat later than other sources of sexual outlet (Table 52, Figures 59–64). In only a small number of cases do they appear at the very beginning of adolescence. Even in those cases where dreams provide the first source of ejaculation, pubic hair and other physical characteristics usually indicate that the individual became adolescent a year or more before the first emission. There are 4 cases of persons who were past 40 before they had their first nocturnal emission. Nevertheless, dreams to climax are primarily a phenomenon of the teens and the twenties.

The highest incidence of nocturnal emissions is about 71 per cent among single males 21 to 25 years of age. By 50, only about a third of the males still experience such dreams. By 60 years of age only 14 per cent still has them. It is interesting to note that dreams as an occasional source of ejaculation still appear in the histories of men as old as 86.

In the youngest age group there are a few individuals who dream to climax with average frequencies which run as high as 12 per week, although there are many males who average only a few times per year. The maximum frequencies drop rapidly in successive age groups. At 30 years of age, the maximum is only a third as high, and by 50 years of age it is only a twelfth as high, as at age 15.

Among single males of the active population, nocturnal emissions occur with the highest frequency between adolescence and 30 years of age. Among the married males the highest frequency is between 16 and 30 years of age. The highest average frequency, for those single males who have any nocturnal emissions at all, is about once in three weeks (0.3 per week); for the married males, it is once in four weeks (0.23 per week). In both groups there is a decline in frequencies after thirty. Beyond 50 years of age, nocturnal emissions do not average more than four or five per year, for those individuals who have any at all.

PETTING TO CLIMAX, AND AGE

| | | PETTING TO CLIMAX: SAMPLE POPULATION | | | | | | | PETTING TO CLIMAX: U. S. POPULATION | | | | |
| | | TOTAL POPULATION | | | ACTIVE POPULATION | | | | TOTAL POPULATION | | ACTIVE POPULATION | | |
AGE GROUP	CASES	Mean Frequency	Median Freq.	% of Total Outlet	Incid. %	Mean Frequency	Median Freq.	% of Total Outlet	Mean Freq.	% of Total Outlet	Incid. %	Mean Freq.	% of Total Outlet
							Single Males						
Adol.–15	3012	0.05 ± 0.00	0.00	1.69	17.3	0.28 ± 0.02	0.075	7.52 ± 0.62	0.04	1.31	18.3	0.22	4.69
16–20	2868	0.12 ± 0.01	0.00	4.17	38.5	0.31 ± 0.02	0.080	9.41 ± 0.49	0.08	2.56	31.8	0.25	6.10
21–25	1535	0.16 ± 0.01	0.00	6.16	42.7	0.38 ± 0.03	0.091	13.61 ± 0.82	0.08	3.02	28.5	0.30	9.26
26–30	550	0.11 ± 0.02	0.00	4.19	33.5	0.32 ± 0.05	0.084	12.29 ± 1.47	0.06	2.12	23.1	0.23	8.37
31–35	195	0.06 ± 0.01	0.00	2.56	23.6	0.25 ± 0.05	0.094	13.65 ± 3.09	0.04	1.58	20.8	0.17	10.03
36–40	97	0.02 ± 0.01	0.00	1.17	11.3	0.21 ± 0.07	0.100	13.00 ± 8.03	0.02	1.31	11.5	0.22	17.51
41–45	56	0.01 ± 0.01	0.00	0.82	10.7	0.13 ± 0.05	0.088	7.17 ± 5.31	....	....	....	....	....
46–50	39	0.01 ± 0.00	0.00	0.14	5.1	0.05	0.075	0.50	....	....	....	....	....

Table 53. Petting to climax, and age

For explanations, see legend with Table 51 on Masturbation.

In the early twenties, the average single male (total population) derives about one-twelfth (8.3%) of his total outlet from nocturnal dreams. From there on, this outlet is of decreasing importance in the total picture. For those single males who have any dreams at all (active population), they are of greatest importance (21.5% of the total outlet) in the middle thirties. Among married males they are of lesser significance, accounting for about 3 per cent of the total ejaculations of the total population throughout the life span. They steadily rise in importance among the males in the active portion of the married population, representing 5 per cent of the outlet of the younger married males, and 10 per cent of the outlet of the older married males who ever do dream to the point of climax.

PETTING TO CLIMAX, AND AGE

Pre-marital heterosexual histories often involve a considerable amount of physical contact without actual intercourse. About 88 per cent of the total male population has such petting experience prior to mariage (Table 134, Figure 117). There are some males (and a smaller number of females) who respond to such stimulation, whether generalized or more specifically genital, to the point of complete orgasm. Such petting, as it is usually called, is not entirely new with the younger generation; but frank and frequent participation in physical stimulation that is openly intended to effect orgasm is definitely more abundant now than it was among older generations. A great deal of the petting does not proceed to orgasm, but more than a quarter of all the males (28%) pet to that point prior to marriage (Table 135, Figure 118). The incidence of the phenomenon is still higher at upper educational levels (Chapters 10 and 16) where more than half of the males (58%) are ultimately involved. The highest incidence in any single age period is 31.8 per cent during the 21 to 25-year period, and the figures drop steadily from there until the time of marriage—or until they disappear in the old age of still unmarried males.

The highest frequencies recorded for any individual male average 7.0 per week, in the 21 to 25-year group, after which the maximum cases drop quickly to 0.5 per week after 35 years of age (Table 49).

The frequencies with which males reach orgasm in pre-marital petting are relatively low, in all age groups (Table 53, Figures 38–43). This is one phenomenon where frequencies are not highest in the youngest group. Calculated in any way (as means, or medians, for the total, or for only the active portion of the population) the maximum performance is in the 21 to 25-year old group, where the mean of the active population is about once in three weeks (0.30 per week). The averages (means for the active population) then drop a bit from 26 to 40 years of age, and more abruptly thereafter.

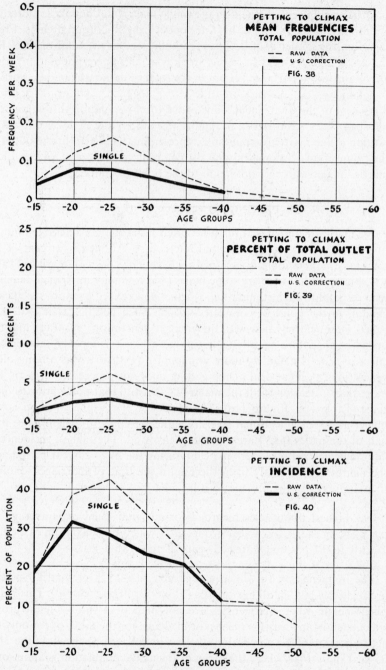

Figures 38–40. Relation of age to frequency, incidence, and significance of petting to climax

Solid lines represent the U. S. Corrections.

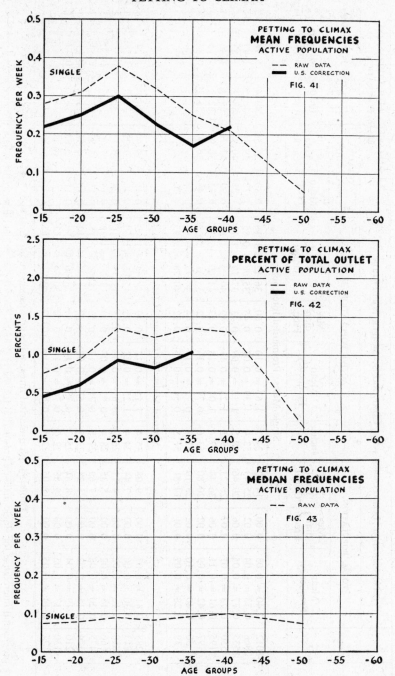

Figures 41–43. Relation of age to frequency and significance of petting to climax

Solid lines represent the U. S. Corrections.

NON-MARITAL INTERCOURSE AND AGE

AGE GROUP	CASES	NON-MARITAL INTERCOURSE WITH COMPANIONS: SAMPLE POPULATION							INTERCOURSE WITH COMPANIONS: U. S. POPULATION				
		TOTAL POPULATION			ACTIVE POPULATION				TOTAL POPULATION		ACTIVE POPULATION		
		Mean Frequency	Median Freq.	% of Total Outlet	Incid. %	Mean Frequency	Median Freq.	% of Total Outlet	Mean Freq.	% of Total Outlet	Incid. %	Mean Freq.	% of Total Outlet
Single Males: Pre-marital Intercourse													
Adol.–15	3012	0.40 ± 0.03	0.00	14.12	24.3	1.67 ± 0.10	0.60	36.12 ± 1.18	0.80	25.56	40.4	1.98	42.18
16–20	2868	0.73 ± 0.04	0.02	25.43	52.4	1.39 ± 0.07	0.45	35.98 ± 0.85	1.32	39.16	70.5	1.87	47.10
21–25	1535	0.77 ± 0.05	0.06	29.46	58.5	1.32 ± 0.09	0.43	37.19 ± 1.14	1.25	40.94	68.3	1.83	47.90
26–30	550	0.73 ± 0.07	0.07	28.23	59.5	1.23 ± 0.11	0.49	40.26 ± 1.88	0.99	33.76	67.3	1.46	44.06
31–35	195	0.61 ± 0.11	0.06	26.44	57.4	1.07 ± 0.18	0.43	44.00 ± 3.32	0.72	30.96	62.2	1.15	44.96
36–40	97	0.42 ± 0.09	0.02	20.80	53.6	0.79 ± 0.16	0.32	35.21 ± 5.08	0.48	26.00	55.2	0.86	38.18
41–45	56	0.40 ± 0.10	0.02	23.10	51.8	0.77 ± 0.17	0.44	46.28 ± 6.86	.....	.....	.....	.....	.....
46–50	39	0.28 ± 0.09	0.01	14.81	51.3	0.54 ± 0.16	0.22	40.88 ± 9.03	.....	.....	.....	.....	.....
Married Males: Extra-marital Intercourse													
16–20	288	0.41 ± 0.07	0.00	9.08	35.4	1.15 ± 0.17	0.40	18.66 ± 1.99	0.45	9.64	36.8	1.23	18.36
21–25	813	0.30 ± 0.06	0.00	7.44	24.4	1.25 ± 0.22	0.25	15.68 ± 1.56	0.40	9.22	31.3	1.28	16.36
26–30	850	0.16 ± 0.02	0.00	4.71	26.0	0.61 ± 0.08	0.15	12.19 ± 1.16	0.24	6.57	32.3	0.72	12.32
31–35	666	0.15 ± 0.02	0.00	5.35	28.4	0.52 ± 0.07	0.19	13.30 ± 1.32	0.15	5.16	30.9	0.50	13.04
36–40	475	0.20 ± 0.05	0.00	7.69	27.8	0.71 ± 0.17	0.22	18.44 ± 2.15	0.15	5.82	27.2	0.54	17.42
41–45	324	0.13 ± 0.02	0.00	5.24	23.5	0.53 ± 0.08	0.22	21.88 ± 3.12	0.10	4.50	23.1	0.41	19.96
46–50	210	0.19 ± 0.04	0.00	8.61	25.2	0.73 ± 0.14	0.34	26.40 ± 3.96	0.11	5.88	30.1	0.43	21.33
51–55	130	0.17 ± 0.05	0.00	9.88	22.3	0.76 ± 0.18	0.42	30.84 ± 5.77	.....	.....	.....	.....	.....
56–60	77	0.14 ± 0.05	0.00	12.05	22.1	0.65 ± 0.16	0.50	40.94 ± 9.25	.....	.....	.....	.....	.....

Table 54. Non-marital intercourse with companions, and age

Showing pre-marital intercourse for single males, extra-marital for married males. For the additional intercourse which those same males have with prostitutes, see Table 55. For further explanations, see the legend with Table 51 on Masturbation.

248

Between 21 and 25 years of age, the average male (total population) derives 3.0 per cent of his total sexual outlet from petting to climax. Leaving out the males who never do reach orgasm in petting, the statement can be made that about 6 per cent of the total outlet is so derived by the average male between 16 and 20 years of age, and this figure builds up to 17.5 per cent at 40 years of age. Since this source drops steadily in importance for the total single population, but rises in importance for individuals who are actively engaged in this activity, it is evident that the percentage of the population which is involved steadily decreases in older age groups. Petting is less important as a source of outlet than any other sexual behavior except intercourse with animals of other species. It is much more significant as a means of education toward the making of socio-sexual adjustments.

The low incidence and frequency of petting to climax in the older single groups may be correlated with the usually low rates of all sexual activities at that age, and with the fact that a large number of older, single males are apathetic, sexually inhibited, socially timid, or heterosexually disinclined. The present data, however, may be merely an expression of the fact that petting as a source of outlet has acquired vogue only in more recent decades. It is possible that some years hence those members of the present younger generation who are still unmarried may account for an increase in the frequency of this activity at older levels.

PRE-MARITAL INTERCOURSE AND AGE

It is probable that heterosexual intercourse would provide the major source of pre-marital outlet if there were no restrictions on the activity of the younger male. There is, however, no other sort of activity that is so markedly affected by the tradition of the social level in which the individual is raised (Chapter 10). The incidence and frequencies of pre-marital intercourse are very low for the more educated portion of the population; but for lower educational levels this remains as the chief source of outlet before marriage. Data on pre-marital intercourse must, therefore, be interpreted in connection with the other factors which are treated in the present volume.

The highest incidence of pre-marital intercourse comes in the late teens, where nearly three-quarters (70.5%) of the total U. S. population is involved (Table 54, Figures 71–76). From that point the incidence drops, but still stays high. In every age group between 16 and 50, more than half (from 70.5% down to 51.3%) of the single males engage in heterosexual intercourse.

The variation in frequency of pre-marital intercourse in any group is at its maximum between adolescence and 25 years of age (Table 49). From that point, the range becomes increasingly restricted in each older popu-

INTERCOURSE WITH PROSTITUTES AND AGE

		INTERCOURSE WITH PROSTITUTES: SAMPLE POPULATION							INTERCOURSE WITH PROSTITUTES: U. S. POPULATION				
		TOTAL POPULATION			ACTIVE POPULATION				TOTAL POPULATION		ACTIVE POPULATION		
AGE GROUP	CASES	Mean Frequency	Median Freq.	% of Total Outlet	Incid. %	Mean Frequency	Median Freq.	% of Total Outlet	Mean Freq.	% of Total Outlet	Incid. %	Mean Freq.	% of Total Outlet
Single Males													
Adol.–15	3012	0.01 ± 0.00	0.00	0.39	5.2	0.21 ± 0.03	0.08	7.13 ± 1.34	0.02	0.61	7.7	0.25	8.79
16–20	2868	0.07 ± 0.01	0.00	2.48	30.8	0.23 ± 0.02	0.07	8.05 ± 0.60	0.12	3.66	41.9	0.29	11.24
21–25	1535	0.10 ± 0.01	0.00	3.92	29.1	0.35 ± 0.03	0.09	15.19 ± 1.21	0.20	6.29	45.5	0.43	20.27
26–30	550	0.16 ± 0.02	0.00	6.14	29.8	0.53 ± 0.06	0.25	22.82 ± 2.23	0.28	9.56	46.8	0.61	26.88
31–35	195	0.22 ± 0.04	0.00	9.67	40.5	0.55 ± 0.08	0.27	28.73 ± 3.36	0.31	12.57	51.6	0.62	32.38
36–40	97	0.26 ± 0.05	0.00	13.03	48.5	0.54 ± 0.09	0.32	39.49 ± 5.17	0.31	16.42	55.5	0.55	41.64
41–45	56	0.18 ± 0.05	0.00	10.65	39.3	0.47 ± 0.10	0.33	48.23 ± 7.93	....	....	....	....	....
46–50	39	0.29 ± 0.11	0.00	15.77	48.7	0.60 ± 0.20	0.27	52.74 ± 8.96	....	....	....	....	....
Married Males													
16–20	272	0.04 ± 0.02	0.00	0.87	14.3	0.28 ± 0.11	0.07	2.87 ± 1.15	0.05	1.17	15.9	0.36	3.58
21–25	751	0.03 ± 0.01	0.00	0.72	12.9	0.21 ± 0.05	0.07	4.03 ± 0.96	0.05	1.15	19.5	0.25	4.29
26–30	737	0.03 ± 0.01	0.00	0.82	11.8	0.23 ± 0.04	0.07	4.95 ± 1.02	0.04	1.30	17.2	0.27	5.89
31–35	569	0.02 ± 0.01	0.00	0.84	11.1	0.20 ± 0.04	0.08	5.42 ± 1.19	0.03	1.12	14.9	0.18	5.76
36–40	390	0.02 ± 0.00	0.00	0.85	10.5	0.20 ± 0.04	0.08	7.33 ± 2.33	0.02	1.12	12.0	0.22	8.52
41–45	272	0.02 ± 0.00	0.00	0.78	8.5	0.18 ± 0.04	0.09	8.00 ± 3.75	0.02	1.11	11.4	0.19	9.84
46–50	175	0.01 ± 0.00	0.00	0.80	5.7	0.25 ± 0.07	0.22	12.25 ± 7.94	0.02	1.01	7.9	0.24	13.58
51–55	109	0.02 ± 0.01	0.00	1.13	7.3	0.24 ± 0.09	0.17	15.19 ± 10.73	0.02	1.65	9.1	0.25	18.43
56–60	67	0.02 ± 0.01	0.00	1.75	7.5	0.25 ± 0.15	0.10	19.50 ± 18.35	....	....	....	....	....

Table 55. Intercourse with prostitutes, and age
For explanations, see the legend with Table 51 on Masturbation.

lation. At 15 years of age, the most active male is having pre-marital intercourse with ejaculation on an average of 25 times per week. At 30 years of
age, the extreme male still has a rate of 16 per week; but by 50 years of
age, the maximum frequency is down to 3.5 per week.

For the total population, the highest frequency of pre-marital intercourse occurs in the 16–20 year group, where the mean is about one and a
third times (1.32) per week. If the calculations are made on the active males
only, the highest average frequency is in the youngest group, between
adolescence and 15 years of age, where the corrected figure is almost
exactly 2 per week. It again becomes evident that the youngest boy has
the greatest capacity and the highest frequency of activity if he has the
opportunity to exercise it. From age 16 on, the frequencies drop, and those
males who are still unmarried at 50 engage in intercourse only a quarter
as often (0.5 per week) as the active teen-age boys.

With advancing age, the average unmarried male draws a somewhat
decreasing proportion of his total outlet from pre-marital intercourse.
The average teen-age boy (of the active population) derives nearly half of
all his outlet from intercourse. The average 50-year old, unmarried male
derives nearer a third of his outlet from heterosexual intercourse (the data
based on interpolations from the uncorrected figures in Table 54). This
follows the now familiar pattern of each outlet beginning at its peak in the
middle teens, and going down in rate with advancing age.

Pre-marital intercourse may be had either with companions or with
professional prostitutes. Among unmarried males, an increasing portion
of the intercourse is derived in later years from paid contacts (Table 55,
Figures 77–82). In the adolescent to 15-year group, less than 1 per cent of
the boys with pre-marital intercourse depend solely upon prostitutes, and
14.6 per cent have intercourse with both companions and prostitutes. By
50 years of age, a seventh of the males (14.3%) who have pre-marital intercourse depend entirely upon prostitutes, and more than a half of them
(62.0%) have intercourse with both companions and prostitutes.

The individual males who have the highest frequencies of pre-marital
intercourse with prostitutes are found in the group between 21 and 25 years
of age (Table 49). In both younger and older age groups, the maximum
frequencies are lower (*i.e.*, the range of variation in those populations is
less).

For this active portion of the population, the frequency of intercourse
with companions is greatest between adolescence and 15, after which the
frequencies drop steadily into the oldest ages; but intercourse with prostitutes increases in frequency until it reaches its maximum (over 0.6 per
week) between 26 and 35 years of age. This increase in frequency is not an
effect of aging, but a social effect. Younger males find it easier to secure
intercourse with girls of their own age and social level. The older male

MARITAL INTERCOURSE AND AGE

AGE GROUP	CASES	MARITAL INTERCOURSE: SAMPLE POPULATION							MARITAL INTERCOURSE: U. S. POPULATION				
		TOTAL POPULATION			ACTIVE POPULATION				TOTAL POPULATION		ACTIVE POPULATION		
		Mean Frequency	Median Freq.	% of Total Outlet	Incid. %	Mean Frequency	Median Freq.	% of Total Outlet	Mean Freq.	% of Total Outlet	Incid. %	Mean Freq.	% of Total Outlet
						Married Males							
16–20	272	3.75 ± 0.24	2.56	81.36	100.0	3.75 ± 0.24	2.56	84.61 ± 1.23	3.92	81.41	100.0	3.92	85.2
21–25	751	3.16 ± 0.12	2.27	81.80	99.6	3.17 ± 0.12	2.28	85.26 ± 0.75	3.34	81.29	99.7	3.35	85.9
26–30	737	2.69 ± 0.10	1.98	83.30	99.7	2.70 ± 0.10	1.98	85.50 ± 0.71	2.89	83.17	99.9	2.89	86.4
31–35	569	2.23 ± 0.10	1.75	82.57	99.6	2.24 ± 0.10	1.76	85.07 ± 0.85	2.45	85.48	99.9	2.46	87.4
36–40	390	1.97 ± 0.11	1.58	81.18	99.2	1.99 ± 0.11	1.59	85.84 ± 1.01	2.05	86.35	99.5	2.22	87.0
41–45	272	1.62 ± 0.10	1.26	82.98	98.9	1.64 ± 0.10	1.28	85.90 ± 1.26	1.74	88.27	98.6	1.77	88.8
46–50	175	1.43 ± 0.14	0.86	80.16	97.1	1.47 ± 0.14	0.88	83.69 ± 1.88	1.80	87.79	98.1	1.83	87.3
51–55	109	1.19 ± 0.16	0.73	77.42	97.2	1.22 ± 0.16	0.76	83.07 ± 2.58	1.33	87.21	97.0	1.38	88.0
56–60	67	0.83 ± 0.11	0.62	78.29	94.0	0.89 ± 0.11	0.68	81.10 ± 3.95	....	....	....	....	....

Table 56. Marital intercourse and age

For explanations, see the legend with Table 51, on Masturbation.

finds it more convenient and less dangerous to secure intercourse from professional sources. This custom may not be followed by succeeding generations, who have been less accustomed to going to prostitutes at any age (Chapter 11).

For the younger males, between 16 and 20, prostitution provides only 4 per cent of the total outlet for the population as a whole, and about 11 per cent of the outlet for those who actually frequent prostitutes. But by 50 years of age, prostitutes provide nearer a sixth (approximately 16%) of the total outlet for the still single males, and more than half (about 53%) of the total outlet for the males who do go to prostitutes. Since payment for sexual contacts is much more frequent among males of particular social levels, the data need the breakdown which will be given them in subsequent chapters on social factors affecting patterns of sexual behavior.

MARITAL INTERCOURSE AND AGE

Marital intercourse is the one activity which is least affected by any of the social factors except marital status itself. The data given here are based on males who are living with either legal or common-law wives.

Between 16 and 40 years of age, practically all of the males (more than 99%) who are married find some outlet in marital intercourse (Table 56, Figures 44–49). From 45 on, there are a few males who discontinue such intercourse even though they remain wedded and live with their wives. By 60 years of age about 6 per cent of the married males are no longer active. Our limited series of older histories shows 83 per cent of the males having intercourse with their wives at ages 60–65, and 70 per cent having it between 66 and 70. We have so few histories of still older married males that we cannot make a further statement.

In all the age groups between 16 and 30, there are individuals who have intercourse with frequencies as high as 25 or more per week (Table 49). Such high frequencies are not found in older groups. There the range of variation becomes narrower; and by 50 years of age the maximum average rate for any individual is 14 per week. By 60 the maximum has cut down to 3 per week.

It is particularly instructive to compare average frequencies in marital intercourse for successive age groups (Table 56, Figures 44–49). Between 16 and 20, the boy who is married has a higher rate of total sexual outlet (4.8 per week) than the males of any other group, and most of that outlet (over 85%) is derived from his marital intercourse. The frequencies of the intercourse in this teen-age group average near 4 (3.9) per week. From there on, the mean frequencies drop in each successive five-year period. The decline is at an astonishingly constant rate, from the youngest to the oldest ages. By 60 years of age, the average frequency is about once (0.9) per week.

MARITAL INTERCOURSE

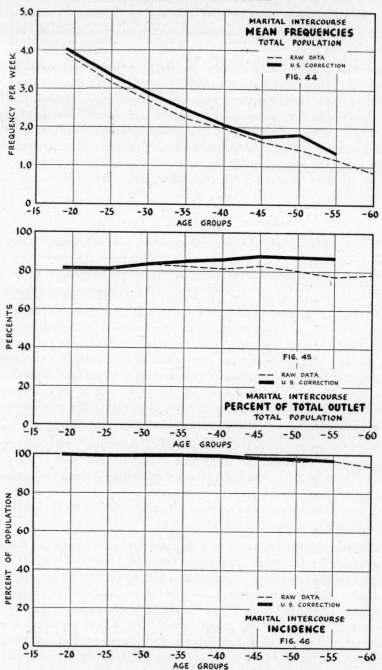

Figures 44–46. Relation of age to marital intercourse

Solid lines represent the U. S. Corrections.

MARITAL INTERCOURSE

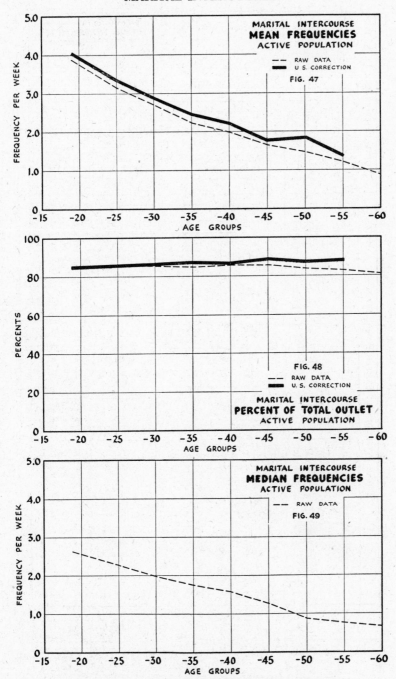

Figures 47–49. Relation of age to marital intercourse

Solid lines represent the U. S. Corrections.

TOTAL INTERCOURSE AND AGE

| | | TOTAL INTERCOURSE: SAMPLE POPULATION | | | | | | | TOTAL INTERCOURSE: U. S. POPULATION | | | | |
| | | TOTAL POPULATION | | | ACTIVE POPULATION | | | | TOTAL POPULATION | | ACTIVE POPULATION | | |
AGE GROUP	CASES	Mean Frequency	Median Freq.	% of Total Outlet	Incid. %	Mean Frequency	Median Freq.	% of Total Outlet	Mean Freq.	% of Total Outlet	Incid. %	Mean Freq.	% of Total Outlet
					Single Males								
Adol.–15	3925	0.34 ± 0.02	0.00	14.51	21.7	1.56 ± 0.09	0.56	36.18 ± 1.61	0.79	26.17	39.9	1.98	43.38
16–20	3739	0.67 ± 0.03	0.02	27.91	53.6	1.25 ± 0.05	0.41	35.41 ± 0.77	1.35	42.82	73.7	1.84	50.97
21–25	2121	0.75 ± 0.04	0.07	33.38	60.7	1.24 ± 0.07	0.43	38.75 ± 0.99	1.37	50.33	75.0	1.82	55.64
26–30	607	1.00 ± 0.08	0.21	34.37	66.1	1.51 ± 0.12	0.73	49.29 ± 1.78	1.34	45.44	75.4	1.77	57.11
31–35	223	1.02 ± 0.13	0.30	36.11	67.7	1.50 ± 0.18	0.78	58.46 ± 2.80	1.11	45.12	72.2	1.53	62.84
36–40	110	0.92 ± 0.16	0.29	33.83	70.0	1.32 ± 0.22	0.57	57.68 ± 4.14	1.00	43.72	80.8	1.23	59.66
41–45	61	0.75 ± 0.17	0.23	33.75	65.6	1.14 ± 0.25	0.49	66.56 ± 5.34	.....	.....	.....	.....	.....
46–50	36	0.61 ± 0.16	0.16	30.58	66.7	0.91 ± 0.22	0.40	66.33 ± 6.77	.....	.....	.....	.....	.....
					Married Males								
16–20	279	4.27 ± 0.27	2.78	91.31	100.0	4.27 ± 0.27	2.78	91.64 ± 0.81	4.51	92.22	100.0	4.51	92.53
21–25	766	3.46 ± 0.14	2.44	89.96	99.9	3.46 ± 0.14	2.44	89.54 ± 0.61	3.73	91.66	100.0	3.73	91.97
26–30	792	2.90 ± 0.11	2.16	88.83	99.7	2.91 ± 0.11	2.16	89.17 ± 0.59	3.17	91.05	99.8	3.18	90.99
31–35	623	2.48 ± 0.10	1.89	88.76	99.7	2.49 ± 0.10	1.89	89.45 ± 0.65	2.72	91.76	99.9	2.72	91.66
36–40	442	2.22 ± 0.11	1.72	89.72	99.1	2.24 ± 0.11	1.73	90.87 ± 0.69	2.28	93.29	99.0	2.32	93.31
41–45	306	1.89 ± 0.11	1.46	89.00	99.7	1.89 ± 0.11	1.46	91.56 ± 0.79	2.04	93.78	99.9	2.04	94.43
46–50	197	1.76 ± 0.14	1.11	89.57	98.0	1.79 ± 0.14	1.16	90.33 ± 1.22	1.87	94.25	98.0	1.91	93.09
51–55	123	1.49 ± 0.16	0.94	88.43	97.6	1.53 ± 0.17	0.97	90.50 ± 1.41	1.48	94.14	96.4	1.54	94.45
56–60	73	1.09 ± 0.13	0.79	92.09	97.3	1.12 ± 0.13	0.82	91.31 ± 2.11	.....	.....	.....	.....	.....

Table 57. Total heterosexual intercourse and age

For explanations, see the legend with Table 51, on Masturbation.

256

On the other hand, the average male draws a nearly constant proportion of his total outlet throughout his life from marital intercourse. He gets from 85 to 89 per cent of his outlet from that source between 16 and 55, after which there is only a slight drop in the significance of marital intercourse. Since his rate has gone down while he continues to draw a constant portion of his total outlet from the intercourse, it is obvious that the decline in frequency of this activity must occur at precisely the same rate as the decline in the frequency of his total outlet.

Although biologic aging must be the main factor involved, it still is not clear how often the conditions of marriage itself are responsible for this decline in frequency of marital intercourse. Long-time marriage provides the maximum opportunity for repetition of a relatively uniform sort of experience. It is not surprising that there should be some loss of interest in the activity among the older males, even if there were no aging process to accelerate it.

EXTRA-MARITAL INTERCOURSE AND AGE

Extra-marital intercourse, partly with companions and partly with prostitutes, occurs among 23 to 37 per cent of the males in each of the five-year periods. It is highest among the teen-age males, where 36.8 per cent of the population is involved (Tables 54, 55, Figures 71–76). The accumulated number of males who have such intercourse at any time in their lives is, of course, much higher (Chapter 19). The active incidence figure stays remarkably constant between 21 and 60 years of age, with only a slight trend toward a decline in the older years. The absence of an aging effect on the incidence of the outlet is unique among all kinds of sexual activity.

The range of variation in any five-year population is greatest between 21 and 25 years of age (18 per week for the most active individuals), and the maximum goes down rapidly after that (Table 49). By 60 years of age, the most active individual has extra-marital intercourse only twice per week.

Mean frequencies for the males who are actively involved in extra-marital intercourse go down more or less steadily from about 1.3 per week in the late twenties to about once in four weeks for the sixty-year olds.

The percentage of the total outlet which is derived from extra-marital intercourse is highest in the 16–20-year period (9.6 per cent of the outlet of the total population), after which there is a drop at least to age 45. Then, only about 5 per cent of the outlet of the total married population comes from this source. Considering only the males who are having some extra-marital intercourse, the figures first drop and then rise—18.4 per cent of the outlet in the teen-age group, 12.3 per cent of the outlet in the 30-year group, and possibly 41 per cent of the outlet in the 60-year group comes from this intercourse with females not their wives. The rise in significance of extra-marital intercourse, both in the total population and particularly

AGE GROUP	CASES	HOMOSEXUAL OUTLET: SAMPLE POPULATION							HOMOSEXUAL OUTLET: U. S. POPULATION				
		TOTAL POPULATION			ACTIVE POPULATION				TOTAL POPULATION		ACTIVE POPULATION		
		Mean Frequency	Median Freq.	% of Total Outlet	Incid. %	Mean Frequency	Median Freq.	% of Total Outlet	Mean Freq.	% of Total Outlet	Incid. %	Mean Freq.	% of Total Outlet
Single Males													
Adol.–15	3012	0.14 ± 0.01	0.00	4.89	24.8	0.56 ± 0.04	0.10	12.13 ± 0.71	0.22	7.03	27.3	0.81	17.46
16–20	2868	0.13 ± 0.01	0.00	4.70	21.6	0.62 ± 0.05	0.11	13.25 ± 0.82	0.26	7.84	31.0	0.85	17.73
21–25	1535	0.16 ± 0.02	0.00	5.98	14.5	1.09 ± 0.12	0.40	25.45 ± 1.95	0.35	11.81	27.5	1.30	30.31
26–30	550	0.37 ± 0.06	0.00	14.31	25.1	1.48 ± 0.21	0.73	37.00 ± 2.80	0.58	19.68	35.8	1.61	35.20
31–35	195	0.51 ± 0.14	0.00	21.94	30.3	1.68 ± 0.42	0.96	46.90 ± 4.31	0.45	22.61	33.0	1.69	45.75
36–40	97	0.44 ± 0.09	0.00	21.74	40.2	1.09 ± 0.18	0.67	42.17 ± 5.32	0.41	22.01	38.7	1.06	40.42
41–45	56	0.44 ± 0.14	0.00	25.51	37.5	1.18 ± 0.32	0.50	42.17 ± 7.24	....	....	....	....	....
46–50	39	0.61 ± 0.20	0.00	32.64	35.9	1.69 ± 0.43	1.25	54.25 ± 9.08	....	....	....	....	....
Married Males													
16–20	272	0.10 ± 0.04	0.00	2.21	8.5	1.20 ± 0.41	0.32	9.20 ± 2.19	0.11	2.31	9.3	1.25	8.25
21–25	751	0.03 ± 0.01	0.00	0.83	7.5	0.43 ± 0.10	0.09	7.60 ± 2.16	0.04	0.86	10.6	0.37	4.69
26–30	737	0.02 ± 0.01	0.00	0.69	4.6	0.48 ± 0.11	0.13	11.38 ± 3.54	0.03	0.75	6.9	0.38	6.91
31–35	569	0.02 ± 0.01	0.00	0.67	3.9	0.47 ± 0.14	0.09	10.50 ± 4.53	0.02	0.72	4.8	0.47	9.11
36–40	390	0.02 ± 0.01	0.00	0.67	2.8	0.57 ± 0.33	0.10	7.55 ± 2.52	0.01	0.53	2.8	0.42	9.04
41–45	272	0.02 ± 0.02	0.00	0.86	2.2	0.76 ± 0.71	0.07	5.50 ± 4.52	0.01	0.33	2.1	0.22	2.34
46–50	175	....	0.00	1.41	1.7	1.47 ± 1.42	0.10	12.17 ± 10.45	0.01	0.40	1.2	0.52	6.07

Table 58. Homosexual outlets and age

For explanations, see the legend with Table 51 on Masturbation.

among males who are actually having such experience, is matched only by the increased significance which pre-marital intercourse plays in the lives of the older single males. Among married males, the rise in importance of extra-marital intercourse is chiefly at the expense of marital intercourse which contributes less and less to the total picture. The other outlets, masturbation, nocturnal dreams, and the homosexual, are not so modified by the extra-marital intercourse.

From about 7.5 per cent to 14.5 per cent of the extra-marital intercourse is had with prostitutes (Table 55, Figures 77–82). The figures on the available histories fluctate from group to group, without a discernible aging effect, at least up to age 60. The percentage of married males involved with prostitutes drops steadily from 19.5 per cent among the young 20-year olds, to 7.9 per cent at age 50. The frequencies among the active males stay quite constant (between 0.18 and 0.27) at all ages, without any definite trend. For males who have any extra-marital intercourse with prostitutes, the contacts account for about 3.6 per cent of the total sexual outlet at earlier ages. The significance of such intercourse increases with advancing age among these males who are actively involved. It finally approaches a figure which is nearly a fifth (18.4%) of the total outlet of these males in their fifties. This increase in percent of total outlet derived from extra-marital intercourse with prostitutes is in striking contrast with the lowered incidences, frequencies, and significances, with advancing age, of most other types of sexual activity. The meaning of this will be discussed in Chapter 20.

The individuals who have extra-marital intercourse with prostitutes most frequently are in the youngest age group, 16 to 20 years of age; but since the percentage of the total sexual outlet which is drawn from that source is lowest in the youngest group, and rises gradually to 50 years of age, it is apparent that prostitutes are important in replacing other sources of outlet among older males.

HOMOSEXUAL ACTIVITY AND AGE

Homosexual activity in the human male is much more frequent than is ordinarily realized (Chapter 21). In the youngest unmarried group, more than a quarter (27.3%) of the males have some homosexual activity to the point of orgasm (Table 58, Figures 83–88). The incidence among these single males rises in successive age groups until it reaches a maximum of 38.7 per cent between 36 and 40 years of age.

High frequencies do not occur as often in the homosexual as they do in some other kinds of sexual activity (Table 49). Populations are more homogeneous in regard to this outlet. This may reflect the difficulties involved in having frequent and regular relations in a socially taboo activity. Nevertheless, there are a few of the younger adolescent males who have homo-

ANIMAL CONTACTS AND AGE

AGE GROUP	CASES	ANIMAL CONTACTS: SAMPLE POPULATION							ANIMAL CONTACTS: U. S. POPULATION					
		TOTAL POPULATION			ACTIVE POPULATION				TOTAL POPULATION		ACTIVE POPULATION		
		Mean Frequency	Median Freq.	% of Total Outlet	Incid. %	Mean Frequency	Median Freq.	% of Total Outlet	Mean Freq.	% of Total Outlet	Incid. %	Mean Freq.	% of Total Outlet
Adol.–15	3012	0.022 ± 0.005	0.00	0.78	5.9	0.38 ± 0.077	0.076	5.88 ± 0.90	0.023	0.74	5.9	0.39	6.92
16–20	2868	0.019 ± 0.005	0.00	0.66	3.5	0.54 ± 0.12	0.094	9.88 ± 1.57	0.029	0.87	4.2	0.69	11.96
21–25	1535	0.003 ± 0.002	0.00	0.13	1.0	0.32 ± 0.12	0.094	11.13 ± 3.71	0.003	0.11	1.2	0.28	14.70
26–30	550	0.002 ± 0.002	0.00	0.063	0.5	0.30 ± 0.25	0.10	4.67 ± 4.17	0.001	0.04	0.7	0.13	1.40
31–35	195	.....	.....	.....	2.1	0.30 ± 0.25	.....	.....	.....	.....	.....	.....	.....

Single Males

Table 59. Animal contacts and age

For explanations, see the legend with Table 51 on Masturbation.

sexual frequencies of 7 or more per week, and between 26 and 30 the maximum frequencies run to 15 per week. By 50 years of age the most active individual is averaging only 5.0 per week.

For single, active populations, the mean frequencies of homosexual contacts (Table 58, Figures 83–88) rise more or less steadily from near once per week (0.8 per week) for the younger adolescent boys to nearly twice as often (1.7 per week) for males between the ages of 31 and 35. They stand above once a week through age 50.

In the population as a whole, among boys in their teens, about 8 per cent of the total sexual outlet is derived from the homosexual. Calculating only for the single males who are actually participating, the average active male in his teens gets about 18 per cent of his outlet from that source, and the figure is increasingly higher until, at 50 years of age, the average male who is still single and actively involved gets 54 per cent of his outlet from the homosexual. This, and pre-marital intercourse with prostitutes, are the only sources of outlet which become an increasing part of the sexual activity of single males. For most other kinds of outlet, as we have shown, the figures drop with advancing age. Since there is a steady decline in frequency of total sexual outlet for the average male, and since there is an increase both in frequencies and in percentage of total outlet derived from the homosexual, it is obvious that this outlet acquires a definitely greater significance, and a very real significance, in the lives of most unmarried males who have anything at all to do with it. There is considerable conflict among younger males over participation in such socially taboo activity, and there is evidence that a much higher percentage of younger males is attracted and aroused than ever engages in overt homosexual activities to the point of orgasm. Gradually, over a period of years, many males who are aroused by homosexual situations become more frank in their acceptance and more direct in their pursuit of complete relations (Chapter 21), although some of them are still much restrained by fear of blackmail.

Homosexual contact as an extra-marital activity is recorded by about 10 per cent of the teen-age and young 20-year old married males. By 50 years of age, it is admitted by only 1 per cent of the still married males, but this latter figure is undoubtedly below the fact. Average frequencies fluctuate between once a week to once in two or three weeks for the married males who have any such contacts; and there is no distinct age trend. From 4 to 9 per cent of the total outlet of these married males is drawn from the homosexual source, but again there is no apparent age trend.

ANIMAL CONTACTS AND AGE

Contacts between the human and animals of other species are largely confined to the rural portions of the male population. Rural-urban backgrounds are, consequently, the most important factors in determining the incidence and frequency of this sort of outlet. Animal contacts include the usual type of heterosexual intercourse and also anal and oral techniques which provide orgasm for the human males. The present calculations include all three types of relations.

There are some data which indicate that the frequency of animal contacts varies tremendously in different parts of the United States. The figures given here apply primarily to the northeastern quarter of the country.

About 6 per cent of the total male population is involved in animal contacts during early adolescence (Table 59). This is the highest incidence figure at any age. The figure drops to about 1 per cent in the single population over 20 years of age. If only the unmarried rural population is considered, the incidence figures range from 11 per cent at 11–15 years of age to 4 per cent at 25 years of age. Differences in social level affect this activity, and the figures need further analyses on that basis (Table 124).

The maximum frequencies in animal intercourse (for the most active individual) go up to 8.0 per week for the population between adolescence and 15 years of age (Table 49). The most active cases in the next age group drop to 4.0 per week, and to 0.1 per week by 30 years of age.

Animal intercourse has the lowest frequencies of all the sources that contribute to sexual outlet. For the total population (including persons who never engage in the activity) the average never rises above once or twice in a year; but for those who actually utilize this source of outlet, the frequency is about twice in three weeks (0.69 per week) in the late teens. There are too few active cases to generalize for older groups. The average boy who is having animal intercourse draws 7 per cent of his total outlet from that source in his early teens, and nearly 15 per cent of his outlet from that source between ages 21 and 25. There are cases of animal intercourse that extend with some frequency into the fifties, and in one case past 80 years of age. In general, the picture is one of decreasing incidence, decreasing frequency, and decreasing significance in the later years; but the cases are so few and the rural-urban factors are so significant, that these data are not readily interpreted without further breakdown.

POST-MARITAL OUTLETS AND AGE

Among the males who have been married, but whose marriages have been terminated by death, separation, or divorce, there is sexual activity which in frequency is considerably above that of the single male, and nearly as high as among the married males. The effects of aging are, of course, apparent in this group. The detailed record is given in Chapter 8 on Marital Status and Sexual Outlet.

Chapter 8

MARITAL STATUS AND SEXUAL OUTLET

Among the social factors affecting sexual activity, marital status is the one that would seem most likely to influence both the frequencies and the sources of the individual's outlet. The data, however, need detailed analyses.

SOCIAL AND LEGAL LIMITATIONS

In social and religious philosophies, there have been two antagonistic interpretations of sex. There have been cultures and religions which have inclined to the hedonistic doctrine that sexual activity is justifiable for its immediate and pleasurable return; and there have been cultures and religions which accept sex primarily as the necessary means of procreation, to be enjoyed only in marriage, and then only if reproduction is the goal of the act. The Hebrews were among the Asiatics who held this ascetic approach to sex; and Christian sexual philosophy and English-American sex law is largely built around these Hebraic interpretations, around Greek ascetic philosophies, and around the asceticism of some of the Roman cults (Angus 1925, May 1931).

A third possible interpretation of sex as a normal biologic function, acceptable in whatever form it is manifested, has hardly figured in either general or scientific discussions. By English and American standards, such an attitude is considered primitive, materialistic or animalistic, and beneath the dignity of a civilized and educated people. Freud has contributed more than the biologists toward an adoption of this biologic viewpoint.

Since English-American moral codes and sex laws are the direct outcome of the reproductive interpretation of sex, they accept no form of socio-sexual activity outside of the marital state; and even marital intercourse is more or less limited to particular times and places and to the techniques which are most likely to result in conception. By this system, no socio-sexual outlet is provided for the single male or for the widowed or divorced male, since they cannot legally procreate; and homosexual and solitary sources of outlet, since they are completely without reproductive possibilities, are penalized or frowned upon by public opinion and by the processes of the law.

Specifically, English-American legal codes restrict the sexual activity of the unmarried male by characterizing all pre-marital, extra-marital, and post-marital intercourse as rape, statutory rape, fornication, adultery, prostitution, association with a prostitute, incest, delinquency, a contribution to delinquency, assault and battery, or public indecency—all of which are offenses with penalties attached. However it is labelled, all intercourse outside of marriage (non-marital intercourse) is illicit and subject to penalty by statute law in most of the states of the Union, or by the precedent of the common law on which most courts, in all states, chiefly depend when sex is involved. In addition to their restrictions on heterosexual intercourse, statute law and the common law penalize all homosexual activity, and all sexual contacts with animals; and they specifically limit the techniques of marital intercourse. Mouth-genital and anal contacts are punishable as crimes whether they occur in heterosexual or homosexual relations and whether in or outside of marriage. Such manual manipulation as occurs in the petting which is common in the younger generation has been interpreted in some courts as an impairment of the morals of a minor, or even as assault and battery. The public exhibition of any kind of sexual activity, including self masturbation, or the viewing of such activity, is punishable as a contribution to delinquency or as public indecency.

There have been occasional court decisions which have attempted to limit the individual's right to solitary masturbation; and the statutes of at least one state (Indiana Acts 1905, ch. 169, § 473, p. 584) rule that the encouragement of self masturbation is an offense punishable as sodomy. Under a literal interpretation of this law, it is possible that a teacher, biologist, psychologist, physician or other person who published the scientifically determinable fact that masturbation does no physical harm might be prosecuted for encouraging some person to "commit masturbation." There have been penal commitments of adults who have given sex instruction to minors, and there are evidently some courts who are inclined to interpret all sex instruction as a contribution to the delinquency of minors. In state controlled penal and mental institutions, and in homes for dependent children, the administrations are authorized to establish rules of sexual behavior which go beyond the definitions of courtroom law It is the usual practice in such institutions to impose penalties, including physical punishment, for masturbation, and we have histories from at least two institutions which imposed equally severe penalties for nocturnal emissions. The United States Naval Academy at Annapolis considers evidence of masturbation sufficient grounds for refusing admission to a candidate (U. S. Naval Acad. Regul., June 1940). It is probable that the courts would defend the right of the administrators of institutions to impose such ultimate restrictions upon the sexual outlets of their charges.

Concepts of sexual perversion depend in part on this same reproductive interpretation of sex. Sodomy laws are usually indefinite in their descriptions of acts that are punishable; perversions are defined as unnatural acts, acts contrary to nature, bestial, abominable, and detestable. Such laws are

interpretable only in accordance with the ancient tradition of the English
common law which, as has already been indicated, is committed to the
doctrine that no sexual activity is justifiable unless its objective is procreation.

Official church attitudes toward contraception and abortion similarly
stem from the demand that there be no interference with reproduction.
They are consistent in denying the use of contraceptives in marriage and in
intercourse which is outside of marriage, for intercourse outside of marriage is illegal and not a legitimate source of procreation. Medical and
presumably scientific data which are adduced in support of the objections
to contraception and abortion, are rationalizations or confusions of the
real issue, which is the reproductive value of any kind of sexual behavior.

In addition to establishing restrictions by way of the statutory and common law, society at large, and each element in it, have developed mores
that even more profoundly affect the frequency of sexual activity and the
general pattern of behavior. Some of the community attitudes fortify certain of the legal interpretations, even though no segment of society accepts
the whole of the legal code, as its behavior and expressed attitudes demonstrate (Chapter 10). Often the social proscriptions involve more than
is in the law, and the individual who conforms with the traditions of the
social level to which he belongs, is restricted in such detail as the written
codes never venture to cover. Group attitudes become his "conscience,"
and he accepts group interpretations, thinking them the product of his
own wisdom. Each type of sex act acquires values, becomes right or wrong,
socially useful or undesirable. Esthetic values are attached: limitations
are set on the times and places where sexual relations may be had; the
social niceties (and the law) forbid the presence of witnesses to sexual acts;
there are standards of physical cleanliness and supposed requirements of
hygiene and sanitation which may become more important than the gratification of sexual drives; the forms of courtesy between men and women
may receive especial attention when sexual relations are involved; the
effect of the relations upon the sexual partner, the effect upon the subsequent sexual, marital, or business relations with the partner, the effect
upon the subject's own self esteem or subsequent mental or physical happiness, or conflict—may all be involved in the decision to have, or not to
have, a socio-sexual relation. While the decision seems to rest upon personal desires, ideals, and concepts of esthetics, the individual's standards
are very largely set by the mores of the social level to which he belongs. In
the end, their effect is strongly to limit his opportunity for intercourse, or
for most other types of sexual activity, especially if he is unmarried, widowed, separated, or divorced.

A lower level male has fewer esthetic demands and social forms to
satisfy. By the time he becomes an adolescent, he has learned that it is

TOTAL OUTLET, MARITAL STATUS, AND AGE

AGE GROUP	TOTAL SAMPLE POPULATION					
	CASES			MEAN FREQUENCY		
	Single	Married	Post-marital	Single	Married	Post-marital
Adol.–15	3012			2.91		
16–20	2868	272	46	2.88	4.67	4.08
21–25	1535	751	119	2.67	3.90	3.70
26–30	550	737	182	2.63	3.27	2.93
31–35	195	569	158	2.38	2.73	1.93
36–40	97	390	128	2.07	2.46	1.69
41–45	56	272	96	1.79	1.95	1.49
46–50	39	175	63	1.88	1.79	1.26
51–55		109	42		1.54	1.17
56–60		67			1.08	

AGE GROUP	ACTIVE CASES IN SAMPLE POPULATION					
	INCIDENCE %			MEAN FREQUENCY		
	Single	Married	Post-marital	Single	Married	Post-marital
Adol.–15	95.1			3.06		
16–20	99.2	100.0	97.8	2.90	4.67	4.17
21–25	99.1	100.0	98.3	2.70	3.90	3.76
26–30	99.3	100.0	97.3	2.65	3.27	3.01
31–35	99.0	100.0	94.9	2.40	2.73	2.04
36–40	97.9	99.7	97.7	2.12	2.47	1.73
41–45	96.4	100.0	93.7	1.85	1.95	1.59
46–50	92.3	98.9	93.7	2.04	1.81	1.35
51–55		98.2	88.1		1.57	1.33
56–60		98.5			1.09	

AGE GROUP	CORRECTED FOR U. S. POPULATION					
	TOTAL POPULATION		ACTIVE POPULATION			
	MEAN FREQUENCY		INCIDENCE %		MEAN FREQUENCY	
	Single	Married	Single	Married	Single	Married
Adol.–15	3.17		94.2		3.36	
16–20	3.30	4.83	98.8	100.0	3.35	4.83
21–25	3.04	4.14	97.9	100.0	3.11	4.14
26–30	2.94	3.51	98.6	100.0	2.98	3.51
31–35	2.44	2.90	99.2	100.0	2.46	2.90
36–40	2.00	2.42	98.5	99.9	2.04	2.42
41–45		1.95		100.0		1.95
46–50		1.80		98.1		1.83
51–55		1.54		97.2		1.58

Table 60. Total outlet in relation to marital status and age

Data for the U. S. population are based on the sample population which is corrected for the distribution of educational levels which is shown in the U. S. Census for 1940. For sigmas of means, median frequencies, etc., see the tables in Chapter 7.

TOTAL OUTLET

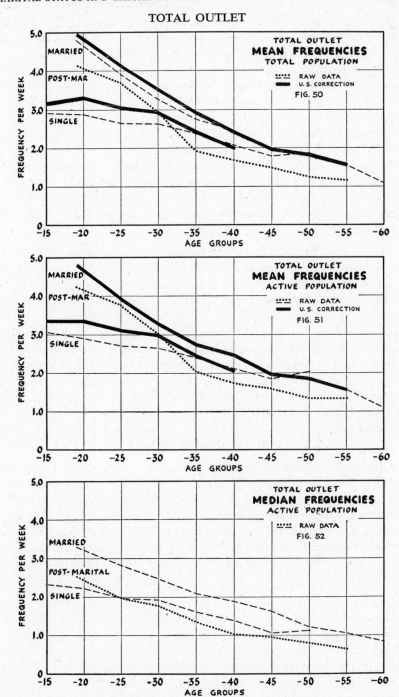

Figures 50–52. Relation of age and marital status to frequency of total outlet

Solid lines represent the U. S. Corrections.

possible to josh any passing girl, ask for a simple social date, and, inside of a few minutes, suggest intercourse. Such financial resources as will provide a drink, tickets for a movie, or an automobile ride, are at that level sufficient for making the necessary approaches. Such things are impossible for most better educated males. Education develops a demand for more elaborate recreation and more extended social contacts. The average college male plans repeated dates, dinners, expensive entertainments, and long-time acquaintances before he feels warranted in asking for a complete sexual relation. There is, in consequence, a definitely greater limitation on the heterosexual activities of the educated portion of the population, and a higher frequency of solitary outlets in that group. Upper level males rationalize their lack of socio-sexual activities in terms of right and wrong, but it is certain that the social formalities have a great deal to do with their chastity.

In any case, at any social level, the human animal is more hampered in its pursuit of sexual contacts than the primitive anthropoid in the wild; and, at any level, the restrictions would appear to be most severe for males who are not married. One should expect, then, that the sexual histories of unmarried males would contrast sharply with the histories of married adults; and that, at the end of two thousand years of social monitoring, at least some unmarried males might be found who follow the custom and the law and live abstinent, celibate, sublimated, and wholly chaste lives. Scientists will, however, want to examine the specific data showing the effect of marital status on the human male's total sexual outlet, and on his choice of particular outlets (if he has any) in his single, married, or post-marital states.

TOTAL SEXUAL OUTLET

The mean frequencies of total sexual outlet for the married males are always, at all age levels, higher than the total outlets for single males; but, as already pointed out (Chapter 6), essentially all single males have regular and usually frequent sexual outlet, whether before marriage, or after being widowed, separated, or divorced. Of the more than five thousand males who have contributed to the present study, only 1 per cent has lived for as much as five years (after the onset of adolescence and outside of old age) without orgasm.

As previously recorded, the mean frequency of the total outlet for the single males between 16 and 20 is (on the basis of the U. S. Corrections) about 3.3 per week (Table 60, Figures 50–52). The mean frequency of total outlet for the married male is about 4.8 per week, which is 47 per cent above the average outlet of the single male At 30, the frequencies for the married males are about 18 per cent above those of the single males, and approximately this relation holds for some period of years. Beyond 40 years of age, tl.e single males may actually exceed the married males in their sexual frequencies. In adolescent years, the restrictions upon the sexual activity of the unmarried male are greatest. He finds it more difficult to locate sources of outlet and he has not learned the techniques for approaching and utilizing those sources when they are available. Nevertheless, his frequency between adolescence and 16 does average about 3.0 per week and between 16 and 20 it amounts to nearly 3.4 per week. This represents arousal that leads to orgasm on an average of about every other day. By the time he is 30, the single male has become much more efficient in his social approaches and does not lag far behind the married individual in his performance. Considering the physical advantage which the married individual has in securing intercourse without going outside of his own home, it is apparent that the older single male develops skills in making social approaches and finding places for sexual contacts which far exceed the skills of married persons. Beau Brummels and Casanovas are not married males. A few of the married males who are involved in promiscuous extra-marital activity are the only ones whose facilities begin to compare with those found among unmarried groups. It is notable that in the male homosexual, where long-time unions are not often maintained and new partners are being continually sought, there are many persons who preserve this same facility for making social contacts for long periods of years.

The differences that exist between the total activities of the younger married male and the younger unmarried male are, to some degree, a measure of the effectiveness of the social pressures that keep the single male's performance below his native capacity; although the lower rates in the single males may depend, in part, upon the possibility that less responsive males may not marry so young, or may never marry. On the other hand, the fact that the single male, from adolescence to 30 years of age, does have a frequency of nearly 3.0 per week is evidence of the ineffectiveness of social restrictions and of the imperativeness of the biologic demands. For those who like the term, it is clear that there is a sexual drive which cannot be set aside for any large portion of the population, by any sort of social convention. For those who prefer to think in simpler terms of action and reaction, it is a picture of an animal who, however civilized or cultured, continues to respond to the constantly present sexual stimuli, albeit with some social and physical restraints.

In addition to the differences in frequencies of total outlet between married and single males, there are minor differences in incidence and in range of variation in the groups. Between adolescence and 15 years of age, 95 per cent of the unmarried boys have some sort of sexual outlet. From 16 to 35 years of age, 99 per cent or more of these males are engaging in some form of sexual activity (Table 60). Among the married males, a full 100 per cent is sexually active between 16 and 35 years of age. Beyond

MASTURBATION

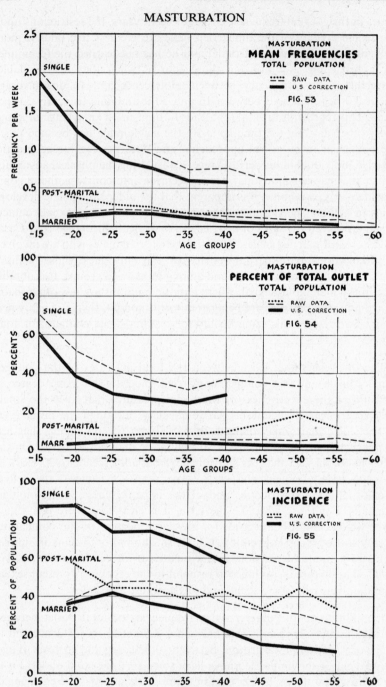

Figures 53–55. Relation of age and marital status to masturbation

Solid lines represent the U. S. Corrections.

MASTURBATION

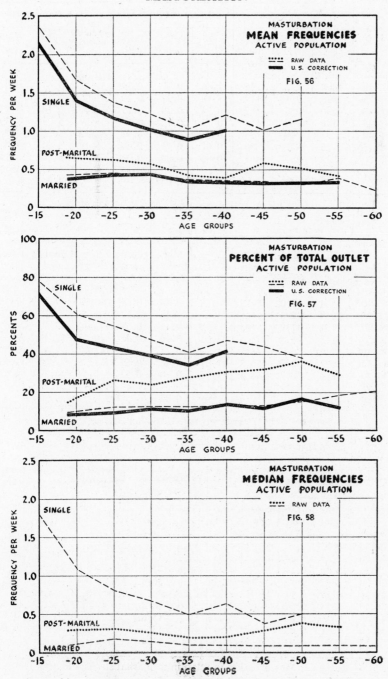

Figures 56–58. Relation of age and marital status to masturbation

Solid lines represent the U. S. Corrections.

TOTAL SAMPLE POPULATION

AGE GROUP	CASES			MEAN FREQUENCY			% OF TOTAL OUTLET		
	Single	Married	Post-mar.	Single	Married	Post-mar.	Single	Married	Post-mar.
Adol.–15	3012			2.02			70.33		
16–20	2868	272	46	1.46	0.17	0.36	51.28	3.63	9.01
21–25	1535	751	119	1.10	0.21	0.28	41.95	5.52	7.61
26–30	550	737	182	0.94	0.20	0.25	36.40	6.19	8.72
31–35	195	569	158	0.73	0.16	0.16	31.29	6.03	8.35
36–40	97	390	128	0.76	0.13	0.17	37.32	5.22	9.71
41–45	56	272	96	0.61	0.11	0.20	35.19	5.64	13.28
46–50	39	175	63	0.62	0.09	0.23	33.13	5.11	18.39
51–55		109	42		0.10	0.14		6.35	11.49
56–60		67			0.04			4.06	

ACTIVE CASES IN SAMPLE POPULATION

AGE GROUP	INCIDENCE %			MEAN FREQUENCY			% OF TOTAL OUTLET		
	Single	Married	Post-mar.	Single	Married	Post-mar.	Single	Married	Post-mar.
Adol.–15	85.4			2.36			77.94		
16–20	88.4	39.0	56.5	1.66	0.43	0.64	60.23	9.91	17.13
21–25	80.7	47.8	44.5	1.37	0.45	0.62	54.40	12.15	26.25
26–30	77.1	47.9	44.0	1.22	0.42	0.58	47.34	12.50	24.00
31–35	71.3	45.5	38.6	1.02	0.36	0.42	40.43	12.44	28.25
36–40	62.9	36.7	42.2	1.20	0.35	0.39	47.06	12.41	30.59
41–45	60.7	32.7	33.3	1.01	0.34	0.59	43.66	12.66	32.06
46–50	53.8	30.9	44.4	1.15	0.30	0.52	37.88	14.94	36.57
51–55		25.7	33.3		0.38	0.41		18.18	29.43
56–60		19.4			0.22			20.86	

CORRECTED FOR U. S. POPULATION

AGE GROUP	TOTAL POPULATION				ACTIVE POPULATION					
	MEAN FREQUENCY		% OF TOTAL OUTLET		INCIDENCE %		MEAN FREQUENCY		% OF TOTAL OUTLET	
	Single	Married	Single	Married	Single	Married	Single	Married	Single	Married
Adol.–15	1.86		60.22		87.2		2.14		71.02	
16–20	1.23	0.14	38.50	2.95	87.7	37.1	1.40	0.38	47.76	8.29
21–25	0.06	0.17	29.52	4.40	73.6	42.1	1.16	0.42	43.12	9.40
26–30	0.75	0.16	26.94	4.57	73.9	36.5	1.02	0.43	39.12	11.34
31–35	0.59	0.11	24.94	3.79	67.6	32.8	0.88	0.34	34.03	10.25
36–40	0.58	0.07	29.09	2.95	57.7	22.2	1.01	0.33	41.30	13.17
41–45		0.05		2.43		15.0		0.32		11.80
46–50		0.05		2.53		13.6		0.33		16.29
51–55		0.03		2.13		11.4		0.34		12.09

Table 61. Masturbation in relation to marital status and age

Data for the U. S. population are based on the sample population which is corrected for the distribution of educational levels shown in the U. S. Census for 1940. For sigmas of means, median frequencies, etc., see the tables in Chapter 7.

35, the incidence figures drop for single males, and at a somewhat faster rate than for married males. The differences are not great.

The range of variation in frequency of outlet in any particular age group is also nearly identical for single and married males. In both populations (Table 49), there are individuals who engage in sexual activity only a few times a year, and there are some who engage in sexual activities regularly 3 or 4 or more times per day (29 or more per week). The lower average rates for single males are not dependent upon the fact that there are no high-rating individuals in that group, but upon the fact that there is a larger number of the single males who have lower rates, and a larger number of married males who have higher rates. At least half of the younger married males have outlets which average 3 or more per week, whereas only a third of the single males fall into that category.

Throughout both single and married histories, there is a steady decline in total sexual outlet in successive age groups (Chapter 7). After 30 years of age this decline in any 5-year period (Figures 50–52) is very nearly as great as the differences between married and single males of the same age group. Age is eventually as important as all of the social, moral, and legal factors which differentiate single from married histories.

SOURCES OF SEXUAL OUTLET

Every one of the possible sources of sexual outlet is to be found in both single and married histories, except as the activities are limited by definition (as in the case of pre-marital intercourse and extra-marital intercourse). The primary forces determining which particular outlets are utilized are the mores of the social level in which the individual is raised (Chapter 10). Nevertheless, marital status is a prime factor in regard to certain of the outlets.

Masturbation, although it is found in practically all male histories, is very much restricted by the conventions of particular social groups. In all groups, however, it is much more frequent in single histories. It provides about three-quarters (71%) of the sexual outlet for about 85 per cent of the single males below 15 years of age (Table 61, Figures 53–58). The figure is lower for lower educational levels (52.3% for boys who never go beyond eighth grade) and higher (79.6%) for boys who will ultimately go to college (Chapter 10). Between 16 and 20, the incidence begins to go down for all levels, although up until marriage masturbation remains the chief source of sexual outlet for unmarried males who belong to that portion of the population that goes to college. The unmarried males who are actually in college draw nearly two-thirds of their total sexual outlet from masturbation, while pre-marital intercourse accounts for little more than a tenth of the outlet of the group (Table 64). On the other hand, for boys who never get beyond the eighth grade in school, masturbation provides a little more

NOCTURNAL EMISSIONS

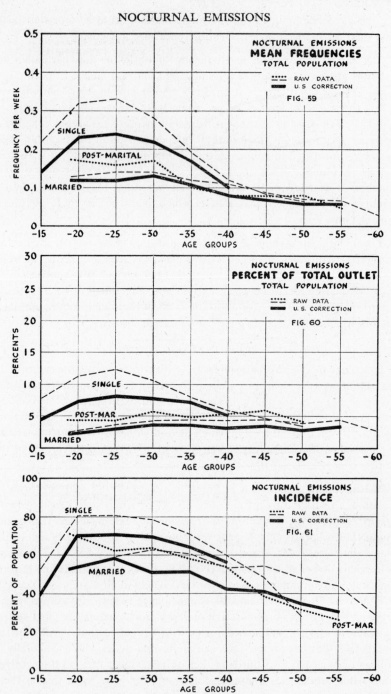

Figures 59–61. Relation of age and marital status to nocturnal emissions

Solid lines represent the U. S. Corrections.

NOCTURNAL EMISSIONS

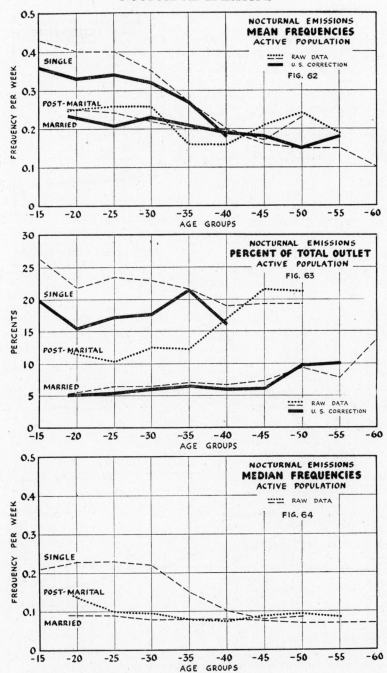

Figures 62–64. Relation of age and marital status to nocturnal emissions

Solid lines represent the U. S. Corrections.

NOCTURNAL EMISSIONS, MARITAL STATUS, AND AGE

AGE GROUP	TOTAL SAMPLE POPULATION								
	CASES			MEAN FREQUENCY			% OF TOTAL OUTLET		
	Single	Married	Post-marital	Single	Married	Post-marital	Single	Married	Post-marital
Adol.–15	3012			0.22			7.80		
16–20	2868	272	46	0.32	0.13	0.17	11.29	2.85	4.27
21–25	1535	751	119	0.33	0.14	0.16	12.40	3.68	4.44
26–30	550	737	182	0.28	0.14	0.17	10.67	4.29	5.79
31–35	195	569	158	0.19	0.12	0.10	8.11	4.54	4.89
36–40	97	390	128	0.12	0.11	0.08	5.93	4.40	4.90
41–45	56	272	96	0.08	0.09	0.08	4.73	4.50	5.53
46–50	39	175	63	0.07	0.07	0.08	3.51	3.91	5.96
51–55		109	42		0.07	0.05		4.42	4.13
56–60		67			0.03			2.73	

AGE GROUP	ACTIVE CASES IN SAMPLE POPULATION								
	INCIDENCE %			MEAN FREQUENCY			% OF TOTAL OUTLET		
	Single	Married	Post-marital	Single	Married	Post-marital	Single	Married	Post-marital
Adol.–15	52.2			0.43			26.49		
16–20	80.3	52.9	69.6	0.40	0.25	0.25	21.72	5.57	11.59
21–25	80.8	59.0	62.2	0.40	0.24	0.26	23.47	6.49	10.33
26–30	78.7	62.6	63.7	0.35	0.22	0.26	22.98	6.49	12.55
31–35	70.8	60.6	58.2	0.27	0.20	0.16	21.68	7.18	12.35
36–40	59.8	53.3	53.9	0.20	0.20	0.16	19.12	6.80	17.09
41–45	48.2	54.4	38.5	0.17	0.16	0.21	19.48	7.49	21.58
46–50	28.2	48.0	31.7	0.23	0.15	0.24	19.59	9.40	21.25
51–55		44.0	26.2		0.15	0.19		7.90	10.27
56–60		28.4			0.10			13.79	

AGE GROUP	CORRECTED FOR U. S. POPULATION									
	TOTAL POPULATION				ACTIVE POPULATION					
	MEAN FREQUENCY		% OF TOTAL OUTLET		INCIDENCE %		MEAN FREQUENCY		% OF TOTAL OUTLET	
	Single	Married	Single	Married	Single	Married	Single	Married	Single	Married
Adol.–15	0.14		4.55		39.1		0.36		19.97	
16–20	0.23	0.12	7.41	2.52	70.2	53.3	0.33	0.23	15.53	5.17
21–25	0.24	0.12	8.28	3.09	70.9	58.4	0.34	0.21	17.36	5.45
26–30	0.22	0.13	7.92	3.65	69.9	50.8	0.32	0.23	17.86	6.00
31–35	0.17	0.11	7.34	3.73	64.3	51.5	0.27	0.21	21.50	6.56
36–40	0.10	0.08	5.17	3.24	56.4	42.1	0.18	0.19	16.17	5.99
41–45		0.07		3.55		41.1		0.18		6.08
46–50		0.06		2.97		34.9		0.15		9.79
51–55		0.06		3.50		30.4		0.18		10.06

Table 62. Nocturnal emissions in relation to marital status and age

Data for the U. S. population are based on the sample population which is corrected for the distribution of educational levels shown in the U. S. Census for 1940. For sigmas of means, median frequencies, etc., see the tables in Chapter 7.

than a quarter (29.2%) of the sexual outlet in their late teens. As soon as marriage occurs, the incidence and frequency of masturbation drop considerably in all social levels. Among college-bred males over two-thirds (69%) of the married men have some self masturbation in their histories. The frequencies in married histories are, however, definitely low, and there are few individuals who have rates that exceed once or twice per week. At lower educational levels only about a third of the married males (29% to 42% in various groups) ever masturbate, and the frequencies are much lower than in upper levels, averaging not a quarter as high as in the corresponding group of single males.

Nocturnal emissions vary in frequency in different social levels, the figures being higher for upper level males and lower for more poorly educated males. They reach their highest incidence in single males between 21 and 30 years of age. About 85 per cent of the single males have at least some experience with nocturnal dreams that lead to climax (Table 133, Figures 138–139). Hardly more than half of the married males (58.4%) have nocturnal emissions in any particular age group. In younger single males (of the total population), the emissions occur twice as often as among married males of the same age (Table 62, Figures 59–64). In older groups, the incidences and frequencies of nocturnal emissions in married males are about two-thirds of what they are in single males. This, in conjunction with the higher rates of total sexual outlet in the married groups, means that nocturnal dreams provide 5 to 15 per cent of the outlet of the single males, but only 2 to 6 per cent of the outlet of the married males. The lower percentages are in lower educational levels, the higher percentages in upper educational levels (Chapter 10).

Pre-marital petting as a source of outlet is, by definition, restricted to the single male. The incentives for petting to the point of climax are chiefly those of avoiding pre-marital intercourse (at the social levels where such intercourse is taboo), and initiating sexual relations by way of an activity which is simpler than actual coitus (Chapter 16). There are some married males who engage in such petting to the point of climax with their wives, and there are some upper level males who engage in extra-marital petting with women other than their wives. At lower social levels, pre-marital petting to the point of climax is relatively rare, and there are few records of the occurrence of such behavior in marriage among the poorly educated groups.

Heterosexual intercourse is the chief pre-marital outlet of the lower social level, although it is a lesser source of outlet for the college-bred portion of the population. Between 16 and 20, it occurs in about 85 per cent of the pre-marital histories of the males who never go beyond eighth grade in school, but it occurs in only 42 per cent of the males who go to college (Table 85, Figure 101). Between 20 and 30, pre-marital intercourse

TOTAL INTERCOURSE

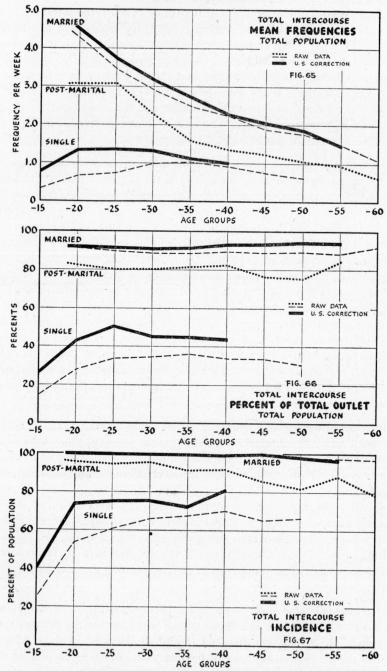

Figures 65–67. Relation of age and marital status to total intercourse
Solid lines represent the U. S. Corrections.

TOTAL INTERCOURSE

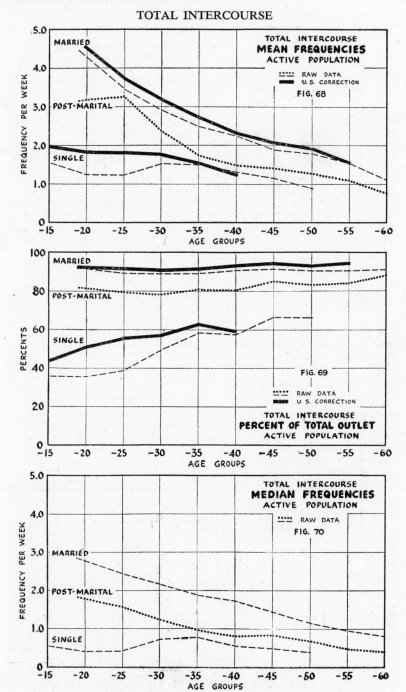

Figures 68–70. Relation of age and marital status to total intercourse
Solid lines represent the U. S. Corrections.

TOTAL INTERCOURSE, MARITAL STATUS, AND AGE

AGE GROUP	TOTAL SAMPLE POPULATION								
	CASES			MEAN FREQUENCY			% OF TOTAL OUTLET		
	Single	Married	Post-marital	Single	Married	Post-marital	Single	Married	Post-marital
Adol.–15	3925			0.34			14.51		
16–20	3739	279	48	0.67	4.27	3.06	27.91	91.31	82.28
21–25	2121	766	150	0.75	3.46	3.08	33.38	89.96	80.12
26–30	607	792	192	1.00	2.90	2.28	34.37	88.83	80.11
31–35	223	623	171	1.02	2.48	1.58	36.11	88.76	81.63
36–40	110	442	146	0.92	2.22	1.37	33.83	89.72	82.45
41–45	61	306	107	0.75	1.89	1.22	33.75	89.00	76.78
46–50	36	197	72	0.61	1.76	1.05	30.58	89.57	75.64
51–55		123	43		1.49	0.96		88.43	84.38
56–60		73	33		1.09	0.62		92.09	

AGE GROUP	ACTIVE CASES IN SAMPLE POPULATION								
	INCIDENCE %			MEAN FREQUENCY			% OF TOTAL OUTLET		
	Single	Married	Post-marital	Single	Married	Post-marital	Single	Married	Post-marital
Adol.–15	21.7			1.56			36.18		
16–20	53.6	100.0	95.8	1.25	4.27	3.19	35.41	91.64	81.64
21–25	60.7	99.9	94.7	1.24	3.46	3.26	38.75	89.54	79.48
26–30	66.1	99.7	95.3	1.51	2.91	2.39	49.29	89.17	78.60
31–35	67.7	99.7	91.2	1.50	2.49	1.73	58.46	89.45	80.92
36–40	70.0	99.1	91.8	1.32	2.24	1.49	57.68	90.87	80.37
41–45	65.6	99.7	86.0	1.14	1.89	1.42	66.56	91.56	85.09
46–50	66.7	98.0	81.9	0.91	1.79	1.28	66.33	90.33	83.25
51–55		97.6	88.4		1.53	1.09		90.50	84.18
56–60		97.3	78.8		1.12	0.79		91.31	88.00

AGE GROUP	CORRECTED FOR U. S. POPULATION								
	TOTAL POPULATION				ACTIVE POPULATION				
	MEAN FREQUENCY		% OF TOTAL OUTLET		INCIDENCE %		MEAN FREQUENCY		% OF TOTAL OUTLET	
	Single	Married	Single	Married	Single	Married	Single	Married	Single	Married
Adol.–15	0.79		26.17		39.9		1.98		43.38	
16–20	1.35	4.51	42.82	92.22	73.7	100.0	1.84	4.51	50.97	92.53
21–25	1.37	3.73	50.33	91.66	75.0	100.0	1.82	3.73	55.64	91.97
26–30	1.34	3.17	45.44	91.05	75.4	99.8	1.77	3.18	57.11	90.99
31–35	1.11	2.72	45.12	91.76	72.2	99.1	1.53	2.72	62.84	91.66
36–40	1.00	2.28	43.72	93.29	80.8	99.0	1.23	2.32	59.66	93.31
41–45		2.04		93.78		99.9		2.04		94.43
46–50		1.87		94.25		98.0		1.91		93.09
51–55		1.48		94.14		96.4		1.54		94.45

Table 63. Total intercourse in relation to marital status and age

Data for the U. S. population are based on the sample population which is corrected for the distribution of educational levels shown in the U. S. Census for 1940. For sigmas of means, median frequencies, etc., see the tables in Chapter 7.

accounts for about two-thirds (57.6% to 68.2%) of the outlet of the males who have not gone beyond eighth grade, although in that same period it accounts for only a fifth (19.4% to 21.4%) of the outlet of the college males.

In marriage, practically 100 per cent of the males of all social levels engage in heterosexual intercourse, except as advancing age limits the activity of some individuals after 45 (Table 56). Among married males of lower educational levels, more than 95 per cent of the total outlet (at 31 to 55 years of age) is derived from intercourse with the spouse or with other females (Table 97, Figures 131–133). Among college-bred males of the same ages, little more than 80 per cent of the total outlet comes from that source. The average for the total married population is about 87 per cent between 31 and 55 years of age. The frequencies of marital coitus are two or three times as high as in the intercourse of the single male (Table 56, Figures 65–70).

For the total married population, of all social levels, about 85 per cent of the sexual outlet comes from the intercourse with the wife (Table 56, Figures 44–49). It will surprise most people that this figure is not higher. Masturbation, nocturnal emissions, heterosexual intercourse with persons other than the wife, homosexual contacts, and animal intercourse provide the remaining 15 per cent of the activity. The proportion derived from marital intercourse varies from 81.4 per cent between 16 and 20 years, to 88.3 per cent at 45 years of age, after which it again drops. In view of the rather high frequency of extra-marital intercourse among lower social levels, it is interesting to find that the highest percentage of outlet derived from the intercourse with the wife (95.5%) is found among those persons who have not gone beyond the twelfth grade in school, and the lowest percentage (61.9%) among older males who have gone to college (Table 97). Whether or not it is true, as some students contend, that marriage as an institution has resulted from the demand for regular intercourse, it is apparent that marriage does provide a more convenient source of sexual activity than is to be had in any other state.

A part of the heterosexual intercourse of the married males is with females other than their wives. This provides 5 to 10 per cent of the total sexual outlet of the married population taken as a whole (Table 64, Figures 71–76). In the youngest age groups, 37 per cent of the males are having extra-marital intercourse, but this figure cuts down to 30 per cent by 50 years of age.

Among single males, in the population as a whole, prostitutes provide 8.6 per cent of the heterosexual intercourse between 16 and 20 years of age. In successive five-year periods, the percentage rises to 13.3, to 22.0, to 28.9 per cent, and (by age 40) to 38.7 per cent. There is some rise in significance of prostitutes among older males of all social levels, although the group that goes to college never derives as much as 1 per cent of its total

NON-MARITAL INTERCOURSE WITH COMPANIONS

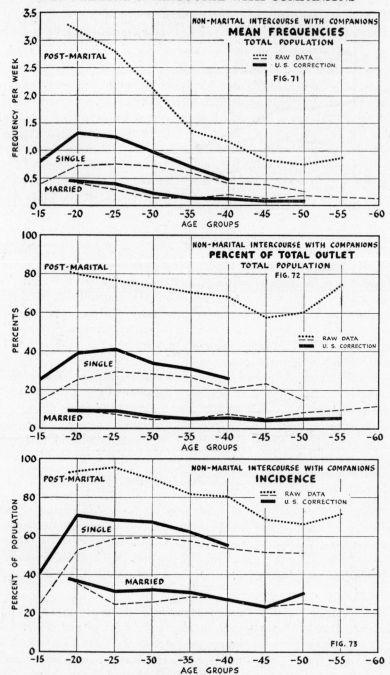

Figures 71–73. Relation of age and marital status to non-marital intercourse with companions

Solid lines represent the U. S. Corrections.

NON-MARITAL INTERCOURSE WITH COMPANIONS

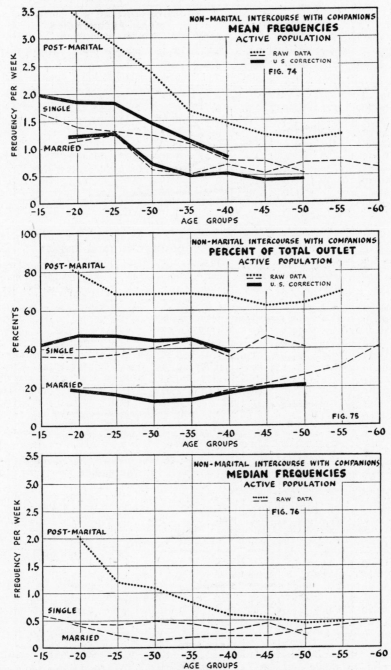

Figures 74–76. Relation of age and marital status to non-marital intercourse with companions

Solid lines represent the U. S. Corrections.

NON-MARITAL INTERCOURSE, MARITAL STATUS, AND AGE

AGE GROUP	TOTAL SAMPLE POPULATION								
	CASES			MEAN FREQUENCY			% OF TOTAL OUTLET		
	Pre-marital	Extra-marital	Post-marital	Pre-marital	Extra-marital	Post-marital	Pre-marital	Extra-marital	Post-marital
Adol.–15	3012			0.40			14.12		
16–20	2868	288	46	0.73	0.41	3.19	25.43	9.08	79.91
21–25	1535	813	119	0.77	0.30	2.79	29.46	7.44	76.87
26–30	550	850	182	0.73	0.16	2.13	28.23	4.71	73.65
31–35	195	666	158	0.61	0.15	1.37	26.44	5.35	70.29
36–40	97	475	128	0.42	0.20	1.17	20.80	7.69	68.64
41–45	56	324	96	0.40	0.13	0.85	23.10	5.24	57.82
46–50	39	210	63	0.28	0.19	0.76	14.81	8.61	60.39
51–55		130	42		0.17	0.88		9.88	74.60
56–60		77			0.14			12.05	

AGE GROUP	ACTIVE CASES IN SAMPLE POPULATION								
	INCIDENCE %			MEAN FREQUENCY			% OF TOTAL OUTLET		
	Pre-marital	Extra-marital	Post-marital	Pre-marital	Extra-marital	Post-marital	Pre-marital	Extra-marital	Post-marital
Adol.–15	24.3			1.67			36.12		
16–20	52.4	35.4	93.5	1.39	1.15	3.41	35.98	18.66	79.34
21–25	58.5	24.4	95.8	1.32	1.25	2.91	37.19	15.68	68.15
26–30	59.5	26.0	89.6	1.23	0.61	2.38	40.26	12.19	68.52
31–35	57.4	28.4	81.6	1.07	0.52	1.68	44.00	13.30	68.27
36–40	53.6	27.8	80.5	0.79	0.71	1.45	35.21	18.44	67.25
41–45	51.8	23.5	68.8	0.77	0.53	1.24	46.28	21.88	62.43
46–50	51.3	25.2	66.7	0.54	0.73	1.15	40.88	26.40	63.71
51–55		22.3	71.4		0.76	1.23		30.84	69.50
56–60		22.1			0.65			40.94	

AGE GROUP	CORRECTED FOR U. S. POPULATION									
	TOTAL POPULATION				ACTIVE POPULATION					
	MEAN FREQUENCY		% OF TOTAL OUTLET		INCIDENCE %		MEAN FREQUENCY		% OF TOTAL OUTLET	
	Pre-marital	Extra-marital	Pre-marital	Extra-marital	Pre-marital	Extra-marital	Pre-marital	Extra-marital	Pre-marital	Extra-marital
Adol.–15	0.80		25.56		40.4		1.98		42.18	
16–20	1.32	0.45	39.16	9.64	70.5	36.8	1.87	1.23	47.10	18.36
21–25	1.25	0.40	40.94	9.22	68.3	31.3	1.83	1.28	47.90	16.36
26–30	0.99	0.24	33.76	6.57	67.3	32.3	1.46	0.72	44.06	12.32
31–35	0.72	0.15	30.96	5.16	62.2	30.9	1.15	0.50	44.96	13.04
36–40	0.48	0.15	26.00	5.82	55.2	27.2	0.86	0.54	38.18	17.42
41–45		0.10		4.50		23.1		0.41		19.96
46–50		0.11		5.88		30.1		0.43		21.33
51–55				6.84						

Table 64. Intercourse with companions in relation to marital status and age

Data for the U. S. population are based on the sample population which is corrected for the distribution of educational levels shown in the U. S. Census for 1940. For sigmas of means, median frequencies, etc., see the tables in Chapter 7.

outlet from this source, while single males who never go beyond high school ultimately get more than 10 per cent of their outlet from prostitutes. The older single males who have never gone beyond grade school may draw nearly a quarter (23.4%) of their outlet from females whom they pay for intercourse (Table 96, Figures 77–82).

Among married males (as a whole group), prostitutes never provide more than one or two per cent of the total sexual outlet. This is true of all social levels and all age groups. Married males are much like single males in finding, as they advance in age, an increasing portion of their hetero-sexual, non-marital outlet with prostitutes. Between 16 and 20, prostitutes provide 10.8 per cent of the extra-marital intercourse and in successive five-year periods the percentages rise to 11.1, to 16.5, to 17.6 per cent (at 35 years of age) and to 22.3 per cent by 55 years of age. Among those married males who go to prostitutes at all (the "active population"), an increasing percentage of the total sexual outlet comes from this source; the figure is 3.6 per cent of the total sexual outlet from prostitutes at 20 years of age, with a steady rise in the figures in older groups, until 18.4 per cent of the total outlet of the 55-year old, prostitute-frequenting, married male is derived from the commercial sources.

The single males at all ages have more frequent paid contacts than the males who have wives. The reported frequencies of intercourse with prosti-tutes for the single males between 16 and 25 (total population) are three or four times as high as among married males of the same age. Between 46 and 50, they are 15 times as high as the frequencies reported by the married males. Marriage is clearly a factor of considerable importance in reducing the frequency of intercourse with prostitutes.

It should, however, be said that we are not entirely confident of the accuracy of these data on extra-marital intercourse, especially among older males from upper social levels. Where social position is dependent upon the maintenance of an appearance of conformity with the sexual conven-tions, males who have had extra-marital intercourse are less inclined to contribute to the present study. Consequently, it is not unlikely that the actual incidence and frequency figures exceed those given here.

Homosexual contacts, as might be expected, are most frequent among unmarried males. The lowest incidence, about 27 per cent, occurs between adolescence and 15 years of age (Table 66, Figures 83–88). The figures steadily rise in older groups of single males. Between 36 and 40 years of age, over a third (38.7% is the corrected figure for the total U. S. popula-tion) of the unmarried males are having some homosexual experience, and uncorrected figures indicate that about half of the unmarried 50-year olds are so involved.

In marriage, the highest recorded incidence is 10.6 per cent, between 21 and 25 years of age. After that, the incidence in the married groups drops

INTERCOURSE WITH PROSTITUTES

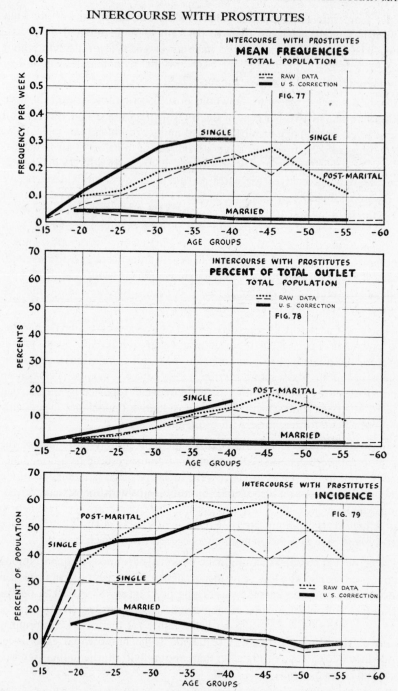

Figures 77–79. Relation of age and marital status to intercourse with prostitutes
Solid lines represent the U. S. Corrections.

INTERCOURSE WITH PROSTITUTES

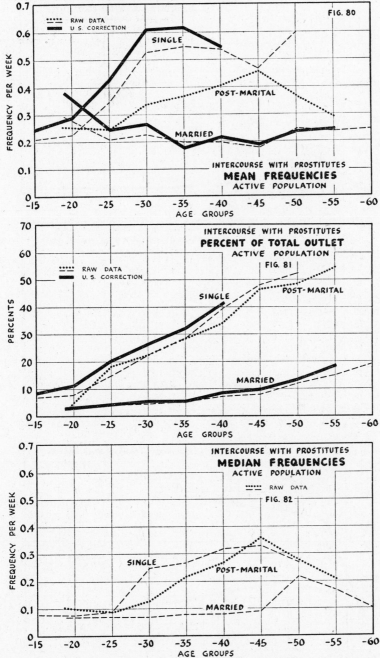

Figures 80–82. Relation of age and marital status to intercourse with prostitutes

Solid lines represent the U. S. Corrections,

INTERCOURSE WITH PROSTITUTES, MARITAL STATUS, AND AGE

AGE GROUP	TOTAL SAMPLE POPULATION								
	CASES			MEAN FREQUENCY			% OF TOTAL OUTLET		
	Pre-marital	Extra-marital	Post-marital	Pre-marital	Extra-marital	Post-marital	Pre-marital	Extra-marital	Post-marital
Adol.–15	3012			0.01			0.39		
16–20	2868	272	46	0.07	0.04	0.10	2.48	0.87	2.37
21–25	1535	751	119	0.10	0.03	0.12	3.92	0.72	3.25
26–30	550	737	182	0.16	0.03	0.19	6.14	0.82	6.46
31–35	195	569	158	0.22	0.02	0.22	9.67	0.84	11.34
36–40	97	390	128	0.26	0.02	0.24	13.03	0.85	13.81
41–45	56	272	96	0.18	0.02	0.28	10.65	0.78	18.96
46–50	39	175	63	0.29	0.01	0.19	15.77	0.80	15.25
51–55		109	42		0.02	0.12		1.13	9.78
56–60		67			0.02			1.75	

AGE GROUP	ACTIVE CASES IN SAMPLE POPULATION								
	INCIDENCE %			MEAN FREQUENCY			% OF TOTAL OUTLET		
	Pre-marital	Extra-marital	Post-marital	Pre-marital	Extra-marital	Post-marital	Pre-marital	Extra-marital	Post-marital
Adol.–15	5.2			0.21			7.13		
16–20	30.8	14.3	37.0	0.23	0.28	0.26	8.05	2.87	5.50
21–25	29.1	12.9	47.1	0.35	0.21	0.25	15.19	4.03	18.36
26–30	29.8	11.8	55.5	0.53	0.23	0.34	22.82	4.95	22.28
31–35	40.5	11.1	60.8	0.55	0.20	0.37	28.73	5.42	28.63
36–40	48.5	10.5	57.0	0.54	0.20	0.41	39.49	7.33	34.23
41–45	39.3	8.5	60.4	0.47	0.18	0.46	48.23	8.00	46.92
46–50	48.7	5.7	52.4	0.60	0.25	0.37	52.74	12.25	48.83
51–55		7.3	40.5		0.24	0.29		15.19	54.91
56–60		7.5			0.25			19.50	

AGE GROUP	CORRECTED FOR U. S. POPULATION								
	TOTAL POPULATION				ACTIVE POPULATION				
	MEAN FREQUENCY		% OF TOTAL OUTLET		INCIDENCE %		MEAN FREQUENCY		% OF TOTAL OUTLET	
	Pre-marital	Extra-marital	Pre-marital	Extra-marital	Pre-marital	Extra-marital	Pre-marital	Extra-marital	Pre-marital	Extra-marital
Adol.–15	0.02		0.61		7.7		0.25		8.79	
16–20	0.12	0.05	3.66	1.17	41.9	15.9	0.29	0.36	11.24	3.58
21–25	0.20	0.05	6.29	1.15	45.5	19.5	0.43	0.25	20.27	4.29
26–30	0.28	0.04	9.56	1.30	46.8	17.2	0.61	0.27	26.88	5.89
31–35	0.31	0.03	12.57	1.12	51.6	14.9	0.62	0.18	32.38	5.76
36–40	0.31	0.02	16.42	1.12	55.5	12.0	0.55	0.22	41.64	8.52
41–45		0.02		1.11		11.4		0.19		9.84
46–50		0.02		1.01		7.9		0.24		13.58
51–55		0.02		1.65		9.1		0.25		18.43

Table 65. Intercourse with prostitutes in relation to marital status and age

Data for the U. S. population are based on the sample population which is corrected for the distribution of educational levels shown in the U. S. Census for 1940. For sigmas of means, median frequencies, etc., see the tables in Chapter 7.

to about 2 per cent at 45 years of age, and still lower in still older married groups. Social factors, particularly the physical and social organization of the family, make it difficult for the married individual to have any sort of sexual relation with anyone except his wife. However, the incidence of the homosexual is probably higher than the available record on the married group shows. Married males who have social position to maintain and who fear that their wives may discover their extra-marital activities, are not readily persuaded into contributing histories to a research study. While it is possible to secure hundred percent samples from younger males, which make the incidence figures for homosexual contacts fairly reliable there, it is rarely possible to get as good a representation of older married males. There are hundreds of younger individuals in the histories who report homosexual contacts with these older, socially established, married males, and the post-marital histories of males who are widowed or divorced include the homosexual in 28.3 per cent of the teen-age group, and still in 10.8 per cent of the 31–35-year old histories. These data make it appear probable that the true incidence of the homosexual in married groups is much higher than we are able to record.

Homosexual relations, both among single and married males, are sometimes a substitute for less readily available heterosexual contacts. This is true at all social levels and at all age groups, especially among isolated, morally restrained, or timid males who are afraid to approach females for sexual relations. On the other hand, it must be recognized that the homosexual is in many instances, among both single and married males, deliberately chosen as the preferred source of outlet; and it is simply accepted as a different kind of sexual outlet by a fair number of persons, whatever their marital status, who embrace both heterosexual and homosexual experiences in the same age period. Consequently, the high incidence of the homosexual among single males is not wholly chargeable to the unavailability of heterosexual contacts. The increased incidence and frequency among older single males are, as previously noted, partly dependent upon the freer acceptance of a socially taboo activity as the individual becomes more experienced and more certain of himself. The very high incidence among the still older males may depend upon the fact that those persons who are not exclusively or primarily homosexual are ordinarily married when younger, and those who have no interest in heterosexual contacts are left in higher proportion in the older, unmarried populations.

Animal contacts in the northeastern quarter of the United States are largely confined to rural populations and are primarily activities of pre-adolescent and younger adolescent boys. Social taboos quickly lead the older individual to cover up his activity, to deny it in giving us a history and, in actuality, to stop such contacts at a rather early age. There are

HOMOSEXUAL OUTLET

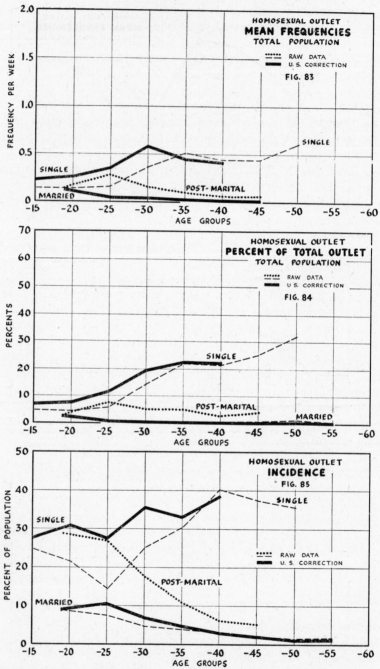

Figures 83–85. Relation of age and marital status to homosexual outlet
Solid lines represent the U. S. Corrections.

HOMOSEXUAL OUTLET

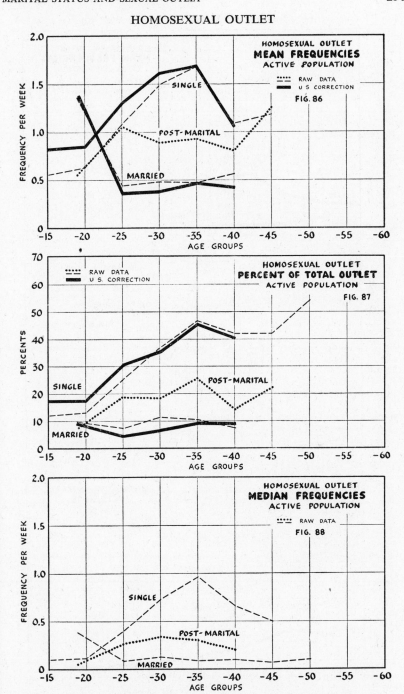

Figures 86–88. Relation of age and marital status to homosexual outlet

Solid lines represent the U. S. Corrections.

HOMOSEXUAL OUTLETS, MARITAL STATUS, AND AGE

AGE GROUP	TOTAL SAMPLE POPULATION								
	CASES			MEAN FREQUENCY			% OF TOTAL OUTLET		
	Single	Married	Post-married	Single	Married	Post-married	Single	Married	Post-married
Adol.–15	3012			0.14			4.89		
16–20	2868	272	46	0.13	0.10	0.18	4.70	2.21	4.44
21–25	1535	751	119	0.16	0.03	0.28	5.98	0.83	7.82
26–30	550	737	182	0.37	0.02	0.16	14.31	0.69	5.38
31–35	195	569	158	0.51	0.02	0.10	21.94	0.67	5.13
36–40	97	390	128	0.44	0.02	0.05	21.74	0.67	2.93
41–45	56	272	96	0.44	0.02	0.07	25.51	0.86	4.40
46–50	39	175	63	0.61			32.64	1.41	
51–55		109	42					0.81	
56–60		67							

AGE GROUP	ACTIVE CASES IN SAMPLE POPULATION								
	INCIDENCE %			MEAN FREQUENCY			% OF TOTAL OUTLET		
	Single	Married	Post-married	Single	Married	Post-married	Single	Married	Post-married
Adol.–15	24.8			0.56			12.13		
16–20	21.6	8.5	28.3	0.62	1.20	0.63	13.25	9.20	9.54
21–25	14.5	7.5	26.9	1.09	0.43	1.06	25.45	7.60	18.94
26–30	25.1	4.6	17.6	1.48	0.48	0.89	37.00	11.38	18.70
31–35	30.3	3.9	10.8	1.68	0.47	0.93	46.90	10.50	25.79
36–40	40.2	2.8	6.2	1.09	0.57	0.80	42.17	7.55	14.56
41–45	37.5	2.2	5.2	1.18	0.76	1.25	42.17	5.50	22.50
46–50	35.9	1.7		1.69	1.47		54.25	12.17	
51–55		1.8			0.68			15.50	

AGE GROUP	CORRECTED FOR U. S. POPULATION									
	TOTAL POPULATION				ACTIVE POPULATION					
	MEAN FREQUENCY		% OF TOTAL OUTLET		INCIDENCE %		MEAN FREQUENCY		% OF TOTAL OUTLET	
	Single	Married	Single	Married	Single	Married	Single	Married	Single	Married
Adol.–15	0.22		7.03		27.3		0.81		17.46	
16–20	0.26	0.11	7.84	2.31	31.0	9.3	0.85	1.25	17.73	8.25
21–25	0.35	0.04	11.81	0.86	27.5	10.6	1.30	0.37	30.31	4.69
26–30	0.58	0.03	19.68	0.75	35.8	6.9	1.61	0.38	35.20	6.91
31–35	0.45	0.02	22.61	0.72	33.0	4.8	1.69	0.47	45.75	9.11
36–40	0.41	0.01	22.01	0.53	38.7	2.8	1.06	0.42	40.42	9.04
41–45				0.33		2.1		0.22		2.34
46–50				0.40		1.2		0.52		6.07
51–55				0.29		1.6		0.20		5.82

Table 66. Homosexual outlets in relation to marital status and age

Data for the U. S. population are based on the sample population which is corrected for the distribution of educational levels shown in the U. S. Census for 1940. For sigmas of means, median frequencies, etc., see the tables in Chapter 7.

differences in incidences and frequencies in different social levels, the activity being highest among those rural boys who ultimately go to college. In this latter group, about 28 per cent has intercourse with animals between adolescence and 15 years of age and 17 per cent engages in the activity sometime between 16 and 20 years of age (Table 59). In this farm population, the incidence drops so rapidly for older single males that we are not warranted in calculating averages on the basis of our present data. Similarly, the active cases are too few to warrant calculations for married males in the northeastern quarter of the United States. Limited data which we have from more western and southwestern portions of the country indicate that such animal intercourse continues as a part of the sexual activity of not a few married adults.

Many of the pre-marital sources of sexual outlet are, to a degree, substitutes for less readily available heterosexual coitus. This is particularly true of masturbation, the homosexual, and intercourse with animals of other species. Sexual activities after marriage are concentrated on heterosexual intercourse and chiefly, but by no means wholly, on marital intercourse. Nevertheless, it would be a mistake to consider that differences in the availability of sources are the sole factors which distinguish the pre-marital from the marital record. It is to be recalled that the younger male, who is in most cases the unmarried male, is the sexually most active individual; and the intensity and frequency of his response to any situation which comes along, particularly if that situation is novel and unexpected, lead to his involvement in more kinds of sexual activity, whether he be single or married. Similarly, among married males it is the younger ones who have the highest frequencies of masturbation, extra-marital intercourse, homosexual relations, and animal contacts. Marriage is undoubtedly an overwhelming force in focusing sexual activity; but the similar concentration of the activities of the older single male upon his particular forms of outlet, particularly intercourse with prostitutes and the homosexual, indicates that marriage is not the only factor involved. It is also a matter of conditioning which leads to a centering of attention on those activities which have proved most satisfactory. It is a matter of a loss in interest in variety, after an initial experimentation with its charms, of concentrating upon the outlets that are most available in our society as it is set up, and of avoiding those things which are most likely to cause social disturbance.

Throughout the record, the effects of marital status are modified and mitigated by the age of the individual (Chapter 7). In spite of all the social and legal distinctions between the rights and privileges of married as opposed to unmarried individuals, age is, at many points, a more significant factor than marital status in determining the frequencies and, indirectly, the sources of sexual outlet.

POST-MARITAL OUTLETS

The sexual lives of previously married males who are no longer living with wives, have been a closer secret than the lives of single or married adults. We now have the post-marital histories of 433 white males. The sample is too small to warrant analyses even by age; and it is to be noted that there are not enough cases to allow corrections in accordance with the age, marital status, and education distribution shown in the U. S. Census. Uncorrected figures based on our particular sample are, therefore, the only ones available on these post-marital histories. Nevertheless, the data do seem to indicate general trends in regard to each of the sources of outlet.

The post-marital histories are, in general, an interesting combination of items which are characteristic of both single and married groups. The total sexual outlet of the previously married males between the ages of 16 and 30 is about 85 to 95 per cent as high as among married males, which means that it is between 40 and 50 per cent higher than among single males (Table 60, Figures 50–52). At these ages, there is little effect on the frequency of the previously married individual's sexual activity when he is deprived of a legalized source of outlet. With advancing age, after 30, however, the post-marital frequencies drop more rapidly than those in marriage, to about three-quarters (69% to 76%) of the marital rates; and this actually places them below the rates of even the single groups after age 30. It is not immediately apparent what is responsible for these differences, but the data should be kept in mind.

Many males who dropped masturbation in marriage, return to it after they have become widowed, separated, or divorced. Masturbation is found in a smaller percentage (56% at 16–20 years, 33% at age 45) of the post-marital cases than was true of the single histories; but the post-marital incidence is somewhat higher than it was in marriage (Table 61, Figures 53–58). The frequency of the post-marital masturbation (total population) is about a quarter to one-half of what it was in the single histories, but a little higher than it was in the married histories. For those persons who engage at all in masturbation, the percentage of the total outlet which comes from this source (17% to 36%) in the post-marital period is about twice as high as it was in marriage; but this is only a half to two-thirds as much as it was in the pre-marital period. As in all other populations, advancing age brings some decline in the incidences and frequencies; but the portion of the outlet which is derived from masturbation increases with the years, among these men who live without wives.

Nocturnal emissions (Table 62, Figures 59–64) occur in approximately the same number of persons in pre-marital, marital, and post-marital histories. The incidence is only slightly higher in single histories. The frequencies are highest among single males, two-thirds as high among married males, and somewhere between the two among previously married persons (where the frequencies range from about 0.26 per week at 16–30, to 0.19 at age 55). Nevertheless, while the incidences and actual frequencies go down, the percentage of the total outlet which is derived from nocturnal dreams (among previously married males who have any at all) rises more or less steadily from 10 per cent or 11 per cent between 16 and 25, to 21 per cent at age 50. Only after that does the significance of the dreams in the post-marital picture show any considerable drop.

Heterosexual intercourse is most important in the marital histories, least important in the histories of single males, and midway or higher in importance in the post-marital group (Table 63, Figures 65–70). The number of previously married males involved in intercourse ranges from about 96 per cent in the younger ages to 82 per cent by age 50. The drop in frequency is a bit faster than among married males. With advancing age, prostitutes provide an increasing part of the intercourse, companions a decreasing part of the post-marital intercourse (Tables 64–65, Figures 71–82).

The actual frequencies and the proportion of the total outlet which is derived from intercourse similarly lie between those of the married and single groups. They lie closer to those of the married males when the post-marital group is younger, and are nearly identical with those of married males when the group is older. Males who have ever become accustomed to the coital activities of marriage, keep coitus as their chief source of outlet (80% to 85% of their outlet) even after their marriages are terminated by the spouse's death, or by separation or divorce. Nearly all males (about 95%), after they have once been initiated into regular coital experience, whether as older single males or as previously married persons, repudiate the doctrine that intercourse should be restricted to marital relations. Nearly all ignore the legal limitation on intercourse outside of marriage. Only age finally reduces the coital activities of those individuals, and thus demonstrates that biological factors are, in the long run, more effective than man-made regulations in determining the patterns of human behavior. The picture probably differs for different social levels, but this breakdown cannot be made with the present-sized sample.

Homosexual activity occurs among many of the males who have been previously married (Table 66, Figures 83–88). It is in 28 per cent of the younger histories, and in a smaller number of the older histories (5.2% at 45 years of age). This group is larger than the group that had homosexual relations during marriage. While the incidence among the younger single and post-marital histories is about the same, it is eight times higher among the older males who have never been married. It is evident in a few of the individual histories that marriages sometimes break up because of the male partner's developing preference for relations with other males; in a few cases the male is induced by the breakdown of the heterosexual marriage to accept his first homosexual experience; but in a larger number of cases it is a matter of the individual returning to the sort of outlet that he had before he was ever married. The mean frequencies of the homosexual contacts (in the active population) among these previously married males are a bit lower than, or of the same order as among single males; and they are twice as high as among those married males who are having homosexual relations. The percentage of the previously married male's total outlet which is derived from the homosexual (19 per cent, rising to 22 per cent at older ages) is similarly double that found among married males, but not nearly so high as is found among older single males (where the figure rises to nearly half of the total sexual outlet). With advancing age, the homosexual in the post-marital group definitely drops in incidence, stays more or less constant in frequency, and slightly increases in its significance as a part of the total sexual outlet.

*   *   *

In summary, it is to be noted that the average male who is widowed or divorced is not left without sexual outlet, as the mores of our society and legal codes would have him. On the contrary, and in spite of customs and laws, he continues to have almost as active a sexual life as when he was married. He depends to a somewhat greater degree upon masturbation and nocturnal dreams, and at younger ages he turns to homosexual activity about as often as the single, previously unmarried male, but in most cases this widowed or divorced individual depends upon heterosexual intercourse for most (80%) of his not inconsiderable outlet. His is not the picture of the single male, unless it be the oldest group of the single males with which the comparison is made. Once married, a male largely retains the pattern of the married male, even after marriage ceases to furnish the physically convenient and legally recognized means for a frequent and regular sexual outlet. These data are in striking contrast to those available for the widowed or divorced female who, in a great many cases, ceases to have any socio-sexual contacts and who, very often, may go for long periods of years without sexual arousal or further sexual experience of any sort.

Chapter 9

AGE OF ADOLESCENCE AND SEXUAL OUTLET

For many centuries, men have wanted to know whether early involvement in sexual activity, or high frequencies of early activity, would reduce one's capacities in later life. It has been suggested that the duration of one's sexual life is definitely limited, and that ultimate high capacity and long-lived performance depend upon the conservation of one's sexual powers in earlier years. The individual's ability to function sexually has been conceived as a finite quantity which is fairly limited and ultimately exhaustible. One can use up those capacities by frequent activity in his youth, or preserve his wealth for the fulfillment of the later obligations and privileges of marriage.

Medical practitioners have sometimes ascribed infertility to wastage of sperm. Erectal impotence is supposed to be the penalty for excessive sexual exercise in youth (*e.g.*, as in Vecki 1901, 1920; Liederman 1926, Efferz in Bilderlexikon 1930 (3):118, Robinson 1933, pp. 61, 135, 142, et al., Rice 1946). The discovery of the hormones has provided ammunition for these ideas, and millions of youths have been told that in order "to be prepared" one must conserve one's virility by avoiding any wastage of vital fluids in boyhood (Boy Scout Manual, all editions, 1911–1945; W. S. Hall 1909; Dickerson 1930: 109ff; 1933: 15ff; U. S. Publ. Health Serv. 1937). Through all of this literature, an amazing assemblage of errors of anatomy, physiology, and endocrinology has been worked together for the good of the conservationist's theories. Why the ejaculation of prostatic and vesicular secretions should involve a greater wastage of gonadal hormones than the outpouring of secretions from any of the other glands—than the spitting out, for instance, of salivary secretions—is something that biologists would need to have explained. The authors of various popular manuals, however, seem able to explain it "so youth may know," and conserve their glandular secretions.

The Greek writers Empedocles and Diocles, and others including Plato after them, are said (Allbutt 1921, May 1931) to have believed that semen came from the brain and spinal marrow and that excessive copulation would, in consequence, injure the senses and the spine. Today, it is not unusual to find exactly the same superstitions about the origin of semen, and the consequently debilitating effects of ejaculation, among adolescent boys and among certain of their elders who want to believe such things. Many teen-age boys, on the contrary, have held to the equally unproved opinions that the exercise of one's sexual functions, either in masturbation or in intercourse, may develop genital size and increase one's erectal capacity, and that abstinence for any long period of time may impair one's capacities for subsequent performance.

There have been few scientific data available to answer these questions, but that has not interfered with their being answered. It not infrequently happens that the volume of discussion on a subject bears an inverse relation to the amount of exact information which is available. The assurance with which generalizations and conclusions are drawn, may reach its maximum when the least effort has been made to investigate the data which are basic to an understanding of the situation. If, as in the present instance, a whole system of moral philosophy is involved, the conclusions become foregone and by dint of much repetition assume the status of axioms which are accepted by laymen and scientists alike. But this is a question of the physical and physiologic outcome of physical and physiologic activities, and as such it is a question which can be investigated only by scientific procedures.

DATE OF FIRST EJACULATION	AGE OF ONSET OF ADOLESCENCE							
	Before 10	10	11	12	13	14	15	16
	%	%	%	%	%	%	%	%
Same year	100	96	92	87	83	78	78	81
Second year	0	2	5	8	11	14	16	11
Third year	0	0	2	3	3	5	4	5
Fourth year	0	2	1	1	1	2	2	3
Still later	0	0	0	1	2	1	1	0
Cases	14	94	309	1059	1510	1233	307	80

Table 67. Lapse between onset of adolescence and first ejaculation

Early in the course of the present study, Dr. Glenn V. Ramsey, while securing the histories of younger boys, noted differences in their then current sexual frequencies which seemed to be correlated with the degree of maturity of each boy. Following that lead, we have subsequently examined the histories of the whole population involved in the present study, and find that there is, in actuality, a relationship between the age at onset of adolescence, the age of first sexual performance, the frequencies of early sexual activity, the frequencies of sexual activity throughout most of the life span of the individual, and the sources on which he depends for his sexual outlet. While chronologic age is of prime importance in determining the mean frequencies of sexual activity for populations in different age groups (Chapter 7), the biologic factors which account for variation in the age of onset of adolescence seem to be of definite importance in effecting variation within any single group. The data which substantiate these generalizations should provide one more instance of the difference between a priori reasoning and conclusions based on statistically accumulated fact.

ONSET OF SEXUAL ACTIVITY

Any consideration of the age of onset of adolescence is made difficult by the fact that there is no single criterion by which that age can be recognized. In Chapter 5, in presenting the statistical data on adolescent developments, it was pointed out that there are a good many physical characters involved, and that they do not all appear and develop at exactly the same time. In the same chapter, it was pointed out that the designation of a particular year, in any individual's history, as the age of onset of adolescence, must, therefore, depend upon judgments which may sometimes be arbitrary and not exactly in accord with all of the details of the fact.

In the present study, the time of onset of adolescence has been fixed as the date of the first ejaculation, unless there has been evidence that ejaculation would have been possible at an earlier age if the individual had been stimulated to the point of orgasm. When the year of first ejaculation coincides with the year in which the first pubic hair appears, and with the time of onset of rapid growth in height, and/or with certain other developments, there is no question that that year may be accepted as the first year of adolescence. Eighty-five per cent of all male histories fall into this category. On the other hand, if the first ejaculation follows these other events by a year or more, and if it is clear that there was no test of the individual's sexual capacity prior to the first ejaculation, and if there seems to be no question of the reliability of the memory in regard to the dates of the other adolescent developments, then the age of onset of adolescence is better established by events other than ejaculation. Where first ejaculation occurs as a nocturnal emission, it usually (though not always) does not come until a year or more after the appearance of the other adolescent developments, and the onset of adolescence should be set a year or more before the first ejaculation.

To define the time of onset of adolescence by any single criterion does not satisfy the reality as well as a judgment based on all of the pertinent data. Even hormones and the 17-ketosteroids cannot be accepted as the sole criteria for determining this event, or any other event. The history of systematic botany and systematic zoology is replete with attempts to discover significant and diagnostic characters which might provide clear-cut and absolute bases for systems of classification; but the modern taxonomist finds that the use of a single character inevitably provides a classificatory system which is artificial and, at least at certain points, in direct conflict with data from other sources. Every aspect of a situation is part of the reality which one must take into account, if one is to understand that reality. In the present instance, the onset of adolescence must be recognized whenever there is any development of any physiologic or physical character that pertains to adolescence. The ages of onset of adolescence used for statistical analyses in the present chapter, and throughout this whole volume, are based upon this use of the multiple characters which are concerned.

SOURCE OF FIRST EJACULATION	PERCENT DEPENDING ON EACH SOURCE				
	WHEN AGE AT ONSET OF ADOLESCENCE IS:				
	8–11	12	13	14	15+ later
Masturbation	71.6	64.8	58.9	55.0	52.1
Nocturnal emissions	21.6	28.2	35.6	38.9	37.1
Petting	0.0	0.3	0.6	0.3	2.2
Intercourse	0.6	1.4	0.9	0.9	3.2
Homosexual	2.6	3.2	1.2	2.0	2.2
Animal	0.3	0.3	0.2	0.3	0.0
Spontaneous	3.3	1.8	2.6	2.6	3.2
Total	100.0	100.0	100.0	100.0	100.0
Cases	306	722	984	650	186

Table 68. Sources of first ejaculation in relation to age at onset of adolescence

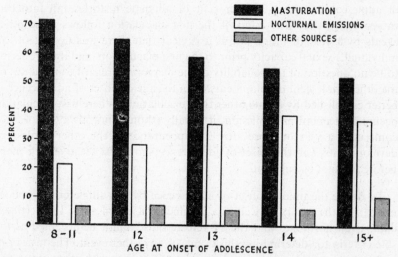

Figure 89. Sources of first ejaculation in relation to age at onset of adolescence

The use of multiple characters in a taxonomic classification inevitably calls for a certain exercise of subjective judgment, and this is the most serious objection to such a procedure; but the errors introduced by judgment are not likely to be as misleading as the artificialities introduced by the use of a single set of criteria in a classification.

In this study, the determination of the age of onset of adolescence has been further complicated by the necessity for depending on the subject's memory for a report of what is supposed to have happened. Considering the indefinite nature of the event itself, and this difficulty of obtaining accurate records by way of memory (Chapter 4), it is surprising that it has been possible to demonstrate correlations between this phenomenon and any aspects of sexual behavior.

It will be recalled that the average age of onset of adolescence for the white male population has been calculated as 13 years and 7 months (Chapter 5). There are very few boys who reach adolescence prior to age 10, and few even before age 11. Consequently, in most of the tables accompanying the present chapter, the males who were adolescent prior to age 11 have, for purposes of calculation, been included in one group with those who began adolescence at 11. In a few instances, the small number of available cases has made it necessary to put all those adolescent before 12 into the 12-year group. Those who were adolescent after age 15 are grouped with those who became adolescent at 15.

In order to make significant comparisons, it has been necessary to confine the analyses to groups that are homogeneous for sex, race, marital status, and educational level, as well as for the age of onset of adolescence. The tables in the present chapter cover all of those segments of the population which are now represented in the sample by enough cases to warrant statistical treatment. There has been no other basis for selecting the groups which are included.

The first difference to be observed between the males who become adolescent at an earlier age, and the males who become adolescent at an older age, is the fact that the younger-adolescent boys begin regular sexual activity of some sort, and begin having a regular outlet, more or less coincidently with the onset of adolescence. Some of them, as a matter of fact, had already experienced regular orgasm in pre-adolescence. On the other hand, the older-adolescent males, despite the fact that they have taken four or five years more in reaching adolescence, often delay a year or two beyond that before they ejaculate for the first time. Sometimes it is still longer before they acquire anything like regular rates of outlet. Early-adolescent males ejaculate in the same year in which they become adolescent in 92 to 100 per cent of the cases (Table 67). The older-adolescent males ejaculate in their first year of adolescence in only about 80 per cent of the cases. Nearly every one (99.5%) of the younger-maturing boys acquires a regular sexual outlet between the time of adolescence and age 15.

There is an interesting correlation of the source of first ejaculation and the age of onset of ejaculation (Table 68, Figure 89). For the boys who become adolescent by 11 years of age, masturbation provides the first

TOTAL OUTLET AND AGE AT ADOLESCENCE

AGE AT ADOL.	CASES	FREQUENCIES AMONG ALL SINGLE MALES						
		TOTAL POPULATION		INDICES, TOTAL POPULATIONS		ACTIVE POPULATION		
		Mean Frequency	Median Freq.	By Means %	By Medians %	Incid. %	Mean Frequency	Median Freq.
Activity between adol.–15								
8–11	395	3.89 ± 0.84	2.98	**184**	**223**	99.5	3.91 ± 0.85	3.00
12	1013	3.53 ± 0.11	2.64	**167**	**197**	98.6	3.58 ± 0.11	2.68
13	1481	2.90 ± 0.07	2.19	**137**	**163**	97.6	2.97 ± 0.08	2.27
14	1175	2.30 ± 0.08	1.51	**109**	**116**	91.1	2.53 ± 0.08	1.80
15+	292	2.11 ± 0.14	1.34	**100**	**100**	85.6	2.46 ± 0.15	1.74
Activity between 16–20								
8–11	361	3.68 ± 0.18	2.89	**149**	**159**	99.7	3.69 ± 0.18	2.90
12	920	3.37 ± 0.11	2.48	**137**	**136**	99.8	3.38 ± 0.11	2.49
13	1359	2.86 ± 0.07	2.25	**116**	**124**	99.6	2.87 ± 0.07	2.26
14	1128	2.54 ± 0.07	1.89	**103**	**104**	99.2	2.56 ± 0.07	1.92
15+	398	2.46 ± 0.12	1.82	**100**	**100**	99.7	2.49 ± 0.12	1.85
Activity between 21–25								
8–11	241	3.30 ± 0.22	2.46	**143**	**149**	100.0	3.30 ± 0.22	2.46
12	515	3.03 ± 0.14	2.16	**132**	**131**	99.8	3.03 ± 0.14	2.16
13	769	2.49 ± 0.08	1.91	**108**	**116**	99.7	2.50 ± 0.08	1.92
14	626	2.40 ± 0.11	1.65	**104**	**100**	98.9	2.43 ± 0.11	1.69
15+	257	2.30 ± 0.14	1.66	**100**	**101**	98.8	2.33 ± 0.14	1.69
Activity between 26–30								
8–11	69	3.84 ± 0.49	2.81	**152**	**178**	100.0	3.84 ± 0.49	2.81
12	122	3.07 ± 0.28	1.95	**136**	**123**	100.0	3.07 ± 0.28	1.95
13	213	2.72 ± 0.20	2.00	**120**	**127**	99.5	2.73 ± 0.20	2.01
14	200	2.26 ± 0.16	1.58	**100**	**100**	99.0	2.28 ± 0.16	1.60
15+	98	2.49 ± 0.27	1.80	**110**	**114**	98.0	2.54 ± 0.27	1.84
Activity between 31–35								
8–12	82	3.30 ± 0.43	2.08	**160**	**144**	100.0	3.30 ± 0.43	2.08
13	86	2.78 ± 0.40	1.81	**135**	**125**	98.8	2.81 ± 0.40	1.82
14	97	2.06 ± 0.20	1.45	**100**	**100**	100.0	2.06 ± 0.20	1.45

Table 69. Total sexual outlet, in single males, as related to age at onset of adolescence

Based on total white male population, including all education levels. The relative sizes of the frequencies are shown in the boldface columns as indices, with the lowest frequency in each 5-year period equalling 100 per cent.

ejaculation in nearly three-quarters of the cases (71.6 per cent); but for the boys who become adolescent last, masturbation is the source of the first outlet in only about half of the cases (52.1 per cent). Nocturnal dreams, on the contrary, are the first source for only 21.6 per cent of the younger-adolescent boys, but for 37.1 per cent of the late-adolescent males. The boys who mature first more often act deliberately in going after their first outlet; the boys who mature last more often depend upon the involuntary reactions which bring nocturnal emissions.

The sexual activities of these boys who start the earliest are far from incidental. Between adolescence and 15 years, their rates are higher than the rates of any other group of single males, of any age, in any segment of the white population. Consequent on their quicker start, there are 16 per cent more of the early-adolescent boys than there are of the late-adolescent boys, who are active between adolescence and 15. Early-adolescent boys have four or five years in which to make a start in that period, while the later-adolescent boys have only one year in the period; but the higher incidence of activity among the early-adolescent boys must depend, in part, upon the generally higher level of performance in the group. This is confirmed by the fact that in all subsequent age periods there is still a slight but consistent difference in incidence in favor of the boys who became adolescent earliest.

FREQUENCIES OF TOTAL OUTLET

The younger-adolescent and the older-adolescent males differ most in respect to the frequencies with which they engage in sexual activities. Tables 69 and 71 give the data for single and married males respectively.

Upon examining the record for the single males it will be seen that the boys who became adolescent first (by 11 years of age) have, on an average, about twice as much sexual outlet per week as the older-adolescent boys have during their early teens. If the means for the total populations are compared, the early-adolescent boys have 1.84 times as high frequencies as the slower males. If the medians are compared, the younger-adolescent boys have 2.23 times as much outlet. This is a material difference, and it is a real difference, since the averages for this age period between adolescence and 15 are calculated for the active years only, and not averaged with the pre-adolescent years (page 110).

These younger-adolescent boys constitute the most active group of single (unmarried) males in the whole population. In Chapter 7 it was concluded that out of all single males, taken as a group, the sexually most active are the 16–20-year old group; and that among the married males the highest frequencies are also in the 16–20-year period. While boys below 16, taken as a group, do not have frequencies as high as do the boys

TOTAL OUTLET AND AGE AT ADOLESCENCE

| AGE AT ADOL. | CASES | FREQUENCIES AMONG SINGLE MALES, BY EDUCATIONAL LEVEL | | | | | | |
| | | TOTAL POPULATION | | INDICES, TOTAL POPULATIONS | | ACTIVE POPULATION | | |
		Mean Frequency	Median Freq.	By Means %	By Medians %	Incid. %	Mean Frequency	Median Freq.
		Educ. level 0–8		Activity between adol.–15				
8–12	131	5.10 ± 0.43	3.75	244	329	97.7	5.22 ± 0.44	3.88
13	180	3.34 ± 0.24	2.38	160	196	97.8	3.41 ± 0.25	2.45
14	270	2.47 ± 0.21	1.25	118	110	87.8	2.82 ± 0.23	1.61
15+	115	2.09 ± 0.22	1.14	100	100	90.4	2.32 ± 0.24	1.34
		Educ. level 0–8		Activity between 16–20				
8–12	114	5.54 ± 0.49	3.85	226	221	100.0	5.54 ± 0.49	3.85
13	165	3.40 ± 0.22	2.71	139	156	99.4	3.42 ± 0.22	2.73
14	266	2.88 ± 0.21	1.96	118	113	97.7	2.95 ± 0.21	2.03
15+	154	2.45 ± 0.20	1.74	100	100	97.4	2.51 ± 0.21	1.79
		Educ. level 0–8		Activity between 21–25				
8–12	46	5.34 ± 0.84	3.25	197	175	97.8	5.46 ± 0.85	3.30
13–14	188	3.00 ± 0.27	2.01	111	108	97.3	3.08 ± 0.28	2.07
15+	84	2.71 ± 0.30	1.86	100	100	98.8	2.74 ± 0.30	1.89
		Educ. level 9–12		Activity between adol.–15				
8–12	170	4.23 ± 0.30	3.11	163	182	98.8	4.28 ± 0.30	3.16
13	197	3.63 ± 0.28	2.35	140	137	98.5	3.69 ± 0.28	2.40
14	213	2.59 ± 0.19	1.78	100	104	91.5	2.83 ± 0.20	2.04
15+	42	2.60 ± 0.46	1.71	100	100	88.1	2.95 ± 0.49	1.92
		Educ. level 9–12		Activity between 16–20				
8–12	162	4.23 ± 0.31	3.25	144	139	99.4	4.25 ± 0.31	3.28
13	196	3.73 ± 0.26	2.80	127	120	100.0	3.73 ± 0.26	2.80
14	207	2.94 ± 0.19	2.38	100	102	99.5	2.95 ± 0.19	2.40
15+	58	3.21 ± 0.45	2.34	109	100	100.0	3.21 ± 0.45	2.34
		Educ. level 9–12		Activity between 21–25				
8–12	63	3.87 ± 0.53	2.92	291	292	100.0	3.87 ± 0.53	2.92
13–14	144	2.91 ± 0.25	2.08	219	208	98.6	2.95 ± 0.26	2.13
15+	25	1.33 ± 0.24	1.00	100	100	96.0	1.38 ± 0.25	1.05

(*Table continued on next page*)

AGE AT ADOL.	CASES	FREQUENCIES AMONG SINGLE MALES, BY EDUCATIONAL LEVEL						
		TOTAL POPULATION		INDICES, TOTAL POPULATIONS		ACTIVE POPULATION		
		Mean Frequency	Median Freq.	By Means %	By Medians %	Incid. %	Mean Frequency	Median Freq.
		Educ. level 13+		Activity between adol.–15				
8–12	893	3.31 ± 0.10	2.57	176	185	98.9	3.35 ± 0.10	2.60
13	896	2.77 ± 0.09	2.27	147	163	97.7	2.84 ± 0.09	2.35
14	600	2.18 ± 0.09	1.56	116	112	92.0	2.37 ± 0.10	1.84
15+	114	1.88 ± 0.21	1.39	100	100	78.1	2.41 ± 0.24	2.00
		Educ. level 13+		Activity between 16–20				
8–12	893	3.00 ± 0.09	2.34	133	134	99.8	3.01 ± 0.09	2.34
13	896	2.56 ± 0.07	2.10	114	121	99.8	2.56 ± 0.07	2.10
14	600	2.26 ± 0.08	1.74	101	100	99.8	2.26 ± 0.08	1.75
15+	170	2.25 ± 0.14	1.86	100	107	99.4	2.26 ± 0.14	1.87
		Educ. level 13+		Activity between 21–25				
8–12	561	2.79 ± 0.11	2.06	129	132	100.0	2.79 ± 0.11	2.06
13	566	2.25 ± 0.07	1.80	104	115	99.5	2.26 ± 0.07	1.81
14	393	2.17 ± 0.10	1.56	100	100	100.0	2.17 ± 0.10	1.56
15+	136	2.23 ± 0.17	1.72	103	110	99.3	2.25 ± 0.17	1.74
		Educ. level 13+		Activity between 26–30				
8–12	176	3.03 ± 0.24	2.17	133	133	100.0	3.03 ± 0.24	2.17
13	179	2.52 ± 0.19	1.87	111	115	99.4	2.53 ± 0.19	1.88
14	152	2.27 ± 0.16	1.63	100	100	100.0	2.27 ± 0.16	1.63
15+	48	2.45 ± 0.41	1.65	108	101	100.0	2.45 ± 0.41	1.65

Table 70. Total outlet, as related to educational level and age at onset of adolescence

in their late teens, we now find that the activities of the early-adolescent individuals of this early teen-age group surpass those of the 16–20-year olds.

The mean frequencies of total outlet for the late teen-age boys, taken as a whole group, are 3.2 per week. The mean frequencies for the early-adolescent boys during the period between 11 and 15 average 3.9 per week. If this early-adolescent population is broken down into three educational levels (Table 70), the mean frequencies become 5.1 per week among the

AGE AT ADOL.	CASES	FREQUENCIES AMONG ALL MARRIED MALES						
		TOTAL POPULATION		INDICES, TOTAL POPULATIONS		ACTIVE POPULATION		
		Mean Frequency	Median Freq.	By Means %	By Medians %	Incid. %	Mean Frequency	Median Freq.
		Activity between 16–20						
8–11	23	7.27 ± 1.31	6.00	220	240	100.0	7.27 ± 1.31	6.00
12	65	5.21 ± 0.64	3.42	158	137	100.0	5.21 ± 0.64	3.42
13	85	4.87 ± 0.52	3.57	147	143	100.0	4.87 ± 0.52	3.57
14	102	4.01 ± 0.39	2.97	121	119	100.0	4.01 ± 0.39	2.97
15+	31	3.30 ± 0.44	2.50	100	100	100.0	3.30 ± 0.44	2.50
		Activity between 21–25						
8–11	70	4.93 ± 0.63	3.41	151	133	100.0	4.93 ± 0.63	3.41
12	183	4.48 ± 0.30	3.37	137	131	100.0	4.48 ± 0.30	3.37
13	245	3.94 ± 0.26	3.05	121	119	100.0	3.94 ± 0.26	3.05
14	278	3.55 ± 0.21	2.67	109	104	100.0	3.55 ± 0.21	2.67
15+	99	3.26 ± 0.25	2.57	100	100	100.0	3.26 ± 0.25	2.57
		Activity between 26–30						
8–11	82	4.32 ± 0.52	3.09	147	134	100.0	4.32 ± 0.52	3.09
12	168	3.68 ± 0.27	2.86	125	124	100.0	3.68 ± 0.27	2.86
13	258	3.26 ± 0.19	2.59	111	112	100.0	3.26 ± 0.19	2.59
14	276	2.93 ± 0.15	2.37	100	103	99.3	2.95 ± 0.15	2.38
15+	97	3.42 ± 0.37	2.31	116	100	100.0	3.42 ± 0.37	2.31
		Activity between 31–35						
8–11	46	3.02 ± 0.34	2.38	112	114	100.0	3.02 ± 0.34	2.38
12	114	3.21 ± 0.30	2.53	120	121	100.0	3.21 ± 0.30	2.53
13	193	2.97 ± 0.20	2.29	111	109	100.0	2.97 ± 0.20	2.29
14	223	2.68 ± 0.17	2.09	100	100	100.0	2.68 ± 0.17	2.09
15+	85	3.14 ± 0.33	2.20	117	105	100.0	3.14 ± 0.33	2.20
		Activity between 36–40						
12	143	2.87 ± 0.25	2.17	121	115	99.3	2.89 ± 0.25	2.18
13	152	2.76 ± 0.21	2.21	116	117	100.0	2.76 ± 0.21	2.21
14	199	2.37 ± 0.16	1.89	100	100	100.0	2.37 ± 0.16	1.89
15+	70	2.53 ± 0.26	1.98	107	105	100.0	2.53 ± 0.26	1.98
		Activity between 41–45						
13	84	2.45 ± 0.26	1.95	121	119	100.0	2.45 ± 0.26	1.95
14	123	2.03 ± 0.20	1.64	100	100	100.0	2.03 ± 0.20	1.64
		Activity between 46–50						
13	52	2.22 ± 0.33	1.63	112	121	100.0	2.22 ± 0.33	1.63
14	92	1.99 ± 0.25	1.35	100	100	98.9	2.02 ± 0.25	1.38

Table 71. Total sexual outlet in married males, as related to age at onset of adolescence

Based on total married population, including all educational levels.

boys who never go beyond eighth grade in school, 4.2 per week for the boys who go into high school but not beyond, and 3.3 per week for the boys who will ultimately go to college. For each educational level, the maximum frequencies for the early-adolescent boys are in the earliest age period (except for the grade school group, where there is a slight increase in rate in the next two age periods; but the samples on these grade school boys are too small to be accepted as final). This location of the peak of sexual activity in the earlier adolescent years is scientifically most interesting, and it may have considerable social significance. The data emphasize the importance of a breakdown by age of onset of adolescence, in any final analysis of the problems of sexual behavior.

Not only do these earlier-developing boys have four years head start, and not only do they have higher rates of activity in those initial years, but they continue to have higher rates throughout the subsequent age periods. In the fifteen years that lie between ages 16 and 30, the younger-developing boys have about half again as much outlet as the later-developing boys. There is still a discernible difference in the age group 31 to 35, which is 20 to 25 years after the time of onset of adolescence! Considering the multiplicity of other factors that may modify the frequencies of sexual activity, it is surprising to find such a long-time correlation with the age of onset of adolescence. In spite of their early start, and in spite of their much higher expenditure of energy in sexual activity, these early-maturing males remain more active than those who were delayed in their adolescence.

In the histories of married males, the age of onset of adolescence proves to be as significant as in the histories of single males (Table 71). This is astounding! It might have been expected that the frequency of sexual activity for a married male would depend, to at least some degree, upon the wife's interest and willingness to engage in marital intercourse; and certainly individual histories provide abundant examples of marital partners having to adjust their rates in accordance with each other's wishes. Nevertheless, during the 16- to 20-year period, the outlets of the married males who were adolescent at an early age are about twice as high as the outlets of the males who were not adolescent until a later age—and this is exactly the difference that would have been found if they had remained unmarried. The effect persists throughout the lives of the married males, as far as data are available. While the differential between the groups decreases with advancing age, the rates of the younger-maturing group in the 46- to 50-year old period are still about 20 per cent higher than the rates of the slower-maturing group. Thirty-five years after the onset of adolescence, there is still a discernible effect, which persists in spite of marriage and in spite of all of the other events that affect sexual frequencies!

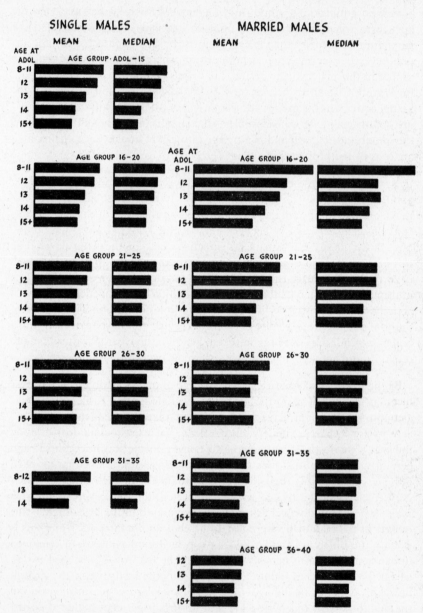

Figure 90. Relation of age at onset of adolescence to frequency of total outlet

Based on the total population. Relative lengths of bars show mean and median frequencies for each adolescent group. Single males in columns 1 and 2; married males in columns 3 and 4. Effects shown as continuing up to 30 years after onset of adolescence.

FACTORS INVOLVED

While the data in Tables 69 to 71 indicate a definite correlation between the ages of adolescence and the frequency of sexual activity, it must not be concluded that a simple causal relationship exists. Such misinterpretations of correlations are too commonly made, both in popular thinking and in technical scientific experiment. In many cases, more basic factors are involved, and two sets of correlated phenomena may be simply end products of the same forces. In the present instance, several basic factors may be operating. It is possible that the fact that an early-adolescent individual becomes sexually mature and erotically responsive at an earlier age, is the significant item. This gives him more years to become conditioned toward sexual experience before he reaches the teen-ages where social restraints become more significant. To put the matter in another way, the boy who becomes adolescent at 10 or 11 has not had as many years to build up inhibitions against sexual activity as the boy who does not mature until 15 or later; and it is quite possible (but not specifically demonstrable from the available data) that the younger boy plunges into sexual activity with less restraint and with more enthusiasm than the boy who starts at a later date. Moreover, it is possible that the patterns which are established by the earliest sexual activity, meaning patterns of higher frequency for younger-maturing boys, and patterns of lower frequency for older-maturing boys, are the patterns by which the individual's subsequent life is ordered. At least part of the long-time effects may depend upon psychologic learning and conditioning.

But it is also probable that there are physiologic bases for the differences. It is difficult to know just what these may be, for, unfortunately, there are next to no studies of physiologic capacities in relation to the age at which individuals become adolescent. There are studies of younger children, adolescents, and older adults which show correlations between their absolute ages and their physiologic performances (Robinson 1938, and the references therein). There is at least one study (Richey 1931) which shows that there is some correlation between age at the onset of adolescence and blood pressures (systolic, diastolic, and pulse), the heights and weights that are ultimately attained, and some anatomic developments. Most significantly, these characters distinguish the various adolescent groups as much as six years before the onset of adolescence, and for at least six years after the beginning of adolescence. Further investigation of a larger number of physiologic characters operating over a longer period of years seems not to have been made. On the psychologic side, Terman (1925), in his study of geniuses, found that the individuals with the highest IQ's were more often those who became adolescent first. It can, therefore, be suggested that the frequency of sexual activity may, to some degree, be dependent upon a general metabolic level which the individual maintains through much of his life. One who functions at a higher level at one period

AGE AT ADOL.	CASES	TOTAL POPULATION			INDICES, TOTAL POPULATIONS		ACTIVE POPULATION		
		Mean Frequency	Me-dian Freq.	% of Total Outlet	By Means %	By Me-dians %	Incid. %	Mean Frequency	Me-dian Freq.
		Educ. level 0–8			Activity between adol.–15				
8–12	131	2.65 ± 0.25	1.70	53.0	**230**	**284**	96.9	2.73 ± 0.25	1.76
13	180	1.71 ± 0.16	1.01	53.8	**149**	**168**	91.7	1.87 ± 0.17	1.19
14	270	1.25 ± 0.11	0.60	53.7	**109**	**100**	80.4	1.55 ± 0.12	0.94
15+	115	1.15 ± 0.14	0.60	58.0	**100**	**100**	79.1	1.45 ± 0.16	0.90
		Educ. level 0–8			Activity between 16–20				
8–12	114	1.47 ± 0.18	0.77	28.3	**179**	**197**	91.2	1.61 ± 0.19	0.92
13	165	0.96 ± 0.09	0.50	31.1	**117**	**128**	86.1	1.11 ± 0.10	0.71
14	266	0.82 ± 0.07	0.39	31.9	**100**	**100**	82.3	1.00 ± 0.08	0.53
15+	154	0.89 ± 0.09	0.47	40.0	**109**	**120**	89.0	1.00 ± 0.10	0.58
		Educ. level 9-12			Activity between adol.–15				
8–12	170	2.32 ± 0.17	1.64	58.2	**157**	**132**	97.1	2.39 ± 0.17	1.72
13	197	2.10 ± 0.19	1.21	60.6	**142**	**115**	91.9	2.28 ± 0.20	1.38
14	213	1.62 ± 0.12	1.06	66.0	**109**	**101**	85.0	1.91 ± 0.13	1.38
15+	42	1.48 ± 0.26	1.05	59.3	**100**	**100**	83.3	1.77 ± 0.28	1.40
		Educ. level 9–12			Activity between 16–20				
8–12	162	1.37 ± 0.11	0.80	34.9	**120**	**154**	92.0	1.49 ± 0.12	0.91
13	196	1.45 ± 0.17	0.74	41.1	**127**	**142**	90.3	1.60 ± 0.19	0.88
14	207	1.14 ± 0.10	0.52	42.5	**100**	**100**	84.5	1.34 ± 0.11	0.77
15+	58	1.34 ± 0.19	0.87	44.4	**117**	**167**	94.8	1.42 ± 0.19	0.92
		Educ. level 13+			Activity between adol.–15				
8–12	893	2.61 ± 0.09	1.98	79.7	**175**	**194**	90.3	2.89 ± 0.10	2.24
13	896	2.15 ± 0.08	1.59	78.8	**144**	**159**	83.4	2.58 ± 0.08	2.01
14	600	1.67 ± 0.09	1.02	78.6	**112**	**100**	73.2	2.29 ± 0.10	1.82
15+	114	1.49 ± 0.19	1.02	80.9	**100**	**100**	60.5	2.46 ± 0.25	1.93
		Educ. level 13+			Activity between 16–20				
8–12	893	2.02 ± 0.08	1.43	67.2	**142**	**164**	91.8	2.20 ± 0.08	1.63
13	896	1.66 ± 0.06	1.08	65.4	**117**	**124**	88.6	1.88 ± 0.06	1.38
14	600	1.45 ± 0.07	0.92	64.2	**102**	**106**	84.5	1.72 ± 0.07	1.31
15+	170	1.42 ± 0.12	0.87	63.6	**100**	**100**	83.5	1.70 ± 0.13	1.23
		Educ. level 13+			Activity between 21–25				
8–12	561	1.46 ± 0.08	0.78	53.1	**128**	**150**	90.4	1.61 ± 0.08	0.92
13	566	1.18 ± 0.06	0.68	52.2	**104**	**131**	85.7	1.38 ± 0.07	0.85
14	393	1.14 ± 0.07	0.52	53.2	**100**	**100**	82.7	1.37 ± 0.08	0.80
15+	136	1.17 ± 0.13	0.55	53.0	**103**	**106**	81.6	1.43 ± 0.15	0.81
		Educ. level 13+			Activity between 26–30				
8–12	176	1.36 ± 0.17	0.58	49.8	**137**	**132**	89.8	1.52 ± 0.18	0.71
13	179	0.99 ± 0.09	0.49	42.7	**100**	**111**	80.4	1.23 ± 0.10	0.78
14	152	1.11 ± 0.13	0.44	52.9	**112**	**100**	82.2	1.35 ± 0.15	0.66

Table 72. Frequency of masturbation, as related to age at onset of adolescence

310

MASTURBATION AND AGE AT ADOLESCENCE

	ACCUMULATIVE INCIDENCE EDUCATIONAL LEVEL 13+								
AGE	ADOLESCENT BY 11		ADOLESCENT AT 12		ADOLESCENT AT 13		ADOLESCENT AT 14		ADOLESCENT AT 15+	
	Cases	% with Exper.	Cases	% with Exper.	Cases	% with Exper.	Cases	% with Exper.	Cases	% with Exper.
8	307	0.3	724	0.0	986	0.0	650	0.0	187	0.0
9	307	2.9	724	0.0	986	0.0	650	0.0	187	0.0
10	307	21.2	724	0.0	986	0.0	650	0.0	187	0.0
11	307	79.8	724	0.0	986	0.0	650	0.0	187	0.0
12	307	87.9	724	71.4	986	0.0	650	0.0	187	0.0
13	307	91.2	724	80.5	986	65.4	650	0.0	187	0.0
14	307	93.2	724	85.5	986	77.5	650	60.2	187	0.0
15	307	93.8	724	89.0	986	82.9	650	71.7	187	39.6
16	307	94.8	724	90.2	986	85.8	650	76.9	187	63.1
17	307	95.1	724	91.3	985	88.6	649	80.3	187	73.3
18	297	95.3	706	92.5	957	89.8	630	84.3	187	78.1
19	282	96.5	660	93.3	897	90.3	593	86.3	180	80.0
20	266	97.0	609	93.8	802	91.4	529	87.7	170	82.4
21	243	97.9	510	95.1	689	91.9	472	88.8	154	85.1
22	205	97.6	407	95.8	568	92.6	401	89.8	126	88.1
23	183	97.3	339	96.5	474	93.2	332	90.1	105	88.6
24	152	97.4	274	96.7	391	93.9	288	88.5	84	88.1
25	131	99.2	238	97.1	345	94.5	246	89.8	77	87.0
26	112	99.1	206	97.1	310	95.8	224	92.0	67	88.1
27	90	98.9	174	97.1	278	96.8	205	91.7	54	90.7
28	86	98.8	155	97.4	248	97.2	188	91.0		
29	74	98.6	144	97.2	223	96.9	174	90.2		
30	64	98.4	125	97.6	206	97.1	162	92.6		
31	60	98.3	110	97.3	188	96.8	156	92.3		
32	55	98.2	100	97.0	171	97.1	149	93.3		
33	53	98.1	91	96.7	154	97.4	135	92.6		
34			85	97.6	142	97.9	124	93.5		
35			77	97.4	131	97.7	119	94.1		
36			70	97.1	119	97.5	114	94.7		
37			64	96.9	105	98.1	103	94.2		
38			60	96.7	100	98.0	100	95.0		
39			57	96.5	89	97.8	93	94.6		
40			50	98.0	83	97.6	87	95.4		

Table 73. Experience in masturbation, as affected by age at onset of adolescence

Accumulative incidence data based on males of the college level.

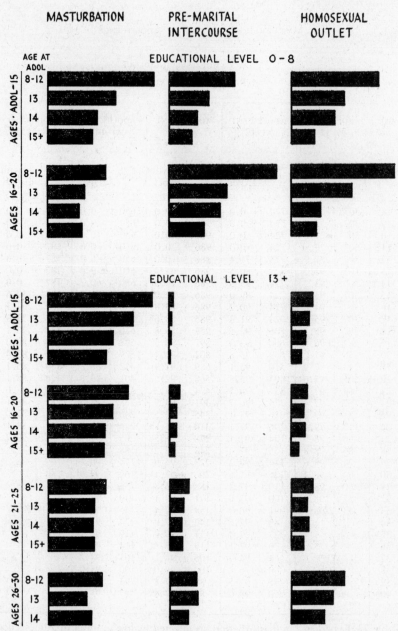

Figure 91. Relation of age at onset of adolescence to frequencies of masturbation, pre-marital intercourse with companions, and homosexual outlet

Based on single males. Relative lengths of bars show mean frequencies for each adolescent group. Effects shown as continuing up to 10 years for a grade school group (0–8); and up to 20 years for a college group (13+).

in his life is likely to function at a higher level through most of his life, barring illness and physical accidents that produce permanent incapacities. Casual observation would suggest that such an individual is not worn down by his quicker and more frequent responses to everyday situations, and there would seem to be no more reason for his being exhausted by his frequent sexual responses. Moreover, it is possible that the factors accounting for these other evidences of high metabolic level also account for early adolescence. Whether this is the correct interpretation is a matter which will have to be investigated through extensive research on the physiologic qualities of sexually high and low rating individuals.

SOURCES OF OUTLET

An examination of the sources of outlet of the younger adolescent males indicates that their higher rates of total outlet are not consequent upon an increased frequency in each and every kind of sexual activity. On the contrary, nearly all of the increased frequency comes from masturbation, pre-marital intercourse, and the homosexual (Tables 72–78).

Masturbation. While 90 per cent of the younger-maturing boys are involved in masturbation during their early teens, only 60 per cent of the late-maturing boys are involved in that same period. In successive five-year periods the number of earlier-adolescent males who are masturbating is 10 per cent to 15 per cent higher than the number of later-adolescent males who are so involved. Ultimately, nearly 99 per cent of the younger-adolescent boys have some experience in masturbation, while only 93 per cent of the later-adolescent boys are ever involved (Table 73, Figure 92). The younger-maturing boys have about twice as much masturbation as the late-maturing males during the early adolescent years, and 50 to 60 per cent more masturbation between 16 and 25 years of age, if they remain single. The frequencies calculated for the active population (*i.e.*, for that portion of the population that is involved in this activity at all) are definitely higher in every age period for the males who matured first (Table 72). At this college level, these higher frequencies in masturbation are the chief source of the higher total outlets of the younger-maturing males.

Pre-marital Intercourse. In their earlier adolescent years, the younger-maturing boys are also much involved in pre-marital intercourse. Their frequencies are much higher than the frequencies for the late-adolescent group in this period (Table 74). In subsequent age periods, the frequencies among the boys who became adolescent first remain 50 per cent to 75 per cent higher.

During this early adolescent period, the younger-maturing boys of the college level are involved in pre-marital intercourse in 11.8 per cent of the cases, while the older-maturing boys are involved in 7.0 per cent of the

AGE AT ADOL.	CASES	PRE-MARITAL INTERCOURSE AND AGE AT ADOLESCENCE							
		TOTAL POPULATION			INDICES, TOTAL POPULATIONS		ACTIVE POPULATION		
		Mean Frequency	Me-dian Freq.	% of Total Outlet	By Means %	By Me-dians %	Incid. %	Mean Frequency	Me-dian Freq.
		Educ. level 0–8			Activity between adol.–15				
8–12	131	1.86 ± 0.33	0.44	37.3	**286**	**220**	66.4	2.80 ± 0.46	1.39
13	180	1.13 ± 0.15	0.20	35.3	**174**	**100**	60.0	1.88 ± 0.23	1.03
14	270	0.80 ± 0.12	0.00	34.7	**123**	——	41.5	1.94 ± 0.25	1.25
15+	115	0.65 ± 0.15	0.00	33.0	**100**	——	31.3	2.08 ± 0.37	1.25
		Educ. level 0–8			Activity between 16–20				
8–12	114	3.06 ± 0.44	1.58	58.8	**306**	**396**	86.0	3.56 ± 0.49	1.98
13	165	1.64 ± 0.16	0.79	53.3	**162**	**198**	89.1	1.84 ± 0.17	1.09
14	266	1.46 ± 0.16	0.47	56.9	**145**	**118**	82.3	1.78 ± 0.18	0.83
15+	154	1.01 ± 0.14	0.40	45.2	**100**	**100**	74.7	1.35 ± 0.17	0.73
		Educ. level 9–12			Activity between adol.–15				
8–12	170	0.91 ± 0.20	0.00	22.7	**162**	——	48.2	1.88 ± 0.39	0.48
13	197	0.96 ± 0.15	0.01	27.7	**171**	——	50.3	1.91 ± 0.27	0.89
14	213	0.56 ± 0.13	0.00	22.9	**100**	——	35.2	1.60 ± 0.35	0.80
		Educ. level 9–12			Activity between 16–20				
8–12	162	1.58 ± 0.24	0.29	40.3	**155**	**161**	71.0	2.23 ± 0.32	0.78
13	196	1.54 ± 0.18	0.57	43.8	**151**	**317**	76.5	2.01 ± 0.22	1.16
14	207	1.02 ± 0.15	0.38	37.9	**100**	**211**	72.5	1.40 ± 0.19	0.77
		Educ. level 13+			Activity between adol.–15				
8–12	893	0.11 ± 0.02	0.00	3.2	**1100**	——	11.8	0.90 ± 0.16	0.29
13	896	0.07 ± 0.02	0.00	2.5	**700**	——	7.8	0.87 ± 0.18	0.34
14	600	0.06 ± 0.02	0.00	2.6	**600**	——	7.7	0.71 ± 0.17	0.29
15+	114	0.01 ± 0.00	0.00	0.4	**100**	——	7.0	0.11 ± 0.04	0.08
		Educ. level 13+			Activity between 16–20				
8–12	893	0.30 ± 0.03	0.00	9.9	**177**	——	43.8	0.68 ± 0.07	0.24
13	896	0.22 ± 0.03	0.00	8.7	**129**	——	35.6	0.62 ± 0.06	0.20
14	600	0.21 ± 0.03	0.00	9.3	**124**	——	35.5	0.59 ± 0.08	0.17
15+	170	0.17 ± 0.05	0.00	7.7	**100**	——	32.9	0.52 ± 0.13	0.21
		Educ. level 13+			Activity between 21–25				
8–12	561	0.54 ± 0.06	0.03	19.6	**154**	**300**	55.3	0.97 ± 0.10	0.36
13	566	0.40 ± 0.05	0.01	17.4	**114**	**100**	51.4	0.77 ± 0.09	0.30
14	393	0.35 ± 0.05	0.01	16.4	**100**	**100**	50.9	0.69 ± 0.09	0.28
15+	136	0.38 ± 0.09	0.01	17.1	**109**	**100**	50.7	0.74 ± 0.16	0.34
		Educ. level 13+			Activity between 26–30				
8–12	176	0.78 ± 0.11	0.13	28.6	**144**	**186**	64.2	1.22 ± 0.15	0.48
13	179	0.80 ± 0.15	0.07	34.4	**148**	**100**	59.2	1.35 ± 0.24	0.51
14	152	0.54 ± 0.08	0.07	25.8	**100**	**100**	58.6	0.92 ± 0.13	0.44

Table 74. Frequency of pre-marital intercourse, as related to age at onset of adolescence

Data cover the pre-marital intercourse which is had with companions.

314

cases. The active incidence figures beyond 15 years of age are more or less the same for each of the adolescent groups; but the accumulative incidence figures (showing the number of males from each adolescent group who are ever involved, in the course of their lives) show some striking differences between the adolescent groups (Table 75, Figure 93). Ultimately 95 per cent of the early-adolescent boys of this college group obtain experience in heterosexual intercourse, either through pre-marital or marital relations, by age 30; but hardly more than 80 per cent of the late-adolescent males have arrived at such experience in intercourse by that age. For the males who become adolescent at intermediate ages, *i.e.*, at 12, 13, or 14 years of age, the accumulative incidence curves are intermediate (Table 75, Figure 93). Ultimately the curves for the groups which are adolescent at 12 to 14 reach the same level (that is, 95%) which is obtained by the earlier-adolescent boys, but the group which does not become adolescent until 15 or later shows no evidence that it will get much beyond the 80 per cent mark. It is amazing that there should be nearly 20 per cent of these late-adolescent males who have not had some sort of heterosexual coitus by age 35. Most of the late-adolescent males who still lack coital experience in their thirties, have depended upon masturbation and nocturnal dreams rather than upon any other socio-sexual source for their outlet. An unusual proportion of these late-adolescent males is introvert and socially timid, and a considerable number is not yet married at 35 years of age (Table 76, Figure 95).

Homosexual Outlet. During the early adolescent years, twice as many of the early-maturing boys of this college level are involved in homosexual activities (Table 78). During subsequent age periods, the differences in incidence are not so great. Ultimately about 45 per cent of the early-adolescent boys of this college level have some homosexual experience, while less than 25 per cent of the late-adolescent males are ever involved. On the other hand, the frequencies with which homosexual contacts occur (Table 77) remain at about twice the height for these single males who first became adolescent, at least through the period between adolescence and 25. As a factor in the development of the homosexual, age of onset of adolescence (which probably means the metabolic drive of the individual) may prove to be more significant than the much discussed Oedipus relation of Freudian philosophy.

Other Outlets. Apart from masturbation, heterosexual coitus, and the homosexual, the other possible sources of sexual outlet are utilized to about an equal degree by the unmarried males from different adolescent groups. A single instance of such conformance is shown in Table 79, which covers the data for nocturnal emissions. Similarly, there are no fundamental differences between the incidences and frequencies in regard to heterosexual petting, and in regard to that part of the heterosexual

FIRST INTERCOURSE AND AGE AT ADOLESCENCE

AGE	ACCUMULATIVE INCIDENCE DATA EDUCATIONAL LEVEL 13+								
	ADOLESCENT BY 11		ADOLESCENT AT 12		ADOLESCENT AT 13		ADOLESCENT AT 14		ADOLESCENT AT 15+
	Cases	% with Exper.	Cases	% with Exper.	Cases	% with Exper.	Cases	% with Exper.	Cases	% with Exper.
8	300	0.0	707	0.0	979	0.0	647	0.0	183	0.0
9	300	0.3	707	0.0	979	0.0	647	0.0	183	0.0
10	300	0.3	707	0.0	979	0.0	647	0.0	183	0.0
11	300	1.7	707	0.0	979	0.0	647	0.0	183	0.0
12	300	3.3	707	2.4	979	0.0	647	0.0	183	0.0
13	300	8.7	707	4.2	979	2.9	647	0.0	183	0.0
14	300	13.0	707	7.5	979	5.0	647	5.0	183	0.0
15	300	15.0	707	11.6	979	8.6	647	7.6	183	4.4
16	300	23.0	707	19.0	979	13.6	646	12.8	183	9.3
17	300	29.0	707	27.4	978	22.2	645	19.5	183	14.8
18	290	37.2	690	35.8	948	28.7	626	28.8	183	21.9
19	275	44.7	646	43.2	886	36.0	590	35.8	176	30.7
20	259	53.7	595	50.1	791	43.9	526	42.4	167	37.1
21	236	57.2	499	54.5	676	50.0	470	47.9	151	43.7
22	198	65.1	397	61.5	555	58.4	398	53.8	123	52.0
23	176	68.2	329	64.4	462	66.7	327	57.2	102	52.9
24	146	74.7	264	72.7	379	71.2	281	62.6	81	58.0
25	126	79.4	229	79.0	334	76.0	239	71.5	73	64.4
26	107	87.9	198	83.8	299	79.6	216	78.2	63	66.7
27	86	90.7	169	85.2	270	81.9	198	81.8	50	70.0
28	82	91.5	150	85.3	240	85.4	182	86.3	44	70.5
29	70	95.7	139	85.6	216	86.1	169	88.8	39	79.5
30	60	95.0	121	87.6	199	89.4	158	91.1	34	82.4
31	56	94.6	107	91.6	181	90.6	153	92.2		
32	51	94.1	97	92.8	166	91.0	146	92.5		
33			89	92.1	148	91.2	131	92.4		
34			83	92.8	137	92.7	120	94.2		
35			76	92.1	126	96.0	115	93.9		
36			70	94.3	114	95.6	110	94.5		
37			64	93.8	101	95.0	99	93.9		
38			60	93.3	96	92.7	96	95.8		
39			57	93.0	85	96.5	90	95.6		
40					79	96.2	84	95.2		

Table 75. Age of first intercourse, as affected by age at onset of adolescence

Accumulative incidence data based on males of college level.

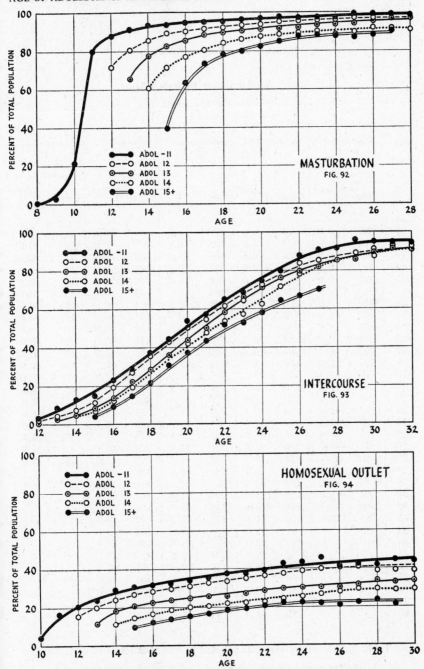

Figures 92–94. Relation of age at onset of adolescence to accumulative incidence
of masturbation, total intercourse, and homosexual outlet

Based on lifetime histories of males of the college level. Each adolescent group maintains its relative position for 20 or more years.

MARRIAGE AND AGE AT ADOLESCENCE

AGE	ACCUMULATIVE INCIDENCE DATA EDUCATIONAL LEVEL 13+									
	ADOLESCENT BY 11		ADOLESCENT AT 12		ADOLESCENT AT 13		ADOLESCENT AT 14		ADOLESCENT AT 15+	
	Cases	% with Exper.	Cases	% with Exper.	Cases	% with Exper.	Cases	% with Exper.	Cases	% with Exper.
8	307	0.0	724	0.0	986	0.0	651	0.0	187	0.0
9	307	0.0	724	0.0	986	0.0	651	0.0	187	0.0
10	307	0.0	724	0.0	986	0.0	651	0.0	187	0.0
11	307	0.0	724	0.0	986	0.0	651	0.0	187	0.0
12	307	0.0	724	0.0	986	0.0	651	0.0	187	0.0
13	307	0.0	724	0.0	986	0.0	651	0.0	187	0.0
14	307	0.0	724	0.0	986	0.0	651	0.0	187	0.0
15	307	0.0	724	0.0	986	0.0	651	0.0	187	0.0
16	307	0.3	724	0.1	986	0.0	651	0.0	187	0.0
17	307	0.3	724	0.1	985	0.2	650	0.0	187	0.0
18	297	0.7	706	0.4	957	0.4	631	0.0	187	0.0
19	282	2.5	660	1.4	897	1.2	594	0.7	180	0.0
20	266	3.4	609	3.1	802	2.9	530	2.8	170	0.0
21	243	5.3	510	6.3	689	4.9	473	5.3	154	0.6
22	205	9.8	407	12.0	568	11.1	402	10.0	126	6.3
23	183	16.9	339	19.8	474	16.5	332	14.8	105	8.6
24	152	28.3	274	32.5	391	23.3	288	20.1	84	15.5
25	131	37.4	238	45.0	345	29.9	246	29.7	77	23.4
26	112	48.2	206	52.4	310	42.3	224	40.6	67	26.9
27	90	55.6	174	60.3	278	51.8	205	49.3	54	37.0
28	86	59.3	155	63.2	248	60.1	188	55.3		
29	74	67.6	144	67.4	223	64.6	174	59.2		
30	64	68.8	125	73.6	206	71.4	162	67.3		
31	60	73.3	110	83.6	188	73.9	156	71.2		
32	55	76.4	100	84.0	171	77.2	149	73.2		
33	53	77.4	91	85.7	154	78.6	135	75.6		
34			85	87.1	142	81.0	124	79.8		
35			77	87.0	131	83.2	119	80.7		
36			70	88.6	119	84.9	114	82.5		
37			64	87.5	105	83.8	103	80.6		
38			60	86.7	100	83.0	100	83.0		
39			57	86.0	89	83.1	93	83.9		
40			50	88.0	83	85.5	87	86.2		

Table 76. Age at marriage, as affected by age at onset of adolescence

Accumulative incidence data based on males of college level.

intercourse which is had with prostitutes. There is some suggestion in the data that the farm boys who became adolescent first have more animal intercourse, but the number of active cases is too small to allow dependable calculations.

For the married males, the rates of total outlet among the early-adolescent individuals are definitely higher. There is some indication that most of this comes from marital intercourse, but the necessity for a six-way breakdown of the population before correlations can be run puts such a strain on the relatively smaller samples now available for married males, that further analyses cannot be made at this time.

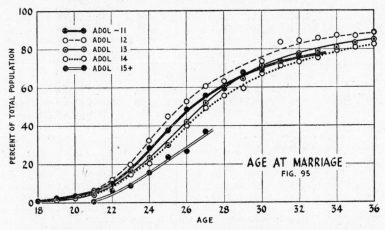

Figure 95. Relation of age at onset of adolescence to age at marriage

Based on males of the college level. A social phenomenon is correlated with the factors which control onset of adolescence.

AGING VERSUS EARLY ACTIVITY

It would be of considerable interest to know whether an early onset of sexual activity and a lifetime of higher frequencies among the early-adolescent males show any correlation with the age at which individuals become sexually unresponsive or impotent, and at which they cease sexual activity altogether.

Some information on these points may be had from Table 71 where the record for married males is shown up to the age of 50. At that time, 100 per cent of the early-adolescent males are still sexually active, and their frequencies are still 20 per cent higher than the frequencies of the later-maturing males. Nearly forty years of maximum activity have not yet worn them out physically, physiologically, or psychologically. On the other hand, some of the males (not many) who were late adolescent and who

AGE AT ADOL.	CASES	FREQUENCIES AMONG SINGLE MALES, BY EDUCATIONAL LEVEL						
		TOTAL POPULATION			INDICES, TOTAL POPULATIONS	ACTIVE POPULATION		
		Mean Frequency	Me-dian Freq.	% of Total Outlet	By Means %	Incid. %	Mean Frequency	Me-dian Freq.
Educ. level 0–8				Activity between adol.–15				
8–12	131	0.44 ± 0.08	0.00	8.8	367	46.6	0.94 ± 0.15	0.40
13	180	0.27 ± 0.06	0.00	8.6	225	25.0	1.09 ± 0.20	0.50
14	270	0.22 ± 0.06	0.00	9.7	183	18.9	1.19 ± 0.28	0.38
15+	115	0.12 ± 0.04	0.00	6.0	100	13.9	0.85 ± 0.24	0.56
Educ. level 0–8				Activity between 16–20				
8–12	114	0.52 ± 0.12	0.00	10.0	400	45.6	1.14 ± 0.22	0.40
13	165	0.31 ± 0.08	0.00	10.1	238	28.5	1.09 ± 0.25	0.39
14	266	0.15 ± 0.04	0.00	6.0	115	22.6	0.68 ± 0.13	0.30
15+	154	0.13 ± 0.03	0.00	5.9	100	22.7	0.58 ± 0.10	0.43
Educ. level 9–12				Activity between adol.–15				
8–12	170	0.54 ± 0.11	0.00	13.4	599	47.1	1.14 ± 0.21	0.45
13	197	0.26 ± 0.06	0.00	7.5	288	31.0	0.85 ± 0.19	0.10
14	213	0.17 ± 0.03	0.00	6.9	130	26.8	0.64 ± 0.10	0.27
15+	42	0.09 ± 0.04	0.00	3.8	100	21.4	0.44 ± 0.12	0.50
Educ. level 9–12				Activity between 16–20				
8–12	162	0.72 ± 0.14	0.03	18.3	480	54.9	1.31 ± 0.24	0.50
13	196	0.31 ± 0.06	0.00	8.7	207	38.8	0.79 ± 0.13	0.17
14	207	0.31 ± 0.06	0.00	11.5	207	37.2	0.83 ± 0.13	0.34
15+	58	0.15 ± 0.05	0.00	4.8	100	34.5	0.43 ± 0.13	0.14
Educ. level 13+				Activity between adol.–15				
8–12	893	0.11 ± 0.02	0.00	3.2	220	27.9	0.38 ± 0.05	0.08
13	896	0.09 ± 0.01	0.00	3.3	180	20.9	0.43 ± 0.05	0.09
14	600	0.07 ± 0.02	0.00	3.3	140	14.0	0.50 ± 0.12	0.09
15+	114	0.05 ± 0.02	0.00	2.8	100	14.0	0.36 ± 0.14	0.23
Educ. level 13+				Activity between 16–20				
8–12	893	0.08 ± 0.01	0.00	2.5	200	16.6	0.46 ± 0.07	0.08
13	896	0.06 ± 0.01	0.00	2.4	150	15.5	0.39 ± 0.06	0.08
14	600	0.07 ± 0.02	0.00	3.0	175	15.3	0.44 ± 0.12	0.09
15+	170	0.04 ± 0.02	0.00	1.7	100	15.9	0.24 ± 0.09	0.08
Educ. level 13+				Activity between 21–25				
8–12	561	0.11 ± 0.02	0.00	4.0	183	9.3	1.18 ± 0.19	0.48
13	566	0.08 ± 0.02	0.00	3.4	133	9.0	0.84 ± 0.20	0.26
14	393	0.09 ± 0.03	0.00	4.4	150	9.7	0.97 ± 0.31	0.23
15+	136	0.06 ± 0.03	0.00	2.5	100	8.8	0.63 ± 0.28	0.30
Educ. level 13+				Activity between 26–30				
8–12	176	0.27 ± 0.06	0.00	9.8	159	17.6	1.52 ± 0.27	1.17
13	179	0.21 ± 0.06	0.00	9.0	123	17.3	1.21 ± 0.26	0.63
14	152	0.17 ± 0.05	0.00	7.9	100	16.4	1.01 ± 0.26	0.37

Table 77. Frequency of homosexual outlet as related to age at onset of adolescence

HOMOSEXUAL OUTLETS AND AGE AT ADOLESCENCE

AGE	ACCUMULATIVE INCIDENCE DATA EDUCATIONAL LEVEL 13+									
	ADOLESCENT BY 11		ADOLESCENT AT 12		ADOLESCENT AT 13		ADOLESCENT AT 14		ADOLESCENT AT 15+	
	Cases	% with Exper.	Cases	% with Exper.	Cases	% with Exper.	Cases	% with Exper.	Cases	% with Exper.
8	307	0.3	724	0.0	986	0.0	651	0.0	187	0.0
9	307	0.7	724	0.0	986	0.0	651	0.0	187	0.0
10	307	4.2	724	0.0	986	0.0	651	0.0	187	0.0
11	307	16.3	724	0.0	986	0.0	651	0.0	187	0.0
12	307	20.5	724	15.2	986	0.0	651	0.0	187	0.0
13	307	23.8	724	19.9	986	11.4	651	0.0	187	0.0
14	307	29.3	724	23.8	986	18.1	651	11.2	187	0.0
15	307	30.6	724	27.1	986	20.5	651	14.3	187	9.6
16	307	31.9	724	28.6	986	22.2	651	16.9	187	12.3
17	307	32.2	724	29.6	985	23.4	650	18.2	187	13.9
18	297	34.0	706	30.6	957	24.7	631	20.1	187	15.5
19	282	35.5	660	32.7	897	25.4	594	20.7	180	16.7
20	266	37.6	609	33.5	802	25.6	530	21.9	170	18.2
21	243	37.4	510	35.1	689	27.0	473	22.2	154	19.5
22	205	39.0	407	36.4	568	28.5	402	22.9	126	21.4
23	183	42.6	339	37.5	474	29.5	332	24.4	105	22.9
24	152	43.4	274	38.7	391	29.9	288	25.3	84	22.6
25	131	45.8	236	39.4	345	29.9	246	27.2	77	22.1
26	112	41.1	206	40.8	310	30.0	224	28.6	67	20.9
27	90	42.2	174	40.8	278	31.7	205	29.3	54	22.2
28	86	41.9	155	38.7	248	33.5	188	29.3		
29	74	44.6	144	38.9	223	32.7	174	28.7		
30	64	43.8	125	38.4	206	33.5	162	29.0		
31	60	46.7	110	37.3	188	34.0	156	29.5		
32	55	43.6	100	37.0	171	32.2	149	28.9		
33	53	43.4	91	38.5	154	33.8	135	29.6		
34			85	40.0	142	33.8	124	30.6		
35			77	39.0	131	32.1	119	30.3		
36			70	40.0	119	31.9	114	28.9		
37			64	42.2	105	30.5	103	28.2		
38			60	43.3	100	30.0	100	28.0		
39			57	42.1	89	31.5	93	28.0		
40			50	42.0	83	28.9	87	27.6		

Table 78. Homosexual outlet as affected by age at onset of adolescence
Accumulative incidence data based on males of the college level.

SEXUAL BEHAVIOR IN THE HUMAN MALE

NOCTURNAL EMISSIONS AND AGE AT ADOLESCENCE

AGE AT ADOL.	CASES	TOTAL POPULATION			INDICES, TOTAL POPULATIONS		ACTIVE POPULATION		
		Mean Frequency	Me-dian Freq.	% of Total Outlet	By Means %	By Me-dians %	Incid. %	Mean Frequency	Me-dian Freq.
Educ. level 0–8				Activity between adol.–15					
8–12	131	0.04 ± 0.01	0.00	0.9	100	—	30.5	0.14 ± 0.04	0.07
13	180	0.07 ± 0.02	0.00	2.3	175	—	37.2	0.20 ± 0.04	0.08
14	270	0.05 ± 0.01	0.00	2.0	125	—	20.4	0.23 ± 0.06	0.07
15+	115	0.06 ± 0.02	0.00	3.0	150	—	14.8	0.40 ± 0.13	0.26
Educ. level 0–8				Activity between 16–20					
8–12	114	0.15 ± 0.03	0.03	2.9	115	300	57.0	0.26 ± 0.05	0.10
13	165	0.17 ± 0.03	0.05	5.5	131	500	66.7	0.25 ± 0.04	0.10
14	266	0.13 ± 0.02	0.01	5.1	100	100	51.5	0.26 ± 0.04	0.08
15+	154	0.20 ± 0.04	0.03	8.9	154	300	56.5	0.35 ± 0.06	0.13
Educ. level 9–12				Activity between adol.–15					
8–12	170	0.23 ± 0.06	0.00	5.7	288	—	46.5	0.49 ± 0.11	0.12
13	197	0.15 ± 0.03	0.00	4.2	188	—	44.7	0.33 ± 0.05	0.16
14	213	0.10 ± 0.03	0.00	4.2	125	—	33.8	0.30 ± 0.07	0.09
15+	42	0.08 ± 0.03	0.00	3.3	100	—	23.8	0.35 ± 0.08	0.33
Educ. level 9–12				Activity between 16–20					
8–12	162	0.25 ± 0.04	0.07	6.5	156	140	74.7	0.34 ± 0.05	0.11
13	196	0.22 ± 0.03	0.07	6.3	137	140	73.0	0.30 ± 0.04	0.16
14	207	0.22 ± 0.03	0.05	8.1	137	100	68.6	0.31 ± 0.05	0.10
15+	58	0.16 ± 0.03	0.05	5.1	100	100	62.1	0.25 ± 0.04	0.18
Educ. level 13+				Activity between adol.–15					
8–12	893	0.37 ± 0.03	0.10	11.4	154	163	73.1	0.51 ± 0.04	0.25
13	896	0.35 ± 0.02	0.13	13.0	146	125	74.2	0.48 ± 0.03	0.28
14	600	0.28 ± 0.02	0.08	13.0	117	100	61.2	0.45 ± 0.03	0.29
15+	114	0.24 ± 0.06	0.00	13.2	100	—	40.4	0.60 ± 0.14	0.34
Educ. level 13+				Activity between 16–20					
8–12	893	0.41 ± 0.02	0.22	13.6	105	100	88.9	0.46 ± 0.02	0.27
13	896	0.43 ± 0.02	0.27	17.0	110	123	93.4	0.46 ± 0.02	0.30
14	600	0.39 ± 0.02	0.24	17.5	100	109	90.7	0.44 ± 0.03	0.28
15+	170	0.47 ± 0.06	0.27	21.2	122	123	91.8	0.52 ± 0.06	0.30
Educ. level 13+				Activity between 21–25					
8–12	561	0.37 ± 0.03	0.19	13.5	100	100	84.7	0.44 ± 0.03	0.27
13	566	0.40 ± 0.03	0.23	17.7	108	121	89.0	0.45 ± 0.03	0.28
14	393	0.37 ± 0.03	0.23	17.2	100	121	91.1	0.40 ± 0.03	0.27
15+	136	0.46 ± 0.06	0.26	21.0	124	137	86.8	0.53 ± 0.07	0.31

FREQUENCIES AMONG SINGLE MALES, BY EDUCATIONAL LEVEL

Table 79. Lack of correlation between nocturnal emissions and age at onset of adolescence

have had five years less of sexual activity, are beginning to drop completely out of the picture; and the rates of this group are definitely lower in these older age periods.

It is unfortunate that the number of histories now on hand from still older males is too small to allow further calculations on these points. It has, however, been possible to calculate correlations between the age of onset of adolescence and the age of onset of impotence for a small group of 69 older males. For these cases, the coefficient of correlation proves to be 0.30. If the results can be trusted on a sample of this size, the low coefficient indicates that there is in actuality no significant correlation. In other words, the fact that an individual has started sexual activity in early life and has had frequent activity throughout a long period of years is not necessarily responsible for the onset of impotence in his old age. Impotence is as likely to occur at the same age among those males who did not start activity until late and whose rates of sexual activity were always low. The ready assumption which is made in some of the medical literature that impotence is the product of sexual excess, is not justified by such data as are now available. Impotence is clearly the product of a great diversity of physical, physiologic, and psychologic factors, and in each individual case a multiplicity of factors is likely to be involved.

It will be recalled (Chapter 7) that impotence is in actuality a relatively rare phenomenon. The clinicians, especially the urologists and endocrinologists, see so many individuals who are badly upset by impotence that they may find it difficult to believe that the incidence of the phenomenon is as low as we find it in the population at large; but again it should be pointed out that a clinic is no place from which to get incidence data.

Impotence in a male under 55 years of age is almost always the product of psychologic conflict, except in those exceedingly few cases where there has been mechanical injury of the genitalia or of the portions of the central nervous system which control erection, or in those similarly few cases where venereal or other disease has interfered with nervous functions. There is even some evidence that much of the impotence which is seen in old age is psychologic in its origin. In a larger number of cases than has ordinarily been realized, there are psychologic problems involving sex which may not develop until the later years of an individual's marriage, either in connection with his marital intercourse, or in connection with other sexual activities which the male begins in his more advanced years. Psychologically, impotence is also predicated among older persons because they so often expect it; and the psychologic fatigue which follows long years of sexual experience is a prominent factor in the development of incapacity in old age. It will be recalled (Chapter 7) that only 27 per cent of the male population becomes impotent by 70 years of age, and that much older histories would be needed to secure any large number of cases for

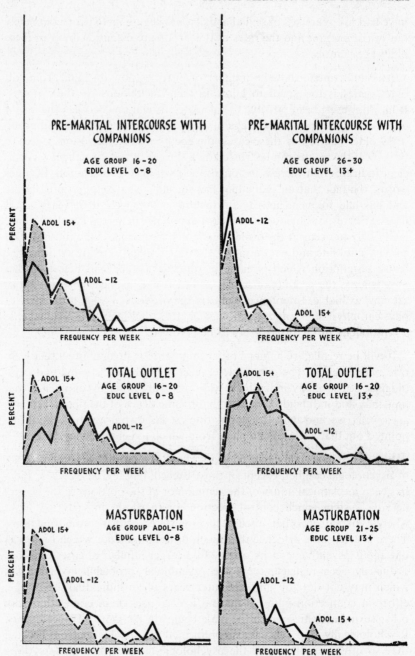

Figure 96. Comparisons of individual variation among early-adolescent and
late-adolescent males

Based on single males. Solid lines show frequency distributions for males who became
adolescent by 12. Broken lines and shaded areas show frequency distributions for males
who did not become adolescent before 15.

a study of the relation of impotence to the age of onset of adolescence. Certain it is that among persons who become impotent by 70, there are histories of males who became adolescent at each and every age; but there are also histories of males who are still active after sixty or more years of sexual activities which were maintained at a maximum rate from the time they first turned adolescent at 10 or 11.

CONCLUSIONS

In fine, the data add up as follows:

1. The males who are first adolescent begin their sexual activity almost immediately and maintain higher frequencies in sexual activity for a matter of at least 35 or 40 years.

2. The factors which contribute to this early adolescence apparently continue to operate for at least these 35 or 40 years.

3. Exercise of the sexual capacities does not seem to impair those capacities, at least as they are exercised by most of the persons who belong in the highest-rating segment of the population. While it is theoretically conceivable that very high rates of activity might contribute to physical impairment, or indirectly to diseased conditions, or to other difficulties in certain cases, the actual record includes exceedingly few high-rating males whose activities have had such an outcome.

4. Those individuals who become adolescent late, however, more often delay the start of their sexual activities and have the minimum frequencies of activity, both in their early years and throughout the remainder of their lives. If any of these individuals have deliberately chosen low frequencies in order to conserve their energies for later use, they appear never to have found the sufficient justification for such a use at any later time. It is probable that most of these low rating individuals never were capable of higher rates and never could have increased their rates to match those of the more active segments of the population.

5. In general, the boys who were first mature are the ones who most often turn to masturbation and, interestingly enough, to pre-marital sociosexual contacts as well. They engage in both heterosexual and homosexual relations more frequently than the boys who are last in maturing.

There is some reason for thinking that these early-adolescent males are more often the more alert, energetic, vivacious, spontaneous, physically active, socially extrovert, and/or aggressive individuals in the population. Actually, 53 per cent of the early-adolescent boys are so described on their histories, while only 33 per cent of the late-adolescent boys received such personality ratings. Conversely, 54 per cent of the males who were last-adolescent were described as slow, quiet, mild in manner, without force, reserved, timid, taciturn, introvert, and/or socially inept, while only 31 per cent of the early-adolescent boys fell under such headings. There are, of course, some individuals who do not fall clearly into either of these classifications. Prior to analyzing these data for the present chapter, we had no indication that we would find this sort of correlation and, consequently, all of the personality notations on the original histories were made without regard for the ages at which adolescence had occurred.

There is, of course, much individual variation on all of these matters, and there is no invariable correlation between personalities and rates of sexual activity. There are some very energetic and socially extrovert individuals who rate low in their sexual frequencies, and there are quiet and even timid individuals who have considerable socio-sexual activity. Behavior is always the product of a multiplicity of factors, no one of which can be identified as the exclusive or predominant agent in more than some small portion of the cases which one studies.

There is evidence that the late-maturing males have more limited sexual capacities which would be badly strained if, through any circumstance, they tried to raise their rates to the levels maintained by the sexually more capable persons. If further studies show that some physiologic quality, such as metabolic rate, works together with or through the hormones to determine the time of onset of adolescence, it may become a matter of clinical importance to exercise some control over that event. If this were done, would the subsequent sexual performance then be affected? Parents and clinicians may properly be concerned with such questions.

Chapter 10

SOCIAL LEVEL AND SEXUAL OUTLET

The sexual behavior of the human animal is the outcome of its morphologic and physiologic organization, of the conditioning which its experience has brought it, and of all the forces which exist in its living and non-living environment. In terms of academic disciplines, there are biologic, psychologic, and sociologic factors involved; but all of these operate simultaneously, and the end product is a single, unified phenomenon which is not merely biologic, psychologic, or sociologic in nature. Nevertheless, the importance of each group of factors can never be ignored.

Without its physical body and its physiologic capacities, there would be no animal to act. The individual's sexual behavior is, to a degree, predestined by its morphologic structure, its metabolic capacities, its hormones, and all of the other characters which it has inherited or which have been built into it by the physical environment in which it has developed. Two of the most important of these distinctively biologic forces, age and the age at onset of adolescence, have been examined in the earlier chapters of the present volume.

But through all of the previous chapters, constant consideration has been given to the significance of the psychologic factors which affect sexual behavior, and it should be apparent by now that the experience of the individual, the satisfactory or unsatisfactory nature of that experience, the conformance or non-conformance of that experience with the individual's personality, attitudes, and rational thinking, and a great variety of other factors make the psychologic bases of behavior even more important than the biologic heritage and acquirements.

It is evident, however, that psychologic processes depend, to a considerable degree, upon the way in which external forces impinge upon the animal. For a creature with as highly organized a central nervous system as is found in the human animal, the most important external force is the social environment in which it lives. In the human species, the environment consists of one's family, his close friends, his neighbors, his business associates, and his mere acquaintances. It also includes the thousands of other persons whom he has never seen but whose attitudes, habits, expressed opinions, and overt activities constitute the culture in which he moves and lives. These are the social forces which contribute to the individual's behavior. There is, of course, no part of the individual himself which is social in nature, in quite the way that morphologic, physiologic, or psychologic capacities may be identified and localized in an organism. Occasionally social forces provide physical restraints on individuals, or facilitate their physical activities; but more often they operate only as they affect the individual psychologically.

EDUC. LEVEL ATTAINED	OCCUPATIONAL CLASS							CASES IN EDUC. LEVEL
	2 DAY LABOR	3 SEMI-SKILLED LABOR	4 SKILLED LABOR	5 LOWER WHITE COLLAR	6 UPPER WHITE COLLAR	7 PRO-FES-SIONAL	8 BUSI-NESS EXECU-TIVE	
	%	%	%	%	%	%	%	
0	4.6	1.1	0.7	0.2				26
1	1.3	0.4	0.0	0.0				7
2	3.8	1.1	0.7	0.2				23
3	4.1	3.2	2.9	0.2				39
4	7.6	4.3	3.6					61
5	7.6	6.1	1.4	0.2				67
6	9.6	6.8	5.8	1.8				92
7	15.2	9.3	12.9	2.0				139
8	22.9	26.4	23.7	6.8	1.6			309
9	8.6	11.1	3.6	4.1	0.4			121
10	8.6	13.7	9.4	6.5	1.0			158
11	2.8	6.3	5.8	6.5	1.6			90
12	3.3	8.6	22.3	27.6	5.0		6.3	239
13		0.7	3.6	12.0	2.7			76
14		0.7	0.7	11.0	5.8			84
15		0.2	0.7	6.3	4.5	0.3		55
16			2.2	8.3	25.3	0.9	18.8	181
17				3.4	22.7	2.0	0.0	145
18				2.0	21.9	6.6	12.5	167
19				0.7	5.2	6.1	18.8	73
20+				0.2	2.3	84.1	43.6	567
Total %	100.0	100.0	100.0	100.0	100.0	100.0	100.0	2719
Cases in oc-cup. class	394	559	139	444	516	651	16	2719
Mean educ.	6.23	7.59	8.57	11.84	15.68	19.20	17.81	
Median educ.	6.78	7.69	7.95	11.80	16.11	19.41	18.69	

Table 80. Relation between educational level and occupational class of subjects in present sample

Based on those males in the present sample who have finished their educational careers.

The present chapter and the three chapters which follow are concerned with the relation of the individual's pattern of sexual behavior to patterns which are followed by other persons in the same social group—in the group in which the individual is raised, or into which he moves and establishes himself in the course of his lifetime.

DEFINING SOCIAL LEVELS

The data now available show that patterns of sexual behavior may be strikingly different for the different social levels that exist in the same city or town, and sometimes in immediately adjacent sections of a single community. The data show that divergencies in the sexual patterns of such social groups may be as great as those which anthropologists have found between the sexual patterns of different racial groups in remote parts of the world. There is no American pattern of sexual behavior, but scores of patterns, each of which is confined to a particular segment of our society. Within each segment there are attitudes on sex and patterns of overt activity which are followed by a high proportion of the individuals in that group; and an understanding of the sexual mores of the American people as a whole is possible only through an understanding of the sexual patterns of all of the constituent groups.

These social levels are, admittedly, intangible divisions of the population which are difficult to define; but they are recognized by everyone as real and significant factors in the life of a community. In the present study, the social level of each subject has been measured by three criteria: 1. The educational level, in years, which the individual has reached by the time he terminates his formal education (Chapter 3). 2. The occupational class to which the individual belongs (as such classes have been defined in Chapter 3). 3. The occupational class of the individual's parents at the time that he lived in the parental home.

There are, of course, certain correlations among these three criteria. The educational level ultimately attained determines, to some degree, the occupation which an individual follows. The nature of the correlation is shown in Table 80, where it will be observed that certain educational levels send people into several of the occupational classes, while other educational levels (e.g., the one which includes those who have done graduate work in a university) send nearly all of their members into a single occupational class. It is understandable, therefore, that analyses of sexual behavior made on the basis of ultimate educational level give results which are close to those obtained by the use of a system of occupational classes.

The ultimate educational level attained by an individual shows a limited correlation with intelligence quotients (Lorge 1942). The correlations have been shown to run about 0.66, which may mean that there is some trend for the more intelligent students to continue in school. It also indicates, however, that there are some perfectly intelligent individuals who stop school long before they have reached the limits of their capacities; and that there are some less intelligent individuals who, by dint of work or fortuitous circumstance, manage to get further along in school than their capacities would predicate. Since there may be some correlation between mental capacity and the nature of the occupation which an individual chooses, here is another reason for one's educational level correlating with his occupational class.

Educational Level as a Criterion. The educational level attained by an individual by the time he terminates his schooling has proved to be the simplest and the best-defined means for recognizing social levels (see Chapter 3 for details of the way in which this criterion has been used). Social level is not necessarily controlled by the amount of schooling that an individual has had, but the amount of schooling does provide a measure of more basic factors which determine one's social level.

Each level has its own attitudes toward education and, consequently, a high proportion of the persons in any level go to about the same point in school. One group allows its children to terminate their schooling at the eighth grade, or as soon thereafter as the law allows; and in that group there is a general acceptance of the idea that it is a waste of time to send children further along in school when they might be earning wages and contributing to the family income. There is no community action which formalizes these things and some individuals in the community may disagree with the general attitude; but by and large the children hear the group opinion so often expressed that they come to accept it and look forward to the time when they will be allowed to quit school. The individuals in another social level believe that their children should go part way, or perhaps fully, through high school. Going to college is the expected and more or less inevitable thing for the children of other social groups.

Persons who depart from the educational trends of their particular level do so against the community opinion and must be ready to defend themselves for their independent action. This is as true of the professor's son who decides to go to work at the end of high school as it is of the lower level boy who strikes out for a college education. The boy or girl who departs from the custom is quickly made aware of the fact that he has done something as unusual as wearing the wrong kind of clothing to a social event, or using his table silver in a fashion which is recognized as not good manners in that group. There are no penalties attached to departures from the custom, except those of being made to feel different from the community of which one has previously considered himself a part. Such penalties, however, may control behavior as effectively as though they were physical restraints.

During the past thirty or forty years, there has been a considerable departure of younger generations from the educational levels attained by their parents (Table 106); but almost always this has been in the direction of an increase in the amount of education which the younger persons receive. The idea of a boy or girl being satisfied with less education than his parents had is so abhorrent as to be rarely accepted, and most people are startled when they find an individual case of such regression.

Educational level is a convenient criterion for statistical use because it provides a well-defined, simple figure which is discrete and does not vary in the individual's lifetime, after he has once finished his schooling. Educational level cannot be used for studying the histories of persons who are still in school, since there is no certainty how far they will go before they finally terminate their education. Educational level is not a satisfactory basis for analysis when the individual changes his social level in the course of his life.

Occupational Class as a Criterion. It has been pointed out (Chapter 3) that a modification of the Chapin and Lloyd Warner schemes of occupational classes (Chapin 1933, Hollingshead 1939, Warner and Lunt 1941, 1942, Warner and Srole 1945) is the basis for the analyses made in the present study. In brief, the following classes are recognized:

0. **Dependents**
1. **Underworld**
2. **Day labor**
3. **Semi-skilled labor**
4. **Skilled labor**
5. **Lower white collar group**
6. **Upper white collar group**
7. **Professional group**
8. **Business executive group**
9. **Extremely wealthy group**

Occupational classes are more poorly defined than educational levels. Whether an individual belongs in one occupational group or the next not infrequently calls for a judgment in which equally skilled investigators might disagree, although experience in the present research indicates that the judgments are not often more than one occupational class apart. Whether a person is a laborer or a semi-skilled workman, whether he is a semi-skilled or a skilled workman, is not always possible to say; but in most cases it is possible to make a definite classification. Labor unions often define the occupational qualities of their members. Whether a person is a mechanic or a white collar worker is rarely in dispute; but whether the white collar worker belongs to class 5 (the lower white collar group) or class 6 (the upper white collar group), is sometimes more difficult to say. This makes occupational class less precise than educational level for measuring social status.

On the other hand, classifications by occupation probably show a closer correlation with the intangible realities of social organization, since this classification is designed to express the social prestige of the work with which the individual is occupied. The use of occupational class provides the best opportunity, and the only opportunity we have had, to take into account the migrations of an individual from one social level to another within his lifetime; and all of the data given in the next chapter on the relation of such migration to changes in patterns of sexual behavior have been derived from this source. With younger persons who are still at home, it will be recalled that their occupational class is derived from that of their parents (their "ascribed status" as some anthropologists have put it). Younger individuals who are just beginning to establish themselves away from their parents' home are often involved in more menial occupations, and sometimes in occupations totally different from those which they will ultimately work into (the latter is "the achieved status" in the anthropological terminology); and in this case, occupational class is not a good means of measuring social level.

In this and the next chapter, references to occupational class are usually made as double entries which include the parental class in which the subject originated, and the ultimate class into which the subject independently migrated.

Realities of Social Levels. If there were invariable correlations between education, occupation, and the social organization of our society, "social levels" would be recognized as realities which could easily be delimited. That there is no invariable relation means that such levels are difficult to define; but that does not prove that they are not realities. Quite on the contrary, each child soon becomes aware of the social classification to which he belongs, and learns the boundaries of the group within which he is allowed to move. Each adult lives and moves and does his thinking, to a considerable degree, in accord with the movements and the thinking of other persons who have about the same education and who usually belong to the same occupational class. While there are no sharp boundaries to social levels, there are obstacles to the crossing of those boundaries.

Social levels are hierarchies which are not supposed to exist in a democratic society, and many people would, therefore, deny their existence. In this country we make it a point that there should be no physical barriers nor legal codes which forbid people to move with almost any social group. But while there are, admittedly, a few persons who do move between groups, most persons do not in actuality move freely with those who belong to other levels. Each group recognizes its unity, and its distinction from every other group.

In their occupations or professional activities, persons of different social levels may have a certain amount of daily contact, but their close friends and companions are more likely to come from their own groups. The white collar executive and the office force may work only a few feet away from the factory laborers and mechanics, but they do not really work with them;

and in their recreations, after hours, the two groups rarely intermingle. Persons in the one group do not invite persons from the other group to their homes for dinner, or for an evening of conversation, games, or other activities. One's companions in a card game or around a fireplace are a better test of one's social position than are one's business contacts, or even one's verbalization of his social philosophy.

Within the white collar groups, for instance, there are several levels of social organization. Store clerks and office staffs do not move freely with the business executive groups, outside of their business relations. Persons in professional groups have few intimates among any but the better business and professional men. Doctors may serve persons on both sides of the tracks, but in off hours they visit and find their recreations with other doctors, with some business men, or with college professors. The professional group is not particularly at home with financially successful business men, nor with persons from the Social Register and the top social strata, unless the professional persons themselves happen to have inherited such financial or social backgrounds. These social stratifications are very real, even though they are difficult to define.

Social levels are not necessarily determined by the economic status of an individual. School teachers belong to a white collar class which is generally looked up to by working classes although the working classes may have considerably higher incomes than school teachers ever will have. The fact that the janitor in the school may earn more than the teacher in the same building does not admit him to the social activities of the teacher's group. Conversely, the lesser salary of the teacher does not give her the entrée into the group with which the janitor finds his recreation. For such reasons, neither the current income nor the general economic status of an individual has been used in the present study as a criterion for establishing social levels.

It is, moreover, difficult to know what an income may be worth in a particular instance. An income of a couple of thousand a year would provide a very comfortable living for certain families, although it might spell poverty for the next family whose esthetic and cultural ideals demand much more to satisfy them. Moreover, the dollar has a different purchasing power in different cities and towns in different parts of the country, and it may vary within a single community, depending upon the standards of dress, of entertainment, and of social front which one must maintain in the particular social level to which he belongs. There are economic rating scales which are designed to take these many items into account; but any such scale, in order to be effective, needs to be so detailed that its use in anything but an economic survey is prohibitive. The better economic rating scales take about as long to administer as the entire interview on which the present case history study has been based.

The U. S. Department of Labor has used a job classification (U. S. Dept. Labor 1939) which assigns each individual in accord with the inherent nature of the occupation or profession in which he engages. Specifically, the classification is as follows:

1. Professional and managerial occupations
2. Service occupations
3. Agricultural, forestry, fisheries, and kindred occupations
4–5. Skilled occupations
6–7. Semi-skilled occupations
8–9. Unskilled occupations

There is obviously a certain amount of agreement between this arrangement and the occupational classes used in the present study, *i.e.*, an economic classification does coincide with one like the Chapin and Warner classification which is based on the social prestige of one's occupation. There are, however, considerable departures between the two systems. For instance, the professional group in the job classification includes college presidents and professors, accountants, actors, newspaper reporters and copy men, all teachers, all social workers, and all trained nurses. The list includes persons who have advanced degrees for several years of university post-graduate work, persons who have had no more than twelfth grade education and, in some cases, those who have had nothing more than grade schooling. Socially the group is not a unit. The persons included do not come together in their strictly social activities. Grade school and high school teachers do not move in the same social groups as college professors. Business managers, who, in many cases, are economically much better off than college professors, are not ordinarily included in the social activities of the professional groups. Trained nurses in most instances have no more than twelve grades of regular schooling. In the same fashion, the several manufacturing groups and the agricultural groups in this classification include persons who are day laborers and persons who are foremen and managers; and these several groups do not mingle socially. Economic and job classifications are set up, of course, to serve a totally different purpose from the one with which a student of the social organization or of the mores is most often concerned. It is unfortunate that so many social studies, including army surveys and most other governmental studies, and even some of the public opinion polls have used this job classification where a social level rating of the sort employed in the present study would have served much better.

The reality of this intangible unit called a social level is further attested by the fact that each group has sexual mores which are, to a degree, distinct from those of all other levels. Most people realize that each group wears clothing of a particular quality and of a particular style, that the styles of their clothing differ especially at social events, that there are differences in food habits, in table manners, in the forms of their social courtesies, in vocabularies and in pronunciations, and in the sorts of things to which they turn for recreation. Among social scientists there has been some recognition of these differences, more particularly in European countries where the social hierarchies are older and more fixed and even legally recognized; but there has been scant recognition of the possibility that the sexual patterns of different social levels might differ in any particular way. The remarkably distinct patterns of sexual behavior which characterize these social levels are the subject of the analyses which follow in the present chapter. It is to be noted that the analyses are made for each criterion, educational level, and occupational class, separately. The close identities of the sexual records thus independently arrived at constitute some of the best evidence yet available that social categories are realities in our Anglo-American culture.

INCIDENCES AND FREQUENCIES OF SEXUAL OUTLET

In the present chapter and the one that follows, comparisons of patterns of sexual behavior in different social levels are made for educational levels and for occupational classes of the parent and of the subject. Comparisons are made for three educational groups: grade school, high school, and college. The sample now at hand is not large enough to allow a finer classification. Preliminary analyses on a two-year educational breakdown indicate that a smoothly graded series lies between each of the three groups utilized in this chapter, but the data are insufficient for final publication. We do have a college population which is large enough to break down into finer educational levels, but it became available at too late a date to be included in the present volume.

The occupational classes utilized in the present analyses are 2, 3, 4, 5, 6, and 7, as defined above. Class 0, the dependents, should not rate as a separate group in such analyses, and classes 1, 8, and 9 are not represented by large enough series in the sample to allow the six-way breakdown needed here.

Total Outlet. The frequencies of total sexual outlet vary somewhat with the educational level to which an individual belongs (Table 81, Figure 97), although they do not differ as much as the frequencies for the several sources of outlet. Among single males, at all ages, and whether the calculations are made as means or as medians, the highest total outlets are found among those boys who go into high school but never beyond. This is true while they are still in grade school, while they are in high school, and after they have left high school. While they are in grade school they may associate with boys who will stop school at every level. Nevertheless, during these school years their outlets average 10 to 20 per cent higher than the outlets of the boys who will stop by the eighth grade, and 20 to 30 per cent higher than the outlets of the boys who will ultimately go to college.

| AGE GROUP | EDUC. LEVEL | CASES | TOTAL OUTLET BY EDUCATIONAL LEVELS | | | | |
| | | | TOTAL POPULATION | | ACTIVE POPULATION | | |
			Mean Frequency	Median Freq.	Incid. %	Mean Frequency	Median Freq.
			Single Males				
Adol.–15	0–8	712	3.02 ± 0.14	1.74	91.3	3.31 ± 0.15	2.08
	9–12	606	3.34 ± 0.15	2.29	95.4	3.51 ± 0.15	2.46
	13+	2799	2.83 ± 0.05	2.20	95.8	2.95 ± 0.05	2.32
16–20	0–8	720	3.22 ± 0.13	2.16	97.5	3.30 ± 0.14	2.24
	9–12	607	3.53 ± 0.14	2.66	99.7	3.54 ± 0.14	2.67
	13+	2861	2.70 ± 0.07	2.12	99.8	2.71 ± 0.07	2.12
21–25	0–8	361	3.15 ± 0.20	1.94	96.7	3.26 ± 0.21	2.03
	9–12	263	3.00 ± 0.20	2.24	99.2	3.02 ± 0.20	2.26
	13+	1898	2.49 ± 0.05	1.87	99.8	2.49 ± 0.05	1.88
26–30	0–8	159	3.01 ± 0.28	1.97	98.7	3.05 ± 0.28	2.00
	9–12	117	2.88 ± 0.26	2.05	99.1	2.91 ± 0.26	2.07
	13+	487	2.57 ± 0.12	1.83	99.8	2.57 ± 0.12	1.83
			Married Males				
16–20	0–8	158	4.67 ± 0.41	3.06	100.0	4.67 ± 0.41	3.06
	9–12	87	5.05 ± 0.52	3.57	100.0	5.05 ± 0.52	3.57
	13+	46	4.13 ± 0.54	3.21	100.0	4.13 ± 0.54	3.21
21–25	0–8	324	4.02 ± 0.25	2.62	100.0	4.02 ± 0.25	2.62
	9–12	164	4.15 ± 0.34	2.86	100.0	4.15 ± 0.34	2.86
	13+	440	3.70 ± 0.13	3.06	100.0	3.70 ± 0.13	3.06
26–30	0–8	292	3.51 ± 0.24	2.42	99.3	3.53 ± 0.24	2.44
	9–12	135	3.55 ± 0.31	2.53	100.0	3.55 ± 0.31	2.53
	13+	532	3.19 ± 0.11	2.64	100.0	3.19 ± 0.11	2.64
31–35	0–8	186	2.58 ± 0.20	1.88	100.0	2.58 ± 0.20	1.88
	9–12	82	3.35 ± 0.39	2.53	100.0	3.35 ± 0.39	2.53
	13+	301	2.65 ± 0.13	2.16	100.0	2.65 ± 0.13	2.16
36–40	0–8	143	2.26 ± 0.18	1.71	100.0	2.26 ± 0.18	1.71
	9–12	58	2.64 ± 0.38	2.04	100.0	2.64 ± 0.38	2.04
	13+	189	2.56 ± 0.20	2.02	99.5	2.57 ± 0.20	2.02
41–45	0–8	100	1.87 ± 0.20	1.43	100.0	1.87 ± 0.20	1.43
	13+	138	1.98 ± 0.14	1.69	100.0	1.98 ± 0.14	1.69

Table 81. Total sexual outlet, as related to educational level

It is obvious that such differences are not the product of something that the school contributes or fails to contribute, for the same school is supporting three very different patterns of sexual behavior at the same time. The differences must be dependent upon something which the boy has acquired from the community in which he was raised before he went to school, in which he lives while he is attending school, and in which he will continue to live after he quits school; or else these higher frequencies must be dependent upon some physical or physiologic capacity which these particular boys have and which is correlated with the progress of their schooling. Either social or biological factors, or both, might conceivably be operating.

A finer educational breakdown than the one which is shown in Table 81 suggests that the sexually most active group is the one that goes into high school but not beyond tenth grade. Since the laws in many states set a minimum age which must be attained before a boy or girl can stop school, it often happens that there is a considerable exodus of students who attain the age of sixteen (or whatever other age the particular state requires), somewhere about the middle of their high school careers. The boys who leave school at that time may represent a group that is not particularly studious, whatever its mental ability may be, and a group which is impatient of such confinement as the school offers and energetic in its pursuit of physical activity and social contacts. These are, however, merely hypotheses which need further investigation.

The single males who have the lowest frequencies of total sexual outlet are those who belong to the college level. The boys who never go beyond eighth grade in school stand intermediate between the high school and the college groups, as far as the calculations in Table 81 show. It is to be recalled, however, that the breakdown in Chapter 9 indicates that early-adolescent males of this lower educational level actually have higher outlets than any other group in the population, in practically every age period. The over-all averages shown for the grade school males as a group are probably pulled down by the large number of undernourished, physically poor, and, therefore, late-maturing males who are in this class. It includes most of the feeble-minded and mentally lower individuals in the population, and many of these are physically poor and sexually inactive. But the physically well-developed and mentally normal individuals among these grade school boys are more active than the boys of any other educational level.

The social level picture for total outlet among married males is quite the same as for single males. The married males who have the highest total outlet are those who went into high school but not beyond. This is true for every age group between 16 and 40 years of age, and may be true at older ages; but the data beyond 45 become too scant for significant calculation. It is impressive to find that what is true of populations in their teens usually holds true for those same populations at later ages, throughout the life span. Only a very few individuals ever depart from their original patterns.

If the record for total outlet is analyzed on the basis of occupational classes (Table 107), it will be seen that there is as sharp and as consistent a differentiation of groups as there is on the basis of educational level. The highest rates of total outlet are to be found among the males who belong to occupational class 3. This is as true of these males when they are boys living at home with their parents as it is of the same persons at older ages, when they are independent of their parents. On the other hand, males who

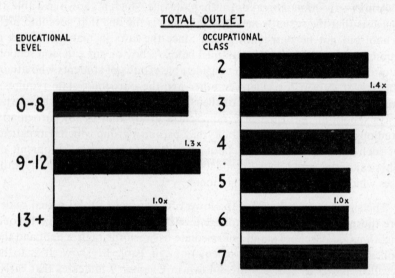

Figure 97. Total outlet, by educational level and occupational class

For single males of the age group 16–20. Relative lengths of bars compare mean frequencies for the groups.

belong to class 3 have about the same rates of total outlet, irrespective of whether their parents belonged to classes 3, 4, or 5. Since occupational class 3 is the one that includes semi-skilled workers, it contains a great many persons who do not go beyond grade school, and almost none of them go beyond high school (Table 80); and the generalizations based on occupational classes agree very well with the generalizations based upon educational levels. Since the occupational classes are not as sharply defined as educational levels, the frequency series are not quite as consistent as the frequencies shown by the educational breakdown.

The lowest rates of total outlet are to be found in occupational class 4. This is the group which includes the skilled mechanics. The group has very diverse educational backgrounds (Table 80), and in Chapter 11 it will be pointed out that it is the most unstable of all occupational classes. Members of this group often aspire to move into higher levels, and they send a high proportion of their children to college.

In general, the white collar groups (classes 5, 6, and 7) are low in their rates; but of these class 7 shows the highest rates. This is the professional group. It usually has 17 to 20 years of schooling. The group has not been calculated separately in the educational breakdowns made in this volume, and it will be interesting to see what such a breakdown ultimately gives.

Masturbation. Ultimately, between 92 and 97 per cent of all males have masturbatory experience (Tables 82, 132, Figures 98, 136). The accumulative incidence figures are hardly different for the high school and college groups, but the lower figure (92%) belongs to the grade school group. The highest active incidence between the ages of adolescence and 15 is to be found among the boys who never go beyond high school. In later age periods the college males have the highest incidence.

The highest frequencies of masturbation among single males, in all age periods, are in the college level, whether the calculations are made for total populations or for the active portions of the populations (that portion of the population which is actually utilizing this source of outlet). Between 16 and 20, for instance, masturbation among the single males of college level occurs nearly twice as frequently as it does among the boys who never go beyond grade school, and the differential is still higher in the twenties. This is the great source of pre-marital sexual outlet for the upper educational levels. For that group, masturbation provides nearly 80 per cent of the orgasms during the earlier adolescent years, as against little more than half the outlet (52%) for the lower educational level. In the late teens it still accounts for two-thirds (66%) of the college male's orgasms, while the lower level has relegated such activity to a low place that provides less than 30 per cent of the total outlet. In all later age periods the relative positions of these groups remain about the same.

Differences in incidences and frequencies of masturbation at different educational levels are even more striking among married males. At the grade school level, there are only 20 to 30 per cent who masturbate in their early marital years, and the accumulative incidence figure climbs only a bit during the later years of marriage. The frequencies are very low. The high school group closely matches the grade school group in this regard. On the other hand, among the married males who have been to college, 60 to 70 per cent masturbate in each of the age periods.

In the grade school group of married males, only 1 to 3 per cent of the total sexual outlet is derived from masturbation. The proportion of the total sexual outlet derived by college males from this source begins at 8.5

AGE GROUP	EDUC. LEVEL	CASES	TOTAL POPULATION			ACTIVE POPULATION			ACCUM. INCID. %
			Mean Frequency	Median Freq.	% of Total Outlet	Incid. %	Mean Freq.	Median Freq.	
Single Males									
Adol. −15	0–8	712	1.55 ± 0.078	0.85	52.25	84.7	1.84	1.12	84
	9–12	606	1.93 ± 0.089	1.22	59.08	89.9	2.15	1.44	90
	13+	2799	2.22 ± 0.048	1.61	79.62	82.4	2.70	2.06	82
16–20	0–8	720	0.93 ± 0.048	0.45	29.15	84.4	1.10	0.61	90
	9–12	607	1.30 ± 0.074	0.69	37.17	89.0	1.46	0.84	94
	13+	2861	1.79 ± 0.038	1.18	66.37	88.6	2.02	1.50	91
21–25	0–8	361	0.63 ± 0.057	0.18	20.15	62.3	1.01	0.50	91
	9–12	263	0.87 ± 0.076	0.37	29.67	76.4	1.13	0.63	95
	13+	1898	1.31 ± 0.039	0.68	53.31	87.0	1.50	0.86	94
26–30	0–8	159	0.59 ± 0.087	0.07	20.68	60.4	0.97	0.48	92
	9–12	117	0.78 ± 0.095	0.35	27.69	78.6	0.99	0.47	97
	13+	487	1.18 ± 0.081	0.48	45.88	83.2	1.42	0.73	96
Married Males									
16–20	0–8	158	0.11 ± 0.031	0.00	2.40	28.5	0.39	0.14	29
	9–12	87	0.14 ± 0.048	0.00	2.75	39.1	0.35	0.08	39
	13+	46	0.35 ± 0.14	0.05	8.53	63.0	0.55	0.19	63
21–25	0–8	324	0.10 ± 0.020	0.00	2.43	28.7	0.34	0.09	29
	9–12	164	0.15 ± 0.037	0.00	3.70	41.5	0.37	0.09	42
	13+	440	0.32 ± 0.030	0.06	8.79	65.9	0.49	0.22	68
26–30	0–8	292	0.09 ± 0.024	0.00	2.44	21.2	0.40	0.08	29
	9–12	135	0.18 ± 0.046	0.00	5.05	37.0	0.48	0.10	42
	13+	532	0.27 ± 0.023	0.06	8.67	66.4	0.41	0.18	69
31–35	0–8	186	0.05 ± 0.019	0.00	1.79	19.4	0.24	0.07	29
	9–12	82	0.13 ± 0.045	0.00	4.04	36.6	0.37	0.10	42
	13+	301	0.24 ± 0.03	0.05	9.28	64.1	0.38	0.13	69
36–40	0–8	143	0.04 ± 0.013	0.00	1.59	11.2	0.32	0.20	29
	9–12	58	0.08 ± 0.030	0.00	3.15	25.9	0.32	0.18	42
	13+	189	0.21 ± 0.036	0.03	8.26	59.3	0.35	0.09	69
41–45	0–8	100	0.03 ± 0.013	0.00	1.41	9.0	0.30	0.23	29
	13+	138	0.19 ± 0.043	0.02	9.71	55.1	0.34	0.09	69

Table 82. Masturbation, as related to educational level

per cent during the early years of marriage, and rises to as much as 18 per cent in the later years. The college group stands out as perfectly distinct on this score.

Among occupational classes, the professional group masturbates most frequently (Table 108, Figure 98). This is true whether the persons in that class originate from parental class 7, or whether they come from parental classes 3, 4, or 6. Since essentially all professional persons have an educational rating of 17+ these data from an occupational class analysis are quite in line with the data based on educational levels. The distinctions between occupational classes are, however, even more extreme than the differences between educational levels, as far as masturbation is concerned.

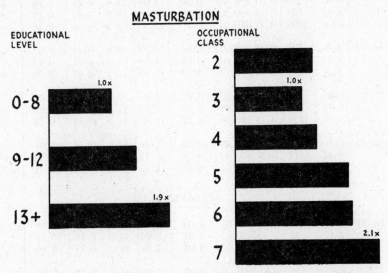

Figure 98. Masturbation, by educational level and occupational class

For single males of the age group 16–20. Relative lengths of bars compare mean frequencies for the groups. Note similarity of data based on educational levels and data based on occupational classes.

Between the ages of 16 and 20, for instance, the males of occupational class 7 have average frequencies of masturbation which run 2.12, 2.17, 2.21, and 1.60 per week, varying with the parental occupational class from which they came. The corresponding groups of occupational classes 2 and 3 have masturbatory frequencies which run very close to 1 per week—sometimes a bit more, sometimes a bit less in the various breakdowns. The educational breakdown for the same age period shows the college level masturbating with frequencies which are about 1.9 times the frequencies of the grade school males. Differences in the frequencies of the occupational classes are more nearly of the order of 2.2 to 2.5. Differences in attitudes on masturbation, pre-marital intercourse, and prostitution are among the most

			NOCTURNAL EMISSIONS, BY EDUCATIONAL LEVELS						
			TOTAL POPULATION			ACTIVE POPULATION			
AGE GROUP	EDUC. LEVEL	CASES	Mean Frequency	Median Freq.	% of Total Outlet	Incid. %	Mean Freq.	Median Freq.	ACCUM. INCID. %
			Single Males						
Adol. −15	0–8	712	0.05 ± 0.01	0.00	1.82	25.4	0.21	0.08	26
	9–12	606	0.15 ± 0.02	0.00	4.44	39.6	0.37	0.12	39
	13+	2799	0.34 ± 0.01	0.10	12.15	69.8	0.48	0.28	70
16–20	0–8	720	0.15 ± 0.01	0.02	4.83	56.4	0.27	0.09	65
	9–12	607	0.22 ± 0.02	0.06	6.33	70.7	0.31	0.13	71
	13+	2861	0.42 ± 0.01	0.25	15.65	91.2	0.46	0.29	94
21–25	0–8	361	0.16 ± 0.02	0.03	5.02	59.6	0.26	0.09	73
	9–12	263	0.24 ± 0.02	0.08	8.10	71.1	0.33	0.20	82
	13+	1898	0.38 ± 0.01	0.22	15.67	87.0	0.44	0.28	96
26–30	0–8	159	0.18 ± 0.03	0.04	6.26	64.8	0.27	0.09	79
	9–12	117	0.21 ± 0.03	0.08	7.48	70.1	0.30	0.20	86
	13+	487	0.31 ± 0.02	0.18	11.93	85.2	0.36	0.25	97
			Married Males						
16–20	0–8	158	0.14 ± 0.03	0.00	3.08	48.1	0.30	0.08	
	9–12	87	0.10 ± 0.02	0.02	2.04	54.0	0.19	0.10	
	13+	46	0.12 ± 0.03	0.03	2.99	58.7	0.21	0.09	
21–25	0–8	324	0.11 ± 0.02	0.00	2.79	45.1	0.25	0.08	
	9–12	164	0.12 ± 0.01	0.04	2.85	63.4	0.18	0.09	
	13±	440	0.17 ± 0.02	0.05	4.65	66.4	0.26	0.09	
26–30	0–8	292	0.12 ± 0.02	0.00	3.41	47.3	0.25	0.08	
	9–12	135	0.11 ± 0.02	0.02	3.22	56.3	0.20	0.09	
	13+	532	0.15 ± 0.01	0.05	4.69	73.5	0.20	0.08	
31–35	0–8	186	0.08 ± 0.02	0.00	3.03	39.8	0.20	0.07	
	9–12	82	0.13 ± 0.03	0.02	3.79	56.1	0.22	0.09	
	13+	301	0.15 ± 0.02	0.05	5.71	74.8	0.20	0.08	
36–40	0–8	143	0.04 ± 0.01	0.00	1.85	29.4	0.14	0.07	
	9–12	58	0.12 ± 0.03	0.01	4.48	51.7	0.23	0.09	
	13+	189	0.15 ± 0.02	0.06	6.06	72.0	0.21	0.09	
41–45	0–8	100	0.04 ± 0.01	0.00	2.25	31.0	0.14	0.07	
	13+	138	0.11 ± 0.01	0.05	5.87	72.5	0.16	0.08	

Table 83. Nocturnal emissions, as related to educational level

marked of all the distinctions between social levels, and this is true whether the calculations are made by educational levels or by occupational classes.

The professional males who originated in parental class 5, becoming members of class 7 as a result of their university training, have masturbatory rates which are 25 per cent lower than those of class 7 males who are derived from any other source. It is a striking situation for which we have no explanation at this time.

Nocturnal Emissions. Masturbation may appear to be volitional behavior, and one may question whether the pattern in masturbation represents the individual's choice, rather than something that has been imposed upon

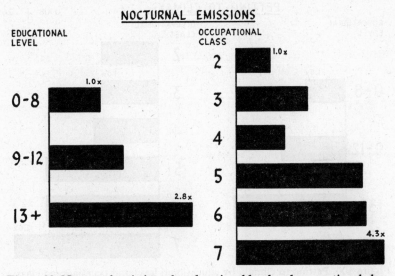

Figure 99. Nocturnal emissions, by educational level and occupational class

For single males of the age group 16–20. Relative lengths of bars compare mean frequencies for the groups. Note similarity of data based on educational levels and data based on occupational classes.

him by the mores of his group. It is, therefore, particularly interesting to find that there are still greater differences between educational levels in regard to nocturnal emissions—a type of sexual outlet which one might suppose would represent involuntary behavior.

Nocturnal emissions occur most often in that segment of the population that goes to college (Table 83, Figure 99). Among males of the college level the emissions begin at earlier ages than among males of lower educational levels. About 70 per cent of the boys who will go to college have such experience by age 15, whereas only about 25 per cent of the grade school group has started by then. Between 16 and 20 years of age, 91 per cent of the single males of the college level experience nocturnal emissions, while only 56 per cent of the lower level boys have such experience in the same period. The active incidence figures are highest for the college males in every other age group. Ultimately, nearly 100 per cent of the better educated males have such experience, whereas the accumulative incidence figure is only 86 per cent for the high school group, and only 75 per cent for the grade school group.

Between adolescence and age 15, upper level males average nocturnal emissions nearly seven times as frequently as the boys of lower educational levels. Between 16 and 20 the frequencies among the upper level males are nearly three times those for the lower level, if the whole population is

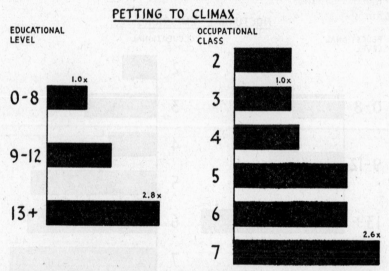

Figure 100. Petting to climax, by educational level and occupational class

For single males of the age group 16–20. Relative lengths of bars compare mean frequencies for the groups. Note similarity of data based on educational levels and data based on occupational classes.

involved in the calculation. For the active populations the frequencies for the college group are still twice as high. About the same differences hold in the older age periods, at least up to 30 years of age.

In marriage there are only minor differences between the educational levels in frequencies of nocturnal emissions, but the highest incidence figures at all ages are to be found among the males who have gone to college. Before marriage, college-bred males draw between 12 and 15 per cent of their outlet from nocturnal emissions, while the males of lower educational levels draw only 5 or 6 per cent of their outlet from that source. After marriage the college males draw 3 to 6 per cent of their outlet from emissions, but the lower educational levels never draw over 3 per cent from that source.

While it is clear that higher frequencies of nocturnal emissions are cor-related with more extended educational histories, the explanation of this correlation is not so apparent. It is evident that nocturnal dreams are not the product of the education in itself, for two groups of boys of different social levels, working together in the same class in grade school or in high school, may have totally different histories of emissions. Is this a measure of some difference in the psychologic or physiologic capacities of the two groups which correlates in some way with factors which determine their educational careers? These are problems which the physiologist and the psychologist will want to investigate in more elaborate detail.

We do know that the frequencies of nocturnal dreams show some corre-lation with the level of erotic responsiveness of an individual. The boys of lower level are not so often aroused erotically, nor aroused by so many items as the boys from the upper educational levels. Nocturnal dreams may depend upon an imaginative capacity, in something of the same way that daytime eroticism is dependent upon the individual's capacity to project himself into a situation which is not a part of his immediate experience. It may be that the paucity of overt socio-sexual experience among upper level males accounts both for their daytime eroticism and for their nocturnal dreaming.

The record on frequencies of nocturnal emissions in different occupa-tional classes is fully as striking as the record based on an educational breakdown, and the two bodies of data lie in exactly the same direction (Table 109, Figure 99). The lowest average frequencies of nocturnal emissions, averaging not more than 2 or 3 per year, are to be found among the males of occupational class 2, which is the group that includes the day laborers, and the frequencies are only a bit higher for the semi-skilled workmen of occupational class 3. The frequencies for occupational classes 6 and 7 (the college and graduate school groups), on the contrary, run nearer once in 2 weeks at practically every age level and irrespective of the nature of the parental occupational class from which these individuals come. This means that there are 10 to 12 times as frequent nocturnal emissions among males of the upper occupational classes as there are among males of the lower classes.

Heterosexual Petting. Petting is pre-eminently an occupation of the high school and college levels. For all social levels, it may begin in high school or even before; but from 16 years of age, the males and the females who are most often involved are the ones who go into high school or ultimately into college (Table 84, Figure 100). About 92 per cent of the males of the high school and college levels engage in at least some kind of petting prior to marriage, and nearly as many (88%) of the grade school group has such experience. These figures are not very far apart, but there are greater differences in the limits to which the petting techniques go in these several groups. In general, males of the grade school and high school levels are more restricted in their petting behavior than males of the college level.

Unfortunately, the data secured in this study do not allow a statistical calculation for each degree of petting experience, but there are precise data on the frequencies of petting which extends to the point of orgasm (Table 84, Figure 100). In the pre-marital histories of college males, about 61 per cent reach orgasm by that means. It is only about 32 per cent of the high school males who ever have such experience, and only about 16 per cent of the grade school group.

AGE GROUP	EDUC. LEVEL	CASES	PETTING TO CLIMAX, SINGLE MALES, BY EDUCATIONAL LEVELS						
			TOTAL POPULATION			ACTIVE POPULATION			ACCUM. INCID. %
			Mean Frequency	Median Freq.	% of Total Outlet	Incid. %	Mean Freq.	Median Freq.	
Adol. −15	0–8	712	0.03 ± 0.01	0.00	1.06	13.3	0.24	0.06	13
	9–12	606	0.05 ± 0.01	0.00	1.46	19.5	0.24	0.07	19
	13+	2799	0.04 ± 0.01	0.00	1.54	13.8	0.31	0.09	14
16–20	0–8	720	0.05 ± 0.01	0.00	1.66	21.2	0.25	0.07	22
	9–12	607	0.08 ± 0.01	0.00	2.37	34.3	0.24	0.07	34
	13+	2861	0.14 ± 0.01	0.00	5.26	45.8	0.31	0.09	46
21–25	0–8	361	0.04 ± 0.01	0.00	1.23	15.5	0.25	0.07	
	9–12	263	0.08 ± 0.02	0.00	2.77	28.5	0.28	0.08	
	13+	1898	0.18 ± 0.01	0.01	7.50	51.9	0.35	0.10	58
26–30	0–8	159	0.06 ± 0.03	0.00	1.96	19.5	0.28	0.07	
	9–12	117	0.05 ± 0.01	0.00	1.82	25.6	0.20	0.08	
	13+	487	0.13 ± 0.02	0.00	5.17	44.6	0.30	0.09	61

Table 84. Heterosexual petting to climax, and educational level

In regard to the frequencies of petting to climax, the differences between educational levels are even more extreme. In the later teens, this source provides nearly three times as frequent orgasm for the males who go to college; and between 21 and 25, there is nearly 5 times as much orgasm from this source for the college males as there is for the males who never go beyond grade school. The lower level males derive something between 1 and 2 per cent of their total outlet from petting in their pre-marital years. The college males derive between 5 and 8 per cent of their outlet from that source.

Analyses of the record by occupational classes confirm the statement made above that petting is most characteristic of the upper social levels. The differences by occupational class (Table 110, Figure 100) are not notable in the early adolescent years, but they become greater between 16 and 20, at which age classes 6 and 7 pet to the point of climax twice as often as classes 2 or 3. In the early twenties there is a 3 to 1 difference between the two ends of the occupational scale, and the distinctions are more or less true irrespective of the occupational classes of the parents.

Pre-marital Intercourse. Pre-marital intercourse may be had either with companions or with prostitutes. In every social level coitus with girls who are not prostitutes is more frequent. In younger age groups there is a 10 to 1 or still higher difference in favor of the non-prostitutes. In older age groups, males of the lower educational level who are not yet married turn to prostitutes more often than they did when they were younger; but non-prostitutes still provide a larger part of the coitus. At the college level, contacts with companions exceed the prostitute relations by some factor which lies between 20 and 100 in every age group, including the older groups.

Pre-marital intercourse, whatever its source, is more abundant in the grade school and high school levels, and less common at the college level (Tables 85–87, Figures 101–102). Even in the period between adolescence and 15 the active incidence includes nearly half (48% and 43%) of the lower educational groups, but only 10 per cent of the boys who will ultimately go to college. In the later teens, 85 per cent of the grade school group and 75 per cent of the high school group is having pre-marital intercourse, while the figure for the college group is still only 42 per cent. In later years the differentials are not so great but, compared with the grade school group, it is still only about two-thirds as many of the college males who have such intercourse.

The accumulative incidence figures for pre-marital intercourse show much the same differences. About 98 per cent of the grade school level has experience before marriage, while only 84 per cent of the high school level and 67 per cent of the college level is involved (Table 136, Figure 145).

The frequency figures show still greater differences between educational levels. In the age period between 16 and 20, the grade school group has 7 times as much pre-marital coitus as the college group. There is not much drop in the differential even in the older age groups. The mother who is afraid to send her boy away to college for fear that he will be morally corrupted there, is evidently unaware of the histories of the boys who stay at home. Moreover, nearly half of the males who have intercourse while in college had their first experience while they were still at home, before they started to college (Table 136, Figure 145). Varying with the age period, the

AGE GROUP	EDUC. LEVEL	CASES	TOTAL NON-MARITAL INTERCOURSE, BY EDUCATIONAL LEVELS						ACCUM. INCID. %
			TOTAL POPULATION			ACTIVE POPULATION			
			Mean Frequency	Median Freq.	% of Total Outlet	Incid. %	Mean Freq.	Median Freq.	
Single Males: Pre-marital Intercourse									
Adol. –15	0–8	630	1.08 ± 0.10	0.00	37.94	48.1	2.24	1.21	48
	9–12	511	0.81 ± 0.10	0.00	25.45	43.2	1.88	0.84	43
	13+	2421	0.08 ± 0.01	0.00	3.73	9.8	0.83	0.29	10
16–20	0–8	635	1.74 ± 0.11	0.73	58.92	85.4	2.04	0.99	86
	9–12	515	1.43 ± 0.12	0.44	42.17	75.5	1.89	0.89	76
	13+	2475	0.25 + 0.02	0.00	11.26	41.8	0.60	0.17	44
21–25	0–8	312	2.00 ± 0.19	0.82	68.23	86.2	2.32	1.06	90
	9–12	217	1.25 ± 0.19	0.38	42.72	74.2	1.69	0.77	84
	13+	1593	0.44 ± 0.03	0.02	19.41	53.9	0.81	0.30	64
26–30	0–8	137	1.82 ± 0.24	0.88	57.60	87.6	2.07	1.16	94
	9–12	95	1.18 ± 0.22	0.41	38.72	71.6	1.64	0.86	85
	13+	373	0.64 ± 0.08	0.05	21.40	56.3	1.14	0.48	68
Married Males: Extra-marital Intercourse									
16–20	0–8	139	0.52 ± 0.11	0.00	11.37	44.6	1.16	0.44	
	9–12	87	0.54 ± 0.16	0.00	10.91	37.9	1.44	0.23	
	13+	46	0.12 ± 0.07	0.00	2.91	19.6	0.61	0.10	
21–25	0–8	284	0.53 ± 0.13	0.00	12.89	34.5	1.53	0.36	
	9–12	144	0.48 ± 0.11	0.00	11.21	43.1	1.11	0.30	
	13+	323	0.05 ± 0.02	0.00	1.57	14.2	0.38	0.11	
26–30	0–8	244	0.26 ± 0.05	0.00	7.66	35.7	0.72	0.25	
	9–12	113	0.36 ± 0.11	0.00	9.75	46.9	0.77	0.19	
	13+	380	0.07 ± 0.02	0.00	2.43	19.5	0.37	0.08	
31–35	0–8	186	0.18 ± 0.04	0.00	6.97	31.7	0.56	0.26	
	9–12	82	0.19 ± 0.06	0.00	5.61	36.6	0.51	0.21	
	13+	301	0.16 ± 0.04	0.00	5.92	24.6	0.63	0.25	
36–40	0–8	143	0.18 ± 0.05	0.00	8.17	26.6	0.68	0.35	
	9–12	58	0.09 ± 0.03	0.00	3.45	32.8	0.27	0.19	
	13+	189	0.26 ± 0.11	0.00	10.38	29.6	0.89	0.21	
41–45	0–8	100	0.12 ± 0.03	0.00	6.30	21.0	0.57	0.44	
	13+	138	0.12 ± 0.03	0.00	6.39	23.9	0.52	0.21	
46–50	0–8	70	0.11 ± 0.04	0.00	6.05	18.6	0.59	0.42	
	13+	81	0.25 ± 0.08	0.00	14.09	27.2	0.93	0.58	

Table 85. Total pre-marital and extra-marital intercourse, as related to educational level

Including the non-marital intercourse with companions and with prostitutes.

college group derives 4 to 21 per cent of its pre-marital outlet from intercourse; the high school group derives 26 to 54 per cent of its outlet from
that source; but the grade school group depends on coitus for 40 to 70 per
cent of its total pre-marital outlet.

The number of college-bred males who have some pre-marital intercourse is high enough to surprise many persons, but the frequencies with
which they have it are very much lower than anywhere else in the population. Between a third and a half of the males at college level have intercourse only once or twice, or half a dozen times, or a matter of two or
three times a year for a few years before they marry. It is about 15 per cent

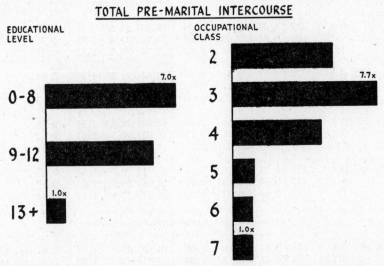

Figure 101. Total pre-marital intercourse, by educational level and occupational
class

For single males of the age group 16–20. Relative lengths of bars compare mean frequencies for the groups. Note similarity of data based on educational levels and data
based on occupational classes.

of the college males who have pre-marital intercourse with weekly regularity for any period of years before marriage. A good many college males
never have pre-marital intercourse with more than the one girl whom they
subsequently marry, and very few of them have pre-marital intercourse
with more than half a dozen girls or so. College males are very slow in
arriving at their first pre-marital intercourse (Figure 146), and a comparison
of the accumulative incidence curves (Table 136, Figure 146) indicates that,
on an average, they do not have their first experience until five or six years
after the lower level males start.

The pre-marital coital pictures for the grade school and high school
groups are much alike. They both differ from the college group in starting

AGE GROUP	EDUC. LEVEL	CASES	NON-MARITAL INTERCOURSE WITH COMPANIONS, BY EDUCATIONAL LEVELS						ACCUM. INCID. %
			TOTAL POPULATION			ACTIVE POPULATION			
			Mean Frequency	Median Freq.	% of Total Outlet	Incid. %	Mean Freq.	Median Freq.	
Single Males: Pre-marital Intercourse									
Adol. −15	0–8	712	1.04 ± 0.09	0.00	35.00	48.5	2.15	1.20	
	9–12	606	0.81 ± 0.09	0.00	24.93	43.4	1.88	0.76	
	13+	2799	0.08 ± 0.01	0.00	2.74	9.3	0.82	0.27	
16–20	0–8	720	1.62 ± 0.11	0.54	50.62	81.2	1.99	0.95	
	9–12	607	1.38 ± 0.11	0.39	39.48	73.1	1.89	0.86	
	13+	2861	0.25 ± 0.02	0.00	9.13	38.8	0.63	0.22	
21–25	0–8	361	1.65 ± 0.16	0.43	52.84	78.1	2.11	0.78	
	9–12	263	1.11 ± 0.16	0.27	38.02	70.7	1.57	0.62	
	13+	1898	0.45 ± 0.03	0.03	18.45	54.6	0.83	0.31	
26–30	0–8	159	1.21 ± 0.19	0.37	42.71	76.7	1.58	0.67	
	9–12	117	0.84 ± 0.16	0.16	29.75	66.7	1.25	0.57	
	13+	487	0.64 ± 0.07	0.06	24.97	57.9	1.11	0.44	
Married Males: Extra-marital Intercourse									
16–20	0–8	146	0.47 ± 0.10	0.00	10.91	41.8	1.14	0.47	42
	9–12	94	0.46 ± 0.13	0.00	9.43	35.1	1.30	0.34	35
	13+	48	0.11 ± 0.06	0.00	2.86	16.7	0.68	0.30	16
21–25	0–8	309	0.54 ± 0.14	0.00	11.62	30.4	1.78	0.38	
	9–12	147	0.41 ± 0.11	0.00	9.35	36.1	1.14	0.28	37
	13+	357	0.05 ± 0.01	0.00	1.86	14.3	0.37	0.10	16
26–30	0–8	278	0.24 ± 0.05	0.00	6.38	28.8	0.82	0.32	
	9–12	124	0.28 ± 0.10	0.00	7.61	38.7	0.71	0.15	39
	13+	448	0.08 ± 0.02	0.00	2.72	20.8	0.38	0.09	23
31–35	0–8	211	0.13 ± 0.03	0.00	5.51	28.4	0.47	0.17	
	9–12	85	0.18 ± 0.05	0.00	4.62	35.3	0.50	0.18	43
	13+	370	0.15 ± 0.03	0.00	5.51	26.8	0.56	0.22	31
36–40	0–8	165	0.14 ± 0.04	0.00	7.24	23.6	0.60	0.27	
	9–12	62	0.11 ± 0.05	0.00	1.76	32.3	0.35	0.12	44
	13+	248	0.26 ± 0.09	0.00	9.85	29.4	0.87	0.25	37
41–45	0–8	114	0.10 ± 0.03	0.00	4.84	20.2	0.47	0.26	
	13+	175	0.16 ± 0.04	0.00	6.07	24.6	0.64	0.12	40

Table 86. Pre-marital and extra-marital intercourse with companions, as related to educational level

their intercourse at a much earlier age—in many cases in pre-adolescence, and in a large number of cases coincidentally with the onset of adolescence. Within two or three years after the onset of adolescence nearly all of those who will ever be involved have started heterosexual relations. Ultimately, 10 to 15 per cent more of the grade school group is involved than of the high school group.

As analyzed by occupational classes, pre-marital intercourse is much more frequently had by males of class 3, which is the group of semi-skilled workmen (Table 111, Figure 101). Between adolescence and 15 years of age there may be 15 times as much intercourse among males of class 3 as there is among the boys who will ultimately go to college and whose occupational ratings will ultimately be in class 6 or 7. If the parental occupational class is 5 (the lower white collar group), there is 122 times as much pre-marital intercourse among the boys who regress to class 3 as there is among those boys who will ultimately go into the professional group. Between 16 and 20, the differences between the extreme groups are somewhat less, but the boys who will end up in occupational class 3 are still having intercourse 4 to 9 times as often as the boys who will move into occupational classes 6 and 7. Even during the twenties, when intercourse becomes more common at the upper levels, there is still 4 times as much of it among the males of occupational class 3.

The males of occupational class 2 have high frequencies of pre-marital intercourse at all age levels, but they do not rate as high as the males of class 3. Just as was pointed out for the lower educational levels, this lower rate of the lowest class is certainly due to the higher incidence of feeble-mindedness, to the low physical state, and to the low social prestige of many of the individuals in the group. It is quite possible that this lower occupational class includes some groups who have very much higher rates than the average for the whole class. They are probably the lower level boys who became adolescent first (Chapter 9). Since class 2 as a group is quite unrestrained sexually, any male in the group who does have any amount of sexual drive would be likely to have relatively high frequencies of pre-marital intercourse.

Intercourse with Prostitutes. Among those males who are not married by age 25, pre-marital intercourse with prostitutes has been had by 74 per cent of the grade school level, and by 54 per cent of the high school group, but by not more than about 28 per cent of those who belong in the college level (Table 87, Figure 102). These striking differences between educational levels were as true in a past generation as they are in the present day (Chapter 11). The active incidence figures in each of the five-year periods indicate that lower level males start relations with prostitutes at a much earlier age, and that three to four times as many of them are having intercourse with prostitutes in each age period.

AGE GROUP	EDUC. LEVEL	CASES	INTERCOURSE WITH PROSTITUTES, BY EDUCATIONAL LEVELS					
			TOTAL POPULATION		ACTIVE POPULATION			ACCUMUL. INCID. %
			Mean Frequency	% of Total Outlet	Incid. %	Mean Freq.	Median Freq.	
			Single Males: Pre-marital Intercourse					
Adol.–15	0–8	712	0.029 ± 0.007	0.97	8.7	0.33	0.10	8
	9–12	606	0.014 ± 0.004	0.44	7.9	0.18	0.07	8
	13+	2799	0.003 ± 0.001	0.11	2.3	0.13	0.07	2
16–20	0–8	720	0.20 ± 0.019	6.21	48.2	0.41	0.14	51
	9–12	607	0.096 ± 0.011	2.75	41.4	0.23	0.08	44
	13+	2861	0.022 ± 0.002	0.80	19.3	0.11	0.06	20
21–25	0–8	361	0.39 ± 0.045	12.55	60.7	0.64	0.33	74
	9–12	263	0.14 ± 0.02	4.66	43.7	0.31	0.10	54
	13+	1898	0.03 ± 0.007	1.27	17.2	0.18	0.07	28
26–30	0–8	159	0.41 ± 0.08	14.34	72.3	0.56	0.37	80
	9–12	117	0.18 ± 0.04	6.46	42.7	0.43	0.17	61
	13+	487	0.08 ± 0.035	3.16	16.4	0.49	0.08	35
			Married Males: Extra-marital Intercourse					
16–20	0–8	158	0.029 ± 0.012	0.61	16.5	0.18	0.07	17
	9–12	87	0.074 ± 0.048	1.48	16.1	0.46	0.07	16
	13+	46	0.002 ± 0.001	0.05	4.3	0.05	0.08	4
21–25	0–8	324	0.032 ± 0.009	0.80	15.1	0.21	0.08	18
	9–12	164	0.061 ± 0.023	1.49	25.0	0.25	0.06	25
	13+	440	0.008 ± 0.003	0.23	5.2	0.16	0.07	6
26–30	0–8	292	0.040 ± 0.011	1.16	17.1	0.24	0.08	20
	9–12	135	0.053 ± 0.021	1.49	20.0	0.26	0.07	25
	13+	532	0.006 ± 0.002	0.20	6.0	0.10	0.07	7
31–35	0–8	186	0.037 ± 0.012	1.46	15.6	0.24	0.09	20
	9–12	82	0.033 ± 0.017	0.99	17.1	0.19	0.08	25
	13+	301	0.011 ± 0.004	0.41	6.6	0.16	0.08	8
36–40	0–8	143	0.021 ± 0.007	0.93	9.8	0.21	0.13	21
	9–12	58	0.044 ± 0.024	1.69	19.0	0.23	0.09	
	13+	189	0.013 ± 0.005	0.53	8.5	0.16	0.08	12
41–45	0–8	100	0.028 ± 0.01	1.46	11.0	0.25	0.23	21
	9–12	34	0.015 ± 0.009	0.70	14.7	0.10	0.08	
	13+	138	0.006 ± 0.003	0.32	5.1	0.12	0.08	12

Table 87. Intercourse with prostitutes, as related to educational level
Median frequencies for the total populations are, for the most part, 0.00.

The percentage of the total sexual outlet which is derived by unmarried males from intercourse with prostitutes steadily rises in all educational levels with advancing age. Between 16 and 40 the percentage for males in the grade school level rises from about 6 to 23 per cent. For the high school level the figures at the same ages rise from less than 3 per cent to about 11 per cent; and for the college males they start at a fraction of 1 per cent and rise no higher than 3 per cent in the later age periods. At 16 years of age, the grade school males derive seven times as much of their outlet from prostitutes as the college males do; and high school males get three or four times as much of their outlet from prostitutes as college males get from

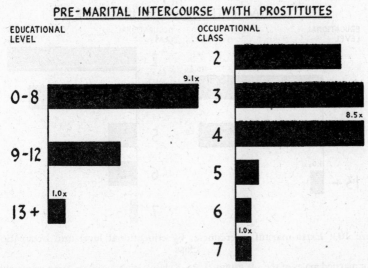

Figure 102. Pre-marital intercourse with prostitutes, by educational level and occupational class

For single males of the age group 16–20. Relative lengths of bars compare mean frequencies for the groups. Note similarity of data based on educational levels and data based on occupational classes.

that source. Among those who are still unmarried between 31 and 35, the lower level individuals have 36 times as much contact with prostitutes as the college males do.

Except for these lower level males of older ages, the actual frequencies of contacts with prostitutes are relatively low. In spite of some opinion that the college male depends primarily on paid contacts for his pre-marital socio-sexual experience, this is the least significant part of all his sexual activities (except for the incidental outlet that he derives from intercourse with animals). The mean frequency of prostitute contacts for the entire male population of all ages and of all educational and occupational groups is 0.093 per week, or approximately 5 times per year. For the lower level groups it may average as high as 0.50 per week (25 times per year) between 31 and 35 years of age. For the unmarried college males taken as a group, it never averages higher than 0.08 per week (4 times per year) in any age period.

Extra-marital intercourse with prostitutes is a still less important item, at all social levels. In any age period, it never constitutes more than 1.5 per cent of the outlet of the grade school level, 1.7 per cent of the outlet of the high school level, and 0.5 per cent of the outlet of the married males of college level.

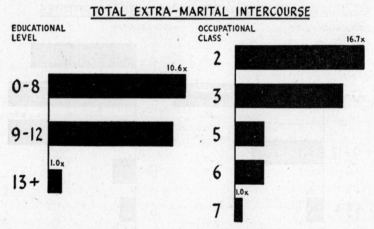

Figure 103. Extra-marital intercourse, by educational level and occupational class

For married males of the age group 21–25. Relative lengths of bars compare mean frequencies for the groups. Note similarity of data based on educational levels and data based on occupational classes.

A breakdown of the population by occupational classes shows that most of the high frequencies of intercourse with prostitutes occur in occupational classes 2 and 3, which are the day labor and semi-skilled workmen groups. The skilled workmen of class 4 show quite as high frequencies in those few instances where we have sufficient material to make calculations. Frequencies even in the lower occupational classes are not more than once in 6 weeks in any particular age group; but the frequencies are rarely more than once or twice in a year in occupational classes 5, 6, and 7. These rates, which represent averages for total populations, are, of course, much lower than the rates for the active members of those populations; but if the analyses are made on the active populations, the differences are still 2 to 1 in most cases, and in some cases nearly 8 to 1, with the higher frequencies occurring in occupational classes 2 and 3. This breakdown by occupational classes is a strict parallel to the breakdown by educational levels.

Marital Intercourse. At all social levels, practically one hundred per cent of the married males have intercourse with their wives (Table 88, Figure 104). There are a few exceptions among the aged, among persons who are married for only brief periods of time, among spouses between whom there are insurmountable incompatibilities on questions of sex, in an occasional case where one or both partners are completely homosexual, or in a very few cases of persons who are religiously much restrained. There are exceedingly few such cases of abstinence, and the number is too small to show any trend by social levels.

There are social differences, however, in regard to the percentage of the total sexual outlet which is derived from marital intercourse. In the age period between 16 and 20, among males of the grade school level, only about 80 per cent of the total sexual outlet comes from marital intercourse, while extra-marital intercourse accounts for another 11 per cent of the total outlet (Tables 86, 97, Figure 103). However, the portion of the outlet coming from marital intercourse in this grade school group rises to approximately 90 per cent in the late forties and early fifties. Among males of the high school group, marital intercourse in the early years accounts for 82 per cent, but rises to 91 per cent of the total outlet by the late forties. For the college level, marital intercourse starts out as a higher portion of the total outlet—nearly 85 per cent; but it drops steadily through the successive years until by the middle fifties it accounts for only 62 per cent of the outlet of these males (Table 97, Figure 133). In comparison with males of the college level, males of the grade school level, in their middle fifties, derive 26 per cent more of their total outlet from intercourse with their wives.

In the course of his marriage, the outlet of the married male of the college level has increasingly included masturbation and nocturnal dreams and, strikingly enough, extra-marital intercourse. On the other hand, the lower level males never have much masturbation in their marital histories, and the amount becomes less in the later years. During their teens and early twenties, lower level males find a considerable outlet in extra-marital intercourse, but with the advancing years they become increasingly faithful to their wives. In short, lower level males take 35 or 40 years to arrive at the marital ideals which the upper level begins with; or, to put it with equal accuracy, upper level males take 35 to 40 years to arrive at the sexual freedom which the lower level accepts in its teens. Some persons may interpret the data to mean that the lower level starts out by trying promiscuity and, as a result of that trial, finally decides that strict monogamy is a better policy; but it would be equally correct to say that the upper level starts out by trying monogamy and ultimately decides that variety is worth having. Of course, neither interpretation is quite correct, for the factors

AGE GROUP	EDUC. LEVEL	CASES	MARITAL INTERCOURSE, BY EDUCATIONAL LEVELS					
			TOTAL POPULATION			ACTIVE POPULATION		
			Mean Frequency	Median Freq.	% of Total Outlet	Incid. %	Mean Frequency	Median Freq.
16–20	0–8	158	3.74 ± 0.35	2.51	79.92	100.0	3.74 ± 0.35	2.51
	9–12	87	4.10 ± 0.44	2.79	82.19	100.0	4.10 ± 0.44	2.79
	13+	46	3.47 ± 0.51	2.58	85.40	100.0	3.47 ± 0.51	2.58
21–25	0–8	324	3.28 ± 0.20	2.22	81.03	99.4	3.30 ± 0.20	2.23
	9–12	164	3.35 ± 0.29	2.53	81.56	100.0	3.35 ± 0.29	2.53
	13+	440	3.07 ± 0.13	2.50	83.93	99.5	3.08 ± 0.13	2.50
26–30	0–8	292	3.00 ± 0.21	2.11	86.15	99.3	3.02 ± 0.21	2.12
	9–12	135	2.88 ± 0.25	2.08	81.67	100.0	2.88 ± 0.25	2.08
	13+	532	2.61 ± 0.10	2.07	82.76	99.2	2.63 ± 0.10	2.08
31–35	0–8	186	2.26 ± 0.18	1.72	88.07	100.0	2.26 ± 0.18	1.72
	9–12	82	2.83 ± 0.34	2.11	85.18	100.0	2.83 ± 0.34	2.11
	13+	301	2.05 ± 0.11	1.73	78.34	99.3	2.07 ± 0.11	1.74
36–40	0–8	143	1.95 ± 0.16	1.56	88.09	99.3	1.97 ± 0.16	1.57
	9–12	58	2.29 ± 0.38	1.70	88.18	100.0	2.29 ± 0.38	1.70
	13+	189	1.89 ± 0.14	1.56	74.41	98.9	1.91 ± 0.15	1.58
41–45	0–8	100	1.72 ± 0.19	1.16	89.97	99.0	1.74 ± 0.19	1.19
	13+	138	1.48 ± 0.10	1.25	76.38	99.3	1.50 ± 0.10	1.26

Table 88. Marital intercourse as related to educational level

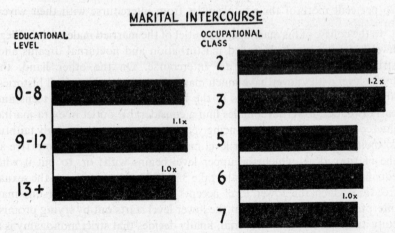

Figure 104. Marital intercourse, by educational level and occupational class

For married males of the age group 21–25. Relative lengths of bars compare mean frequencies for the groups. Note similarity of data based on educational levels and data based on occupational classes.

involve differences in sexual adjustment in marriages at the different levels, as well as the force of the mores which lie at the base of most of these class differences.

Unfortunately, the available data are not sufficient for any detailed analysis of the frequencies of marital intercourse by occupational classes. There are only a few instances where comparisons can be made. It is rather notable, however, that even in those instances there is a differentiation in the direction of slightly higher frequencies and higher percentages of the total outlet derived from marital intercourse among those males who belong to class 6, and slightly lower figures for class 7. If the calculations are based upon the active members of the population, the differences between these two classes are a bit more marked.

Homosexual Contacts. Among single males homosexual relations occur most often in the group that goes into high school but not beyond, and least often in the group that goes to college.

The active incidence figures for single males of the high school group begin at 32 per cent in the early adolescent years and rise to 46 per cent by age 30 (Table 90, Figure 105). The accumulative incidence figure is 54 per cent for those who are not married by age 30. Allowing for the fact that males of this high school group usually marry early, it is something less than 50 per cent which has experience in the homosexual, to the point of orgasm, between the onset of adolescence and marriage. It should be noted that a high proportion of the males in the Army, Navy, Merchant Marine, CCC camps, and other such organizations belong to this educational level. During the age periods in which these men are actually in these services, about 40 per cent have at least incidental homosexual relations. After marriage, the high school level continues to have homosexual relations in something between 9 and 13 per cent of the cases. The active incidence figures during marriage gradually drop in successive age periods.

Among single males of the high school level, frequencies in the homosexual (for the total group) average about once in three weeks between the ages of adolescence and twenty. The averages for that portion of the population which is actually having experience range from a little under once a week in the teens, to about three times in two weeks if the males are still unmarried by their thirties. In early adolescence this high school group draws nearly 9 per cent of its total outlet from the homosexual, and the percentage increases in subsequent age periods until it accounts for a quarter of the total sexual outlet of the high school males who are still unmarried at age 30. While considerable attention has been given to the amount of sexual activity which males in general, and this high school group in particular, have with prostitutes, comparisons of Tables 87 and

AGE GROUP	EDUC. LEVEL	CASES	TOTAL INTERCOURSE, MARRIED MALES, BY EDUCATIONAL LEVELS, INCLUDING MARITAL INTERCOURSE AND ALL EXTRA-MARITAL INTERCOURSE					
			TOTAL POPULATION			ACTIVE POPULATION		
			Mean Frequency	Median Freq.	% of Total Outlet	Incid. %	Mean Frequency	Median Freq.
16–20	0–8	140	4.18 ± 0.38	2.73	90.97	100.0	4.18 ± 0.38	2.73
	9–12	92	4.73 ± 0.50	3.06	93.10	100.0	4.73 ± 0.50	3.06
	13+	47	3.63 ± 0.53	2.63	88.31	100.0	3.63 ± 0.53	2.63
21–25	0–8	297	3.75 ± 0.25	2.41	93.17	100.0	3.75 ± 0.25	2.41
	9–12	143	3.90 ± 0.37	2.63	92.44	100.0	3.90 ± 0.37	2.63
	13+	326	3.01 ± 0.14	2.38	85.27	99.7	3.02 ± 0.14	2.39
26–30	0–8	265	3.23 ± 0.23	2.27	93.94	99.6	3.24 ± 0.23	2.28
	9–12	117	3.32 ± 0.33	2.32	90.80	100.0	3.32 ± 0.33	2.32
	13+	410	2.56 ± 0.11	2.04	84.42	99.8	2.57 ± 0.11	2.04
31–35	0–8	201	2.67 ± 0.20	1.87	95.04	100.0	2.67 ± 0.20	1.87
	9–12	83	2.96 ± 0.36	2.10	90.79	100.0	2.96 ± 0.36	2.10
	13+	338	2.24 ± 0.11	1.87	84.26	99.4	2.25 ± 0.11	1.87
36–40	0–8	154	2.32 ± 0.18	1.74	96.26	99.4	2.34 ± 0.18	1.75
	9–12	60	2.28 ± 0.37	1.71	91.63	98.3	2.32 ± 0.37	1.73
	13+	228	2.14 ± 0.15	1.72	84.79	99.1	2.16 ± 0.15	1.73
41–45	0–8	109	2.09 ± 0.22	1.46	96.27	100.0	2.09 ± 0.22	1.46
	9–12	33	2.07 ± 0.43	1.70	92.93	100.0	2.07 ± 0.43	1.70
	13+	164	1.71 ± 0.11	1.39	82.77	99.4	1.72 ± 0.11	1.40
46–50	0–8	74	1.99 ± 0.29	1.18	96.01	97.3	2.04 ± 0.30	1.25
	9–12	24	1.66 ± 0.44	0.95	94.28	100.0	1.66 ± 0.44	0.95
	13+	99	1.61 ± 0.15	1.15	82.59	98.0	1.64 ± 0.15	1.20
51–55	0–8	53	1.50 ± 0.30	0.85	95.26	96.2	1.56 ± 0.31	0.88
	13+	58	1.36 ± 0.18	0.98	79.27	98.3	1.38 ± 0.18	1.00

Table 89. Total intercourse among married males, in relation to educational level

The data cover the total outlet derived from marital intercourse plus the extra-marital intercourse which is had with both companions and prostitutes.

90 will show that the sexual outlet which is provided by homosexual relations amounts to three or four times the outlet which is provided by prostitutes.

Among the males who ultimately go to college, homosexual relations are less frequent, but they are still a material part of the total sexual picture. Between adolescence and 15 years of age, 21 per cent of the single males of the college level is actively involved, at least in incidental experience to the point of orgasm. The active incidence figure drops to 17 per cent by age 30. The number of college-bred males who ultimately have experience is 40 per cent, if they are not married by age 30.

Frequencies for the college males are much lower than for any of the other educational levels. They average only about once in ten weeks for the population as a whole, and less than once in two weeks for the active population. For those males who are not yet married by 30, the mean frequencies rise to as much as 1.3 per week for the active portion of the population. Only about 3 per cent of the outlet of the college males is derived from the homosexual between adolescence and age 25, but in the next age period they derive nearly 9 per cent of their outlet from such contacts.

After marriage only 2 or 3 per cent of the college males engage in homosexual relations, according to the histories that are now available. There is no doubt, however, that this is one of the points on which there has been considerable cover-up, and it is certain that a good many married males who are having homosexual relations have deliberately avoided contributing their histories to this study. The 3 per cent incidence figure and the low frequencies shown here are, consequently, absolute minima, and they should be increased by some unknown quantity if they are to represent the reality.

The data on the incidence, frequency, and total significance of homosexual relations among grade school males are intermediate between the data for the high school and the college males. In any single age period, about one-fourth of all the males of grade school level have some homosexual relations. This is true for all the years between adolescence and 30. Ultimately, about 45 per cent of the grade school group is involved. Frequencies of homosexual contacts are about once in four weeks for the group taken as a whole, and nearly once a week for those who are actively involved between the ages of 16 and 20. In marriage, the grade school group continues its homosexual relations in 10 per cent of the cases, but the incidence figures drop to about 3 per cent by age 45. The frequencies of homosexual contacts for homosexually active married males of the grade school level begin at about 1.4 per week and drop to a few times per year, or once in a year or two, in the older groups.

| | | | HOMOSEXUAL OUTLET, BY EDUCATIONAL LEVELS | | | | | | |
| AGE GROUP | EDUC. LEVEL | CASES | TOTAL POPULATION | | | ACTIVE POPULATION | | | ACCUMUL. INCID. % |
			Mean Frequency	% of Total Outlet	Incid. %	Mean Freq.	Median Freq.		
				Single Males					
Adol.–15	0–8	712	0.24 ± 0.03	8.03	23.7	1.01	0.42		25
	9–12	606	0.29 ± 0.04	8.73	32.5	0.88	0.30		33
	13+	2799	0.09 ± 0.01	3.14	21.5	0.41	0.09		22
16–20	0–8	720	0.22 ± 0.03	6.85	26.1	0.84	0.34		32
	9–12	607	0.38 ± 0.05	10.81	40.9	0.93	0.31		48
	13+	2861	0.07 ± 0.01	2.43	16.0	0.41	0.08		27
21–25	0–8	361	0.25 ± 0.05	8.06	22.4	1.12	0.41		38
	9–12	263	0.48 ± 0.08	16.31	37.6	1.26	0.68		53
	13+	1898	0.09 ± 0.01	3.72	9.5	0.96	0.30		33
26–30	0–8	159	0.40 ± 0.14	14.04	27.7	1.44	0.48		45
	9–12	117	0.73 ± 0.18	25.95	46.2	1.58	0.73		55
	13+	487	0.23 ± 0.04	8.82	17.2	1.31	0.66		40
				Married Males					
16–20	0–8	158	0.14 ± 0.06	3.08	10.1	1.43	0.35		10
	9–12	87	0.11 ± 0.08	2.11	9.2	1.14	0.39		12
	13+	46		0.16	2.2				3
21–25	0–8	324	0.05 ± 0.02	1.33	9.3	0.58	0.09		
	9–12	164	0.04 ± 0.02	1.05	13.4	0.32	0.10		
	13+	440	0.02 ± 0.01	0.53	2.7	0.72	0.58		3
26–30	0–8	292	0.02 ± 0.01	0.46	4.8	0.34	0.09		
	9–12	135	0.03 ± 0.01	0.96	8.1	0.41	0.30		
	13+	532	0.03 ± 0.01	0.96	2.6	1.16	1.25		4
31–35	0–8	186		0.14	4.3	0.08	0.06		
	9–12	82	0.05 ± 0.02	1.38	6.1	0.75	0.70		
	13+	301	0.02 ± 0.01	0.75	3.0	0.66	0.10		4
36–40	0–8	143		0.30	2.8	0.24	0.08		
	9–12	58	0.02 ± 0.01	0.73	3.4	0.55	0.75		
	13+	189		0.89	2.8		0.10		
41–45	0–8	100		0.08	3.0	0.05	0.07		
	13+	138		1.64	2.2	1.47	0.10		

Table 90. Homosexual outlet, as related to educational level

Median frequencies for the total populations are uniformly 0.00.

A breakdown of the homosexual data for the several occupational classes does not show marked or consistent differences between occupational classes 2, 3, and 5 (Table 114, Figure 105). On most items of sexual activity class 5 is closer to classes 6 and 7, but in regard to the incidences and frequencies of the homosexual, it is closer to the semi-skilled and skilled labor groups. The active incidence figures for homosexual contacts among the lower occupational classes may be as high as 35 or 40 per cent in different groups at particular age periods, but they never go higher than 14 per cent for the males of class 7, except during the period of earliest adolescence for that portion of class 7 which originates from parental class 5.

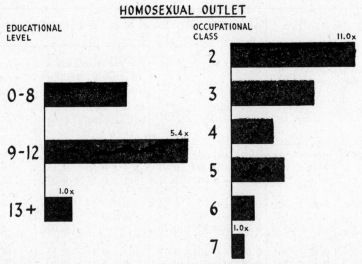

Figure 105. Homosexual outlet, by educational level and occupational class

For single males of the age group 16–20. Relative lengths of bars compare mean frequencies for the groups.

The frequencies of homosexual activity among the males of class 6 are a bit lower than the frequencies in the lower occupational levels. Class 7 is the most distinct. Its frequencies are very much below those of every other occupational class. In practically every age group, and irrespective of the parental occupational class from which these class 7 males may have come, the frequencies average only about one-fourth or one-fifth of those for the lower occupational classes. If the calculations are made only for those males who do become actively involved, the mean frequencies for class 7 are still only half as high as the mean frequencies for the active males of classes 3 and 5. Males of occupational class 6 are intermediate between the males of the lower levels and those of class 7.

The situation portrayed by frequencies in the homosexual is more or less paralleled by the calculations showing the percent of the total sexual outlet which is derived from this source in each of the occupational classes. An average of 10 per cent or more of the total sexual outlet may be derived from the homosexual by males of classes 2 and 5, while among males of class 7 the average of the total outlet which is so derived is never more than 2 per cent. The males of class 6 are rather intermediate in this regard, or more nearly approach the males of class 5 in deriving upward of 10 per cent (in one group slightly more than 10 per cent) of their orgasms in contacts with other males.

Animal Intercourse. Intercourse with animals other than the human is almost entirely confined to males raised in rural areas. Only an occa-

AGE GROUP	EDUC. LEVEL	CASES	ANIMAL CONTACTS, SINGLE MALES, BY EDUCATIONAL LEVEL						ACCUMUL. INCID. RURAL MALES ONLY %
			TOTAL POPULATION			ACTIVE POPULATION			
			Mean Frequency	% of Total Outlet	Incid. %	Mean Freq.	Median Freq.		
Adol.–15	0–8	712	0.026 ± 0.007	0.86	5.8	0.45	0.14		10
	9–12	606	0.030 ± 0.009	0.91	5.9	0.50	0.16		9
	13+	2799	0.020 ± 0.005	0.71	5.3	0.37	0.07		23
16–20	0–8	720	0.022 ± 0.007	0.68	4.0	0.54	0.17		14
	9–12	607	0.038 ± 0.012	1.08	4.6	0.82	0.24		17
	13+	2861	0.010 ± 0.004	0.36	2.5	0.39	0.09		25
21–25	0–8	361	0.005 ± 0.003	0.15	1.1	0.43	0.33		14
	9–12	263	0.014 ± 0.010	0.47	2.7	0.51	0.10		20
	13+	1898	0.002 ± 0.001	0.09	0.7	0.32	0.10		26

Table 91. Animal contacts, as related to educational level

The active population is almost wholly rural and the active frequencies are essentially those for that portion of the rural population which has animal contacts. Median frequencies for the total populations are uniformly 0.00.

sional contact is had by city boys, unless they visit farms in vacation periods. Consequently, averages of animal contacts for the total American population are so low that they cannot be calculated with an accuracy which means anything in terms of the actualities of human behavior. For the rural males who are actively involved in such contacts, animal intercourse is more significant (Table 91).

The accumulative incidence figures for animal intercourse go to about 14 per cent for the farm boys who do not go beyond grade school, to about 20 per cent for the group which goes into high school but not beyond, and to 26 per cent for the males who will ultimately go to college. The boys of college level who are ever involved in animal intercourse number nearly twice as many, relatively, as the boys who never go beyond grade school.

On the other hand, the boys of lower educational levels who are actually involved are the ones who have the highest frequencies in animal contacts (Table 91). For them the frequencies average close to once in two weeks, plus or minus. The frequencies for the boys of the college level who are actually having any animal contacts average nearer once in three weeks.

ATTITUDES ON SEXUAL TECHNIQUES

In addition to differences in frequencies and sources of sexual outlet, social levels differ in their attitudes on other matters of sex. Their sources of erotic interest, attitudes toward nudity, and techniques utilized in coitus are the items on which we have sufficient data to warrant some treatment here.

Sources of Erotic Arousal. The upper level male is aroused by a considerable variety of sexual stimuli. He has a minimum of pre-marital or extra-marital intercourse (Tables 96, 97). The lower level male, on the other hand, is less often aroused by anything except physical contact in coitus; he has an abundance of pre-marital intercourse, and a considerable amount of extra-marital intercourse in the early years of his marriage. How much of this difference is simply the product of psychologic factors and how much represents a community pattern which can be properly identified as the mores, it is difficult to say. The very fact that upper level males fail to get what they want in socio-sexual relations would provide a psychologic explanation of their high degree of erotic responsiveness to stimuli which fall short of actual coitus. The fact that the lower level male comes nearer having as much coitus as he wants (Table 92) would make him less susceptible to any stimulus except actual coitus.

The higher degree of eroticism in the upper level male may also be consequent on his greater capacity to visualize situations which are not immediately at hand. In consequence, he is affected by thinking about females, and/or by seeing females or the homosexual partner, by burlesque shows, obscene stories, love stories in good literature, love stories in moving pictures, animals in coitus, and sado-masochistic literature. Upper level males are the ones who most often read erotic literature, and the ones who most often find erotic stimulation in pictures and other objects. None of these are significant sources of stimulation for most lower level males, who may look on such a thing as the use of pictures or literature to augment masturbatory fantasies as the strangest sort of perversion.

While these group differences may be primarily psychologic in origin, there is clearly an element of tradition involved. Each community more or less accepts the idea that there will be or will not be erotic arousal under particular sorts of circumstances. The college male who continuously talks about girls does so with a certain consciousness that the other persons in his group are also going to be aroused by such conversation, and that they accept such arousal as natural and desirable. The homosexual male, and the heterosexual male who does not approve of such deliberately induced

RESTRAINTS ON INTERCOURSE	EDUC. LEVEL	ATTITUDES ON PRE-MARITAL INTERCOURSE AT THREE EDUCATIONAL LEVELS							
		ALL AGES		ADOL.–25		26–45		46+	
		Cases	%	Cases	%	Cases	%	Cases	%
Moral objections	0–8	814	20.8	317	18.9	338	16.2	159	33.9
	9–12	650	25.5	369	22.8	232	28.5		
	13+	3161	61.4	2016	62.5	969	56.6	176	76.2
Fear of public opinion	0–8	775	13.5	300	14.4	322	11.5	153	16.3
	9–12	615	14.3	343	12.0	224	17.0		
	13+	2847	22.8	1756	21.5	918	24.1	173	28.9
Fear of pregnancy	0–8	814	20.4	318	19.2	336	20.6	160	22.5
	9–12	645	17.5	364	18.6	232	15.5		
	13+	3136	27.6	1995	28.0	964	27.5	177	23.7
Fear of venereal disease	0–8	811	28.6	317	27.1	335	29.0	159	30.8
	9–12	641	25.3	361	23.8	231	26.8		
	13+	3143	24.8	2001	25.1	965	23.9	177	25.4
Lack opportunity	0–8	785	34.6	312	36.9	323	33.8	150	32.0
	9–12	627	38.0	358	37.5	225	39.6		
	13+	3104	51.6	1980	51.4	950	55.5	174	33.4
Lack of interest in having more	0–8	327	41.9	155	35.5	117	45.3	55	52.7
	9–12	279	44.5	153	45.1	111	45.9		
	13+	1831	18.8	1041	18.7	688	19.2	102	17.6
Male desires to marry a virgin	0–8	595	43.3	215	40.9	267	38.5	113	59.3
	9–12	523	39.2	309	40.8	176	32.4		
	13+	2972	46.5	1943	50.7	880	36.2	149	41.6

Table 92. Attitudes on pre-marital intercourse, at three educational levels

eroticism, considers this public display of elation over females as a group activity which is more or less artificially encouraged. The lower level male who talks about girls quite as frequently, or even more so, is less often aroused by such talk and may be inclined to consider a listener who is so aroused as somewhat aberrant. There is an element of custom involved in these styles of erotic response.

Nudity. In many cultures, the world around, people have been much exercised by questions of propriety in the public exposure of portions or the whole of the nude body. There are few matters on which customs are more specific, and few items of sexual behavior which bring more intense reactions when the custom is transgressed. These customs vary tremendously between cultures and nations, and even between the individual communities in particular countries. The inhabitant of the Central American tropics has one custom, the Indian who comes down from his mountain home to trade in the lowland has totally different customs. There is neither rhyme nor reason to the custom—there is nothing but tradition to explain it. The mountain Indian of the warmer country of Southern Mexico is thoroughly clothed, the mountain Indian of the coldest part of Northern Mexico is more completely nude than the natives of the hottest Mexican tropics. But there are probably no groups in the world who are free of taboos of some sort on this point. The history of the origin of clothing is more often one of taboos on nudity than a story of the utility of body coverings.

The English are more or less justly reputed to be the most completely clothed people in the world, and Americans have been slow in breaking away from the English tradition. The American visitor to foreign lands is often amazed at the exposure which is allowed in some other cultures, and he criticizes it on moral grounds. The nudity of the French burlesque is ascribed to the "low morality" of Frenchmen as a group; and although an approach is made to the same sort of display in American burlesque, the institution here does not achieve the same free acceptance of complete nudity which the original French has. The German nudist movement is assumed by the average American to be immoral in intent, and its counterpart in this country survives only after considerable public discussion and continual wrangling in court over the obscenity of such activity. Although Anglo-American law has tried for six or seven centuries to define indecent exposure, there is no legal agreement on the decency or indecency of nude art, nor on the rights of art schools, photographers, magazines, and books to portray the nude human form. Public sentiment, backed by sporadic police action, has dictated the styles of bathing suits, from the gay nineties down to the present. It is only within the last decade or two that the male's right to appear in swimming trunks without tops has been established for public swimming beaches and pools.

More definite limits may be set on nudity than on more overtly sexual activities. The kissing which is commonplace in American films is considered most immoral in some of the foreign countries to which the films are distributed. A completely nude art production may be shown in a Latin American moving picture theatre to an audience which takes the film complacently, for its artistic value, although it will hiss the next picture off the screen because it contains a Hollywood kissing scene.

The acceptance of nudity may even vary with the hour and the place of the exposure. The costume which is accepted on the swimming beach is strictly forbidden in most other places. In the middle of the day, the female may safely expose her arms in public, although she is then limited in regard to the exposure of her back. At the formal affair in the evening, she may expose the whole of her back, but she is then most proper if she covers her arms with long gloves. In a Latin American tropic town, inside a public building, there may be considerable objection when one rolls his shirt sleeves to the elbow, even on the hottest summer day; but out of doors both men and women may go stripped to the waist through the streets of the town, and all of them may come together for nude bathing in the nearby stream. It would require a considerable treatise to portray the reactions of the peoples of the world to nudity, and a larger treatise to explain the origins of those customs.

Most amazing of all, customs in regard to nudity may vary between the social levels of a single community. In our American culture, there is a greater acceptance of nudity at upper social levels, and greater restraint at lower social levels. Compared with previous generations, there is a more general acceptance of nudity in the upper social level today (Table 95). There is an increasing amount of nudity within the family circle in this upper level. There is rather free exposure in the home for both sexes, including the parents and the children of all ages, at times of dressing and at times of bathing. Still more significant, there is an increasing habit among upper level persons of sleeping in partial or complete nudity (Table 95). This is probably more common among males, though there is a considerable number of upper level females who also sleep nude. Among the males of the college level, nearly half (41%) frequently sleep nude, about one-third (34%) of the high school males do so, but only one-sixth (16%) of the males of the grade school level sleep that way.

Finally, the upper level considers nudity almost an essential concomitant of intercourse. About 90 per cent of the persons at this level regularly have coitus nude (Table 95). The upper level finds it difficult to comprehend that anyone should regularly and as a matter of preference have intercourse while clothed. This group uses clothing only under unusual circumstances, or when variety and experimentation are the desired objectives in the intercourse. On the other hand, nude coitus is regularly had by only 66 per cent of those who never go beyond high school, and by 43 per cent of those who never go beyond grade school.

This intercourse with clothing is not a product of the inconveniences of the lower level home, nor is it dependent upon the difficulties of securing privacy in a small home, as too many sociologists have gratuitously assumed. It is primarily the product of the lower level's conviction that nudity is obscene. It is obscene in the presence of strangers, and it is even obscene in the presence of one's spouse. Some of the older men and women in this group take pride in the fact that they have never seen their own spouses nude.

Many persons at this level strictly avoid nudity while dressing or undressing. They acquire a considerable knack of removing daytime clothing and of putting on night clothing, without ever exposing any part of the body. This is less often true of the younger generation which has been exposed to the mixture of social levels encountered in the CCC camps, the Y.M.C.A., and the Army and the Navy. Exposure of the upper half of the male body on swimming beaches started as an upper level custom, but the democracy of the public beach has fostered a much wider acceptance of nudity among lower social levels today. Compare the three generations of the educational level 0–8 in Table 95. Younger males, even of the laboring groups, are often seen at work, out of doors, in public view, while stripped to the waist; but older males of the same social level still keep their arms covered to the wrist, even on the hottest of days and while engaged in the most uncomfortable of jobs. These inroads on the traditions against nudity are reflected in the sleeping and coital customs of younger persons of these lower levels, but the older members of these groups still observe the traditions. There are some cases of lower level males who have been highly promiscuous, who have had intercourse with several hundred females, and who emphasize the fact that they have never turned down an opportunity to have intercourse except "on one occasion when the girl started to remove her clothing before coitus. She was too indecent to have intercourse with!"

Manual Manipulation. At upper social levels there may be considerable manual petting between partners, particularly on the part of the male who has been persuaded by the general talk among his companions, and by the codification of those opinions in the marriage manuals, that the female needs extended sensory stimulation if she is to be brought to simultaneous orgasm in coitus. Upper level petting involves the manual stimulation of all parts of the female body.

Manual manipulation of the female breast occurs regularly in 96 per cent of the histories of the married males of the upper level, and manual manipulation of the female genitalia is regularly found in about 90 per cent of the histories (Table 93). The upper level believes that this petting is necessary for successful coital adjustment; but preliminary calculations indicate that the frequency of orgasm is higher among lower level females than it is among upper level females, even though the lower level coitus involves a minimum of specific physical stimulation (Table 93).

The manual manipulation of the female breast occurs in only 79 per cent of the married male histories at lower levels, and the manipulation of the female genitalia occurs in only 75 per cent of the cases (Table 93). Even

TECHNIQUE	EDUC. LEVEL	UTILIZATION OF PETTING TECHNIQUES AT THREE EDUCATIONAL LEVELS							
		ALL AGES		ADOL.–25		26–45		46+	
		Cases	%	Cases	%	Cases	%	Cases	%
Kissing, lip. Marital. Frequent	0–8	457	88.4	73	95.9	252	90.1	132	81.1
	9–12	267	93.2	80	98.7	149	94.0		
	13+	1071	97.7	225	99.6	689	97.5	157	95.5
Kissing, deep. Marital. Frequent	0–8	455	40.5	73	54.8	252	42.4	130	28.5
	9–12	267	56.2	80	60.0	149	58.4		
	13+	1069	77.3	225	86.7	687	78.3	157	59.2
Breast, manual. Marital. Frequent	0–8	458	78.6	74	85.1	252	81.4	132	69.7
	9–12	266	90.6	80	92.5	148	93.9		
	13+	1071	96.3	225	99.0	689	96.5	157	91.1
Breast, oral. Marital. Frequent	0–8	458	33.2	74	32.4	252	36.1	132	28.0
	9–12	266	57.5	80	57.5	148	62.9		
	13+	1071	81.6	225	92.5	689	81.1	157	67.5
Female genitalia, manual. Pre-m. Frequent	0–8	235	79.1	151	82.2	63	76.2		
	9–12	224	85.3	173	87.3				
	13+	566	91.0	439	91.8	118	90.7		
Female genitalia, manual. Marital. Frequent	0–8	457	74.8	74	74.3	252	78.2	131	68.7
	9–12	266	79.7	80	77.4	148	85.1		
	13+	1071	89.6	225	94.6	689	89.2	157	83.4
Male genitalia, manual. Pre-m. Frequent	0–8	235	66.4	151	65.6	63	69.9		
	9–12	224	71.0	173	74.0				
	13+	566	75.1	439	74.7	118	78.0		
Male genitalia, manual. Marital. Frequent	0–8	457	57.1	74	54.1	252	58.0	131	57.3
	9–12	266	60.9	80	65.0	148	63.5		
	13+	1069	75.3	225	84.0	687	74.5	157	66.2
Female genitalia, oral. Pre-marital. Ever	0–8	235	8.5	151	9.3	63	7.9		
	9–12	224	10.3	173	11.6				
	13+	564	18.4	438	15.5	117	25.6		
Female genitalia, oral. Marital. Ever	0–8	458	4.1	74	5.4	252	4.0	132	3.8
	9–12	267	15.4	80	13.7	149	16.8		
	13+	1070	45.3	225	35.1	688	49.6	157	41.4
Male genitalia, oral. Pre-marital. Ever	0–8	235	22.1	151	21.8	63	25.4		
	9–12	224	29.9	173	27.7	45	37.8		
	13+	564	38.6	438	34.5	117	51.3		
Male genitalia, oral. Marital. Ever	0–8	458	6.6	74	9.5	252	6.8	132	4.6
	9–12	267	15.3	80	12.5	149	18.1		
	13+	1070	42.7	225	38.7	688	45.5	157	36.3

Table 93. Utilization of pre-coital petting techniques at three educational levels, in three generations

Ages shown represent ages of subjects at time of reporting.

when there is such stimulation, it is usually restricted in its extent and in its duration. The lower level female agrees to manipulate the male genitalia in only 57 per cent of the cases. The record is, therefore, one of more extended pre-coital play at the upper levels, and of a minimum of play at the lower levels. Many persons at the lower level consider that intromission is the essential activity and the only justifiable activity in a "normal" sexual relation.

Oral Eroticism. Many persons in the upper levels consider a certain amount of oral eroticism as natural, desirable, and a fundamental part of love making. Simple lip kissing is so commonly accepted that it has a minimum of erotic significance at this level. The college male may expect to kiss his date the first time they go out together. Most college students understand there will be good night kisses as soon as their dating becomes regular. Many a college male will have kissed dozens of girls, although he has had intercourse with none of them. On the other hand, the lower level male is likely to have had intercourse with hundreds of girls, but he may have kissed few of them. What kissing he has done has involved simple lip contacts, for he is likely to have a considerable distaste for the deep kiss which is fairly common in upper level histories.

Deep kissing is utilized as a prime source of erotic arousal by many persons in the better educated and top social levels. A deep kiss may involve considerable tongue contacts, deep lip contacts, and extended explorations of the interior of the partner's mouth. Such behavior is, as noted before, a regular concomitant of coital activity among many of the vertebrates, and particularly among the mammals (Beach 1947, and original observations which we have). In the human mammal, at the upper level, oral eroticism may still be considered a bit sophisticated, but deep kissing is in the experience of 87 per cent of the group (Table 93). Its sanitary implications seem no obstacle to its acceptance. This group accepts mouth contacts in its erotic play, although it objects to the use of a common drinking glass.

On the other hand, the lower level male considers such oral contacts to be dirty, filthy, and a source of disease, although he may drink from a common cup which hangs in the water pail, and he may utilize common utensils in eating and drinking. Obviously, the arguments, at both levels, have nothing to do with the real issues. They are rationalizations of mores which place taboos upon mouth contacts for reasons which only the student of custom can explain. Once again, it is the upper level which first reverted, through a considerable sophistication, to behavior which is biologically natural and basic.

Mouth-breast contact does occur at all social levels, but it is most elaborately developed again in the upper social level (Table 93). Almost

		ORAL CONTACTS: ACCUMULATIVE INCIDENCE BY PERCENTS OF TOTAL POPULATION										
		HETEROSEXUAL									HOMO-SEXUAL	
AGE GROUP	CASES	Any Type	Ever, Male Active	Ever, Male Passive	Pre-Marital, Any	Pre-Marital, Male Active	Pre-Marital, Male Passive	Marital, Any	Marital, Male Active	Marital, Male Passive	Male Active	Male Passive
All Educational Levels: U. S. Correction												
16–20	1208	46.2	8.2	22.8	23.7	7.7	22.8				12.0	38.3
21–25	1502	49.1	8.4	27.2	26.7	6.9	26.5	16.7	12.1	12.6	14.1	36.3
26–30	653	55.9	12.3	40.0				22.3	15.8	21.3	13.5	36.6
31–35	370	55.2	15.3	40.6				19.2	15.8	13.8	15.4	32.0
36–40	317	58.9	16.7	46.7							11.5	29.8
Educational Level 0–8												
16–20	176	44.9	8.0	22.2	21.0	8.0	21.0				15.2	38.2
21–25	123	41.5	4.9	22.8	21.0	6.5	21.0	8.2	3.3	6.6	10.6	30.9
26–30	109	45.0	5.5	37.6				9.3	2.7	9.3	4.6	33.0
31–35	74	40.5	6.8	29.7				10.5	7.0	7.0	10.8	27.0
36–40	88	44.8	9.1	35.2				10.8	6.2	9.2	5.7	24.1
41–45	67	34.3	1.5	28.8					0.0	0.0	5.9	13.2
46–55	84	22.6	1.2	16.7					3.0	4.5	6.0	14.5
56+	77	23.1	5.2	18.2					4.5	4.5	6.3	15.2
Educational Level 9–12												
16–20	228	54.8	9.6	26.8	28.9	8.8	27.5				12.4	46.5
21–25	142	57.0	9.1	30.1	31.0	6.9	31.0	14.3	10.7	8.9	18.0	45.8
26–30	104	64.4	10.6	40.4				21.7	15.0	21.7	21.4	45.7
31–35	62	66.1	14.8	47.5							21.3	42.6
36–40	49	77.6	16.3	61.2							20.4	42.9
Educational Level 13+												
16–20	802	15.8	3.2	8.8	9.5	3.0	8.7				3.6	6.6
21–25	1237	34.9	13.5	25.7	22.1	8.0	20.9	44.1	36.2	39.9	6.5	11.5
26–30	440	57.0	34.8	44.8	29.1	12.6	28.1	56.9	51.5	50.6	11.4	17.1
31–35	234	70.5	42.7	55.1				48.7	43.5	36.8	13.8	18.9
36–40	180	71.7	49.4	58.9				54.2	50.3	47.7	13.7	21.3
41–45	118	74.6	51.7	55.1				62.1	55.3	46.6	11.9	17.8
46–55	122	63.9	43.4	50.8				47.2	42.5	36.8	9.8	10.7
56+	55	54.5	41.8	40.0				43.1	39.2	35.3	9.1	12.7

Table 94. Oral techniques at three educational levels

Showing accumulative incidences. Data not calculated as described for accumulative incidence curves in Chapter 3, but derived from experience of each subject up to time of reporting. Lower incidences in some older age groups may be due to small size of samples and to possible cover-up, but most probably to the fact that incidences were actually a bit lower in that generation.

invariably it is a matter of the male manipulating the female breast with his mouth. It is interesting that females rarely attempt to manipulate male breasts (Chapter 18).

The upper level male considers it natural that the female breast should interest him, and that he should want to manipulate it, both by hand and by mouth. The biologic origin of this interest is, however, open to question, because many lower level males do not find the female breast similarly interesting and have little inclination to manipulate it, either by hand or by mouth. Many lower level males rate such mouth-breast contacts as perversions, and some of them dismiss the idea with considerable disgust, as something that only a baby does when nursing from the mother's breast. Considering these opposite reactions to a single type of situation, it must be apparent that a considerable psychic element is involved in the development of individual patterns on this point. The concentration of these patterns in whole social levels indicates that the mores, the long-time customs of the groups, are the fundamental factors in the picture.

Mouth-genital contacts of some sort, with the subject as either the active or the passive member in the relationship, occur at some time in the histories of nearly 60 per cent of all males (Table 94). As noted elsewhere (Chapter 18), these are quite common in the sexual activity of many of the other mammals, particularly among the other anthropoids (Beach 1947). There have been some other human cultures which have accepted such contacts as usual behavior, and even as a part of their religious service. The suggestion that such techniques in our present-day society are a recent development among sophisticated and sexually exhausted individuals is curiously contrary to the specific record, for the figures for at least three generations do not show significant changes in this respect (Table 93).

Mouth-genital contacts (of any kind) occur much more often at high school and college levels (Table 94), less often in the grade school group. In the histories of the college group, about 72 per cent of the males have at least experimented with such contacts, and about 65 per cent of the males who have gone into high school but not beyond. Among those males who have never gone beyond eighth grade in school the accumulative incidence figure is only 40 per cent.

The percentages for males who have made mouth contacts with female genitalia prior to marriage are 9, 10, and 18 for grade school, high school, and college levels, respectively (Table 93). In marriage, such contacts are in 4, 15, and 45 per cent of the histories, for the three groups. Before marriage, the percentages of males with histories which included mouth stimulation of the male genitalia during heterosexual relations were 22, 30, and 39, for the three educational levels. In marriage, such relations have been had in 7, 15, and 43 per cent of the cases, for the three levels, respectively.

POSITIONS IN MARITAL COITUS	EDUC. LEVEL	COITAL TECHNIQUES AND NUDITY AT THREE EDUCATIONAL LEVELS							
		ALL AGES		ADOL.–25		26–45		46+	
		Cases	%	Cases	%	Cases	%	Cases	%
Female above; frequent	0–8	457	17.1	74	24.3	251	20.3	132	6.8
	9–12	265	28.3	80	31.2	148	20.4		
	13+	1071	34.6	226	42.9	688	34.4	157	23.6
Side; frequent	0–8	457	16.4	74	32.4	251	16.4	132	7.6
	9–12	263	22.8	80	20.0	147	27.2		
	13+	1066	26.0	225	22.7	684	27.2	157	25.5
Rear; frequent	0–8	456	7.6	74	12.2	250	8.4	132	3.8
	9–12	265	11.3	80	7.5	148	14.9		
	13+	1068	10.6	225	9.8	686	11.1	157	9.6
Sitting; frequent	0–8	457	7.7	74	17.6	251	7.2	132	3.0
	9–12	265	9.4	80	6.2	148	11.5		
	13+	1065	6.1	224	6.7	684	6.1	157	5.0
Standing; frequent	0–8	455	7.5	74	17.5	249	7.2	132	2.3
	9–12	263	9.1	80	7.5	146	11.0		
	13+	1062	3.6	224	2.6	683	3.6	155	4.5
NUDITY									
In sleep; frequent	0–8	724	16.1	271	19.6	296	14.5	157	13.4
	9–12	486	34.1	256	34.8	187	34.2		
	13+	2407	41.1	1412	34.9	832	52.2	163	37.4
In coitus. Premarital. Frequent	0–8	436	31.7	198	32.8	181	32.6	57	24.5
	9–12	366	45.1	217	52.1	126	37.3		
	13+	894	54.9	456	52.2	407	58.7		
In coitus. Marital. Frequent	0–8	383	42.8	54	63.0	208	43.3	121	33.1
	9–12	205	66.3	55	81.8	118	67.0		
	13+	924	89.2	184	92.4	598	90.8	142	78.1

Table 95. Coital techniques and nudity at three educational levels, in three generations

The most frequently used coital position is the one in which the male is above. It is not shown in the table because its use does not significantly vary between educational levels. Ages shown represent ages of subjects at time of reporting. Consequently it may be expected that the incidence data for the youngest generation, although they are already higher than any other on most items, will go still higher before this group reaches the age of the oldest generation shown in the table.

Most of the mouth-genital contacts are had between spouses. Prostitutes provide a portion of such contacts. However, it should be noted that most prostitutes are from the lower social levels, and consequently that few of them engage freely in oral activities. Even among those who make such contacts professionally, few of them would accept the same type of relationship with their boy friends. In her private life, even the prostitute does not depart from the mores of her social level, although she may do anything for pay.

Mouth-genital contacts in homosexual relations occur most commonly among the males of the high school level, and not quite so often in the males of the college and grade school groups (Table 94). Of the entire male population (U. S. Corrections), about 30 per cent has been brought to climax at least once in such relations with other males, and 14 per cent has brought other males to climax by the same techniques. The total of those who have had any type of oral relation in the homosexual is something over 30 per cent.

Positions in Intercourse. Universally, at all social levels in our Anglo-American culture, the opinion is held that there is one coital position which is biologically natural, and that all others are man-devised variants which become perversions when regularly engaged in. However, the one position which might be defended as natural because it is usual throughout the Class Mammalia, is not the one commonly used in our culture. The usual mammalian position involves, of course, rear entrance, with the female more or less prone, face down, with her legs flexed under her body, while the male is above or to the rear. Among the anthropoids this mammalian position is still the most common, but some variety of positions also occurs (Bingham 1928, Yerkes and Elder 1936, Beach 1947, Nowlis ms.).

Most persons will be surprised to learn that positions in intercourse are as much a product of human cultures as languages and clothing, and that the common English-American position is rare in some other cultures. Among the several thousand portrayals of human coitus in the art left by ancient civilizations, there is hardly a single portrayal of the English-American position. It will be recalled that Malinowski (1929) records the nearly universal use of a totally different position among the Trobrianders in the Southwestern Pacific; and that he notes that caricatures of the English-American position are performed around the communal camp-fires, to the great amusement of the natives who refer to the position as the "missionary position."

The origin of our present custom is involved in early and later Church history, and needs clarification before it can be presented with any authority; but certain it is that there was a time in the history of the Christian Church when the utilization of any other except the present-day position was made a matter for confession. What has been taken to be a question of biologic normality proves, once again, to be a matter of cultural development.

Since this is so, it is not surprising to find that within our American culture there is some variation in coital positions among the social levels. Throughout the population as a whole, a high proportion of all the intercourse is had in a position with the female supine, on her back, with the male above and facing the female. Only a part of the intercourse is had with the female above the male. This occurs in about 35 per cent of the college level histories, in 28 per cent of the high school histories, but in only 17 per cent of the grade school histories (Table 95). At the upper level 26 per cent of the males may use a position in which the partners lie on their sides, facing each other, but only 23 and 16 per cent of the high school and grade school males try such a technique. Rear entrance into the vagina is found in 11 per cent of college and high school histories, but in less than 8 per cent of the grade school histories. The lower level experiments more often than the upper level only in sitting and standing positions, but no group uses these two positions very often.

It should be emphasized that the most common variant position is the one with the female above. It is used, at least occasionally, by more than a third (34.6%) of the upper level males. The position was more nearly universal in Ancient Greece and Rome (vide the art objects and materials, as well as the literature from that period). It is shown in the oldest known depiction of human coitus, dating between 3200 and 3000 B.C., from the Ur excavations in Mesopotamia (Legrain 1936). The position with the female above is similarly the commonest in the ancient art of Peru, India, China, Japan, and other civilizations. In spite of its ancient history, many persons at lower social levels consider the position a considerable perversion. It is associated in their rationalizations with the idea that the female becomes masculine while the male becomes effeminate in assuming such a position, and that it destroys the dignity of the male and his authority in the family relationship. There may be a feeling that a male who accepts this position shows homosexual tendencies. One of the older psychiatrists goes so far as to insist that the assumption of such a dominating position by the female in coitus may lead to neurotic disturbances and, in many cases, to divorce. Even the scientifically trained person is inclined to use such rationalizations to defend his custom.

PATTERNS OF BEHAVIOR

Within any single social level there are, of course, considerable differences between individuals in their choice of sexual outlets, and in the frequencies with which they engage in each type of activity. The range of individual variation in any level is not particularly different from the range of variation in each other level. Within each group, each individual pattern is more or less duplicated by the patterns of individuals in every one of the other social levels. Nevertheless, the frequencies of each type of variant are so different for different social levels that the means and the medians and the general shapes of the frequency curves for the several groups are perfectly distinct. Translated into everyday thinking, this means that a large proportion of all the individuals in any group follows patterns of sexual behavior which are typical of the group, and which are followed by only a smaller number of the individuals in other groups.

If the mean or median frequencies for each type of sexual activity, at each social level, are brought together in a single chart (Figures 106, 107), it becomes possible to see what material differences there are in these patterns of behavior. Each horizontal line, followed across the chart, epitomizes the story for one social level. It is, as it were, a silhouette, a profile representing the essence of the group's attitudes on matters of sex, and the translation of those attitudes into overt sexual activity.

Even a child would comprehend that the creature represented in each of these silhouettes is distinct and unlike the creatures represented in the other silhouettes.

It is, of course, of prime concern to ask why patterns of sexual behavior differ as they do in different social levels. It is of scientific importance to understand how such patterns originate, how they are passed on to each individual, and how they become standards of behavior for such a high proportion of all the individuals in each group. It is of equal importance to understand the social significances of these patterns of sexual behavior. Few of us have been aware that there were such differences in patterns in the various subdivisions of our culture. An understanding of the facts may contribute something toward easing the tensions that arise because individuals and whole segments of the population fail to understand the sexual philosophies and the sexual behavior of groups in which they have not been raised.

We do not yet understand, to the full, the origins of these diverse sexual philosophies; but it will be possible to record what the thinking of each group is in regard to each type of activity.

Masturbation. At lower social levels, and particularly among the older generations of the lowest levels, masturbation may be looked down upon as abnormal, a perversion, and an infantile substitute for socio-sexual contacts. Although most lower level boys masturbate during their early adolescence, many of them never have more than a few experiences or, at the most, regular masturbation for a short period of months or years, after which they rarely again depend on such self-induced outlets. Among many of these lower level males, masturbation stops abruptly and immediately after the first experiences in heterosexual coitus. The lower level boy who

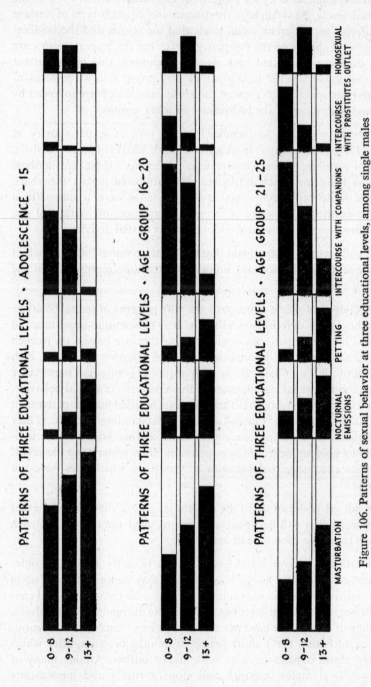

PATTERNS OF THREE EDUCATIONAL LEVELS · ADOLESCENCE - 15

PATTERNS OF THREE EDUCATIONAL LEVELS · AGE GROUP 16-20

PATTERNS OF THREE EDUCATIONAL LEVELS · AGE GROUP 21-25

MASTURBATION   NOCTURNAL   PETTING   INTERCOURSE WITH COMPANIONS   INTERCOURSE   HOMOSEXUAL
                EMISSIONS   WITH PROSTITUTES   OUTLET

Figure 106. Patterns of sexual behavior at three educational levels, among single males

For 3 age groups. Each horizontal line extending across the page summarizes the pattern for one of the educational levels. Relative lengths of bars in each outlet show average mean frequencies for the group. The scales vary for different sources of outlet, but there is an approximate indication of the relative importance of each source in the total outlet.

continues to draw any material portion of his sexual outlet from masturbation after his middle teens may be much ashamed of it, and he may become the object of community jokes and of more serious disapproval if his history becomes known. In many instances, these attitudes are bolstered by rationalizations to the effect that masturbation does physical harm; but the objections are in reality based on the idea that masturbation is either abnormal, or else an admission that one is incapable of securing heterosexual intercourse and, therefore, socially inadequate. Among some primitive peoples (*e.g.*, Bryk 1933), there is a somewhat similar attitude toward masturbation—an attitude which does not involve moral evaluations as much as it involves amusement at the social incapacity of the individual who has to resort to self stimulation for his sexual outlet. The better educated portion of the population which so largely depends upon masturbation for its pre-marital outlet, and which draws a not insignificant portion of its outlet from masturbation after marriage, will be surprised to learn what the less educated segments of the population think of one who masturbates instead of having intercourse.

The upper level more or less allows masturbation as not exactly desirable nor exactly commendable, but not as immoral as a socio-sexual contact. Older generations of the upper level were not so ready to accept masturbation. As many males were involved in the older generations, but the frequencies were definitely lower (Chapter 11), and there was considerable moral conflict over the rightness or wrongness of the "habit" (Chapter 14). Upper level males have accepted masturbation more freely within the last two or three decades, and today a high proportion of the teen-age boys of the college group frankly and openly admit this form of pre-marital outlet. During their years in college about 70 per cent of these males depend upon masturbation as their chief source of outlet. They derive about 66 per cent of their orgasms from this source during their college years.

The upper level's pre-marital experience leads it to include masturbation as a source of outlet after marriage. The coital adjustments of this group in marriage are frequently poor, particularly because of the low degree of erotic responsiveness which exists among many of the college-bred females. This offers some excuse for masturbation among the married males of the group; but their early acceptance of masturbation in their pre-marital histories, and their tardy acceptance of heterosexual coitus, are prime determinants in the marital patterns. There are few things in all human sexual behavior which will surprise the poorly educated groups more than this considerable utilization of masturbation by the college-bred male as an outlet after marriage.

Petting. The social levels are furthest apart in their attitudes on petting and on pre-marital intercourse. The two items are related, for petting,

SOURCES	SOURCES OF ORGASM: SINGLE MALES % OF TOTAL OUTLET					
	ADOL.–15	16–20	21–25	26–30	31–35	36–40
Educational Level 0–8						
Masturbation	52.26	29.15	20.15	20.68	24.24	28.95
Nocturnal emissions	1.82	4.83	5.02	6.26	5.49	5.97
Petting to climax	1.06	1.66	1.23	1.96	0.68	0.05
Intercourse with companions	35.00	50.62	52.84	42.71	23.74	23.08
Intercourse with prostitutes	0.97	6.21	12.55	14.34	18.42	23.35
Homosexual outlet	8.03	6.85	8.06	14.04	27.43	18.60
Animal contacts	0.86	0.68	0.15	0.01		
Total outlet	100.00	100.00	100.00	100.00	100.00	100.00
Number of cases	712	720	361	159	61	47
Total solitary outlets	54.08	33.98	25.17	26.94	29.73	34.92
Total heterosexual outlets	37.03	58.49	66.62	59.01	42.84	46.48
Total homosexual outlet	8.03	6.85	8.06	14.04	27.43	18.60
Educational Level 9–12						
Masturbation	59.09	37.17	29.67	27.69	18.48	
Nocturnal emissions	4.44	6.33	8.10	7.48	8.21	
Petting to climax	1.46	2.37	2.77	1.82	1.35	
Intercourse with companions	24.93	39.49	38.02	29.75	42.81	
Intercourse with prostitutes	0.44	2.75	4.66	6.46	10.32	
Homosexual outlet	8.73	10.81	16.31	25.95	18.83	
Animal contacts	0.91	1.08	0.47	0.85		
Total outlet	100.00	100.00	100.00	100.00	100.00	
Number of cases	606	607	263	117	41	
Total solitary outlets	63.53	43.50	37.77	35.17	26.69	
Total heterosexual outlets	26.83	44.61	45.45	38.03	54.48	
Total homosexual outlet	8.73	10.81	16.31	25.95	18.83	
Educational Level 13+						
Masturbation	79.61	66.37	53.30	45.88	44.28	
Nocturnal emissions	12.15	15.65	15.67	11.93	10.67	
Petting to climax	1.54	5.26	7.50	5.17	4.98	
Intercourse with companions	2.74	9.13	18.45	24.97	21.52	
Intercourse with prostitutes	0.11	0.80	1.27	3.16	0.65	
Homosexual outlet	3.14	2.43	3.72	8.82	17.90	
Animal contacts	0.71	0.36	0.09	0.07		
Total outlet	100.00	100.00	100.00	100.00	100.00	
Number of cases	2799	2861	1898	487	87	
Total solitary outlets	91.76	82.02	68.97	57.81	54.95	
Total heterosexual outlets	4.39	15.19	27.22	33.30	27.15	
Total homosexual outlet	3.14	2.43	3.72	8.82	17.90	

Table 96. Sources of sexual outlet for single males, at three educational levels
Showing percentages of total outlet derived by each group from each source.

among males of the college level, is more or less a substitute for actual coitus.

In the upper level code of sexual morality, there is nothing so important as the preservation of the virginity of the female and, to a somewhat lesser degree, the similar preservation of the virginity of the male until the time of marriage. The utilization of pre-marital petting at this level is fortified by the emphasis which the marriage manuals place upon the importance of pre-coital techniques in married relations; and the younger generation considers that its experience before marriage may contribute something to the development of satisfactory marital relations. Compared with coitus, petting has the advantage of being accessible under conditions where coitus would be impossible; it provides a simpler means of achieving both arousal and orgasm, it makes it possible to experience orgasm while avoiding the possibility of a pregnancy, and, above all, it preserves one's "virginity." Whether consciously or unconsciously, petting is chosen by the upper level because intercourse destroys virginity and is, therefore, unacceptable. It is significant to note what different values are attached, at that level, to erotic arousal and orgasm achieved through the union of genitalia, and to erotic arousal and orgasm achieved through physical contact of other portions of the body, or even through genital contact or genital manipulation which does not involve actual copulation. There are many males in the upper level who develop a fine art of achieving orgasm by petting techniques which avoid intercourse. The youth who may have experienced orgasm scores or hundreds of times in petting, and who may have utilized every type of petting technique, including mouth-genital contacts, still has the satisfaction of knowing that he is still a virgin, as his level defines virginity. There are even cases of males who effect genital union; but because they avoid orgasm while in such union they persuade themselves that they are still virgins. The illogic of the situation emphasizes the fact that the basic issue is one of conforming with a code (the avoidance of pre-marital intercourse, the preservation of one's virginity), which is of paramount importance in the mores of this social level.

The lower educational levels see no sense in this. They have nothing like this strong taboo against pre-marital intercourse and, on the contrary, accept it as natural and inevitable and a desirable thing. Lower level taboos are more often turned against an avoidance of intercourse, and against any substitution for simple and direct coitus. Petting involves a considerable list of techniques which may be acceptable to the college group, and to some degree to the high school group, but which are quite taboo at lower levels (as discussed above). It is just because petting involves these techniques, and because it substitutes for actual intercourse, that it is considered a perversion by the lower level.

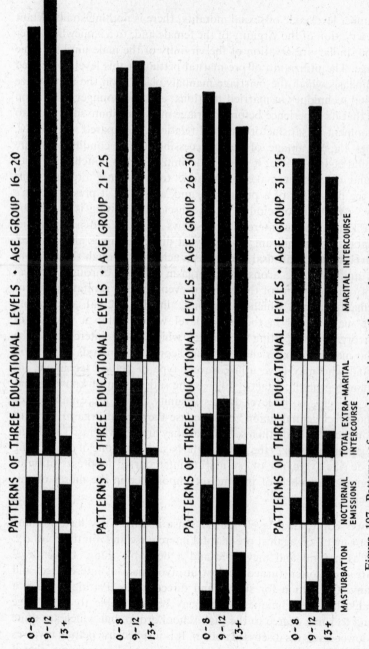

Figure 107. Patterns of sexual behavior at three educational levels, among married males

For 4 age groups. Each horizontal line extending across the page summarizes the pattern for one of the educational levels. Relative lengths of bars in each outlet show average mean frequencies for the group. The scales vary for different sources of outlet, but there is an approximate indication of the relative importance of each source in the total outlet.

In particular cases, older persons, even at upper levels, have objected to pre-marital petting; but individual objections do not have the force of long-established mores. Pre-marital intercourse is condemned by mores which go back hundreds and thousands of years. Such taboos are very different from the criticisms which lone individuals have levied against petting within the last few decades, and for the most part the younger generation has paid little attention to such criticisms.

There is nothing in the behavior of the upper level which is more responsible than petting is for the general opinion that college students are sexually wild. The lower level has many times as much pre-marital intercourse as the college male has, and it is not the intercourse of the college student which is the source of the lower level's criticism. It is the fact that petting may be engaged in for many hours without arriving at intercourse—it is the fact that intercourse itself is not more often accepted as a pre-marital outlet by the upper social level.

Pre-marital Intercourse. With the upper educational level, the question of pre-marital intercourse is largely one of morals. Some of the younger generation find it modern to insist that they do not avoid pre-marital intercourse because it is wrong, but because they consider intercourse too precious to have with anyone except the girl that they marry, or because they consider that marriages work out better when there has been no pre-marital intercourse. To this extent the younger generation is "emancipated"; but the change in the form of its rationalizations has not affected its overt behavior one whit (Chapter 11).

A large portion of the 85 per cent of the population which never goes to college accepts pre-marital intercourse as normal and natural. Most of this group would insist that there is no question of right or wrong involved. Even some lower level clergymen, of the group that has never gone beyond grade school or high school, may react as the rest of the community of which they are a part, preaching against profanity, smoking, drinking, gambling, and extra-marital intercourse, but considering that no moral issue is involved in pre-marital intercourse. So nearly universal is pre-marital intercourse among grade school groups that in two or three lower level communities in which we have worked we have been unable to find a solitary male who had not had sexual relations with girls by the time he was 16 or 17 years of age. In such a community, the occasional boy who has not had intercourse by that age is either physically incapacitated, mentally deficient, homosexual, or ear-marked for moving out of his community and going to college.

Lower level males may have a certain respect for virginity, and this may lead them to insist (in 41 per cent of the cases) that they would not marry a girl who had had previous intercourse (Table 92); but this may be more of a profession than a matter on which they will stand when it comes to the

SOURCES	SOURCES OF ORGASM: MARRIED MALES % OF TOTAL OUTLET						
	16–20	21–25	26–30	31–35	36–40	41–45	46–50
Educational Level 0–8							
Masturbation	2.40	2.43	2.44	1.79	1.59	1.41	1.4
Nocturnal emissions	3.08	2.79	3.41	3.03	1.85	2.25	2.6
Intercourse, marital	79.92	81.03	86.15	88.07	88.09	89.96	89.9
Interc., extra-m., comp.	10.91	11.62	6.38	5.51	7.24	4.84	4.7
Interc., extra-m., prost.	0.61	0.80	1.16	1.46	0.93	1.46	1.4
Homosexual outlet	3.08	1.33	0.46	0.14	0.30	0.08	0.0
Total outlet	100.00	100.00	100.00	100.00	100.00	100.00	100.0
Number of cases	158	324	292	186	143	100	70
Total solitary outlets	5.48	5.22	5.85	4.82	3.44	3.66	4.0
Total hetero. outlets	91.44	93.45	93.69	95.04	96.26	96.26	96.0
Total homo. outlet	3.08	1.33	0.46	0.14	0.30	0.08	0.0
Educational Level 9–12							
Masturbation	2.75	3.70	5.05	4.04	3.15	1.68	2.8
Nocturnal emissions	2.04	2.85	3.22	3.79	4.48	5.29	2.9
Intercourse, marital	82.19	81.56	81.67	85.18	88.19	89.18	91.0
Interc., extra-m., comp.	9.43	9.35	7.61	4.62	1.76	3.15	3.1
Interc., extra-m., prost.	1.48	1.49	1.49	0.99	1.69	0.70	0.2
Homosexual outlet	2.11	1.05	0.96	1.38	0.73		
Total outlet	100.00	100.00	100.00	100.00	100.00	100.00	100.0
Number of cases	87	164	135	82	58	34	24
Total solitary outlets	4.79	6.55	8.27	7.83	7.63	6.97	5.7
Total hetero. outlets	93.10	92.40	90.77	90.79	91.64	93.03	94.3
Total homo. outlet	2.11	1.05	0.96	1.38	0.73		
Educational Level 13+							
Masturbation	8.53	8.79	8.67	9.28	8.26	9.71	9.0
Nocturnal emissions	2.99	4.65	4.69	5.71	6.06	5.87	5.4
Intercourse, marital	85.41	83.94	82.76	78.34	74.41	76.39	68.5
Interc., extra-m., comp.	2.86	1.86	2.72	5.51	9.85	6.07	13.7
Interc., extra-m., prost.	0.05	0.23	0.20	0.41	0.53	0.32	0.4
Homosexual outlet	0.16	0.53	0.96	0.75	0.89	1.64	3.0
Total outlet	100.00	100.00	100.00	100.00	100.00	100.00	100.0
Number of cases	46	440	532	301	189	138	81
Total solitary outlets	11.52	13.44	13.36	14.99	14.32	15.58	14.4
Total hetero. outlets	88.32	86.03	85.68	84.26	84.79	82.78	82.6
Total homo. outlet	0.16	0.53	0.96	0.75	0.89	1.64	3.0

Table 97. Sources of sexual outlet for married males, at three educational levels

Showing percentages of total outlet derived by each group from each source.

actual choice of a mate. Lower level males are likely to acquire weekly or more than weekly frequencies in intercourse soon after they start in early adolescence, or at least by the middle teens. They are often highly promiscuous in their choice of pre-marital partners, and there are many who have no interest in having intercourse with the same girl more than once. This strikingly parallels the promiscuity which is found among those homosexual males who are "oncers," as the vernacular term puts it. Some lower level males may have pre-marital intercourse with several hundred or even a thousand or more different girls before marriage, and here their behavior is most different from the behavior of the college-bred males.

Extra-marital Intercourse. In lower social levels there is a somewhat bitter acceptance of the idea that the male is basically promiscuous and that he is going to have extra-marital intercourse, whether or not his wife or society objects. There is some continuation of the group attitude on pre-marital intercourse into the realm of extra-marital intercourse, at least in the early years of marriage. On the other hand, the upper level male who has been heterosexually restrained for 10 or 15 years before marriage does not freely let down and start extra-marital intercourse as soon as he has learned to have coitus with his wife. As a matter of fact, a male who has been so restrained often has difficulty in working out a sexual adjustment with his wife, and it is doubtful whether very many of the upper level males would have any facility in finding extra-marital intercourse, even if they were to set out deliberately after it. The lower level's extra-marital intercourse does cause trouble, but we do not yet understand all the factors which account for the fact that with advancing age there is a steady decline and finally a near disappearance of extra-marital intercourse from lower level marital histories (Chapter 7).

The development of extra-marital intercourse in the histories of the older males of the upper level (Chapter 7) is done with a certain deliberation which in some cases may be acceded to and encouraged by the wife.

Homosexual Contacts. The considerable differences which exist in the incidences and frequencies of the homosexual in the three educational levels (Table 90) would seem to indicate basic differences in attitudes toward such activity; but we are not sure that we yet understand what these differences are.

The fewest objections to the homosexual are found in the very lowest of the social levels, in the best educated groups, and in top society. At the lowest social levels sex, whether it be heterosexual or homosexual, is more or less accepted as inevitable. The children here are the least restrained sexually and usually become involved in both heterosexual and homosexual activities at an early age (Chapter 5). Since this is the group in which pre-adolescent behavior most often carries over into adult behavior

(Table 29), it is not surprising to find a fair number of the males at this level continuing both types of activity through the major portion of their lives. It is notable, however, that there are few individuals in this group who become exclusively homosexual. There are some who definitely condemn the homosexual, but there are many who accept it simply as one more form of sex. Rarely do they interfere with other persons who are involved, even though they themselves may not enter into such activities.

The acceptance of the homosexual in top educational and social levels is the product of a wider understanding of realities, some comprehension of the factors involved, and more concern over the mental qualities and social capacities of an individual than over anything in his sexual history.

The highest incidences of the homosexual, however, are in the group which most often verbalizes its disapproval of such activity. This is in the group that goes into high school but never beyond in its educational career. These are the males who most often condemn the homosexual, most often ridicule and express disgust for such activity, and most often punish other males for their homosexuality. And yet, this is the group which has the largest amount of overt homosexual activity. Their involvement may be due to curiosity, to the fact that one may profit financially by accepting homosexual relations, or to the fact that one may derive a sadistic satisfaction from beating up the partner after orgasm has been achieved in the homosexual activity. In a certain segment of this group the idea is more or less accepted that one may uphold the heterosexual mores while "playing the queers," provided one punishes them after orgasm is achieved in the homosexual relation. As a group these males may strenuously deny that their sexual contacts have anything to do with homosexuality; but the full and complete record indicates that many of them have stronger psychic reactions to other males than they care to admit. When they no longer find themselves being paid for such contacts, many of them begin paying other males for the privilege of sexual relations.

If there are group attitudes in regard to the homosexual, they are not as freely discussed at most social levels. It may be that this explains why community thinking is not so well crystallized on this subject as it is in regard to other forms of sexual activity.

SOCIAL IMPLICATIONS

Each social level is convinced that its pattern is the best of all patterns; but each level rationalizes its behavior in its own way.

The upper level rationalizes on the basis of what is right or wrong. For this group, all socio-sexual behavior becomes a moral issue. Morality and sexual morality become more or less synonymous terms. Many persons at this level believe that there are few types of immorality which are more enormous than sexual immorality. Proper, straight, upright, honorable, clean, fine, wholesome, manly, and pure refer primarily to abstinence from socio-sexual relations. Their opposites refer to participation in non-marital sexual relations. Honor, fidelity, and success in marriage are understood to involve the complete absorption of the individual's sexual urge in coitus with his wife. There is nothing of which persons at this level are more afraid than a charge of immorality, as immorality is defined by the group. There is no disgrace that is more feared than that which may result from sexual scandal. Sex is so clearly a moral issue that many persons in the group consider it a religious obligation to impose their code upon all other segments of the population.

Lower social levels, on the contrary, rationalize their patterns of sexual behavior on the basis of what is natural or unnatural. Pre-marital intercourse is natural, and it is, in consequence, acceptable. Masturbation is not natural, nor is petting as a substitute for intercourse, nor even petting as a preliminary to intercourse.

There are some individuals at lower levels who do see moral issues in sexual behavior, but by and large even they recognize that nature will triumph over morals. They may "know that intercourse is wrong," but "they expect to have it anyway, because it is human and natural to have it." It is not at all unusual to find middle class persons who have had intercourse with scores or even hundreds of girls, still insisting that they would never marry a girl who was not a virgin (Table 92). If the upper level male departs from his code and has intercourse, he is most likely to have it with the fiancée. His excuse is that "it is not wrong when love is involved." The middle class or lower level male, on the contrary, may frankly state that "I didn't think anything of her, so we had intercourse. But when I find the girl that I really love, I won't touch her until I marry her." To many persons in the upper level, and to some in the middle class, the moral issues are matters of divine revelation and mandate. As a fundamentalist professor of philosophy put it, "There are some things that one innately understands to be right or wrong, and about which there is no need for logical discussion."

For both upper and lower levels, these matters do lie deeper than logic. There are, in consequence, no rational arguments, no cool discussions, no initial presentations of data, no investigations after the fact when diverse sexual patterns come into conflict. Like matters of religion, the mores are simply accepted and defended. For many persons, the mores are even more implicit than religious tenets. The arguments that are produced in their defense are the veriest sorts of rationalizations. If they cannot be defended in any other way, they are accepted as products of the experience of the past which has culminated in the wisdom of the present custom.

Most of the tragedies that develop out of sexual activities are products of this conflict between the attitudes of different social levels. Sexual activities in themselves rarely do physical damage, but disagreements over the significance of sexual behavior may result in personality conflicts, a loss of social standing, imprisonment, disgrace, and the loss of life itself.

In Clinical Practice. Wherever professionally trained persons try to direct the behavior of lower level individuals, conflicts are likely to arise because of these diverse sexual philosophies. Clinicians of all groups, including physicians, clinical psychologists, school psychologists, nurses, psychiatrists—particularly if they work in public clinics—have a portion and sometimes a major portion of their contacts with lower social levels. The sexual advice which the upper level clinician gives will mean most when it takes into account the background of the community from which the client comes. The upper level physician or nurse who expects the lower level patient to disrobe for physical examination should understand that he outrages the mores of the group in which the patient has been raised. The physician who mixes moral advice with his medical prescription should realize that the applicability of his advice will vary with the social level from which the patient comes. The woman physician in a prison may never become reconciled to the fact that every one of the inmates in the institution proves to have had coital experience before reaching the institution; but she must comprehend that her effectiveness as a physician is impaired when she proffers moral advice which has no relation to the realities of the world from which the inmate comes.

Marriage counseling, as set up today, is based upon concepts of marriage, goals, and ideals which may appear right to the educational level from which the marriage counselors come, and from which most of the counselor's clients also come, but which mean something else in the communities from which a lower level client may come. The sexual techniques which marriage councils and marriage manuals recommend are designed to foster the sort of intellectual eroticism which the upper level esteems. It depends on prolonged pre-coital play, a considerable variety in techniques, a maximum of stimulation before coital union, some delay after effecting such union, and, finally, orgasm which is simultaneous for the male and the female. Most of this, however, would be anathema to a large portion of the population, and an outrage to their mores. Many marriage counselors would like to impose their own upper level patterns on their clients, without regard to the complications which may develop when an individual is educated into something that puts him at discord with the mores of the society in which he was raised and in which he may still be living.

In industry, some of the conflicts which arise between the better educated management and the more poorly educated labor may depend on failures to comprehend the diverse sexual patterns which are involved. Trained persons are increasingly used for personnel staffs in industrial plants. These persons, however, are not always aware of the viewpoints of lower level groups. Personnel managers, social workers, psychologists, physicians who try to comprehend and accept the patterns by which these other levels live, might aid in establishing a better rapport between labor and management.

In Social Service. Wherever people of different social levels come into contact, conflicts between sexual patterns, and failures to understand the patterns of other groups and the philosophies that lie back of them, provide considerable impediments to any cooperation between the groups. Administrators of institutions need to understand the patterns of the communities from which their inmate populations come. This is especially true in penal institutions, in homes for the feeble-minded, in children's homes, in homes for the aged, in hospitals, and in other institutions whose populations come mostly from lower social levels. Heads of boarding schools and of colleges are not so often concerned with this problem, because their populations come largely from their own social level; but teachers in public grade schools and in public high schools are regularly confronted with the problem of understanding cultures other than their own. The unmarried college graduate who is an eighth grade teacher will find it difficult to understand how her eighth grade boy, from the laborer's or mechanic's home, could be so evil as to have had intercourse with one of her fourteen-year old girls. Her reaction, based upon her upper level standards, may result in the boy's expulsion from school, and in public disgrace for both the boy and the girl. The teacher does not realize that more than a fourth (28%) of all her other eighth grade boys have similarly had intercourse (Table 136). The boy who was caught might have been handled differently if the teacher had known more about the boy's background.

Social workers are involved with sexual problems even more often than physicians. There are cases of pre-marital pregnancies, of rape, of divorce resulting from sexual conflicts between the parents of the children in whom the social worker is interested. There may be coitus, and sometimes incestuous relations, between the children and the adults in the community. These last are things that may offend the community as well as the social worker. But everywhere the social worker runs into a record of sexual contacts among children, pre-marital intercourse, and extra-marital intercourse; and although the community accepts these things as inevitable, the social worker sees the behavior in terms of her own mores, and may be outraged and vindictive in her reactions. She may refuse welfare allowances to a family in which there is such "delinquency." In many cases, it is the welfare worker who brings the case of sexual activity to the attention of the court. Often it is she who initiates the moves to have such "neglected" children taken away from their parents and made wards of the court, for placement in other families or in children's homes or in juvenile disciplinary institutions. The untrained, less educated individual who enters social work, particularly in smaller communities, sometimes has a better understanding of the realities of these lower level groups. Some of the graduates of some of the better schools for social workers may also have some comprehension of these differences between levels. The least comprehending are the well intentioned, upper level women who turn to social work as a contribution to civic welfare. Some of the most poorly understood groups are in lower level Negro communities, and it takes a social worker who is capable of comprehending a great deal more than her own social level to work effectively with such a group. It is sometimes suggested that Negro communities should be handled only by Negro social workers; but educated, upper level Negroes may have as little comprehension of a lower level Negro community's attitudes as upper level white persons would have. In fact, the upper level Negro worker may be even more intent upon "raising" the pattern of the lower level community, in a move designed to bring credit to Negroes as a race.

In the Army and Navy. Officers in the Army and Navy are faced with the problem of dealing with persons of diverse social levels who are brought together into a single, closely knit community. Since most of the population has not gone beyond the tenth grade in school, most of the men in the armed forces have lower level patterns of sexual behavior. Some of the officers come out of the ranks and comprehend these patterns. Professionally trained officers who are products of West Point or Annapolis, or of some other special school, are more likely to come from better educated levels. Some of the incongruities which exist between Army and Navy rules and the administration of those rules are products of these differences in the backgrounds of officers and enlisted men. American armies of occupation have found themselves in cultures that are different from our own in their attitudes on matters of sex. The upper level officer who establishes the law for the country he is temporarily ruling may try to impose "moral standards" which reflect the mores of only a limited portion of our American population, upon the whole of a foreign people who have none of the sexual patterns of any of our social levels.

During times of peace, the better educated segments of the population are sufficiently isolated to be unaware of the sexual patterns in the mass of the population. In times of war, when these upper level groups are suddenly thrust into close contact with these other levels, they are startled to discover the realities of human behavior. They are inclined to blame all of the sexual activity which enlisted men have upon the organization of the Army and Navy itself. The specific data which we have indicate that very few of the men in the armed forces are as active sexually as they would have been at home in times of peace, but the upper level, especially the older generation of the upper level, is unaware of this. Considerable pressure, in consequence, is brought upon military officials to establish and enforce rules, and upon Congress to enact laws which are designed to force all of the heterogeneous group which constitutes a draft army into an upper level pattern of sexual behavior. The demand is fortified by an emphasis upon the dangers of venereal disease; but it is certain that many of the persons who discuss disease are more concerned over the morals of the men for whom the government has suddenly become responsible. Such an issue could be grasped more intelligently if more people understood the origins of the sexual patterns of the men in uniform.

In Everyday Contacts. In general, the upper level feels that "lower level morality" lacks the ideals and the righteousness of the upper level philosophy. The lower level, on the other hand, feels that educated and upper level society has an artificial and insincere pattern of sexual behavior which is all the more obnoxious because the upper level tries to force its pattern upon all other levels. Legends about the immorality of the lower level are matched by legends about the perversions of the upper level. One is inclined to accept the particular legends that apply to the group to which one does not belong. Such legends reach their maximum proportions when they concern whole racial or national groups: "The French do this, the Chinese do that." Primitive peoples and pagans are always believed to be aberrant in their sexual lives. There are exaggerated legends concerning the Negro's sexual behavior, and Negro leaders are much disturbed over such popular beliefs (Cobb 1947). Sexual propaganda against the Jews as a race was a cornerstone of the Hitlerian attack on that group in Germany. Both Nazi and Japanese propaganda included attacks on the sexual behavior of Americans at home. There are traditions concerning the sexual behavior of the Italian, Spanish, Latin American, and other groups, even though there are no objective data to establish any generalizations. There are, of course, endless variations in sexual patterns in each of these populations, just as there are in our own American population. What data we have so far on these other groups indicate that there is at least some stratification of social levels in all of them; and this would lead one to presuppose that each group would, therefore, have a variety of sexual patterns.

In the Law. Anglo-American sex laws are a codification of the sexual mores of the better educated portion of the population. While they are rooted in the English common law, their maintenance and defense lie chiefly in the hands of state legislators and judges who, for the most part, come from better-educated levels.

Consequent on this fact, the written codes severely penalize all nonmarital intercourse, whether it occurs before or after marriage; but they do not make masturbation a crime, even though there are a few courts which have tried to read such interpretations into the law (Chapter 8).

However, the enforcement of the law is placed in the hands of police officials who come largely from grade school and high school segments of the population. For that reason, the laws against non-marital intercourse are rarely and only capriciously enforced, and then most often when upper level individuals demand such police action. It is difficult for a lower level policeman or detective to feel that much of a crime is being committed when he finds a boy and a girl involved in the sort of sexual activity which was part of his own adolescent history, and which he knows was in the histories of most of the youth in the community in which he was raised. If the behavior involves persons against whom the policeman has a grudge (probably for some totally non-sexual reason), if the relation involves too public an exhibition, if it involves a contact between a much older and a younger person (which under the policeman's code is more or less taboo), if it involves a relation between persons belonging to different racial groups (which under his code may be exceedingly taboo), then the laws against pre-marital intercourse become convenient tools for punishing these other activities. But if it is the routine sort of relationship that the officer very well knows occurs regularly in the lower level community, then he may pay little attention to the enforcement of the laws. The policeman's behavior may appear incongruous or hypocritical to the citizen from the other side of the town, but it is based on a comprehension of realities of which the other citizen is not often aware. There are policemen who frankly state that they consider it one of their functions to keep the judge from knowing things that he simply does not understand.

On the other hand, if it is the case of a boy who is found masturbating in a back alley, the policeman is likely to push the case through court and see that the boy is sent to an institution for indecent exposure, for moral degeneracy, or for perversion. When the boy arrives in the reformatory, the small-town sheriff may send a letter urging that the administration of the institution pay especial attention to curing the boy of the perversion. However, the educated superintendent of the institution is not much impressed by the problem, and he may explain to the boy that masturbation does him no harm, even though the law penalizes him for his public exposure. The superintendent may let it be known among his officers that masturbation seems to him to be a more acceptable form of sexual outlet than the homosexual activity which involves some of the inmates of the institution, and he may even believe that he has actually provided for the sexual needs of his wards by making such a ruling. On the other hand, the guards in the institution, who are the officials most often in contact with the inmates, have lower level backgrounds and lower level attitudes toward masturbation. In consequence, they continue to punish inmates who are discovered masturbating as severely as they would punish them for homosexual activity.

On sex cases, the decisions of the judge on the bench are often affected by the mores of the group from which he originated. Judges often come from better educated groups, and their severe condemnation of sex offenders is largely a defense of the code of their own social level. Lower level individuals simply do not understand the bitter denunciations which many a judge heaps upon the lower level boy or girl who has been involved in sexual relations. They cannot see why behavior which, to them, seems perfectly natural and humanly inevitable should be punishable under the law. For them, there is no majesty in laws which are as unrealistic as the sex laws. Life is a maze. The sex laws and the upper level persons who defend them are simply hazards about which one has to learn to find his way. Like the rough spots in a sidewalk, or the traffic on a street, the sex laws are things that one learns to negotiate without getting into too much trouble; but that is no reason why one should not walk on sidewalks, or cross streets, or have sexual relations.

The influence of the mores is strikingly shown by a study of the decisions which are reached by judges with different social backgrounds. There is still a portion of the legal profession that has not gone to college and, particularly where judges are elected by popular vote, there are some instances of judges who have originated in lower social levels and acquired their legal training by office apprenticeship or night school courses. The significance of the background becomes most apparent when two judges, one of upper level and one of lower level, sit in alternation on the same bench. The record of the upper level judge may involve convictions and maximum sentences in a high proportion of the sex cases, particularly those that involve non-marital intercourse or prostitution. The judge with the lower level background may convict in only a small fraction of the cases. The lower level community recognizes these differences between judges, and expresses the hope that when it is brought to trial it will come before the second judge, because "he understands." The experienced attorney similarly sees to it that his case is set for trial when the understanding judge is on the bench. Parole officers and social workers who investigate cases before they are decided in court may have a good deal to do with setting a particular case before a particular judge, in order to get a verdict that accords with the philosophy of their (the parole officers') background.

Judges who are ignorant of the way in which the other three-quarters of the population lives, naively believe that the police officials are apprehending all of those who are involved in any material infraction of the sex laws. If the community has been aroused by a sex case which has involved a forceful rape or a death following a sexual relation, the judge may lead the other public officials in demanding the arrest of all sex offenders in the community. Newspapers goad the police, and there is likely to be a wave of arrests and convictions which carry maximum sentences, until the wide scope of the problem becomes apparent to even the most unrealistic official. It will be recalled that 85 per cent of the total male population has pre-marital intercourse (Table 136), 59 per cent has some experience in mouth-genital contacts (Table 94), nearly 70 per cent has relations with prostitutes (Table 138), something between 30 and 45 per cent has extra-marital intercourse (Tables 85, 111), 37 per cent has some homosexual experience (Table 139), 17 per cent of the farm boys have animal inter-course (Table 151). All of these, and still other types of sexual behavior (Chapter 8), are illicit activities, each performance of which is punishable as a crime under the law. The persons involved in these activities, taken as a whole, constitute more than 95 per cent of the total male population. Only a relatively small proportion of the males who are sent to penal institutions for sex offenses have been involved in behavior which is materially different from the behavior of most of the males in the population. But it is the total 95 per cent of the male population for which the judge, or board of public safety, or church, or civic group demands apprehension, arrest, and conviction, when they call for a clean-up of the sex offenders in a community. It is, in fine, a proposal that 5 per cent of the population should support the other 95 per cent in penal institutions. The only possible defense of the proposal is the fact that the judge, the civic leader, and most of the others who make such suggestions, come from that segment of the population which is most restrained on nearly all types of sexual behavior, and they simply do not understand how the rest of the population actually lives.

The penalties visited upon persons who are convicted of sex offense may be peculiarly severe, just because the judge does not comprehend the lower level background of the offender. The judge may give a long sentence because he believes that such a stay in prison will reform the ways of the particular individual who is being punished; but again he fails to understand the deep origins of sexual behavior. Data which we have on more than 1200 persons who have been convicted of sex offenses indicate that there are very few who modify their sexual patterns as a result of their contacts with the law, or, indeed, as a result of anything that happens to them after they have passed their middle teens. This is not because convicted sex offenders are peculiarly degenerate or different from the mass of the population. It is simply because all persons have their sexual patterns laid down for them by the custom of the communities in which they are raised.

The sex offender is a marked individual in the penal institution to which he is sent. He is lectured on the heinous nature of his crime by the prison official who receives him, even though in many cases he has not been involved in sex behavior which is fundamentally different from that of the institutional official himself. There is a mystery connected with the nature of the specific sexual activity for which a sex offender is convicted, and this brings emotional reactions from all persons concerned.

When it comes to a question of releasing sex offenders, parole boards are loath to take action. The inmate is judged by the standards of the upper level community from which most parole board members come. Women on prison boards are especially likely to come from a social level where the loss of virginity before marriage is an unforgivable moral offense. The girl whose future they are deciding comes from a community where three-fourths of the girls have intercourse before marriage. Persons who attempt to control the behavior of other persons might more properly be concerned with determining the extent of the departure of the individual from the behavior of the community of which he is a part.

Conflicts between social levels are as intense as the conflicts between nations, between cultures, between races, and between the most extreme of the religious groups. The existence of the conflict between sexual patterns is, however, not recognized by the parties immediately concerned, because neither of them understands the diversity of patterns which exist at different social levels. Each thinks that he is in a conflict with a particular individual. He is, however, more often in conflict with a whole culture.

SOCIAL LEVELS AMONG NEGROES

As already explained, we do not yet have enough histories of Negroes to warrant their inclusion in the analyses that have been made in the present volume. Any fair comparison of Negroes and whites will have to be made for groups that are homogeneous in regard to age, education, social level, religious background, and still other factors. It is impossible to generalize concerning the behavior of a whole race. Analyses of any complex population, to be scientific, must be confined to particular segments of that population. Preliminary findings show that there are as many patterns of behavior among Negroes of different social levels as there are among whites. It is already clear that Negro and white patterns for comparable social levels are close if not identical. Since erroneous conclusions to the contrary have been drawn by certain persons who have seen some of our data prior to publication, it is important to emphasize here that final generalizations will be warranted only after a sufficient body of histories has been obtained at each and every social level among Negro groups.

Chapter 11

STABILITY OF SEXUAL PATTERNS

Before going further in discussing the stability of patterns of sexual behavior, it should be emphasized again (as in Chapter 10) that there is, inevitably, a considerable variation among the individuals in any social group. This variation involves the frequencies of total sexual outlet, the choice of activities in which each individual may engage, and his frequencies in each type of activity. There is similar variation in attitudes on all other matters of sex.

The frequency curves (*e.g.*, in Chapters 14 to 21) show how far individuals in any particular educational level or occupational class may depart from the averages which are the bases for most of the discussions in the present chapters on social levels. These same curves, however, show that 80 to 85 per cent of each population is likely to lie within an area close to the calculated means or medians. This is true for each of the outlets involved; but if an individual is rather far removed from the average in regard to any one outlet, he is still likely to fit the generalizations made for his group for most of the other outlets. He is much less likely to depart from the pattern of his social group in regard to each and all of the individual outlets.

How often individuals conform in every regard, how often they depart in some respects, how often they are in discord with their social group on all items, are matters which we shall have to follow up with more precise calculations at some later date. For the present we shall have to be satisfied with comparisons of such general pictures as may be recognized for whole groups, through calculations of means, medians, incidences, and other statistics.

PATTERNS IN SUCCESSIVE GENERATIONS

In order to ascertain how much stability there may be in patterns of sexual behavior, and something of the changes that may occur in patterns within the lives of individuals and between successive generations of individuals, we have made two sorts of calculations for the present chapter. The first has involved a comparison of the incidences and average frequencies in two generations of the same educational level. The second has concerned the patterns of behavior of individuals, compared with the patterns of behavior in the occupational classes to which their parents belonged and in which these individuals have either stayed or from which they have moved into some other occupational class.

Many persons, of course, believe that patterns of sexual behavior have changed considerably within the last generation or two. Some persons seem to find a masochistic satisfaction in believing that the world is continuously becoming more evil. The upper level critic believes that the younger generation is having an increasing amount of pre-marital intercourse, that fewer men are faithful to their wives, that promiscuous petting, embodying mysteries which older persons do not well understand, is lowering standards among youth, and that more unmentionable things are steadily on the increase (*e.g.*, Cooper 1939, Rice 1946, McPartland 1947). The lower level critic has fewer opportunities to voice his opinions in print, but he is as certain that young people are sexually more precocious, and (above all) he is convinced that the younger generation of the better educated segment of the population is becoming perverted beyond all previous imagining. As already indicated (Chapter 10), "perversion," to this lower level, refers to masturbation in an adult, involvement in petting, oral eroticism, the use of variety in coital positions, and the homosexual.

If it were not for the fact that there have been similar Cassandras throughout the history of the world, one could almost be persuaded to believe that these persons possessed scientifically adequate data on the sexual behavior of previous generations, which they have been able to compare with equally adequate data on the behavior of the present generation. There is, certainly, a considerable amount of sexual literature which has been kept carefully concealed from laymen and scientists alike; but it is also to be emphasized that nine years of research has failed to disclose statistically sound data which would justify any objective comparison of the behavior of any previous generation with the present one. One is inclined to suspect that the amazement of the older generation at the present-day behavior is dependent, at least in part, upon the fact that the older generation knew very little about the behavior of the world in which it lived when it was young, and that it has only more recently become acquainted with the long-established facts of life. Certainly it becomes highly desirable to confine any statements about trends in sexual behavior to such generalizations as can be established by statistically adequate data.

We have, therefore, undertaken to make a precise comparison of the older and younger generations which have contributed to the present study. We have divided the entire male sample into two groups of more or less equal size. One group has included all of those persons who were 33 years of age or older at the time they contributed their histories. Its median age is 43.1 years. The other group has included all the cases of persons who were younger than 33 at the time of contributing. Its median age is 21.2 years. The difference between the median ages of the two groups is about

22 years. The older group represents the generation that was in its youth and therefore sexually most active from 1910 to 1925. These are the individuals who fought World War I and were responsible for the reputation of the "roaring twenties." It is quite generally believed by many people that this was a period of such sexual laxity as America is supposed never to have known before (Allen 1931). Nevertheless, this is the generation that is quite convinced that youth today is still wilder in its behavior. Most of the younger group used in the present calculation was at its peak of activity between 1930 and the present time.

A more precise comparison would involve a successive breakdown of the population according to the year in which each individual was born, and a grouping into generations separated by twenty-year spans. This finer analysis is not possible with the number of histories now at hand, but should be undertaken as this project expands.

Comparisons of Accumulative Incidences. Tables 98 to 103 and Figures 108 to 121 compare the accumulative incidence data for the older and younger segments of the population in regard to masturbation, nocturnal emissions, pre-marital petting experience, petting to the point of orgasm, total pre-marital intercourse, pre-marital intercourse with prostitutes, extra-marital intercourse, and the homosexual. Tables 104–105 and Figures 122–123 show the average frequencies and the active incidences in comparable age periods and at comparable social levels of the older and the younger segments of the population.

An examination of the accumulative incidence curves (Figures 108–114) will show that the number of persons ultimately involved, and the ages at which they became involved, are almost exactly the same for the older and the younger generations in the following groups and for the following types of behavior:

> College level—masturbation
> College level—nocturnal emissions
> College level—heterosexual intercourse
> College level—total pre-marital intercourse
> College level—intercourse with prostitutes
> Grade school level—intercourse with prostitutes
> College level—homosexual outlet

Comparisons of the accumulative incidence curves (Figures 115, 116) indicate that the same number of persons is ultimately involved in the two generations, but that the younger generation appears to become active a year or two earlier, in the following cases:

> Grade school level—heterosexual intercourse
> Grade school level—pre-marital intercourse

Comparisons of the accumulative incidence curves (Figures 117–121) indicate that more individuals of the younger generation are involved, and that these individuals begin their activity at an earlier age, in the following cases:

> College level—petting experience
> College level—petting to climax
> Grade school level—masturbation
> Grade school level—nocturnal emissions
> Grade school level—petting experience

In general, the sexual patterns of the younger generation are so nearly identical with the sexual patterns of the older generation in regard to so many types of sexual activity that there seems to be no sound basis for the widespread opinion that the younger generation has become more active in its socio-sexual contacts. The only instances in which a larger number of the younger generation is involved at an earlier age apply to such activities (masturbation, nocturnal emissions, and petting) as are not ordinarily considered when the charge is made that the younger generation is becoming increasingly immoral. The charge more often concerns pre-marital intercourse with companions and with prostitutes, and homosexual contacts. On all of these latter points, however, the records for the older and the younger generation are, by the admission of the older generation when it contributes its own histories, so nearly identical that no significant differences can be found in the accumulative incidence curves. And as for the homosexual, if a larger number of the younger generation is becoming involved, we have failed to find any evidence of it. These questions are of such social significance that it is high time that scientific data replace the loose statements and easy conclusions drawn by persons who find some sort of advantage in bewailing the ways of the world.

It is notable that in those instances where the younger generation seems to become involved at an earlier age, it is the lower educational level that is concerned, and this is probably the product of the better sanitation, better medical care, and better standards of nutrition which have brought improvements in the general health of that group within the last thirty years. It will be recalled (Chapter 5) that there is evidence that the younger generation of the lower social level is becoming adolescent a year or so sooner than the boys of the same level a generation or two ago. There is no evidence that the better educated portion of the population is becoming adolescent any earlier, probably because the upper level was not so poorly nourished in the past.

Finally, it should be emphasized that the younger generation has materially modified its behavior only in respect to items (masturbation and petting) which were first accepted by the upper social levels, whose attitudes

398   SEXUAL BEHAVIOR IN THE HUMAN MALE

	ACCUMULATIVE INCIDENCE, TWO GENERATIONS EDUCATIONAL LEVEL 13+							
	MASTURBATION				NOCTURNAL EMISSIONS			
AGE	Older Generation		Younger Generation		Older Generation		Younger Generation	
	Cases	% with Exper.	Cases	% with Exper.	Cases	% with Exper.	Cases	% with Exper.
8	382	0.0	2433	0.0	381	0.0	2430	0.0
9	382	0.5	2433	0.3	381	0.0	2430	0.0
10	382	2.9	2433	2.2	381	0.0	2430	0.6
11	382	9.9	2433	8.8	381	3.9	2430	3.0
12	382	22.8	2433	28.6	381	12.9	2430	11.4
13	382	47.9	2433	53.7	381	32.5	2430	28.6
14	382	72.5	2433	72.2	381	57.7	2430	51.3
15	382	78.5	2433	80.5	381	73.5	2430	68.2
16	382	83.2	2432	84.4	381	85.3	2429	80.0
17	382	85.6	2430	87.2	381	89.5	2427	86.7
18	382	88.0	2354	89.1	381	91.6	2351	90.9
19	382	88.7	2190	90.3	381	92.7	2187	92.6
20	382	90.6	1955	91.2	381	94.2	1952	93.5
21	382	91.1	1649	92.2	381	95.3	1646	94.3
22	382	92.1	1288	93.0	381	95.8	1287	94.4
23	382	92.7	1014	93.6	381	96.1	1014	94.4
24	382	92.7	769	93.4	381	96.9	769	95.2
25	382	93.2	620	94.4	381	97.9	620	95.2
26	382	93.7	502	95.8	381	97.9	502	95.4
27	382	94.5	392	96.2	381	97.9	392	94.6
28	382	94.8	317	95.9	381	97.9	317	95.0
29	382	94.8	252	95.2	381	97.9	252	95.2
30	382	95.3	191	96.3	381	98.4	191	94.8
31	382	95.3	147	95.2	381	98.4	147	94.6
32	382	95.5	110	95.5	381	98.4	110	94.5
33	382	95.5	66	93.9	381	98.4	66	92.4

Table 98. Comparisons of older and younger generations of the college level: masturbation, and nocturnal emissions

Accumulative incidence data based on the life span. Median difference of age between the two generations is 22 years.

seem to have infiltrated into the younger generation of the lower level today. There is considerable evidence at many other points that ideas and attitudes may be modified long before there are differences in overt behavior, and especially in overt socio-sexual contacts.

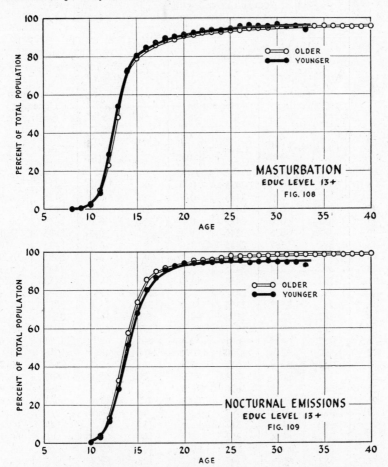

Figures 108–109. Comparisons of accumulative incidence for older and younger generations of college level: masturbation, nocturnal emissions

Showing percentage of males with experience at any time in the life-span. Median age difference between the two generations is 22 years.

Comparisons of Frequencies. In regard to frequencies in each of these types of sexual activity, the comparisons of the two generations are more complex. An examination of Table 104 and Figure 122 leads to the following generalizations:

1. TOTAL SEXUAL OUTLET. The frequencies of total outlet are very close for the college level of the population among single males at every age

AGE	ACCUMULATIVE INCIDENCE, TWO GENERATIONS EDUCATIONAL LEVEL 13+							
	TOTAL INTERCOURSE				PRE-MARITAL INTERCOURSE			
	Older Generation		Younger Generation		Older Generation		Younger Generation	
	Cases	% with Exper.	Cases	% with Exper.	Cases	% with Exper.	Cases	% with Exper.
8	382	0.0	2435	0.0	382	0.0	2435	0.0
9	382	0.0	2435	0.0	382	0.0	2435	0.0
10	382	0.0	2435	0.0	382	0.0	2435	0.0
11	382	0.0	2435	0.2	382	0.0	2435	0.3
12	382	0.5	2345	1.1	382	0.5	2435	1.1
13	382	3.7	2435	3.0	382	3.7	2435	3.0
14	382	6.3	2435	5.9	382	6.3	2435	5.9
15	382	9.4	2435	9.5	382	9.4	2435	9.5
16	382	14.9	2434	15.6	382	14.9	2434	15.6
17	382	21.5	2432	23.4	381	21.3	2431	23.4
18	382	27.2	2356	31.5	381	27.0	2353	31.4
19	382	32.5	2192	39.3	380	31.8	2185	39.0
20	382	40.1	1957	46.8	376	38.8	1932	45.4
21	382	44.5	1651	52.4	369	42.5	1611	50.6
22	382	52.4	1290	60.0	363	48.2	1218	55.8
23	382	58.9	1015	64.5	342	52.9	907	58.4
24	382	66.0	770	70.3	320	55.3	647	61.2
25	382	72.8	620	76.5	292	62.0	469	65.9
26	382	79.3	502	80.7	262	63.0	341	66.9
27	382	82.5	392	82.7	214	64.0	218	66.1
28	382	84.8	317	85.5	185	65.9	144	67.4
29	382	87.4	252	86.5	164	67.7	96	66.7
30	382	89.3	191	90.1	142	69.7	60	63.3
31	382	90.8	147	91.2	123	69.1		
32	382	91.9	110	89.1	106	69.8		
33	382	92.1	66	84.8	96	69.8		

Table 99. Comparisons of older and younger generations of the college level: total intercourse, and total pre-marital intercourse

Accumulative incidence data. Pre-marital intercourse based on single males, including intercourse with companions and with prostitutes. Total intercourse based on life span, including pre-marital, marital, extra-marital, and post-marital relations with companions and with prostitutes. Median difference of age between the two generations is 22 years.

between adolescence and thirty, and among married males of the college level between the ages of 21 and 30 (which is as far as the sufficient data go).

Among single males of the lower educational levels, the frequencies of total outlet are rather materially higher for the younger generation at

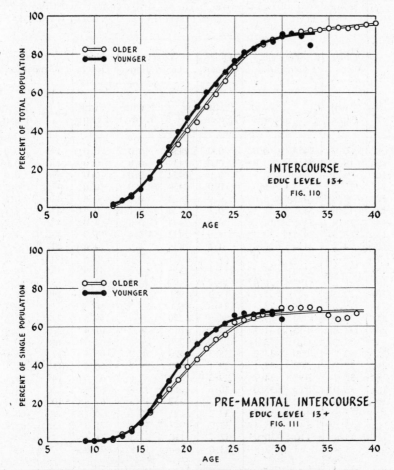

Figures 110–111. Comparisons of accumulative incidence for older and younger generations of college level: total and pre-marital intercourse

Data for total intercourse include all coital experience, regardless of marital status. Median age difference between the two generations is 22 years.

every age between adolescence and 30; and they similarly are higher for the married males of the younger generation at all ages for which there are sufficient data. The increase in the reported frequency is greatest for the grade school group, and not so great for the high school group. It is possible that these data represent a reality—that the younger generation

AGE	ACCUMULATIVE INCIDENCE, TWO GENERATIONS								
	HOMOSEXUAL OUTLET EDUC. LEVEL 13+			INTERC. WITH PROSTITUTES EDUC. LEVEL 13+			INTERC. WITH PROSTITUTES EDUC. LEVEL 0–8		
	Older Gener.	Younger Generation		Older Gener.	Younger Generation		Older Gener.	Younger Generation	
	% with Exper.	Cases	% with Exper.	% with Exper.	Cases	% with Exper.	% with Exper.	Cases	% with Exper.
8	0.0	2435	0.0	0.0	2434	0.0	0.0	476	0.0
9	0.3	2435	0.0	0.0	2434	0.0	0.0	476	0.0
10	1.3	2435	0.3	0.0	2434	0.0	0.0	476	0.0
11	3.7	2435	1.6	0.0	2434	0.0	0.0	475	0.2
12	7.6	2435	6.0	0.0	2434	0.0	0.6	475	0.6
13	12.6	2435	11.5	0.3	2434	0.1	0.9	475	1.1
14	19.9	2435	17.7	0.5	2434	0.8	4.0	472	3.2
15	23.3	2435	20.8	1.6	2434	2.4	7.7	466	7.5
16	24.3	2434	22.8	4.2	2433	4.9	19.4	447	15.9
17	25.4	2432	23.9	9.7	2431	9.0	30.6	405	25.9
18	27.2	2356	25.3	13.1	2355	13.7	42.6	373	38.3
19	28.5	2192	26.4	15.2	2191	17.8	47.5	333	42.9
20	29.3	1957	27.3	18.3	1956	21.0	51.9	299	47.8
21	29.8	1651	28.3	21.2	1650	22.5	56.8	274	50.4
22	30.9	1290	29.5	24.9	1290	24.9	59.3	243	55.6
23	31.4	1015	31.5	25.7	1015	25.7	61.4	222	55.4
24	32.2	770	32.1	27.0	770	26.5	62.3	198	60.1
25	32.7	620	33.2	28.3	620	28.9	65.7	173	63.6
26	32.7	502	33.1	29.1	502	29.7	66.4	158	67.1
27	32.7	392	34.7	29.3	392	31.6	67.0	141	68.1
28	33.0	317	35.0	30.6	317	33.8	67.3	126	68.3
29	33.0	252	34.5	31.2	252	33.3	67.9	100	66.0
30	33.8	191	33.5	32.2	191	35.1	70.7	80	66.3
31	33.8	147	35.4	32.2	147	38.8	71.3	58	63.8
32	33.8	110	30.0	32.7	110	37.3	71.3		
33	33.8	66	34.8	33.0	66	34.8	71.6		

Table 100. Comparisons of older and younger generations: homosexual outlet, and intercourse with prostitutes

Accumulative incidence data based on total life span, including pre-marital, extra-marital, and post-marital contacts. Median difference in age between the two generations is 22 years. In the older generation, for the homosexual data and for the data on intercourse with prostitutes at "Educ. Level 13+" there are 382 cases for each and every age. In the older generation for intercourse with prostitutes at "Educ. Level 0–8" there are 324 cases.

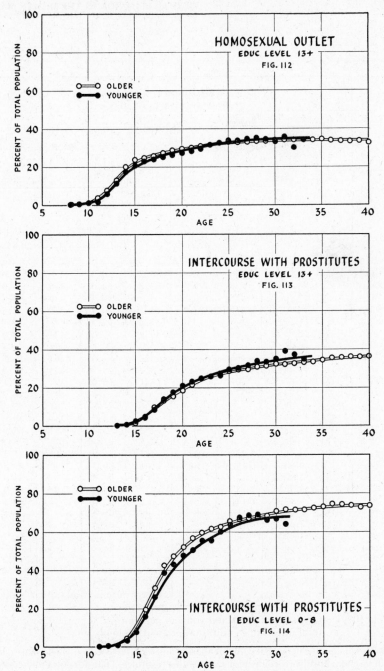

Figures 112–114. Comparisons of accumulative incidence for older and younger generations: homosexual outlet, intercourse with prostitutes

All curves based on total life span, irrespective of marital status. The first two figures, 112 and 113, show the homosexual outlet and intercourse with prostitutes for males of the college level (13+). Figure 114 shows intercourse with prostitutes for males of the grade school level (0–8).

AGE	ACCUMULATIVE INCIDENCE, TWO GENERATIONS EDUCATIONAL LEVEL 0–8							
	TOTAL INTERCOURSE				PRE-MARITAL INTERCOURSE			
	Older Generation		Younger Generation		Older Generation		Younger Generation	
	Cases	% with Exper.	Cases	% with Exper.	Cases	% with Exper.	Cases	% with Exper.
8	324	0.0	476	0.0	322	0.0	476	0.0
9	324	0.0	476	0.0	322	0.0	476	0.0
10	324	0.3	476	0.0	322	0.3	476	0.0
11	324	0.9	475	1.5	322	0.9	475	1.5
12	324	2.5	475	10.3	322	2.5	475	10.1
13	324	6.2	475	21.1	322	6.2	474	20.9
14	324	20.7	472	35.0	322	20.8	471	34.8
15	324	34.3	466	51.5	322	34.5	464	51.1
16	324	48.5	447	67.1	322	48.1	443	66.8
17	324	60.8	405	76.3	321	60.4	394	75.1
18	324	74.7	373	83.9	315	73.3	343	81.9
19	324	79.6	333	87.7	296	77.7	287	85.4
20	324	84.9	299	89.6	275	82.2	231	86.6
21	324	88.0	274	90.5	252	83.7	192	85.9
22	324	91.4	243	91.8	215	83.3	142	85.9
23	324	92.6	222	92.3	177	85.9	115	85.2
24	324	94.4	198	95.5	161	86.3	94	89.4
25	324	96.0	173	95.4	144	90.3	72	88.9
26	324	96.9	158	96.2	122	91.8	62	88.7
27	324	97.8	141	96.5	112	92.0	54	90.7
28	324	98.1	126	96.0	98	93.9		
29	324	98.1	100	95.0	86	93.0		
30	324	98.5	80	95.0	80	93.8		
31	324	98.8	58	93.1	73	94.5		
32	324	98.8			71	94.4		
33	324	98.8			67	94.0		
34	324	98.8			67	94.0		

Table 101. Comparisons of older and younger generations of grade school level: total intercourse, and total pre-marital intercourse

Accumulative incidence data for pre-marital intercourse based on single males, including intercourse with companions and with prostitutes. Data for total intercourse based on life span, including pre-marital, marital, extra-marital, and post-marital relations with companions and with prostitutes.

of the lower level is actually more active, again because of its improved nutrition. On the other hand, it is to be noted that older individuals of these lower educational levels, especially of the grade school group, are often in very poor condition physically and mentally by the time they reach 45 or 50 years of age, and their reports of past events are not as reliable as those

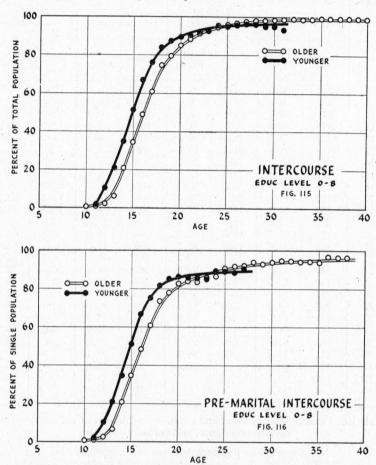

Figures 115–116. Comparisons of accumulative incidence for older and younger generations of grade school level: total and pre-marital intercourse

The first figure, 115, is based on the total male population, irrespective of the marital status, and shows the percentage of males with any coital experience. Figure 116 shows the percentage of single males with experience in pre-marital intercourse.

of the teen-age boys. Again, it is not impossible that there is more cover-up among older males of a generation in which the social pretense appears to have departed further from the actual behavior than it does today. It will take a larger sample than we yet have to enable final analysis to be made of these data.

	ACCUMULATIVE INCIDENCE, TWO GENERATIONS EDUCATIONAL LEVEL 13+							
	TOTAL PETTING EXPERIENCE				PETTING TO CLIMAX			
AGE	Older Generation		Younger Generation		Older Generation		Younger Generation	
	Cases	% with Exper.	Cases	% with Exper.	Cases	% with Exper.	Cases	% with Exper.
8	381	0.0	2433	0.0	306	0.0	1290	0.0
9	381	0.0	2433	0.0	306	0.0	1290	0.0
10	381	0.3	2433	0.3	306	0.0	1290	0.0
11	381	0.8	2433	1.4	306	0.0	1290	0.0
12	381	3.7	2433	6.1	306	0.7	1290	0.2
13	381	12.9	2433	17.6	306	2.9	1290	1.3
14	381	25.5	2433	35.0	306	4.2	1290	4.0
15	381	36.5	2433	48.9	306	6.9	1290	8.4
16	381	47.8	2432	66.7	306	13.4	1290	16.0
17	380	55.8	2429	78.4	305	19.3	1288	23.9
18	380	64.7	2351	85.8	305	24.6	1229	32.8
19	379	71.8	2183	90.4	305	31.5	1169	40.2
20	375	75.7	1930	92.7	304	37.2	1085	48.5
21	368	77.4	1609	93.7	299	41.5	941	52.8
22	362	80.4	1217	94.3	294	44.2	753	56.2
23	341	83.3	906	94.2	281	44.8	591	59.2
24	319	86.5	646	94.3	264	48.1	424	61.3
25	291	86.9	468	95.7	240	53.3	303	62.0
26	261	88.9	340	95.3	216	56.0	221	65.2
27	213	87.3	217	94.9	177	55.9	144	57.6
28	184	86.4	144	93.1	153	56.9	102	55.9
29	163	87.1	96	93.8	137	59.9	67	58.2
30	141	87.2	60	93.3	115	59.1		
31	123	86.2			99	59.6		
32	106	84.9			86	58.1		
33	96	83.3			80	57.5		

Table 102. Comparisons of older and younger generations of college level: total petting experience, and petting to climax

Accumulative incidence data based on single males.

2. MASTURBATION. Among males of the college level, and among all but the youngest group of high school males, frequencies of masturbation in the two generations are, again, close. However, for the younger generations of the lower educational levels they are distinctly higher. There seems in actuality to be a greater utilization of masturbation in these lower levels today.

3. NOCTURNAL EMISSIONS. The frequencies of nocturnal emissions as recorded by both upper and lower educational groups are nearly identical

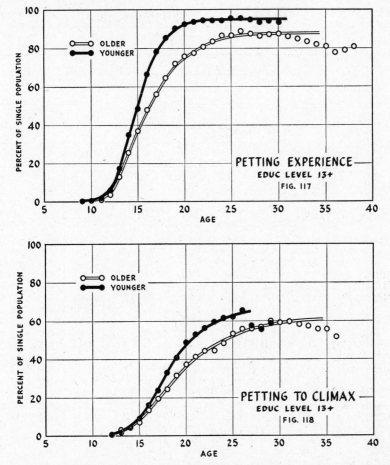

Figures 117–118. Comparisons of accumulative incidence for older and younger
generations of college level: petting

The first figure, 117, shows the data for any kind of petting experience. Figure 118
shows petting experience to the point of orgasm. Median age difference between the two
generations is 22 years.

in every age group. If one notes that the older group had to recall the events
of a period which extended, on an average, over 22 years more than the
younger groups were recalling, it is all the more impressive to secure such
similar results.

4. PETTING. Petting to climax shows a slight increase in frequency for
all social levels in the younger age groups, when the calculation is based
upon the total populations in each group. The frequencies are still more
nearly identical when the calculations are based upon the persons who are
actively involved.

	ACCUMULATIVE INCIDENCE, TWO GENERATIONS EDUCATIONAL LEVEL 0–8									
	MASTURBATION			NOCTURNAL EMISSIONS			PETTING EXPERIENCE			
AGE	Older Gener.	Younger Generation		Older Gener.	Younger Generation		Older Generation		Younger Generation	
	% with Exper.	Cases	% with Exper.	% with Exper.	Cases	% with Exper.	Cases	% with Exper.	Cases	% with Exper.
8	0.0	476	0.0	0.0	476	0.0	320	0.0	476	0.0
9	0.0	476	0.2	0.0	476	0.0	320	0.0	476	0.0
10	0.0	476	1.5	0.0	476	0.0	320	0.3	476	0.0
11	1.2	475	4.6	0.0	475	0.6	320	0.9	475	1.7
12	8.7	475	20.4	0.9	475	1.3	320	3.4	475	10.7
13	23.0	475	44.0	1.6	475	5.1	320	8.4	474	27.0
14	49.7	472	70.1	9.7	472	13.8	320	25.3	471	45.9
15	67.4	466	86.7	23.2	466	28.3	320	40.3	464	62.7
16	77.3	447	91.9	35.1	447	42.7	320	54.4	443	75.2
17	80.7	405	93.1	40.8	405	52.8	319	64.6	394	81.0
18	84.2	373	94.9	50.8	373	61.7	314	72.6	343	85.4
19	85.1	333	94.6	53.3	333	66.1	295	74.9	287	87.5
20	85.4	299	95.0	58.6	299	70.9	274	78.8	231	86.1
21	85.4	274	95.3	59.9	274	73.4	251	79.3	192	88.0
22	85.4	243	95.5	61.4	243	77.0	214	78.5	142	88.7
23	85.4	222	95.9	62.4	222	79.7	176	77.8	115	87.8
24	85.7	198	96.5	63.3	198	82.8	160	78.8	94	90.4
25	86.0	173	96.5	65.8	173	83.2	143	80.4	72	90.3
26	86.0	158	96.2	66.8	158	84.2	121	78.5	62	88.7
27	86.0	141	96.5	67.4	141	85.1	111	77.5	54	88.9
28	86.0	126	96.0	69.3	126	83.3	98	77.6		
29	86.3	100	95.0	70.2	100	86.0	86	75.6		
30	86.3	80	95.0	72.1	80	86.3	80	76.3		
31	86.3	58	93.1	72.1	58	86.2	73	76.7		
32	86.3			72.7			71	76.1		
33	86.3			73.0			67	74.6		
34	86.3			73.4			67	76.1		

Table 103. Comparisons of older and younger generations of grade school level: masturbation, nocturnal emissions, and heterosexual petting

Accumulative incidence data for masturbation and nocturnal emissions based on the life span. Data for petting experience, with or without climax, based on single males. Data for older generation on masturbation are based on 322 cases, on nocturnal emissions on 319 cases, at each and every age.

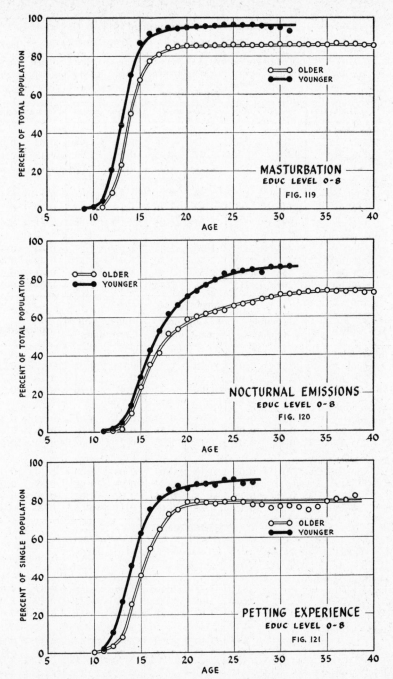

Figures 119–121. Comparisons of accumulative incidence for older and younger generations of grade school level: masturbation, nocturnal emissions, petting

The first two figures, 119 and 120, show masturbation and nocturnal emissions during the life span. Figure 121 shows any kind of pre-marital petting experience.

409

EDUCATIONAL LEVEL AND AGE GROUP	COMPARISONS OF FREQUENCIES IN TWO GENERATIONS MEAN FREQUENCIES FOR TOTAL POPULATION							
	OLDER GENER.	YOUNG. GENER.	OLDER GENER.	YOUNG. GENER.	OLDER GENER.	YOUNG. GENER.	OLDER GENER.	YOUNG. GENER.
Single Males								
Outlet	No. of cases		Total outlet		Masturbation		Nocturn. emiss.	
Educ. level 0–8								
Adol.–15	315	397	2.07	3.77	1.07	1.94	0.05	0.06
16–20	346	374	2.31	4.05	0.78	1.08	0.13	0.17
21–25	229	132	2.35	4.53	0.59	0.69	0.12	0.21
Educ. level 9–12								
Adol.–15	144	462	2.49	3.61	1.58	2.04	0.13	0.15
16–20	146	461	2.82	3.76	1.15	1.35	0.20	0.23
21–25	109	154	2.41	3.42	0.70	0.98	0.21	0.25
Educ. level 13+								
Adol.–15	462	2337	2.76	2.84	1.97	2.27	0.44	0.32
16–20	476	2385	2.69	2.70	1.71	1.81	0.49	0.41
21–25	456	1442	2.57	2.47	1.30	1.31	0.41	0.38
26–30	269	218	2.68	2.43	1.24	1.09	0.34	0.27

Single Males								
Outlet	Petting to climax		Total pre-marit. interc.		Interc. with prostitutes		Homosexual	
Educ. level 0–8								
Adol.–15	0.02	0.05	0.70	1.35	0.04	0.02	0.17	0.30
16–20	0.03	0.08	1.20	2.39	0.23	0.17	0.16	0.27
21–25	0.01	0.08	1.36	3.22	0.41	0.36	0.22	0.30
Educ. level 9–12								
Adol.–15	0.03	0.06	0.47	0.94	0.03	0.01	0.18	0.32
16–20	0.06	0.09	1.17	1.58	0.16	0.08	0.18	0.44
21–25	0.07	0.09	1.13	1.33	0.22	0.08	0.24	0.64
Educ. level 13+								
Adol.–15	0.03	0.05	0.12	0.07	0.00	0.00	0.14	0.08
16–20	0.11	0.15	0.28	0.27	0.03	0.02	0.09	0.06
21–25	0.18	0.18	0.58	0.45	0.07	0.02	0.10	0.09
26–30	0.12	0.15	0.81	0.62	0.11	0.05	0.20	0.26

Married Males								
Outlet	No. of cases		Total outlet		Marit. interc.		Extra-marit. interc.	
Educ. level 0–8								
16–20	75	83	3.75	5.50	3.07	4.35	0.37	0.69
21–25	204	120	3.08	5.61	2.70	4.28	0.19	1.04
26–30	227	65	3.02	5.22	2.65	4.21	0.16	0.61
Educ. level 9–12								
21–25	71	93	3.89	4.35	3.24	3.43	0.37	0.50
26–30	83	52	3.43	3.76	2.76	3.07	0.32	0.32
Educ. level 13+								
21–25	144	296	3.86	3.62	3.25	2.98	0.16	0.04
26–30	317	215	3.33	2.99	2.76	2.40	0.12	0.05

Table 104. Comparisons of mean frequencies of sexual activities in older and younger generations

Median difference of age between the two groups is 22 years.

5. PRE-MARITAL INTERCOURSE WITH COMPANIONS. Among males of the upper educational levels, coitus before marriage occurs with frequencies that are, again, duplicates for the two generations. The only marked differences come in early adolescence, where the record is rather materially higher for the younger generation. For pre-marital intercourse at lower educational levels, the younger generation reports definitely higher frequencies in every age group, although the differences are more marked for the younger ages. As noted above, this increased activity among younger males of the lower educational level is apparently correlated with the earlier maturation of the boys of that group in the present day; but all of these lower level data may be affected by the poor memory of the older men who supply the record for the older group.

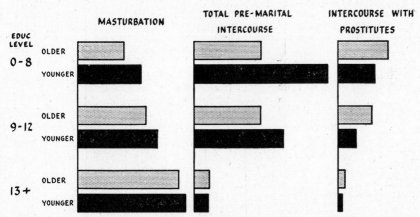

Figure 122. Comparisons of frequencies of sexual activity in older and younger generations

Comparisons of mean frequencies for males 16–20 years of age, showing data for masturbation, total pre-marital intercourse, and intercourse with prostitutes, for three educational levels. Median age difference between the two generations is 22 years.

6. PRE-MARITAL INTERCOURSE WITH PROSTITUTES. The frequencies of pre-marital sexual relations with prostitutes are more or less constantly lower in the younger generations of all educational levels. There are no exceptions to be observed in Table 104. In most cases the average frequencies of intercourse with prostitutes are down to two-thirds or even to one-half of what they were in the generation that was most active 22 years ago. This is undoubtedly the result of the extensive educational campaigns which have associated the prostitute with venereal disease, and of the legal drives which have been made against organized prostitution. In the 22-year period which has elapsed between the two generations which are involved here, most of the state laws against prostitution have come into existence or have been considerably strengthened. In particular localities, there has been an increasing public interest in controlling organized prostitution.

EDUCATIONAL LEVEL AND AGE GROUP	COMPARISONS OF INCIDENCES IN TWO GENERATIONS PERCENTS OF TOTAL POPULATION INVOLVED							
	OLDER GENER.	YOUNG. GENER.	OLDER GENER.	YOUNG. GENER.	OLDER GENER.	YOUNG. GENER.	OLDER GENER.	YOUNG. GENER.

Single Males

Outlet	No. of cases		Total outlet		Masturbation		Nocturn. emiss.	
Educ. level 0–8								
Adol.–15	315	397	85.4	96.0	76.8	90.9	22.9	27.5
16–20	346	374	96.2	98.7	78.0	90.4	55.2	57.5
21–25	229	132	96.1	97.7	59.4	67.4	57.6	62.9
Educ. level 9–12								
Adol.–15	144	462	92.4	96.3	84.7	91.6	41.0	39.2
16–20	146	461	100.0	99.6	84.9	90.2	69.2	71.1
21–25	109	154	98.2	100.0	67.0	83.1	70.6	71.4
Educ. level 13+								
Adol.–15	462	2337	95.5	95.8	80.3	82.8	72.7	69.3
16–20	476	2385	99.8	99.7	85.7	89.2	92.2	91.0
21–25	456	1442	99.6	99.9	83.6	88.1	90.1	86.1
26–30	269	218	99.6	100.0	81.0	85.8	86.6	83.5

Single Males

Outlet	Petting to climax		Interc. with companions		Interc. with prostitutes		Homosexual	
Educ. level 0–8								
Adol.–15	6.7	18.6	37.1	57.4	9.8	7.8	17.1	29.0
16–20	13.0	28.9	74.3	87.7	51.7	44.9	17.9	33.7
21–25	11.4	22.7	72.5	87.9	65.5	52.3	16.6	32.6
Educ. level 9–12								
Adol.–15	12.5	21.6	31.3	47.2	9.7	7.4	23.6	35.3
16–20	32.2	34.9	71.2	73.8	45.2	40.1	26.7	45.3
21–25	32.1	26.0	73.4	68.8	54.1	36.4	29.4	43.5
Educ. level 13+								
Adol.–15	9.7	14.6	9.3	9.3	1.7	2.4	25.1	20.8
16–20	39.3	47.1	37.0	39.2	18.7	19.4	16.4	15.9
21–25	51.8	51.9	56.4	54.1	23.7	15.1	12.7	8.5
26–30	46.1	42.7	59.9	55.5	20.4	11.5	16.4	18.3

Married Males

Outlet	No. of cases		Total outlet		Marit. interc.		Extra-marit. interc.	
Educ. level 0–8								
16–20	75	83	100.0	100.0	100.0	100.0	32.0	55.4
21–25	204	120	100.0	100.0	99.5	99.2	27.9	45.0
26–30	227	65	100.0	96.9	100.0	96.9	32.2	44.6
Educ. level 9–12								
21–25	71	93	100.0	100.0	100.0	100.0	36.6	46.2
26–30	83	52	100.0	100.0	100.0	100.0	38.6	53.8
Educ. level 13+								
21–25	144	296	100.0	100.0	98.6	100.0	18.8	13.2
26–30	317	215	100.0	100.0	99.1	99.5	24.3	18.1

Table 105. Comparisons of incidences of sexual activities in older and younger generations

Median difference of age between the two groups is 22 years.

412

There is no doubt that the openly run organized house of prostitution has thereby been eliminated in a great many instances, although our specific data make it doubtful that the number of girls involved in prostitution has been very much decreased. As indicated above (Table 100, Figures 113, 114), the number of males going to prostitutes at some time in their lives seems not to have been affected by these restrictive measures, but the frequency data do indicate that they do not return as often as they did before these educational and legal moves were made against prostitution.

7. TOTAL PRE-MARITAL INTERCOURSE. Comparing frequencies among the older and the younger generations, the sum total of the pre-marital intercourse which is had with companions and with prostitutes today remains about the same in the college level, has definitely increased in the grade school group, and has somewhat increased in the high school group. The

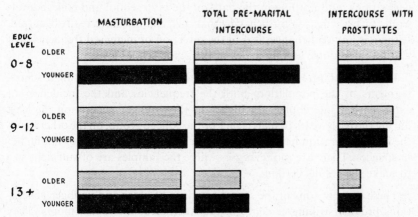

Figure 123. Comparisons of active incidence data for older and younger generations

Data for the age period 16–20. Median age difference between the two generations is 22 years.

drives against prostitution have succeeded in diverting a third to a half of the intercourse that males used to have with prostitutes to pre-marital activities with other girls.

8. HOMOSEXUAL OUTLETS. Frequencies in the homosexual show, on the whole, very little change in older age groups of the two generations (Table 104 and other data not in the table). In the youngest adolescent period there seems to be a definite increase in frequencies for the younger groups, but after 16 or 20 years of age there are no constant changes. There are particular educational levels at particular ages where the younger generation seems to be more active, and there are other groups where the older generation seems to have had the lead. There is, at best, only a slight substantiation for the oft-repeated assertion that "sexual perversion" is on the increase. It is difficult to understand what sufficient basis there can be

for that opinion. It cannot be due to any increase in the obvious public display of homosexuality; for if there is one change between generations which is certainly established by the data, it is to the effect that public displays were more frequent in an older day. Certainly the police in many of the larger cities have made particular efforts to reduce street and tavern exhibitions of such activity. Evidently many individuals of the older generation were unaware of the extent of homosexual activity during their younger years. It is possible that the freer discussion of the homosexual today, both in technical and in popular print, has made the public more conscious of sexual activity that has always been a part of the pattern of the human animal.

9. MARITAL INTERCOURSE. One would presume that the frequencies of marital intercourse should show no material differences between the two generations, and nothing in the data on the high school and college levels would give any reason for believing that such changes have really occurred. If there is any real change, it is in the direction of increased frequencies of marital intercourse among males of the grade school level.

10. EXTRA-MARITAL INTERCOURSE. In the grade school and high school segments of the population, both the frequencies and the incidences of extra-marital intercourse are higher in the younger generation, at least during the early years of marriage. For the college group, on the other hand, the older generation has much the higher frequencies and somewhat higher incidences. There are too few cases where the samples are of sufficient size to make the results certain.

These comparisons of the sexual activities of older and younger generations provide striking evidence of the stability of the sexual mores. They provide scant justification for the opinion harbored by some persons that there are constant changes in such mores, or at least a constant flux—perhaps an "evolution" toward something better, or a constant degeneration in behavior.

Some persons have expressed a fear that a long-time sex study of the sort in which we are currently engaged will fall into error if it averages histories obtained early in the study with histories obtained ten or twenty years later. There are persons who have regretted the fact that it was not possible to complete this study before World War II. They indicate that it is not correct to compare data obtained before the war and data obtained since, for patterns change so much in times of war and during post-war adjustments that we probably should begin the study anew. Not only do the press, propaganda agencies, and moral and law enforcement groups encourage this notion, but scientists have been inclined to accept it. There are persons who have suggested that we should rule out all histories of men who have been in the armed forces, inasmuch as their patterns of behavior have, inevitably, been so changed that they are no longer representative of a peace-time population. There are persons who have thought that the publication of the present volume might so affect the patterns of behavior for whole segments of the population that we could no longer find histories that would be representative of the conditions that existed before these data were made available. There are more persons who have thought that it would be important for us to get re-takes on histories of subjects who had previously given histories—not for the sake of testing the validity of memory and the extent of the cover-up (as we have in actuality used such re-takes), but for the sake of recording the presumably great changes in behavior that must follow such discussions of sexual matters as are involved in the contribution of one's history.

These persons do not seem to have realized the ancient origins of our current patterns and their deep foundations in the basic thinking of each cultural group. We have repeatedly pointed out that many of our present-day attitudes on sex are matters which were settled in the religious philosophy of the authors of the Old Testament and even among more ancient peoples, and there is no evidence that scientific analyses will quickly modify such deep-rooted behavior.

The changes that have occurred in 22 years, as measured by the data given in the present chapter, concern attitudes and minor details of behavior, and nothing that is deeply fundamental in overt activity. There has been nothing as fundamental as the substitution of one type of outlet for another, of masturbation for heterosexual coitus, of coitus for the homosexual, or vice versa. There has not even been a material increase or decrease in the incidences and frequencies of most types of activity. In these 20 to 30 years, there appear to have been as material social changes as in any period of history. The expansion of manufactured utilities, the extension of means of locomotion and of all types of communication, the increase in educational programs, the political upheavals, the changes of attitude on matters of religion, have been extreme in this period. There have been two wars on such a world-wide scale as has never before been known. Twice in this period a high percentage of the young men of the country was drafted into military service and brought into contact with the sexual patterns of persons representing the full range of social levels in our own nation, and with the sexual patterns of many of the other nations of the world. Following these two wars there have been periods in which many persons thought they saw unprecedented moral breakdowns. There have been periods of wild inflation, the jazz age, periods of prosperity, periods of depression. Millions of dollars have been spent by certain organizations for the express purpose of changing the sexual habits of the nation. This period has seen much new legislation on matters of sex. For the first time in American history, Federal agents have been used to enforce sex laws on a national scale. And the sum total of the measurable effects on

American sexual behavior are slight changes in attitudes, some increase in the frequency of masturbation among boys of the lower educational levels, more frequent nocturnal emissions, increased frequencies of pre-marital petting, earlier coitus for a portion of the male population, and the transference of a percentage of the pre-marital intercourse from prostitutes to girls who are not prostitutes.

There is not even evidence that patterns of sexual behavior are materially altered among men in the armed forces during a period of war. Precise calculations will have to come later, but the available data now indicate that it is a small portion of the men who go into the Army or the Navy who materially modify their patterns of behavior after they leave home. The data are conclusive that such patterns in the case of the male are largely established by the age of 16, and no sort of circumstance, however catastrophic, materially alters them for more than a very few persons in their later years. It is true that many a man has had his first experience in heterosexual coitus after he got into the armed forces; but most of these men would have begun coitus at about that age if they had stayed at home. The men who have the most coitus after getting into the armed forces are, for the most part, the men who would have had the most coitus if they had stayed at home. The men who find most of their war-time coitus with prostitutes are the men who would have found most of their experience with prostitutes at home; and the men who avoid prostitutes in the Army avoid them for the same reasons that they would have avoided them at home.

The public is much more conscious of the behavior of a man in uniform than it is of a man in civilian clothes. The civilian who walks down the street with a girl does not attract nearly so much attention as the uniformed male who walks down the same street with the same girl. The high officer who complained that too many mothers thought that the Army had invented sex had considerable justification for his complaint.

There is a ready assumption that men in segregated groups, as in the Army and the Navy, turn to the homosexual more often than they would at home; but it is to be recalled that the active incidence of the homosexual in the peace-time U. S. population among men of Army and Navy age is nearly 30 per cent (Table 90), and one would have to show that the incidence among men in the Army and the Navy is higher than that, or that the frequencies of contact are higher, in order to prove that patterns for these men had been changed in any way. There are, of course, men who have their first homosexual experience while in the Army or the Navy, but there are men of the same age who would have had their first experience at home if there had never been a war.

Similarly, the married men in the armed forces turn to extra-marital intercourse, or avoid extra-marital intercourse, largely in accord with the patterns that have guided their behavior previously in their lives.

Patterns of sexual behavior may persist in a social group even though many persons may move into it from other groups that have totally different patterns of behavior (Table 106). Twenty-five or thirty years ago, about 5 per cent of the American males went to college. The 1940 census shows about 15 per cent of the males of this younger generation receiving such advanced education. In the 22 years which have elapsed between our older and younger generations, the college population has increased three times. But in spite of the fact that the original college population has been enlarged by a group twice as large as its original self, the college pattern of sexual behavior has remained practically unchanged. In fact, the nearest identities between the older and the younger generations (Tables 98–105) are at this college level. This is a remarkable tribute to the stability of the sexual mores.

With the return of the veterans from the recent war, and with the subsidization of their education from public funds, there has come such a sudden invasion of the college group as has never before been known. The research investigator concerned with human behavior today needs to be especially careful to understand the background of the college student whom he is interviewing. Many of the veterans who are now attending college would have done so if there had been no war, and this is the group which, by and large, has sexual histories of the sort that have been reported here for the college level. But there are many others who would never have gone beyond high school except for the present governmental program. Many males of this group are contributing histories of a sort which is not usually found within college halls. There are high frequencies of premarital intercourse with large numbers of companions. There are lower level attitudes about masturbation in this group. What will the outcome be upon the patterns of sexual behavior among college levels? Will this sudden influx of lower level patterns overwhelm the traditions of the upper level groups? Will the lower level individuals have their patterns changed by their college contacts? Certainly no scientist could have conceived a more remarkable experiment for testing the effect of the intermingling of social groups. We have found that patterns are largely determined by the time of adolescence or at some still earlier age. We find (as reported later in this chapter) that, in such migrations as do occur between social levels, the changes in patterns do not come in the lifetime of an individual, but by way of the next generation. In the light of these considerations, it will be interesting to observe what the outcome of this GI invasion of the colleges may be.

VERTICAL MOBILITY: AT AN EARLY AGE

There are, of course, persons who are born into one social level and who move into some other level or levels in the course of their lives. Sorokin (1927) and other writers in the social sciences have referred to this as social or vertical mobility. Increasingly common instances are to be found today in lower level homes from which children go on to high school and in some cases to college. As noted in the previous chapter, such an improvement of social position has been an increasingly common phenomenon for some decades now in this country. The data (Table 106) show that about 39 per cent of the subjects in the present study have stayed in the same occupational class as their parents, 21 per cent of the population regressed to

OCCUP. CLASS OF SUBJECT	OCCUPATIONAL CLASS OF PARENT							CASES IN OCCUP. CLASS OF SUBJECT
	2	3	4	5	6	7	8	
	%	%	%	%	%	%	%	
2	56	21	6	3	1	0	0	430
3	29	44	23	11	1	1	2	609
4	4	7	14	5	1	0	0	162
5	6	14	24	28	16	9	7	500
6	3	7	17	24	40	23	24	556
7	2	7	16	29	40	65	46	671
8	0	0	0	0	1	2	21	17
Total %	100	100	100	100	100	100	100	2945
Cases in parental class	419	673	485	566	567	193	42	2945

Table 106. Stability and mobility of occupational classes

Showing (in bold face) percent of each parental class whose male offspring stay within the same class. And showing (in regular type) what percent of the offspring of each parental class moves into other occupational classes. Parental classes represent all ratings held by parent while subject lived in the home. Subject classes represent only the highest rating ever held by subject up to time of reporting.

occupational classes lower than those in which their parents raised them, and 40 per cent have risen to social positions superior to those held by their parents. There is, obviously, a considerable shifting of occupational classes and social position in our American society, and it is of interest to know how sexual patterns are affected when such changes occur in social classes.

Two sorts of situations are involved. The first includes those cases where the subject breaks with the parental patterns while he is still living with his parents. This is much the commoner sort of case, accounting for nearly all of the movement of the 61 per cent of the population which does not stay in its parental class. On this type of case we have an abundance of data.

The second type is one in which the individual stays within his parental class until some later time in his life, at least until his late teens, and only finally moves into some other occupational group. This is the rarer type of case. Consequently there are only a few instances of this sort on which we can draw for illustration. It is unwarranted, at the present time, to attempt statistical analyses of these few data.

From the tabulations in Tables 107 to 114, it is possible to compare the sexual histories of males who have stayed in the parental occupational class with the histories of males who have moved out of the parental class into some other group which is either higher or lower. In Table 115 it is possible to compare the sexual histories of males who have arrived at the same occupational class, even though the parents of these several males belonged to a variety of occupational classes.

In general, it will be seen that the sexual history of the individual accords with the pattern of the social group into which he ultimately moves, rather than with the pattern of the social group to which the parent belongs and in which the subject was placed when he lived in the parental home. Individuals originating from different parental classes have much the same histories, if they ultimately arrive at the same occupational rating. A half dozen persons who come from the same parental occupational class may have a half dozen different sorts of histories if they finally locate in that many different classes. These statements are, of course, based on averages for whole groups, and it may be anticipated that particular individuals in each and every one of these groups will depart from any average. Nevertheless, so many individuals do fit into this general description that the means and medians calculated for these several populations are quite distinct.

The most significant thing shown by these calculations (Tables 107–115) is the evidence that an individual who is ever going to depart from the parental pattern is likely to have done so by the time he has become adolescent. (See Chapter 5 on pre-adolescent sexual development.) In comparing the sexual histories with the educational backgrounds of each individual (Chapter 10), we have already reached the conclusion that the patterns of behavior are largely laid down by age 16, and that relatively few persons change their patterns of behavior at any later time in their lives. Now the analyses made for the occupational classes of the parent and the subject fully and abundantly confirm this generalization. The patterns of the several occupational classes are remarkably distinct in the group that is 16 to 20 years of age. It is evident that a high proportion of the individuals are conforming to the general pattern. Between adolescence and 15 years of age, the groups are not yet as distinct. Nevertheless, it is amazing that distinctions are at all evident in these early adolescent years. These facts have considerable scientific and social significance.

Unfortunately, analyses that are based upon frequencies of orgasm do not provide a basis for measuring pre-adolescent activity. It will, however, be of the utmost significance to obtain a considerable number of histories

AGE GROUP	OCCUP. CLASS REACHED BY SUBJECT	CASES	TOTAL OUTLET AND OCCUPATIONAL CLASS				
			TOTAL POPULATION		ACTIVE POPULATION		
			Mean Frequency	Median Freq.	Incid. %	Mean Frequency	Median Freq.

Parental Occupational Class 2

AGE GROUP	OCCUP. CLASS	CASES	Mean Frequency	Median Freq.	Incid. %	Mean Frequency	Median Freq.
Adol.–15	2	231	2.71 ± 0.19	1.83	95.7	2.83 ± 0.19	1.92
	3	126	2.68 ± 0.30	1.40	90.5	2.96 ± 0.33	1.69
16–20	2	198	3.08 ± 0.18	2.36	99.5	3.10 ± 0.18	2.38
	3	116	3.46 ± 0.37	2.11	99.1	3.49 ± 0.37	2.14
21–25	2	92	2.50 ± 0.24	1.89	98.9	2.53 ± 0.24	1.93

Parental Occupational Class 3

AGE GROUP	OCCUP. CLASS	CASES	Mean Frequency	Median Freq.	Incid. %	Mean Frequency	Median Freq.
Adol.–15	2	140	2.67 ± 0.27	1.73	91.4	2.92 ± 0.29	1.95
	3	384	3.10 ± 0.18	1.95	93.0	3.33 ± 0.19	2.20
	5	205	2.85 ± 0.19	2.06	95.1	2.99 ± 0.19	2.19
	6 + 7	92	2.88 ± 0.30	2.19	96.7	2.97 ± 0.30	2.28
16–20	2	138	2.85 ± 0.24	2.20	97.1	2.93 ± 0.24	2.30
	3	318	3.50 ± 0.21	2.45	98.1	3.57 ± 0.21	2.51
	5	201	2.88 ± 0.20	2.05	99.5	2.89 ± 0.20	2.06
	6 + 7	94	3.12 ± 0.26	2.54	98.9	3.15 ± 0.26	2.57
21–25	2	64	2.45 ± 0.41	1.55	98.4	2.49 ± 0.42	1.60
	3	120	3.41 ± 0.41	2.07	97.5	3.50 ± 0.42	2.14
	5	124	2.73 ± 0.22	1.93	99.2	2.75 ± 0.22	1.95
	6 + 7	87	2.67 ± 0.20	2.40	100.0	2.67 ± 0.20	2.40

Parental Occupational Class 4

AGE GROUP	OCCUP. CLASS	CASES	Mean Frequency	Median Freq.	Incid. %	Mean Frequency	Median Freq.
Adol.–15	3	107	3.62 ± 0.35	2.50	95.3	3.80 ± 0.35	2.68
	4	158	2.56 ± 0.21	1.85	94.3	2.71 ± 0.21	1.95
	5	304	3.00 ± 0.17	2.29	94.1	3.18 ± 0.17	2.49
	6	109	2.85 ± 0.25	2.36	96.3	2.96 ± 0.25	2.50
	7	74	3.14 ± 0.39	1.96	97.3	3.23 ± 0.40	2.06
16–20	3	105	3.82 ± 0.34	2.64	99.0	3.86 ± 0.34	2.68
	4	104	2.73 ± 0.24	2.09	100.0	2.73 ± 0.24	2.09
	5	305	2.97 ± 0.16	2.36	99.0	3.00 ± 0.16	2.40
	6	111	3.01 ± 0.24	2.32	100.0	3.01 ± 0.24	2.32
	7	75	3.23 ± 0.32	2.43	100.0	3.23 ± 0.32	2.43
21–25	5	183	2.86 ± 0.22	2.09	99.5	2.87 ± 0.22	2.10
	6	98	2.55 ± 0.21	1.94	100.0	2.55 ± 0.21	1.94
	7	71	2.51 ± 0.23	2.00	100.0	2.51 ± 0.23	2.00

(*Table continued on next page*)

AGE GROUP	OCCUP. CLASS REACHED BY SUBJECT	CASES	TOTAL OUTLET AND OCCUPATIONAL CLASS				
			TOTAL POPULATION		ACTIVE POPULATION		
			Mean Frequency	Median Freq.	Incid. %	Mean Frequency	Median Freq.
Parental Occupational Class 5							
Adol.–15	3	65	3.38 ± 0.48	2.33	93.8	3.60 ± 0.49	2.50
	5	563	2.77 ± 0.10	2.21	94.1	2.95 ± 0.11	2.37
	6	228	2.86 ± 0.21	2.15	95.6	2.99 ± 0.22	2.26
	7	152	2.70 ± 0.23	1.81	95.4	2.83 ± 0.24	1.96
16–20	3	64	3.03 ± 0.42	2.42	95.3	3.17 ± 0.43	2.56
	5	516	2.63 ± 0.10	2.05	99.0	2.65 ± 0.10	2.08
	6	230	2.72 ± 0.16	1.98	99.6	2.73 ± 0.16	1.98
	7	155	2.50 ± 0.17	1.89	100.0	2.50 ± 0.17	1.89
21–25	5	262	2.32 ± 0.13	1.76	99.2	2.33 ± 0.13	1.78
	6	178	2.56 ± 0.18	1.86	100.0	2.56 ± 0.18	1.86
	7	143	2.43 ± 0.18	1.84	100.0	2.43 ± 0.18	1.84
Parental Occupational Class 6							
Adol.–15	5	98	3.76 ± 0.34	3.03	98.0	3.84 ± 0.34	3.09
	6	1048	2.86 ± 0.09	2.29	96.2	2.97 ± 0.09	2.41
	7	244	3.00 ± 0.22	2.07	98.4	3.05 ± 0.22	2.13
16–20	5	100	3.80 ± 0.31	3.19	99.0	3.84 ± 0.31	3.22
	6	1021	2.58 ± 0.07	2.11	99.7	2.58 ± 0.07	2.12
	7	246	3.18 ± 0.19	2.66	100.0	3.18 ± 0.19	2.66
21–25	5	71	3.13 ± 0.32	2.86	98.6	3.17 ± 0.32	2.89
	6	554	2.38 ± 0.08	1.88	100.0	2.38 ± 0.08	1.88
	7	236	2.88 ± 0.19	2.03	100.0	2.88 ± 0.19	2.03
26–30	6	103	2.34 ± 0.21	1.73	100.0	2.34 ± 0.21	1.73
	7	97	2.90 ± 0.38	1.89	100.0	2.90 ± 0.38	1.89
Married 21–25	6	113	3.73 ± 0.27	2.97	100.0	3.73 ± 0.27	2.97
	7	76	4.41 ± 0.40	3.71	100.0	4.41 ± 0.40	3.71
26–30	6	112	3.11 ± 0.27	2.48	100.0	3.11 ± 0.27	2.48
	7	135	3.54 ± 0.25	2.97	100.0	3.54 ± 0.25	2.97
Parental Occupational Class 7							
Adol.–15	7	414	3.05 ± 0.14	2.46	96.6	3.16 ± 0.14	2.54
16–20	7	416	3.04 ± 0.13	2.49	99.8	3.04 ± 0.13	2.50
21–25	7	266	2.71 ± 0.15	2.09	100.0	2.71 ± 0.15	2.09
Married 21–25	7	63	3.64 ± 0.26	3.27	100.0	3.64 ± 0.26	3.27
26–30	7	72	3.46 ± 0.24	3.17	100.0	3.46 ± 0.24	3.17

Table 107. Total outlet in relation to occupational class of parent and of subject

All data based on single males, except where indicated as "married."

AGE GROUP	OCCUP. CLASS REACHED BY SUBJECT	CASES	MASTURBATION AND OCCUPATIONAL CLASS					
			TOTAL POPULATION			ACTIVE POPULATION		
			Mean Frequency	Median Freq.	% of Total Outlet	Incid. %	Mean Frequency	Median Freq.
	Parental Occupational Class 2
Adol.–15	2	231	1.47 ± 0.11	0.91	56.07	89.6	1.65 ± 0.12	1.04
	3	126	1.40 ± 0.15	0.90	53.07	87.3	1.60 ± 0.16	1.18
16–20	2	198	1.15 ± 0.10	0.63	38.06	84.8	1.36 ± 0.11	0.83
	3	116	1.01 ± 0.12	0.48	28.95	89.7	1.13 ± 0.13	0.65
21–25	2	92	0.72 ± 0.10	0.33	29.86	72.8	0.99 ± 0.13	0.58
	Parental Occupational Class 3
Adol.–15	2	140	1.61 ± 0.18	0.84	61.87	86.4	1.87 ± 0.20	1.04
	3	384	1.57 ± 0.10	0.95	51.99	88.8	1.77 ± 0.10	1.16
	5	205	2.07 ± 0.17	1.38	73.84	82.4	2.52 ± 0.18	1.80
	6 + 7	92	2.25 ± 0.26	1.61	81.23	83.7	2.69 ± 0.29	2.11
16–20	2	138	0.99 ± 0.12	0.43	35.15	83.3	1.19 ± 0.14	0.61
	3	318	1.00 ± 0.07	0.48	29.02	86.8	1.16 ± 0.08	0.64
	5	201	1.57 ± 0.14	0.85	55.57	87.6	1.79 ± 0.15	1.02
	6 + 7	94	2.13 ± 0.22	1.66	68.47	88.3	2.41 ± 0.24	2.00
21–25	2	64	0.47 ± 0.12	0.09	19.49	62.5	0.75 ± 0.18	0.35
	3	120	0.56 ± 0.08	0.17	16.91	65.0	0.86 ± 0.12	0.42
	5	124	1.09 ± 0.13	0.49	41.00	87.9	1.24 ± 0.14	0.68
	6 + 7	87	1.40 ± 0.16	0.73	53.00	90.8	1.54 ± 0.17	0.88
	Parental Occupational Class 4
Adol.–15	3	107	1.94 ± 0.21	1.29	54.63	86.9	2.24 ± 0.22	1.54
	4	158	1.84 ± 0.15	1.31	72.58	88.6	2.07 ± 0.16	1.61
	5	304	2.18 ± 0.13	1.64	73.93	84.5	2.57 ± 0.14	2.08
	6	109	2.18 ± 0.21	1.71	77.39	82.6	2.64 ± 0.22	2.18
	7	74	2.56 ± 0.38	1.38	82.13	82.4	3.11 ± 0.40	2.25
16–20	3	105	0.98 ± 0.12	0.49	25.58	85.7	1.14 ± 0.13	0.66
	4	104	1.21 ± 0.14	0.70	44.31	89.4	1.35 ± 0.15	0.89
	5	305	1.64 ± 0.11	1.02	55.86	88.2	1.86 ± 0.12	1.43
	6	111	1.71 ± 0.17	0.98	57.31	85.6	2.00 ± 0.18	1.50
	7	75	2.21 ± 0.24	1.60	68.38	96.0	2.31 ± 0.24	1.75
21–25	5	183	1.17 ± 0.12	0.62	41.50	84.2	1.39 ± 0.14	0.86
	6	98	1.10 ± 0.13	0.65	43.15	84.7	1.30 ± 0.14	0.80
	7	71	1.37 ± 0.16	0.96	54.04	95.8	1.43 ± 0.17	1.03

(*Table continued on next page*)

AGE GROUP	OCCUP. CLASS REACHED BY SUBJECT	CASES	MASTURBATION AND OCCUPATIONAL CLASS					
			TOTAL POPULATION			ACTIVE POPULATION		
			Mean Frequency	Median Freq.	% of Total Outlet	Incid. %	Mean Frequency	Median Freq.
			Parental Occupational Class 5					
Adol.–15	3	65	1.81 ± 0.24	1.18	54.18	92.3	1.96 ± 0.25	1.30
	5	563	2.13 ± 0.09	1.62	78.07	85.1	2.51 ± 0.10	1.94
	6	228	2.17 ± 0.15	1.69	76.69	83.3	2.60 ± 0.17	2.08
	7	152	2.05 ± 0.22	1.10	78.48	80.3	2.55 ± 0.25	1.67
16–20	3	64	0.88 ± 0.12	0.57	29.35	89.1	0.99 ± 0.13	0.68
	5	516	1.68 ± 0.08	1.10	64.37	88.8	1.90 ± 0.09	1.36
	6	230	1.82 ± 0.13	1.27	67.29	88.3	2.06 ± 0.14	1.57
	7	155	1.60 ± 0.16	0.85	64.24	86.5	1.86 ± 0.17	1.16
21–25	5	262	1.22 ± 0.10	0.64	52.95	84.4	1.45 ± 0.11	0.85
	6	178	1.43 ± 0.14	0.65	57.18	85.4	1.67 ± 0.16	0.91
	7	143	1.18 ± 0.12	0.57	49.68	85.3	1.38 ± 0.14	0.79
			Parental Occupational Class 6					
Adol.–15	5	98	2.74 ± 0.28	1.83	74.71	91.8	2.98 ± 0.29	1.98
	6	1048	2.29 ± 0.08	1.72	81.20	85.1	2.69 ± 0.09	2.13
	7	244	2.24 ± 0.19	1.34	76.23	79.1	2.84 ± 0.22	2.00
16–20	5	100	1.94 ± 0.20	1.55	52.46	90.0	2.16 ± 0.20	1.72
	6	1021	1.73 ± 0.06	1.18	66.93	90.0	1.92 ± 0.06	1.44
	7	246	2.17 ± 0.17	1.58	68.26	89.0	2.44 ± 0.19	1.81
21–25	5	71	1.27 ± 0.16	0.78	41.97	81.7	1.56 ± 0.18	1.25
	6	554	1.27 ± 0.07	0.68	54.80	87.5	1.45 ± 0.07	0.87
	7	236	1.38 ± 0.13	0.74	48.66	86.9	1.59 ± 0.14	0.91
26–30	6	103	0.94 ± 0.13	0.46	39.84	84.5	1.11 ± 0.14	0.64
	7	97	1.17 ± 0.25	0.44	39.22	79.4	1.48 ± 0.30	0.67
			Parental Occupational Class 7					
Adol.–15	7	414	2.39 ± 0.12	1.85	79.29	79.0	3.03 ± 0.13	2.42
16–20	7	416	2.12 ± 0.11	1.66	70.34	88.9	2.39 ± 0.12	1.87
21–25	7	266	1.51 ± 0.11	0.82	56.56	88.3	1.71 ± 0.11	0.99

Table 108. Masturbation in relation to occupational class of parent and of subject

All data based on single males.

AGE GROUP	OCCUP. CLASS REACHED BY SUBJECT	CASES	NOCTURNAL EMISSIONS AND OCCUPATIONAL CLASS					
			TOTAL POPULATION			ACTIVE POPULATION		
			Mean Frequency	Me-dian Freq.	% of Total Outlet	Incid. %	Mean Frequency	Me-dian Freq.
Parental Occupational Class 2								
Adol.–15	2	231	0.05 ± 0.01	0.00	1.81	26.0	0.18 ± 0.05	0.08
	3	126	0.06 ± 0.03	0.00	2.46	21.4	0.30 ± 0.14	0.09
16–20	2	198	0.10 ± 0.02	0.01	3.28	52.5	0.19 ± 0.03	0.08
	3	116	0.16 ± 0.03	0.03	4.62	59.5	0.27 ± 0.05	0.10
21–25	2	92	0.12 ± 0.02	0.03	4.81	58.7	0.20 ± 0.03	0.10
Parental Occupational Class 3								
Adol.–15	2	140	0.05 ± 0.02	0.00	1.99	25.7	0.20 ± 0.05	0.08
	3	384	0.11 ± 0.02	0.00	3.76	31.3	0.36 ± 0.07	0.09
	5	205	0.27 ± 0.04	0.02	9.64	54.1	0.50 ± 0.07	0.24
	6 + 7	92	0.35 ± 0.07	0.09	12.55	71.7	0.49 ± 0.09	0.24
16–20	2	138	0.11 ± 0.02	0.02	3.95	56.5	0.20 ± 0.03	0.09
	3	318	0.21 ± 0.02	0.05	6.12	65.1	0.33 ± 0.03	0.13
	5	201	0.35 ± 0.04	0.14	12.48	82.6	0.43 ± 0.04	0.24
	6 + 7	94	0.47 ± 0.07	0.26	15.08	93.6	0.50 ± 0.07	0.29
21–25	2	64	0.13 ± 0.03	0.04	5.39	64.1	0.20 ± 0.05	0.09
	3	120	0.19 ± 0.03	0.04	5.74	63.3	0.30 ± 0.05	0.11
	5	124	0.31 ± 0.04	0.11	11.82	73.4	0.43 ± 0.06	0.27
	6 + 7	87	0.38 ± 0.06	0.22	14.45	90.8	0.42 ± 0.06	0.26
Parental Occupational Class 4								
Adol.–15	3	107	0.07 ± 0.02	0.00	2.08	31.8	0.23 ± 0.06	0.11
	4	158	0.07 ± 0.02	0.00	2.77	36.1	0.19 ± 0.04	0.09
	5	304	0.28 ± 0.04	0.06	9.64	63.2	0.45 ± 0.06	0.21
	6	109	0.33 ± 0.05	0.08	11.75	67.0	0.50 ± 0.07	0.32
	7	74	0.45 ± 0.09	0.19	14.39	81.1	0.55 ± 0.10	0.29
16–20	3	105	0.24 ± 0.05	0.06	6.22	65.7	0.36 ± 0.06	0.18
	4	104	0.14 ± 0.03	0.04	5.07	64.4	0.21 ± 0.03	0.10
	5	305	0.38 ± 0.04	0.15	12.87	87.2	0.43 ± 0.04	0.22
	6	111	0.48 ± 0.06	0.29	16.20	88.3	0.55 ± 0.06	0.35
	7	75	0.55 ± 0.09	0.29	17.04	90.7	0.61 ± 0.10	0.33
21–25	5	183	0.35 ± 0.05	0.15	12.38	84.2	0.42 ± 0.06	0.23
	6	98	0.46 ± 0.07	0.25	17.85	86.7	0.53 ± 0.07	0.32
	7	71	0.39 ± 0.07	0.19	15.41	83.1	0.47 ± 0.08	0.28

(*Table continued on next page*)

AGE GROUP	OCCUP. CLASS REACHED BY SUBJECT	CASES	NOCTURNAL EMISSIONS AND OCCUPATIONAL CLASS					
			TOTAL POPULATION			ACTIVE POPULATION		
			Mean Frequency	Median Freq.	% of Total Outlet	Incid. %	Mean Frequency	Median Freq.
			Parental Occupational Class 5					
Adol.–15	3	65	0.05 ± 0.02	0.00	1.38	30.8	0.15 ± 0.04	0.08
	5	563	0.31 ± 0.03	0.05	11.24	60.9	0.50 ± 0.05	0.23
	6	228	0.43 ± 0.08	0.12	15.04	68.9	0.62 ± 0.12	0.30
	7	152	0.43 ± 0.06	0.22	16.47	78.3	0.55 ± 0.08	0.33
16–20	3	64	0.14 ± 0.04	0.03	4.53	60.9	0.22 ± 0.05	0.08
	5	516	0.37 ± 0.03	0.17	14.17	85.1	0.44 ± 0.03	0.25
	6	230	0.47 ± 0.05	0.26	17.25	89.6	0.52 ± 0.05	0.31
	7	155	0.47 ± 0.06	0.29	18.70	92.3	0.51 ± 0.06	0.32
21–25	5	262	0.30 ± 0.03	0.16	13.01	82.4	0.36 ± 0.04	0.24
	6	178	0.43 ± 0.05	0.24	16.99	86.0	0.49 ± 0.05	0.30
	7	143	0.40 ± 0.06	0.23	16.70	86.7	0.46 ± 0.07	0.29
			Parental Occupational Class 6					
Adol.–15	5	98	0.20 ± 0.04	0.04	5.54	59.2	0.34 ± 0.06	0.19
	6	1048	0.28 ± 0.02	0.08	10.09	66.9	0.43 ± 0.02	0.26
	7	244	0.44 ± 0.04	0.25	15.07	84.0	0.53 ± 0.04	0.33
16–20	5	100	0.35 ± 0.05	0.17	9.52	85.0	0.41 ± 0.06	0.24
	6	1021	0.38 ± 0.02	0.23	14.77	90.8	0.42 ± 0.02	0.27
	7	246	0.54 ± 0.04	0.33	16.88	93.5	0.58 ± 0.04	0.35
21–25	5	71	0.31 ± 0.05	0.16	10.23	78.9	0.39 ± 0.06	0.26
	6	554	0.37 ± 0.02	0.22	15.85	87.5	0.42 ± 0.02	0.28
	7	236	0.43 ± 0.04	0.26	15.12	88.1	0.49 ± 0.04	0.32
26–30	6	103	0.31 ± 0.04	0.20	13.17	84.5	0.37 ± 0.04	0.27
	7	97	0.30 ± 0.04	0.20	10.18	83.5	0.36 ± 0.04	0.27
			Parental Occupational Class 7					
Adol.–15	7	414	0.40 ± 0.04	0.18	13.30	76.6	0.52 ± 0.05	0.30
16–20	7	416	0.43 ± 0.03	0.27	14.38	88.9	0.49 ± 0.03	0.32
21–25	7	266	0.43 ± 0.04	0.26	15.95	86.8	0.49 ± 0.05	0.31

Table 109. Nocturnal emissions in relation to occupational class of parent and of subject

All data based on single males.

from very young boys, in order to examine the possibility that movements between social classes begin in pre-adolescence. It is now certain that such movements are well under way by the earliest adolescent years, and that they are completed long before most boys ever leave the parental home.

More detailed analyses of the data shown in Tables 107 to 115 may be summed up as follows:

Occupational Classes 2 and 3. Class 2 includes the day laborers and class 3 includes the semi-skilled laborers. It will be seen that the sexual patterns of these two groups are very similar, whether measured by incidences or frequencies for particular sources of outlet. Class 3 does have somewhat higher frequencies of total outlet, primarily because class 2 (like the grade school group in Chapter 10) has its averages pulled down by the undue number of physically poor and mentally dull individuals who are in the group.

Occupational class 2 is one of the most stable in the social organization. About 56 per cent of the males who were born in class 2 stay in that class throughout their lives (Table 106). The median number of years of schooling which this group has is 6.8 (Table 80), and it is only 23 per cent of the group which ever goes into high school. Consequently, the sexual pattern for most of the group is very close to that which has been described previously (Chapter 10) for those boys who never go beyond grade school. The single males of the group depend primarily upon heterosexual intercourse, utilize masturbation to a lesser degree, have an absolute minimum of nocturnal emissions, rarely pet to the point of climax, and are involved in the homosexual more frequently than the males in any other occupational class (Tables 107–115).

To apply the description to a specific age period, namely that between ages 16 and 20, the statement is that these males who never belong to any occupational class that is higher than a 2 or a 3 average pre-marital intercourse with frequencies that are 6 to 8 times as high as the frequencies among boys who go further along in school and who ultimately belong to occupational class 6 (Figures 101–102). Between 16 and 20 they masturbate only about half as often as the boys who end up in occupational class 6 (Figure 98). The nocturnal emissions of the males of class 2 occur one-quarter as often as nocturnal emissions among the males of class 6 or 7 (Figure 99). Class 3 has emissions more frequently than class 2. Petting to climax between ages 16 and 20 occurs only a half or a third as often among these boys who are in class 2 and class 3 (Figure 100). Frequencies of the homosexual among males of class 2, between the ages of 16 and 20, are 11 times higher than among the males who ultimately arrive in occupational class 7; and, next to class 2, the males of class 3 have the highest frequencies in the homosexual (Figure 105).

About 90 per cent of the males of occupational class 2 who have contributed to the present study had parents who belonged to either occupational class 2 or 3 (Table 106). There has not been much movement between classes here. On the other hand, the males of occupational class 3, which includes the semi-skilled workmen, were derived from parents of the same occupational class in 44 per cent of the cases (Table 106), and in the remainder of the cases derived more or less equally from parents of occupational class 2 and from parents of higher social rating. About 38 per cent of the males of occupational class 3 represent individuals who regressed from the level reached by their parents. In a number of cases, the fathers were skilled workmen whose offspring were not equally skilled, but in 15 per cent of the cases these males in class 3 were derived from parents who belonged to white collar classes, even including professional and top business groups. However, in spite of the diverse origins of the males in class 3, there is most remarkable agreement between the sexual histories of those who came from occupational class 2 and those who came from occupational classes 4 and 5. This agreement becomes striking by the time the male has reached his late teens, but it is already quite apparent in the histories of the youngest adolescent boys.

Occupational Class 4. This class includes the skilled workmen. It is the least stable of all the occupational classes. There is a continual influx into the group from persons who originated in occupational classes 2 and 3. On the other hand, the offspring of the group move on into higher occupational ratings in 57 per cent of the cases. The group has a much better economic status than most of the other laboring groups, and includes a good many persons of superior ability. The group continuously aspires to higher levels and a considerable proportion of its children go to college. About 40 per cent of the group stops with some high school education, and 7 per cent gets some work in college. Next to the white collar and professional classes, this is the class that supplies the largest number of college students (Table 80). Because of this migration the group does not perpetuate itself. It has been a considerable problem in industry to persuade the sons of skilled workmen to become interested in the trades in which their fathers work.

In their patterns of sexual behavior, the males of occupational class 4 seem to be more or less intermediate between males of the lower occupational classes and males of the lower white collar group (Tables 107–115). The children in the homes which belong to occupational class 4 present an amazing assemblage of patterns of behavior, because some of them finally regress to class 3, and a great many of them move on to occupational classes 5 and 6, and, in a fair number of cases, to the professional class 7. By early adolescence, the boys from class 4 homes who are destined to reach class 7 may already be identified by their high frequencies of masturbation

AGE GROUP	OCCUP. CLASS REACHED BY SUBJECT	CASES	PETTING TO CLIMAX, AND OCCUPATIONAL CLASS					
			TOTAL POPULATION			ACTIVE POPULATION		
			Mean Frequency	Me-dian Freq.	% of Total Outlet	Incid. %	Mean Frequency	Me-dian Freq.
			Parental Occupational Class 2					
Adol.–15	2	231	0.05 ± 0.02	0.00	1.83	14.3	0.34 ± 0.11	0.07
	3	126	0.03 ± 0.01	0.00	0.95	14.3	0.18 ± 0.10	0.06
16–20	2	198	0.07 ± 0.02	0.00	2.13	25.8	0.25 ± 0.08	0.07
	3	116	0.04 ± 0.02	0.00	1.14	24.1	0.17 ± 0.07	0.06
21–25	2	92	0.07 ± 0.04	0.00	2.72	17.4	0.38 ± 0.20	0.09
			Parental Occupational Class 3					
Adol.–15	2	140	0.03 ± 0.02	0.00	1.24	11.4	0.28 ± 0.14	0.08
	3	384	0.04 ± 0.01	0.00	1.27	17.4	0.22 ± 0.06	0.06
	5	205	0.03 ± 0.01	0.00	0.95	12.2	0.22 ± 0.07	0.08
	6 + 7	92	0.02 ± 0.01	0.00	0.74	14.1	0.15 ± 0.04	0.09
16–20	2	138	0.08 ± 0.03	0.00	2.89	22.5	0.36 ± 0.11	0.09
	3	318	0.07 ± 0.02	0.00	2.10	29.6	0.25 ± 0.06	0.06
	5	201	0.10 ± 0.02	0.00	3.57	34.8	0.29 ± 0.05	0.11
	6 + 7	94	0.15 ± 0.03	0.00	4.66	45.7	0.32 ± 0.05	0.21
21–25	2	64	0.07 ± 0.05	0.00	3.05	14.1	0.52 ± 0.36	0.08
	3	120	0.07 ± 0.03	0.00	2.02	17.5	0.38 ± 0.19	0.07
	5	124	0.11 ± 0.02	0.00	4.01	36.3	0.29 ± 0.06	0.10
	6 + 7	87	0.21 ± 0.04	0.06	7.92	67.8	0.31 ± 0.05	0.14
			Parental Occupational Class 4					
Adol.–15	3	107	0.04 ± 0.02	0.00	1.14	25.2	0.16 ± 0.06	0.06
	4	158	0.04 ± 0.02	0.00	1.58	13.9	0.29 ± 0.12	0.07
	5	304	0.03 ± 0.01	0.00	1.01	11.8	0.25 ± 0.06	0.08
	6	109	0.04 ± 0.02	0.00	1.46	9.2	0.45 ± 0.23	0.09
	7	74	0.04 ± 0.03	0.00	1.21	8.1	0.47 ± 0.27	0.30
16–20	3	105	0.06 ± 0.02	0.00	1.53	36.2	0.16 ± 0.05	0.06
	4	104	0.08 ± 0.03	0.00	2.91	24.0	0.33 ± 0.13	0.08
	5	305	0.11 ± 0.02	0.00	3.72	43.9	0.25 ± 0.03	0.08
	6	111	0.20 ± 0.05	0.01	6.75	51.4	0.39 ± 0.10	0.09
	7	75	0.12 ± 0.04	0.00	3.82	41.3	0.30 ± 0.10	0.10
21–25	5	183	0.14 ± 0.03	0.00	4.94	47.0	0.30 ± 0.06	0.08
	6	98	0.27 ± 0.07	0.02	10.37	56.1	0.47 ± 0.11	0.09
	7	71	0.17 ± 0.04	0.03	6.53	56.3	0.29 ± 0.06	0.20

(*Table continued on next page*)

AGE GROUP	OCCUP. CLASS REACHED BY SUBJECT	CASES	PETTING TO CLIMAX, AND OCCUPATIONAL CLASS					
			TOTAL POPULATION			ACTIVE POPULATION		
			Mean Frequency	Me-dian Freq.	% of Total Outlet	Incid. %	Mean Frequency	Me-dian Freq.

Parental Occupational Class 5

Adol.–15	3	65	0.03 ± 0.01	0.00	0.83	16.9	0.16 ± 0.07	0.08
	5	563	0.04 ± 0.01	0.00	1.57	13.1	0.33 ± 0.06	0.09
	6	228	0.04 ± 0.02	0.00	1.50	10.5	0.40 ± 0.12	0.13
	7	152	0.06 ± 0.02	0.00	2.12	12.5	0.44 ± 0.11	0.32
16–20	3	64	0.05 ± 0.03	0.00	1.79	21.9	0.25 ± 0.13	0.07
	5	516	0.14 ± 0.02	0.00	5.19	40.3	0.34 ± 0.04	0.09
	6	230	0.15 ± 0.03	0.00	5.42	40.4	0.36 ± 0.06	0.09
	7	155	0.17 ± 0.03	0.003	6.62	50.3	0.33 ± 0.06	0.16
21–25	5	262	0.14 ± 0.02	0.00	6.04	45.8	0.30 ± 0.04	0.09
	6	178	0.21 ± 0.04	0.01	8.35	52.8	0.40 ± 0.06	0.09
	7	143	0.17 ± 0.03	0.02	7.08	53.1	0.32 ± 0.05	0.21

Parental Occupational Class 6

Adol.–15	5	98	0.03 ± 0.02	0.00	0.86	12.2	0.26 ± 0.12	0.08
	6	1048	0.05 ± 0.01	0.00	1.84	16.7	0.31 ± 0.04	0.09
	7	244	0.02 ± 0.01	0.00	0.74	9.0	0.24 ± 0.10	0.08
16–20	5	100	0.12 ± 0.04	0.00	3.36	34.0	0.37 ± 0.10	0.08
	6	1021	0.14 ± 0.01	0.00	5.47	46.4	0.30 ± 0.02	0.09
	7	246	0.14 ± 0.02	0.00	4.48	48.0	0.30 ± 0.04	0.09
21–25	5	71	0.21 ± 0.07	0.00	6.96	42.3	0.50 ± 0.15	0.09
	6	554	0.16 ± 0.02	0.00	7.02	46.2	0.35 ± 0.03	0.09
	7	236	0.23 ± 0.03	0.04	7.93	61.0	0.37 ± 0.05	0.10
26–30	6	103	0.10 ± 0.03	0.00	4.36	39.8	0.26 ± 0.06	0.08
	7	97	0.15 ± 0.03	0.004	5.15	50.5	0.31 ± 0.05	0.09

Parental Occupational Class 7

Adol.–15	7	414	0.07 ± 0.02	0.00	2.21	15.0	0.45 ± 0.08	0.13
16–20	7	416	0.18 ± 0.03	0.00	5.99	49.5	0.37 ± 0.05	0.09
21–25	7	266	0.23 ± 0.05	0.02	8.73	55.6	0.42 ± 0.08	0.15

Table 110. Petting to climax, in relation to occupational class of parent and of subject

All data based on single males.

AGE GROUP	OCCUP. CLASS REACHED BY SUBJECT	CASES	NON-MARITAL INTERCOURSE AND OCCUPATIONAL CLASS						
			TOTAL POPULATION				ACTIVE POPULATION		
			Mean Frequency	Me-dian Freq.	% of Total Outlet		Incid. %	Mean Frequency	Me-dian Freq.
			Parental Occupational Class 2						
Adol.–15	2	231	0.59 ± 0.08	0.00	22.57		46.8	1.27 ± 0.15	0.75
	3	126	0.90 ± 0.17	0.00	34.33		46.0	1.95 ± 0.31	1.13
16–20	2	198	1.20 ± 0.12	0.51	39.74		79.3	1.52 ± 0.14	0.88
	3	116	1.90 ± 0.32	0.55	54.47		85.3	2.23 ± 0.36	0.86
21–25	2	92	0.95 ± 0.17	0.34	39.28		77.2	1.23 ± 0.21	0.50
			Parental Occupational Class 3						
Adol.–15	2	140	0.56 ± 0.11	0.00	21.39		41.4	1.35 ± 0.22	0.83
	3	384	1.00 ± 0.11	0.00	32.95		45.6	2.19 ± 0.22	1.13
	5	205	0.22 ± 0.07	0.00	7.81		17.1	1.29 ± 0.33	0.37
	6 + 7	92	0.06 ± 0.03	0.00	2.05		5.4	1.05 ± 0.43	1.00
16–20	2	138	1.20 ± 0.12	0.56	42.45		79.0	1.52 ± 0.14	1.11
	3	318	1.76 ± 0.17	0.50	50.81		77.4	2.27 ± 0.20	1.07
	5	201	0.46 ± 0.11	0.00	16.17		42.8	1.07 ± 0.24	0.31
	6 + 7	94	0.29 ± 0.09	0.00	9.46		41.5	0.71 ± 0.19	0.19
21–25	2	64	1.19 ± 0.22	0.38	49.33		75.0	1.58 ± 0.27	0.88
	3	120	1.90 ± 0.31	0.58	57.40		81.7	2.33 ± 0.37	0.92
	5	124	0.65 ± 0.13	0.04	24.50		55.6	1.17 ± 0.21	0.39
	6 + 7	87	0.58 ± 0.11	0.10	21.79		64.4	0.89 ± 0.15	0.44
			Parental Occupational Class 4						
Adol.–15	3	107	1.17 ± 0.20	0.16	32.87		53.3	2.19 ± 0.31	1.38
	4	158	0.48 ± 0.12	0.00	18.97		36.1	1.33 ± 0.32	0.43
	5	304	0.29 ± 0.09	0.00	9.69		20.1	1.42 ± 0.44	0.34
	6	109	0.03 ± 0.02	0.00	0.89		4.6	0.55 ± 0.44	0.10
	7	74	0.002 ± 0.001	0.00	0.06		4.1	0.05 ±	0.07
16–20	3	105	2.17 ± 0.28	1.00	56.84		92.4	2.35 ± 0.29	1.50
	4	104	1.01 ± 0.20	0.14	37.24		66.3	1.53 ± 0.28	0.63
	5	305	0.56 ± 0.11	0.00	19.14		47.2	1.19 ± 0.22	0.31
	6	111	0.29 ± 0.08	0.00	9.62		37.8	0.76 ± 0.18	0.21
	7	75	0.30 ± 0.13	0.00	9.34		38.7	0.78 ± 0.33	0.16
21–25	5	183	0.78 ± 0.18	0.06	27.50		59.0	1.32 ± 0.29	0.35
	6	98	0.44 ± 0.08	0.06	17.07		62.2	0.70 ± 0.11	0.33
	7	71	0.58 ± 0.14	0.07	22.94		56.3	1.03 ± 0.22	0.46

(Table continued on next page)

AGE GROUP	OCCUP. CLASS REACHED BY SUBJECT	CASES	NON-MARITAL INTERCOURSE AND OCCUPATIONAL CLASS						
			TOTAL POPULATION			ACTIVE POPULATION		
			Mean Frequency	Median Freq.	% of Total Outlet	Incid. %	Mean Frequency	Median Freq.
Parental Occupational Class 5								
Adol.–15	3	65	1.22 ±0.32	0.10	36.51	53.8	2.26 ± 0.53	1.25
	5	563	0.08 ±0.01	0.00	2.74	14.9	0.50 ± 0.08	0.25
	6	228	0.06 ±0.03	0.00	2.14	7.5	0.81 ± 0.30	0.33
	7	152	0.01 ±0.004	0.00	0.40	7.9	0.13 ± 0.04	0.08
16–20	3	64	1.52 ±0.33	0.53	50.76	79.7	1.91 ± 0.39	0.94
	5	516	0.25 ±0.03	0.00	9.39	38.8	0.63 ± 0.07	0.27
	6	230	0.16 ±0.03	0.00	5.86	40.4	0.39 ± 0.06	0.19
	7	155	0.20 ±0.04	0.00	8.08	39.4	0.51 ± 0.09	0.25
21–25	5	262	0.37 ±0.06	0.001	15.87	50.0	0.73 ± 0.10	0.34
	6	178	0.32 ±0.05	0.05	12.97	59.0	0.55 ± 0.08	0.27
	7	143	0.55 ±0.09	0.14	23.29	67.1	0.82 ± 0.12	0.39
Parental Occupational Class 6								
Adol.–15	5	98	0.21 ±0.07	0.00	5.78	20.4	1.04 ± 0.28	0.65
	6	1048	0.09 ±0.02	0.00	3.06	10.1	0.85 ± 0.21	0.26
	7	244	0.12 ±0.07	0.00	4.20	7.8	1.59 ± 0.81	0.20
16–20	5	100	0.58 ±0.15	0.00	15.70	49.0	1.19 ± 0.29	0.46
	6	1021	0.23 ±0.03	0.00	9.04	39.4	0.59 ± 0.07	0.20
	7	246	0.23 ±0.04	0.00	7.10	37.8	0.60 ± 0.09	0.27
21–25	5	71	0.53 ±0.15	0.02	17.57	52.1	1.02 ± 0.26	0.54
	6	554	0.39 ±0.04	0.02	16.72	52.2	0.74 ± 0.07	0.32
	7	236	0.71 ±0.11	0.07	24.89	63.1	1.12 ± 0.16	0.36
26–30	6	103	0.68 ±0.17	0.05	28.76	55.3	1.22 ± 0.28	0.46
	7	97	1.15 ±0.21	0.26	38.35	63.9	1.80 ± 0.31	1.08
Married 21–25	6	113	0.11 ±0.09	0.00	3.05	15.9	0.70 ± 0.54	0.13
	7	76	0.16 ±0.12	0.00	3.55	17.1	0.93 ± 0.66	0.23
26–30	6	112	0.05 ±0.01	0.00	1.46	27.7	0.16 ± 0.03	0.08
	7	135	0.18 ±0.07	0.00	5.02	28.1	0.63 ± 0.23	0.15
Parental Occupational Class 7								
Adol.–15	7	414	0.08 ±0.03	0.00	2.62	7.5	1.06 ± 0.40	0.19
16–20	7	416	0.23 ±0.05	0.00	7.59	35.3	0.65 ± 0.14	0.21
21–25	7	266	0.46 ±0.09	0.003	17.20	50.4	0.91 ± 0.17	0.22

Table 111. Non-marital intercourse in relation to occupational class of parent
and of subject

All data based on single males except where indicated as "married." Data for single males cover pre-marital intercourse with companions only. Data for married males cover extra-marital intercourse with both companions and prostitutes.

AGE GROUP	OCCUP. CLASS REACHED BY SUBJECT	CASES	MARITAL INTERCOURSE AND OCCUPATIONAL CLASS					
			TOTAL POPULATION			ACTIVE POPULATION		
			Mean Frequency	Me-dian Freq.	% of Total Outlet	Incid. %	Mean Frequency	Me-dian Freq.
Parental Occupational Class 5								
21-25	5	57	2.94 ± 0.32	2.33	83.52	100.0	2.94 ± 0.32	2.33
	6	67	3.23 ± 0.42	2.36	87.60	100.0	3.23 ± 0.42	2.36
26-30	6	70	2.78 ± 0.36	2.04	85.57	100.0	2.78 ± 0.36	2.04
	7	92	2.74 ± 0.21	2.35	87.24	100.0	2.74 ± 0.21	2.35
31-35	6	57	2.63 ± 0.38	1.90	85.42	100.0	2.63 ± 0.38	1.90
	7	77	2.49 ± 0.23	2.04	81.71	98.7	2.52 ± 0.23	2.06
Parental Occupational Class 6								
21-25	6	113	3.08 ± 0.25	2.54	83.90	99.1	3.11 ± 0.25	2.55
	7	76	3.70 ± 0.40	2.87	82.45	100.0	3.70 ± 0.40	2.87
26-30	6	112	2.57 ± 0.25	1.95	83.74	100.0	2.57 ± 0.25	1.95
	7	135	2.88 ± 0.21	2.39	81.59	100.0	2.88 ± 0.21	2.39
31-35	6	82	2.47 ± 0.34	1.78	82.08	100.0	2.47 ± 0.34	1.78
	7	114	2.34 ± 0.17	1.97	80.22	100.0	2.34 ± 0.17	1.97
36-40	6	51	2.31 ± 0.43	1.57	82.16	96.1	2.41 ± 0.44	1.64
	7	88	2.03 ± 0.16	1.78	73.96	97.8	2.08 ± 0.16	1.82
Parental Occupational Class 7								
21-25	7	63	2.93 ± 0.24	2.50	81.85	98.4	2.97 ± 0.24	2.56
26-30	7	72	2.71 ± 0.22	2.36	79.73	98.6	2.75 ± 0.22	2.39
31-35	7	57	2.25 ± 0.19	2.13	72.41	100.0	2.25 ± 0.19	2.13
36-40	7	50	2.01 ± 0.26	1.60	66.57	100.0	2.01 ± 0.26	1.60

Table 112. Marital intercourse in relation to occupational class of parent and of subject

and by their very low frequencies of intercourse. Conversely, the boys from class 4 homes who will ultimately drop back into a group of semi-skilled workmen, masturbate less frequently and have a considerable amount of pre-marital intercourse before they are 15 (Tables 108, 111). Because group 4 is so unstable, it should provide the very best material to be found for the study of the forces which control the development of sexual patterns, and particularly those forces which lead an individual to diverge from the patterns of his parents.

Occupational Class 5. This is the lower white collar group. It includes persons who work for the most part indoors at positions demanding some mental ability but usually not a great deal of training. The educational background of the group (Table 80) is a high school education of some sort in a high proportion of the cases, and at least some college work in 44 per cent of the cases. The group is more stable than occupational class 4, but it is less stable than any other white collar group. About 19 per cent of its children drop back into laboring groups and into the trades. However, 53 per cent of the homes in class 5 send their children on to college and into occupations which give them higher social status.

The sexual patterns of class 5 represent close approximations to the patterns of the upper white collar classes 6 and 7, as regards masturbation and nocturnal emissions (Tables 108, 109). The group has a good deal more pre-marital intercourse than the males of occupational classes 6 and 7 (Table 111) and it has a great deal more homosexual activity than classes 6 and 7 (Table 114), but it does not match the high frequencies which lower occupational classes have in heterosexual coitus and in the homosexual.

Occupational Class 6. This is an upper white collar group whose members have college or graduate school training in about 90 per cent of the cases. Obviously, this was not so in past generations, but there will be an increasing amount of college training for this group in the future. Class 6 is a remarkably stable group, with 40 per cent of its offspring remaining in the same class and another 40 per cent moving up into professional class 7 (Table 106). Since the group is so exclusively college in its educational background, its pattern is typical of that described in Chapter 10 for the college level. This means that it depends primarily upon masturbation for its pre-marital outlet, but has pre-marital intercourse with frequencies that are only one-sixth or one-eighth as high as those among the boys of corresponding age in class 3 (Tables 108, 111). The males of occupational class 6 are derived from parental homes which rate anything from 2 to 8; but irrespective of the origins of these males, the fact that they are headed for class 6 is abundantly evident in their early adolescent years, if not before.

AGE GROUP	OCCUP. CLASS REACHED BY SUBJECT	CASES	INTERCOURSE WITH PROSTITUTES AND OCCUPATIONAL CLASS						
			TOTAL POPULATION				ACTIVE POPULATION		
			Mean Frequency	Me-dian Freq.	% of Total Outlet	Incid. %	Mean Frequency	Me-dian Freq.

AGE GROUP	OCCUP. CLASS REACHED BY SUBJECT	CASES	Mean Frequency (Total)	Median Freq. (Total)	% of Total Outlet	Incid. %	Mean Frequency (Active)	Median Freq. (Active)
Parental Occupational Class 2								
Adol.–15	2	231	0.03 ±0.02	0.00	1.26	6.1	0.55 ± 0.28	0.09
	3	126	0.01 ±0.007	0.00	0.41	5.6	0.19 ± 0.11	0.08
16–20	2	198	0.14 ±0.03	0.00	4.60	39.4	0.35 ± 0.06	0.10
	3	116	0.16 ±0.04	0.00	4.53	40.5	0.39 ± 0.09	0.13
21–25	2	92	0.39 ±0.09	0.07	15.99	66.3	0.58 ± 0.12	0.31
Parental Occupational Class 3								
Adol.–15	2	140	0.04 ±0.03	0.00	1.62	6.4	0.66 ± 0.40	0.30
	3	384	0.01 ±0.004	0.00	0.47	8.1	0.18 ± 0.04	0.08
	5	205	0.01 ±0.005	0.00	0.35	2.9	0.34 ± 0.10	0.35
	6 + 7	92	0.004 ±0.003	0.00	0.13	2.2	0.18 ± 0.13	0.30
16–20	2	138	0.15 ±0.03	0.00	5.41	41.3	0.37 ± 0.07	0.12
	3	318	0.17 ±0.03	0.00	4.85	45.3	0.37 ± 0.06	0.10
	5	201	0.05 ±0.01	0.00	1.82	25.9	0.20 ± 0.05	0.07
	6 + 7	94	0.02 ±0.01	0.00	0.70	17.0	0.13 ± 0.05	0.07
21–25	2	64	0.32 ±0.09	0.01	13.25	51.6	0.62 ± 0.17	0.28
	3	120	0.35 ±0.08	0.03	10.66	55.8	0.63 ± 0.14	0.30
	5	124	0.07 ±0.02	0.00	2.51	21.0	0.32 ± 0.09	0.08
	6 + 7	87	0.02 ±0.01	0.00	0.80	25.3	0.08 ± 0.02	0.06
Parental Occupational Class 4								
Adol.–15	3	107	0.01 ±0.02	0.00	0.34	10.3	0.12 ± 0.04	0.08
	4	158	0.01 ±0.007	0.00	0.52	4.4	0.30 ± 0.14	0.10
	5	304	0.003 ±0.002	0.00	0.10	3.0	0.11 ± 0.04	0.07
	6	109	0.003 ±0.003	0.00	0.09	0.9	0.30 ±	0.50
16–20	3	105	0.10 ±0.02	0.02	2.62	57.1	0.18 ± 0.03	0.08
	4	104	0.17 ±0.05	0.00	6.28	44.2	0.39 ± 0.09	0.09
	5	305	0.04 ±0.01	0.00	1.46	27.2	0.16 ± 0.04	0.07
	6	111	0.03 ±0.01	0.00	0.89	17.1	0.16 ± 0.07	0.07
	7	75	0.01 ±0.006	0.00	0.43	14.7	0.10 ± 0.03	0.07
21–25	5	183	0.06 ±0.02	0.00	2.25	26.2	0.24 ± 0.07	0.08
	6	98	0.03 ±0.01	0.00	1.09	15.3	0.18 ± 0.05	0.09
	7	71	0.01 ±0.004	0.00	0.38	12.7	0.08 ± 0.01	0.06

(*Table continued on next page*)

AGE GROUP	OCCUP. CLASS REACHED BY SUBJECT	CASES	INTERCOURSE WITH PROSTITUTES AND OCCUPATIONAL CLASS					
			TOTAL POPULATION			ACTIVE POPULATION		
			Mean Frequency	Median Freq.	% of Total Outlet	Incid. %	Mean Frequency	Median Freq.
Parental Occupational Class 5								
Adol.–15	3	65	0.01 ±0.007	0.00	0.32	6.2	0.18 ± 0.08	0.20
	5	563	0.006±0.003	0.00	0.22	3.6	0.18 ± 0.07	0.08
	6	228	0.001 ± 0.0004	0.00	0.02	1.3	0.05	0.07
	7	152	0.0003 ± 0.0003	0.00	0.01	0.7	0.05	0.10
16–20	3	64	0.11 ±0.03	0.01	3.75	53.1	0.21 ± 0.04	0.09
	5	516	0.03 ±0.004	0.00	1.04	23.8	0.12 ± 0.02	0.06
	6	230	0.02 ±0.01	0.00	0.75	14.8	0.14 ± 0.06	0.06
	7	155	0.02 ±0.01	0.00	0.60	14.2	0.11 ± 0.06	0.06
21–25	5	262	0.06 ±0.02	0.00	2.40	24.8	0.22 ± 0.06	0.08
	6	178	0.01 ±0.005	0.00	0.53	12.9	0.10 ± 0.04	0.06
	7	143	0.02 ±0.01	0.00	0.98	18.9	0.12 ± 0.06	0.06
Parental Occupational Class 6								
Adol.–15	5	98	0.005±0.003	0.00	0.12	4.1	0.11 ± 0.07	0.08
	6	1048	0.005±0.003	0.00	0.18	2.5	0.21 ± 0.09	0.06
	7	244	0.001 ± 0.0005	0.00	0.04	2.5	0.05	0.06
16–20	5	100	0.02 ±0.005	0.00	0.54	25.0	0.08 ± 0.02	0.06
	6	1021	0.02 ±0.004	0.00	0.90	20.4	0.11 ± 0.02	0.06
	7	246	0.04 ±0.01	0.00	1.11	17.9	0.20 ± 0.05	0.08
21–25	5	71	0.03 ±0.01	0.00	0.99	25.4	0.12 ± 0.03	0.07
	6	554	0.03 ±0.005	0.00	1.15	18.2	0.15 ± 0.02	0.07
	7	236	0.08 ±0.05	0.00	2.87	21.6	0.38 ± 0.22	0.07
26–30	6	103	0.04 ±0.02	0.00	1.84	18.4	0.23 ± 0.10	0.08
	7	97	0.20 ±0.16	0.00	6.63	16.5	1.20 ± 0.96	0.09
Parental Occupational Class 7								
Adol.–15	7	414	0.004±0.002	0.00	0.12	2.9	0.13 ± 0.04	0.08
16–20	7	416	0.02 ±0.005	0.00	0.70	15.9	0.13 ± 0.03	0.06
21–25	7	266	0.02 ±0.006	0.00	0.78	13.5	0.15 ± 0.04	0.07

Table 113. Intercourse with prostitutes in relation to occupational class of parent and of subject

All data based on single males.

Occupational Class 7. This is the professional group which, by definition, has better than college training in 99 per cent of the cases (Table 106). About 65 per cent of the offspring of this group go into the professions, and consequently belong to the same occupational class as their parents; but nearly one-fourth of the offspring of the group drops back to occupational class 6. Only a small portion of the persons in occupational class 7 are derived from homes which are anything but class 6 or 7 (Table 106). It is, nevertheless, intensely interesting to find that those males who do get into class 7 out of parental homes which rated 4 and 5, have class 7 patterns early in their teens. Indeed, the class 4 males who ultimately arrive at class 7 have the most restrained socio-sexual histories in this whole group, and depend upon masturbation more exclusively than the class 7 males who are derived from any other parental background (Table 115). It is as though the bigger the move which the boy makes between his parental class and the class toward which he aims, the more strict he is about lining up his sexual history with the pattern of the group into which he is going to move. If this were done consciously, it would be more understandable; but considering that the boy in actuality knows very little about the sexual behavior of the social group into which he is moving, it is all the more remarkable to find that these patterns are laid down at such an early age.

VERTICAL MOBILITY: AT LATER AGES

It is a relatively small number of individuals who start with the sexual pattern of the parental social level, stay with it through their teens and perhaps for some years beyond, and finally move into some other social level.

There are some cases of males who have dropped back into a distinctly lower social level, after they had been well started in the parental class. Such cases are relatively few. These males are the "black sheep" of the community, who amount to something less than what was expected of them, or the persons who become involved in some maze of social circumstances which brings economic or social disaster. Men in Salvation Army homes or over-night hotels have supplied a number of histories of this sort. The underworld occasionally contributes the history of a man with a degree of Ph.D. or of M.D. who has turned to illicit activities and to loafing for an occupation.

Vertical mobility which did not start upward until after the late teens is found occasionally among males who stop school, find employment as laborers or in the trades for a period of years, and only later decide to go to college. These are the individuals who come into contact with some person or persons, or with some particular circumstance which encourages them to go back to school some time after they have left it. These are the persons who have enough ability to succeed in business and who are thus able to achieve social position because of their acquired financial status.

These are the persons who are encouraged or forced, by some particular circumstance, to consider the future in terms which had never appeared in their previous thinking, and who may be given specific aid for such an undertaking. Many GI's who are attending the colleges and universities of the country would not be going to college now if they were not subsidized by public funds, and many of them would still not be going to college if there were not a considerable public sentiment in this country for the GI to utilize the most of his opportunities.

The sexual records of these males are most significant, but we do not yet have enough cases to warrant a statistical manipulation of the data. However, it is safe to generalize so far as to say that males who have lower level patterns in their early adolescent years, and who keep their lower level patterns through their teens, usually retain their lower level patterns when they finally go to college or professional school, and throughout the rest of their lives. Even though they may subsequently engage in the professions and acquire considerable social position, they do not usually adopt the upper level sexual patterns. A male from this group may keep his lower level pattern even though he may subsequently become a judge on the bench, a physician, a psychiatrist, or a successful business man. This is, of course, exactly in line with the conclusions drawn for those males who departed from the parental pattern in their early years. In both cases, it is a matter of patterns of behavior being laid down by early or middle adolescence; and of practically nothing, either in the parental background or in the subsequent migration of the individual to other social levels, modifying those patterns in subsequent years. The judge with the lower level background excuses pre-marital intercourse and objects to mastur-bation, even though all of his colleagues on the same bench may have different, upper level ideas on the subject. The successful business man who has risen from lower levels never gives up his early acceptance of pre-marital intercourse, but continues to condemn what he calls the sophisti-cated sexual techniques of the upper level into which he has moved. The physician whose own history began with a lower level pattern expects to find pre-marital intercourse in the histories of his patients, and may recom-mend intercourse to them as a matter of therapy. He has a greater tolerance of extra-marital intercourse; but he may lecture before the local high school on the dangers of masturbation. He may assure his patients that petting as a substitute for coitus is likely to lead to all sorts of nervous dis-orders and neurotic disturbances. He condemns mouth-genital contacts, and insists that simple and direct heterosexual coitus provides the only normal sex life. Such physicians may imply that they have scientific author-ity for these opinions, when in actuality they are merely verbalizing the standards of the social level in which they were raised.

AGE GROUP	OCCUP. CLASS REACHED BY SUBJECT	CASES	HOMOSEXUAL OUTLET AND OCCUPATIONAL CLASS					
			TOTAL POPULATION			ACTIVE POPULATION		
			Mean Frequency	Median Freq.	% of Total Outlet	Incid. %	Mean Frequency	Median Freq.
	Parental Occupational Class 2
Adol.–15	2	231	0.37 ± 0.06	0.00	14.25	32.9	1.14 ± 0.14	0.73
	3	126	0.20 ± 0.08	0.00	7.51	27.0	0.73 ± 0.30	0.23
16–20	2	198	0.33 ± 0.05	0.00	10.85	34.3	0.96 ± 0.11	0.66
	3	116	0.21 ± 0.08	0.00	6.06	26.7	0.79 ± 0.27	0.23
21–25	2	92	0.18 ± 0.05	0.00	7.29	26.1	0.68 ± 0.16	0.36
	Parental Occupational Class 3
Adol.–15	2	140	0.27 ± 0.07	0.00	10.50	30.0	0.91 ± 0.21	0.36
	3	384	0.26 ± 0.05	0.00	8.66	29.4	0.89 ± 0.15	0.37
	5	205	0.16 ± 0.04	0.00	5.53	25.4	0.61 ± 0.15	0.10
	6 + 7	92	0.09 ± 0.05	0.00	3.05	22.8	0.37 ± 0.22	0.08
16–20	2	138	0.23 ± 0.06	0.00	8.27	29.0	0.81 ± 0.17	0.41
	3	318	0.22 ± 0.05	0.00	6.32	27.4	0.80 ± 0.16	0.27
	5	201	0.27 ± 0.09	0.00	9.67	24.4	1.12 ± 0.35	0.28
	6 + 7	94	0.04 ± 0.02	0.00	1.41	13.8	0.32 ± 0.14	0.10
21–25	2	64	0.21 ± 0.10	0.00	8.93	15.6	1.38 ± 0.52	0.66
	3	120	0.23 ± 0.13	0.00	6.95	15.0	1.53 ± 0.80	0.45
	5	124	0.43 ± 0.14	0.00	16.13	21.8	1.97 ± 0.57	1.00
	6 + 7	87	0.05 ± 0.03	0.00	2.00	8.0	0.66 ± 0.26	0.50
	Parental Occupational Class 4
Adol.–15	3	107	0.31 ± 0.10	0.00	8.80	28.0	1.12 ± 0.30	0.33
	4	158	0.09 ± 0.02	0.00	3.49	31.0	0.28 ± 0.06	0.09
	5	304	0.16 ± 0.03	0.00	5.32	22.7	0.69 ± 0.12	0.24
	6	109	0.22 ± 0.08	0.00	7.78	26.6	0.83 ± 0.29	0.20
	7	74	0.05 ± 0.03	0.00	1.47	10.8	0.43 ± 0.27	0.17
16–20	3	105	0.27 ± 0.11	0.00	7.08	31.4	0.86 ± 0.32	0.22
	4	104	0.11 ± 0.06	0.00	4.15	28.8	0.39 ± 0.19	0.08
	5	305	0.20 ± 0.04	0.00	6.77	21.6	0.92 ± 0.16	0.27
	6	111	0.27 ± 0.10	0.00	9.18	20.7	1.32 ± 0.39	0.30
	7	75	0.03 ± 0.02	0.00	0.90	12.0	0.24 ± 0.14	0.08
21–25	5	183	0.32 ± 0.09	0.00	11.40	21.3	1.51 ± 0.38	0.83
	6	98	0.27 ± 0.10	0.00	10.43	18.4	1.45 ± 0.44	0.35
	7	71	0.02 ± 0.01	0.00	0.66	5.6	0.30 ± 0.18	0.30

(*Table continued on next page*)

AGE GROUP	OCCUP. CLASS REACHED BY SUBJECT	CASES	HOMOSEXUAL OUTLET AND OCCUPATIONAL CLASS					
			TOTAL POPULATION			ACTIVE POPULATION		
			Mean Frequency	Median Freq.	% of Total Outlet	Incid. %	Mean Frequency	Median Freq.
Parental Occupational Class 5								
Adol.–15	3	65	0.15 ± 0.06	0.00	4.47	29.2	0.51 ± 0.18	0.10
	5	563	0.15 ± 0.02	0.00	5.31	26.6	0.55 ± 0.06	0.18
	6	228	0.09 ± 0.03	0.00	3.21	19.7	0.46 ± 0.14	0.09
	7	152	0.06 ± 0.02	0.00	2.37	22.4	0.28 ± 0.08	0.08
16–20	3	64	0.23 ± 0.09	0.00	7.50	35.9	0.63 ± 0.24	0.10
	5	516	0.14 ± 0.02	0.00	5.34	21.5	0.65 ± 0.09	0.12
	6	230	0.07 ± 0.03	0.00	2.69	15.2	0.48 ± 0.15	0.09
	7	155	0.04 ± 0.02	0.00	1.65	11.6	0.36 ± 0.13	0.08
21–25	5	262	0.21 ± 0.06	0.00	9.07	15.6	1.34 ± 0.36	0.50
	6	178	0.10 ± 0.04	0.00	3.84	9.6	1.01 ± 0.34	0.34
	7	143	0.05 ± 0.03	0.00	2.22	7.7	0.69 ± 0.29	0.30
Parental Occupational Class 6								
Adol.–15	5	98	0.45 ± 0.12	0.00	12.34	41.8	1.08 ± 0.25	0.32
	6	1048	0.08 ± 0.01	0.00	2.77	22.7	0.34 ± 0.04	0.08
	7	244	0.10 ± 0.03	0.00	3.37	22.1	0.45 ± 0.12	0.10
16–20	5	100	0.62 ± 0.15	0.00	16.85	44.0	1.42 ± 0.29	0.88
	6	1021	0.06 ± 0.01	0.00	2.24	16.7	0.35 ± 0.06	0.09
	7	246	0.07 ± 0.03	0.00	2.10	14.2	0.47 ± 0.20	0.08
21–25	5	71	0.67 ± 0.19	0.00	22.21	32.4	2.08 ± 0.47	1.70
	6	554	0.10 ± 0.02	0.00	4.20	10.6	0.91 ± 0.19	0.28
	7	236	0.01 ± 0.005	0.00	0.49	6.8	0.21 ± 0.07	0.09
26–30	6	103	0.27 ± 0.09	0.00	11.68	24.3	1.13 ± 0.30	0.42
	7	97	0.01 ± 0.01	0.00	0.43	5.2	0.25 ± 0.15	0.10
Parental Occupational Class 7								
Adol.–15	7	414	0.07 ± 0.01	0.00	2.38	23.2	0.31 ± 0.05	0.09
16–20	7	416	0.03 ± 0.01	0.00	0.94	13.7	0.21 ± 0.05	0.07
21–25	7	266	0.02 ± 0.01	0.00	0.74	5.6	0.35 ± 0.25	0.07

Table 114. Homosexual outlet in relation to occupational class of parent and of subject

All data based on single males.

TRANSMISSION OF SEXUAL MORES

When we understand the processes by which the sexual mores are stabilized in each social group, and transmitted to each and all of the members of the group, we shall have gone a considerable way toward understanding some of the most fundamental of social phenomena. If we understood the forces which lead some boys to ignore the attitudes and expressed sexual philosophies of their parents, and even of their companions in the community in which they are raised, we should have the key to problems that are basic in genetic psychology. If we knew by what processes a boy acquires the patterns of a social level in which he is not living and into which he will only ultimately move, we should know a great deal more than we do today.

It is a far simpler matter to understand how children acquire their habits in regard to dressing, eating, and other behavioral activities. It is much simpler to discern the processes by which they learn to speak the mother tongue. But since there is a minimum of verbal instruction on matters of sex, since the child is rarely lectured in regard to attitudes on sex, and since it almost never observes adult sexual activity, sex education is a subtle process which, nevertheless, is powerful enough to force most children, somewhere during pre-adolescent or early adolescent years, into becoming conforming machines which rarely fail to perpetuate the mores of the community.

We can record the fact of vertical mobility in the social organization; we can figure statistics on the number of persons who make such moves and the directions in which they move. In all of psychology and sociology there is, however, next to no information on the factors which affect this movement from out of a parental group into a new social status. That a considerable number of individuals should aspire to move into levels that have greater prestige is quite understandable; but that does not explain why certain individuals rather than others are the ones who make these moves. We have been able to show that sexual attitudes and overt experience in sexual activities are closely correlated with the educational and occupational class into which an individual ultimately moves, after he has broken with his parental background but very often before he has ever left the parental home. But this still falls short of identifying the impetus which stirs that individual to make such moves.

As yet we have only hypotheses about the sources of the inspiration which leads this boy to make the break with his parental pattern, and as yet we can only cite specific instances in support of our preliminary thinking. We can point to the father whose contacts with the upper level lead him to associate upper level sexual patterns with upper level success in social and business affairs. His contacts may not affect his own sexual performance, but they may be significant enough to lead him to encourage a pattern for his son which differs from his own. It is probable that the mother is even more often responsible for the boy's sexual restraint. It is often she who encourages him to associate with proper, well-behaved, and similarly restrained upper level companions. On the other hand, there are cases of boys who make these moves in the face of parental objections. Some boys complete high school only over the parental protest and ultimately go to college without parental support and sometimes in the face of considerable opposition from their homes. The boy's companions in school, in church, and elsewhere, may take him away from his companions in the community in which he actually lives. Sometimes adults other than the parents have something to do with the boy's acquisition of new attitudes and ideals. We shall need a great deal of additional information before we can appraise the relative significances of these several sources of influence, and of still others which we may not yet have recognized.

Psychologists and psychiatrists will be inclined to suggest that the beginnings of this conditioning should be searched for in very early childhood, and what few data we do have confirm such a theory. As noted earlier in the present volume (Chapter 5), we have recently undertaken to secure sexual data from very young children and plan to publish a volume concerned entirely with these processes of learning. Although the data are not yet abundant enough to analyze statistically, we can make the following generalizations at this time:

1. Some of the most fundamental distinctions between the social levels are already discernible in pre-adolescents as young as 3 and 4. The ease or embarrassment with which such a child discusses genitalia, excretory functions, anatomical distinctions between males and females, the possibility that there has been self manipulation of genitalia, the possibility that there has been genital exhibition or genital play with other children, the question of the origin of babies, the merely social companionship with his own or the opposite sex, questions about kissing his parents and about kissing companions of his own or of the opposite sex—and kindred items —indicate in practically every instance that the 3- or 4-year old child has already acquired something of the social attitudes on at least some of these issues.

Social approval or disapproval means a great deal to a child of that age. It may not take more than a single adverse experience to make a child feel that he must not expose himself again to the laughter, the specific reprimand, or physical punishment which accompanied his first performance. The disdainful ridicule of other children, the angry withdrawal of companions who disapprove of the child's overt activity, the nervous amusement of adults, are things that even the 3-year old does not wish to experience again.

AGE GROUP	PAREN-TAL OCCUP. CLASS	CASES	OUTLETS AND PARENTAL OCCUPATIONAL CLASS MEAN FREQUENCIES, TOTAL POPULATION						
			Total Outlet	Mastur-bation	Noctur-nal Emis-sions	Petting to Climax	Coitus, Com-panions	Coitus, Pros-titutes	Homo-sexual
Subject: Occupational Class 3									
Adol.–15	2	126	2.68	1.40	0.06	0.03	0.90	0.01	0.20
	3	384	3.10	1.57	0.11	0.04	1.00	0.01	0.26
	4	107	3.62	1.94	0.07	0.04	1.17	0.01	0.31
	5	65	3.38	1.81	0.05	0.03	1.22	0.01	0.15
16–20	2	116	3.46	1.01	0.16	0.04	1.90	0.16	0.21
	3	318	3.50	1.00	0.21	0.07	1.76	0.17	0.22
	4	105	3.82	0.98	0.24	0.06	2.17	0.10	0.27
	5	64	3.03	0.88	0.14	0.05	1.52	0.11	0.23
Subject: Occupational Class 5									
Adol.–15	3	205	2.85	2.07	0.27	0.03	0.22	0.01	0.16
	4	304	3.00	2.18	0.28	0.03	0.29	0.003	0.16
	5	563	2.77	2.13	0.31	0.04	0.08	0.006	0.15
	6	98	3.76	2.74	0.20	0.03	0.21	0.005	0.45
16–20	3	201	2.88	1.57	0.35	0.10	0.46	0.05	0.27
	4	305	2.97	1.64	0.38	0.11	0.56	0.04	0.20
	5	516	2.63	1.68	0.37	0.14	0.25	0.03	0.14
	6	100	3.80	1.94	0.35	0.12	0.58	0.02	0.62
21–25	3	124	2.73	1.09	0.31	0.11	0.65	0.07	0.43
	4	183	2.86	1.17	0.35	0.14	0.78	0.06	0.32
	5	262	2.32	1.22	0.30	0.14	0.37	0.06	0.21
	6	71	3.13	1.27	0.31	0.21	0.53	0.03	0.67
Subject: Occupational Class 6									
Adol.–15	4	109	2.85	2.18	0.33	0.04	0.03	0.003	0.22
	5	228	2.86	2.17	0.43	0.04	0.06	0.001	0.09
	6	1048	2.86	2.29	0.28	0.05	0.09	0.005	0.08
16–20	4	111	3.01	1.71	0.48	0.20	0.29	0.03	0.27
	5	230	2.72	1.82	0.47	0.15	0.16	0.02	0.07
	6	1021	2.58	1.73	0.38	0.14	0.23	0.02	0.06
21–25	4	98	2.55	1.10	0.46	0.27	0.44	0.03	0.27
	5	178	2.56	1.43	0.43	0.21	0.32	0.01	0.10
	6	554	2.38	1.27	0.37	0.16	0.39	0.03	0.10
Subject: Occupational Class 7									
Adol.–15	4	74	3.14	2.56	0.45	0.04	0.002		0.05
	5	152	2.70	2.05	0.43	0.06	0.01	0.0003	0.06
	6	244	3.00	2.24	0.44	0.02	0.12	0.001	0.10
	7	414	3.05	2.39	0.40	0.07	0.08	0.004	0.07
16–20	4	75	3.23	2.21	0.55	0.12	0.30	0.01	0.03
	5	155	2.50	1.60	0.47	0.17	0.20	0.02	0.04
	6	246	3.18	2.17	0.54	0.14	0.23	0.04	0.07
	7	416	3.04	2.12	0.43	0.18	0.23	0.02	0.03
21–25	4	71	2.51	1.37	0.39	0.17	0.58	0.01	0.02
	5	143	2.43	1.18	0.40	0.17	0.55	0.02	0.05
	6	236	2.88	1.38	0.43	0.23	0.71	0.08	0.01
	7	266	2.71	1.51	0.43	0.23	0.46	0.02	0.02

Table 115. Similarity of sexual frequencies of persons belonging to the same occupational class

Emphasizing near identity of histories of subjects who reach the same occupational class, irrespective of the diverse occupational classes of their parents. Showing mean frequencies for total populations. Medians, incidences, data on active populations, standard deviations of means, etc., shown for same populations in previous tables in this chapter.

Questioned concerning his behavior, the young child may deny that he has ever kissed or been kissed, that he has exposed his genitalia, that he has touched his own genitalia, that he has allowed other persons to touch his genitalia, or that he has touched the genitalia of other children. His denials are made with a nervous haste and apparent discomfort which make it apparent that he wants to leave the subject and not discuss such things further. The history of the army colonel who denied that he had ever had homosexual experience unless it happened at night, when he did not know anything about it, is matched by the history of the 4-year old boy who insisted that no other boys had touched him except when he was asleep. One is concerned not so much with ascertaining the actuality of the child's overt experience, but rather with getting some measure of the nature of his emotional responses; for in those responses one may learn what values the child has already acquired, and how those values will shape his future behavior.

2. Social attitudes are acquired long before the child may know that there is any significance to genital stimulation, much less intercourse. The so-called sex instruction which is given by parents and schools usually consists of a certain amount of information concerning the anatomy and mechanics of reproduction. As far as our present information goes, this has a minimum of any effect upon the development of patterns of sexual behavior and, indeed, it may have no effect at all. Patterns of behavior are the products of attitudes; and attitudes may begin shaping long before the child has acquired very much, if any, factual information.

3. Traditional attitudes toward heterosexual and homosexual relationships have been apparent in some of the 3- and 4-year old histories. The older pre-adolescent boys from upper social levels, however, were often more willing to admit their homosexual experience, less often willing to admit their heterosexual relationships. It is apparent that the attitudes of companions who consider it sissy to play with girls are predominant factors, both in the development of the child's attitudes and in the shaping of his overt activity. By early adolescence, however, it is more difficult to obtain homosexual data from an upper level group, and simpler to obtain data of heterosexual contacts. The group has begun to attach values to heterosexuality, it has begun to recognize the taboos which older persons place on the homosexual. It is the attitude of the group that has changed, and not the independent thinking of the child.

4. The lower level interest in heterosexual intercourse and frank acceptance of it as a pre-marital activity is apparent in the histories of a high proportion of the 7- and 8-year old boys from those groups; and in some instances it is well developed as early as age 4. By ages 7 or 8 the lower level boy knows that intercourse is one of the activities in which most of his companions, at least his slightly older companions, are engaging; and

SUBJECT OCCUPATIONAL CLASS 3

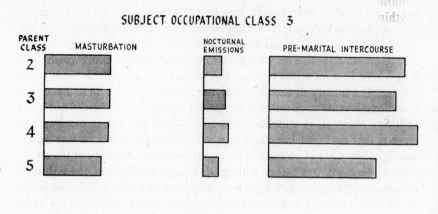

SUBJECT OCCUPATIONAL CLASS 5

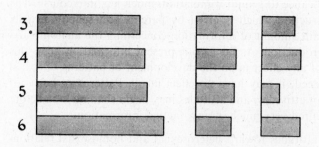

SUBJECT OCCUPATIONAL CLASS 7

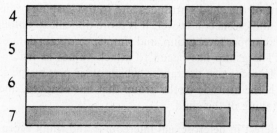

Figure 124. Comparisons of sexual patterns of males of same occupational class but originating from diverse parental classes

Comparing mean frequency data for the age period 16–20, for three sources of outlet, for single males of three occupational classes.

he has already learned that intercourse is one of the things that are considered highly desirable by those companions. Meanwhile, the 10-year old boy from the upper level home is likely to confine his pre-adolescent sex play to the exhibition and manual manipulation of genitalia, and he does not attempt intercourse because, in many instances, he has not yet learned that there is such a possibility.

5. Children are the most frequent agents for the transmission of the sexual mores. Adults serve in that capacity only to a smaller extent. This will not surprise sociologists and anthropologists, for they are aware of the great amount of imitative adult activity which enters into the play of children, the world around. In this activity, play though it may be, children are severe, highly critical, and vindictive in their punishment of a child who does not do it "this way," or "that way." Even before there has been any attempt at overt sex play, the child may have acquired a considerable schooling on matters of sex. Much of this comes so early that the adult has no memory of where his attitudes were acquired.

6. The mores may be imposed by the children of the community in defiance of the attempts of adults to impose other patterns. Lower level parents may punish their children for attempting intercourse, but the lower level 7-year old assures us with wide open eyes that he cannot understand why his mother should punish him, and he does not consider it wrong to attempt intercourse, because all of the other boys are doing it. Upon securing the history of the boy's mother, it becomes apparent that the punishment she gave was quite perfunctory, and that deep in her own thinking she does not exactly disapprove of pre-marital sexual relations, anyway. Even when the parents are sincere in their attempts to impose ideas that differ from those of the community, the children may triumph over the parents. Sometimes parents attempt to impose patterns which are stricter than those in the community. Sometimes they attempt to be more liberal, and try to raise the child without having it acquire fears and inhibitions concerning sex. In some cases the parents succeed, but in many cases they do not. In the further study of this problem it will be important to accumulate specific data in such abundance that it will be possible, ultimately, to measure the relative importance of companions, parents, and other adults in the establishment of the child's attitudes and patterns of overt behavior.

Children are, on the whole, conformists. Their initial experiences with a particular object or event lead them to believe that the world is made in a particular way, and they are likely to conclude that the whole world should be made that way. Any departure in the placement of furniture, in the style of clothing which is worn, in the way in which food is served, or in the schedule of the day—the routine which is followed upon getting up in the morning or upon going to bed at night—may bring protests that "that is not the way to do it." This is the sort of conformance that children are continually forcing upon each other in regard to all matters, including sex.

7. The record given in this chapter makes it clear that exceedingly few males modify their attitudes on matters of sex or change their patterns of overt behavior in any fundamental way after their middle teens. Many individuals do acquire certain details of activity in their later years, and some individuals think that they have acquired entirely new attitudes on matters of sex, at some late period in their lives. Upper level individuals like to think that they have become more liberal, sexually emancipated, free of their former inhibitions, rational instead of traditional in their behavior, ready to experiment with anything. It is notable, however, that such emancipated persons rarely engage in any amount of actual behavior which is foreign to the pattern laid down in their youth. Such an individual may publicly discuss his changed attitudes, and may go so far as to engage in such a public display of petting as leads the community to believe that there is considerably more going on; but the actual history is not likely to contain more than a minimum of non-marital intercourse. The upper level male who comes back from an army experience with tales of the wild places where he has been, the freedom of the girls in the tropics, the endless chances he had for experience of every sort, the record of the particular girl with whom he became acquainted in this station, and the girl with whom he got in trouble in another station—may have to admit, when he contributes an objective record to a scientific study, that he never did bring himself to having actual intercourse with a single one of the girls. This is a long way from the sort of promiscuous pattern which is common-place in lower level histories.

8. While the behavior of the adult is thus controlled by what he calls his conscience, he is also influenced by such social forces as public opinion. Among adults, this operates in much the same subtle way that community attitudes are passed on to the children. The tone of voice in which gossip is relayed warns the individual to avoid becoming a subject for similar gossip. The care and circumlocution with which certain matters of sex are avoided in books, in the press, and in other public communications, constantly remind the individual of the state of public opinion on these things. Discussions of such things as divorce, marital discord, the sexual scandals of the community, and the gossip about public characters probably have more influence in controlling the individual's behavior than any specific action that society may take or any legal penalties that are attached to those things.

9. The church and the other organizations that are chiefly concerned with problems of morals are, basically, the source of a good deal of the sexual philosophy of the community (Chapter 13). On occasion the church specifically condemns departures from its sex code, but more often it

depends upon the less tangible concepts of purity, cleanliness, sin, un-cleanliness, degradation. The very indefiniteness of these characterizations makes them more inclusive. Each individual categorizes himself in accordance with the standards that are set up. He is often more severe to himself than his fellows would be if they were judging his record. To the religiously devout, moral values are considerable forces. Nevertheless, the patterns of the social levels are even more influential than the mandates of a religion (Chapter 13).

10. The written legal codes and the proscriptions of the common law are much less influential in controlling the sexual behavior of the human animal. Patterns of behavior are established long before the child is likely to have any comprehension of the nature of the legal formalization of our codes.

These observations may contribute to our understanding of the fact that individuals in our American society rarely adopt totally new patterns of sexual behavior after their middle teens. It would appear that the changes that do occur represent departures made by pre-adolescent and adolescent children from the patterns of their parents. We have at least progressed in our understanding of social forces when we have recognized these very early years as fundamental in the development of both individual and community patterns of sexual behavior.

AGE GROUP	RURAL-URBAN GROUP	CASES	TOTAL OUTLET: RURAL, URBAN				
			TOTAL POPULATION		ACTIVE POPULATION		
			Mean Frequency	Median Freq.	Incid. %	Mean Frequency	Median Freq.
Single Males: Educational Level 0–8							
Adol.–15	Rural	245	2.41 ± 0.18	1.33	89.4	2.69 ± 0.20	1.70
	Urban	401	3.40 ± 0.21	1.98	92.0	3.69 ± 0.22	2.34
16–20	Rural	259	2.81 ± 0.20	1.85	96.5	2.91 ± 0.20	1.95
	Urban	397	3.43 ± 0.19	2.37	98.2	3.49 ± 0.19	2.43
21–25	Rural	141	2.80 ± 0.29	1.56	95.0	2.95 ± 0.30	1.78
	Urban	188	3.29 ± 0.30	1.97	97.9	3.36 ± 0.31	2.01
26–30	Rural	61	3.01 ± 0.53	1.40	98.4	3.06 ± 0.54	1.45
	Urban	88	3.04 ± 0.34	2.08	98.9	3.07 ± 0.34	2.10
Single Males: Educational Level 9–12							
Adol.–15	Rural	124	2.81 ± 0.30	1.70	94.4	2.98 ± 0.31	1.86
	Urban	459	3.50 ± 0.16	2.51	95.6	3.66 ± 0.17	2.64
16–20	Rural	124	3.17 ± 0.27	2.43	99.2	3.20 ± 0.27	2.45
	Urban	458	3.60 ± 0.15	2.82	99.8	3.61 ± 0.15	2.82
21–25	Rural	50	2.53 ± 0.37	1.55	98.0	2.58 ± 0.37	1.60
	Urban	209	3.17 ± 0.21	2.55	99.5	3.19 ± 0.21	2.56
Single Males: Educational Level 13+							
Adol.–15	Rural	352	2.94 ± 0.16	2.28	96.3	3.05 ± 0.16	2.38
	Urban	2587	2.84 ± 0.06	2.20	95.9	2.96 ± 0.06	2.32
16–20	Rural	363	2.52 ± 0.10	2.01	99.7	2.53 ± 0.11	2.02
	Urban	2640	2.77 ± 0.05	2.18	99.7	2.78 ± 0.05	2.19
21–25	Rural	266	2.17 ± 0.11	1.64	99.2	2.19 ± 0.11	1.66
	Urban	1753	2.59 ± 0.06	1.93	99.9	2.59 ± 0.06	1.93
26–30	Rural	85	2.17 ± 0.23	1.46	98.8	2.20 ± 0.23	1.48
	Urban	445	2.64 ± 0.13	1.91	100.0	2.64 ± 0.13	1.91
Married Males: Educational Level 0–8							
21–25	Rural	128	3.36 ± 0.34	2.31	100.0	3.36 ± 0.34	2.31
	Urban	162	4.41 ± 0.38	2.85	100.0	4.41 ± 0.38	2.85
26–30	Rural	117	3.29 ± 0.38	2.09	100.0	3.29 ± 0.38	2.09
	Urban	148	3.35 ± 0.26	2.58	98.6	3.40 ± 0.26	2.63
31–35	Rural	93	2.75 ± 0.33	1.74	100.0	2.75 ± 0.33	1.74
	Urban	109	2.98 ± 0.27	2.34	100.0	2.98 ± 0.27	2.34
36–40	Rural	84	2.48 ± 0.31	1.70	100.0	2.48 ± 0.31	1.70
	Urban	75	2.53 ± 0.25	2.19	100.0	2.53 ± 0.25	2.19
Married Males: Educational Level 13+							
21–25	Rural	63	3.85 ± 0.46	3.06	100.0	3.85 ± 0.46	3.06
	Urban	428	3.70 ± 0.12	3.12	100.0	3.70 ± 0.12	3.12
26–30	Rural	86	3.01 ± 0.35	2.41	100.0	3.01 ± 0.35	2.41
	Urban	516	3.36 ± 0.11	2.76	100.0	3.36 ± 0.11	2.76
31–35	Rural	76	2.73 ± 0.29	2.24	100.0	2.73 ± 0.29	2.24
	Urban	402	2.96 ± 0.12	2.35	100.0	2.96 ± 0.12	2.35
36–40	Rural	50	2.26 ± 0.26	2.09	98.0	2.31 ± 0.26	2.11
	Urban	281	2.70 ± 0.15	2.09	100.0	2.70 ± 0.15	2.09

Table 116. Total outlet and rural-urban background

Chapter 12

RURAL-URBAN BACKGROUND AND SEXUAL OUTLET

The city boy's failure to understand what life can mean to a boy who is raised on a farm, and the farm boy's idea that there is something glamorous about the way in which the city boy lives, apply to every avenue of human activity, including the sexual. This popular interest in knowing how another group lives is projected into the sociologist's invariable search for basic differences between the mores of city groups and the mores of farm groups; and this accounts for the fact that the few data which have been available on the sexual life of the rural male have commanded widespread attention.

Unfortunately, the only specific comparisons of the sexual activities of rural versus urban groups come from a small study made by Pearl in 1925. The study covered a limited number of sexual items on 174 older males, of whom 39 were farmers. The calculations derived from these few cases seemed to show that the farmers were sexually more active than the merchants and the bankers, and they in turn were more active than the professional men. These conclusions have been quoted many times in the sociological literature, although the data are, of course, altogether too scant to warrant any generalizations concerning such a tremendous population as the rural American group constitutes. It is unfortunate that such poorly established conclusions should have gained such wide credence, and particularly unfortunate because the conclusions are diametrically opposed to what now appears to be the fact. The Pearl series was not broken down for educational backgrounds or any other social measures of the individuals involved. Since lower social levels have higher frequencies of total sexual outlet, particularly of marital intercourse (Table 88), and since marital intercourse was the only sexual outlet for which Pearl had data, it is probable that the farmers in the Pearl study rated high in sexual activity because they belonged to lower educational levels. Conversely, the merchants, bankers, and professional groups, which constituted the major portion of Pearl's urban sample, were from upper white collar and professional classes, and these always have lower rates of marital outlet.

Reference to Chapter 3 in the present volume will show the definitions by which the subjects in the present study have been classified as rural or urban. It is unfortunate that the limited rural sample which is now available has made it impossible to make the complete breakdowns which are shown in Chapter 3, and the analyses in the present chapter have been made

AGE GROUP	RURAL-URBAN GROUP	CASES	MASTURBATION: RURAL, URBAN					
			TOTAL POPULATION			ACTIVE POPULATION		
			Mean Frequency	Me-dian Freq.	% of Total Outlet	Incid. %	Mean Frequency	Me-dian Freq.

Single Males: Educational Level 0–8

AGE GROUP	RURAL-URBAN GROUP	CASES	Mean Frequency	Me-dian Freq.	% of Total Outlet	Incid. %	Mean Frequency	Me-dian Freq.
Adol.–15	Rural	245	1.28 ± 0.11	0.75	55.0	80.8	1.59 ± 0.13	1.05
	Urban	401	1.76 ± 0.11	0.94	52.3	86.8	2.03 ± 0.13	1.19
16–20	Rural	259	0.94 ± 0.07	0.48	33.6	84.9	1.11 ± 0.08	0.66
	Urban	397	0.98 ± 0.07	0.45	28.7	84.6	1.16 ± 0.08	0.62
21–25	Rural	141	0.67 ± 0.09	0.21	24.3	63.8	1.05 ± 0.13	0.57
	Urban	188	0.64 ± 0.08	0.18	19.5	63.3	1.01 ± 0.12	0.48
26–30	Rural	61	0.58 ± 0.12	0.05	19.6	54.1	1.07 ± 0.19	0.71
	Urban	88	0.65 ± 0.13	0.11	22.0	64.8	1.01 ± 0.19	0.48

Single Males: Educational Level 9–12

AGE GROUP	RURAL-URBAN GROUP	CASES	Mean Frequency	Me-dian Freq.	% of Total Outlet	Incid. %	Mean Frequency	Me-dian Freq.
Adol.–15	Rural	124	1.66 ± 0.19	0.94	60.8	88.7	1.87 ± 0.20	1.19
	Urban	459	2.07 ± 0.11	1.34	60.3	90.2	2.29 ± 0.11	1.56
16–20	Rural	124	1.13 ± 0.15	0.61	35.8	85.5	1.32 ± 0.17	0.82
	Urban	458	1.33 ± 0.07	0.74	37.2	90.2	1.47 ± 0.07	0.87
21–25	Rural	50	0.68 ± 0.16	0.24	27.4	66.0	1.03 ± 0.23	0.61
	Urban	209	0.92 ± 0.09	0.41	30.0	78.9	1.17 ± 0.10	0.66

Single Males: Educational Level 13+

AGE GROUP	RURAL-URBAN GROUP	CASES	Mean Frequency	Me-dian Freq.	% of Total Outlet	Incid. %	Mean Frequency	Me-dian Freq.
Adol.–15	Rural	352	2.28 ± 0.13	1.76	79.1	84.1	2.71 ± 0.14	2.17
	Urban	2587	2.24 ± 0.05	1.60	79.9	82.1	2.73 ± 0.06	2.08
16–20	Rural	363	1.67 ± 0.08	1.18	67.3	89.0	1.88 ± 0.09	1.44
	Urban	2640	1.86 ± 0.04	1.22	67.0	88.9	2.09 ± 0.05	1.54
21–25	Rural	266	1.19 ± 0.08	0.79	56.4	86.1	1.38 ± 0.08	0.95
	Urban	1753	1.35 ± 0.04	0.67	52.9	87.5	1.54 ± 0.05	0.85
26–30	Rural	85	1.09 ± 0.16	0.48	50.6	78.8	1.39 ± 0.19	0.94
	Urban	445	1.15 ± 0.08	0.49	43.5	85.6	1.34 ± 0.09	0.68

Table 117. Masturbation and rural-urban background

on a simpler basis. They must be taken as indications of trends which will have to be analyzed more precisely when more material is available.

Throughout this chapter persons have been classified as rural if they ever belonged to the rural-urban group which is numbered 3 (Chapter 3), either alone or in conjunction with some other rating which they held at some other period of their lives. This means that they have been considered rural if they lived on an operating farm for an appreciable portion of the years between 12 and 18. This is the late pre-adolescent and adolescent period which is so important in the shaping of sexual patterns (Chapter 11). Persons have been classified as urban if they ever belonged to rural-urban groups 0, 1, or 4, or to some combination of these groups, without ever belonging to class 3. This means they have been rated as urban if they never had more than incidental residence in rural areas, or if their rural residence occurred only after the age of 18, which is the age by which most of the patterns of sexual behavior are already laid down (Chapter 11). Rural-urban group 2 was not used because the sample was too small. As treated in the present chapter, the rural group is very definitely rural, but the urban group involves some individuals who have had chiefly city residence but some less significant rural contacts. It is unfortunate that no finer breakdown could be made with the material available at this time.

FREQUENCIES OF TOTAL OUTLET

For the population as a whole, it has been shown that frequencies of sexual outlet depend upon the age of the individual, the age at which he became adolescent, his educational background and occupational class, and his religious background. This is equally true of the rural portion of the population and of the urban portion of the population, and no comparison of the frequencies of total sexual outlet or of the sexual outlet from the several sorts of sexual activity can mean much unless there is a preliminary breakdown on most of these other factors.

An examination of Table 116 will show that the differences between the total outlet of the rural males and the total outlet of the urban males are never very great. In general, the differences would not be particularly significant if they did not all lie in the same direction, which is almost without exception in the direction of a lower frequency of total sexual outlet for the rural males. The differences are most marked in the lower educational level, where the rural males may not have more than three-fourths as frequent activity as the urban males. Differences are less for the males of the high school level and among the boys who go to college.

City-bred persons might expect the farm boy to have higher rates of outlet, inasmuch as he sees sexual activity among animals and hears free discussion of sex from the time he is very young; but the specific data do

AGE GROUP	RURAL-URBAN GROUP	CASES	NOCTURNAL EMISSIONS: RURAL, URBAN					
			TOTAL POPULATION			ACTIVE POPULATION		
			Mean Frequency	Me-dian Freq.	% of Total Outlet	Incid. %	Mean Frequency	Me-dian Freq.

Single Males: Educational Level 0–8

AGE GROUP	RURAL-URBAN GROUP	CASES	Mean Frequency	Me-dian Freq.	% of Total Outlet	Incid. %	Mean Frequency	Me-dian Freq.
Adol.–15	Rural	245	0.05 ± 0.015	0.00	2.3	22.9	0.24 ± 0.056	0.08
	Urban	401	0.06 ± 0.011	0.00	1.7	27.4	0.21 ± 0.038	0.08
16–20	Rural	259	0.13 ± 0.019	0.01	4.8	53.3	0.25 ± 0.033	0.08
	Urban	397	0.17 ± 0.019	0.03	5.0	58.2	0.29 ± 0.030	0.09
21–25	Rural	141	0.17 ± 0.030	0.03	6.3	57.4	0.30 ± 0.049	0.10
	Urban	188	0.16 ± 0.024	0.03	4.7	60.1	0.26 ± 0.038	0.09
26–30	Rural	61	0.18 ± 0.041	0.05	5.9	65.6	0.27 ± 0.059	0.10
	Urban	88	0.19 ± 0.039	0.04	6.3	63.6	0.29 ± 0.059	0.09

Single Males: Educational Level 9–12

AGE GROUP	RURAL-URBAN GROUP	CASES	Mean Frequency	Me-dian Freq.	% of Total Outlet	Incid. %	Mean Frequency	Me-dian Freq.
Adol.–15	Rural	124	0.11 ± 0.025	0.00	4.0	34.7	0.31 ± 0.063	0.15
	Urban	459	0.17 ± 0.026	0.00	4.9	41.8	0.40 ± 0.057	0.12
16–20	Rural	124	0.20 ± 0.031	0.06	6.3	71.8	0.28 ± 0.039	0.11
	Urban	458	0.24 ± 0.022	0.07	6.6	71.0	0.33 ± 0.029	0.14
21–25	Rural	50	0.21 ± 0.047	0.07	8.5	74.0	0.29 ± 0.059	0.13
	Urban	209	0.25 ± 0.026	0.08	8.1	70.3	0.35 ± 0.034	0.23

Single Males: Educational Level 13+

AGE GROUP	RURAL-URBAN GROUP	CASES	Mean Frequency	Me-dian Freq.	% of Total Outlet	Incid. %	Mean Frequency	Me-dian Freq.
Adol.–15	Rural	352	0.27 ± 0.031	0.06	9.3	61.9	0.43 ± 0.047	0.25
	Urban	2587	0.36 ± 0.014	0.12	12.7	71.8	0.50 ± 0.019	0.28
16–20	Rural	363	0.44 ± 0.035	0.26	17.6	92.0	0.47 ± 0.038	0.29
	Urban	2640	0.42 ± 0.012	0.25	15.2	90.7	0.47 ± 0.013	0.29
21–25	Rural	266	0.39 ± 0.038	0.25	18.7	89.5	0.44 ± 0.041	0.29
	Urban	1753	0.39 ± 0.014	0.22	15.2	86.0	0.45 ± 0.016	0.28
26–30	Rural	85	0.29 ± 0.030	0.22	13.6	85.9	0.34 ± 0.033	0.08
	Urban	445	0.32 ± 0.022	0.18	12.0	84.0	0.38 ± 0.025	0.25

Table 118. Nocturnal emissions and rural-urban background

not bear out such an idea. In fact, it might be possible to theorize to the effect that early and constant acquaintance with sex would reduce the farm boy's erotic responses and leave him less interested; but this still remains unproved theory. The average city dweller thinks of the farm boy as having more privacy than the city boy has for carrying on socio-sexual activities, but the theory does not seem to fit the fact. There is a general opinion that rural communities are in general stricter in their religious adherence than city communities, and this may be one of the explanations of the slightly lower rates of rural groups, but this is not demonstrable with the present data. It might be suggested that the city boy has more opportunity for making social contacts in general, for dating girls and, consequently, for obtaining sexual relations with girls; and this may, or may not, be an explanation of the fact that socio-sexual contacts are in actuality less frequent for the boy who is raised on the farm. There are other possible explanations of the lower rates of the rural males, but none of these is more than a possibility which will need investigation when sufficient series of cases become available.

SPECIFIC SEXUAL OUTLETS

Masturbation. Self-induced orgasm occurs in almost exactly the same proportions of the rural and of the urban populations (Table 117). Frequencies are rather lower for the youngest adolescent group of farm boys who never go beyond eighth grade or high school; but at all ages the frequencies among the boys who will ultimately go to college are practically identical for the rural and for the urban groups. Since the total outlet of the rural male is a bit lower, and since the actual frequencies of masturbation are about the same as those of the urban group, the part of the total outlet which the farm boy derives from masturbation is a bit higher at all ages and in all educational levels.

Nocturnal Emissions. These occur with much the same incidences and frequencies among the rural and the urban groups. This is true at all ages, and in all social levels (Table 118). In the few places where the table indicates some differences, there are no consistent trends.

Petting to Climax. Orgasm achieved through heterosexual petting occurs in a definitely higher percentage of the urban males (Table 119). The frequencies are somewhat higher for the urban males who do not go beyond eighth grade or high school, but at the college level the frequencies of petting are 2.5 to 3 times as high among the urban males. Perhaps the farm boy is not so often involved because girls simply are not so available in a rural community; or perhaps he is not so often involved because the smaller community has not yet acquired the newer customs that are found in the city. The fact will have to be determined by a detailed examination of more histories.

AGE GROUP	RURAL-URBAN GROUP	CASES	PETTING TO CLIMAX: RURAL, URBAN					
			TOTAL POPULATION			ACTIVE POPULATION		
			Mean Frequency	Me-dian Freq.	% of Total Outlet	Incid. %	Mean Frequency	Me-dian Freq.
Single Males: Educational Level 0–8								
Adol.–15	Rural	245	0.017±0.006	0.00	0.7	11.8	0.14 ± 0.043	0.06
	Urban	401	0.037±0.011	0.00	1.1	13.7	0.27 ± 0.078	0.07
16–20	Rural	259	0.043±0.012	0.00	1.5	17.8	0.24 ± 0.059	0.07
	Urban	397	0.058±0.015	0.00	1.7	22.4	0.26 ± 0.064	0.07
21–25	Rural	141	0.031±0.013	0.00	1.1	12.8	0.24 ± 0.085	0.08
	Urban	188	0.047±0.023	0.00	1.4	16.5	0.28 ± 0.070	0.07
26–30	Rural	61	0.11 ±0.065	0.00	3.8	21.3	0.53 ± 0.28	0.20
	Urban	88	0.017±0.009	0.00	0.6	17.0	0.10 ± 0.049	0.06
Single Males: Educational Level 9–12								
Adol.–15	Rural	124	0.021±0.008	0.00	0.8	17.7	0.12 ± 0.038	0.06
	Urban	459	0.059±0.013	0.00	1.7	19.6	0.30 ± 0.060	0.07
16–20	Rural	124	0.040±0.011	0.00	1.3	30.6	0.13 ± 0.029	0.07
	Urban	458	0.095±0.015	0.00	2.7	34.3	0.28 ± 0.038	0.08
21–25	Rural	50	0.034±0.012	0.00	1.4	28.0	0.12 ± 0.032	0.08
	Urban	209	0.094±0.019	0.00	3.0	29.2	0.32 ± 0.072	0.08
Single Males: Educational Level 13+								
Adol.–15	Rural	352	0.019±0.006	0.00	0.7	11.1	0.17 ± 0.053	0.07
	Urban	2587	0.045±0.005	0.00	1.6	13.9	0.33 ± 0.027	0.09
16–20	Rural	363	0.074±0.013	0.00	3.0	35.5	0.21 ± 0.034	0.07
	Urban	2640	0.15 ±0.008	0.00	5.6	47.7	0.32 ± 0.016	0.09
21–25	Rural	266	0.081±0.012	0.00	3.8	43.6	0.19 ± 0.025	0.07
	Urban	1753	0.20 ±0.012	0.02	7.9	54.5	0.37 ± 0.021	0.11
26–30	Rural	85	0.063±0.014	0.00	2.9	43.5	0.14 ± 0.026	0.08
	Urban	445	0.16 ±0.019	0.00	5.9	47.2	0.33 ± 0.037	0.10

Table 119. Petting to climax and rural-urban background

Pre-marital Intercourse. The differences between rural and urban groups are greater in regard to pre-marital intercourse than they are for any of the preceding activities. In most age groups and at all educational levels, more of the city boys are involved and fewer of the farm boys (Table 120). At the grade school level, 91 per cent of the city boys may be involved between the ages of 21 and 25, but only 80 per cent of the farm boys. At the college level in the same age period, 55 per cent of the city boys have some pre-marital intercourse and about 47 per cent of the farm boys. The differences in frequencies of pre-marital intercourse between rural and urban groups are of about the same order.

Intercourse with Prostitutes. Pre-marital relations with prostitutes are even more distinctively an activity of the city group (Table 121). While it is commonly believed that farm boys are particularly interested in securing intercourse with prostitutes when they go into the city, the record indicates that fewer of them ever arrive at such experience. The frequency with which they have relations with prostitutes is definitely lower than the frequency with which city boys have such relations.

Marital Intercourse. In marital relations, the rural male again has a slightly lower rate of outlet than the city male (Table 122). The differences are not great but are consistent in several groups, as far as our limited data apply.

Homosexual Outlet. Orgasm effected by contacts with other males is, on the whole, less frequent among the farm boys who have contributed histories to this study, more frequent among the urban males (Table 123). The two groups are most distinct at the grade school and high school levels. The differences in incidence are very minor at the college level. Among the boys who have not gone beyond grade school, 32 per cent of the city boys may be involved between the ages of 16 and 20, but only 21 per cent of the farm boys. Among males of the high school level, at a corresponding age, the figures are 46 per cent for the city boys, 26 per cent for the rural. For the boys of the college level, in the same age group, the figures are very nearly identical, 16 or 17 per cent in both groups. Differences in frequencies are of the same general order, with the city boy having the most frequent contacts.

There is a wide-spread theory among psychologists and psychiatrists that the homosexual is a product of an effete and over-organized urban civilization. The failure to make heterosexual adjustments is supposed to be consequent on the complexities of life in our modern cities; or it is a product of a neuroticism which the high speed of living in the city imposes upon an increasing number of individuals. The specific data on the particular rural and urban groups which are shown in Table 123 do seem to suggest that there is something in city life which encourages the develop-

AGE GROUP	RURAL-URBAN GROUP	CASES	TOTAL POPULATION			ACTIVE POPULATION		
			Mean Frequency	Me-dian Freq.	% of Total Outlet	Incid. %	Mean Frequency	Me-dian Freq.

<table>

TOTAL NON-MARITAL INTERCOURSE: RURAL, URBAN

AGE GROUP	RURAL-URBAN GROUP	CASES	Mean Frequency	Me-dian Freq.	% of Total Outlet	Incid. %	Mean Frequency	Me-dian Freq.
Single Males: Educational Level 0–8
Adol.–15	Rural	199	0.67 ± 0.12	0.00	31.3	39.2	1.72 ± 0.27	0.91
	Urban	414	1.26 ± 0.14	0.03	39.9	51.4	2.45 ± 0.24	1.39
16–20	Rural	208	1.26 ± 0.15	0.43	50.2	81.3	1.55 ± 0.17	0.72
	Urban	406	1.99 ± 0.16	0.89	60.2	87.4	2.27 ± 0.17	1.25
21–25	Rural	106	1.40 ± 0.24	0.49	56.2	80.2	1.75 ± 0.29	0.83
	Urban	195	2.35 ± 0.26	0.96	69.5	90.8	2.59 ± 0.28	1.43
Single Males: Educational Level 9–12
Adol.–15	Rural	91	0.57 ± 0.12	0.00	21.4	38.5	1.47 ± 0.26	0.86
	Urban	405	0.87 ± 0.12	0.00	26.6	44.2	1.97 ± 0.25	0.81
16–20	Rural	95	1.48 ± 0.18	0.70	46.2	87.4	1.69 ± 0.20	1.00
	Urban	405	1.40 ± 0.14	0.41	40.8	72.6	1.92 ± 0.18	0.87
Single Males: Educational Level 13+
Adol.–15	Rural	265	0.08 ± 0.03	0.00	2.9	10.6	0.77 ± 0.23	0.31
	Urban	2126	0.08 ± 0.01	0.00	4.2	9.7	0.84 ± 0.10	0.29
16–20	Rural	272	0.19 ± 0.04	0.00	8.0	36.4	0.53 ± 0.11	0.10
	Urban	2172	0.26 ± 0.02	0.00	13.8	42.5	0.62 ± 0.04	0.18
21–25	Rural	200	0.34 ± 0.07	0.00	16.7	47.0	0.73 ± 0.13	0.25
	Urban	1377	0.45 ± 0.03	0.03	19.3	55.0	0.82 ± 0.06	0.30
26–30	Rural	58	0.48 ± 0.15	0.00	23.4	44.8	1.06 ± 0.31	0.54
	Urban	308	0.68 ± 0.09	0.06	21.4	58.8	1.16 ± 0.15	0.47
Married Males: Educational Level 0–8
21–25	Rural	128	0.14 ± 0.042	0.00	4.1	25.0	0.55 ± 0.14	0.27
	Urban	162	0.73 ± 0.21	0.00	16.1	40.7	1.78 ± 0.50	0.30
26–30	Rural	117	0.15 ± 0.047	0.00	4.6	29.9	0.51 ± 0.14	0.22
	Urban	148	0.23 ± 0.066	0.00	7.0	35.1	0.67 ± 0.17	0.12
31–35	Rural	93	0.18 ± 0.061	0.00	6.5	22.6	0.78 ± 0.23	0.43
	Urban	109	0.10 ± 0.024	0.00	3.5	36.7	0.28 ± 0.06	0.10
Married Males: Educational Level 13+
21–25	Rural	63	0.16 ± 0.14	0.00	4.0	9.5	1.68 ± 1.42	0.35
	Urban	428	0.05 ± 0.011	0.00	1.4	15.7	0.32 ± 0.06	0.10
26–30	Rural	86	0.12 ± 0.092	0.00	3.9	9.3	1.27 ± 0.94	0.40
	Urban	516	0.09 ± 0.016	0.00	2.8	25.2	0.37 ± 0.06	0.09
31–35	Rural	76	0.07 ± 0.045	0.00	2.5	10.5	0.64 ± 0.39	0.30
	Urban	402	0.16 ± 0.032	0.00	5.6	34.1	0.48 ± 0.09	0.17

</table>

Table 120. Total non-marital intercourse and rural-urban background

ment of the homosexual. But the distinctive thing about homosexuality in the city is the development of a more or less organized group activity which is unknown in any rural area.

Large cities have taverns, night clubs, restaurants, and baths which may become frequented almost exclusively by persons interested in meeting homosexual friends, or interested in finding opportunities for discussions with others who do not object to the known homosexuality of their companions. In this city group, the development of an elaborate argot gives a sense of belonging which may defend a minority group against the rest of society; but it also intensifies a feeling which the group has that it stands apart from the rest of the population. Moreover, it is this city group which exhibits all the affectations, the mannerisms, the dress, and the other displays which the rest of the population take to be distinctive of all homosexual persons, even though it is only a small fraction of the males with homosexual histories who ever display such characteristics. None of these city-bred homosexual institutions is known in rural areas, and this may well acount for a somewhat lower rate of the homosexual among farm boys.

On the other hand, the highest frequencies of the homosexual which we have ever secured anywhere have been in particular rural communities in some of the more remote sections of the country. The boy on the isolated farm has few companions except his brothers, the boys on an adjacent farm or two, visiting male cousins, and the somewhat older farm hand. His mother may see to it that he does not spend much time with his sisters, and the moral codes of the rural community may impose considerable limitations upon the association of boys and girls under other circumstances. Moreover, farm activities call for masculine capacities, and associations with girls are rated sissy by most of the boys in such a community. All of these things are conducive to a considerable amount of homosexuality among the teen-age males in the most isolated of the rural areas. There is much less of it in the smaller farm country of the Eastern United States.

Beyond this, there is a fair amount of sexual contact among the older males in Western rural areas. It is a type of homosexuality which was probably common among pioneers and outdoor men in general. Today it is found among ranchmen, cattle men, prospectors, lumbermen, and farming groups in general—among groups that are virile, physically active. These are men who have faced the rigors of nature in the wild. They live on realities and on a minimum of theory. Such a background breeds the attitude that sex is sex, irrespective of the nature of the partner with whom the relation is had. Sexual relations are had with women when they are available, or with other males when outdoor routines bring men together into exclusively male groups. Such a pattern is not at all uncommon among pre-adolescent and early adolescent males in such rural areas, and it continues in a number of histories into the adult years and through marriage.

			INTERCOURSE WITH PROSTITUTES: RURAL, URBAN					
AGE GROUP	RURAL-URBAN GROUP	CASES	TOTAL POPULATION			ACTIVE POPULATION		
			Mean Frequency	Median Freq.	% of Total Outlet	Incid. %	Mean Frequency	Median Freq.
Single Males: Educational Level 0–8								
Adol.–15	Rural	245	0.012±0.005	0.00	0.5	5.3	0.22 ± 0.08	0.09
	Urban	401	0.041±0.012	0.00	1.2	10.0	0.41 ± 0.11	0.15
16–20	Rural	259	0.15 ±0.025	0.00	5.4	42.5	0.35 ± 0.05	0.09
	Urban	397	0.23 ±0.029	0.01	6.6	50.9	0.45 ± 0.05	0.20
21–25	Rural	141	0.31 ±0.067	0.003	11.1	50.4	0.61 ± 0.12	0.25
	Urban	188	0.46 ±0.067	0.12	14.0	66.5	0.69 ± 0.10	0.36
26–30	Rural	61	0.50 ±0.14	0.07	16.9	65.6	0.76 ± 0.20	0.32
	Urban	88	0.57 ±0.095	0.25	19.2	75.0	0.76 ± 0.12	0.42
Single Males: Educational Level 9–12								
Adol.–15	Rural	124	0.004±0.003	0.00	0.2	4.8	0.09 ± 0.041	0.07
	Urban	459	0.017±0.005	0.00	0.5	8.1	0.21 ± 0.046	0.08
16–20	Rural	124	0.10 ±0.031	0.00	3.3	41.1	0.25 ± 0.070	0.07
	Urban	458	0.097±0.013	0.00	2.7	40.8	0.24 ± 0.029	0.08
21–25	Rural	50	0.19 ±0.071	0.00	7.8	48.0	0.40 ± 0.14	0.13
	Urban	209	0.12 ±0.019	0.00	3.9	40.7	0.29 ± 0.040	0.11
Single Males: Educational Level 13+								
Adol.–15	Rural	352	0.002±0.001	0.00	0.1	2.0	0.12 ± 0.045	0.08
	Urban	2587	0.003±0.001	0.00	0.1	2.2	0.12 ± 0.033	0.06
16–20	Rural	363	0.011±0.002	0.00	0.4	12.9	0.08 ± 0.012	0.06
	Urban	2640	0.021±0.002	0.00	0.8	19.9	0.11 ± 0.008	0.06
21–25	Rural	266	0.013±0.003	0.00	0.6	15.8	0.08 ± 0.013	0.06
	Urban	1753	0.032±0.007	0.00	1.3	17.6	0.18 ± 0.040	0.07
26–30	Rural	85	0.007±0.004	0.00	0.3	7.1	0.09 ± 0.041	0.07
	Urban	445	0.097±0.040	0.00	3.7	19.1	0.51 ± 0.20	0.08

Table 121. Intercourse with prostitutes and rural-urban background

Such a group of hard-riding, hard-hitting, assertive males would not tolerate the affectations of some city groups that are involved in the homosexual; but this, as far as they can see, has little to do with the question of having sexual relations with other men. This type of rural homosexuality contradicts the theory that homosexuality in itself is an urban product.

AGE GROUP	RURAL-URBAN GROUP	CASES	MARITAL INTERCOURSE: RURAL, URBAN					
			TOTAL POPULATION			ACTIVE POPULATION		
			Mean Frequency	Me-dian Freq.	% of Total Outlet	Incid. %	Mean Frequency	Me-dian Freq.
Educational Level 0–8								
21–25	Rural	128	3.03 ± 0.31	1.99	90.6	100.0	3.03 ± 0.31	1.99
	Urban	162	3.44 ± 0.28	2.38	76.3	98.1	3.51 ± 0.28	2.42
26–30	Rural	117	2.90 ± 0.36	1.83	88.5	100.0	2.90 ± 0.36	1.83
	Urban	148	2.86 ± 0.21	2.33	86.0	98.6	2.90 ± 0.21	2.35
31–35	Rural	93	2.39 ± 0.29	1.58	88.1	100.0	2.39 ± 0.29	1.58
	Urban	109	2.73 ± 0.25	2.18	91.9	100.0	2.73 ± 0.25	2.18
36–40	Rural	84	2.21 ± 0.28	1.54	91.4	100.0	2.21 ± 0.28	1.54
	Urban	75	2.23 ± 0.24	1.95	89.2	98.7	2.26 ± 0.24	1.98
Educational Level 13+								
21–25	Rural	63	3.34 ± 0.47	2.65	84.6	100.0	3.34 ± 0.47	2.65
	Urban	428	3.07 ± 0.11	2.58	84.1	99.5	3.08 ± 0.11	2.59
26–30	Rural	86	2.49 ± 0.29	1.93	82.9	100.0	2.49 ± 0.29	1.93
	Urban	516	2.77 ± 0.10	2.23	83.1	99.2	2.79 ± 0.10	2.25
31–35	Rural	76	2.22 ± 0.24	1.85	82.2	100.0	2.22 ± 0.24	1.85
	Urban	402	2.38 ± 0.11	1.91	81.1	99.5	2.40 ± 0.11	1.92
36–40	Rural	50	1.77 ± 0.22	1.53	79.2	98.0	1.81 ± 0.22	1.56
	Urban	281	2.06 ± 0.12	1.66	76.6	98.9	2.09 ± 0.12	1.67

Table 122. Marital intercourse and rural-urban background

Animal Contacts. Sexual relations with animals of other species are, of necessity, most often found in rural areas. Ultimately about 17 per cent of the farm boys have complete sexual relations with other animals (Table 124), and perhaps as many more have relations which are not carried through to climax.

AGE GROUP	RURAL-URBAN GROUP	CASES	HOMOSEXUAL OUTLET: RURAL, URBAN					
			TOTAL POPULATION			ACTIVE POPULATION		
			Mean Frequency	Median Freq.	% of Total Outlet	Incid. %	Mean Frequency	Median Freq.
Single Males: Educational Level 0–8								
Adol.–15	Rural	245	0.18 ± 0.039	0.00	7.7	18.4	0.98 ± 0.17	0.46
	Urban	401	0.32 ± 0.051	0.00	9.5	28.4	1.12 ± 0.16	0.44
16–20	Rural	259	0.21 ± 0.054	0.00	7.4	21.2	0.97 ± 0.23	0.37
	Urban	397	0.26 ± 0.037	0.00	7.6	32.0	0.81 ± 0.10	0.34
21–25	Rural	141	0.26 ± 0.11	0.00	9.4	17.0	1.52 ± 0.61	0.43
	Urban	188	0.26 ± 0.058	0.00	7.9	28.7	0.91 ± 0.17	0.41
26–30	Rural	61	0.53 ± 0.33	0.00	18.0	19.7	2.71 ± 1.57	0.75
	Urban	88	0.34 ± 0.097	0.00	11.6	35.2	0.98 ± 0.24	0.44
Single Males: Educational Level 9–12								
Adol.–15	Rural	124	0.26 ± 0.13	0.00	9.6	20.2	1.30 ± 0.60	0.10
	Urban	459	0.32 ± 0.037	0.00	9.3	37.9	0.84 ± 0.09	0.33
16–20	Rural	124	0.10 ± 0.031	0.00	3.2	25.8	0.39 ± 0.10	0.08
	Urban	458	0.50 ± 0.060	0.00	14.1	46.7	1.07 ± 0.12	0.37
21–25	Rural	50	0.10 ± 0.051	0.00	3.9	24.0	0.40 ± 0.19	0.09
	Urban	209	0.69 ± 0.13	0.00	22.4	42.6	1.61 ± 0.27	0.89
Single Males: Educational Level 13+								
Adol.–15	Rural	352	0.08 ± 0.019	0.00	2.7	21.3	0.36 ± 0.08	0.09
	Urban	2587	0.09 ± 0.008	0.00	3.2	21.8	0.41 ± 0.03	0.09
16–20	Rural	363	0.05 ± 0.013	0.00	2.1	16.8	0.32 ± 0.07	0.09
	Urban	2640	0.07 ± 0.008	0.00	2.4	15.8	0.42 ± 0.04	0.08
21–25	Rural	266	0.06 ± 0.022	0.00	2.8	9.4	0.62 ± 0.21	0.15
	Urban	1753	0.09 ± 0.012	0.00	3.4	10.1	0.85 ± 0.10	0.24
26–30	Rural	85	0.10 ± 0.042	0.00	4.9	15.3	0.68 ± 0.22	0.39
	Urban	445	0.22 ± 0.036	0.00	8.3	16.9	1.30 ± 0.16	0.63

Table 123. Homosexual outlet and rural-urban background

AGE GROUP	RURAL-URBAN GROUP	CASES	ANIMAL CONTACTS: RURAL					
			TOTAL POPULATION			ACTIVE POPULATION		
			Mean Frequency	Me-dian Freq.	% of Total Outlet	Incid. %	Mean Frequency	Me-dian Freq.
Educational Level 0–8								
Adol.–15	Rural	245	0.054±0.018	0.00	2.3	8.6	0.63 ± 0.16	0.50
	Urban	401	0.011±0.006	0.00	0.3	4.0	0.28 ± 0.13	0.08
16–20	Rural	259	0.034±0.012	0.00	1.2	7.3	0.46 ± 0.13	0.26
	Urban	397	0.012±0.008	0.00	0.3	2.0	0.58 ± 0.35	0.09
Educational Level 9–12								
Adol.–15	Rural	124	0.038±0.020	0.00	1.4	10.5	0.36 ± 0.17	0.10
	Urban	459	0.018±0.008	0.00	0.5	3.7	0.48 ± 0.19	0.09
16–20	Rural	124	0.092±0.040	0.00	2.9	10.5	0.88 ± 0.32	0.40
	Urban	458	0.017±0.010	0.00	0.5	2.6	0.65 ± 0.33	0.09
21–25	Rural	50	0.013±0.008	0.00	0.5	6.0	0.22 ± 0.08	0.30
	Urban	209	0.014±0.013	0.00	0.5	1.9	0.74 ± 0.69	0.08
Educational Level 13+								
Adol.–15	Rural	352	0.14 ±0.039	0.00	4.7	27.8	0.49 ± 0.13	0.08
	Urban	2587	0.003±0.001	0.00	0.1	1.9	0.14 ± 0.05	0.06
16–20	Rural	363	0.070±0.028	0.00	2.8	15.4	0.46 ± 0.18	0.10
	Urban	2640	0.001±0.001	0.00	0.02	0.7	0.12 ± 0.07	0.06
21–25	Rural	266	0.015±0.008	0.00	0.7	3.8	0.40 ± 0.17	0.25
	Urban	1753	0.0001± 0.0004	0.00	0.002	0.1	0.05	0.08
26–30	Rural	85	0.009±0.009	0.00	0.4	1.2	0.80	1.00
	Urban	445	0.0002± 0.00011	0.00	0.0004	0.4	0.05	0.08

Table 124. Animal contacts and rural-urban background

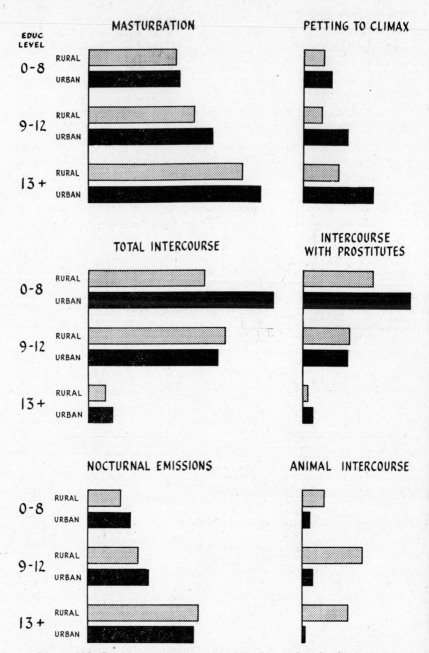

Figure 125. Comparisons of sexual activity in rural and urban groups

Comparing mean frequency data for the age period 16–20, for three educational levels. Black bars for urban population, shaded bars for rural groups.

There is, of course, a considerable amount of pre-adolescent contact with animals (Chapter 5). Among adolescent and older males of the rural groups, the lowest incidences of animal contacts are to be found in Eastern areas. The incidences increase considerably in the ranch country of the West. For the available rural sample, which is largely Eastern in origin, the active incidence figures begin at about 9 per cent in the early adolescent years of the group which never goes beyond grade school, and grades down to about 3 per cent for males of that educational level who are not yet married between the ages of 21 and 25. Among the rural boys who go into high school but not beyond, the active incidence figures stand at about 11 per cent between adolescence and 20 years of age. For the rural boys who will ultimately go to college, about 28 per cent have animal contacts between adolescence and 15, about 15 per cent in the late teens, and 4 per cent in the early twenties. Sexual contacts with animals are, it will be seen, most abundant among boys of the college level during their early and later teens.

Surprisingly enough, in the grade school portion of the urban population the boys have an appreciable amount of animal intercourse. About 4 per cent of these boys are involved between adolescence and 15. However, the frequencies for the city boys are very low, not amounting to more than a half to a fifth of the frequencies found among rural males. At the high school level, and particularly at the college level, there are fewer (1 to 4 per cent) of the city boys who are involved, and the discrepancies between the rural and the urban histories become very great on this point. For instance, the incidence among males of the college level, at 16–20 years of age, is 0.7 per cent for the city-bred boys and 15.4 per cent for the farm group. The differences in frequencies are even greater, the farm boys having 30 to 70 experiences for every one which the city boy has.

It is, of course, surprising to find that the city boy is ever involved, because he does not have such access to animals as the farm boy has. The city boy's contacts usually occur when he is visiting on a farm, and so in actuality this still remains rural behavior. In the city itself he may have contact with horses or ponies in some stable, or with some other animal in a city stockyard; but most of his contacts are with the household pets, particularly with pet dogs.

The absolute frequencies of animal contact are, in actuality, low. In a high proportion of the histories they are isolated occurrences, or events that happen two or three or a half dozen times in the boy's early adolescence. With a few individuals they may occur several times a week, and there are some cases of farm boys who depend upon this source for their major outlet. In Western farm areas there are more boys who have animal contacts with weekly or bi-weekly regularity through their early and perhaps later teens, and occasionally into their early twenties.

In summary, it may be emphasized again that there are few material differences between the histories of farm boys and the histories of boys raised in the city, or between adult males living in the two places. In general there are slightly lower frequencies of total sexual activity in the rural population, and lower frequencies in most of the particular sources of outlet. Nocturnal emissions occur with nearly identical incidences and frequencies in rural and in urban groups. The rural population is most distinct in having fewer socio-sexual contacts (meaning pre-marital hetero-sexual petting, pre-marital and extra-marital intercourse, and homosexual relations), and in its much higher frequencies of animal intercourse. But the city boy's interest in animal contacts as soon as they are available makes it clear that it is simply a question of opportunity which differentiates the rural and urban groups on this latter point.

Chapter 13

RELIGIOUS BACKGROUND AND SEXUAL OUTLET

In the broadest sense, the mores may become systems of morals and systems of morals are formalizations of the mores. It is no accident that the two words, *mores* and *morals*, stem from the same Latin root. Throughout history all peoples have defended their mores as stoutly as they have defended their religions, and their moral systems have determined the custom of the land. Sexual mores and systems of sexual morality are no exceptions to this general rule.

This means that there is nothing in the English-American social structure which has had more influence upon present-day patterns of sexual behavior than the religious backgrounds of that culture. It would require long research and a complete volume to work out the origins of the present-day religious codes which apply to sex, of the present-day sex mores, of the coded sex laws, and to trace the subtle ways in which these have influenced the behavior of individuals (Northcote 1916, Angus 1925, May 1931). Our particular systems certainly go back to the Old Testament philosophy on which the Talmud is based, and which was the philosophy of those Jews who first followed the Christian faith. In many details, the proscriptions of the Talmud are nearly identical with those of our present-day legal codes governing sexual behavior. Back of the Jewish formulations were the older codes of such peoples as the Hittites (Barton 1925), Babylonians (Harper 1904), Assyrians (Barton 1925), and Egyptians (Budge 1895), all of whom probably had a part in shaping the sexual systems of the early Jews. Several Roman ascetic cults had a considerable influence on the asceticism of the early Christian church, and Greek philosophy in a more general way contributed to Christian ethics, both in the early days of the church and in the middle ages.

Ecclesiastic law governing sexual matters set the pattern from which the sex law of English common courts was derived between the twelfth and fifteenth centuries, and irrespective of the specific statutes which the several states have written to control sexual behavior, the decisions of American criminal courts today are primarily based upon the precedents of those common courts. This is no place to work out the details of the historic development, but it is important at this point to realize that these present-day codes are quite ancient, that they are the product of still older religious systems, and that throughout their history they have been

465

RELIGIOUS GROUP	CASES	TOTAL OUTLET AND RELIGION				
		TOTAL POPULATION		ACTIVE POPULATION		
		Mean Frequency	Median Freq.	Incid. %	Mean Frequency	Median Freq.
Single Males: Educational Level 0–8						
Age: Adol.–15						
Protestant, active	89	2.65 ± 0.40	1.30	83.1	3.18 ± 0.46	1.89
Protestant, inactive	481	3.09 ± 0.17	1.78	93.8	3.29 ± 0.18	2.03
Catholic, inactive	106	3.21 ± 0.34	2.04	90.6	3.55 ± 0.36	2.46
Age: 16–20						
Protestant, active	91	2.73 ± 0.37	1.50	93.4	2.93 ± 0.39	1.71
Protestant, inactive	493	3.31 ± 0.17	2.24	98.2	3.37 ± 0.17	2.29
Catholic, inactive	105	3.42 ± 0.30	2.57	98.1	3.49 ± 0.30	2.64
Age: 21–25						
Protestant, inactive	234	3.22 ± 0.27	2.03	97.9	3.29 ± 0.27	2.08
Catholic, inactive	60	3.27 ± 0.40	2.21	98.3	3.33 ± 0.40	2.25
Single Males: Educational Level 9–12						
Age: Adol.–15						
Protestant, active	93	2.61 ± 0.27	1.71	92.5	2.83 ± 0.28	1.85
Protestant, inactive	375	3.38 ± 0.18	2.33	95.2	3.55 ± 0.19	2.48
Catholic, inactive	103	3.85 ± 0.43	2.58	98.1	3.93 ± 0.43	2.67
Age: 16–20						
Protestant, active	95	2.52 ± 0.23	1.69	100.0	2.52 ± 0.23	1.69
Protestant, inactive	315	3.53 ± 0.19	2.67	99.0	3.57 ± 0.19	2.71
Catholic, inactive	101	4.36 ± 0.40	3.15	100.0	4.36 ± 0.40	3.15
Single Males: Educational Level 13+						
Age: Adol.–15						
Protestant, active	547	2.48 ± 0.10	1.98	95.4	2.60 ± 0.10	2.10
Protestant, inactive	1471	3.04 ± 0.07	2.45	96.0	3.17 ± 0.08	2.58
Catholic, devout	132	2.44 ± 0.26	1.60	97.7	2.50 ± 0.26	1.65
Catholic, inactive	165	3.03 ± 0.23	2.16	95.2	3.19 ± 0.24	2.26
Jewish, Orthodox	58	1.96 ± 0.27	1.28	91.4	2.14 ± 0.28	1.40
Jewish, inactive	601	2.91 ± 0.13	2.17	96.0	3.03 ± 0.13	2.29
Age: 16–20						
Protestant, active	557	2.31 ± 0.08	1.83	99.6	2.32 ± 0.08	1.83
Protestant, inactive	1513	2.87 ± 0.06	2.36	99.7	2.88 ± 0.06	2.37
Catholic, devout	136	2.42 ± 0.20	1.70	100.0	2.42 ± 0.20	1.70
Catholic, inactive	168	2.79 ± 0.19	2.18	99.4	2.81 ± 0.19	2.19
Jewish, Orthodox	59	1.97 ± 0.21	1.57	100.0	1.97 ± 0.21	1.57
Jewish, inactive	607	2.98 ± 0.11	2.30	100.0	2.98 ± 0.11	2.30

(*Table continued on next page*)

| RELIGIOUS GROUP | CASES | TOTAL OUTLET AND RELIGION | | | | |
| | | TOTAL POPULATION | | ACTIVE POPULATION | | |
		Mean Frequency	Median Freq.	Incid. %	Mean Frequency	Median Freq.
Single Males: Educational Level 13+ (Continued)						
Age: 21–25						
Protestant, active	384	2.02 ± 0.10	1.43	99.7	2.02 ± 0.10	1.43
Protestant, inactive	1000	2.62 ± 0.07	1.99	99.8	2.62 ± 0.07	1.99
Catholic, devout	94	1.85 ± 0.16	1.32	100.0	1.85 ± 0.16	1.32
Catholic, inactive	125	2.86 ± 0.23	2.09	100.0	2.86 ± 0.23	2.09
Jewish, inactive	331	3.09 ± 0.15	2.44	100.0	3.09 ± 0.15	2.44
Age: 26–30						
Protestant, active	100	1.85 ± 0.21	1.25	100.0	1.85 ± 0.21	1.25
Protestant, inactive	279	2.56 ± 0.15	1.82	99.6	2.57 ± 0.15	1.83
Jewish, inactive	104	3.23 ± 0.35	2.42	100.0	3.23 ± 0.35	2.42
Married Males: Educational Level 13+						
Age: 21–25						
Protestant, active	91	3.29 ± 0.26	2.71	100.0	3.29 ± 0.26	2.71
Protestant, inactive	280	3.85 ± 0.18	3.19	100.0	3.85 ± 0.18	3.19
Jewish, inactive	86	4.02 ± 0.23	3.44	100.0	4.02 ± 0.23	3.44
Age: 26–30						
Protestant, active	123	2.67 ± 0.15	2.50	100.0	2.67 ± 0.15	2.50
Protestant, inactive	346	3.45 ± 0.16	2.76	100.0	3.45 ± 0.16	2.76
Jewish, inactive	109	3.50 ± 0.21	2.86	100.0	3.50 ± 0.21	2.86
Age: 31–35						
Protestant, active	109	2.31 ± 0.13	2.17	100.0	2.31 ± 0.13	2.17
Protestant, inactive	270	3.10 ± 0.17	2.37	100.0	3.10 ± 0.17	2.37
Jewish, inactive	84	3.05 ± 0.26	2.43	100.0	3.05 ± 0.26	2.43
Age: 36–40						
Protestant, active	73	1.98 ± 0.12	1.90	100.0	1.98 ± 0.12	1.90
Protestant, inactive	187	2.88 ± 0.22	2.20	99.5	2.89 ± 0.22	2.21
Jewish, inactive	62	2.67 ± 0.26	2.13	100.0	2.67 ± 0.26	2.13

Table 125. Total sexual outlet as related to religious background

the bases for the law which has formally expressed society's interest in controlling human sexual behavior.

It has already been pointed out (Chapter 6) that average frequencies of sexual outlet for the human male are distinctly below those which are normal among some other anthropoids and which would probably be normal in the human animal if there were no restrictions upon his sexual activity. Averages for the single males begin at 3.3 per week and drop with old age, and averages for the married males begin at 4.8 per week and drop with age; but the averages in non-restrained human animals would probably be nearer 7 per week, and in 10 to 15 per cent of the population would probably run higher than that (Chapter 6). It has been stated (Chapter 8) that the differences between these higher figures and the actual rates of the male population provide some measure of the effectiveness of the social pressures, of the specific laws, and of the attitudes, ideals, esthetic values, physical interferences, and other restraints which the social organization imposes upon the sexual activity of the individual.

That these social pressures are primarily religious in their origin is confirmed by the comparisons which can now be made between the frequencies of total sexual outlet and the incidences and frequencies of outlet from the various sexual sources, among persons who are actively concerned with religious organizations, and among persons who are less closely concerned with the teachings and practices of any church group.

In attempting to measure these present-day influences of the church on the sexual behavior of the American population, three religious groups, Protestant, Catholic, and Jewish, are recognized in the present chapter. These faiths embrace most of those Americans who recognize any church affiliation. Within each group a still more important classification has, however, been made. This involves the degree of adherence of the individual to the doctrines and to the activities of the religious group in which he is at least nominally placed. Of course, every degree of adherence exists among various individuals, and as the data have been recorded in our original histories, several such degrees have been recognized (Chapter 3). However, the limited size of the present sample has made it necessary to base the analyses in the present chapter on two groups of Protestants, two groups of Catholics, and two groups of those of the Jewish faith. These groups have included, on the one hand, the less active (or less devout) members of each faith, and on the other hand the more active (or more devout) members of those same faiths. Active or devout in this classification has been taken to mean regular attendance and/or active participation in organized church activities, and/or frequent attendance at the Catholic confessional or the Jewish synagogue. Inactive or non-devout in the immediate analysis has been applied to all persons who have not qualified as active or devout under the above definitions.

It is hardly necessary to add that all comparisons made in the present chapter are based on a preliminary breakdown of each population for sex, race, marital status, age, and educational levels. With the additional breakdowns on the religious group and on the degree of adherence of each subject to that religious group, all of the calculations given in the present chapter are based on 7-way breakdowns. Any analysis short of this would have proven inadequate; but it is only a limited list of religious groups for which we have samples that are adequate for such elaborate treatment (Chapter 3). All conclusions which are drawn in the present chapter should be limited to these particular groups. In the interest of scientific fact and of such social and moral applications as others may wish to draw from the scientific fact, it is to be hoped that religious groups which are not yet sufficiently represented may be included in the future development of this survey.

TOTAL SEXUAL OUTLET

Considering the frequencies of total sexual outlet (Table 125), the sexually least active individuals in any age and educational group are the Orthodox Jews (who are the least active of all), the devout Catholics, and the active Protestants (in that order). Conversely, the sexually most active individuals are the non-church-going Catholics, with the inactive Protestants and the inactive Jewish males intermediate in the system. At various educational levels and in different age groups there is some variation in this ordering, but there is only one group, namely the single males of the college level, where the data are abundant enough to compare all six religious classifications.

Between adolescence and 15 years of age, the boys who will ultimately go to college are arranged in the following religious groups, beginning with those who are sexually least active and building the list in the direction of those who are most active:

> Jewish Orthodox
> Catholic devout
> Protestant active
> Jewish inactive
> Catholic inactive
> Protestant inactive

This order remains constant whether the calculations are made as means or as medians, and whether for total populations or for active populations. The order is somewhat different when it is based on the number of persons involved in sexual activity (the active incidence figures). In this latter case, the smallest number of sexually active individuals (91%) is to be found among the Orthodox Jews, while the largest number of active individuals (98%) is to be found among the devout Catholics.

Between 16 and 20 years of age the boys who will go to college, or who are already in college, are arranged in the following order, beginning with

| | | MASTURBATION AND RELIGION | | | | | |
| | | TOTAL POPULATION | | | ACTIVE POPULATION | | |
RELIGIOUS GROUP	CASES	Mean Frequency	Median Freq.	% of Total Outlet	Incid. %	Mean Freq.	Median Freq.
		Single Males: Educational Level 0-8					
Age: Adol.–15							
Protestant, active	89	1.30 ± 0.22	0.50	52.9	70.8	1.83	1.13
Protestant, inactive	481	1.58 ± 0.10	0.89	51.1	88.1	1.79	1.08
Catholic, inactive	106	1.66 ± 0.20	0.93	52.6	85.8	1.94	1.21
Age: 16–20							
Protestant, active	91	0.77 ± 0.11	0.34	28.6	81.3	0.95	0.49
Protestant, inactive	493	0.94 ± 0.06	0.46	28.4	85.8	1.10	0.60
Catholic, inactive	105	1.04 ± 0.13	0.49	30.9	84.8	1.22	0.72
Age: 21–25							
Protestant, inactive	234	0.60 ± 0.07	0.18	18.7	62.4	0.96	0.50
Catholic, inactive	60	0.61 ± 0.15	0.20	18.9	66.7	0.91	0.42
		Single Males: Educational Level 9-12					
Age: Adol.–15							
Protestant, active	93	1.75 ± 0.19	1.32	68.2	87.1	2.01	1.60
Protestant, inactive	375	1.88 ± 0.11	1.13	55.8	90.4	2.08	1.35
Catholic, inactive	103	2.22 ± 0.23	1.46	58.8	95.1	2.33	1.57
Age: 16–20							
Protestant, active	95	1.15 ± 0.14	0.58	45.9	88.4	1.30	0.72
Protestant, inactive	315	1.20 ± 0.09	0.66	34.4	88.9	1.35	0.83
Catholic, inactive	101	1.56 ± 0.18	0.89	36.1	91.1	1.71	1.03
		Single Males: Educational Level 13+					
Age: Adol.–15							
Protestant, active	547	1.88 ± 0.08	1.42	75.6	80.8	2.33	1.88
Protestant, inactive	1471	2.40 ± 0.06	1.82	78.8	84.7	2.83	2.30
Catholic, devout	132	1.96 ± 0.25	0.96	81.9	78.8	2.49	1.61
Catholic, inactive	165	2.33 ± 0.21	1.65	78.4	80.6	2.89	1.98
Jewish, Orthodox	58	1.56 ± 0.26	1.03	79.3	72.4	2.15	1.47
Jewish, inactive	601	2.34 ± 0.12	1.58	80.6	80.0	2.93	2.16
Age: 16–20							
Protestant, active	557	1.50 ± 0.07	1.00	65.0	85.6	1.75	1.33
Protestant, inactive	1513	1.95 ± 0.05	1.41	67.8	91.5	2.13	1.62
Catholic, devout	136	1.53 ± 0.19	0.75	63.3	87.8	1.82	0.95
Catholic, inactive	168	1.65 ± 0.15	1.06	58.7	86.3	1.91	1.50
Jewish, Orthodox	59	1.18 ± 0.19	0.64	59.4	78.0	1.52	0.93
Jewish, inactive	607	2.09 ± 0.11	1.41	70.2	88.1	2.38	1.68

(*Table continued on next page*)

| RELIGIOUS GROUP | CASES | MASTURBATION AND RELIGION | | | | | |
| | | TOTAL POPULATION | | | ACTIVE POPULATION | | |
		Mean Frequency	Median Freq.	% of Total Outlet	Incid. %	Mean Freq.	Median Freq.
Single Males: Educational Level 13+ (*Continued*)							
Age: 21–25							
Protestant, active	384	1.10 ± 0.07	0.60	54.5	83.6	1.32	0.81
Protestant, inactive	1000	1.46 ± 0.06	0.80	55.6	90.3	1.61	0.93
Catholic, devout	94	0.82 ± 0.12	0.36	45.1	78.7	1.04	0.52
Catholic, inactive	125	1.10 ± 0.15	0.50	39.4	81.6	1.35	0.75
Jewish, inactive	331	1.58 ± 0.12	0.73	51.4	86.4	1.83	1.03
Age: 26–30							
Protestant, active	100	1.00 ± 0.14	0.49	54.3	82.0	1.22	0.72
Protestant, inactive	279	1.32 ± 0.10	0.63	51.8	88.2	1.50	0.81
Jewish, inactive	104	1.02 ± 0.21	0.38	31.2	79.8	1.27	0.57
Married Males: Educational Level 13+							
Age: 21–25							
Protestant, active	91	0.22 ± 0.04	0.04	6.9	60.4	0.37	0.21
Protestant, inactive	280	0.34 ± 0.04	0.08	8.9	69.6	0.49	0.24
Jewish, inactive	86	0.45 ± 0.10	0.07	11.4	64.0	0.71	0.28
Age: 26–30							
Protestant, active	123	0.27 ± 0.06	0.05	10.1	64.2	0.41	0.10
Protestant, inactive	346	0.33 ± 0.03	0.08	9.6	71.1	0.46	0.24
Jewish, inactive	109	0.25 ± 0.05	0.04	7.0	57.8	0.43	0.21
Age: 31–35							
Protestant, active	109	0.22 ± 0.06	0.03	9.7	59.6	0.37	0.09
Protestant, inactive	270	0.29 ± 0.04	0.08	9.5	71.1	0.41	0.21
Jewish, inactive	84	0.20 ± 0.05	0.01	6.5	52.4	0.37	0.14
Age: 36–40							
Protestant, active	73	0.22 ± 0.07	0.02	11.2	54.8	0.41	0.09
Protestant, inactive	187	0.27 ± 0.04	0.07	9.6	71.1	0.38	0.17
Jewish, inactive	62	0.14 ± 0.05	0.00	5.1	41.9	0.34	0.10

Table 126. Masturbation as related to religious background

the sexually least active group and building the list in the direction of the most active group:

Jewish Orthodox	Catholic inactive
Catholic devout	Protestant inactive
Protestant active	Jewish inactive

This order varies somewhat with the calculations as means or as medians, and for total populations and for active populations.

Between 21 and 25 years of age, the single males who have gone to college are arranged in the following order, beginning with the sexually least active group and ending with the most active group:

Catholic devout	Catholic inactive
Protestant active	Jewish inactive
Protestant inactive	

This order is more or less constant, whatever the method of calculating.

For the less adequate series of religious groups among males of other educational levels the story appears to be much the same. In both grade school and high school groups, the persons most actively connected with church activities are, again, the least active sexually, and the males who are sexually most active are those Catholics who have least to do with their church.

The differences between the frequencies of these several religious groups are, in most instances, not large but rather constant. There is a 25 per cent difference between groups at certain ages in certain educational levels, and in some instances the most extreme groups have rates of total outlet which are 75 per cent higher than the rates of the least active groups of the same age and educational levels. To put it another way, devout acceptance of the church's teaching is correlated with sexual frequencies which are two-thirds or less than two-thirds of the frequencies which are found among males of corresponding age and educational levels who are not actively connected with the church. Either this is the direct effect of church teachings, or else those individuals who become most actively associated with the church are a select group which would not have had high frequencies of sexual outlet if they had never belonged to a church. It will take more elaborate analyses of a much larger series of histories to determine which explanation is correct, but there is some evidence now at hand (Chapter 6) that some portion of the devoutly religious individuals have repressed rather than sublimated sex histories.

MASTURBATION

At various places in the foregoing chapters it has been pointed out that masturbation and intercourse are the chief sources of pre-marital outlet. It is, therefore, to be expected that there should be certain correlations between the frequencies of masturbation and the frequencies of inter course, and thus indirectly of total sexual outlet. In upper and lower social levels (Chapter 10) the frequencies of masturbation do bear an inverse relation to the frequencies of pre-marital intercourse, and it might be anticipated that the suppression of one of these activities by the rules of any religious group would provide some direct impetus to the development of the other activity.

This, however, proves not to be so. The least frequent experience in masturbation is found among the more devout members of each and every one of the religious groups (Table 126), and these are the very groups which have the lowest rates of total outlet. The incidence figures for masturbation are not constantly different, but the mean frequencies are always lower for the more devout groups. This is true for both single and married males of every age group on which there are sufficient data and, strikingly enough, it is true of every educational level in each religious group. In some age and educational groups the masturbatory rates of the active Protestants, the devout Catholics, and the Orthodox Jews do not average more than two-thirds or three-fourths as high as the rates of the inactive members of those same churches. Even in those segments of the population where the differences between devout and inactive groups are more minor, it is significant that they always stand in the same order: the religiously active persons masturbate less frequently than the persons who are less concerned with their religion. At the other end of the picture, the males who most often masturbate are the religiously inactive Protestants, sometimes the non-church-going members of the Catholic faith, and in some cases the inactive Jewish males.

The objections to masturbation have originated from religious creeds which go back to the most remote beginnings of our Western European-American civilization. Elsewhere in the world masturbation may be looked upon as a childish performance, or as evidence of the incapacity of an individual to make socio-sexual adjustments (Chapter 14); but few other peoples have condemned masturbation as severely as the Jews have. The Talmudic references and discussions make masturbation a greater sin than non-marital intercourse. There were excuses for pre-marital intercourse and for extra-marital intercourse with certain persons under the Jewish code, but no extenuation for masturbation (Bible, Talmud *passim*). The logic of this proscription depended, of course, upon the reproductive motive in the sexual philosophy of the Jews. This made any act which offered no possibility of a resulting conception unnatural, a perversion, and a sin. Whatever other sources may have contributed to the Christian church's objections to masturbation, certainly the Jewish traditions must have provided a considerable impetus to the perpetuation of this taboo in the Christian religion. In the Orthodox church today, the Jewish boy is definitely affected by the old-time Hebraic laws on this point, and the often

RELIGIOUS GROUP	CASES	NOCTURNAL EMISSIONS AND RELIGION					
		TOTAL POPULATION			ACTIVE POPULATION		
		Mean Frequency	Median Freq.	% of Total Outlet	Incid. %	Mean Freq.	Median Freq.
Single Males: Educational Level 0–8							
Age: Adol.–15							
Protestant, active	89	0.022±0.007	0.00	0.9	21.3	0.10	0.067
Protestant, inactive	481	0.057±0.010	0.00	1.8	26.0	0.22	0.078
Catholic, inactive	106	0.035±0.010	0.00	1.1	23.6	0.15	0.076
Age: 16–20							
Protestant, active	91	0.14 ±0.04	0.01	5.0	52.7	0.26	0.077
Protestant, inactive	493	0.14 ±0.02	0.02	4.4	56.6	0.26	0.087
Catholic, inactive	105	0.17 ±0.03	0.03	5.0	57.1	0.30	0.16
Age: 21–25							
Protestant, inactive	234	0.15 ±0.02	0.03	4.6	59.0	0.25	0.087
Catholic, inactive	60	0.21 ±0.04	0.07	6.6	65.0	0.33	0.23
Single Males: Educational Level 9–12							
Age: Adol.–15							
Protestant, active	93	0.16 ±0.05	0.00	6.3	40.9	0.39	0.15
Protestant, inactive	375	0.14 ±0.03	0.00	4.1	40.0	0.35	0.10
Catholic, inactive	103	0.13 ±0.04	0.00	3.4	35.0	0.36	0.15
Age: 16–20							
Protestant, active	95	0.18 ±0.03	0.06	7.3	71.6	0.26	0.10
Protestant, inactive	315	0.22 ±0.02	0.06	6.4	72.7	0.31	0.10
Catholic, inactive	101	0.18 ±0.03	0.04	4.1	60.4	0.29	0.17
Single Males: Educational Level 13+							
Age: Adol.–15							
Protestant, active	547	0.34 ±0.03	0.12	13.6	70.7	0.48	0.29
Protestant, inactive	1471	0.33 ±0.02	0.02	10.8	68.0	0.48	0.27
Catholic, devout	132	0.30 ±0.04	0.15	12.4	75.0	0.40	0.27
Catholic, inactive	165	0.32 ±0.04	0.10	10.8	65.5	0.49	0.31
Jewish, Orthodox	58	0.25 ±0.06	0.09	12.5	77.6	0.32	0.18
Jewish, inactive	601	0.41 ±0.03	0.15	14.1	75.4	0.54	0.29
Age: 16–20							
Protestant, active	557	0.41 ±0.02	0.27	17.9	92.5	0.45	0.30
Protestant, inactive	1513	0.42 ±0.02	0.24	14.5	91.7	0.45	0.28
Catholic, devout	136	0.48 ±0.06	0.30	19.9	94.1	0.51	0.32
Catholic, inactive	168	0.43 ±0.04	0.26	15.3	91.1	0.47	0.30
Jewish, Orthodox	59	0.37 ±0.06	0.23	18.6	89.8	0.41	0.28
Jewish, inactive	607	0.44 ±0.03	0.24	14.9	86.2	0.51	0.31

(*Table continued on next page*)

RELIGIOUS GROUP	CASES	NOCTURNAL EMISSIONS AND RELIGION					
		TOTAL POPULATION			ACTIVE POPULATION		
		Mean Frequency	Median Freq.	% of Total Outlet	Incid. %	Mean Freq.	Median Freq.
Single Males: Educational Level 13+ (Continued)							
Age: 21–25							
Protestant, active	384	0.42 ±0.03	0.26	20.8	90.1	0.47	0.30
Protestant, inactive	1000	0.36 ±0.02	0.20	13.8	86.9	0.42	0.26
Catholic, devout	94	0.48 ±0.07	0.31	26.6	90.4	0.53	0.34
Catholic, inactive	125	0.40 ±0.05	0.24	14.3	88.0	0.45	0.29
Jewish, inactive	331	0.40 ±0.04	0.19	13.1	81.0	0.50	0.29
Age: 26–30							
Protestant, active	100	0.41 ±0.05	0.27	21.9	95.0	0.43	0.29
Protestant, inactive	279	0.29 ±0.02	0.17	11.2	85.3	0.34	0.24
Jewish, inactive	104	0.31 ±0.06	0.12	9.6	75.0	0.42	0.24
Married Males: Educational Level 13+							
Age: 21–25							
Protestant, active	91	0.17 ±0.03	0.053	5.2	67.0	0.25	0.12
Protestant, inactive	280	0.19 ±0.03	0.051	5.0	67.9	0.28	0.10
Jewish, inactive	86	0.13 ±0.03	0.033	3.3	60.5	0.22	0.09
Age: 26–30							
Protestant, active	123	0.16 ±0.02	0.067	6.1	78.9	0.20	0.09
Protestant, inactive	346	0.16 ±0.02	0.056	4.7	71.7	0.22	0.09
Jewish, inactive	109	0.17 ±0.03	0.043	4.7	66.1	0.25	0.09
Age: 31–35							
Protestant, active	109	0.17 ±0.02	0.073	7.6	78.9	0.22	0.10
Protestant, inactive	270	0.14 ±0.02	0.050	4.6	72.2	0.19	0.08
Jewish, inactive	84	0.12 ±0.04	0.017	4.0	56.0	0.21	0.08
Age: 36–40							
Protestant, active	73	0.16 ±0.02	0.079	7.9	75.3	0.21	0.16
Protestant, inactive	187	0.12 ±0.02	0.042	4.4	66.8	0.19	0.08
Jewish, inactive	62	0.11 ±0.03	0.028	3.9	61.3	0.18	0.07

Table 127. Nocturnal emissions as related to religious background

lower rates of the religiously inactive Jewish boys indicate that even they are not entirely free of the ancestral codes.

The Catholic boy is told that masturbation is a carnal sin, particularly because it is so often accompanied by erotic fantasies which represent an improper use of functions which should be reserved for contacts which might lead to reproduction (Davis 1946). Some priests go to considerable lengths to impress a confessant with the idea that masturbation is one of the more serious sins, and earlier church writers sometimes specifically declared it more sinful than fornication (Northcote 1916).

Through most of its past history the Protestant church has been as severe in its condemnation of "self-abuse" as either the Jewish or the Catholic groups, and some Protestant clergymen maintain such attitudes today. However, many Protestant clergymen now accept medical, psychologic, and biologic opinion that masturbation does no physical harm. Perhaps as a result of this, we find the religiously active Protestants of the better educated groups more often involved in masturbation than the devout Catholics or Orthodox Jews. Some Protestant groups now lay less emphasis upon the physical harm supposed to result from masturbation, and attach more importance to the undesirability of allowing oneself to become subject to such a habit. Whatever the issues, however, the record is clear that religious influences do succeed in reducing both the incidence and the frequency of masturbation among the more devout members of each church group.

NOCTURNAL EMISSIONS

Nocturnal emissions represent the one type of sexual outlet to which there is a minimum of religious objection. One might, therefore, have anticipated that there would be higher frequencies of nocturnal emissions among males who are more closely allied to the church; but this is not consistently so. What differences there are between the frequencies and the incidences of emissions among religiously more active and religiously less active groups, are quite minor (Table 127). The means differ from the medians calculated for the same groups, nearly as often as the averages for devout groups differ from the averages for inactive groups.

This result is significant. Persons who are interested in moral interpretations in sex education insist that the frequencies of nocturnal emissions rise to sufficient heights to provide all of the necessary sexual outlet for a boy who abstains from other sexual activities. But although the record indicates that those who have been most interested in the church have actually reduced their total outlets, the frequencies of nocturnal emissions in these groups have not been raised (Chapter 15). The relative importance of the emissions is raised by the reduction of the rates of total outlet, but the absolute frequencies of the emissions are not altered.

PRE-MARITAL PETTING TO CLIMAX

There are some slight differences in the incidences and frequencies of pre-marital petting in the several religious groups (Table 128) but, as we have already seen, there are much greater differences between the several social levels (Tables 84, 110, Figure 100). The deliberate elaboration of pre-marital petting first emerged as an activity of a particular educational level (the college group), and religious backgrounds seem to have had little to do with the individual's acceptance or rejection of such activity. Many individuals in lower level groups, whatever their religious connections, consider that petting is a perversion because it is a substitute for actual coitus. At the college level, however, petting is much more often accepted, with little distinction on account of the religious background of the group. There may be some tendency for the more devout Catholics of the college level to avoid petting during the younger adolescent years, but there is no consistent trend in the arrangement of religious groups at any older age level.

In all religious groups, older persons have been disturbed over this petting behavior. In Catholic philosophy, the general principles concerning venial and carnal sins certainly apply to many of the techniques that are utilized in petting (Davis 1946). It is surprising, therefore, that there has not been more specific religious objection to petting, and that young people of all faiths have so uniformly ignored what objections they have heard. That petting is not still more abundant must, however, depend upon the more general inhibitions on sex which religious teachings have built into the very body of our culture.

PRE-MARITAL INTERCOURSE

As already pointed out (Chapter 10), there are material differences between the attitudes on pre-marital intercourse in lower social levels and the attitudes in better educated segments of the population. There may be 7 times (700 per cent) as much pre-marital intercourse among lower social levels as there is in the group that goes to college (Tables 85–87, Figures 101–103). But within any particular social level, the differences between Protestants, Catholics, and Jews, and the differences between the most active and least devout members of each of these religious groups, are very much less (Table 129). Rarely do they amount to more than 50 or 100 per cent. Lower level, religiously active Protestants average only two-thirds as much pre-marital intercourse as religiously inactive Protestants of the same level; but the same lower level Protestants average 6 or 8 times as much pre-marital intercourse as the religiously inactive Protestants of the college level. It is true that within each and every educational level it is the religiously devout group which has the least pre-marital intercourse; and the differences in incidence and frequency figures are enough to appear

		PETTING TO CLIMAX, AND RELIGION					
RELIGIOUS GROUP	CASES	TOTAL POPULATION			ACTIVE POPULATION		
		Mean Frequency	Median Freq.	% of Total Outlet	Incid. %	Mean Freq.	Median Freq.
Single Males: Educational Level 0–8							
Age: Adol.–15							
Protestant, active	89	0.022 ± 0.013	0.00	0.9	11.2	0.20	0.069
Protestant, inactive	422	0.027 ± 0.010	0.00	0.9	13.5	0.20	0.060
Catholic, inactive	106	0.025 ± 0.011	0.00	0.8	16.0	0.15	0.064
Age: 16–20							
Protestant, active	91	0.026 ± 0.013	0.00	1.0	18.7	0.14	0.060
Protestant, inactive	431	0.043 ± 0.012	0.00	1.3	21.6	0.20	0.063
Catholic, inactive	105	0.052 ± 0.020	0.00	1.5	22.9	0.23	0.074
Age: 21–25							
Protestant, inactive	234	0.040 ± 0.018	0.00	1.2	15.4	0.26	0.066
Catholic, inactive	60	0.053 ± 0.031	0.00	1.7	23.3	0.23	0.075
Single Males: Educational Level 9–12							
Age: Adol.–15							
Protestant, active	93	0.013 ± 0.005	0.00	0.5	16.1	0.08	0.062
Protestant, inactive	311	0.038 ± 0.009	0.00	1.1	20.6	0.19	0.069
Catholic, inactive	103	0.010 ± 0.041	0.00	2.7	21.4	0.47	0.088
Age: 16–20							
Protestant, active	95	0.058 ± 0.018	0.00	2.3	31.6	0.18	0.070
Protestant, inactive	315	0.072 ± 0.014	0.00	2.1	33.3	0.22	0.071
Catholic, inactive	101	0.13 ± 0.040	0.00	3.0	35.6	0.36	0.080
Single Males: Educational Level 13+							
Age: Adol.–15							
Protestant, active	484	0.06 ± 0.14	0.00	2.3	13.6	0.43	0.086
Protestant, inactive	1178	0.05 ± 0.007	0.00	1.7	17.0	0.29	0.082
Catholic, devout	132	0.02 ± 0.008	0.00	0.8	8.3	0.23	0.180
Catholic, inactive	165	0.03 ± 0.009	0.00	1.1	13.3	0.24	0.130
Jewish, Orthodox	58	0.07 ± 0.034	0.00	3.6	20.7	0.34	0.081
Jewish, inactive	377	0.02 ± 0.007	0.00	0.9	10.3	0.24	0.091
Age: 16–20							
Protestant, active	492	0.14 ± 0.020	0.00	6.1	39.6	0.35	0.082
Protestant, inactive	1210	0.14 ± 0.011	0.00	5.2	46.9	0.31	0.084
Catholic, devout	136	0.15 ± 0.032	0.00	6.2	43.4	0.35	0.097
Catholic, inactive	168	0.11 ± 0.019	0.001	4.0	50.0	0.23	0.087
Jewish, Orthodox	59	0.14 ± 0.046	0.00	6.9	45.8	0.30	0.088
Jewish, inactive	379	0.13 ± 0.019	0.00	5.0	47.8	0.28	0.093
Age: 21–25							
Protestant, active	339	0.20 ± 0.036	0.000	10.0	48.1	0.42	0.090
Protestant, inactive	841	0.18 ± 0.018	0.004	7.6	50.9	0.36	0.093
Catholic, devout	94	0.15 ± 0.032	0.013	8.2	53.2	0.28	0.098
Catholic, inactive	125	0.16 ± 0.039	0.008	5.9	52.0	0.32	0.087
Jewish, inactive	331	0.23 ± 0.023	0.060	7.5	68.6	0.34	0.150

Table 128. Heterosexual petting to climax as related to religious background

478

significant if they were not dwarfed by the differences which are effected by the mores of the social groups which are involved.

Heterosexual coitus is, in many ways, the most important aspect of human sexual behavior. Its occurrence in non-marital histories has been condemned by every religious group, practically without exception, in our Western European-American culture. But this is one more type of sexual activity where religious restraints have had less direct effect than the mores of the several groups which constitute our society.

On the other hand, the origins of these sexual mores must be credited to the long-time effects which religious teachings have had through the many hundreds of years in which our cultural patterns have been developing. Religiously active members of the upper social level know that they are rejecting pre-marital intercourse on purely moral grounds (Chapter 10). Religiously inactive persons at this same level reject pre-marital intercourse almost as often, but they insist that they do so as a matter of plain decency. There is, however, little difference in meaning between these two verbalizations of what are basically the same religious philosophies.

Among males of the lower social levels, those who are least active in the church rather freely accept pre-marital intercourse without conflicts of conscience. The religiously more devout individuals at the same level may accept coitus almost as often, although they "know that it is a sin," and they may occasionally be disturbed by their recognition of its moral significance. Nevertheless, both church-going and non-church-going males of the lower social levels continue to have pre-marital coitus with frequencies that average far above those of any upper level group, because all lower level groups, whatever the degree of their religious affiliation, believe that it is human nature to have intercourse, and an inevitable activity for man as he is made.

The church may even have more influence on the masturbatory behavior of a male than it does upon his pre-marital coital behavior. The acceptance or rejection of masturbation is not so difficult an issue to so many persons; but the very fact that coitus is a more significant activity socially makes its acceptance or rejection a matter of greater importance in the mores of a group. It would appear that in order to go further in changing overt behavior in regard to pre-marital intercourse, the church will have to affect the thinking of whole social levels; and that is a long-time process.

MARITAL INTERCOURSE

The available data are inadequate for analyzing the frequencies of marital intercourse in more than a few of the religious groups which have contributed to this study. It is interesting to note, however, that in these particular groups marital intercourse is consistently affected by the degree

RELIGIOUS GROUP	CASES	TOTAL POPULATION			ACTIVE POPULATION		
		Mean Frequency	Median Freq.	% of Total Outlet	Incid. %	Mean Freq.	Median Freq.

Single Males: Educational Level 0–8							
Age: Adol.–15							
Protestant, active	83	0.68 ± 0.21	0.00	28.7	33.7	2.01	0.79
Protestant, inactive	431	1.18 ± 0.13	0.07	40.1	52.4	2.24	1.25
Catholic, inactive	89	1.22 ± 0.25	0.00	40.1	44.9	2.72	2.06
Age: 16–20							
Protestant, active	81	1.24 ± 0.30	0.24	48.6	70.4	1.76	0.56
Protestant, inactive	442	1.88 ± 0.14	0.90	60.0	90.5	2.08	1.12
Catholic, inactive	88	1.81 ± 0.28	0.53	57.0	80.7	2.25	1.25
Age: 21–25							
Protestant, inactive	200	2.23 ± 0.25	0.94	69.5	92.0	2.42	1.18
Catholic, inactive	53	1.97 ± 0.38	0.93	61.3	84.9	2.32	1.38

Single Males: Educational Level 9–12							
Age: Adol.–15							
Protestant, active	86	0.45 ± 0.13	0.00	18.6	31.4	1.42	0.75
Protestant, inactive	318	0.98 ± 0.13	0.00	29.3	47.8	2.04	0.97
Catholic, inactive	72	0.59 ± 0.34	0.00	16.8	37.5	1.58	0.45
Age: 16–20							
Protestant, active	89	0.88 ± 0.16	0.21	34.8	67.4	1.31	0.67
Protestant, inactive	322	1.60 ± 0.15	0.55	46.9	80.4	1.99	0.94
Catholic, inactive	69	1.34 ± 0.40	0.50	31.3	68.1	1.97	1.00

Single Males: Educational Level 13+							
Age: Adol.–15							
Protestant, active	493	0.06 ± 0.02	0.00	2.5	7.1	0.84	0.32
Protestant, inactive	1205	0.09 ± 0.02	0.00	3.1	11.5	0.77	0.29
Catholic, devout	103	0.04 ± 0.02	0.00	1.8	4.8	0.85	1.00
Catholic, inactive	117	0.24 ± 0.09	0.00	6.3	16.2	1.48	0.50
Jewish, inactive	412	0.03 ± 0.02	0.00	1.2	7.0	0.49	0.13
Age: 16–20							
Protestant, active	502	0.15 ± 0.03	0.00	6.8	27.3	0.56	0.09
Protestant, inactive	1235	0.27 ± 0.03	0.00	10.4	45.0	0.61	0.20
Catholic, devout	107	0.18 ± 0.06	0.00	6.0	39.3	0.46	0.12
Catholic, inactive	120	0.54 ± 0.13	0.04	19.5	59.2	0.91	0.27
Jewish, Orthodox	54	0.24 ± 0.08	0.00	13.4	38.9	0.62	0.30
Jewish, inactive	416	0.21 ± 0.03	0.00	7.2	45.9	0.46	0.10

(*Table continued on next page*)

RELIGIOUS GROUP	CASES	TOTAL NON-MARITAL INTERCOURSE AND RELIGION					
		TOTAL POPULATION			ACTIVE POPULATION		
		Mean Frequency	Median Freq.	% of Total Outlet	Incid. %	Mean Freq.	Median Freq.

Single Males: Educational Level 13+ (*Continued*)

Age: 21–25							
Protestant, active	348	0.20 ± 0.04	0.00	10.4	32.5	0.63	0.16
Protestant, inactive	867	0.41 ± 0.04	0.04	17.8	59.1	0.70	0.28
Catholic, devout	71	0.27 ± 0.09	0.00	11.0	38.0	0.71	0.30
Catholic, inactive	180	0.98 ± 0.20	0.25	31.7	75.0	1.31	0.45
Age: 26–30							
Protestant, active	88	0.19 ± 0.05	0.00	9.2	35.2	0.54	0.30
Protestant, inactive	187	0.39 ± 0.06	0.05	16.2	59.9	0.65	0.34
Jewish, inactive	77	1.69 ± 0.32	0.65	50.9	84.4	2.00	0.95

Married Males: Educational Level 13+

Age: 21–25							
Protestant, active	91	0.04 ± 0.03	0.00	1.2	7.7	0.51	0.10
Protestant, inactive	280	0.09 ± 0.03	0.00	2.2	17.9	0.48	0.18
Jewish, inactive	86	0.04 ± 0.02	0.00	0.9	16.3	0.23	0.08
Age: 26–30							
Protestant, active	123	0.04 ± 0.02	0.00	1.3	8.1	0.43	0.08
Protestant, inactive	346	0.11 ± 0.03	0.00	3.1	26.3	0.40	0.10
Jewish, inactive	109	0.15 ± 0.05	0.00	4.3	27.5	0.55	0.23
Age: 31–35							
Protestant, active	109	0.03 ± 0.03	0.00	1.4	12.8	0.25	0.06
Protestant, inactive	270	0.20 ± 0.04	0.00	6.4	34.8	0.56	0.27
Jewish, inactive	84	0.18 ± 0.07	0.00	5.8	40.5	0.43	0.09
Age: 36–40							
Protestant, active	73	0.02 ± 0.01	0.00	1.1	16.4	0.13	0.08
Protestant, inactive	187	0.34 ± 0.12	0.00	12.1	40.6	0.84	0.27
Jewish, inactive	62	0.23 ± 0.08	0.00	8.2	41.9	0.54	0.13

Table 129. Total pre-marital and extra-marital intercourse as related to religious background

of church affiliation. In practically every instance the religiously active groups engage in marital intercourse less frequently than the religiously inactive groups (Table 130). There are frequencies in the inactive groups which are between 20 and 30 per cent higher than the frequencies in the religiously active groups of the same age and educational level. What effect

RELIGIOUS GROUP	CASES	MARITAL INTERCOURSE AND RELIGION					
		TOTAL POPULATION			ACTIVE POPULATION		
		Mean Frequency	Median Freq.	% of Total Outlet	Incid. %	Mean Freq.	Median Freq.
Educational Level 13+							
Age: 21–25							
Protestant, active	91	2.80 ± 0.25	2.19	86.6	98.9	2.83	2.22
Protestant, inactive	280	3.19 ± 0.17	2.51	83.3	99.6	3.20	2.52
Jewish, inactive	86	3.34 ± 0.22	2.88	84.3	100.0	3.34	2.88
Age: 26–30							
Protestant, active	123	2.15 ± 0.14	1.85	82.1	99.2	2.17	1.86
Protestant, inactive	346	2.80 ± 0.14	2.13	82.1	99.7	2.81	2.14
Jewish, inactive	109	2.92 ± 0.20	2.47	83.2	99.1	2.95	2.49
Age: 31–35							
Protestant, active	109	1.84 ± 0.11	1.75	80.8	98.2	1.87	1.78
Protestant, inactive	270	2.43 ± 0.14	1.86	78.7	100.0	2.43	1.86
Jewish, inactive	84	2.54 ± 0.24	2.12	83.8	100.0	2.54	2.12
Age: 36–40							
Protestant, active	73	1.58 ± 0.11	1.56	79.8	98.6	1.61	1.57
Protestant, inactive	187	2.07 ± 0.16	1.59	73.1	98.4	2.11	1.61
Jewish, inactive	62	2.28 ± 0.22	1.90	82.8	100.0	2.28	1.90

Table 130. Marital intercourse as related to religious background

this may have upon the quality of marital adjustments among religiously active persons is a matter that will merit further investigation.

HOMOSEXUAL OUTLETS

There is much more homosexual activity among males of lower educational levels than there is among males of the college level (Table 90, Figure 105). Within any particular educational level the differences between religious groups are not so great (Table 131). Between grade school and college males of the same religious group there may be a 200 to 500 per cent difference. Between religiously active and religiously inactive groups of the same denomination in the same educational level, the differences are ordinarily not more than 50 to 150 per cent, and sometimes they are not even 10 per cent. Such differences as do occur lie in the direction of less homosexual activity among devout groups, whether they be Protestant, Catholic, or Jewish, and more homosexual activity among religiously less active groups.

The Hebrews, in contrast to some of their neighbors, attached a severe religious condemnation to homosexual activity (May 1931, Westermarck 1936, Genesis 19, Leviticus 18: 7, 22, Leviticus 20: 13, Judges 19, I Kings 22:46, II Kings 23:7, Romans 1:27, I Corinthians 6:9, I Timothy 1:9–10, Talmud *passim*). There has, in consequence, been a continuous history of condemnation of the homosexual in the Christian church from its very beginning. Nevertheless, there has not been so frequent or so free discussion of the sinfulness of the homosexual in religious literature as there has been of the sinfulness of masturbation and of pre-marital intercourse. Consequently, it is not unusual to find even devoutly religious persons who become involved in the homosexual without any clear understanding of the church's attitude on the subject.

In general, however, the highest incidences of the homosexual are among the non-devout groups, and the lowest incidences are to be found among the more devout groups. In upper educational levels, among religiously inactive groups, something between 10 and 50 per cent more individuals may be involved than in the active groups; and in lower educational levels the differences in incidences are even greater. The differences in frequencies between the devout and non-devout groups are ordinarily much less, except that the homosexual among Orthodox Jewish groups appears to be phenomenally low.

RELIGIOUS BASES OF THE MORES

There are only minor differences in the emphases which the several religious groups have placed upon sexual morality. The strictly Orthodox Jewish code and the strict Catholic interpretations differ somewhat, but both of them accept the reproductive philosophy of sex, and both of them consider sexual activities which do not offer the possibility of fruition in reproduction as morally wrong. Consequently both of them vigorously condemn masturbation, and both of them attach a tremendous importance to the value of virginity at the time of marriage. The Jewish church maintains its stand on the basis of Biblical and Talmudic interpretations. The Catholic church more often bases its interpretations on a natural philosophy which may be re-interpreted from time to time but which has always emphasized the abnormality or the perverseness of sexual behavior which occurs outside of marriage.

RELIGIOUS GROUP	CASES	HOMOSEXUAL OUTLET AND RELIGION					
		TOTAL POPULATION			ACTIVE POPULATION		
		Mean Frequency	Median Freq.	% of Total Outlet	Incid. %	Mean Freq.	Median Freq.
Single Males: Educational Level 0–8							
Age: Adol.–15							
Protestant, active	89	0.38 ± 0.09	0.00	15.3	22.5	1.68	1.69
Protestant, inactive	481	0.21 ± 0.03	0.00	6.9	22.5	0.95	0.36
Catholic, inactive	106	0.31 ± 0.11	0.00	9.9	30.2	1.03	0.35
Age: 16–20							
Protestant, active	91	0.33 ± 0.12	0.00	12.2	23.1	1.43	0.81
Protestant, inactive	493	0.20 ± 0.03	0.00	6.1	24.5	0.83	0.30
Catholic, inactive	105	0.34 ± 0.08	0.00	10.2	35.2	0.97	0.37
Age: 21–25							
Protestant, inactive	234	0.21 ± 0.05	0.00	6.4	18.8	1.10	0.46
Catholic, inactive	60	0.36 ± 0.13	0.00	11.1	40.0	0.89	0.30
Single Males: Educational Level 9–12							
Age: Adol.–15							
Protestant, active	93	0.11 ± 0.05	0.00	4.3	15.1	0.73	0.09
Protestant, inactive	375	0.28 ± 0.04	0.00	8.1	34.1	0.81	0.29
Catholic, inactive	103	0.52 ± 0.15	0.00	13.7	46.6	1.11	0.41
Age: 16–20							
Protestant, active	95	0.20 ± 0.06	0.00	8.0	30.5	0.65	0.10
Protestant, inactive	315	0.30 ± 0.05	0.00	8.7	37.1	0.81	0.21
Catholic, inactive	101	0.85 ± 0.19	0.06	19.7	59.4	1.43	0.63
Single Males: Educational Level 13+							
Age: Adol.–15							
Protestant, active	547	0.09 ± 0.019	0.00	3.7	23.8	0.38	0.09
Protestant, inactive	1471	0.10 ± 0.011	0.00	3.4	25.6	0.41	0.09
Catholic, devout	132	0.08 ± 0.041	0.00	3.4	16.7	0.48	0.08
Catholic, inactive	165	0.13 ± 0.040	0.00	4.3	20.0	0.64	0.21
Jewish, inactive	601	0.07 ± 0.015	0.00	2.2	14.6	0.44	0.10
Age: 16–20							
Protestant, active	557	0.07 ± 0.017	0.00	2.8	17.4	0.37	0.09
Protestant, inactive	1513	0.07 ± 0.010	0.00	2.4	18.0	0.39	0.08
Catholic, devout	136	0.04 ± 0.015	0.00	1.6	14.6	0.26	0.10
Catholic, inactive	168	0.13 ± 0.037	0.00	4.8	19.6	0.69	0.28
Jewish, Orthodox	59	0.02 ± 0.014	0.00	1.1	11.9	0.19	0.08
Jewish, inactive	607	0.06 ± 0.015	0.00	2.0	10.7	0.55	0.09
Age: 21–25							
Protestant, active	384	0.04 ± 0.015	0.00	2.0	6.2	0.63	0.23
Protestant, inactive	1000	0.09 ± 0.016	0.00	3.5	11.5	0.79	0.24
Catholic, devout	94	0.08 ± 0.037	0.00	4.3	10.6	0.73	0.30
Catholic, inactive	125	0.26 ± 0.081	0.00	9.2	15.2	1.68	1.50
Jewish, inactive	331	0.07 ± 0.025	0.00	2.3	7.9	0.89	0.13

Table 131. Homosexual outlet as related to religious background

These restraints on sexual activities are well recognized among devout Catholics, and often have major effects on the personalities of these individuals. Devout Catholics are restrained in regard to the frequencies of their total outlet, and in regard to their acceptance of any variety of sexual outlets. Non-devout Catholics are much more active sexually. As the church might well contend, the Catholics who are most active sexually are those who are not good Catholics. There will be persons who will suggest that the higher rates of sexual activity among non-devout Catholics depend upon the fact that many poorly educated and immigrant groups belong to that church; but it should be pointed out again that all comparisons between religious groups have been made for populations that are homogeneous in regard to five other biologic and social items, and that Catholic groups of particular educational levels have been compared only with other groups of exactly the same levels. We have no sufficient data for explaining these high rates of sexual activity among the non-devout Catholic groups.

The intermediate positions of the Protestant groups are again in line with our understanding of the intermediate effectiveness of the control which the Protestant church attempts to exercise on sexual behavior. There are, of course, considerable differences between Protestant sects on this matter and often greater differences in the interpretations of sexual moralities among clergymen of the same sect. In general, the more literal groups of the Protestant church make sexual appraisals which are close to those of the Talmud and of the Catholic natural law; but a more liberal portion of the Protestant clergy is inclined to re-interpret all types of sexual behavior in terms of the total social adjustment of the individual.

Even though the differences between the sexual philosophies of these three religious groups are not great, one might have expected greater differences than those which actually exist between the histories of the adherents of the three groups. With one exception, there are surprisingly few differences between the behavior of equally devout or non-devout members of the three religious faiths. The one exception lies among the Orthodox Jewish males. Of all religious groups they are the sexually least active, both in regard to the frequencies of their total sexual outlet, and in regard to the incidences and frequencies of masturbation, nocturnal emissions, and the homosexual. They are closer to the males of other groups in regard to pre-marital petting and pre-marital intercourse.

This relative inactivity of the Orthodox Jewish males is especially interesting, in view of the diametrically opposite opinion which recently stirred a considerable portion of Europe against the Jews as a race. It is further significant to note here that while the non-Orthodox are much more active than the Orthodox Jewish males, the sexually most active groups are religiously non-active Protestants or Catholics as often as they are Jewish.

These data on the lower frequencies of sexual activity among the Ortho-dox Jews will occasion no surprise to those who understand the pervading asceticism of Hebrew philosophy. Non-devout Jewish groups, even includ-ing those who observe none of the Orthodox customs and who may be removed by several generations from ancestors who ever attended the synagogue, may still be controlled to a considerable degree by the Talmudic interpretations of sexual morality. There is a general opinion that Jewish groups discuss sexual matters publicly with less restraint than most other groups, and this opinion may provide some basis for the general im-pression that Jews are sexually more active. It has been notable, however, in a high proportion of our Jewish histories, that the freedom with which they record the details of their own sexual activities and the freedom with which they discuss those details, not only with us but with many of their fellows and with utter strangers, has surprisingly little relation to the extent of the overt activity in their individual sexual his-tories. The influence of the several thousand years of Jewish sexual philos-ophy is not to be ignored in the search for any final explanation of these data.

The differences between religiously devout persons and religiously in-active persons of the same faith are much greater than the differences between two equally devout groups of different faiths. In regard to total sexual outlet the religiously inactive groups may have frequencies that are 25 to 75 per cent higher than the frequencies of the religiously devout groups. Among religiously inactive males there are definitely higher frequencies of masturbation, pre-marital intercourse, marital intercourse, and the homosexual.

The church, however, exerts a wider influence on even non-devout individuals, by way of the influence which it has had throughout the centuries upon the development of the sexual mores of our Western European-American culture. The religious codes have always and every-where been the prime source of those social attitudes which, in their aggregate, represent the sexual mores of all groups, devout or non-devout, church-going or non-church-going, rational, faithful to a creed, or merely following the custom of the land. It is, of course, often contended that social attitudes are the product of experience and that the wisdom thus acquired becomes the basis of the formalized systems of ethics which are recognized by various religious bodies. In theological terms, such systems are ascribed to divine revelation. Whether the religious, social, and legal systems came before the social experience, or the social experience before the formulations of the rules of behavior, is, however, a matter that needs careful historical investigation before any final conclusions are reached.

In an older day, when church courts had authority over the life and death of each and every individual, departures from the expressed sexual codes made the culprit painfully aware of the source of the sexual mores. In the present day, when most of the population refuses to recognize the jurisdiction of religious courts, the influence of the church is more indirect; but the ancient religious codes are still the prime sources of the attitudes, the ideas, the ideals, and the rationalizations by which most individuals pattern their sexual lives.

No social level accepts the whole of the original Judaeo-Christian code, but each level derives its taboos from some part of the same basic religious philosophy. Whether sexual acts are evaluated in terms of what is right or wrong (as the upper social level puts it), or of what is natural or unnatural (as the lower social level considers it), the Hebraic and Christian concept of the reproductive function of sex lies back of both interpretations. The lower social level's taboo on nudity (Chapter 10) has a long history in Jewish codes and in Catholic church rulings, and the upper level's freer acceptance of nudity is in direct violation of church opinion. On the other hand, the upper level accepts the church's restrictions on pre-marital and extra-marital intercourse (Chapter 10), while the lower level largely ignores the religious objections on those items. Particular individuals may come nearer to accepting the whole of the sexual code of the particular religious group to which they belong, but the patterns of every social level depart at some point from every church code.

These apparent conflicts between the religious codes and the patterns of sexual behavior may lead one to overlook the religious origins of the social patterns. Nevertheless, the individual who denies that he is in any way influenced by church rulings still stoutly defends the church's system of natural law, recognizes certain behavior as normal and other activities as unnatural, abnormal, and perverse, or considers that certain things (but only certain things) are fine, esthetically satisfactory, socially expedient, and decent for a mature and intelligent male to engage in. In so contending, he perpetuates the tradition of the Judaic law and the Christian precept.

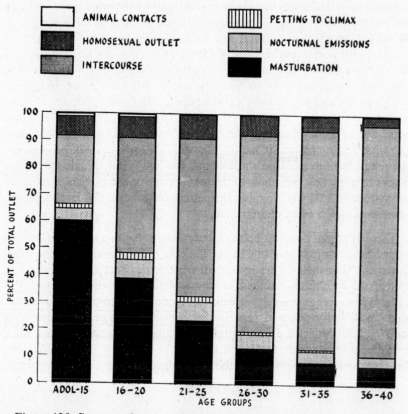

Figure 126. Sources of orgasm for total U. S. population, by age groups

Summary data, corrected for distribution of age, marital status, and educational level shown in U. S. Census of 1940. Figures 126–133 on same scale, so percents of total outlet derived from each source may be seen by direct comparisons of all these figures.

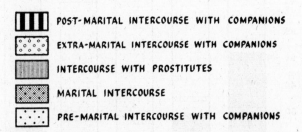

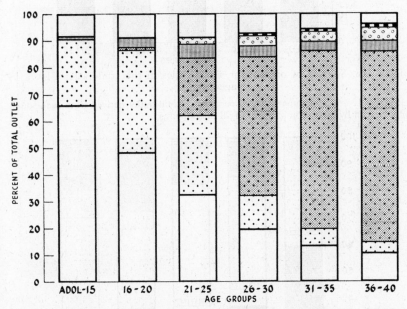

Figure 127. Types of heterosexual coitus contributing to outlet of total U. S.
population in each age period

Summary data, corrected for distribution of age, marital status, and educational level
shown in U. S. Census for 1940. Identical with Figure 126, except that the area of the
total heterosexual intercourse is subdivided into its several sources. Figures 126 and
127 on same scale, so direct comparisons can be made between figures.

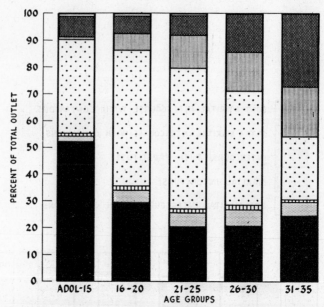

Figure 128. Sources of orgasm for single males of the grade school level, by age groups

Figures 126–133 on same scale, so percents of total outlet derived from each source may be seen by direct comparisons of all these figures.

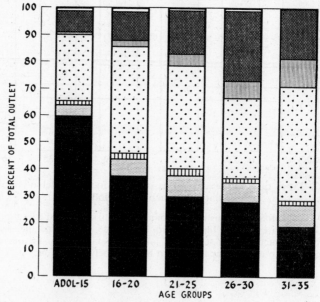

Figure 129. Sources of orgasm for single males of the high school level, by age groups

Figures 126–133 on same scale, so percents of total outlet derived from each source may be seen by direct comparisons of all these figures.

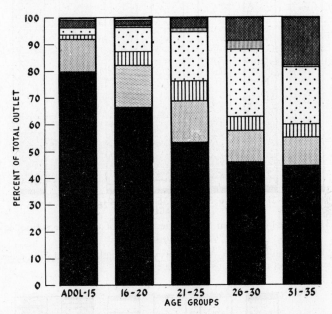

Figure 130. Sources of orgasm for single males of the college level, by age groups

Figures 126–133 on same scale, so percents of total outlet derived from each source may be seen by direct comparisons of all these figures.

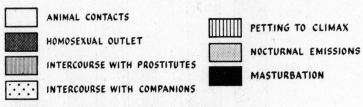

Key to Figures 128–130

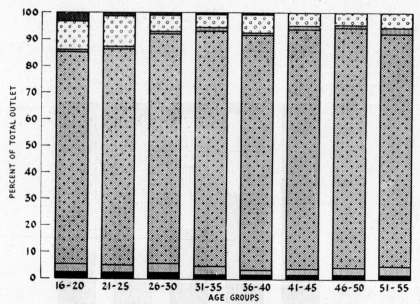

Figure 131. Sources of orgasm for married males of the grade school level, by age groups

Figures 126–133 on same scale, so percents of total outlet derived from each source may be seen by direct comparisons of all these figures.

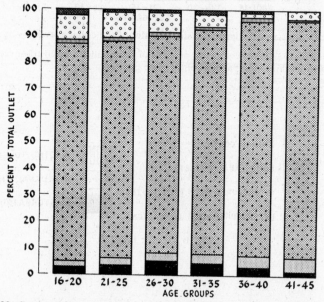

Figure 132. Sources of orgasm for married males of the high school level, by age groups

Figures 126–133 on same scale, so percents of total outlet derived from each source may be seen by direct comparisons of all these figures.

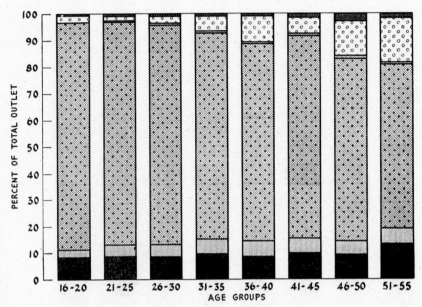

Figure 133. Sources of orgasm for married males of the college level, by age groups

Figures 126–133 on same scale, so percents of total outlet derived from each source may be seen by direct comparisons of all these figures.

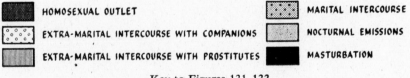

	HOMOSEXUAL OUTLET			MARITAL INTERCOURSE
	EXTRA-MARITAL INTERCOURSE WITH COMPANIONS			NOCTURNAL EMISSIONS
	EXTRA-MARITAL INTERCOURSE WITH PROSTITUTES			MASTURBATION

Key to Figures 131–133

Part III

SOURCES OF SEXUAL OUTLET

Chapter 14

MASTURBATION

The previous section of this volume has been occupied with an examination of the factors which affect human sexual behavior. Such biologic items as age and the age at onset of adolescence, and such social factors as educational level, occupational class of the subject and of the subject's parents, the rural-urban backgrounds of the individual, and the religious backgrounds have been analyzed as factors affecting the total sexual outlet and each of the particular types of sexual outlet. The remainder of this volume will summarize the record for each source of outlet: masturbation (in the present chapter), and nocturnal emissions, pre-marital intercourse, homosexual contacts, and other sources of outlet (in the subsequent chapters). Although many of the specific data in this section will be drawn from material presented elsewhere in the book, these chapters will be especially concerned with interpretations of the data, and will summarize the nature of each type of behavior, emphasize the individual variation that occurs, discuss the correlations of each type of activity with each other source of outlet, and show something of the significance of these factors to the individual and to the society of which he is a part.

DEFINITION

The term masturbation may be applied to any sort of self stimulation which brings erotic arousal. Since, as we have already seen (Chapter 5), all tactile responses and still others of the sensory responses are basic to sexual activity, there is considerable justice in extending the concept of masturbation to all situations in which there is tactile stimulation. Freud (1938) and many of the analysts and other clinicians (Meagher 1924, Meagher and Jelliffe 1936, Mowrer and Kluckhohn in Hunt 1944, Lorand 1944, Carmichael 1946, Landis and Bolles 1946) use the word in this way, especially in connection with the behavior of younger children. When so defined, the phenomenon of masturbation is recognizable as universal among both males and females, from the youngest child to the oldest adult; but this is not the concept of masturbation held by the public in general, nor by most clinicians who inquire about it or report it in the histories of their patients. As more usually employed, the word "masturbation" refers to any self stimulation which is deliberate and designed to effect erotic arousal. By such a definition, the accidental touching of oneself is not masturbation because it is not deliberate. As so defined, not only tactile stimulation, but all other sorts of sensory and psychic stimulation, if deliberate and designed to bring satisfaction, fall under this head. Rubbing or scratching one's body, even one's genitalia, is not masturbation when it serves some other function than that of effecting erotic arousal. Throughout this volume the word has not been applied to anything except deliberate self stimulation.

When so strictly defined, masturbation cannot be taken to be as universal as some of the psychiatrists and psychologists would have it. The extension of the meaning of the word has, unfortunately, distorted the interpretation of the actual data on the phenomenon; and it is to be suggested that the analysts would do better to describe a good deal of what they observe, especially among younger children, as tactile experience, which is exactly what it is, and not call it masturbation until there is evidence that the child is reaping an erotic reward for his activity, and that the behavior has been inspired by some anticipation of such a reward.

REFERENCES

Data on the occurrence of masturbation, its incidences and frequencies in various segments of the male population, have already been detailed in this volume in the following tables and figures:

PAGE	TABLE	FIGURE	NATURE OF DATA
190, 191	38	30	Sources of first ejaculation
234	49	136–137	Range of variation and age
238–243	51	53–58	Age and masturbation
273–277	61	53–58	Marital status and masturbation
300–303	68	89	Sources of first ejaculation versus age at onset of adolescence
310–313	72, 73	91–92	Age at onset of adolescence as related to masturbation
339–343	82, 108, 115	98, 124	Social level and masturbation
375–380	96–97	106–107	Masturbation in patterns of behavior at different educational levels
396–399, 407–413	98, 103–105	108, 119, 122, 123	Older and younger generations and masturbation
450–453, 462	117	125	Rural and urban groups and masturbation
470–476	126		Religious backgrounds and masturbation
488–493		126, 128–133	Significance of masturbation as one source of total outlet
499–502	4, 17, 22, 132	8, 16, 24, 134–135	Accumulative incidence of masturbation
504–506		7, 136–137	Individual variation in masturbation

INCIDENCES AND FREQUENCIES

Incidences. By even the stricter definition, masturbation may be identified in the histories of a very high proportion of the human males. Ultimately about 92 per cent of the total population is involved in masturbation which leads to orgasm (Table 132, Figures 134, 135). More individuals (96%) of the college level and 95 per cent of the high school group, are ultimately included, fewer (89%) of the males who never go beyond grade school. The general opinion that all males masturbate at some time in their lives, and the easy acceptance of this opinion among many clinicians and educators, are not warranted by the actual record. There are some individuals who do not masturbate for the simple reason that they do not have sufficient sex drive to cause them to go out of their way to find any sort of outlet, and who depend on nocturnal emissions for most of their orgasms. There are some boys, particularly at lower social levels, who do not masturbate because they become involved in heterosexual coitus at such an early age that they have little need for other sources of outlet. There are some duller and slower reacting individuals who find it impossible to effect orgasm in masturbation, and who in consequence make no attempt to masturbate after their first experiments. Thus there is a group of males who definitely do not have masturbatory histories, although the percentage is as small as is indicated above.

In several of the previous studies on human male sexual behavior (Merrill 1918, Peck and Wells 1923, 1925, Hughes 1926, Hamilton 1929, Dickinson and Beam 1931, Peterson 1938, Wile 1941, Ramsey 1943, Finger 1947, Hohman and Schaffner 1947), similar incidence figures have been obtained. It is interesting to find that a number of the European studies report comparable incidences (85% to 96%) among European males (Rohleder 1902, 1921; also summary in Haire 1937). There is every reason to believe that the lower figures obtained in some of the other American studies (Brockman 1902, Exner 1915, Achilles 1923, Taylor 1933, Bromley and Britten 1938) represent failures to obtain the fact. It must be realized that masturbation is taboo and even strongly condemned among certain groups (Chapter 10); and while college men more often admit their experience, there are males in some other groups who would admit almost any other kind of sexual activity before they would give a record of masturbatory experience. On the other hand, the high incidence of masturbation in the male should not be taken as warrant for believing that there is a similarly high incidence in the female. The data on the female will be presented in a later volume.

Pre-adolescent Activity. For two-thirds (68.4%) of the boys, self masturbation provides the first ejaculation. For most of the other boys, nocturnal emissions and heterosexual coitus provide the first ejaculation. There is little variation in these data for different social levels. Masturbation is more

| | MASTURBATION: ACCUMULATIVE INCIDENCE DATA | | | | | | |
| AGE | TOTAL POPULATION U. S. CORRECTIONS | | EDUC. LEVEL 0–8 | | EDUC. LEVEL 9–12 | | EDUC. LEVEL 13+ | |
	Cases	% with Exper.	Cases	% with Exper.	Cases	% with Exper.	Cases	% with Exper.
8	3960	0.1	661	0.0	484	0.2	2815	0.0
9	3960	0.3	661	0.0	484	0.6	2815	0.3
10	3960	2.0	661	0.8	484	2.5	2815	2.3
11	3959	6.1	660	3.2	484	7.0	2815	8.9
12	3959	21.2	660	15.5	484	22.7	2815	27.9
13	3959	44.9	660	34.4	484	48.6	2815	52.9
14	3956	71.7	657	60.3	484	77.9	2815	72.2
15	3950	82.2	651	77.3	484	85.5	2815	80.2
16	3929	87.6	634	84.5	481	90.2	2814	84.3
17	3870	90.2	597	86.6	461	93.1	2812	87.0
18	3735	91.8	573	89.4	426	93.9	2736	88.9
19	3504	92.1	543	89.5	389	94.1	2572	90.0
20	3200	92.1	515	89.7	348	93.7	2337	91.1
21	2827	92.6	491	89.6	305	94.4	2031	92.0
22	2425	92.7	472	89.6	283	94.3	1670	92.8
23	2110	93.5	456	89.7	258	95.7	1396	93.3
24	1819	93.8	436	89.9	232	96.1	1151	93.1
25	1634	93.4	416	89.7	216	96.3	1002	93.9
26	1491	93.3	405	89.4	202	96.0	884	94.9
27	1356	93.1	391	89.0	191	95.8	774	95.3
28	1250	92.8	377	88.6	174	95.4	699	95.3
29	1141	92.3	353	88.1	154	94.8	634	95.0
30	1047	91.5	337	87.8	137	94.2	573	95.6
31	971	90.9	317	87.1	125	93.6	529	95.3
32	913	91.2	305	87.2	116	94.0	492	95.5
33	854	90.8	293	86.7	113	93.8	448	95.3
34	802	90.9	285	86.3	105	94.3	412	95.9
35	745	90.2	271	86.3	92	94.6	382	95.8
36	701	90.6	258	87.2	87	94.3	356	95.8
37	639	90.0	240	86.7	76	93.4	323	95.7
38	609	89.6	232	86.2	70	92.9	307	95.8
39	554	89.1	210	85.7	64	92.2	280	95.4
40	507	88.3	192	85.4	58	91.4	257	96.1
41	472	87.5	181	84.5	53	90.6	238	95.8
42	444	87.3	173	84.4	50	90.0	221	95.5

Table 132. Accumulative incidence data on masturbation

Covering the life span, including both single and married histories. In three educational levels, and in the total population corrected for the U. S. Census of 1940.

likely to provide the first experience (72%) for the boys who become adolescent at an early age, less likely (52%) for the boys who are slowest in development (Table 68, Figure 89).

The inspiration for the first experimentation in masturbation is a matter which will need more extensive consideration in a later study on sex education. It may be stated now that nearly all boys have heard about masturbation before they attempt it themselves, and a high proportion has observed companions masturbating. This is particularly true in the grade school and high school levels of society; but some males of the college level will be surprised that there are so few boys who discover masturbation on their own initiative, because it is chiefly at that level that masturbation is independently discovered by some boys. After early adolescence, there are many males who never have an opportunity to observe another male in sexual performance, and consequently it is notable that so many boys do observe masturbation in connection with their initial experiences. The female more often discovers masturbation independently and without any previous knowledge that any other person has ever been involved in similar activity.

However extensive the incidental touching of genitalia may be, specific masturbation is quite rare among younger boys. Of course, there are cases of infants under a year of age who have learned the advantage of specific manipulation, sometimes as a result of being so manipulated by older persons; and there are some boys who masturbate quite specifically and with some frequency from the age of two or three. But most young boys, in attempting masturbation, engage in such desultory motions and so quickly cease their efforts that no satisfaction is obtained and they are, therefore, not interested in trying again. When an older person provides the more specific sort of manipulation which is usual among adults, the same child may be much aroused, and in a high proportion of the cases may be brought to actual orgasm (Chapter 5).

As far as the available data indicate it is, then, a relatively small number of the younger pre-adolescents who, in any strict sense, masturbate. Not more than 10 per cent seems to have done so before the age of nine, and 13 per cent before the age of ten. Most boys are ten, eleven or twelve years old before they become involved. These are minimum data, derived chiefly from the memories of adults, and adults sometimes forget their childhood experiences. Comparisons of records from children and from adults (Chapter 5) indicate that the actual figures may be somewhat higher, but not more than 20 per cent higher, *i.e.*, instead of 13 per cent it may be as many as 16 per cent of the boys who masturbate before age ten.

There appear to be some differences between social levels in the incidences of pre-adolescent masturbation, but such differences are fewer than are ordinarily found between social levels in adolescence. Actually, few boys begin masturbation until they are near the age when regular erotic responses are recognizable, which means not more than a year or two before adolescence for most of them, even though a larger proportion would be capable of definite response at a much earlier age if sufficient contacts

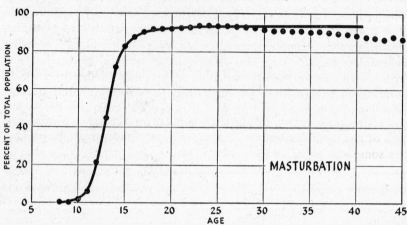

Figure 134. Masturbation: accumulative incidence, in total U. S. population

Showing percent of total population that has ever had masturbatory experience by each of the indicated ages. All data based on total population, irrespective of marital status, and corrected for the U. S. Census distribution.

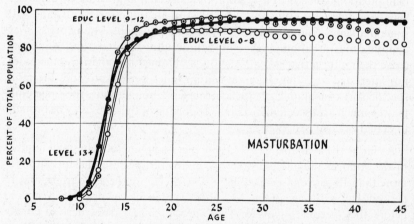

Figure 135. Masturbation: accumulative incidence in three educational levels

Showing percent of each population that has ever had masturbatory experience by each of the indicated ages. All data based on total population, irrespective of marital status.

were had. It is, of course, quite understandable that the boy should not be interested until there is a sufficient return for his efforts.

Some of the pre-adolescents carry their masturbation through to a definite and satisfactory orgasm, although in some instances the boy may not recognize what is happening, and does not identify the experience by either name or description as something that other boys have had. Nevertheless, masturbation in the younger boy is usually a definite sort of performance which is often limited to a few minutes in time, and which ceases abruptly when, as he may report, he has had enough of it. This means either that he has reached orgasm, or that he has found at least some sort of release from the tension which initiated the activity and which may have been augmented in the course of the performance. Some adolescent boys and many adults recall specific orgasm with all of its adult characteristics occurring before they had acquired the ability to ejaculate; and there are definite records (Chapter 5) on several hundred boys who have been observed in pre-adolescent orgasm which was achieved either through self masturbation or through socio-sexual contacts. Among the older psychiatrists there are some who go so far as to state, dogmatically, that no pre-adolescent ever experienced orgasm unless he was neurotic. Such a statement smacks of something other than scientific objectivity and is, of course, unacceptable in view of the observations now at hand.

Adults are often disturbed when they discover young children masturbating, and many a clinician supports the parents' fears and lends little comfort to the child who is taken to the doctor to be cured of his biologically normal capacities. Inasmuch as nearly all boys arrive at masturbation sooner or later, it may be asked why one should worry over pre-adolescent or even infantile masturbation. If it is a moral issue, the answer must come from someone else than the scientists, and be treated as a question of morals (as it is in Kirsch 1930, Ruland and Rattler 1934, Fleege 1945, Davis 1946 vol. 2). If it is a question of physical outcome, the issue is for the biologist; and it should be made clear that there is no evidence, among the thousands of histories now at hand, that the boy who begins masturbating at an early age suffers any more harm than the boy who delays the beginning of his experience until some time in adolescence or later. And most scientists and clinicians are now agreed that masturbation does no harm at the later ages.

If the question is one of social values, it may be stated that there is no record of early masturbation disturbing the child's adjustments except in some of the cases where adults discovered the activity, reprimanded or punished the youngster, made a public exhibition of the offense, or upset the child's peace of mind in some other way. Even the parents who try to avoid reprimands may cause some disturbance in the child because they, the parents themselves, are inhibited, or because they are not accustomed to observing sexual behavior of any sort. It takes no more than a show of surprise on the part of the parent, a supercilious smile, or even a studied avoidance of the issue to make it apparent to the child that the parent is emotionally upset, and that sexual activity is in a different category from

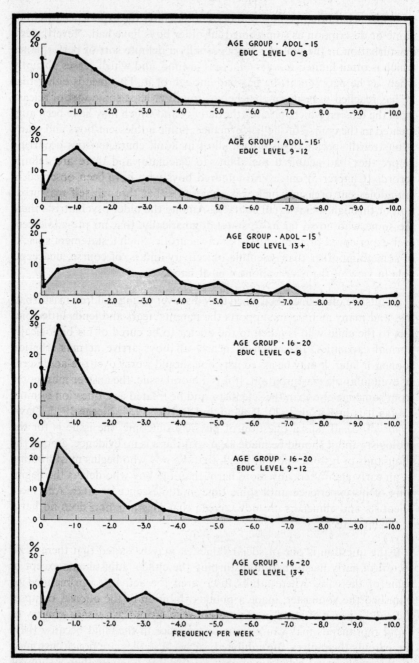

Figure 136. Masturbation: individual variation in frequencies, at ages adolescent–15 and 16–20, for three educational levels

Showing percent of each population (vertical line) which masturbates with each type of frequency (horizontal line).

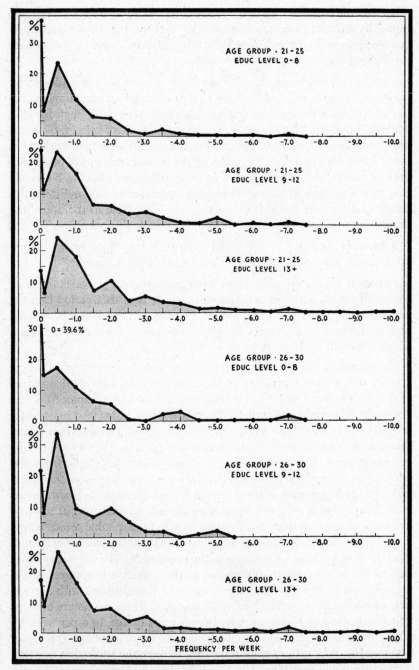

Figure 137. Masturbation: individual variation in frequencies, at ages 21–25 and 26–30, for three educational levels

Showing percent of each population (vertical line) which masturbates with each type of frequency (horizontal line).

other everyday affairs. Children, even infants and very young children, are especially sensitive to the reactions of other persons. If the child is seriously disturbed over his behavior, the disturbance may color his personality throughout life, as the psychiatrist and psychologist well know.

For the parent who intends that the child, or even the older adolescent, shall not be upset over masturbation, it is a matter of accepting the behavior without allowing it to appear important (Weiss and English 1943), while still making it clear that such activity in front of other individuals may bring social difficulties. The careful adjustments which are worked out in the home may be completely upset by the violent reactions of other children or adults who become aware of the child's masturbation. Nevertheless, there are cases of parents who have succeeded in accomplishing this delicate adjustment between things that are acceptable in the home and things that other people outside the home "just don't understand."

Adolescent Activity. When specific masturbation does occur in pre-adolescence, it is almost invariably continued into adolescence.

For most males, of every social level, masturbation provides the chief source of sexual outlet in early adolescence. It is at that period that the activity reaches its highest frequencies. For those males who subsequently turn to socio-sexual contacts for their pre-marital outlet, masturbatory frequencies will never again be so high.

Masturbation and pre-marital intercourse are the only types of sexual activity which show something of the same range of individual variation (Table 49, Figures 136, 137) as is shown by total outlet (Chapter 6). There are males who never masturbate. There are a few males who masturbate only once or twice in their lives; and there are others who have frequencies that may average seven to fourteen or twenty or more per week for long periods of years. There are males whose high frequencies extend from pre-adolescence through all of the pre-marital years, and males who may maintain average frequencies of three or four a week through the marital years into old age. There are a few males who are still masturbating at seventy-five years of age, but there are no older ones in the available record whose masturbation results in orgasm. Some males may masturbate several thousand times as often as some others in the population. The statement about lack of harmful outcome still applies to these most active cases. In the present records, the highest-rating males were masturbating with average frequencies of 23 per week in early adolescence. These maximum average frequencies drop to 15 per week by twenty years of age, to 6 per week by fifty years of age, and to once in two weeks at sixty years of age. It is about then that the older males are most inclined to warn the adolescent boy that masturbation will certainly harm him if he does it to excess.

For the active population, average frequencies of masturbation in early adolescence are nearly two and a half (2.4) per week, but a goodly number

(17%) of the boys at that age may average four to seven times a week, or oftener (Table 51). A much larger number of the boys reach these higher frequencies on occasion, even though they do not regularly average such rates.

From the early teens, the frequencies of masturbation drop steadily into old age. They drop more abruptly in the lower social levels, where there is the most intercourse, and less abruptly in the upper social levels, where there is less intercourse before marriage.

In all groups, masturbation after marriage occurs only with reduced frequencies (Table 82). It occurs most often among the married males of the college level, where 69 per cent is ultimately involved, and where the frequencies may average about once in two weeks in early marriage, dropping a bit in the later years. It is, however, much less frequent in the marital histories of the lower levels. Less than a third (29%) of the grade school level, and less than half (42%) of the high school level, ever masturbate after marriage, and then the frequencies do not average more than once in three weeks. In most cases, the experience after marriage is confined to those periods when the husband is away from his wife. Some married males will go for years without masturbation, but come back to it as an outlet when they are separated from their wives for some period of time, as many men were during the recent war. This was most often true of the college male. Sometimes masturbation in the marital histories is the product of the fact that the wife does not want as frequent sexual relations as the male would like to have, or that periods of pregnancy, menstruation, or illness interfere with the regular intercourse. There are, however, some males who deliberately turn to self stimulation as a source of sexual variety, and who masturbate irrespective of the amount of marital intercourse they may have.

In Various Groups. Males with the highest frequencies of masturbation are most often those who become adolescent first. These are the males who have the maximum total outlet throughout their lives (Chapter 9). During the early adolescent years these younger-maturing males masturbate about twice as frequently as the boys who became adolescent last, and between sixteen and twenty-five years of age they still masturbate with rates that are 50 to 60 per cent higher than those of the late-adolescent males (Table 73). The highest incidence (99%) of masturbation in any segment of the population is among these younger-adolescent boys. It is only 93 per cent of the late-adolescent boys who ever masturbate.

At all ages, in all religious groups and in nearly all other subdivisions of the population, the highest incidences and frequencies of masturbation are to be found among boys of the college level, and the lowest incidences and frequencies among boys of lower educational levels. The accumulative incidence figures for the two groups are not very different, but the active incidence figures for any particular age period may differ more materially

(Table 82). At the college level, masturbation involves most of the males (96%) and continues to be the chief source (about 60%) of the outlet up until the time of marriage. More than two-thirds (69%) of the college-bred males have some masturbation in their histories after marriage, and this provides no small part (about 9%) of the total outlet of the group after marriage. On the other hand, masturbation in the more poorly educated groups may begin to drop out almost immediately after it is begun. There are lower level males who have masturbated only a single time or two, or a few times in their lives. Some of them may masturbate for a year or two, but then stop. By sixteen years of age 16 per cent of them has stopped masturbating, and nearly 40 per cent has stopped by the time age twenty has been passed. In these late teens masturbation supplies only about a fourth (29.2%) of the outlet for the lower level males. Most males of this level find it difficult to understand how a grown man could think of masturbating, particularly if he is married and living with his wife.

The average frequencies of masturbation differ between social levels, more than the incidences. Average frequencies (active population) for the boys of the grade school level, between adolescence and fifteen years of age, are 1.8 per week; for the corresponding high school level, 2.2 per week; for the boys who will ultimately go to college, 2.7 per week (Table 82). The differences in frequencies become greater in the later age groups, and between adolescence and marriage the males of the college level masturbate more than twice as frequently as the males of the grade school level.

At lower levels there are definite taboos against masturbation. These may be fortified with the explanation that masturbation will drive one crazy, give one pimples, make one weak, or do some other sort of physical harm. More often masturbation is simply rejected because it is considered unnatural. The entire sexual philosophy at this level is turned around the acceptance of what is natural and the rejection of activities that are unnatural. The upper level's wider acceptance of masturbation is rationalized on the ground that scientific investigation shows that it does no physical harm. Actually, however, the acceptance of masturbation in the upper level is probably the result of the very strong taboos which that group has against pre-marital intercourse. It is not a case of liking masturbation more, so much as it is a case of liking non-marital heterosexual relations less.

The masturbatory records of older and younger generations of males from the college level are practically identical, both as to the percentage of persons involved and the frequencies of the activity (Tables 98, 104). The present-day masturbatory pattern of the college level male goes back at least twenty-two years; but there is a more conscious, more generally verbalized acceptance of the reality among college-bred males today. Moreover, the upper level attitude and its scientific acceptance of masturbation seems to have extended to at least some of the more poorly edu-

cated males in the population. For the younger generation of the grade
school level, for instance, masturbation begins earlier, includes more persons, and is had nearly twice as frequently as it was had in the older generation.

Boys in rural areas masturbate less often than boys raised in cities or
towns, especially during adolescence (Table 117). But since the farm boy
has a somewhat lower total outlet than the city boy, and since the farm boy
has definitely lower rates of socio-sexual contacts, masturbation provides
a higher percentage of his total outlet than it does for the city boy.

Masturbation occurs with the lowest incidences and frequencies among
Jewish males who are Orthodox and among devout Catholics, and it occurs
with the highest frequencies among religiously inactive Protestants (Table
126). The religious codes, both Jewish and Christian, have been the prime
source of the taboos on masturbation (Chapter 13).

TECHNIQUES

In the human male, masturbatory techniques are largely manual. They
usually constitute a deliberate attempt to provide genital stimulation which
will result in the satisfaction of orgasm. There are very few males who deliberately avoid orgasm as the conclusion of the activity, although a few
of them may deliberately prolong the act into a matter of several minutes
or more—sometimes to half an hour or an hour or more, in order to extend the sensory satisfaction. Most males carry the activity through to
climax as rapidly as is possible, which means it does not ordinarily continue
for more than a minute or two. Some males, indeed, are able to achieve
orgasm quite regularly in a half minute or so, sometimes in ten or twenty
seconds.

There are some boys who attempt to masturbate by moving the penis
against a bed or against some other object; but for most males this technique is rare and confined to an incidental experience or two. Surprisingly
enough, this method seems to be common only among the males of a particular group; but the specific data are insufficient to present at this time,
and it has been impossible to get any clue as to the origin or significance
of this pattern. Many of the persons who depend upon this mode of masturbation think of the act as a substitute for heterosexual coitus, and there
are some clinicians who specifically recommend such a technique, in conjunction with fantasy, on the ground that it may provide some carry-over
into later heterosexual activity. But however good the theory may appear
to be, it finds no substantiation in the specific record, for the great majority of the boys use simpler manual techniques in masturbation, and make
perfectly satisfactory heterosexual adjustments anyway. It is also to be
noted that males have been known to masturbate against a bed while
fantasying frictation or anal relations in the homosexual.

Self fellation is an anatomic impossibility for most human males, but it is a common means of masturbation among rhesus monkeys, the macaque, mandrille, chimpanzees and other primates (Carpenter 1942, National Research Council Conference on Mammalian Sex Behavior, 1943), and occurs quite widely among mammals of many other groups (Beach 1947). Throughout vertebrate sexual behavior there is such a close tie-up between oral eroticism and genital stimulation that oral activity of any sort must be accepted by the scientist as a biologically normal aspect of sexuality. Its tremendous suppression in the human animal must be taken to be the outcome of cultural developments. Consequently, it is not surprising to find that the human male, with his animal background, does sometimes attempt self fellation. It has taken special interviewing techniques (Chapter 2) to get adults to admit such experience, but a considerable portion of the population does record attempts at self fellation, at least in early adolescence. Only two or three males in a thousand are able to achieve the objective, but there are three or four histories of males who had depended upon self fellation as a masturbatory technique for some appreciable period of time—in the case of one thirty-year old male, for most of his life. In his psychic drive, the human animal is more mammalian than even his anatomy allows him to be.

Only a limited number of individuals extend their masturbatory techniques to involve any variety of other procedures. Such experimentation is most often found among better educated individuals who have well developed imaginative capacities and who are, of course, the ones most likely to have a minimum of overt socio-sexual contacts. The manual techniques of genital manipulation are elaborated by a few individuals. The use of literature and erotic pictures for stimulation during masturbation is not really common, and it is largely confined to better educated individuals. Urethral insertions and other masochistic techniques, and anal stimulation and anal insertions occur only very occasionally. Sometimes devices which simulate the female genitalia may be used for masturbation, but they are rarely employed. Most males restrict themselves to a limited series of particular techniques to which they have been erotically conditioned.

Nearly, but not quite, all males experience sexual fantasies during masturbation. The female fantasies much less often while masturbating. Masturbatory fantasies accord with the general psychiatric and psychologic understanding of the matter. The fantasies are heterosexual when the primary interests of the individual are heterosexual, homosexual when the individual's overt experience or psychic reactions are homosexual. They may be alternately heterosexual and homosexual in the case of the individual who reacts definitely in both directions. The fantasies may include animal contacts for boys who have had such animal experience as some farm boys have. There are occasional sadistic or masochistic fantasies. Just as with nocturnal dreams (Chapter 15), there may be some striking disparities between the nature of the fantasies accompanying masturbation and the overt experience of the male, and one cannot discover the history of an individual merely by finding out what he thinks about when he masturbates.

Where the masturbatory techniques are manual, many individuals find some additional stimulation in observing their own genitalia; and this may have some homosexual significance, although most persons with such histories may deny any other homosexual interests. A considerable portion of the pre-eminently homosexual males whose homosexual activities involve mutual masturbation or oral techniques do observe their own genitalia during self masturbation; but not even all of them do so. Some of the most vigorously heterosexual males, however, carefully avoid any observation of their genitalia during masturbation, and their performances depend primarily upon involved heterosexual fantasies. Many of these persons masturbate in the dark, in order to concentrate the better upon the imagery. It is an important question whether masturbation should be interpreted as a narcissistic performance or a socio-sexual activity, and one is not warranted in considering that all masturbation is a matter of self interest. There are some individuals for whom masturbation is a distinctly heterosexual or a distinctly homosexual experience, depending upon the strength of the fantasy and the abundance of the associations which complement the activity.

CORRELATIONS WITH OTHER OUTLETS

It has not been possible to make precise correlations between the frequencies of the various types of sexual outlet for the present study; and at this time the relations between masturbation and the other outlets may only be suggested in the most general terms.

There may be some correlation between the frequencies of masturbation and the frequencies of nocturnal dreams. In general, the males who have the highest frequencies of nocturnal emissions may have somewhat lower rates of masturbation. Some of these males credit the frequent emissions to the fact that they do not masturbate; but it is just as likely that the reverse relationship is true, namely, that they do not masturbate because they have frequent emissions.

On the other hand, there is little evidence that high frequencies of masturbation reduce the frequencies of nocturnal emissions (Chapter 15). Even where there are high masturbatory frequencies and low frequencies of nocturnal emissions, the possibility should not be overlooked that those particular males never would have had frequent emissions, even if they had stopped masturbating.

There may be some relationship between masturbation and pre-marital petting with females. Both of these activities are most frequent at upper levels, but it is probable that both are the products of the upper level sexual philosophy, rather than the products of each other. Nevertheless, the genital manipulations which are employed in masturbation may provide some introduction to the techniques of heterosexual petting.

Masturbation sometimes shows a complementary relationship with pre-marital coitus. Where the one is high, the other is likely to be lower. Where there is sufficient coitus, it may be that there is not much need for masturbation. On the other hand, it remains to be demonstrated that a sufficiency of masturbation reduces the incentive to find a socio-sexual outlet. There are those who believe so, and recommend masturbation as a means of controlling what they consider the more immoral pre-marital activity. There are also those, including not a few psychiatrists, who feel that it would be unfortunate if pre-marital masturbation reduced the urge to make a heterosexual adjustment. It will take a carefully objective study to show what the real relationships may be.

Any relation which may exist between masturbation and the homosexual similarly needs to be studied in detail (Taylor 1933). It has already been suggested that an interest in one's own genitalia may be transferred to an interest in the genitalia of another individual of the same sex. Certainly there are some records of the sort in the histories now at hand; but the number of clear-cut cases is not large. Careful analyses of a considerable series of individual histories should be made before any conclusion is reached on these matters.

Even some of the animal contacts which the farm boy has may have been inspired by his own masturbatory experience, for the masturbation of farm animals and of household pets is about as frequent as coitus or oral relations with the animals. In a considerable number of cases the boy's relation is had with a male animal which he masturbates. If the boy is erotically aroused in such a case, the relationship may involve some homosexual element, as well as the zoöphilic.

SIGNIFICANCE OF MASTURBATION

There are no other sexual activities which involve anywhere near so many individuals as are involved in heterosexual coitus and masturbation; and there are no other activities which provide so large a proportion of the total orgasms which the average male experiences in his lifetime. For most males, coitus is primary, masturbation secondary in importance; but for males of the college level masturbation is, as we have seen, the chief source of outlet up to the time of marriage. It is a question whether activities which are as important as these can be altogether ignored, easily regulated, or completely ruled out of the lives of any large number of people. Unmarried youths who had neither masturbation nor coitus (nor the homosexual) in their histories would be left with essentially no outlet except nocturnal emissions. That would nearly amount to abstinence, for such emissions do not ordinarily account for more than 10 or 12 per cent of the orgasms of any group of males, and there is no evidence that the frequencies of such emissions can be materially increased by avoiding other sexual activities (Chapter 15). The moral desirability of eliminating masturbation is, of course, an issue whose merits scientists are not qualified to judge. Whether such a program is psychologically or socially desirable or physically possible for any large number of males is a question that can be submitted to scientific examination (Chapter 6).

Throughout history, both the Jewish and Christian churches have condemned masturbation as either immoral or unnatural (Chapter 13). In more recent years, with an increase in public respect for science, the moral arguments have been supported with statements concerning the physical and mental harm supposed to come from the continuance of such a habit. The older males who have contributed to the present study were adolescent in a day in which there was widespread teaching against the sin of self-abuse (e.g., Vecki 1901, 1920, G. S. Hall 1904, W. S. Hall 1907, 1909, 1920, Boy Scout Manual, all editions 1911–1945, Jefferis and Nichols 1912, Wulffen 1913, Lieber 1920, U. S. Public Health Service 1921, 1934, Coppens and Spalding 1921, Forel 1922, Meyer 1927, 1929a, 1929b, Weatherhead 1932, Bloch 1933, Crisp 1939, T. V. Moore 1945). Every conceivable ill from pimples to insanity, including stooped shoulders, loss of weight, fatigue, insomnia, general weakness, neurasthenia, loss of manly vigor, weak eyes, digestive upsets, stomach ulcers, impotence, feeble-mindedness, genital cancer, and the rest, was ascribed to masturbation. Feeble-minded and insane individuals in the neighborhood were held up as horrid examples of the result of masturbation, and the authorities in mental institutions maintained separate wards for those whose insanity was supposed to have originated from such practices. Patients in such institutions were observed to engage in frequent masturbation, and this seemed sufficient proof that the insanity was a product of the sexual behavior. Since the lives of university scholars were not so easily observed, it was not so generally known that masturbation occurred quite as frequently among them. Thousands of patients in mental institutions were put into strait jackets or other restraints, on the assumption that they had no chance of recovery unless the masturbation was controlled and cured. There are mental institutions which are operated on the same theory today. In many penal institutions inmates may still be punished severely if found masturbating, and in some homes for children and in some other institutions the older attitudes are still enforced. The United States Naval Academy at Annapolis rules that a candidate "shall be rejected by the examining surgeon for . . . evidence of . . . masturbation" (U. S. Navy Dpt. 1940).

Millions of boys have lived in continual mental conflict over this problem. For that matter, many a boy still does. Many boys pass through a periodic succession of attempts to stop the habit, inevitable failures in those attempts, consequent periods of remorse, the making of new resolutions—and a new start on the whole cycle. It is difficult to imagine anything better calculated to do permanent damage to the personality of an individual.

For several decades now, educators, clinical psychologists and psychiatrists, and some of the general medical practitioners have come to agree that the physical effects of masturbation are not fundamentally different from the physical effects of any other sexual activity, and that any mental harm resulting from masturbation is an outcome of the conflicts introduced by the condemnation of the boy's activity (*e.g.*, Tenenbaum in Robinson 1936, Willoughby 1937, Haire 1937, Butterfield 1939, Himes 1940, Kirkendall 1940, Allen 1940, Weiss and English 1943, Sadler and Sadler 1944, English and Pearson 1945, Frank 1946, Seward 1946).

In the present study we have examined the histories of 5300 males, of which about 5100 record experience in masturbation. It would be difficult to show that the masturbatory activities have done measurable damage to any of these individuals, with the very rare exception of the psychotic who is compulsive in his behavior. On the other hand, the record does include thousands of cases of boys living in continual conflict, fearful of social disgrace, oftentimes disturbed over the effect of such behavior on their ultimate sexual capacities, occasionally attempting suicide—as a result of the teachings concerning masturbation. For the boys who have not been too disturbed psychically, masturbation has, however, provided a regular sexual outlet which has alleviated nervous tensions; and the record is clear in many cases that these boys have on the whole lived more balanced lives than the boys who have been more restrained in their sexual activities (Chapter 6). The resolution adopted at an American Medical Association convention in 1917 asserting that there is no evidence that abstinence from sex activity is "inconsistent with the highest physical, mental and moral efficiency" would be questioned by most clinical psychologists and psychiatrists today, and is definitely contrary to the findings in the present study (Chapter 6).

The scientific judgments are, however, not fully accepted by the persons who have been most interested in sex education (Bigelow 1916, Eddy 1928a, 1928b, Elliott and Bone 1929, Amer. Soc. Hyg. Assoc. 1930, Dickerson 1930, 1933, Rice 1933, Strain 1934, Ellis 1936, Snow 1937, Henry 1938, Rosanoff 1938, Stone and Stone 1937, Laton and Bailey 1940, Lovell 1940, Gruenberg and Kaukonen 1940, Corner and Landis 1941, Boys Club Amer. 1946, Hyman 1946, Landis and Bolles 1946, Thornton 1946, Popenoe 1946).

In this literature it has become customary to admit that the earlier teachings greatly exaggerated the possible harms of masturbation; but the conclusion is nevertheless reached that no manly youth will want to accept such a habit as part of his lifelong pattern. The boy is advised that a limited amount of masturbation may do him no harm, but that in excess it is something which needs the attention of a physician. Since the point at which excess begins is never defined, the conscientious boy is left uncertain whether his own rate is going to harm him; and psychiatrists will quickly recognize that such subtle and indirect condemnation can do as much damage to the boy's personality as the more extreme teaching of the older day. One needs to be reminded again (as in Chapter 6) that there is tremendous individual variation in the human male's capacity to engage in sexual activity without undue fatigue or other physical harm. Some individuals reach their limits when they experience orgasm once in a week or two. The average adolescent boy is quite capable of three or four ejaculations per week, and there are boys who are capable of seven to fourteen or more per week without incurring any greater disturbance than that which accompanies the infrequent activities of less capable males. Like many other physiologic functions, erotic response depends upon a remarkably foolproof mechanism. When one reaches the limit of physiologic endurance he no longer responds erotically. He is no longer capable of erection and finds little incentive to force the situation. Once or twice in a lifetime a few of the males may try to establish a record of repeated orgasms, and extreme fatigue and even some local pain may result; but, except by a few psychotics, this type of performance is not likely to be repeated.

Many of the persons who are responsible for the compromised attitudes found in the sex literature cited above are physicians. Even psychiatrists are divided on this question. In general, those who were raised in Europe, as were many of the psychiatrists who are now in this country, consider masturbation an infantile substitute for heterosexual coitus, which latter activity they take to be synonymous with a good sexual adjustment. Often these clinicians are amazed to find masturbation persisting into the adult lives of American males, and look upon masturbation in the history of the married male as nothing short of pathologic. This is, of course, merely a rationalization of their own European mores. American psychiatrists, on the contrary, with their American backgrounds, are much more acceptant of the same activity.

Although masturbation may do no physical harm, and although it may do no mental harm unless psychic conflicts are involved, it still remains to be determined what relations there may be between masturbation and socio-sexual adjustments (Henry 1938). It is now clear that masturbation is relied upon by the upper level primarily because it has an insufficient outlet through heterosexual coitus. This is, to a degree, an escape from reality, and the effect upon the ultimate personality of the individual is something that needs consideration. It is to be noted again (Chapter 11) that at age fifty-five the college-bred males derive only 62 per cent of their total outlet from marital intercourse, and that 19 per cent of the outlet at that age is derived from the dream world which accompanies masturbation or nocturnal emissions. Any final assay of the significance of masturbation should take these and still other specific data into account.

Chapter 15

NOCTURNAL EMISSIONS

It is possible that the first sexual responses of an infant or younger pre-adolescent could be evoked by physical stimulation alone; but the human animal is always conditioned by its experiences, and its reactions may come to depend as much upon the previous experience as upon any immediate stimuli. The evidence accumulates that the physical is usually a minor element in evoking sexual responses among older males, and there are few of the responses of an experienced adult which would be possible without a sufficient psychologic accompaniment.

Time and again a male may fail to respond to particular physical contacts, while responding almost instantly to more minor stimulation which comes under other circumstances (Vecki 1920, Haire 1937, Lovell 1940, Weiss and English 1943). His responses in the heterosexual may be immediate, while he experiences a minimum of arousal, or none at all, when subjected to identical techniques in contact with another male. The next male's responses, on the contrary, may be immediate in the homosexual, and completely fail in the heterosexual. Some males are impotent when they attempt extra-marital intercourse, although they may be perfectly potent with their own wives. Other males may become impotent with their wives and capable of performing only with extra-marital partners. There are a few males who are impotent when they attempt to masturbate, although they are potent enough under other circumstances. There are males who are potent and respond to the point of orgasm in petting, although they block and become incapable of performing when they attempt actual coitus. Such differential impotency emphasizes the importance of the psychic element in sexual activities.

Except for inexperienced children, most males come to erection if there is any considerable arousal, even before they have made physical contacts. The exceptions include those males who have had such an abundance of sexual activity (as among certain lower level groups) that they are psychologically satisfied or even fatigued; and among upper level groups, where psychic stimulation means most to the individual, there are some males who do not erect in anticipation of a sexual situation because they are inhibited by moral or social training. This further emphasizes the importance of the psychic factor in a sexual relation.

Three or four adult males, out of the more than 5000 in the present study, have been able to ejaculate by deliberately concentrating on sexual fantasies, without any genital manipulation. In such a case the psychic stimulation is entirely responsible for the result. Spontaneous ejaculation occurs most often among young adolescent boys. A list of situations which bring spontaneous ejaculation in the younger male has already been given (Chapter 5). Some of the climaces reached in heterosexual petting may amount to spontaneous ejaculation without genital stimulation. Orgasm from purely psychic sources may occur more often in the female.

Psychic stimulation during sleep is a more familiar phenomenon. It results in orgasm much more often than does psychic stimulation during waking hours. This is probably due to the fact that one is not so inhibited during sleep. Orgasm as the product of nocturnal dreams is well known in the male, but it is not so generally understood that similar orgasm during sleep is not uncommon in the female, especially in the older and sexually more experienced female (Ellis 1936). In the male, nocturnal emissions or wet dreams are generally accepted as a usual part of the sexual picture.

There are many nocturnal sex dreams which do not result in orgasm for the male. There are some males who may have sex dreams with considerable frequency, even every night, without ever experiencing orgasm, unless it be in their early years. On the other hand, there are some who regularly have nocturnal emissions but are unable to recall that such experiences were ever accompanied by dreams. If the absence of the dreams could be absolutely established in these cases, they would be perfect instances of orgasm from physical or physiologic stimulation alone. Most psychologists and psychiatrists, however, hesitate to believe that emissions ever result from internal forces which do not have psychosexual backgrounds. Generally such emissions are considered to be products of dreams that are forgotten by their author, and we incline to this interpretation. Proving that an emission could occur without a psychic accompaniment would, however, be of such great importance that a series of experiments should be devised for testing these unusual individuals.

Throughout the present volume, nocturnal dreams have been recorded as outlets only when they have led to actual ejaculation; but all ejaculation during sleep has been recorded, whether reported with or without dreams.

REFERENCES

Specific data on the incidences and frequencies of nocturnal emissions, in various age groups and in various social divisions of the population, have already been given in tables and charts, and in earlier discussions in this volume, as follows:

PAGE	TABLE	FIGURE	NATURE OF DATA
190–191	38	30	Sources of first ejaculation
234	49	139–140	Range of variation and age
243–245	52	59–64	Age and nocturnal emissions

INCIDENCES AND FREQUENCIES

A high percentage of all males experience nocturnal emissions at some time in their lives. Ultimately, about 83 per cent is involved (Table 133, Figure 138). There is 17 per cent of the male population that never seems to have nocturnal emissions. Somewhat similar data have been reported by some other investigators (Achilles 1923, Peck and Wells 1923, 1925, Hughes 1926, Hamilton 1929, Willoughby 1937). The figures differ considerably for different social levels, the highest incidence being among those males who go to college and the lowest among males of the grade school level.

Over 99 per cent of the males who go to college have nocturnal emissions at some time in their lives, but only 85 per cent of the high school males, and only 75 per cent of the males who never go beyond grade school (Table 133, Figure 139). The high incidence figures given in some of the previous studies (e.g., Peterson 1938) apply, obviously, only to the college populations on which the data were based.

Nocturnal emissions never account for any large portion of the total number of orgasms experienced by the male population (Table 52, Figures 60, 63). For instance, the single males of the college level who are in their twenties, derive about one-sixth (12% to 16%) of their total outlet from this source. For the high school level it is about 8 per cent, but at the grade school level less than 6 per cent of the outlet is so derived. Among married males, emissions account for something between 2 per cent and 6 per cent of the total outlet.

	NOCTURNAL EMISSIONS: ACCUMULATIVE INCIDENCE						
AGE	TOTAL POPULATION U. S. CORRECTIONS		EDUC. LEVEL 0-8		EDUC. LEVEL 9-12		EDUC. LEVEL 13+
	Cases	% with Exper.	Cases	% with Exper.	Cases	% with Exper.	Cases	% with Exper.
8	3986	0.1	681	0.0	494	0.2	2811	0.0
9	3986	0.1	681	0.0	494	0.2	2811	0.0
10	3986	0.2	681	0.0	494	0.2	2811	0.5
11	3985	0.8	680	0.3	494	0.4	2811	3.2
12	3985	3.3	680	1.0	494	2.4	2811	11.6
13	3985	9.8	680	3.7	494	8.1	2811	29.1
14	3982	25.3	677	11.8	494	25.7	2811	52.2
15	3976	39.6	671	25.3	494	39.9	2811	68.9
16	1955	54.1	654	39.1	491	55.6	2810	80.7
17	3896	63.1	617	47.5	471	65.6	2808	87.0
18	3758	71.4	590	56.9	436	74.3	2732	91.0
19	3527	73.6	560	60.2	399	76.2	2568	92.6
20	3222	77.0	532	65.8	357	79.0	2333	93.6
21	2848	78.7	508	67.5	313	80.8	2027	94.5
22	2446	80.0	488	70.1	290	81.7	1668	94.7
23	2131	81.8	472	70.8	264	84.5	1395	94.8
24	1839	81.5	452	71.9	237	83.1	1150	95.7
25	1654	81.5	432	73.1	221	83.7	1001	96.2
26	1510	81.6	420	73.8	207	83.1	883	96.5
27	1374	81.9	405	73.6	196	84.2	773	96.2
28	1268	82.9	391	74.2	179	85.5	698	96.6
29	1159	83.2	367	74.9	159	85.5	633	96.8
30	1064	82.8	351	76.1	141	85.1	572	97.2
31	988	82.7	331	75.5	129	85.3	528	97.3
32	929	82.9	319	76.2	119	84.9	491	97.6
33	868	82.5	305	75.7	116	84.5	447	97.5
34	814	82.6	296	75.3	107	85.0	411	98.1
35	757	81.2	282	74.8	94	85.1	381	98.4
36	713	81.0	269	74.3	89	85.4	355	98.6
37	651	80.6	251	74.1	78	84.6	322	98.4
38	620	81.1	242	74.8	72	84.7	306	98.7
39	565	80.3	220	74.1	66	83.3	279	98.6
40	516	78.8	200	73.5	60	81.7	256	99.2
41	480	78.0	188	72.9	55	80.0	237	99.6
42	452	77.2	180	72.2	52	78.8	220	99.5
43	405	77.0	164	71.3	50	80.0	191	99.5

Table 133. Accumulative incidence data on nocturnal emissions

Covering the life span, including both single and married histories. In three educational levels, and in the total population corrected for the U. S. Census of 1940.

As might be expected, there is considerable variation among individuals in the frequencies with which they have nocturnal emissions (Figure 140). There are males who never ejaculate in their sleep, and more males who have only a few wet dreams in their lives. There are also some who experience orgasm practically every time they awaken from sleep, even though that may be two or three times in a single night. Sometimes emissions may accompany daytime naps. Among men who have been suddenly deprived of some drug to which they have been addicted, emissions may occur several times in each twenty-four hours, for two or three weeks or more. For most males during their earlier years, nocturnal emissions are usually monthly or bi-monthly, rarely weekly or more than weekly events.

The frequencies of nocturnal emissions are, as might have been anticipated, highest among males of the college level (Table 83, Figure 99). They occur less frequently among the males who never go beyond high school, and even less often among the males who never go beyond grade school (Chapter 10). In their younger adolescent years, the boys who will go to college have 7 times as frequent dreams as the boys who never go beyond grade school. In the later teens the differences are nearly 3 to 1 in favor of the college males. They are almost 2 to 1 among the males who are still single at 30 years of age. The frequencies of nocturnal dreams of any sort, sexual or otherwise, appear to have some correlation with the imaginative capacities of an individual. The sexual life of a male of a lower educational level is primarily dependent upon actual physical contacts. He is aroused during his waking hours by relatively few psychic stimuli, and he rarely utilizes such secondhand sources of stimulation as art, literature, nude pictures, stories, or specifically pornographic materials to accompany or substitute for overt sex acts. At night he probably does less dreaming, of any sort, than the better educated male, and his sex dreams are certainly not frequent.

At all social levels, nocturnal emissions occur most abundantly before marriage. Ultimately about 85 per cent of the unmarried males are involved. After marriage a number of the males have their nocturnal emissions reduced or altogether stopped, and the accumulative incidence figure for the married population is something under 60 per cent. At most ages in marriage the frequencies are only two-thirds as high as they are among unmarried males. Since the total outlets of married males are much higher than those of the single males, nocturnal emissions provide only a small part, 2 to 6 per cent, of the outlet after marriage (Chapter 8). Among those males who have been previously married but who have been divorced or otherwise separated from their wives, nocturnal emissions may begin again, even though they were absent during the married years; but the average frequencies in the post-marital group remain at the same low levels as among married males.

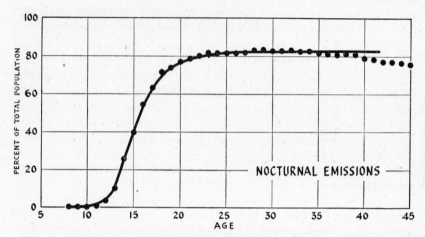

Figure 138. Nocturnal emissions: accumulative incidence in total U. S. population

Showing percent of total population that has ever experienced nocturnal emissions by each of the indicated ages. All data based on total population, irrespective of marital status, and corrected for the U. S. Census distribution.

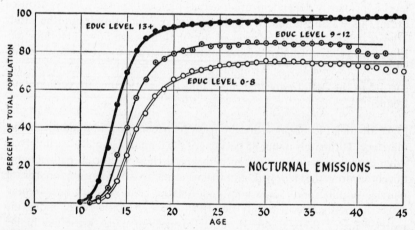

Figure 139. Nocturnal emissions: accumulative incidence in three educational levels

Showing percent of each population that has ever had nocturnal emissions by each of the indicated ages. All data based on total population, irrespective of marital status.

In all social groups, nocturnal emissions are primarily an outlet of younger adolescent and older teen-age boys. It is interesting to find that they ordinarily do not begin with the first signs of adolescence (Chapters 5, 9). Most boys obtain their first orgasms through self stimulation or from physical contacts with other individuals, either in late pre-adolescence or immediately with the onset of adolescence. It is probable that all boys are capable of such orgasm as soon as they turn adolescent, and most of them would be capable at least a year or two before the onset of adolescence. However, the first orgasms resulting from dreams ordinarily do not come until a year or more after the onset of adolescence (Chapter 10). Even in those cases where nocturnal emissions provide the very first experiences in orgasm, they almost invariably begin a year or more after the other adolescent developments (pubic hair, voice change, growth in height, etc.) are under way.

These data provide some measure of the relative positions of the physical and the psychic in the sex life of the human animal. It is for a similar reason that fantasies often do not begin to accompany masturbation until a year or more after such self stimulation has begun. Although the psychic may play a considerable part in even the earliest sexual experiences of pre-adolescent males, and becomes important soon after the onset of adolescence, it ordinarily does not become very significant until there has been a certain amount of physical experience.

The highest incidence and frequency figures of nocturnal emissions (for the population taken as a whole) come in the late teens, during which period fully 70 per cent of the males experience orgasm in sleep (Table 52). The frequencies then average about once in four weeks. If the experienced males alone are used in the calculations, the highest frequencies of nocturnal emissions occur between adolescence and fifteen, at rates of about once in three weeks. From that point, both the incidence and frequency figures go down, and the dreams become few after age thirty and are largely out of the picture after age forty. Beyond fifty years of age nocturnal emissions rarely occur more often than four or five times a year, if they occur at all. There are, however, a few cases of nocturnal emissions occurring among still older males, even between the ages of seventy-six and eighty.

Among boys of the high school and college levels, the emissions between adolescence and age fifteen occur most frequently among those who became adolescent before eleven or twelve. On the other hand, they provide a higher percentage of the total outlet for those boys who reach adolescence last, and some of these males depend largely or exclusively on nocturnal emissions for their total sexual outlet. The early-adolescent boys more frequently depend on masturbation, heterosexual coitus, and the homosexual.

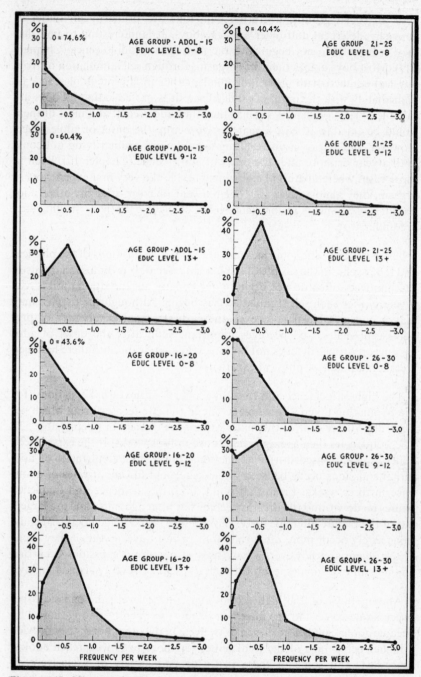

Figure 140. Nocturnal emissions: individual variation in frequencies, in four
age groups, at three educational levels

Showing percent of each population (vertical line) which has nocturnal emissions with
each type of frequency (horizontal line).

In younger generations of the social level that goes to college, the number of males having nocturnal emissions is almost identical with the number involved (in the corresponding social level) twenty-two years ago (Chapter 11). On the other hand, in the grade school groups, the younger generations appear to have emissions at an earlier age, and more of them are ultimately involved than was true in older generations. At all levels, however, the frequencies today are almost precisely what they were twenty-two years ago. These data are important to note, even if their explanation is not immediately apparent.

Nocturnal emissions occur with about the same incidences and frequencies among rural and urban males (Chapter 12).

The incidences and frequencies of nocturnal emissions are almost exactly the same among the active and inactive members of each religious group (Chapter 13).

Among the several sources of sexual outlet, there is none that is less significant than nocturnal emissions, unless it be intercourse with animals of other species. Intercourse with prostitutes and the homosexual both contribute more to the total sexual picture. There are some males who draw the whole of their sexual outlet from nocturnal emissions, and this is true of 8 per cent of the younger, adolescent boys, but it is not true of more than 5 per cent of the males at any later age. It is, in consequence, interesting to find so much attention given to the significance of nocturnal emissions in certain literature. This undoubtedly reflects a wish that involuntary emissions were a more important part of the pre-marital outlet.

On the whole, the males who are most dependent upon nocturnal emissions are those who are slow in developing physically, those who are slow in their nervous reactions or unresponsive to the usual sexual stimuli, or those who are timid and awkward in making social contacts. They are the males who are most often restrained for moral reasons. There are some outstanding exceptions to this, proving that a multiplicity of factors may be involved in determining the frequencies of nocturnal emissions; but, by and large, emissions are most often depended upon by the male who has not made what the psychiatrist would call a good socio-sexual adjustment.

CONTENT OF NOCTURNAL SEX DREAMS

Considering the importance which Freud (1938, 1945) and others have attached to the interpretation of dreams, and considering the considerable literature which has in consequence developed on this subject (e.g., Moll 1899, Ellis 1936, Weiss and English 1943, Meyer in Lorand 1944), we will attempt to add nothing at this time except certain factual data that have been accumulated in the course of the present investigation.

The parallel between the content of the nocturnal dream and one's overt daytime experience has been recognized by all peoples, primitive and civilized, since the dawn of history. The present study confirms the usual interpretations, although it has nothing to contribute on the question of symbolism in dreams. The dream is usually a reflection of the individual's overt experience or of his desire for experience. It often involves other persons, usually persons who are obscure and unidentifiable. Sometimes the actors are engaged in non-sexual daytime activities, more often they are about to make sexual contacts, or to engage in actual coitus or other relations. Sometimes the dreamer is a participant in the activities, and sometimes the dreamer does not participate but merely observes. The dream situations are most often heterosexual when the overt experience or daytime reactions of the individual are heterosexual, and the dreams are most often homosexual when the overt experience of the individual is homosexual. Persons who have both things in their histories have dreams that are sometimes homosexual, sometimes heterosexual, and sometimes both homosexual and heterosexual in the same event. In such cases, the predominance of heterosexual or homosexual dreams may reflect the individual's preference for one or the other sort of experience, but this is not always so.

A number of males dream of females who have male genitalia, and this is particularly interesting in the light of the fact that most of these males have not heard of the classic Greek concept of the hermaphrodite (Licht 1925–1928), nor are they acquainted with the psychoanalytic treatments of such combinations of male and female characters. Sometimes dreams of hermaphrodites occur among males who have had neither heterosexual nor homosexual experience, and we are inclined to interpret them as primarily heterosexual (as also in Näcke 1908, Ellis 1936). The maleness of the genitalia in the dream may depend upon the fact that an individual who has not actually seen female genitalia may have some difficulty in imagining an anatomy or a genital performance which is different from that which he has experienced in his own person.

There are a few males who dream of masturbation, but this is not common. Boys who have had animal contacts, or thought about having them, quite regularly dream of such experiences. There are occasional sadistic or masochistic dreams which may reflect some phase of the thinking of the individual, or of his actual experience.

Finally, it must be emphasized that there are some dreams which simply do not correlate with any overt experience. Such dreams are not frequent, but they do seem to occur, for they are sometimes reported under circumstances which make one feel that the record is thoroughly reliable. For instance, a male who reports an extensive homosexual history would appear to have little reason for distorting the fact when he says that all of his dreams are heterosexual. He may emphasize that he wishes they were not so, because he has no use for the heterosexual, and would enjoy the experience of having homosexual dreams. Explanations of such contradictory dreams should be based on more detail than anyone seems yet to have obtained. It is difficult to believe that suppressed desires are always involved. It is not at all impossible that familiarity with the experiences of other persons would be sufficient to generate a dream, even though it included events which were totally distasteful to the individual and in which he had no desire to participate.

Often the actual experience of orgasm is not realized in a dream. Even when the subject wakes to find himself ejaculating, he may not have reached the fulfillment of his activity in the dream itself. Most individuals wake up when there is an orgasm, but there are some who continue to sleep through it. Even in those cases, however, the dream may not include any realization of the activity which produced the orgasm.

RELATION TO OTHER OUTLETS

By nearly all moral philosophies, nocturnal emissions provide the one form of sexual outlet for which the individual is least responsible. Masturbation, heterosexual petting or coitus, and homosexual and animal contacts may all be penalized as the product of the individual's deliberate intent and conscious performance. There is some contention that one should control the frequencies of his emissions by controlling his thoughts before going to sleep (*e.g.*, W. S. Hall 1920, Lieber 1920, Amer. Soc. Hyg. Assoc. 1930, Kirsch 1930. See Ellis 1936, Vol. 1 (1):188 ff. for a history of the Church's attitudes). It is suggested that dreams may be controlled by regulating the position in which one sleeps, or by choosing one's night clothing (*e.g.*, W. S. Hall 1907, Jefferis and Nichols 1921, Exner 1932, Kirkendall 1940). But the condemnation of nocturnal emissions has not been great. They have been looked upon as involuntary and spontaneous releases of pressure, and as a means of avoiding other sexual activities. Since there are several biologic problems involved in these interpretations, a scientist is justified in asking for objective data on the physiology of the several processes concerned, and on the relation between nocturnal emissions and the frequencies of other sexual outlets.

On the physiologic origin of these emissions, the information is exceedingly scant, and investigations are much needed. Certainly no interpretation is tenable which depends upon the idea that the testes are the sources of the semen, and that they or other glands become so engorged with accumulating secretions that involuntary ejaculation is the result. The semen is chiefly composed of secretions from the seminal vesicles and the prostate gland, and the testes contribute nothing but sperm which, of course, constitute only the most minute part of the semen (*e.g.*, Hotchkiss

1944). There is no evidence that the testes have any part in effecting erotic arousal or ejaculation, except indirectly as they supply hormones which influence the male metabolism. If there are any pressures involved, they must arise in the seminal vesicles or in the prostate gland; but data on this point are lacking. It is more tenable to think of nervous tensions which are built up until, periodically, they precipitate an orgasm; but again the physiology is not understood. We are, in consequence, almost completely in the dark as to the possibility of a biologic mechanism which could force nocturnal emissions when other sexual outlets were insufficient.

Neither are there objective data on the mechanical factors that may effect nocturnal emissions. It has been known for some time that the nerve centers that control ejaculation are in the lower spinal cord, and this has lent some substantiation to the theory that sleeping on one's back, especially if there are pressures on the lower spine, may increase the frequencies of emissions; but there seem to be no sound data to substantiate this. Genital stimulation from tight clothing, more general stimulation from too warm a bed, or still other conditions may have some effect; but such relationships are not yet scientifically established.

It has frequently been said that persons who are celibate, or at least abstinent before marriage, will find an increased outlet through involuntary emissions, and that the emissions will provide a sufficient release to keep an individual physically and mentally balanced (e.g., W. S. Hall 1907, 1909, Eddy 1928a, 1928b, Elliott and Bone 1929, Ruland and Rattler 1934, Frank 1946). It would, in consequence, be of exceeding scientific importance to have histories from a sufficient sample of highly restrained individuals, particularly of those who are celibate. Without such data it is, of course, impossible to depend upon general statements which have been made on this point, especially when they come from persons who are interested in defending moral or social philosophies.

It can, however, be noted again that the frequencies of emissions among the religiously more devout males are neither higher nor lower than the frequencies among the non-church-going males in the population (Chapter 13). The rates of masturbation, pre-marital intercourse, and the homosexual are much reduced in the devout group and, in consequence, the total sexual outlets are reduced; but this merely increases the percentage of the total outlet which is derived from nocturnal emissions. Among these histories of the religiously devout, the absolute frequencies of such emissions are not altered by the abstinence.

Lacking a sufficient series of histories of celibates, the best data now available on persons largely deprived of other outlets come from men who have been confined to penal institutions and who are cut off from their outside sexual activities. Among such men there is a slightly higher frequency of nocturnal emissions, but the increases are not great (Plättner 1930). Even though there are some men who have their first emissions after entering an institution, their subsequent experiences rarely occur more often than a few times a year or, at most, once in a month or two.

While it is commonly believed that males in a prison find an abundant release through the homosexual, and while it is in actuality a fact that a high percentage of them do become involved in such activity after they have been in a penal institution for some length of time, neither the homosexual nor masturbation ever provides any frequent outlet for more than a small proportion of a prison population. Many males do not begin their homosexual activity for some years after entering an institution. Perhaps half of the men in a short-time institution never do arrive at such activity during the period of their stay. Consequently for a fair number of the inmates either nocturnal emissions provide the total outlet, or these men have none at all. Considering that most prison inmates come from social levels where the frequencies of marital intercourse often average six or seven times a week, nocturnal emissions at the rate of three to six per year do not provide much compensation.

There are some records of persons who report an increase in the frequencies of nocturnal emissions when there has been a minimum of other activity; but there are some who never have emissions unless they have engaged in heterosexual petting or unless they have experienced orgasm in heterosexual coitus or in homosexual relations during the preceding evening. In the latter instance, it would appear that the psychic stimulation resulting from the overt contacts had been carried over into sleep. If there are, in some cases, physiologic mechanisms which produce emissions when there is an insufficiency of other outlets, there may be psychologic mechanisms which work in exactly the opposite way. In some individuals the physiologic factors may predominate; in others, the psychologic factors may be more significant. It is quite probable that in still other cases, still other factors are involved.

There are individuals who have high rates of total outlet and who have infrequent nocturnal emissions, or none at all; and there are individuals with low rates of total outlet who similarly have infrequent emissions. On the other hand, there are individuals of both high and low rates who have an abundance of nocturnal emissions. The situation cannot be simply summarized. When precise correlations are run they must not only relate the emissions with the several other sources of outlet, but must also take into account the nature of the socio-sexual contacts which each individual is making, the significance of his personality, and those psychic capacities which might influence his daytime imaginations and his nighttime dreaming.

Most boys have learned from current opinion and from printed literature that nocturnal emissions are usual and normal sources of sexual outlet (as in G. S. Hall 1904, Bigelow 1916, Liederman 1926, Exner 1932,

Weatherhead 1932, Rice 1933, Dickerson 1933, Ellis 1936, Bruckner 1937, U. S. Public Health Service 1937, Crisp 1939, Klemer 1939, Gruenberg and Kaukonen 1940, Lovell 1940, Corner and Landis 1941, Kelly 1941, Sadler and Sadler 1944, Boys Club Amer. 1946). Males of an older generation more often worried over the emissions, and an occasional boy may still become disturbed over the question of the frequency of his experience. Writers who advise one who has "frequent" emissions to consult his physician or his confessor, do not help in allaying the boy's fears. Authorities in some schools, especially in some religious schools and in some penal institutions, may reprimand the individual who "allows" emissions to occur, and there are records of at least two disciplinary schools where the boys were punished for having nocturnal emissions.

There are some individuals who report some feeling of lassitude after experiencing a nocturnal emission, but this is a possible outcome of any type of sexual activity. It is the more usual experience that such emissions do not have even this after-effect. As a matter of fact, nocturnal emissions are accepted by most of the boys of the present generation as a usual part of male experience.

Chapter 16

HETEROSEXUAL PETTING

During the past few decades, particularly at upper social levels, pre-marital physical contacts between males and females have been consider-ably elaborated without any increase in the frequency of actual intercourse (Chapter 11). These contacts may go far beyond the hugging and kissing which occurred in older generations. In their maximum extensions they may involve all of the techniques of the pre-coital play in which sophisti-cated married partners engage.

In general this behavior is known to the younger generation as petting, although other terms are applied to certain types of contacts. Those which are confined to latitudes not lower than the neck are sometimes known as necking, and petting is distinguished from the heavy petting which involves a deliberate stimulation of the female breast, or of the male or female gen-italia. While most of the younger generation of high school and college-bred males and females more or less accepts petting as usual and proper in pre-marital behavior, some of those who have doubts about the morality of their activities ease their consciences by avoiding the term petting for anything except the more extended forms of contact.

In the present volume the term "petting" has been applied to any sort of physical contact which does not involve a union of genitalia but in which there is a deliberate attempt to effect erotic arousal. Accidental touching is not petting, even though it may bring an erotic response. Simple lip kissing may or may not be petting, depending on the intent and earnestness of the procedure. Petting is not always effective in achieving an arousal, but if there has been a deliberate attempt it satisfies the definition. Soul kissing, smooching, necking, mild petting, and heavy petting are basically one thing, even though there may be differences in the limits to which the tech-niques are carried. The extent of the petting is not necessarily related to the degree of arousal. Relatively simple contacts—which in some cases may not involve more than a touch or a kiss—may be as effective for certain indi-viduals, under certain circumstances, as the most extreme genital manipula-tions. If the erotic significance is being considered, a classification of petting should be based on the degree of arousal and the success of the activity in effecting orgasm, rather than upon the nature of the mechanics employed. Obviously, the psychic components are, again (Chapter 15), more im-portant than the physical in this sort of sexual activity.

531

Until quite recently the deliberate elaboration of petting techniques has been confined largely to pre-marital and marital relationships, and all of the data which are given in the present chapter apply to the pre-marital petting activities of single males. Within much more recent years there has been an increasing tendency to accept petting as an extra-marital relationship among persons who would not think of having extra-marital intercourse, and who more or less persuade themselves that they are still faithful to their spouses if they engage in nothing but petting with other partners. At many an upper level social affair, at cocktail parties, at dances, during automobile rides, after dinner parties, and on other occasions, married males may engage in such flirtations and physical contacts with other men's wives, sometimes quite openly and often without being restrained by the presence of the other spouses. Unfortunately, the extent of this extra-marital petting was not comprehended in the earlier years of the present study, and we have not yet accumulated sufficient material for reporting on this aspect of human sexual behavior.

REFERENCES

Specific data on the incidences and frequencies of pre-marital heterosexual petting have already been given in the following tables and charts, and in earlier discussions in this volume, as follows:

PAGE	TABLE	FIGURE	NATURE OF DATA
174	29		Continuity of pre-adolescent sex play with adolescent activity
190–191	38	30	Sources of first ejaculation
234	49	144	Range of variation and age
244–249	53	38–43	Age and petting to climax
277			Petting as an activity of single males
300	68		Age at onset of adolescence and petting
345–347	84,96,110,115	100	Social level and petting
376–381	93–95		Attitudes toward petting in various social levels
399, 406–412	102, 103, 105	117–118, 121	Older and younger generations and petting
453–454, 462	119	125	Rural and urban populations and petting
477–478	128		Religious backgrounds and petting
488–493		126, 128–130	Significance of petting as one source of total outlet
511–512			Masturbation and pre-marital petting
533–535	134	141, 142	Accumulative incidence of total petting experience
533–539	5, 135	10, 143	Accumulative incidence of petting to climax
533–539		144	Individual variation in petting to climax

INCIDENCES AND FREQUENCIES

In pre-adolescence there is, in actuality, very little behavior which can properly be classified as petting; but with the onset of adolescence the boy increasingly realizes the significance of sexual arousal and, with the example set by his older companions, he is likely to begin more specific manipulation of the girls with whom he has social contact. Petting provides the first ejaculation for only one-third of one per cent of the boys at the turn of adolescence, but by the age of 15 a number (8.4%) find a specific sexual outlet in such activity. There is a steady increase in the amount of petting that is done in the later teens.

On the exact incidences and frequencies of petting, few data have been available (Hamilton 1929, Willoughby 1937, Bromley and Britten 1938, Wile 1941, Ramsey 1943, Seward 1946). The histories in the present study show that about 88 per cent of the total male population has engaged in some sort of petting, or (in the case of the younger males) will engage in at least some petting prior to marriage (Table 134, Figure 141). The activity is extensive enough to result in orgasm for the males in over a quarter (28%) of this population prior to the time of marriage. However, since petting is more extensive in the present generation than it was in the older generation, the more significant accumulative incidence calculations on males of the college level show over 85 per cent of the younger groups with some petting experience, and something over 50 per cent of the younger males petting to climax prior to marriage (Table 135, Figure 143).

Something between 18 and 32 per cent of the younger population may be involved in petting which leads to climax in each age period prior to marriage (Table 53, Figure 40). The highest active incidence occurs between the ages of 16 and 20. At that time, about a third of the males are securing a portion of their outlet through petting.

Among those who engage in petting, the frequencies vary considerably (Figure 144). There are males who have petting experiences practically every night in the week and on other occasions in the day. The most active male in the series averaged orgasm about 7 times per week throughout the five-year period between 21 and 25. There are, of course, males who go for weeks and months without dating girls with whom they may engage in petting, and there are some males who may have lapses of a year or two or more between such dates. There are some males who have petting experience with dozens or even hundreds of girls prior to marriage, and there are a few males who have such experience with only two or three girls, and sometimes with no more than the one whom they subsequently marry. These are tremendous differences to be found in any sort of behavior; and since the social significance of petting is much greater than the social significance of masturbation or of some other types of sexual activity, one

| AGE | TOTAL PETTING EXPERIENCE: ACCUMULATIVE INCIDENCE | | | | | | | |
| | TOTAL POPULATION U. S. CORRECTIONS | | EDUC. LEVEL 0–8 | | EDUC. LEVEL 9–12 | | EDUC. LEVEL 13+ | |
	Cases	% with Exper.	Cases	% with Exper.	Cases	% with Exper.	Cases	% with Exper.
8	3989	0.0	682	0.0	493	0.0	2814	0.0
9	3989	0.0	682	0.0	493	0.0	2814	0.0
10	3989	0.2	682	0.1	493	0.2	2814	0.3
11	3988	1.8	681	1.2	493	2.2	2814	1.4
12	3988	7.7	681	6.9	493	8.7	2814	5.8
13	3987	21.4	680	18.7	493	24.1	2814	17.0
14	3984	43.2	677	35.5	493	50.0	2814	33.7
15	3977	57.0	670	51.2	493	62.9	2814	47.2
16	3952	71.3	651	64.5	488	77.0	2813	64.2
17	3882	79.1	607	71.7	466	84.3	2809	75.3
18	3704	83.7	559	77.5	414	87.4	2731	82.9
19	3413	85.9	500	79.6	351	88.9	2562	87.7
20	3026	87.0	437	80.5	284	89.8	2305	89.9
21	2592	87.9	384	81.8	231	90.5	1977	90.6
22	2074	88.4	309	81.6	186	91.4	1579	91.1
23	1658	89.0	256	80.9	155	92.9	1247	91.2
24	1313	88.6	223	82.5	125	91.2	965	91.7
25	1057	88.7	188	83.5	110	91.8	759	92.4
26	857	88.5	164	82.3	92	92.4	601	92.5
27	659	88.3	149	81.9	80	92.5	430	91.2
28	528	90.3	131	82.4	69	97.1	328	89.3
29	432	89.8	113	81.4	60	96.7	259	89.6
30	351	88.5	100	82.0	50	96.0	201	89.1
31	282	88.0	83	81.9			155	87.1
32	242	86.8	77	80.5			127	85.0
33	212	86.4	68	77.9			110	84.5
34	180	86.1	64	78.1			87	82.8
35	155	84.9	59	79.7			73	80.8
36	140	85.0	58	81.0			63	77.8
37	121	84.7	52	80.8			53	79.2
38	114	86.2	50	84.0			51	80.4

Table 134. Accumulative incidence data on total petting experience

Covering pre-marital activity, whether with or without orgasm. In three educational levels and in the total population corrected for the U. S. Census of 1940.

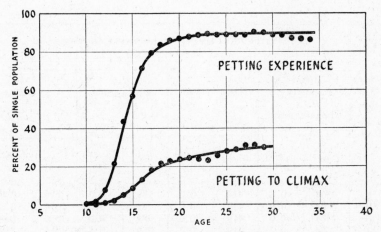

Figure 141. Pre-marital petting experience (of any kind), and petting to climax:
accumulative incidence among single males

Showing percent of the single males that has ever had petting experience by each of
the indicated ages. Based on pre-marital histories of population corrected for U. S.
Census distribution.

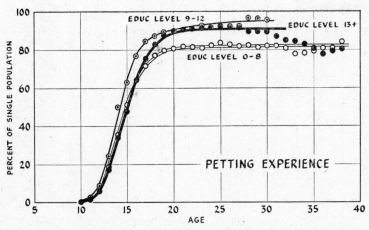

Figure 142. Pre-marital petting experience of any kind: accumulative incidence
in three educational levels

Showing percent of each population that has had any kind of petting experience by
each of the indicated ages. All data based on unmarried males.

| AGE | PETTING TO CLIMAX: ACCUMULATIVE INCIDENCE | | | | | | | |
| | TOTAL POPULATION U. S. CORRECTIONS | | EDUC. LEVEL 0–8 | | EDUC. LEVEL 9–12 | | EDUC. LEVEL 13+ | |
	Cases	% with Exper.	Cases	% with Exper.	Cases	% with Exper.	Cases	% with Exper.
8	2304	0.0	419	0.0	289	0.0	1596	0.0
9	2304	0.0	419	0.0	289	0.0	1596	0.0
10	2304	0.0	419	0.0	289	0.0	1596	0.0
11	2304	0.2	419	0.2	289	0.3	1596	0.0
12	2304	1.0	419	1.4	289	1.0	1596	0.3
13	2303	2.0	418	2.6	289	1.7	1596	1.6
14	2301	5.1	416	5.3	289	5.2	1596	4.1
15	2295	8.4	410	8.8	289	8.3	1596	7.6
16	2271	12.8	392	10.5	283	13.4	1596	15.5
17	2213	17.9	356	12.1	264	19.7	1593	23.0
18	2097	21.3	322	14.6	241	22.4	1534	31.2
19	1969	22.6	285	14.7	210	22.9	1474	38.4
20	1816	23.6	249	14.1	178	23.0	1389	46.0
21	1616	24.0	220	12.3	156	23.7	1240	50.1
22	1347	23.7	174	11.5	126	23.0	1047	52.8
23	1123	23.1	139	11.5	112	21.4	872	54.6
24	903	25.8	121	14.0	94	24.5	688	56.3
25	729	27.9	103	16.5	83	27.7	543	58.2
26	595	28.5	84	13.1	74	31.1	437	60.6
27	465	30.8	75	16.0	69	34.8	321	56.7
28	382	31.1	66	15.2	61	36.1	255	56.5
29	315	29.9	59	15.3	52	32.7	204	59.3
30	254	26.9	55	14.5			161	61.5
31	206	25.6					122	60.7
32	178	23.1					100	57.0
33	154	23.4					89	56.2
34	132	24.9					72	55.6
35	115	20.3					61	55.7
36	105	19.4					54	51.9

Table 135. Accumulative incidence data on petting to climax

Covering pre-marital petting experience which leads to orgasm without coitus. In three educational levels, and in the total population corrected for the U. S. Census of 1940.

who attempts to understand human society must allow for wide variations between males on this point.

Petting is pre-eminently an activity of youth of the high school and college levels. In both of these groups about 92 per cent of all the males are involved before marriage (Table 135, Figure 142), and the figure is still higher for the younger generations. It is only a slightly smaller number (84%) of the males of the grade school level which has experience of the sort, but this level is restricted in the nature of its activity. Such petting as does occur in the grade school group is often incidental, confined to a few minutes of hugging and kissing prior to actual coitus, and quite without the elaborations which are usual among college students. Petting at upper social levels may be indefinitely prolonged, even into hours of intensive

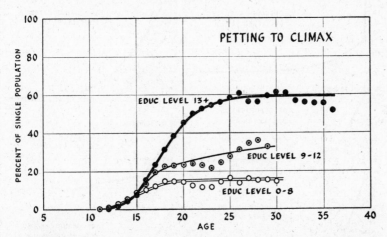

Figure 143. Pre-marital petting to climax: accumulative incidence in three educational levels

Showing percent of each population that has ever engaged in pre-marital petting to the point of climax, at each of the indicated ages. All data based on unmarried males.

erotic play, and usually never arrives at coitus. Orgasm as a product of petting occurs among 16 per cent of the males of the grade school level, 32 per cent of the males of the high school level, and over 61 per cent of the college-bred males who are not married by the age of 30. The social issues involved in petting are, therefore, matters that chiefly concern the high school and college groups.

Thirty years ago, petting involved fewer persons and was a less highly elaborated activity than it often is today. In regard to most other types of sexual activity, the behavior of the older generations (during their youth) was so nearly identical with the behavior of the present-day youth that no significant differences are shown in statistical analyses of the data obtained from the two groups (Chapter 11). The records for petting, however, show

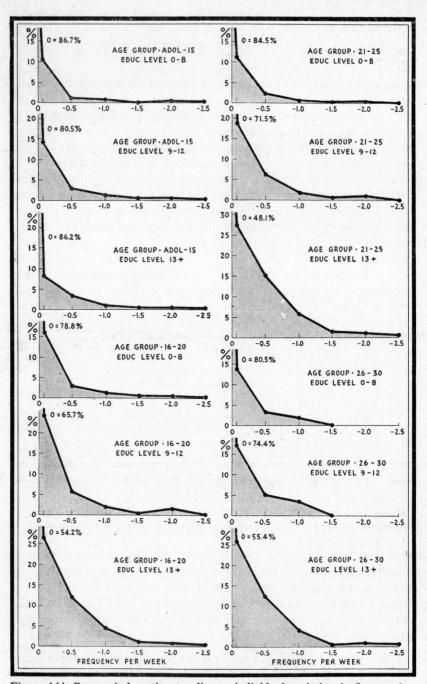

Figure 144. Pre-marital petting to climax: individual variation in frequencies, in four age groups, at three educational levels

Showing percent of each population (vertical line) which engages in pre-marital petting to the point of climax, with each type of frequency (horizontal line). Based on unmarried males.

actual differences between the generations (Table 102, Figures 117, 118, 121). Even at the college level petting has increased within these thirty years. In the older generation of this group, about 87 per cent of the males were involved; nearly 95 per cent has such experience today. Moreover, the younger generation of college males is starting its petting activity at an earlier age. Among those males who never go beyond grade school, only 78 per cent of the older generation had any petting experience, in contrast to 94 per cent in the present day.

The frequencies of petting activities reach their height between the ages of 21 and 25 (Table 53, Figures 38, 41). Calculating averages for the total population, including both those who do and those who do not engage in petting, the mean frequency of orgasm from this source, between 21 and 25, is about once in six weeks. For those males who are actually reaching orgasm, the average frequencies are something more than once in three weeks. It is, of course, only a small part of the petting which actually reaches climax, and the frequencies of petting without climax are many times higher than the frequencies of petting to climax. Males who remain unmarried into still older age periods pet to climax less frequently, partly because they carry more of their heterosexual contacts through to coitus, partly because some of them are sexually apathetic, and partly because some of them have homosexual histories.

Petting never accounts for more than 3 per cent of the total outlet for any segment of the total male population (Table 53, Figures 39, 42). This is in the age period between 21 and 25. Considering only those who do reach orgasm in petting (the active population), about 6 per cent of the total outlet is derived from this source during the late teens. While the incidence and frequency figures in the total population drop in later years, the frequencies for those who go as far as orgasm gradually increase. In this active population, among those males who are still unmarried in their thirties, as much as 10 per cent of the outlet is derived from petting.

Petting provides somewhat fewer orgasms than nocturnal emissions, and only animal intercourse is less important as a source of outlet. The real importance of petting, however, lies in the education it provides in making socio-sexual contacts. On this score, pre-marital petting is one of the most significant factors in the sexual lives of high school and college males and females.

Among all urban groups, of all educational levels, petting to climax occurs 2 to 3 times as often as it does among rural boys of the same levels (Table 119). This is one of the most marked distinctions between rural and urban populations. These differences are more marked than the differences between the social levels within each area.

While there has been a fair amount of moral objection to petting, it has already been shown (Chapter 13) that religiously devout males are involved as often as those who are religiously inactive. The differences in patterns of petting in the several social levels outweigh any religious influences within any single social level.

TECHNIQUES IN PETTING

Petting techniques may include all the conceivable forms of physical contact between two individuals of the opposite sex, except that they do not include the actual union of genitalia. Petting usually starts with general body contacts, and with kissing. While kissing under any circumstances is more or less taboo for some individuals of the lower social levels (Chapter 10), it is the most widely distributed form of contact among males and females of the high school and college levels. In these groups it may occur among casual acquaintances who are having their first date. So common is kissing at this level that it has relatively little sexual significance unless it becomes specifically elaborated. Simple lip kissing may be extended into a deep kiss (a French kiss or soul kiss, in the college parlance) which may involve more or less extensive tongue contacts, contacts of the inner lips, and a considerable stimulation of the interior of the mouth by the other individual's tongue. From the reptiles, down through the birds and the mammals, such tongue and mouth contacts are common concomitants of other sexual activities (Beach 1947). For the other vertebrates, tongue contacts are definitely erotic, and they are naturally so for the human animal that is not too inhibited by its esthetic and cultural backgrounds. Deep kissing may effect orgasm, even though no other physical contacts are involved.

Petting techniques usually expand in a more or less standard sequence, as the partners become better acquainted. Beginning with general body contact, lip kissing, and the deep kiss, it advances to a deliberate manipulation of the female breast, to mouth contacts with the female breast, to manual stimulation of the female genitalia, less often to the manual stimulation of the male genitalia, to the apposition of naked genitalia, to oral stimulation of the male genitalia, and finally to oral stimulation of the female genitalia (Tables 93, 94). Petting techniques at the grade school level rarely go beyond incidental breast and genital contacts; but a goodly portion of the petting at high school and college levels does arrive at more specific genital manipulation. A great many engaged couples go that far before they marry. It is a smaller portion of the population which includes mouth-genital contacts in its pre-marital history (Table 94).

Most of the action in a petting relationship originates with the male. Most of it is designed to stimulate the female. It is doubtful if a sufficient biologic basis could be shown for such a one-sided performance, and it may be that this great difference in the activity of the male and the female is, at least in part, another outcome of the patterns by which females are raised in our culture. The male in the petting relationship derives his stimulation through his own activity in contact with the female, and this is often suffi-cient, as already indicated, to lead to spontaneous ejaculation.

The astonishment of the lower level at the petting behavior of the better educated groups has been recorded in Chapter 10. As there noted, petting is the particular activity which has led many persons to conclude that col-lege students are sexually wild and perverted. On the other hand, the college level disapproves of the heterosexual intercourse which the lower level has, in some abundance, before marriage. The conflict is obviously one between two systems of mores, between two cultural patterns, only one of which seems right to a person who accepts the traditions of the group in which he has been raised. With the better educated groups, intercourse versus petting is a question of morals. For the lower level, it is a problem of un-derstanding how a mentally normal individual can engage in such highly erotic activity as petting and still refrain from actual intercourse.

There is some indication that younger generations have become freer in making these contacts. They also seem to be becoming freer in petting in public places. On doorsteps and on street corners, and on high school and college campuses, general body contacts and more specific hugging and kissing may be observed in the daytime as well as in the evening hours. Similar contacts may be observed in automobiles, on double dates, at cock-tail parties, at parties of other sorts, in taverns and in restaurants, in drug stores and inns, in reception rooms in college dormitories, in high school corridors, in the homes of many of the students, and wherever else young people congregate. More specific contacts may call for more privacy. On occasion, some nudity may be involved, and there are a few records of males who sleep nude with partners with whom they become involved in intensive petting, while never having genital intercourse. Sometimes naked genitalia are placed in apposition, again without effecting coitus.

To some extent, petting is the outcome of the upper level's attempt to avoid pre-marital intercourse. The condemnation of petting on the ground that it may lead to something that is worse is quite unfounded, for there is no evidence that the frequency of pre-marital intercourse has increased during recent generations (Chapter 11), even though petting has increased. In a number of cases, the specific record indicates that there would have been intercourse if petting had not supplied an outlet.

The physical outcome of petting has been a matter of some concern to educators, to parents, and to high school and college students themselves (as in Elliott and Bone 1929, Butterfield 1939, Rice 1946, Frank 1946). There is probably no sex question which is asked more often by the younger generation than this one concerning the physical outcome of their petting behavior. Consequently, it has been important to secure data on this point. The evidence is now clear that such arousal as petting provides may seriously disturb some individuals, leaving them in a more or less extended nervous state unless the activity has proceeded to the point of orgasm. If orgasm results, there seem to be no after-effects other than those which follow any other type of sexual activity. On the other hand, there is a portion of the males, perhaps as many as a third of those in the present sample, who may become involved in extensive petting which stops short of orgasm, and who are able to calm down without the specific release that sexual climax would provide. Many males who do not reach orgasm while in contact with the female resort to masturbation soon after they leave the girl. Pain which is ordinarily said to occur in the testes or in the groin (but which probably involves some other structures instead) is not uncommonly experienced by the male who fails to reach climax during the petting. It occasionally happens that a male who has gone through a prolonged period of arousal, extending perhaps for an hour or more, finds difficulty in achieving orgasm or, if that point is finally reached, may find that there is an insufficient nervous release, or that there is some localized pain following ejaculation.

SOCIAL SIGNIFICANCE OF PETTING

Throughout the animal kingdom, and to some extent in the plant kingdom as well, it is normal for an organism to respond to physical contact by pressing against the stimulating object. Unless high temperatures are involved, or pain is adduced by some other quality of the situation, pressure by an object normally leads the animal or some part of its body to move toward that object. The human babe so responds from the time of birth, and it soon learns that such responses are rewarded by the warmth of a contact with another human body, by additional satisfaction which it may receive from the petting and cuddling which its mother or others may give it, sometimes by food, and sometimes by protection from unpleasant situations. These early contacts bring such arousal as would be called erotic in an adult, and which are undoubtedly so in the younger animal (Chapter 5).

Throughout the first years of its life, most parents provide a considerable amount of stimulation for the child, and aid and abet the development of its emotional responses. To love a babe and to teach it to love in return is an accepted part of the mores. But as the child grows still older, most parents in our English-American culture begin to restrain its physical contacts, whether with themselves or with other persons. The small girl is taught that she should not allow contacts if they come from persons who are not relatives and, in particular, that she should avoid contacts with males. The boy learns that he is not supposed to touch girls, at least "until he gets older." Any show of affection is deliberately controlled, and the growing boy is taught not to expect mothering or much sympathy when he faces difficult situations. As some of the psychiatrists (e.g., English and Pearson 1945) have pointed out, the child is brought into a world that is filled with affection and physical love; but as it grows up it is taught to resist its bio- logically normal responses and to pull away when it is touched by any other person. After fifteen or twenty years of such training, a marriage ceremony is supposed to correct all of the negative responses which have been drilled into the boy or girl, and in their marital relations they are sup- posed to become as natural and unrestrained as when they were babes. This, of course, is just too much to expect, and it is not surprising that a considerable portion of the best drilled persons in the population (males and females of the college level) is awkward and ineffective in developing affectional relations after marriage.

The female is, on the average, slower in developing sexually, and less re- sponsive than the male. She is, in consequence, more easily affected by this training in the niceties of restraint. It is, therefore, not surprising to find sexually unresponsive wives in a startlingly high proportion of the mar- riages, especially in the better educated segments of the population.

Within recent years, younger generations have come to realize something of the significance of pre-marital restraint. Although there is, of course, no doubt that many of the boys and girls who engage in petting do so for the sake of the immediate satisfaction to be obtained, a surprising number of them have consciously considered the relation of such experience to their subsequent marital adjustments. Their understanding of the situation has been helped by the numerous marriage manuals that have been published within the last twenty years, and by courses in psychology, home econom- ics, marriage, and child development, and in other fields of the social sciences. This explains, at least in part, why this younger generation has been more or less oblivious to the not inconsiderable criticisms made by older persons about its petting behavior (Jefferis and Nichols 1912, For- bush 1919, Liederman 1926, Meyer 1927, 1929, 1934, 1935, Eddy 1928a, 1928b, Elliott and Bone 1929, Kirsch 1930, Weatherhead 1932, Edson 1936, Bruckner 1937, Dickerson 1937, Clarke 1938, A Catholic Woman Doctor 1939, Kirkendall 1940, Kelly 1941, Bowman 1942, Moffett 1942, Morgan 1943, Moore 1943, Popenoe 1943, Sadler and Sadler 1944, Fleege 1945, Griffin 1945, 1946, Davis 1946, Rice 1946, Boys Club Amer. 1946, Tanner 1946, A Redemptorist Father 1946, H. Frank 1946, R. Frank 1946, McGill 1946a, 1946b, Gartland 1946).

It is amazing to observe the mixture of scientifically supported logic, and of utter illogic, which shapes the petting behavior of most of these youths. That some of them are in some psychic conflict over their activities is evi- denced by the curious rationalizations which they use to satisfy their con- sciences. They are particularly concerned with the avoidance of genital union. The fact that petting involves erotic contacts which are as effective as genital union, and that it may even involve contacts which have been more taboo than genital union, including some that have been considered perversions, does not disturb the youth so much as actual intercourse would. By petting, they preserve their virginities, even though they may achieve orgasm while doing so. They still value virginity, much as the previous generations valued it. Only the list of most other activities has had new values placed on it.

The younger generation considers that its type of behavior is more natural than the restrained courting of the Victorian generations. It sees logic in the Freudian interpretations of the outcome of such restraint on the total personality of an individual. And it is impressed by the evidence which marriage counselors and psychiatrists have that the long periods of premarital restraint are the source of some of the difficulties which many persons find in making sexual adjustments in marriage.

While our data on the sexual factor in marital adjustment must be presented in a later volume, it may now be stated that there are always many factors which are involved in the success or failure of a marriage. It is usually difficult to understand which factors came first in the chain of events, and the persons immediately concerned in any discord are often the ones least capable of understanding the sources of the difficulties in which they find themselves. Sexual adjustments are not the only problems involved in marriage, and often they are not even the most important factors in marital adjustments. A preliminary examination of the six thousand marital histories in the present study, and of nearly three thousand divorce histories, suggests that there may be nothing more important in a marriage than a determination that it shall persist. With such a determination, individuals force themselves to adjust and to accept situations which would seem sufficient grounds for a break-up, if the continuation of the marriage were not the prime objective.

Nevertheless, sexual maladjustments contribute in perhaps three-quarters of the upper level marriages that end in separation or divorce, and in some smaller percentage of the lower level marriages that break up. Where the sexual adjustments are poor, marriages are maintained with difficulty. It takes a considerable amount of idealism and determination to keep a marriage together when the sexual adjustments are not right. Sexual factors are, in consequence, very important in a marriage.

Specifically, the sexual factors which most often cause difficulty in the upper level marriages are (1) the failure of the male to show skill in sexual approach and technique, and (2) the failure of the female to participate with the abandon which is necessary for the successful consummation of any sexual relation. Both of these difficulties stem from the same source, namely, the restraints which are developed in pre-marital years, and the impossibility of freely releasing those restraints after marriage. On this point Freud, the psychoanalysts, and the psychiatrists in general are largely agreed. On this point, our own data provide abundant evidence. The de-

tails of the several thousand marital histories that substantiate this conclusion must be given later, but the matter needs to be brought up at this
time because of its bearing on the significance of pre-marital petting.

The male's difficulties in his sexual relations after marriage include a lack
of facility, of ease, or of suavity in establishing rapport in a sexual situation. Marriage manuals are mistaken in considering that the masculine
failure lies in an insufficient knowledge of techniques. Details of techniques
come spontaneously enough when the male is at ease in his own mind
about the propriety of his sexual behavior. But as an educated youth he
has acquired ideas concerning esthetic acceptability, about the scientific
interpretations of actions as clean or hygienic, about techniques that should
be effective, mechanically, when he has intercourse. He has decided that
there are sexual activities which are right and sexual activities which are
wrong, or at least indecent—perhaps abnormal and perverted. Even though
these things may not be consciously considered at the moment of intercourse, they are part of the subconscious which controls his performance.
Few males achieve any real freedom in their sexual relations even with their
wives. Few males realize how badly inhibited they are on these matters. In
extreme cases these inhibitions may result in impotence for the male; and
most instances of impotence (prior to old age, and outside of those few
cases where there is physical damage to the genitalia) are to be found
among upper level, educated males. The psychiatrist well understands that
such impotence is the product of inhibitions. The hesitancy of the inhibited
male even to try to secure coitus is reflected in the fact that marital coitus
in the more religiously inclined males (Chapter 13) and among upper level
males in general (Chapter 10) occurs with significantly lower frequencies
than marital coitus in the lower educational levels.

The inhibitions of the upper level female are more extreme than those of
the average male. There are some of these females who object to all intercourse with their newly married husbands, and a larger number of the
wives who remain uninterested in intercourse through the years of their
marriage, who object to each new technique which the male tries, who
charge their husbands with being lewd, lascivious, lacking in consideration,
and guilty of sex perversion in general. There are numerous divorces which
turn on the wife's refusal to accept some item in coital technique which may
in actuality be commonplace in human behavior. The female who has lived
for twenty or more years without learning that any ethically or socially decent male has ever touched a female breast, and the female who has no
comprehension of the fact that sexual contacts may involve a great deal
more than genital union, find it difficult to give up their ideas about the
right and wrong of these matters and accept sexual relations with any
abandon after marriage. The girl who, as a result of pre-marital petting relations, has learned something about the significance of tactile stimulation

and response, has less of a problem in resolving her inhibitions after marriage.

There is, then, considerable evidence that pre-marital petting experience contributes definitely to the effectiveness of the sexual relations after marriage. The correlations will be given in a later volume. Some of those who have not had pre-marital petting experience do make satisfactory marital adjustments, but in many cases they make poorer adjustments. Although this conclusion is contrary to the usual statements in the sex education literature (*e.g.*, Dickerson 1930, 1937, 1944, Popenoe 1938), it is in line with Terman's findings (Terman 1938), and there have been some others (*e.g.*, Rice 1933, 1946, Taylor 1933, Himes 1940, Laton and Bailey 1940, Corner and Landis 1941, English and Pearson 1945, Adams 1946) who have arrived at more or less the same conclusion. Whether pre-marital petting is right or wrong is, of course, a moral issue which a scientist has no capacity to decide. What the relations of pre-marital petting may be to a subsequent marital adjustment, is a matter that the scientist can measure.

Chapter 17

PRE-MARITAL INTERCOURSE

Throughout history, in all cultures, primitive, classic, and modern, the matter of non-marital intercourse has been one of social concern; but in nearly all cultures extra-marital intercourse has been considered more important than pre-marital intercourse. In the ancient Hittite, Assyrian, and Babylonian codes (Harper 1904, Barton 1925), the issue was more often one of property rights, rather than one of ethics or morals. The married male's ownership of his wife and his rights to all of the privileges that she could grant, were the primary concern. In most of the codes, pre-marital intercourse was rarely mentioned, unless it occurred after the time of betrothal. Then the first property rights emerged, there were laws against the infringement of those rights by another male, and considerable attention was given to the nature of those rights when an engagement was broken. In all history there are few instances of such concern over pre-marital intercourse as exists in the Jewish and Anglo-American codes.

There is an almost universal acceptance of pre-marital intercourse among so-called primitive peoples today, throughout the world (*e.g.*, Ratzel 1896, Malinowski 1929, Thurnwald 1931, Wissler 1922, Fortune 1932, Murdock 1934, Blackwood 1935, Linton 1936, Landes 1938, Mead 1939, Reichard 1938, Schapera 1941, Chapple and Coon 1942, Bryk 1944, Ford 1945, Fehlinger 1945). Sometimes the pre-marital activity has certain restrictions put on it, often it is accepted quite without reservation. In only a few instances is there any outright condemnation of the intercourse (Murdock 1934, Mead 1939, Fehlinger 1945, Ford 1945, Morley 1946).

Pre-marital relations have also been more or less openly accepted in most of the other civilizations of the world, in the Orient, in the Ancient World, and among most European groups apart from the Anglo-American stocks.

It would be significant to examine the origins of our current attitudes on coitus before marriage. Explanations of the codes as products of experience, as instruments designed to protect children born out of wedlock, and as devices for protecting the institution of marriage cannot represent the whole of the history. Part of it must stem from the tremendous importance which is attached in Jewish codes to the virginity of the female at the time of marriage.

Even among the Jews, however, the virginity of the male was a matter of less concern, and most of the Continental European codes are closer to the Talmud than they are to Anglo-American attitudes in this respect. Certain it is that in our own culture, today, there is a considerable group of devoutly religious persons who consider the pre-marital loss of virginity as a cardinal sin for the male, as well as for the female.

In the case of the female, the unbroken hymen was depended upon in the Jewish code and subsequently among many European peoples as evidence of virginity at marriage, and marriage ceremonies in many Eastern European and other groups still require the demonstration of such virginity for the sake of the public record. First generation immigrants in some parts of this country today may still send the blood-stained napkin back to relatives in Europe, as evidence of the valid consummation of the marriage. Among present-day youth in our own culture, an individual may still be rated as a virgin, even though there have been other sorts of sexual relations, such as petting and all types of manual and oral contacts, as long as they do not involve intercourse which breaks the hymen (Chapter 16).

Scientifically, popularly, and legally, the term "sexual intercourse" refers to genital union, and it is in that sense that the term is used here. The present chapter summarizes the data on the occurrence of all types of pre-marital intercourse, whether it is had with companions or with prostitutes. A later chapter (Chapter 20) is concerned with the record on that part of the intercourse which is had with prostitutes.

REFERENCES

Data on the occurrence of pre-marital intercourse, and on the factors affecting the incidence and frequencies of pre-marital intercourse, have already been presented in this volume in tables and charts, and in discussions in the text, as follows:

PAGE	TABLE	FIGURE	NATURE OF DATA
116–118	12	14	Accumulative incidence data: intercourse with prostitutes
162–174	24, 25, 27–29	25, 26	Pre-adolescent sex play
190–191	38, 68	30	Sources of first ejaculation
234	49		Range of variation and pre-marital intercourse
248–253, 277–288	54, 63–65, 77–82	71–76, 65–82	Age and pre-marital intercourse
312–315	68, 74, 75	91	Age at onset of adolescence and pre-marital intercourse
347–355	85–87, 96, 111, 113, 115	101–102, 145, 146	Social level and pre-marital intercourse
364	92		Attitudes on pre-marital intercourse at different social levels

INCIDENCES AND FREQUENCIES

In all other anthropoids effective coitus develops out of pre-adolescent attempts at heterosexual relations and begins as soon as the animal is physically capable and psychically oriented toward socio-sexual contacts. While there are families of a sort among anthropoids in the wild, where the male's right to his females may be defended against outsiders, there is, of course, nothing to demark pre-marital from marital chapters in the coital history. Among some of the most poorly educated groups in our own culture the distinctions between pre-marital and marital experience are hardly greater than those among the sub-human anthropoids; and there is no doubt that all males in an uninhibited society would have pre-adolescent and adolescent intercourse before marriage if there were no social restraints to prevent them. The only conceivable exceptions would be found among those few individuals who were either physically incapable or physically so weak that they could not assert themselves against competing males.

It is, in consequence, not surprising to find that most human males do have intercourse prior to marriage. Twenty-two per cent of all the pre-adolescents attempt coitus, chiefly between age ten and adolescence (Table 27, Chapter 5). Having once begun, the childhood activity carries over into adolescence in more than half of all the cases—among three-quarters of all the boys of the lower educational levels (Table 29). Heterosexual coitus provides the first ejaculation for an eighth (12.5%) of all the boys (Table 38), for a higher percentage (18.5%) of the boys who will not go beyond grade school, and for a much lower percentage (1.4%) of those who will ultimately go to college.

The accumulative incidence figures for pre-marital intercourse vary considerably for different social levels (Figure 146). Among the males who go

	TOTAL PRE-MARITAL INTERCOURSE: ACCUMULATIVE INCIDENCE						
AGE	TOTAL POPULATION U. S. CORRECTIONS		EDUC. LEVEL 0–8		EDUC. LEVEL 9–12		EDUC. LEVEL 13+
	Cases	% with Exper.	Cases	% with Exper.	Cases	% with Exper.	Cases	% with Exper.
8	3994	0.0	683	0.0	494	0.0	2817	0.0
9	3994	0.0	683	0.0	494	0.0	2817	0.0
10	3994	0.0	683	0.1	494	0.0	2817	0.0
11	3993	1.0	682	1.3	494	1.0	2817	0.2
12	3993	4.9	682	6.5	494	5.1	2817	1.0
13	3992	13.8	681	14.5	494	16.2	2817	3.1
14	3989	27.8	678	28.0	494	33.4	2817	6.0
15	3982	38.8	671	42.2	494	44.7	2817	9.5
16	3957	51.6	652	56.9	489	58.1	2816	15.5
17	3887	61.3	608	66.8	467	68.3	2812	23.1
18	3709	68.2	560	76.1	415	73.7	2734	30.8
19	3418	71.5	501	80.0	352	75.6	2565	38.0
20	3031	73.1	438	82.9	285	75.1	2308	44.4
21	2597	74.9	385	83.6	232	76.7	1980	49.1
22	2078	76.6	310	83.5	187	78.6	1581	54.1
23	1662	78.7	257	85.2	156	80.8	1249	56.9
24	1317	80.2	224	87.1	126	81.7	967	59.3
25	1061	83.3	189	89.9	111	83.8	761	64.4
26	861	83.1	165	91.5	93	81.7	603	65.2
27	663	84.3	150	92.0	81	84.0	432	65.0
28	530	86.1	131	93.9	70	85.7	329	66.6
29	434	85.5	113	92.9	61	85.2	260	67.3
30	353	86.4	100	94.0	51	84.3	202	67.8
31	283	86.4	83	94.0			155	67.1
32	243	86.6	77	94.8			127	65.4
33	213	85.4	68	94.1			110	64.5
34	181	85.3	64	95.3			87	67.8
35	156	87.5	59	94.9			73	65.8
36	140	89.4	58	98.3			63	63.5
37	121	90.4	52	98.1			53	64.2
38	114	92.2	50	98.0			51	66.7

Table 136. Accumulative incidence data on total pre-marital intercourse

Including pre-marital intercourse with companions and with prostitutes. In three educational levels, and in the total population corrected for the U. S. Census of 1940.

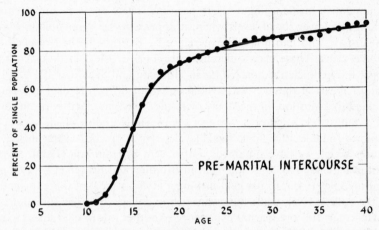

Figure 145. Total pre-marital intercourse: accumulative incidence among single
males

Includes pre-marital intercourse with companions and pre-marital intercourse with
prostitutes. Based on pre-marital histories of population corrected for U. S. Census
distribution.

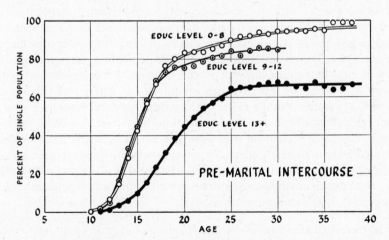

Figure 146. Total pre-marital intercourse: accumulative incidence in three
educational levels

Showing percent of each population that has ever had pre-marital experience by each
of the indicated ages. Data based on unmarried males.

to college, about 67 per cent has coital experience before marriage; among those who go into high school but not beyond, about 84 per cent has such intercourse; and among the boys who never go beyond grade school the accumulative incidence figure is 98 per cent. There are even some groups among the lower social levels where it appears to be impossible to find a single male who had not had experience by the time he had reached his middle teens. These class differences account for the fact that many an upper level clinician is amazed (as in Hohman and Schaffner 1947) at the coital records of the men with whom he is called upon to deal in a penal or mental institution, in the Army or in the Navy, in a factory or on some other industrial assignment. Most of the previous studies which have been confined to males of a single social level arrive at much the same incidence figures which we have obtained: 54 per cent in Hamilton (1929), 55 per cent in Peterson (1938), 52 per cent in Bromley and Britten (1938), 60 per cent in Wile (1941), 45 per cent in Finger (1947)—most of these for males of the college level, while they were still in college and therefore short of having their full pre-marital experience. Another group of studies (Exner 1915, Achilles 1923, Willoughby 1937, Terman 1938, Butterfield 1939) has involved populations of mixed social levels, and other sources of error which make the data uninterpretable.

The frequencies of pre-marital intercourse vary between social levels even more than do the incidences (Tables 86, 111). Coitus, either with companions or with prostitutes, never accounts for more than 21 per cent of the total outlet of the unmarried males of the college level, but it may constitute as much as 68 per cent of the outlet for males of the lower educational levels. For the better educated portion of the population, the significance of pre-marital intercourse lies not in the number of the orgasms which it provides, but in the fact that such orgasms as do come from this source represent a break with the mores of the group. An upper level male who is not married thinks of sex as masturbation, nocturnal emissions, petting, and a continual excitement over girls with whom he would like relations, but with whom he rarely effects actual coitus. The lower level male, on the other hand, may find it difficult to understand that a sex study should be concerned with anything except heterosexual coitus, unless perchance he is interested in homosexual relations.

In the population as a whole, the frequencies of pre-marital intercourse reach their maximum (for those males who have any such experience) in the earlier adolescent years, where coitus averages about 2.0 per week, and where it provides nearly half of the total sexual outlet (Table 57). The frequencies gradually drop with age, but not so fast as the total outlet drops. Consequently the significance of pre-marital intercourse rises, and by the middle forties it accounts for two-thirds (66.6%) of the total outlet of the unmarried males who are having any coitus at all (Table 57).

Since masturbation and intercourse are the two chief sources of pre-marital orgasm for the population as a whole, they are, as previously noted, the only outlets which show the same range of individual variation. There are some males, chiefly at the upper level, whose pre-marital inter-course is confined to a single experience, and then only with the fiancée immediately before marriage. There are some males, chiefly at the lower levels, who have much higher frequencies of intercourse, even up to ten or more times per week. In every age group between adolescence and 25 there are males who reach frequencies which may average as much as 25 times per week continuously for five or more years; but the rates of the extreme individuals are lower in the later years. For the total population the frequencies average 1.4 per week in the late teens and early twenties, and less than that thereafter. Boys of the lower level are more likely to av-erage pre-marital intercourse with frequencies of two to four times a week, which is close to the average frequencies in marriage for many of the popu-lation. The rates for any particular individual may vary considerably, de-pending upon the accessibility of female partners.

The highest incidences and highest average frequencies of pre-marital intercourse occur among those males of the grade school level who became adolescent by ten or eleven (Table 74). By the late teens, 86 per cent of this lower level and early-adolescent group is having intercourse, as against less than 33 per cent of the college-bred males who were late in becoming adolescent. The highest frequencies of pre-marital intercourse are reached by this same grade school group in their late teens, where the averages are over 3.0 per week for the whole group, or 3.6 per week for those individuals who are actively involved in intercourse. In the same age period (16–20), the frequencies for the high school group average about 1.5 per week, and for the college group about 0.3 per week (once in three weeks).

At all social levels, pre-marital intercourse occurs much less frequently among males who are devoutly religious, whether they be Protestant or Catholic (Table 128). Conversely, it occurs most frequently among the males who are least concerned with the Church. The frequencies are low for all Jewish groups but, interestingly enough, the incidences and fre-quencies seem to be higher for Orthodox Jews than for inactive Jews. This may be a result of the considerable condemnation which the Jewish faith puts upon masturbation as an outlet. The differences between devout and inactive Catholics are much greater. There may be three times as much pre-marital intercourse among inactive Catholics as there is among those who follow the Church teachings more strictly. The differences between active and inactive Protestants are not so great.

Pre-marital intercourse occurs much more often among boys who live in cities and towns, less often among farm boys (Table 120). This is true at all

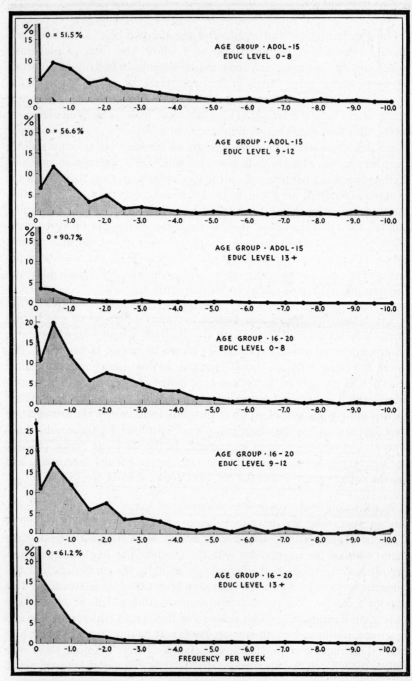

Figure 147. Pre-marital intercourse with companions: individual variation in frequencies, at ages adolescent–15 and 16–20, for three educational levels

Showing percent of each population (vertical line) which engages in pre-marital intercourse with companions with each type of frequency (horizontal line).

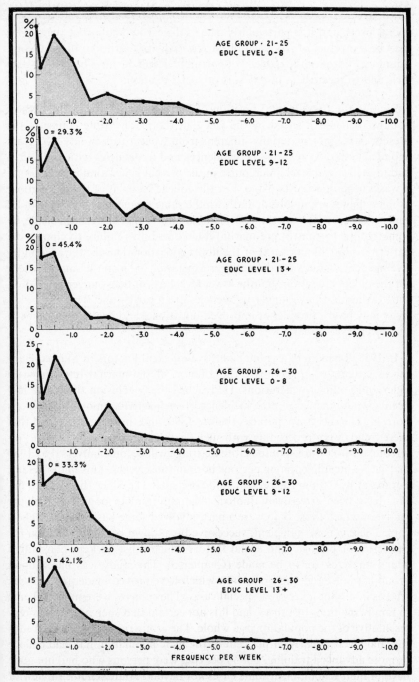

Figure 148. Pre-marital intercourse with companions: individual variation in frequencies, at ages 21–25 and 26–30, for three educational levels

Showing percent of each population (vertical line) that has pre-marital intercourse with each type of frequency (horizontal line).

social levels, and it is particularly true in the earlier adolescent years. This may be a product of the generally stricter religious attitudes in rural communities, and/or of the reduced opportunity which the farm boy has to date girls and to meet them in any sort of social relation.

Finally, the fundamental position of heterosexual coitus in the lives of younger males is attested by the fact that the place of intercourse in the present day is not materially different from what it was twenty-two years ago (Table 99). As regards the incidences and frequencies with which it is had in each social level, intercourse in the present generation is about what it was a generation or two ago. For the college segment of the population, as many males are involved, and with the same frequencies, as in the older generations. In view of the considerable efforts that have been made by some groups to control pre-marital intercourse, this failure to change the pattern is most significant. For the lower educational levels, the accumulative incidence figures for the younger generation are also the same as those for the older generation; but the lower level boys of the younger generation start earlier and have higher frequencies at an earlier age. This earlier activity may be the product of improved nutritional and health conditions in the lower levels today.

In 1938, Terman, in a volume on Psychological Factors in Marital Happiness, attempted to compare the amount of pre-marital intercourse in older and younger generations. He reached the conclusion that there had been a steady increase in the incidence of such activity among the persons born in four successive decades (before 1890, and through 1910), and that these trends were proceeding with such "extraordinary rapidity" that "intercourse with future spouse before marriage will become universal by 1950 or 1955"—meaning among persons born in those years. This finding is not borne out by data in the present study (Chapter 11). Since the Terman figures have been extensively quoted, it is important to point out that the study, of which those data were a part, involved some basic procedural errors. There was no sufficient, successive breakdown of the population for the series of biologic and social factors which must be kept constant if sound analyses are to be made (Chapter 3). The study was based upon group-administered questionnaires, which have proved inadequate for sex studies in all but a very few special cases. The subjects were mostly clients of family relations institutes, and it is not certain that such a sample is representative of the population as a whole. The group represented mixed educational levels. Nearly 71 per cent of the male population had had college or more advanced training, but 30 per cent were persons who had not gone beyond high school, or in some cases not beyond grade school. In view of the considerable differences which our present data show to exist between these several educational levels (Chapter 10), it is obvious that any mixed population is inadequate for analyzing pre-marital intercourse.

It should also be emphasized that the most strategic population in the Terman series, the sample which established the last point (for 1910) on the curve, included only 22 males. Such a sample is, of course, totally insufficient for representing any large portion of the American population (Chapter 3). The data which we now have on pre-marital intercourse would lead us to predict that there will always be a segment of the population which will, as a moral issue, avoid such activity. While the incidence of pre-marital intercourse has remained stable within each social level in the last twenty or thirty years, it should be pointed out that the number of persons who go to college has materially increased in that period. Since this is the group that has the least pre-marital coitus, this means that there is now a distinctly larger portion of the population which is going without pre-marital coitus than there was when Terman made his prediction ten years ago.

NATURE OF PRE-MARITAL INTERCOURSE

A detailed analysis of the varying situations under which pre-marital intercourse is had will have to be made in a later publication. It should, however, be emphasized now that the intercourse varies considerably not only in frequencies but also in regard to the number of partners involved, in regard to the nature of the partners, and in regard to the times and places where the activity is had.

There are males, particularly of the upper social level, who may confine their pre-marital intercourse to a single girl, who is often the fiancée. There are males who have some dozens or scores of partners before they marry. In some cases, lower level males may have intercourse with several hundred or even a thousand or more girls in pre-marital relations. There are quite a few individuals, especially of the grade school and high school levels, who find more interest in the pursuit and conquest, and in a variety of partners, than they do in developing long-time relations with a single girl. Some males avoid all repetitions of experience with the same girl. Sometimes the interest which such a promiscuous male has in heterosexual coitus does not involve any interest in the girls themselves. Many a lower level male states quite frankly that he does not like girls, and that he would have nothing to do with them if it were not for the fact that they are sources of intercourse. There are vernacular phrases which precisely sum up this situation. Until such attitudes are comprehended by clinicians, and especially by public health officials, and until such professional groups understand the lower level's ability to effect frequent contacts with such a variety of partners, the control of venereal disease is not likely to become more effective.

Unfortunately, data on the social levels of the girls with whom males have their pre-marital relations have not been systematically gathered in the present study. There is a popular opinion that most pre-marital intercourse is had with girls who are below the social status of the male. Such information as we have does not seem to confirm this opinion. Certainly, at the college level today, males find a great deal of their pre-marital intercourse within their own level. Although there is some reason for believing that older generations of college males more often resorted to town girls for their sexual contacts, the specific data are not available. Of course, the educationally lower level males have most of their pre-marital intercourse with lower level girls.

The upper level male has only a very small portion of his pre-marital contacts with professional prostitutes. The lower level male depends to a much greater degree upon the commercial source.

Most males have intercourse with girls of about their own age, or with girls who are only a few years younger. Only a few males have intercourse with very young girls, except when they themselves are equally young. There are not many males who have intercourse with women who are much older than themselves, although there are some cases of teen-age and even pre-adolescent boys who have intercourse with married women in their twenties, their thirties, or older. A few males develop long-time relations with older women, either single, married, or divorced women; but nearly all of the intercourse which the young, unmarried male has is with unmarried females.

Heterosexual incest occurs more frequently in the thinking of clinicians and social workers than it does in actual performance. There may be a good many males who have thought of the possibilities of sexual relations with sisters or mothers or with other close female relatives, but even this is by no means universal, and is usually confined to limited periods in the boy's younger years. There are some psychoanalysts who contend that they have never had a patient who has not had incestuous relations; but such a statement is totally out of line with the specific records which have been obtained in this study or which, for that matter, have been obtained in any other survey of the general population. The clinician must beware that the select group of persons who come to a clinic does not color his thinking concerning the population as a whole. In the present study, such incestuous relations as have been recorded represent every social level, including males of the lower levels and males who belong to the socially top levels. Because the cases are so few, it would be misleading to suggest where the highest incidences lie. The most frequent incestuous contacts are between pre-adolescent children, but the number of such cases among adolescent or older males is very small.

The circumstances under which pre-marital intercourse is had differ again for social levels. Some of the intercourse which the college male has before marriage may be had on the college grounds, or in college buildings, but more of it occurs during vacation periods, often in the girl's home town, and often under the girl's parental roof. For all levels, intercourse is had in cars, some of it outdoors in the open, some in tourist camps and hotels, some in the homes of friends or in rented apartments, some in the male's home, but much of it in the home of the girl. Special provisions for pre-marital intercourse are almost as commonly accepted in certain segments of the population as communal bachelors' huts are in some primitive societies (Malinowski 1929, Murdock 1934, Reichard 1938, Mead 1939, Bryk 1944, Fehlinger 1945, Morley 1946).

While the upper social level has a high portion (90%) of its marital intercourse without clothing, not much more than half (55%) of its pre-marital intercourse is had under circumstances where that is possible (Table 95). The lower social level, which has less than half (43%) of its marital intercourse without clothing, has even less (32%) of its pre-marital intercourse in that fashion.

SIGNIFICANCE OF PRE-MARITAL INTERCOURSE

To have or not to have pre-marital intercourse is a more important issue for more males than any other aspect of sex. Heterosexual intercourse is the ultimate goal of all sexual thought and of all deliberately planned sexual activity for perhaps half or more of the unmarried male population; and it is a matter of considerable importance for a high proportion of the remaining males who, nevertheless, may get their actual outlet from other sources. Except for the 15 per cent of the population which goes to college, most males actually accept pre-marital intercourse, and believe it to be a desirable part of a normal human development. Even among those who publicly uphold the taboos against pre-marital relations, including legislators and the law enforcement officers who sporadically impose legal penalties upon non-marital activities, there are many who demonstrate through their own histories that they consider pre-marital and extra-marital intercourse acceptable and desirable. There is a not inconsiderable portion of the population which openly defends the value of such intercourse. This is particularly true at the lower educational levels, but it is sometimes true at top social levels. The general impression which is held by many students of social affairs that the middle class is the one which most rigorously upholds the social traditions is obviously based on the expressed opinions of this group, rather than upon the record of its actual behavior.

In Continental Europe, the acceptance of pre-marital intercourse is more general than it is in our American population, and European clinicians have contributed materially to an increasing opinion among professional groups in this country that there are social values to be obtained by pre-marital experience in intercourse. There are some clinicians who advise their patients to this effect, and there are histories of individuals who would have found it difficult to have made socio-sexual adjustments without such experience.

On the other hand, of course, there is no sort of sexual behavior which has been more often condemned than pre-marital intercourse. It has usually been condemned on strictly moral grounds (as in Jefferis and Nichols 1912, Armitage 1913, Exner 1914, Gallichan 1916, Bigelow 1916, Forbush 1919, W. S. Hall 1920, Coppens and Spalding 1921, U. S. Public Health Service 1921, 1937, Meyer 1927, 1929, 1934, Eddy 1928a, Clark 1928, Elliott and Bone 1929, Kirsch 1930, Gillis 1930, Amer. Soc. Hygiene Association 1930, Ruland and Rattler 1934, Hildebrand 1935, Martindale 1925, Bruckner 1937, Lowry 1938, A Catholic Woman Doctor 1939, Kelly 1941, H. Frank 1941, Moore 1943, Dickerson 1944, Griffin 1945, 1946, Davis 1946, Wood in Chivers 1946, Gartland 1946, McGill 1946, Redemptorist Father 1946).

More scientific issues are raised when pre-marital intercourse is condemned on the ground that it leads to unwanted pregnancies, to the birth of offspring outside of wedlock, to the acquirement and spread of venereal disease, to psychic upset for the individual, to social and legal difficulties, and to maladjustments with one's spouse after marriage (W. S. Hall 1907, 1909, Liederman 1926, Eddy 1928a, 1928b, Amer. Soc. Hygiene Association 1930, Dickerson 1930, 1937, 1944, 1946, Exner 1932, Rice 1933a, 1933b, 1946, Meagher and Jelliffe 1936, Popenoe 1936, 1940, 1943, 1944, Stone and Stone 1937, Snow 1937, Clarke 1938, Butterfield 1939, Crisp 1939, Kirkendall 1940, Bowman 1942, Sadler and Sadler 1944, Adams 1946, Boys Club Amer. 1946, R. Frank 1946). The questions involved here represent physical situations and measurable social relationships which can be subjected to scientific investigation. Unfortunately, the few scientists who have written on these matters have treated them in much the same subjective fashion as have persons without scientific backgrounds. There have been pleas for polygamy and promiscuity and there have been pleas for chastity, written by biologists, by physicians, by psychologists, and by psychiatrists, quite without benefit from the scientific training on which they traded for their reputations.

In a later volume we shall endeavor to make an objective study of pre-marital intercourse in its several social relations, and particularly in regard to its effect on subsequent marital adjustments. It may be pointed out now that simple correlations (as used in Terman 1938, Burgess and Cottrell 1939) cannot suffice to measure the effects of pre-marital experience upon marital histories. Simple two-way correlations are never wholly adequate for showing cause and effect. At the best they show a relation, but not necessarily a causal relationship. They are always inadequate unless the items that are correlated are well-defined units, rather than complexes of units which have varied effects as their ingredients vary.

It does not suffice to show that the persons who have had or who have not had pre-marital experience are the ones who make the best or do not make the best adjustments after marriage. For pre-marital intercourse is always a complexity of things. It is, in part, a question of the sort of individual who has the intercourse and the degree to which the pre-marital activity is acceptable or unacceptable in the individual's whole pattern of behavior. It depends upon the extent of the psychic conflict which may be evoked for an individual who transgresses the ideals and philosophies by which he has been raised, and to which he may still subconsciously adhere. For a person who believes that pre-marital intercourse is morally wrong there may be, as the specific histories show, conflicts which can do damage not only to marital adjustments, but to the entire personality of the individual. For a person who really accepts pre-marital intercourse, and who in actuality is not in conflict with himself when he engages in such behavior, the outcome may be totally different.

Again, the effects of pre-marital intercourse depend upon the nature of the partners with whom it is had, and the degree to which the activity becomes promiscuous. It is a question of the nature of the female partners, whether it is had with girls of the same social level or with girls of lower social levels, whether it is had as a social relationship or as a commercial relation, whether or nor it is had with the fiancée before marriage. The effect of pre-marital intercourse upon the marital adjustment may depend upon the extent to which the female partner accepts the intercourse, and the extent to which the male accepts the idea of his wife's having had intercourse before he married her. Even in those cases where both the spouses believe that they accept the idea, situations of stress after marriage may bring the issue up for recriminations.

The significance of pre-marital intercourse depends upon the situations under which it is had. If it is had under conditions which are physically uncomfortable and not conducive to a mutually satisfactory relationship, if it is had under conditions which leave the individuals disturbed for fear that they have been or will be detected, the outcome is one thing. If it is had under satisfying circumstances and without fear, the outcome may be very different.

The meaning of the pre-marital intercourse will vary with its relation to venereal disease. At the college level, nearly all of the relations are had with a condom. Most of the pre-marital intercourse is had with girls of the same level. Consequently the incidence of venereal disease acquired by these persons is exceedingly low. On the other hand, the incidence of venereal disease resulting from pre-marital intercourse at the lower social levels, where condoms are not often used, is as high as and probably higher than is ordinarily indicated in the social hygiene literature.

The significance of pre-marital intercourse depends upon the success or failure with which the couple avoids an unwanted pregnancy. It is much affected even by the fear of such a pregnancy. At the college level where contraceptives are almost universally used, the incidence of pre-marital pregnancies is phenomenally low. Those pregnancies that do occur almost invariably represent instances where contraceptives were not employed. In segments of the population which rarely use contraceptives, the frequencies of pre-marital pregnancies are quite high.

At the other end of the correlation, it is, of course, equally inadequate to treat marital happiness as a unit character. There are many factors which may affect marital adjustment, and the identification of the part which the sexual factor plays must depend on an exceedingly acute understanding of the effects of all these other factors.

It is sometimes asserted that all persons who have pre-marital intercourse subsequently regret the experience, and that such regrets may constitute a major cloud on their lives. There are a few males whose histories seem to indicate that they have so reacted to their pre-marital experience, but a very high proportion of the thousands of experienced males whom we have questioned on this point indicated that they did not regret having had such experience, and that the pre-marital intercourse had not caused any trouble in their subsequent marital adjustments. It is notable that most of the males who did regret the experience were individuals who had had very little pre-marital intercourse, amounting in most cases to not more than one or two experiences. It will, of course, be particularly significant at some later time to compare the responses of the females who have had pre-marital experience.

For the individual who is particularly concerned with the moral values of sexual behavior, none of these scientific issues are, of course, of any moment. For such individuals, moral issues are a very real part of life. They are as real as the social values of a heterosexual adjustment, and the happiness or unhappiness of a marital adjustment. They should not be overlooked by the scientist who attempts to make an objective measure of the outcome of pre-marital intercourse.

Chapter 18

MARITAL INTERCOURSE

Marital intercourse is the one type of sexual activity which is approved by our Anglo-American mores and legal codes. For those males who are married and living with their wives, marital intercourse accounts for most of the sexual outlet; and to them, a successful sexual adjustment means sufficiently frequent and emotionally effective intercourse with their wives. It is, in consequence, inevitable in any study of human sexual behavior that especial attention be given to the nature of marital relationships.

Sociologists and anthropologists generally consider that the family is the basis of human society, and at least some students believe that the sexual attraction between the anthropoid male and female has been fundamental in the development of the human and infra-human family. Supporting data for these opinions are adduced from a study of the anthropoid family (*e.g.*, Miller 1928, 1931). But whatever the phylogenetic history of the human family, the evidence is clear that the sexual factor contributes materially to its maintenance today. We have already emphasized (Chapter 16) that the success or failure of a marriage usually depends upon a multiplicity of factors, of which the sexual are only a part. Nevertheless, as we have further pointed out, where the sexual adjustments are poor, marriages are maintained with difficulty.

Society is interested in the nature of marital intercourse because it is interested in the maintenance of the family. Society is interested in maintaining the family as a way for men and women to live together in partnerships that may make for more effective functioning than solitary living may allow. Society is interested in maintaining the family as a means of providing homes for children that result from coitus; and in Jewish and many Christian philosophies, this is made a prime end of marriage. Society is also interested in maintaining families as a means of providing a regular sexual outlet for adults, and as a means of controlling promiscuous sexual activity. While these latter interests are not so often formulated in the thinking of our culture, these functions of marriage are more evident in some primitive cultures. Whatever other interests are involved, the sexual factor is one which is of considerable concern to any group that is interested in the maintenance of the family.

While it is not the function of the present chapter to measure the significance of the sexual factors in the success or failure of a marriage, it will summarize the data which have been given in the present volume on the

563

nature of sexual relations in marriage. With this as a starting point, it should be possible, in a subsequent volume, to make more understanding analyses of the data which we are gathering on the sexual factor in marital adjustments.

That the present volume has been so largely concerned with types of sexual activity other than marital intercourse is due to the fact that only a portion of the male population is married at any one time. There are, of course, males who never marry; and every male spends a considerable part of his life outside of marriage. All males must depend, at times, on some other source than marital intercourse for their sexual outlets. Moreover, even those males who are married derive a not inconsiderable portion of their orgasms from sources other than intercourse with their wives. It is one of the functions of the present chapter to show the place of marital intercourse among the many sexual activities which contribute to the total sexual life of the human male.

REFERENCES

The term marital intercourse as used in the present volume applies to intercourse which is had between spouses. Specific data on the incidences and frequencies of marital intercourse, and the factors affecting that intercourse, have been presented previously in this volume as follows:

PAGE	TABLE	FIGURE	NATURE OF DATA
234	49		Range of variation and marital intercourse
252–257	56	44–49	Age and marital intercourse
277–281	63		Total intercourse in relation to marital status and age
306–308	71		Total sexual outlet in married males, as related to age at onset of adolescence
355–358, 432	88, 112	104	Social level and marital intercourse
363–369	93		Petting techniques at three educational levels
368–373	94		Oral techniques at three educational levels
365–367, 372–374	95		Coital techniques and nudity at three educational levels
380, 382	97	107	Patterns of sexual behavior among married males
410, 414	104		Frequencies of marital intercourse in older and younger generations
455, 459	122		Marital intercourse and rural-urban backgrounds
479–482	130		Marital intercourse and religious backgrounds
382, 488–489	97	126–127, 131–133	Significance of marital intercourse as one source of total outlet
564–566		149–150	Accumulative incidence for total intercourse
564–565, 570		151	Individual variation in marital intercourse

INCIDENCE AND SIGNIFICANCE

Marital intercourse is the one sort of sexual activity which involves practically 100 per cent of the eligible males in the population. There are exceedingly few who marry and then fail to have any intercourse with their wives. Exceptions occur only among those who never live with their spouses after marriage, among those very few who are physically incapable of even attempting intercourse, among a few of those who are primarily homosexual and whose wives may be similarly homosexual, and among the still fewer males who are so inhibited by religious, esthetic, or other philosophies that they are incapable of performance or deliberately choose to avoid coitus even with their wives. Under forty years of age, these abstinent males are so few that they never account for more than a fraction of 1 per cent of the married population. At later ages, there are a few more males who do not engage in marital intercourse: as many as 2 per cent in the late forties and as many as 6 per cent in the late fifties (Table 56). No other type of sexual activity is found in the histories of such a high proportion of an eligible population.

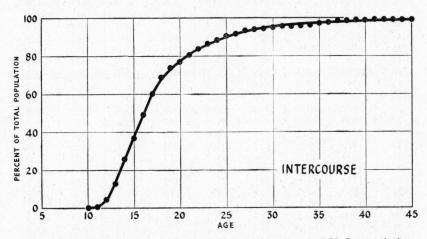

Figure 149. All intercourse: accumulative incidence in total U. S. population

Showing percent of total population that has ever had experience in any kind of intercourse by each of the indicated ages. All data based on total population irrespective of marital status, and corrected for the U. S. Census distribution.

But although marital intercourse thus provides the chief source of outlet for married males, immediately from the time of onset of marriage, it falls considerably short of constituting the total outlet of those individuals. In the married population taken as a whole, it does not ordinarily provide more than about 85 per cent of the total sexual outlet (Table 56). The remaining orgasms of the married male are derived from masturbation, nocturnal emissions, petting and heterosexual coitus with partners other than wives, the homosexual, and, especially in some Western rural areas, from intercourse with other animals (Figures 131–133). There is no pre-marital sexual activity which may not continue into marriage, although the frequencies of all these other activities are almost invariably reduced.

	TOTAL INTERCOURSE: ACCUMULATIVE INCIDENCE						
AGE	TOTAL POPULATION U. S. CORRECTIONS		EDUC. LEVEL 0–8		EDUC. LEVEL 9–12		EDUC. LEVEL 13+	
	Cases	% with Exper.	Cases	% with Exper.	Cases	% with Exper.	Cases	% with Exper.
8	4148	0.0	663	0.0	668	0.0	2817	0.0
9	4148	0.0	663	0.0	668	0.0	2817	0.0
10	4148	0.1	663	0.2	668	0.0	2817	0.0
11	4148	0.8	663	1.4	668	0.7	2817	0.2
12	4148	4.4	663	6.8	668	4.0	2817	1.0
13	4147	12.9	662	15.0	668	14.2	2817	3.1
14	4143	25.6	659	28.2	667	29.2	2817	6.0
15	4115	36.8	653	42.7	645	40.6	2817	9.5
16	4047	49.2	636	57.2	595	53.4	2816	15.5
17	3939	60.1	599	67.6	526	65.6	2814	23.1
18	3769	68.3	575	78.1	456	72.6	2738	30.9
19	3516	73.9	545	82.4	397	78.3	2574	38.3
20	3206	77.1	517	86.1	350	80.3	2339	45.7
21	2832	80.5	493	88.4	306	83.7	2033	50.9
22	2430	83.9	474	91.4	284	86.3	1672	58.3
23	2114	86.5	458	92.6	259	89.2	1397	63.0
24	1823	88.6	438	95.0	233	90.1	1152	68.8
25	1637	90.7	418	95.7	217	91.7	1002	75.0
26	1494	91.8	407	96.6	203	91.6	884	80.1
27	1359	93.6	393	97.5	192	93.8	774	82.6
28	1253	94.2	379	97.6	175	94.3	699	85.1
29	1144	94.7	355	97.5	155	94.8	634	87.1
30	1050	95.2	339	97.9	138	94.2	573	89.5
31	973	95.9	319	98.1	125	95.2	529	90.9
32	915	96.0	307	98.7	116	94.8	492	91.3
33	856	95.9	295	98.6	113	94.7	448	91.1
34	804	96.5	287	99.0	105	95.2	412	92.5
35	747	97.4	273	99.3	92	95.7	382	93.2
36	703	97.9	260	99.6	87	96.6	356	93.8
37	641	98.5	242	99.6	76	98.7	323	93.5
38	611	98.6	234	99.6	70	98.6	307	94.1
39	556	98.6	212	99.5	64	98.4	280	95.4
40	509	98.8	194	99.5	58	98.3	257	96.1
41	474	99.3	183	99.5	53	100.0	238	96.2
42	445	99.2	174	99.4	50	100.0	221	95.9
43	399	99.1	159	99.4			192	95.3
44	369	99.1	146	99.3			177	95.5
45	340	99.0	135	99.3			161	95.0

Table 137. Accumulative incidence data on total heterosexual intercourse

Covering the life span, including pre-marital, marital, extra-marital, and post-marital coitus with companions and with prostitutes. In three educational levels, and in the total population corrected for the U. S. Census of 1940.

The percentage of the total outlet which the married male derives from intercourse with his spouse varies considerably with different social levels. For the lower level group it provides 80 per cent of the outlet during the early years of marriage, but an increasing proportion of the outlet as the marriage continues (Table 97). By 50 years of age the lower level male is deriving 90 per cent of his outlet from marital intercourse. On the other hand, males of the college level derive a larger proportion of their outlet (85%) from intercourse with their wives during the early years of marriage, but a smaller proportion of their outlet in later years. **Not more than 62 per cent of the upper level male's outlet is derived from marital intercourse by the age of 55.** At no time in their lives do college-bred males depend on marital intercourse to the extent that lower level males do throughout most of their marriages.

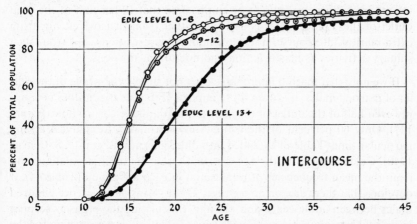

Figure 150. All intercourse: accumulative incidence in three educational levels

Showing percent of total population that has ever had experience in intercourse of any kind, by each of the indicated ages. All data based on total population, irrespective of marital status, and corrected for the U. S. Census distribution.

These data will surprise most persons because there seems to have been very little comprehension that marital intercourse provided anything less than the total outlet for married males at all levels. Several scientific and sociologic investigations have been based on the assumption that a study of marital intercourse was the equivalent of studying the sexual lives of at least the married portion of the population. This accords, of course, with the emphasis placed in Anglo-American ethical systems on marital intercourse as the goal of all sexual development; although there are some cultures in which a history of sexuality would be primarily a history of non-marital sexual activities.

The general opinion that males become increasingly interested in extra-marital relations as they grow older, thus proves to be true only of the upper level male. The explanation of these differences between upper and lower educational levels is not immediately available.

It is possible that the increased frequencies of extra-marital intercourse among older males of the upper level are based on a conclusion that the early restraints on their sexual lives were not justified, and on an interest in securing extra-marital experience before old age has interfered with their capacities to do so. It sometimes happens that the decrease in the frequency of marital intercourse at this upper level is due to an increasing dissatisfaction with the relations which are had with restrained upper level wives. There are some who will ascribe the decrease in marital intercourse to the preoccupation of the educated male with the professional or business affairs of his life; but this explanation does not account for the fact that he finds a third of his total sexual outlet through channels other than marital intercourse. Moreover, it is to be emphasized that 19 per cent of the total outlet of these older males is derived neither from their wives, nor from extra-marital intercourse, nor from homosexual relations, but from such solitary activities as masturbation and nocturnal emissions.

If we note that marital intercourse does not supply the whole of the outlet of married males, it is even more important to note that it does not supply even half of the outlet of the male population taken as a whole (Figure 127). Only 60 per cent of the white American males are married at any particular time (Table 11 extended into older age groups, and U. S. Census 1940). Calculating from the age distribution of the total population, and from the mean frequencies of total outlet in each age group (Table 44), it develops that there are, on an average, 231 orgasms per week per hundred males between adolescence and old age. Calculating the orgasms secured in marital intercourse in each age group (Table 56), and correcting for the incidence of married males in the total population (Table 11), there prove to be, on an average, 106 orgasms per week which are derived from coitus with spouses, per hundred males of the total population (single and married). This means that only 45.9 per cent of the total outlet of the total population is derived from marital intercourse.

Thus it will be seen that marital intercourse, although it is the most important single source of sexual outlet, does not provide even half of the total number of orgasms experienced by the males in our American population. Allowing for the socially and legally accepted 5 or 6 per cent of the outlet which is secured from nocturnal emissions (Figure 126), it is to be concluded that approximately half of the sexual outlet of the total male population is being secured from sources which are socially disapproved and in large part illegal and punishable under the criminal codes. Marital intercourse, important as it is in the lives of most of the population, falls far short of constituting the whole of the sexual history of the American male.

FREQUENCIES

In the population as a whole, and in all of its subdivisions, the highest frequencies of marital intercourse occur in the youngest age groups. Males who are married between 16 and 20 start with frequencies which average 3.9 for the population as a whole (Table 56), and many individuals at that age have intercourse on an average of 5, 7, 10 or more times per week. There is considerable individual variation, and the 15 per cent of the group who are capable of multiple orgasm (Table 48, Figure 36) may regularly secure 14, 21, or more climaces per week from intercourse with their wives. Frequencies drop steadily from the teens to about 2.9 at age 30, to 1.8 at age 50, and to 0.9 at age 60. Among all the calculations in the present study, there is none which falls along straighter lines.

At the high school level the beginning frequencies of marital intercourse may be as high as 4.1 per week; but here, too, the frequencies drop to about 2.9 per week by age 30, and to similarly low rates at 60 years of age (Table 88).

It is significant to find that the married males who have the highest total outlets, most of which depend upon high frequencies of marital intercourse, are, for every social level, those who became adolescent first (Table 71, Figure 90). Married males who became adolescent as early as 10 or 11 average mean total outlets of 5 to 7 per week, if they are married during the age period 16 to 20, as against mean outlets of 3.3 per week for the married males who did not become adolescent until fifteen or later. It has already been pointed out (Chapter 9) that this indicates that the wife's part in determining the frequency of marital intercourse is not as important as one might expect. The age at which the male became adolescent or, more strictly speaking, the general metabolic level which probably determines both the age of onset of adolescence and the intensity of a male's sex drive, appears to be the prime factor in fixing the frequency of marital intercourse.

There are no significant differences between older and younger generations in the frequencies of their marital intercourse, in the same age periods.

Contrary to previous suggestions (Pearl 1925), frequencies of marital intercourse prove to be slightly but consistently lower among rural males than they are among city-bred males (Table 122), if corrections are made for age and social level in making such comparisons. This is in accord with the observation (Chapter 12) that the rural male has fewer chances to make socio-sexual contacts of any sort, and is more inept in making sexual advances even to his wife after marriage. It is also possible that there is more religious restraint on sexual activity among rural groups.

It is significant to find that frequencies of marital intercourse are lower among religiously active Protestants and higher among inactive Protestants

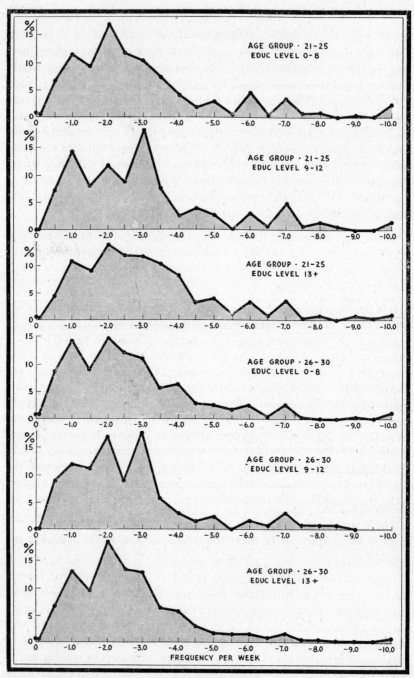

Figure 151. Marital intercourse: individual variation in frequencies, at ages 21–25 and 26–30, for three educational levels

Showing percent of each population (vertical line) which has marital intercourse with each type of frequency (horizontal line).

(Table 130). The differences may amount to as much as 20 or 30 per cent. There are not sufficient data on Catholic or Jewish marriages to warrant any statements for those groups. The data on the Protestant groups are, however, particularly interesting because the restraints which the church has placed upon pre-marital relations, upon extra-marital relations, and upon all other types of sexual activity outside of marital intercourse, are justified by the explanation that the whole of one's emotional and overt sexual life should be developed around one lifelong partner in marriage. It would appear, however, that the effect of inhibitions on pre-marital sexual activity are carried over into inhibitions upon coitus with the married partner. Psychologically, this is quite what might have been expected.

Beyond these several factors which affect the frequencies of marital intercourse, the restraint of the wife constantly lowers the frequencies in all segments of the population, but chiefly among better educated groups. A great many husbands wish their coitus were more frequent, and believe it would be if their wives were more interested. That this may be an expression of fact is peculiarly corroborated (Chapter 4) by the large number of wives who report that they consider their coital frequencies already too high and wish that their husbands did not desire intercourse so often. A very few wives wish for more frequent coitus; only a very few husbands wish their wives were not so desirous.

These differences in interest inevitably cause difficulties in marital adjustment, and there is no sexual factor which causes more difficulty at upper social levels. The situation depends upon basic differences in the sexual characteristics of males and females throughout the class Mammalia, and it should be realized that they do not arise in the perversities of the particular individuals who happen to be united in a particular marriage. If clinicians are to provide the maximum help in individual instances of marital maladjustment, it is fundamental that we learn as much as possible about the diverse origins of the sexual responses of males and females among higher animals in general, and among human males and females in particular. A considerable body of data on these points will be reported in subsequent volumes from the present research.

COITAL TECHNIQUES IN MARRIAGE

Individual variations that occur in the frequencies of marital intercourse are matched and possibly exceeded by variations in the techniques employed in that intercourse. There are differences in the extent and the techniques of the pre-coital play. There are differences in the positions employed in the intercourse. There are differences in the duration of the coital unions. There are differences in the desire for nudity or for clothing during intercourse. There are differences in preferences for light or dark. There are differences in places and circumstances under which the intercourse is had. There are some experimental individuals who may be involved in group activities in connection with their marital intercourse.

There has been an insistence under our English-American codes that the simpler and more direct a sexual relation, the more completely it is confined to genital coitus, and the less the variation which enters into the performance of the act, the more acceptable the relationship is morally. This is the basis of much of our sex law, of a large portion of the sexual mores, and of the lower level's frequent avoidance of any variety in sexual relations—particularly if those relations are had with marital partners (Chapter 10).

On the other hand, the educated portion of the population, especially within more recent generations, includes a good many persons who feel that any sort of activity which contributes to the significance of an emotional relationship between spouses is justified, and that no sort of sexual act is perverse if it so contributes to the marital relationship, even though exactly the same act between two persons who were not spouses might be considered a perversion. Even persons in high church positions have defended this thesis, with restrictions in certain cases that variety is acceptable only when the techniques are not an end in themselves, but a means of increasing the possibility and probability of conception as an outcome of the marriage. In the last two decades, marriage manuals have more or less uniformly emphasized the value of variety in coital techniques, and have probably encouraged an increasing proportion of the population to experiment. It is to be noted, however, that the English-American common law under which our courts still operate, and the specific statutes of our several states, make no distinctions between acts that are "contrary to nature" in marriage, and acts that are "contrary to nature" outside of marriage.

There is, however, a considerable portion of the population, totalling perhaps a half or more of all persons, which is not interested in prolonging a sexual relationship. This is true, for the most part, of the more poorly educated portions of the population, although there are not a few upper level individuals who react similarly. It is a mistake to assume that a sophistication of techniques would be equally significant to all persons. For most of the population, the satisfaction to be secured in orgasm is the goal of the sexual act, and the more quickly that satisfaction is attained, the more effective the performance is judged to be. These attitudes among lower educational levels may depend upon their generally lower imaginative and emotional capacities, but they are probably as dependent upon a sexual philosophy which makes any departure from the direct union of genitalia a perversion.

Extent of Petting. Pre-coital petting is limited in many of the lower level histories to the most perfunctory sort of body contact, or to a single kiss or two. In some cases even that much show of affection may be omitted. When

this occurs at upper levels it is usually assumed to indicate some lack of affection, but it is unwarranted to make such an assumption for the great
body of the population which regularly limits its pre-coital play (Chapter
10). The average college-bred male is more likely to extend the pre-coital
petting for a matter of five to fifteen minutes or more. Some individuals,
especially younger persons in recent generations, may extend the pre-coital
play regularly to a half hour, or to an hour or more—occasionally for several hours—before attempting coitus. In such a case the petting becomes
the chief source of the satisfaction in the relationship, and the orgasm in
which the activity finally culminates becomes significant as the climax,
rather than as the whole of the relationship.

Mouth Stimulation. If it is understood that sexual stimulation and response may involve, and usually do involve, a major portion of the nervous
system (Chapter 5), and not merely that portion of the system which is located in or connected with the genitalia, it will be seen that any area of the
body which is abundantly supplied with end organs of touch may become
a center for erotic arousal and response. Such "erogenous zones" are most
prominent on the lips, in the interior of the mouth and on the tongue, on
the breasts of certain individuals, on certain portions of the genitalia of
both males and females, and sometimes in the anal area.

There is, however, no part of the surface of the human body which may
not be a source of sexual stimulation and response, for there is no appreciable area of the skin which is without end organs of touch. For different
individuals, the erotic responsiveness of different areas may vary, depending in part on the psychologic conditioning of the individual as a result of
his previous experience, but probably as often depending upon differences
in the innervation of the same area in different individuals. The statement
has been made by some psychiatrists that there is probably no portion of
the body which could not be made an erotic area if there were sufficient
psychologic conditioning for that area. While this is doubtful as applied to
all individuals, our record shows that there is no part of the human body
which is not sufficiently sensitive to effect erotic arousal and even orgasm
for at least some individuals in the population.

While the genitalia include the areas that are most often involved in sexual stimulation and response, it is a mistake to think of the genitalia as the
only "sex organs," and a considerable error to consider a stimulation or
response which involves any other area as biologically abnormal, unnatural, contrary to nature, and perverse. Mouth, breast, anal, or other stimulations involve the same nervous system (namely the whole nervous system)
which is involved in a genital response, and the arousal and orgasm which
are effected by stimulation of the other areas involve the same physiology
(as far as we yet understand them) which is involved in arousal and orgasm
effected through the stimulation of genital areas. That this is not generally

understood is due to the considerable taboo in our culture on all non-genital sexual activity. As already noted (Chapters 10, 16), the lower mammals, unrestricted by social convention, know and utilize oral and anal stimulations as well as genital (Beach 1947); and even the most restrained of the human animals give evidence of their positive response by blocking and becoming violently upset at the mere suggestion of such activities. The violence of our social and legal condemnations of these phenomena is testimony to the psychologist and to the biologist that it is a basic biologic urge that is being repressed. The "sophisticate" who utilizes non-genital stimulations is, like the "sophisticate" who accepts nudity in a sexual relation, returning to basic mammalian patterns of behavior (Chapter 6).

In actuality, as American custom goes, genital stimulation is most often utilized, but mouth stimulation is involved to at least some degree among a considerable portion of the males and, to a somewhat lesser degree, among the females in the population. That the full possibilities of deep mouth and tongue stimulation are not more often utilized, is a measure of the extent to which the cultural restraints have modified human sexual behavior.

At upper social levels lip kissing is an almost invariable concomitant (in 99.6%) of heterosexual relations (Table 93). At this level, there is a considerable amount of kissing as a show of affection between spouses throughout the day's activities, and it is inevitable that the kissing should be still further extended in actual sexual relations. Kissing is involved both as an element in the pre-coital play, and as an accompaniment to actual coitus. At lower social levels taboos on all oral contacts are much stronger (Chapters 10, 16), and even simple lip kissing is reduced to a minimum. While it does occur in many (96%) of the lower level histories (Table 93), it is usually limited in amount.

Deep kissing, which may involve contacts of the inner lips, tongue contacts, and the stimulation of the interior of the partner's mouth, is a frequent element (in 87%) of the pre-coital contacts at upper levels; but only a smaller portion (55%) of the lower social level engages in such activities (Table 93). Among less restrained couples deep kissing is a simultaneous accompaniment of actual coitus, especially at the moment of orgasm. In such groups mouth eroticism is developed to a considerable degree, and it may be fully as significant as the actual union of genitalia, or even more significant in effecting arousal to the point of climax.

Breast Stimulation. Manual and oral manipulations of the female breast are elaborated to a considerable degree among many persons of upper social levels (Table 93). There is at least incidental touching of the female breast in nearly all (99%) of the upper level histories, and in a considerable proportion (85%) of the lower level histories. Oral manipulations of the female breast occur in 93 per cent of the upper level histories, but in only

63 per cent of the histories of the married males who belong to the high school level, and in only 36 per cent of the histories of the married males who have never gone beyond grade school.

Breast manipulation of the sort in which the upper level engages is a source of considerable arousal to the male who provides the manipulation. There is reason to believe that more males in our culture are psychically aroused by contemplation of the female breast than by the sight of female genitalia. In the light of this fact, it is interesting to observe the lengths to which censors and law enforcement agencies go to prohibit the exhibition of genitalia, although they frequently allow the display of the nude female breast. How much of the American male's interest in female breasts is cultural, and how much of it is biologically based, would be an interesting matter to investigate, especially in view of the frequent display of breasts among primitive peoples elsewhere in the world.

There are many females who find some specific arousal in breast stimulation, but there may be even more who are not particularly aroused by breast contacts. Only a few females, perhaps not more than a few percent, are ever brought to orgasm by breast stimulation unaccompanied by genital contacts.

It is important to note that females rarely attempt to manipulate male breasts. This may be due to the greater prominence of the female breast and to the wider knowledge of its eroticism. Conversely it may be due to the lesser prominence of the male breast and to the general lack of knowledge of its erotic capacities. It may also be due to the fact that the female is generally less responsive than the male erotically, and for that reason as well as because of social custom less often takes the initiative in any sex play. At any rate, most males whose experiences are confined to the heterosexual have never had their breast eroticism tested, and it has, therefore, been impossible to obtain data on the percentage in the population as a whole who have particularly sensitive breasts. Among males with extensive homosexual histories, however, breast manipulation is fairly frequent and it is commonly known in such groups that many males have highly sensitive breasts. The data from such cases indicate that there may be as many males as there are females who are sensitive to breast stimulation.

Genital Stimulation, Manual. Hand manipulation of the female genitalia by the male occurs at least incidentally in all social levels, but its elaboration is more characteristic of the better educated groups (Table 93). With the anatomic information supplied by current marriage manuals, most upper level males have become aware of the existence of the clitoris in the female, and studied techniques of stimulation of the vulva in general and of the clitoris in particular are becoming more frequent accompaniments of upper level coitus (in 95%). In such groups it is now generally believed (again, in consequence of marriage manual instruction), that the female should be aroused to a considerable height before there is an actual union of genitalia. The biologic and psychologic desirability of this is something that needs further study; but the fact remains that upper level males of younger generations often operate on this theory.

The most common error which the male makes concerning female sexuality is the assumption that stimulation of the interior of the vagina is necessary to bring maximum satisfaction to the female. This is obviously based upon the fact that vaginal insertion of the penis during coitus may result in orgasm for the female. It is a considerable question, however, how significant the stimulation of the interior of the vagina may be. It is certain that most of the physical stimulation which the female receives from actual coitus comes from contact of the external areas of the vulva, of the areas immediately inside the outer edges of the labia, and of the clitoris, with the pubic area of the male during genital union.

There is a great deal of anatomic and clinical evidence that most of the interior of the vagina is without nerves. A considerable amount of surgery may be performed inside the vagina without need for anesthetics. Nerves have been demonstrated inside the vagina only in an area in the anterior wall, proximate to the base of the clitoris. There is need for much further research in this field, especially because there is a widespread but certainly unfounded opinion among psychiatrists, which is repeated among other clinicians involved in marriage counseling, that there is such a thing as a vaginal orgasm which is something different from an orgasm achieved through clitoral stimulation. The whole question will be reviewed in detail in our subsequent volume on the female.

Beyond the occasional consciousness of stimulation of this limited vaginal area which is known to have nerves, the female may be conscious of the intrusion of an object into the vagina, particularly if vaginal muscles are tightened; but the satisfaction so obtained is probably related more to muscle tonus than it is to erotic nerve stimulation. This interpretation is confirmed by the fact that there are exceedingly few females who masturbate by inserting objects into the vagina, and most of them who do so are novices, exhibitionistic prostitutes, or women who have had such procedures recommended to them by male clinicians. Most of the female masturbatory techniques are labial or, more often, clitoral. A high proportion of the female homosexual relations similarly depend upon stimulating the vulva or the clitoris. The male who attempts to simulate coital intromission in his petting techniques is probably not so effective as the male who depends primarily on external stimulation of the genital labia, or of the clitoris.

Genital Stimulation, Oral. In marital relations, oral stimulation of male or female genitalia occurs in about 60 per cent of the histories of persons who have been to college, although it is in only about 20 per cent of the histories of the high school level and in 11 per cent of the histories of the grade school level (Table 94). Because of the long-standing taboos in our culture on mouth-genital activity, it is quite probable that there has been more cover-up on this point than on most others in the present study, and the above figures must, therefore, represent minimum incidences. In nearly all of the upper level histories which involve oral contacts the males make contacts with the female genitalia. In about 47 per cent of the histories, the females make similar contacts with the male genitalia. The frequencies of such contacts range from a single experimental instance to regular and abundant elaborations of oral techniques in connection with nearly every sexual relation.

Since an appreciable portion of the male homosexual contacts, and some part of the female homosexual contacts, may involve mouth-genital techniques, oral activities between males and females have sometimes been considered "homosexual." There is, of course, no scientific justification for such a use of the term, and an analysis of oral contacts in the heterosexual does not show any homosexual element involved. It is the basic, oral eroticism of the mammal which is concerned in all mouth-genital relations, whatever the sex of the partner.

The English-American common law and most of the American written codes condemn all mouth-genital contacts, whether they occur between partners of the same sex, or between partners of the opposite sex, and whether they occur within marriage or outside of marriage. While the laws are more commonly enforced in regard to such relations outside of marriage, there are instances of spouses whose oral activities became known to their children and through them to the neighborhood, and ultimately led to prosecution and penal sentences for both husband and wife. Because of the taboos in this country, not even psychiatrists have comprehended the considerable incidence of such relations among married partners. Such activities have been more freely discussed in certain European cultures, and they have, of course, been recorded from every culture in the history of the world, including the most ancient from which there are documentary or pictorial records, pottery, or other materials (from Greece, Rome, India, China, Japan, Peru, Bali, etc.).

Because of the widespread taboos on the subject, the contemplation of participation in oral-genital activities often results in blocked emotional responses which erupt in bitter condemnations of the partner who initiated the activity, and sometimes produce alimentary peristalsis resulting in nausea or diarrhea. This is, of course, the clearest sort of evidence that the affected individual's initial responses were positive, for it demands a blockage of a definite reaction to produce such a violent disturbance. The male, with his higher level of sexual responsiveness, is the one who is more often interested in making oral contacts, and it is the wife who is more often offended. This may lead to guilt feelings on the part of both of the partners. The refusal of the wife to accept such contacts, or the husband's hesitancy to risk his wife's refusal, may lead some upper level males to seek oral contacts with prostitutes.

There is a not inconsiderable list of histories in which dissension over oral relations has caused serious disagreements in marriage, and a fair number of divorces have revolved around this question, although the contesting partners rarely disclose the real source of their difficulty when they come to court action. There are several instances of wives who have murdered their husbands because they insisted on mouth-genital contacts. Unfortunately, marriage counselors, clinical psychologists, and psychiatrists have not known enough about the basic biology of these contacts, nor enough about the actual frequencies of such behavior in the population, to be able to help their patients as often as they might, and they have not been able to supply courts with adequate scientific data when such cases have come up. The clinician who advises a patient that oral contacts are rare and abnormal and that they constitute sexual perversions is merely epitomizing the mores. He is not supplying scientific data. On the other hand, the clinician who freely advises acceptance of such contacts must not overlook the deep emotional values which are rooted in the long-time customs of our society, and which for many persons are prime factors in determining their individual behavior.

A list of the social problems which most often arise out of human sexual activity would give first places to venereal disease, bastardy, rape, and the contribution by adults to the delinquency of minor children. On the other hand, personal conflicts most often develop over masturbation, oral contacts, and the homosexual. These are the three that need especial help—not because they are rare, but because they are widespread, and because nearly every male in the population is at one time or other involved in one or more of them. These are the three that are most often encountered by the clinician, not because men are frequently abnormal or recently become perverse, but because all three of these are part of the basic biologic pattern of mammalian sexual behavior, and because no legislation or social taboos have been able to eliminate them from the history of the human animal.

Positions in Intercourse. As previously indicated (Chapter 10), nearly all coitus in our English-American culture occurs with the partners lying face to face, with the male above the female. There may be as much as 70 per cent of the population (estimated from Table 95) which has never attempted to use any other position in intercourse. It is the better educated portions of the population which experiment with other positions most frequently. Only about half as many persons of the grade school level ever depart from the one position which they consider most natural. We have pointed out (Chapter 10) that other positions are, from any biologic standpoint, more natural, and that the standardization of a particular position in our society is the product of cultural forces which more often control the behavior of lower levels, less often of upper levels.

The incidences and frequencies with which variant positions are employed are shown in Table 95, where it will be observed that the second most common position is the one in which the female is above, facing the male; and among most persons who have used it, this position is found to be the one which most often results in orgasm for the female. Sitting positions, standing positions, and rear entrance into the vagina as the female lies face down or kneels are much rarer in American patterns. Variety in coital position is regularly suggested by marriage manuals, but once again it is the male who is most often interested in experimenting.

Anal Eroticism. There are some individuals for whom anal stimulation is definitely erotic, and there are a few who may be brought to orgasm by such stimulation.

The mechanisms involved in such responses are the same as those which account for erotic response to oral, breast, or genital stimulation, and there is no need for special theories to explain anal reactions. It would appear, however, that there is considerable variation in these reactions, probably due to differences in the nerve supply in different individuals, as well as to considerable differences in psychologic conditioning on this point. There is some anal play in some of the marital histories, usually as an additional source of stimulation during vaginal coitus; and there is an occasional instance of anal coitus. However, anal activity in the heterosexual is not frequent enough to make it possible to determine the incidence of individuals who are specifically responsive to such stimulation. Among males who have been stimulated anally in the homosexual, there are only a few who are particularly aroused, and only an occasional individual who is brought to orgasm by such techniques.

Speed of Male Orgasm. There may be a considerable amount of intercourse which is had without orgasm for the female, and some males may fail to reach orgasm in pre-marital or extra-marital coitus or in some other types of sexual activity; but failures to achieve climax are almost never found among married males in intercourse with their wives.

Throughout the population it is customary for the male to reach a single orgasm and not to attempt to continue intercourse beyond that point. Exceptions are found chiefly among younger married males who are still in their teens. At that age 15 per cent of the population is capable of experiencing two or more ejaculations during a limited period of time and during continuous erotic activity (Table 48). The number of males who are capable of such multiple orgasm decreases with advancing age. Not more than 7 per cent remain so capable by age 35.

At lower educational levels, it is usual for the male to try to achieve an orgasm as soon as possible after effecting genital union. Upper level males more often attempt to delay orgasm. For perhaps three-quarters of all males, orgasm is reached within two minutes after the initiation of the sexual relation, and for a not inconsiderable number of males the climax may be reached within less than a minute or even within ten or twenty seconds after coital entrance. Occasionally a male may become so stimulated psychically or through physical petting that he ejaculates before he has effected genital union.

This quick performance of the typical male may be most unsatisfactory to a wife who is inhibited or natively low in response, as many wives are; and such disparities in the speed of male and female response are frequent sources of marital conflict, especially among upper social levels where the female is most restrained in her behavior. Nevertheless, the idea that the male who responds quickly in a sexual relation is neurotic or otherwise pathologically involved is, in most cases, not justified scientifically. There are clinicians who insist that ejaculation should be considered premature if a male is incapable of delaying until the female is ready to reach orgasm. Considering the many upper level females who are so adversely conditioned to sexual situations that they may require ten to fifteen minutes of the most careful stimulation to bring them to climax, and considering the fair number of females who never come to climax in their whole lives, it is, of course, demanding that the male be quite abnormal in his ability to prolong sexual activity without ejaculation if he is required to match the female partner.

Interpretations of human behavior would benefit if there were a more general understanding of basic mammalian behavior. On the present issue, for instance, it is to be emphasized that in many species of mammals the male ejaculates almost instantly upon intromission, and that this is true of man's closest relatives among the primates. Students of sexual activity among chimpanzees, for instance, report that ten to twenty seconds is all the time which is ordinarily needed to effect ejaculation in that species. Far from being abnormal, the human male who is quick in his sexual response is quite normal among the mammals, and usual in his own species. It is curious that the term "impotence" should have ever been applied to such rapid response. It would be difficult to find another situation in which an individual who was quick and intense in his responses was labeled anything but superior, and that in most instances is exactly what the rapidly ejaculating male probably is, however inconvenient and unfortunate his qualities may be from the standpoint of the wife in the relationship.

A portion of the upper level males do deliberately learn to delay ejaculation, and it is probable that most males could learn to control urethral convulsions, primarily through a tightening of anal muscles, so they could prolong sexual activity before orgasm. But it is only a portion of the male population that would consider the acquirement of such an ability as a desirable substitute for direct and rapidly effected intercourse.

In the female, variations in the speed with which orgasm is achieved are much greater than in the male. These variations in the female will be considered in a later volume.

Nudity. It may again be noted that 90 per cent of the upper level males have intercourse without clothing (Table 95), and still others would prefer it so, if circumstances allowed. The female is more often inhibited on this point than the male, but at upper social levels she usually comes to accept this as the normal accompaniment of coitus. Not more than 43 per cent of the grade school level ever has intercourse without clothing, for nudity is more commonly taboo at those levels. There is evidence (Table 95) that nudity has been accepted by upper level groups more freely within more recent generations. This is one point in human sexual behavior to which arguments as to what is natural and what is unnatural have never been applied, for there can be no question of the fact that intercourse without clothing is biologically normal, and that the custom of having intercourse with clothing is a distinctly cultural acquirement. But the upper social level returns to what is biologically normal behavior only after a considerable rationalization and a reasoned break with the mores.

Preferences for Light or Dark. Among married partners, there may be considerable differences in preferences for having intercourse in full light, in subdued light, or in the dark. In general, more males prefer to have intercourse in the light, and more females prefer it in the dark. Such differences may be ascribed to different levels of "modesty" in the two sexes, but the basic explanation probably lies much deeper. These preferences for light or dark are closely correlated with differences between males and females in the erotic significances of objects that are visually observed.

Most males, particularly in upper segments of the population, are definitely aroused upon seeing things that are associated with sex, and most females are not so aroused. To have intercourse in the light increases the sources of erotic stimulation for most males, and means very little erotically to most females. In consequence, moral considerations of the sort that are associated with modesty may very well control the female in her behavior, but they do not mean so much to the male. It is probable that these differences between the sexes are, again, dependent upon basic differences in the neural organizations which are involved in sexual responses (Beach 1947). These matters must have more elaborate consideration in a later volume on the female, and always the nature of the patterns that are basic among the other mammals must be taken into account, if we are to understand the relative effects of heredity and culture on human behavior.

* * *

Marital intercourse, the most extensive of all sexual activities of the human male, thus furnishes some insight into his sexual capacities. But more remarkable than the variation which occurs in marital intercourse is the fact that so much of it is stereotyped and restricted to the age-old patterns which are an established part of the mores. The variety that is recorded does no more than allow the scientist to glimpse the extent of the variation that might occur in the human animal's sexual behavior.

Chapter 19

EXTRA-MARITAL INTERCOURSE

In the history of most human cultures, extra-marital intercourse has more often been a matter for regulation than has intercourse before marriage. Frequently this has taken the form of denying the married female intercourse with anyone except her husband; less often it has included a restriction of the male's right to have intercourse outside of his home. While various issues have been involved, such regulations have been particularly concerned with the property rights which the male has had in his wife, and there is no question that the extra-marital activities of the female became objects of concern in such early codes as the Babylonian (Harper 1904), Hittite (Barton 1925), Assyrian (Barton 1925), Jewish (Bible, Talmud), and others, because of these property rights, rather than because moral issues were recognized.

In so-called primitive groups in various parts of the world today much the same distinctions are made between intercourse before and after marriage, and between the male's right and the female's right to have such relations (Malinowski 1929, Hartland 1931, Thurnwald 1931, Wissler 1922, Fortune 1932, Murdock 1934, Blackwood 1935, Linton 1936, Lips 1938, Reichard 1938, Mead 1939, Schapera 1941, Chapple and Coon 1942, Bryk 1944, Ford 1945). Similar distinctions have been made throughout the history of Western European civilization, and the rights of the male in the female who is married to him have been a basic part of English and American law. It is only within the last few decades that material changes have been effected in this country in legal viewpoints on the relationship of the husband and wife.

In line with these ancient distinctions, there are still various segments of our population in this country today which more or less freely accept pre-marital relations, while objecting strenuously to extra-marital intercourse. In fact it may be said that there is no segment of our American population which, as a whole, really accepts extra-marital activities in anything like the way that masturbation is accepted at upper social levels, or in the way that pre-marital intercourse is accepted at lower social levels. In some segments of the population, relatively little attention is paid to the pre-marital intercourse which occurs among young people; but at all social levels, extra-marital intercourse is a subject for gossip—often malicious gossip—often for peremptory and outraged community reaction, and quite often for legal penalties. The offended spouse who takes the law into his or her

583

own hands, and assaults and even murders the competitor in the sexual relation, is, in many parts of the country today, likely to be backed by a certain amount of public sympathy. Juries are loath to convict in such cases. It does not alter the fact that society knows that extra-marital intercourse does occur, and that it occurs with some frequency; and it seems not to matter that it is generally known that such intercourse usually goes unpunished. Society is still outraged when confronted with the specific case on which it is challenged to pass judgment.

These social attitudes are particularly interesting in view of the fact that a considerable proportion of those who react most violently against the known instances of extra-marital relations, may have similar experience in their own histories. Nearly three-quarters (72%) of the males in the Terman study (Terman 1938) admitted that they wished on occasion to have extra-marital intercourse, and a similarly high proportion of the males in our present study have expressed the same desire. Furthermore, many of them actually have such extra-marital relations. The pretense that these persons make in defending the codes clearly indicates a conflict in their own minds concerning the social significance of such relations. If our society is ever to act more intelligently on these matters, it will need more factual data. Even the scant data that we can offer here may prove of some significance.

REFERENCES

Specific material on the occurrence of extra-marital intercourse in various age groups and in various social divisions of the population, has already been given in tables and charts, and in earlier discussions in the present volume, as follows:

PAGE	TABLE	FIGURE	NATURE OF DATA
248, 257–259, 281–285	54, 64	71–76	Age, marital status, and non-marital intercourse with companions
250–253, 281–289	55, 65	77–82	Age, marital status, and intercourse with prostitutes
348, 354	85	103	Total extra-marital intercourse as related to social level
350, 383	86		Extra-marital intercourse with companions, and social level
351–354	87		Intercourse with prostitutes, as related to educational level
456	120		Total non-marital intercourse and rural-urban background
480–481	129		Total extra-marital intercourse and religious background
382, 489, 492–493	97	127, 131–133	Extra-marital intercourse as part of the total sexual outlet

INCIDENCES AND FREQUENCIES

We have found a great many persons who would like to know how many males have extra-marital intercourse. Obviously this considerable interest depends upon the fact that most of the married males who ask the question have already had such experience, or would like to have it if they could reconcile it with their consciences and if it could be managed without involving them in legal difficulties or public scandal.

At the same time, this considerable interest also indicates that many individuals fear that their extra-marital histories may become known. In consequence, it has been peculiarly difficult, in the present study, to secure anything like adequate data on this aspect of human sexual activity. There is probably nothing in the histories of older married males who belong to better educational and social levels that has more often been responsible for their refusal to contribute to the present research. Many of the persons who have contributed only after some months or years of refusal to do so, prove to have nothing in their histories that would explain their original hesitancy except their extra-marital intercourse. Even those who have contributed more readily have probably covered up on this more often than on any other single item. We have reason for believing that most of the persons who have criticized the adequacy of the present study, on the ground that they were able to go through a history "without telling everything," were individuals who failed to record their own extra-marital experience. Considering that the legal penalties for such sexual activity are rarely enforced, and that most males feel that such activity is highly desirable and not exactly wrong, it is particularly interesting to observe this considerable disturbance over the issue. Only the fear of the social (as opposed to the legal) consequences can explain this reticence about extra-marital sexual performance.

It has so far been impossible to secure hundred percent samples from men of the type that belongs to business organizations, business executive groups, and service clubs; and we have every reason for believing that extra-marital intercourse is the source of the hesitance of many of the individuals in such groups to cooperate. Consequently, the incidence and frequency figures which are given here must represent the absolute minimum, and it is not at all improbable that the actuality may lie 10 to 20 per cent above the figures now given.

Hamilton (1929) found 28 per cent of his hundred men with records of extra-marital intercourse. His figure would have been higher if he had dealt with older men. In the present study, something over a third (27% to 37%) of the married males in each of the five-year age periods have admitted some experience in extra-marital intercourse (Table 64, Figure 73). Since these are active incidence data, the accumulative figure must amount to something more than that. Because of the inadequacy of the record it has been impossible to construct accumulative incidence curves by the usual techniques (Chapter 3), and we can only estimate from these active incidence figures.

On the basis of these active data, and allowing for the cover-up that has been involved, it is probably safe to suggest that about half of all the married males have intercourse with women other than their wives, at some time while they are married.

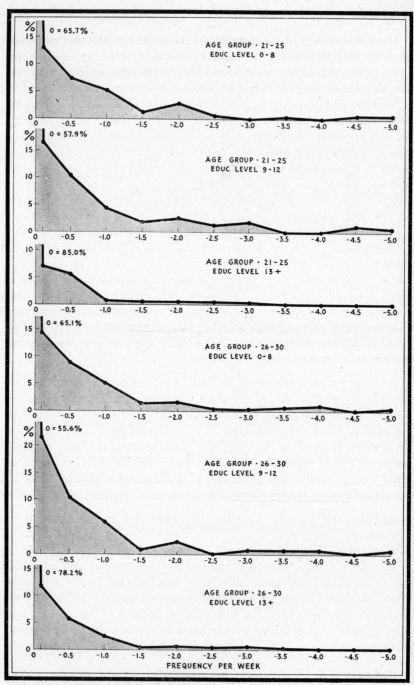

Figure 152. Total extra-marital intercourse: individual variation in frequencies,
at ages 21–25 and 26–30, for three educational levels

Showing percent of each population (vertical line) which has extra-marital intercourse
with each type of frequency (horizontal line).

586

About 40 per cent of the high school and college males have admitted extra-marital relations (Tables 85, 86). For the grade school group, a higher percentage of the younger males have given such records, but only a smaller percentage (19%) of the older males. There are several possible explanations of this discrepancy, but there is so much likelihood of cover-up here that the question cannot be resolved at this time.

The most striking thing about the occurrence of extra-marital intercourse is the fact that the highest incidences for the lower social levels occur at the younger ages, and that the number of persons involved steadily decreases with advancing age (Table 85). Lower level males who were married in the late teens have given a record of extra-marital intercourse in 45 per cent of the cases, whereas not more than 27 per cent is actively involved by age 40 and not more than 19 per cent by age 50. In striking contrast, the lowest incidences of extra-marital intercourse among males of the college level are to be found in the youngest age groups, where not more than 15 to 20 per cent is involved, and the incidence increases steadily until about 27 per cent is having extra-marital relations by age 50.

Similarly, the highest frequencies of extra-marital intercourse are to be found among the younger males of the lower educational levels, but the frequencies drop steadily with advancing age (Tables 85, 97). Between 16 and 20, males of the lower educational level who are actually involved in extra-marital intercourse average such contacts more than once (1.2) per week; but by age 55 the frequencies have dropped to hardly more than once in two weeks (0.6 per week). On the other hand, college males of the active population begin with frequencies of a little more than once in two or three weeks between the ages of 16 and 30, but finally arrive at frequencies that are nearer once a week by the time they are 50.

We have previously suggested (Chapters 10, 18) possible explanations for these diverse patterns in the extra-marital intercourse of different social levels, of which explanations the most likely is the fact that lower level males have an abundance of pre-marital intercourse, and there is some carry-over of that type of promiscuity after marriage. On the other hand, upper level individuals are the ones with the most restrained pre-marital histories, and they lose that restraint only gradually and do not so often embark on extra-marital relations until later years. We cannot explain why there should be a cessation of extra-marital activity among so many older males of the lower level. It cannot be entirely due to their generally poorer physical condition at older ages, for it is the percent of their total outlet from extra-marital relations which has dropped, from an original of 12 per cent to 6 per cent. Meanwhile, among males of the college level, the percent of the total outlet which is derived from extra-marital intercourse has increased from an original 3 per cent in the earlier years to 14 per cent by age 50 (Table 97).

Between 16 and 20, married males of the grade school level have 10.6 times as much extra-marital intercourse as males of the college level. To make another comparison, married males of occupational classes 2 and 3 (the laborers and semi-skilled workmen) have 16.7 times as much extra-marital intercourse during their late teens as males of occupational class 7 (the future professional group).

For most males, at every social level, extra-marital intercourse is usually sporadic, occurring on an occasion or two with this female, a few times with the next partner, not happening again for some months or a year or two, but then occurring several times or every night for a week or even for a month or more, after which that particular affair is abruptly stopped. The averaged data may show mean frequencies of once a week or two, but the whole of the year's total is likely to have been accumulated on a single trip or in a few weeks of the summer vacation. There are extreme instances of younger males whose orgasms, achieved in extra-marital relations, have averaged as many as eighteen per week for periods of as long as five years; but these are unusual cases. Lower level males are the ones who are most likely to have more regularly distributed experience, often with some variety of females. Among males of the college level extra-marital relations are almost always infrequent, often with not more than one or two or a very few partners in all of their lives, and usually with a single partner over a period of some time—in some cases for a number of years.

Extra-marital intercourse occasionally accounts for a fair portion of the outlet of the married males of certain segments of the population. It accounts for 11 per cent of the outlet of married males of the grade school level during their late teens (Table 86). But more often it is a smaller part of the total picture. It ultimately accounts for something between 5 and 10 per cent of the total orgasms of all the married males in the population (Table 64).

Prostitutes supply something between 8 and 15 per cent of all extra-marital intercourse (Chapter 20). Obviously, most of the extra-marital activities are had with companions. For lower level males, these may be semi-professional pick-ups, but are often married women of their own class. For the upper level males, the contacts may be had with females of any social level, but many of them are had with their own social level.

Extra-marital intercourse occurs most frequently among males who live in cities or towns; less frequently in rural populations (Table 120). At the grade school level, the number of urban males involved may be 20 to 60 per cent higher than the number of rural males who are having extra-marital experience, and the frequencies in this lower educational level are higher among urban males, especially in the early twenties. Among the college-bred males, the city-raised individuals are involved two or three times as often as the rural males, but the frequencies seem to be higher in the rural group.

To judge from those few groups on which religious data are available (Table 129), extra-marital intercourse seems to occur much more frequently among those who are less actively concerned with the church, and much less frequently among males who are devoutly religious. The differences between devout and inactive members of any religious group are, however, nowhere near so great as the differences between social levels. The community acceptance or non-acceptance of extra-marital intercourse is much more effective than the immediate restraints provided by the present-day religious organization. But since the sex mores originated in religious codes (Chapter 13), it is, in the last analysis, the church which is the origin of the restrictions on extra-marital intercourse.

RELATION TO OTHER OUTLETS

There seems to be no question but that the human male would be promiscuous in his choice of sexual partners throughout the whole of his life if there were no social restrictions. This is the history of his anthropoid ancestors, and this is the history of unrestrained human males everywhere. The human male almost invariably becomes promiscuous as soon as he becomes involved in sexual relations that are outside of the law. This is true to a degree in pre-marital and in extra-marital intercourse, and it is true of those who are most involved in homosexual activities.

The human female is much less interested in a variety of partners. This is true in her pre-marital and extra-marital histories and, again, it is strikingly true in her homosexual relations. The easy explanation that the female is basically more moral, and the male less moral, does not suffice. These differences must be more dependent upon differences in the sexual responsiveness of males and females, and particularly upon differences in the conditionability of the two sexes. The average female is not aroused by nearly so many stimuli as is the male, and finds much less sexual excitement in psychic associations or in any sensory stimulations outside of the purely tactile. These differences are similar to those found between males and females in the lower mammals, and there is a good deal of evidence (Beach 1947) that they depend upon differences in the nervous organization on which sexual behavior depends.

In practical terms this means that there are a great many human females who find it incomprehensible that so many human males should look for sexual relations with women other than their wives. On the other hand, most males see some force to the argument that variety is attractive in any sort of situation, whether it concerns the literature that one reads, the music that one hears, the recreation in which one engages, the food which one eats, the type of sex relations which one has, or the sexual partners with whom the relations are had. This philosophy has been frankly expressed by a considerable number of males who have contributed histories to the present study, even though some of them immediately add that for moral and social reasons they have not had extra-marital intercourse and will not have extra-marital intercourse, however much they may desire it.

There is, of course, a smaller portion of the females, the number of whom we have not yet calculated, who find variety in sexual relations as interesting as any of the males find it.

Extra-marital intercourse, then, may occur irrespective of the availability or frequency of other sorts of sexual outlet, and without respect to the satisfactory or unsatisfactory nature of the sexual relations at home. Most of the male's extra-marital activity is undoubtedly a product of his interest in a variety of experience. On the other hand, there is certainly a portion of his extra-marital intercourse which is the product of unsatisfactory relations with his wife. When she fails to be interested in sexual relations with her husband, when she is less interested than he is, when she refuses to have intercourse as frequently as he would like it, when she refuses to allow the variety in pre-coital techniques that the male would like to have, or when she accedes to such techniques without evidencing an interest equal to that of the male, she is encouraging him to find extra-marital relations. The wife's refusal of mouth-genital contacts (Chapter 18) with her husband is a factor in sending some males elsewhere for such experience.

All of these same factors may, of course, operate to lead a sexually responsive wife into extra-marital intercourse; but that is not so often true as is the reverse situation.

It is not yet clear how much relation there is between experience in pre-marital intercourse and experience in extra-marital intercourse. Exact correlations will have to be published later. Certainly there are histories of males who had an abundance of pre-marital intercourse and who never have any sort of extra-marital intercourse; and there are histories of males who had no pre-marital intercourse but who begin a considerable amount of extra-marital intercourse as soon as they are married. There are histories of males who are examples of every other type of relationship between these two phenomena. A multiplicity of factors must be involved, and it will take careful analyses to identify what correlations may exist.

It is true, as just noted, that males of the lower educational levels are the ones who have the most pre-marital intercourse, and they are the ones who have the most extra-marital intercourse in early marriage. And it is also true that the college level males have the least pre-marital intercourse, and the least extra-marital intercourse in early marriage. But the correlations lie in the basic attitudes of the social groups which are involved, and they are not a direct effect of pre-marital behavior on extra-marital patterns.

SOCIAL SIGNIFICANCE

Throughout the literature of the world, extra-marital intercourse has provided an overwhelming abundance of material for biography, drama, fiction, and serious essay. There is probably no sexual theme that has appeared more often in the world's literature, both great and small, in all ages and among all nations. Most often the relationships have been portrayed as highly desirable, intrinsically sinful, certain of obstruction by a conspiracy of social forces, and doomed to tragic failure which becomes most tragic when it appears that the illicit relations would have been the higher destiny if social conventions had not interfered. That extra-marital relations are generally desired has, evidently, been known to all men throughout the ages. That they seldom work out in society as it is constructed has been at least believed by the writers of all ages.

Current sociologic, clinical, sex educational, and religious literature repeats, for the most part, this conviction that extra-marital intercourse always does damage to marriages (*e.g.*, Armitage 1913, Forel 1922, Meyer 1927, Eddy 1928, Hamilton 1929, Lindsey and Evans 1929, Amer. Soc. Hyg. Assoc. 1930, Rice 1933, 1946, Ruland and Rattler 1934, Robinson 1936, Ellis 1936, Clark 1937, Benjamin 1939, Popenoe 1943, Rockwood and Ford 1945, Seward 1946). In this literature, the judgment against extra-marital intercourse is almost uniform. Only an occasional writer suggests that there may be values in such experience which can be utilized for human needs.

The public record is replete with instances of marital infidelities which have wrecked homes and destroyed individuals. The counselor and clinician see a stream of cases in which marital difficulties turn around the extra-marital activities of the husband or of the wife. The scientist can add little that is new in the record of such cases, and he cannot minimize their significance in our social organization.

There is, nevertheless, room for a scientific examination of the real bases of the difficulties that develop out of extra-marital sexual relations. Is it inevitable that extra-marital intercourse should lead to difficulties, or do the difficulties originate in the mores of the group? What proportion of all extra-marital relations lead to marital disturbances? The publicly known clinical cases may, like clinical cases of other sorts, represent only the disturbed segment of the group that has extra-marital experience, and may not adequately represent the situation as a whole. Do extra-marital relations ever contribute to the effectiveness of a marriage? What effect does such activity ultimately have upon the personalities of those who are involved? Certainly society may be concerned with securing objective answers to these questions.

In gathering the thousands of married histories which have entered into the present study, we have begun the accumulation of a considerable body of material on the factors that contribute to marital stability and, conversely, to marital discord. With the further continuation of this study, analyses of these data will be undertaken in a later publication. For the present, only fragments can be offered that bear on the social significance of extra-marital intercourse.

Certainly many different sorts of situations are involved. There are many factors that may affect the outcome of the extra-marital activities, and the record is much more diverse than has generally been believed.

At lower social levels, where the most extra-marital intercourse occurs, wives rather generally expect their husbands to "step out," and some of them rather frankly admit that they do not object provided they do not learn of the specific affairs which are carried on. Nevertheless, extra-marital intercourse is the sexual factor which is most often involved in marital discord at that level. Diversion of the interest and affection of the spouse who has the extra-marital relation results in jealousy and bitter hatreds, and these lead to endless quarrels and vicious fighting with, occasionally, murder as the outcome. A portion of the non-support which is so common at this level is the result of the male's distraction by females other than his wife. Desertions, separations, and divorce, in this group, are frequently the outcome of these extra-marital attractions.

Nevertheless, a portion of the extra-marital intercourse at lower levels is had without apparent interference with the affection between the spouses, or with the stability of the marriage. The data are as yet insufficient to warrant a statistical measure of the frequency of each type of situation.

Extra-marital intercourse is less often accepted in middle class groups. While it may not involve as much quarreling and fighting, it often leads to divorce. How often it occurs without causing trouble is a matter that still needs to be determined.

The extra-marital intercourse of the upper social level much less often causes difficulty, because it is usually unknown to anyone except the two persons immediately involved. On occasion it does become known and causes marital discord and divorce. On the other hand, it is sometimes had with the knowledge of the other spouse who may even aid and encourage the arrangement. Such a frank and open acceptance of the partner's non-marital sexual relations is practically unknown at lower social levels, and at all levels is a source of astonishment to persons with strict moral codes.

Wives, at every social level, more often accept the non-marital activities of their husbands. Husbands are much less inclined to accept the non-marital activities of their wives. It has been so since the dawn of history. The biology and psychology of this difference need more careful analysis than the available data yet afford.

The significance of extra-marital intercourse may more often depend upon the attitudes of the spouses and of the social groups to which they belong, than upon the effect of the actual intercourse upon the participating individuals. Few difficulties develop out of extra-marital intercourse when the relationships are unknown to anyone but the two persons having the intercourse. There are histories of long-continued extra-marital relationships which seem to have interfered in no way with the marriages, until the other partner or partners discovered the infidelity. Then they immediately filed suit for divorce.

Extra-marital intercourse most often causes difficulty when it involves emotional and affectional relations with the new partner who takes precedence over the spouse. Conversely, the extra-marital contacts most often avoid trouble when they are social affairs without too much emotional content. There are a few males who can carry on emotional relationships with two or more partners simultaneously, but there are many more who do not succeed at such an arrangement.

There are some individuals among our histories whose sexual adjustments in marriage have undoubtedly been helped by extra-marital experience. Sometimes this depends upon their learning new techniques or acquiring new attitudes which reduce inhibitions in their marital relations. Some women who have had difficulty in reaching orgasm with their husbands, find the novelty of the situation with another male stimulating them to their first orgasm; and with this as a background they make better adjustments with their husbands. Extra-marital intercourse has had the effect of convincing some males that the relationships with their wives were more satisfactory than they had realized.

There are a few cases of married couples who have ceased sexual relations with each other, but who maintain happy and socially successful homes while each of the partners finds the whole of his or her sexual outlet outside of marriage. There are cases of males who are totally impotent with their wives, although they are successful in extra-marital relations which they may carry on throughout the whole of their marital histories, while the wives similarly maintain lifelong relations with men other than their husbands.

In both lower and upper level histories, there are cases where the children in the home are the offspring of the extra-marital relationships. Both spouses may accept the situation, and it may cause no difficulty as long as the neighbors and the law are unaware of the fact.

The histories of persons born and raised in Continental Europe usually involve a great deal of extra-marital intercourse, and such histories should be carefully studied in any scientific analysis of the outcome of such relations.

* * *

By and large, it is not a large proportion of the population that accepts an unlimited amount of extra-marital intercourse. Even those individuals who publicly defend the desirability of such relationships usually have notably few experiences in their actual histories. Whether this is a tribute to the effectiveness of the mores in controlling the behavior of persons who think that they are emancipated, or whether it is evidence that extra-marital intercourse entails difficulties that they did not anticipate, or whether it merely indicates that successful extra-marital relations are carried on with difficulty under our present social organization, it is impossible to say at this time. Certainly the psychologist and social scientist, and society in general, need a great many more specific data before there can be any final evaluation of the effects of extra-marital intercourse on individuals and on their relations to their homes and to the society of which they are a part.

Chapter 20

INTERCOURSE WITH PROSTITUTES

By sociological and legal definition a prostitute is an individual who indiscriminately provides sexual relations in return for money payments. The practical interpretation of the term emphasizes the fact that a prostitute accepts a sexual relation with almost anyone, stranger or acquaintance, who offers to pay, and that the payment is in currency rather than in goods or services.

It is impractical to confine the term to those persons who derive their whole living or any particular part of it from prostitution, for a very high number of the females who engage in such activities do so as a minor adjunct to their regular occupations. The person who is specifically paid for a single sexual relation is, for that particular occasion, a prostitute.

The definition requires that payment for a sexual relation be in currency and be made for each particular contact. If the term prostitution were to be applied to all sexual acts for which either participant received some valuable consideration, it would be impossible to draw a line between the most obvious sort of commercialized prostitution and the relationships of every husband and wife. The girl who has to be taken to dinner or to an evening's entertainment before she will agree to intercourse with her boy friend or fiancé is engaged in a more commercialized relationship than she would like to admit. The gifts that are bestowed by males of all social levels upon girls with whom they keep company may be cloaked with fine sentiments, but they are, to a considerable degree, payment for the intercourse that is expected.

At lower social levels there is often an elaborate arrangement by which the girl in the pre-marital or extra-marital relation is provided with stockings, dresses, fur coats, and other materials of value, for sexual relations which would be immediately stopped if the male failed to provide such gifts as the girl considered commensurate with her contribution, and with his ability to pay. In some lower levels it is quite customary for the male to share his pay envelope with the girl from whom he is securing regular intercourse, and at all social levels there may be some sort of regular contribution to the support of the girl's home, if the sexual relation is continued over any period of time. It is difficult to characterize such relationships as prostitution. It is even more misleading to apply the term to the case of the wife who demands payment in coin of the realm each time she engages in intercourse with her husband (and such arrangements are recorded in the histories). But it is only rarely that there is any difficulty in recognizing the situations that do deserve to be called prostitution.

There are four types of prostitution. The commonest involves heterosexual relations for which the female is paid. This is the type of prostitution with which the present chapter is concerned.

There is, however, a homosexual prostitution among males who provide sexual relations for other males; and such homosexual prostitutes are, in many large cities, not far inferior in number to the females who are engaged in heterosexual prostitution. Male homosexual prostitutes less often derive their main income from such activities, and less often engage in prostitution for any long period of years.

There is also a heterosexual prostitution in which females pay males for sexual relations, but this situation is not common.

The rarest of the four types of prostitution involves females who are paid for the homosexual relations with which they supply other females.

Any extensive treatment of the subject should cover all four types of prostitution, and should analyze the basic elements in all of them. But the present chapter is not concerned with prostitution as a social institution, nor with prostitutes. Those subjects will provide the material for a later volume. The present chapter deals only with the behavior of the males who pay female prostitutes for a portion of their sexual outlet.

REFERENCES

Data on the part which intercourse with prostitutes plays in the sexual lives of males in various segments of the population have already been detailed in this volume in tables and charts, and in discussions in the text, as follows:

PAGE	TABLE	FIGURE	NATURE OF DATA
67, 68			Items on prostitution covered in interview
116, 117	12	14	Calculation of accumulative incidence curve on coitus with prostitutes
234	49		Range of variation in intercourse with prostitutes
251, 253	55, 65	77–82	Age and marital status affecting intercourse with prostitutes
353–357	87, 113, 115	102, 106, 154	Relation of social level to intercourse with prostitutes
404, 413	100, 104, 105	113, 114, 122, 123	Comparisons of two generations, in intercourse with prostitutes
455	121	125	Rural-urban backgrounds and intercourse with prostitutes
488–493	96, 97	127–133	Portion of total outlet derived from prostitutes
597–600	138	153, 154	Accumulative incidence of intercourse with prostitutes
601–603		155	Individual variation in frequencies of intercourse with prostitutes

INCIDENCES AND FREQUENCIES

There is a widespread opinion, both in the public at large and among social scientists, that prostitution provides the major source of non-marital sexual outlet for most of the male population. However, though it may play a more important part in the sexual patterns of some other countries, in the United States the number of males who go to prostitutes is not so high as is generally believed, and the frequencies with which they go are very much lower than almost anyone has realized.

There have been very few attempts to obtain statistical data on the incidence of contacts with prostitutes (Eddy 1928, Taylor 1934, Reitman in Robinson 1936, Bromley and Britten 1938), and these data have been inadequate. Similarly, it would appear that the frequencies of such contacts in any large segment of the population have never been investigated (although there are reports on isolated cases), and this is astounding in view of the tremendous interest that so many agencies have had in controlling the frequencies of such contacts. Law enforcement officers, the reports of vice societies, popular sex books and pamphlets, novels, and even the best of the literature written in this country have made prostitution appear much more significant than it actually proves to be in the total sexual life of the American male.

We find that about 69 per cent of the total white male population ultimately has some experience with prostitutes (Table 138, Figure 153). Many of these males, however, never have more than a single experience or two, and not more than 15 or 20 per cent of them ever have such relations more often than a few times a year, over as much as a five-year period in their lives. This means that there is nearly a third (31%) of the population that never has any sort of sexual contact with prostitutes. There are, of course, a few males who never have heterosexual relations except with prostitutes, but this happens very rarely.

Ultimately, something between 3.5 and 4 per cent of the total outlet of the total male population (single and married) is drawn from relations with female prostitutes (Tables 96, 97, Figures 126, 127). This is not a very large portion of the total outlet. Nocturnal emissions are more important (Chapter 15), and the homosexual accounts for two or three times as many orgasms among males (Chapter 21). Only petting to climax (Chapter 16) and animal intercourse (Chapter 22) account for smaller parts of the outlet. In the college group, where intercourse with prostitutes is at its lowest, the homosexual may provide ten to twenty times as much of the outlet as prostitutes do. Many groups interested in controlling non-marital sexual activities have centered their attention upon prostitution when, in actuality, it accounts for less than a tenth of the non-marital outlet of the male population. Intercourse with prostitutes is much more important socially than it is as a means of outlet.

	TOTAL INTERCOURSE WITH PROSTITUTES: ACCUMULATIVE INCIDENCE							
AGE	TOTAL POPULATION U. S. CORRECTIONS		EDUC. LEVEL 0–8		EDUC. LEVEL 9–12		EDUC. LEVEL 13+	
	Cases	% with Exper.	Cases	% with Exper.	Cases	% with Exper.	Cases	% with Exper.
8	3995	0.0	685	0.0	494	0.0	2816	0.0
9	3995	0.0	685	0.0	494	0.0	2816	0.0
10	3995	0.0	685	0.0	494	0.0	2816	0.0
11	3994	0.0	684	0.1	494	0.0	2816	0.0
12	3994	0.3	684	0.6	494	0.2	2816	0.0
13	3994	0.7	684	1.0	494	0.6	2816	0.1
14	3991	2.6	681	3.5	494	2.6	2816	0.8
15	3985	7.4	675	7.7	494	8.5	2816	2.3
16	3964	16.1	658	18.4	491	17.7	2815	4.8
17	3905	26.0	621	28.8	471	28.9	2813	9.1
18	3767	36.7	594	40.6	436	40.6	2737	13.6
19	3536	42.1	564	45.6	399	46.6	2573	17.4
20	3231	45.3	536	50.9	357	48.5	2338	20.6
21	2857	48.6	512	54.7	313	52.1	2032	22.2
22	2454	51.4	492	58.3	290	54.5	1672	24.9
23	2137	54.5	476	59.5	264	59.1	1397	25.7
24	1845	55.9	456	61.6	237	60.3	1152	26.6
25	1659	58.6	436	65.1	221	62.9	1002	28.6
26	1515	59.9	424	66.5	207	64.3	884	29.4
27	1379	61.2	409	67.5	196	65.8	774	30.5
28	1273	63.3	395	67.6	179	69.8	699	32.0
29	1164	64.0	371	67.7	159	71.1	634	32.0
30	1069	65.5	355	69.6	141	73.0	573	33.2
31	993	66.1	335	70.1	129	73.6	529	34.0
32	934	65.9	323	70.9	119	72.3	492	33.7
33	873	66.4	309	71.2	116	73.3	448	33.3
34	819	66.7	300	72.0	107	72.9	412	33.7
35	762	68.0	286	72.7	94	73.4	382	34.6
36	718	70.0	273	74.4	89	76.4	356	35.7
37	656	69.8	255	73.7	78	76.9	323	35.6
38	625	69.6	246	73.6	72	76.4	307	36.2
39	570	68.2	224	72.3	66	74.2	280	36.4
40	521	68.8	204	73.5	60	71.7	257	36.6
41	485	68.9	192	74.0	55	70.9	238	37.0
42	456	68.1	183	73.8	52	69.2	221	35.3
43	409	67.2	167	73.1	50	68.0	192	34.4
44	379	66.8	154	72.7			177	36.2
45	348	68.7	141	73.0			161	38.5

Table 138. Accumulative incidence data on total intercourse with prostitutes

Covering the life span, including pre-marital, extra-marital, and post-marital histories. In three educational levels, and in the total population corrected for the U. S. Census of 1940.

Among single males, the percentage of the total outlet derived from contacts with prostitutes increases markedly with age (Table 65, Figure 78), beginning at 3.7 per cent in the late teens, rising to nearly 10 per cent by age 30, and going still higher for those relatively few males who are still unmarried in the later years. For married males (Table 65, Figure 78), hardly more than 1 per cent of the outlet is derived from extra-marital intercourse with prostitutes, and this lowers the average for all males, single and married.

Prostitutes provide only about a tenth of the male's total pre-marital intercourse: 8.6 per cent between ages 16 and 20, 13.3 per cent between

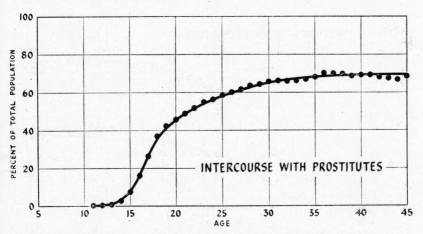

Figure 153. Intercourse with prostitutes: accumulative incidence in total U. S. population

Showing percent of total population that has ever had intercourse with prostitutes by each of the indicated ages. All data based on total population, irrespective of marital status, and corrected for the U. S. Census distribution.

21 and 25, and even more of the pre-marital intercourse of the males who are still unmarried at later ages (Tables 64, 65). It is to be noted that an increasing proportion of the extra-marital intercourse comes from prostitutes as the male grows older. This is partly due to his decreasing ability to find sexual partners, particularly partners of attractive, younger ages. It is also due, however, to the fact that the older male finally reaches the point where he considers it simpler to go to prostitutes than to try to court and win the favors of a girl who is not a prostitute.

In the same fashion, and for the same reasons, intercourse with prostitutes supplies an increasing proportion of the outlet of the males who have been previously married, but who are now widowed, separated from their wives, or divorced (Table 65, Figure 78).

Among married males, prostitutes provide about 11 per cent of the extra-marital outlet between ages 16 and 20, over 16 per cent of that outlet by age 30, and 22 per cent of the extra-marital outlet at age 55 (Tables 64, 65). This apparent increase, however, is not due to any increase in actual frequencies, but to the fact that the total outlet drops steadily through the years, while intercourse with prostitutes is maintained with more or less constant frequencies over a period of several decades.

The incidence and frequency figures vary tremendously for different segments of the population, and it is misleading to discuss the place of prostitution in the population as a whole. Contacts with prostitutes are most frequently had by males of the lowest social levels. By 25 years of

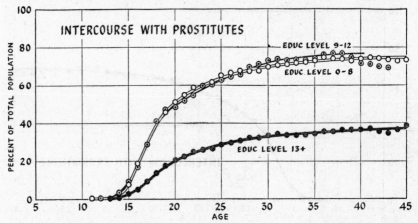

Figure 154. Intercourse with prostitutes: accumulative incidence in three educational levels

Showing percent of each population that has ever had intercourse with prostitutes by each of the indicated ages. All data based on total population, irrespective of marital status.

age, 74 per cent of the males who never went beyond grade school have had some intercourse with prostitutes (Table 87), while only 54 per cent of the males of the high school level, and only 28 per cent of the males of the college level, have had such experience. Among single males of the group that never goes beyond the eighth grade, as much as 6 per cent of the total sexual outlet is derived from prostitutes in the late teens, 14.3 per cent by the late twenties, and 23.4 per cent by the late thirties, if the male is not yet married by that time (Table 96). Among the boys who go to high school the figures start at 3 per cent in the late teens and climb to 10.3 per cent in the middle thirties. For males of the college level less than 1 per cent of the total sexual outlet is derived from prostitutes in the late teens, and only 3 per cent in the late twenties. This is one of the most striking differences between the patterns of college males and the patterns of all other groups.

Among all married males, it is never more than 1.7 per cent of the total sexual outlet which is derived from prostitutes in any particular age period (Table 97) and, again, it is the married male of the college level who draws the lowest percentage of his outlet from professional sources.

The actual frequencies of intercourse with prostitutes begin at very low levels in the early adolescent years, but they do begin there. Law enforcement officers are especially interested in trying to prevent young boys from having such relations, and it is very difficult to get a prostitute to admit that she has ever had relations with any boy under 18. But nearly 8 per cent of the males who have contributed to the present study have reported that they had such relations before or by the time they were 15 years of age. Frequencies of contacts steadily rise until they average about once in three weeks (0.3 per week) for the total population of un-married males in their thirties (Table 65, Figure 77). For those males who actually have such relations, the frequencies start in the earliest adolescent years at once in four weeks and rise to twice in three weeks (0.6 per week) by the thirties. If these calculations are broken down by social levels (Table 87, Figure 102), the active frequencies for those boys who never go beyond the eighth grade in school start at about once in three weeks and rise to once in two weeks or twice in three weeks. For the boys who go to high school but not beyond, the frequencies (of the active population) start at some lower level and rise to once in four weeks by age 20, once in three weeks by age 25, and somewhat higher in the later years for the males who remain unmarried. For the males who belong to the college level, those who have any intercourse at all with prostitutes average only once in six to ten weeks, unless they remain unmarried past the age of 25, when the frequencies rise rather considerably.

Between 16 and 20, males of the grade school level have intercourse with prostitutes 9 times as often, and males of the high school level have it more than 4 times as often as males of the college level (Table 87, Figure 102). By the early thirties, males of the grade school level have intercourse with prostitutes about 36 times as frequently as males of the college level. Making the comparisons by occupational classes, the record is that males of classes 2 and 3 (the laboring group and the semi-skilled workmen) and possibly class 4 (the skilled workmen) have 5 to 10 times as many contacts with prostitutes during their late teens as males of occupational class 7 (the future professional group) (Table 113, Figure 102). The differences become even greater in later years. Public health officials who are inter-ested in controlling the spread of venereal disease might profitably give maximum attention to educating the groups which have the most frequent contacts with prostitutes and with other girls.

For the population taken as a whole, including single and married males of all social levels and of all ages above adolescence, the mean

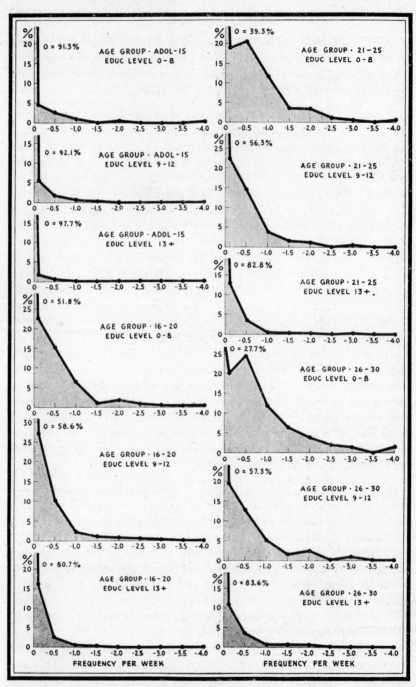

Figure 155. Pre-marital intercourse with prostitutes: individual variation in
frequencies, in four age groups, at three educational levels

Showing percent of each population (vertical line) which has pre-marital intercourse
with prostitutes with each type of frequency (horizontal line).

average frequency of intercourse with prostitutes is 0.093 per week, which is a little less than 5 times per year. With this average figure, which has been very carefully calculated on the basis of all of our available data, it is possible to estimate the average number of contacts that are being made with prostitutes in any particular city or state, per week or per year. Infrequent as such contacts are in relation to the total sexual activity of the average male, they amount to a good deal in absolute frequencies in any population as a whole.

In the total U. S. population 34.3 per cent (calculated from U. S. Census 1940) consists of males who are above the age of onset of adolescence and under the age of impotence and, therefore, eligible for intercourse with prostitutes. The frequencies of contacts per million of total population should then total close to 1,659,000 per year. In terms of the town of 100,000 inhabitants, the contacts average about 3,190 per week. If the police force in such a community fails to make that many arrests each week for association with prostitutes, this may be taken as a measure of the difficulty of facing the actualities of human behavior. With such data, it should be possible to sense the magnitude of the problem of eliminating prostitution. And yet contacts with prostitutes, as just noted, represent only a small part of the non-marital (and therefore largely taboo or illegal) sexual activity of the community.

In view of the efforts that have been made in the last decade or two to control heterosexual prostitution, it is important to note that the data show (Table 100, Figures 113, 114) that the percentage of males in each social level who are frequenting prostitutes today is almost precisely the same as the percentage which had such experience twenty or more years ago (Chapter 11). While there are considerable differences in frequencies for males of the different social levels which may live together in the same town, there are practically no differences between the males of two generations which are as far apart as the two world wars.

The frequencies of contacts with prostitutes have, however, been significantly reduced, undoubtedly as a result of the educational campaigns and the legal moves which have more recently been made against prostitution. The present-day male is making such contacts only two-thirds, or even half, as often as the older generation did (Table 104). In compensation, however, there has been a definite increase in the amount of intercourse with girls who are not prostitutes, and the totals for pre-marital intercourse have not been materially changed.

Moreover, prostitution does not now occupy the thinking of males as it did in past generations. Males of the older generation visited houses of prostitution, not only in search of intercourse, but on sightseeing trips and in social groups as well. They were more often involved in the non-sexual activities that occurred in the established houses, such as drinking, gambling, etc. Present day prostitution is more often a matter of dealing with an individual girl who operates on her own. In practically every large city in the United States, those who are acquainted with conditions can locate prostitutes easily enough; but since organized houses have been eliminated in most of these cities, the stranger in town may have considerable difficulty in making such contacts. It is our impression, which will need more statistical support before it is established, that the number of girls who are now involved in prostitution is not materially smaller than the number which was so engaged ten or twenty years ago. Their manner of operation, however, has been materially changed, and the number of contacts they make per week has been appreciably reduced.

TECHNIQUES

This is not the place to make any detailed study of the way in which prostitution is managed, how its contacts are made, and the types of relations which it offers. It is appropriate in this volume, however, to note certain situations that arise when persons of diverse social levels, the prostitute and her client, undertake to have sexual relations together. Most prostitutes originate in lower social levels, from which they have acquired lower level patterns of behavior (Chapter 10). These lower level attitudes still persist even after a girl goes into prostitution. Some of her trade comes from her own social level, and then her own patterns of coitus suffice; but a large part of her trade is, as we have seen, from the high school level, and a smaller but financially very significant part of it comes from the college level. In their pre-coital and coital techniques, both the high school and college groups want something that is usually foreign to the prostitute's background. For the sake of her trade, she may agree to such overt activity as these males desire but, interesting to note, she still would refuse to use such techniques with her husband or boy friend.

Specifically, elaborated pre-coital petting, kissing, oral manipulation of the breast, and mouth-genital contacts are taboo in the level from which the girl comes (Chapter 10). The introduction of nudity in intercourse is often foreign to her previous experience. Variety in coital positions and, in fact, all techniques which involve anything except simple genital union may be, in her estimation, perversions, "freakish," or "queer." Even the prostitute who goes furthest in supplying variety for the upper level male, may never accept such things as normal or right. She may not be particularly worried about her own behavior—that is a necessary part of the business—but she does not respect the male who wants such things. There are, of course, exceptions. A few of the lower level prostitutes consider that a male should be allowed any sort of sexual activity for which he pays, and a few prostitutes become erotically interested in the full variety of activities in which they engage. There are a few who are better educated, with high school or even college backgrounds; and there are some who are physically energetic, mentally alert, and intelligent. They more readily accept and provide the variety of techniques which the upper level males find most satisfactory, and some of these girls may develop long-time relations which make them full-fledged mistresses.

The lower level prostitute more often learns to accept the high school or college male's desire for nudity during intercourse, and his desire for intercourse in the light. These things are usual in relations with prostitutes today, although they were far from being so in past generations. In a certain number of cases, the prostitute may provide mouth-genital contacts.

The cheaper prostitute restricts each sexual relation to a minimum of time. This, again, is part of the pattern of her social level and is, of course, more convenient for her. In the days of established houses, contacts were often limited to five minutes or less, and extra payment was demanded for any extension of activity. The educated male's interest in protracted relationships which involve social contacts and pre-coital petting is likely to go unsatisfied with most prostitutes. Only the occasional girl in the more expensive house of prostitution, or the still more expensive partner maintained by the financially richer male, has been willing to make a prolonged social performance of each contact.

As a result of the more recent drives against organized prostitution, many of the better houses have been closed. The poorest houses have been the ones that have most often survived. As noted previously, most prostitution has become a matter of an individual girl operating on her own. These girls often have no place to take the men except to the back alley, to their own very poor homes, or to the cheap hotels to which they have entrance. Consequently, the conditions under which the sex relations are now had are still less satisfactory to the upper level male than they were in the older generation. The sexually expert and socially more effective girl who remains in prostitution operates for very high fees and restricts her contacts to a very limited clientele with which she has had long-time acquaintance.

SIGNIFICANCE OF PROSTITUTION

The world's literature contains hundreds of volumes whose authors have attempted to assay the social significance of prostitution. For an activity which contributes no more than this does to the sexual outlet of the male population, it is amazing that it should have been given such widespread consideration. Some of the attention which the subject has received, and certainly many of the books that have been written about it, have undoubtedly been inspired by erotic interest; but a major part of the interest has centered around this question of the social significance of prostitution. The extent of the attention which the subject still receives in this country today is, as we have shown, all out of proportion to its significance in the lives of most males, and this makes one skeptical of using the older literature as a source of information on the place of prostitution in past generations and past centuries. Certainly the older accounts would make it appear that prostitution was much more important in the life of the male who lived any time between the dawn of history and World War I than we have evidence of its having been since then.

There has always been a considerable relation between prostitution and other underworld activities, including gambling, bootlegging, dope peddling, robbery, and other activities. A very high percentage of the prostitutes rob their clients whenever the opportunity affords. Often strong-arm robbery, assault, and occasionally murder are involved. These activities, more than the sexual relations themselves, have concerned law enforcement officers and all others who have been interested in maintaining orderly communities. The relation of prostitution and venereal disease has supplied the argument most often used in recent decades for the suppression of organized prostitution (*e.g.*, W. S. Hall 1907, 1909, Exner 1914, Bigelow 1916, Coppens and Spalding 1921, U. S. Public Health Service 1921, 1937, Forel 1922, Martindale 1925, Eddy 1928, Meyer 1929, Dickerson 1930, Weatherhead 1932, Rice 1933, Ruland and Rattler 1934, Ellis 1936, Robinson in Robinson 1936, Stone and Stone 1937, Haire 1937, Clarke 1938, Rosanoff 1938, Crisp 1939. Kirkendall 1940, Snow 1941, Bowman 1942, Dickerson 1944, 1946, Koch and Wilbur 1944, Popenoe 1946, McPartland 1947). This is not the place to discuss the scientific data which are available on these social problems.

Throughout history, there have been few social institutions which have been objects of as continuous condemnation and concentrated attack as the institution of heterosexual prostitution; and this undoubtedly reflects a widespread judgment that there are basic faults in the institution. On the other hand, prostitution continues to exist, and one may well ask why men continue to go to prostitutes. It is probable that prostitution is no exception to the economic laws, and it continues to exist because there is a sufficient demand for what it offers (see, for instance, Forel 1922, Weatherhead 1932, Ellis 1936, Benjamin 1939, Faris in Hunt 1944, Popenoe 1944, Sadler and Sadler 1944).

First of all, men go to prostitutes because they have insufficient sexual outlets in other directions, or because prostitution provides types of sexual activity which are not so readily available elsewhere. Many men go to prostitutes to find the variety that sexual experience with a new partner may offer. Some men go because they feel that the danger of contracting venereal disease from a prostitute is actually less than it would be with a girl who was not in an organized house of prostitution. Some males experiment with prostitution just to discover what it means. In many cases some social psychology is involved as groups of males go together to look for prostitutes.

At all social levels men go to prostitutes because it is simpler to secure a sexual partner commercially than it is to secure a sexual partner by courting a girl who would not accept pay. Even at lower social levels, where most males find it remarkably simple to make frequent contacts with girls who are not prostitutes, there are still occasions when they desire intercourse immediately and find it much simpler to obtain it from a prostitute. As for college-bred males, a great majority of them are utterly ineffective in securing intercourse from any girl whom they have not dated for long periods of time and at considerable expense; and in some cases, their only chance to secure coital experience is with a prostitute. This is, of course, particularly true if the male is away from home in a strange town.

Hundreds of males have insisted that intercourse with a prostitute is cheaper than intercourse with any other girl. The cost of dating a girl, especially at the upper social level, may mount considerably through the weeks and months, or even years, that it may take to arrive at the first intercourse. There are flowers, candy, "coke dates," dinner engagements, parties, evening entertainments, moving pictures, theatres, night clubs, dances, picnics, week-end house parties, car rides, longer trips, and all sorts of other expensive entertainment to be paid for, and gifts to be made to the girl on her birthday, at Christmas, and on innumerable other special occasions. Finally, after all this the girl may break off the whole affair as soon as she realizes that the male is interested in intercourse. Before the recent war the average cost of a sexual relation with a prostitute was one to five dollars. This was less than the cost of a single supper date with a girl who was not a prostitute; and even at the inflated prices of prostitution which prevailed during the war, the cost did not amount to more than many a soldier or sailor was obliged to spend on another girl from whom he might or might not be able to obtain the intercourse which he wanted.

Men go to prostitutes because they can pay for the sexual relations and forget other responsibilities, whereas coitus with other girls may involve them socially and legally beyond anything which they care to undertake.

Men go to prostitutes to obtain types of sexual activity which they are unable to obtain easily elsewhere. Few prostitutes offer any variety of sexual techniques, but many of them do provide mouth-genital contacts. The prostitute offers the readiest source of experience for the sadist or the masochist, and for persons who have developed associations with non-sexual objects (fetishes) which have come to have sexual significance for them because of some contact they have had in the past. Most males who have participated in sexual activities in groups have found the opportunity to do so with prostitutes. Nearly all of the opportunity that males have to observe sexual activity is connected with prostitutes, and such experiences are in the history of many more persons than is ordinarily realized.

Some men go to prostitutes because they are more or less ineffective in securing sexual relations with other girls. This may be true of males who are unusually timid. Persons who are deformed physically, deaf, blind, severely crippled, spastic, or otherwise handicapped, often have considerable difficulty in finding heterosexual coitus. The matter may weigh heavily upon their minds and cause considerable psychic disturbance. There are instances where prostitutes have contributed to establishing these individuals in their own self esteem by providing their first sexual contacts.

Finally, at the lower social levels there are persons who are feeble-minded, physically deformed, and so repulsive and offensive physically that no girl except a prostitute would have intercourse with them. Without such outlets, these individuals would become even more serious social problems than they already are.

The exclusively homosexual male, however, is not the person to be helped by a prostitute. There are numerous histories of such males being advised by clinicians, or led by some friend, or forced by some hilarious group of male companions into attempting intercourse with a prostitute. In a high proportion of such cases the male proves impotent, and his psychic problem is thereby intensified. Even when the intercourse is more or less successful, it is likely to prove distasteful because of the unesthetic conditions under which it is had. The introduction of the homosexual male to heterosexual experience should come through friendships which lead to affection and spontaneously erotic developments.

There is constant rumor of an increase in the frequency of forced intercourse or outright rape among the girls of a community where prostitution has been suppressed. We have no adequate data to prove the truth or falsity of such reports.

Neither are we convinced that there has been any sufficiently objective study of the place of prostitution in the spread of venereal disease, as compared with the spread of such disease through sexual contacts with lower level girls who are not prostitutes.

The significance of prostitution to the male who goes to the prostitute must depend very much upon the sort of person who is involved and the social background from which he comes. At lower social levels there are some who find intercourse with prostitutes distasteful, but in a much larger number of cases there are no objections to the type of relation that is had. In not a few cases, the male insists that intercourse with a prostitute is superior to intercourse with most other girls. The lower level male is not particularly concerned with the responsiveness or unresponsiveness of his female partner, and he is not interested in a particularly emotional experience in coitus, does not want any elaboration of pre-coital petting, and does not object esthetically to the sorts of situations under which most of the intercourse occurs. He likes a matter-of-fact performance in which there are no emotional and no social obligations incurred. Most often he prefers the prostitute, however, because she expects that there will be intercourse, and does not offer the objections that other girls, even his wife, may offer against sexual relations.

On the other hand, the upper level males who have contributed to the present study have almost unanimously agreed that intercourse with a prostitute is not nearly so satisfactory as the intercourse which may be had with other girls. This is undoubtedly the prime reason why most upper level males do not return to prostitutes more often than they do. The complaints turn largely around the fact that a sexual relation which is commercialized lacks the affection which makes a sexual relation significant in marriage, or even in non-marital relations with girls who are not prostitutes. The upper level male dislikes the limitation on petting in his relations with prostitutes. He commonly complains about the genital inadequacies of the prostitute, and this in most instances means that she is not responding erotically. In consequence, she does not stimulate the emotionally sensitive, upper level male. There is a fair number of upper level males who find themselves impotent in attempting intercourse with prostitutes, and this means that they are not psychically satisfied by the situation.

What effect intercourse with prostitutes may have upon the personality of the male who is involved, is a matter which will need careful investigation by a qualified psychologist or psychiatrist.

Chapter 21

HOMOSEXUAL OUTLET

In the total male population, single and married, between adolescence and old age, 24 per cent of the total outlet is derived from solitary sources (masturbation and nocturnal emissions), 69.4 per cent is derived from heterosexual sources (petting and coitus), and 6.3 per cent of the total number of orgasms is derived from homosexual contacts. It is not more than 0.3 per cent of the outlet which is derived from relations with animals of other species.

Homesexual contacts account, therefore, for a rather small but still significant portion of the total outlet of the human male. The significance of the homosexual is, furthermore, much greater than the frequencies of outlet may indicate, because a considerable portion of the population, perhaps the major portion of the male population, has at least some homosexual experience between adolescence and old age. In addition, about 60 per cent of the pre-adolescent boys engage in homosexual activities (Chapter 5), and there is an additional group of adult males who avoid overt contacts but who are quite aware of their potentialities for reacting to other males.

The social significance of the homosexual is considerably emphasized by the fact that both Jewish and Christian churches have considered this aspect of human sexuality to be abnormal and immoral (Chapter 13). Social custom and our Anglo-American law are sometimes very severe in penalizing one who is discovered to have had homosexual relations. In consequence, many persons who have had such experience are psychically disturbed, and not a few of them have been in open conflict with the social organization.

It is, therefore, peculiarly difficult to secure factual data concerning the nature and the extent of the homosexual in Western European or American cultures, and even more difficult to find strictly objective presentations of such data as are available. Most of the literature on the homosexual represents either a polemic against the heinous abnormality of such activity, or a biased argument in defense of an individual's right to choose his patterns of sexual behavior.

Until the extent of any type of human behavior is adequately known, it is difficult to assess its significance, either to the individuals who are involved or to society as a whole; and until the extent of the homosexual is known, it is practically impossible to understand its biologic or social origins. It is one thing if we are dealing with a type of activity that is unusual, without precedent among other animals, and restricted to peculiar types of individuals within the human population. It is another thing if the phenomenon proves to be a fundamental part, not only of human sexuality, but of mammalian patterns as a whole. The present chapter is, therefore, wholly confined to an analysis of the data which we now have on the incidence and the frequencies of homosexual activity in the white male population in this country. Analyses of the factors which affect the development of both heterosexual and homosexual patterns of behavior will be presented in a subsequent volume in this series.

REFERENCES

Specific data on the incidences and frequencies of overt homosexual contacts in various segments of the male population have already been detailed in this volume in tables and charts, and in discussions in the text, as follows:

PAGE	TABLE	FIGURE	NATURE OF DATA
68–70			Homosexual items covered in the interview
84–88	2	4, 155–162	Size of sample necessary to establish homosexual data
94–102	3, 6	13	Comparisons of data obtained from hundred percent and partial samples
121–125, 129, 130	13		Comparisons of data on original histories and retakes
133–143	16, 20	21	Comparisons of data obtained by three interviewers
143–147	21, 23	24	Comparisons of data obtained in successive periods
162, 167– 168	24	25	Ages involved in pre-adolescent homosexual play
166–167	25		Number of years involved in pre-adolescent homosexual play
168	26		Sex of companions of pre-adolescent boys
169–171	27		Techniques in pre-adolescent sex play
168, 171– 172	28	26	Age of first pre-adolescent sex play
171, 174	29		Continuity of pre-adolescent sex play with adolescent activity
175–181	30–34		Pre-adolescent eroticism and orgasm
190–191	38	30	Sources of first ejaculation
196		31	Examples of combinations of sources of outlet
211–213	42		Sexual outlet in a restrained group of males
232–233	48		Capacity for multiple orgasm in sexual contacts
234–235	49		Range of variation in homosexual contacts
258–261, 285–293	58, 66	83–88	Homosexual contacts in relation to marital status and age

PAGE	TABLE	FIGURE	NATURE OF DATA
300, 312, 315, 317, 320–321	68, 77–78	91, 94	Homosexual contacts in relation to age at onset of adolescence
357–362, 382–384	90, 94, 96–97, 114–115, 141–146	105–106	Homosexual contacts and social level
369–373	94		Oral techniques in sexual contacts
402–403, 410–413	100, 104–105	112	Comparisons of incidences and frequencies of the homosexual in two successive generations
455–460	123		Homosexual contacts and rural-urban backgrounds
482–484	131		Homosexual outlets and religious backgrounds
378, 382, 488–493	96, 97	126, 128–133	Portion of total outlet derived from homosexual contacts
512			Relation of masturbation and the homosexual
523–527			Significance of dream content
617–629	139–140	3, 6, 156–158	Accumulative incidence of homosexual contacts
631–636		159–160	Individual variation in frequencies of homosexual contacts
636–650		161	Heterosexual-homosexual rating scale
640–656	141–150	162–169	Distribution of heterosexual-homosexual ratings in the male population
658		170	Development of heterosexuality and homosexuality, by age periods

DEFINITION

For nearly a century the term homosexual in connection with human behavior has been applied to sexual relations, either overt or psychic, between individuals of the same sex. Derived from the Greek root *homo* rather than from the Latin word for man, the term emphasizes the *sameness* of the two individuals who are involved in a sexual relation. The word is, of course, patterned after and intended to represent the antithesis of the word heterosexual, which applies to a relation between individuals of different sexes.

The term homosexual has had an endless list of synonyms in the technical vocabularies and a still greater list in the vernaculars. The terms homogenic love, contrasexuality, homo-erotism, similisexualism, uranism and others have been used in English (Legman in Henry 1941). The terms sexual inversion, intersexuality, transsexuality, the third sex, psychosexual hermaphroditism, and others have been applied not merely to designate the nature of the partner involved in the sexual relation, but to emphasize the general opinion that individuals engaging in homosexual activity are neither male nor female, but persons of mixed sex. These latter terms are, however, most unfortunate, for they provide an interpretation in anticipation of any sufficient demonstration of the fact; and consequently they prejudice investigations of the nature and origin of homosexual activity.

The term Lesbian, referring to such female homosexual relations as were immortalized in the poetry of Sappho of the Greek Isle of Lesbos, has gained considerable usage within recent years, particularly in some of the larger Eastern cities where the existence of female homosexuality is more generally recognized by the public at large. Although there can be no objection to designating relations between females by a special term, it should be recognized that such activities are quite the equivalent of sexual relations between males.

It is unfortunate that the students of animal behavior have applied the term homosexual to a totally different sort of phenomenon among the lower mammals. In most of the literature on animal behavior it is applied on the basis of the general conspectus of the behavior pattern of the animal, its aggressiveness in seeking the sexual contact, its postures during coitus, its position relative to the other animal in the sex relation, and the conformance or disconformance of that behavior to the usual positions and activities of the animal during heterosexual coitus (Ball, var. titles; Beach, var. titles, espec. 1947).

In most mammals the behavior of the female in a heterosexual performance usually involves the acceptance of the male which is trying to make intromission. The female at such a moment is less aggressive than the male, even passive in her acceptance of the male's approaches, and subordinate in position to him during actual coitus. This means that the female usually lies beneath the male or in front of him during copulation, either submitting from the very beginning of the sexual relation or (as in the cats, ferret, mink, and some other animals) being forced into submission by the assault of the male. In the case of the mink, the female is far from being passive during the initial stages of the contact, and the courting performances involve as strenuous fighting as the most extreme non-sexual circumstances could produce. There is no sexual relation, however, until the female has been sufficiently subdued to allow the male to effect coitus. In the case of the rat, the female which is in heat as the result of the hormones which her ovaries secrete near the time of ovulation, is more readily induced to crouch on the floor, arch her back (in lordosis) so her body is raised posteriorly, and pass into a nervous state which is characterized by a general rigidity of most of the body, but by a constant and rapid trembling of the ears and by peculiar hopping movements. This is the behavior which is characteristic of the female in a heterosexual contact, and this is what the students of animals describe as typically feminine behavior.

Throughout the mammals it is the male which more often (but not always) pursues the female for a sexual contact. In species where there is a struggle before the female submits to coitus, the male must be physically dominant and capable of controlling the female. In the ultimate act it is the male which more often mounts in back of the female and makes the active pelvic thrusts which effect intromission. This is the behavior that students of the lower mammals commonly refer to as typically masculine behavior.

But among many species of mammals and, indeed, probably among all of them, it not infrequently happens that males and females assume other than their usual positions in a sexual contact. This may be dependent upon individual differences in the physiology or anatomy of certain individuals, on differences in hormones, on environmental circumstances, or on some previous experience which has conditioned the animal in its behavior.

In a certain number of cases the assumption of the attitudes and positions of the opposite sex, among these lower mammals, seems to depend upon nothing more than the accident of the position in which the individual finds itself. The same male rat that has mounted a female in typical heterosexual coitus only a few moments before, may crouch on the floor, arch its back, and rear its posterior when it is approached by another rat from the rear. The same female which rises from the floor where she has been crouching in front of a copulating male may bump into another rat as she runs around the cage, rear on her haunches in front of the decumbent partner, and go through all of the motions that a male ordinarily goes through in heterosexual copulation. She may move her pelvis in thrusts which are quite like those of the male. She may strike her genital area against the genital area of the rat in front, quite as she would if she had a penis to effect entrance. And, what is most astounding, she may double up her body as she pulls back from the genital thrusts and manipulate her own genitalia with her mouth (Beach 1947), exactly as the male rat ordinarily manipulates his penis between the thrusts that he makes when he is engaged in the masculine role in the usual type of heterosexual relation.

The assumption by a male animal of a female position in a sexual relation, or the assumption by a female of a position which is more typical of the male in a heterosexual relation, is what the students of animal behavior have referred to as homosexuality. This, of course, has nothing whatsoever to do with the use of the term among the students of human behavior, and one must be exceedingly careful how one transfers the conclusions based on these animal studies.

In studies of human behavior, the term inversion is applied to sexual situations in which males play female roles and females play male roles in sex relations. Most of the data on "homosexuality" in the animal studies actually refer to inversion. Inversion, of course, may occur in either heterosexual or homosexual relations, although there has been a widespread opinion, even among students of human psychology, and among some persons whose experience has been largely homosexual, that inversion is an invariable accompaniment of homosexuality. However, this generalization is not warranted. A more elaborate presentation of our data would show that there are a great many males who remain as masculine, and a great many females who remain as feminine, in their attitudes and their approaches in homosexual relations, as the males or females who have nothing but heterosexual relations. Inversion and homosexuality are two distinct and not always correlated types of behavior.

More recently some of the students of animal behavior (*e.g.*, Beach in later papers) have used the term *bisexual* to apply to individuals which assume sometimes male and sometimes female roles during sexual activities. This, however, is not a happy correction of the terminology, because the term bisexual has a long-standing meaning in biology which is totally different than the meaning intended here. Moreover, in regard to human behavior, the term bisexual has already been misapplied to persons who include both heterosexual and homosexual activities in their current histories. (See the discussion on "Bisexuality" in a later section in this chapter.) The student of animal behavior is observing an inversion of behavior patterns, and this is a phenomenon apart from either homosexuality or bisexuality, as those terms have ordinarily been used.

The inappropriate use of the term homosexual in the literature on animal behavior has led to unfortunate misinterpretations of the data. Thus, for instance, several investigators (*e.g.*, Ball, Beach, Stone, Young, et al.) have shown that the injection of gonadal hormones may modify the frequency with which an animal shows an inversion of behavior of the sort described above. Among many clinicians this work has been taken to mean that the sex hormones control the heterosexuality or homosexuality of an individual's behavior. This, of course, is a totally unwarranted interpretation. The animal work merely shows that there may be an inversion of female and male roles as a result of hormonal injections. It points to a relationship between the amount of hormone and the aggressiveness of an individual in approaching other animals for sexual relations. The injection of male hormones quite generally increases the frequency and intensity of an animal's reactions, but there is no evidence that it affects its choice of a partner in a sexual relation (Kinsey 1941). Beach (1947) makes the significant observation that the males who must often assume the female type of behavior are the ones who "invariably prove to be the most vigorous copulators," when they assume the more usual masculine role in coitus. There is clinical experience with the human male which similarly shows that the intensity of his sexual activity is increased when male hormones are administered, while his choice of a partner (*i.e.*, his heterosexuality or his homosexuality) is not modified.

If the term homosexual is restricted as it should be, the homosexuality or heterosexuality of any activity becomes apparent by determining the sexes of the two individuals involved in the relationship. For instance, mouth-genital contacts between males and females are certainly heterosexual, even though some persons may think of them as homosexual. And although one may hear of a male "who has sex relations with his wife in a homosexual way," there is no logic in such a use of the term, and analyses of the behavior and of the motivations of the behavior in such cases do not show them necessarily related to any homosexual experience.

On the other hand, the homosexuality of certain relationships between individuals of the same sex may be denied by some persons, because the situation does not fulfill other criteria that they think should be attached to the definition. Mutual masturbation between two males may be dismissed, even by certain clinicians, as not homosexual, because oral or anal relations or particular levels of psychic response are required, according to their concept of homosexuality. There are persons who insist that the active male in an anal relation is essentially heterosexual in his behavior, and that the passive male in the same relation is the only one who is homosexual. These, however, are misapplications of terms, which are often unfortunate because they obscure the interpretations of the situation which the clinician is supposed to help by his analysis.

These misinterpretations are often encouraged by the very persons who are having homosexual experience. Some males who are being regularly fellated by other males without, however, ever performing fellation themselves, may insist that they are exclusively heterosexual and that they have never been involved in a truly homosexual relation. Their consciences are cleared and they may avoid trouble with society and with the police by perpetrating the additional fiction that they are incapable of responding to a relation with a male unless they fantasy themselves in contact with a female. Even clinicians have allowed themselves to be diverted by such pretensions. The actual histories, however, show few if any cases of sexual relations between males which could be considered anything but homosexual.

Many individuals who have had considerable homosexual experience, construct a hierarchy on the basis of which they insist that anyone who has not had as much homosexual experience as they have had, or who is less exclusively aroused by homosexual stimuli, is "not really homosexual." It is amazing to observe how many psychologists and psychiatrists have accepted this sort of propaganda, and have come to believe that homosexual males and females are discretely different from persons who merely have homosexual experience, or who react sometimes to homosexual stimuli. Sometimes such an interpretation allows for only two kinds of males and two kinds of females, namely those who are heterosexual and those who are homosexual. But as subsequent data in this chapter will show, there is only about half of the male population whose sexual behavior is exclusively heterosexual, and there are only a few percent who are exclusively homosexual. Any restriction of the term homosexuality to individuals who are exclusively so demands, logically, that the term heterosexual be applied only to those individuals who are exclusively heterosexual; and this makes no allowance for the nearly half of the population which has had sexual contacts with, or reacted psychically to, individuals of their own as well as of the opposite sex. Actually, of course, one must learn to recognize every combination of heterosexuality and homosexuality in the histories of various individuals.

It would encourage clearer thinking on these matters if persons were not characterized as heterosexual or homosexual, but as individuals who have had certain amounts of heterosexual experience and certain amounts of homosexual experience. Instead of using these terms as substantives which stand for persons, or even as adjectives to describe persons, they may better be used to describe the nature of the overt sexual relations, or of the stimuli to which an individual erotically responds.

PREVIOUS ESTIMATES OF INCIDENCE

Many persons have recognized the importance of securing specific information on the incidence of the homosexual. The clinician needs to know how far the experience of his patient departs from norms for the remainder of the population. Counselors, teachers, clergymen, personnel officers, the administrators of institutions, social workers, law enforcement officers, and still others who are concerned with the direction of human behavior, may completely misinterpret the meaning of the homosexual experience in an individual's history, unless they understand the incidence and frequency of such activity in the population as a whole.

Administrators in prisons, mental institutions, public and private schools, colleges and universities, the Army and the Navy, Y.M.C.A. and scouting activities, and of all other sorts of groups, must understand the part which the homosexual plays in the life of the total male population, before they can understand the significance of the behavior of the particular individuals with whom they are called upon to deal. Scientific explanations of the origin and development of the homosexual, and, for that matter, of the heterosexual, will not be on any sound basis until we know the number of persons who are involved in each type of activity, the ages at which they first become involved, and the ages at which they are most frequently involved. There is no other aspect of human sexual activity about which it has been more important to have some precise knowledge of the incidences and frequencies.

There are many persons who believe the homosexual to be a rare phenomenon, a clinical curiosity, and something which one may never meet among the sorts of persons with whom he would associate. On the other hand, there are some clinicians and some persons who have had first-hand contacts in the homosexual, who have estimated that something between 50 and 100 per cent of the population has such experience.

There is undoubtedly a tendency on the part of some males who have had frequent homosexual contacts to exaggerate in their estimates. Some of these more promiscuous males have actually tested the responses of hundreds and sometimes of thousands of males whom they have invited to have homosexual relations. Many of them insist that a very high proportion of all the males whom they have approached have accepted such relations, and it is upon this fact that they base their opinion that most males are "homosexual" or that they are "partly homosexual," or that they "are really homosexual even though they may not be aware of it and may not have had actual experience." But they overlook the fact that the experienced male does not actually invite anyone to have sexual relations until he has had such social contact as may indicate the final success of his sexual approach. His contacts are, therefore, really confined to a very select portion of the males whom he meets.

Satisfactory incidence figures on the homosexual cannot be obtained by any technique short of a carefully planned population survey. The data should cover every segment of the total population. There is no other aspect of human sexual behavior where it is more fundamental that the sample be secured without any selection of cases which would bias the results. Many persons with homosexual experience very naturally hesitate to expose their histories. On the other hand, there are some who are so upset by personal conflicts or social difficulties that have developed out of their homosexual activities that they are anxious to discuss their problems with an investigator whom they have come to trust. In consequence, if one depends only upon volunteers in a survey, it is impossible to know whether homosexual histories are represented in an undue proportion, or less often than their actual incidence would demand. In order to secure data that have any relation to the reality, it is imperative that the cases be derived from as careful a distribution and stratification of the sample as the public opinion polls employ, or as we have employed in the present study.

Unfortunately, no previous attempts to assess the incidence of the homosexual have begun to satisfy these demands for statistical adequacy. The incidence figures which are most often quoted are derived from the 2 to 5 per cent estimate which Havelock Ellis made for England (Ellis 1936), and from the more elaborate calculations made by Hirschfeld, chiefly for Germany (as finally summarized in Hirschfeld 1920). The professional literature, if it does not cite these studies, rarely quotes any other sources except "the best informed students of the subject" (*e.g.*, Haire 1937, Rosanoff 1938, Squier in Folsom 1938, Painter 1941, Moore 1945, et al.); and through devious channels these data have become general property among people who have no idea of their origin. Terman and Miles (1936) do credit a 4 per cent estimate to "the university medical staff in one of the largest of American universities." And there is a bare statement in McPartland (1947) which reports a current "guess" that "the number of potential homosexuals in the United States is in the neighborhood of 8,000,000 or higher"—a figure that represents about 6 per cent of the total male and female population.

As for Ellis' estimate of a 2 to 5 per cent incidence figure for males, and double that figure for females, it is to be noted that this follows a review of the Hirschfeld data, and is made without any support other than the statement that "considering those individuals with whom I have been brought in contact by the ordinary circumstances of life . . . I am still led to the conclusions that . . . there must be a distinct percentage which may sometimes be . . . slightly over 2 per cent." As a matter of fact, Ellis never made any sort of systematic survey of any aspect of sex in any segment of the population. He had a minimum of face to face contact with his subjects, and depended largely upon information which was supplied him by correspondents. It is, of course, only a very select portion of the population that will send sex histories through the mails, and such histories are rarely more than partial accounts, usually of specific episodes that have been high lights in the life of the individual.

More elaborate attempts to obtain estimates of the extent of homosexual activity have been made by some of the Central European students. At the turn of the century, Römer in Holland got 595 of his fellow students to give written answers to questions concerning their erotic reactions to females and to males. In 1903 and 1904, Magnus Hirschfeld conducted a much more extensive investigation (finally summarized in Hirschfeld 1920).

Through the mails, Hirschfeld distributed forms to 3000 students at the Charlottenburg Institute of Technology, and to 5721 metal workers in Berlin, asking each recipient to indicate whether his "libido had always been directed only to females . . . only to males . . . or to both males and females." Of the 7481 persons who apparently received the letters, about 49 per cent answered. On the basis of these replies, Hirschfeld concluded that 94.3 per cent of the males were exclusively heterosexual, 2.3 per cent homosexual, and the remainder bisexual. The survey is open to the very severe criticism that it involved only a highly selected sample of the total population. What is more serious, one is left guessing as to the histories of the 51 per cent that failed to answer the questionnaire.

In a more elaborate attempt to secure estimates of the incidence of the homosexual, Hirschfeld contacted persons who, because they had homosexual histories, could supply some information concerning the extent of such activity in the business or professional groups in which they moved. Persons in the Army and Navy were asked to estimate how many in their whole company or among the officers in their group were known as homosexual. College students were asked to estimate how many of the men in their fraternities were known to have homosexual histories. Similar reports were obtained from groups of Protestant clergymen and from Catholic priests, from postal employees, railroad employees, a group of court judges, bakers, bank employees, draftsmen, butchers, actors, hotel employees, the recorded histories of English kings, etc.—from a total of 34 different groups. Hirschfeld concluded that 525 out of the 23,771 persons in these groups were "homosexual." Calculations give an incidence figure of approximately 2.2 per cent, and this is the figure on which Hirschfeld subsequently depended.

Obviously this method of sampling falls far short of the demands of a scientific population analysis. It depends upon the ability of an informant to know the sexual histories of all the persons in a group, without collecting actual histories from any of them. It depends upon the informant's ability to recognize homosexual males (other than those with whom he has had actual contact) on the basis of their physical characters and mannerisms, or of their public reputations. Very often such reputations are nothing more than mere gossip. Moreover, there are many persons in any group whose homosexual histories are never known publicly. In brief, such sources of information are little better than the gossip and general impressions on which many persons depended before public opinion polls showed what can be accomplished in a statistically well-organized survey.

Hirschfeld deserves considerable credit for having tried on a larger scale than anyone had before to ascertain the facts on a matter that has always been difficult to survey. Down to the beginning of the present study, no more serious attempt has been made. Nevertheless, the uncritical acceptance of these inadequate calculations has delayed the recognition of the magnitude of the medical, psychiatric, social, and legal problems involved in homosexuality, and delayed scientific interpretations of the bases of such behavior.

In later years, Hirschfeld had the opportunity to obtain the histories of persons who visited his Sex Institute at Berlin, some of them as patients, some of them merely as visitors who filled out the questionnaire supplied by the Institute. Some 10,000 of these were accumulated in the course of the years; but the data were uninterpretable because they were derived from such a select portion of the total population. Moreover, all of the Hirschfeld conclusions were biased by his opinion that a person is really homosexual only when his psychic or overt contacts are more or less exclusively so, and consequently his estimates may come nearer representing the incidence of certain degrees of homosexuality, rather than the totality of homosexual activity.

There have been other European studies that have been modelled on the Hirschfeld techniques, but all of them were based on smaller populations, and none of them has had as great influence on the thinking of clinicians.

In this country, three investigators have obtained data on the incidence of the homosexual in our American male population. It is notable that all three of them have secured figures which are remarkably higher than the European studies have given—not because there is any likelihood that the American picture is particularly different from that in Europe, but because all of these studies have come nearer satisfying the demands of a population survey. All of them involved a more thorough coverage of particular groups, and all of them were based on direct interviews with persons with whom the interviewer had had enough contact to have developed some rapport. Hamilton (1929) found that 17 per cent of the hundred men in his study had had homosexual experience after they were eighteen years old. Ramsey (1943), in a study of 291 younger boys, one-half of whom constituted a hundred percent sample of a seventh and eighth grade group in a junior high school, found that 30 per cent had had adolescent homosexual experience to the point of orgasm. More recently (1947), Finger has reported 27 per cent of a college class of 111 males admitting "at least one overt homosexual episode involving orgasm." These figures come remarkably close to those which we have obtained in the present study.

One other source of data on the extent of "homosexuality" among American males has recently become available through statistics gathered by Selective Service Boards and at induction centers during the last war. Theoretically, this should have been a splendid opportunity to gain information that would have been of considerable scientific use and of considerable practical use to the armed forces. From these sources, the over-all figures show that about one-tenth of 1 per cent of all the men were rejected by draft boards (Selective Service Bull. 1-4), about 0.4 per cent were turned down at induction centers (e.g., Hohman and Schaffner 1947), and about as many more were subsequently discharged for homosexual activity while they were in active service. The total gives about 1 per cent officially identified as "homosexual." These figures are so much lower than any which case history studies have obtained that they need critical examination.

The most obvious explanation of these very low figures lies in the fact that both the Army and Navy had precluded the possibility of getting accurate data on these matters by announcing at the beginning of the war that they intended to exclude all persons with homosexual histories. The American Army and Navy have always been traditionally opposed to homosexual activity, and in the last war, for the first time, they turned to psychiatrists to provide expert help in eliminating individuals with such histories.

Physicians on draft boards and psychiatrists at induction centers were charged with the responsibility of detecting and eliminating men with such records, and many of the psychiatrists at induction centers paid especial attention to identifying these men. While the reasons for elimination of any man were supposed to be kept confidential, they were in actuality not infrequently known to the whole community in which he lived. The mere fact that he was rejected under a particular classification, or discharged from the Army or Navy on a particular discharge form, often made him a subject for suspicion, and in a large number of instances practically precluded the possibility of his securing employment as a civilian. Consesequently, few men with any common sense would admit their homosexual experience to draft boards or to psychiatrists at induction centers or in the services.

It is amazing that some of the psychiatrists (e.g., Hohman and Schaffner 1947) apparently believed that they were getting a true record under these circumstances. Only a naive individual, one who was badly neurotic and upset over his experience, or an effeminate type of male who freely exhibited his homosexual interests, was ordinarily detected through the official channels. Many of the psychiatrists were less experienced in identifying the obviously homosexual male than several million untrained persons who had had actual contact with homosexual activities. Many psychiatrists realized this, and some of them recognized the fact that the incidence of homosexual activity in the armed forces must have been high—even involving as many as 10 per cent or more of the men.

It is also to be noted that at induction centers the average interview was limited to less than three minutes. Considering that the psychoanalysts and many of the other psychiatrists have heretofore insisted that one could not expect to obtain data on socially taboo items of sexual behavior in anything less that a hundred hours of analysis, it is the more surprising that the results of these short interviews at induction centers should have been taken seriously.

Discharges from the Army and Navy similarly have not provided any adequate source of information on the actual incidence of homosexual activity. Many psychiatrists in the armed forces were aware of the great social damage done to an individual who was discharged for such reasons, and they considered it desirable to help him by showing flat feet, stomach ulcers, shock, or some other non-sexual item as the immediate cause of the discharge. Consequently, no one anywhere in official circles in the Army and the Navy will ever be able to obtain any adequate estimate of the number of men with homosexual activity who were identified and discharged from the services during the war.

The estimates on the incidence of the homosexual, range, then, from these Selective Service figures of one-tenth of 1 per cent to the 100 per cent estimates of some of the psychoanalysts and of some promiscuous homosexual males. It has, therefore, been especially important in our present study to apply all of the techniques of a statistically sound population survey to obtaining data on this particular matter.

INCIDENCE DATA IN PRESENT STUDY

The statistics given throughout this volume on the incidence of homosexual activity, and the statistics to be given in the present section of this chapter, are based on those persons who have had physical contacts with other males, and who were brought to orgasm as a result of such contacts. By any strict definition such contacts are homosexual, irrespective of the extent of the psychic stimulation involved, of the techniques employed, or of the relative importance of the homosexual and the heterosexual in the history of such an individual. These are not data on the number of persons who are "homosexual," but on the number of persons who have had at least some homosexual experience—even though sometimes not more than one experience—up to the ages shown in the tables and curves. The incidences of persons who have had various amounts of homosexual experience are presented in a later section of this chapter.

An individual who engages in a sexual relation with another male without, however, coming to climax, or an individual who is erotically aroused by a homosexual stimulus without ever having overt relations, has certainly had a homosexual experience. Such relations and reactions are, however, not included in the incidence data given here nor in most other places in this volume, because the volume as a whole has been concerned with the number and sources of male orgasms. On the other hand, the data on the heterosexual-homosexual ratings which are presented later in the present chapter, do take into account these homosexual contacts in which the subject fails to reach climax. Accumulative incidence curves based upon heterosexual-homosexual ratings may, therefore, be somewhat higher than the accumulative incidence curves based upon overt contacts carried through to the point of actual orgasm.

Data on the homosexual activity of the pre-adolescent boy have been presented in another chapter (Chapter 5) and no male is included in any of the calculations shown in the present chapter unless he has had homosexual experience beyond the onset of adolescence.

In these terms (of physical contact to the point of orgasm), the data in the present study indicate that at least 37 per cent of the male population has some homosexual experience between the beginning of adolescence and old age (U. S. Corrections. See Table 139, Figure 156). This is more than one male in three of the persons that one may meet as he passes along a city street. Among the males who remain unmarried until the age of 35, almost exactly 50 per cent have homosexual experience between the beginning of adolescence and that age. Some of these persons have but a single experience, and some of them have much more or even a lifetime of experience; but all of them have at least some experience to the point of orgasm.

TOTAL HOMOSEXUAL OUTLET: ACCUMULATIVE INCIDENCE

AGE	TOTAL POPULATION U. S. CORRECTIONS		EDUC. LEVEL 0–8		EDUC. LEVEL 9–12		EDUC. LEVEL 13+	
	Cases	% with Exper.	Cases	% with Exper.	Cases	% with Exper.	Cases	% with Exper.
8	3969	0.0	662	0.0	490	0.0	2817	0.0
9	3969	0.1	662	0.0	490	0.2	2817	0.1
10	3969	0.5	662	0.2	490	0.6	2817	0.5
11	3968	1.7	661	1.2	490	2.0	2817	1.8
12	3968	6.1	661	5.6	490	6.3	2817	6.2
13	3968	12.6	661	11.0	490	13.7	2817	11.6
14	3965	21.3	658	17.8	490	24.1	2817	18.0
15	3957	27.7	652	24.8	488	31.1	2817	21.1
16	3934	31.6	635	27.7	483	36.0	2816	23.0
17	3874	34.5	598	27.8	462	40.9	2814	24.1
18	3738	36.7	574	29.3	426	43.7	2738	25.6
19	3507	37.5	544	29.0	389	45.0	2574	26.7
20	3203	36.7	516	28.9	348	43.4	2339	27.6
21	2830	37.0	492	29.1	305	43.6	2033	28.6
22	2428	37.1	473	29.0	283	43.5	1672	29.8
23	2113	37.3	458	29.0	258	43.4	1397	31.5
24	1822	36.5	438	29.2	232	41.8	1152	32.1
25	1636	35.4	418	28.0	216	42.1	1002	33.0
26	1493	35.6	407	28.0	202	42.6	884	32.9
27	1358	35.6	393	28.5	191	41.9	774	33.7
28	1252	35.5	379	28.2	174	42.0	699	33.9
29	1143	33.7	355	27.3	154	39.0	634	33.6
30	1049	32.4	339	26.5	137	38.7	573	33.7
31	973	31.3	319	25.4	125	36.8	529	34.2
32	915	30.5	307	26.1	116	34.5	492	32.9
33	856	31.0	295	25.4	113	36.3	448	33.9
34	804	29.9	287	23.7	105	35.2	412	34.7
35	747	27.5	273	22.3	92	33.7	382	34.0
36	703	27.2	260	22.7	87	32.2	356	33.7
37	641	26.1	242	21.9	76	30.3	323	33.4
38	611	25.4	234	20.9	70	30.0	307	33.2
39	556	25.3	212	20.8	64	29.7	280	33.6
40	509	25.0	194	21.6	58	29.3	257	32.7
41	474	23.3	183	20.2	53	26.4	238	31.9
42	445	23.3	174	19.5	50	28.0	221	31.2
43	399	22.9	159	20.1			192	32.8
44	369	23.5	146	21.9			177	31.1
45	340	22.9	135	21.5			161	32.9

Table 139. Accumulative incidence data on total homosexual outlet

Covering the life span, including pre-marital, extra-marital, and post-marital experience. In three educational levels, and in the total population corrected for the U. S. Census of 1940.

These figures are, of course, considerably higher than any which have previously been estimated; but as already shown (Chapter 4) they must be understatements, if they are anything other than the fact.

We ourselves were totally unprepared to find such incidence data when this research was originally undertaken. Over a period of several years we were repeatedly assailed with doubts as to whether we were getting a fair cross section of the total population or whether a selection of cases was biasing the results. It has been our experience, however, that each new group into which we have gone has provided substantially the same data.

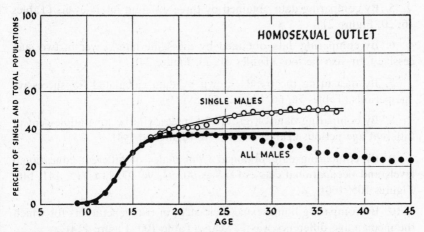

Figure 156. Homosexual outlet: accumulative incidence in total U. S. population and in single population alone

Black line shows percent of total population which has ever had homosexual experience by each of the indicated ages. Hollow line shows percent of the population of single males which has ever had experience. All data corrected for U. S. Census distribution. The incidence for the total population is lower than the incidence for the single population because the males who marry have less homosexual experience and bring down the averages when they are included in the calculations with the single males.

Whether the histories were taken in one large city or another, whether they were taken in large cities, in small towns, or in rural areas, whether they came from one college or from another, a church school or a state university or some private institution, whether they came from one part of the country or from another, the incidence data on the homosexual have been more or less the same.

While the validity of the data on all of the sexual outlets has been tested and retested throughout the study (Chapters 3 and 4), especial attention has been given to testing the material on the homosexual. This means, specifically, that we have checked these homosexual data in the following ways:

1. By comparing samples of various size, taken by a strict randomization out of the whole of the accumulation of histories (Tables 2, 155–162, Figure 4).

2. By carefully providing cross-checks and other techniques in the interviewing which would check memory and the accuracy of the data (Chapters 2, 4).

3. By comparing data obtained from hundred percent and partial samples (Tables 3, 6, Figure 13).

4. By comparing data on originals and re-takes of histories (Table 13).

5. By comparing data obtained by three different interviewers (Tables 16, 20, Figure 21).

6. By comparing data obtained by the same interviewer in two successive four-year periods (Tables 21, 23, Figure 24).

7. By measuring the trends shown by data calculated for successive age periods (Tables 58, 66, Figures 83–88).

8. By comparing data on groups of males who became adolescent at different age periods (Tables 68, 77–78, Figures 91, 94).

9. By comparing data obtained from males of different educational levels and occupational classes (Tables 90, 94, 96–97, 114–115, 141–146, Figures 105–106).

10. By comparing homosexual incidences in two generations for which the median age difference was 22 years (Table 100, Figure 114).

11. By comparing the incidences in rural and in urban groups (Table 123).

12. By comparing the data on various religious groups (Table 131).

If we had arrived at the present incidence figures by a single calculation based on a single population, one might well question their validity. But the determination of the extent of the homosexual in the population is too important a matter to be settled on anything but an elaborately devised system of samples. When twelve ways of obtaining data give results that are as consistent as those which are to be found in the tables and charts listed above, there can be no question that the actual incidence of the homosexual is at least 37 and 50 per cent as given above. The tests show that the actual figures may be as much as 5 per cent higher, or still higher.

Those who have been best acquainted with the extent of homosexual activity in the population, whether through clinical contacts with homosexual patients, through homosexual acquaintances, or through their own firsthand homosexual experience, will not find it too difficult to accept the accumulative incidence figures which are arrived at here. There are many who have been aware of the fact that persons with homosexual histories are to be found in every age group, in every social level, in every conceivable occupation, in cities and on farms, and in the most remote areas in the country. They have known the homosexual in young adolescents and in persons of every other age. They have known it in single persons and in the histories of males who were married. In large city communities they know that an experienced observer may identify hundreds of persons in a day whose homosexual interests are certain. They have known the homosexuality of many persons whose histories were utterly unknown to most of their friends and acquaintances. They have repeatedly had the experience of discovering homosexual histories among

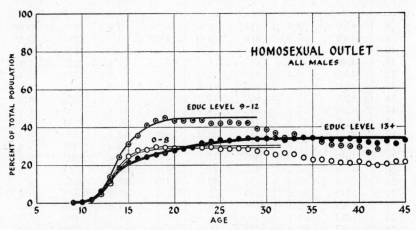

Figure 157. Homosexual outlet: accumulative incidence in total U. S. population for three educational levels

Showing percent of each population that has ever had homosexual experience by each of the indicated ages. All data based on total population, irrespective of marital status.

persons whom they had known for years before they realized that they had had anything except heterosexual experience.

On the other hand, the incidence of the homosexual is not 100 per cent, as some persons would have it. There is no doubt that there are males who have never been involved in any sexual contact with any other male, and who have never been conscious of any erotic arousal by another male. For while some of the psychoanalysts will contend to the contrary, it is to be pointed out that there are several dozen psychoanalysts who have contributed histories to this study who have insisted that they have never identified homosexual experience or reactions in their own histories.

The number of males who have any homosexual experience after the onset of adolescence (the accumulative incidence) is highest in the group that enters high school but never goes beyond in its educational career.

	PRE-MARITAL HOMOSEXUAL OUTLET: ACCUMULATIVE INCIDENCE							
AGE	TOTAL POPULATION U. S. CORRECTIONS		EDUC. LEVEL 0–8		EDUC. LEVEL 9–12		EDUC. LEVEL 13+	
	Cases	% with Exper.	Cases	% with Exper.	Cases	% with Exper.	Cases	% with Exper.
8	4301	0.0	814	0.0	632	0.0	2855	0.0
9	4301	0.1	814	0.0	632	0.2	2855	0.1
10	4301	0.4	814	0.2	632	0.5	2855	0.5
11	4300	1.8	813	1.2	632	2.1	2855	1.8
12	4300	6.4	813	5.5	632	7.0	2855	6.1
13	4299	13.1	812	11.0	632	14.6	2855	11.6
14	4296	21.5	809	17.8	632	24.5	2855	18.0
15	4289	28.0	802	24.7	632	31.6	2855	21.1
16	4261	32.1	781	28.0	626	36.7	2854	23.0
17	4177	35.8	731	28.7	596	42.8	2850	24.1
18	3981	37.8	674	30.1	535	45.4	2772	25.5
19	3657	39.8	598	30.1	457	48.6	2602	26.6
20	3238	40.3	518	31.7	376	48.4	2344	27.4
21	2782	40.4	456	32.0	312	48.1	2014	28.5
22	2233	40.6	367	32.7	251	47.8	1615	29.8
23	1795	42.1	298	35.9	215	48.4	1282	31.2
24	1433	44.1	260	36.5	178	51.7	995	31.2
25	1157	44.4	221	38.0	154	53.2	782	33.0
26	945	46.9	189	42.3	135	54.8	621	33.7
27	736	48.1	171	45.0	119	54.6	446	35.0
28	593	48.9	150	47.3	105	53.3	338	38.8
29	491	48.0	131	45.8	91	52.7	269	38.7
30	397	48.1	117	45.3	72	54.2	208	40.4
31	324	48.6	99	45.5	64	54.7	161	41.6
32	281	50.2	93	46.2	56	57.1	132	43.9
33	242	49.7	80	45.0			113	44.2
34	207	50.9	75	42.7			90	46.7
35	180	49.8	70	40.0			76	47.4
36	163	50.5	69	40.6			66	50.0
37	141	48.8	62	40.3			56	55.4
38	132	53.7	58	41.4			54	53.7
39	114	50.8	51	37.3				

Table 140. Accumulative incidence data on homosexual outlet in single males

In three educational levels, and in the total population corrected for the U. S. Census of 1940.

In that group 55 per cent of the males who are still single by 30 years of age have had the experience of being brought to climax through a physical contact with another male (Table 90). Among the boys who never go beyond grade school the corresponding figure is 45 per cent, and for the males who belong to the college level, 40 per cent. The accumulative incidence figures for the whole of the life span (Table 140, Figure 157) are a bit higher for all of these groups, inasmuch as there are some males who do not have their first homosexual experience until after they are 30 years of age.

Among single males in the population, the highest active incidence figures occur in the older age groups. Between adolescence and 15 years of age about 1 male in 4 (27%) has some homosexual experience (Table 58).

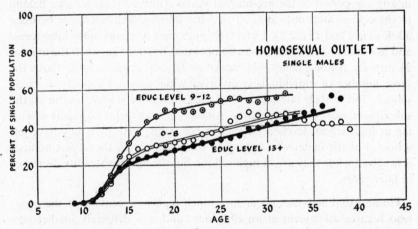

Figure 158. Homosexual outlet: accumulative incidence among single males, in three educational levels

The figures rise to nearly 1 male in 3 in the later teens and appear to drop a bit in the early twenties. Among those who are not married by the latter part of their twenties, the incidence is about 1 male in 3, and the figures increase slightly among older unmarried males (39%). There are some minor differences in the trends in the different social levels.

The drop in the active incidence figures between 21 and 25 appears so consistently through all of the calculations, that there is reason for believing that it represents an actual fact in the behavior of the population. During their late teens, many males experience considerable personal conflict over their homosexual activities, because they have become more conscious of social reactions to such contacts. Particularly in that period, many individuals attempt to stop their homosexual relations, and try to make the heterosexual adjustments which society demands. Some of these individuals are, of course, successful, but in a certain number of cases they finally reach the point, somewhere in their middle twenties, where they conclude that it is too costly to attempt to avoid the homosexual, and consciously, deliberately and sometimes publicly decide to renew such activities. Another factor which certainly contributes to the decrease in active incidence in the early twenties is the fact that heterosexually oriented males are then marrying in great numbers, and this leaves an increasingly select group at older ages in the single population.

The active incidence figures are highest among single males of the high school level (Table 90). In the late teens nearly every other male of this level (41%) is having some homosexual contact, and between the ages of 26 and 30 it is had by 46 per cent of the group. Among the males of the grade school level about 1 in 4 (22 to 27%) has any homosexual experience in any age period of the pre-marital years. Among the males who belong to the college level only about 1 in 5 has homosexual experience between adolescence and 15 (22%), 1 in 6 (16%) has such relations in the later teens, and less than 1 in 10 (10%) has homosexual relations between the ages of 21 and 25. Among males who never go beyond grade school, about the same number of individuals is involved while they are actually in grade school, during their late teens when they are out of school, and in all the subsequent years until they marry. Among the males who stop their schooling at high school levels a larger number is involved after they have left school. For the males who belong to the college level, the largest number is involved while they are in high school, but the number steadily decreases in later years.

Homosexual activities occur in a much higher percentage of the males who became adolescent at an early age; and in a definitely smaller percentage of those who became adolescent at later ages (Tables 77, 78, Figure 94). For instance, at the college level, during early adolescence about 28 per cent of the early-adolescent boys are involved, and only 14 per cent of the boys who were late in becoming adolescent. This difference is narrowed in successive age periods, but the boys who became adolescent first are more often involved even ten and fifteen years later. It is to be recalled (Chapter 9) that these early-adolescent boys are the same ones who have the highest incidences and frequencies in masturbation and in heterosexual contacts. It is the group which possesses on the whole the greatest sex drive, both in early adolescence and throughout most of the subsequent periods of their lives.

Homosexual activities occur less frequently among rural groups and more frequently among those who live in towns or cities (Table 123). On the other hand, it has already been pointed out (Chapter 12) that this is a product not only of the greater opportunity which the city may provide for certain types of homosexual contacts, but also of the generally lower rate of total outlet among males raised on the farm. It has also been pointed out that in certain of the most remote rural areas there is considerable homosexual activity among lumbermen, cattlemen, prospectors, miners, hunters, and others engaged in out-of-door occupations. The homosexual activity rarely conflicts with their heterosexual relations, and is quite without the argot, physical manifestations, and other affectations so often found in urban groups. There is a minimum of personal disturbance or social conflict over such activity. It is the type of homosexual experience which the explorer and pioneer may have had in their histories.

On the whole, homosexual contacts occur most frequently among the males who are not particularly active in their church connections. They occur less frequently among devout Catholics, Orthodox Jewish groups, and Protestants who are active in the church. The differences are not always great, but lie constantly in the same direction.

Among married males the highest incidences of homosexual activity appear to occur between the ages of 16 and 25, when nearly 10 per cent of the total population of married males (U.S. Correction) is involved (Table 66, Figure 85). The available data seem to indicate that the percentage steadily drops with advancing age, but we have already suggested that these figures are probably unreliable. Younger, unmarried males have regularly given us some record of sexual contacts with older, married males.

Many married males with homosexual experience currently in their histories have, undoubtedly, avoided us, and it has usually been impossible to secure hundred percent groups of older married males, especially from males of assured social position, primarily because of the extra-marital intercourse which they often have, and sometimes because some of them have active homosexual histories. About 10 per cent of the lower level married males have admitted homosexual experience between the ages of 16 and 20. About 13 per cent of the high school level has admitted such experience after marriage and between the ages of 21 and 25. Only 3 per cent of the married males of college level have admitted homosexual experience after marriage—mostly between the ages of 31 and 35. It has been impossible to calculate accumulative incidence figures for these several groups, but they must lie well above the active incidence figures just cited.

Finally, it should be noted that there is no evidence that the homosexual involves more males or, for that matter, fewer males today than it did among older generations, at least as far back as the specific record in the present study goes (Chapter 11, Tables 100, 104, Figure 112).

FREQUENCIES

Since the incidence of the homosexual is high, and since it accounts for only 8 to 16 per cent of the total orgasms of the unmarried males (Tables 66, 96, 97, Figures 84, 126, 128-130) and for a rather insignificant portion of the outlet of the married males (Figures 131-133), it is obvious that the mean frequencies must be low in the population as a whole. Even when the calculations are confined to those males who are having actual experience, the average frequencies are never high.

These low rates are in striking discord with the fact that homosexual contacts could in actuality be had more abundantly than heterosexual contacts, if there were no social restraints or personal conflicts involved. The sexual possibilities of the average male in his teens or twenties are probably more often assayed by males than by females, and younger males who are attractive physically or who have attractive personalities may be approached for homosexual relations more often than they themselves would ever approach females for heterosexual relations. A homosexually experienced male could undoubtedly find a larger number of sexual partners among males than a heterosexually experienced male could find among females. It is, of course, only the experienced male who understands that homosexual contacts are so freely available. The considerable taboo which society places upon these activities and upon their open discussion leaves most people in ignorance of the channels through which homosexual contacts are made; and even among males who desire homosexual relations, there are only a relatively few who have any knowledge of how to find them in abundance. Consequently, many homosexual individuals may go for months and even for years at a stretch without a single contact which is carried through to orgasm.

The heterosexual male finds a regular outlet if he locates a single female who is acceptable as a wife in marriage. The homosexual male is more often concerned with finding a succession of partners, no one of whom will provide more than a few contacts, or perhaps not more than a single contact. Some promiscuous males with homosexual histories become so interested in the thrill of conquest, and in the variety of partners and in the variety of genital experiences that may be had, that they deliberately turn down opportunities for repetitions of contacts with any one person. This necessity for finding new partners may result in their going for some days or weeks without sexual relations.

Even the most experienced homosexual males may be inhibited from making all the contacts that are available because of preferences for particular sorts of partners. A male who has highly developed esthetic tastes, one who is emotionally very sensitive, one who over-reacts to situations which do not entirely please him, one who develops a preference for a partner of a particular age or a particular social level, of a particular height or weight, with hair of a particular color, with particular genital qualities, or with other particular physical aspects—a male who refuses to have sexual relations except under particular circumstances, at particular hours of the day, and in particular sorts of environments—may turn down hundreds of opportunities for contacts before he finds the one individual with whom he accepts a relation.

Many of the males who have homosexual histories are acutely aware that they are transgressing social custom and engaging in activity which has a certain amount of peril attached to it if it becomes known to the society in which they live. Consequently, many such males become over-sensitive to the precise situations under which they accept relationships. All of these handicaps make for discord between homosexual partners, and this lessens the number of opportunities for successful relations.

Long-time relationships between two males are notably few. Long-time relationships in the heterosexual would probably be less frequent than they are, if there were no social custom or legal restraints to enforce continued relationships in marriage. But without such outside pressures to preserve homosexual relations, and with personal and social conflicts continually disturbing them, relationships between two males rarely survive the first disagreements.

There are some males whose homosexuality is undoubtedly the product of inherent or acquired timidity or other personality traits which make it difficult for them to approach other persons for any sort of social contact. Such males find it easier to make contacts with individuals of their own sex. Their homosexuality may be the direct outcome of their social inadequacies. Even with their own sex, however, these timid individuals may find it very difficult to approach strangers. They may resort to taverns, clubs, and other places where they know that homosexual contacts may be easily obtained, but are likely to go alone, and may go regularly for weeks and months without speaking to anyone in the assemblage. The low rates of outlet of some of these individuals are as extreme as any in the whole male population.

There are some males who are primarily or even exclusively homosexual in their psychic responses, but who may completely abstain from overt relations for moral reasons or for fear of social difficulties. Left without any socio-sexual contacts, some of these persons have essentially no outlet, and some of them are, therefore, very badly upset.

For these several reasons, average frequencies among males with homosexual histories are usually low, and there are very few high frequencies. In any particular age group, in any segment of the population, it is never more than about 5.5 per cent of the males who are having homosexual relations that average more than once every other day (3.5 per week). Calculating only for the males who actually have homosexual experience, there are never more than 5.2 per cent that have frequencies averaging more than 6.0 per week during their most active years. Considering that it is 25 per cent of the entire population which has total sexual outlets which

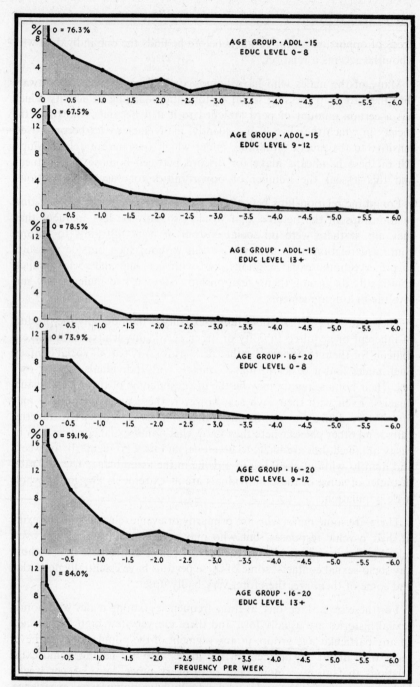

Figure 159. Homosexual outlet: individual variation in frequencies, among single males, at ages adolescent–15 and 16–20, for three educational levels

Showing percent of each population (vertical line) which has homosexual experience with each type of frequency (horizontal line).

634

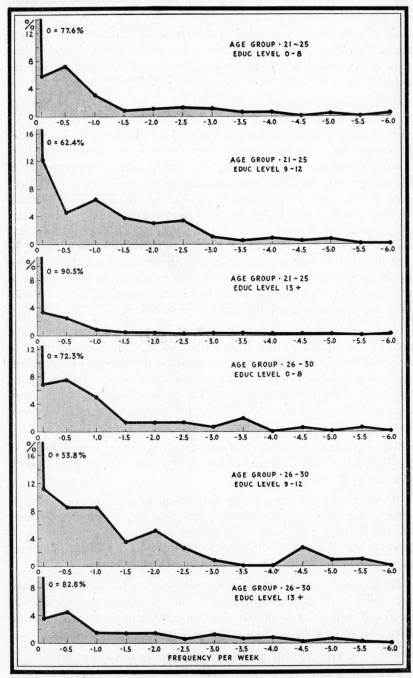

Figure 160. Homosexual outlet: individual variation in frequencies among single males, at ages 21–25 and 26–30, for three educational levels

Showing percent of each population (vertical line) which has homosexual experience with each type of frequency (horizontal line).

average more than 3.5 per week, and considering that 24 per cent of the married males have outlets that average more than 6.0 per week in their most active period, it is apparent that outlets from the homosexual are definitely low.

Among single males who are having homosexual experience the average frequencies rise from 0.8 per week in early adolescence to about 1.3 per week at age 25 and 1.7 per week by age 35 (Table 58). Since the frequencies of total sexual outlet steadily decrease with advancing age (Chapter 7), it is to be noted that the homosexual supplies an increasing proportion of the orgasms for the single males who are having such contacts: 17.5 per cent of the orgasms in early adolescence, 30.3 per cent in the early twenties, 40.4 per cent by age 40 (Table 58). This increased dependence of this older male upon his homosexual outlet parallels the increased dependence which the heterosexual male places upon coitus as a source of outlet (Chapter 7). The situation is, however, accentuated in the case of the homosexual because the younger male may be restrained by considerable doubts as to the advisability of continuing in a socially taboo activity (Figures 162–167). See the discussion in this chapter on *Incidences*.

The frequencies of homosexual contacts differ considerably at different social levels (Tables 90, 114, Figure 105). The least frequent activity is to be found in the college level. Comparing active populations of college and high school levels, there is 50 to 100 per cent more frequent activity among the males of the high school group. The grade school level stands intermediate between the other two groups. The differences between the social levels are most marked in the early age periods.

The considerable amount of homosexual experience among males of the high school level is a matter for especial note. See the discussion in Chapter 10 (p. 384).

Between rural and urban groups the frequencies of homosexual contacts differ in the same way that the incidences differ (*cf.* above). The contacts are less frequent among the farm boys of grade school and high school level (Table 123); but for the college level there are almost no differences between the two groups (Chapter 12).

Homosexual contacts, among those males who are having such relations, occur less frequently (in most groups) among persons who are actively interested in the church (Table 131), more frequently among those who have least to do with religious activities (Chapter 13).

THE HETEROSEXUAL-HOMOSEXUAL BALANCE

Concerning patterns of sexual behavior, a great deal of the thinking done by scientists and laymen alike stems from the assumption that there are persons who are "heterosexual" and persons who are "homosexual," that these two types represent antitheses in the sexual world, and that there is only an insignificant class of "bisexuals" who occupy an inter-mediate position between the other groups. It is implied that every in-dividual is innately—inherently—either heterosexual or homosexual. It is further implied that from the time of birth one is fated to be one thing or the other, and that there is little chance for one to change his pattern in the course of a lifetime.

It is quite generally believed that one's preference for a sexual partner of one or the other sex is correlated with various physical and mental qualities, and with the total personality which makes a homosexual male or female physically, psychically, and perhaps spiritually distinct from a heterosexual individual. It is generally thought that these qualities make a homosexual person obvious and recognizable to any one who has a sufficient understanding of such matters. Even psychiatrists discuss "the homosexual personality" and many of them believe that preferences for sexual partners of a particular sex are merely secondary manifestations of something that lies much deeper in the totality of that intangible which they call the personality.

It is commonly believed, for instance, that homosexual males are rarely robust physically, are uncoordinated or delicate in their movements, or perhaps graceful enough but not strong and vigorous in their physical expression. Fine skins, high-pitched voices, obvious hand movements, a feminine carriage of the hips, and peculiarities of walking gaits are sup-posed accompaniments of a preference for a male as a sexual partner. It is commonly believed that the homosexual male is artistically sensitive, emotionally unbalanced, temperamental to the point of being unpredict-able, difficult to get along with, and undependable in meeting specific obligations. In physical characters there have been attempts to show that the homosexual male has a considerable crop of hair and less often be-comes bald, has teeth which are more like those of the female, a broader pelvis, larger genitalia, and a tendency toward being fat, and that he lacks a linea alba. The homosexual male is supposed to be less interested in athletics, more often interested in music and the arts, more often engaged in such occupations as bookkeeping, dress design, window display, hair-dressing, acting, radio work, nursing, religious service, and social work. The converse to all of these is supposed to represent the typical hetero-sexual male. Many a clinician attaches considerable weight to these things in diagnosing the basic heterosexuality or homosexuality of his patients. The characterizations are so distinct that they seem to leave little room for doubt that homosexual and heterosexual represent two very distinct types of males.

The Terman-Miles scale for determining the degree of masculinity or femininity of an individual (Terman and Miles 1936) is largely based upon these preconceptions. Some other psychology scales have utilized very much the same principles. While these scales have made it more apparent that there may be gradations between exclusively heterosexual and exclusively homosexual individuals, or between the extremes of masculinity and the extremes of femininity, the implication is always present that an individual's choice of a sexual partner is closely related to the masculinity or femininity of his personality.

It should be pointed out that scientific judgments on this point have been based on little more than the same sorts of impressions which the general public has had concerning homosexual persons. But before any sufficient

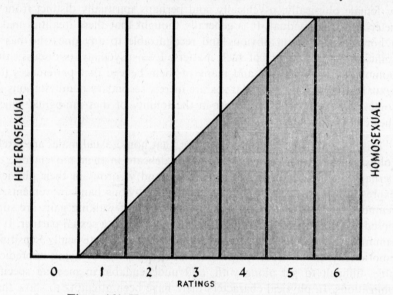

Figure 161. Heterosexual-homosexual rating scale

Based on both psychologic reactions and overt experience, individuals rate as follows:

0. Exclusively heterosexual with no homosexual
1. Predominantly heterosexual, only incidentally homosexual
2. Predominantly heterosexual, but more than incidentally homosexual
3. Equally heterosexual and homosexual
4. Predominantly homosexual, but more than incidentally heterosexual
5. Predominantly homosexual, but incidentally heterosexual
6. Exclusively homosexual

study can be made of such possible correlations between patterns of sexual behavior and other qualities in the individual, it is necessary to understand the incidences and frequencies of the homosexual in the population as a whole, and the relation of the homosexual activity to the rest of the sexual pattern in each individual's history.

The histories which have been available in the present study make it apparent that the heterosexuality or homosexuality of many individuals is not an all-or-none proposition. It is true that there are persons in the population whose histories are exclusively heterosexual, both in regard to their overt experience and in regard to their psychic reactions. And there are individuals in the population whose histories are exclusively homosexual, both in experience and in psychic reactions. But the record also shows that there is a considerable portion of the population whose members have combined, within their individual histories, both homosexual and hetero-sexual experience and/or psychic responses. There are some whose hetero-sexual experiences predominate, there are some whose homosexual ex-periences predominate, there are some who have had quite equal amounts of both types of experience.

Some of the males who are involved in one type of relation at one period in their lives, may have only the other type of relation at some later period. There may be considerable fluctuation of patterns from time to time. Some males may be involved in both heterosexual and homosexual activities within the same period of time. For instance, there are some who engage in both heterosexual and homosexual activities in the same year, or in the same month or week, or even in the same day. There are not a few indi-viduals who engage in group activities in which they may make simulta-neous contact with partners of both sexes.

Males do not represent two discrete populations, heterosexual and homosexual. The world is not to be divided into sheep and goats. Not all things are black nor all things white. It is a fundamental of taxonomy that nature rarely deals with discrete categories. Only the human mind invents categories and tries to force facts into separated pigeon-holes. The living world is a continuum in each and every one of its aspects. The sooner we learn this concerning human sexual behavior the sooner we shall reach a sound understanding of the realities of sex.

While emphasizing the continuity of the gradations between exclusively heterosexual and exclusively homosexual histories, it has seemed desirable to develop some sort of classification which could be based on the relative amounts of heterosexual and of homosexual experience or response in each history. Such a heterosexual-homosexual rating scale is shown in Figure 161. An individual may be assigned a position on this scale, for each age period in his life, in accordance with the following definitions of the various points on the scale:

0. Individuals are rated as **0's** if they make no physical contacts which result in erotic arousal or orgasm, and make no psychic responses to individuals of their own sex. Their socio-sexual contacts and responses are exclusively with individuals of the opposite sex.

1. Individuals are rated as **1's** if they have only incidental homosexual con-tacts which have involved physical or psychic response, or incidental psychic responses without physical contact. The great preponderance of their socio-sexual experience and reactions is directed toward individuals of the opposite sex. Such homosexual experiences as these individuals have may occur only a single

AGE	CASES	HETEROSEXUAL-HOMOSEXUAL RATING: ACTIVE INCIDENCE SINGLE WHITE MALES—EDUC. LEVEL 0-8							
		X	0	1	2	3	4	5	6
		%	%	%	%	%	%	%	%
5	820	92.6	2.3	0.1	0.4	1.5	0.2	0.1	2.8
6	820	87.1	2.9	0.5	1.2	2.8	0.2	0.1	5.2
7	819	81.8	4.2	1.5	2.2	3.2	0.9	0.2	6.0
8	819	73.7	6.2	1.8	3.5	4.3	0.7	0.4	9.4
9	819	70.5	6.6	1.8	4.3	4.6	0.7	0.5	11.0
10	819	62.9	8.5	2.2	5.1	5.9	1.0	0.5	13.9
11	818	59.9	10.0	2.3	5.4	6.4	1.1	0.5	14.4
12	815	54.1	13.3	2.8	6.5	7.1	1.2	0.6	14.4
13	814	49.8	20.8	2.3	5.7	6.0	1.6	0.9	12.9
14	811	41.2	31.4	1.7	5.3	6.3	2.1	1.4	10.6
15	803	32.0	42.1	2.7	6.2	5.1	2.7	1.5	7.7
16	774	24.1	50.1	3.7	7.6	5.0	3.1	1.4	5.0
17	708	17.5	56.4	4.0	8.1	5.1	3.1	1.4	4.4
18	635	11.5	61.6	4.6	7.9	5.7	2.4	1.7	4.6
19	550	10.7	62.5	4.5	8.0	6.0	2.5	1.3	4.5
20	473	9.3	65.1	3.2	7.6	5.7	2.5	1.5	5.1
21	386	8.8	63.0	4.1	7.8	6.7	2.9	2.3	4.4
22	306	7.8	63.9	4.2	6.9	7.8	2.6	2.6	4.2
23	269	8.2	61.7	4.5	8.2	7.4	3.3	2.6	4.1
24	231	6.1	62.3	4.3	9.1	8.2	3.5	1.3	5.2
25	187	4.8	59.9	7.0	9.1	9.1	3.2	1.6	5.3
26	172	2.3	60.5	5.8	9.9	10.5	3.5	1.7	5.8
27	152	2.6	57.3	7.2	10.5	11.2	3.3	2.6	5.3
28	134	2.2	55.3	6.0	11.2	13.4	3.7	1.5	6.7
29	121	2.5	54.5	5.8	12.4	13.2	4.1	1.7	5.8
30	107	1.9	53.2	6.5	11.2	13.1	4.7	1.9	7.5
31	95	2.1	54.7	5.3	8.4	11.6	7.4	4.2	6.3
32	87	2.3	54.2	5.7	8.0	11.5	5.7	4.6	8.0
33	78	2.6	56.4	5.1	10.3	11.5	2.6	5.1	6.4
34	72	2.8	58.2	1.4	11.1	12.5	2.8	5.6	5.6
35	68	2.9	58.8	1.5	11.8	13.2	1.5	5.9	4.4
36	65	3.1	58.5	1.5	10.8	13.8	1.5	4.6	6.2
37	59	1.7	57.5	1.7	11.9	15.3	1.7	3.4	6.8
38	57	1.8	57.8	1.8	12.3	15.8	0.0	3.5	7.0
39	50	2.0	64.0	2.0	8.0	18.0	0.0	0.0	6.0

Table 141. Heterosexual-homosexual ratings for single white males of grade school level (0–8)

These are active incidence figures for each rating at each age. For an explanation of the meanings of the ratings X, 0, 1, etc., see the accompanying text. If the percentages are added from the right-hand side of each line, the cumulated percents will show the portion of the population which rates 1 or more, or 2 or more, etc., in each age period.

time or two, or at least infrequently in comparison to the amount of their hetero-sexual experience. Their homosexual experiences never involve as specific psychic reactions as they make to heterosexual stimuli. Sometimes the homosexual activities in which they engage may be inspired by curiosity, or may be more or less forced upon them by other individuals, perhaps when they are asleep or when they are drunk, or under some other peculiar circumstance.

2. Individuals are rated as **2's** if they have more than incidental homosexual experience, and/or if they respond rather definitely to homosexual stimuli. Their heterosexual experiences and/or reactions still surpass their homosexual experi-ences and/or reactions. These individuals may have only a small amount of homosexual experience or they may have a considerable amount of it, but in every case it is surpassed by the amount of heterosexual experience that they have within the same period of time. They usually recognize their quite specific arousal by homosexual stimuli, but their responses to the opposite sex are still stronger. A few of these individuals may even have all of their overt experience in the homosexual, but their psychic reactions to persons of the opposite sex indicate that they are still predominantly heterosexual. This latter situation is most often found among younger males who have not yet ventured to have actual intercourse with girls, while their orientation is definitely heterosexual. On the other hand, there are some males who should be rated as 2's because of their strong reactions to individuals of their own sex, even though they have never had overt relations with them.

3. Individuals who are rated **3's** stand midway on the heterosexual-homo-sexual scale. They are about equally homosexual and heterosexual in their overt experience and/or their psychic reactions. In general, they accept and equally enjoy both types of contacts, and have no strong preferences for one or the other. Some persons are rated 3's, even though they may have a larger amount of experience of one sort, because they respond psychically to partners of both sexes, and it is only a matter of circumstance that brings them into more frequent contact with one of the sexes. Such a situation is not unusual among single males, for male contacts are often more available to them than female contacts. Married males, on the other hand, find it simpler to secure a sexual outlet through intercourse with their wives, even though some of them may be as interested in males as they are in females.

4. Individuals are rated as **4's** if they have more overt activity and/or psychic reactions in the homosexual, while still maintaining a fair amount of hetero-sexual activity and/or responding rather definitely to heterosexual stimuli.

5. Individuals are rated **5's** if they are almost entirely homosexual in their overt activities and/or reactions. They do have incidental experience with the opposite sex and sometimes react psychically to individuals of the opposite sex.

6. Individuals are rated as **6's** if they are exclusively homosexual, both in regard to their overt experience and in regard to their psychic reactions.

It will be observed that this is a seven-point scale, with 0 and 6 as the extreme points, and with 3 as the midpoint in the classification. On opposite sides of the midpoint the following relations hold:

> 0 is the opposite of 6
> 1 is the opposite of 5
> 2 is the opposite of 4

AGE	CASES	HETEROSEXUAL-HOMOSEXUAL RATING: ACTIVE INCIDENCE SINGLE WHITE MALES—EDUC. LEVEL 9–12							
		X	0	1	2	3	4	5	6
		%	%	%	%	%	%	%	%
5	631	90.8	4.4	0.3	0.3	0.8	0.3	0.2	2.9
6	631	83.0	7.4	0.8	0.8	2.2	0.5	0.2	5.1
7	631	77.7	9.0	1.1	1.7	3.0	1.1	0.2	6.2
8	631	72.0	10.9	1.0	2.2	3.6	1.1	0.3	8.9
9	631	68.7	9.7	1.1	2.7	4.8	1.1	0.3	11.6
10	631	59.3	11.9	1.7	3.2	5.5	1.4	0.5	16.5
11	631	56.0	12.7	3.2	4.1	5.5	1.4	1.1	16.0
12	631	46.1	18.9	4.0	5.5	6.0	2.2	1.1	16.2
13	631	40.3	26.1	4.0	5.2	6.0	2.2	1.6	14.6
14	631	27.9	40.5	3.6	5.5	4.8	3.0	3.0	11.7
15	629	19.9	48.6	4.3	6.5	4.8	4.6	3.5	7.8
16	619	9.7	56.6	6.5	8.1	4.7	4.7	3.6	6.5
17	577	4.9	56.2	7.3	11.1	4.5	5.2	4.0	6.8
18	502	3.0	57.0	6.6	10.8	6.0	5.4	4.6	7.0
19	420	2.4	55.2	6.9	11.7	5.0	5.2	6.0	7.6
20	350	2.0	57.0	5.4	10.9	4.6	4.9	6.6	8.6
21	274	1.5	56.9	6.6	8.8	3.6	5.8	7.3	9.5
22	232	1.7	56.5	6.9	8.2	3.9	5.2	7.3	10.3
23	197	1.5	55.4	7.1	6.1	5.1	7.1	9.1	8.6
24	166	1.8	51.4	7.8	6.6	6.0	8.4	8.4	9.6
25	140	0.7	50.8	6.4	5.7	5.7	9.3	10.7	10.7
26	125	1.6	50.4	6.4	5.6	2.4	10.4	9.6	13.6
27	113	0.9	52.3	6.2	4.4	3.5	8.8	9.7	14.2
28	97	1.0	52.5	5.2	2.1	3.1	12.4	9.3	14.4
29	82	1.2	48.8	7.3	2.4	3.7	11.0	8.5	17.1
30	67	1.5	46.2	9.0	3.0	3.0	10.4	9.0	17.9
31	58	0.0	48.3	6.9	5.2	3.4	6.9	8.6	20.7

Table 142. Heterosexual-homosexual ratings for single white males of high school level (9–12)

These are active incidence figures for each rating at each age. For an explanation of the meanings of the ratings X, 0, 1, etc., see the accompanying text. If the percentages are added from the right-hand side of each line, the cumulated percents will show the portion of the population which rates 1 or more, or 2 or more, etc., in each age period.

AGE	CASES	HETEROSEXUAL-HOMOSEXUAL RATING: ACTIVE INCIDENCE SINGLE WHITE MALES—EDUC. LEVEL 13+							
		X	0	1	2	3	4	5	6
		%	%	%	%	%	%	%	%
5	2846	85.8	7.3	0.2	0.2	2.2	0.6	0.2	3.5
6	2846	82.5	7.7	0.3	0.6	3.0	0.7	0.2	5.0
7	2846	79.5	8.0	0.3	0.7	3.1	1.0	0.5	6.9
8	2846	73.1	9.5	0.5	1.2	4.1	1.2	0.6	9.8
9	2846	72.2	9.1	0.6	1.3	4.3	1.3	0.6	10.6
10	2846	63.9	11.3	0.9	1.9	5.5	1.7	0.7	14.1
11	2846	61.7	12.4	1.1	2.1	5.0	1.9	0.8	15.0
12	2846	51.5	19.7	1.4	2.5	5.2	2.4	1.0	16.3
13	2846	42.5	31.8	1.9	2.5	5.1	3.0	1.4	11.8
14	2846	30.0	47.6	3.0	3.0	3.7	3.0	1.5	8.2
15	2846	22.3	59.1	3.3	2.9	2.8	2.7	1.4	5.5
16	2843	13.8	68.9	4.0	3.0	2.5	2.5	1.7	3.6
17	2839	8.9	75.7	3.9	2.8	2.0	2.2	1.7	2.8
18	2755	5.7	79.5	4.8	2.5	1.6	1.8	1.8	2.3
19	2579	4.3	81.0	5.2	2.3	1.6	1.8	1.8	2.2
20	2306	3.9	80.6	5.6	2.6	1.3	1.8	1.9	2.3
21	1961	3.6	81.4	5.2	2.5	1.0	1.9	2.0	2.4
22	1527	3.2	80.4	5.4	2.3	1.0	2.2	2.4	3.1
23	1201	2.9	80.5	4.5	2.2	0.9	2.4	2.9	3.7
24	895	3.2	77.5	5.1	2.1	1.3	3.4	3.0	4.4
25	687	3.3	75.5	5.5	2.3	1.3	3.3	4.1	4.7
26	517	3.7	71.9	5.8	2.9	1.4	3.1	5.0	6.2
27	381	3.7	68.3	7.1	1.8	1.3	3.9	5.5	8.4
28	303	4.3	67.0	6.6	0.3	1.7	3.6	6.6	9.9
29	240	4.2	67.4	5.0	0.4	1.3	2.1	7.5	12.1
30	179	4.5	64.7	4.5	0.6	0.6	2.8	9.5	12.8
31	140	5.7	64.9	3.6	0.7	0.0	2.9	7.9	14.3
32	119	6.7	63.1	4.2	0.8	0.0	3.4	8.4	13.4
33	100	7.0	59.0	5.0	1.0	0.0	4.0	7.0	17.0
34	80	6.3	56.2	5.0	0.0	0.0	5.0	7.5	20.0
35	71	7.0	55.0	5.6	0.0	1.4	2.8	8.5	19.7
36	58	6.9	48.4	5.2	0.0	1.7	3.4	10.3	24.1
37	56	7.1	48.2	5.4	0.0	1.8	3.6	10.7	23.2
38	51	5.9	51.0	3.9	0.0	0.0	3.9	9.8	25.5

Table 143. Heterosexual-homosexual ratings for single white males of college level (13 +)

These are active incidence figures for each rating at each age. For an explanation of the meanings of the ratings X, 0, 1, etc., see the accompanying text. If the percentages are added from the right-hand side of each line, the cumulated percents will show the portion of the population which rates 1 or more, or 2 or more, etc., in each age period.

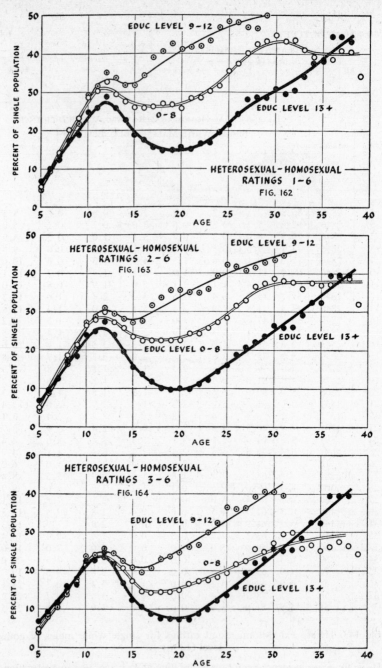

Figures 162–164. Active incidence curves: heterosexual-homosexual ratings, by age and educational level, among single males

Top figure, 162, shows percent of single males who have at least incidental (or more) homosexual reactions or experience (ratings 1–6) in each year. Middle figure, 163, shows percent of single males who have more than incidental homosexual reactions or experience (ratings 2–6). Bottom figure, 164, shows percent of single males who have as much as or more homosexual than heterosexual reactions or experience (ratings 3–6), in each year.

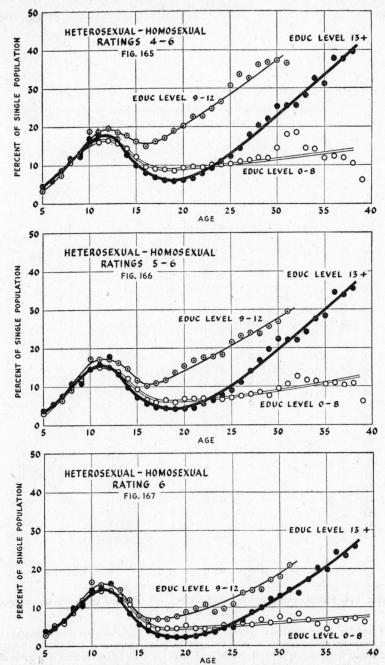

Figures 165–167. Active incidence curves: heterosexual-homosexual ratings, by age and educational level, among single males

Top figure, 165, shows percent of single males who have more homosexual than heterosexual reactions or experience (ratings 4–6) in each year. Middle figure, 166, shows percent of single males who have more or less exclusively homosexual reactions or experience (ratings 5–6). Bottom figure, 167, shows percent of single males who are exclusively homosexual (rating 6) in each year.

AGE	CASES	HETEROSEXUAL-HOMOSEXUAL RATING: ACTIVE INCIDENCE MARRIED WHITE MALES—EDUC. LEVEL 0-8					
		X	0	1	2	3	4
		%	%	%	%	%	%
18	68	0.0	85.3	4.4	7.4	2.9	0.0
19	103	0.0	91.3	1.9	3.9	2.9	0.0
20	134	0.0	90.3	2.2	3.0	4.5	0.0
21	181	0.0	90.1	2.2	5.5	2.2	0.0
22	223	0.0	88.8	3.6	5.8	1.8	0.0
23	222	0.0	91.8	2.3	4.1	1.8	0.0
24	228	0.0	91.2	3.1	3.5	2.2	0.0
25	238	0.0	92.0	1.7	4.2	1.7	0.4
26	223	0.0	96.0	1.8	1.8	0.4	0.0
27	232	0.0	92.7	3.4	3.0	0.9	0.0
28	232	0.0	92.7	2.2	4.7	0.4	0.0
29	209	0.0	93.3	1.4	4.3	1.0	0.0
30	207	0.0	94.7	1.4	2.9	1.0	0.0
31	194	0.0	92.8	3.1	3.1	1.0	0.0
32	192	0.0	91.2	3.6	3.6	1.6	0.0
33	179	0.0	92.7	1.7	3.9	1.7	0.0
34	177	0.0	93.8	1.7	4.5	0.0	0.0
35	162	0.0	95.7	0.6	3.7	0.0	0.0
36	157	0.6	93.0	3.2	3.2	0.0	0.0
37	146	0.7	93.8	1.4	3.4	0.0	0.7
38	139	0.7	94.3	1.4	2.9	0.0	0.7
39	126	0.8	92.8	1.6	4.0	0.0	0.8
40	125	0.8	92.8	1.6	4.0	0.0	0.8
41	113	0.9	94.6	1.8	1.8	0.0	0.9
42	111	0.9	94.6	1.8	1.8	0.0	0.9
43	99	1.0	93.8	2.0	2.0	0.0	1.0
44	84	1.2	95.2	1.2	1.2	0.0	1.2
45	75	1.3	96.1	1.3	1.3	0.0	0.0
46	75	1.3	96.1	1.3	1.3	0.0	0.0
47	74	1.4	95.9	0.0	2.7	0.0	0.0
48	71	1.4	97.2	0.0	1.4	0.0	0.0
49	65	1.5	97.0	0.0	1.5	0.0	0.0

Table 144. Heterosexual-homosexual ratings for married white males of grade school level (0-8)

These are active incidence figures for each rating at each age. For an explanation of the meanings of the ratings X, 0, 1, etc., see the accompanying text. If the percentages are added from the right-hand side of each line, the cumulated percents will show the portion of the population which rates 1 or more, or 2 or more, etc., in each age period.

It will be observed that the rating which an individual receives has a dual basis. It takes into account his overt sexual experience and/or his psychosexual reactions. In the majority of instances the two aspects of the history parallel, but sometimes they are not in accord. In the latter case, the rating of an individual must be based upon an evaluation of the relative importance of the overt and the psychic in his history.

In each classification there are persons who have had no experience or a minimum of overt sexual experience, but in the same classification there may also be persons who have had hundreds of sexual contacts. In every case, however, all of the individuals in each classification show the same balance between the heterosexual and homosexual elements in their histories. The position of an individual on this scale is always based upon the relation of the heterosexual to the homosexual in his history, rather than upon the actual amount of overt experience or psychic reaction.

Finally, it should be emphasized again that the reality is a continuum, with individuals in the population occupying not only the seven categories which are recognized here, but every gradation between each of the categories, as well. Nevertheless, it does no great injustice to the fact to group the population as indicated above.

From all of this, it should be evident that one is not warranted in recognizing merely two types of individuals, heterosexual and homosexual, and that the characterization of the homosexual as a third sex fails to describe any actuality.

It is imperative that one understand the relative amounts of the heterosexual and homosexual in an individual's history if one is to make any significant analysis of him. Army and Navy officials and administrators in schools, prisons, and other institutions should be more concerned with the degree of heterosexuality or homosexuality in an individual than they are with the question of whether he has ever had an experience of either sort. It is obvious that the clinician must determine the balance that exists between the heterosexual and homosexual experience and reactions of his patient, before he can begin to help him. Even courts of law might well consider the totality of the individual's history, before passing judgment on the particular instance that has brought him into the hands of the law.

Everywhere in our society there is a tendency to consider an individual "homosexual" if he is known to have had a single experience with another individual of his own sex. Under the law an individual may receive the same penalty for a single homosexual experience that he would for a continuous record of experiences. In penal and mental institutions a male is likely to be rated "homosexual" if he is discovered to have had a single contact with another male. In society at large, a male who has worked out

AGE	CASES	HETEROSEXUAL-HOMOSEXUAL RATING: ACTIVE INCIDENCE MARRIED WHITE MALES—EDUC. LEVEL 9–12					
		0	1	2	3	4	5
		%	%	%	%	%	%
18	51	84.3	3.9	9.8	2.0	0.0	0.0
19	73	84.9	4.1	4.1	4.1	1.4	1.4
20	84	83.2	4.8	4.8	4.8	1.2	1.2
21	99	80.0	4.0	9.0	6.0	1.0	0.0
22	101	85.1	1.0	7.9	5.0	1.0	0.0
23	104	84.7	1.9	9.6	3.8	0.0	0.0
24	102	90.2	2.0	4.9	2.9	0.0	0.0
25	107	92.5	1.9	4.7	0.9	0.0	0.0
26	107	90.6	1.9	5.6	1.9	0.0	0.0
27	99	91.0	2.0	5.0	0.0	2.0	0.0
28	96	88.5	4.2	5.2	0.0	2.1	0.0
29	90	89.0	4.4	3.3	0.0	3.3	0.0
30	80	88.7	3.8	2.5	0.0	5.0	0.0
31	79	91.2	2.5	2.5	0.0	3.8	0.0
32	74	91.7	1.4	1.4	1.4	4.1	0.0
33	69	92.9	1.4	1.4	1.4	2.9	0.0
34	63	93.6	3.2	0.0	0.0	3.2	0.0
35	58	91.5	3.4	0.0	1.7	3.4	0.0
36	58	93.2	3.4	0.0	0.0	3.4	0.0
37	53	90.5	3.8	0.0	0.0	3.8	0.0
38	50	90.0	4.0	0.0	0.0	4.0	0.0

Table 145. Heterosexual-homosexual ratings for married white males of high school level (9–12)

These are active incidence figures for each rating at each age. For an explanation of the meanings of the ratings 0, 1, etc., see the accompanying text. If the percentages are added from the right-hand side of each line, the cumulated percents will show the portion of the population which rates 1 or more, or 2 or more, etc., in each age period.

AGE	CASES	HETEROSEXUAL-HOMOSEXUAL RATING: ACTIVE INCIDENCE MARRIED WHITE MALES—EDUC. LEVEL 13+							
		X	0	1	2	3	4	5	6
		%	%	%	%	%	%	%	%
20	59	0.0	96.6	0.0	3.4	0.0	0.0	0.0	0.0
21	97	0.0	91.7	5.2	2.1	1.0	0.0	0.0	0.0
22	172	0.0	90.1	5.8	2.3	0.6	0.0	1.2	0.0
23	221	0.0	90.9	4.5	1.8	1.4	0.9	0.5	0.0
24	278	0.4	91.9	3.6	2.2	0.7	0.4	0.4	0.4
25	330	0.0	91.3	4.8	1.8	0.9	0.6	0.3	0.3
26	378	0.0	93.4	4.2	0.8	0.5	0.5	0.3	0.3
27	391	0.0	91.5	5.9	0.5	0.8	0.3	0.5	0.5
28	392	0.0	90.0	5.9	1.5	1.3	0.3	0.5	0.5
29	385	0.0	90.4	6.2	1.6	1.0	0.3	0.5	0.0
30	386	0.0	89.9	7.3	1.0	0.8	0.5	0.5	0.0
31	387	0.0	91.0	5.9	1.1	0.8	0.8	0.5	0.0
32	366	0.0	90.7	6.6	1.1	0.8	0.5	0.0	0.0
33	340	0.0	91.1	5.9	1.8	0.6	0.6	0.0	0.0
34	323	0.0	89.8	7.1	1.9	0.6	0.6	0.0	0.0
35	300	0.0	90.2	5.7	2.7	0.7	0.7	0.0	0.0
36	283	0.0	90.5	5.3	2.8	0.7	0.7	0.0	0.0
37	248	0.0	90.8	4.8	2.8	0.8	0.8	0.0	0.0
38	235	0.0	90.1	5.1	3.0	0.9	0.9	0.0	0.0
39	218	0.0	89.0	5.5	3.2	1.4	0.9	0.0	0.0
40	205	0.0	89.2	4.9	3.4	1.5	1.0	0.0	0.0
41	190	0.0	90.5	4.7	2.6	1.1	1.1	0.0	0.0
42	182	0.0	90.2	5.5	2.7	0.5	1.1	0.0	0.0
43	154	0.6	89.7	5.8	2.6	0.0	1.3	0.0	0.0
44	145	0.7	91.0	4.1	2.8	0.0	1.4	0.0	0.0
45	128	0.8	91.3	4.7	1.6	0.0	1.6	0.0	0.0
46	117	0.9	92.2	4.3	1.7	0.0	0.9	0.0	0.0
47	113	0.9	92.0	4.4	1.8	0.0	0.9	0.0	0.0
48	97	1.0	90.7	6.2	2.1	0.0	0.0	0.0	0.0
49	93	2.2	90.2	5.4	2.2	0.0	0.0	0.0	0.0

Table 146. Heterosexual-homosexual ratings for married white males of the college level (13+)

These are active incidence figures for each rating at each age. For an explanation of the meanings of the ratings X, 0, 1, etc., see the accompanying text. If the percentages are added from the right-hand side of each line, the cumulated percents will show the portion of the population which rates 1 or more, or 2 or more, etc., in each age period.

a highly successful marital adjustment is likely to be rated "homosexual" if the community learns about a single contact that he has had with another male. All such misjudgments are the product of the tendency to categorize sexual activities under only two heads, and of a failure to recognize the endless gradations that actually exist.

From all of this, it becomes obvious that any question as to the number of persons in the world who are homosexual and the number who are heterosexual is unanswerable. It is only possible to record the number of those who belong to each of the positions on such a heterosexual-homosexual scale as is given above. Summarizing our data on the incidence of overt homosexual experience in the white male population (Tables 139–140, and Figures 156–158) and the distribution of various degrees of heterosexual-homosexual balance in that population (Tables 141–150, Figures 162–170), the following generalizations may be made:

37 per cent of the total male population has **at least some overt homosexual experience** to the point of orgasm between adolescence and old age (Figure 156). This accounts for nearly 2 males out of every 5 that one may meet.

50 per cent of the males **who remain single until age 35** have had overt homosexual experience to the point of orgasm, since the onset of adolescence (Figure 156).

58 per cent of the males who belong to the group that goes into **high school** but not beyond, **50 per cent of the grade school level**, and **47 per cent of the college level** have had homosexual experience to the point of orgasm if they remain single to the age of 35 (Figure 158).

63 per cent of all males **never have overt** homosexual experience to the point of orgasm after the onset of adolescence (Figure 156).

50 per cent of all males (approximately) **have neither overt nor psychic** experience in the homosexual after the onset of adolescence (Figures 162–167).

13 per cent of the males (approximately) **react erotically** to other males **without having overt** homosexual contacts after the onset of adolescence.

30 per cent of all males **have at least incidental homosexual experience** or reactions (*i.e.*, rate 1 to 6) over at least a three-year period between the ages of 16 and 55. This accounts for one male out of every three in the population who is past the early years of adolescence (Table 150, Figure 168).

25 per cent of the male population **has more than incidental homosexual experience** or reactions (*i.e.*, rates 2–6) for at least three years between the ages of 16 and 55. In terms of averages, one male out of approximately every four has had or will have such distinct and continued homosexual experience.

18 per cent of the males have at least **as much of the homosexual as the heterosexual** in their histories (*i.e.*, rate 3–6) for at least three years between the ages of 16 and 55. This is more than one in six of the white male population.

13 per cent of the population **has more of the homosexual than the heterosexual** (*i.e.*, rates 4–6) for at least three years between the ages of 16 and 55. This is one in eight of the white male population.

10 per cent of the males are **more or less exclusively homosexual** (*i.e.*, rate 5 or 6) for at least three years between the ages of 16 and 55. This is one male in ten in the white male population.

8 per cent of the males are **exclusively homosexual** (*i.e.*, rate a 6) for at least three years between the ages of 16 and 55. This is one male in every 13.

4 per cent of the white males are **exclusively homosexual throughout their lives,** after the onset of adolescence (Table 150, Figure 168).

None of those who have previously attempted to estimate the incidence of the homosexual have made any clear-cut definition of the degree of homosexuality which they were including in their statistics. As a matter of fact, it seems fairly certain that none of them had any clear-cut concep-

AGE	CASES	HETEROSEXUAL-HOMOSEXUAL RATING: ACTIVE INCIDENCE TOTAL POPULATION—U. S. CORRECTIONS							
		X	0	1	2	3	4	5	6
		%	%	%	%	%	%	%	%
5	4297	90.6	4.2	0.2	0.3	1.2	0.3	0.2	3.0
10	4296	61.1	10.8	1.7	3.6	5.6	1.3	0.5	15.4
15	4284	23.6	48.4	3.6	6.0	4.7	3.7	2.6	7.4
20	3467	3.3	69.3	4.4	7.4	4.4	2.9	3.4	4.9
25	1835	1.0	79.2	3.9	5.1	3.2	2.4	2.3	2.9
30	1192	0.5	83.1	4.0	3.4	2.1	3.0	1.3	2.6
35	844	0.4	86.7	2.4	3.4	1.9	1.7	0.9	2.6
40	576	1.3	86.8	3.0	3.6	2.0	0.7	0.3	2.3
45	382	2.7	88.8	2.3	2.0	1.3	0.9	0.2	1.8

Table 147. Heterosexual-homosexual ratings for all white males

These are active incidence figures for the entire white male population, including single, married, and post-marital histories, the final figure corrected for the distribution of the population in the U. S. Census of 1940. For further explanations see the legend for Table 141.

tion of what they intended, other than their assurance that they were in-cluding only those "who were really homosexual." For that reason it is useless to compare the 2 or 3 per cent figure of Havelock Ellis, or the 2 to 5 per cent figure of Hirschfeld, or the 0.1 per cent figure of the Army induction centers with any of the data given above. The persons who are identified as "homosexuals" in much of the legal and social practice have rated anything between 1 and 6 on the above scale. On the other hand, there are some persons who would not rate an individual as "really homosexual" if he were anything less than a 5 or 6. Nevertheless, it should be emphasized again that there are persons who rate 2's or 3's who, in terms of the number of contacts they have made, may have had more homosexual experience than many persons who rate 6, and the clinician, the social

AGE	CASES	HETEROSEXUAL-HOMOSEXUAL RATING: ACTIVE INCIDENCE CUMULATED PERCENTS							
		X	0	1+	2+	3+	4+	5+	6
Single Males—Educ. Level 0–8									
		%	%	%	%	%	%	%	%
15	803	32.0	42.1	25.9	23.2	17.0	11.9	9.2	7.7
20	473	9.3	65.1	25.6	22.4	14.8	9.1	6.6	5.1
25	187	4.8	59.9	35.3	28.3	19.2	10.1	6.9	5.3
30	107	1.9	53.2	44.9	38.4	27.2	14.1	9.4	7.5
35	68	2.9	58.8	38.3	36.8	25.0	11.8	10.3	4.4
Single Males—Educ. Level 9–12									
15	629	19.9	48.6	31.5	27.2	20.7	15.9	11.3	7.8
20	350	2.0	57.0	41.0	35.6	24.7	20.1	15.2	8.6
25	140	0.7	50.8	48.5	42.1	36.4	30.7	21.4	10.7
30	67	1.5	46.2	52.3	43.3	40.3	37.3	26.9	17.9
Single Males—Educ. Level 13+									
15	2846	22.3	59.1	18.6	15.3	12.4	9.6	6.9	5.5
20	2306	3.9	80.6	15.5	9.9	7.3	6.0	4.2	2.3
25	687	3.3	75.5	21.2	15.7	13.4	12.1	8.8	4.7
30	179	4.5	64.7	30.8	26.3	25.7	25.1	22.3	12.8
35	71	7.0	55.0	38.0	32.4	32.4	31.0	28.2	19.7
Married Males—Educ. Level 0–8									
20	134	0.0	90.3	9.7	7.5	4.5	0.0	0.0	0.0
25	238	0.0	92.0	8.0	6.3	2.1	0.4	0.0	0.0
30	207	0.0	94.7	5.3	3.9	1.0	0.0	0.0	0.0
35	162	0.0	95.7	4.3	3.7	0.0	0.0	0.0	0.0
40	125	0.8	92.8	6.4	4.8	0.8	0.8	0.0	0.0
45	75	1.3	96.1	2.6	1.3	0.0	0.0	0.0	0.0
Married Males—Educ. Level 13+									
20	59	0.0	96.6	3.4	3.4	0.0	0.0	0.0	0.0
25	330	0.0	91.3	8.7	3.9	2.1	1.2	0.6	0.3
30	386	0.0	89.9	10.1	2.8	1.8	1.0	0.5	0.0
35	300	0.0	90.2	9.8	4.1	1.4	0.7	0.0	0.0
40	205	0.0	89.2	10.8	5.9	2.5	1.0	0.0	0.0
45	128	0.8	91.3	7.9	3.2	1.6	1.6	0.0	0.0
Total Population: Single, Married—All Educ. Levels									
15	4284	23.6	48.4	28.0	24.4	18.4	13.7	10.0	7.4
20	3467	3.3	69.3	27.4	23.0	15.6	11.2	8.3	4.9
25	1835	1.0	79.2	19.8	15.9	10.8	7.6	5.2	2.9
30	1192	0.5	83.1	16.4	12.4	9.0	6.9	3.9	2.6
35	844	0.4	86.7	12.9	10.5	7.1	5.2	3.5	2.6
40	576	1.3	86.8	11.9	8.9	5.3	3.3	2.6	2.3
45	382	2.7	88.8	8.5	6.2	4.2	2.9	2.0	1.8

Table 148. Cumulated percents of heterosexual-homosexual ratings

Based on Tables 141–147, cumulated from the right-hand end of each line. See accompanying text for definitions of ratings X, 0, 1, 2, etc. Data for adult males (at ages 15, 20, 25, 30, etc.), for single and married groups of each educational level and of total population. Shows percent of each group which rates 1 or more, 2 or more, 3 or more, etc., in each of the given years.

AGE PERIOD	CASES	HETEROSEXUAL-HOMOSEXUAL RATINGS: ACCUMULATIVE INCIDENCE ALL MALES, SINGLE AND MARRIED							
		CURRENT RATING	HIGHEST RATINGS FOR ANY 3 YEARS SINCE 16						
		X	0	1	2	3	4	5	6
Educ. Level 0–8									
		%	%	%	%	%	%	%	%
16–20	712	11.2	64.4	2.9	8.2	5.2	2.2	1.7	4.2
16–25	557	3.8	73.7	2.9	7.5	5.9	1.4	1.4	3.4
16–30	462	1.1	77.7	2.8	7.6	4.5	1.3	1.1	3.9
16–35	357	0.8	80.1	2.8	6.2	4.2	1.4	1.1	3.4
16–40	288	0.3	83.7	1.4	5.9	3.5	1.0	0.7	3.5
16–45	205	0.5	84.8	1.0	5.4	2.4	1.5	0.5	3.9
16–50	147	0.7	84.9	1.4	4.8	2.0	0.7	0.7	4.8
16–55	98	1.0	84.8	0.0	5.1	2.0	1.0	1.0	5.1
Educ. Level 9–12									
16–20	584	2.7	61.2	5.3	10.4	4.8	5.0	3.4	7.2
16–25	347	0.9	63.4	4.9	8.1	4.9	4.9	4.0	8.9
16–30	238	0.4	67.2	4.6	5.9	3.4	4.2	3.4	10.9
16–35	148	0.0	70.3	4.7	6.1	3.4	2.7	2.0	10.8
16–40	92	0.0	72.8	4.3	4.3	3.3	3.3	1.1	10.9
16–45	61	0.0	77.1	3.3	3.3	1.6	3.3	1.6	9.8
Educ. Level 13+									
16–20	2979	5.3	80.3	3.8	2.4	1.7	2.1	1.9	2.5
16–25	1635	2.1	80.1	4.3	2.5	1.3	2.9	2.7	4.1
16–30	876	1.4	77.8	4.6	2.1	1.7	2.6	3.4	6.4
16–35	552	1.1	80.7	4.2	2.4	1.1	2.5	2.0	6.0
16–40	375	0.5	81.4	4.5	1.3	0.8	2.1	2.2	7.2
16–45	218	0.5	82.1	6.0	1.8	0.9	0.9	1.8	6.0
16–50	132	0.0	87.1	4.5	2.3	1.5	0.8	0.0	3.8
16–55	74	0.0	86.5	4.1	2.7	1.3	1.3	0.0	4.1
Total Population—U. S. Correction									
16–20	4275	5.7	64.8	4.4	8.6	4.5	3.7	2.7	5.6
16–25	2539	2.0	69.0	4.2	7.1	4.7	3.5	3.0	6.5
16–30	1576	0.8	72.7	3.9	6.0	3.6	2.9	2.5	7.6
16–35	1057	0.5	76.3	3.8	5.6	3.4	2.1	1.6	6.7
16–40	755	0.2	79.9	2.7	4.8	3.1	1.9	1.0	6.4
16–45	484	0.4	82.3	2.2	4.4	2.0	1.9	1.0	5.8
16–50	318	0.5	83.8	2.6	4.0	2.1	1.1	0.5	5.4
16–55	191	0.7	85.0	1.4	4.9	1.5	0.8	0.7	5.0

Table 149. Heterosexual-homosexual ratings: accumulative incidence for each rating

Showing percents of each population which have ever held the shown rating for at least three years between 16 and the age shown in column 1. By eliminating both pre-adolescent and early adolescent years from the calculations, and by limiting the table to cases which have had at least three years of homosexual ratings, the table has been limited to definitely adult and pronouncedly homosexual experience of the degree shown by each rating. See Table 150 for cumulated percents derived from this table.

AGE PERIOD	CASES	HETEROSEXUAL-HOMOSEXUAL RATINGS: ACCUMULATIVE INCIDENCE ALL MALES, SINGLE OR MARRIED							
		CURRENT RATING		CUMULATED PERCENTS HIGHEST RATINGS FOR ANY 3 YEARS SINCE 16					
		X	0	1–6	2–6	3–6	4–6	5–6	6
Educ. Level 0–8									
		%	%	%	%	%	%	%	%
16–20	712	11.2	64.4	24.4	21.5	13.3	8.1	5.9	4.2
16–25	557	3.8	73.7	22.5	19.6	12.1	6.2	4.8	3.4
16–30	462	1.1	77.7	21.2	18.4	10.8	6.3	5.0	3.9
16–35	357	0.8	80.1	19.1	16.3	10.1	5.9	4.5	3.4
16–40	288	0.3	83.7	16.0	14.6	8.7	5.2	4.2	3.5
16–45	205	0.5	84.8	14.7	13.7	8.3	5.9	4.4	3.9
16–50	147	0.7	84.9	14.4	13.0	8.2	6.2	5.5	4.8
16–55	98	1.0	84.8	14.2	14.2	9.1	7.1	6.1	5.1
Educ. Level 9–12									
16–20	584	2.7	61.2	36.1	30.8	20.4	15.6	10.6	7.2
16–25	347	0.9	63.4	35.7	30.8	22.7	17.8	12.9	8.9
16–30	238	0.4	67.2	32.4	27.8	21.9	18.5	14.3	10.9
16–35	148	0.0	70.3	29.7	25.0	18.9	15.5	12.8	10.8
16–40	92	0.0	72.8	27.2	22.9	18.6	15.3	12.0	10.9
16–45	61	0.0	77.1	22.9	19.6	16.3	14.7	11.4	9.8
Educ. Level 13+									
16–20	2979	5.3	80.3	14.4	10.6	8.2	6.5	4.4	2.5
16–25	1635	2.1	80.1	17.8	13.5	11.0	9.7	6.8	4.1
16–30	876	1.4	77.8	20.8	16.2	14.1	12.4	9.8	6.4
16–35	552	1.1	80.7	18.2	14.0	11.6	10.5	8.0	6.0
16–40	375	0.5	81.4	18.1	13.6	12.3	11.5	9.4	7.2
16–45	218	0.5	82.1	17.4	11.4	9.6	8.7	7.8	6.0
16–50	132	0.0	87.1	12.9	8.4	6.1	4.6	3.8	3.8
16–55	74	0.0	86.5	13.5	9.4	6.7	5.4	4.1	4.1
Total Population—U. S. Corrections									
16–20	4275	5.7	64.8	29.5	25.1	16.5	12.0	8.3	5.6
16–25	2539	2.0	69.0	29.0	24.8	17.7	13.0	9.5	6.5
16–30	1576	0.8	72.7	26.5	22.6	16.6	13.0	10.1	7.6
16–35	1057	0.5	76.3	23.2	19.4	13.8	10.4	8.3	6.7
16–40	755	0.2	79.9	19.9	17.2	12.4	9.3	7.4	6.4
16–45	484	0.4	82.3	17.3	15.1	10.7	8.7	6.8	5.8
16–50	318	0.5	83.8	15.7	13.1	9.1	7.0	5.9	5.4
16–55	191	0.7	85.0	14.3	12.9	8.0	6.5	5.7	5.0
Total U. S. Population—Corrected for All Ages									
16–55	4275	1.5	75.6	**22.9**	**19.6**	**13.7**	**10.4**	**8.0**	**6.2**

Table 150. Heterosexual-homosexual rating: cumulated percents on each rating

Derived from Table 149. Showing percents of each population which have rated "at least a 1," "at least a 2," "at least a 3," etc., **for at least 3 years** between 16 and the age shown in column 1. The final line of figures, for the total U. S. population corrected for all ages, shows how many males in any population may be expected to have ratings of each sort.

worker, court officials, and society in general are not infrequently concerned with persons who rate no more than 2's or 3's. Many who rate only 1 or 2 are much disturbed over their homosexual experience, and they are frequently among those who go to clinicians for help.

Finally, it should be emphasized that the social significance of an individual's history may or may not have any relation to his rating on the above scale. An older male who has never before had homosexual contact, may

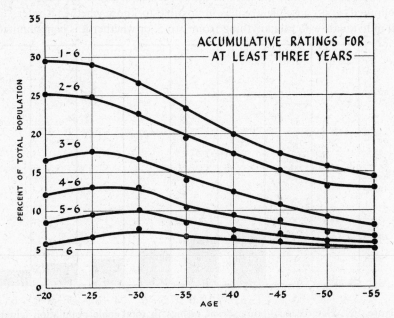

Figure 168. Accumulative incidence of heterosexual-homosexual ratings in total male population (single and married), by age periods

Based on U. S. Corrected data. Based only on ratings held by each individual for a period of at least three years. All accumulative incidence curves should rise; these drop in older age periods because (1) younger males today may be more often involved in homosexual activity, or (2) older males forget their earlier experience, or (3) older males deliberately cover up their homosexual experience. Certainly the data for the earlier age periods are the most reliable.

force a sexual relation with a small boy; and although he rates only a 1, he may so outrage the community that the full force of the law may be stirred up against him. On the contrary, most persons who rate 1's have histories which do not disturb anybody. At the other end of the scale, some of the exclusively homosexual males may so confine their overt contacts that no social problems are raised, while others who also rate 6 are active wolves who are in continual trouble because of their open affronts to social conventions.

BISEXUALITY

Since only 50 per cent of the population is exclusively heterosexual throughout its adult life, and since only 4 per cent of the population is exclusively homosexual throughout its life, it appears that nearly half (46%) of the population engages in both heterosexual and homosexual activities, or reacts to persons of both sexes, in the course of their adult lives. The term bisexual has been applied to at least some portion of this group. Unfortunately, the term as it has been used has never been strictly delimited, and consequently it is impossible to know whether it refers to all individuals who rate anything from 1 to 5, or whether it is being limited

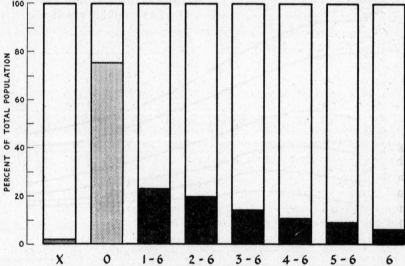

Figure 169. Heterosexual-homosexual ratings in total male population (single and married) in any single year

Based on U. S. Corrected data (last line of Table 150). Passing experiences eliminated from data by showing only ratings which have involved a period of at least three years after the males turned 16. Percent shown as "X" have no socio-sexual contacts or reactions.

to some smaller number of categories, perhaps centering around group 3. If the latter is intended, it should be emphasized that the 1's, 2's, 4's, and 5's have not yet been accounted for, and they constitute a considerable portion of the population.

In any event, such a scheme provides only a three-point scale (heterosexual, bisexual, and homosexual), and such a limited scale does not adequately describe the continuum which is the reality in nature. A seven-point scale comes nearer to showing the many gradations that actually exist.

As previously pointed out, it is rather unfortunate that the word bisexual should have been chosen to describe this intermediate group. The term is used as a substantive, designating individuals—persons; and the root meaning of the word and the way in which it is usually used imply that these persons have both masculine qualities and feminine qualities within their single bodies. We have objected to the use of the terms heterosexual and homosexual when used as nouns which stand for individuals. It is similarly untenable to imply that these "bisexual" persons have an anatomy or an endocrine system or other sorts of physiologic or psychologic capacities which make them partly male and partly female, or of the two sexes simultaneously.

The term bisexual has been used in biology for structures or individuals or aggregates of individuals that include the anatomy or functions of both sexes. There are unisexual species which are exclusively female and reproduce parthenogenetically (from eggs that are not fertilized). In contrast, there are bisexual species which include both males and females and which commonly reproduce through fertilization of the eggs produced by the females. Among plants and animals which have an alternation of generations, there are unisexual or parthenogenetic generations in which there are only females, and bisexual generations in which there are both males and females. In regard to the embryonic structures from which the gonads of some of the vertebrates develop, the term bisexual is applied because these embryonic structures have the potentialities of both sexes and may develop later into either ovaries or testes. Hermaphroditic animals, like earthworms, some snails, and a rare human, may be referred to as bisexual, because they have both ovaries and testes in their single bodies. These are the customary usages for the term bisexual in biology.

On the other hand, as applied to human sexual behavior, the term indicates that there are individuals who choose to have sexual relations with both males and females; and until it is demonstrated, as it certainly is not at the present time, that such a catholicity of taste in a sexual relation is dependent upon the individual containing within his anatomy both male and female structures, or male and female physiologic capacities, it is unfortunate to call such individuals bisexual. Because of its wide currency, the term will undoubtedly continue in use among students of human behavior and in the public in general. It should, however, be used with the understanding that it is patterned on the words heterosexual and homosexual and, like them, refers to the sex of the partner, and proves nothing about the constitution of the person who is labelled bisexual.

There has been a very considerable confusion of the concept of bisexuality and the concept of intersexuality by persons who are unacquainted with the exact nature of the work that has been done on intersexual forms among animals. As the term was originally used by Goldschmidt, and subsequently among geneticists and students in other fields of biology, an individual is recognized as an intersex if it shows secondary sexual characters that are intermediate between those of the typical male and the typical female in the population. Where a single individual combines in its one person the primary sex characters of two sexes (namely, the ovaries and the testes), it is recognized as a *hermaphrodite*. Where the secondary sexual characters of an individual are in part the unmodified characters of one sex, and in part the characters of the other sex, the individual is known as a *gynandromorph*. A gynandromorphic insect may have the head coloration that is typical of one sex and the thoracic coloration that is typical of the other sex. An *intersex*, on the contrary, has a portion or the whole of its structures intermediate in character between the structures of the typical male or the female of the species. In the case of Goldschmidt's gypsy moths, the females are typically large, the males

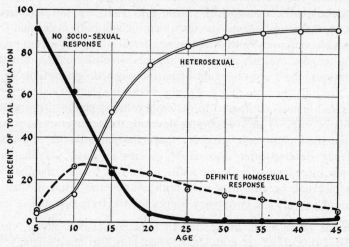

Figure 170. Development of heterosexuality and homosexuality by age periods

Active incidence curves, corrected for U. S. population. Males with no socio-sexual response (rating X) rapidly disappear between the ages of 5 and 20. Males whose responses are chiefly heterosexual (rating 0 or 1) rapidly increase in number until they ultimately account for 90 per cent of the whole population. Males who are more than incidentally homosexual in response or overt activity (ratings 2–6) are most abundant in pre-adolescence and through the teens, gradually becoming less abundant with advancing age.

typically smaller. The intersexual individuals show gradations in size between the larger female and smaller male. The typical female of the gypsy moth is buff yellow, the male is white. The intersexes show various grades of color between yellow and white. A gynandromorph might have one wing yellow and one wing white, one wing large and one wing small, but the intersexes have wings that are intermediate in size and color.

In spite of the fact that Goldschmidt himself (1916) accepted the idea that the homosexual human male or female was an intersex, there is no adequate basis for reaching any such conclusion. Those who have accepted this interpretation have assumed without asking for specific evidence that an individual's choice of a sexual partner is affected by some basic physiologic capacity. No work that has been done on hormones or on any other physiologic capacities of the human animal justifies such a conclusion (Kinsey 1941). Goldschmidt and others who have thought of the homosexual individual as an intersex have relied upon incidence figures which were pure guesses and which, as the data in the present chapter will show, bear little relation to the fact as it has now been ascertained.

There are a few males in whom the urethra opens on the under surface of the penis. Such a condition is known as a *hypospadia*. The most extreme confusion of biological ideas has come from the identification of these hypospadiac males as intersexes who are predisposed to be homosexual in their behavior. However, an investigation of the embryonic development of the male penis (Arey 1924, 1946, Patten 1946) will show that a hypospadia is nothing more than a failure in the closure of the urethra at the end of normal embryonic development, and has no relation whatsoever to the genetic maleness or femaleness of the individual, nor to the endocrine constitution of the individual. As our own histories of hypospadiac individuals definitely show, such malformations have nothing to do with their choice of sexual partners unless, as in some extreme cases among ignorant and uneducated persons, the sexual identity of the individual is confused and he is raised in the clothing and the traditions of the opposite sex. In popular parlance such individuals are commonly called "morphodites," but the designation is incorrect, for a true hermaphrodite, as we have already pointed out, has functioning gonads of both sexes within its one body. It is, of course, in the same way that a female with a large clitoris is sometimes called a hermaphrodite. Sometimes the term intersex has been applied to such females (Dickinson 1933); but until more is known about the biological basis of this situation, it is not certain that the term intersex should be applied even in these cases.

SCIENTIFIC AND SOCIAL IMPLICATIONS

In view of the data which we now have on the incidence and frequency of the homosexual, and in particular on its co-existence with the heterosexual in the lives of a considerable portion of the male population, it is difficult to maintain the view that psychosexual reactions between individuals of the same sex are rare and therefore abnormal or unnatural, or that they constitute within themselves evidence of neuroses or even psychoses.

If homosexual activity persists on as large a scale as it does, in the face of the very considerable public sentiment against it and in spite of the severity of the penalties that our Anglo-American culture has placed upon it through the centuries, there seems some reason for believing that such activity would appear in the histories of a much larger portion of the population if there were no social restraints. The very general occurrence of the homosexual in ancient Greece (Licht 1925, 1926, 1928, 1932), and its wide occurrence today in some cultures in which such activity is not as taboo as it is in our own, suggests that the capacity of an individual to respond erotically to any sort of stimulus, whether it is provided by another person of the same or of the opposite sex, is basic in the species. That patterns of heterosexuality and patterns of homosexuality represent learned behavior which depends, to a considerable degree, upon the mores of the particular culture in which the individual is raised, is a possibility that must be thoroughly considered before there can be any acceptance of the idea that homosexuality is inherited, and that the pattern for each individual is so innately fixed that no modification of it may be expected within his lifetime.

The opinion that homosexual activity in itself provides evidence of a psychopathic personality is materially challenged by these incidence and frequency data. Of the 40 or 50 per cent of the male population which has homosexual experience, certainly a high proportion would not be considered psychopathic personalities on the basis of anything else in their histories. It is argued that an individual who is so obtuse to social reactions as to continue his homosexual activity and make it any material portion of his life, therein evidences some social incapacity; but psychiatrists and clinicians in general might very well re-examine their justification for demanding that all persons conform to particular patterns of behavior. As a matter of fact, there is an increasing proportion of the most skilled psychiatrists who make no attempt to re-direct behavior, but who devote their attention to helping an individual accept himself, and to conduct himself in such a manner that he does not come into open conflict with society.

There are, of course, some persons with homosexual histories who are neurotic and in constant difficulty with themselves and not infrequently with society. That is also true of some persons with heterosexual histories. Some homosexual individuals are so upset that they have difficulty in the accomplishment of their business or professional obligations and reach the point where they find it difficult to make the simplest sort of social contact without friction. It is, however, a considerable question whether these persons have homosexual histories because they are neurotic, or whether their neurotic disturbances are the product of their homosexual activities and of society's reaction to them. These are matters that must be investigated in more detail in a later volume; but they are questions that become more significant when one realizes the actual extent of homosexual behavior.

Factors Accounting for the Homosexual. Attempts to identify the biologic bases of homosexual activity, must take into account the large number of males who have demonstrated their capacity to respond to stimuli provided by other persons of the same sex. It must also be taken into account that many males combine in their single histories, and very often in exactly the same period of time, or even simultaneously in the same moment, reactions to both heterosexual and homosexual stimuli. They must take into account that in these combinations of heterosexual and homosexual experience, there is every conceivable gradation between exclusively heterosexual histories and exclusively homosexual histories. It must be shown that the fluctuations in preferences for female or male partners are related to fluctuations in the hormones, the genes, or the other biologic factors which are assumed to be operating (Kinsey 1941). It must be shown that there is a definite correlation between the degree in which the biologic factor operates, and the degree of the heterosexual-homosexual balance in the history of each individual.

If psychologic or social forces are considered as agents in the origin of the homosexual, the same sorts of correlations must be shown before any causal relationship is established. An infrequent phenomenon might be accounted for by factors of one sort, but the factors which account for the homosexual must be of such an order as the incidence and frequency data show this phenomenon to be in our culture. Moreover, it should be emphasized that it is one thing to account for an all-or-none proposition, as heterosexuality and homosexuality have ordinarily been taken to be. But it is a totally different matter to recognize factors which will account for the continuum which we find existing between the exclusively heterosexual and the exclusively homosexual history.

Whatever factors are considered, it must not be forgotten that the basic phenomenon to be explained is an individual's preference for a partner of one sex, or for a partner of the other sex, or his acceptance of a partner of either sex. This problem, is after all, part of the broader problem of choices in general: the choice of the road that one takes, of the clothes that one wears, of the food that one eats, of the place in which one sleeps, and of the endless other things that one is constantly choosing. A choice of a partner in a sexual relation becomes more significant only because society demands that there be a particular choice in this matter, and does not so often dictate one's choice of food or of clothing.

Hereditary Bases of Homosexuality. Through a brilliant series of studies, Goldschmidt showed the hereditary bases of intersexes among insects. It is unfortunate, however, that he identified homosexual males and females in the human species as intersexes, and thereby reached the conclusion that there must be a hereditary basis for homosexuality (Goldschmidt 1916). The argument in his original paper was based on nothing more than an analogy between the intermediate secondary sexual characters which he found in the insects, and what he assumed to be intermediate characters in the psychology of the homosexual human individual. From this analogy he reasoned that there must be an inheritance of the human behavior phenomenon, just as there is inheritance of the morphologic structures which constitute the intersexuality of moths. With this idea of the inheritance of heterosexuality or homosexuality, a number of other workers have agreed. We are not ready at this time to discuss these data in detail, but we may point out that the incidence data and the record of gradations between exclusively heterosexual and exclusively homosexual histories which have been presented in the present chapter, have considerable significance in this question of heredity.

In order to prove that homosexual patterns of behavior are inherited in the human animal, the following conditions would need to be fulfilled:

1. It would be necessary to define strictly what is meant in the study by the term homosexual. The term should be limited to persons of particular position on the heterosexual-homosexual scale; but whatever the restrictions of the original study the conclusions should finally be applicable to all persons who have ever had any homosexual experience.

2. There should be a determination of the incidence of the phenomenon in groups of siblings in which the complete sexual history of every individual in each family is known. It would be very desirable to secure complete histories of all the siblings in each family for at least two successive generations. As far as we are aware, such an accumulation of complete histories has never been available in any study of the inheritance of the homosexual.

3. Especial attention should be paid to the balance between the homosexual and the heterosexual behavior in the histories of each of the siblings in such a study.

4. The recognition of homosexuality in any individual should not be considered sufficient unless a complete sexual history is available. In considering the histories of relatives and ancestors, the published studies have put too much reliance upon suspicion, gossip, or the accidental public disclosure of homosexual activity. In no instance has there been any sufficient regard for the fact that these relatives, who may, indeed, have had homosexual experience, may also have had heterosexual experience and rated anything between 1 and 6 on the heterosexual-homosexual scale.

5. Similarly, the heterosexuality of any individual who enters into the calculations should be determined through complete sex histories. In nearly all studies to date, heterosexuality has been assumed where there was marriage or other known relations with the opposite sex, and when there was no public knowledge of homosexuality. These are, of course,

untrustworthy sources of information on such a socially taboo item of behavior as is involved here.

6. There should be data on enough cases of siblings to be statistically significant. In view of the experience in the present study (Chapter 3), it may be necessary to have histories from several hundred individuals in order to obtain satisfactory results.

7. The incidence of the homosexual, as it is defined in the study, should be shown to be higher among siblings than it is in the histories of the non-siblings in the study. Inasmuch as our present data indicate that more than a third (37%) of the white males in any population (or probably, for that matter, among anyone's ancestors) have had at least some homosexual experience, and inasmuch as the data indicate that a quarter of the males in the population (and a quarter of the males in anyone's ancestry) may have more than incidental homosexual experience in the course of their lives, it would be necessary to show that the incidence of the homosexual in groups of siblings is higher than that. This, of course, has never been shown in any study on the inheritance of the homosexual.

8. Whatever the hereditary mechanisms which are proposed, they must allow for the fact that some individuals change from exclusively heterosexual to exclusively homosexual patterns in the course of their lives, or vice versa, and they must allow for frequent changes in ratings of individuals on the heterosexual-homosexual scale.

Social Applications. It is obvious that social interpretations of the homosexual behavior of any individual may be materially affected by a consideration of what is now known about the behavior of the population as a whole. Social reactions to the homosexual have obviously been based on the general belief that a deviant individual is unique and as such needs special consideration. When it is recognized that the particular boy who is discovered in homosexual relations in school, the business man who is having such activity, and the institutional inmate with a homosexual record, are involved in behavior that is not fundamentally different from that had by a fourth to a third of all of the rest of the population, the activity of the single individual acquires a somewhat different social significance.

One of the factors that materially contributes to the development of exclusively homosexual histories, is the ostracism which society imposes upon one who is discovered to have had perhaps no more than a lone experience. The high school boy is likely to be expelled from school and, if it is in a small town, he is almost certain to be driven from the community. His chances for making heterosexual contacts are tremendously reduced after the public disclosure, and he is forced into the company of other homosexual individuals among whom he finally develops an exclusively homosexual pattern for himself. Every school teacher and principal who is faced with the problem of the individual boy should realize that something between a quarter and a third of all the other boys in the same high school have had at least some homosexual experience since they turned adolescent.

Community gossip and reactions to rumors of homosexual activity in the history of some member of the community would probably be modified if it were kept in mind that the same individual may have a considerable heterosexual element in his history as well. The social worker who is inclined to label a particular boy or older male in her case load as homosexual, because he is known to have had some such activity, should keep in mind that there is every gradation between complete homosexuality and complete heterosexuality. Administrators in institutions, officials in the Army and Navy, and many other persons in charge of groups of males may profitably consider the balance between the heterosexual and homosexual in an individual's history, rather than the homosexual aspects alone.

Administrators of penal and mental institutions are often much disturbed over the problem presented by a male who is committed for a homosexual offense. Such an individual is likely to receive especially severe treatment from the officials in the institution, and he may be segregated as a potential menace to the rest of the inmate body. If it is an institution in which trained psychologists or psychiatrists are employed, they are likely to give especial attention to the half dozen cases who are sent to the institution each year, on such charges. Our surveys in institutions, however, indicate that 25 or 30 per cent of all the inmates have had homosexual experience before admission. It is obvious that the male who happens to be sent in on a homosexual charge may present no more special problem to the institution in this regard than the other quarter or third of the inmate body, who might just as well have been sent in on such a charge. As far as the administration of a custodial institution is concerned, the problem of discipline does not depend upon the control of individuals who have some homosexual experience in their history, as much as it does upon the control of men who are particularly aggressive in forcing other individuals into homosexual relations.

The judge who is considering the case of the male who has been arrested for homosexual activity, should keep in mind that nearly 40 per cent of all the other males in the town could be arrested at some time in their lives for similar activity, and that 20 to 30 per cent of the unmarried males in that town could have been arrested for homosexual activity that had taken place within that same year. The court might also keep in mind that the penal or mental institution to which he may send the male has something between 30 and 85 per cent of its inmates engaging in the sort of homosexual activity which may be involved in the individual case before him.

On the other hand, the judge who dismisses the homosexual case that has come before him, or places the boy or adult on probation, may find himself the subject of attack from the local press which charges him with releasing dangerous "perverts" upon the community. Law enforcement officers can utilize the findings of scientific studies of human behavior only to the extent that the community will back them. Until the whole community understands the realities of human homosexual behavior, there is not likely to be much change in the official handling of individual cases.

The difficulty of the situation becomes still more apparent when it is realized that these generalizations concerning the incidence and frequency of homosexual activity apply in varying degrees to every social level, to persons in every occupation, and of every age in the community. The police force and court officials who attempt to enforce the sex laws, the clergymen and business men and every other group in the city which periodically calls for enforcement of the laws—particularly the laws against sexual "perversion"—have given a record of incidences and frequencies in the homosexual which are as high as those of the rest of the social level to which they belong. It is not a matter of individual hypocrisy which leads officials with homosexual histories to become prosecutors of the homosexual activity in the community. They themselves are the victims of the mores, and the public demand that they protect those mores. As long as there are such gaps between the traditional custom and the actual behavior of the population, such inconsistencies will continue to exist.

There are those who will contend that the immorality of homosexual behavior calls for its suppression no matter what the facts are concerning the incidence and frequency of such activity in the population. Some have demanded that homosexuality be completely eliminated from society by a concentrated attack upon it at every point, and the "treatment" or isolation of all individuals with any homosexual tendencies. Whether such a program is morally desirable is a matter on which a scientist is not qualified to pass judgment; but whether such a program is physically feasible is a matter for scientific determination.

The evidence that we now have on the incidence and frequency of homosexual activity indicates that at least a third of the male population would have to be isolated from the rest of the community, if all those with any homosexual capacities were to be so treated. It means that at least 13 per cent of the male population (rating 4 to 6 on the heterosexual-homosexual scale), would have to be institutionalized and isolated, if all persons who were predominantly homosexual were to be handled in that way. Since about 34 per cent of the total population of the United States are adult males, this means that there are about six and a third million males in the country who would need such isolation.

If all persons with any trace of homosexual history, or those who were predominantly homosexual, were eliminated from the population today, there is no reason for believing that the incidence of the homosexual in the next generation would be materially reduced. The homosexual has been a significant part of human sexual activity ever since the dawn of history, primarily because it is an expression of capacities that are basic in the human animal.

Chapter 22

ANIMAL CONTACTS

To many persons it will seem almost axiomatic that two mating animals should be individuals of the same species. This is so often true, from one end of the animal kingdom to the other, that exceptions to the rule seem especially worthy of note. To those who believe, as children do, that conformance should be universal, any departure from the rule becomes an immorality. The immorality seems particularly gross to an individual who is unaware of the frequency with which exceptions to the supposed rule actually occur.

No biologist exactly understands why males of a species are attracted primarily, even if not exclusively, to females of the same species. What is there to prevent insects of one species from mating with insects of many other species? What is there to prevent a frog from mating with frogs of other species? Why should mammals mate only with mammals of their own kind? In the animal kingdom as a whole, is it to be believed that the sources of sexual attraction are of such a nature that they provide stimuli only for other individuals of the same species? For the scientist it does not suffice to be told that nature allows nothing else but intraspecific mating because she considers reproduction to be the objective of all sexual activities, and because the production of offspring is supposed to be impossible as a product of an interspecific cross. It does not suffice to think of inner forces which draw individuals together in their sexual relations. Such concepts concern intangibles with which science can have no dealing and, in the last analysis, the biologist and psychologist must look for material stimuli which, originating in one individual, may so affect other individuals that mating is the inevitable consequence.

For instance, such specific stimuli are recognized in the odors emitted by female moths; and they have been demonstrated to be the sources of attraction for the males who come from considerable distances to congregate around the female that emits the odors. Such specific stimuli are recognized in the mating calls of toads and frogs, probably in the songs of birds, in the odors which some female mammals produce and, among the higher mammals, in the visual stimuli which the mere presence of an individual may provide. There is a considerable literature on this subject, but it needs to be analyzed with caution because so much of it is anthropomorphic, arriving at the sort of interpretation that a human intelligence

667

would expect to find if intraspecific mating were the only possibility in nature.

Even the scientists have been considerably biased in their investigations in this field, for they too have accepted the traditions. Even they have believed that matings between individuals of different species occur only rarely. Within the last few decades, however, students of taxonomy, genetics, and evolution have had the existence of interspecific hybrids increasingly drawn to their attention. These, of course, predicate the existence of interspecific matings. Some biologists are clearly uncomfortable in the face of these data, and are inclined to argue them away as they would argue away blots on their philosophy or theology. Even among the higher animals, interspecific crosses, or crosses between distinct varieties, have increasingly become known. The bird banding work has shown that birds respect the limits of their own species much less often than the old-time naturalists would have insisted. And, finally, the students of sexual behavior among the higher mammals are beginning to report an increasing number of instances of animals mating, or trying to mate, with individuals of totally distinct and sometimes quite remote species (Nat. Res. Council Conf. on Mammalian Sex Behav. 1943, Beach 1947).

Fertile crosses between very distinct species are limited by microscopic mechanisms which the students of genetics and of cell structure have investigated in considerable detail. There is, however, no comparable knowledge of factors which might prevent matings between specifically distinct individuals. When one examines the observed cases of such crosses, and especially the rather considerable number of instances in which primates, including man, have been involved, one begins to suspect that the rules about intraspecific matings are not so universal as tradition would have it. Indeed, one is struck anew with the necessity for better reasons than biologists and psychologists have yet found, for expecting that animal matings should invariably be limited to individuals of the same species.

In light of the above, it is particularly interesting to note the degree of abhorrence with which intercourse between the human and animals of other species is viewed by most persons who have not had such experience. The biologist and the psychologist, and the anthropologist and the student of history, will have made a significant contribution when they can expound the development of our taboos on such contacts.

It is known, of course, that these taboos were well-established in the Old Testament and in the Talmud. Attention is also to be drawn to the fact that in the older Hittite code (Barton 1925), which may have had some influence on the Hebrew codes, the taboos on animal intercourse were not clearly the moral issues that they subsequently came to be. Specifically, in the Hittite code it is decreed that "if a man lie with a cow the punishment is death." "If a man lies with a hog or dog, he shall die."

"If a man . . . lies [with another, unidentified animal] the punishment is death." "If a bull rear upon a man, the bull shall die, but the man shall not die." "If a boar rear upon a man, there is no penalty." "If a man lies with a horse or mule, there is no penalty, but he shall not come near the king, and he shall not become a priest." These are proscriptions against contacts with certain animals, while contacts with certain other animals are more or less accepted. Such distinctions are strikingly paralleled by the taboos which made certain foods clean and other foods unclean. The student of human folkways is inclined to see a considerable body of superstition in the origins of all such taboos, even though they may ultimately become religious and moral issues for whole nations and whole races of people.

In any event, it is certain that human contacts with animals of other species have been known since the dawn of history, they are known among all races of people today, and they are not uncommon in our own culture, as the data in the present chapter will show. Far from being a matter for surprise, the record simply substantiates our present understanding that the forces which bring individuals of the same species together in sexual relations, may sometimes serve to bring individuals of different species together in the same types of sexual relations.

REFERENCES

Data on the incidence and frequency of sexual contacts between the human male and animals of other species have already been detailed in this volume in tables and charts, and in discussions in the text, as follows:

PAGE	TABLE	FIGURE	NATURE OF DATA
174			Pre-adolescent experience with animals
234	49		Range of variation in frequency of animal contacts
260–262	59		Age affecting animal contacts
362–363	91	172	Educational level and animal contacts
378,	96	126, 128–130	Importance of animal intercourse as one
488–491			source of sexual outlet for single males
459–463	124	125	Relation of rural-urban background to animal contacts
512			Masturbation, self and animal
669–673	151	171	Accumulative incidence of animal contacts among single, rural males
670–674		173	Individual variation in frequencies of animal contacts among rural males

INCIDENCES AND FREQUENCIES

The significance of animal contacts in the history of the human male lies largely in the field of social values; for there is no other type of sexual activity which accounts for a smaller proportion of the total outlet of the total population (Figures 126, 128–130). For that population, including both single and married males, only a fraction of 1 per cent of the total number of orgasms is derived from animal intercourse. In the period when such contacts are most frequent, namely between adolescence and 20 years of age, a little less than 1 per cent of the total outlet is so derived; but the figure drops rapidly in successive age groups, and it amounts to only 0.04 per cent among those males who remain single after the age of 25 (Table 59).

In the total population, only one male in twelve or fourteen (estimated at about 8%) ever has sexual experience with animals (Table 59). In this total population, it is not more than 6 per cent which is involved in the

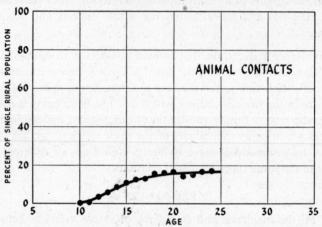

Figure 171. Animal contacts: accumulative incidence in single rural population

Showing percent of single rural males who have ever had sexual contacts with animals to the point of orgasm, by each of the indicated ages. All data corrected for U. S. Census distribution.

most active period (between adolescence and 20). The percentage drops in successive age groups to a little more than 1 per cent in the early twenties, and to a still lower figure at older ages.

Frequencies of animal contacts are similarly low in the population taken as a whole. For most individuals, they do not occur more than once or twice, or a few times in a lifetime.

On the other hand, the significance of such interspecific relationships becomes more apparent if we confine the calculations simply to that segment of the population which has access to animals, namely to the males who are raised on farms. For that group, the incidences and frequencies of animal contacts are more nearly comparable to the incidences and frequencies of contacts with prostitutes, or of homosexual contacts, in the population. There are a number of city-bred boys (4% between adolescence and age 15 alone) who have animal contacts in their histories (Table 124), and the fact that most of their experiences occur when they visit on farms suggests that the entire human male population might have animal contacts as frequently as farm boys do if animals were available to all of them.

Among boys raised on farms, about 17 per cent experience orgasm as the product of animal contacts which occur sometime after the onset of adolescence (Table 151, Figure 171). As many more have contacts which do not result in orgasm, and there are still others who have pre-adolescent experience which is not included in the above calculations. It is, in consequence, something between 40 and 50 per cent of all farm boys who have some sort of animal contact, either with or without orgasm, in their pre-adolescent, adolescent, and/or later histories. These must be minimum data, for there has undoubtedly been some cover-up in the reports of these activities. The data given in the remainder of this chapter are confined to those contacts which have resulted in orgasm for the human subject; but all of these figures may be doubled if one wishes to determine the total number of persons involved in any sort of relation, whether with or without orgasm. Such data begin to show what the significance of animal intercourse might be if conditions were more favorable for such activity.

In fact, in certain Western areas of the United States, where animals are most readily available and social restraints on this matter are less stringent, we have secured incidence figures of as high as 65 per cent in some communities, and there are indications of still higher incidences in some other areas. The cases, however, are still too few to warrant a specific statement on these regional differences.

Ultimately, 14 to 16 per cent of the rural males of the grade school level, 20 per cent of the rural males of the high school level, and 26 to 28 per cent of the rural males of the college level have some animal experience to the point of orgasm (Tables 91, 151). In this upper educational level, nearly one rural male in three has such contacts to the point of orgasm, and well over half of these upper level males have some kind of sexual contact with animals.

Frequencies of animal contacts vary from once or twice in a lifetime to regular rates of several times a week over a considerable period of years. Maximum regular frequencies for a few individuals may go as high as 8 per week between adolescence and 15, and 4 per week between 16 and 20, but not above once per week between ages 21 and 25 (Table 49). For most males, however, the frequencies come nearer averaging once in 2 or 3 weeks, in that portion of the population which is having any contacts at all (Table 124). In most histories the contacts with animals are limited to a matter of 2 or 3 years, but in some cases they may extend over a 10- or 15-year period or even throughout the whole of a life span.

Animal contacts are most frequent during the late pre-adolescent years (Chapter 5) while ejaculation is still impossible for the human subject and

	ANIMAL CONTACTS: ACCUMULATIVE INCIDENCE DATA						
AGE	TOTAL POPULATION U. S. CORRECTIONS		EDUC. LEVEL 0–8		EDUC. LEVEL 9–12		EDUC. LEVEL 13+	
	Cases	% with Exper.	Cases	% with Exper.	Cases	% with Exper.	Cases	% with Exper.
10	749	0.04	203		110		436	0.7
11	749	0.4	203	0.5	110		436	1.1
12	749	3.7	203	4.4	110	2.7	436	4.8
13	749	5.7	203	5.9	110	4.5	436	10.8
14	749	8.1	203	8.4	110	6.4	436	17.2
15	749	10.4	203	9.9	110	9.1	436	22.7
16	745	12.2	201	10.0	109	12.8	435	25.5
17	728	12.8	190	10.0	105	14.3	433	26.1
18	700	15.4	179	13.4	93	16.1	428	26.6
19	646	15.9	166	13.9	79	16.5	401	26.4
20	567	16.5	145	14.5	63	17.5	359	26.2
21	500	14.0	128	14.1	51	11.8	321	28.0
22	366	15.0	101	12.9			265	29.4
23	290	16.7	76	15.8			214	29.0
24	253	17.2	67	14.9			186	28.0
25	217		60	13.3			157	27.4
26	176		50	12.0			126	25.4
27	96						96	24.0
28	72						72	23.6
29	59						59	23.7

Table 151. Accumulative incidence data on animal contacts among rural males

Data confined to single males who lived on farms for some period between 12 and 18 years of age, or for longer periods. Data shown for three educational levels, and for the total farm population corrected for the U. S. Census of 1940.

when, in actuality, the boy almost never reaches orgasm in his animal contacts. One-third of the males who will ever have such contacts have had them by the age of 9. Between 10 and 12 there is a rapid increase in the number of boys involved and the peak of such activity is reached just before the onset of adolescence. In a third of the cases, boys with pre-adolescent experience continue their activities with animals into adolescent years. In terms of actual orgasms achieved by the human participant, the highest frequencies occur in the earliest adolescent years; but in some rural areas, especially in the West, there is a considerable amount of regular activity in the later teens and even through the early twenties. Cases become relatively rare among single males in later years. There are, nevertheless, occasional individuals who have regular contacts from adolescence into

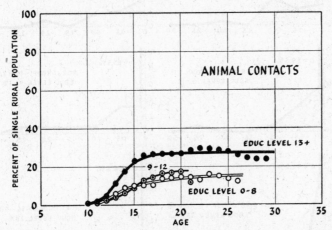

Figure 172. Animal contacts: accumulative incidence in three educational levels of single rural population

Showing percent of each level of single rural males who have ever had sexual contacts with animals to the point of orgasm, by each of the indicated ages.

their fifties, and there is one case of a male past 80 years of age who had had such contacts regularly throughout the whole of his life.

In most parts of the country animal intercourse is extremely rare among married males; but, again, such experiences are not unknown among married adults in some rural areas of the West.

Younger adolescent boys who are having animal contacts, derive, on an average, 7 per cent of their total outlet from that source. The males who are still having such contacts in their early twenties may derive as much as 15 per cent of their outlet from that source (Table 59).

As already indicated, a fair number of city boys have sexual relations with animals (Table 124). Some of this is had with household pets, particularly with dogs, and some of it is had with ponies or with animals in the city stockyards. More of it, however, is had with animals with which the city boy comes into contact when he visits a farm during a vacation period. Since their opportunities for contacts are infrequent, city-bred males may not have more than a few experiences, and the frequencies of contacts among farm boys may average thirty to seventy times as high as the frequencies among city-bred groups.

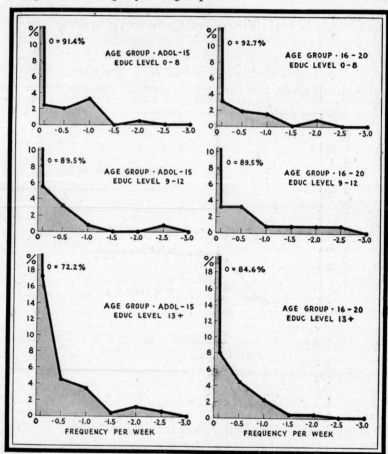

Figure 173. Animal contacts: individual variation in frequencies, in two age periods, at three educational levels

NATURE OF CONTACTS

The animals that are involved in these human contacts include practically all of the species that are domesticated on the farm or kept as pets in the household. Because of their convenient size, animals like calves or, in the West, burros and sheep are most often involved. Practically every other mammal that has ever been kept on a farm enters into the record, and a few of the larger birds, like chickens, ducks, and geese. Vaginal coitus is the most frequent technique in the relations, but in at least parts of the country the fellation of the boy by the calf is not uncommon, and occasionally the household pets, particularly the dog and even the cat, may be induced to so perform. There is some anal intercourse. In some cases the boy masturbates by frictation against the body of the animal. There is an occasional record of the human male fellating the male animal.

Masturbation of the animal by the human subject is almost as frequent as vaginal coitus. Masturbation may be either on the male or female animal, but it is most common with the male animal, particularly with the male dog. Very often whole groups of boys may be involved in such activities. If a boy is alone, he may masturbate himself while he masturbates the animal, and there may be considerable erotic stimulation to the boy involved in such a performance.

SOCIAL SIGNIFICANCE

A considerable portion of the animal activity of the farm boy is the product of his erotic arousal upon contemplating the coitus that occurs among the animals themselves, and of his constant association with animals that he knows have been recently involved in sexual activity. Such sympathetic emotional responses are natural enough and not fundamentally different from those which would be expected if the boy were to observe coitus among human subjects. His attempt to replace the male animal in such relations is the obvious outcome of an identification of his own capacities with those of the animal he has observed. His initial attempts are sometimes inspired by a quite understandable curiosity to try what he has discovered to be a possible sort of activity. Whatever moral issues may be involved, and however long-standing the social condemnation of animal contacts may have been throughout the history of Western European civilizations, the easy dismissal of such behavior by characterizing it as abnormal shows little capacity for making objective analyses of the basic psychology that is involved.

In a considerable number of instances the farm boy's initiation into animal contacts is inspired by his knowledge of similar activity among his companions. This is particularly true in Western areas where adults as well as adolescents are not infrequently engaged in animal intercourse, and where there may be frequent conversation in the community about such activities. It is not unusual in some rural areas to find individuals who openly admit that such contacts have provided them with some erotic satisfaction.

To a considerable extent contacts with animals are substitutes for heterosexual relations with human females. In rural areas where both social and sexual relations with girls may be more or less limited, the boy is often left alone or with his brothers, his male cousins, or the adult males who are working on the farm. We share the general impression, although we have no significant data to establish it, that rural communities are on the whole more traditional in their moral condemnation of pre-marital sexual relations, and the boy on the farm is often strictly forbidden to associate with girls. This cannot help but encourage substitutional behavior of the sort which the animals may afford. There are histories of extremely religious males who, even in their twenties and in later years, continue to derive practically the whole of their outlet from animals because of their conviction that heterosexual coitus with a human female is morally unacceptable.

In not a few cases the animal contacts become homosexual activities. Masturbating the male animal, whether it is a dog, horse, bull, or some other species, may provide considerable erotic excitement for the boy or older adult. He senses the genital similarities between the male animal and himself, and he recognizes the relationship between the animal's performance and reactions and his own capacities. His enjoyment of the relationship is enhanced by the fact that the male animal responds to the point of orgasm, and in at least some cases he is disappointed that the female animal (with rare exceptions) shows no erotic arousal and fails to experience orgasm. For these reasons, many a farm boy has as much contact with male animals as he does with female animals. There is considerable basis for calling such activity homosexual, but since it is not recognized as such by most of the boys who are involved, they are in no conflict over that fact.

Psychically, animal relations may become of considerable significance to the boy who is having regular experience. While his initial contacts may involve little more than the satisfaction which is to be obtained from physical stimulation, the situation becomes quite different for the boy who is having frequent contacts with particular animals. The depth of the boy's psychic response is evidenced by his quick erection and by the ease with which he may reach orgasm in his relations with the animal. The psychic significance of his experience is particularly evidenced by the fact that animal contacts may become a regular part of his nocturnal dreams. Moreover, many a farm boy, while masturbating, develops erotic fantasies of himself in contact with some animal. In some cases the boy may develop an affectional relation with the particular animal with which he has his contacts, and there are males who are quite upset emotionally, when situations force them to sever connections with the particular animal. If this seems a strange perversion of human affection, it should be recalled that exactly the same sort of affectional relationship is developed in many a household where there are pets; and it is not uncommon for persons, everywhere in our society, to become considerably upset at the loss of a pet dog or cat which has been in the home for some period of time. The elements that are involved in sexual contacts between the human and animals of other species are at no point basically different from those that are involved in erotic responses to human situations.

On the other side of the record, it is to be noted that male dogs who have been masturbated may become considerably attached to the persons who provide the stimulation; and there are records of male dogs who completely forsake the females of their own species in preference for the sexual contacts that may be had with a human partner.

With most males, animal contacts represent a passing chapter in the sexual history. They are replaced by coitus with human females as soon as that is available. On the other hand, the male who has had any considerable amount of animal experience may become so conditioned that he still finds himself erotically aroused by contemplating such possibilities, even years after he has stopped having actual contacts.

Anglo-American legal codes rate sexual relations between the human and animals of other species as sodomy, punishable under the same laws which penalize homosexual and mouth-genital contacts. The city-bred judge who hears such a case is likely to be unusually severe in his condemnation, and is likely to give the maximum sentence that is possible. Males who are sent to penal institutions on such charges are likely to receive unusually severe treatment both from the administrations and from the inmates of the institutions. All in all, there is probably no type of human sexual behavior which has been more severely condemned by that segment of the population which happens not to have had such experience, and which accepts the age-old judgment that animal intercourse must evidence a mental abnormality, as well as an immorality.

On the other hand, in rural communities where animal contacts are not infrequent, and where there is some general knowledge that they do commonly occur, there seem to be few personal conflicts growing out of such activity, and very few social difficulties. It is only when the farm-bred male migrates to a city community and comes in contact with city-bred reactions to these activities, that he becomes upset over the contemplation of what he has done. This is particularly true if he learns through some psychology course or through books that such behavior is considered abnormal. There are histories of farm-bred males who have risen to positions of importance in the business, academic, or political world in some large urban center, and who have lived for years in constant fear that their early histories will be discovered. The clinician who can reassure these individuals that such activities are biologically and psychologically part of the normal mammalian picture, and that such contacts occur in as high a percentage of the farm population as we have already indicated, may contribute materially toward the resolution of these conflicts.

* * *

Viewed objectively, human sexual behavior, in spite of its diversity, is more easily comprehended than most people, even scientists, have previously realized. The six types of sexual activity, masturbation, spontaneous nocturnal emissions, petting, heterosexual intercourse, homosexual contacts, and animal contacts, may seem to fall into categories that are as far apart as right and wrong, licit and illicit, normal and abnormal, acceptable and unacceptable in our social organization. In actuality, they all prove to originate in the relatively simple mechanisms which provide for erotic response when there are sufficient physical or psychic stimuli.

To each individual, the significance of any particular type of sexual activity depends very largely upon his previous experience. Ultimately, certain activities may seem to him to be the only things that have value, that are right, that are socially acceptable; and all departures from his own particular pattern may seem to him to be enormous abnormalities. But the scientific data which are accumulating make it appear that, if circumstances had been propitious, most individuals might have become conditioned in any direction, even into activities which they now consider quite unacceptable. There is little evidence of the existence of such a thing as innate perversity, even among those individuals whose sexual activities society has been least inclined to accept. There is an abundance of evidence that most human sexual activities would become comprehensible to most individuals, if they could know the background of each other individual's behavior.

The social values of human activities must be measured by many scales other than those which are available to the scientist. Individual responsibilities toward others in the social organization, and the long-range outcome of behavior which represents the individual's response to the stimuli of the immediate moment, are things that persons other than scientists must evaluate. As scientists, we have explored, and we have performed our function when we have published the record of what we have found the human male doing sexually, as far as we have been able to ascertain that fact.

CLINICAL TABLES

Chapter 23

CLINICAL TABLES

This chapter is primarily designed for use by the clinician and some others concerned with directing human behavior. It will be of particular use to psychiatrists, physicians, clinical psychologists, personnel officers, counselors in schools, marriage counselors, court judges, probation and parole officers, institutional directors, social workers, clergymen, teachers, and parents. By means of the tables included in this chapter, it should be possible to compare the sexual history of the individual who comes for help, with averages for other persons of the same age group, educational level, and religious or rural-urban background. Many persons should be interested in comparing their histories with the group patterns.

It is often important to know how far an individual's sexual behavior departs from the pattern of the group in which he has been raised or in which he may now live. Personality conflicts more often depend upon the individual's departure from the pattern of the social group to which he belongs, less often upon his failure to conform to the publicly pretended social code or to the formulated laws. Many clinicians feel that any re-direction of behavior should be limited to fitting the individual into the pattern of the particular group to which he belongs, rather than trying to place him in a pattern which the upper social level considers socially or morally desirable. An increasing number of clinicians have come to realize that attempts to re-direct behavior into patterns which are foreign to the background of the individual may introduce even more conflicts.

Many persons who are disturbed over items in their sexual histories may be put at ease when they learn what the patterns of the rest of the population are, and when they realize that their own behavior has not departed fundamentally from the behavior of most persons in their social group.

It may well be questioned how far an individual is responsible for his behavior when he conforms to the pattern of his social level, even though he may thereby be involved in a transgression of the law. Court officers and other law enforcement officials, administrators of penal, mental, and other institutions, and social workers might well distinguish between departures from the law and departures from the pattern which is common in a whole social group. The clinician who is interested in modifying the pattern of a particular individual should realize that this must ultimately involve a transformation of the pattern of the whole group from which the individual comes.

DEFINITIONS

Terms in these tables have been used with the same meanings that have been applied to them throughout the present volume. Specifically, the following definitions have been used:

1. White males. These tables are based entirely upon white males. The data for Negro males are not included.

2. Marital status. There are three sets of tables (Tables 152, 153, 154) covering single males, married males, and previously married males. Persons who have lived openly as man and wife for a full year in a common law relationship are treated as married persons.

3. Age. Summaries are given for each age group, beginning with a period which extends from adolescence through 15, and continuing with groups that extend beyond that by 5-year periods.

4. Educational level. This represents the amount of schooling which the subject ultimately attains before leaving school. There are three classifications: **0–8** are the males who never have more than grade school education; **9–12** are the males who go into high school but not beyond; **13+** are the males who at least start to college. For those individuals who are still in grade school or high school, the ratings must not be taken to represent the grades in which they are currently located. For a male who is still in grade school or in high school, the clinician may sometimes predict, on the basis of his home background, the amount of his future schooling. All males who are still in college may be considered of college level and located in the tables along with the males who have completed college.

5. Urban. Persons who have lived in cities or towns for the major portion of the period between 12 and 18 years of age.

6. Rural. Persons who have lived on operating farms for an appreciable portion of the time between ages 12 and 18.

7. Protest., active. Persons regularly attendant or actively involved in organizational work in a Protestant church, during the age period presented on the tables.

8. Protest., inactive. Persons with Protestant church background, but not regular attendants or active participants in church activities, during the period shown.

9. Cath., devout. Persons who are members and frequent attendants in the Catholic church, and/or who regularly attend confession.

10. Cath., inactive. Persons with Catholic backgrounds but not regular attendants and not regularly going to confession during the age period shown in the tables.

11. Jewish, Orthod. Persons who are regular attendants at the synagogue and/or more or less strict in their observance of the Orthodox customs.

12. Jewish, inactive. Persons with Jewish backgrounds but not regular attendants at the synagogue or strict in their observance of the Orthodox customs.

13. Source of outlet.

Total. The total number of orgasms (given as averages per week) which result from any and all types of sexual activity, added together

Mast. Masturbation. Orgasms experienced from deliberate self-stimulation by any technique, whether manual, frictional, or other.

Emiss. Nocturnal emissions. Orgasms experienced during sleep, whether with or without accompanying dreams.

Pet. Petting to climax. Orgasms experienced as a result of heterosexual contacts which do not include the actual union of genitalia.

Interc. Intercourse. Orgasms resulting from heterosexual coitus. For single males this represents the total of all pre-marital intercourse, irrespective of whether it is had with companions or with prostitutes, or with both. For married males this represents only that portion of the heterosexual intercourse which is had with the wife. In post-marital histories this is again the total of all heterosexual intercourse, whether with companions or with prostitutes or with both.

Extra. Extra-marital intercourse. The total number of orgasms secured by the married male from coitus with females other than his wife, whether the partners are companions or prostitutes.

Prost. Intercourse with prostitutes. The record of orgasms derived from heterosexual intercourse with prostitutes, in the single, extra-marital, or post-marital histories.

Homo. Homosexual outlet. Orgasms resulting from physical contacts with other males, irrespective of the techniques employed, and irrespective of whether the relation is had with companions or with male prostitutes.

Anim. Animal contacts. Orgasms resulting from sexual contacts with animals other than human, and irrespective of techniques employed.

14. Cases. Showing the size of the population on which the data in the tables are based. It is to be recalled (Chapter 3) that a sample of 50 has proven adequate for establishing incidence data, that samples of 100 or 200 are fairly adequate for means and medians, and that samples of 300 or more are quite adequate for determining means and medians. The larger the sample, the more adequate the data on the range of variation. The clinician may make some allowance for error in data which are shown here when they are based on samples which are smaller than those prescribed above; but such smaller samples may still be taken as indicative of results that may be obtained from larger samples.

15. Incid. %. Showing the percentage of that particular group (the *incidence*) which has any experience with that particular outlet. This provides a figure for calculating the size of the active population.

16. Freq. per week. Data showing the average frequencies per week from each particular source of outlet, for each segment of the population. These data are all based on "active populations," as the term has been used throughout the present volume. They are averages for those persons who derive any of their outlet from that particular source, and they are not averaged with data from those who do not draw an outlet from that source.

17. Range. The ranges given under **Freq. per week** represent the maximum frequencies which have been recorded for the individuals available in the present study, except that the one most extreme individual in each population has not been included. An individual whose rates of outlet average higher than the rates shown in this column, represents a more extreme case than the present investigators have found in a population of the size used here. How far these most extreme individuals depart from the average for the particular population may be seen by comparing the size of the range with the size of the means and the medians.

18. Mean. The means shown under **Freq. per week** represent the average number of orgasms from each particular source in the particular population. They represent one sort of average which should be taken into account in judging the particular individual, but they should be compared with the averages shown as medians in the next column.

19. Median. The medians shown under **Freq. per week** represent the average number of orgasms derived by the average individual (the individual who stands mid-way) in the particular population. In many instances this is the most important sort of average for comparisons. The figures for the median become meaningless, however, when they become too small, in which case the data for the means will have to be relied upon.

20. % of total outlet. These data show the proportion of the total sexual outlet which is derived from each source, in each active population. These do not total 100% for the whole population, because each calculation is based only on those individuals whose histories include the particular outlet (see Chapter 3).

21. Range. The range under **% of total outlet** shows the maximum percentage which any individual in the available sample has derived from a particular source, except that the one most extreme individual is not included in the calculations.

22. Mean. The means under **% of total outlet** show the proportion of the total number of orgasms which, on an average, is derived from the particular source. This is one kind of average, but it should be compared with the averages shown as medians in the next column.

23. Median. The medians under **% of total outlet** show the percentages of the total number of orgasms which are derived from each particular source by the average individual in the active population (the individual who stands mid-way in the whole population).

HOW TO USE THE TABLES

1. After the sexual history of an individual is secured by the clinician, the extent to which the history agrees or disagrees with averages for the particular social group to which he belongs, and the question of whether he falls within or outside of the range of variation now known within that group, may be determined by the use of these clinical tables. Data which the clinician needs for such comparisons should include average frequencies of orgasms experienced by the individual (averaged per week) from each of the possible sources (masturbation, nocturnal emissions, heterosexual petting, total heterosexual intercourse, heterosexual intercourse with prostitutes, marital intercourse, homosexual outlets, and animal contacts), during each of the 5-year periods of the history. The total sexual outlet for the individual in each of the 5-year periods may then be determined by an addition of the above outlets. It is then possible to compute the percentages of the total outlet which the individual has derived from each of these sources, during each of these 5-year periods.

2. The group to which a particular individual belongs may be determined as follows:

  A. Locate the individual in Table 152, 153, or 154, depending on whether he is single, married, or previously married.

  B. Under one of these Tables, pick the age group to which the individual now belongs.

  C. Under each of the ages, locate the section which covers groups whose maximum amount of schooling corresponds with that of the subject.

  D. Under the particular educational levels, locate the individual as urban or rural, and belonging to one or another of the religious groups shown. If the proper rural-urban or religious group is not shown, the history of the particular individual will have to be compared with the data for that educational level taken as a whole.

  E. For further information, examine the data given under each of the age groups which the individual has previously passed through.

3. It is then possible to consider the extent to which the individual's pattern agrees with or departs from the pattern shown for his group in the tables. Remember that in any group there is always considerable individual variation, and that no individual may be expected to conform to averages for the group (see Figures 136 to 160). The extent to which the clinician allows a departure from any average will depend upon his interpretation of the significance of a strict conformance to the group pattern, and his acceptance of some latitude of individual variation. In any event, the judgment of the individual's behavior will have been based upon an understanding of the patterns of sexual behavior which lie in the background from which the individual comes.

4. A generalized statement concerning the nature of the sexual pattern in each of these social groups is given on the right-hand page and directly opposite the corresponding data in the tables. If statistical calculations on the individual's sexual history are not available, or do not seem sufficiently important to secure, his history can at least be compared with the generalized statements given on the right-hand pages throughout this chapter.

TABLE 152. CLINICAL TABLES
SINGLE WHITE MALES

AGE: ADOL.–15	SOURCE OF OUTLET	CASES	INCID. %	FREQ. PER WEEK			% OF TOTAL OUTLET		
				Range	Mean	Med.	Range	Mean	Med.
Educ. level 0–8									
1. Whole group	Total	712	91	25.0	3.3	2.1	—	—	—
	Mast.	712	85	14.0	1.8	1.1	100	66.9	75.8
	Emiss.	712	25	2.5	0.2	0.1	100	17.1	2.7
	Pet.	712	13	3.0	0.2	0.1	30	2.5	0.6
	Interc.	630	48	22.0	2.2	1.2	100	50.8	48.5
	Prost.	712	9	2.0	0.3	0.1	85	12.3	2.5
	Homo.	712	24	7.0	1.0	0.4	100	19.4	9.3
	Anim.	712	6	2.0	0.5	0.1	25	5.2	0.9
2. Urban	Total	401	92	25.0	3.7	2.3	—	—	—
	Mast.	401	87	14.0	2.0	1.2	100	65.6	74.2
	Emiss.	401	27	2.5	0.2	0.1	100	14.1	1.9
	Pet.	401	14	2.5	0.3	0.1	15	2.4	0.6
	Interc.	414	51	22.0	2.5	1.4	100	50.2	48.8
	Prost.	401	10	2.0	0.4	0.2	70	11.4	3.3
	Homo.	401	28	7.0	1.1	0.4	75	17.6	8.1
	Anim.	401	4	1.5	0.3	0.1	25	4.1	0.8
3. Rural	Total	245	89	17.0	2.7	1.7	—	—	—
	Mast.	245	81	14.0	1.6	1.1	100	70.2	84.3
	Emiss.	245	23	2.0	0.2	0.1	100	24.4	4.8
	Pet.	245	12	1.0	0.1	0.1	30	3.1	0.7
	Interc.	199	39	14.0	1.7	0.9	100	52.0	48.1
	Prost.	245	5	1.0	0.2	0.1	85	20.2	3.0
	Homo.	245	18	3.5	1.0	0.5	100	24.9	12.5
	Anim.	245	9	2.0	0.6	0.5	20	7.2	5.8
4. Protest., active	Total	89	83	14.0	3.2	1.9	—	—	—
	Mast.	89	71	10.0	1.8	1.1	100	69.4	87.5
	Emiss.	89	21	0.5	0.1	0.1	100	29.5	4.0
	Pet.	89	11	1.0	0.2	0.1	10	4.4	0.7
	Interc.	83	34	7.0	2.0	0.8	100	51.8	47.5
	Prost.	89	4	0.5	1.1	0.4	30	28.6	17.5
	Homo.	89	22	3.5	1.7	1.7	100	37.1	27.5
	Anim.	78	4	1.0	1.1	1.0	15	13.0	15.0
5. Protest., inactive	Total	481	94	25.0	3.3	2.0	—	—	—
	Mast.	481	88	14.0	1.8	1.1	100	66.3	73.1
	Emiss.	481	26	2.5	0.2	0.1	100	13.6	2.2
	Pet.	422	14	3.0	0.2	0.1	15	2.5	0.6
	Interc.	431	52	22.0	2.2	1.3	100	51.3	49.2
	Prost.	422	10	2.0	0.3	0.1	85	12.2	2.0
	Homo.	481	23	6.0	1.0	0.4	75	17.3	5.4
	Anim.	422	5	1.0	0.2	0.1	20	4.0	0.9
6. Cath., inactive	Total	106	91	14.0	3.6	2.5	—	—	—
	Mast.	106	86	9.0	1.9	1.2	100	64.1	75.0
	Emiss.	106	24	0.5	0.2	0.1	100	17.3	3.0
	Pet.	106	16	1.0	0.2	0.1	10	1.7	0.6
	Interc.	89	45	9.0	2.7	2.1	100	52.6	56.3
	Prost.	106	7	0.5	0.3	0.3	15	7.1	6.3
	Homo.	106	30	3.5	1.0	0.4	55	17.3	6.3
	Anim.	77	8	Scant	0.1	0.1	Scant	4.3	0.7
Educ. level 9–12									
7. Whole group	Total	606	95	25.0	3.5	2.5	—	—	—
	Mast.	606	90	15.0	2.2	1.4	100	70.5	78.5
	Emiss.	606	40	5.0	0.4	0.1	100	16.7	3.7
	Pet.	606	20	2.5	0.2	0.1	40	4.5	0.7
	Interc.	511	43	25.0	1.9	0.8	100	39.9	33.9
	Prost.	606	8	1.0	0.2	0.1	60	7.0	0.9
	Homo.	606	32	7.0	0.9	0.3	100	18.1	4.9
	Anim.	606	6	2.5	0.5	0.2	45	7.8	2.8

TABLE 152. CLINICAL TABLES

SINGLE WHITE MALES

1. Adol.–15. Educ. level 0–8. Whole group. Most boys (91%) immediately active upon onset of adolescence, mean weekly rates 3.3 but often 7 or more. Regular masturbation for 85%, but ½ of total outlet from intercourse for ½ of group. This level accepts intercourse as the great desideratum, often begins it in pre-adolescence. Nocturnal emissions in only ¼ of boys. Homosexual in ¼, accounting for 1/10 of their outlet. Other outlets less frequent.

2. Adol.–15. Educ. level 0–8. Urban. Essentially as described above (Group 1). City-bred boys are somewhat more often involved than rural boys in every type of sexual activity except animal contacts. Masturbation ¾ of outlet for 87% of boys; intercourse important, providing ½ of outlet for ½ of boys. Homosexual in 28%, accounting for 8% of their outlet. All other sources more minor.

3. Adol.–15. Educ. level 0–8. Rural. Essentially as described under Group 1. In most sexual activities, farm boys are less often involved than city boys (Group 2). Masturbation in 81%, intercourse in 39%, homosexual in 18%. Masturbation accounts for 84% of total outlet of those who masturbate at all, intercourse for 48%, homosexual for 13%. Animal contacts to orgasm in 9%, attempts in as many more.

4. Adol.–15. Educ. level 0–8. Protest., active. Somewhat more restrained boys of lower level (Group 1). Fewer individuals involved in any type of activity; only a few of these upset by conflict between religious backgrounds and lower level's acceptance of sex. Boys who do engage in any activity, may have as high frequencies as the rest of the community. Masturbation, intercourse, and the homosexual are the most common, in that order.

5. Adol.–15. Educ. level 0–8. Protest., inactive. A sexually active group of lower level boys (Group 1). Acceptant of most types of sexual activity. Masturbation in 88%, intercourse in 52%, prostitutes in 10%, the homosexual in 23%. Frequencies highest in masturbation and intercourse. Quite aware that their companions and older boys are similarly involved, and not impressed by persons who interfere with such nearly universal activity.

6. Adol.–15. Educ. level 0–8. Cath., inactive. Of Catholic background, but sexual activities little affected by religious teaching. Closely duplicating the group pattern (Group 1), and pattern of inactive Protestant boys (Group 5). Accept masturbation (86% of boys), intercourse (45%), and homosexual relations (30%). Few conflicts. Predominantly heterosexual in psychic response, overt activity, and public pretense; but a full third have some homosexual relations.

7. Adol.–15. Educ. level 9–12. Whole group. Most active of all educational levels, nearly every boy sexually active immediately at adolescence, with high frequencies—3.5 per week, often 10 or more. Nearly all (90%) masturbate; nearly half (43%) have intercourse before 15, many before adolescence; a third (32%) ejaculate in homosexual before 15. Nocturnal emissions (40%) higher than among boys of grade school level; petting more often than in grade school or even college levels.

TABLE 152. CLINICAL TABLES (*continued*)

SINGLE WHITE MALES

AGE: ADOL.–15	SOURCE OF OUTLET	CASES	INCID. %	FREQ. PER WEEK			% OF TOTAL OUTLET		
				Range	Mean	Med.	Range	Mean	Med.
Educ. level 9–12									
8. Urban	Total	459	96	23.0	3.7	2.6	—	—	—
	Mast.	459	90	12.0	2.3	1.6	100	69.1	77.2
	Emiss.	459	42	5.0	0.4	0.1	100	16.7	3.9
	Pet.	459	20	2.5	0.3	0.1	40	5.0	0.7
	Interc.	405	44	25.0	2.0	0.8	100	40.0	35.0
	Prost.	459	8	1.0	0.2	0.1	30	5.1	0.9
	Homo.	459	38	5.0	0.8	0.3	100	18.8	7.9
	Anim.	459	4	2.0	0.5	0.1	20	6.3	3.0
9. Rural	Total	124	94	18.0	3.0	1.9	—	—	—
	Mast.	124	89	9.0	1.9	1.2	100	77.9	92.5
	Emiss.	124	35	2.0	0.3	0.2	100	17.6	3.0
	Pet.	124	18	0.5	0.1	0.1	10	2.6	0.6
	Interc.	91	38	4.5	1.5	0.9	100	37.4	32.0
	Prost.	124	5	Scant	0.1	0.1	Scant	20.0	0.8
	Homo.	124	20	7.0	1.3	0.1	45	12.6	2.3
	Anim.	124	10	1.0	0.4	0.1	45	11.5	3.0
10. Protest., active	Total	93	92	12.0	2.8	1.9	—	—	—
	Mast.	93	87	9.0	2.0	1.6	100	72.0	81.3
	Emiss.	93	41	2.5	0.4	0.2	100	25.8	11.3
	Pet.	93	16	0.5	0.1	0.1	10	3.3	0.7
	Interc.	86	31	4.5	1.4	0.8	80	40.5	40.0
	Prost.	93	5	Scant	0.1	0.1	Scant	1.0	0.8
	Homo.	93	15	2.5	0.7	0.1	75	21.9	3.0
	Anim.	83	5	0.5	0.2	0.2	15	16.8	12.5
11. Protest., inactive	Total	375	95	23.0	3.6	2.5	—	—	—
	Mast.	375	90	12.0	2.1	1.4	100	69.6	77.8
	Emiss.	375	40	4.0	0.4	0.1	100	13.2	2.7
	Pet.	311	21	1.5	0.2	0.1	30	3.7	0.7
	Interc.	318	48	14.0	2.0	1.0	100	42.4	36.1
	Prost.	311	8	0.5	0.2	0.1	15	2.6	0.8
	Homo.	375	34	5.0	0.8	0.3	95	15.6	4.4
	Anim.	311	8	2.0	0.5	0.2	55	7.4	2.7
12. Cath., inactive	Total	103	98	23.0	3.9	2.7	—	—	—
	Mast.	103	95	11.0	2.3	1.6	100	73.9	81.0
	Emiss.	103	35	1.5	0.4	0.2	90	13.1	4.3
	Pet.	103	21	2.5	0.5	0.1	40	7.1	0.7
	Interc.	72	38	3.0	1.6	0.5	85	26.1	22.5
	Prost.	103	9	Scant	0.1	0.1	5	6.5	1.0
	Homo.	103	47	5.0	1.1	0.4	75	23.2	12.5
Educ. level 13+									
13. Whole group	Total	2799	96	29.0	3.0	2.3	—	—	—
	Mast.	2799	82	29.0	2.7	2.1	100	82.2	92.7
	Emiss.	2799	70	12.0	0.5	0.3	100	30.0	11.6
	Pet.	2799	14	3.5	0.3	0.1	80	9.1	0.8
	Interc.	2421	10	9.5	0.8	0.3	100	23.6	9.4
	Prost.	2799	2	0.5	0.1	0.1	35	4.2	0.7
	Homo.	2799	21	6.0	0.4	0.1	90	9.4	1.1
	Anim.	2799	5	8.0	0.4	0.1	75	6.6	0.8
14. Urban	Total	2587	96	29.0	3.0	2.3	—	—	—
	Mast.	2587	82	29.0	2.7	2.1	100	81.8	92.6
	Emiss.	2587	72	12.0	0.5	0.3	100	28.9	10.7
	Pet.	2587	14	3.5	0.3	0.1	70	9.3	0.9
	Interc.	2126	10	9.5	0.8	0.3	100	21.9	9.0
	Prost.	2587	2	0.5	0.1	0.1	15	2.6	0.7
	Homo.	2587	22	6.0	0.4	0.1	85	10.1	1.4
	Anim.	2587	2	2.0	0.1	0.1	51	0.7	0.6

SINGLE WHITE MALES

8. Adol.–15. Educ. level 9–12. Urban. Often very energetic and socially active. Sexually more involved than farm boys (Group 9), especially those city boys who become adolescent by 12. Mean total frequencies 3.7 per week (often to 10 or more). Chief outlets masturbation (among 90%), intercourse (44%), nocturnal emissions (42%), and homosexual (38%). Early becoming proficient at socio-sexual contacts, relatively uninhibited except in a few of the religiously devout.

9. Adol.–15. Educ. level 9–12. Rural. Less active than city-bred boys (Group 8), more active than farm boys of grade school level (Group 3). Most (89%) masturbate, a third (38%) have coitus, another third (35%) nocturnal emissions. In contrast to city boys, only one in five (20%) has homosexual, but one in ten (10%) completes animal intercourse, as many more may attempt it. For those actively involved, 92% of outlet from masturbation, 32% from intercourse.

10. Adol.–15. Educ. level 9–12. Protest., active. Slightly less active, but actually very close to other young adolescent boys of high school level (Group 7). Masturbation in 87% of histories, intercourse in one-third, these the chief sources of outlet. Nevertheless, petting and homosexual in one in seven histories. An occasional individual may be in conflict with religious backgrounds, but more affected by group pattern than by religion.

11. Adol.–15. Educ. level 9–12. Protest., inactive. Data almost exactly as described for urban group of high school level (Group 8). Incidences highest in masturbation (90%), intercourse (48%), nocturnal emissions (40%), and the homosexual (34%). Chief outlets from masturbation (78% of total for masturbating males) and intercourse (36% of total for males who have any coitus). Group accepts sex with little conflict.

12. Adol.–15. Educ. level 9–12. Cath., inactive. Most active of younger adolescent boys, 98% having some outlet by 15. This a reflection of community acceptance of sex, and of minimum attention to religious teaching. Incidences highest in masturbation (95%), homosexual (47%), intercourse (38%). Chief outlets masturbation (81%), intercourse (22%). Intercourse considered highly desirable. Homosexual often condemned, but nearly one-half (47%) draw 12.5% of their outlet from it.

13. Adol.–15. Educ. level 13+. Whole group. Boys who ultimately go to college become active early, depend chiefly on masturbation and nocturnal emissions. Masturbation often accepted, occasionally causes worry, not as often as among older generations. Pre-adolescent play chiefly exhibitionistic, with little carry-over. Much inhibited socio-sexually, from adolescence and on. Much less affected than lower level boys by sexual activities of older companions, but soon acquire community judgment that intercourse is wrong. More often pet to climax. 21% have homosexual contacts (infrequently); this not often causing conflicts at this age.

14. Adol.–15. Educ. level 13+. Urban. More or less precisely matches description given above (Group 13) for whole college level at this age; but animal intercourse rare in this city-bred group.

TABLE 152. CLINICAL TABLES (*continued*)
SINGLE WHITE MALES

AGE: ADOL.–15	SOURCE OF OUTLET	CASES	INCID. %	FREQ. PER WEEK			% OF TOTAL OUTLET		
				Range	Mean	Med.	Range	Mean	Med.
Educ. level 13+									
15. Rural	Total	352	96	20.0	3.1	2.4	—	—	—
	Mast.	352	84	14.0	2.7	2.2	100	84.8	94.4
	Emiss.	352	62	4.0	0.4	0.3	100	28.0	11.1
	Pet.	352	11	1.0	0.2	0.1	25	3.6	0.6
	Interc.	265	11	4.5	0.8	0.3	100	35.7	20.0
	Prost.	352	2	0.5	0.1	0.1	10	3.8	0.9
	Homo.	352	21	2.5	0.4	0.1	40	6.4	2.4
	Anim.	352	28	8.0	0.5	0.1	75	9.1	1.0
16. Protest., active	Total	547	95	12.0	2.6	2.1	—	—	—
	Mast.	547	81	12.0	2.3	1.9	100	81.2	90.4
	Emiss.	547	71	7.0	0.5	0.3	100	33.5	17.2
	Pet.	484	14	3.0	0.4	0.1	60	11.3	0.9
	Interc.	493	7	4.5	0.8	0.3	100	21.3	8.6
	Prost.	484	2	Scant	0.1	0.1	Scant	0.8	0.6
	Homo.	547	24	4.0	0.4	0.1	80	8.8	1.7
	Anim.	484	9	2.0	0.3	0.1	30	6.2	0.8
17. Protest., inactive	Total	1471	96	25.0	3.2	2.6	—	—	—
	Mast.	1471	85	20.0	2.8	2.3	100	81.6	92.1
	Emiss.	1471	68	7.0	0.5	0.3	100	29.2	11.5
	Pet.	1178	17	2.5	0.3	0.1	70	8.2	0.8
	Interc.	1205	11	7.0	0.8	0.3	100	22.6	10.0
	Prost.	1178	2	0.5	0.1	0.1	15	2.5	0.7
	Homo.	1471	26	5.0	0.4	0.1	85	7.8	1.0
	Anim.	1178	7	2.5	0.4	0.1	35	5.2	0.8
18. Cath., devout	Total	132	98	16.0	2.5	1.7	—	—	—
	Mast.	132	79	16.0	2.5	1.6	100	83.4	91.7
	Emiss.	132	75	3.0	0.4	0.3	100	40.1	19.5
	Pet.	132	8	0.5	0.2	0.2	25	9.9	5.5
	Interc.	103	5	1.5	0.9	1.0	45	37.0	40.0
	Prost.	132	2	0.1	0.1	0.1	1	4.3	5.5
	Homo.	132	17	2.5	0.5	0.1	40	14.2	5.0
	Anim.	98	3	0.1	0.1	0.1	1	1.3	1.0
19. Cath., inactive	Total	165	95	15.0	3.2	2.3	—	—	—
	Mast.	165	81	14.0	2.9	2.0	100	77.9	89.4
	Emiss.	165	65	3.5	0.5	0.3	100	33.9	12.0
	Pet.	165	13	1.0	0.2	0.1	50	17.7	6.3
	Interc.	117	16	3.0	1.5	0.5	95	33.9	25.0
	Prost.	165	4	0.5	0.1	0.1	5	8.0	3.0
	Homo.	165	20	2.5	0.6	0.2	50	16.6	10.8
20. Jewish, Orthod.	Total	58	91	7.0	2.1	1.4	—	—	—
	Mast.	58	72	6.0	2.2	1.5	100	76.5	95.0
	Emiss.	58	78	2.5	0.3	0.2	100	37.7	15.0
	Pet.	58	21	1.5	0.3	0.1	50	14.0	0.9
	Interc.	53	11	1.0	0.6	0.3	50	26.3	20.0
	Prost.	58	5	0.1	0.1	0.1	Scant	0.5	0.7
	Homo.	58	10	0.5	0.1	0.1	5	10.9	2.0
21. Jewish, inactive	Total	601	96	29.0	3.0	2.3	—	—	—
	Mast.	601	80	29.0	2.9	2.2	100	81.2	93.9
	Emiss.	601	75	6.5	0.5	0.3	100	36.5	19.6
	Pet.	377	10	1.0	0.2	0.1	45	9.1	1.7
	Interc.	412	7	3.0	0.5	0.1	75	13.2	5.0
	Prost.	377	2	0.5	0.3	0.1	10	7.7	1.0
	Homo.	601	15	4.5	0.4	0.1	55	9.9	2.8
	Anim.	377	1	Scant	0.1	0.1	Scant	0.5	1.0

SINGLE WHITE MALES

15. Adol.–15. Educ. level 13+. Rural. Closely matches whole college level of this age (Group 13). But animal intercourse with orgasm occurs among more than a quarter (28%), attempts with animals may occur in nearly as many more, so about half of these boys may be involved, with frequencies that average once in ten weeks. Conflicts rarely develop out of this, unless some city-bred clinician or other adult becomes disturbed in dealing with the boy.

16. Adol.–15. Educ. level 13+. Protest., active. Closely similar to whole group of boys of college level (Group 13), with only a slightly more inhibited pattern. Differing chiefly in being still less often involved in intercourse (7%) and still more often in the homosexual (24%). Some individuals in the group, however, in conflict over what sexual activity they do have.

17. Adol.–15. Educ. level 13+. Protest., inactive. Sexual pattern a close duplicate of that described for whole group of young boys of college level (Group 13). Only a bit more active in each type of sexual activity. Not so often in conflict over their sexual activity, but boys of college level rarely come to consider pre-marital socio-sexual contacts as right.

18. Adol.–15. Educ. level 13+. Cath., devout. A slightly more restrained version of pattern typical of all college level at this age (Group 13). This identity emphasizes that it is group pattern rather than immediate religious background that is most significant (Chapter 10). Religious teaching, however, may introduce conflicts which are not infrequently observed among boys in this group. Emissions supply 20% of outlet for ¾ of boys.

19. Adol.–15. Educ. level 13+. Cath., inactive. Not particularly different from pattern followed by all younger boys of college level (Group 13). Differing chiefly from devout Catholics in having 3 times as many (16%) involved in intercourse. Still as restrained as rest of college level, irrespective of lack of religious background (Chapter 10).

20. Adol.–15. Educ. level 13+. Jewish, Orthodox. Most restrained of all younger adolescents of college level, mean outlet only 2.1. Slower in getting started, depending more often on involuntary emissions; only 72% start masturbation, against which there are strong taboos. Petting more often than any other college level group, but intercourse in only 11% of cases. Compared with rest of college level, one-half as many (10%) with homosexual. The pattern lays groundwork for personality conflicts which are frequent in next age group of these males.

21. Adol.–15. Educ. level 13+. Jewish, inactive. Closer to average for all college level boys (Group 13), in some respects less restrained than Orthodox Jewish boys, but taboos on heterosexual petting (10%) and intercourse (7%) apparently more severe. Sometimes involved in conflicts over sexual codes, even though not actively connected with church.

TABLE 152. CLINICAL TABLES (*continued*)
SINGLE WHITE MALES

AGE: 16–20	SOURCE OF OUTLET	CASES	INCID. %	FREQ. PER WEEK			% OF TOTAL OUTLET		
				Range	Mean	Med.	Range	Mean	Med.
Educ. level 0–8									
22. Whole group	Total	720	97	29.0	3.3	2.2	—	—	—
	Mast.	720	84	8.0	1.1	0.6	100	42.0	34.0
	Emiss.	720	56	2.5	0.3	0.1	100	12.4	3.7
	Pet.	720	21	3.0	0.3	0.1	40	3.3	0.6
	Interc.	635	85	22.0	2.0	1.0	100	57.3	59.7
	Prost.	720	48	4.0	0.4	0.1	100	15.7	4.8
	Homo.	720	26	7.0	0.8	0.3	75	16.7	5.2
	Anim.	720	4	2.5	0.5	0.2	20	4.1	1.0
23. Urban	Total	397	98	26.0	3.5	2.4	—	—	—
	Mast.	397	85	8.0	1.2	0.6	100	39.2	31.0
	Emiss.	397	58	2.5	0.3	0.1	100	10.4	3.1
	Pet.	397	22	3.0	0.3	0.1	25	3.0	0.7
	Interc.	406	87	22.0	2.3	1.3	100	60.2	64.0
	Prost.	397	51	4.0	0.5	0.2	100	17.3	6.0
	Homo.	397	32	5.5	0.8	0.3	75	15.6	5.2
	Anim.	397	2	1.5	0.6	0.1	20	4.9	1.0
24. Rural	Total	259	96	16.0	2.9	2.0	—	—	—
	Mast.	259	85	7.0	1.1	0.7	100	50.7	48.8
	Emiss.	259	53	2.0	0.3	0.1	100	14.1	4.0
	Pet.	259	18	1.5	0.2	0.1	30	4.1	0.7
	Interc.	208	81	14.0	1.6	0.7	100	51.1	48.9
	Prost.	259	42	3.0	0.4	0.1	95	14.1	3.8
	Homo.	259	21	7.0	1.0	0.4	70	18.1	7.5
	Anim.	259	7	2.0	0.5	0.3	5	2.2	1.4
25. Protest., active	Total	91	93	15.0	2.9	1.7	—	—	—
	Mast.	91	81	5.0	1.0	0.5	100	51.1	43.3
	Emiss.	91	53	2.0	0.3	0.1	100	14.2	1.6
	Pet.	91	19	1.0	0.1	0.1	5	0.9	0.7
	Interc.	81	70	14.0	1.8	0.6	100	53.0	52.5
	Prost.	91	37	1.0	0.3	0.1	75	14.8	5.0
	Homo.	91	23	3.0	1.4	0.8	70	29.6	27.5
26. Protest., inactive	Total	493	98	29.0	3.4	2.3	—	—	—
	Mast.	493	86	8.0	1.1	0.6	100	40.9	33.7
	Emiss.	493	57	2.5	0.3	0.1	100	10.3	2.6
	Pet.	431	22	3.0	0.2	0.1	30	3.1	0.7
	Interc.	442	90	22.0	2.1	1.1	100	58.1	61.1
	Prost.	431	49	4.0	0.4	0.2	100	16.9	5.2
	Homo.	493	24	7.0	0.8	0.3	75	14.4	4.1
	Anim.	431	4	2.5	0.4	0.1	20	3.1	0.9
27. Cath., inactive	Total	105	98	12.0	3.5	2.6	—	—	—
	Mast.	105	85	7.0	1.2	0.7	100	45.1	36.9
	Emiss.	105	57	1.0	0.3	0.2	40	11.6	6.3
	Pet.	105	23	1.0	0.2	0.1	10	1.9	0.7
	Interc.	88	81	10.0	2.3	1.3	100	57.5	60.0
	Prost.	105	59	3.0	0.5	0.2	100	14.1	5.6
	Homo.	105	35	4.0	1.0	0.4	60	17.1	4.6
Educ. level 9–12									
28. Whole group	Total	607	100	26.0	3.5	2.7	—	—	—
	Mast.	607	89	15.0	1.5	0.8	100	45.4	39.2
	Emiss.	607	71	3.0	0.3	0.1	100	13.6	3.9
	Pet.	607	34	2.0	0.2	0.1	50	5.5	0.7
	Interc.	515	76	25.0	1.9	0.9	100	51.7	55.8
	Prost.	607	41	2.5	0.2	0.1	100	9.5	0.9
	Homo.	607	41	11.0	0.9	0.3	100	19.0	5.3
	Anim.	607	5	3.5	0.8	0.2	65	15.5	5.8

SINGLE WHITE MALES

22. Age 16–20. Educ. level 0–8. Whole group. Most boys sexually most active at this age, mean frequencies 3.3 per week, often 10, or more. Masturbation still in 84%, becoming strongly taboo at this level, constituting only 34% of outlet. Intercourse expected, freely accepted (Chapter 10), in 85%, contributing 60% of outlet; males often promiscuous, often with venereal disease, often in conflict with society because of sexual activity. Petting in 21%, a very minor outlet. Homosexual in a quarter (26%), but publicly condemned and infrequent. Nocturnal emissions in half (56%), very minor outlet. Individuals who were adolescent by 12 most active of all single males (Chapter 9); but mentally and physically poorer individuals often with low rates. Little psychic eroticism. Often strong taboos against nudity, oral eroticism, and some petting techniques.

23. Age 16–20. Educ. level 0–8. Urban. Typical of whole grade school level (Group 22). More active than corresponding rural males (Group 24), more often involved in intercourse and homosexual, less often with animals. A third of outlet from solitary sources, two-thirds from socio-sexual contacts.

24. Age 16–20. Educ. level 0–8. Rural. Typical of whole grade school level (Group 22), not quite so active. Not so many (81%) with intercourse, only 21% with homosexual. Masturbation and intercourse account for most of outlet, equally important. Animal intercourse still in 7%, of minor significance at this age.

25. Age 16–20. Educ. level 0–8. Protest., active. Somewhat less active than average of grade school level (Group 22), much more active than any college group. Intercourse still accepted in 70%, accounting for 53% of outlet. Masturbation in 81% but taboo, accounting for only 43% of outlet. Homosexual in nearly a quarter (23%), accounting for 28% of their outlet. Other activities minor.

26. Age 16–20. Educ. level 0–8. Protest., inactive. Very close to average for whole lower level (Group 22), in most outlets somewhat more active. Intercourse now in 90% for whom it provides nearly two-thirds (61%) of outlet. Masturbation still in 86%, but taboo and provides only a third of outlet. All else very minor. Rarely any conflict over behavior.

27. Age 16–20. Educ. level 0–8. Cath., inactive. A rather active group of lower level boys, averaging 3.5 per week, often 7 or more. Intercourse in 81%, accounting for 60% of outlet. Masturbation in 85%, accounting for only 37% of outlet. All other activities minor. Homosexual in 35%, but accounting for less than 5% of orgasms even for those males. Quite acceptant of this pattern, not often with conflicts.

28. Age 16–20. Educ. level 9–12. Whole group. This age at high school and grade school levels (Group 22) more active than any other single males (especially if adolescent by 12). Masturbation in 89% but more or less taboo, accounting for 39% of outlet. Intercourse in three-quarters (76%), accounting for 56% of outlet. Often highly promiscuous, not infrequently acquiring venereal disease. Nocturnal emissions, petting, prostitutes, homosexual in many histories, but minor as sources of outlet. 41% experiment with homosexual, often severely condemning it but clearly aroused by it. Otherwise little conflict over their pattern. Especially acceptant of heterosexual activity, although this may bring difficulty with police. More erotic psychically than grade school level; more or less accept nudity and oral eroticism; involved in petting as often as college males.

TABLE 152. CLINICAL TABLES (*continued*)
SINGLE WHITE MALES

AGE: 16-20	SOURCE OF OUTLET	CASES	INCID. %	FREQ. PER WEEK Range	FREQ. PER WEEK Mean	FREQ. PER WEEK Med.	% OF TOTAL OUTLET Range	% OF TOTAL OUTLET Mean	% OF TOTAL OUTLET Med.
Educ. level 9-12									
29. Urban	Total	520	100	26.0	3.6	2.7	—	—	—
	Mast.	520	90	8.0	1.5	0.9	100	45.4	39.7
	Emiss.	520	71	3.0	0.3	0.1	100	13.4	4.2
	Pet.	458	34	2.0	0.3	0.1	50	6.0	0.8
	Interc.	405	73	25.0	1.9	0.9	100	51.6	55.6
	Prost.	458	41	2.0	0.2	0.1	85	9.5	1.0
	Homo.	520	46	11.0	1.0	0.4	100	20.6	6.6
	Anim.	458	3	3.0	0.7	0.1	25	7.0	1.0
30. Rural	Total	124	99	17.0	3.2	2.5	—	—	—
	Mast.	124	85	7.0	1.3	0.8	100	47.0	39.2
	Emiss.	124	72	2.0	0.3	0.1	100	12.3	2.3
	Pet.	124	31	1.0	0.1	0.1	30	3.6	0.7
	Interc.	95	87	7.0	1.7	1.0	100	51.8	56.3
	Prost.	124	41	2.5	0.3	0.1	25	5.2	0.8
	Homo.	124	26	2.0	0.4	0.1	55	9.4	0.8
	Anim.	124	10	2.5	0.9	0.4	65	27.8	25.0
31. Protest., active	Total	95	100	9.5	2.5	1.7	—	—	—
	Mast.	95	88	6.0	1.3	0.7	100	51.8	50.0
	Emiss.	95	72	2.0	0.3	0.1	100	19.4	6.4
	Pet.	95	32	1.0	0.2	0.1	35	6.5	0.8
	Interc.	89	67	6.0	1.3	0.7	100	49.8	55.8
	Prost.	95	32	1.0	0.2	0.1	20	3.6	0.8
	Homo.	95	31	3.0	0.7	0.1	80	14.8	0.9
32. Protest., inactive	Total	315	99	21.0	3.6	2.7	—	—	—
	Mast.	315	89	7.0	1.4	0.8	100	43.4	37.3
	Emiss.	315	73	3.0	0.3	0.1	100	11.5	3.2
	Pet.	315	33	2.0	0.2	0.1	60	6.3	0.7
	Interc.	322	80	20.0	2.0	0.9	100	52.9	57.0
	Prost.	315	44	2.0	0.2	0.1	100	8.9	0.9
	Homo.	315	37	6.0	0.8	0.2	100	16.4	4.7
	Anim.	315	6	3.5	0.9	0.4	65	16.2	6.7
33. Cath., inactive	Total	101	100	19.0	4.4	3.2	—	—	—
	Mast.	101	91	8.0	1.7	1.0	100	44.0	39.6
	Emiss.	101	60	2.0	0.3	0.2	50	10.1	5.0
	Pet.	101	36	2.0	0.4	0.1	30	6.5	0.8
	Interc.	69	68	13.0	2.0	1.0	100	54.6	57.5
	Prost.	101	45	1.5	0.2	0.1	75	9.2	0.9
	Homo.	101	59	6.0	1.4	0.6	85	29.3	22.5
Educ. level 13+									
34. Whole group	Total	2861	100	24.0	2.7	2.1	—	—	—
	Mast.	2861	89	23.0	2.0	1.5	100	68.3	76.0
	Emiss.	2861	91	6.5	0.5	0.3	100	25.4	12.7
	Pet.	2861	46	5.0	0.3	0.1	100	10.7	0.9
	Interc.	2475	42	12.0	0.6	0.2	100	18.5	4.9
	Prost.	2861	19	1.5	0.1	0.1	50	2.4	0.6
	Homo.	2861	16	7.0	0.4	0.1	90	10.1	1.1
	Anim.	2861	2	2.0	0.4	0.1	50	10.1	2.8
35. Urban	Total	2762	100	24.0	2.8	2.2	—	—	—
	Mast.	2762	89	23.0	2.1	1.6	100	66.2	71.8
	Emiss.	2762	91	6.5	0.5	0.3	100	25.1	11.8
	Pet.	2762	48	5.0	0.3	0.1	95	12.1	0.9
	Interc.	2172	43	12.0	0.6	0.2	100	18.9	5.4
	Prost.	2640	20	1.5	0.1	0.1	40	2.0	0.6
	Homo.	2762	1	7.0	0.4	0.1	70	10.3	1.0
	Anim.	2640	1	Scant	0.1	0.1	10	5.5	0.8

* ## SINGLE WHITE MALES

29. Age 16–20. Educ. level 9–12. Urban. Fits description given above for high school level in late teens (Group 28). More often (46%) experiments with homosexual; but intercourse the accepted source, accounting for 56% of outlet. Often highly promiscuous, often (in 41%) with prostitutes.

30. Age 16–20. Educ. level 9–12. Rural. Not significantly different from whole high school level (Group 28). Differs from corresponding urban groups in being involved in intercourse in more cases (87%), less often in homosexual (26%). Animal intercourse in 10%, this a rather material outlet (25%) for males involved.

31. Age 16–20. Educ. level 9–12. Protest., active. Pattern typical of whole high school level (Group 28). Showing little effect of church connections, unless an occasional individual is disturbed by conflicts between religious teaching and group pattern which he actually follows. Intercourse in somewhat fewer histories (67%), homosexual in fewer (31%).

32. Age 16–20. Educ. level 9–12. Protest., inactive. Pattern typical of whole high school level (Group 28). The group pattern predominates. Not materially different from active Protestant group, except more (80%) involved in intercourse; 44% with prostitutes; 37% with homosexual experience. Intercourse chief source (57%) of outlet, masturbation next (37%).

33. Age 16–20. Educ. level 9–12. Cath., inactive. Most unrestrained and sexually most active of all high school level (Group 28), with almost double the outlet of active Protestants. Mean rate totals 4.4, higher than in any other single males except individuals who become adolescent at early ages. Incidences and rates high in masturbation, petting, intercourse with prostitutes, and homosexual (59%). Incidences and rates lower for nocturnal emissions and (strangely enough) for intercourse (68%). Few sexual conflicts, though often social difficulties from sexual activity.

34. Age 16–20. Educ. level 13+. Whole group. Highly restrained (Chapter 10), largely avoiding socio-sexual contacts on moral grounds (often rationalized as "sensible" or "decent"). Even those who pet to climax (46%), have intercourse (42%), or homosexual (16%), derive less than 7% of total outlet from such sources, over 90% from solitary sources (masturbation, nocturnal emissions). Few partners in socio-sexual contacts. Much psychic eroticism that does not lead to intercourse. Many individuals appear to accept such a regime, but many actually tense in socio-sexual situations. Some much disturbed over few contacts they do have. Masturbation, petting, oral eroticism, nudity more often accepted. Most American-trained clinicians come from this group, and may therefore need to make special effort to recognize inhibitions and conflicts inherent in such asocial patterns.

35. Age 16–20. Educ. level 13+. Urban. Typical of whole college level (Group 34).

TABLE 152. CLINICAL TABLES (*continued*)
SINGLE WHITE MALES

AGE: 16–20	SOURCE OF OUTLET	CASES	INCID. %	FREQ. PER WEEK			% OF TOTAL OUTLET		
				Range	Mean	Med.	Range	Mean	Med.
Educ. level 13+									
36. Rural	Total	363	100	13.0	2.5	2.0	—	—	—
	Mast.	363	89	8.0	1.9	1.4	100	73.3	79.0
	Emiss.	363	92	5.0	0.5	0.3	100	24.5	13.7
	Pet.	363	35	2.0	0.2	0.1	75	5.1	0.7
	Interc.	272	36	5.5	0.5	0.1	95	16.6	3.0
	Prost.	363	13	0.5	0.1	0.1	10	1.7	0.6
	Homo.	363	17	2.0	0.3	0.1	50	7.7	2.0
	Anim.	363	16	2.0	0.5	0.1	50	11.7	4.2
37. Protest., active	Total	557	100	11.0	2.3	1.8	—	—	—
	Mast.	557	86	10.0	1.8	1.3	100	71.3	77.4
	Emiss.	557	92	5.0	0.5	0.3	100	29.2	16.7
	Pet.	492	40	3.5	0.4	0.1	100	12.7	1.0
	Interc.	502	27	7.0	0.6	0.1	100	15.2	2.4
	Prost.	492	11	0.5	0.1	0.1	20	2.5	0.6
	Homo.	557	17	4.0	0.4	0.1	75	8.3	1.3
	Anim.	492	4	1.0	0.3	0.2	40	10.1	3.4
38. Protest., inactive	Total	1513	100	21.0	2.9	2.4	—	—	—
	Mast.	1513	91	14.0	2.1	1.6	100	68.9	76.2
	Emiss.	1513	92	6.0	0.5	0.3	100	24.3	12.3
	Pet.	1210	47	4.0	0.3	0.1	90	9.3	0.9
	Interc.	1235	45	9.0	0.6	0.2	100	18.1	6.1
	Prost.	1210	20	0.5	0.1	0.1	25	1.4	0.6
	Homo.	1513	18	5.0	0.4	0.1	90	8.9	0.9
	Anim.	1210	3	2.0	0.6	0.1	50	9.7	2.3
39. Cath., devout	Total	136	100	12.0	2.4	1.7	—	—	—
	Mast.	136	84	12.0	1.8	1.0	100	66.4	75.6
	Emiss.	136	94	4.5	0.5	0.3	100	34.2	24.2
	Pet.	136	43	2.0	0.4	0.1	60	14.0	5.0
	Interc.	107	39	2.0	0.5	0.1	100	19.7	5.4
	Prost.	136	16	0.5	0.2	0.1	10	2.0	0.7
	Homo.	136	15	1.0	0.3	0.1	15	5.5	2.2
40. Cath., inactive	Total	168	100	13.0	2.8	2.2	—	—	—
	Mast.	168	86	11.0	1.9	1.5	100	56.2	58.8
	Emiss.	168	91	3.0	0.5	0.3	100	29.2	14.0
	Pet.	168	50	1.0	0.2	0.1	50	9.5	1.0
	Interc.	120	59	5.5	0.9	0.3	100	29.1	13.8
	Prost.	168	30	1.0	0.2	0.1	30	3.5	0.7
	Homo.	168	20	3.0	0.7	0.3	70	19.7	10.0
41. Jewish, Orthod.	Total	59	100	6.0	2.0	1.6	—	—	—
	Mast.	59	78	6.0	1.5	0.9	100	64.3	72.5
	Emiss.	59	90	2.0	0.4	0.3	100	37.0	23.8
	Pet.	59	46	1.5	0.3	0.1	60	11.0	1.0
	Interc.	54	39	2.5	0.6	0.3	85	28.0	15.0
	Prost.	59	20	Scant	0.1	0.1	Scant	0.7	0.6
	Homo.	59	12	0.5	0.2	0.1	15	9.8	0.8
42. Jewish, inactive	Total	607	100	23.0	3.0	2.3	—	—	—
	Mast.	607	88	23.0	2.4	1.7	100	70.4	78.2
	Emiss.	607	86	6.0	0.5	0.3	100	29.6	15.7
	Pet.	379	48	3.5	0.3	0.1	80	9.9	2.6
	Interc.	416	46	5.5	0.5	0.1	95	14.6	2.8
	Prost.	379	22	1.5	0.1	0.1	50	3.8	0.6
	Homo.	607	11	3.5	0.6	0.1	70	12.7	2.0

SINGLE WHITE MALES

36. Age 16–20. Educ. level 13+. Rural. Close to pattern for whole college level (Group 34), a bit less active. Incidences, frequencies, and percents of total outlet a bit lower in petting, total intercourse, intercourse with prostitutes. Animal intercourse in 16%, attempts in still others; but provides only 4% of outlet.

37. Age 16–20. Educ. level 13+. Protest., active. Pattern close to that for whole college level (Group 34), but still lower incidences, frequencies, and percents of total outlet. Intercourse in only 27%, lower than in any other group of this age, as against 80% to 91% incidence figures in other educational levels at this same age.

38. Age 16–20. Educ. level 13+. Protest., inactive. Typical of whole college level (Group 34). Because they are not active in church, many of this group consider themselves emancipated sexually, and a few more (45%) do have intercourse, but even they derive only 6% of outlet therefrom. Actually about as restrained as actively religious groups; and clinician should realize these males are equally capable of being disturbed over the few socio-sexual contacts they do have.

39. Age 16–20. Educ. level 13+. Cath., devout. Close to pattern for whole college level (Group 34), showing remarkably little effect of devoutly religious background. Slightly lower incidences in most outlets, this raising importance but not actual frequencies of nocturnal emissions. Group pattern (Chapter 10) more important than immediate religious influences (Chapter 13).

40. Age 16–20. Educ. level 13+. Cath., inactive. Close to pattern for whole college level (Group 34), not nearly as distinct as religiously inactive groups are at lower educational levels. Hardly differs from devout Catholic group except in lower percent of outlet from masturbation and emissions, higher incidence (59%) of intercourse, and higher rates and percent of outlet from that source.

41. Age 16–20. Educ. level 13+. Jewish, Orthodox. Most restrained and sexually least active among all groups of college level (Group 34). Total outlet only 2.0 per week. Incidences lower in masturbation (78%), intercourse (39%), homosexual (12%). Total outlet largely from masturbation (73%) and nocturnal emissions (24%). Relation of sexual restraint and neuroses should be given especial attention by clinician handling individual cases in this group.

42. Age 16–20. Educ. level 13+. Jewish, inactive. Very similar to pattern of whole college level (Group 34). Much restraint still to be recognized here. Remarkably close to Orthodox pattern (Group 41), even though present group not actively connected with synagogue. A few more (46%) have intercourse, but percent of total outlet from intercourse (3%) actually lower than in Orthodox group (15%); much of intercourse commercially secured from prostitutes.

TABLE 152. CLINICAL TABLES (*continued*)
SINGLE WHITE MALES

AGE: 21–25	SOURCE OF OUTLET	CASES	INCID. %	FREQ. PER WEEK			% OF TOTAL OUTLET		
				Range	Mean	Med.	Range	Mean	Med.
Educ. level 0–8									
43. Whole group	Total	361	97	26.0	3.3	2.0	—	—	—
	Mast.	361	62	7.0	1.0	0.5	100	37.5	24.8
	Emiss.	361	60	2.0	0.3	0.1	100	13.2	4.0
	Pet.	361	16	2.0	0.3	0.1	25	2.8	0.6
	Interc.	312	86	18.0	2.3	1.1	100	66.4	76.3
	Prost.	361	61	7.0	0.6	0.3	100	28.2	16.3
	Homo.	361	22	6.0	1.1	0.4	90	21.7	9.0
	Anim.	361	1	1.0	0.4	0.3	Scant	9.3	10.5
44. Urban	Total	188	98	26.0	3.4	2.0	—	—	—
	Mast.	188	63	7.0	1.0	0.5	100	34.2	22.5
	Emiss.	188	60	2.0	0.3	0.1	100	11.8	3.5
	Pet.	188	16	2.0	0.3	0.1	15	2.4	0.6
	Interc.	195	91	18.0	2.6	1.4	100	68.4	78.8
	Prost.	188	66	5.5	0.7	0.4	100	29.6	18.1
	Homo.	188	29	5.0	0.9	0.4	100	20.6	10.0
45. Rural	Total	141	95	19.0	3.0	1.8	—	—	—
	Mast.	141	64	5.5	1.1	0.6	100	48.0	45.0
	Emiss.	141	57	2.0	0.3	0.1	100	16.4	4.8
	Pet.	141	13	1.0	0.2	0.1	15	5.7	0.9
	Interc.	106	80	14.0	1.8	0.8	100	62.8	68.0
	Prost.	141	50	4.5	0.6	0.3	100	27.3	13.8
	Homo.	141	17	3.5	1.5	0.4	70	32.8	25.0
	Anim.	141	3	1.0	0.4	0.3	Scant	6.3	1.0
46. Protest., inactive	Total	234	98	26.0	3.3	2.1	—	—	—
	Mast.	234	62	6.0	1.0	0.5	100	38.2	25.0
	Emiss.	234	59	2.0	0.3	0.1	95	11.4	3.0
	Pet.	234	15	1.5	0.3	0.1	40	4.3	0.7
	Interc.	200	92	18.0	2.4	1.2	100	67.4	77.7
	Prost.	234	64	5.0	0.6	0.3	100	28.1	16.5
	Homo.	234	19	4.0	1.1	0.5	70	20.7	11.3
47. Cath., inactive	Total	60	98	12.0	3.3	2.3	—	—	—
	Mast.	60	67	4.0	0.9	0.4	100	32.7	22.5
	Emiss.	60	65	1.5	0.3	0.2	50	13.4	8.5
	Pet.	60	23	0.5	0.2	0.1	10	3.5	0.8
	Interc.	57	86	10.0	2.3	1.3	100	68.9	75.0
	Prost.	60	63	5.5	0.9	0.4	100	39.9	30.0
	Homo.	60	40	3.5	0.9	0.3	90	21.1	4.6
Educ. level 9–12									
48. Whole group	Total	263	99	25.0	3.0	2.3	—	—	—
	Mast.	263	76	7.0	1.1	0.6	100	40.9	35.4
	Emiss.	263	71	2.0	0.3	0.2	100	16.5	7.1
	Pet.	263	28	2.0	0.3	0.1	65	8.9	0.8
	Interc.	217	74	25.0	1.7	0.8	100	53.9	58.3
	Prost.	263	44	2.0	0.3	0.1	100	15.6	2.9
	Homo.	263	38	11.0	1.3	0.7	100	33.7	29.2
	Anim.	263	3	0.5	0.5	0.1	15	17.2	15.0
49. Urban	Total	209	100	17.0	3.2	2.6	—	—	—
	Mast.	209	79	7.0	1.2	0.7	100	41.5	37.5
	Emiss.	209	70	2.0	0.4	0.2	80	15.4	7.5
	Pet.	209	29	2.0	0.3	0.1	65	9.8	0.8
	Interc.	172	72	25.0	1.6	0.7	100	51.7	52.5
	Prost.	209	41	2.0	0.3	0.1	90	15.0	2.5
	Homo.	209	43	14.0	1.6	0.9	100	36.9	35.0
	Anim.	209	2	Scant	0.7	0.1	Scant	0.5	1.0

698

SINGLE WHITE MALES

43. Age 21–25. Educ. level 0–8. Whole group. Lower level males are usually married by this age. If single, total outlets still average 3.3 per week. Most males ignore the law and have intercourse (86%), some (61%) with prostitutes, 62% still masturbate, 60% have emissions, 22% have homosexual. ¾ of outlet from intercourse (including 16% from prostitutes), highly promiscuous. Only ¼ of outlet from masturbation. All other outlets minor. Personality disturbances over sex rare, more often products of inadequate personalities rather than of sex. Inhibited only in regard to nudity, oral eroticism, and other petting techniques.

44. Age 21–25. Educ. level 0–8. Urban. More active than average of whole lower level (Group 43). Intercourse accepted by 91%, 66% having some with prostitutes, nearly 80% of outlet from intercourse. Masturbation once every two weeks for 63%, homosexual nearly as often for 29%. Group accepts sex, may be promiscuous, is often infected with venereal disease.

45. Age 21–25. Educ. level 0–8. Rural. Rather less active than city males (Group 44), having notably fewer socio-sexual contacts; intercourse, petting, prostitutes, and homosexual all lower. Intercourse supplies 68% of outlet for 80% of farm-bred males, masturbation supplies 45% for 64%, homosexual supplies 25% of outlet for 17%. At this age, animal intercourse minor for Eastern rural males, often a distinct part of Western rural histories.

46. Age 21–25. Educ. level 0–8. Protest., inactive. Typical of lower level group, as described above (Group 43).

47. Age 21–25. Educ. level 0–8. Cath., inactive. Not differing from whole lower level group (Group 43), except in an apparently higher incidence (40%) of homosexual contacts. At this age, inactive Protestants and inactive Catholics are so far away from their churches that religion does not have enough direct effect to differentiate two groups.

48. Age 21–25. Educ. level 9–12. Whole group. Active, with mean total outlet of 3.0, but this lower than in younger males (mean of 3.3). Many involved in wide variety of activities. Most important is intercourse (for 74% this averages 58% of outlet), masturbation (for 76%, averages 35% of outlet), and homosexual (for 38%, averages 29% of outlet). Homosexual attractive to group, but many evidence conflict by condemning it and punishing the homosexual partner. This and next age group includes the street-walking, tavern-frequenting, exhibitionistic city homosexual group. Masturbation often shunned, not really accepted. All other outlets minor. Many accept nudity, oral eroticism, and petting; others as inhibited as grade school level (Group 43) on these points.

49. Age 21–25. Educ. level 9–12. Urban. Adequately covered by description of whole high school level (Group 48). A larger number (43%) has some homosexual experience, drawing ⅓ of their outlet from that source.

TABLE 152. CLINICAL TABLES (*continued*)
SINGLE WHITE MALES

AGE: 21–25	SOURCE OF OUTLET	CASES	INCID. %	FREQ. PER WEEK			% OF TOTAL OUTLET		
				Range	Mean	Med.	Range	Mean	Med.
Educ. level 9–12									
50. Protest., inactive	Total	130	99	14.0	2.9	2.1	—	—	—
	Mast.	130	75	5.0	1.1	0.7	100	39.8	35.0
	Emiss.	130	72	2.0	0.4	0.2	80	15.9	7.5
	Pet.	130	26	2.0	0.2	0.1	35	7.0	0.8
	Interc.	132	80	11.0	1.6	0.7	100	55.3	60.0
	Prost.	130	46	1.0	0.2	0.1	100	14.1	1.6
	Homo.	130	32	5.0	1.2	0.8	100	32.2	30.8
Educ. level 13+									
51. Whole group	Total	1898	100	21.0	2.5	1.9	—	—	—
	Mast.	1898	87	15.0	1.5	0.9	100	59.4	65.2
	Emiss.	1898	87	7.0	0.4	0.3	100	26.6	13.6
	Pet.	1898	52	7.0	0.4	0.1	100	14.6	2.3
	Interc.	1593	54	17.0	0.8	0.3	100	27.4	15.3
	Prost.	1898	17	3.0	0.2	0.1	40	3.5	0.7
	Homo.	1898	9	7.0	1.0	0.3	95	24.5	9.6
	Anim.	1898	1	1.0	0.3	0.1	35	10.1	3.0
52. Urban	Total	1844	100	21.0	2.6	2.0	—	—	—
	Mast.	1844	87	15.0	1.6	0.9	100	57.5	61.4
	Emiss.	1844	86	6.5	0.5	0.3	100	28.4	16.4
	Pet.	1753	54	7.0	0.4	0.1	100	14.8	3.7
	Interc.	1377	55	17.0	0.8	0.3	100	27.6	15.8
	Prost.	1753	18	3.0	0.2	0.1	40	4.4	0.8
	Homo.	1844	10	7.0	0.9	0.3	100	25.9	15.0
	Anim.	1753	1	Scant	0.1	0.1	Scant	0.5	0.7
53. Rural	Total	266	99	9.0	2.2	1.7	—	—	—
	Mast.	266	86	7.0	1.4	1.0	100	66.2	73.6
	Emiss.	266	89	4.5	0.4	0.3	100	29.1	14.4
	Pet.	266	44	1.5	0.2	0.1	45	6.2	0.7
	Interc.	200	47	6.0	0.7	0.3	100	26.0	9.7
	Prost.	266	16	0.5	0.1	0.1	5	1.1	0.6
	Homo.	266	9	2.5	0.6	0.2	60	15.1	6.3
	Anim.	266	4	1.0	0.4	0.3	35	14.3	12.5
54. Protest., active	Total	384	100	11.0	2.0	1.4	—	—	—
	Mast.	384	84	6.0	1.3	0.8	100	63.5	68.8
	Emiss.	384	90	5.0	0.5	0.3	100	35.3	23.7
	Pet.	339	48	3.0	0.4	0.1	90	14.6	1.4
	Interc.	348	32	7.5	0.6	0.2	95	19.7	5.8
	Prost.	339	7	0.5	0.1	0.1	30	5.0	0.8
	Homo.	384	6	3.5	0.6	0.2	40	15.5	6.9
	Anim.	339	1	0.5	0.2	0.2	25	16.8	13.0
55. Protest., inactive	Total	1000	100	17.0	2.6	2.0	—	—	—
	Mast.	1000	90	12.0	1.6	0.9	100	59.9	65.2
	Emiss.	1000	87	6.0	0.4	0.3	100	24.6	12.4
	Pet.	841	51	4.5	0.4	0.1	95	13.0	1.1
	Interc.	867	59	9.0	0.7	0.3	100	26.1	13.9
	Prost.	841	19	1.0	0.1	0.1	30	2.6	0.7
	Homo.	1000	11	6.5	0.8	0.2	100	22.6	8.1
	Anim.	841	1	1.0	0.4	0.1	20	8.6	5.0
56. Cath., devout	Total	94	100	7.0	1.9	1.3	—	—	—
	Mast.	94	79	5.0	1.0	0.5	100	53.6	52.5
	Emiss.	94	90	3.5	0.5	0.3	100	41.4	34.2
	Pet.	94	53	1.5	0.3	0.1	55	15.4	6.3
	Interc.	71	38	4.0	0.7	0.3	100	26.2	20.0
	Prost.	94	12	0.5	0.3	0.1	Scant	3.6	0.8
	Homo.	94	11	2.0	0.7	0.3	35	16.8	3.0

SINGLE WHITE MALES

50. Age 21–25. Educ. level 9–12. Protest., inactive. Almost exactly as described for whole high school level at this age (Group 48).

51. Age 21–25. Educ. level 13+. Whole group. Many college level males are still unmarried at this age. They often disclaim moral restraints, but are most inhibited of all social levels. Highly erotic, often involved in social relations and petting with females, and highly aroused but still avoiding coitus. Some upset when they do have intercourse or (particularly) the homosexual. Hardly more than ½ attempt intercourse, and they derive only 15% of outlet from it. 87% still depend on masturbation for ⅔ of outlet, rarely upset over that. 87% derive 14% of outlet from emissions. Other outlets minor. About 69% of outlet from solitary sources. In contrast to grade school group, this college group freely accepts nudity and elaborate petting techniques. Oral techniques in experience of 35%, more often in next age period.

52. Age 21–25. Educ. level 13+. Urban. Almost exactly as described for whole college level of this age (Group 51).

53. Age 21–25. Educ. level 13+. Rural. Very close to their urban equivalents (Group 52), therefore closely matching the description given for whole college level at this age (Group 51). A little less often in socio-sexual contacts—petting in 44%, intercourse in 47%, homosexual in 9%. 86% of group derives ¾ of outlet from masturbation. Animal intercourse remains in histories of 4%, who derive 12.5% of their outlet therefrom.

54. Age 21–25. Educ. level 13+. Protest., active. Definitely restrained version of college group (Group 51). Even more likely to present cases of conflict over sexual activities they do have. Masturbation in 84%, provides 69% of outlet. Depend on emissions (average 24% of outlet for 90% of males) more often than non-religious males. Petting in only 48%, intercourse in 32%, prostitutes in 7%, homosexual in 6%—all minor sources of outlet.

55. Age 21–25. Educ. level 13+. Protest., inactive. Definitely less restrained than corresponding group of active Protestants (Group 54). More (90%) accept masturbation; emissions are less important. Petting (51%), intercourse (59%), with prostitutes (19%), and homosexual (11%) are decidedly more frequent, and all had with less disturbance than in religious group.

56. Age 21–25. Educ. level 13+. Cath., devout. College level pattern (Group 51), more restrained than average, but less restrained than active Protestants. Sometimes in serious conflict over sex (although often claiming to be examples of sublimation). Mean total outlet (1.9), petting (53%) same as in non-devout, but intercourse in only half as many (38%).

TABLE 152. CLINICAL TABLES (*continued*)
SINGLE WHITE MALES

AGE: 21-25	SOURCE OF OUTLET	CASES	INCID. %	FREQ. PER WEEK			% OF TOTAL OUTLET		
				Range	Mean	Med.	Range	Mean	Med.
Educ. level 13+									
57. Cath., inactive	Total	125	100	14.0	2.9	2.1	—	—	—
	Mast.	125	82	8.5	1.4	0.8	100	42.0	40.0
	Emiss.	125	88	3.0	0.5	0.3	100	27.9	14.2
	Pet.	125	52	3.0	0.3	0.1	90	13.8	3.0
	Interc.	80	75	6.0	1.3	0.5	100	40.8	32.5
	Prost.	125	27	1.5	0.2	0.1	35	6.4	1.5
	Homo.	125	15	4.5	1.7	1.5	90	45.1	47.5
58. Jewish, inactive	Total	331	100	17.0	3.1	2.4	—	—	—
	Mast.	331	86	15.0	1.8	1.0	100	54.3	54.0
	Emiss.	331	81	6.5	0.5	0.3	100	26.9	16.4
	Pet.	331	69	3.0	0.3	0.2	90	15.0	5.6
	Interc.	182	67	12.0	1.1	0.4	100	30.8	21.9
	Prost.	331	24	2.0	0.3	0.1	10	1.7	0.7
	Homo.	331	8	3.5	0.9	0.1	75	42.0	47.5
AGE: 26-30									
59. Whole group	Total	550	99	17.0	2.7	1.9	—	—	—
	Mast.	550	77	9.0	1.2	0.7	100	47.3	45.3
	Emiss.	550	79	4.0	0.4	0.2	100	23.0	10.7
	Pet.	550	34	4.0	0.3	0.1	90	12.3	0.9
	Interc.	607	66	16.0	1.5	0.7	100	49.3	46.8
	Prost.	550	30	4.0	0.5	0.3	100	22.8	10.8
	Homo.	550	25	15.0	1.5	0.7	100	37.0	28.9
Educ. level 0-8									
60. Whole group	Total	159	99	19.0	3.1	2.0	—	—	—
	Mast.	159	60	7.0	1.0	0.5	100	33.9	24.6
	Emiss.	159	65	2.0	0.3	0.1	100	14.4	4.6
	Pet.	159	19	1.0	0.3	0.1	40	4.8	0.6
	Interc.	137	88	4.0	2.1	1.2	100	67.5	74.4
	Prost.	159	72	5.5	0.6	0.4	100	30.2	20.8
	Homo.	159	28	5.5	1.4	0.5	100	29.9	20.0
61. Urban	Total	88	99	16.0	3.1	2.1	—	—	—
	Mast.	88	65	7.0	1.0	0.5	100	29.3	21.0
	Emiss.	88	64	2.0	0.3	0.1	60	12.0	3.8
	Pet.	88	17	Scant	0.1	0.1	Scant	3.2	0.6
	Interc.	92	90	13.0	2.1	1.5	100	67.8	73.3
	Prost.	88	75	4.0	0.8	0.4	100	27.7	21.1
	Homo.	88	35	4.5	1.0	0.4	100	25.5	12.5
62. Protest., inactive	Total	77	100	13.0	2.7	2.1	—	—	—
	Mast.	77	68	3.5	0.8	0.4	100	30.7	21.9
	Emiss.	77	70	1.5	0.3	0.1	95	14.3	5.4
	Pet.	77	20	1.0	0.4	0.1	40	6.7	0.7
	Interc.	80	93	13.0	1.9	1.1	100	67.8	75.8
	Prost.	77	75	3.0	0.6	0.3	100	28.7	20.3
	Homo.	77	19	3.5	1.3	0.6	75	29.8	25.0
Educ. level 9-12									
63. Whole group	Total	117	99	14.0	2.9	2.1	—	—	—
	Mast.	117	79	5.0	1.0	0.5	100	37.8	36.9
	Emiss.	117	70	2.0	0.3	0.2	85	16.9	8.2
	Pet.	117	26	1.0	0.2	0.1	45	7.9	0.7
	Interc.	95	72	11.0	1.6	0.9	100	51.7	51.3
	Prost.	117	43	2.0	0.4	0.2	80	24.2	8.0
	Homo.	117	46	11.0	1.6	0.7	95	36.9	36.7

SINGLE WHITE MALES

57. Age 21–25. Educ. level 13+. Cath., inactive. One of less restrained college groups. Incidence of coitus half again as high (75%) as in whole college group; prostitutes in 27%. Nevertheless, the restraint of whole college group (Group 51) is still evident, and masturbation provides largest portion of outlet for 82%. Homosexual provides nearly ½ of outlet for 15% of males.

58. Age 21–25. Educ. level 13+. Jewish, inactive. Highest total outlet (3.1) among college groups (Group 51), definitely less restrained than average college male in socio-sexual activities. Masturbation still provides 54% of outlet for 86%, petting in 69% of histories. Intercourse in 67%, provides 22% of outlet therefrom. Prostitutes in 24%, but very minor outlet; homosexual in a few.

59. Age 26–30. Whole group. Shows some effect of aging, mean total outlet averaging only 2.7. Males of grade and high school levels who are unmarried by this age begin to be a select group. Some are prevented from marrying by untoward circumstances, some are actively and promiscuously heterosexual and disinclined to settle down to a single partner in marriage, and ¼ to nearly ½ have homosexual histories, a fair number of which are now so pronounced as to interfere with marriage. Clinician might well determine reason for delay in marriage in each case. College level males more often unmarried because of custom of group or because of demands of an extended education, less often because of sexual situations. Patterns now well fixed, not liable to re-direction.

60. Age 26–30. Educ. level 0–8. Whole group. Least inhibited of social levels. Nearly all actively involved in intercourse (88%), prostitutes increasingly important (in 72%) because easier to secure. 74% of outlet from intercourse, practically unaffected by moral arguments. Masturbation quite taboo, but still in 60% for whom it supplies 25% of outlet. Homosexual in 28%, for many of whom it constitutes a material source and sometimes the sole source of outlet.

61. Age 26–30. Educ. level 0–8. Urban. The city-bred portion of this lower educational level is almost exactly as described for whole group above (Group 60), except that even a larger number (35%) has homosexual which, however, is not an important outlet. Quite unrestrained, often carefree and promiscuous.

62. Age 26–30. Educ. level 0–8. Protest., inactive. Pattern close to that of whole lower level at this age (Group 60). Quite unrestrained, with 93% having intercourse. Apparently fewer males (19%) involved in homosexual.

63. Age 26–30. Educ. level 9–12. Whole group. Single males of this level quite unrestrained in late twenties. Masturbation 79%, emissions 70%, petting in 26%, intercourse in 72% of whom 43% have some with prostitutes. Incidence of homosexual apparently higher (46%) than in any other segment of entire male population, because many heterosexual males have left the group for marriage. Some of most active homosexual cases here, sometimes upset, over-react to social pressures, this and previous age group including street-walking, tavern-frequenting, exhibitionistic city groups.

TABLE 152. CLINICAL TABLES (*continued*)
SINGLE WHITE MALES

AGE: 26–30	SOURCE OF OUTLET	CASES	INCID. %	FREQ. PER WEEK			% OF TOTAL OUTLET		
				Range	Mean	Med.	Range	Mean	Med.
Educ. level 9–12									
64. Urban	Total	73	97	14.0	3.1	2.3	—	—	—
	Mast.	73	81	4.5	1.0	0.5	100	40.3	41.3
	Emiss.	73	70	1.5	0.3	0.2	85	15.0	7.9
	Pet.	73	25	0.5	0.1	0.1	45	8.3	0.7
	Interc.	77	68	9.0	1.4	0.8	100	48.1	42.5
	Prost.	73	34	2.0	0.5	0.3	80	26.3	10.0
	Homo.	73	52	11.0	1.8	0.8	95	38.3	37.5
65. Protest., inactive	Total	51	98	12.0	3.1	2.3	—	—	—
	Mast.	51	75	3.0	0.9	0.6	100	36.4	38.8
	Emiss.	51	73	2.0	0.4	0.3	75	18.2	11.0
	Pet.	51	18	0.5	0.1	0.1	15	4.7	0.8
	Interc.	53	72	9.0	1.6	0.9	100	50.9	51.3
	Prost.	51	39	1.0	0.3	0.2	80	19.8	6.9
	Homo.	51	49	5.5	1.7	0.9	85	38.9	42.5
Educ. level 13+									
66. Whole group	Total	487	100	17.0	2.6	1.8	—	—	—
	Mast.	487	83	10.0	1.4	0.7	100	53.9	55.8
	Emiss.	487	85	4.0	0.4	0.3	100	26.7	13.3
	Pet.	487	45	3.0	0.3	0.1	90	14.2	2.6
	Interc.	373	56	15.0	1.1	0.5	100	37.6	28.4
	Prost.	487	16	6.0	0.5	0.1	25	4.5	0.9
	Homo.	487	17	5.0	1.3	0.7	100	41.3	37.5
	Anim.	487	1	Scant	0.4	0.6	Scant	6.8	8.0
67. Urban	Total	479	100	17.0	2.7	1.9	—	—	—
	Mast.	479	86	10.0	1.4	0.7	100	51.6	51.4
	Emiss.	479	85	4.0	0.4	0.3	100	26.2	13.0
	Pet.	445	47	3.0	0.3	0.1	90	15.7	4.1
	Interc.	308	59	15.0	1.2	0.5	100	36.6	26.7
	Prost.	445	19	6.0	0.5	0.1	25	4.6	0.9
	Homo.	479	17	5.0	1.4	0.6	100	43.4	46.3
68. Rural	Total	85	99	8.0	2.2	1.5	—	—	—
	Mast.	85	79	7.0	1.4	0.9	100	63.1	75.0
	Emiss.	85	86	1.0	0.3	0.3	100	30.6	14.7
	Pet.	85	43	0.5	0.1	0.1	35	7.1	0.8
	Interc.	58	45	5.0	1.1	0.5	100	43.5	38.8
	Prost.	85	7	Scant	0.1	0.1	Scant	0.5	1.0
	Homo.	85	15	1.5	0.7	0.4	35	25.1	10.0
69. Protest., active	Total	100	100	7.0	1.9	1.3	—	—	—
	Mast.	100	82	5.5	1.2	0.7	100	59.5	62.5
	Emiss.	100	95	2.5	0.4	0.3	100	37.1	30.7
	Pet.	100	42	2.5	0.4	0.1	75	14.4	1.5
	Interc.	88	35	2.5	0.5	0.3	90	24.5	16.3
	Prost.	100	9	0.5	0.1	0.1	10	3.4	0.8
	Homo.	100	10	3.5	1.1	0.4	30	23.3	14.2
70. Protest., inactive	Total	279	100	16.0	2.6	1.8	—	—	—
	Mast.	279	88	9.0	1.5	0.8	100	57.0	62.0
	Emiss.	279	85	1.5	0.3	0.2	100	23.8	10.7
	Pet.	279	44	2.0	0.3	0.1	75	12.3	0.9
	Interc.	187	60	3.0	0.7	0.3	100	28.9	18.6
	Prost.	279	15	5.5	0.4	0.1	15	3.5	0.9
	Homo.	279	21	5.0	1.1	0.5	100	36.4	29.2

SINGLE WHITE MALES

64. Age 26–30. Educ. level 9–12. Urban. Typical of whole high school level (Group 63). Heterosexual slightly lower, homosexual rather higher. Intercourse in $\frac{2}{3}$ of cases accounting for 43% of outlet, half as many cases with some prostitute contacts. Masturbation in 81% accounting for 41% of their outlet. Homosexual in more than half, accounting for more than $\frac{1}{3}$ of their outlet.

65. Age 26–30. Educ. level 9–12. Protest., inactive. Pattern very close to that described for whole high school level (Group 63).

66. Age 26–30. Educ. level 13+. Whole group. Even in late twenties males of college level are remarkably restrained. Restrained individuals increase with advancing age because more social individuals have already married. Many highly erotic, nearly half (45%) involved in heterosexual petting, most with fantasies during masturbation and in nocturnal dreams, but hardly more than half (56%) yet attempting overt intercourse, and then not often, and with few partners. Much disturbed by blockage of sexual response, and those not having intercourse may need special consideration from clinician. Masturbation accepted, providing 56% of outlet. Petting of social value, but provides very minor outlet. Homosexual (17%) is much lower than in high school group, but sometimes serious disturbance over it. Nudity accepted, oral erotic techniques now in 57%. Prostitutes largely avoided, providing less than 1% of outlet. No particular VD problem.

67. Age 26–30. Educ. level 13+. Urban. Pattern for this city-bred group almost exactly as described for whole college level at this age (Group 66).

68. Age 26–30. Educ. level 13+. Rural. A somewhat less active portion of college level (Group 66), differing from corresponding urban population (Group 67) in having lower incidences in most of outlets. 79% derive $\frac{3}{4}$ of total outlet from masturbation, 45% derive a little more than $\frac{1}{3}$ from intercourse. Other outlets more minor. Animal intercourse now very rare in rural histories from Eastern part of U. S., not uncommon in histories of this and older ages from Western areas.

69. Age 26–30. Educ. level 13+. Protest., active. Most restrained segment of college level in late twenties (Group 66). Mean total outlet only $\frac{3}{4}$ as high as average for whole college group. Incidences lower on every outlet except nocturnal emissions, 82% deriving 63% of outlet from masturbation, 95% with emissions giving 31% of outlet. Coitus in only $\frac{1}{3}$ of group. Homosexual in 10%, which is lowest among all groups at this age. Clinician may expect sexual conflicts here.

70. Age 26–30. Educ. level 13+. Protest., inactive. Not materially different from average for whole college level of this age (Group 66).

TABLE 152. CLINICAL TABLES (*continued*)
SINGLE WHITE MALES

AGE: 26–30	SOURCE OF OUTLET	CASES	INCID. %	FREQ. PER WEEK			% OF TOTAL OUTLET		
				Range	Mean	Med.	Range	Mean	Med.
Educ. level 13+									
71. Jewish, inactive	Total	104	100	15.0	3.2	2.4	—	—	—
	Mast.	104	80	6.0	1.3	0.6	100	39.9	31.7
	Emiss.	104	75	4.0	0.4	0.2	100	16.3	8.8
	Pet.	104	57	1.5	0.3	0.2	35	10.0	3.8
	Interc.	77	84	15.0	2.0	1.0	100	53.6	56.7
	Prost.	104	28	2.0	0.8	0.1	45	11.4	1.0
AGE: 31–35	Homo.	104	8	3.0	1.4	1.0	100	53.8	65.0
72. Whole group	Total	195	99	14.0	2.4	1.6	—	—	—
	Mast.	195	71	7.0	1.0	0.5	100	40.4	33.3
	Emiss.	195	71	1.5	0.3	0.2	100	21.7	8.3
	Pet.	195	24	1.0	0.3	0.1	80	13.7	1.0
	Interc.	223	68	13.0	1.5	0.8	100	58.5	63.0
	Prost.	195	41	3.0	0.6	0.3	100	28.7	20.7
	Homo.	195	30	4.5	1.7	1.0	100	46.9	50.0
Educ. level 0–8									
73. Whole group	Total	67	99	9.5	2.8	1.7	—	—	—
	Mast.	67	70	4.0	0.9	0.5	90	30.6	20.0
	Emiss.	67	61	1.5	0.3	0.1	100	17.0	6.7
	Pet.	67	8	0.5	0.3	0.1	5	2.5	1.0
	Interc.	70	84	7.0	1.4	0.8	100	61.4	70.0
	Prost.	67	66	3.0	0.8	0.5	100	37.8	31.3
	Homo.	67	30	4.0	2.5	1.1	100	48.3	37.5
Educ. level 13+									
74. Whole group	Total	87	99	13.0	2.2	1.6	—	—	—
	Mast.	87	77	7.0	1.2	0.7	100	51.0	48.8
	Emiss.	87	83	1.5	0.3	0.2	100	22.8	8.6
	Pet.	87	32	1.0	0.3	0.2	80	17.7	9.2
	Interc.	107	58	13.0	1.5	0.6	100	49.9	46.3
	Prost.	87	16	0.5	0.1	0.1	15	4.1	0.9
	Homo.	87	26	4.5	1.4	1.0	100	48.5	56.7
75. Urban	Total	72	100	13.0	2.2	1.5	—	—	—
	Mast.	72	78	7.0	1.1	0.6	100	48.6	47.5
	Emiss.	72	86	1.5	0.3	0.2	100	23.2	9.1
	Pet.	72	32	1.0	0.3	0.2	50	16.4	10.0
	Interc.	89	61	13.0	1.6	0.6	100	51.4	48.8
	Prost.	72	17	0.5	0.1	0.1	15	4.7	1.7
	Homo.	72	28	4.5	1.6	1.3	90	50.4	54.2
76. Protest., inactive	Total	53	98	7.0	2.2	1.7	—	—	—
	Mast.	53	81	7.0	1.2	0.7	100	49.5	40.0
	Emiss.	53	79	1.0	0.2	0.1	90	20.4	7.5
	Pet.	53	34	1.0	0.3	0.1	45	12.9	3.0
	Interc.	59	59	3.0	0.8	0.5	100	40.6	35.0
	Prost.	53	23	0.5	0.1	0.1	15	4.7	1.7
	Homo.	53	28	3.0	1.5	1.0	85	52.7	60.0

SINGLE WHITE MALES

71. Age 26–30. Educ. level 13+. Jewish, inactive. Socio-sexually most active of all college groups (Group 66). Many Jewish males are slow in starting sexual activity and inhibited during their earlier years (Groups 21, 42); but those who are unmarried in late twenties become distinctly freer. Clinician will do well to examine possibility of maladjustment due to change of pattern. 84% now have intercourse, which accounts for 57% of outlet. Only ⅓ of these have any intercourse with prostitutes. Masturbation still accounts for ⅓ of outlet for 80%. Homosexual incidence low.

72. Age 31–35. Whole group. Males who are unmarried by this age often have special problems in socio-sexual adjustment. Only ⅔ are having intercourse, deriving ⅔ of total outlet therefrom, ⅔ of these depend in part on prostitutes—a further indication of difficulty in making socio-sexual advances. This is particularly true at lower educational levels. Masturbation still in ¾ of histories, accounting for ⅓ of outlet of those males. Homosexual in nearly ⅓ of histories, accounting for ½ of their outlet, many individuals primarily or exclusively homosexual by this age. Rates of outlet lowered by advancing age. A fair number of individuals derive their total outlet now from a single source.

73. Age 31–35. Educ. level 0–8. Whole group. Similar to whole age group described above (Group 72). More intercourse, especially with prostitutes. 84% draw 70% of outlet from intercourse, but 66% get ⅓ of outlet from intercourse with prostitutes. Petting nearly absent. Many lower level males have increasing difficulty in finding sexual partners as they grow older. Some persons physically handicapped, mentally dull, and physically unattractive, and a satisfactory adjustment with prostitutes is about all that can be hoped for. Masturbation in 70% but not really accepted by group. Often with strong taboos against nudity and variety of techniques. ⅓ of group with some homosexual history, many exclusively homosexual, this not leading to conflict as often as in upper social levels.

74. Age 31–35. Educ. level 13+. Whole group. As described for whole age group above (Group 72), except for a somewhat higher dependence on masturbation and emissions, and a lower utilization of intercourse. Contacts with prostitutes rare. These males still in conflict over moral aspects of socio-sexual contacts. ⅓ have never yet had intercourse, and little possibility of most of them ever developing facility in securing such contacts. Only a portion is homosexual.

75. Age 31–35. Educ. level 13+. Urban. Almost exactly as described for whole college-bred portion of this age group (Group 74).

76. Age 31–35. Educ. level 13+. Protest., inactive. Almost exactly as described for whole college-bred portion of this age group (Group 74).

TABLE 152. CLINICAL TABLES (*concluded*)

SINGLE WHITE MALES

SOURCE OF OUTLET	CASES	INCID. %	FREQ. PER WEEK			% OF TOTAL OUTLET		
			Range	Mean	Med.	Range	Mean	Med.

AGE: 36–40

77. Whole group

SOURCE OF OUTLET	CASES	INCID. %	Range	Mean	Med.	Range	Mean	Med.
Total	97	98	9.0	2.1	1.4	—	—	—
Mast.	97	63	7.0	1.2	0.6	100	47.1	45.0
Emiss.	97	60	1.5	0.2	0.1	100	19.1	6.4
Pet.	97	11	0.5	0.2	0.1	35	13.0	1.0
Interc.	110	70	8.5	1.3	0.6	100	57.7	60.0
Prost.	97	49	2.5	0.5	0.3	100	39.5	35.0
Homo.	97	40	4.0	1.1	0.7	100	42.2	37.5

AGE: 41–45

78. Whole group

SOURCE OF OUTLET	CASES	INCID. %	Range	Mean	Med.	Range	Mean	Med.
Total	56	96	7.5	1.9	1.1	—	—	—
Mast.	56	61	7.0	1.0	0.4	100	43.7	32.5
Emiss.	56	48	0.5	0.2	0.1	100	19.5	8.3
Pet.	56	11	0.5	0.1	0.1	10	7.2	0.9
Interc.	61	66	6.5	1.1	0.5	100	66.6	73.8
Prost.	56	39	1.5	0.5	0.3	100	48.2	47.5
Homo.	56	38	5.0	1.2	0.5	100	42.2	35.0

SINGLE WHITE MALES

77. Age 36–40. Whole group. Frequencies of total outlet have been declining since late teens, now average 2.1. Males unmarried by this age include some who are heterosexually very active but unwilling to settle down with a single partner; some who are timid or otherwise handicapped for making socio-sexual contacts, and some who are primarily or exclusively homosexual. Group rather too old to modify patterns, and clinician's function primarily one of helping individual accept whatever pattern he now has. Occasionally marriage at this or later age is successful, usually not.

78. Age 41–45. Whole group. A continuation of all trends described for previous age group (Group 77). Remarks made there apply in even greater force to this older group.

TABLE 153. CLINICAL TABLES
MARRIED WHITE MALES

	SOURCE OF OUTLET	CASES	INCID. %	FREQ. PER WEEK.			% OF TOTAL OUTLET		
AGE: 16–20				Range	Mean	Med.	Range	Mean	Med.
79. Whole group	Total	272	100	28.0	4.7	3.2	—	—	—
	Mast.	272	39	3.0	0.4	0.1	65	9.9	2.3
	Emiss.	272	53	2.5	0.3	0.1	65	5.6	1.3
	Interc.	272	100	25.0	3.8	2.6	100	84.6	95.3
	Extra.	272	38	7.5	1.2	0.3	75	18.0	9.7
	Prost.	272	14	2.0	0.3	0.1	15	2.9	0.7
	Homo.	272	9	6.0	1.2	0.3	30	9.2	4.1
Educ. level 0–8									
80. Whole group	Total	158	100	29.0	4.7	3.1	—	—	—
	Mast.	158	29	2.5	0.4	0.1	50	10.1	2.6
	Emiss.	158	48	2.5	0.3	0.1	50	5.3	1.0
	Interc.	158	100	28.0	3.7	2.5	100	83.9	95.3
	Extra.	158	44	7.0	1.2	0.5	60	18.4	12.5
	Prost.	158	17	0.5	0.2	0.1	10	2.1	0.8
	Homo.	158	10	4.5	1.4	0.4	30	10.1	4.5
81. Urban	Total	97	100	20.0	4.7	3.0	—	—	—
	Mast.	97	32	2.0	0.4	0.1	50	9.5	2.1
	Emiss.	97	54	2.5	0.4	0.1	50	6.4	1.2
	Interc.	97	100	18.0	3.5	2.3	100	81.5	95.1
	Extra.	97	47	7.0	1.4	0.5	60	20.6	14.2
	Prost.	97	19	0.5	0.2	0.1	10	2.4	0.8
	Homo.	97	12	4.0	1.5	0.4	30	11.5	7.5
82. Protest., inactive	Total	96	100	24.0	4.7	3.0	—	—	—
	Mast.	96	31	2.5	0.5	0.2	50	10.8	2.4
	Emiss.	96	53	2.0	0.2	0.1	40	4.4	0.9
	Interc.	96	100	18.0	3.8	2.4	100	84.5	95.6
	Extra.	96	44	4.5	1.2	0.5	60	18.2	12.5
	Prost.	96	17	0.5	0.2	0.1	10	2.5	0.8
	Homo.	96	7	4.0	1.4	0.1	30	9.8	3.0
Educ. level 9–12									
83. Whole group	Total	87	100	24.0	5.1	3.6	—	—	—
	Mast.	87	39	3.0	0.4	0.1	50	7.1	1.0
	Emiss.	87	54	1.0	0.2	0.1	30	5.0	1.8
	Interc.	87	100	17.0	4.1	2.8	100	85.9	95.9
	Extra.	87	38	6.0	1.4	0.2	60	18.6	10.0
	Prost.	87	16	2.0	0.5	0.1	10	4.4	0.8
	Homo.	87	9	1.0	1.1	0.4	15	7.1	3.8
84. Urban	Total	61	100	20.0	4.7	3.6	—	—	—
	Mast.	61	39	3.0	0.4	0.1	50	7.4	1.3
	Emiss.	61	57	1.0	0.2	0.1	30	5.3	1.0
	Interc.	61	100	16.0	3.6	2.8	100	83.3	95.5
	Extra.	61	43	6.0	1.6	0.4	60	21.1	15.8
	Prost.	61	20	0.5	0.4	0.1	5	4.5	0.7
	Homo.	61	11	1.0	1.3	0.4	15	7.6	4.0
85. Protest., inactive	Total	60	100	20.0	4.5	3.3	—	—	—
	Mast.	60	35	1.0	0.2	0.1	10	3.1	0.9
	Emiss.	60	52	0.5	0.2	0.1	20	4.1	1.4
	Interc.	60	100	16.0	3.8	2.8	100	88.5	96.4
	Extra.	60	40	6.0	1.3	0.1	60	17.9	4.0
	Prost.	60	12	0.5	0.6	0.1	5	7.3	1.0
	Homo.	60	5	0.5	0.2	0.3	5	2.2	3.0

TABLE 153. CLINICAL TABLES

MARRIED WHITE MALES

79. Age 16–20. Whole group. Males married at this age have maximum sexual performance of any group in total population. Mean total outlet 4.7, frequencies for many individuals going to 10, 14, or even 20 per week, with no ill effects. 95% of outlet from marital intercourse, more in high school level; not enough males of college level married at this age to warrant generalizations, but some proportion of grade school males marrying before twenty.

80. Age 16–20. Educ. level 0–8. Whole group. 95% of total outlet of group derived from marital intercourse, but nearly ½ of lower level males have extramarital intercourse which accounts for 13% of their outlet. Frequencies of all other outlets low, although a fair number involved in masturbation, emissions, and the homosexual, even while living with wives. Group often irresponsible, many quickly deserting wives, some not self-supporting, becoming drifters, sometimes involved in petty underworld activities. Many promiscuous in extramarital relations, VD rates rather high.

81. Age 16–20. Educ. level 0–8. Urban. Almost precisely as described for the whole lower educational level (Group 80).

82. Age 16–20. Educ. level 0–8. Protest., inactive. Almost precisely as described for the whole lower educational level (Group 80).

83. Age 16–20. Educ. level 9–12. Whole group. Remarkably close to grade school group of same age (Group 80). 96% of total outlet of whole group from marital intercourse, 38% get 10% from extra-marital intercourse, 9% get 4% from homosexual. More acceptant of extra-marital intercourse at this age than later. All other outlets very minor. Group probably more reliable, more balanced than corresponding grade school group. Considerable diversity in mental ability and educational background, similar diversity in regard to religious restraint and sexual inhibition. Devoutly religious persons often traditional in respect to sexual mores, but group as a whole nowhere near as restrained as college level.

84. Age 16–20. Educ. level 9–12. Urban. Almost precisely as described for whole high school level (Group 83). 43% having extra-marital intercourse, which accounts for 16% of total outlet, and some marital discord may grow out of this. Extra-marital relations for this group are reduced in later age periods.

85. Age 16–20. Educ. level 9–12. Protest., inactive. Not materially different from whole high school level as described above (Group 83). Not closely enough connected with church backgrounds to have behavior materially affected, unless in regard to extra-marital intercourse which accounts for only 4% of total outlet of 40% of males.

TABLE 153. CLINICAL TABLES (*continued*)

MARRIED WHITE MALES

AGE: 21–25	SOURCE OF OUTLET	CASES	INCID. %	FREQ. PER WEEK			% OF TOTAL OUTLET		
				Range	Mean	Med.	Range	Mean	Med.
86. Whole group	Total	751	100	29.0	3.9	2.8	—	—	—
	Mast.	751	48	4.0	0.5	0.2	90	12.2	4.0
	Emiss.	751	59	4.0	0.2	0.1	70	6.5	1.7
	Interc.	751	100	29.0	3.2	2.3	100	85.3	95.2
	Extra.	751	27	18.0	1.2	0.3	95	16.0	5.4
	Prost.	751	13	2.0	0.2	0.1	50	4.0	0.8
	Homo.	751	8	3.0	0.4	0.1	50	7.6	1.4
Educ. level 0–8									
87. Whole group	Total	324	100	29.0	4.0	2.6	—	—	—
	Mast.	324	29	3.0	0.3	0.1	75	8.5	2.4
	Emiss.	324	45	2.0	0.3	0.1	45	5.3	1.0
	Interc.	324	99	28.0	3.3	2.2	100	87.7	96.0
	Extra.	324	34	18.0	1.5	0.3	90	19.5	11.9
	Prost.	324	15	2.0	0.2	0.1	40	4.5	0.9
	Homo.	324	9	3.5	0.6	0.1	25	3.9	1.0
88. Urban	Total	162	100	29.0	4.4	2.9	—	—	—
	Mast.	162	33	3.0	0.4	0.1	50	7.9	2.7
	Emiss.	162	48	2.0	0.3	0.1	45	5.8	1.0
	Interc.	162	98	20.0	3.5	2.4	100	86.4	95.8
	Extra.	162	41	18.0	1.8	0.3	90	20.5	10.0
	Prost.	162	20	1.0	0.2	0.1	30	4.5	0.9
	Homo.	162	14	3.5	0.6	0.1	25	4.9	2.2
89. Rural	Total	128	100	17.0	3.4	2.3	—	—	—
	Mast.	128	25	1.0	0.3	0.1	40	8.7	2.7
	Emiss.	128	40	1.5	0.2	0.1	20	3.7	0.9
	Interc.	128	100	16.0	3.0	2.0	100	90.9	96.5
	Extra.	128	25	2.0	0.6	0.3	40	15.5	13.3
	Prost.	128	9	0.5	0.2	0.1	5	5.5	1.0
	Homo.	128	6	0.5	0.4	0.1	5	1.3	0.9
90. Protest., inactive	Total	206	100	29.0	4.2	2.7	—	—	—
	Mast.	206	30	3.0	0.4	0.1	50	8.4	2.0
	Emiss.	206	47	2.0	0.2	0.1	35	4.4	1.0
	Interc.	206	100	17.0	3.3	2.3	100	87.8	96.0
	Extra.	206	35	18.0	1.8	0.4	75	19.7	15.6
	Prost.	206	16	1.0	0.2	0.1	40	4.7	0.9
	Homo.	206	10	1.0	0.4	0.1	10	3.9	2.0
Educ. level 9–12									
91. Whole group	Total	164	100	26.0	4.2	2.9	—	—	—
	Mast.	164	42	3.0	0.4	0.1	75	7.6	1.0
	Emiss.	164	63	1.0	0.2	0.1	30	4.8	1.0
	Interc.	164	100	25.0	3.4	2.5	100	85.7	95.2
	Extra.	164	42	7.0	1.1	0.3	70	16.0	5.5
	Prost.	164	25	2.0	0.3	0.1	30	4.4	0.7
	Homo.	164	13	2.0	0.3	0.1	15	3.8	1.0
92. Urban	Total	107	100	20.0	4.1	3.0	—	—	—
	Mast.	107	41	3.0	0.4	0.1	70	8.6	1.0
	Emiss.	107	64	1.0	0.2	0.1	30	5.0	1.0
	Interc.	107	100	15.0	3.1	2.6	100	83.4	94.1
	Extra.	107	46	7.0	1.3	0.4	70	19.2	10.0
	Prost.	107	29	2.0	0.2	0.1	30	4.6	0.7
	Homo.	107	16	0.5	0.2	0.1	15	3.6	0.9

MARRIED WHITE MALES

86. Age 21–25. Whole group. A very high proportion of males at this age are now married except in college level. Mean total outlet only 3.9, which is definitely below mean for males who are married in late teens. Extra-marital intercourse in $\frac{1}{4}$ accounting for 5% of outlet, homosexual in 8%, masturbation in 48%, but most masturbation among males of college level. Marital intercourse accounting for 95% of total outlet. All other outlets minor except for extra-marital intercourse in certain groups.

87. Age 21–25. Educ. level 0–8. Whole group. Mean total outlet 4.0. Most from marital intercourse, frequencies commonly 7 and in many cases 14 and 20 per week. Intercourse with minimum of pre-coital petting, entire relation usually completed in 2 to 5 minutes. Males give little consideration to female orgasm, but females in actuality more often reaching orgasm and sexual relation satisfactory for them more often than in college level. Marital discord rarely originating from unsatisfactory sexual relations, but often resulting from extra-marital intercourse which involves $\frac{1}{3}$ of group and supplies 12% of their outlet. Drinking, non-support, physical cruelty to wife are most common sources of marital difficulty. Masturbation, emissions, and homosexual in limited number of histories and supplying only minor portion of outlet.

88. Age 21–25. Educ. level 0–8. Urban. Much as described for whole grade school level (Group 87). City-bred males are, however, somewhat more active sexually, with mean total outlet 4.4. 41% with extra-marital intercourse, 14% with homosexual. Often considerable irresponsibility in marriage.

89. Age 21–25. Educ. level 0–8. Rural. General pattern as described above for whole grade school level (Group 87), but definitely less active. Not a product of restraint as much as of less developed social interest and facility, even with wife. Mean rate of marital intercourse 3.0, and rates of 7 and more much less frequent. Marital intercourse supplying 97% of outlet. Extra-marital intercourse in only $\frac{1}{4}$, supplying 13% of their outlet. Masturbation, emissions, and homosexual in fewer instances than in city group.

90. Age 21–25. Educ. level 0–8. Protest., inactive. Closely matching description given for whole grade school level (Group 87). Less active than urban group (Group 88), with fewer persons involved in extra-marital intercourse or homosexual. Religious backgrounds too remote to have much direct influence.

91. Age 21–25. Educ. level 9–12. Whole group. Most active group of males of this age, with mean total outlet 4.2, with high frequencies of marital intercourse in individual cases, and with highest incidences of extra-marital intercourse and homosexual experience after marriage. 95% of outlet from marital intercourse, all other outlets minor, but masturbation, emissions, extra-marital intercourse, experience with prostitutes, and homosexual in a considerable portion of all histories.

92. Age 21–25. Educ. level 9–12. Urban. A rather active group, with general pattern as described above for whole high school level (Group 91), nearly $\frac{1}{2}$ with extra-marital intercourse, which accounts for 10% of their outlet. One in six with homosexual activity, averaging one in two months. Masturbation and emissions with about same frequency as homosexual but with higher incidences.

TABLE 153. CLINICAL TABLES (*continued*)
MARRIED WHITE MALES

AGE: 21–25	SOURCE OF OUTLET	CASES	INCID. %	FREQ. PER WEEK			% OF TOTAL OUTLET		
				Range	Mean	Med.	Range	Mean	Med.
Educ. level 9–12									
93. Protest., inactive	Total	108	100	21.0	3.8	2.7	—	—	—
	Mast.	108	41	3.0	0.4	0.1	75	7.6	0.9
	Emiss.	108	63	1.0	0.2	0.1	25	4.5	0.9
	Interc.	108	100	20.0	3.1	2.3	100	85.1	95.3
	Extra.	108	47	7.0	1.0	0.3	70	16.9	5.0
	Prost.	108	29	2.0	0.2	0.1	30	4.5	0.7
	Homo.	108	12	0.5	0.2	0.1	10	2.8	1.0
Educ. level 13+									
94. Whole group	Total	440	100	22.0	3.7	3.1	—	—	—
	Mast.	440	66	4.0	0.5	0.2	85	14.9	5.8
	Emiss.	440	66	4.0	0.3	0.1	70	7.9	2.7
	Interc.	440	100	20.0	3.1	2.5	100	82.9	91.9
	Extra.	440	15	3.0	0.5	0.1	50	8.4	2.4
	Prost.	440	5	0.5	0.2	0.1	10	2.3	0.7
	Homo.	440	3	2.0	0.7	0.6	50	24.8	10.0
95. Urban	Total	460	100	22.0	3.7	3.1	—	—	—
	Mast.	428	67	4.0	0.5	0.2	85	15.1	6.3
	Emiss.	460	66	4.0	0.3	0.1	70	8.3	3.0
	Interc.	460	100	20.0	3.1	2.6	100	82.5	91.2
	Extra.	460	16	3.0	0.5	0.1	50	8.7	2.6
	Prost.	428	5	0.5	0.2	0.1	10	2.4	0.8
	Homo.	428	3	2.0	0.6	0.5	50	24.8	10.0
96. Protest., active	Total	91	100	15.0	3.3	2.7	—	—	—
	Mast.	91	60	2.0	0.4	0.2	70	14.4	4.9
	Emiss.	91	67	1.5	0.3	0.1	25	6.5	2.7
	Interc.	91	99	11.0	2.8	2.2	100	86.7	95.3
	Extra.	91	8	0.5	0.5	0.1	5	7.2	0.9
97. Protest., inactive	Total	280	100	22.0	3.9	3.2	—	—	—
	Mast.	280	70	4.0	0.5	0.2	70	13.9	6.0
	Emiss.	280	68	4.0	0.3	0.1	70	8.5	2.7
	Interc.	280	100	20.0	3.2	2.5	100	82.1	90.3
	Extra.	280	18	2.5	0.5	0.2	30	7.9	3.3
	Prost.	280	5	0.5	0.1	0.1	10	3.3	0.8
	Homo.	280	3	2.0	0.7	0.7	50	34.3	30.0
AGE: 26–30									
98. Whole group	Total	737	100	29.0	3.3	2.5	—	—	—
	Mast.	737	48	4.0	0.4	0.1	90	12.5	4.2
	Emiss.	737	63	3.0	0.2	0.1	65	6.5	1.8
	Interc.	737	100	25.0	2.7	2.0	100	85.5	95.0
	Extra.	737	29	6.0	0.6	0.1	75	12.2	4.2
	Prost.	737	12	2.0	0.2	0.1	40	5.0	0.8
	Homo.	737	5	2.0	0.5	0.1	50	11.4	2.8
Educ. level 0–8									
99. Whole group	Total	292	99	29.0	3.5	2.4	—	—	—
	Mast.	292	21	4.0	0.4	0.1	70	7.7	0.8
	Emiss.	292	47	2.0	0.3	0.1	50	6.2	1.0
	Interc.	292	99	25.0	3.0	2.1	100	88.8	96.1
	Extra.	292	35	6.0	0.8	0.3	60	14.9	8.3
	Prost.	292	17	2.0	0.2	0.1	30	5.3	1.0
	Homo.	292	5	1.0	0.3	0.1	10	2.8	0.9

MARRIED WHITE MALES

93. Age 21–25. Educ. level 9–12. Protest., inactive. Almost exactly as described for whole high school level (Group 91). Total outlet a bit lower, a mean of 3.8, but individual outlets only slightly less than described for Group 91.

94. Age 21–25. Educ. level 13+. Whole group. This is the most active age period for college males, but among both single and married males this is much the most restrained of all social levels. Only 92% of total outlet from marital intercourse, and in successive age periods the proportion steadily drops. $\frac{2}{3}$ of males still draw outlets from masturbation and nocturnal emissions. Only 1 in 7 has extra-marital intercourse, 3% with homosexual. Even in marriage, years of pre-marital restraint continue to affect sexual adjustment. Lack of facility in approaching even the wife for sexual relations. An occasional male with occasional impotence because of such inhibitions, and many avoid frequencies of intercourse higher than 3 or 4 per week on moral, ethical, or other grounds. Group does accept nudity, variety of techniques in pre-coital play, including some oral erotic play, and these may aid in development of satisfactory sexual relations. Females of group more restrained than males, poorly responsive or completely unresponsive in a fair proportion of cases; this difference between male and female the chief sexual factor in marital discord. Since group assumes marital obligations with considerable sense of responsibility, and since higher level of education provides esthetic and other cultural interests, marriages on a whole more stable here than in any other group.

95. Age 21–25. Educ. level 13+. Urban. Almost precisely as described for whole college level above (Group 94).

96. Age 21–25. Educ. level 13+. Protest., active. Pattern much as described for whole college level (Group 94); but somewhat more restrained. Mean frequency of marital intercourse down to 2.8, often because of doubts as to propriety of more frequent sexual relations even with wife. All other socio-sexual contacts, both heterosexual and homosexual, very minor. Masturbation, however, in 60% for whom it provides 5% of outlet.

97. Age 21–25. Educ. level 13+. Protest., inactive. Essentially as described for whole college level (Group 94). Group little affected by religious background, but restraint derived from mores of social level.

98. Age 26–30. Whole group. While still in prime of life by various criteria, group has aged sexually; mean total outlet no higher than that of average younger adolescent boy (3.3 per week)—a drop of about 1.5 per week from rate of married teen-age males. Marital intercourse supplies 95% of total outlet and all other outlets minor; but considerable differences at different social levels, and description for each group should be consulted.

99. Age 26–30. Educ. level 0–8. Whole group. Grade school and high school segments of this age a bit more active socio-sexually than college segment (Group 106). Mean total outlet 3.5 per week. 96% of total outlet from marital intercourse, mean average frequencies 3.0, but rates of 7, 14, and more not infrequent. Extra-marital intercourse in more than $\frac{1}{3}$ but frequency reduced, $\frac{1}{2}$ of these contacts with prostitutes. Number of companions may be high. Masturbation in $\frac{1}{5}$ but rates low; all other outlets definitely minor. Group uninhibited in simple intercourse, often inhibited on nudity, pre-coital petting, oral eroticism, etc.

TABLE 153. CLINICAL TABLES (*continued*)

MARRIED WHITE MALES

AGE: 26–30	SOURCE OF OUTLET	CASES	INCID. %	FREQ. PER WEEK			% OF TOTAL OUTLET		
				Range	Mean	Med.	Range	Mean	Med.
Educ. level 0–8									
100. Urban	Total	148	99	20.0	3.4	2.6	—	—	—
	Mast.	148	23	2.0	0.3	0.1	20	5.5	0.7
	Emiss.	148	50	2.0	0.3	0.1	50	7.3	1.0
	Interc.	148	99	15.0	2.9	2.4	100	88.0	96.0
	Extra.	148	35	5.0	0.7	0.1	60	15.7	9.7
	Prost.	148	18	0.5	0.1	0.1	15	4.4	1.4
	Homo.	148	7	0.5	0.3	0.1	5	1.8	0.8
101. Rural	Total	117	100	25.0	3.3	2.1	—	—	—
	Mast.	117	24	3.5	0.5	0.1	45	9.3	1.0
	Emiss.	117	42	1.0	0.2	0.1	20	3.9	1.0
	Interc.	117	100	24.0	2.9	1.8	100	91.0	96.5
	Extra.	117	30	3.5	0.5	0.2	50	11.6	4.0
	Prost.	117	14	1.0	0.3	0.1	30	6.5	0.9
	Homo	117	4	0.5	0.3	0.3	5	4.9	4.0
102. Protest., inactive	Total	166	100	23.0	3.4	2.4	—	—	—
	Mast.	166	27	2.5	0.3	0.1	45	6.7	0.8
	Emiss.	166	51	2.0	0.2	0.1	40	5.8	1.0
	Interc.	166	100	20.0	2.9	2.1	100	88.4	96.0
	Extra.	166	39	4.0	0.7	0.3	60	15.0	9.1
	Prost.	166	19	1.0	0.2	0.1	30	5.7	1.0
	Homo.	166	4	0.5	0.2	0.1	5	3.4	2.0
Educ. level 9–12									
103. Whole group	Total	135	100	20.0	3.6	2.5	—	—	—
	Mast.	135	37	3.0	0.5	0.1	60	11.8	4.3
	Emiss.	135	56	1.0	0.2	0.1	30	5.4	1.8
	Interc.	135	100	15.0	2.9	2.1	100	85.4	94.5
	Extra.	135	44	5.0	0.7	0.1	60	12.4	5.0
	Prost.	135	20	2.0	0.3	0.1	30	6.5	0.8
	Homo.	135	8	1.0	0.4	0.3	15	6.9	4.0
104. Urban	Total	81	100	17.0	3.3	2.6	—	—	—
	Mast.	81	36	3.0	0.5	0.2	60	13.6	5.0
	Emiss.	81	57	1.0	0.2	0.1	20	4.6	1.6
	Interc.	81	100	7.5	2.6	2.1	100	84.0	93.6
	Extra.	81	48	5.0	0.9	0.2	60	15.1	7.5
	Prost.	81	21	1.0	0.2	0.1	30	8.2	0.8
	Homo.	81	11	1.0	0.3	0.1	15	6.6	3.0
105. Protest., inactive	Total	77	100	17.0	3.3	2.5	—	—	—
	Mast.	77	36	2.0	0.4	0.1	60	11.5	3.0
	Emiss.	77	60	1.0	0.2	0.1	30	5.5	1.2
	Interc.	77	100	14.0	2.7	1.9	100	85.3	95.1
	Extra.	77	51	2.0	0.5	0.1	60	12.0	3.0
	Prost.	77	21	1.0	0.2	0.1	30	8.5	0.8
	Homo.	77	8	1.0	0.5	0.4	15	9.3	4.3
Educ. level 13+									
106. Whole group	Total	532	100	22.0	3.2	2.6	—	—	—
	Mast.	532	66	3.5	0.4	0.2	90	13.7	4.9
	Emiss.	532	73	3.0	0.2	0.1	65	6.9	2.1
	Interc.	532	99	20.0	2.6	2.1	100	83.4	91.1
	Extra.	532	22	3.5	0.4	0.1	70	8.9	1.2
	Prost.	532	6	0.5	0.1	0.1	10	2.6	0.7
	Homo.	532	3	2.5	1.2	1.3	50	25.3	15.0

MARRIED WHITE MALES

100. Age 26–30. Educ. level 0–8. Urban. Almost exactly as described for total grade school level of this age (Group 99).

101. Age 26–30. Educ. level 0–8. Rural. Almost exactly as described for total grade school group of this age (Group 99). Not particularly distinct from urban males (Group 100), although this rural group at earlier age levels is a bit less active sexually. Extra-marital intercourse not so frequent.

102. Age 26–30. Educ. level 0–8. Protest., inactive. Almost precisely as described for whole grade school level of this age (Group 99).

103. Age 26–30. Educ. level 9–12. Whole group. Most active of all social levels in this age period. Mean total outlet 3.6 per week, but frequencies of marital intercourse of 7, 10, or more in 10%. Relative lack of restraint in group further shown by nearly ½ having extra-marital intercourse in this period, half of these with prostitutes. Nevertheless, marital intercourse accounts for 95% of total outlet, all other outlets definitely minor except extra-marital intercourse. Over ⅓ still with masturbation. Group closer to college level in its acceptance of nudity, precoital petting, and mouth-genital eroticism, but closer to grade school level in its acceptance of frequent marital intercourse and of extra-marital intercourse.

104. Age 26–30. Educ. level 9–12. Urban. Almost precisely as described for whole high school level at this age (Group 103). All differences minor.

105. Age 26–30. Educ. level 9–12. Protest., inactive. Group almost exactly as described for whole high school level (Group 103). 95% of total outlet coming from marital intercourse, over ½ having extra-marital intercourse, 21% of group having some intercourse with prostitutes, but outlets from this and all other sources minor.

106. Age 26–30. Educ. level 13+. Whole group. Sexually less active than males of other educational levels at this age, mean total outlet 3.2. Only 91% of outlet from marital intercourse, with mean frequency of 2.6. Long period of pre-marital restraint reflected in restraint on marital intercourse in this group. See younger age group of same college level (Group 94). ⅔ of males masturbating, drawing 5% of outlet from that source. Extra-marital intercourse in ¼, but exceedingly infrequent and usually with only 1 or 2 partners. Very few married males in this group with homosexual experience at this age.

TABLE 153. CLINICAL TABLES (*continued*)
MARRIED WHITE MALES

AGE: 26–30	SOURCE OF OUTLET	CASES	INCID. %	FREQ. PER WEEK			% OF TOTAL OUTLET		
				Range	Mean	Med.	Range	Mean	Med.
Educ. level 13+									
107. Urban	Total	561	100	22.0	3.4	2.7	—	—	—
	Mast.	516	68	3.0	0.4	0.2	90	13.6	5.3
	Emiss.	561	72	3.0	0.2	0.1	65	6.3	2.0
	Interc.	561	99	20.0	.8	2.2	100	83.3	90.8
	Extra.	561	25	3.5	0.4	0.1	70	9.1	1.0
	Prost.	516	6	1.5	0.2	0.1	10	2.8	0.8
	Homo.	516	2	2.5	1.2	1.3	50	27.8	20.0
108. Rural	Total	86	100	9.0	3.0	2.4	—	—	—
	Mast.	86	57	2.0	0.4	0.2	75	15.3	4.1
	Emiss.	86	73	1.0	0.2	0.1	50	9.8	2.3
	Interc.	86	100	9.0	2.5	1.9	100	83.3	95.0
	Extra.	86	9	1.0	1.3	0.4	10	6.0	5.0
109. Protest., inactive	Total	346	100	22.0	3.5	2.8	—	—	—
	Mast.	346	71	3.0	0.5	0.2	80	13.6	7.1
	Emiss.	346	72	1.5	0.2	0.1	60	7.0	2.4
	Interc.	346	100	20.0	2.8	2.1	100	82.5	88.6
	Extra.	346	26	3.5	0.4	0.1	70	9.4	1.8
	Prost.	346	7	0.5	0.2	0.1	10	3.2	0.8
	Homo.	346	3	2.0	0.7	0.1	5	16.6	1.0
AGE: 31–35									
110. Whole group	Total	569	100	21.0	2.7	2.1	—	—	—
	Mast.	569	45	4.0	0.4	0.1	95	12.4	3.9
	Emiss.	569	61	3.0	0.2	0.1	90	7.2	1.7
	Interc.	569	100	20.0	2.2	1.8	100	85.1	95.0
	Extra.	569	29	4.0	0.6	0.2	75	15.0	8.0
	Prost.	569	11	1.5	0.2	0.1	40	5.4	0.9
	Homo.	569	4	2.0	0.5	0.1	30	10.5	2.5
Educ. level 0–8									
111. Whole group	Total	186	100	16.0	2.6	1.9	—	—	—
	Mast.	186	19	1.0	0.2	0.1	35	5.7	0.8
	Emiss.	186	40	2.0	0.2	0.1	65	6.2	0.9
	Interc.	186	100	15.0	2.3	1.7	100	90.5	96.4
	Extra.	186	32	3.5	0.6	0.3	70	15.3	10.6
	Prost.	186	16	1.0	0.2	0.1	25	5.8	1.0
	Homo.	186	4	Scant	0.1	0.1	5	2.1	0.9
112. Urban	Total	109	100	19.0	3.0	2.3	—	—	—
	Mast.	109	17	0.5	0.1	0.1	15	2.2	0.7
	Emiss.	109	49	2.0	0.2	0.1	65	7.5	0.9
	Interc.	109	100	17.0	2.7	2.2	100	89.9	96.2
	Extra.	109	37	1.0	0.3	0.1	50	13.0	8.8
	Prost.	109	20	0.5	0.2	0.1	15	5.3	1.0
	Homo.	109	4	Scant	0.1	0.1	Scant	2.0	0.8
113. Rural	Total	93	100	16.0	2.8	1.7	—	—	—
	Mast.	93	16	1.0	0.4	0.1	20	9.5	3.0
	Emiss.	93	32	1.0	0.2	0.1	15	3.3	0.9
	Interc.	93	100	14.0	2.4	1.6	100	92.1	96.7
	Extra.	93	23	3.5	0.8	0.4	50	19.7	20.0
	Prost.	93	9	1.0	0.5	0.3	10	5.9	3.0
	Homo.	93	4	Scant	0.1	0.1	5	2.2	3.0

MARRIED WHITE MALES

107. Age 26–30. Educ. level 13+. Urban. A bit more active than corresponding rural group of this level (Group 108). Mean total outlet of 3.4. Otherwise almost exactly as described for whole college level at this age (Group 106).

108. Age 26–30. Educ. level 13+. Rural. Slightly less active than average for whole college level of this age (Group 106), consequently a bit more distinct from urban population (Group 107). Draws more of its outlet (95%) from marital intercourse and less from masturbation and extra-marital intercourse, thus approaching lower educational levels more than urban college segment.

109. Age 26–30. Educ. level 13+. Protest., inactive. Slightly more active than any other segment of college level at this age (Group 106), as far as available data go. A mean total outlet of 3.5, with only 89% of that outlet from marital intercourse. Somewhat higher incidence (71%) and higher frequency of masturbation, and 26% with experience in extra-marital intercourse.

110. Age 31–35. Whole group. Males in "prime of life," but with mean total outlet averaging only 2.7 per week, which is nearly 20% below mean for boys who have just turned adolescent. 95% of outlet drawn from marital intercourse. 29% of males with extra-marital intercourse which accounts for 8% of total outlet. All other outlets minor except masturbation in college level.

111. Age 31–35. Educ. level 0–8. Whole group. Grade school level of married males at this age definitely slowing up sexually, mean total outlet only 2.6, high frequencies of marital intercourse no longer common. This a product of poorer physical condition of many males at this level, and not of sexual maladjustment. 96% of total outlet from marital intercourse, figure increasing for group in later age periods. Extra-marital intercourse still in 1/3, accounting for 11% of their outlet, 1/2 of these having contacts with prostitutes. Masturbation taboo, definitely rare; less than 1/2 with nocturnal emissions and that outlet minor. Homosexual fairly common at younger ages in this group, now reduced to low incidence and scant frequencies.

112. Age 31–35. Educ. level 0–8. Urban. A bit more active than average for whole grade school level at this age (Group 111), with a slightly higher percentage having extra-marital intercourse. Otherwise as described for whole group (Group 111).

113. Age 31–35. Educ. level 0–8. Rural. Very close to pattern described for whole grade school level (Group 111), with somewhat lower incidences in masturbation, nocturnal emissions, extra-marital intercourse, and contacts with prostitutes. Marital intercourse much the most important aspect of sex life of this group, constituting 97% of total outlet.

TABLE 153. CLINICAL TABLES (*continued*)
MARRIED WHITE MALES

AGE: 31–35	SOURCE OF OUTLET	CASES	INCID. %	FREQ. PER WEEK			% OF TOTAL OUTLET		
				Range	Mean	Med.	Range	Mean	Med.
Educ. level 0–8									
114. Protest., inactive	Total	119	100	16.0	2.6	2.0	—	—	—
	Mast.	119	25	1.0	0.3	0.1	35	6.3	0.8
	Emiss.	119	45	1.5	0.2	0.1	35	5.6	0.8
	Interc.	119	100	14.0	2.2	1.8	100	89.4	96.3
	Extra.	119	37	2.5	0.5	0.3	70	15.0	10.4
	Prost.	119	19	1.0	0.2	0.1	25	5.8	0.9
	Homo.	119	3	Scant	0.1	0.1	5	1.8	2.0
Educ. level 9–12									
115. Whole group	Total	82	100	20.0	3.4	2.5	—	—	—
	Mast.	82	37	2.0	0.4	0.1	35	10.6	4.3
	Emiss.	82	56	1.0	0.2	0.1	40	6.3	1.6
	Interc.	82	100	15.0	2.8	2.1	100	86.1	95.2
	Extra.	82	37	2.0	0.5	0.2	50	14.4	4.6
	Prost.	82	17	0.5	0.2	0.1	30	5.9	0.8
	Homo.	82	6	1.0	0.8	0.7	20	13.5	15.0
116. Urban	Total	58	100	7.0	3.0	2.4	—	—	—
	Mast.	58	40	2.0	0.4	0.1	30	9.2	2.3
	Emiss.	58	52	1.0	0.2	0.1	35	6.2	1.4
	Interc.	58	100	7.0	2.5	2.1	100	85.3	94.6
	Extra.	58	36	2.0	0.6	0.2	50	17.5	10.0
	Prost.	58	16	0.5	0.3	0.1	30	8.8	1.0
	Homo.	58	7	1.0	0.7	0.8	20	14.9	17.5
117. Protest., inactive	Total	54	100	14.0	3.2	2.6	—	—	—
	Mast.	54	32	1.0	0.3	0.2	30	11.8	7.5
	Emiss.	54	65	1.0	0.2	0.1	40	5.9	1.0
	Interc.	54	100	14.0	2.7	2.0	100	86.7	95.6
	Extra.	54	35	1.5	0.4	0.2	35	12.6	4.0
	Prost.	54	17	0.5	0.2	0.1	30	8.6	0.8
	Homo.	54	6	1.0	1.0	1.0	25	21.3	25.0
Educ. level 13+									
118. Whole group	Total	301	100	18.0	2.7	2.2	—	—	—
	Mast.	301	64	4.0	0.4	0.1	95	14.0	4.8
	Emiss.	301	75	3.0	0.2	0.1	75	7.7	2.3
	Interc.	301	99	16.0	2.1	1.7	100	81.4	90.5
	Extra.	301	25	3.5	0.6	0.3	70	15.0	7.8
	Prost.	301	7	0.5	0.2	0.1	15	4.5	0.9
	Homo.	301	3	2.0	0.7	0.1	25	16.3	3.0
119. Urban	Total	438	100	20.0	3.0	2.3	—	—	—
	Mast.	402	67	5.0	0.4	0.1	95	13.0	4.5
	Emiss.	438	69	3.0	0.2	0.1	75	7.6	2.4
	Interc.	438	100	18.0	2.4	1.9	100	81.4	90.0
	Extra.	438	34	4.5	0.5	0.2	70	15.6	8.1
	Prost.	402	8	0.5	0.2	0.1	15	4.7	0.9
	Homo.	402	2	2.5	0.9	0.3	25	20.5	5.0
120. Protest., active	Total	109	100	6.0	2.3	2.2	—	—	—
	Mast.	109	60	3.5	0.4	0.1	90	16.0	4.1
	Emiss.	109	79	1.0	0.2	0.1	55	10.5	4.0
	Interc.	109	98	5.5	1.9	1.8	100	82.1	91.3
	Extra.	109	13	Scant	0.3	0.1	10	5.5	0.9

MARRIED WHITE MALES

114. Age 31–35. Educ. level 0–8. Protest., inactive. Very closely matches urban section of whole grade school level, as described above (Group 112).

115. Age 31–35. Educ. level 9–12. Whole group. Definitely more active than either grade school or college level at this age, with mean total outlet 3.4. 90% of total outlet from marital intercourse, $\frac{1}{3}$ of males with some masturbation, $\frac{1}{3}$ with extra-marital intercourse ($\frac{1}{2}$ of these with prostitutes), and $\frac{1}{2}$ with some nocturnal emissions; but all of these other outlets very minor. Wives at this level fairly responsive and sexual adjustments with them fairly good; but extra-marital intercourse may cause some difficulty.

116. Age 31–35. Educ. level 9–12. Urban. Almost exactly as described for whole high school level (Group 115).

117. Age 31–35. Educ. level 9–12. Protest., inactive. Very closely matching description given for whole high school level (Group 115).

118. Age 31–35. Educ. level 13+. Whole group. College males still reflect restraint of pre-marital years, even at this age in marriage. Mean total outlet only 2.7 per week, only 91% of that from marital intercourse. For $\frac{2}{3}$ of males, masturbation supplies 5% of outlet and $\frac{1}{4}$ draw 8% from extra-marital intercourse. This extra-marital intercourse, very little of which is had with prostitutes, gradually becoming more common, in incidence and in frequency, as these college level males grow older. Correspondingly, percentage of outlet from marital intercourse gradually decreasing. On both of these items group is quite opposite to lower level groups. Sexual problems concern unresponsiveness of wives and, increasingly with advancing age, problems arise from extra-marital intercourse.

119. Age 31–35. Educ. level 13+. Urban. Slightly more active group of married males of college level (Group 118), with $\frac{1}{3}$ drawing 8% of their outlet from extra-marital intercourse and $\frac{2}{3}$ drawing 5% from masturbation. All other outlets except marital intercourse minor.

120. Age 31–35. Educ. level 13+. Protest., active. Most restrained segment of college group of married males (Group 118) on which data are available. Total outlet only 2.3 per week, marital intercourse averaging less than 2 per week, never more than 5.5 in most extreme case. Group definitely restrained and allowing significance of sex in marriage to become gradually less. Both marital and extra-marital intercourse less frequent than in remainder of college group at this age (Group 118). Many individuals in group not well satisfied with this sexual arrangement, although they are not always conscious of that.

Table 153. Clinical Tables (*continued*)

MARRIED WHITE MALES

AGE: 31–35	SOURCE OF OUTLET	CASES	INCID. %	FREQ. PER WEEK			% OF TOTAL OUTLET		
				Range	Mean	Med.	Range	Mean	Med.
Educ. level 13+									
121. Protest., inactive	Total	270	100	20.0	3.1	2.4	—	—	—
	Mast.	270	71	5.0	0.4	0.2	80	14.3	6.6
	Emiss.	270	72	1.0	0.2	0.1	50	6.2	2.0
	Interc.	270	100	18.0	2.4	1.9	100	79.6	87.9
	Extra.	270	35	3.5	0.6	0.3	70	17.7	10.0
	Prost.	270	8	0.5	0.2	0.1	15	5.5	3.0
	Homo.	270	5	2.5	0.6	0.1	20	15.5	2.0
AGE: 36–40									
122. Whole group	Total	390	100	22.0	2.5	1.9	—	—	—
	Mast.	390	37	3.0	0.4	0.1	100	12.4	3.7
	Emiss.	390	53	2.0	0.2	0.1	55	6.8	2.2
	Interc.	390	99	20.0	2.0	1.6	100	85.8	95.2
	Extra.	390	29	4.0	0.7	0.2	100	18.8	9.0
	Prost.	390	11	1.0	0.2	0.1	50	7.3	0.9
	Homo.	390	3	1.0	0.6	0.1	20	7.6	5.0
Educ. level 0–8									
123. Whole group	Total	143	100	13.0	2.3	1.7	—	—	—
	Mast.	143	11	1.0	0.3	0.2	35	12.2	5.6
	Emiss.	143	29	1.0	0.1	0.1	20	4.0	0.9
	Interc.	143	99	12.0	2.0	1.6	100	90.3	96.5
	Extra.	143	27	3.5	0.7	0.4	90	23.6	17.2
	Prost.	143	10	0.5	0.2	0.1	20	9.1	2.5
	Homo.	143	3	Scant	0.2	0.1	5	3.0	3.0
124. Urban	Total	75	100	7.0	2.5	2.2	—	—	—
	Mast.	75	8	0.5	0.3	0.2	10	18.0	0.9
	Emiss.	75	33	0.5	0.2	0.1	20	5.3	1.0
	Interc.	75	99	7.0	2.3	2.0	100	87.9	96.2
	Extra.	75	33	3.5	0.6	0.2	90	24.7	16.3
	Prost.	75	16	0.5	0.2	0.1	20	10.3	3.0
125. Rural	Total	84	100	15.0	2.5	1.7	—	—	—
	Mast.	84	12	1.0	0.3	0.3	15	6.1	6.7
	Emiss.	84	31	1.0	0.2	0.1	10	2.7	0.8
	Interc.	84	100	14.0	2.2	1.5	100	93.1	96.8
	Extra.	84	19	1.5	0.6	0.5	50	22.6	22.5
	Homo.	84	5	0.5	0.3	0.3	5	3.8	5.0
126. Protest., inactive	Total	93	100	13.0	2.5	1.8	—	—	—
	Mast.	93	16	1.0	0.3	0.2	35	12.2	5.0
	Emiss.	93	37	1.0	0.2	0.1	20	3.9	0.8
	Interc.	93	99	12.0	2.1	1.6	100	89.6	96.3
	Extra.	93	29	3.5	0.7	0.4	80	22.9	15.7
	Prost.	93	11	0.5	0.2	0.1	20	11.3	2.0
	Homo.	93	3	Scant	0.3	0.1	5	3.8	5.0
Educ. level 9–12									
127. Whole group	Total	58	100	10.0	2.6	2.0	—	—	—
	Mast.	58	26	1.0	0.3	0.2	35	14.8	8.3
	Emiss.	58	52	1.0	0.2	0.1	30	7.0	2.5
	Interc.	58	100	10.0	2.3	1.7	100	87.7	95.4
	Extra.	58	33	1.0	0.3	0.2	35	11.4	5.0
	Prost.	58	19	0.5	0.2	0.1	30	8.7	0.9

MARRIED WHITE MALES

121. Age 31–35. Educ. level 13+. Protest., inactive. Pattern typical of married males of college level (Group 118). Group definitely less inhibited than actively religious males of same level (Group 120). Mean total outlet 3.1, only 88% from marital intercourse, remainder supplied by masturbation (for 71% it provides 7% of outlet) and extra-marital intercourse (10% of total outlet for 35% of males). Developing an increasing dependence upon masturbation and extra-marital intercourse as substitute for sexual relations with wives who are unresponsive or inhibited in accepting such variety of techniques as average male at this level would like. In spite of their expressed desires, however, these males themselves are inhibited.

122. Age 36–40. Whole group. Married males at this age on a steady decline sexually. Mean total outlet 2.5, 95% of total from marital intercourse; masturbation in $1/3$ but mostly at college level and quite taboo at lower levels. Nocturnal emissions in more than $1/2$, but very minor and chiefly in high school and college levels. Extra-marital intercourse in nearly $1/3$, at this age as abundant or more abundant in college level than in lower level.

123. Age 36–40. Educ. level 0–8. Whole group. Married males of grade school level with mean total outlet 2.3. Males of this level often begin to show physical effects of aging, with mean frequencies of marital intercourse down to 2.0 and frequencies above 7 now rare. With advancing age, an increasing proportion of outlet (97%) from marital intercourse (in contrast to decreasing proportion among males of college level). Extra-marital intercourse in not more than $1/4$, accounting for 17% of their outlet. All other outlets infrequent and of minor significance.

124. Age 36–40. Educ. level 0–8. Urban. Pattern much as described for whole grade school level of this age (Group 123), but city males more often have extra-marital intercourse (in 33%) and more often go to prostitutes (in 16%).

125. Age 36–40. Educ. level 0–8. Rural. Closely fitting description given for whole grade school level (Group 123). Incidence of extra-marital intercourse (19%) not as high as in city group; otherwise closer to city group than was true among rural populations at earlier ages.

126. Age 36–40. Educ. level 0–8. Protest., inactive. Closely fitting description given for whole grade school level at this age (Group 123).

127. Age 36–40. Educ. level 9–12. Whole group. Even this high school group begins to show effects of aging; now not more active than any other social level. 95% of total sexual outlet from marital intercourse. $1/4$ masturbate, $1/4$ have extra-marital intercourse, more than $1/2$ having some with prostitutes. All outlets except marital intercourse infrequent and a minor part of total outlet.

TABLE 153. CLINICAL TABLES (continued)
MARRIED WHITE MALES

AGE: 36-40	SOURCE OF OUTLET	CASES	INCID. %	FREQ. PER WEEK			% OF TOTAL OUTLET		
				Range	Mean	Med.	Range	Mean	Med.
Educ. level 13+									
128. Whole group	Total	189	100	22.0	2.6	2.0	—	—	—
	Mast.	189	5)	3.0	0.4	0.1	95	12.1	3.3
	Emiss.	189	72	2.0	0.2	0.1	55	7.6	3.1
	Interc.	189	99	12.0	1.9	1.6	100	81.9	90.2
	Extra.	189	30	3.5	0.9	0.2	100	18.1	7.1
	Prost.	189	9	0.5	0.2	0.1	20	4.9	0.9
	Homo.	189	3	0.5	0.9	0.1	10	7.0	5.0
129. Urban	Total	281	100	22.0	2.7	2.1	—	—	—
	Mast.	281	62	4.0	0.4	0.1	95	11.0	3.0
	Emiss.	281	67	2.0	0.2	0.1	55	7.0	3.0
	Interc.	281	99	12.0	2.1	1.7	100	82.3	90.1
	Extra.	281	37	6.0	0.7	0.2	100	19.3	7.5
	Prost.	281	8	1.0	0.5	0.1	20	4.9	0.9
130. Protest., active	Total	73	100	4.5	2.0	1.9	—	—	—
	Mast.	73	55	3.0	0.4	0.1	95	18.8	4.6
	Emiss.	73	75	1.0	0.2	0.1	50	10.3	4.2
	Interc.	73	99	4.0	1.6	1.6	100	81.5	89.6
	Extra.	73	16	0.5	0.1	0.1	15	5.3	2.0
131. Protest., inactive	Total	187	99	22.0	2.9	2.2	—	—	—
	Mast.	187	71	3.0	0.4	0.2	70	10.4	3.9
	Emiss.	187	67	1.0	0.2	0.1	40	6.8	3.1
	Interc.	187	98	12.0	2.1	1.6	100	80.0	88.3
	Extra.	187	41	6.0	0.8	0.3	100	22.0	9.5
	Prost.	187	10	1.0	0.5	0.1	2)	5.5	0.9
	Homo.	187	3	0.5	0.7	0.1	10	7.0	5.0
AGE: 41-45									
132. Whole group	Total	272	100	15.0	2.0	1.6	—	—	—
	Mast.	272	33	3.0	0.3	0.1	90	12.7	4.3
	Emiss.	272	54	1.0	0.2	0.1	60	7.5	2.0
	Interc.	272	99	14.0	1.6	1.3	100	85.9	95.4
	Extra.	272	24	2.0	0.5	0.3	100	24.3	16.3
	Prost.	272	9	0.5	0.2	0.1	35	8.0	1.0
	Homo.	272	2	Scant	0.8	0.1	5	5.5	0.9
Educ. level 0-8									
133. Whole group	Total	100	100	9.5	1.9	1.4	—	—	—
	Mast.	100	9	1.0	0.3	0.2	10	5.2	5.0
	Emiss.	100	31	1.0	0.1	0.1	20	4.4	0.9
	Interc.	100	99	9.0	1.7	1.2	100	90.8	96.7
	Extra.	100	21	2.0	0.6	0.4	100	32.2	19.0
	Prost.	100	11	0.5	0.3	0.2	20	12.3	5.0
	Homo.	·100	3	0.1	0.1	0.1	Scant	1.3	1.0
·134. Rural	Total	52	100	9.5	2.1	1.4	—	—	—
	Mast.	52	12	1.0	0.4	0.4	10	7.6	7.5
	Emiss.	52	27	0.5	0.2	0.1	10	3.0	0.9
	Interc.	52	100	9.0	2.1	1.3	100	93.7	97.0
	Extra.	52	12	1.0	0.6	0.6	50	26.3	27.5
	Prost.	52	4	Scant	0.2	0.3	Scant	1.8	3.0
	Homo.	52	4	Scant	0.1	0.1	Scant	1.8	3.0

128. Age 36–40. Educ. level 13+. Whole group. Married males of this college level usually in fair condition physically and sexually capable enough. Not materially different from college level in preceding 5-year period (Group 118). Whole group shows effect of pre-marital restraint which is characteristic of this level. 90% of total outlet from marital intercourse. 59% masturbate, usually with low frequencies; 30% have extra-marital intercourse, usually not with prostitutes; other outlets of minor significance. Problems of sexual adjustment in marriage not as frequent as at an earlier age because male rates have dropped, and female has lost some of previous inhibitions and is now near prime of her responsiveness. Occasionally this erotic development of female comes too late to correct a maladjustment that developed earlier in the marriage; and male's extra-marital intercourse may become a source of difficulty.

129. Age 36–40. Educ. level 13+. Urban. Very well described by paragraph above for whole college level (Group 128).

130. Age 36–40. Educ. level 13+. Protest., active. Most restrained segment of college level, as far as data are available. General pattern that of whole level (Group 128), but mean total outlet down to 2.0 per week. Mean frequency of marital intercourse 1.6, in no individual more than 4 per week, supplying only 90% of total sexual outlet. More than $\frac{1}{2}$ of males masturbate but infrequently, $\frac{3}{4}$ have emissions but infrequently. Extra-marital intercourse in only 16%, supplying only 2% of outlet, but even then a likely source of conflict. Marked contrast to inactive Protestants of same level (Group 131). Clinician may well examine possibility that maladjusted individual from this group is in sexual conflict, even when he asserts otherwise.

131. Age 36–40. Educ. level 13+. Protest., inactive. Most active segment of college level at this age. General pattern quite like that described for whole college level (Group 128), but mean total outlet 2.9 per week, marital intercourse 2.1 per week, with maximum frequencies still up to 12 per week. 88% of outlet from marital intercourse. 41% with extra-marital intercourse, which supplies 10% of outlet, prostitutes in only $\frac{1}{4}$ of these cases. Masturbation in nearly $\frac{3}{4}$, but not frequent.

132. Age 41–45. Whole group. Sexual activity continues to drop, mean total outlet averaging only 2.0 by this age. 95% of total outlet from marital intercourse, mean frequency 1.6, but some individuals still averaging 7, 10, or more per week. Masturbation still in $\frac{1}{3}$, chiefly, however, at college level; frequencies low. Nocturnal emissions in $\frac{1}{2}$ but of no great significance. Extra-marital intercourse in $\frac{1}{4}$, other outlets very minor.

133. Age 41–45. Educ. level 0–8. Whole group. Males of this level in early forties so affected by age that their rates for first time are now lower than rates of college level. Early aging probably a product of poor nutrition, hard work, or original physical or mental incapacity. Marital intercourse supplies 97% of outlet, but mean frequencies down to 1.7, and for $\frac{1}{2}$ of population not more often than 1.2 per week. Very few individuals with frequencies to 7 per week. Extra-marital intercourse in only 21%, all other outlets very minor. Problems of sexual adjustment less significant because of lowered interest of these males in sexual activity, and particularly because of decrease in frequency of extra-marital intercourse.

134. Age 41–45. Educ. level 0–8. Rural. Married males of rural group drawing 97% of total outlet from marital intercourse, mean frequency 2.1 per week, median 1.3. Extra-marital intercourse in only 12%, all other outlets very minor.

TABLE 153. CLINICAL TABLES (*continued*)
MARRIED WHITE MALES

AGE: 41–45	SOURCE OF OUTLET	CASES	INCID. %	FREQ. PER WEEK			% OF TOTAL OUTLET		
				Range	Mean	Med.	Range	Mean	Med.
Educ. level 0–8									
135. Protest., inactive	Total	60	100	9.5	1.9	1.3	—	—	—
	Mast.	60	13	0.5	0.2	0.2	10	4.9	3.0
	Emiss.	60	42	1.0	0.2	0.1	20	4.5	0.9
	Interc.	60	98	9.0	1.8	1.0	100	87.8	96.5
	Extra.	60	27	2.0	0.6	0.5	100	36.4	27.5
	Prost.	60	12	0.5	0.3	0.2	20	17.3	7.5
	Homo.	60	3	Scant	0.1	0.1	Scant	1.8	3.0
Educ. level 13+									
136. Whole group	Total	138	100	9.5	2.0	1.7	—	—	—
	Mast.	138	55	3.0	0.3	0.1	90	13.2	4.3
	Emiss.	138	73	1.0	0.2	0.1	45	7.5	2.5
	Interc.	138	99	8.0	1.5	1.3	100	82.0	91.0
	Extra.	138	24	2.0	0.5	0.2	85	21.4	15.0
	Prost.	138	5	0.5	0.1	0.1	5	1.9	0.8
137. Urban	Total	112	100	9.5	2.1	1.8	—	—	—
	Mast.	112	55	3.0	0.4	0.1	90	13.0	4.4
	Emiss.	112	74	1.0	0.2	0.1	45	7.0	2.4
	Interc.	112	99	8.0	1.6	1.3	100	82.1	91.2
	Extra.	112	23	2.0	0.6	0.3	85	23.0	12.5
	Prost.	112	6	0.5	0.1	0.1	5	1.9	0.8
	Homo.	112	3	Scant	1.5	0.1	Scant	9.7	1.0
138. Protest., inactive	Total	83	100	9.5	2.1	1.7	—	—	—
	Mast.	83	60	2.0	0.3	0.1	55	11.0	5.8
	Emiss.	83	72	1.0	0.1	0.1	30	6.4	2.0
	Interc.	83	100	8.0	1.5	1.3	100	80.0	87.2
	Extra.	83	31	2.0	0.6	0.4	85	25.9	22.5
	Prost.	83	7	0.5	0.1	0.1	5	2.2	0.9
	Homo.	83	4	Scant	1.5	0.1	Scant	9.7	1.0
AGE: 46–50									
139. Whole group	Total	175	99	14.0	1.8	1.2	—	—	—
	Mast.	175	31	1.5	0.3	0.1	70	14.9	6.8
	Emiss.	175	48	1.0	0.2	0.1	80	9.4	2.2
	Interc.	175	97	14.0	1.5	0.9	100	83.7	95.8
	Extra.	175	24	2.5	0.7	0.4	95	29.1	18.8
	Prost.	175	6	0.5	0.3	0.2	10	12.3	5.6
	Homo.	175	2	Scant	1.5	0.1	5	12.2	5.0
Educ. level 0–8									
140. Whole group	Total	70	97	14.0	1.9	1.2	—	—	—
	Mast.	70	7	1.0	0.4	0.1	10	6.5	1.0
	Emiss.	70	29	1.0	0.2	0.1	20	5.1	1.0
	Interc.	70	97	14.0	1.7	0.9	100	90.1	96.8
	Extra.	70	19	1.5	0.6	0.4	80	33.6	35.0
	Prost.	70	9	0.5	0.3	0.3	10	17.2	6.3
Educ. level 13+									
141. Whole group	Total	81	100	7.5	1.8	1.3	—	—	—
	Mast.	81	57	1.5	0.3	0.1	70	14.5	6.9
	Emiss.	81	68	1.0	0.1	0.1	50	9.2	2.5
	Interc.	81	98	5.5	1.3	0.9	100	78.2	92.5
	Extra.	81	27	2.5	0.9	0.6	95	30.3	22.5

MARRIED WHITE MALES

135. Age 41–45. Educ. level 0–8. Protest., inactive. Pattern well covered by description for whole grade school level at this age (Group 133).

136. Age 41–45. Educ. level 13+. Whole group. Married males of college level usually in good condition physically at this age, although mean total outlet has continued to drop since late teens, now down to 2.0. Marital intercourse 91% of total outlet, extra-marital intercourse in $\frac{1}{4}$ of group accounting for 15% of their outlet. Masturbation still in more than $\frac{1}{2}$, nocturnal emissions in $\frac{3}{4}$, but these and other outlets of minor significance. Group offers no special sexual problems other than those which are the product of general restraint characteristic of college group throughout their histories.

137. Age 41–45. Educ. level 13+. Urban. Pattern almost exactly as described in whole college level (Group 136).

138. Age 41–45. Educ. level 13+. Protest., inactive. Very close to pattern described for whole college level (Group 136). Marital intercourse accounting for only 87% of total outlet. Somewhat higher incidence (31%) of extra-marital intercourse, accounting for 23% of outlet. Masturbation in 60%, accounting for 6% of their outlet. Other sexual activities less significant.

139. Age 46–50. Whole group. General level of sexual activity continues to decline with age. In these late forties, mean total outlet is 1.8 per week, about 96% of that from marital intercourse. $\frac{1}{4}$ of males with extra-marital intercourse which provides 19% of their outlet, masturbation in $\frac{1}{3}$, other outlets minor. First cases of permanent impotence from age, although healthy males may not expect impotence for another 10 or 20 years, if ever. Some impotence now appearing is product of inhibition or loss of interest in sexual activity. Some problems of marital adjustment now develop because of waning interest in sexual activity, although not generally so for another 10 years for most males.

140. Age 46–50. Educ. level 0–8. Whole group. Males of grade school level derive higher proportion of total outlet from marital intercourse, with incidence of extra-marital intercourse (19%) definitely lower than in corresponding college level (Group 141). Aging problems more acute in this lower level at this age, than in college level (see Group 139).

141. Age 46–50. Educ. level 13+. Whole group. General pattern as described for all married males of this age (Group 139). Aging problems less acute than with lower social levels. Intercourse accounting for only 93% of outlet, extra-marital intercourse increasing, with incidence now 27%. Masturbation increasing, now in 57%, accounting for 7% of outlet. Emissions still in 68%, accounting for only 3% of outlet.

TABLE 153. CLINICAL TABLES (*concluded*)

MARRIED WHITE MALES

AGE: 46–50	SOURCE OF OUTLET	CASES	INCID. %	FREQ. PER WEEK			% OF TOTAL OUTLET		
				Range	Mean	Med.	Range	Mean	Med.
Educ. level 13+									
142. Urban	Total	64	100	7.5	2.0	1.5	—	—	—
	Mast.	64	58	1.5	0.3	0.1	70	15.4	7.5
	Emiss.	64	69	1.0	0.2	0.1	45	7.9	3.0
	Interc.	64	97	5.5	1.4	1.0	100	79.3	91.9
	Extra.	64	27	2.5	1.0	0.5	9 ϡ	29.0	15.0
	Prost.	64	3	0.5	0.3	0.4	5	5.5	7.5
AGE: 51–55									
143. Whole group	Total	109	98	7.0	1.6	1.0	—	—	—
	Mast.	109	26	1.5	0.4	0.1	50	18.2	11.3
	Emiss.	109	44	1.0	0.2	0.1	50	7.9	0.9
	Interc.	109	97	6.0	1.2	0.8	100	83.1	96.1
	Extra.	109	22	2.0	0.8	0.5	90	33.3	32.5
	Prost.	109	7	0.5	0.2	0.2	25	15.2	3.0
	Homo.	109	2	Scant	0.7	0.8	5	15.5	17.5
Educ. level 0–8									
144. Whole group	Total	50	96	6.0	1.4	0.9	—	—	—
	Mast.	50	6	Scant	0.3	0.1	Scant	3.0	1.0
	Emiss.	50	20	1.0	0.2	0.1	50	12.0	0.9
	Interc.	50	96	6.0	1.2	0.7	100	88.3	97.0
	Extra.	50	20	1.5	0.5	0.3	90	32.5	22.5
	Prost.	50	10	0.5	0.3	0.3	25	23.5	5.0
AGE: 56–60									
145. Whole group	Total	67	99	4.5	1.1	0.8	—	—	—
	Mast.	67	19	0.5	0.2	0.1	60	20.9	7.8
	Emiss.	67	28	0.5	0.1	0.1	60	13.8	1.0
	Interc.	67	94	3.0	0.9	0.7	100	81.1	96.3
	Extra.	67	25	2.0	0.6	0.4	100	37.0	15.0
	Prost.	67	8	0.5	0.3	0.1	5	19.5	1.0

MARRIED WHITE MALES

142. Age 46–50. Educ. level 13+. Urban. Very close to pattern described for whole college level at this age (Group 141).

143. Age 51–55. Whole group. Steady decline in sexual activity continues, as it has since late teens. Mean total outlet now 1.6, 2% of total population no longer experiences orgasm. Maximum frequencies for any male 7 per week, although median frequencies are only 1 per week. Nearly all total outlet still from marital intercourse, more true of lower levels, less true of upper levels. Masturbation practically out for lower educational level, on increase for upper level. Extra-marital intercourse steadily increasing for upper level. Among males of college level, marital intercourse may not account for more than 62% of total outlet at this age. Decline of sexual interest between spouses only occasionally causing serious trouble at this age. Impotence slightly more frequent but still in not more than 9% of population.

144. Age 51–55. Educ. level 0–8. Whole group. Some differences from whole group described above (Group 143). Mean total outlet (1.4) lower. Percentage derived from marital intercourse steadily increasing, now totals 97%. Only 20% having extra-marital intercourse, from which they derive 23% of outlet. Masturbation exceedingly scant at this lower level, other outlets not important. 4% of group inactive, no longer experiencing orgasm.

145. Age 56–60. Whole group. The aging process leads to a mean frequency of only 1.1 per week for this group. The most extreme male experiences orgasm only 4.5 per week. Nearly all outlet of lower educational level derived from marital intercourse, not ⅔ of it so derived by college level. Extra-marital intercourse infrequent at lower level, more frequent at upper level. Masturbation and nocturnal emissions account for very little of lower level's outlet, may account for as much as 22% of outlet of college level at this age. Impotence now in 18%.

TABLE 154. CLINICAL TABLES
PREVIOUSLY MARRIED WHITE MALES

	SOURCE OF OUTLET	CASES	INCID. %	FREQ. PER WEEK			% OF TOTAL OUTLET		
AGE: 21–25				Range	Mean	Med.	Range	Mean	Med.
146. Whole group	Total	119	98	23.0	3.8	2.0	—	—	—
	Mast.	119	45	3.0	0.6	0.3	100	26.3	17.5
	Emiss.	119	62	2.0	0.3	0.1	50	10.3	2.7
	Interc.	150	96	28.0	3.3	1.6	100	79.5	95.1
	Comp.	119	96	20.0	2.9	1.2	100	68.2	85.4
	Prost.	119	47	1.5	0.3	0.1	100	18.4	2.7
	Homo.	119	27	4.0	1.1	0.3	85	18.9	4.6
Educ. level 0–8									
147. Whole group	Total	93	96	23.0	3.7	1.8	—	—	—
	Mast.	93	34	2.0	0.5	0.3	100	22.2	10.8
	Emiss.	93	50	2.0	0.3	0.2	50	10.1	4.8
	Interc.	93	94	28.0	3.4	1.5	100	86.5	95.6
	Comp.	93	88	20.0	3.3	1.2	100	74.0	89.2
	Prost.	93	46	1.0	0.4	0.3	100	31.7	17.5
	Homo.	93	14	1.0	0.5	0.2	15	9.7	5.0
148. Protest., inactive	Total	69	97	18.0	3.4	1.7	—	—	—
	Mast.	69	36	2.0	0.6	0.3	100	26.9	18.3
	Emiss.	69	48	2.0	0.3	0.2	40	9.4	4.4
	Interc.	69	94	20.0	3.2	1.5	100	86.4	95.7
	Comp.	69	87	18.0	3.1	1.2	100	73.2	88.2
	Prost.	69	51	1.0	0.4	0.3	100	32.4	20.0
	Homo.	69	12	1.0	0.3	0.2	10	4.6	4.0
Educ. level 9–12									
149. Whole group	Total	57	100	22.0	4.2	2.3	—	—	—
	Mast.	57	56	3.0	0.6	0.2	65	19.1	11.3
	Emiss.	57	72	1.0	0.2	0.1	50	10.7	1.9
	Interc.	56	91	20.0	3.4	1.8	100	77.6	93.8
	Comp.	57	91	20.0	3.3	1.7	100	73.9	90.8
	Prost.	57	46	2.0	0.2	0.1	30	6.7	0.8
AGE: 26–30	Homo.	57	39	3.5	1.4	0.6	80	25.8	12.5
150. Whole group	Total	182	97	23.0	3.0	1.8	—	—	—
	Mast.	182	44	4.0	0.6	0.3	100	24.0	12.5
	Emiss.	182	64	2.0	0.3	0.1	100	12.6	3.7
	Interc.	192	95	20.0	2.4	1.3	100	78.6	94.0
	Comp.	182	90	20.0	2.4	1.1	100	68.5	81.7
	Prost.	182	56	2.0	0.3	0.1	100	22.3	6.4˙
	Homo.	182	18	4.0	0.9	0.3	85	18.7	6.9
Educ. level 0–8									
151. Whole group	Total	108	95	17.0	2.9	1.6	—	—	—
	Mast.	108	35	2.0	0.5	0.2	100	24.4	13.8
	Emiss.	108	58	2.0	0.3	0.1	50	10.6	4.6
	Interc.	117	94	17.0	2.3	1.0	100	83.3	95.4
	Comp.	108	86	17.0	2.4	0.9	100	68.3	81.0
	Prost.	108	63	1.5	0.4	0.3	100	29.6	14.6
	Homo.	108	14	3.0	0.7	0.2	—	—	—
152. Urban	Total	68	99	17.0	3.2	1.7	—	—	—
	Mast.	68	38	1.5	0.4	0.2	60	19.4	11.3
	Emiss.	68	62	2.0	0.3	0.1	50	10.0	3.6
	Interc.	75	97	17.0	2.6	1.2	100	82.9	95.4
	Comp.	68	93	17.0	2.6	1.0	100	68.2	80.0
	Prost.	68	69	1.5	0.4	0.3	100	27.5	15.0
	Homo.	68	19	3.0	0.7	0.2	25	11.3	6.3

Table 154. Clinical Tables

PREVIOUSLY MARRIED WHITE MALES

146. Age 21–25. Whole group. Males who have been previously married but who no longer live with wives, have patterns closer to those of married males than to those of single males. 96% of whole population continues heterosexual coitus, ½ having some with prostitutes, but most frequently with other females. Masturbation in less than ½, but accounting for 18% of their outlet. Nocturnal emissions in nearly ⅔. Homosexual activities much more frequent than among married males, less frequent than among some groups of single males, now in 27% accounting for 5% of outlet. Often present personality problems which not infrequently involve sexual maladjustments. Many come from lower educational levels where there is considerable irresponsibility, incapacity, unwillingness or ineffectiveness in securing and holding jobs, failure to support wives, cruelty, and problems arising from drinking. While married, were promiscuous in extramarital relations and had a fair amount of homosexual activity, and these sometimes caused divorce. This, however, a personality problem rather than a sexual problem in origin.

147. Age 21–25. Educ. level 0–8. Whole group. Pattern well described in paragraph above (Group 146). Apparently somewhat lower incidence of masturbation and of homosexual. Few inhibitions on socio-sexual contacts in this group, but more inhibitions against masturbation, nudity, petting techniques, and oral eroticism. Promiscuous, and VD often high.

148. Age 21–25. Educ. level 0–8. Protest., inactive. Pattern covered by descriptions in two paragraphs above (Groups 146, 147).

149. Age 21–25. Educ. level 9–12. Whole group. Most active males of this age group, with mean total outlet 4.2. 91% have intercourse which accounts for 94% of their outlet. ½ of these have some intercourse with prostitutes, which accounts for less than 1% of outlet. 56% masturbate, so deriving 11% of their outlet, 39% have homosexual relations which account for 13% of their outlet. In heterosexual promiscuity and high incidence of homosexual, this group a close duplicate of single males of same educational level and age (Group 48). Marriage a passing episode to many of these individuals; many present basic personality problems. Others more balanced. Clinicians will do well to make a sharp distinction between persons with these diverse backgrounds.

150. Age 26–30. Whole group. Males who have been previously married but are no longer living with wives, have patterns closer to those of married males than to those of single males. 95% have intercourse which provides 94% of total outlet, nearly 60% have some of that intercourse with prostitutes; and considerable promiscuity for grade school and high school males of this group. Masturbation in 44%, accounting for 13% of their outlet, but more of this in upper educational levels, less in lower educational levels. Homosexual in 18%, accounting for 7% of outlet. Compare younger age level of previously married males (Group 146). A larger number of these males have made a real attempt at marital adjustment and have encountered more serious difficulties, which in many cases have involved sexual problems.

151. Age 26–30. Educ. level 0–8. Whole group. Remarks made in paragraph above (Group 150) applicable to grade school level of this age group. Masturbation less frequently a source of outlet (in 35% of males), prostitutes providing a larger portion of intercourse (for 63% of males); homosexual of minor significance but in 14% of histories. Few inhibitions on socio-sexual contacts in this group, but more against masturbation, nudity, petting techniques, and oral eroticism.

TABLE 154. CLINICAL TABLES (*continued*)
PREVIOUSLY MARRIED WHITE MALES

AGE: 26–30	SOURCE OF OUTLET	CASES	INCID. %	FREQ. PER WEEK			% OF TOTAL OUTLET		
				Range	Mean	Med.	Range	Mean	Med.
Educ. level 13+									
153. Protest., inactive	Total	86	97	17.0	3.0	1.7	—	—	—
	Mast.	86	38	2.0	0.5	0.2	100	26.0	15.0
	Emiss.	86	62	2.0	0.3	0.1	50	9.2	3.5
	Interc.	91	96	17.0	2.5	1.3	100	84.8	95.5
	Comp.	86	85	17.0	2.6	1.1	100	68.3	82.0
	Prost.	86	65	1.5	0.4	0.3	100	31.1	17.5
	Homo.	86	11	1.0	0.5	0.1	15	6.1	3.7
AGE: 31–35									
154. Whole group	Total	158	95	15.0	2.0	1.3	—	—	—
	Mast.	158	39	3.0	0.4	0.2	100	28.3	15.0
	Emiss.	158	58	1.0	0.2	0.1	100	12.4	1.4
	Interc.	171	91	11.0	1.7	1.0	100	80.9	95.3
	Comp.	158	82	10.0	1.7	0.8	100	68.3	81.4
	Prost.	158	61	2.0	0.4	0.2	100	28.6	9.2
	Homo.	158	11	4.0	0.9	0.3	100	25.8	8.3
Educ. level 0–8									
155. Whole group	Total	102	95	15.0	1.8	1.1	—	—	—
	Mast.	102	32	1.0	0.3	0.1	95	24.1	15.0
	Emiss.	102	55	1.0	0.2	0.1	95	13.4	3.0
	Interc.	108	94	11.0	1.6	0.8	100	83.0	95.5
	Comp.	102	81	10.0	1.5	0.6	100	65.6	76.3
	Prost.	102	66	2.0	0.4	0.3	100	37.7	25.0
	Homo.	102	7	0.5	0.7	0.2	15	9.8	8.3
156. Urban	Total	67	99	15.0	1.9	1.0	—	—	—
	Mast.	67	34	0.5	0.2	0.1	50	12.9	0.9
	Emiss.	67	60	0.5	0.1	0.1	95	14.9	1.0
	Interc.	71	97	11.0	1.7	0.9	100	85.1	95.9
	Comp.	67	87	10.0	1.7	0.7	100	64.5	73.8
	Prost.	67	72	1.0	0.4	0.3	100	38.2	24.5
	Homo.	67	9	0.5	0.8	0.3	15	10.9	8.5
157. Protest., inactive	Total	78	95	15.0	1.9	1.0	—	—	—
	Mast.	78	36	1.0	0.4	0.1	95	26.9	16.3
	Emiss.	78	58	1.0	0.2	0.1	75	11.2	1.4
	Interc.	81	93	11.0	1.6	0.8	100	83.3	95.8
	Comp.	78	78	10.0	1.6	0.6	100	65.2	77.5
	Prost.	78	67	1.5	0.4	0.3	100	39.5	29.2
	Homo.	78	4	Scant	1.3	0.1	10	13.0	10.0
AGE: 36–40									
158. Whole group	Total	128	98	16.0	1.7	1.0	—	—	—
	Mast.	128	42	2.0	0.4	0.2	100	30.6	16.9
	Emiss.	128	54	0.5	0.2	0.1	100	17.1	5.0
	Interc.	146	92	7.5	1.5	0.8	100	80.4	95.5
	Comp.	128	81	10.0	1.5	0.6	100	67.3	85.0
	Prost.	128	57	1.5	0.4	0.3	100	34.2	15.0
	Homo.	128	6	1.0	0.8	0.2	35	14.6	7.8
Educ. level 0–8									
159. Whole group	Total	82	98	16.0	1.6	0.9	—	—	—
	Mast.	82	37	1.0	0.4	0.2	95	23.8	10.0
	Emiss	82	46	0.5	0.1	0.1	100	18.0	4.0
	Interc.	86	94	5.0	1.1	0.7	100	80.9	95.9
	Comp.	82	78	10.0	1.2	0.5	100	64.8	77.5
	Prost.	82	70	1.5	0.5	0.3	100	40.0	30.0
	Homo.	82	6	0.5	1.1	0.3	15	12.5	10.0

PREVIOUSLY MARRIED WHITE MALES

152. Age 26–30. Educ. level 0–8. Urban. A somewhat more active segment of grade school level (Group 151). Mean total outlet 3.2 with frequencies of 10, 14, or more not uncommon, 97% with intercourse which provides 95% of total outlet, 69% with some intercourse with prostitutes, 19% with homosexual outlet. Group heterosexually almost as active as married males and homosexually more so.

153. Age 26–30. Educ. level 0–8. Protest., inactive. Almost exactly as described above (Group 152).

154. Age 31–35. Whole group. Males who have been previously married very little less active than married males of same age, with mean total outlet 2.0. Intercourse in 91%, accounting for 95% of their total outlet. 61% have some intercourse with prostitutes, 11% have homosexual relations, 39% have masturbation which accounts for only 15% of outlet. 5% apparently without sexual outlet, these the individuals most likely to be disturbed and most often involved in basic personality difficulties. Any individual among previously married males who is having outlets much less frequently than those given here, needs especial consideration.

155. Age 31–35. Educ. level 0–8. Whole group. Pattern very close to that described for whole group above (Group 154). Mean total outlet 1.8, 94% deriving 96% of outlet from intercourse, over ⅔ of these having some intercourse with prostitutes, masturbation in only ⅓ of histories, 5% apparently without any sexual outlet.

156. Age 31–35. Educ. level 0–8. Urban. A less restrained segment of grade school group (Groups 154, 155). Only 1% without any sexual outlet. 97% with some intercourse accounting for 96% of outlet, about ¾ of these with some of intercourse with prostitutes. Masturbation very minor source of outlet.

157. Age 31–35. Educ. level 0–8. Protest., inactive. Record very close to description given for whole grade school level (Group 155).

158. Age 36–40. Whole group. Aging effect on males who have been previously married somewhat sharper than on married males. Mean total outlet down to 1.7, but nearly all males (98%) with active histories. 92% of group deriving 96% of outlet from intercourse, nearly ⅔ of these having some with prostitutes, 6% with homosexual, masturbation in 42% accounting for 17% of total outlet.

159. Age 36–40. Educ. level 0–8. Whole group. Available data do not show this group significantly different from description given above (Group 158), except that 70% have intercourse with prostitutes, which accounts for 30% of outlet.

TABLE 154. CLINICAL TABLES (concluded)
PREVIOUSLY MARRIED WHITE MALES

AGE: 36-40	SOURCE OF OUTLET	CASES	INCID. %	FREQ. PER WEEK			% OF TOTAL OUTLET		
				Range	Mean	Med.	Range	Mean	Med.
Educ. level 0-8									
160. Protest., inactive	Total	62	97	16.0	1.7	1.0	—	—	—
	Mast.	62	44	1.0	0.4	0.2	95	25.8	15.0
	Emiss.	62	48	0.5	0.1	0.1	100	13.9	0.9
	Interc.	66	92	5.0	1.1	0.7	100	80.3	96.1
	Comp.	62	76	10.0	1.4	0.5	100	65.8	87.5
	Prost.	62	69	1.5	0.4	0.3	100	39.1	35.0
	Homo.	62	5	Scant	1.6	0.1	10	13.8	10.0
AGE: 41-45									
161. Whole group	Total	96	94	12.0	1.6	1.0	—	—	—
	Mast.	96	33	2.0	0.6	0.3	95	32.1	17.5
	Emiss.	96	39	1.0	0.2	0.1	100	21.6	5.0
	Interc.	107	86	10.0	1.4	0.8	100	85.1	96.2
	Comp.	96	69	10.0	1.2	0.6	100	62.4	69.4
	Prost.	96	60	1.5	0.5	0.4	100	46.9	47.5
	Homo.	96	5	1.0	1.3	0.5	35	22.5	15.0
Educ. level 0-8									
162. Whole group	Total	69	93	12.0	1.5	0.9	—	—	—
	Mast.	69	26	1.5	0.6	0.3	95	33.3	15.0
	Emiss.	69	32	0.5	0.1	0.1	100	18.1	2.0
	Interc.	71	87	10.0	1.3	0.8	100	87.0	96.5
	Comp.	69	68	10.0	1.2	0.5	100	62.1	70.0
	Prost.	69	68	1.5	0.5	0.4	100	49.1	48.0
	Homo.	69	6	0.5	1.4	0.4	15	13.6	12.5
AGE: 46-50									
163. Whole group	Total	63	94	6.0	1.4	0.8	—	—	—
	Mast.	63	44	2.0	0.5	0.4	100	36.6	32.5
	Emiss.	63	32	1.0	0.2	0.1	100	21.3	5.8
	Interc.	72	82	5.0	1.3	0.7	100	83.3	96.3
	Comp.	63	67	4.5	1.2	0.5	100	63.7	77.5
	Prost.	63	52	1.0	0.4	0.3	100	48.8	50.0

PREVIOUSLY MARRIED WHITE MALES

160. Age 36–40. Educ. level 0–8. Protest., inactive. The relatively scant data available on this group do not show it significantly different from description given above (Group 159).

161. Age 41–45. Whole group. Aging effects continue to mount; apparently 6% of group without sexual outlet. Only 86% have intercourse, which accounts for 96% of their outlet, 60% have some of this with prostitutes, but this probably more true of lower educational level which is chief source of present sample. Only ⅓ masturbate. Homosexual in 5%.

162. Age 41–45. Educ. level 0–8. Whole group. Scant data available on this group do not show it significantly different from description given above (Group 161).

163. Age 46–50. Whole group. A continued decline in sexual activity evident in this group. Mean total outlet 1.4, with 6% of males apparently inactive. Only 82% in limited sample with any intercourse, which contributes 96% of their outlet. 52% with some intercourse with prostitutes, which contributes ½ of their total outlet—this a measure of their social maladjustments. Nearly ½ of group masturbates, so deriving ⅓ of their outlet. Homosexual too minor to record on this small sample.

APPENDIX ON SAMPLE SIZE

The problem involved in determining the number of cases necessary in the present study to provide an adequate sample of any larger population, has already been discussed in Chapter 3. The generalizations made there have been based upon a series of pragmatic tests of the values of calculations derived from samples of various sizes. The specific data derived from those tests are shown in the tables presented in this Appendix.

As previously explained (Chapter 3), calculations have been made systematically for samples of 50, 100, 200, 300, 400, and (where the material is available) 600, 1000, and still larger numbers of cases. In all, 698 different populations have been used in these tests. Each population has been homogeneous for sex, race, marital status, age, educational level, and either the rural-urban background or the religious background of the included individuals. The samples of various size have all been selected by a strict randomization performed on an IBM sorter; and in each instance the sample has been drawn directly from the total number of histories available in each population. In no case has a larger sample been built up by adding cases to an originally smaller sample of 50, 100, or other size.

In the tables given here, the statistics which are shown **in boldface** represent calculations which lie **within 5 per cent,** plus or minus, of the calculations obtained from the largest sample available in that group; except that comparisons of incidence data have been made with an allowance of 2 per cent, plus or minus. The boldface figures therefore represent results that are adequate, as judged by the results obtained from the use of the largest sample, and within the allowed range of error. Of course, an error of any other size might have been arbitrarily selected as a basis for judging adequacy in these tables. See Chapter 3 (Table 2) for a summary tabulation of the number of adequate samples which are shown here in these tables.

The eight tables which follow present the following statistics on each of the sample populations:

> Table 155: Mean frequencies per week (and the standard deviation) on the total population in each sample
> Table 156: Mean frequencies per week (and the standard deviation) for the active population in each sample
> Table 157: Median frequencies per week for the total population in each sample

Wherever all of the medians in an entire section of any table have fallen into a zero frequency class, they have not been shown in these tables.

In column one, in each of the following tables, these abbreviations have been used:

S	=	single
M	=	married
U	=	urban
Px	=	Protestant, inactive
P√	=	Protestant, devout
Jx	=	Jewish, inactive

MEAN OF TOTAL POPULATION: SIZE OF ADEQUATE SAMPLE
CALCULATIONS WITH SAMPLES OF VARIOUS SIZES

Total Outlet

GROUP	EDUC. LEVEL	AGE	50	100	200	300	400	600	LARGEST SAMPLE	CASES IN LARGEST SAMPLE
S-U	0-8	11-15	4.77 ± 0.73	3.65 ± 0.52	3.12 ± 0.26	3.34 ± 0.24	3.32 ± 0.20		3.35 ± 0.18	490
S-U	0-8	16-20	3.16 ± 0.35	3.30 ± 0.38	3.29 ± 0.22	3.53 ± 0.19	3.41 ± 0.19		3.45 ± 0.17	486
S-U	9-12	11-15	3.26 ± 0.44	3.54 ± 0.39	3.37 ± 0.24	3.52 ± 0.22	3.52 ± 0.18		3.49 ± 0.16	521
S-U	9-12	16-20	3.74 ± 0.55	4.20 ± 0.50	3.42 ± 0.23	3.54 ± 0.20	3.61 ± 0.18		3.62 ± 0.16	520
S-U	13+	11-15	3.28 ± 0.59	3.11 ± 0.35	2.97 ± 0.19	2.87 ± 0.18	2.77 ± 0.13	2.91 ± 0.12	2.84 ± 0.05	2708
S-U	13+	16-20	2.80 ± 0.58	2.50 ± 0.22	2.77 ± 0.17	2.76 ± 0.16	3.10 ± 0.14	2.68 ± 0.09	2.77 ± 0.05	2762
S-U	13+	21-25	2.69 ± 0.36	2.80 ± 0.21	2.63 ± 0.20	2.55 ± 0.12	2.61 ± 0.12	2.51 ± 0.10	2.60 ± 0.06	1844
S-U	13+	26-30	2.55 ± 0.36	3.03 ± 0.30	2.79 ± 0.24	2.61 ± 0.14	2.67 ± 0.14		2.67 ± 0.13	479
M-U	13+	21-25	3.38 ± 0.34	3.83 ± 0.29	3.88 ± 0.20	3.56 ± 0.15	3.77 ± 0.14		3.74 ± 0.13	460
M-U	13+	26-30	3.66 ± 0.29	3.03 ± 0.23	3.26 ± 0.20	3.35 ± 0.16	3.41 ± 0.14		3.36 ± 0.11	561
M-U	13+	31-35	2.87 ± 0.25	2.80 ± 0.23	3.12 ± 0.20	3.05 ± 0.14			2.98 ± 0.12	438
S-Px	0-8	11-15	3.80 ± 0.60	2.85 ± 0.31	3.49 ± 0.31	2.77 ± 0.19	3.17 ± 0.20		3.09 ± 0.17	481
S-Px	0-8	16-20	3.02 ± 0.62	3.23 ± 0.39	3.16 ± 0.26	3.37 ± 0.23	3.45 ± 0.19		3.31 ± 0.17	493
S-Px	9-12	11-15	3.12 ± 0.43	3.45 ± 0.34	3.32 ± 0.25	3.35 ± 0.21			3.38 ± 0.18	375
S-Jx	13+	11-15	2.80 ± 0.38	3.28 ± 0.44	2.74 ± 0.22	2.91 ± 0.19	3.03 ± 0.17		2.91 ± 0.13	601
S-Jx	13+	16-20	2.44 ± 0.29	3.22 ± 0.24	2.94 ± 0.18	2.94 ± 0.15	3.09 ± 0.14		2.98 ± 0.11	607
S-P√	13+	11-15	2.86 ± 0.36	2.49 ± 0.21	2.58 ± 0.15	2.56 ± 0.13	2.48 ± 0.12		2.48 ± 0.10	547
S-P√	13+	16-20	2.49 ± 0.27	2.43 ± 0.18	2.28 ± 0.15	2.25 ± 0.11	2.35 ± 0.10		2.31 ± 0.08	557
S-P√	13+	21-25	1.83 ± 0.26	2.01 ± 0.16	1.88 ± 0.12	1.97 ± 0.10			2.02 ± 0.10	384
S-Px	13+	11-15	2.81 ± 0.47	3.15 ± 0.32	3.17 ± 0.18	3.14 ± 0.18	3.13 ± 0.14	2.93 ± 0.10	3.04 ± 0.07	1471
S-Px	13+	16-20	3.32 ± 0.43	2.71 ± 0.19	2.77 ± 0.15	2.99 ± 0.14	2.87 ± 0.12	2.90 ± 0.10	2.87 ± 0.06	1513
S-Px	13+	21-25	2.74 ± 0.33	2.61 ± 0.24	2.58 ± 0.16	2.62 ± 0.13	2.63 ± 0.12	2.56 ± 0.09	2.62 ± 0.07	1000

Masturbation

S-U	0–8	11–15	2.30 ± 0.45	1.92 ± 0.27	1.53 ± 0.13	1.71 ± 0.14	1.70 ± 0.11		1.71 ± 0.10	490
S-U	0–8	16–20	0.97 ± 0.15	0.97 ± 0.14	0.96 ± 0.09	1.05 ± 0.08	0.92 ± 0.07		0.95 ± 0.06	486
S-U	9–12	11–15	2.13 ± 0.31	1.98 ± 0.23	1.94 ± 0.16	2.03 ± 0.13	2.00 ± 0.11		2.02 ± 0.10	521
S-U	9–12	16–20	1.25 ± 0.21	1.41 ± 0.27	1.43 ± 0.16	1.38 ± 0.12	1.29 ± 0.09	2.27 ± 0.11	1.35 ± 0.08	520
S-U	13+	11–15	2.56 ± 0.52	2.44 ± 0.34	2.40 ± 0.18	2.29 ± 0.16	2.18 ± 0.12	1.77 ± 0.08	2.23 ± 0.05	2708
S-U	13+	16–20	1.95 ± 0.58	1.70 ± 0.19	1.80 ± 0.14	1.95 ± 0.15	2.04 ± 0.12	1.35 ± 0.07	1.85 ± 0.04	2762
S-U	13+	21–25	1.20 ± 0.20	1.48 ± 0.18	1.42 ± 0.15	1.26 ± 0.09	1.28 ± 0.08		1.35 ± 0.04	1844
S-U	13+	26–30	0.92 ± 0.19	1.24 ± 0.16	1.30 ± 0.16	1.15 ± 0.11	1.22 ± 0.09		1.17 ± 0.08	479
S-Px	0–8	11–15	1.85 ± 0.33	1.60 ± 0.22	1.74 ± 0.16	1.39 ± 0.10	1.61 ± 0.11		1.58 ± 0.10	481
S-Px	0–8	16–20	0.90 ± 0.27	0.98 ± 0.15	0.96 ± 0.10	0.92 ± 0.08	0.98 ± 0.07		0.94 ± 0.06	493
S-Px	9–12	11–15	2.06 ± 0.36	1.79 ± 0.19	2.03 ± 0.17	1.80 ± 0.12			1.88 ± 0.11	375
S-Jx	13+	11–15	2.48 ± 0.36	2.67 ± 0.42	2.23 ± 0.22	2.33 ± 0.18	2.47 ± 0.16		2.34 ± 0.12	601
S-Jx	13+	16–20	1.67 ± 0.26	2.21 ± 0.20	2.01 ± 0.16	1.99 ± 0.14	2.16 ± 0.13		2.09 ± 0.11	607
S-P√	13+	11–15	2.11 ± 0.29	1.88 ± 0.18	2.04 ± 0.14	1.95 ± 0.11	1.86 ± 0.10		1.88 ± 0.08	547
S-P√	13+	16–20	1.89 ± 0.26	1.55 ± 0.15	1.53 ± 0.12	1.40 ± 0.09	1.56 ± 0.08		1.50 ± 0.07	557
S-P√	13+	21–25	1.08 ± 0.18	1.17 ± 0.12	1.11 ± 0.09	1.05 ± 0.07			1.10 ± 0.07	384
S-Px	13+	11–15	2.10 ± 0.37	2.59 ± 0.29	2.65 ± 0.17	2.44 ± 0.16	2.47 ± 0.12	2.27 ± 0.09	2.40 ± 0.06	1471
S-Px	13+	16–20	2.41 ± 0.35	2.00 ± 0.18	1.86 ± 0.13	2.02 ± 0.13	1.93 ± 0.10	2.05 ± 0.08	1.95 ± 0.05	1513
S-Px	13+	21–25	1.58 ± 0.29	1.46 ± 0.21	1.44 ± 0.12	1.41 ± 0.11	1.48 ± 0.09	1.34 ± 0.07	1.46 ± 0.06	1000

Nocturnal Emissions

S-U	0–8	11–15	0.02 ± 0.01	0.08 ± 0.04	0.04 ± 0.01	0.05 ± 0.01	0.06 ± 0.01		0.05 ± 0.01	490
S-U	0–8	16–20	0.15 ± 0.05	0.13 ± 0.03	0.18 ± 0.03	0.17 ± 0.02	0.16 ± 0.02		0.16 ± 0.02	486
S-U	9–12	11–15	0.07 ± 0.02	0.12 ± 0.02	0.16 ± 0.04	0.13 ± 0.02	0.16 ± 0.03		0.16 ± 0.02	521
S-U	9–12	16–20	0.15 ± 0.03	0.22 ± 0.04	0.24 ± 0.03	0.24 ± 0.03	0.23 ± 0.02		0.23 ± 0.02	520
S-U	13+	11–15	0.43 ± 0.11	0.33 ± 0.05	0.33 ± 0.04	0.35 ± 0.05	0.37 ± 0.04	0.35 ± 0.03	0.35 ± 0.01	2708
S-U	13+	16–20	0.35 ± 0.06	0.37 ± 0.05	0.47 ± 0.05	0.43 ± 0.03	0.44 ± 0.03	0.42 ± 0.02	0.42 ± 0.01	2762
S-U	13+	21–25	0.37 ± 0.05	0.37 ± 0.04	0.38 ± 0.04	0.37 ± 0.03	0.38 ± 0.03	0.39 ± 0.02	0.39 ± 0.01	1844
S-U	13+	26–30	0.23 ± 0.05	0.30 ± 0.04	0.30 ± 0.03	0.35 ± 0.03	0.31 ± 0.02		0.31 ± 0.02	479
M-U	13+	21–25	0.15 ± 0.04	0.14 ± 0.03	0.18 ± 0.03	0.19 ± 0.02	0.17 ± 0.02		0.17 ± 0.02	460

(Table continued on next page)

MEAN OF TOTAL POPULATION: SIZE OF ADEQUATE SAMPLE
CALCULATIONS WITH SAMPLES OF VARIOUS SIZES

GROUP	EDUC. LEVEL	AGE	50	100	200	300	400	600	LARGEST SAMPLE	CASES IN LARGEST SAMPLE
					Nocturnal Emissions (*continued*)					
M-U	13+	26–30	0.16 ± 0.03	0.17 ± 0.03	0.11 ± 0.01	0.16 ± 0.02	0.16 ± 0.02		0.16 ± 0.01	561
M-U	13+	31–35	0.13 ± 0.03	0.16 ± 0.02	0.14 ± 0.02	0.15 ± 0.02			0.14 ± 0.01	438
S-Px	0–8	11–15	0.05 ± 0.02	0.06 ± 0.02	0.05 ± 0.01	0.06 ± 0.01	0.06 ± 0.01		0.06 ± 0.01	481
S-Px	0–8	16–20	0.15 ± 0.06	0.14 ± 0.04	0.14 ± 0.03	0.13 ± 0.02	0.15 ± 0.02		0.14 ± 0.02	493
S-Px	9–12	11–15	0.15 ± 0.04	0.13 ± 0.04	0.13 ± 0.03	0.14 ± 0.03			0.14 ± 0.03	375
S-Jx	13+	11–15	0.23 ± 0.07	0.41 ± 0.07	0.37 ± 0.04	0.39 ± 0.04	0.41 ± 0.04		0.41 ± 0.03	601
S-Jx	13+	16–20	0.40 ± 0.08	0.42 ± 0.05	0.44 ± 0.05	0.47 ± 0.04	0.47 ± 0.04		0.44 ± 0.03	607
S-P√	13+	11–15	0.39 ± 0.11	0.29 ± 0.03	0.32 ± 0.04	0.35 ± 0.04	0.36 ± 0.05		0.34 ± 0.03	547
S-P√	13+	16–20	0.31 ± 0.04	0.41 ± 0.05	0.41 ± 0.05	0.41 ± 0.04	0.40 ± 0.03		0.41 ± 0.02	557
S-P√	13+	21–25	0.38 ± 0.10	0.39 ± 0.06	0.36 ± 0.03	0.42 ± 0.04			0.42 ± 0.03	384
S-Px	13+	11–15	0.32 ± 0.06	0.36 ± 0.07	0.22 ± 0.03	0.32 ± 0.04	0.35 ± 0.03	0.32 ± 0.03	0.33 ± 0.02	1471
S-Px	13+	16–20	0.42 ± 0.13	0.34 ± 0.04	0.39 ± 0.04	0.36 ± 0.03	0.39 ± 0.03	0.41 ± 0.03	0.42 ± 0.02	1513
S-Px	13+	21–25	0.38 ± 0.08	0.31 ± 0.04	0.37 ± 0.04	0.35 ± 0.03	0.34 ± 0.03	0.38 ± 0.03	0.36 ± 0.02	1000
					Pre-marital Intercourse with Companions					
S-U	0–8	11–15	2.02 ± 0.65	1.42 ± 0.39	1.14 ± 0.17	1.21 ± 0.16	1.19 ± 0.13		1.17 ± 0.12	490
S-U	0–8	16–20	1.40 ± 0.23	1.66 ± 0.27	1.58 ± 0.17	1.65 ± 0.14	1.76 ± 0.15		1.76 ± 0.13	486
S-U	9–12	11–15	0.25 ± 0.21	0.92 ± 0.22	0.81 ± 0.14	0.87 ± 0.14	0.88 ± 0.12		0.83 ± 0.10	521
S-U	9–12	16–20	1.87 ± 0.51	1.67 ± 0.36	1.02 ± 0.12	1.09 ± 0.13	1.36 ± 0.14		1.34 ± 0.12	520
S-U	13+	11–15	0.19 ± 0.14	0.15 ± 0.10	0.04 ± 0.01	0.06 ± 0.02	0.05 ± 0.02	0.10 ± 0.03	0.07 ± 0.01	2708
S-U	13+	16–20	0.27 ± 0.09	0.16 ± 0.05	0.26 ± 0.07	0.20 ± 0.03	0.29 ± 0.05	0.25 ± 0.03	0.25 ± 0.02	2762

Pre-marital Intercourse with Companions *(continued)*

S-U	13+	21–25	0.78 ± 0.35	0.54 ± 0.12	0.44 ± 0.07	0.58 ± 0.07	0.58 ± 0.07	0.46 ± 0.04	0.49 ± 0.03	1844
S-U	13+	26–30	0.86 ± 0.32	0.87 ± 0.21	0.66 ± 0.11	0.65 ± 0.07	0.66 ± 0.08		0.70 ± 0.07	479
S-Px	0–8	11–15	1.43 ± 0.41	0.91 ± 0.18	1.40 ± 0.24	0.95 ± 0.12	1.19 ± 0.14		1.13 ± 0.12	481
S-Px	0–8	16–20	1.79 ± 0.60	1.68 ± 0.32	1.65 ± 0.22	1.84 ± 0.18	1.83 ± 0.16		1.74 ± 0.13	493
S-Px	9–12	11–15	0.46 ± 0.16	0.99 ± 0.20	0.80 ± 0.16	0.98 ± 0.14			0.91 ± 0.12	375
S-Jx	13+	11–15	0.02 ± 0.01	0.00 ± 0.00	0.03 ± 0.03	0.02 ± 0.01	0.02 ± 0.01		0.02 ± 0.01	601
S-Jx	13+	16–20	0.16 ± 0.06	0.20 ± 0.04	0.21 ± 0.05	0.23 ± 0.04	0.21 ± 0.03		0.20 ± 0.03	607
S-P√	13+	11–15	0.14 ± 0.08	0.10 ± 0.05	0.04 ± 0.02	0.07 ± 0.03	0.06 ± 0.02		0.06 ± 0.02	547
S-P√	13+	16–20	0.03 ± 0.02	0.26 ± 0.11	0.14 ± 0.04	0.22 ± 0.05	0.15 ± 0.03		0.16 ± 0.03	557
S-P√	13+	21–25	0.10 ± 0.08	0.18 ± 0.06	0.21 ± 0.06	0.21 ± 0.05			0.21 ± 0.04	384
S-Px	13+	11–15	0.03 ± 0.02	0.02 ± 0.01	0.06 ± 0.03	0.11 ± 0.04	0.10 ± 0.03	0.08 ± 0.02	0.08 ± 0.02	1471
S-Px	13+	16–20	0.22 ± 0.09	0.21 ± 0.05	0.22 ± 0.04	0.35 ± 0.06	0.26 ± 0.04	0.21 ± 0.03	0.25 ± 0.02	1513
S-Px	13+	21–25	0.47 ± 0.17	0.46 ± 0.10	0.43 ± 0.07	0.49 ± 0.07	0.43 ± 0.05	0.46 ± 0.05	0.46 ± 0.04	1000

Marital Intercourse

M-U	13+	21–25	2.78 ± 0.33	3.19 ± 0.28	3.25 ± 0.19	2.91 ± 0.15	3.15 ± 0.14		3.11 ± 0.12	460
M-U	13+	26–30	2.80 ± 0.26	2.43 ± 0.22	2.67 ± 0.17	2.74 ± 0.14	2.78 ± 0.13		2.75 ± 0.11	561
M-U	13+	31–35	2.25 ± 0.23	2.25 ± 0.22	2.54 ± 0.18	2.35 ± 0.12			2.37 ± 0.11	438

Total Extra-marital Intercourse

M-U	13+	21–25	0.10 ± 0.06	0.04 ± 0.02	0.10 ± 0.05	0.09 ± 0.03	0.08 ± 0.03		0.08 ± 0.02	460
M-U	13+	26–30	0.13 ± 0.07	0.13 ± 0.05	0.12 ± 0.05	0.11 ± 0.03	0.11 ± 0.03		0.11 ± 0.02	561
M-U	13+	31–35	0.16 ± 0.08	0.13 ± 0.05	0.16 ± 0.04	0.19 ± 0.04			0.17 ± 0.03	438

(Table continued on next page)

741

MEAN OF TOTAL POPULATION: SIZE OF ADEQUATE SAMPLE
CALCULATIONS WITH SAMPLES OF VARIOUS SIZES

Homosexual Outlet

GROUP	EDUC. LEVEL	AGE	50	100	200	300	400	600	LARGEST SAMPLE	CASES IN LARGEST SAMPLE
S-U	0–8	11–15	0.57 ± 0.19	0.27 ± 0.10	**0.29** ± 0.07	**0.28** ± 0.06	0.26 ± 0.04		0.29 ± 0.04	490
S-U	0–8	16–20	0.44 ± 0.14	0.17 ± 0.05	**0.26** ± 0.05	0.28 ± 0.04	0.24 ± 0.04		0.26 ± 0.04	486
S-U	9–12	11–15	0.47 ± 0.16	**0.34** ± 0.15	0.29 ± 0.06	**0.32** ± 0.06	0.29 ± 0.04		0.32 ± 0.04	521
S-U	9–12	16–20	0.25 ± 0.10	0.64 ± 0.21	**0.45** ± 0.08	0.58 ± 0.09	**0.48** ± 0.07		0.46 ± 0.05	520
S-U	13+	11–15	0.06 ± 0.04	0.03 ± 0.01	0.13 ± 0.03	0.10 ± 0.03	0.08 ± 0.02	0.10 ± 0.02	0.09 ± 0.01	2708
S-U	13+	16–20	0.08 ± 0.04	0.11 ± 0.05	**0.07** ± 0.02	0.05 ± 0.02	0.05 ± 0.01	**0.07** ± 0.02	0.07 ± 0.01	2762
S-U	13+	21–25	0.02 ± 0.00	0.08 ± 0.05	**0.09** ± 0.03	0.06 ± 0.02	0.11 ± 0.03	0.07 ± 0.02	0.09 ± 0.01	1844
S-U	13+	26–30	**0.25** ± 0.11	0.27 ± 0.08	**0.25** ± 0.06	0.21 ± 0.05	0.22 ± 0.04		0.24 ± 0.04	479
S-Px	0–8	11–15	0.34 ± 0.12	0.14 ± 0.05	0.24 ± 0.06	0.23 ± 0.05	0.23 ± 0.04		0.21 ± 0.03	481
S-Px	0–8	16–20	0.13 ± 0.06	0.23 ± 0.08	0.17 ± 0.05	**0.20** ± 0.04	**0.19** ± 0.04		0.20 ± 0.03	493
S-Px	9–12	11–15	0.31 ± 0.10	0.31 ± 0.10	0.19 ± 0.04	0.25 ± 0.05			0.28 ± 0.04	375
S-Jx	13+	11–15	0.05 ± 0.04	0.15 ± 0.08	0.03 ± 0.02	0.09 ± 0.03	0.06 ± 0.02		0.07 ± 0.02	601
S-Jx	13+	16–20	0.01 ± 0.01	0.10 ± 0.05	0.07 ± 0.02	**0.06** ± 0.03	0.04 ± 0.02		0.06 ± 0.02	607
S-P√	13+	11–15	0.11 ± 0.06	0.11 ± 0.04	0.06 ± 0.04	0.07 ± 0.02	0.10 ± 0.03		0.09 ± 0.02	547
S-P√	13+	16–20	0.02 ± 0.01	0.05 ± 0.02	0.09 ± 0.04	**0.06** ± 0.02	0.07 ± 0.02		0.06 ± 0.02	557
S-P√	13+	21–25	0.03 ± 0.03	0.02 ± 0.01	0.02 ± 0.01	0.03 ± 0.01			0.04 ± 0.02	384
S-Px	13+	11–15	0.04 ± 0.01	**0.10** ± 0.03	**0.11** ± 0.03	**0.11** ± 0.02	0.12 ± 0.02	0.13 ± 0.02	0.10 ± 0.01	1471
S-Px	13+	16–20	0.13 ± 0.10	0.03 ± 0.01	0.12 ± 0.05	0.05 ± 0.01	0.09 ± 0.02	0.09 ± 0.02	0.07 ± 0.01	1513
S-Px	13+	21–25	0.10 ± 0.05	0.06 ± 0.03	0.10 ± 0.04	0.11 ± 0.04	0.10 ± 0.03	0.10 ± 0.02	0.09 ± 0.02	1000

Table 155. Size of sample necessary to secure stable means on total population. Means are frequencies per week.

Boldface figures designate calculations that lie within 5 per cent, plus or minus, of the calculations obtained from the largest sample. Means are frequencies per week.

MEAN OF ACTIVE POPULATION: SIZE OF ADEQUATE SAMPLE
CALCULATIONS WITH SAMPLES OF VARIOUS SIZES

Total Outlet

GROUP	EDUC. LEVEL	AGE	50	100	200	300	400	600	LARGEST SAMPLE	CASES IN LARGEST SAMPLE
S-U	0-8	11-15	5.18 ± 0.76	4.06 ± 0.56	3.38 ± 0.28	3.61 ± 0.26	3.63 ± 0.21		3.62 ± 0.19	490
S-U	0-8	16-20	3.16 ± 0.35	3.37 ± 0.39	3.34 ± 0.22	3.59 ± 0.20	3.48 ± 0.19		3.53 ± 0.17	486
S-U	9-12	11-15	3.55 ± 0.46	3.73 ± 0.40	3.48 ± 0.24	3.65 ± 0.22	3.67 ± 0.19		3.66 ± 0.16	521
S-U	9-12	16-20	3.74 ± 0.55	4.20 ± 0.50	3.42 ± 0.23	3.57 ± 0.20	3.62 ± 0.18		3.64 ± 0.16	520
S-U	13+	11-15	3.34 ± 0.60	3.21 ± 0.36	3.11 ± 0.20	2.98 ± 0.18	2.92 ± 0.14	3.06 ± 0.12	2.97 ± 0.06	2708
S-U	13+	16-20	2.80 ± 0.58	2.52 ± 0.22	2.77 ± 0.17	2.76 ± 0.16	3.10 ± 0.14	2.68 ± 0.09	2.78 ± 0.05	2762
S-U	13+	21-25	2.69 ± 0.36	2.80 ± 0.21	2.63 ± 0.20	2.55 ± 0.12	2.61 ± 0.12	2.51 ± 0.10	2.60 ± 0.06	1844
S-U	13+	26-30	2.55 ± 0.36	3.03 ± 0.30	2.79 ± 0.24	2.61 ± 0.16	2.67 ± 0.14		2.67 ± 0.13	479
M-U	13+	21-25	3.38 ± 0.34	3.83 ± 0.29	3.88 ± 0.20	3.56 ± 0.15	3.77 ± 0.14		3.74 ± 0.13	460
M-U	13+	26-30	3.66 ± 0.29	3.03 ± 0.23	3.26 ± 0.20	3.35 ± 0.16	3.41 ± 0.14		3.36 ± 0.11	561
M-U	13+	31-35	2.87 ± 0.25	2.80 ± 0.23	3.12 ± 0.20	3.05 ± 0.14			2.98 ± 0.12	438
S-Px	0-8	11-15	4.04 ± 0.62	3.03 ± 0.32	3.64 ± 0.32	2.97 ± 0.20	3.38 ± 0.21		3.29 ± 0.18	481
S-Px	0-8	16-20	3.02 ± 0.62	3.29 ± 0.40	3.22 ± 0.27	3.40 ± 0.23	3.52 ± 0.20		3.37 ± 0.17	493
S-Px	9-12	11-15	3.47 ± 0.45	3.67 ± 0.35	3.47 ± 0.26	3.50 ± 0.21			3.55 ± 0.19	375
S-Jx	13+	11-15	2.80 ± 0.38	3.42 ± 0.45	2.86 ± 0.23	3.00 ± 0.19	3.11 ± 0.17		3.03 ± 0.13	601
S-Jx	13+	16-20	2.44 ± 0.29	3.22 ± 0.24	2.94 ± 0.18	2.94 ± 0.15	3.09 ± 0.14		2.98 ± 0.11	607
S-P√	13+	11-15	3.04 ± 0.36	2.65 ± 0.22	2.70 ± 0.15	2.67 ± 0.13	2.58 ± 0.13		2.60 ± 0.10	547
S-P√	13+	16-20	2.49 ± 0.27	2.43 ± 0.18	2.29 ± 0.15	2.26 ± 0.11	2.35 ± 0.10		2.32 ± 0.08	557
S-P√	13+	21-25	1.87 ± 0.27	2.03 ± 0.16	1.89 ± 0.12	1.97 ± 0.10			2.02 ± 0.10	384
S-Px	13+	11-15	2.98 ± 0.48	3.28 ± 0.33	3.23 ± 0.18	3.35 ± 0.19	3.26 ± 0.14	3.04 ± 0.10	3.17 ± 0.08	1471
S-Px	13+	16-20	3.32 ± 0.43	2.71 ± 0.19	2.77 ± 0.15	2.99 ± 0.14	2.88 ± 0.12	2.92 ± 0.10	2.88 ± 0.06	1513
S-Px	13+	21-25	2.74 ± 0.33	2.61 ± 0.24	2.58 ± 0.16	2.64 ± 0.13	2.64 ± 0.12	2.56 ± 0.09	2.62 ± 0.07	1000

744

Masturbation

S-U	0-8	11-15	2.61 ± 0.49	2.23 ± 0.30	1.78 ± 0.15		1.99 ± 0.13	2.01 ± 0.16	1.98 ± 0.11	490
S-U	0-8	16-20	1.05 ± 0.16	1.18 ± 0.16	1.12 ± 0.10		1.10 ± 0.08	1.22 ± 0.09	1.12 ± 0.07	486
S-U	9-12	11-15	2.48 ± 0.33	2.31 ± 0.25	2.10 ± 0.17		2.20 ± 0.12	2.21 ± 0.14	2.24 ± 0.10	521
S-U	9-12	16-20	1.35 ± 0.22	1.59 ± 0.30	1.56 ± 0.17		1.44 ± 0.10	1.57 ± 0.13	1.50 ± 0.09	520
S-U	13+	11-15	3.28 ± 0.62	2.87 ± 0.38	2.88 ± 0.19	2.79 ± 0.12	2.68 ± 0.13	2.75 ± 0.17	2.72 ± 0.05	2708
S-U	13+	16-20	2.11 ± 0.62	1.93 ± 0.21	2.09 ± 0.15	1.95 ± 0.09	2.24 ± 0.13	2.21 ± 0.17	2.08 ± 0.04	2762
S-U	13+	21-25	1.28 ± 0.21	1.76 ± 0.20	1.65 ± 0.17	1.53 ± 0.08	1.47 ± 0.09	1.40 ± 0.10	1.55 ± 0.05	1844
S-U	13+	26-30	0.98 ± 0.20	1.39 ± 0.17	1.61 ± 0.19		1.42 ± 0.10	1.37 ± 0.12	1.37 ± 0.09	479
S-Px	0-8	11-15	2.10 ± 0.36	1.87 ± 0.25	1.88 ± 0.17		1.81 ± 0.12	1.58 ± 0.10	1.79 ± 0.10	481
S-Px	0-8	16-20	1.10 ± 0.32	1.18 ± 0.17	1.10 ± 0.11		1.13 ± 0.07	1.07 ± 0.09	1.10 ± 0.07	493
S-Px	9-12	11-15	2.40 ± 0.40	1.96 ± 0.20	2.25 ± 0.18			1.98 ± 0.12	2.08 ± 0.12	375
S-Jx	13+	11-15	2.88 ± 0.38	3.34 ± 0.49	2.86 ± 0.26		3.09 ± 0.18	2.94 ± 0.21	2.93 ± 0.14	601
S-Jx	13+	16-20	2.04 ± 0.29	2.35 ± 0.21	2.36 ± 0.17		2.43 ± 0.14	2.24 ± 0.15	2.38 ± 0.12	607
S-P√	13+	11-15	2.57 ± 0.31	2.41 ± 0.20	2.54 ± 0.15		2.28 ± 0.10	2.46 ± 0.12	2.33 ± 0.09	547
S-P√	13+	16-20	2.06 ± 0.27	1.89 ± 0.15	1.78 ± 0.13		1.79 ± 0.08	1.68 ± 0.10	1.75 ± 0.07	557
S-P√	13+	21-25	1.25 ± 0.20	1.35 ± 0.13	1.31 ± 0.09			1.26 ± 0.08	1.32 ± 0.07	384
S-Px	13+	11-15	2.63 ± 0.43	3.08 ± 0.31	2.97 ± 0.17	2.66 ± 0.10	2.93 ± 0.13	3.01 ± 0.18	2.83 ± 0.07	1471
S-Px	13+	16-20	2.61 ± 0.37	2.08 ± 0.18	1.99 ± 0.14	2.21 ± 0.09	2.08 ± 0.10	2.17 ± 0.13	2.13 ± 0.05	1513
S-Px	13+	21-25	1.88 ± 0.33	1.65 ± 0.23	1.66 ± 0.13	1.48 ± 0.07	1.66 ± 0.10	1.57 ± 0.12	1.61 ± 0.06	1000

Nocturnal Emissions

S-U	0-8	11-15	0.09 ± 0.03	0.28 ± 0.12	0.13 ± 0.02		0.17 ± 0.04	0.22 ± 0.04	0.20 ± 0.03	490
S-U	0-8	16-20	0.23 ± 0.07	0.25 ± 0.05	0.31 ± 0.05		0.28 ± 0.03	0.26 ± 0.03	0.27 ± 0.03	486
S-U	9-12	11-15	0.18 ± 0.04	0.27 ± 0.04	0.36 ± 0.09		0.30 ± 0.05	0.40 ± 0.07	0.38 ± 0.05	521
S-U	9-12	16-20	0.24 ± 0.05	0.32 ± 0.05	0.32 ± 0.04		0.33 ± 0.04	0.32 ± 0.03	0.32 ± 0.03	520
S-U	13+	11-15	0.52 ± 0.14	0.45 ± 0.06	0.47 ± 0.06	0.47 ± 0.04	0.50 ± 0.07	0.50 ± 0.05	0.49 ± 0.02	2708
S-U	13+	16-20	0.37 ± 0.06	0.43 ± 0.06	0.52 ± 0.05	0.46 ± 0.02	0.47 ± 0.04	0.49 ± 0.04	0.47 ± 0.01	2762
S-U	13+	21-25	0.43 ± 0.06	0.44 ± 0.06	0.43 ± 0.05	0.45 ± 0.03	0.44 ± 0.04	0.43 ± 0.03	0.45 ± 0.02	1844
S-U	13+	26-30	0.28 ± 0.05	0.35 ± 0.05	0.36 ± 0.03		0.40 ± 0.03	0.37 ± 0.03	0.37 ± 0.02	479
M-U	13+	21-25	0.22 ± 0.06	0.21 ± 0.03	0.27 ± 0.04		0.28 ± 0.03	0.25 ± 0.03	0.26 ± 0.02	460

(Table continued on next page)

MEAN OF ACTIVE POPULATION: SIZE OF ADEQUATE SAMPLE
CALCULATIONS WITH SAMPLES OF VARIOUS SIZES

GROUP	EDUC. LEVEL	AGE	50	100	200	300	400	600	LARGEST SAMPLE	CASES IN LARGEST SAMPLE
					Nocturnal Emissions (*continued*)					
M-U	13+	26-30	0.21 ± 0.04	0.22 ± 0.03	0.16 ± 0.02	0.22 ± 0.03	0.22 ± 0.02		0.21 ± 0.02	561
M-U	13+	31-35	0.18 ± 0.04	0.22 ± 0.03	0.21 ± 0.03	0.22 ± 0.03			0.21 ± 0.02	438
S-Px	0-8	11-15	0.18 ± 0.06	0.25 ± 0.07	0.19 ± 0.04	0.21 ± 0.05	0.22 ± 0.04		0.22 ± 0.04	481
S-Px	0-8	16-20	0.29 ± 0.12	0.24 ± 0.07	0.24 ± 0.04	0.22 ± 0.03	0.26 ± 0.03		0.26 ± 0.03	493
S-Px	9-12	11-15	0.36 ± 0.08	0.33 ± 0.10	0.31 ± 0.06	0.35 ± 0.07			0.35 ± 0.06	375
S-Jx	13+	11-15	0.32 ± 0.09	0.55 ± 0.08	0.49 ± 0.06	0.49 ± 0.04	0.55 ± 0.05		0.54 ± 0.04	601
S-Jx	13+	16-20	0.45 ± 0.09	0.48 ± 0.06	0.52 ± 0.06	0.54 ± 0.04	0.53 ± 0.04		0.51 ± 0.03	607
S-P√	13+	11-15	0.55 ± 0.14	0.41 ± 0.04	0.47 ± 0.05	0.49 ± 0.05	0.51 ± 0.06		0.48 ± 0.05	547
S-P√	13+	16-20	0.37 ± 0.05	0.45 ± 0.05	0.46 ± 0.05	0.43 ± 0.04	0.43 ± 0.03		0.45 ± 0.03	557
S-P√	13+	21-25	0.41 ± 0.11	0.46 ± 0.06	0.41 ± 0.04	0.47 ± 0.04			0.47 ± 0.03	384
S-Px	13+	11-15	0.46 ± 0.08	0.54 ± 0.10	0.34 ± 0.03	0.47 ± 0.05	0.53 ± 0.05	0.47 ± 0.04	0.48 ± 0.03	1471
S-Px	13+	16-20	0.51 ± 0.15	0.37 ± 0.05	0.44 ± 0.05	0.40 ± 0.03	0.43 ± 0.03	0.45 ± 0.03	0.45 ± 0.02	1513
S-Px	13+	21-25	0.44 ± 0.10	0.35 ± 0.05	0.45 ± 0.05	0.41 ± 0.03	0.40 ± 0.03	0.44 ± 0.03	0.42 ± 0.02	1000
					Pre-marital Intercourse with Companions					
S-U	0-8	11-15	3.05 ± 0.94	3.22 ± 0.81	2.09 ± 0.29	2.30 ± 0.27	2.38 ± 0.24		2.29 ± 0.21	490
S-U	0-8	16-20	1.71 ± 0.26	1.89 ± 0.30	1.83 ± 0.19	2.00 ± 0.16	2.12 ± 0.18		2.11 ± 0.15	486
S-U	9-12	11-15	0.58 ± 0.50	2.00 ± 0.43	1.69 ± 0.25	1.98 ± 0.30	2.00 ± 0.26		1.92 ± 0.22	521
S-U	9-12	16-20	2.40 ± 0.63	2.35 ± 0.49	1.39 ± 0.15	1.68 ± 0.18	1.92 ± 0.19		1.91 ± 0.16	520
S-U	13+	11-15	3.22 ± 1.81	1.48 ± 0.92	0.38 ± 0.09	0.77 ± 0.20	0.57 ± 0.17	1.06 ± 0.32	0.81 ± 0.11	2708
S-U	13+	16-20	0.63 ± 0.19	0.53 ± 0.14	0.66 ± 0.17	0.53 ± 0.07	0.70 ± 0.12	0.61 ± 0.08	0.64 ± 0.04	2762

Pre-marital Intercourse with Companions (*continued*)

Pattern	Educ.	Age								Cases
S-U	13+	21–25	1.34 ± 0.58	0.92 ± 0.18	0.73 ± 0.11	0.92 ± 0.11	0.98 ± 0.11	0.85 ± 0.07	0.87 ± 0.05	1844
S-U	13+	26–30	1.65 ± 0.57	1.52 ± 0.35	1.23 ± 0.19	1.03 ± 0.11	1.12 ± 0.12		1.16 ± 0.11	479
S-Px	0–8	11–15	2.47 ± 0.64	1.63 ± 0.28	2.66 ± 0.41	1.89 ± 0.22	2.29 ± 0.24		2.16 ± 0.20	481
S-Px	0–8	16–20	2.08 ± 0.68	1.91 ± 0.36	1.95 ± 0.25	2.03 ± 0.20	2.10 ± 0.18		2.02 ± 0.15	493
S-Px	9–12	11–15	1.66 ± 0.45	1.83 ± 0.33	1.89 ± 0.35	2.02 ± 0.25			1.98 ± 0.23	375
S-Jx	13+	11–15	0.15 ± 0.06	0.05	0.65 ± 0.52	0.29 ± 0.14	0.23 ± 0.09		0.34 ± 0.15	601
S-Jx	13+	16–20	0.44 ± 0.15	0.45 ± 0.07	0.51 ± 0.11	0.53 ± 0.08	0.51 ± 0.07		0.48 ± 0.06	607
S-P✓	13+	11–15	1.40 ± 0.51	1.24 ± 0.53	0.62 ± 0.21	0.91 ± 0.28	0.81 ± 0.24		0.86 ± 0.21	547
S-P✓	13+	16–20	0.15 ± 0.08	1.15 ± 0.43	0.60 ± 0.15	0.88 ± 0.18	0.66 ± 0.13		0.66 ± 0.11	557
S-P✓	13+	21–25	0.61 ± 0.46	0.54 ± 0.17	0.66 ± 0.17	0.63 ± 0.13		0.73 ± 0.17	0.64 ± 0.11	384
S-Px	13+	11–15	0.26 ± 0.12	0.26 ± 0.03	0.55 ± 0.23	1.06 ± 0.39	0.89 ± 0.27	0.52 ± 0.06	0.81 ± 0.14	1471
S-Px	13+	16–20	0.51 ± 0.21	0.55 ± 0.12	0.47 ± 0.07	0.82 ± 0.12	0.64 ± 0.09		0.62 ± 0.05	1513
S-Px	13+	21–25	0.74 ± 0.26	0.83 ± 0.17	0.78 ± 0.12	0.83 ± 0.11	0.77 ± 0.09	0.80 ± 0.09	0.78 ± 0.06	1000

Marital Intercourse

Pattern	Educ.	Age							Cases
M-U	13+	21–25	2.78 ± 0.33	3.19 ± 0.28	3.27 ± 0.19	2.93 ± 0.15	3.16 ± 0.14	3.12 ± 0.12	460
M-U	13+	26–30	2.80 ± 0.26	2.46 ± 0.22	2.69 ± 0.17	2.76 ± 0.15	2.81 ± 0.13	2.77 ± 0.11	561
M-U	13+	31–35	2.25 ± 0.23	2.27 ± 0.22	2.55 ± 0.18	2.36 ± 0.12		2.38 ± 0.11	438

Total Extra-marital Intercourse

Pattern	Educ.	Age							Cases
M-U	13+	21–25	0.55 ± 0.29	0.28 ± 0.13	0.66 ± 0.31	0.54 ± 0.19	0.50 ± 0.15	0.47 ± 0.13	460
M-U	13+	26–30	0.60 ± 0.28	0.58 ± 0.18	0.46 ± 0.17	0.44 ± 0.12	0.47 ± 0.10	0.44 ± 0.08	561
M-U	13+	31–35	0.63 ± 0.27	0.48 ± 0.15	0.50 ± 0.10	0.53 ± 0.11		0.50 ± 0.08	438

Homosexual Outlet

Pattern	Educ.	Age							Cases
S-U	0–8	11–15	1.51 ± 0.41	1.17 ± 0.38	1.10 ± 0.25	1.09 ± 0.20	0.94 ± 0.13	1.04 ± 0.14	490
S-U	0–8	16–20	1.16 ± 0.31	0.64 ± 0.17	0.77 ± 0.11	0.84 ± 0.11	0.77 ± 0.10	0.85 ± 0.10	486
S-U	9–12	11–15	1.25 ± 0.37	1.15 ± 0.47	0.79 ± 0.14	0.85 ± 0.15	0.81 ± 0.10	0.87 ± 0.10	521

(*Table continued on next page*)

MEAN OF ACTIVE POPULATION: SIZE OF ADEQUATE SAMPLE

CALCULATIONS WITH SAMPLES OF VARIOUS SIZES

Homosexual Outlet (continued)

GROUP	EDUC. LEVEL	AGE	50	100	200	300	400	600	LARGEST SAMPLE	CASES IN LARGEST SAMPLE
S-U	9-12	16-20	0.57 ± 0.20	1.46 ± 0.44	**1.06 ± 0.18**	1.28 ± 0.17	1.07 ± 0.13		1.01 ± 0.11	520
S-U	13+	11-15	0.28 ± 0.17	0.18 ± 0.05	**0.43 ± 0.11**	**0.45 ± 0.10**	0.36 ± 0.06	0.48 ± 0.08	0.43 ± 0.03	2708
S-U	13+	16-20	0.35 ± 0.17	0.52 ± 0.20	0.51 ± 0.13	0.36 ± 0.12	0.29 ± 0.07	**0.41 ± 0.10**	0.43 ± 0.04	2762
S-U	13+	21-25	0.20 ± 0.06	0.75 ± 0.46	**0.89 ± 0.28**	0.68 ± 0.19	0.94 ± 0.23	0.77 ± 0.18	0.89 ± 0.10	1844
S-U	13+	26-30	1.25 ± 0.44	1.21 ± 0.28	**1.45 ± 0.26**	**1.41 ± 0.24**	1.26 ± 0.17		1.39 ± 0.16	479
S-Px	0-8	11-15	1.12 ± 0.34	0.64 ± 0.21	**0.99 ± 0.20**	**1.00 ± 0.18**	**0.96 ± 0.15**		0.95 ± 0.13	481
S-Px	0-8	16-20	0.63 ± 0.26	1.06 ± 0.33	0.68 ± 0.19	**0.81 ± 0.14**	0.76 ± 0.12		0.83 ± 0.12	493
S-Px	9-12	11-15	0.96 ± 0.23	1.03 ± 0.29	0.64 ± 0.11	0.76 ± 0.12			0.81 ± 0.10	375
S-Jx	13+	11-15	0.37 ± 0.24	0.91 ± 0.45	0.26 ± 0.11	0.55 ± 0.16	**0.43 ± 0.14**		0.44 ± 0.10	601
S-Jx	13+	16-20	0.11 ± 0.07	1.27 ± 0.46	0.62 ± 0.18	0.48 ± 0.19	0.48 ± 0.18		0.55 ± 0.13	607
S-P√	13+	11-15	0.71 ± 0.32	0.41 ± 0.14	0.29 ± 0.09	0.32 ± 0.07	0.46 ± 0.10		0.38 ± 0.08	547
S-P√	13+	16-20	0.11 ± 0.04	0.23 ± 0.07	0.51 ± 0.23	**0.35 ± 0.14**	0.40 ± 0.11		0.37 ± 0.09	557
S-P√	13+	21-25	0.43 ± 0.30	0.26 ± 0.18	0.36 ± 0.15	0.41 ± 0.13			0.63 ± 0.21	384
S-Px	13+	11-15	0.15 ± 0.04	0.33 ± 0.10	0.44 ± 0.10	**0.43 ± 0.08**	0.45 ± 0.08	0.46 ± 0.06	0.41 ± 0.04	1471
S-Px	13+	16-20	0.63 ± 0.47	0.14 ± 0.04	0.61 ± 0.23	0.33 ± 0.07	0.44 ± 0.10	0.49 ± 0.09	0.39 ± 0.05	1513
S-Px	13+	21-25	0.69 ± 0.30	0.53 ± 0.18	**0.79 ± 0.31**	1.04 ± 0.32	**0.82 ± 0.18**	**0.83 ± 0.16**	0.79 ± 0.13	1000

Table 156. Size of sample necessary to secure stable means on active population

Boldface figures designate calculations that lie within 5 per cent, plus or minus, of the calculations obtained from the largest sample. Means are frequencies per week.

GROUP	EDUC. LEVEL	AGE	MEDIAN OF TOTAL POPULATION: SIZE OF ADEQUATE SAMPLE. CALCULATIONS WITH SAMPLES OF VARIOUS SIZES								CASES IN LARGEST SAMPLE
			50	100	200	300	400	600	1000	LARGEST SAMPLE	
Total Outlet											
S-U	0–8	11–15	2.94	1.93	2.02	1.87	1.88			2.03	490
S-U	0–8	16–20	2.46	2.29	2.33	2.54	2.30			2.37	486
S-U	9–12	11–15	2.13	2.47	2.55	2.47	2.53			2.49	521
S-U	9–12	16–20	2.65	2.47	2.81	2.75	2.66			2.73	520
S-U	13+	11–15	2.42	2.33	2.48	2.19	2.22	2.22	2.25	2.21	2708
S-U	13+	16–20	1.85	2.02	2.12	2.26	2.48	2.07	2.24	2.19	2762
S-U	13+	21–25	2.04	2.47	2.14	1.95	1.99	1.86	2.07	1.95	1844
S-U	13+	26–30	1.94	2.19	1.75	1.90	1.91			1.92	479
M-U	13+	21–25	2.88	3.38	3.26	2.98	3.14			3.11	460
M-U	13+	26–30	3.04	2.48	2.68	2.72	2.77			2.74	561
M-U	13+	31–35	2.31	2.40	2.35	2.47				2.33	438
S-Px	0–8	11–15	2.75	2.03	2.02	1.60	1.88			1.78	481
S-Px	0–8	16–20	2.03	2.25	2.14	2.23	2.32			2.24	493
S-Px	9–12	11–15	2.55	2.41	2.25	2.26				2.33	375
S-Jx	13+	11–15	1.88	2.19	2.11	2.03	2.30			2.17	601
S-Jx	13+	16–20	2.08	2.63	2.30	2.28	2.34			2.30	607
S-P√	13+	11–15	2.21	2.11	2.22	2.08	1.93			1.98	547
S-P√	13+	16–20	1.96	1.93	1.79	1.74	1.86			1.83	557
S-P√	13+	21–25	1.16	1.61	1.36	1.43				1.43	384
S-Px	13+	11–15	2.11	2.29	2.75	2.34	2.58	2.45	2.55	2.45	1471
S-Px	13+	16–20	2.56	2.29	2.27	2.41	2.26	2.39	2.40	2.36	1513
S-Px	13+	21–25	2.54	1.94	1.99	1.98	1.98	1.91	1.99	1.99	1000
Masturbation											
S-U	0–8	11–15	1.25	1.03	0.82	0.81	0.92			0.93	490
S-U	0–8	16–20	0.62	0.42	0.48	0.50	0.43			0.44	486
S-U	9–12	11–15	1.46	1.16	1.28	1.29	1.27			1.30	521
S-U	9–12	16–20	0.59	0.69	0.71	0.69	0.67			0.71	520
S-U	13+	11–15	1.69	1.67	1.78	1.67	1.61	1.63	1.67	1.60	2708
S-U	13+	16–20	0.91	1.17	1.24	1.26	1.51	1.10	1.19	1.23	2762
S-U	13+	21–25	0.47	0.89	0.71	0.69	0.69	0.69	0.70	0.68	1844
S-U	13+	26–30	0.41	0.59	0.45	0.49	0.52			0.49	479
S-Px	0–8	11–15	1.32	0.94	1.01	0.87	0.91			0.89	481
S-Px	0–8	16–20	0.33	0.45	0.47	0.45	0.49			0.46	493
S-Px	9–12	11–15	1.15	1.10	1.14	1.10				1.13	375
S-Jx	13+	11–15	1.75	1.72	1.63	1.47	1.72			1.58	601
S-Jx	13+	16–20	1.13	1.71	1.53	1.27	1.55			1.41	607
S-P√	13+	11–15	1.64	1.55	1.49	1.52	1.37			1.42	547
S-P√	13+	16–20	1.28	1.25	0.97	0.90	1.09			1.00	557
S-P√	13+	21–25	0.53	0.74	0.65	0.58				0.60	384
S-Px	13+	11–15	1.66	1.89	2.14	1.73	1.88	1.78	1.90	1.82	1471
S-Px	13+	16–20	1.88	1.42	1.21	1.37	1.39	1.58	1.39	1.41	1513
S-Px	13+	21–25	0.64	0.72	0.75	0.74	0.83	0.76		0.80	1000
Nocturnal Emissions											
S-U	0–8	11–15	0.00	0.00	0.00	0.00	0.00			0.00	490
S-U	0–8	16–20	0.05	0.01	0.03	0.03	0.03			0.03	486
S-U	9–12	11–15	0.00	0.00	0.00	0.00	0.00			0.00	521
S-U	9–12	16–20	0.04	0.07	0.08	0.07	0.07			0.06	520
S-U	13+	11–15	0.22	0.12	0.11	0.10	0.10	0.11	0.10	0.11	2708

(*Table continued on next page*)

GROUP	EDUC. LEVEL	AGE	MEDIAN OF TOTAL POPULATION: SIZE OF ADEQUATE SAMPLE. CALCULATIONS WITH SAMPLES OF VARIOUS SIZES								CASES IN LARGEST SAMPLE
			50	100	200	300	400	600	1000	LARGEST SAMPLE	
Nocturnal Emissions (*continued*)											
S-U	13+	16–20	**0.24**	0.22	**0.25**	**0.25**	**0.25**	**0.25**	**0.25**	0.25	2762
S-U	13+	21–25	0.27	0.24	0.24	**0.22**	0.20	**0.22**	**0.23**	0.22	1844
S-U	13+	26–30	0.13	**0.17**	0.16	0.20	**0.17**			0.18	479
M-U	13+	21–25	0.04	0.04	0.04	**0.05**	**0.05**			0.05	460
M-U	13+	26–30	**0.06**	0.07	0.04	0.05	**0.06**			0.06	561
M-U	13+	31–35	**0.05**	0.06	0.04	**0.05**				0.05	438
S-Px	0–8	11–15	0.00	0.00	0.00	0.00	0.00			0.00	481
S-Px	0–8	16–20	0.00	**0.02**	**0.02**	**0.02**	0.03			0.02	493
S-Px	9–12	11–15	0.00	0.00	0.00	0.00				0.00	375
S-Jx	13+	11–15	0.08	0.12	0.10	0.17	0.12			0.15	601
S-Jx	13+	16–20	0.22	0.27	**0.23**	0.26	0.26			0.24	607
S-P√	13+	11–15	0.14	0.16	0.10	0,14	**0.12**			0.12	547
S-P√	13+	16–20	0.25	**0.27**	0.23	**0.26**	**0.26**			0.27	557
S-P√	13+	21–25	0.21	0.17	0.23	**0.26**				0.26	384
S-Px	13+	11–15	0.11	0.12	0.07	**0.09**	0.10	**0.09**	**0.09**	0.09	1471
S-Px	13+	16–20	0.17	0.21	**0.24**	0.21	**0.25**	0.23	**0.24**	0.24	1513
S-Px	13+	21–25	0.15	0.21	0.18	**0.20**	**0.20**	**0.20**	**0.20**	0.20	1000
Pre-marital Intercourse with Companions											
S-U	0–8	11–15	0.63	0.00	**0.07**	0.06	0.00			0.02	490
S-U	0–8	16–20	0.88	0.74	**0.72**	**0.68**	**0.69**			0.69	486
S-U	9–12	11–15	0.00	0.00	0.00	0.00	0.00			0.00	521
S-U	9–12	16–20	0.52	0.41	**0.34**	0.27	**0.35**			0.34	520
S-U	13+	11–15	0.00	0.00	0.00	0.00	0.00	0.00	0.00	0.00	2708
S-U	13+	16–20	0.00	0.00	0.00	0.00	0.00	0.00	0.00	0.00	2762
S-U	13+	21–25	0.06	0.06	0.06	0.07	0.06	0.03	0.05	0.04	1844
S-U	13+	26–30	0.04	0.05	0.03	0.09	0.06			0.08	479
S-Px	0–8	11–15	0.22	0.09	0.08	0.00	0.05			0.06	481
S-Px	0–8	16–20	0.63	**0.73**	0.51	**0.70**	0.77			0.70	493
S-Jx	13+	11–15	0.00	0.00	0.00	0.00	0.00			0.00	601
S-Jx	13+	16–20	0.00	0.00	0.00	0.00	0.00			0.00	607
S-P√	13+	11–15	0.00	0.00	0.00	0.00	0.00			0.00	547
S-P√	13+	16–20	0.00	0.00	0.00	0.00	0.00			0.00	557
S-Px	13+	11–15	0.00	0.00	0.00	0.00	0.00	0.00	0.00	0.00	1471
S-Px	13+	16–20	0.00	0.00	0.00	0.00	0.00	0.00	0.00	0.00	1513
S-Px	13+	21–25	0.06	0.03	0.02	**0.05**	0.04	0.04	**0.05**	0.05	1000
Marital Intercourse											
M-U	13+	21–25	2.36	**2.58**	2.77	2.41	**2.59**			2.57	460
M-U	13+	26–30	2.46	1.99	**2.22**	**2.20**	**2.22**			2.19	561
M-U	13+	31–35	**1.92**	**1.91**	**1.92**	**1.91**				1.88	438
Total Extra-marital Intercourse											
M-U	13+	21–25	0.00	0.00	0.00	0.00	0.00			0.00	460
M-U	13+	26–30	0.00	0.00	0.00	0.00	0.00			0.00	561
M-U	13+	31–35	0.00	0.00	0.00	0.00				0.00	438

Table 157. Size of sample necessary to secure stable medians on total population

Boldface figures designate calculations that lie within 5 per cent, plus or minus, of the calculations obtained from the largest sample. Medians are frequencies per week.

GROUP	EDUC. LEVEL	AGE	MEDIAN OF ACTIVE POPULATION: SIZE OF ADEQUATE SAMPLE. CALCULATIONS WITH SAMPLES OF VARIOUS SIZES								CASES IN LARGEST SAMPLE
			50	100	200	300	400	600	1000	LARGEST SAMPLE	
Total Outlet											
S-U	0–8	11–15	3.38	2.22	**2.31**	2.22	**2.26**			2.36	490
S-U	0–8	16–20	**2.46**	**2.33**	**2.37**	2.60	**2.36**			2.44	486
S-U	9–12	11–15	**2.63**	**2.67**	**2.61**	2.56	**2.63**			2.61	521
S-U	9–12	16–20	**2.65**	2.47	**2.81**	**2.77**	2.67			2.74	520
S-U	13+	11–15	2.50	**2.40**	2.63	**2.29**	**2.37**	**2.35**	**2.35**	2.34	2708
S-U	13+	16–20	1.85	2.05	**2.12**	**2.26**	2.48	2.07	**2.25**	2.20	2762
S-U	13+	21–25	**2.04**	2.47	2.14	**1.95**	**1.99**	**1.86**	2.08	1.95	1844
S-U	13+	26–30	**1.94**	2.19	1.75	**1.90**	**1.91**			1.92	479
M-U	13+	21–25	2.88	3.38	**3.26**	2.98	**3.14**			3.11	460
M-U	13+	26–30	3.04	2.48	**2.68**	**2.72**	**2.77**			2.74	561
M-U	13+	31–35	**2.31**	**2.40**	**2.35**	2.47				2.33	438
S-Px	0–8	11–15	3.10	2.18	2.15	1.88	**2.13**			2.03	481
S-Px	0–8	16–20	2.03	**2.29**	**2.19**	**2.26**	2.37			2.29	493
S-Px	9–12	11–15	2.80	**2.58**	**2.38**	**2.40**				2.48	375
S-Jx	13+	11–15	1.88	**2.31**	**2.21**	2.12	**2.39**			2.29	601
S-Jx	13+	16–20	2.08	2.63	**2.30**	**2.28**	**2.34**			2.30	607
S-P√	13+	11–15	2.33	2.32	2.34	**2.18**	**2.02**			2.10	547
S-P√	13+	16–20	1.96	1.93	**1.80**	**1.76**	**1.86**			1.83	557
S-P√	13+	21–25	1.19	1.64	**1.38**	**1.43**				1.43	384
S-Px	13+	11–15	2.21	**2.46**	2.81	**2.50**	2.72	**2.56**	**2.67**	2.58	1471
S-Px	13+	16–20	2.56	**2.29**	**2.27**	**2.41**	2.28	**2.41**	**2.40**	2.37	1513
S-Px	13+	21–25	2.54	**1.94**	**1.99**	**1.99**	1.98	**1.91**	**1.99**	1.99	1000
Masturbation											
S-U	0–8	11–15	1.46	1.47	1.04	1.05	**1.19**			1.18	490
S-U	0–8	16–20	0.68	**0.61**	0.64	0.69	**0.56**			0.59	486
S-U	9–12	11–15	1.80	**1.48**	1.41	**1.48**	**1.46**			1.52	521
S-U	9–12	16–20	0.72	**0.83**	0.81	**0.86**	0.81			0.86	520
S-U	13+	11–15	2.30	1.96	2.33	1.97	**2.07**	**2.10**	**2.11**	2.09	2708
S-U	13+	16–20	1.04	1.40	**1.58**	**1.61**	1.69	1.41	**1.56**	1.55	2762
S-U	13+	21–25	0.50	1.54	0.92	**0.83**	**0.86**	**0.86**	**0.89**	0.87	1844
S-U	13+	26–30	0.44	0.74	0.73	**0.70**	0.73			0.69	479
S-Px	0–8	11–15	1.55	1.28	1.15	**1.05**	**1.12**			1.08	481
S-Px	0–8	16–20	0.43	**0.61**	**0.61**	0.58	0.64			0.60	493
S-Px	9–12	11–15	1.50	1.24	**1.38**	**1.30**				1.35	375
S-Jx	13+	11–15	2.50	2.28	**2.12**	2.01	**2.27**			2.16	601
S-Jx	13+	16–20	**1.75**	1.83	1.80	1.56	**1.73**			1.68	607
S-P√	13+	11–15	**1.89**	**1.92**	2.09	1.99	**1.81**			1.88	547
S-P√	13+	16–20	1.41	1.56	**1.36**	1.21	**1.38**			1.33	557
S-P√	13+	21–25	0.70	0.92	**0.83**	0.79				0.81	384
S-Px	13+	11–15	1.97	2.46	2.47	**2.42**	2.45	**2.24**	**2.36**	2.30	1471
S-Px	13+	16–20	2.25	1.48	1.39	1.53	**1.56**	1.72	**1.59**	1.62	1513
S-Px	13+	21–25	0.86	**0.90**	**0.93**	0.88	**0.98**	**0.88**	**0.93**	0.93	1000
Nocturnal Emissions											
S-U	0–8	11–15	0.06	0.07	0.07	0.07	**0.08**			0.08	490
S-U	0–8	16–20	0.10	**0.09**	**0.09**	0.10	**0.09**			0.09	486
S-U	9–12	11–15	0.09	0.16	0.09	0.10	0.10			0.12	521

(Table continued on next page)

752

GROUP	EDUC. LEVEL	AGE	MEDIAN OF ACTIVE POPULATION: SIZE OF ADEQUATE SAMPLE. CALCULATIONS WITH SAMPLES OF VARIOUS SIZES								CASES IN LARGEST SAMPLE
			50	100	200	300	400	600	1000	LARGEST SAMPLE	

Nocturnal Emissions (*continued*)

GROUP	EDUC. LEVEL	AGE	50	100	200	300	400	600	1000	LARGEST SAMPLE	CASES IN LARGEST SAMPLE
S-U	9–12	16–20	**0.13**	0.20	**0.14**	**0.15**	**0.14**			0.14	520
S-U	13+	11–15	0.31	**0.28**	**0.28**	0.27	0.27	0.27	0.27	0.28	2708
S-U	13+	16–20	0.26	**0.28**	0.30	0.29	0.29	0.30	0.29	0.29	2762
S-U	13+	21–25	0.33	0.31	**0.29**	**0.29**	0.27	**0.29**	**0.29**	0.28	1844
S-U	13+	26–30	0.20	**0.24**	**0.24**	0.26	0.24			0.25	479
M-U	13+	21–25	**0.09**	0.08	**0.09**	0.10	**0.09**			0.09	460
M-U	13+	26–30	**0.09**	**0.09**	0.08	0.08	**0.09**			0.09	561
M-U	13+	31–35	**0.08**	0.10	0.09	0.09				0.08	438
S-Px	0–8	11–15	**0.08**	0.10	**0.08**	0.07	**0.08**			0.08	481
S-Px	0–8	16–20	0.07	0.07	0.08	0.08	0.09			0.09	493
S-Px	9–12	11–15	0.26	0.13	**0.10**	0.09				0.10	375
S-Jx	13+	11–15	0.18	**0.29**	0.26	**0.29**	0.28			0.29	601
S-Jx	13+	16–20	0.28	0.34	**0.30**	0.33	0.32			0.31	607
S-P√	13+	11–15	0.34	0.33	**0.29**	**0.29**	**0.29**			0.29	547
S-P√	13+	16–20	**0.31**	**0.31**	0.28	0.28	**0.29**			0.30	557
S-P√	13+	21–25	0.23	0.26	0.28	**0.30**				0.30	384
S-Px	13+	11–15	0.33	0.29	0.24	0.25	0.31	**0.26**	**0.27**	0.27	1471
S-Px	13+	16–20	**0.27**	0.26	**0.29**	0.26	**0.29**	**0.27**	**0.27**	0.28	1513
S-Px	13+	21–25	0.23	**0.25**	**0.27**	**0.27**	**0.26**	**0.27**	**0.26**	0.26	1000

Pre-marital Intercourse with Companions

GROUP	EDUC. LEVEL	AGE	50	100	200	300	400	600	1000	LARGEST SAMPLE	CASES IN LARGEST SAMPLE
S-U	0–8	11–15	**1.25**	1.69	1.13	**1.26**	1.34			1.27	490
S-U	0–8	16–20	1.50	0.89	0.98	1.18	**1.05**			1.06	486
S-U	9–12	11–15	0.44	0.98	**0.75**	**0.75**	0.81			0.74	521
S-U	9–12	16–20	0.77	1.06	0.68	0.91	**0.85**			0.83	520
S-U	13+	11–15	3.50	0.20	0.18	0.43	**0.27**	0.31	0.29	0.26	2708
S-U	13+	16–20	0.34	0.20	0.20	**0.23**	0.24	**0.22**	0.24	0.22	2762
S-U	13+	21–25	0.41	**0.33**	**0.32**	**0.33**	0.36	**0.34**	**0.33**	0.32	1844
S-U	13+	26–30	0.69	0.69	**0.49**	**0.48**	0.45			0.47	479
S-Px	0–8	11–15	**1.20**	0.98	1.29	1.08	1.30			1.19	481
S-Px	0–8	16–20	0.80	**0.98**	0.83	0.89	1.04			0.97	493
S-Px	9–12	11–15	1.17	0.93	**0.89**	**0.86**				0.87	375
S-Jx	13+	11–15	0.10	0.06	0.09	0.09	**0.08**			0.08	601
S-Jx	13+	16–20	0.20	0.27	0.14	0.20	**0.17**			0.16	607
S-P√	13+	11–15	1.50	0.75	**0.38**	0.43	**0.34**			0.36	547
S-P√	13+	16–20	0.07	0.28	0.12	0.26	**0.16**			0.16	557
S-P√	13+	21–25	**0.17**	0.15	0.14	0.14				0.17	384
S-Px	13+	11–15	0.20	0.30	0.09	0.32	0.29	**0.27**	0.20	0.27	1471
S-Px	13+	16–20	**0.22**	**0.23**	0.19	0.28	0.28	0.21	0.26	0.23	1513
S-Px	13+	21–25	0.28	0.34	**0.30**	**0.30**	**0.32**	**0.31**	**0.31**	0.31	1000

Marital Intercourse

GROUP	EDUC. LEVEL	AGE	50	100	200	300	400	600	1000	LARGEST SAMPLE	CASES IN LARGEST SAMPLE
M-U	13+	21–25	2.36	**2.58**	2.78	2.43	**2.60**			2.58	460
M-U	13+	26–30	2.46	2.00	**2.24**	**2.21**	2.24			2.20	561
M-U	13+	31–35	**1.92**	**1.92**	1.93	**1.92**				1.88	438

(*Table continued on next page*)

GROUP	EDUC. LEVEL	AGE	Median of Active Population: Size of Adequate Sample. Calculations with Samples of Various Sizes								Cases in Largest Sample
			50	100	200	300	400	600	1000	Largest Sample	
Total Extra-marital Intercourse											
M-U	13+	21–25	0.10	0.08	0.14	0.10	**0.11**			0.12	460
M-U	13+	26–30	0.34	0.23	0.08	**0.09**	**0.11**			0.10	561
M-U	13+	31–35	0.10	0.21	**0.19**	0.21				0.18	438
Homosexual Outlet											
S-U	0–8	11–15	0.75	0.46	**0.41**	0.34	0.36			0.42	490
S-U	0–8	16–20	0.50	0.32	**0.35**	**0.37**	**0.33**			0.35	486
S-U	9–12	11–15	0.42	**0.30**	0.28	0.26	0.29			0.32	521
S-U	9–12	16–20	0.28	0.30	**0.37**	0.49	**0.37**			0.35	520
S-U	13+	11–15	0.08	**0.09**	0.08	**0.09**	0.10	0.10	**0.09**	0.09	2708
S-U	13+	16–20	0.08	0.08	0.19	0.08	0.08	0.08	0.08	0.09	2762
S-U	13+	21–25	0.23	0.30	0.50	0.28	0.22	0.17	0.21	0.26	1844
S-U	13+	26–30	0.75	0.88	0.75	0.65	0.57			0.75	479
S-Px	0–8	11–15	0.75	0.10	0.44	0.32	**0.34**			0.36	481
S-Px	0–8	16–20	0.43	0.46	0.21	**0.30**	**0.29**			0.30	493
S-Px	9–12	11–15	0.88	0.38	0.23	0.20				0.29	375
S-Jx	13+	11–15	0.10	0.08	0.08	**0.09**	0.08			0.09	601
S-Jx	13+	16–20	0.08	1.25	0.26	0.07	0.08			0.09	607
S-P√	13+	11–15	**0.09**	**0.09**	**0.09**	**0.09**	**0.09**			0.09	547
S-P√	13+	16–20	0.07	0.08	0.07	0.08	**0.09**			0.09	557
S-P√	13+	21–25	0.30	0.08	0.10	0.20				0.23	384
S-Px	13+	11–15	**0.09**	**0.09**	0.18	0.13	0.10	0.10	0.10	0.09	1471
S-Px	13+	16–20	0.15	0.07	0.09	**0.08**	**0.08**	**0.08**	**0.08**	0.08	1513
S-Px	13+	21–25	0.50	0.38	**0.24**	**0.25**	0.32	0.22	**0.24**	0.24	1000

Table 158. Size of sample necessary to secure stable medians on active population

Boldface figures designate calculations that lie within 5 per cent, plus or minus, of the calculations obtained from the largest sample. Medians are frequencies per week.

GROUP	EDUC. LEVEL	AGE	INCIDENCE: SIZE OF ADEQUATE SAMPLE CALCULATIONS WITH SAMPLES OF VARIOUS SIZES								CASES IN LARGEST SAMPLE
			50	100	200	300	400	600	1000	LARGEST SAMPLE	
						Total Outlet					
S-U	0–8	11–15	92.0	90.0	92.5	92.3	91.5			92.4	490
S-U	0–8	16–20	100.0	98.0	98.5	98.3	98.0			97.7	486
S-U	9–12	11–15	92.0	95.0	97.0	96.7	95.7			95.4	521
S-U	9–12	16–20	100.0	100.0	100.0	99.3	99.7			99.6	520
S-U	13+	11–15	98.0	97.0	95.5	96.3	95.0	94.8	96.6	95.8	2708
S-U	13+	16–20	100.0	99.0	100.0	100.0	100.0	100.0	99.8	99.7	2762
S-U	13+	21–25	100.0	100.0	100.0	100.0	100.0	100.0	99.9	99.9	1844
S-U	13+	26–30	100.0	100.0	100.0	100.0	100.0			100.0	479
M-U	13+	21–25	100.0	100.0	100.0	100.0	100.0			100.0	460
M-U	13+	26–30	100.0	100.0	100.0	100.0	100.0			100.0	561
M-U	13+	31–35	100.0	100.0	100.0	100.0				100.0	438
S-Px	0–8	11–15	94.0	94.0	96.0	93.3	93.7			93.8	481
S-Px	0–8	16–20	100.0	98.0	98.0	99.0	98.0			98.2	493
S-Px	9–12	11–15	90.0	94.0	95.5	95.7				95.2	375
S-Jx	13+	11–15	100.0	96.0	96.0	97.0	97.2			96.0	601
S-Jx	13+	16–20	100.0	100.0	100.0	100.0	100.0			100.0	607
S-P√	13+	11–15	94.0	94.0	95.5	96.0	96.0			95.4	547
S-P√	13+	16–20	100.0	100.0	99.5	99.3	100.0			99.6	557
S-P√	13+	21–25	98.0	99.0	99.5	100.0				99.7	384
S-Px	13+	11–15	94.0	96.0	98.0	93.7	96.0	96.5	96.3	96.0	1471
S-Px	13+	16–20	100.0	100.0	100.0	100.0	99.5	99.5	99.8	99.7	1513
S-Px	13+	21–25	100.0	100.0	100.0	99.3	99.7	99.8	99.8	99.8	1000
						Masturbation					
S-U	0–8	11–15	88.0	86.0	86.0	85.0	85.7			86.7	490
S-U	0–8	16–20	92.0	82.0	85.5	86.3	84.2			84.8	486
S-U	9–12	11–15	86.0	86.0	92.5	91.7	90.7			90.0	521
S-U	9–12	16–20	92.0	89.0	92.0	88.0	90.0			89.8	520
S-U	13+	11–15	78.0	85.0	83.5	83.3	81.2	81.2	82.8	82.0	2708
S-U	13+	16–20	92.0	88.0	86.0	88.3	91.2	90.7	88.4	88.7	2762
S-U	13+	21–25	94.0	84.0	86.5	90.0	87.0	87.8	87.3	87.3	1844
S-U	13+	26–30	94.0	89.0	81.0	84.0	85.5			85.4	479
S-Px	0–8	11–15	88.0	86.0	92.5	88.0	88.5			88.1	481
S-Px	0–8	16–20	82.0	83.0	87.5	85.7	86.7			85.8	493
S-Px	9–12	11–15	86.0	91.0	90.5	90.7				90.4	375
S-Jx	13+	11–15	86.0	80.0	78.0	79.3	80.0			80.0	601
S-Jx	13+	16–20	82.0	94.0	85.5	88.7	88.7			88.1	607
S-P√	13+	11–15	82.0	78.0	80.5	79.3	81.7			80.8	547
S-P√	13+	16–20	92.0	82.0	86.0	83.7	87.5			85.6	557
S-P√	13+	21–25	86.0	87.0	84.5	83.3				83.6	384
S-Px	13+	11–15	80.0	84.0	89.5	81.0	84.5	85.5	85.5	84.7	1471
S-Px	13+	16–20	92.0	96.0	93.5	93.0	93.0	92.7	92.0	91.5	1513
S-Px	13+	21–25	84.0	88.0	86.5	90.0	89.0	90.5	90.3	90.3	1000

(*Table continued on next page*)

GROUP	EDUC. LEVEL	AGE	INCIDENCE: SIZE OF ADEQUATE SAMPLE CALCULATIONS WITH SAMPLES OF VARIOUS SIZES								CASES IN LARGEST SAMPLE
			50	100	200	300	400	600	1000	LARGEST SAMPLE	
			Nocturnal Emissions								
S-U	0–8	11–15	28.0	27.0	27.5	29.0	25.2			26.9	490
S-U	0–8	16–20	68.0	53.0	59.0	58.7	59.5			58.4	486
S-U	9–12	11–15	40.0	44.0	45.0	42.0	40.7			41.8	521
S-U	9–12	16–20	62.0	69.0	76.0	72.3	71.7			70.6	520
S-U	13+	11–15	82.0	74.0	70.0	70.7	73.7	73.2	72.7	71.4	2708
S-U	13+	16–20	96.0	87.0	89.5	91.0	90.2	90.8	90.7	90.8	2762
S-U	13+	21–25	88.0	84.0	87.5	83.0	86.7	85.7	86.3	86.3	1844
S-U	13+	26–30	82.0	84.0	84.0	86.7	85.0			84.6	479
M-U	13+	21–25	66.0	68.0	65.5	67.3	66.2			66.3	460
M-U	13+	26–30	76.0	78.0	66.5	70.3	74.7			72.4	561
M-U	13+	31–35	74.0	72.0	65.5	69.7				68.7	438
S-Px	0–8	11–15	28.0	22.0	25.0	26.7	25.5			26.0	481
S-Px	0–8	16–20	50.0	56.0	57.5	57.7	58.5			56.6	493
S-Px	9–12	11–15	42.0	39.0	43.5	40.3				40.0	375
S-Jx	13+	11–15	72.0	75.0	75.5	78.7	74.7			75.4	601
S-Jx	13+	16–20	88.0	86.0	86.0	87.0	87.7			86.2	607
S-P√	13+	11–15	70.0	71.0	69.0	72.0	70.0			70.7	547
S-P√	13+	16–20	84.0	91.0	90.0	94.7	92.5			92.5	557
S-P√	13+	21–25	94.0	85.0	88.0	90.7				90.1	384
S-Px	13+	11–15	70.0	67.0	64.0	68.7	66.0	67.3	66.6	68.0	1471
S-Px	13+	16–20	82.0	90.0	89.0	89.0	91.2	91.5	92.1	91.7	1513
S-Px	13+	21–25	86.0	89.0	81.5	85.7	86.7	86.5	86.9	86.9	1000
			Pre-marital Intercourse with Companions								
S-U	0–8	11–15	66.0	44.0	54.5	52.7	50.0			51.2	490
S-U	0–8	16–20	82.0	88.0	86.5	82.7	83.0			83.1	486
S-U	9–12	11–15	42.0	46.0	48.0	43.7	44.0			43.2	521
S-U	9–12	16–20	78.0	71.0	73.5	65.0	70.7			70.4	520
S-U	13+	11–15	6.0	10.0	11.5	7.7	8.2	9.0	7.3	9.0	2708
S-U	13+	16–20	42.0	30.0	39.5	36.7	41.5	40.3	38.6	39.1	2762
S-U	13+	21–25	58.0	59.0	60.0	63.3	58.7	54.5	57.9	57.0	1844
S-U	13+	26–30	52.0	57.0	54.0	63.3	58.7			60.5	479
S-Px	0–8	11–15	58.0	56.0	52.5	50.0	52.0			52.4	481
S-Px	0–8	16–20	86.0	88.0	84.5	90.3	87.5			86.4	493
S-Px	9–12	11–15	28.0	54.0	42.0	48.7				45.9	375
S-Jx	13+	11–15	10.0	4.0	5.0	6.3	7.7			6.5	601
S-Jx	13+	16–20	36.0	44.0	41.5	43.0	41.5			41.5	607
S-P√	13+	11–15	10.0	8.0	7.0	8.0	7.5			7.1	547
S-P√	13+	16–20	20.0	23.0	23.0	25.0	23.0			23.9	557
S-P√	13+	21–25	16.0	34.0	32.5	33.0				32.6	384
S-Px	13+	11–15	12.0	7.0	11.5	10.3	10.7	10.8	9.7	10.3	1471
S-Px	13+	16–20	42.0	38.0	46.5	42.7	40.7	39.5	41.2	41.1	1513
S-Px	13+	21–25	64.0	55.0	54.5	59.0	56.7	57.8	58.6	58.6	1000

(*Table continued on next page*)

GROUP	EDUC. LEVEL	AGE	INCIDENCE: SIZE OF ADEQUATE SAMPLE CALCULATIONS WITH SAMPLES OF VARIOUS SIZES								CASES IN LARGEST SAMPLE
			50	100	200	300	400	600	1000	LARGEST SAMPLE	
			Marital Intercourse								
M-U	13+	21–25	100.0	100.0	99.5	99.3	99.5			99.6	460
M-U	13+	26–30	100.0	99.0	99.0	99.3	99.0			99.3	561
M-U	13+	31–35	100.0	99.0	99.5	99.7				99.5	438
			Total Extra-marital Intercourse								
M-U	13+	21–25	18.0	14.0	14.5	16.7	16.0			16.3	460
M-U	13+	26–30	22.0	23.0	26.0	24.0	23.5			25.0	561
M-U	13+	31–35	26.0	27.0	32.5	36.0				34.0	438
			Homosexual Outlet								
S-U	0–8	11–15	38.0	23.0	26.5	26.0	28.0			27.3	490
S-U	0–8	16–20	38.0	26.0	33.0	34.0	31.5			30.2	486
S-U	9–12	11–15	38.0	30.0	36.5	37.7	36.0			36.5	521
S-U	9–12	16–20	44.0	44.0	42.0	45.3	45.0			45.6	520
S-U	13+	11–15	20.0	18.0	29.0	23.0	22.2	21.2	22.6	21.9	2708
S-U	13+	16–20	22.0	22.0	14.0	13.0	17.7	16.3	15.0	16.0	2762
S-U	13+	21–25	10.0	10.0	9.5	9.3	11.2	9.0	11.2	10.2	1844
S-U	13+	26–30	20.0	22.0	17.0	14.7	17.7			16.9	479
S-Px	0–8	11–15	30.0	22.0	24.0	23.3	23.7			22.5	481
S-Px	0–8	16–20	20.0	22.0	25.5	24.7	25.0			24.5	493
S-Px	9–12	11–15	32.0	30.0	29.5	33.3				34.1	375
S-Jx	13+	11–15	14.0	16.0	13.0	16.7	14.2			14.6	601
S-Jx	13+	16–20	8.0	8.0	10.5	12.3	9.2			10.7	607
S-P√	13+	11–15	16.0	26.0	22.0	20.7	22.7			23.8	547
S-P√	13+	16–20	18.0	22.0	17.0	16.7	18.2			17.4	557
S-P√	13+	21–25	8.0	7.0	6.5	6.0				6.2	384
S-Px	13+	11–15	24.0	31.0	26.0	25.3	25.5	28.2	26.8	25.6	1471
S-Px	13+	16–20	20.0	19.0	19.0	16.7	21.0	18.0	19.2	18.0	1513
S-Px	13+	21–25	14.0	12.0	13.0	11.0	12.2	11.8	11.5	11.5	1000

Table 159. Size of sample necessary to secure stable incidence data

Boldface figures designate calculations that lie within 2 per cent, plus or minus, of the calculations obtained from the largest sample.

GROUP	EDUC. LEVEL	AGE	Locus of Mode: Size of Adequate Sample — Calculations with Samples of Various Sizes								CASES IN LARGEST SAMPLE
			50	100	200	300	400	600	1000	LARGEST SAMPLE	
Total Outlet											
S-U	0–8	11–15	2.0	0.5	1.0	0.5	0.5			0.5	490
S-U	0–8	16–20	2.5	2.5	2.0	..	1.0			1.0	486
S-U	9–12	11–15	2.0	3.5	3.0	1.0	..			1.0	521
S-U	9–12	16–20	1.0	1.5	1.0	1.5	..			1.0	520
S-U	13+	11–15	0.5	0.5	0.5	0.5	1.0	0.5	0.5	0.5	2708
S-U	13+	16–20	1.0	1.0	1.0	1.0	2.0	2.0	1.5	1.0	2762
S-U	13+	21–25	2.0	1.0	1.0	1.0	1.5	1.0	1.0	1.0	1844
S-U	13+	26–30	1.5	2.0	0.5	1.0	1.0			1.0	479
M-U	13+	21–25	3.0	3.0	3.0	3.0	3.5			3.0	460
M-U	13+	26–30	3.0	2.0	3.0	3.0	3.0			3.0	561
M-U	13+	31–35	2.0	2.5	2.0	2.0				2.0	438
S-Px	0–8	11–15	1.5	1.0	1.0	0.5	0.5			1.0	481
S-Px	0–8	16–20	1.0	2.5	1.0	1.0	1.0			1.0	493
S-Px	9–12	11–15	..	2.0	1.0	1.0				1.0	375
S-Jx	13+	11–15	0.5	0.5	0.5	0.5	0.5			0.5	601
S-Jx	13+	16–20	..	3.0	1.5	0.5	2.5			0.5	607
S-P√	13+	11–15	..	0.5	0.5	0.5	0.5			0.5	547
S-P√	13+	16–20	3.5	2.0	1.0	1.5	1.0			1.0	557
S-P√	13+	21–25	1.0	1.0	1.0	1.0				1.0	384
S-Px	13+	11–15	1.0	2.0	3.5	0.5	0.5	0.5	3.5	3.5	1471
S-Px	13+	16–20	..	2.0	2.0	1.5	1.0	1.0	1.0	1.5	1513
S-Px	13+	21–25	0.5	0.5	1.0	1.0	1.0	1.0	1.0	1.0	1000
Masturbation											
S-U	0–8	11–15	1.0	0.5	0.5	0.5	0.5			0.5	490
S-U	0–8	16–20	0.5	0.5	0.5	0.5	0.5			0.5	486
S-U	9–12	11–15	0.0	1.0	1.0	1.0	1.0			1.0	521
S-U	9–12	16–20	0.5	0.5	0.5	0.5	0.5			0.5	520
S-U	13+	11–15	0.0	0.0	0.0	0.0	0.0	0.0	0.0	0.0	2708
S-U	13+	16–20	0.5	0.5	1.0	0.5	0.5	0.5	1.0	1.0	2762
S-U	13+	21–25	0.5	0.5	0.5	0.5	0.5	0.5	0.5	0.5	1844
S-U	13+	26–30	0.5	0.5	0.5	0.5	0.5			0.5	479
S-Px	0–8	11–15	1.5	0.5	1.0	0.5	0.5			0.5	481
S-Px	0–8	16–20	0.5	0.5	0.5	0.5	0.5			0.5	493
S-Px	9–12	11–15	1.0	1.0	1.0	1.0				1.0	375
S-Jx	13+	11–15	..	0.0	0.0	0.0	0.0			0.0	601
S-Jx	13+	16–20	0.5	..	..	0.5	2.0			0.5	607
S-P√	13+	11–15	..	0.0	0.0	0.0	0.0			0.0	547
S-P√	13+	16–20	..	0.0	1.0	1.0	1.0			1.0	557
S-P√	13+	21–25	0.5	0.5	0.5	0.5				0.5	384
S-Px	13+	11–15	0.0	0.0	2.0	0.0	0.0	0.0	0.0	0.0	1471
S-Px	13+	16–20	0.5	1.0	1.0	1.0	1.0	0.5	1.0	1.0	1513
S-Px	13+	21–25	0.5	0.5	0.5	0.5	0.5	0.5	0.5	0.5	1000
Nocturnal Emissions											
S-U	0–8	11–15	0.0	0.0	0.0	0.0	0.0			0.0	490
S-U	0–8	16–20	0.1	0.0	0.0	0.0	0.0			0.0	486
S-U	9–12	11–15	0.0	0.0	0.0	0.0	0.0			0.0	521
S-U	9–12	16–20	0.0	0.5	0.1	0.1	0.1			0.1	520

(*Table continued on next page*)

GROUP	EDUC. LEVEL	AGE	LOCUS OF MODE: SIZE OF ADEQUATE SAMPLE CALCULATIONS WITH SAMPLES OF VARIOUS SIZES								CASES IN LARGEST SAMPLE
			50	100	200	300	400	600	1000	LARGEST SAMPLE	
Nocturnal Emissions (*continued*)											
S-U	13+	11–15	0.5	0.5	0.5	0.5	0.5	0.5	0.5	0.5	2708
S-U	13+	16–20	0.5	0.5	0.5	0.5	0.5	0.5	0.5	0.5	2762
S-U	13+	21–25	0.5	0.5	0.5	0.5	0.5	0.5	0.5	0.5	1844
S-U	13+	26–30	0.5	0.5	0.5	0.5	0.5			0.5	479
M-U	13+	21–25	0.1	0.1	0.1	0.1	0.1			0.1	460
M-U	13+	26–30	0.1	0.1	0.1	0.1	0.1			0.1	561
M-U	13+	31–35	0.1	0.1	0.1	0.1				0.1	438
S-Px	0–8	11–15	0.0	0.0	0.0	0.0	0.0			0.0	481
S-Px	0–8	16–20	0.0	0.0	0.0	0.0	0.0			0.0	493
S-Px	9–12	11–15	0.0	0.0	0.0	0.0				0.0	375
S-Jx	13+	11–15	0.5	0.5	0.5	0.5	0.5			0.5	601
S-Jx	13+	16–20	0.5	0.5	0.5	0.5	0.5			0.5	607
S-P√	13+	11–15	..	0.5	0.0	0.5	0.5			0.5	547
S-P√	13+	16–20	0.5	0.5	0.5	0.5	0.5			0.5	557
S-P√	13+	21–25	0.5	0.5	0.5	0.5				0.5	384
S-Px	13+	11–15	0.0	0.5	0.0	0.5	0.0	0.0	0.0	0.0	1471
S-Px	13+	16–20	0.5	0.5	0.5	0.5	0.5	0.5	0.5	0.5	1513
S-Px	13+	21–25	0.5	0.5	0.5	0.5	0.5	0.5	0.5	0.5	1000
Pre-marital Intercourse with Companions											
S-U	0–8	11–15	0.0	0.0	0.0	0.0	0.0			0.0	490
S-U	0–8	16–20	..	0.5	0.5	0.5	0.5			0.5	486
S-U	9–12	11–15	0.0	0.0	0.0	0.0	0.0			0.0	521
S-U	9–12	16–20	0.5	0.0	0.0	0.0	0.0			0.0	520
S-U	13+	11–15	0.0	0.0	0.0	0.0	0.0	0.0	0.0	0.0	2708
S-U	13+	16–20	0.0	0.0	0.0	0.0	0.0	0.0	0.0	0.0	2762
S-U	13+	21–25	0.0	0.0	0.0	0.0	0.0	0.0	0.0	0.0	1844
S-U	13+	26–30	0.0	0.0	0.0	0.0	0.0			0.0	479
S-Px	0–8	11–15	0.0	0.0	0.0	0.0	0.0			0.0	481
S-Px	0–8	16–20	..	0.5	0.5	0.5	0.5			0.5	493
S-Px	9–12	11–15	0.0	0.0	0.0	0.0				0.0	375
S-Jx	13+	11–15	0.0	0.0	0.0	0.0	0.0			0.0	601
S-Jx	13+	16–20	0.0	0.0	0.0	0.0	0.0			0.0	607
S-P√	13+	11–15	0.0	0.0	0.0	0.0	0.0			0.0	547
S-P√	13+	16–20	0.0	0.0	0.0	0.0	0.0			0.0	557
S-P√	13+	21–25	0.0	0.0	0.0	0.0				0.0	384
S-Px	13+	11–15	0.0	0.0	0.0	0.0	0.0	0.0	0.0	0.0	1471
S-Px	13+	16–20	0.0	0.0	0.0	0.0	0.0	0.0	0.0	0.0	1513
S-Px	13+	21–25	0.0	0.0	0.0	0.0	0.0	0.0	0.0	0.0	1000
Marital Intercourse											
M-U	13+	21–25	2.5	2.0	3.0	3.0	2.0			2.0	460
M-U	13+	26–30	1.5	2.0	3.0	2.0	2.0			2.0	561
M-U	13+	31–35	2.0	2.0	2.0	2.0				2.0	438

Table 160. Size of sample necessary to fix the locus of the mode

Boldface figures designate calculations that lie within 5 per cent, plus or minus, of the calculations obtained from the largest sample.

GROUP	EDUC. LEVEL	AGE	HEIGHT OF MODE: SIZE OF ADEQUATE SAMPLE — CALCULATIONS WITH SAMPLES OF VARIOUS SIZES								CASES IN LARGEST SAMPLE
			50	100	200	300	400	600	1000	LARGEST SAMPLE	
						Total Outlet					
S-U	0–8	11–15	14.0	16.0	12.0	13.3	12.3			12.0	490
S-U	0–8	16–20	14.0	13.0	11.5	9.7	11.0			10.5	486
S-U	9–12	11–15	14.0	13.0	12.0	10.7	10.3			9.6	521
S-U	9–12	16–20	20.0	13.0	15.0	10.7	11.5			11.2	520
S-U	13+	11–15	18.0	16.0	12.5	13.7	12.3	12.0	12.7	12.4	2708
S-U	13+	16–20	18.0	14.0	15.0	15.3	11.0	13.8	12.3	11.9	2762
S-U	13+	21–25	18.0	15.0	15.0	15.0	14.5	15.3	14.0	14.8	1844
S-U	13+	26–30	16.0	15.0	17.0	17.0	16.0			16.3	479
M-U	13+	21–25	20.0	12.0	15.0	17.3	13.8			14.1	460
M-U	13+	26–30	22.0	19.0	17.5	13.3	14.3			13.9	561
M-U	13+	31–35	20.0	18.0	18.5	16.3				17.1	438
S-Px	0–8	11–15	14.0	16.0	16.0	14.3	12.5			13.3	481
S-Px	0–8	16–20	22.0	13.0	13.0	12.3	10.5			11.1	493
S-Px	9–12	11–15	10.0	13.0	11.5	11.7				10.9	375
S-Jx	13+	11–15	22.0	14.0	17.0	16.0	14.3			13.8	601
S-Jx	13+	16–20	16.0	14.0	12.0	12.0	12.3			11.2	607
S-P√	13+	11–15	12.0	14.0	12.0	13.0	14.0			13.7	547
S-P√	13+	16–20	16.0	17.0	15.0	14.7	14.5			14.2	557
S-P√	13+	21–25	20.0	17.0	20.0	18.7				19.3	384
S-Px	13+	11–15	22.0	15.0	12.5	10.3	11.0	11.0	9.9	9.9	1471
S-Px	13+	16–20	12.0	17.0	14.5	11.7	12.5	11.3	11.7	11.8	1513
S-Px	13+	21–25	16.0	16.0	17.0	14.7	15.5	15.8	14.7	14.7	1000
						Masturbation					
S-U	0–8	11–15	18.0	19.0	18.5	18.3	17.5			18.0	490
S-U	0–8	16–20	32.0	29.0	29.5	28.3	30.5			29.2	486
S-U	9–12	11–15	14.0	17.0	18.0	19.0	18.3			17.3	521
S-U	9–12	16–20	28.0	23.0	25.5	24.3	26.0			25.0	520
S-U	13+	11–15	22.0	15.0	16.5	16.7	18.8	18.8	17.2	18.0	2708
S-U	13+	16–20	28.0	20.0	18.5	19.3	15.5	18.8	16.6	16.5	2762
S-U	13+	21–25	44.0	20.0	22.0	24.3	23.3	24.5	24.7	24.5	1844
S-U	13+	26–30	40.0	26.0	22.5	25.3	26.3			26.5	479
S-Px	0–8	11–15	14.0	20.0	20.0	19.7	18.0			18.3	481
S.Px	0–8	16–20	36.0	27.0	29.5	31.3	30.8			31.2	493
S-Px	9–12	11–15	20.0	26.0	22.0	22.3				21.3	375
S-Jx	13+	11–15	14.0	20.0	22.0	20.7	20.0			20.0	601
S-Jx	13+	16–20	20.0	13.0	14.5	16.0	15.0			15.3	607
S-P√	13+	11–15	18.0	22.0	19.5	20.7	18.3			19.2	547
S-P√	13+	16–20	16.0	18.0	20.0	19.7	18.5			18.7	557
S-P√	13+	21–25	36.0	25.0	25.5	26.0				25.8	384
S-Px	13+	11–15	20.0	16.0	12.5	19.0	15.5	14.5	14.5	15.3	1471
S-Px	13+	16–20	20.0	23.0	19.5	16.7	18.5	16.0	17.4	17.6	1513
S-Px	13+	21–25	24.0	21.0	25.0	24.3	21.5	23.3	22.4	22.4	1000

(Table continued on next page)

GROUP	EDUC. LEVEL	AGE	HEIGHT OF MODE: SIZE OF ADEQUATE SAMPLE CALCULATIONS WITH SAMPLES OF VARIOUS SIZES								CASES IN LARGEST SAMPLE
			50	100	200	300	400	600	1000	LARGEST SAMPLE	
			Nocturnal Emissions								
S-U	0–8	11–15	72.0	73.0	72.5	71.0	74.8			73.1	490
S-U	0–8	16–20	36.0	47.0	41.0	41.3	40.5			41.6	486
S-U	9–12	11–15	60.0	56.0	55.0	58.0	59.3			58.2	521
S-U	9–12	16–20	38.0	32.0	35.0	32.7	33.3			32.7	520
S-U	13+	11–15	42.0	33.0	35.0	33.0	30.5	34.3	31.7	33.8	2708
S-U	13+	16–20	48.0	47.0	40.5	42.0	47.0	45.3	44.6	44.7	2762
S-U	13+	21–25	36.0	42.0	49.5	45.0	41.8	44.5	43.7	43.5	1844
S-U	13+	26–30	46.0	46.0	42.0	45.3	42.5			44.3	479
M-U	13+	21–25	40.0	42.0	35.5	34.0	36.0			35.2	460
M-U	13+	26–30	42.0	43.0	42.0	42.0	40.3			40.8	561
M-U	13+	31–35	48.0	37.0	38.5	40.3				40.9	438
S-Px	0–8	11–15	72.0	78.0	75.0	73.3	74.5			74.0	481
S-Px	0–8	16–20	50.0	44.0	42.5	42.3	41.5			43.4	493
S-Px	9–12	11–15	58.0	61.0	56.5	59.7				60.0	375
S-Jx	13+	11–15	34.0	30.0	29.5	37.0	31.8			33.6	601
S-Jx	13+	16–20	42.0	41.0	39.0	37.7	40.5			38.9	607
S-P√	13+	11–15	30.0	35.0	31.0	37.3	35.3			35.8	547
S-P√	13+	16–20	56.0	48.0	43.5	51.0	49.0			48.8	557
S-P√	13+	21–25	48.0	35.0	48.0	47.7				45.8	384
S-Px	13+	11–15	30.0	37.0	36.0	32.3	34.0	32.7	33.4	32.0	1471
S-Px	13+	16–20	38.0	45.0	44.0	44.7	46.3	44.7	43.6	45.3	1513
S-Px	13+	21–25	38.0	51.0	41.5	43.3	45.0	43.7	44.5	44.5	1000
			Pre-marital Intercourse with Companions								
S-U	0–8	11–15	34.0	56.0	45.5	47.3	50.0			48.8	490
S-U	0–8	16–20	18.0	21.0	19.0	20.3	19.5			19.3	486
S-U	9–12	11–15	58.0	54.0	52.0	56.3	56.0			56.8	521
S-U	9–12	16–20	24.0	29.0	26.5	35.0	29.3			29.6	520
S-U	13+	11–15	94.0	90.0	88.5	92.3	91.8	91.0	92.7	91.0	2708
S-U	13+	16–20	58.0	70.0	60.5	63.3	58.5	59.7	61.4	60.9	2762
S-U	13+	21–25	42.0	41.0	40.0	36.7	41.3	45.5	42.1	43.0	1844
S-U	13+	26–30	48.0	43.0	46.0	36.7	41.3			39.5	479
S-Px	0–8	11–15	42.0	44.0	47.5	50.0	48.0			47.6	481
S-Px	0–8	16–20	20.0	24.0	24.0	24.3	22.0			22.3	493
S-Px	9–12	11–15	72.0	46.0	58.0	51.3				54.1	375
S-Jx	13+	11–15	90.0	96.0	95.0	93.7	92.3			93.5	601
S-Jx	13+	16–20	64.0	56.0	58.5	57.0	58.5			58.5	607
S-P√	13+	11–15	90.0	92.0	93.0	92.0	92.5			92.9	547
S-P√	13+	16–20	80.0	77.0	77.0	75.0	77.0			76.1	557
S-P√	13+	21–25	84.0	66.0	67.5	67.0				67.4	384
S-Px	13+	11–15	88.0	93.0	88.5	89.7	89.3	89.2	90.3	89.7	1471
S-Px	13+	16–20	58.0	62.0	53.5	57.3	59.3	60.5	58.8	58.9	1513
S-Px	13+	21–25	36.0	45.0	45.5	41.0	43.3	42.2	41.4	41.4	1000

(*Table continued on next page*)

GROUP	EDUC. LEVEL	AGE	HEIGHT OF MODE: SIZE OF ADEQUATE SAMPLE — CALCULATIONS WITH SAMPLES OF VARIOUS SIZES								CASES IN LARGEST SAMPLE
			50	100	200	300	400	600	1000	LARGEST SAMPLE	
Marital Intercourse											
M-U	13+	21–25	18.0	**13.0**	**13.5**	**13.3**	**13.5**			13.5	460
M-U	13+	26–30	**16.0**	**17.0**	14.5	14.0	**15.8**			16.4	561
M-U	13+	31–35	18.0	19.0	24.5	18.0				20.3	438
Total Extra-marital Intercourse											
M-U	13+	21–25	**82.0**	**86.0**	**85.5**	**83.3**	**84.0**			83.7	460
M-U	13+	26–30	**78.0**	**77.0**	**74.0**	**76.0**	**76.5**			75.0	561
M-U	13+	31–35	**74.0**	**73.0**	67.5	64.0				66.0	438
Homosexual Outlet											
S-U	0–8	11–15	62.0	**77.0**	**73.5**	**74.0**	**72.0**			72.7	490
S-U	0–8	16–20	62.0	**74.0**	**67.0**	66.0	**68.5**			69.8	486
S-U	9–12	11–15	**62.0**	**70.0**	**63.5**	**62.3**	**64.0**			63.5	521
S-U	9–12	16–20	**56.0**	**56.0**	58.0	54.7	55.0			54.4	520
S-U	13+	11–15	**80.0**	**82.0**	71.0	**77.0**	**77.8**	**78.8**	**77.4**	78.1	2708
S-U	13+	16–20	78.0	78.0	**86.0**	**87.0**	**82.3**	**83.7**	**85.0**	84.0	2762
S-U	13+	21–25	**90.0**	**90.0**	**90.5**	**90.7**	**88.8**	**91.0**	**88.8**	89.8	1844
S-U	13+	26–30	**80.0**	78.0	**83.0**	**85.3**	**82.3**			83.1	479
S-Px	0–8	11–15	70.0	**78.0**	**76.0**	**76.7**	**76.3**			77.5	481
S-Px	0–8	16–20	**80.0**	**78.0**	**74.5**	**75.3**	**75.0**			75.5	493
S-Px	9–12	11–15	**68.0**	**70.0**	**70.5**	66.7				65.9	375
S-Jx	13+	11–15	**86.0**	**84.0**	**87.0**	**83.3**	**85.8**			85.4	601
S-Jx	13+	16–20	**92.0**	**92.0**	**89.5**	**87.7**	**90.8**			89.3	607
S-P√	13+	11–15	84.0	**74.0**	**78.0**	**79.3**	**77.3**			76.2	547
S-P√	13+	16–20	**82.0**	78.0	**83.0**	**83.3**	**81.8**			82.6	557
S-P√	13+	21–25	92.0	**93.0**	**93.5**	**94.0**				93.8	384
S-Px	13+	11–15	**76.0**	69.0	**74.0**	**74.7**	**74.5**	**71.8**	**73.2**	74.4	1471
S-Px	13+	16–20	**80.0**	**81.0**	**81.0**	**83.3**	**79.0**	**82.0**	**80.8**	82.0	1513
S-Px	13+	21–25	**86.0**	**88.0**	**87.0**	**89.0**	**87.8**	**88.2**	**88.5**	88.5	1000

Table 161. Size of sample necessary to fix the height of the mode

Boldface figures designate calculations that lie within 5 per cent, plus or minus, of the calculations obtained from the largest sample.

GROUP	EDUC. LEVEL	AGE	RANGE: MAXIMUM FREQUENCY MINUS 1: SIZE OF ADEQUATE SAMPLE / CALCULATIONS WITH SAMPLES OF VARIOUS SIZES								CASES IN LARGEST SAMPLE
			50	100	200	300	400	600	1000	LARGEST SAMPLE	
			Total Outlet								
S-U	0–8	11–15	14.0	25.0	18.0	22.0	22.0			25.0	490
S-U	0–8	16–20	9.0	16.0	16.0	17.0	26.0			26.0	486
S-U	9–12	11–15	11.0	19.0	23.0	25.0	25.0			25.0	521
S-U	9–12	16–20	18.0	26.0	16.0	26.0	26.0			26.0	520
S-U	13+	11–15	14.0	13.0	15.0	29.0	18.0	26.0	26.0	29.0	2708
S-U	13+	16–20	7.5	12.0	14.0	20.0	20.0	17.0	23.0	24.0	2762
S-U	13+	21–25	6.5	8.0	17.0	11.0	14.0	18.0	21.0	21.0	1844
S-U	13+	26–30	8.0	16.0	17.0	17.0	17.0			17.0	479
M-U	13+	21–25	8.0	16.0	15.0	15.0	22.0			22.0	460
M-U	13+	26–30	10.0	11.0	12.0	22.0	22.0			22.0	561
M-U	13+	31–35	8.0	14.0	20.0	18.0				20.0	438
S-Px	0–8	11–15	17.0	14.0	25.0	22.0	25.0			25.0	481
S-Px	0–8	16–20	12.0	17.0	21.0	26.0	29.0			29.0	493
S-Px	9–12	11–15	11.0	16.0	19.0	23.0				23.0	375
S-Jx	13+	11–15	9.0	26.0	25.0	25.0	26.0			29.0	601
S-Jx	13+	16–20	7.5	11.0	12.0	15.0	20.0			23.0	607
S-P√	13+	11–15	9.5	8.0	9.5	12.0	12.0			13.0	547
S-P√	13+	16–20	7.5	7.5	9.0	9.5	11.0			11.0	557
S-P√	13+	21–25	6.5	7.5	8.0	10.0				11.0	384
S-Px	13+	11–15	14.0	10.0	14.0	22.0	20.0	15.0	23.0	25.0	1471
S-Px	13+	16–20	13.0	10.0	11.0	14.0	14.0	15.0	14.0	21.0	1513
S-Px	13+	21–25	11.0	11.0	13.0	14.0	15.0	15.0	17.0	17.0	1000
			Masturbation								
S-U	0–8	11–15	10.0	12.0	10.0	14.0	14.0			14.0	490
S-U	0–8	16–20	4.0	7.0	7.0	7.0	7.0			8.0	486
S-U	9–12	11–15	7.0	10.0	12.0	12.0	12.0			12.0	521
S-U	9–12	16–20	4.0	8.0	8.0	8.0	8.0			8.0	520
S-U	13+	11–15	14.0	10.0	14.0	14.0	15.0	15.0	15.0	29.0	2708
S-U	13+	16–20	7.0	10.0	10.0	20.0	18.0	16.0	23.0	23.0	2762
S-U	13+	21–25	5.0	7.0	11.0	7.0	10.0	15.0	15.0	15.0	1844
S-U	13+	26–30	5.0	7.0	10.0	10.0	10.0			10.0	479
S-Px	0–8	11–15	7.0	14.0	14.0	10.0	14.0			14.0	481
S-Px	0–8	16–20	7.0	7.0	7.0	7.0	7.0			8.0	493
S-Px	9–12	11–15	10.0	9.0	12.0	10.0				12.0	375
S-Jx	13+	11–15	7.0	25.0	25.0	25.0	25.0			29.0	601
S-Jx	13+	16–20	7.0	8.5	10.0	15.0	20.0			23.0	607
S-P√	13+	11–15	7.0	7.0	7.5	7.0	8.0			12.0	547
S-P√	13+	16–20	7.0	5.5	8.5	9.0	10.0			10.0	557
S-P√	13+	21–25	4.5	5.0	5.5	6.0				6.0	384
S-Px	13+	11–15	10.0	10.0	14.0	14.0	14.0	14.0	20.0	20.0	1471
S-Px	13+	16–20	8.0	10.0	10.0	14.0	14.0	14.0	14.0	14.0	1513
S-Px	13+	21–25	7.0	10.0	8.0	11.0	12.0	12.0	12.0	12.0	1000

(*Table continued on next page*)

GROUP	EDUC. LEVEL	AGE	RANGE: MAXIMUM FREQUENCY MINUS 1: SIZE OF ADEQUATE SAMPLE CALCULATIONS WITH SAMPLES OF VARIOUS SIZES								CASES IN LARGEST SAMPLE
			50	100	200	300	400	600	1000	LARGEST SAMPLE	

Nocturnal Emissions

GROUP	EDUC. LEVEL	AGE	50	100	200	300	400	600	1000	LARGEST SAMPLE	CASES IN LARGEST SAMPLE
S-U	0–8	11–15	0.5	2.0	0.5	2.0	2.5			2.5	490
S-U	0–8	16–20	0.5	1.5	2.5	2.5	2.5			2.5	486
S-U	9–12	11–15	0.5	1.0	3.0	4.0	5.0			5.0	521
S-U	9–12	16–20	1.0	2.0	3.0	3.0	3.0			3.0	520
S-U	13+	11–15	2.5	2.5	3.0	5.0	6.0	7.0	6.5	12.0	2708
S-U	13+	16–20	1.5	2.5	4.0	3.0	5.5	5.0	6.0	6.5	2762
S-U	13+	21–25	1.5	2.0	3.0	3.5	5.0	5.0	6.5	6.5	1844
S-U	13+	26–30	1.5	2.0	2.0	4.0	4.0			4.0	479
M-U	13+	21–25	1.0	1.5	2.5	4.0	4.0			4.0	460
M-U	13+	26–30	1.0	1.5	1.0	3.0	3.0			3.0	561
M-U	13+	31–35	1.0	1.0	1.5	3.0				3.0	438
S-Px	0–8	11–15	0.5	1.0	1.0	2.0	2.5			2.5	481
S-Px	0–8	16–20	2.0	2.5	2.5	2.5	2.5			2.5	493
S-Px	9–12	11–15	1.5	1.5	2.0	4.0				4.0	375
S-Jx	13+	11–15	1.0	3.5	3.0	3.5	6.5			6.5	601
S-Jx	13+	16–20	2.5	2.5	4.5	3.5	6.0			6.0	607
S-P√	13+	11–15	2.5	1.5	3.0	5.0	7.0			7.0	547
S-P√	13+	16–20	1.5	2.0	2.5	5.0	3.5			5.0	557
S-P√	13+	21–25	2.5	2.5	2.5	5.0				5.0	384
S-Px	13+	11–15	1.5	3.0	2.0	5.0	4.0	6.0	6.0	7.0	1471
S-Px	13+	16–20	2.5	2.5	4.0	3.0	3.5	5.5	6.0	6.0	1513
S-Px	13+	21–25	2.5	2.0	3.5	4.0	3.5	6.0	6.0	6.0	1000

Pre-marital Intercourse with Companions

GROUP	EDUC. LEVEL	AGE	50	100	200	300	400	600	1000	LARGEST SAMPLE	CASES IN LARGEST SAMPLE
S-U	0–8	11–15	12.0	20.0	14.0	15.0	17.0			20.0	490
S-U	0–8	16–20	7.0	14.0	12.0	16.0	20.0			20.0	486
S-U	9–12	11–15	2.0	12.0	10.0	25.0	25.0			25.0	521
S-U	9–12	16–20	14.0	20.0	10.0	12.0	25.0			25.0	520
S-U	13+	11–15	3.5	3.0	1.0	3.0	3.0	9.5	9.5	10.0	2708
S-U	13+	16–20	2.0	3.0	6.0	3.0	12.0	7.0	12.0	12.0	2762
S-U	13+	21–25	5.0	5.5	6.0	9.0	9.0	8.5	17.0	17.0	1844
S-U	13+	26–30	5.5	14.0	9.5	6.0	14.0			14.0	479
S-Px	0–8	11–15	11.0	6.0	20.0	15.0	20.0			20.0	481
S-Px	0–8	16–20	8.0	16.0	16.0	20.0	25.0			25.0	493
S-Px	9–12	11–15	3.5	9.5	10.0	14.0				14.0	375
S-Jx	13+	11–15	0.5	0.1	0.5	0.5	0.5			3.0	601
S-Jx	13+	16–20	2.0	1.5	5.0	5.5	5.5			7.0	607
S-P√	13+	11–15	2.5	2.5	2.0	3.0	3.0			4.5	547
S-P√	13+	16–20	0.5	6.0	2.5	7.0	6.0			7.0	557
S-P√	13+	21–25	0.5	3.5	6.0	7.5				7.5	384
S-Px	13+	11–15	0.5	0.5	3.0	7.0	5.0	6.0	6.0	10.0	1471
S-Px	13+	16–20	3.0	2.5	3.0	6.5	7.0	7.0	7.0	9.0	1513
S-Px	13+	21–25	3.0	4.5	5.5	9.0	8.0	9.0	9.0	9.0	1000

(*Table continued on next page*)

GROUP	EDUC. LEVEL	AGE	RANGE: MAXIMUM FREQUENCY MINUS 1: SIZE OF ADEQUATE SAMPLE — CALCULATIONS WITH SAMPLES OF VARIOUS SIZES								CASES IN LARGEST SAMPLE
			50	100	200	300	400	600	1000	LARGEST SAMPLE	
						Marital Intercourse					
M-U	13+	21–25	8.0	16.0	15.0	15.0	**20.0**			20.0	460
M-U	13+	26–30	8.0	10.0	11.0	**20.0**	**20.0**			20.0	561
M-U	13+	31–35	7.0	13.0	**18.0**	16.0				18.0	438
						Total Extra-marital Intercourse					
M-U	13+	21–25	2.0	1.0	2.5	**3.0**	3.0			3.0	460
M-U	13+	26–30	1.0	3.0	**3.5**	2.5	3.5			3.5	561
M-U	13+	31–35	2.5	3.0	3.5	**4.5**				4.5	438
						Homosexual Outlet					
S-U	0–8	11–15	4.0	6.0	6.0	**7.0**	7.0			7.0	490
S-U	0–8	16–20	4.0	2.5	3.5	5.5	5.5			6.0	486
S-U	9–12	11–15	5.0	4.5	5.0	**7.0**	5.0			7.0	521
S-U	9–12	16–20	1.5	**11.0**	6.0	**11.0**	**11.0**			11.0	520
S-U	13+	11–15	0.5	0.5	3.0	4.0	2.5	5.0	**6.0**	6.0	2708
S-U	13+	16–20	1.0	2.5	2.0	3.0	2.5	5.0	2.5	7.0	2762
S-U	13+	21–25	0.5	1.0	3.0	3.5	4.5	4.5	**7.0**	7.0	1844
S-U	13+	26–30	3.5	4.0	4.5	**5.0**	5.0			5.0	479
S-Px	0–8	11–15	3.5	3.0	**6.0**	**6.0**	**6.0**			6.0	481
S-Px	0–8	16–20	1.0	3.0	6.0	5.5	6.0			7.0	493
S-Px	9–12	11–15	3.0	4.5	3.0	**5.0**				5.0	375
S-Jx	13+	11–15	0.5	**4.5**	1.0	**4.5**	4.5			4.5	601
S-Jx	13+	16–20	0.1	2.5	2.5	**3.5**	3.0			3.5	607
S-P√	13+	11–15	2.0	2.5	2.0	2.0	**4.0**			4.0	547
S-P√	13+	16–20	0.5	1.0	**4.0**	2.0	**4.0**			4.0	557
S-P√	13+	21–25	0.5	0.5	1.5	1.5				3.5	384
S-Px	13+	11–15	0.5	2.0	3.0	3.0	3.5	4.0	**5.0**	5.0	1471
S-Px	13+	16–20	0.5	0.5	**5.0**	2.0	3.5	**5.0**	**5.0**	5.0	1513
S-Px	13+	21–25	2.0	1.0	5.0	**6.5**	4.5	5.0	**6.5**	6.5	1000

Table 162. Size of sample necessary to secure stable data on range of variation

The figures shown represent maximum frequencies minus one case. Boldface figures designate calculations that lie within 5 per cent, plus or minus, of the calculations obtained from the largest sample.

BIBLIOGRAPHY

The following bibliography includes items which are cited in the text of the present volume, and some additional references to the more important general studies on sex. It does not purport to be a general bibliography on human sexual behavior.

Achilles, P. S. 1923. The effectiveness of certain social hygiene literature. New York, Amer. Soc. Hyg. Assoc., pp. 116.

Ackerson, L. 1931. Children's behavior problems. A statistical study based upon 5000 children examined consecutively at the Illinois Institute for Juvenile Research. I. Incidence, genetic and intellectual factors. Chicago, University of Chicago Press, pp. xxi + 268.

— 1942. Children's behavior problems. A statistical study based upon 2113 boys and 1181 girls examined consecutively at the Illinois Institute for Juvenile Research. II. Relative importance and interrelations among traits. Chicago, University of Chicago Press, pp. xix + 570.

Adams, C. R., and Packard, V. O. 1946. How to pick a mate. The guide to a happy marriage. New York, E. P. Dutton & Co., pp. 215.

Ahlstrom, E. H. 1937. Studies on variability in the genus Dinobryon (Mastigophora). Trans. Amer. Micro. Soc. 56:139–159.

Allbutt, T. C. 1921. Greek medicine in Rome. London, Macmillan & Co., pp. xiv + 633.

Allen, C. 1940. The sexual perversions and abnormalities. London, Oxford University Press, pp. xii + 193.

Allen, E., et al. 1939. Sex and internal secretions. A survey of recent research. Baltimore, Williams & Wilkins Co., pp. xxxvi + 1346.

Allen, F. L. 1931. Only yesterday. An informal history of the nineteen-twenties. New York, Bantam Books, pp. 413.

Allport, G. W. 1942. The use of personal documents in psychological science. New York, Soc. Sci. Res. Council, Bull. 49, pp. xix + 210.

American Social Hygiene Association. 1930. From boy to man. Amer. Soc. Hyg. Assoc. Publ. 626:1–20.

Ananga-Ranga (A.F.F. and B.F.R., transl.). 1885. Ananga-Ranga; (stage of the bodiless one) or, the Hindu art of love. (Ars amoris indica.) Cosmopoli, Kama Shastra Soc., pp. xvi + 144.

Angus, S. 1925. The mystery-religions and Christianity. A study in the religious background of early Christianity. New York, Charles Scribner's Sons, pp. xvi + 359.

Arey, L. B. 1924. Developmental anatomy. A text-book and laboratory manual of embryology. Philadelphia, W. B. Saunders Co., pp. vii + 433.

— 1946. Developmental anatomy (5th edit.). A textbook and laboratory manual of embryology. Philadelphia, W. B. Saunders Co., pp. ix + 616.

Armitage, R. B. 1913. Private lessons in the cultivation of sex force. Chicago, Franklin Publ., pp. 202.

Asdell, S. A. 1946. Patterns of mammalian reproduction. Ithaca, N. Y., Comstock Publishing Co., pp. xi + 437.

Baldwin, B. T. 1916. A measuring scale for physical growth and physiological age. Yrbk. Nat. Soc. Study Educ. 1916:11–22.

— 1928. The determination of sex maturation in boys by a laboratory method. J. Comp. Psych. 8:39–43.

Baldwin, B. T., Busby, L. M., and Gatside, H. V. 1928. The anatomic growth of children. A study of some bones of the hand, wrist, and lower forearm, by means of roentgenograms. Univ. Iowa Studies in Child Welfare 4, pp. 88.

Ball, J. 1937. Sex activity of castrated male rats increased by estrin administration. J. Comp. Psych. 24:135–144.

    1939. Male and female mating behavior in pre-pubertally castrated male rats receiving estrogens. J. Comp. Psych. 28:273–283.

    1940. The effect of testosterone on the sex behavior of female rats. J. Comp. Psych. 29:151–165.

Barton, G. A. 1925 (4th edit.). Archaeology and the Bible. Philadelphia, American Sunday School Union, pp. xv + 561 + 122 pl.

Barton, R. F. 1938. Philippine pagans; the autobiographies of three Ifugaos. London, George Routledge & Sons, pp. xxi + 271.

Bateson, W. 1894. Materials for the study of variation treated with especial regard to discontinuity in the origin of species. London, New York, Macmillan Co., pp. xvi + 598.

Bauer, J. 1944. The male climacteric—a misnomer. J. Amer. Medic. Assoc. 126:914.

Beach, F. A. 1937. The neural basis of innate behavior. 1. Effects of cortical lesions upon the maternal behavior pattern in the rat. J. Comp. Psych. 24:393–439.

    1938. Sex reversals in the mating pattern of the rat. J. Genet. Psych. 53:329–334.

    1939. The neural basis of innate behavior. III. Comparison of learning ability and instinctive behavior in the rat. J. Comp. Psych. 28:225.

    1940. Effects of cortical lesions upon the copulatory behavior of male rats. J. Comp. Psych. 29:193–245.

    1941. Copulatory behavior of male rats raised in isolation and subjected to partial decortication prior to the acquisition of sexual experience. J. Comp. Psych. 31:457 ff.

    1941. Female mating behavior shown by male rats after administration of testosterone propionate. Endocr. 29:409–412.

    1942. Male and female mating behavior in prepuberally castrated female rats treated with androgens. Endocr. 31:673–678.

    1942. Copulatory behavior in prepuberally castrated male rats and its modification by estrogen administration. Endocr. 31:679–683.

    1942. Analysis of the stimuli adequate to elicit mating behavior in the sexually inexperienced male rat. J. Comp. Psych. 33:163–207.

    1942. Effects of testosterone propionate upon the copulatory behavior of sexually inexperienced male rats. J. Comp. Psych. 33:227–247.

    1942. Sexual behavior of prepuberal male and female rats treated with gonadal hormones. J. Comp. Psych. 34:285–292.

    1942. Comparison of copulatory behavior of male rats raised in isolation, cohabitation, and segregation. J. Genet. Psych. 60:121–136.

    1942. Execution of the complete masculine copulatory pattern by sexually receptive female rats. J. Genet. Psych. 60:137–142.

    1942. Central nervous mechanisms involved in the reproductive behavior of vertebrates. Psych. Bull. 39:200–226.

    1942. Analysis of factors involved in the arousal, maintenance and manifestation of sexual excitement in male animals. Psychosom. Med. 4:173–198.

    1943. Effects of injury to the cerebral cortex upon the display of masculine and feminine mating behavior by female rats. J. Comp. Psych. 36:169–199.

    1944. Effects of injury to the cerebral cortex upon sexually-receptive behavior in the female rat. Psychosom. Med. 6:40–55.

    1944. Experimental studies of sexual behavior in male mammals. J. Clin. Endocr. 4:126–134.

    1944. Relative effects of androgen upon the mating behavior of male rats subjected to forebrain injury or castration. J. Exp. Zool. 97:249–295.

    1945. Hormonal induction of mating responses in a rat with congenital absence of gonadal tissue. Anat. Rec. 92:289–292.

    1945. Bisexual mating behavior in the male rat; effects of castration and hormone administration. Physiol. Zool. 18:390–402.

1947. A review of physiological and psychological studies of sexual behavior in mammals. Physiol. Rev. 27:240–307.

Beach, F. A., and **Holz, A. M. 1946.** Mating behavior in male rats castrated at various ages and injected with androgen. J. Exper. Zool. 101:91–142.

Beach, F. A., and **Rasquin, P. 1942.** Masculine copulatory behavior in intact and castrated female rats. Endocr. 31:393–409.

Beers, C. W. 1908. A mind that found itself. New York, Longmans, Green & Co., pp. ix + 363.

Bell, S. 1902. A preliminary study of the emotion of love between the sexes. Amer. J. Psych. 13:325–354.

Benedict, R. 1934. Patterns of culture. New York, Penguin Books, pp. xiii + 272.

Benjamin, H. 1939. Prostitution and venereal disease. Med. Rev. of Rev., Sept. 1935: 5–40.

1944. The sex problem in the armed forces. Urol. & Cutan. Rev. 48:231–244.

Bigelow, M. A. 1916. Sex-education. New York, The Macmillan Co., pp. xi + 251.

Bilder-Lexikon (Schidrowitz, L., edit.). **1928–1931.** Bilder-Lexikon. Vol. 1: Kulturgeschichte, pp. 942. Vol. 2: Literatur und Kunst, pp. 944. Vol. 3: Sexualwissenschaft, pp. 916. Wien & Leipzig, Verlag für Kulturforschung.

Bingham, H. C. 1928. Sex development in apes. Comp. Psych. Monogr. 5 (1):1–165.

Biskind, M. S., and **Falk, H. C. 1943.** Nutritional therapy of infertility in the male, with special reference to the vitamin B complex and vitamin E. J. Clin. Endocr. 3:148–153.

Blackwood, B. 1935. Both sides of Buka passage. An ethnographic study of social, sexual, and economic questions in the north-western Solomon Islands. Oxford, Clarendon Press, pp. xvi + 624.

Blankenship, A. B. 1943. Consumer and opinion research. The questionnaire technique. New York and London, Harper & Brothers, pp. x + 238.

Blanton, M. G. 1917. The behavior of the human infant during the first thirty days of life. Psych. Rev. 24:456–483.

Bloch, I. 1903. Beiträge zur Aetiologie der Psychopathia sexualis. (Second part.) Dresden, H. R. Dohrn Verlag, pp. xviii + 400.

1908. (ex 6th edit.). (Paul, M. E., transl.). The sexual life of our time in its relations to modern civilization. London, Rebman, pp. xvi + 790.

1909. Das Sexualleben unserer Zeit in seinen Beziehungen zur modernen Kultur. Berlin, L. Marcus Verlagsbuchhandlung, pp. xii + 850 + xix.

1912. Die Prostitution. (Vol. 1). Berlin, Louis Marcus Verlagsbuchhandlung, pp. xxxvi + 870.

1933. Anthropological studies in the strange sexual practises of all races in all ages. New York, Anthropol. Press, pp. ix + 246 + xxiii.

1934. Sex life in England. New York, Panurge Press, pp. 356.

Bloch, I., and **Loewenstein, G. 1925.** Die Prostitution. (Vol. II, pt. 1). Berlin, Louis Marcus Verlagsbuchhandlung, pp. viii + 728.

Blos, P. A. 1941. The adolescent personality. A study of individual behavior. New York, D. Appleton-Century Co., pp. xiii + 517.

Boas, F. 1932. Studies in growth. Human Biol. 4:307–350.

Boas, F. (edit.). **1938.** General anthropology. New York, D. C. Heath & Co., pp. xi + 718.

Bonnar, A. 1937 (1941). The Catholic doctor. New York, P. J. Kenedy & Sons, pp. xvii + 184.

Bowman, H. A. 1942. Marriage for moderns. New York and London, McGraw-Hill Co., pp. ix + 493.

Boys' Clubs of America. 1946. Social hygiene in a boys' club. New York, Boys' Clubs Amer., pp. 19.

Boy Scouts of America. 1911. The official handbook for boys. Garden City, N. Y., Doubleday, Page & Co., pp. xiv + 400.

Boy Scouts of America. 1945 (38th printing). Revised handbook for boys. New York, Boy Scouts Amer., pp. 570.

Bridges, K. B. 1936. Le développement des émotions chez le jeune enfant. J. Psychol. Norm. et Path. 33:45 ff.

Briffault, R. 1927. The mothers. A study of the origins of sentiments and institutions. New York, The Macmillan Co., Vol. 1, pp. xix + 781; Vol. 2, pp. xx + 789; Vol. 3, pp. xv + 841.

Brill, A. A. 1944. Freud's contribution to psychiatry. New York, W. W. Norton & Co., pp. 244.

Brockman, F. S. 1902. A study of the moral and religious life of 251 preparatory school students in the United States. Pedag. Sem. & J. Genet. Psych. 9:255–273.

Bromley, D. D., and **Britten, F. H. 1938.** Youth and sex. A study of 1300 college students. New York and London, Harper & Brothers, pp. xiii + 303.

Brown, H. C. 1937. A mind mislaid. New York, E. P. Dutton & Co., pp. 219.

Brown, J. F. 1940. The psychodynamics of abnormal behavior. New York and London, McGraw-Hill Book Co., pp. xvi + 484.

Bruckner, S. J. 1937. How to give sex instructions. A guide for parents, teachers and others responsible for the training of young people. St. Louis, The Queen's Work, pp. 64.

Bryk, F. 1933. Voodoo eros. New York, priv. printed, Falstaff Press, pp. 251.

Bryk, F. (Norton, A. J., transl.). 1944. Dark rapture. The sex-life of the African Negro. Forest Hills, N. Y., Juno Books, pp. xvi + 167.

Budge, E. A. W. 1895. The book of the dead. The papyrus of Ani in the British Museum. The Egyptian text with interlinear transliteration and translation, a running translation, introduction, etc. London, Brit. Mus., pp. clv + 377.

Bühler, C. 1930. The first year of life. New York, John Day Co.

   1931. [Sexual development in children.] Ztschr. Kinderh. 51:612–642.

   1931. Kindheit und Jugend. Leipzig.

Burgess, E. W., and **Cottrell, L. S. 1939.** Predicting success or failure in marriage. New York, Prentice-Hall, pp. xxiii + 472.

Burns, H., and **Watson, B. F. 1942.** Annotated Indiana statutes 1933. 1942 replacement volume. Indianapolis, Bobbs-Merrill Co., pp. viii + 1155.

Butterfield, O. M. 1939. Love problems of adolescence. New York, Emerson Books, pp. viii + 212.

Calverton, V. F. 1926. Sex expression in literature. New York, Boni & Liveright, pp. xxviii + 337.

Calverton, V. F. (edit.). 1931. The making of man. An outline of anthropology. New York, Modern Library, pp. xv + 879.

   1937. The making of society. An outline of sociology. New York, Modern Library, pp. xviii + 923.

Calverton, V. F., and **Schmalhausen, S. D. (edit.). 1929.** Sex in civilization. New York, Macaulay Co., pp. 719.

   1930. The new generation. The intimate problems of modern parents and children. New York, Macaulay Co., pp. 717.

Campbell, E. H. 1939. The social-sex development of children. Genet. Psych. Monogr. 21:461–552.

Cantril, H. 1944. Gauging public opinion. Princeton, N. J., Princeton University Press, pp. xiv + 318.

Carlson, E. R. 1941. Born that way. New York, John Day Co., pp. ix + 174.

Carmichael, L. (edit.). 1946. Manual of child psychology. New York, John Wiley & Sons; London, Chapman & Hall, pp. viii + 1068.

Carpenter, C. R. 1939. Behavior and social relations of free-ranging primates. Sci. Month. 47:319–325.

   1940. A field study in Siam of the behavior and social relations of the gibbon (Hylobates lar). Comp. Psych. Monogr. 16:3–12.

   1942. Characteristics of social behavior in non-human primates. Trans. N. Y. Acad. Sci. (2) 4:248–258.

   1942. Sexual behavior of free ranging Rhesus monkeys (Macaca mulatta). I. Specimens, procedures and behavioral characteristics of estrus. J. Comp. Psych. 33:113–142.

   1942. Sexual behavior of free ranging Rhesus monkeys (Macaca mulatta). II.

Periodicity of estrus, homosexual, autoerotic and nonconformist behavior. J. Comp. Psych. 33:143–162.

1942. Societies of monkeys and apes. Biol. Sympos. 8:177–204.

Carpenter, E. 1897. An unknown people. London, pp. 31.

1911. Love's coming-of-age. A series of papers on the relations of the sexes. New York and London, Mitchell Kennerley, pp. 199.

1914. Intermediate types among primitive folk. A study in social evolution. New York, Mitchell Kennerley, pp. 185.

1930. The intermediate sex. A study of some transitional types of men and women. London, Allen & Unwin, pp. 176.

Carpenter, E. (edit.). 1902. Iolӓus. An anthology of friendship. London, Swan Sonnenschein & Co.; Manchester, by the author; Boston, Chas. E. Goodspeed, pp. vi + 191.

1935. An anthology of friendship. New York, A. and C. Boni, pp. vi + 295.

Catholic Woman Doctor. 1939. Growing up. A book for girls. New York, Benziger Bros., pp. ix + 47.

Chapin, F. S. 1933. The measurement of social status by the use of the social status scale 1933. Minneapolis, University of Minnesota Press, pp. 16.

Chapple, E., and Coon, C. 1942. Principles of anthropology. New York, Henry Holt & Co., pp. xi + 718.

Chesire, L., Saffir, M., and Thurstone, L. L. 1933. Computing diagrams for the tetrachoric correlation coefficient. Chicago, University of Chicago Bookstore, pp. 59.

Chivers, W. R. (edit.). 1946. Successful marriage and family living. Atlanta, Ga., Morehouse College, pp. 47.

Chlenov. 1907. [The sex life of Moscow students.] Trud. pirog. Syezd, Spb. (acc. to Willoughby, 1937).

Chlenov (Feldhusen, M., transl.). 1908. [The questionnaire on sex among the students of the University of Moscow. Rpt. to Dermat. and Hyg. Sect. 10th Pirogov Congress.] Ztschr. f. Bekämpfung der Geschlechtskrankheiten 8:211–224, 245–255.

Clark, L. 1937. Emotional adjustment in marriage. St. Louis, C. V. Mosby Co., pp. 261.

Clark, P. L., Jr. 1928. Sex education. Why? Where? When? By whom? Ithaca, N.Y., Rational Life Publishing Co., pp. 104.

Clarke, E. L. 1938. Petting. Wise or otherwise? New York, Association Press, pp. 30.

Cobb, M. 1947. Are Negroes oversexed? Our World, May 1947:18–20.

Committee on Education and Labor. 1946. Hearing before a subcommittee of the Committee on Education and Labor, United States Senate, Seventy-ninth Congress, second session on S. 1779. A bill to authorize the Federal Security administrator to assist the states in matters relating to social protection, and for other purposes. Washington, U. S. Govt. Print. Off., pp. 51.

Committee on Judiciary. 1946. Hearings before Subcommittee No. 3 of the Committee on the Judiciary, House of Representatives, Seventy-ninth Congress, second session on H. R. 5234. A bill to authorize the Federal Security administrator to assist the states in matters relating to social protection, and for other purposes. Washington, U. S. Govt. Print. Off., pp. iv + 63.

Conn, J. H. 1939. Factors influencing development of sexual attitudes and sexual awareness in children. Amer. J. Dis. Child. 58:738–745.

1940. Sexual curiosity of children. Amer. J. Dis. Child. 60:1110–1119.

Conwell, C. 1937. The professional thief. Chicago, University of Chicago Press, pp. xiii + 256.

Cooper, C. R. 1939. Designs in scarlet. Boston, Little, Brown & Co., pp. 372.

Coppens, C., and Spalding, H. S. 1921. Moral principles and medical practice. The basis of medical jurisprudence. New York, Benziger Bros., pp. 320.

Corner, G. W. 1938. Attaining manhood. A doctor talks to boys about sex. New York, Harper & Brothers, pp. xi + 67.

1939. Attaining womanhood. A doctor talks to girls about sex. New York, Harper & Brothers, pp. xiii + 95.

1942. The hormones in human reproduction. Princeton, N. J., Princeton University Press, pp. xix + 265.

Corner, G. W., and **Landis, C. 1941.** Sex education for the adolescent. Hygeia, July 1941, reprint pp. 18.

Crampton, C. W. 1908. Physiological age—a fundamental principle. I. Amer. Physic. Educ. Rev. 13:141–147.

1944. Physiological age—a fundamental principle. Child Develop. 15:3–52.

Crampton, H. E. 1925. Studies on the variation, distribution, and evolution of the genus Partula. The species of the Mariana Islands, Guam and Saipan. Carnegie Inst. Wash., Publ. 228A, pp. viii + 116.

Crisp, K. B. 1939. Growing into maturity. Chicago, J. B. Lippincott Co., pp. 38.

Curry, E. T. 1940. The pitch characteristics of the adolescent male voice. Speech Monogr. 7:48–62.

Davis, H. 1946. Moral and pastoral theology. In four volumes. Vol. 1: Human acts, law, sin, virtue, pp. xix + 361. Vol. 2: Commandments of God, precepts of the Church, pp. x + 463. Vol. 3: The sacraments in general, baptism, confirmation, holy eucharist, penance, indulgences, censures, pp. xviii + 504. Vol. 4: Extreme unction, holy orders, marriage, the clerical state, the religious state, duties of lay people, pp. xiii + 432. New York, Sheed & Ward.

Davis, K. B. 1929. Factors in the sex life of twenty-two hundred women. New York and London, Harper & Brothers, pp. xx + 430.

Dearborn, W. F., and **Rothney, J. W. M. 1941.** Predicting the child's development. Cambridge, Mass., Sci-Art. Publishers, pp. 360.

Dice, L. R. 1932. Variation in a geographic race of the deermouse, Peromyscus maniculatus bairdii. Univ. Mich. Mus. Zool., Occ. Papers 239:1–26.

Dickerson, R. E. 1930. So youth may know. New York, Association Press, pp. x + 255.

1933. Growing into manhood. New York, Association Press, pp. vii + 100.

1937. Getting ready to fall in love. New York, Association Press, pp. 16.

1937. Getting started in marriage. New York, Association Press, pp. 11.

1937. When a couple are engaged. New York, Association Press, pp. 12.

1944. Some problems in adolescence. Los Angeles, Amer. Inst. Family Rel., Home Study Course 5:45–60.

1944. Looking ahead to marriage. Los Angeles, Amer. Inst. Family Rel., Home Study Course 6:61–72.

1946. Straight from the shoulder. New York, Association Press, pp. 32.

Dickinson, R. L. 1933. Human sex anatomy. Baltimore, Williams & Wilkins Co., pp. xiii + 145 + 175 figs.

Dickinson, R. L., and **Beam, L. 1931.** A thousand marriages. A medical study of sex adjustment. Baltimore, Williams & Wilkins Co., pp. xxv + 482.

1934. The single woman. A medical study in sex education. Baltimore, Williams & Wilkins Co., pp. xix +469.

Dimock, H. S. 1937. Rediscovering the adolescent. A study of personality development in adolescent boys. New York, Association Press, pp. xx + 287.

Dobkowsky, T. 1923. Gebissuntersuchungen an homosexuellen Männern. Ztschr. f. Sexualwiss. 10:199–200.

Dobzhansky, T. 1937. Genetics and the origin of species. New York, Columbia University Press, pp. xvi + 364.

1941. (2nd edit.). Genetics and the origin of species. New York, Columbia University Press, pp. xviii + 446.

Du Bois, C. A. 1944. The people of Alor. A social-psychological study of an East Indian Island. Minneapolis, University of Minnesota Press, pp. xvi + 654.

Dudycha, G. J. and **M. M. 1933.** Adolescents' memories of preschool experiences. Pedag. Sem. & J. Genet. Psych. 42:468–480.

Dyk, W. 1938. Son of Old Man Hat. A Navaho autobiography. New York, Harcourt, Brace & Co., pp. xiv + 378.

Eddy, S. 1928. Sex and youth. Garden City, N. Y., Doubleday, Doran & Co., pp. xii + 338.

1928. Sex and youth. Garden City, N. Y., Doubleday, Doran & Co., pp. 102.

Edson, N. W. 1936. Love, courtship and marriage. Amer. Soc. Hyg. Assoc., pp. 18, Publ. No. 932.

Elder, J. H., and Yerkes, R. M. 1936. The sexual cycle of the chimpanzee. Anat. Rec. 67:119–143.

Elliott, G. L., and Bone, H. 1929. The sex life of youth. New York, Association Press, pp. xi + 142.

Ellis, A. 1945. The sexual psychology of human hermaphrodites. Psychosom. Med. 7:108–125.

Ellis, H. 1910 (orig. 1900). Studies in the psychology of sex. Vol. 1: The evolution of modesty. The phenomena of sexual periodicity. Auto-erotism. Philadelphia, F. A. Davis Co., pp. xv + 352.

1915 (orig. 1901). Studies in the psychology of sex. Vol. 2: Sexual inversion. Philadelphia, F. A. Davis Co., pp. xi + 391.

1913 (orig. 1903). Studies in the psychology of sex. Vol. 3: Analysis of the sexual impulse. Love and pain. The sexual impulse in women. Philadelphia, F. A. Davis Co., pp. xii + 353.

1905. Studies in the psychology of sex. Vol. 4: Sexual selection in man. I. Touch. II. Smell. III. Hearing. IV. Vision. Philadelphia, F. A. Davis Co., pp. xi + 270.

1906. Studies in the psychology of sex. Vol. 5: Erotic symbolism. The mechanism of detumescence. The psychic state in pregnancy. Philadelphia, F. A. Davis Co., pp. x + 285.

1910. Studies in the psychology of sex. Vol. 6: Sex in relation to society. Philadelphia, F. A. Davis Co., pp. xvi + 656.

1936 (also 1897, 1901, etc.). Studies in the psychology of sex. New York, Random House, Vol. 1, pp. xxxix + 353, xii + 353, xi + 270, xi + 391; Vol. 2, pp. x + 285, vii + 539, xvi + 750.

Engle, E. T. (edit.). **1943** (1944). Proceedings of the conference on problems of human fertility. Sponsored by the National Committee on Maternal Health, January 15–16, 1943, New York City. Menasha, Wis., Geo. Banta Publishing Co., pp. xi + 182.

1946. The problem of fertility. Proceedings of the conference on fertility held under the auspices of the National Committee on Maternal Health. Princeton, N. J., Princeton University Press, pp. viii + 254.

English, O. S., and Pearson, G. H. J. 1945. Emotional problems of living. Avoiding the neurotic pattern. New York, W. W. Norton & Co., pp. 438.

Erickson, R. O. 1941. Mass collections: Camassia scilloides. Ann. Mo. Bot. Garden 28:293–298.

Exner, M. J. 1914. The rational sex life for men. New York and London, Association Press, pp. xiii + 95.

1915. Problems and principles of sex education. A study of 948 college men. New York, Association Press, pp. 39.

1932. The sexual side of marriage. New York, W. W. Norton and Co., pp. 187. Reprint by Eugenics Press, N. Y.

Family Life Education (Popenoe, P., edit.). **1946.** Divorce does not solve the problem! Los Angeles, Amer. Inst. Family Rel., 6 (7):1–10.

Fehlinger, H. (Herbert and Herbert transl.). **1945.** Sexual life of primitive people. New York, United Book Guild, pp. 133.

Féré, C. S. 1904. The evolution and dissolution of the sexual instinct. Paris, Chas. Carrington, pp. xxiv + 358.

Féré, C. S. (Horst, U. van der, transl.). **1932.** Scientific and esoteric studies in sexual degeneration in mankind and in animals. New York, Anthropol. Press, pp. xix + 325.

Finger, F. W. 1947. Sex beliefs and practices among male college students. J. Abn. & Soc. Psych. 42:57–67.

Fleege, U. H. 1945. Self-revelation of the adolescent boy. A key to understanding the modern adolescent. Milwaukee, Bruce Publishing Co., pp. xiv + 384.

Folsom, J. K. (edit.). 1938. Plan for marriage. An intelligent approach to marriage and parenthood. Proposed by members of the staff of Vassar College. New York, Harper & Brothers, pp. xii + 305.

Forbush, W. B. 1919. The sex-education of children. New York and London, Funk & Wagnalls Co., pp. 224.

Ford, C. S. 1941. Smoke from their fires. New Haven, Conn., Yale University Press, pp. xiii + 248.

    1945. A comparative study of human reproduction. New Haven, Conn., Yale University Press, pp. 111.

Ford, F. R., and Guild, H. 1937. Precocious puberty following measles, encephalomyelitis and epidemic encephalitis. Bull. Johns Hopkins Hosp. 60:192–203.

Forel, A. (Marshall, C. F., transl.). 1906 (1922 edit.). The sexual question. A scientific, psychological, hygienic and sociological study. Brooklyn, N. Y., Physicians and Surgeons Book Co., pp. xv + 536.

Fortune, R. F. 1932. Sorcerers of Dobu. The social anthropology of the Dobu Islanders of the Western Pacific. New York, E. P. Dutton & Co., pp. xxviii + 318. London, George Routledge & Sons.

Frank, H. 1941. A guide for confession. Huntington, Ind., Our Sunday Visitor Press, pp. 40.

Frank, R. 1946. Personal counsel. A supplement to morals. New York, Informative Books, pp. 306.

Freud, S. (Brill, A. A., transl.). 1938. The basic writings of Sigmund Freud. New York, Modern Library, pp. vi + 1001.

Freud, S. 1945. Die Traumdeutung. Wien, F. Deuticke, pp. vii + 478.

Gallichan, W. M. 1916. The great unmarried. New York, Frederick A. Stokes Co., pp. 224.

Gallup, G. H. 1944. A guide to public opinion polls. Princeton, N. J., Princeton University Press, pp. xviii + 103.

Gallup, G. H., and Rae, S. F. 1940. The pulse of democracy. New York, Simon & Schuster, pp. 335.

Gantt, W. H. 1944. Experimental basis for neurotic behavior. Origin and development of artificially produced disturbances of behavior in dogs. New York and London, Paul B. Hoeber, pp. xv + 211.

Gartland, F. E. 1945. Fight first: Marry later. Advice to men in the service and to their fiancées. Huntington, Ind., Our Sunday Visitor Press, pp. 29.

    1946. Boy meets girl the Christian way. An exhortation to chaste Christian courtship. Huntington, Ind., Our Sunday Visitor Press, pp. 20.

Geis, R. (Bruehl, C., transl.). 1930. Principles of Catholic sex morality. New York, Joseph F. Wagner, pp. xix + 105.

Geschlecht und Gesellschaft (Vanselow, K., edit.). 1906–1914. Volumes 1–9. Berlin, Leipzig, Wien, Verlag der Schönheit.

Gilbert, J. G. 1941. Memory loss in senescence. J. Abn. & Soc. Psych. 36:73–86.

Gillis, J. M. 1930. The moral law (In the heart of man and on the tablets of stone). Huntington, Ind., Our Sunday Visitor Press, pp. 85.

Glass, S. J., Deuel, H. J., and Wright, C. A. 1940. Sex hormone studies in male homosexuality. Endocr. 26:590–594.

Glass, S. J., and Johnson, R. H. 1944. Limitations and complications of organotherapy in male homosexuality. J. Clin. Endocr. 11:540–544.

Glass, S. J., and Makennon, B. J. 1937. The hormonal aspects of sex reversals. Western J. Surg. 45:467–473.

Goldschmidt, R. 1916. Die biologischen Grundlagen der konträren Sexualität und des Hermaphroditismus beim Menschen. Arch. f. Rassen- und Gesellschaftsbiol. 12:1–14.

Goodland, R. 1931. A bibliography of sex rites and customs. An annotated record of books, articles, and illustrations in all languages. London, George Routledge & Sons, pp. v +752.

Greulich, W. W., et al. 1938. A handbook of methods for the study of adolescent children. Washington, Soc. Res. Child Develop., Nat. Res. Counc., Monogr. 15, pp. xvii + 406.

Greulich, W. W. 1938. Some anatomical aspects. *In* Greulich, W. W., et al.: A handbook of methods for the study of adolescent children. Washington, Soc. Res. Child Develop., Nat. Res. Counc., Monogr. 15:1–70.

Griffin, L. F. 1945. The Catholic boy examines his conscience. Huntington, Ind., Our Sunday Visitor Press, pp. 22.

1946. The Catholic girl examines her conscience. Huntington, Ind., Our Sunday Visitor Press, pp. 24.

Groves, E. R. 1940. The family and its social functions. Chicago, Philadelphia, and New York, J. B. Lippincott and Co., pp. xvi + 631.

Gruenberg, B. C., and Kaukonen, J. L. 1940. High schools and sex education. Washington, U. S. Govt. Print. Off., pp. xix + 110.

Guttman, L. 1942. A revision of Chapin's social status scale. Amer. Soc. Rev. 7:362–369.

Haire, N., Costler, A., Willy, A., et al. 1937. Encyclopaedia of sexual knowledge. New York, Eugenics Publishing Co., pp. xx + 567.

Hall, G. S. 1904. Adolescence. Its psychology and its relations to physiology, anthropology, sociology, sex, crime, religion and education. New York, D. Appleton and Co., Vol. 1, pp. xx + 589; Vol. 2, pp. vi + 784.

Hall, W. S. 1907. The biology, physiology and sociology of reproduction. Also sexual hygiene with special reference to the male. Chicago, Wynnewood Publishing Co., pp. 149.

1909. From youth into manhood. New York, Association Press, pp. 106.

1920. Sex training in the home. Chicago, Midland Press, pp. 128.

Halverson, H. M. 1938. Infant sucking and tensional behavior. Pedag. Sem. & J. Genet. Psych. 53:365–430.

1940. Genital and sphincter behavior of the male infant. Pedag. Sem. & J. Genet. Psych. 56:95–136.

Hamilton, G. V. 1914. A study of sexual tendencies in monkeys and baboons. J. Anim. Behav. 4:295–318.

1929. A research in marriage. New York, A. and C. Boni, pp. xiii + 570.

Hamilton, G. V., and MacGowan, K. 1929. What is wrong with marriage. New York, A. and C. Boni, pp. xxi + 319.

Hamilton, J. B. 1937. Treatment of sexual underdevelopment with synthetic male hormone substance. Endocr. 21:649–654.

1937. Induction of penile erection by male hormone substances. Endocr. 21:744–749.

Hamilton, V. C. (transl.). 1940. Report on the sex question by the Swedish population commission. Baltimore, Williams & Wilkins Co., pp. xx + 182.

Harper, R. F. 1904 (edit. 2). The code of Hammurabi, King of Babylon. Chicago, University of Chicago Press, pp. xv + 192 + 103 pl.

Hartland, E. 1931. Motherright. *In* Calverton, V., 1931, The making of man. New York, Modern Library, pp. xv + 879.

Hatt, E. D. 1931. Turi's book of Lappland. London, Jonathan Cape, pp. 293.

Hattendorf, K. W. 1932. A study of the questions of young children concerning sex: A phase of an experimental approach to parent education. J. Soc. Psych. 3:37–65.

Heidel, A. 1946. The Gilgamesh epic and Old Testament parallels. Chicago, University of Chicago Press, pp. ix + 269.

Heller, C. G., and Myers, G. B. 1944. The male climacteric, its symptomology, diagnosis and treatment. Use of urinary gonadotropins, therapeutic test with testosterone propionate and testicular biopsies in delineating the male climacteric from psychoneurosis and psychogenic impotence. J. Amer. Medic. Assoc. 126:472–477.

Heller, C. G., Nelson, W. O., and Roth, A. A. 1943. Functional prepuberal castration in males. J. Clin. Endocr. 3:573–588.

Henry, G. W. 1938. Essentials of psychiatry. Baltimore, Williams & Wilkins Co., pp. xii + 465.

1941. Sex variants. A study of homosexual patterns. New York and London, Paul B. Hoeber, 2 vols., pp. xx + vi + 1179.

Henry, N. B., et al. 1944. The forty-third yearbook of the National Society for the Study of Education. Part 1, Adolescence. Chicago, University of Chicago Press, pp. x + 358.

Hildebrand, D. V. 1935 (orig. 1927). In defence of purity. New York, Sheed & Ward, pp. 196.

Hile, R. 1937. Morphometry of the cisco, Leucichthys artedi (Le Seur), in the lakes of Northeastern Highlands, Wisconsin. Int. Rev. ges. Hydrobiol. u. Hydrogr. 36:57–130.

Hillyer, J. 1927. Reluctantly told. New York, The Macmillan Co., pp. xvii + 205.

Himes, N. E. 1940. Your marriage. A guide to happiness. New York, Farrar & Rinehart, pp. xvi + 430.

Hirschfeld, M. (edit.). 1899–1922. Jahrbuch für sexuelle Zwischenstufen. Unter besonderer Berücksichtigung der Homosexualität. Leipzig, Max Spohr, Volumes 1–22.

Hirschfeld, M. 1903. Ursachen und Wesen des Uranismus. Jahrb. f. sex. Zwisch. 5:1–193.

1910. Die Transvestiten, eine Untersuchung über den erotischen Verkleidungstrieb, mit umfangreichem casuistischen und historischen Material. Berlin, Alfred Pulvermacher & Co., pp. vi + 562.

1912. Naturgesetze der Liebe. Eine gemeinverständliche Untersuchung über den Liebes-Eindruck, Liebes-Drang und Liebes-Ausdruck. Berlin, Verlag A. Pulvermacher & Co., pp. 281.

1916, 1921, 1920. Sexualpathologie. Ein Lehrbuch für Ärzte und Studierende. Part 1: Geschlechtliche Entwicklungsstörungen mit besonderer Berücksichtigung der Onanie. Part 2: Sexuelle Zwischenstufen. Das männliche Weib und der weibliche Mann. Part 3: Störungen im Sexualstoffwechsel mit besonderer Berücksichtigung der Impotenz. Bonn, Marcus & Webers Verlag, Vol. 1, pp. xv + 211; Vol. 2, pp. x + 279; Vol. 3, pp. xi + 340.

1920 (edit. 2). Die Homosexualität des Mannes und des Weibes. Berlin, L. Marcus Verlagsbuchhandlung, pp. xvii + 1067.

1926–1930. Geschlechtskunde auf Grund dreiszigjähriger Forschung und Erfahrung bearbeitet. Vol. 1 (1926): Die Körperseelischen Grundlagen, pp. xv + 638. Vol. 2 (1928): Folgen und Folgerungen, pp. 659. Vol. 3, pp. 755. Vol. 4 (1930): Index volume. Stuttgart, J. Püttmann Verlagsbuchhandlung.

1935. Men and women. The world journey of a sexologist. New York, G. P. Putnam's Sons, pp. xix + 325.

1936. Magnus Hirschfeld. In: Robinson, Encyclopaedia sexualis, pp. 317–321. New York, Dingwall-Rock.

1936. Homosexuality. In: Robinson, Encyclopaedia sexualis, pp. 321–334. New York, Dingwall-Rock.

1940. Sexual pathology. A study of derangements of the sexual instinct. New York, Emerson Books, pp. xii + 368.

1944. Sexual anomalies and perversions. Physical and psychological development and treatment. London, Francis Aldor Publ., pp. 630.

Hirschfeld, M., and Götz, B. 1929. Sexualgeschichte der Menschheit. Berlin, P. Langenscheidt, pp. vii + 385.

Hodann, M. 1928. Sexualelend und Sexualberatung. Briefe aus der Praxis. Rudolstadt, Greifenverlag (W. Geissler), pp. 302.

Hoddan, M. (Gibbs, J., transl.). 1932. Sex life in Europe. A biological and sociological survey. New York, Julian Press, pp. 252.

Hohman, L. B., and Schaffner, B. 1947. The sex lives of unmarried men. Amer. J. Soc. 52:501–507.

Hollingshead, A. B. 1939. Human ecology and the social sciences. In: Park, R. E. et al., An outline of the principles of sociology. New York, Barnes & Noble, pp. 65–168.

Hoopes, G. G. 1939. Out of the running. Springfield, Ill., Charles C Thomas, pp. xvii + 158.

Hotchkiss, R. S. 1944. Fertility in men. Philadelphia, J. B. Lippincott Co., pp. xiii + 216.

Hubbs, C. L., Hubbs, L. C., and Johnson, R. E. 1943. Hybridization in nature between species of catostomid fishes. Contrib. Lab. Vert. Biol. 22:1–76.

Hubbs, C. L., and Miller, R. R. 1942. Mass hybridization between two genera of cyprinid fishes in the Mohave Desert, California. Papers Mich. Acad. Sci., Arts, Letters 28:343–378.

Hughes, W. L. 1926. Sex experiences of boyhood. J. Soc. Hyg. 12:262–273.

Hunt, J. McV., et al. 1944. Personality and the behavior disorders. A handbook based on experimental and clinical research. New York, Ronald Press Co., 2 vols.: pp. xii + v + 1242.

Huxley, J. (edit.). 1940. The new systematics. Oxford, Clarendon Press, pp. viii + 583.

Hyman, H. T. 1946–47. An integrated practice of medicine. A complete general practice of medicine from differential diagnosis by presenting symptoms to specific management of the patient. Philadelphia, W. B. Saunders Co., 4 Vols. + Index.

Inmate, Ward 8. 1932. Behind the door of delusion. New York, The Macmillan Co., pp. xvi + 325.

Isaacs, S. 1933. Social development of young children. A study of beginnings. London, George Routledge & Sons, pp. xii + 480.

Jackson, C. M. 1925. The effect of inanition and malnutrition upon growth and structure. Philadelphia, P. Blakiston's Son & Co., pp. xii + 616.

Jahrbuch für sexuelle Zwischenstufen. 1899–1922. Unter besonderer Berücksichtigung der Homosexualität. (Hirschfeld, M., edit.) Volumes 1–22. Leipzig, Max Spohr.

Jefferis, B. G. and Nichols, J. L. 1912. Search lights on health. Light on dark corners. A complete sexual science and a guide to purity and physical manhood. Advice to maiden, wife, and mother. Love, courtship, and marriage. Naperville, Ill., J. L. Nichols, pp. 487.

Jerome, E. K. 1937. Change of voice in male adolescents. Quart. J. Speech 23:648–653.

Johnson, W. 1930. Because I stutter. New York and London, D. Appleton & Co., pp. xv + 127.

Jones, H. E. 1944. The development of physical abilities. *In*: Henry, N. B., Adolescence, pp. 100–122. Chicago, Nat. Soc. Study Educ. (University of Chicago Press).

Judge Baker Foundation. 1922. 20 case studies. Boston, Judge Baker Fnd. [no contin. paginat.].

Jung, F. T., and Shafton, A. L. 1935. The mammary gland in the normal adolescent male. Proc. Soc. Exp. Biol. Med. 33:455–458.

Kahn, F. 1939. Our sex life. A guide and counsellor for everyone. New York, Alfred A. Knopf, pp. xxxviii + 459.

Karpman, B. 1935. The individual criminal; studies in the psychogenetics of crime. Vol. 1, cases 1–5. Washington, Nerv. & Ment. Dis. Publ. Co.

1944. Case studies in the psychopathology of crime. A reference source for research in criminal material. Vol. II. Washington, Medic. Sci. Press, pp. viii + 738.

Katz, D. 1941. The public opinion polls and the 1940 election. Publ. Opin. Quart. 5:52–78.

Kellogg, W. N., and Kellogg, L. A. 1933. The ape and the child. A study of environmental influence upon early behavior. New York and London, Whittlesey House, pp. xiv + 341.

Kelly, G. 1941. Modern youth and chastity. St. Louis, The Queen's Work, pp. 104.

Kempf, E. J. 1917. The social and sexual behavior of infra-human primates with some comparable facts in human behavior. Psychoanal. Rev. 4:127–154.

Kinsey, A. C. 1941. Criteria for a hormonal explanation of the homosexual. J. Clin. Endocr. 1:424–428.

1942. Isolating mechanisms in gall wasps. Biol. Symposia 6:251–269.

1947. Sex behavior in the human animal. Ann. N. Y. Acad. Sci. 47:635–637.

Kirkendall, L. A. 1940. Building a program of sex education for the secondary school. J. Soc. Hyg. 26:305–311.

1940. Sex adjustments of young men. New York and London, Harper & Brothers, pp. xiii + 215.

Kirsch, F. M. 1930. Sex education and training in chastity. New York, Benziger Bros., pp. xxxix + 540.

1935. The sex problem. A challenge and an opportunity. New York, Paulist Press, pp. 32.

1945. Training in chastity. Huntington, Ind., Our Sunday Visitor Press, pp. 27.

Klemer, D. H. 1939. The other sex. A frank statement, addressed to both boys and girls, of the essential facts that young people want and need to know about sex. New York, Association Press, pp. 42.

Koch, R. A., and Wilbur, R. L. 1944. Promiscuity as a factor in the spread of venereal disease. J. Soc. Hyg. 30:517–529.

Krafft-Ebing, R. (Rebman, F. J., transl.). 1922 (ex edit. 12). Psychopathia sexualis, with especial reference to the antipathic sexual instinct. A medico-forensic study. Brooklyn, N. Y., Physicians and Surgeons Book Co., pp. xiii + 617.

Krafft-Ebing, R. (Moll, A., edit.). 1924 (edit. 16–17). Psychopathia sexualis. Mit besonderer Berücksichtigung der konträren Sexualempfindung. Eine medizinisch-gerichtliche Studie für Ärzte und Juristen. Stuttgart, Ferdinand Enke, pp. v + 832.

Krauss, F. S. (edit.). 1904–1913. Anthropophyteia. Jahrbücher für folkloristische Erhebungen und Forschungen zur Entwicklunggeschichte der geschlechtlichen Moral. Leipzig, Deutsche Verlagsactiengesellschaft & ethnologischer Verlag. Volumes 1–10.

Kubitschek, P. E. 1932. Sexual development of boys with special reference to the appearance of the secondary sexual characters and their relationship to structural and personality types. J. Nerv. & Ment. Dis. 76:425–451.

Landes, R. 1938. The Ojibwa woman. New York, Columbia University Press, pp. viii + 247.

Landis, C., et al. 1940. Sex in development. A study of the growth and development of the emotional and sexual aspects of personality together with physiological, anatomical, and medical information on a group of 153 normal women and 142 female psychiatric patients. New York and London, Paul B. Hoeber, pp. xx + 329.

Landis, C., and Bolles, M. M. 1942. Personality and sexuality of the physically handicapped woman. New York and London, Paul B. Hoeber, pp. xii + 171.

1946. Textbook of abnormal psychology. New York, The Macmillan Co., pp. xii + 576.

Laton, A. D., and Bailey, E. W. 1940. Suggestions for teaching selected material from the field of sex responsiveness, mating and reproduction. New York, Bur. Publ. Teachers Coll. Columbia Univ., Monogr. 2, pp. xviii + 118.

Legrain, L. 1936. Ur excavations. Vol. III: Archaic seal-impressions. Publ. Brit. Mus. and Univ. Pa. Mus., pp. viii + 51 + 58 pl.

Levey, H. B. 1939. Critique of the theory of sublimation. Psychiatry 2:239–270.

Levy, D. M. 1940. "Control-situation" studies of children's responses to the difference in genitalia. Amer. J. Orthopsychiat. 10:755–762.

Licht, H. 1925, 1926, 1928. Sittengeschichte Griechenlands. Dresden, Zürich, Paul Aretz Verlag. Vol. 1: Die griechische Gesellschaft, pp. 319. Vol. 2: Das Liebesleben der Griechen, pp. 263. Vol. 3: Ergänzungsband. Die Erotik in der griechischen Kunst. Ergänzungen zu Band I und II, pp. viii + 279.

Licht, H. (Freese, J. H., transl.). 1932. Sexual life in ancient Greece. London, George Routledge & Sons, pp. xv + 557.

Lieber, E. 1920. From boyhood to manhood. Indianapolis, Ind. State Bd. Health, pp. 8.

Liederman, E. E. 1926. Sexual guidance. New York, E. E. Liederman, pp. 172.

Linderman, F. B. 1930. American, the life story of a great Indian. New York, John Day Co., pp. xi + 313.

1932. Red mother. New York, John Day Co., pp. 256.

Lindsey, B. B., and Evans, W. 1929. The companionate marriage. Garden City, N. Y., Garden City Publishing Co., pp. xxxiv + 396.

Linton, R. 1936. The study of man. An introduction. New York, D. Appleton-Century Co., pp. ix + 503.

Lips, J. 1938. Government. *In:* Boas, F., 1938, General anthropology. New York, D. C. Heath & Co., pp. xi + 718.

Lisser, H., and Curtis, L. E. 1943. Testosterone therapy of male eunuchoids. IV. Results from methyl testosterone linguets. J. Clin. Endocr. 3:389–399.

Lisser, H., Escamilla, R. F., and Curtis, L. E. 1942. Testosterone therapy of male eunuchoids. III. Sublingual administration of testosterone compounds. J. Clin. Endocr. 2:351–360.

Lorand, S. (edit.). 1944. Psychoanalysis today. New York, International Universities Press, pp. xvi + 404.

1946. Technique of psychoanalytic therapy. New York, International Universities Press, pp. viii + 251.

Lorge, I. 1942. The "last school grade completed" as an index of intellectual level. School and Society 56:529–532.

Lovell, P. M. 1940. Sex and you. Los Angeles, Lovell Publ., pp. 98.

Lowry, O. 1938. A virtuous woman. Sex life in relation to the Christian life. Grand Rapids, Mich., Zondervan Publishing House, pp. 160.

Lundberg, G. A., and Friedman, P. 1943. A comparison of three measures of socio-economic status. Rural Soc. 8:227–242.

Malamud, W., and Palmer, G. 1932. The role played by masturbation in the causation of mental disturbances. J. Nerv. & Ment. Dis. 76:220–233, 366–379.

Malinowski, B. 1929. The sexual life of savages in North-western Melanesia. An ethnographic account of courtship, marriage and family life among the natives of the Trobriand Islands, British New Guinea. New York, Halcyon House, pp. xxviii + 603.

Mantegazza, P. (Putnam, S., transl.). 1935. The sexual relations of mankind. New York, Eugenics Publishing Co., pp. xvi + 335.

Mantegazza, P. (Alexander, H., transl.). 1936. Physiology of love. New York, Eugenics Publishing Co., pp. xviii + 237.

Martindale, C. C. 1925. The difficult commandment. New York, P. J. Kenedy & Sons, pp. 80.

Maslow, A. H. 1940. A test for dominance-feeling (self-esteem) in college women. J. Soc. Psych. 12:255–270.

1942. Self-esteem (dominance-feeling) and sexuality in women. J. Soc. Psych. 16:259–294.

1942. Manual for social personality inventory for college women. Stanford University, Stanford University Press.

Maslow, A. H., Hirsh, E., Stein, M., and Honigmann, I. 1945. A clinically derived test for measuring psychological security-insecurity. J. Gen. Psych. 33:21–41.

May, G. 1931. Social control of sex expression. New York, William Morrow & Co., pp. xi + 307.

Mayr, E. 1942. Systematics and the origin of species. From the viewpoint of a zoologist. New York, Columbia University Press, pp. xiv + 334.

McGill, M. E. 1946. Company keeping: when is it a sin? Huntington, Ind., Our Sunday Visitor Press, pp. 27.

1946. Does that man love you? Huntington, Ind., Our Sunday Visitor Press, pp. 27.

McGraw, M. B. 1935. Growth, A study of Johnny and Jimmy. New York, D. Appleton-Century Co., pp. xxi + 319.

McLean, D., and Hubbell, C. 1934. Male impotence. Publ. by author, pp. 16.

McNemar, Q. 1940. Sampling in psychological research. Psych. Bull. 37:331–365.
1946. Opinion-attitude methodology. Psych. Bull. 43:289–374.
McPartland, J. 1947. Sex in our changing world. New York, Rinehart & Co., pp. 280.
Mead, M. 1939. From the South Seas. Studies of adolescence and sex in primitive societies. New York, William Morrow & Co., pp. xxxv + iii + 304 + 384 + xiv + 335.
Mead, W. R., and Stith, R. 1940. Male climacteric. J. So. Car. Medic. Assoc. 36:222–226.
Meagher, J. F. W. 1924. A study of masturbation and the psychosexual life. Baltimore, William Wood & Co.
Meagher, J. F. W., and Jelliffe, S. E. 1936. A study of masturbation and the psychosexual life. Baltimore, William Wood & Co., pp. xii + 149.
Menzies, K. 1921. Autoerotic phenomena in adolescence. An analytical study of the psychology and psychopathology of onanism. New York, Paul B. Hoeber, pp. 100.
Meredith, H. V. 1935. The rhythm of physical growth. A study of eighteen anthropometric measurements on Iowa City white males ranging in age between birth and eighteen years. Iowa City, Univ. Iowa Studies in Child Welfare 11:1–128.
1939. Stature of Massachusetts children of North European and Italian ancestry. Amer. J. Physic. Anthrop. 24:301–346.
Merrill, L. 1918. A summary of findings in a study of sexualism among a group of one hundred delinquent boys. J. Juv. Res. 3:255–267.
Meyer, F. 1927. Plain talks on marriage. Cincinnati, St. Francis Book Shop, pp. 181.
1927. Youth's pathfinder. Heart to heart chats with Catholic young men and women. Cincinnati, St. Francis Book Shop, pp. 421.
1929. Helps to purity. A frank, yet reverent instruction on the intimate matters of personal life for adolescent girls. Cincinnati, St. Francis Book Shop, pp. 90.
1929. Safeguards of chastity. A frank, yet reverent instruction on the intimate matters of personal life for young men. Cincinnati, St. Francis Book Shop, pp. vii + 84.
1934. I'm keeping company now! Cincinnati, St. Francis Book Shop, pp. 32.
1935. On or off with the dance? Cincinnati, St. Francis Book Shop, pp. 16.
Miles, W. R. 1919. The sex expression of men living on a lowered nutritional level. J. Nerv. & Ment. Dis. 49:208–224.
1942. Psychological aspects of ageing. In: Cowdry, E. V., 1942. Problems of ageing, pp. 756–784.
Miller, A. H. 1941. Speciation in the avian genus Junco. Univ. Calif. Publ. Zool. 44:173–434.
Miller, G. S. 1928. Some elements of sexual behavior in primates and their possible influence on the beginnings of human social development. J. Mammal. 9:273–293.
1931. The primate basis of human sexual behavior. Quart. Rev. Biol. 6:379–410.
Moffett, M. 1942. Youth looks at marriage. A guide for the study of marriage and family life. New York, Association Press, pp. 48.
Moll, A. 1893 (2d edit.). Die konträre Sexualempfindung. Mit Benutzung amtlichen Materials. Berlin, Fischer's Medicin. Buchhandlung, pp. xiv + 394.
1893. Les perversions de l'instinct génital. Étude sur l'inversion sexuelle basée sur des documents officiels. Paris, G. Carré, pp. ix + 327.
1897. (edit. 6). Les perversions de l'instinct génital. Étude sur l'inversion sexuelle basée sur des documents officiels. Paris, G. Carré et C. Naud, pp. xxxvi + ix + 327.
1898. Untersuchungen über die Libido sexualis. Berlin, Fischer's Medicin. Buchhandlung, pp. xv + 872.
1899 (edit. 3). Die konträre Sexualempfindung. Berlin, Fischer's Medicin. Buchhandlung, pp. xvi + 652.
1912. The sexual life of the child. New York, The Macmillan Co., pp. xv + 339.
1933. Libido sexualis. Studies in the psychosexual laws of love verified by clinical sexual case histories. New York, Amer. Ethnol. Press, pp. 384.

Moll, A. (edit.). **1921.** Handbuch der Sexualwissenschaften mit besonderer Berücksichtigung der kulturgeschichtlichen Beziehungen. Leipzig, F. C. W. Vogel, pp. xxiv + 1046.

Moll, A. (Popkin, M., transl.). **1931.** Perversions of the sex instinct. A study of sexual inversion based on clinical data and official documents. Newark, N. J., Julian Press, pp. 237.

Moore, C. R. 1942. Comparative biology of testicular and ovarian hormones. Biol. Symposia 9:3–10.

   1942. The physiology of the testis and application of male sex hormone. J. Urol. 47:31–44.

   1943. Sexual differentiation in the opossum after early gonadectomy. J. Exper. Zool. 94:415–461.

   1944. Gonad hormones and sex differentiation. Amer. Nat. 78:97–130.

   1944. Sex endocrines in development and prepuberal life. J. Clin. Endocr. 4:135–141.

Moore, T. V. 1943. The nature and treatment of mental disorders. New York, Grune & Stratton, pp. viii + 312.

   1943. Principles of ethics. Philadelphia, J. B. Lippincott Co., pp. xii + 405.

   1945. The pathogenesis and treatment of homosexual disorders: A digest of some pertinent evidence. J. Personality. 14:47–83.

Morgan, W. H., and **Morgan, M. I. 1943.** Planning for marriage. Outlines for discussion by young men and women. New York, Association Press, pp. 85.

Morley, S. G. 1946. The ancient Maya. Stanford University, Stanford University Press; London, Oxford University Press, pp. xxxii + 520.

Moses, J. 1922. Konstitution und Erlebnis in der Sexualpsychologie und -pathologie des Kindesalters. Ztschr. f. Sexualwiss. 8:305–319.

Mowrer, O. H., and **Kluckhohn, C. 1944.** Dynamic theory of personality. *In:* Hunt, J. McV., 1944, Personality and the behavior disorders. New York, Ronald Press Co., Vol. 1:69–135.

Murdock, G. 1934. Our primitive contemporaries. New York, The Macmillan Co., pp. xxii + 614.

Näcke, P. 1908. Beiträge zu den sexuellen Träumen. Archiv f. Kriminalanthropologie 20:366.

National Research Council Conference on Mammalian Sex Behavior. 1943. Conference on patterns and problems of primate sex-behavior. New York, mimeo. rpt., pp. 6.

Neugebauer, F. L. von. 1908. Hermaphroditismus beim Menschen. Leipzig, Werner Klinkhardt, pp. vii + 748.

Norbury, E. P. 1934. The climacteric period from the viewpoint of mental disorders. Med. Rec. 140:605–609, 657–662.

Northcote, H. 1916. Christianity and sex problems. Philadelphia, F. A. Davis Co., pp. xvi + 478.

Nowlis, V. 1941. Companionship preference and dominance in the social interaction of young chimpanzees. Compar. Psychol. Monogr. 17:1–57.

Painter, T. 1941. Male homosexuals and their prostitutes in contemporary America. New York, unpubl. ms., 2 vols.

Park, R. E., et al. 1939. An outline of the principles of sociology. New York, Barnes & Noble, pp. viii + 353.

Patten, B. M. 1946. Human embryology. Philadelphia, The Blakiston Co., pp. xv + 776.

Pearl, R. 1925 (revis. 1930). The biology of population growth. New York, Alfred A. Knopf, pp. xiv + 260.

   1940. Introduction to medical biometry and statistics. Philadelphia, W. B. Saunders Co., pp. xv + 537.

   1946. Man the animal. Bloomington, Ind., Principia Press, pp. ix + 128.

Peck, M. W., and **Wells, F. L. 1923.** On the psycho-sexuality of college graduate men. Ment. Hyg. 7:697–714.

1925. Further studies in the psycho-sexuality of college graduate men. Ment. Hyg. 9:502–520.

Pedrey, C. P. 1945. A study of voice change in boys between the ages of eleven and sixteen. Speech Monogr. 12:30–36.

Peterson, K. M. 1938. Early sex information and its influence on later sex concepts. Unpublished thesis in library of College of Education, University of Colorado, pp. vii + 136.

Plättner, K. 1930. Eros im Zuchthaus. Sehnsuchtsschreie gequälter Menschen nach Liebe. Eine Beleuchtung der Geschlechtsnot der Gefangenen bearbeitet auf der Grundlage von Eigenerlebnissen, Beobachtungen und Mitteilungen in achtjähriger Haft. Hannover, P. Witte Verlag, pp. 226.

Popenoe, P. 1936. Betrothal. Amer. Soc. Hyg. Assoc., Publ. 972:1–15.

1938. If your daughter pets. Your Life 1938:(reprint pp. 1–6).

1940. Eugenics and family relations. J. Hered. 31:532–536.

1940. Modern marriage. A handbook for men. New York, The Macmillan Co., pp. xi + 299.

1943. Marriage before and after. New York, Wilfred Funk, pp. xiv + 246.

1944. Building sex into your life. Los Angeles, Amer. Inst. Family Rel., pp. 22.

1946. Sexual inadequacy of the male. A manual for counselors. Los Angeles, Amer. Inst. Family Rel., pp. 41.

Popenoe, P. (edit.). 1946. Family life education. Los Angeles, Amer. Inst. Fam. Rel. 6, pp. 10.

Pratt, J. P. 1942. A personal note on methyl testosterone in hypogonadism. J. Clin. Endocr. 2:460–464.

Prince, M. 1905. The dissociation of a personality. A biographical study in abnormal psychology. London, Longmans, Green, & Co., pp. x + 569.

Radin, P. 1920. The autobiography of a Winnebago Indian. Univ. Calif. Publ. Amer. Archaeol. Ethnol. 16:381–473.

1926. Crashing Thunder. The autobiography of an American Indian. New York, D. Appleton and Co., pp. xxv + 203.

Rado, S. 1940. A critical examination of the concept of bisexuality. Psychosom. Med. 2:459–467.

Ramsey, G. V. 1943. The sexual development of boys. Amer. J. Psych. 56:217–234.

1943. The sex information of younger boys. Amer. J. Orthopsychiat. 13:347–352.

Ratzel, F. (Butler, A. J., transl.). 1896. The history of mankind. New York, The Macmillan Co., Vol. 1, pp. xxiv + 486.

Redemptorist Father. 1946. Aids to purity. Huntington, Ind., Our Sunday Visitor Press, pp. 32.

Reich, W. 1942. The function of the orgasm. Sex-economic problems of biological energy. (Running title: The discovery of the orgone). New York, Orgone Inst. Press, pp. xxxvi + 368.

Reichard, G. 1938. Social life. *In:* Boas, F., 1938, General anthropology. New York, D. C. Heath & Co., pp. xi + 718.

Rice, T. B. 1933. How life goes on and on. A story for girls of high school age. Chicago, American Medical Association, pp. 39.

1933. In training, for boys of high school age. Chicago, American Medical Association, pp. 48.

1933. The age of romance. Chicago, American Medical Association, pp. 44.

1933. The venereal diseases. Chicago, American Medical Association, pp. 39.

1946. Sex, marriage and family. Philadelphia, J. B. Lippincott Co., pp. 272.

Richey, H. G. 1931. The blood pressure in boys and girls before and after puberty. Its relation to growth and to maturity. Amer. J. Dis. Child. 42:1281–1330.

Robie, W. F. 1924. Sex and life. What the experienced should teach and what the inexperienced should learn. Ithaca, N. Y., Rational Life Publishing Co., pp. 424.

1925. The art of love. London, Medic. Res. Soc., pp. vi + 386.

1927. Rational sex ethics and further investigations. A psychological and physiological study of the sex lives of normal men and women. Ithaca, N. Y., Rational Life Publishing Co., pp. 333.

Robinson, S. 1938. Experimental studies of physical fitness in relation to age. Arbeitsphysiol. 10:251–323.

Robinson, V. (edit.). 1936. Encyclopaedia sexualis. New York, Dingwall-Rock, pp. xx + 819.

Robinson, W. J. 1933. Medical and sex dictionary. New York, Eugenics Publishing Co., pp. 187.

—— 1936. Sexual ethics. In: Robinson, V., Encylopaedia sexualis, pp. 209–221. New York, Dingwall-Rock.

Rockwood, L. D., and Ford, M. E. N. 1945. Youth, marriage, and parenthood. The attitudes of 364 university juniors and seniors toward courtship, marriage, and parenthood. New York, John Wiley & Sons, pp. xiii + 298.

Rogers, C. R. 1942. Counseling and psychotherapy. Newer concepts in practice. New York, Houghton Mifflin Co., pp. xiv + 450.

Rohleder, H. 1902 (edit. 2). Die Masturbation. Eine Monographie für Ärzte, Pädagogen und gebildete Eltern. Berlin, Fischer's Medicin. Buchhandlung, pp. xxiii + 336.

—— 1907. Vorlesungen über Geschlechtstrieb und gesamtes Geschlechtsleben des Menschen. Vol. 1: Das normale, anormale und paradoxe Geschlechtsleben. Berlin, Fischer's Medicin. Buchhandlung, pp. xvi + 600.

—— 1907. Vorlesungen über Geschlechtstrieb und gesamtes Geschlechtsleben des Menschen. Vol. 2: Das perverse Geschlechtsleben des Menschen, auch vom Standpunkte der lex lata und der lex ferenda. Berlin, Fischer's Medicin. Buchhandlung, pp. vi + 545.

—— 1918. Normale, pathologische und künstliche Zeugung beim Menschen. Volume I of: Monographien über die Zeugung beim Menschen. Leipzig, G. Thieme Verlag, pp. xvi + 317.

—— 1913. Die Funktionsstörungen der Zeugung beim Manne (Samenflüsse, Impotenz, Sterilität). Volume III of: Monographien über die Zeugung beim Menschen. Leipzig, G. Thieme Verlag, pp. ix + 235.

—— 1914. Die libidinösen Funktionsstörungen der Zeugung beim Weib. Volume IV of: Monographien über die Zeugung beim Menschen. Leipzig, G. Thieme Verlag, pp. viii + 99.

—— 1921. Die künstliche Zeugung (Befruchtung) im Tierreich. Volume VII (supplementary volume) of: Monographien über die Zeugung beim Menschen. Leipzig, G. Thieme Verlag, pp. x + 128.

—— 1921 (4th edit.). Die Masturbation. Eine Monographie für Ärzte, Pädagogen und gebildete Eltern. Berlin, Fischer's Medicin. Buchhandlung, pp. xxvii + 384.

—— 1923. Sexualphilosophie und Sexualethik. Volume IV of Monographien zur Sexualwissenschaft. Leipzig, E. Oldenburg Verlag, pp. 104.

—— 1923–1925. Vorlesungen über das gesamte Geschlechtsleben des Menschen. Bd. 1. 1923. Das normale, anormale und paradoxe Geschlechtsleben. Bd. 2. 1923. Die normale und anormale Kohabitation und Konzeption (Befruchtung). Pp. xiii + 357. Bd. 3. 1925. Das perverse heterosexuelle und automonosexuelle Geschlechtsleben. Pp. xv + 421. Bd. 4. 1925. Die homosexuellen Perversionen des Menschen auch vom Standpunkt der lex lata und lex ferenda. Pp. xii + 403. Berlin, Fischer's Medicin. Buchhandlung.

Rosanoff, A. J. 1938. Manual of psychiatry and mental hygiene. New York, John Wiley & Sons, pp. xviii + 1091.

Rosenzweig, S., and Hoskins, R. G. 1941. A note on the ineffectualness of sex-hormone medication in a case of pronounced homosexuality. Psychosom. Med. 3:87–89.

Ruland, L. (Rattler, T. A., transl.). 1934. Pastoral medicine. St. Louis and London, B. Herder Book Co., pp. viii + 344.

Sadler, W. S., and Sadler, L. K. 1944 (orig. 1938). Living a sane sex life. New York and Chicago, Wilcox & Follett, pp. xii + 344.

Schapera, I. 1941. Married life in an African tribe. New York, Sheridan House, pp. xvii + 364.

Schapiro, B. 1943. Premature ejaculation. A review of 1130 cases. J. Urol. 50:374–379.

Schonfeld, W. A. 1943. Management of male pubescence. J. Amer. Med. Assoc. 121: 177–182.

——— 1943. Primary and secondary sexual characteristics. Study of their development in males from birth through maturity, with biometric study of penis and testes. Amer. J. Dis. Child. 65:535–549.

Schonfeld, W. A., and Beebe, G. W. 1942. Normal growth and variation in the male genitalia from birth to maturity. J. Urol. 48:759–777.

Sears, R. R. 1943. Survey of objective studies of psychoanalytic concepts. Soc. Sci. Res. Council Bull. 51, pp. xiv + 156.

Selective Service System. 1941. Analysis of reports of physical examination. Summary of data from 19,923 reports of physical examination. Washington, Select. Serv. Syst., Med. Statis. Bull. 1, pp. 31.

——— 1943. Causes of rejection and incidence of defects. Local board examinations of Selective Service registrants in peacetime. An analysis of reports of physical examination from 21 selected states. Washington, Select. Serv. Syst., Medic. Statis. Bull. 2, pp. 41.

——— 1944. Physical examinations of Selective Service registrants during wartime. An analysis of reports for the continental United States and each state. April 1942–December 1943. Washington, Select. Serv. Syst., Medic. Statis. Bull. 3, pp. iv + 137.

——— 1946. Physical examinations of Selective Service registrants in the final months of the war. An analysis of national and state data. January 1944–August 1945. Washington, Select. Serv. Syst., Medic. Statis. Bull. 4, pp. 102.

Severinghaus, E. L., and Chornyak, J. 1945. A study of homosexual adult males. Psychosom. Med. 7:302–305.

Seward, G. H. 1946. Sex and the social order. New York, McGraw-Hill Book Co., pp. ix + 301.

Sewell, W. H. 1942. The development of a sociometric scale. Sociometry 5:279–297.

Shaw, C. R. 1930. The jack-roller. A delinquent boy's own story. Chicago, University of Chicago Press, pp. xv + 205.

Shuttleworth, F. K. 1937. Sexual maturation and the physical growth of girls age six to nineteen. Washington, Soc. Res. Child Develop., Nat. Res. Council 12, pp. xx + 253.

——— 1939. The physical and mental growth of girls and boys age six to nineteen in relation to age at maximum growth. Washington, Soc. Res. Child Develop., Nat. Res. Council 22, pp. vi + 291.

——— 1941. Sampling errors involved in incomplete returns to mail questionnaires. J. Appl. Psych. 25:588–591.

Simmons, L. W. 1942. Sun Chief. The autobiography of a Hopi Indian. New Haven, Conn., Yale University Press, pp. xi + 460.

Snedecor, G. W. 1946. Statistical methods applied to experiments in agriculture and biology. Ames, Iowa State College Press, pp. xvi + 485.

Snow, W. F. 1933, 1937, 1941. Marriage and parenthood. Amer. Soc. Hyg. Assoc., Publ. No. A-54, A-329, pp. 15.

——— 1937, 1941. Health for man and boy. New York, Amer. Soc. Hyg. Assoc., pp. 16.

Sokolowsky, A. 1923. The sexual life of the anthropoid apes. Urol. & Cutan. Rev. 27:612–615.

Sorokin, P. 1927. Social mobility. New York, Harper & Brothers, pp. xvii + 559.

Spott, R., and Kroeber, A. L. 1942. Yurok narratives. Univ. Calif. Publ. Amer. Archaeol. & Ethnol. 35:143–256.

Squier, R. 1938. The medical basis of intelligent sexual practice. In: Folsom, J. K., Plan for marriage. New York, Harper & Brothers, pp. 113–137.

Stekel, W. 1920. Onanie und Homosexualität. (Die homosexuelle Neurose). Volume II of: Störungen des Trieb- und Affektlebens. (Die parapathischen Erkrankungen). Berlin und Wien, Urban & Schwarzenberg, pp. xii + 527.

——— 1920. Die Geschlechtskälte der Frau. (Eine Psychopathologie des weiblichen

Liebeslebens). Volume III of: Störungen des Trieb- und Affektlebens. (Die parapathischen Erkrankungen). Berlin und Wien, Urban & Schwarzenberg, pp. xii + 402.

1920. Die Impotenz des Mannes. (Die psychischen Störungen der männlichen Sexualfunktion). Volume IV of: Störungen des Trieb- und Affektlebens. (Die parapathischen Erkrankungen). Berlin, Urban & Schwarzenberg, pp. xi + 484.

1922. Psychosexueller Infantilismus. (Die seelischen Kinderkrankheiten der Erwachsenen). Volume V of: Störungen des Trieb- und Affektlebens. (Die parapathischen Erkrankungen). Berlin und Wien, Urban & Schwarzenberg, pp. xii + 616.

1927. Zwang und Zweifel (für Ärzte und Mediziner dargestellt). First part. Volume IX of: Störungen des Trieb- und Affektlebens. (Die parapathischen Erkrankungen). Berlin und Wien, Urban & Schwarzenberg, pp. 633.

1928. Zwang und Zweifel (für Ärzte und Mediziner dargestellt). Second part. Volume X of: Störungen des Trieb- und Affektlebens. (Die parapathischen Erkrankungen). Berlin und Wien, Urban & Schwarzenberg, pp. 672.

Stekel, W. (van Teslaar, J. S., transl.). 1922. Bi-sexual love. The homosexual neurosis. Boston, R. G. Badger, pp. viii + 359.

1924. Peculiarities of behavior. Wandering mania, dipsomania, cleptomania, pyromania and allied acts. New York, Liveright Publishing Co., Vol. 1, pp. xiv + 328; Vol. 2, pp. x + 341.

1926. Frigidity in woman in relation to her love life. New York, Liveright Publishing Co., Vol. 1, pp. viii + 304; Vol. 2, pp. vii + 314.

Stekel, W. (Boltz, O. H., transl.). 1927. Impotence in the male. The psychic disorders of sexual functions in the male. New York, Liveright Publishing Co., Vol. 1, pp. viii + 329; Vol. 2, pp. viii + 350.

Stekel, W. (Brink, L., transl.). 1929. Sadism and masochism. The psychology of hatred and cruelty. New York, Liveright Publishing Co., Vol. 1, pp. xvii + 441; Vol. 2, pp. xiii + 473.

Stekel, W. (Parker, S., transl.). 1930. Sexual abberations. The phenomena of fetishism in relation to sex. New York, Liveright Publishing Co., Vol. 1, pp. ix + 369; Vol. 2, pp. vi + 355.

Stekel, W. (Tannenbaum, S. A., transl.). 1932. Twelve essays on sex and psychoanalysis. New York, Eugenics Publishing Co., pp. 320.

Stephan, F. F., Deming, W. E., and Hansen, M. H. 1940. The sampling procedure of the 1940 population census. J. Amer. Stat. Assoc. 35:615–630.

Stone, C. P. 1924. A note on "feminine" behavior in adult male rats. Amer. J. Physiol. 68:39.

1926. The effects of cerebral destruction on the sexual behavior of male rabbits. III. The frontal, parietal, and occipital regions. J. Comp. Psych. 6:435–448.

1932. The retention of copulatory activity in male rabbits following castration. Pedag. Semin. & J. Genet. Psych. 40:296–305.

1939. Sex drive. In: Allen, E., Sex and internal secretions. Baltimore, Williams & Wilkins Co., pp. 1213–1262.

Stone, C. P., Tomilin, M. I., and Barker, R. G. 1935. A comparative study of the sexual drive in adult male rats as measured by direct copulatory tests and by the Columbia obstruction apparatus. J. Comp. Psych. 19:215–241.

Stone, C. P., and Ferguson, L. W. 1940. Temporal relationships in the copulatory acts of adult male rats. J. Comp. Psych. 30:419–433.

Stone, H. M., and Stone, A. 1937. A marriage manual. A practical guide-book to sex and marriage. New York, Simon & Schuster, pp. xi + 334.

Strain, F. B. 1934. New patterns in sex teaching. The normal sex interests of children and their guidance from infancy to adolescence. New York, D. Appleton-Century Co., pp. xvi + 242.

Strakosch, F. M. 1934. Factors in the sex life of seven hundred psychopathic women. Utica, New York, State Hospitals Press, pp. 102.

Talmud (Rodkinson, M. L., edit.). **1896, 1899, 1903, 1916.** New edition of the Baby-
    lonian Talmud. Original text, edited, corrected, formulated, and translated
    into English. Boston, Talmud Soc., Vols. 1–10.
Talmud (Epstein, I., and Simon, M. edit.). **1936** edit. The Babylonian Talmud. Seder
    Nashim. Gittin. London, Soncino Press, pp. xv + 474.
Talmud (Epstein, I., Daiches, S., and Slotki, I. W., edit.). **1936** edit. The Babylonian
    Talmud. Seder Nashim. Kethuboth. London, Soncino Press, Vol. I, pp.
    xvii + 432; Vol. II, pp. 433–771.
Talmud (Epstein, I., and Freedman, H., edit.). **1936** edit. The Babylonian Talmud.
    Seder Nashim. Kiddushin. London, Soncino Press, pp. xiii + 463.
Talmud (Epstein, I., and Klien, B. D., edit.). **1936** edit. The Babylonian Talmud. Seder
    Nashim. Nazir. London, Soncino Press, pp. xiii + 300.
Talmud (Epstein, I., and Freedman, H., edit.). **1936** edit. The Babylonian Talmud. Seder
    Nashim. Nedarim. London, Soncino Press, pp. xiv + 312.
Talmud (Epstein, I., edit., Slotki, I. W., transl.). **1936.** The Babylonian Talmud. Seder
    Nashim. Yebamoth. London, Soncino Press, Vol. 1, pp. xlviii + 440; Vol. 2,
    pp. 441–930.
Tanner, P. **1946.** Youth and chastity. (Adapted from "Marriage and the family" by Dr.
    Jacques Leclercq). Huntington, Ind., Our Sunday Visitor Press, pp. 24.
Taylor, W. S. **1933.** A critique of sublimation in males. A study of forty superior single
    men. Genet. Psych. Monogr. 13:1–115.
Terman, L. M. **1930.** Talent and genius in children. *In:* Calverton, V. F. The new genera-
    tion. New York, Macaulay Co., pp. 405–423.
Terman, L. M., and Miles, C. C. **1936.** Sex and personality. Studies in masculinity and
    femininity. New York, McGraw-Hill Book Co., pp. xi + 600.
Terman, L. M., et al. **1938.** Psychological factors in marital happiness. New York,
    McGraw-Hill Book Co., pp. xiv + 474.
Thomas, W. I., and Znaniecki, F. **1918–1920.** The Polish peasant in Europe and America.
    Boston, Gorham Press, Vols. 1–5.
    1927. The Polish peasant in Europe and America. New York, Alfred A. Knopf.
    Vol. 1, pp. xv + 1115; Vol. 2, pp. vi + 1116–2250.
Thorndike, E. L. **1940.** Human nature and the social order. New York, The Macmillan
    Co., pp. xx + 1019.
Thorndike, E. L., Bregman, E. O., Tilton, J. W., and Woodyard, E. **1928.** Adult learning.
    New York, The Macmillan Co., pp. x + 335.
Thornton, N. **1946.** Problems in abnormal behaviour. Philadelphia, The Blakiston Co.,
    pp. x + 244.
Thurnwald, R. **1931.** Banaro society. *In:* Calverton, V., The making of man. New York,
    Modern Library, pp. xv + 879.

Underhill, R. M. **1936.** The autobiography of a Papago woman. Menasha, Wis., Amer.
    Anthrop. Assoc. Memoirs 46:1–64.
U. S. Census Bureau. **1943.** Sixteenth census of the U. S.: 1940. Population. Vol. IV:
    Characteristics by age, marital status, relationship, education, and citizenship.
    Pt. 1: U. S. Summary. Washington, U. S. Govt. Print. Off., pp. xii + 183.
    1943. Sixteenth census of the U. S.: 1940. Population. Special report on institu-
    tional population 14 years old and over. Characteristics of inmates in penal
    institutions, and in institutions for the delinquent, defective, and dependent.
    Washington, U. S. Govt. Print. Off., pp. iv + 361.
    1946. Prisoners in state and federal prisons and reformatories. 1943. Washington,
    U. S. Govt. Print. Off., pp. v + 72.
U. S. Department of Labor. **1939.** Dictionary of occupational titles. Part I: Definitions
    of titles. Washington, U. S. Govt. Print. Off., pp. xxxii + 1287.
    1939. Dictionary of occupational titles. Part II: Group arrangement of occupational
    titles and codes, Washington, U. S. Govt. Print. Off., pp. xxvi + 330.
    1945. Dictionary of occupational titles. Supplement. Edition III. Washington,
    U. S. Govt. Print. Off., pp. viii + 747.
U. S. Navy Department. **1940.** Regulations governing the admission of candidates into

the United States Naval Academy as midshipmen and sample examination papers. Washington, U. S. Govt. Print. Off., pp. 101.

U. S. Public Health Service. 1921. Keeping fit (for boys). Indianapolis, Ind., State Board of Health, pp. 16.

1934. Keeping fit. A pamphlet for adolescent boys. Washington, U. S. Publ. Health Serv., pp. 15.

1937. Man-power. Washington, U. S. Publ. Health Serv., V. D. Pamphl. 6: pp. 15.

Van de Velde, T. H. 1930. Ideal marriage. Its physiology and technique. New York, Covici, Friede, pp. xxvi + 336.

Vatsyayana (Burton, R. F., and Arbuthnot, F. F., transl.). 1883–1925. The Kama Sutra of Vatsyayana. Translated from the Sanscrit by The Hindoo Kama Shastra Society. Benares-New York, Printed for Society of Friends of India, priv. circulat. [Guy d'Isère], pp. xxi + 175.

Vecki, V. G. 1901. The pathology and treatment of sexual impotence. Philadelphia and London, W. B. Saunders Co., pp. 329.

1920. Sexual impotence. Philadelphia and London, W. B. Saunders Co., pp. viii + 424.

Walker, K., and Strauss, E. B. 1939. Sexual disorders in the male. Baltimore, Williams & Wilkins Co., pp. xiv + 248.

Warner, W. L., and Lunt, P. S. 1941. The social life of a modern community. New Haven, Conn., Yale University Press, pp. xx + 460.

1942. The status system of a modern community. New Haven, Conn., Yale University Press, pp. xx + 246.

Warner, W. L., and Srole, L. 1945. The social systems of American ethnic groups. New Haven, Conn., Yale University Press, pp. xii + 318.

Washburne, H. C. 1940. Land of the good shadows. The life story of Anauta, an Eskimo woman. New York, John Day Co., pp. xix + 329.

Weatherhead, L. D., and Greaves, M. 1932. The mastery of sex through psychology and religion. New York, The Macmillan Co., pp. xxv + 246.

Wechsler, D. 1935. The range of human capacities. Baltimore, Williams & Wilkins Co., pp. ix + 159.

Weinberger, L. M., and Grant, F. C. 1941. Precocious puberty and tumors of the hypothalamus. Arch. Int. Med. 67:762–792.

Weisman, A. I. 1941. Spermatozoa and sterility. A clinical manual. New York, Paul B. Hoeber, pp. xvi + 314.

Weiss, E., and English, O. S. 1943. Psychosomatic medicine. The clinical application of psychopathology to general medical problems. Philadelphia, W. B. Saunders Co., pp. xxiii + 687.

Weissenberg, S. 1924. Das Geschlechtsleben der russischen Studentinnen. Ztschr. f. Sexualwiss. 11:7–14.

1924. Das Geschlechtsleben des russischen Studententums der Revolutionszeit. Ztschr. f. Sexualwiss. 11:209–216.

Werner, A. A. 1945. The male climacteric: Report of fifty-four cases. J. Amer. Medic. Assoc. 127:705–710.

Westermarck, E. 1922. The history of human marriage. New York, Allerton Book Co., Vol. 1, pp. xxiii + 571; Vol. 2, pp. xi + 595; Vol. 3, pp. viii + 587.

1934. Three essays on sex and marriage. London, Macmillan & Co., pp. ix + 353.

1936. The future of marriage in western civilization. New York, The Macmillan Co., pp. xiv + 281.

Whelpton, P. K., and Kiser, C. V. 1943. Social and psychological factors affecting fertility. I. Differential fertility among 41,498 native-white couples in Indianapolis. Milbank Mem. Fnd. Quart. 21:221–280.

1944. Social and psychological factors affecting fertility. II. Variations in the size of completed families of 6551 native-white couples in Indianapolis. Milbank Mem. Fnd. Quart. 22:72–105.

1945. Social and psychological factors affecting fertility. III. The completeness and accuracy of the household survey of Indianapolis. Milbank Mem. Fnd. Quart. 23:254–296.

Wile, I. S. 1941. Concerning a pamphlet on sex hygiene. Report to 1941 Nat. Interfraternity Conf.

1941. Sex in terms of personal and social hygiene. Nat. Interfraternity Conf., pp. 32.

Willoughby, R. R. 1937. Sexuality in the second decade. Monogr. Soc. Res. Child Develop. 10, pp. iv + 57.

Wissler, C. 1922. (edit. 2). The American Indian. An introduction to the anthropology of the New World. New York, Oxford University Press, pp. xxi + 474.

Witschi, E., and Mengert, W. F. 1942. Endocrine studies on human hermaphrodites and their bearing on the interpretation of homosexuality. J. Clin. Endocr. 2:279–286.

Wolf, C. 1934. Die Kastration bei sexuellen Perversionen und Sittlichkeitsverbrechen des Mannes. Basel, Benno Schwabe & Co. Verlag, pp. xii + 300.

Wolfe, T. P. 1942. [Review of] P. Schilder "Types of anxiety neuroses." Inter. J. Psychoanal., 1941. Inter. J. Sex-econ. and Orgone-Res. 1:185–186.

Wright, C. A. 1935. Endocrine aspects of homosexuality. Med. Rec. 142:407–410.

1938. Further studies of endocrine aspects of homosexuality. Med. Rec. 147:449–452.

1939. The sex offender's endocrines. Med. Rec. 149:399–402.

1941. Results of endocrine treatment in a controlled group of homosexual men. Med. Rec. 154:60–61.

1942. Endocrine treatment in homosexual men. Therap. Notes, Feb. 1942:65.

Wright, R. 1945. Blackboy; a record of childhood and youth. Cleveland, World Publishing Co., pp. viii + 228.

Wulffen, E. 1913. Das Kind. Sein Wesen und seine Entartung. Berlin, P. Langenscheidt Verlag, pp. xxiv + 542.

Yerkes, R. M. 1939. Sexual behavior in the chimpanzee. Human Biol. 11:78–111.

1939. Social dominance and sexual status in the chimpanzee. Quart. Rev. Biol. 14:115–136.

1940. Social behavior of chimpanzees: dominance between mates, in relation to sexual status. J. Comp. Psych. 30:147–186.

1941. Conjugal contrasts among chimpanzees. J. Abn. & Soc. Psych. 36:175–199.

1943. Chimpanzees. A laboratory colony. New Haven, Conn., Yale University Press, pp. xv + 321.

Yerkes, R. M., and Elder, J. H. 1936. Oestrus, receptivity, and mating in chimpanzee. Compar. Psych. Monogr. 13 (5):1–39.

1936. The sexual and reproductive cycles of chimpanzee. Proc. Nat. Acad. Sci. 22:276–283.

Yerkes, R. M., and Yerkes, A. W. 1929. The great apes. A study of anthropoid life. New Haven, Conn., Yale University Press, pp. xix + 652.

1935. Social behavior in infrahuman primates. Handbk. Soc. Psych. pp. 973–1033.

Young, H. H. 1937. Genital abnormalities, hermaphroditism and related adrenal diseases. Baltimore, William & Wilkins Co., pp. xli + 649.

Young, K. 1940. Personality and problems of adjustment. New York, F. S. Crofts & Co., pp. x + 868.

Young, W. C., and Orbison, W. D. 1944. Changes in selected features of behavior in pairs of oppositely sexed chimpanzees during the sexual cycle and after ovariectomy. J. Comp. Psych. 37:107–143.

Young, W. C., and Rundlett, B. 1939. The hormonal induction of homosexual behavior in the spayed female guinea pig. Psychosom. Medic. 1:449–460.

Zeitschrift für Sexualwissenschaft (Eulenburg, A., and Bloch, I., edit.). 1914–1932. Vols. 1–18. Bonn, Marcus & Webers Verlag.

Zuckerman, S. 1933. Functional affinities of man, monkeys, and apes. A study of the bearings of physiology and behaviour on the taxonomy and phylogeny of lemurs, monkeys, apes, and man. New York, Harcourt, Brace and Co., pp. xviii + 203.

INDEX

All numbers refer to pages. **Bold face** entries refer to more extended treatments of each subject. Names of authors cited are *italicized*.

Abnormal, defined, 7, 37, **199–203**, 385–386, **572–581**

Abstinence, **205–213**, 297–298, **319–326**, 528–529

Accumulative incidence
Animal contacts, **669–673**
Calculating, **114–119**
Extra-marital intercourse, **584–588**
Homosexual, 100–101, 140–141, 145–146, 317, 321, 402–403, 617–631, **623**, **650–651, 653–655**
Marital coitus, 253, 281, **564–567**
Marriage, **318–319**
Masturbation, 96–97, 136–137, 144–145, 311, 317, 398–399, 408–409, **499–502**
Nocturnal emissions, 96–97, 137–138, 144–145, 398–399, 408–409, **519–522**
Oral contacts, **370–371**, 373
Petting, 97–98, 406–409, **533–537**
Pre-marital intercourse, 139, 141, 145–146, 397, 400–401, 404–405, **549–551**
Prostitute intercourse, 100–101, 116–118, 139, 141, 402–403, **597–600**
Total intercourse, 98, 101, 137–138, 316–317, 396, 400–401, 404–405, **565–567**

Achilles, P. S., 23, 28, 499, 519, 552, 766
Ackerson, L., 53, 766
Active incidence. *See* Incidence, active.
Adams, C. R., 546, 560, 766
Adolescence, **182–192,** 297–326
Defined, 182–183, **298–301**
Female, 183, 187
Mean age, **187–189**
Physical developments, **130–131, 184–185**
Precocious, 185–186
School grade, **186–187**
Sexual activity, **219–225,** 506–507, 523
Variation, **182–192**
Adolescence, age at onset vs.
First intercourse, **315–317**
Homosexual, 312, **315,** 317, **320–321,** 630
Marital intercourse, 306–308, 569
Marriage, 315, 318–319
Masturbation, **310–313,** 317, 324, 507
Nocturnal emissions, 315, 322, 523
Onset of activity, **298–303**

Adolescence, age at onset vs., *Continued*
Pre-marital intercourse, **312–315,** 324, 553
Social level, 188–189
Source of first ejaculation, 300–301, 303
Total outlet, **302–308,** 324
Age, determination of, 76–77
Age, old, 226–227, **235–238,** 319–326
Aging, **218–262,** 319–325
Animal contacts, **260–262,** 671–673
Erotic response, 229–230
Extra-marital intercourse, **248, 250, 257, 259,** 568, 587–588
Homosexual, **258–261, 290–292,** 629–630, 636
Marital intercourse, **252–257, 278–281,** 285, 567–569
Masturbation, **238–243, 270–272,** 506–507
Nocturnal emissions, **242–245, 274–276,** 521, 523
Petting, **244–249,** 539
Post-marital outlets, 262–292, **294–296**
Pre-marital intercourse, **248–253, 277–288,** 552–553
Prostitute intercourse, **250–253,** 281, **285–288,** 601
Total activity, **218–262**
Total outlet, **219–221, 226–230, 266–267**
Allbutt, T. C., 297, 766
Allen, C., 207, 514, 766
Allen, F. L., 39, 766
American Social Hygiene Association, 514, 527, 560, 591
Anal contacts, children, **170–171**
Anal eroticism, 170–171, 579
Angus, S., 202, 263, 465, 766
Animal contacts, **667–678**
Accumulative incidence, **669–673**
Active incidence, 260–262, 362–363, **461–464,** 670
Aging effects, **260–262,** 671–673
Data in interview, 65, 70
Frequencies, **260–262,** 293, 362–363, **461–464, 671–673**
Marital status, **289, 293,** 673
Pre-adolescent, **174,** 671, 673
Psychologic basis, **675–678**
Rural–urban, **459–464,** 670–674